ROUTLEDGE LIBRARY EDITIONS:
THE ECONOMY OF THE MIDDLE EAST

Volume 15

THE ECONOMIES OF THE ARAB WORLD

THE ECONOMIES OF THE ARAB WORLD
Development Since 1945

YUSIF A. SAYIGH

LONDON AND NEW YORK

First published in 1978

This edition first published in 2015
by Routledge
2 Park Square, Milton Park, Abingdon, Oxon, OX14 4RN

and by Routledge
711 Third Avenue, New York, NY 10017

Routledge is an imprint of the Taylor & Francis Group, an informa business

© 1978 Yusif A. Sayigh

All rights reserved. No part of this book may be reprinted or reproduced or utilised in any form or by any electronic, mechanical, or other means, now known or hereafter invented, including photocopying and recording, or in any information storage or retrieval system, without permission in writing from the publishers.

Trademark notice: Product or corporate names may be trademarks or registered trademarks, and are used only for identification and explanation without intent to infringe.

British Library Cataloguing in Publication Data
A catalogue record for this book is available from the British Library

ISBN: 978-1-138-78710-0 (Set)
eISBN: 987-1-315-74408-7 (Set)
ISBN: 978-1-138-81004-4 (Volume 15)
eISBN: 978-1-315-74634-0 (Volume 15)
Pb ISBN: 978-1-138-82017-3 (Volume 15)

Publisher's Note
The publisher has gone to great lengths to ensure the quality of this reprint but points out that some imperfections in the original copies may be apparent.

Disclaimer
The publisher has made every effort to trace copyright holders and would welcome correspondence from those they have been unable to trace.

Middle East & North Africa

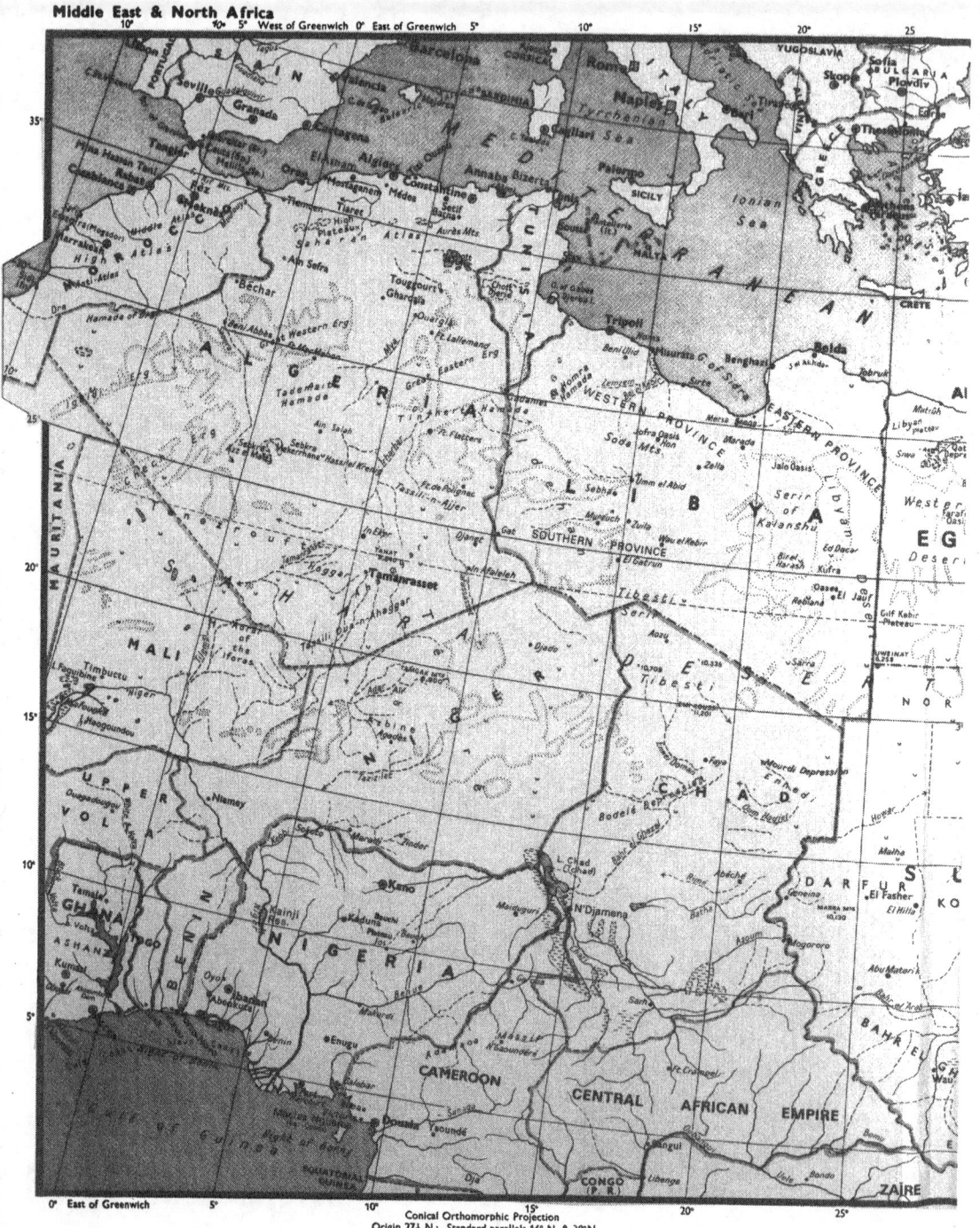

Conical Orthomorphic Projection
Origin 27½ N; Standard parallels 16° N. & 38° N.

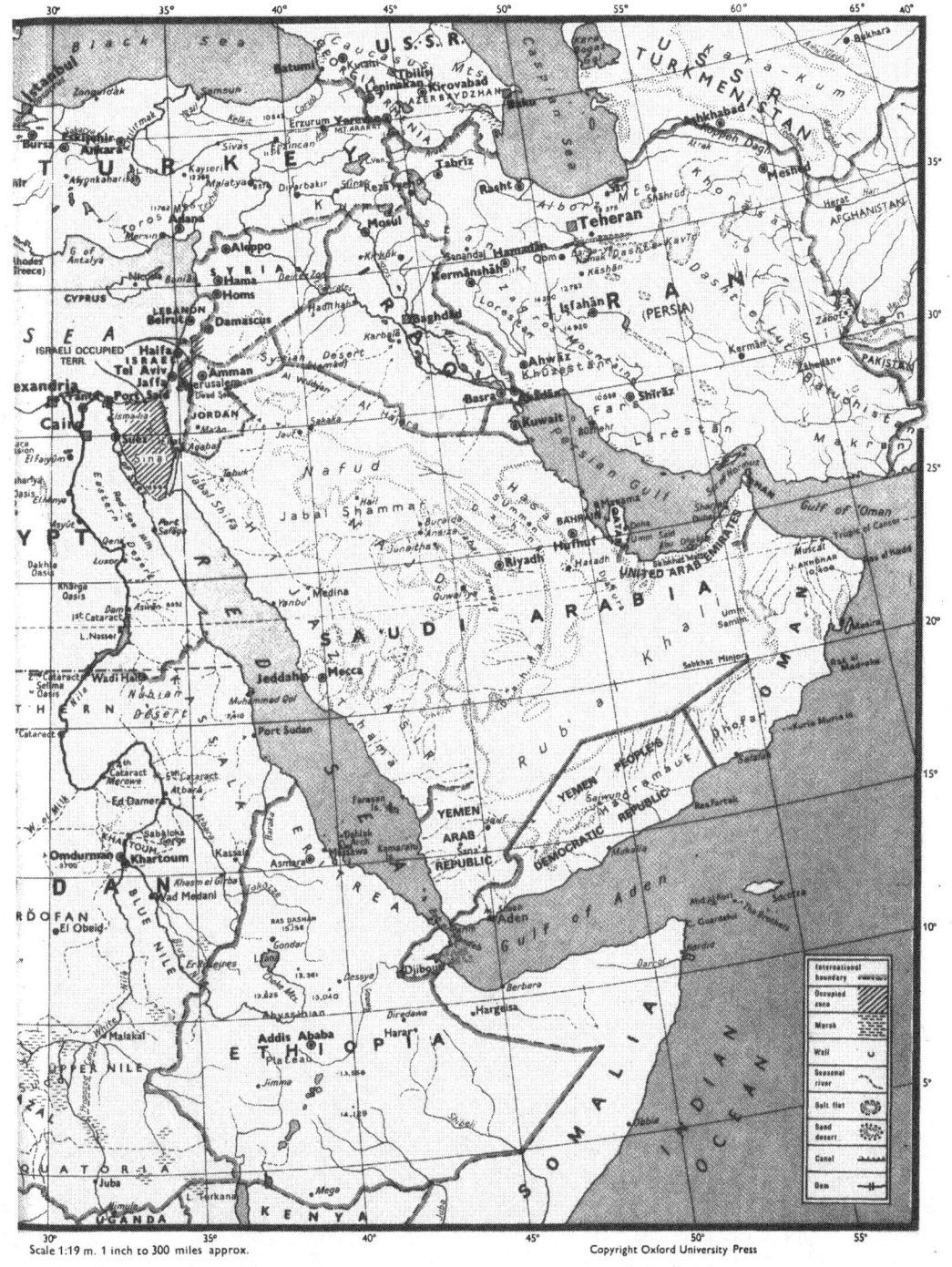

THE ECONOMIES OF THE ARAB WORLD

DEVELOPMENT SINCE 1945

Yusif A. Sayigh

CROOM HELM LONDON

©1978 Yusif A. Sayigh
Croom Helm Ltd, 2-10 St John's Road, London SW11

British Library Cataloguing in Publication Data

Sayigh, Yusif Abdalla
   The economies of the Arab world.
   1. Economic development 2. Arab countries –
   Economic conditions
   I. Title
   330.9'17'4927   HC498   77-3844

ISBN 0-85664-474-9

Printed in Great Britain by Biddles Ltd, Guildford, Surrey

CONTENTS

Acknowledgements
1. Introduction   11
2. Iraq   17
3. Kuwait   81
4. Saudi Arabia   127
5. Jordan   187
6. Syria   229
7. Lebanon   281
8. Egypt   317
9. Sudan   377
10. Libya   419
11. Tunisia   471
12. Algeria   521
13. Morocco   579
14. Arab Development in its Regional Framework   665
Index   719

ACKNOWLEDGEMENTS

I would like to record my enormous debt to the Kuwait Fund for Arab Economic Development which gave me a generous grant to enable me to take long leave from the American University of Beirut, on whose faculty I served at the time, in order to undertake the research, travel, and writing called for by the two volumes of this study, and to finance the research and secretarial assistance required.* While my debt to the Board of Directors of the Fund is heavy, it is particularly so to Mr Abdul-Latif Al-Hamad, the Director-General of the Fund, for his appreciation of the importance of the study and his sympathetic understanding when the study took much longer to complete than originally planned.

It is to be stressed, in this connection, that the views and judgements made, and there are many, are mine. The Management of the Fund is not to blame for any of these. On the contrary, it is to be thanked for allowing me the freedom to express my views. I trust I have not abused of this privilege, but have used it responsibly, and hope that the Fund will not in any way have reason to regret either the award of the grant, or the liberty it accorded me in expressing myself, whether in the survey or analysis undertaken, in the judgements made, or in the conclusions reached.

The manuscript was read by some of the economists serving on the staff of the Fund. As a result, I have benefited from a number of comments and suggestions made. While expressing my gratitude to those who took the trouble to read the manuscript, I would like to extend my apologies for not accepting all the comments and suggestions offered. It may be an author's failing to resort to his own judgement in the final analysis, but this is at the same time a privilege that he enjoys.

It is my pleasure likewise to thank the very large number of persons in the twelve countries covered — about 350 in all — whom I interviewed for the study in the course of my field work, and who gave me the benefit of their wisdom and experience, and the many who supplied me with published reports, studies, and statistics of relevance to my research. To all of these, who must remain unnamed, I extend my gratitude and appreciation. I hope they will feel that I have made proper use of the help they accorded me, and that the study reflects their opinions correctly and responsibly.

Finally, I would like to record my warm thanks to Mrs Sana' Najjar Izzeddin who alone typed and re-typed the very long manuscript, and organised the many tables, always with cheer, precision, and perfect cooperativeness. Without her the task would have been much more demanding and less manageable.

Beirut, 31 January, 1977   Y.A.S.

---

*A companion volume to the present one appears simultaneously under the title *The Determinants of Arab Economic Development*.

1 INTRODUCTION

This book is the product of two interests of which I became strongly aware in the late fifties, and which have become more intense and absorbing over the years. The first was an interest in the economic conditions and development of the Arab world after the close of World War Two, when, one after another, the Arab countries freed themselves of foreign domination. With the exception of Saudi Arabia and North Yemen, they had been under some form of Western colonial rule, but were now entering an exciting era of independence. The process of political liberation was completed between 1946 and 1962 for the countries that were at the centre of my attention, namely those lying between Iraq east and Morocco west. But it was to take another decade for the Arabian Gulf sheikhdoms (then formally known as the Trucial States) stretching south of Kuwait along the eastern coastline of the Arabian Peninsula down to Muscat-Oman, for the Aden colony and the rest of South Yemen, and for Mauritania and Somalia to join the Arab community of independent states – while Palestine, which was taken over by the Zionists in 1948 and turned into the state of Israel has yet to be liberated and to join this community.

Though not comprising the whole Arab region, my focus was very wide, with the twelve countries falling within it constituting 82 per cent of the region's total area, 90 per cent of its aggregate population, and 90 per cent of its combined GNP. These twelve countries were Iraq, Kuwait, Saudi Arabia, Jordan, Syria, Lebanon, Egypt, Sudan, Libya, Tunisia, Algeria and Morocco -- moving from east to west. I was not aware in the late fifties, nor indeed now, of any work that examined economic conditions and development in these countries, let alone the other Arab countries, except for a small number of reference works. These consist mainly of: The Royal Institute of International Affairs' *The Middle East – A Political and Economic Survey,* Europa's annual publication, *The Middle East and North Africa,* and the work put out by the General Union of the Chambers of Commerce, Industry, and Agriculture in the Arab Countries under the title *Economic Development in the Arab Countries 1950-1965,* as well as the Union's annual *Arab Economic Report.* All these publications are of the survey type, with little analysis and with concentration on the economic indicators of growth. However, two works of greater analytical value have appeared in the seventies: *Population Growth and Economic Development in the Middle East,* edited by Charles A. Cooper and Sydney S. Alexander (which leaves out all of the Arab countries in Africa except Egypt), and Galal A. Amin's *The Modernization of Poverty: A Study in the Political Economy of Growth in Nine Arab Countries, 1945-1970.*

Many of the departments of economics in universities in the Arab world offer undergraduate courses, and some graduate seminars, on development in the region. However, none of these embrace more than a few of the countries. The only course of 'area economics' given by the Department of Economics at the American University of Beirut, on whose faculty I served for 21 years until the summer of 1974, was restricted to a few of the Mashreq countries – usually Lebanon, Syria and Jordan, with the occasional addition of Egypt and Iraq. The width or narrowness of the focus depended on the predilections of the members of faculty who happened to be in charge of the course. Although pioneering work had been undertaken in the thirties by Professor Sa'id B. Himadeh of the American University of Beirut, who wrote or edited several works on five of the Asian Arab countries, this endeavour was pursued neither by him nor by any of his many students, beyond a few uncertain starts.

Several reasons explain the failure of the many centres of higher learning in the region to make an attempt to study development in its wide, regional context. Some of these were objective, such as the insufficiency of research material and the paucity of resources to finance travel and field-work. Some were subjective, such as extremely limited familiarity with the Arab community of peoples and the weakness of interest in this wide community. The interest usually went with an Arab nationalist feeling, and the nebulousness of such a feeling among those scholars who were professionally capable of undertaking regional studies may provide the basic explanation of the gap.

These observations are meant much less to claim credit for a book comprising a critical survey and analysis of most of the region's development experience in the three decades since World War Two, than to explain and justify the coverage of the book, its length, and the detail permitted. In addition, they are meant to underline the favourable circumstances which, by contrast, facilitated the translation of the writer's interest in the region's development into the present study.

This interest was not an isolated feeling. It derived from two sources of concern: concern with the development of underdeveloped countries in general, which by the late forties was becoming a magnet for the attention of academic economists, civil servants and politicians alike, and was replacing business cycle theory as the subject of much of the economic literature pouring out of the presses of the Western world; and concern with the necessary and complementary association between the political independence of Arab countries and their economic development. This latter concern was heightened by the energy with which a number of the region's countries were reshaping their political and socio-economic systems to achieve speedier development, among other things. The fact that the Arab world had had a brilliant past economically, culturally and politically, and that its present contained great promise in spite of the heavy legacy left by Ottoman and Western domination and exploitation, constituted a further urge to an exploration of the region's outlook and the factors influencing its future development.

The translation of my interest into concrete research was accelerated by the impetus of having to prepare for a course on development in the Arab world during the year 1960/1 which I spent at Princeton University as Visiting Associate Professor. The impetus was sustained when I was charged with the same kind of course on my return to the American University of Beirut. In both instances, I included the twelve countries listed earlier in the coverage of the course, though the library material then available was far from uniform and thus resulted in widely different degrees of difficulty and imperfection in the treatment of the various countries.

A second interest converged on the first and prompted me not only to prepare a book on the economic development of the Arab world, but to explore the bulk of the iceberg beneath the surface — namely, to explore the main determinants and deterrents to development, both in the economic and non-economic realms. For a few years beginning with the mid-fifties, dissatisfaction had been mounting among a small number of scholars with the very narrow focus of the concept of development then in circulation, and the almost monolithic approach to the factors or determinants of development by United Nations agencies, governments and academic economists alike. The concept was largely restricted to economic growth measured in terms of annual rates of increase in real national income or GNP; the factors were on the whole in the realm of economics, sometimes with main emphasis on capital, sometimes on technical assistance, with non-economic factors lumped together in the basket of 'other factors' and assigned a very small proportion of responsibility. As a student of the phenomenon of underdevelopment in the Arab world, I could not for long fail to see the limitations both of the concept and of the explanation of the phenomenon as well as of the process of development.

Schumpeter had given us valuable lessons with regard to the difference between mere growth and development, and of the factors behind them, in his early work, *The Theory of Economic Development*. But economists, with greater and more minute specialisation, and with more elaborate mathematical models to build, which of necessity had to be manageable and therefore to incorporate as few non-economic factors as possible, were becoming much more sophisticated and more expert, but also more impatient with broad social thought, and less convincing as interpreters of development. This trend continued for quite a number of years. By the mid-sixties, many economists in the Anglo-Saxon world probably felt that capable economists like Everett Hagen, W. W. Rostow, J. J. Spengler, Irma Adelman and Cynthia Morris, to name a few who turned their talent to exploring development in wider fields than just economics, had become a 'misallocated resource'. But the widening of horizons continued, and it is quite accepted now for an economist to take into *explicit* account salient non-economic factors in his interpretation of the process of development, rather than smuggle them shyly and surreptitiously under some such phrase as 'other things being equal', or lumping them together into a 'residual factor'. The 'Invisible Hand' which we had been taught to consider sufficiently long to reach and to transform underdevelopment, has been weighed in the scales and found wanting.

I do not propose in this rather personal Introduction to go into these matters more probingly; that will occupy me in the first chapter of the companion volume (Volume II), entitled *The Determinants of Arab Economic Development*. It is my purpose for the present merely to indicate that the curiosity leading me to investigate the non-economic terrain through which the drive for development had to be steered in the Arab world was a strong factor in prompting the undertaking of the present study. Naturally, personal predilections were strong in influencing the approach and method used in the study, even in determining its scope and content. The present writer feels much more at home with *economie politique* than with dry, mathematicised economics. This runs parallel with an absence of fear of value judgements; for how can the examination of the underdevelopment and development of societies and real human beings remain a value-free matter in a world of poverty, disease, misery, social injustice and international imbalance?

Initially, this study was to centre around the determinants of development in the Arab world, with only occasional references to the actual course of development. Ambitious though that undertaking would have been, it would still have been more manageable than what the study developed into, namely development *and* its determinants in the Arab world. The widening of the focus was not accidental. As my library research and field-work widened and matured I found, first, that I had to devote adequate attention to the developmental efforts and performance of the Arab countries if my investigation of the factors promoting or inhibiting development was to have practical relevance. Second, the mass of material I was collecting on actual development achieved (or *not* achieved, as the case may be) turned out to be enormous, and considering the scarcity (even the absence) of analytical studies on development in the region, it became compelling to make full use of the material and provide a badly needed book of wide geographical and subject coverage.

Specifically, the book as it stands has three broad objectives: to record the developmental achievements, and failings, of the twelve countries encompassed; to examine the main issues arising in the drive for development; and to assess the future outlook for development via the examination of the major determinants identified in the course of the study. Organisationally, the three objectives have been pursued in sequence. Thus, the first objective is sought in Chapters 2 to 14 of the present volume; the second engages our attention explicitly in Chapter 1 of the companion volume (Volume II), but it also receives some consideration in both volumes. The third objective, though engaging some of the critical questioning and analysis of the present volume, occupies the centre of attention in the companion volume, particularly in Chapters 2 and 3. It is hoped that the overlapping will not be thought by the reader to have reached serious dimensions; to have avoided it altogether would have resulted in arid compartmentalisation and lesser readability.

Two approaches are followed in the study. The first is a country approach; hence the present volume consists of an examination of the record of development, with Chapters 2 to 13 taking up one country after another and recording the state and process of development in each. (It is timely to state here that we have designated the countries by their public, not their formal, names for the sake of brevity.) This is essentially done not through a detailed survey of what has been done, but through an examination of a few basic economic and social indicators like national product, sectoral structure, education and manpower development, transformation in the socio-economic (and political) system, and degree of seriousness of planning. Throughout, economic development is placed in its broad sociopolitical context. Chapter 14, with which this volume ends, looks at development from a wide regional angle. Regional generalisations are attempted, and emphasis is placed on Arab economic co-operation in its various modalities and institutions, including the shortcomings as well as the achievements experienced.

A subject approach has been adopted for the companion volume, which centres around the determinants of development in the Arab world. Chapter 1 is introductory; it is concerned first with some conceptual considerations focused on the meaning of development as it is taken in the book, and second, with the notion of 'determinants', and which determinants have been selected for examination in the study. In this latter respect, the methodology adopted for examination is described and justified. Following this, Chapter 2 investigates the actual operation of the determinants selected in the countries covered. Though making use of the library research relevant to these determinants, the investigation essentially draws on the field-work undertaken for the purpose.

This field-work occupied a whole year in the early seventies, and included some 350 interviews with responsible government officials (including many Ministers), the heads of public and semi-public agencies, planning authorities, university professors, leaders of business in the various sectors (usually via the chambers of commerce, industry and agriculture), bankers, trade unionists, journalists and intellectuals. As far as possible, a wide spectrum of spokesmen with different ideologies, views and interests was reached.

Chapter 3, the final chapter of the companion volume, incorporates an attempt to gather the many strands of the study in both volumes, and to draw conclusions from it, basically with regard to the outlook for development for the countries concerned and the region as a whole. Assessment of the outlook is far from crystal ball-gazing; the occasional intuitive tone is in fact an echo of objective research and field-work, but it naturally also draws on the intimate knowledge of the region I have been fortunate to build up over twenty-two

Introduction

years of frequent travel and study in the countries from Iraq east to Morocco west. I make no apology for drawing on the insights acquired through many years of intensified study and interaction with the region's countries and its leaders in many walks of life.

This brief Introduction is sufficient, I trust, to acquaint the reader with the general concern embodied in the study with development and its determinants in the Arab world. However, I do not want to close before emphasising three matters with regard to the 'reader', 'development' and 'determinants' — the key words in the first sentence of this paragraph. The reader I am addressing myself to is not necessarily the specialised student of economics, although I hope I do not alienate the latter or fail to have him read the book. I have tried to write for the undergraduate and graduate students of economics, and for the professors looking for reading material with a wide coverage. But I hope at the same time that the book will prove useful to the general reader with at least secondary education. As the book appears simultaneously in Arabic, it may fill a gap in the Arabic and English libraries in the contemporary Arab world.

Development as understood by me is explained at some length in Chapter 1 of the companion volume. But an indication of the content of development is necessary at this point so that the reader will be aware of what I am examining in Chapters 2 to 14 of this volume; otherwise the dissatisfaction that surfaces in many places with seemingly satisfactory rates of growth will be baffling. As considered here, development does involve an improvement in the rate of real growth achieved, but additionally involves certain necessary and important conditions. These are that the economic performance leading to growth must be the result of the activity of the society and economy itself, not of islands of foreign technology and capital inside it; that the improved rate of growth must be sustained and not a passing windfall; that the improved conditions must be accompanied, if not even preceded, by social and political changes that give significance to, and supplement and sustain the conditions; that the improved performance must be accompanied by wide economic participation by the population, and that the social and political decisions involved in the design of development strategies and policies and in the allocation and use of development resources must be themselves accompanied by wide social and political participation by the population, and finally, that the marked increases in production and productivity must be accompanied by a large measure of distributive justice, such that the sharing of the national product may adequately benefit those that created it. In the last sense, development should be mass- and need-oriented, as against 'statistical' development which satisfies itself with the notion of the arithmetic mean but remains silent about what happens to the real human beings in the urban slums and destitute countryside. (The reader who prefers to have a fuller view of the conceptual framework of the study can read Chapter 1 in the companion volume before proceeding with the book.)

Finally, the determinants. These, as indicated earlier, fall in the economic as well as the socio-cultural and political realms. I had set out to survey a large number of determinants, and only when my research had been initiated did I restrict my choice and select the ones that seemed most relevant to my enquiry. Without anticipating the analysis and the findings which emerge in the companion volume, I want still to warn the reader, especially the one trained in economics and accustomed through professional bias to ascribe primary significance to economics, not to be startled if he was told, and I trust, shown, that what determines the course of economic development in the Arab world is not primarily economic forces. What is more, this is probably true of the Third World as a whole.

The two volumes of this book would have been published a year earlier, had it not been for the Arab-Israeli war of October 1973 and the steep increase in oil prices (and in Arab oil revenues) brought about by the Organization of Petroleum Exporting Countries in October and again in December 1973. Quantitative changes occurred in resource availability and the expansion of development opportunities for the Arab world, which are of such massive dimensions that they can be said to be major qualitative changes. These developments have necessitated a rewriting of much of the book, not just an updating of data. The task took over a year.

But the delay, which may have exasperated the generous sponsors and supporters of the study, and which put me under yet greater pressure to finish a book which had been under preparation since late 1970, is well worth it. The facts, the issues and the outlook for development are today vastly unlike 1972 or 1973, and to have left the transformation out of the account would have been unfair to the reader, and would have made the book grossly out of date even before going to press. But now, towards the end of 1975, with October 1973 behind, and with good fortune, this writer feels he is standing on the hilltop that commands the panorama of Arab development far into the horizon.

The reader's indulgence is sought if the drawing on the canvas of this book betrays many shortcomings; the landscape is vast and the terrain complicated. But the undertaking had to be attempted in its ambitious frontiers. A start had to be made that encompassed most of the Arab world, and explored the determinants of development in their delicate and intricate interaction. It is now up to younger Arab researchers to look more closely at the landscape and go more deeply into the examination of development and its determinants in their homeland. If this study can stir serious discussion and prompt better research to follow, it will have eminently succeeded.

2 IRAQ

The recent economic history of Iraq over the past quarter-century presents the most glaring contrast in the Arab world between abundance of endowments and modesty of achievement — or, as one Iraqi economist summed it up, between richness of the country and poverty of the people.[1] Many things have changed, some drastically, between 1946, our starting point, and 1975, but the contrast remains essentially the same. More than in the case of any other Arab country, the story of Iraq's economic development belies the simplistic approach to development which explains it mostly in terms of the availability of capital and labour and throws all the other factors, which fall outside the economic realm, into a 'residual' basket. In the case of Iraq it is essentially this residual which can explain why not much more has been done in most of the thirty years 1946-75. Yet although an investigation of the determinants of development will occupy us in the companion volume (Volume II), we will have occasion in this chapter to relate the process of development, even if passingly, to some of the non-economic factors in an attempt to suggest how they have acted upon this process and influenced its course and results.

Alone in the Arab world, Iraq has a combination of abundant water, a vast area of cultivable land coupled with a relatively small population, vast oil resources and a large number of educated men and women. It has also exerted an organised developmental effort since 1951. Yet GNP per head was in 1971 still less than ID100* (that is, less than $280 at the rate prevailing prior to the devaluation of the dollar). By the end of the sixties, the large oil revenues and the enormous spending on major projects had neither resulted in a significant horizontal spread of income nor in activating the non-oil sectors substantially.

Until the revolution of 14 July 1958 occurred, the rich were becoming richer faster than the poor were becoming less poor. This was the result of the concentration of power and wealth in relatively few hands, of the skewed pattern of land ownership and the exploitative share-tenancy conditions, of the minimal concern with the social content of development projects in the ruling circles of that period, and of the low taxes generally exacted and the non-taxation of the rich landlords who were the major beneficiaries of major irrigation projects. These conditions were made possible, and allowed to continue, thanks to the socio-political structure which favoured the powerful and the rich. However, though socially vulnerable to severe criticism, the old system provided political continuity and thus succeeded in initiating and sustaining a relatively large works programme down to the middle of 1958.

The system that followed in the summer of 1958 has been much more socially conscious, but much less stable. As a result, there have been notable social changes in favour of the under-privileged and poor, but insufficient parallel economic changes. Only after the latest in a series of political eruptions, on 17 July 1968, has the political management of the economy taken a steady course which promises a marked and balanced social and economic development.[2] Perhaps here more than anywhere else lies the key to the understanding of

* Iraqi dinars.

Iraq's contrasts between rich endowments and poor performance. The key is the political management of the economy which, through discontinuity and frequent violent change, has inhibited growth and confused decision-making in the public sector and the private sector alike.

Yet, disturbed as it has been, the political management has had other complicating factors that have further retarded the healthy progress of the economy. Most conspicuously there have been the fighting with the Kurds in the north of the country and the protracted dispute with the Iraq Petroleum Company, the oil concessionary company. (Unless otherwise indicated, the reference to IPC will apply equally to the Mosul Petroleum Company, MPC, and the Basrah Petroleum Company, BPC — affiliates that have the same owners and fall under the same control of IPC.) The relation between the political factor and economic development has been so close that it deserves to be brought out a little more specifically in the next section.

1. THE MAIN LANDMARKS[3]

The first landmark of significance is 1951, since it was beginning with January of this year that the government started to receive half the net profits arising from the export of crude petroleum under the 'fifty-fifty' formula of profit-sharing. (The agreement under which the formula was adopted was reached in February 1952, but was made retroactive to the beginning of 1951.) In the preceding year, a Development Board had been set up, which in 1951 drew up the first five-year plan. The structure, content and quality of this plan need not detain us at present, but it must be pointed out that it marked a notable departure for the economy, thanks to the steeply increased oil revenues which provided the means for substantial developmental expenditure, and to the new institutional framework which channelled this expenditure.

The period preceding 1951 was mainly one of normalisation following the war years. A survey prepared for the Board of Trade of the United Kingdom in 1949[4] sums up the economic features of the years 1946-9. This survey is particularly enlightening in presenting certain indicators regarding economic and social activity and well-being, and in evaluating economic and administrative policies relating to development in 1946. These indicators help to show how much the economy and society have moved since then. But what is more significant is that some evaluations and judgements in the survey reveal how certain basic problems remain almost as intractable today as they were then. Indeed, in one or two respects, a deterioration seems to have set in since that time. To specify, before oil revenues became the major source of revenue for the state budget, this budget was in 'a healthy state', with the non-oil sectors providing the major part of revenue — and of national income, as we shall see later upon examination of the first set of national accounts estimated by Dr K. G. Fenelon. This budgetary healthiness has never recurred, if it is ceded that over-dependence on oil revenues and the slackening of budgetary effort in the non-oil sectors are symptoms of unhealthiness. In the second place, government machinery, judged strictly on grounds of efficacy and technical performance and not on social orientation, seems to have been more adequate and effective than it was to be for many years after 1958. Lastly, the waste in land and water resources became more glaring as the years went by; paradoxically, with major irrigation and land settlement projects attempted later on, there followed a less provident use of land and water, and the land ownership pattern became even more inequitable as early attempts at land reform unfolded.

The next major landmark, and no doubt the most significant in the whole post-war period, was the revolution of 14 July 1958. The intervening years 1951-8 witnessed three significant processes: a steep increase in oil revenues and therefore in financial resources for capital and recurrent expenditure; the initiation of organised planning and the execution of several major public projects; and the equipping of the public administration with new departments and services, and with personnel at a distinctly higher level of education and training. However, the period also witnessed the gathering of ominous social and political clouds over the horizon. Paradoxically, these clouds were in part the direct outcome of some of the measures taken presumably in order to improve the well-being of the people — measures which proved counter-productive through directing the benefits to the already privileged and powerful, or through being of very indirect benefit or being very slow in fruition. In so doing, they added weight to factors and forces of discontent and even anger already in operation, which culminated in the very violent overthrow of the monarchy and the destruction of its supports, and in the installation of a republican system resting on new supports.

The pre-1958 system rested mainly on the alliance of the Palace (where the real force was the Regent Abdul Ilah, and not the youthful King Faisal II), the tribal chiefs whose loyalty to the throne was as undiluted as their interests were amply served by the alliance, and the strong man of the political system, Nuri es-Said. The army was more of an instrument than an ally, and for a few decades had shown strong Arab nationalist as well as Iraqi patriotic sentiments that often clashed with the orientation and policies of the three-angled alliance. Consistent opposition came from large segments of the urban intelligentsia — students, professionals, unemployed degree-holders, radicalised minor officials — and, less vocally or consistently, from the poor peasantry. The peasants were oppressed by onerous terms of land tenancy imposed by the landlords and their agents, the *sirkals*, and became more like hostages or slaves with the introduction of legislation in 1933 which forbade them from leaving the land while in debt to the landlords. As being in debt was almost a permanent way of life for most of the peasants, their bondage was virtually irredeemable under normal circumstances. The fate of tribesmen was no better, despite the traditionally egalitarian tribal structure. Settlement operations since 1932, which were heavily shaped by the dominant influence of tribal sheikhs, and subsequently two misdirected pieces of land reform legislations (in 1945 and 1951), which, under the guise of land settlement operations and ostensibly for the sake of convenience, registered the title of hitherto tribal land under the name of tribal sheikhs, in effect turned the tribesmen into serfs and empowered the sheikhs to impose very inequitable terms of tenancy. The few outbursts in the countryside, angry and bloody as they were, failed to make a dent in the system, and the alliance survived all attempts to explode it prior to July 1958.

The July revolution has permitted the change of many things in Iraq. It has virtually completely rearranged the social and political structure, altered the locus of power, brought social affairs and welfare into the forefront of political concern and policies, drastically altered the pattern of ownership of the means of production between the private and the public sectors (as in the case of banking, insurance and large industry) and within the private sector itself (as in the case of agricultural land as a result of land reform laws). It has also created the climate that led first to a limitation of the power and privilege of the oil companies and finally to the nationalisation of the IPC (Kirkuk fields) on 1 June 1972. (Further partial nationalisation in the BPC followed the Arab-Israeli war of October 1973.) That there has been a near-complete rearrangement of the structure of political, social and economic power, and that this rearrangement has had the declared objective *inter alia* of developing the country and raising the level of well-being of its people, but that the results have fallen short of the expectations, stands as strong evidence that the intentions have been beyond the capability of the political system. Since this system is the main designer and manager of the economy's and society's policies, it stands to reason that its shortcomings should be of decisive effect. These shortcomings are both subjective and objective, in the sense that they derive from inside (insufficient experience, struggle for personal power, inability to achieve consensus through discussion and argument, frequent political change — often with violence, factionalism) and from circumstances outside (political disputes with neighbouring countries like Iran, Syria and Jordan, civil war between the Kurds and the government forces, and the Arab-Israeli conflict). The sum total of these various influences has had a strong adverse effect on the economy and its growth and modernisation.

The year 1964 is the next major landmark. The period between 1958 and 1964 was very disturbed and deserves at least some brief reporting. Abdul-Karim Qassim, the strong man of the revolution and head of the state, had a troubled and bloody relationship at one time or another with all four groups which had been against the monarchy and supported the revolution: the Arab nationalists, the Ba'ath party, the Communists and the Army. In the end he was overpowered in February 1963 and executed. This was not all, for there was another dimension of strife: the Arab-Kurdish war, which stretched from March 1961 to February 1964, when a lull prevailed. At another level, there was controversy, though no bloodshed, between the government and the Iraq Petroleum Company. The controversy centred around several financial questions, and also around the scale of operations of the company and its concession area. Finally, in December 1961 the now-famous Decree No. 80 was issued which reclaimed more than 99.5 per cent of the concession area and left to the company only the areas actually under exploitation. The loss most felt by the IPC was that of the oilfield of North Rumeila which had been explored by the IPC and found to be extremely rich.

By 14 July 1964, the new President, who was a staunch Arab nationalist and under whom the Arab nationalist elements were effectively in power, had prepared the stage for a series of decrees that intensified the process of change in the socio-economic system. This process had been initiated in September 1958 when land reform was legislated, but — apart from Decree 80 regarding the oil concession area — nothing much else had been done. The 1964 decrees aligned the country's system with Egypt's, with which country the Iraqi President and his associates were in great nationalistic, political and ideological sympathy. Six such decrees were issued and they dealt with the formation of an economic organisation (or institution) to own and operate establishments which the public sector was to nationalise or establish; the nationalisation of insurance and re-insurance companies, and of large industrial and trading firms; the nationalisation of all private banks; the manner of allocation of the net profits of corporations and a number of other large establishments, including the setting aside of a specific share (25 per cent) for labourers and employees; the representation of labourers and employees of all industrial corporations on the boards of directors; and the limitation of the maximum size of capital ownership by any one subscriber in a corporation, as well as the incorporation of all limited liability companies whose capital went beyond a certain minimum size. These decrees paralleled the 'socialisation' decrees of Egypt of July 1961. (See chapter on Egypt.)

More political trouble, and therefore more inhibitions for the economy, were in store for the country between July 1964, when the socialisation decrees were issued, and July 1968, when the next major turning point or landmark was reached. In the intervening four years the struggle for power took a new shape by occurring now within the same political camp, as two *coups* of this nature were attempted but failed. The war with the Kurds, which had experienced a lull in February 1964, was resumed later in 1964 and continued till June 1966, when an imaginative prime minister succeeded in elaborating a reconciliation formula acceptable to both parties. The President was killed in an air crash in April 1966. His brother, who was chosen to replace him, had less popular appeal and power, thus opening the way subsequently in July 1968 to a new take-over by the Ba'ath party.

The oil sector had its share of turmoil and indecision. The areas reclaimed by Decree 80 of December 1961 were still lying idle by 1967 and the rich field at North Rumeila was not being exploited. In 1964 the Iraq National Oil Company, INOC, was formed, and it elaborated and drafted an agreement in 1965 which seemed to have a fair chance of being acceptable to the government and the IPC, but it was not signed because at the political level it was thought to be less advantageous than desired, and because of opposition outside government. And in 1967, INOC was given exclusive rights for oil exploration and exploitation in the whole of the country outside the area left for the IPC. INOC entered into agreement with ERAP, l'Entreprise de Recherches et d'Activités Petroliers of France, empowering the latter to explore for oil in four areas where the presence of oil had not been established. ERAP started exploration work in 1968. The oil sector experienced a serious set-back in the period under consideration. The oil flow across Syria was stopped by the Syrians in December 1966 subsequent to an unresolved dispute with IPC over transit dues, and was only resumed in March 1967. Soon afterwards, the flow to the United States and the United Kingdom was stopped as a result of the Arab-Israeli war of June 1967; the embargo was lifted in August of the same year.

The next turning point was July 1968. Since then the Ba'ath party has been in power, first all by itself but after the announcement of the Charter of National Action in November 1971, in association with other radical elements outside the ranks of the party. The period between July 1968 and the present has been more normal than the preceding decade, in the sense of witnessing more political stability and determination. It has thus been marked by improved economic performance and institutional organisation. Yet it has had its political and economic disruptions, particularly during the first two years. Thus, the war with the Kurds was resumed again in the second half of 1968, and remained active until a new settlement was reached in March 1970. (However, the new lull was short-lived. The strife was still at a heated level by the summer of 1974, and only ended in 1975.) Factionalism within the ruling group necessitated a few changes in government among some of its very senior members. The long search for a partner to help INOC with the exploitation of the North Rumaila oilfield ended in failure; finally INOC decided to exploit the field itself, with the help of the USSR, which signed an agreement with Iraq to that effect in July 1969. The rest of the story of oil with regard to prices and profit-sharing is the common story of all Arab and non-Arab members of OPEC, the Organization of Petroleum Exporting Countries. It culminated in agreements between OPEC and the oil companies in Teheran in February 1971 and Geneva in January 1972. As a result of these agreements the oil revenues to the Arab countries rose considerably. However, the development of Iraqi production and revenues up to October 1973 did not keep pace with the rest of the region, as we shall see later. This led to the nationalisation by Iraq of the IPC, except for the share of France (but not MPC or BPC) on 1 June 1972. This act ended a long process of indecisive irritation, always pregnant with the menace of nationalisation, that had lasted for over a decade. (The developments following October 1973 will be referred to later.)

This last period under examination has been marked by a number of major steps in the areas of land reform, social security, education and planning through the implementation of a new plan of development which is the most ambitious ever attempted. Thus, although the nationalisation of the IPC initially injected a new element of uncertainty with respect to the marketing of oil and the compensation of IPC, the pressure of world demand for oil has reversed the situation and created a 'sellers' market'. The economy began in 1972/3 on the whole to be tangibly healthier than it had been for many years, and seemed to stand with its horizons clear and its landscape in order. Since then, the situation has become much more promising with the vastly increased oil revenues after October 1973, and the intelligent and determined efforts to achieve development speedily and with balance. Perhaps we can sum up the management of the economy today as being realistic and pragmatic, though the leadership is steeped in ideology in the political and social realms. The marriage between realism and ideology does not seem to be uneasy. If it lasts, Iraq can bring much of its economic promise to fruition in a relatively short period. The crucial question remains the quality of political management and the intelligent mobilisation of manpower skills.

2. THE RECORD

The thirty years since World War Two have witnessed important change on a wide front in the Iraqi economy, although this change has not been translated into equally tangible change in the level of personal income and well-being. As we proceed with the examination of the record of the economy and society, and more particularly as we examine the determinants of development in the second volume of this book, we will have a firmer grasp of the causes for the discrepancy. Our present examination will move from the particular, that is from specific sectors or areas, to the general or global manifest mainly in the national accounts.

Population and Manpower

The first modern population census relates to the year 1947 (but was published in 1955), according to which the population then numbered over 4.8 million. According to FAO experts,[5] the returns of this census cannot be accepted and have to be corrected. After rectification, the total reaches 5.2m, and becomes consistent with the findings of the more accurate census of 1957 which returned a total population of 6.5m. The number rose to 8.097m according to the census of 1965. Since then there have been yearly estimates, the latest being that for mid-1973, set at 10.41m. The rate of population increase has varied over time, according to certain Iraqi economists.[6] It is thus believed that the rate rose from a range of 1.3–1.77 per cent for the period 1867–1935, to about 1.94 per cent for the period lying between the first two censuses, to 2.79 per cent for the late fifties, to 3.1 or 3.2 per cent currently. The last two rates quoted are very high indeed.

The Iraqis are divided into three categories: urban, rural and nomadic. According to the first census, the urban population (defined as those living in centres having more than 5,000 inhabitants) accounted for 36 per cent of the total; while the rural population accounted for 59 per cent and the nomadic population for 5 per cent. Obviously, since the whole census is under question, these ratios must be taken as very tentative. Nevertheless there is a clear trend of urbanisation between 1947 and 1973, with the ratio of rural (including bedouin) to urban changing from 64:36 per cent for the year 1947, to 38.6:61.4 per cent for 1973.[7] Again according to FAO estimates, the urban population has been growing at a rate distinctly higher than the rural population, which would explain both the fast rise in the rate of growth and that in the rate of urbanisation — the latter being also influenced by the movement from the countryside to the cities and towns. The age distribution is more skewed than that of other fast-growing Arab countries; Iraqis in the age groups 0–19 years constitute about three-fifths of the population (58.6 per cent to be exact).

Illiteracy is high in Iraq, but the country is making fast progress in the field of education. In the early sixties the rate of illiteracy was 70 per cent for both sexes among Iraqis between 15 and 24 years of age (55 per cent for males and 84 per cent for females) — only Jordan, Lebanon, Libya and Syria having lower rates of illiteracy.[8] However, according to more recent information, by 1965 the rate had dropped to 56.4 per cent for both sexes (38.2 per cent for males, 75.0 per cent for females).[9] It would seem that despite the growing acceptance of women's education, their level is still lower than men's, judging by the greater drop in male than in female illiteracy.

The earliest data on manpower and the labour force relate to 1947. According to the census of that year, the size of manpower can be deduced from the number of inhabitants between 10 and 49 years of age. The labour force actually employed is considerably smaller than the manpower. According to the same census, this force numbered 1.315m, of whom 57 per cent were in the primary, 7.3 per cent in the secondary, and 35.7 per cent in the tertiary sectors or activities.[10] Neither the definition of manpower adopted nor the actual count are satisfactory, and reliance on these data must therefore be qualified. Another account of 'persons engaged' relating to 1956 adopted another definition according to which 'housewives and other women engaged in domestic duties, children below school age, soldiers and retired persons not in receipt of government pensions' were excluded.[11] This account set the number of persons engaged at 2.046m. In addition, students at all levels and government pensioners and disabled persons together totalled 570,000. The grand total of 2.616m represents about 41 per cent of the population estimated at 6.35m for 1956. Later, more reliable estimates suggest that this ratio is too high. The estimate for 1956 is based on data obtained in a number of censuses conducted between 1952 and 1956, as well as on estimates made by Fenelon, the author of the source to which the manpower data relate.

Two sets of data on the labour force and the number actually employed for the decade of the sixties are available. The one appears in the *Annual Abstract of Statistics 1970* for the years 1960 to 1970;[12] the other appears in the authoritative three-volume study of Jawad Hashim, Hussein Omar and Ali al-Manoufi.[13] The discrepancy between the two sources is not negligible, but we have an explanation at hand. Both series suggest that the size of the labour force as a proportion of population has been rising very slightly over the years, from 28.2 per cent to just over 29 per cent. This is more tenable than earlier estimates, and probably the confusion between a mechanistic definition of manpower as all people within a certain age range and the actual labour force has been avoided. The number actually engaged according to the two series suggests that the unemployed constitute a small fraction of the labour force, somewhere between 3 and 5 per cent. This low rate suggests at the same time that data on employment do not take into account the various degrees of fullness of employment, and that Iraq is not overpopulated, even given its low level of technology and capital availability.

More recent information (relating to 1973) became available in 1974. It is useful to record it side by side with information averaged for the years 1960-9, in tabular form. The original data on which the first column in Table 2.1 has been based show that very little absolute change occurred in any of the sectors over the decade 1960-9. Likewise, no dramatic change has occurred in 1973. Indeed, the margin of error in the estimates (and they are nothing else) is on the whole larger than the differences registered over the fourteen years covered. It would be unwarranted and unsafe therefore to comment on the variations from one column to the other. Two observations can be made. The first is the modesty of the proportion of the labour force engaged in manufacturing, despite the efforts made in the

Table 2.1: Distribution of the Labour Force by Sector Averaged for the Years 1960-9, and for 1973 (per cent)

Sector	Average 1960-9	1973
Agriculture	53.45	52.00
Quarrying and mining	0.58	0.63
Manufacturing	5.98	5.74
Electricity, water and gas	0.54	0.48
Construction	2.54	2.46
Trade	5.35	5.54
Transport and communications	5.56	5.47
Services (including government), and others	21.87	20.93
Persons actually employed	95.87	93.25
Unemployment	4.13	6.75
Total labour force	100.00	100.00

Sources: Average calculated from Jawad Hashem, Hussein Omar and Ali Al-Menoufi, *Evaluation of Economic Growth in Iraq 1950-1970* (Baghdad, 1971, Arabic), Vol. 1, Table 13; p. 278. *Annual Abstract of Statistics 1973*, p. 358, for 1973.

sixties and early seventies to expand this sector. It is probable that the new manufacturing units are highly capital-intensive. The second observation is the rise in the proportion of the unemployed, despite increased activity in the economy. One possible explanation is improved reporting; another is increased urbanisation parallel with the sluggish increase in job opportunities to match.

Land, Water and Agriculture

1. *Land:* The total land area of Iraq is 438,446 square kilometres (including territorial waters of 924 sq. km.). Out of this total, some 167,000 sq. km. are desert land along the western and southern extremities of the country, while 92,000 sq. km. are mountainous to the north and east of the country, and some 175,000 sq. km. are hills and flat areas in between the two major rivers, the Tigris and the Euphrates. Broadly speaking, from the point of view of type of agriculture, the country is divided into three categories: uncultivated desert, rain-fed area, lying in the north and north-east, down approximately to the centre of the country, and irrigated area between the two rivers. The examination of land use will clarify this division further.

It is interesting that studies a quarter of a century apart, like Doreen Warriner's, which used data from an Iraqi source published in 1944, Hashem *et al.* writing in 1970, and reports written in the intervening years like the World Bank's *The Economic Development of Iraq*[14] should quote approximately the same figures regarding the areas of cultivable land and very similar figures regarding areas of cultivated land. This would suggest that nothing has happened to turn more of the non-cultivable into cultivable land, and much more of the cultivable into actually cultivated land. The total cultivated and cultivable areas, according to Warriner, stood then as shown in Table 2.2.

Table 2.2: Estimate of Land Use, 1947 (sq. km.)

Rainfall zone	
Cultivable and cultivated	41,000
Cropped	6,000
Irrigation zone	
Cultivable and cultivated	80,000
Cropped	17,000
Total cultivable land	121,000
Total cropped land	23,000

Source: Doreen Warriner, *Land and Poverty in the Middle East* (London, 1948), p. 101.

The figures in the World Bank report, and in Hashem *et al.*, are very close to each other in so far as cultivable and cropped areas are concerned, but vary with regard to cultivated area (namely cropped plus lying fallow under the system prevailing in much of the country). A comparison in Table 2.3 of the two sets of figures shows the similarity and the difference.

Table 2.3: 1952 and 1971 Estimates of Land Use (sq. km.)

	IBRD	Hashem *et al.*
Cultivable area	120,250	120,250
Irrigation zone	80,250	
Rain-fed zone	40,000	
Area actually in crops	27,750	29,500
Irrigation zone	19,000	
Rain-fed zone	8,750	
Area under cultivation	43,750	57,500

Source: IBRD, *Economic Development of Iraq* (Baltimore, 1952), p. 137; Hashem *et al.*, *Evaluation of Economic Growth in Iraq*, pp. 3-6 and 26.

A quick glance at the three sets of data (and more sets can be cited, as for instance in Hassan's *Studies in the Iraqi Economy*) reveals that the estimate of cultivable area has remained static, while that of the area actually under crops has risen and that of the cultivated area has risen even more. However, the increase in the area cropped remains far behind the increase in population during the same quarter-century. Despite this lag, the land-man ratio in Iraq is better than in most Arab countries, particularly if it is kept in mind that Iraq is in addition richly endowed with water resources, and with petroleum to provide the finance for agricultural development.

The area of cultivable land per person now amounts to 1.233 hectares, contrasted with 0.1 ha in Egypt. Perhaps a more significant ratio would be that of actually cropped area to rural inhabitant, which would give us 0.7 ha per person, or 1.4 ha if total cultivated area (that is, actually cropped plus lying fallow) is taken as the base instead of actually cropped area. In any case, the land-man account is favourable on the strength of area. But serious qualifications have to be introduced. One, favourable to the account, relates to the large proportion of cultivable to total land area, which is over a quarter, and of irrigable to cultivable area, which is roughly two-thirds. Unfavourable qualifications relate to the current faulty practices which permit a great deal of wastage in land and in water, and result in the curtailment of the area cultivable and increase in salinity — to say nothing of primitive farming techniques and the application of extensive farming practices where intensive farming is both called for and possible. Finally, it remains to be pointed out that the area actually cropped is just under a quarter of the cultivable area, a fact which underlines the wastage in land resources.

The land tenure system is rather complicated in Iraq. The complication has not been cleared upon the completion of land settlement operations. Between 1933 and the end of 1969, when the old land settlement system was abolished upon the issue of the new Law of Agrarian Reform No. 117 of 1970, a total of 97,484,469 Iraqui dunoms, or mesharas, each of which is equal to 2.5 metric dunoms or .25 of one hectare, had been covered by settlement operations. This area is equivalent to 243,711 sq. km., or about 54 per cent of the total area of the country. The distribution of the area by type of land tenure is given in Table 2.4.

Table 2.4: Land Settlement, 1969

Type	Area (sq. km.)
Mulk	4,157
Matruka	18,391
Waqf	2,221
Miri granted in Tapu	33,400
Miri granted in Lazmah	30,417
Miri Sirf	155,124
Total settled	243,710

Source: *Annual Abstract of Statistics 1970*, Table 14, p.41.

An explanation of the various categories of land tenure is in order at this point. The definition goes back in 1932 when a new law, meant to give clarity to the cadastral survey about to be inaugurated, recognised the following types of tenure:[15]

Mamloukah or *Mulk*: land held in absolute private ownership.

Matruka: land reserved for public purposes.

Waqf or *Mawqufa*: land which is administered in trust (1) for the benefit of religious institutions by the state *Awqaf* administration, or (2) for the benefit of private persons by *mutawallis* appointed by religious courts. This type of *Waqf* must be distinguished from so-called untrue *Waqf*, namely property from which the taxes or revenue were in the past assigned to religious institutions by the Turkish government.

Miri Tapu: land held in permanent tenure from the state under conditions enabling the holder to sell or mortgage it and leave it to his successors. Proof of such tenure may be supplied by documentary evidence or by factual evidence that the land has been used productively by the holder or his predecessor for ten years during which no land rent was paid or that it has been planted with trees meeting specified conditions.

Miri Lazmah: land held under generally the same conditions as *Miri Tapu*, but with the stipulation that the government may veto the transfer of such land if it tends to disturb the peace, a precaution designed to prevent, where necessary, the transfer of tribal lands to people outside the tribe. *Lazmah* grants are made upon proof that a person has made productive use of the land within the preceding fifteen years.

Miri Sirf: particularly vacant or idle land, definitely acknowledged as belonging *de facto* or *de jure* to the state.

These categories have remained more or less unaltered since then, although new land laws have been put into effect in 1938 and in each of the succeeding decades.

A great deal has been written about the very inequitable pattern of land distribution in Iraq before the measures of agrarian reform of September 1958, and further back still, and of the very harsh conditions of tenancy and land exploitation imposed on tenants and tribesmen. Perhaps Doreen Warriner has contributed most to an exposition of the situation in her early study, *Land and Poverty in the Middle East,* and in subsequent studies. Mohammad Salman Hassan has also ably analysed land problems in his *Studies in the Iraqi Economy*. However, the fullest and most recent treatment of the subject of land tenure, distribution of land holdings and land reform is contained in Abdul-Wahhab Mutar al-Dahiri's *The Economics of Agrarian Reform.*[16] Doreen Warriner in her *Land Reform and Development in the Middle East*[17] presents the distribution by size of holding of 125,045 holdings, while the IBRD report, already cited, presents the distribution of private land holdings according to the cadastral survey, where the various sizes of holdings are given as a proportion of the total area surveyed. According to Miss Warriner's data (taken from the *Report on the Agricultural and Livestock Census of Iraq, 1952-3),* out of a total 125,045 holdings, 24,270 were under 1 hectare in area, while 104 were 5,000 ha or over. Unfortunately, the total area owned in each category of holdings is not given, as the case is in al-Dahiri's (and Hashem's) data. Because the latter sources are the most instructive, as well as the most comprehensive, we reproduce their table on land distribution below in Table 2.5. From this table it can be seen that the average holding consisted of about 31.7 ha, but around this average there is very wide dispersion. Thus, owners (or holdings) with over 250 ha represented 1.7 per cent of total owners (or holdings), but 63.1 per cent of the total area involved. On the other hand, 83.9 per cent of owners (holdings) fell below the average area of holdings, ranging between a fraction of one hectare and 30 ha. In all, this category represented only 15.3 per cent of total area involved.

The table is very expressive in itself. However, the source cited goes on to indicate that the peasants who own no land but work as share tenants or agricultural labourers number some 3 million. The obvious overstatement in this number notwithstanding, it underlines the very inequitable pattern of land distribution in Iraq. (It remains to be added that this source uses the terms 'holding' and 'landowner' interchangeably, though this need not be the case.) The area covered by the table, 80,412 sq. km., is only 18 per cent of the total land area of the country, but 28 per cent of the non-desert area. It is therefore a very large sample and is representative of the whole pattern of land-holding. It must be pointed out, however, that large land-holding was (in 1957) more characteristic of the irrigated south than of the rain-fed areas of Mosul, Suleimaniyah and Erbil.

The picture of the share tenant's situation adds grimness to that of his minute land holding. Until the first serious agrarian reform measure was decreed in 1958, the picture was

Table 2.5: Distribution of Land Holdings (Landowners) by Size, 1957

Siz Intervals (ha)	No. of Holdings (Owners)	Per Cent of Total	Total Area (ha)	Per Cent of Total
Less than 0.25	23,089	9.12	2,130	0.03
0.25— 1.00	50,021	19.75	23,430	0.29
1.25— 2.50	40,475	15.98	60,751	0.76
2.75— 7.50	48,469	19.14	207,576	2.58
7.75— 15.00	30,367	11.99	313,271	3.90
15.25— 30.00	20,184	7.97	622,826	7.74
30.25— 75.00	29,137	11.51	845,194	10.51
75.25— 125.00	4,284	1.69	395,221	4.92
125.25— 250.00	2,916	1.15	498,108	6.19
250.25— 500.00	1,832	0.72	640,047	7.96
500.25— 1,000.00	1,293	0.51	895,993	11.14
1,000.25— 2,500.00	835	0.33	1,241,598	15.44
2,500.25— 5,000.00	224	0.09	757,693	9.42
5,000.25—12,500.00	95	0.04	749,652	9.32
12,500.25—25,000.00	25	0.01	431,497	5.37
Over 25,000.00	8	0.00	356,206	4.43
Total	253,254	100.00	8,041,193	100.00

Note: Percentage columns not included in al-Dahiri. We have re-arranged the size intervals to be in terms of hectares, not Iraqi dunoms.
Source: Abdul Wahab M. al-Dahiri, *Economics of Agrarian Reform* (Baghdad, 1970; Arabic), p.168, and Hashem *et al.*, Vol.II, p.29.

one of exploitation, oppression, poverty and helplessness. Thus, although the tenant's share of the produce varied from one type of cultivation to another, being lowest where the landlord's outlay was largest, it was invariably small, ranging between one-fifth or one-fourth for his labour, to a mere one-fourteenth or even one-twentieth in pump-irrigated areas, always assuming the peasant has contributed nothing but his manual labour.[18] The tenant was oppressed by the landlord himself or his agent, the *sirkal*, both of whom required the tenant to perform, free of charge, certain functions for them, and generally addressed and treated the tenant as a serf. This landlord-serf relationship existed *de facto*, but had been formalised in 1933 by a law which prohibited the labourer from leaving the land while in debt to the landlord.[19] Few tenants could be found free of debt, except in years of specially good harvests or in periods of inflation, as for instance during World War Two.

The poverty is the result of low productivity, unduly small share in the final produce, weakness in the face of the landowner and *sirkal*, and the absence of benefits in kind that could reduce the dependence on cash or share income. The political power of the landlords and the ignorance and low productivity of the tenants made sure that the situation remained unalleviated. Their helplessness was almost complete, and the few outbreaks of violence were too ineffectual to weaken the grip of the landlords. This power had been strengthened after the introduction in 1932 of a new land settlement law, under which the old system where the tribal sheikhs held land in the name of the tribe and got a certain share of the produce to enable them to perform certain functions (law and order, hospitality, justice, representation) on behalf of the tribe, was disturbed. Thereafter, land was registered in the personal name of the sheikh, supposedly as a continuation of the old system, but in effect as an expression of the new awareness of the sheikhs of the power of a money economy. This awareness grew as new irrigation schemes were implemented and the value of land rose, whetting their appetite for more land. The more land they thus obtained, the stronger politically they became and the less challengeable. Initially, the tribe was not eager for the land to be registered in individual tribesmen's names, for fear that this would lead to military conscription of their males once their names were in the books. By the time the tribesmen had become wiser and more fully aware of the implications of the new development, it was too late and the registration in the names of the sheikhs far advanced.

The sheikhs added to the strength of their hold by making investments in the land, mostly in the form of pumps and other machines, and irrigation canals. But, as Miss Warriner puts it, they were on the whole mere miners of the land, concerned that it should give them the maximum produce with the minimum outlay within a very short-sighted time horizon. 'Thus', she concludes in 1948, 'the bulk of the land has come into the hands of a class from whom no leadership in agricultural methods can be expected and which is tyrannous, callous, and oppressive.'[20] The situation seemed hopeless to the tenants and agricultural labourers in the summer of 1958. This was the setting to the serious reform measures which were introduced soon after the revolution of that summer.

2. Water: The abundance of river water in Iraq, valuable as it is, instead of providing a palliative to the land problem, in some respects accentuated it. It weakened the urgency of this problem and made the search for solutions less insistent. It also adversely influenced land use, as we have already indicated, and we will discuss this further when we come to the subject of irrigation.

Iraq's major rivers are the Tigris and the Euphrates, with an average annual flow of 38.8 billion cubic metres and 26.4 billion cubic metres respectively. The Diala, Lesser Zab, Greater Zab and Adhaim rivers flow into the Tigris between Mosul and Baghdad. The attempt to harness and utilise this great water wealth is millennia old, and the remains of irrigation canals from the days of antiquity are still in evidence, reflecting great engineering knowledge and sound planning. The old network was finally destroyed by the Mongols in 1257.

It is true of the days of antiquity, as of today, that irrigation from river water is necessary because rainfall is inadequate. Thus, normal rainfall, that is the average for the years 1940-70, is 392mm, or under 16 inches, with the months June to September having an overall average of 0.4 in. each.[21] The bad distribution of rainfall is not merely from month to month, but also from region to region. Rainfall is mostly concentrated in the mountainous region in the north and north-east. Serious reconstruction work of dams and barrages to harness the rivers and utilise their waters started early in the twentieth century. Thus, the Hindiya barrage which required the diversion of the Euphrates was built over the years 1911-15. The Kut barrage on the Tigris was completed in 1919. Other major works had to wait until the fifties when increased oil revenues made construction work possible. Table 2.6 below presents an up-to-date summary of the dams and regulators in Iraq. Three new reservoirs were included in the development plan for the years 1965-9. One of these is the Mosul dam on the Tigris (capacity 13.5 billion cm), Haditha dam on the Euphrates (made necessary by the building of a dam in Turkey and another in Syria), and the Himrin dam on Diala River for a reallocation of the Der-Bendi-Khan dam waters after the electrification of the last dam.

The purpose of waterworks is multiple: to regulate the flow of the rivers, to control floods (such as the Habbaniya Lake and the Abu Dibis depression), to act as reservoirs to

Table 2.6: Dams and Regulators in Iraq

Dam or Regulator	Type of Construction	Capacity of Reservoir to Discharge Water (cms/second)	Height (metres)	Length (metres)
Hindiya barrage	Bricks	2,900	7.7	248
Diyala dam	Concrete	4,000	12.0	472
Kut barrage	Concrete	6,000	10.5	692
Al-Majarra regulator	Concrete	1,700	12.0	67
Dibban regulator	Concrete	400	12.0	42
Warrar regulator	Concrete	2,850	10.0	196
Ramadi barrage	Concrete	3,600	10.0	209
Samarra barrage	Concrete	10,000	12.0	252
Dokan dam	Concrete	4,600	116.5	360
Der-Bendi Khan dam	Rockfill	11,400	128.0	535
Al-Gharraf regulator	Concrete	450	9.0	68
Tharthar regulator	Concrete	9,000	7.0	502

Notes: The capacity of each of the five major water reservoirs at the level indicated is detailed below:

	Capacity in billion cm	Area in sq. km.
Der-Bendi Khan	3.00 at level of 485 metres	120
Dokan	6.80 at level of 511 metres	270
Tharthar	85.00 at level of 65 metres	2,700
Habbaniya Lake	3.25 at level of 51 metres	430
Abu Dibis	25.50 at level of 40 metres	1,850

Source: *Annual Abstract of Statistics 1973*, Table 86 and Table 87, p.147.

even out the flow of water over the year and from year to year, and to generate electricity. They have been very useful in all four functions. The shortcomings accompanying the irrigation system arise later on, through the improper use of water and land in combination, and the inadequacy of drainage. The water thus stored provides flow irrigation. In addition to dams, there were 25,482 artesian wells and 13,769 pumps (with a total horsepower of 366,751) by 1970, and 15,734 pumps by 1973. The pumps have increased considerably over the years, from 143 in 1921, and 3,775 in 1950/1, to the present high level. The irrigation system as a whole has led to the vast expansion in the area irrigated. Thus, while in 1953 some 5.6m ha were under irrigation (or five times the area in 1918), the irrigation area rose to 8m ha in 1970. Out of this total, approximately 2.8m ha are actually cropped from year to year, which shows that huge potential exists for the expansion of irrigated agriculture. (Out of the area cropped, some 1.7m ha are irrigated by flow, and 1.1m ha by pump.) A further 2.25m ha can be brought under irrigation if more projects are undertaken to bring flow water into maximum utilisation.[22]

However, concern with irrigation has not, until recently, been matched by equal concern with drainage. This has proved near catastrophic for two reasons: the high level of salinity in the soil and water, and the flatness of the irrigation zone which militates against natural drainage. Failure to attend to drainage, or inhibition because of its high cost per unit of land, have resulted in the neglect of drainage and therefore in the impairment of much of the land which has become highly encrusted with salt. But whatever the reasons, to neglect drainage has meant an invitation to agricultural disaster or near disaster in many areas. Furthermore, nobody can claim to have been surprised by events, since the ancient Iraqis seem to have been aware of the need for drainage and to have installed the necessary networks.

In recent years, many writers have drawn attention to the need for drainage and to the dire consequences if the need were to be left unsatisfied: Lord Salter in his *Development of Iraq*, Doreen Warriner, especially in *Land Reform and Development in the Middle East*, the Food and Agriculture Organization in *Iraq: Country Report*, the World Bank's *The Economic Development of Iraq*, Hashem et al. in their *Evaluation of Economic Growth in Iraq, 1950-1970*, and many official reports mainly for internal circulation. The growing awareness and concern with drainage are being increasingly reflected in development plans, as well as in the deliberations of the competent authorities. In spite of the handicaps which the flatness of the land constitutes, a master plan for drainage has been conceived and is presently under implementation, with the existing unco-ordinated drainage works feeding into it.[23] The significance of drainage cannot be overemphasised. Estimates of the damage done because of failure to undertake drainage vary, but conservatively they refer to 20 – 30 per cent of the irrigation area having been deserted and become derelict after its salination surpassed the limit at which even as hardy a crop as barley could be grown. In addition, other areas are still being exploited, but salinity is rising dangerously in them. It would seem that drainage work must now acquire a higher place in the ladder of priorities than irrigation.

3. Agriculture: The performance of the agricultural sector (which contributes 19.1 per cent of gross domestic product, or 22.5 of gross national product) accords it second place in the economy on the basis of contribution. However, as in the case of other agricultural countries, the sector's significance must be understood via the employment it provides and the size of the community engaged in it, in addition to the contribution. This would place agriculture at the head of the list of sectors. Yet the performance itself must be related to the expanse of land under the plough, the availability of water, the institutional set-up relating to the sector, the investments made in agriculture, the degree of mechanisation and the use of fertilisers, and the number and technical skills of the rural population.

Some of these factors would suggest that the performance has been poor; some others, such as the low technical level of the farmers, that it has been fairly good. On balance, we are inclined to consider the performance as distinctly poor, if we are not to take a fatalistic attitude which would suggest that the determining factors being what they are, the performance cannot but be what it is. This would ignore the impact of human will which could vary the factors involved. This is true at the level of the policy-makers who influence the institutional framework and the availability of credit and selected seeds, and of tractors and fertilisers, as at the level of the farmers themselves who could organise themselves in co-operatives and could, through being more open to new ideas, help raise their productivity and improve the marketability of their produce.

Probably an examination of the average production per unit of land is as good a criterion of performance as any. This could be done for various crops over time for Iraq, or for the same year for Iraq and other countries. Comparisons over time are not easy to make, as the quality of the produce may vary, or the price structure may change in such a way as to make the comparison of little significance. However, notwithstanding these difficulties and others relating to insufficient statistical information, we find, on a rule-of-thumb basis (by comparing data for the years 1947/8—1949/50 with data for the first three years of the seventies) that there have been improvements in the produce per unit of land for most crops. Likewise, the area planted has increased for most crops. Yet population has grown parallel with agricultural expansion, such that on balance the lot of Iraqi peasants is only a little better than it was a quarter of a century ago.

A more convenient comparison to conduct would be over the decade of the sixties, since comparable data exist for the years in question. Leaving wheat and barley aside, it would seem that both winter and summer crops have a tendency to have been grown on a wider area of land and to have produced an increasing output per unit of land, although there is variation — in some instances wide — within the decade. (In the case of wheat and barley, the evidence is not conclusive, and the expansion can only be moderate.) A more precise way of summing up the course is by presenting index number series for the main crops. A number of these exist, with different base years or coming from different sources. They will be grouped together into Table 2.7 below. From this table we can see that on the whole there is progress in unit production, despite the variations within groups and within the decade. (The most recent *Annual Abstract of Statistics* for 1973 does not present such series as the 1970 edition did.)

However important these index numbers are, we are at least equally interested in the welfare aspect of agricultural development. This necessitates an examination of the progress of total agricultural and animal production. A summary of the change in the value of the major components of these two categories is reproduced in Table 2.8 in the form of index numbers for the years 1962-9, with 1962 as the base year.

Comparison of performance spanning a longer period of time but in less detail is possible through the perusal of the annual editions of the FAO *Production Yearbook*. (In the present instance, the editions of 1967 and 1972 have been used.) The performance of the economy is tabulated in index numbers in Table 2.9.

The two tabulations read together show that the performance in the period 1961-5 to 1972 has been uniformly better than that for the period 1952-6 to 1966. (It is necessary to point out however that the first tabulation is in terms of monetary value of produce, whereas the second is in terms of volume of production. The latter is distinctly more useful for our purposes, both on grounds of performance and of welfare.)

It would seem legitimate to conclude from both sets of data that the progress is not spectacular if Iraq's potential is borne in mind. It is also obvious that the increase in production has not kept pace with the natural increase in population. In the case of the value of agricultural production, the category of foodstuffs, vegetables, fruits and dates has shown an average compound growth rate of about 3 per cent per annum, which is about equal to the growth rate of the population over the years 1962-9. Animal products show a better record with an average rate of growth of 5 per cent per annum. The overall average, which is the most significant for our purposes, is just under 4 per cent and is uncomfortably close to the rate of natural increase of population. The latter set of data shows a more comfortable situation, with distinct gains even on a *per capita* basis. This analysis attempts to establish that the sector of agriculture was rather stagnant for a number of years following 1958, but that it has become more productive since then. But this judgement is inconclusive by itself, since it does not relate total production to total area cropped and yield per unit of land. Regrettably, enough detailed information is not available to permit such multi-dimensional examination.

Iraq

Table 2.7: Index Numbers of the Yield per Dunom, 1960-9

Crop	1960	1961	1962	1963	1964	1965	1966	1967	1968	1969
			(A) 1960 = 100							
1. Field crops	100.0	117.6	127.3	103.6	90.9	110.1	98.6	106.3	121.3	128.3
(a) Winter	100.0	122.4	131.9	104.6	88.8	109.8	97.6	103.1	119.0	127.8
(b) Summer	100.0	76.7	88.1	95.1	108.5	112.6	107.3	133.9	141.3	133.3
2. Vegetables	100.0	98.6	106.8	107.5	106.2	115.0	113.3	126.5	114.4	116.2
(a) Winter	100.0	123.6	156.2	157.5	112.1	169.0	159.2	181.6	161.9	158.7
(b) Summer	100.0	93.6	96.9	97.5	105.0	104.2	104.1	115.5	104.9	107.7
3. Four principal crops (wheat, barley, shelled rice, and cotton)[a]	100.0	118.8	129.0	103.9	89.1	109.0	97.3	104.9	120.8	128.9
4. Dates	100.0	109.5	126.0	101.6	92.8	56.4	73.9	75.2	60.1	—
		(B) 1966 = 100								
1. Field crops	101.4	119.8	130.0	105.5	92.9	112.3	100.0	107.9	125.2	129.8
(a) Winter	101.9	125.7	135.2	107.1	92.3	113.5	100.0	105.0	123.3	129.5
(b) Summer	92.9	70.1	81.7	89.7	101.2	104.6	100.0	125.7	131.6	120.0
2. Vegetables	90.5	87.2	94.2	95.1	96.0	101.5	100.0	110.5	100.9	102.6
(a) Winter	67.0	77.1	99.7	101.8	73.9	107.2	100.0	109.7	103.1	101.5
(b) Summer	95.7	89.5	93.0	93.6	100.9	100.2	100.0	110.7	100.4	102.9
3. Dates	135.4	148.2	170.6	137.6	125.6	76.4	100.0	101.8	81.4	—
4. Four principal crops[b]	—	—	—	—	—	—	100.0	109.8	134.8	118.3
5. Four principal crops[c]	102.1	121.5	132.1	106.5	92.9	112.8	100.0	107.9	125.9	131.6

Notes: a. According to data of Ministry of Agriculture.
b. According to data of the Central Statistical Organization.
c. According to data of Ministry of Agriculture.

Source: *Annual Abstract of Statistics, 1970,* Table 39, p. 95 (as Section (A) above), and Table 40, p. 96 (as Section (B) above).

Table 2.8: Relative Values of Agricultural and Animal Production, 1962 and 1969

	1962	1969
1. Foodstuffs, vegetables, fruits and dates		
(a) Foodstuffs	100.0	101.8
(b) Vegetables	100.0	209.5
(c) Fruits and dates	100.0	97.0
Sub-total of category 1	100.0	124.0
2. Animal products		
(a) Dairy products	100.0	134.2
(b) Meat	100.0	146.8
(c) Hides, wool, eggs	100.0	174.2
(d) Other items	100.0	100.5
Sub-total of category 2	100.0	140.5
Total	100.0	130.8

Source: Hashem et al., *Evaluation of Economic Growth in Iraq*, Vol. II, Table 15, p. 41.

Table 2.9: Economic Performance 1952-72

	1952-56 Average	1966	1961-65 Average	1972
Total agricultural production	Base (100)	127	Base (100)	180
Total food production	Base (100)	127	Base (100)	184
Per capita total production	Base (100)	89	Base (100)	133
Per capita food production	Base (100)	89	Base (100)	135

Source: FAO, *Production Yearbook 1967*, pp. 27-30, and *Production Yearbook 1972*, pp. 28, 30, 32 and 34.

When we come to the study of the national accounts of Iraq, we will find out that until the end of the sixties agriculture was the second among the three slowest-growing sectors — along with ownership of dwellings, which was the slowest, and crude oil. (That the crude oil sector should be among the slow-moving sectors should not come as a surprise, considering the tribulations of the oil industry and its untypical course if the other oil-producing Arab countries are taken as the reference group.) The stagnation, or even the modest progress of agriculture, seen against its vast potential, suggests that attention must first be turned to this sector for the solution of its problems and the acceleration of its growth.

The problems are economic, technical, institutional and organisational. But above all, they are political, in the sense that what is first needed is the correct vision, at the policy-maker's level, of the entirety of the problem, and the understanding of the right type of action needed. Considering that the state plays an even greater role now than it did before 1958 with regard to the management of the agricultural sector (and, indeed, of the whole economy) in the fields of ownership and reallocation of ownership, the provision of more credit and other inputs, the setting up of machine workshops, the founding of co-operatives, the provision of extension and marketing services, as well as in the fields of research, planning and follow-up, and finally in irrigation and drainage, it becomes of primary importance to relate the quality of government, particularly in connection with continuity and stability, to agriculture. It is essential to point out here that a distinction ought to be made between government's technical and administrative role, and its political role as the creator of the framework within which the technical and administrative functions are to be performed. It is this latter role which has been especially defective.

Because of the accumulation of misjudgement and mismanagement in the past, and particularly because of the bias of government before the revolution of 1958 in favour of the landlord and against the poor tenant, the government has until recently had low credibility as an initiator and vehicle of reform. It is precisely this credibility that should be raised, and it can only be raised if the government succeeds through its planning, policies and acts in carrying conviction in the eyes of the farmers. Then it can also enjoy authority and solicit co-operation. Up till now, the farmer's attitude has been mainly one of disbelief in the government's intentions and capability; he extends the minimum of co-operation yet expects a great deal from the very government he suspects. It may sound paradoxical, yet it is true that more self-help on the part of the farmers will only come if the government itself has first undertaken a great deal of corrective work and has succeeded in carrying it through. Only then will the efforts to draw out more self-reliance succeed, because only then will the plea for more effort by the farmers themselves be plausible, since the plea would have been preceded by convincingly effective work on the part of government.

The agricultural problems of Iraq fall into two broad categories with respect to the locus of these problems: those problems relating to agricultural land which has not been touched by agrarian reform; and those relating to agrarian reform areas. The first category comprises the conventional weaknesses of primitive technology,[24] incorrect crop rotation (or the non-existence altogether of such rotation), incorrect utilisation of water, incorrect degree of intensity of agriculture in the irrigated zone, insufficient development of the co-operative movement and therefore the absence or inadequacy of co-operative credit, extension and marketing services, and inadequate draining in the irrigation zone. The government can be instrumental in the correction of all these defects, even those that mostly or totally reflect shortcomings of the farmers themselves. As to the second category of problems, these will be discussed within the context of the evaluation to be made of agrarian reform undertaken since 1958. But it can be said at the outset that some of the problems are common and some specific, but that in both categories, the key to the correction of the defects is the government. We cannot overestimate the importance of the political management of the economy in Iraq.

Before we move on to the next sector, we should indicate that the government has made considerable investment in the agricultural sector since 1951, when the Development Board began operations, until the present. These investments were mostly in flood control schemes, regulators, dams and reservoirs, as well as in irrigation networks and to a much lesser extent in drainage networks. A more modest investment was made in agricultural machinery and workshops for maintenance and repair, in laboratories, experimental farms and state farms, in rural roads and similar items. The preponderant share has gone to projects which require a very long time for fruition. Furthermore, substantial as the investments have been, they invariably fell far short of the financial allocations made for agriculture. These allocations in turn varied in size, depending on the availability of funds for the whole plan and on the system of priorities adopted at the time. (See section 4 below.) That the investments made have not resulted in a more spectacular rise in the returns of the sector is partly caused by the failure to spend as much effort and money on other necessary purposes (like drainage), partly because in their nature these investments require a long gestation period, and partly because the more subtle and elusive administrative, organisational and technical improvements did not move as fast and grow in as large a volume as physical investments.[25]

Petroleum[26]

Examined against gross national product (or gross domestic product), public revenue and foreign exchange earnings, petroleum is very important in the economic life of Iraq, but not as significant as it is in Kuwait, Saudi Arabia or Libya. This is mainly because, relatively speaking, Iraq enjoys more resources, has other not unimportant sectors, and has developed these resources and sectors in such a way as to have a less unbalanced economy than these other countries. Furthermore, its population attained a higher level of education and technical skill at an earlier stage than the other countries. Yet the Iraqi economy remains heavily dependent on petroleum. The degree of this dependence has increased since the steep rise in oil prices after the October War 1973, and the resulting vast expansion in revenues. To reduce the dependence tangibly in relative terms will now necessitate very far-reaching development efforts outside of the area of crude oil exports. However, the growth of the non-oil sectors at a rapid pace in absolute terms has become feasible.

The search for oil in Iraq was started earlier than anywhere else in the Arab world. What later (in 1929) became the Iraq Petroleum Company, IPC, has two sister (or daughter) companies, the Mosul Petroleum Company and the Basrah Petroleum Company, which have the same composition as the IPC. Their concessions relate to different years, and covered, until Decree 80 of 12 December 1961 was issued, vast concession areas. Oil was found and later went into export by the IPC in 1927, by the BPC in 1948, and by MPC in 1952.

The significance of oil became prominent only beginning with 1951, when the new 50-50 profit-sharing formula was applied. That year the revenue to government rose to ID13.3m, from 5.3m for 1950. Thus began the upward course of revenues which, though not as steep as for the other major Arab producers and not as consistently upward, was still rising fast by the end of 1971. The years 1972-4 were influenced by new factors which changed the whole course of the sector. Although these three years will be dealt with later, Table 2.10 includes the production and revenue data for 1972, 1973 and 1974 in the series. The oil revenue as recorded in Table 2.10 differs from the contribution of the crude oil sector to national product as it is presented in Table 2.12 below (p. 50). The latter includes the share of the oil companies, which has to be deducted under the item entitled 'net factor income payments abroad'. It also includes local payments by the oil companies not in the form of revenue to government — salaries and local purchases of services and goods. Obviously, most of the purchases appear under their appropriate sectors, but the salaries paid and retained in the country appear as part of the sector's contribution. This contribution should therefore normally be larger than the revenue to government, after factor payments abroad have been deducted.

Table 2.12 below shows that the oil sector contributed 48.6 per cent of GNP (39.9 per

Table 2.10 : Oil Production and Revenue 1946-74

Year	Production Million Tons	Revenue ID Million
1946	4.6	2.3
1947	4.7	2.6
1948	3.4	2.0
1949	4.1	3.2
1950	6.5	5.3
1951	8.6	13.3
1952	18.4	32.4
1953	28.0	49.9
1954	30.0	65.4
1955	33.0	84.4
1956	31.0	68.8
1957	22.0	48.6
1958	35.8	79.9
1959	41.8	86.7
1960	47.5	95.1
1961	49.0	94.8
1962	49.2	95.1
1963	56.7	110.1
1964	61.6	126.1
1965	64.4	131.4
1966	68.0	140.8
1967	60.1	124.6
1968	74.0	174.0
1969	74.9	179.6
1970	76.9	186.1
1971	83.5	276.3
1972	72.1	189.9
1973	97.1	562.1
1974	94.6	1,982.2

Notes: (a) Production figures for the years 1953 through 1957 are available only in rounded form.

(b) Production data vary slightly between sources, such as Hashem *et al.*, *Evaluation of Economic Growth in Iraq*, Vol. I, p. 20, and The British Petroleum Company Limited, *Statistical Review of the World Oil Industry*.

(c) Revenue data also vary, but more widely than production data, as between sources, such as the *Annual Reports* of the Central Bank of Iraq and the *Annual Reports* of the Organization of Petroleum Exporting Countries.

Source: For production: For the years 1946-52, Stephen H. Longrigg, *Oil in the Middle East: its Discovery and Development* (RIIA, Oxford University Press, 3rd edition, 1968), Appendix II (B), p. 277; for the years 1953-7, The British Petroleum Company Limited, *Statistical Review . . . 1960;* for the years 1958-73, different issues of British Petroleum *Statistical Review;* for 1974, Nicolas Sarkis, 'The Energy Crisis and the Challenge of Development in the Arab Countries', Paper No. 132 (A-1) for the Ninth Arab Petroleum Congress, Dubai, 10-16 March 1975, p. 16. For revenue: for the years 1946-64, Abbas Alnasrawi, *Financing Economic Development in Iraq: The Role of Oil in a Middle Eastern Economy* (New York, 1968), p. 23 (see his original sources); for the years 1965-9, Hashem *et al.*, *Evaluation of Economic Growth in Iraq*, Vol. I, p. 20; for 1970-4, Sarkis, op.cit., p.17.

cent of GDP) in 1953, the first year for which the national accounts appear in enough detail to permit the presentation of the sectoral structure of national product. By 1969, the contribution had dropped to 37.9 per cent of GNP or 32.1 per cent of GDP. A similar notable drop has only occurred elsewhere in Kuwait, while in Saudi Arabia and in Libya the oil sector continues to claim to itself a very large and undiminished share of national product. The relative shrinkage in the contribution of oil in Iraq till the beginning of the seventies is explained mainly in the relative expansion in other non-oil sectors (particularly public administration and defence; trade, banking, insurance and other services; and industry, including oil-refining), and partly in the relative drop in the size of net factor income payments abroad. The expansion in the sectors listed has made up for the drop not only in the share of oil, but of agriculture as well. It must be noted, however, that the largest compensatory movement has been in public administration and defence, which is not as healthy a development as if the compensation had come from truly productive sectors. (Beginning with 1971, but most markedly in 1974, the sector's contribution rose. It stood at 43.6 per cent of GNP, or 37 per cent of GDP, for 1971, and it is estimated here at 60-65 per cent of GNP for 1974.) In absolute terms, the oil sector (at pre-1973 level) provided Iraq with a revenue which was below that for Kuwait, Saudi Arabia and Libya, although Iraq was the Arab pioneer in oil production and has substantial reserves. These reserves were estimated at 4,864m tons by the beginning of 1974, representing 5.66 per cent of world reserves. They are lower than Kuwait's and Saudi Arabia's reserves, but greater than Libya's (and those of the United Arab Emirates).[27] The reason why production and revenue have lagged considerably since the beginning of the sixties lies in the severe and protracted controversy which the government has had with the IPC.

The issues involved included: equity participation, profit-sharing arrangements, relinquishment of unexploited acreage, natural gas utilisation, cost components deductible from gross sales, posted price determination, marketing allowances, appointment of an Iraqi managing director, Iraqisation of staff, use of Iraqi tankers, foreign exchange deliveries and Basrah port and cargo dues.[28] But essentially the controversy was the result of Iraqi unease over the fact that the oil was being exploited by a foreign concern, not the country itself. Thus the issues have always been at the base political-ideological, relating to the desire to have complete mastery of one's resources and to put these in the service of nationalistic ends. If viewed in this light, the controversy, and the financial loss sustained by Iraq as a result, can be better understood. Indeed, certain Iraqi economists and thinkers argue that nothing has really been lost to the country; revenue has merely been deferred. The critics of the official oil policy in the sixties argue, on the other hand, that the loss is real and substantial, and that keeping the oil in its underground reservoirs for future exploitation cannot be certain to compensate for revenue forgone in a fast-moving technology.

The revenue forgone has been variously estimated. One detailed estimate attempts to assess the losses incurred until the end of 1965, the year in which an agreement was very close to being reached and signed. The tangible losses are placed at $221.4m, apart from capital investments by the IPC group of $171.0m, or a total of $392.4m of income or investment forgone. The intangible losses include the forgoing of the entry of new companies and the derivation of additional income, as well as the loss of investment and reinvestment income. This calculation goes on to estimate the would-be gains had the 1965 agreement been accepted and implemented. The tangible gains until the end of 1970 would have amounted to $1,129.7m of income plus $139m of investment that would have been made both by the IPC group and jointly with government. Likewise, intangible gains would have been made. These losses, or gains forgone, are all considered the result of Decree 80 of 1961.

A second set of estimates proceeds from the assumption that Decree 80 had not been issued. The would-be gains for the decade in that case are estimated to amount to $1,264.7m of income and $286m of capital investment, or a total of $1,550.7m.[29] In either case, and disregarding the details of the calculation and possible disagreement over the estimates, it remains true that the income forgone is substantial. The tangible long-term gains of the policy actually adopted by the government, which resulted in the non-exploitation for several years of the area removed from the confines of the concession, remain to be seen. Furthermore, the nationalistic, intangible significance of the assumption of control over the country's oil — a control which was completed with regard to IPC proper (Kirkuk fields) on 1 June 1972 by the nationalisation of the IPC interests (except for the French share) — could not by then be given precise translation in economic terms. But fairness requires that the nationalist counter-argument be given respectful hearing. This will be made on the premises warranted by conditions before the war of October 1973 and the subsequent steep increases in oil prices.

Condensed to an extreme degree, this argument runs somewhat as follows. In principle, the country ought fully to control the exploitation of its oil resources and the use to which they will be put, whether this is the sale of crude petroleum, oil-refining and the exports of refined products, the manufacture and export of fertilisers, plastics and other petrochemicals, or any combination of these that promises to serve the country best. Control should mean the ownership of the capital of the industry and its management. It should extend beyond the national frontiers, in the sense that local tankers should be used to a certain limit. Since oil remains in reserve if not exploited, the country should not be attracted by the lure of immediate benefits, if withholding the oil for a calculated time promises, in total, a larger net profit flow coupled with greater control.

The argument can be carried further to the point where it can be claimed that a slightly smaller net profit (per year or within a longer time horizon) with greater control might be preferable, from the national point of view, to a larger profit with lesser control. In other words, petroleum is a 'strategic' commodity, and it should be exploited and developed not merely as a source of revenue and foreign exchange, but also as an instrument of national policy, however this is defined. Looked at in this manner, Iraq's national oil policy has potency and commands consideration, even if it still provokes disagreement. For Iraq refuses the claim made by the foreign oil interests that oil exploitation is a purely commercial undertaking, and that politics should be barred entry into the petroleum domain. The nature of this resource, for its owners and foreign users alike, makes such a claim utterly simplistic, if not outright hypocritical. (Events following the October War 1973 have given sharper relevance to these arguments, which had been originally marshalled and written late in 1972. At the time of updating in 1975, the government's position is stronger in effect than even its logic had earlier suggested.)

Though of lesser importance for the economy of Iraq than for the economies of the other major Arab producers, oil is of crucial importance for development. We refer to it here, as we will do in these other countries, as a leading sector. But the designation is mainly restricted to the financial implications of petroleum. Until 1974, it had not been a leading sector the way iron and steel was for, say, Sweden, or railroads for England, or the car industry for the United States. Nevertheless the revenues arising from the export of crude have made the difference between extreme backwardness for Kuwait, Saudi Arabia, Libya, and to a lesser extent Iraq and Algeria, and advances in many economic and social areas.

Iraq was the first country to utilise the increased oil revenues productively in a systematic manner, first in the 1949-53 plan, and subsequently under the plans initiated by the Development Board and by successor agencies. Since the system of government had been established and organised well before the advent of the oil era, and budgetary practices had already become rigorous, the revenue went neither to the private purses of ruling families nor flagrantly to fancy projects or questionable contractors, but to the public treasury. Indeed, the government first allotted the whole of this revenue to the financing of the development plan, but subsequently reduced the allotment to 70 and later to 50 per cent, as the demands of the ordinary budget grew and political pressures intensified by the established conventional ministries. The examination of allotment and actual expenditure will be undertaken further below, but for the moment it is enough to present the global picture. Thus, over the years 1951/2—1969/70 (as will be detailed in section 4 below) a total of ID1,947.5m was allotted to the various plans, of which ID959.4m was actually spent. The actual state revenue set aside for development work over the same period was ID1,093.7m. To this last sum must be added the allocations made by the central government sector in the 1970-4 plan (before its 1971 and 1974 amendments). Thus a grand total of ID2,484.4m has been allotted for the years 1951-74 (apart from the 1974 amendment) though the revenue actually made available is about ID1.63 billion.[30] (The amendments raised the allocation by ID415.6m.) Approximately 90 per cent of the actual revenue came from the oil sector. It is obvious that oil revenue has been a *sine qua non* for development since 1949.[31] The fact that oil revenue in recent years (down to 1972) has represented 33-40 per cent of general state revenue (around 50 per cent in earlier years) underlines the significance for development of oil revenue, since it indicates that the pattern of allocation of oil revenues favours development spending.

In conclusion, mention must be made of other aspects of Iraq's mineral wealth. The existence in the north of several minerals has long been suspected, such as iron ore, copper, chromite, lead and zinc. Recent surveys have confirmed the hopes of the authorities, though the size of the deposits is yet to be estimated. However, it now seems certain that the country has substantial deposits of limestone, gypsum, dolomite, phosphates and sulphur. The Iraq National Minerals Company has been formed to explore and develop these minerals, and priority has been given to sulphur. Firm information is not available, but it has been suggested to this writer that about a quarter of a million tons of sulphur were mined in 1971. The target a few years hence is 1.5m tons a year. The other proven deposits are yet to be developed. Phosphates are expected to become of major significance for fertiliser production.

Manufacturing Industry[32]

Manufacturing industry had very modest beginnings by the time the post-war period started. The industries that had been developed were related to local raw materials and/or needs. The most important of these were cotton-ginning, spinning and weaving and construction industries. Other industries that existed then or were to follow in the early post-war years were date-processing, cigarettes, wool-pressing, tanning, printing, flour-milling, soap, matches, shoes and simple foods and beverages. With Egypt and Syria, this placed Iraq among the 'more advanced' Arab countries in the field of industry for those days.

The sector of industry benefited from certain promotive policy measures taken in the inter-war years. Thus, Law 14 of 1929, and subsequent amendments, helped to encourage the establishment of industries. The years 1932-45, as Langley and Hashem *et al.* maintain, can be considered as the period during which the climate was being made suitable for industrialisation. Thus protection was introduced, in addition to certain other privileges included in the promotive legislation. In total, 96 factories were benefiting from the 1929 Industry Law by 1945 (71 on the eve of World War Two).[33] A combined agricultural and industrial bank was established in 1936, but with the modest capital of half a million Iraqi dinars. Industrial entrepreneurship, though on a modest scale, began to emerge in the inter-war and subsequent years. However, as can be expected, most of the new industrial entrepreneurs came from a mercantile background and carried with them notions of business and expectations of quick returns more appropriate to mercantile enterprise.[34]

The years 1945-50 witnessed a new trend: indirect governmental intervention following encouragement through remote influence on the industrial climate. The most notable measure taken in this direction was the effecting of the separation between the agricultural and the industrial sections of the bank into two independent banks, a measure which had been decreed in 1940 but implemented only after the war in 1946. Then the capital of the Industrial Bank was made ID500,000. The war years had given an impetus to industry, owing to a scarcity of imports and increased purchasing power.

The next period, 1950-8, witnessed an acceleration of the factors influencing the course of industrialisation. As has been summed up by writers already cited, acceleration was urged by the rise in oil revenues to government (which in turn activated public works and construction and, as a derived effect, intensified demand for construction materials and, at a later round, for consumer goods thanks to the increased purchasing power). It was also urged on by the establishment of the Development Board and its setting up of several large industries, such as bitumen, an oil refinery, cement, spinning and weaving. And finally, it was speeded up by the introduction of certain structural changes in the governmental machinery dealing with industry. Thus, a directorate-general of industry was set up in the Ministry of National Economy, the Industry Law was amended in 1950 (and again in 1956), and the Industrial Bank entered a new phase of increased activity, thanks mainly to its increased resources, as its capital was raised several times within the present period, to reach ID7m in 1957/8 (and later ID10m in 1958/9).

The introduction of planning, albeit modest in its reach and tentative in its methodology and rigour, also helped industry in this period. (It ought to be mentioned that planning, or programming, had been introduced earlier on in Iraq, in the thirties and forties. The precursor plan for the series of plans beginning with the fifties was the 1949-53 plan, which assigned a modest share for industry.) The 1951-5 plan set 20 per cent of its total allocations (ID31m) for industry; its amendment for the years 1951-6 reduced this share in absolute and in relative terms, to ID14m or 15.7 per cent. We need not pursue this stock-taking of plans and the share of industry in them, since the section on planning below is a more appropriate place for this examination. In any case, the allocations do not have great significance, since actual implementation fell below the level of allocations by over half. All through the period under consideration industry was subordinate in place, priority being given to irrigation and flood control works, agriculture and communications. Taking the public and the private sectors together, and their mixture through the Industrial Bank which promoted projects owned jointly by the government (via the Bank) and private investors, it can be said that several new industries emerged in this period. Foremost among these were woollens, artificial silk, paper, metal products and many new establishments — some quite large — in the industries already in existence, such as sugar, foodstuffs and beverages, cement, bricks and other building materials, leather goods and the like.

The 1958 revolution, with what accompanied it in the realm of new socio-economic ideas, was not immediately reflected in the structure of the economy. Thus, the first plan formulated, the Provisional Plan for the years 1959-61, assigned only ID38.3m or 10.2 per cent of total allocations to industry, whereas the Detailed Plan, 1961-5, allocated ID166.8m or 30 per cent to industry, thus pushing it to first place. The much more modest allocation in the Provisional Plan is probably a reflection of the insufficiency of studies on hand of industries to be promoted, as well as the desire to proceed with projects in process which had been started by the previous régime. Generally speaking, the post-revolution period saw larger concern with industrialisation as part of the desire to break with the past and to consolidate independence and challenge the ideas inherited from the era of foreign rule which insisted that agriculture should be emphasised, and not industry. The share of the public sector rose during this period, owing to government's investments in industry. But it was 14 July 1964 which marked a sudden expansion in this share, because it was on this day that far-reaching nationalisation measures were taken which meant the transfer of over twenty large industrial establishments from private to public ownership. This also meant the acceleration of projects already under execution, although the process continued to be slow. Then, as earlier, and to some extent as things stand today, the major bottlenecks to industrial expansion were the shortage of skilled manpower — managerial-administrative and technical, the insufficiency of pre-investment and feasibility studies, and generally the low absorptive capacity for industrial investment.

The nationalisations were to mean a setback for the Industrial Bank, since they meant the exit from its portfolio of the shares of most of the companies in the creation of which it had participated, or to the capital of which it had subscribed. It was left with only a few establishments, and it even had in subsequent years to turn to mercantile and real-estate lending. The mixed sector can thus be said to have suffered. However, the private sector, in spite of ambiguity in the delineation of its frontiers (which continues till the present) expanded noticeably. But, quite understandably, the expansion was in the direction of small establishments, both in new fields and in fields already in existence. One of the factors which led to this was a change in the Industry Law, which was amended in 1961 to encourage private industry.

The last period that can be identified stretches from 1965 to the present. Once again industry was given first place in the 1965-9 plan, with allocations of ID187.2m or 28 per cent of the total. However, the allocations for industry in the current plan for the years 1970-4 (as amended on 1 April 1971) place it after agriculture, with ID207.2m or 21.8 per cent of the total. Emphasis has been placed since 1965 on the public sector, which now comprises all the large establishments in the country, such as petrochemicals, petroleum and gas, spinning and weaving, artificial silk, paper, sulphur extraction from gas, rubber, refineries, leather, fertilisers, medicaments, metal products, glass and agricultural machinery and equipment. Electricity is included in the sector broadly defined, and it has important allocations in the current plan. The Industrial Bank and the mixed sector continued to be of minor importance, since the Bank could only promote small establishments. The private sector also continued to invest in industry, but with the same limitations and handicaps as before.

The whole of the industrial sector (excluding petroleum and electricity and water) produced goods valued at ID123.8m in the year 1971, the last year for which data are available. (Electricity and water contributed ID19.2m to GDP.) A total of 1,330 larger establishments were in operation in 1971, with a labour force of 94,141. In addition, there were 208 electricity and water establishments, with 15,069 employees. On the other hand, small establishments totalled 29,940 with 67,481 employees (with just over 2 employees per establishment on the average). In order of importance based on production and sales, foodstuffs top the list of industries, followed by chemicals and chemical products, non-metallic mineral products, textiles, tobacco, beverages and drinks — all with production and sales in excess of ID10m — followed down the line by the other industries. The index number for industrial production reached 141.3 for 1969, with 1962 as the base year. This means an average compound rate of growth of about 5.5 per cent per year. The fastest-growing industries were the chemical industry, clothing and shoes and oil-refining, while the slowest-growing were foodstuffs, beverages and tobacco (with an index of 120.8 in 1969) and textiles (with an index of 137.5).[35]

The public sector industries underwent some important organisational changes in the decade 1964-74. Thus, as a result of nationalisation in July 1964, an Economic Organization was set up to take over nationalised establishments, industrial and otherwise. Then, in 1965 a first reorganisation was undertaken, whereby the establishments were regrouped on functional grounds, which meant the setting up of a General Organization for Industry. This agency took over 27 manufacturing establishments plus 10 general industrial services that had been under the wing of the public sector before July 1964. Then again in 1965 the merger of similar establishments within the same region was undertaken. And finally, under Law 90 of 1970, the General Organization was again reorganised by splitting it on the basis of specialisation into five institutions for: textiles; clothing, leather and cigarettes; chemicals and foodstuffs; construction materials; and engineering industries. (The labelling of the sections itself suggests little homogeneity in such cases as the second institution which groups together clothing, leather and cigarettes.) The establishments, under the law of 1970, were deprived of their boards of directors and now have advisory committees. Actual administration is controlled by the General Organization. Thus, whereas the Economic Organization had been a co-ordinator, the General Organization for Industry (like the other institutions for other nationalised establishments in other fields) has administrative responsibility.

Finally, the year 1973 witnessed further institutional change. Thus many Orders were issued purporting to organise and promote industry, and to place production under better control and inspection. The General Authority for Industrial Development was formed for the purpose. Special efforts were made to encourage private enterprise in the sector, as a result of which 542 projects with an aggregate capital of ID21m were approved. Law 22 of 1973 was issued in February 1973 with the aim of promoting and organising industrial investment, and it was meant to correct the shortcomings in Law 164 of 1964 or otherwise amend it.

The years 1971-4 witnessed vast expansion and diversification in industrial investment. The new or significantly expanded projects involve electrical equipment, refining, pipelines, electricity, steel rolling, fertilisers and other petrochemicals, artificial fibres, tyres, rubber hose, engineering, chemical, construction and foodstuff industries. Electricity generation likewise shared in the general advance. Production rose from 1.9 billion kwh in 1970 to 2.26 billion in 1971, and 2.36 billion in 1972. New generation plants under construction by the end of 1973 had a total capacity of 360 Megawatts. The expansion in manufacturing industry and electricity was made possible thanks to sizeable investment. Allocations for these areas of activity in the 1970-4 Plan total ID391m, and valuable technical assistance has been received from the USSR and some other socialist countries.[36] (However, the last year of the Plan received a considerably increased allocation in March 1974. Industry was thus allotted ID225m for the year 1974/5, while it had been allotted less than that for the whole Plan period originally. The allocation for 1973/4 was ID45m.)

An interesting comparison of productivity of labourers is made in Hashem et al.[37] According to this analysis, labourers in the public sector had a much higher productivity than those in the private sector of industry, and productivity in both sectors fell below wage levels. However, the public sector in a number of industries suffers from a low level of sales, compared with production. This should come as no surprise in a system where the achievement of physical targets of production features very importantly, perhaps even more so than profitability. Nevertheless, profits have been registered in several industries.

This conceptual question is by no means the only major problem which faces Iraqi industry. Hashem et al. undertake a thorough stock-taking and analysis of the problems, and divide them under general problems afflicting the public as well as the private sector (such as smallness of market, low quality of product, and the shortage of administrative and technical cadres); problems peculiar to the public sector (production problems relating to the misplanning of production and the insufficiency of cost-benefit studies, and the difficulty of setting prices; investment problems involving low implementation as represented in a low percentage of execution of allocations;[38] and organisation problems such as weakness of execution agencies, poor distribution of authority, poor follow-up of projects, lax supervision by officers in charge of projects who are not held responsible for their acts); and problems afflicting the private sector (non-clarity of the frontiers of the sector; poor co-ordination between import programmes and the needs of the sector in inputs and spare parts; complexity of procedures of laws purporting to promote industry; weakness of the role of the Industrial Bank; and weakness of the spirit of industrial enterprise).[39]

Education, Health, Public Housing and Community Facilities

The discussion so far has centred around the prominent sectors of the Iraqi economy: agriculture, oil and industry. None of the other economic sectors will receive separate treatment here, not because of their insignificance, but because they have not had a singularly prominent role to play and because the approach in this book is not that of a survey which deals with the sectors one by one. The growth of the sectors which are not singled out, as of those already discussed, will emerge from Table 2.12 below, via the size of their contribution to national product and how it has evolved over the years.

It is appropriate therefore to move to a major area of interest in the development of the country: the area of public services in the fields of education, public health, housing and community facilities. Government effort in this area, particularly in education, has been outstanding by regional standards. Indeed, it is precisely the existence of a reasonably large reservoir of educated and trained cadres, coupled with the availability of petroleum, water and extensive land without a heavy population pressure that adds poignancy to the regret that Iraq's development should have moved erratically, and on the whole slowly. But taking all these public services together, the government had expended considerable effort right from the thirties towards accelerating education, improving health and housing conditions, and providing the country with basic community facilities. However, housing and community facilities received, and still receive, less attention and public funds, and show less results, than education and health.

The World Bank mission reported[40] that over the two decades preceding the visit of the mission, say between 1930 and 1950, the number of schools rose from 262 to 1,100, and the number of schoolchildren from 32,750 to 175,000. The rate of increase in the latter is 9 per cent per annum — which is more than three times higher than population increase. In the years 1950-73 the number of schoolchildren in the first two cycles of education rose even faster. Thus, enrolment for the year 1972/3 in nurseries, elementary, intermediate and secondary schools totalled 1,915,234 pupils, a figure which represents more than 12 per cent increase per annum on the average. In addition the student body includes a university enrolment of 49,936 (undergraduate and graduate), enrolment at teacher training colleges and institutes of 7,405, and at vocational schools and institutes of 11,426. The total of all these categories outside the first two cycles is thus 68,767.[41] The contrast between 1950 and 1973 is striking, whether looked at from the angle of elementary and secondary education, university education (where only 781 students had been sent abroad to train in universities in the whole decade of the forties), or vocational education (the total number of trainees being some 750 in 1950). Expenditure on education out of the general budget (excluding expenditure on the college of medicine, which was then shown under the Directorate General of Public Health) in 1949/50 amounted to ID2.6m out of recurrent expenditure which totalled ID20.7m, or 12.5 per cent. By 1972/3, the budget of education (including higher education and the grant to the Local Administration for Primary Education) rose to ID73m in a total budget of ID352.2m — or 20.1 per cent.[42] Thus the allocations to education rose 28-fold, while the general ordinary budget rose 17-fold over the 24 years.

These global indicators are not sufficient to convey an adequate picture of the educational effort of Iraq since 1946. Thus, whereas immediately after World War Two there were only five university colleges in Baghdad — for law, commerce and economics, for arts and sciences (established in 1949/50), medicine and pharmacy and engineering — plus a 'junior college' for girls, with total enrolment of 4,582 for 1949, by 1972/3 enrolment in the third cycle of education totalled 49,936 men and women (23.9 per cent women), spread over five universities at Baghdad, Mosul, Basrah, Sulaimaniya and Mustansiriya (the last situated in Baghdad), with a large number of fields of specialisation. And, although probably some of the complaints made early in the post-war period with regard to the quality of education at all its levels (emphasis on memorising, excessive lecturing by the instructors and professors, insufficient scope for discovery and the unfolding of creativity, insufficient experimentation, extremely narrow acquaintance with the literature outside textbooks, poor mastery of foreign languages) are still valid today, yet there is a very clear awareness of the problem and an insistent probing for solutions and answers. Many enquiries have been conducted and reports written in an attempt to diagnose the ills and prescribe proper treatment. The fact that after a quarter of a century qualitative advances have not been greater is to be blamed mainly on political discontinuity as well as the introduction of non-academic considerations into some key appointments in the two ministries of education and of higher education, and into the colleges and universities. However, it must be pointed out that technical education has received a high boost in the early seventies. A university of technology has been established, and the old faculty of engineering has been considerably strengthened, in addition to the faculty of medicine which has always been at a relatively high level.

Vast strides have been taken towards the improvement of health conditions, both through preventive social medicine and through curative medicine. The progress achieved is partly reflected in the statistics. But it is also reflected in the generally improved quality of sanitation, individual health and physical resistance to disease, and the greater control over certain previously endemic diseases such as malaria. However, on the other side of the account, certain major health problems seem to be persistent, though they do not blight the population's well-being today as they did a quarter-century ago.

Descriptive statements on health conditions made in the early post-war period find a sinister familiar echo in statements made currently. The World Bank mission reporting at the beginning of the fifties says:

> There is still a very high incidence of such endemic diseases as trachoma, hookworm, bilharzia, malaria and the dysenteries. Many of the prevailing diseases are the by-product of polluted water, and unsanitary, congested living conditions which in turn are traceable largely to poverty and ignorance.[43]

Two decades later, in a broad survey of the physical and social geography of the Middle East, published in 1971, the reader is told that

> there are a few local areas in the riverine districts of Iraq, the Lebanon, Syria, Turkey, and northern Iran, where the incidence of malaria reaches over 50 percent and not long ago up to 90 percent ... The riverine areas of Egypt and Iraq are notorious for parasitic infestations — hookworm, bilharzia, and ankylostomiasis ...

The survey further describes dysentery (usually of a relatively mild form) as 'an almost ubiquitous feature'[44] in the region as a whole, including Iraq.

The present writer feels that the such recent judgements on health conditions are not as much the result of a careful perusal of statistical evidence as an impressionistic verdict inspired mainly by mental inertia, since impressions regarding the prevalence of 'poverty, disease, and ignorance' seem to be tenacious and have a tendency to be repeated and passed on like the stick in a relay race, being handed on from writer to writer, and from one survey to another. My judgement is based on a comparison of the health statistics for the years 1946/7—1949/50 with those for the years 1971 and 1972. Without presenting a long set of figures, we can firmly establish that the incidence of the major diseases (those which have been cited), and of minor diseases and ailments is distinctly and drastically smaller today than it used to be in the immediate post-war years. This observation is all the more telling in view of the fact that statistical recording today is much more comprehensive than it used to be a quarter-century ago. Furthermore, deaths arising out of diseases constitute a much smaller percentage of the cases recorded.[45]

The tangible progress in public and private health conditions is the direct result of expansion in the relevant facilities and personnel, as well as the improvement in the quality of services offered and the skill of the manpower working in the sector. We can only present evidence of the quantitative advances made, in Table 2.11.

Advances made in the fields of community facilities, social welfare and housing are no less real and tangible. However, the official statistics do not present numerical information on the subject and descriptive reports on activities in these fields are not available. But from interviews made with well-informed Iraqis in government and outside, and from personal observation, it seems evident without doubt both that a great deal of achievement has been attained, and a great deal remains to be attained. Most of the work so far done has been in Baghdad and the other large population centres. This is most true of housing, where the depressing problem of the *sarifa* dwellers (more appropriately squatters)[46] who had come to Baghdad in their tens of thousands, mainly from the distressingly poor and stagnant districts of the south, was largely solved during the early sixties by the construction of many thousands of housing units west of the city for the *sarifa* community and the transportation of this community there. (The transfer was not always voluntary or conducted by the poor dwellers themselves with joy, since even poverty and squalor to which man has been

Iraq

Table 2.11: Health Facilities, 1949/50 and 1972

	1949 or 1950	1972
Hospitals	82	153
of which private	11	14
Hospital beds	4,901	18,913
of which in private hospitals	418	379
Hospitals in Baghdad	21	41
Hospital beds in Baghdad	2,086	8,460
Dispensaries and other health institutions		
(excluding hospitals)	n.a.	1,522
of which in Baghdad	n.a.	237
Inhabitants per hospital	58,734 a	65,843
Inhabitants per hospital bed	983 b	533
Medical doctors	797	3,513
Dentists	85 c	497
Inhabitants per medical doctor	6,043 d	2,868
Inhabitants per dentist	56,661 e	20,270
Pharmacies[f]	201	652
of which in Baghdad	109	388
Medical and para-medical professions		
(including doctors and dentists)		
in government service	3,147 g	12,402

a. 64,024 on basis of adjusted population of 5,250,000, as per reference made further above to FAO, *Production Yearbook 1972*, Annex II-1.
b. 1,071, on basis of adjusted population.
c. Figure relates to 1951.
d. 6,587 on basis of adjusted population.
e. 61,764 on basis of adjusted population.
f. Apart from pharmacies attached to hospitals.
g. Figure relates to 1951.

accustomed often seems more attractive than the more promising but unfamiliar mode of living.) Equally creditable effort has been exerted to provide credit for housing for middle-income government officials, though the scope of the achievement is smaller than that for the very low-income groups.[47]

Evolution of National Product

The first estimate of national income for Iraq was made by the World Bank mission in its report of 1952; it was stated in the Introduction that the *per capita* income was 'probably at most ID30'. However, the report does not explain the method used in the calculation, nor does it give any details. Thus credit for the first detailed estimate, and the one which indicates the method employed and the degree of reliability of each of the figures, must go to Kevin G. Fenelon who, in 1957, while adviser to the Bureau of Central Statistics, produced an estimate of national income for the years 1950-6.[48] According to Fenelon, national income was ID158m for 1950, and rose to ID303m for 1956 at current prices. This represents growth at the highly creditable compound rate of 11.5 per cent per annum.

(At 1956 prices, national income rose from ID165m to ID303m, or at an annual rate of growth of 11 per cent.) Most of this performance is imputable to the steep rise in oil revenue beginning with 1951, and to the brisk investment policy pursued by the Development Board which since 1951 had been engaged in a large public works programme. However, the research sources available made the author of this estimate himself qualify it with caution. A subsequent, more comprehensive study, and one which attempted to correct the short-comings and lacunae in the Fenelon estimates, was conducted by Khair-el-Din Haseeb. This study first covered the years 1953-6, but was subsequently extended to cover the years 1953-61 and later 1962 and 1963 as well.[49]

A third set of estimates was made in 1961 by V. Maniakin, a Soviet expert advising the government at the time. His findings appeared in a report entitled 'Introduction to National Accounting in Iraq for 1956-1960'.[50] The three estimates differ, although Haseeb's and Maniakin's are very close for the year 1960. Subsequently, the Central Statistical Organization at the Ministry of Planning undertook the task of estimating the national product, and as a result we now have an uninterrupted series for GDP, GNP and national income for the years 1953 to 1971. The official estimates for the years 1953 to 1963 are very close to Haseeb's estimates, which suggests that the latter have been adopted apart from very minor adjustments. Table 2.12 below presents the national accounts for the nineteen years.

The national product is given at current prices, as no estimates at constant prices are published. However, the results can be deflated by the wholesale or consumer price index for Iraq. The first index rose from 90 for 1953 to 130.3 for 1971 and to 130.9 for 1973 (1962=100) for the city of Baghdad, while the second index rose from 77 to 121.0 for 1971 and 133.5 for 1973 for Baghdad. In adjusting for price increases, we use the index for the year 1971, which was 130.3 for wholesale prices for Baghdad, and 121 for consumer prices for the whole of Iraq.[51] To be on the safe side, and to account for the usual underestimation of price increases, we deflate the current prices by the wholesale index. Accordingly, the record of growth is qualified to a minor degree. Thus, while at current prices GDP at factor cost rose by 332.7 per cent from 1953 to 1971, it rose by about 200 per cent at constant (1963) prices. The annual rate of growth is 8.5 per cent in the first instance, and 6.5 per cent in the second, on the basis of the use of the wholesale price index as deflator. This is a good record of achievement if we consider the severe political upheavals and the frequent periods of instability which intervened, and which forced investment to be shy and growth to be sluggish.

Growth of GNP was slightly higher than that of GDP, owing to the fact that net factor payments abroad constituted a slightly declining proportion of GDP, on the average. And growth of NNP or national income was also slightly higher than that of GNP. National income rose by about 8.0 per cent on the average, at current prices, or by about 6.5 per cent at constant prices. On a *per capita* basis, national income rose by about 5.5 per cent per annum at current prices (or 3.5 per cent at constant prices), assuming a population rate of increase of 3 per cent for the whole period.[52] Assuming also the population to have been about 5.5 million in 1953, and that it stood at 9.75 million for 1971, then GNP *per capita* would have risen from ID48.24 ($135.07) to ID121.3 ($368.7) at current prices, or from ID44.4 ($124.3) to ID83.8 ($254.7) for the two years respectively for national income *per capita*.

Examination of Table 2.12 reveals that there has been very wide fluctuation in the year-to-year rate of growth of GDP (and of GNP and NNP). This fluctuation has primarily been caused by the very erratic course of the agricultural sector which, though characterised by irrigation to a considerable extent, manifests the uncertainties that normally go with rain-fed cultivation. The second sector responsible for fluctuation is the crude oil sector which, owing to the extended controversy between the government and the oil companies, did not benefit from an even course of growth. In addition, the course of growth reflected the impact of political events in 1956/7 (the Suez war) and in 1967 the June Arab-Israeli war), of policy decisions taken by the government such as Decree 80 of 1961, and of the stoppage of the flow of oil by Syria in 1966. The table also shows wide differences in the overall growth of the various sectors between 1953 and 1971, as the summary in Table 2.13 shows. (The 1971 figures are shown as index numbers, with 1953 equal to 100.)

This summary attributes the fastest growth to the sectors of quarrying, electricity, water and gas, administration, manufacturing proper, banking and insurance and petroleum refining. However, not much should be read into the various rates, since by themselves and without linkage to the absolute size of the sector's contribution little significance can attach to the index numbers. Furthermore, the comparison is seriously vulnerable to accident, since either of the index years could happen to be unusually small or unusually large. Finally, it ought to be pointed out that the three sectors which together contribute between 50 and 75 per cent of GDP — namely agriculture, manufacturing and crude oil — achieved a rate of growth below that for the whole economy represented in GDP or GNP. That the economy marked the growth it did is attributable to the rates of growth achieved by some other substantial sectors such as manufacturing, trade, other services and public administration and defence. It is worth emphasising that the index for the commodity-producing sectors as a group was 386.92 for 1971, which is distinctly below the index for the service sectors which stood at 552.70. The most important single factor in the higher rate of growth of the service sectors is public administration and defence, a sector which surpasses other service sectors in absolute terms and in terms of rate of growth. In view of this fact, the rosy picture of the course of growth ought to be qualified considerably, since the 'contribution' to GDP of the sector in question is more of a definitional than a substantive nature.

Three observations can be made with regard to the internal structure of the economy, that is, the relative importance of the various sectors. First, that the commodity-producing sectors constitute a larger proportion than the service-producing sectors, but that their significance has dropped from about 72 per cent to about 65 per cent over the nineteen years under review. Most of the drop has been picked up by the sector of public administration and defence. Second, petroleum, though in absolute terms 3.9 times as significant as it was at the start of the period, in relative terms now contributes 36.07 per cent, against its initial contribution of 39.92 per cent. This is a clear indication of the faster rate of growth achieved in certain other large sectors than in crude petroleum, as it is an indication that all in all, even in the early fifties, petroleum was not an overwhelmingly large sector as it was in countries like Kuwait, Saudi Arabia, the oil-producing sheikhdoms of the Gulf, or Libya in the early sixties. What supplements this optimistic note with regard to diversification is that industry has picked up the loss in the relative position of petroleum. Furthermore, the fact that public administration and defence, a sector whose growth is probably only of illusory economic significance to the economy, has made substantial gains is qualified by the more important fact that other vital sectors have also made significant gains. The third observation relates to agriculture and industry. The first has lost considerably in relative importance in spite of an absolute expansion to about 2.6 times its original size. The drop is to be expected in a developing economy becoming more advanced and more sophisticated. However industry has gained much less than agriculture has lost in relative terms, raising its contribution from 6.11 to 8.86 per cent while that of

Table 2.12: Distribution of Gross Domestic Product by Economic Sectors at Current Prices 1953-71 (ID million)

Year	Agriculture Forestry and Fisheries	Mining and Quarrying			Manufacturing Industries			Construction	Electricity Water and Gas	Transport Communications and Storage	Trade
		Crude Oil	Others	Total	Oil Products	Other	Total				
1953	71.50	128.91	0.89	129.80	1.91	17.83	19.74	11.27	1.46	21.37	17.85
1954	84.72	149.53	0.93	150.46	2.46	19.42	21.88	17.21	1.78	22.06	20.67
1955	65.33	161.16	1.56	162.72	3.45	23.47	26.92	21.29	2.17	24.56	21.48
1956	89.23	152.45	1.64	154.09	4.19	27.88	32.07	24.83	2.53	27.55	26.90
1957	111.57	113.10	1.74	114.84	4.99	30.26	35.25	27.68	2.68	29.92	29.67
1958	92.76	175.43	1.85	177.28	5.74	31.05	36.79	29.83	2.78	30.16	27.52
1959	82.01	190.00	1.81	191.81	6.45	38.38	44.83	28.72	2.97	34.29	26.23
1960	97.84	208.07	1.68	209.75	7.79	46.61	54.40	23.08	3.62	39.72	32.55
1961	116.98	209.03	2.15	211.18	9.39	50.12	59.51	23.88	4.96	45.95	36.58
1962	140.38	210.23	1.86	212.09	9.67	55.41	65.08	19.64	5.54	47.02	38.56
1963	109.30	242.50	1.90	244.40	10.10	54.10	64.20	20.30	5.20	48.80	35.90
1964	148.10	266.90	1.90	268.80	10.40	53.00	63.40	18.70	7.70	54.90	44.50
1965	162.70	283.62	4.90	288.52	13.26	52.53	65.79	3.93	9.80	56.10	50.65
1966	172.73	298.66	5.77	304.43	14.27	57.63	71.90	27.91	12.35	57.82	56.43
1967	181.39	264.41	5.44	269.85	14.58	68.42	83.00	26.69	13.38	60.60	56.55
1968	190.46	328.16	5.65	333.81	16.41	71.01	87.42	29.36	15.79	64.58	60.28
1969	198.08	333.08	5.95	339.03	17.72	76.70	94.42	32.29	18.14	67.68	64.26
1970	206.90	362.60	7.90	370.50	9.60	106.40	116.00	40.60	17.80	71.20	98.60
1971	188.00	504.00	14.40	518.40	11.50	123.80	135.30	43.60	19.20	79.70	103.40

Note: * Net factor income payments abroad.

Source: *Annual Abstract of Statistics 1970,* Table 159, pp. 344/5 for 1953-1969 and *Abstract 1973*, Table 191, p. 336 for 1970 and 1971. Important adjustments have been made since the appearance of the former source.

agriculture dropped from 22.14 to 13.45 per cent. This means that the responsibility for the overall decline in relative terms of the commodity-producing sectors has been largely shared by agriculture and crude petroleum.

All in all, the internal sectoral structure has not undergone major change. A more consistently energetic development policy, within the framework of a stable government, could have witnessed a larger shift in favour of manufacturing industry though not necessarily at the expense of agriculture, since such a policy could probably have led to further expansion in this latter sector as well.

Changes in the size of the labour force were mentioned earlier during the discussion of population and manpower. We have no information regarding changes in productivity; we can only assume that it rose thanks to better education and training and better business organisation. The other major factor to which growth in national product must be imputed is investment.[53] From 1953 to 1971, a total of ID2,428.5m of gross domestic investment

Banking Insurance and Real Estate	Ownership of Dwellings	Public Administration and Defence	Services	GDP at Factor Cost	N.F.I.P.A.*	GNP at Factor Cost	Depreciation	NNP at Factor Cost (National Income)
3.23	11.61	18.29	16.83	322.95	57.63	265.32	21.37	243.95
3.63	11.91	20.80	19.25	374.37	67.66	306.71	22.69	284.02
4.49	12.20	24.34	21.26	386.76	71.24	315.52	26.24	289.28
6.28	12.47	28.12	24.83	428.90	65.49	363.41	28.65	334.76
6.60	12.80	32.06	26.99	430.06	46.40	383.66	30.94	352.72
7.40	12.51	37.57	29.65	484.70	78.45	406.25	32.21	374.04
8.20	11.58	45.65	33.33	509.62	85.73	423.89	32.27	391.62
8.69	11.89	45.71	38.11	565.36	95.33	470.03	32.90	437.13
11.06	12.13	51.46	41.37	615.06	94.20	520.86	36.62	484.24
11.38	12.45	59.76	46.52	658.42	93.87	564.55	38.06	526.49
12.80	12.40	67.40	49.90	670.60	108.10	562.50	37.20	525.30
7.70	14.80	81.20	51.40	761.20	123.70	637.50	41.70	595.80
12.03	14.19	97.85	49.42	830.98	129.60	701.38	42.09	659.29
14.60	14.54	104.17	51.33	888.21	137.70	750.51	44.98	705.53
14.73	15.10	105.54	55.86	882.69	122.60	760.09	45.30	714.79
15.04	15.85	116.53	60.59	989.71	156.80	832.91	50.00	782.91
16.26	16.65	128.56	63.58	1,038.95	159.40	879.55	52.74	826.81
18.60	51.00	124.30	86.90	1,202.40	166.00	1,036.40	74.40	962.00
20.00	54.50	137.40	97.90	1,397.40	214.90	1,182.50	78.80	1,103.70

was effected, of which ID1,302.8m came from the public sector and ID1,125.7m from the private sector, including the oil companies. At the same time, GDP rose by ID1,074.4m (ID917.2m for GNP). Thus, globally, and disregarding time lags, the capital-output ratio averages 2.25:1 for the period if GDP is considered, or 2.65:1 for GNP. This range of ratios is quite tenable despite the fact that the country is at an early stage of development necessitating heavy investment in slowly fructifying infrastructural projects. The explanation of the apparent paradox lies in the presence and significance of the crude oil sector whose contribution is large and has risen considerably in absolute terms against a small investment. Thus, for the oil sector alone and for the years 1957-71 for which data are available, gross investment effected amounted to ID94m, while increase in contribution totalled ID390.9m, which amounts to a ratio of 0.24:1.

Gross aggregate domestic investment for the period 1953-71 amounts to 18.1 per cent of aggregate GDP at current prices, or 21.4 per cent of GNP. However, on a year-by-year basis, the trend is for gross domestic investment as a proportion of GDP or GNP to drop.

Table 2.13: Economic Growth between 1953 and 1971 (1953=100)

	1971
Agriculture, forestry and fisheries	262.93
Crude oil	390.97
Other mining	1,617.98
Total mining and quarrying	399.38
Petroleum refining	602.09
Other manufacturing	694.33
Total manufacturing	685.41
Construction	386.87
Electricity, water and gas	1,315.07
Transport, communications and storage	372.95
Wholesale and retail trade	572.27
Banking, insurance and real estate	619.19
Ownership of dwellings	469.42
Public administration and defence	751.23
Services	581.70
GDP at factor cost	432.70
Net factor income payments abroad	372.90
GNP at factor cost	445.69
Depreciation	368.74
NNP (=national income)	452.43

Thus, while the proportion was over 25 per cent of GDP in 1953 (about 31 per cent of GNP), it declined to 13.9 per cent of GDP for 1971 (or 16.5 per cent of GNP). We witness here what looks like a paradox: the rise of GDP (and of GNP) by much more than gross domestic investment over the years, the rise in GDP being from 100 as an index in 1953 to 432.7 in 1971 (445.7 for GNP), while the index for investment rose from 100 to about 239. The explanation is only in small part to be found in the increase in the size and productivity of the labour force, but in much larger part in the increase in oil revenue which has been effected with a very small investment.

Another interesting observation that can be made on the subject of investment is that the share of the private sector has been rising in absolute terms, and at about the same rate as that of the public sector. Thus the relative shares of the two sectors have largely remained unchanged, especially between 1964 and 1971, with the public sector ahead by 15-20 per cent. This pattern does not adequately reflect the claims regarding the shift in the socio-economic system in 1964. Indeed, even in 1956, the public sector had provided 49 per cent of investment, and the share subsequently dropped to 43.1, 43.4 and 48.7 per cent for 1960, 1961 and 1962 respectively. It must be admitted, however, that the rise was marked for 1964, the year of major nationalisations. In brief, the examination of politico-economic developments and pronouncements down to the end of 1971 does not supply us with a satisfactory explanation of the relative investment performance by the two sectors.

The pattern of purposes (types of assets) for which investments have been made has not undergone drastic change over the years. Thus construction (other than buildings) and public works have accounted on the average for about 38 per cent, followed by residential and other building with about 33 per cent. The balance went to machines, equipment, furniture and fixtures (about 22 per cent), and means of transport (about 7 per cent). On a sectoral basis, the largest volume of investment went to transport, communications and storage, followed closely by residential housing and manufacturing industry. Agriculture, a laggard initially, gained substantially beginning with the mid-sixties. This pattern reflects customary investment in developing countries of similar conditions as Iraq, where transport and communications are usually given a very large (if not the largest) share, in a desire to open up the country to economic activity and raise its degree of monetisation and increase market transactions. Likewise, residential housing is a major beneficiary, both because there is normally a shortage of housing and because residential housing is a status symbol. Finally, manufacturing and agriculture, as the backbone of most economies, receive important investments. The petroleum sector, while of extreme importance, is not the receiver of vast investments for reasons already explained.

The External Sector[54]

The external trade of Iraq has grown considerably since World War Two. Thus, while imports for 1946 amounted to ID28m, they rose to ID270.3m for 1973. On the other hand, exports have grown even faster, from ID12.7m to ID689.6m, including petroleum. A closer look, however, reveals that the picture is not as dramatic as these figures suggest. Thus, in spite of the steep rise in the value of imports, the leading categories are still the same: machines, metals, automobiles, spare parts and building materials, textiles, clothing materials and foodstuffs, especially tea and sugar.

On the side of exports the picture is depressing, for exports excluding petroleum totalled only ID32.8m for 1973, or 2.6 times their value for 1946. But here again the composition of exports has not changed radically, since dates, grains, raw wool, tobacco and hides and skins were and still are major exports. The only difference of consequence is the emergence of cement and sulphur as large export items. The extremely slow growth of exports and the virtual freezing of their composition over 28 years constitute a harsh but earned judgement on the failure of the economy to rise to the challenge of development in its external sector and to generate new exportable commodities. The import and export of services, or invisible trade, cannot be compared with visible trade for the same years, since data are available only beginning with 1950. Examination of the record reveals that the export of services, or the earnings of foreign exchange for the sale of services, have risen moderately, from ID10.2m for 1950 to ID63m for 1972, while payments have risen from ID26.6m to ID197.4m.[55]

It is thanks to petroleum exports that the balance of payments has in most years shown a surplus — though modest on the whole — on current account. The modesty of the surplus, and the fact that a deficit developed in certain years, is another indication that the oil sector has not contributed as much to the national economy as Iraqi oil reserves and the clement world oil situation would suggest, and that the non-oil sectors have been slower to emerge and to generate exportable goods and services than one has a right to expect.

Money, Banking and Public Finance[56]

Finally, it is necessary to discuss the association of finance — private and public — with the course of development, although reference will again be made to public finance in connection with the forthcoming discussion of the planning experience of Iraq.

First, with regard to money and banking. Here it is found that the degree of monetisation was very low in the year 1950. Thus, money in circulation amounted to ID6.6 *per capita*, while total bank deposits by the private sector averaged ID2.8 per inhabitant. Together, these components of money supply amounted to ID9.4 *per capita,* a figure which is approximately 30 per cent of their counterpart in Lebanon or in Egypt for the same year. By July 1974, money in circulation had risen to ID30.7 *per capita,* and bank deposits (demand, time and savings) to ID22.1 *per capita,* or a total of ID52.8. While in relative terms a noticeable growth can be seen to have occurred, in absolute terms the money supply remains very small *per capita,* amounting for the same year to a mere 11 per cent of its counterpart in Lebanon and 56 per cent of that for Jordan, but just about equal to its counterpart in Egypt.[57] However, the vast expansion of the public sector in Egypt, and the steep rise of its deposits in the banking system disguise the real magnitude of the money supply in this country. The deposits of the public sector in Iraq do not change the picture of the distribution of deposits between the private and the public sector respectively as much as for Egypt.

Naturally, the expansion of money supply and its lag behind its counterpart in Lebanon and Jordan are both a reflection not only of the degree of monetisation but also of the expansion of national product over the years and, at the same time, the income velocity of money in Iraq compared with the two other countries.

The banking system in Iraq today comprises three categories: commercial banks, specialised banks and the Central Bank. The first two categories had 233 head offices and branches in the country, with Baghdad containing about 40 per cent of the total. The commercial banks have all been amalgamated after nationalisation in July 1964 into two banks: the Commercial Bank and the Rafidain Bank (which took over the Mortgage Bank in 1970). The specialised banks include the Agricultural Bank and the Industrial Bank, already referred to briefly, and the Estate Bank (founded in 1949, which acquired the Co-operative Bank in 1970). The Central Bank was founded in 1947 as the National Bank of Iraq. The consolidated statement of the commercial banks totalled ID504m in July 1974, while that of the specialised banks totalled ID118.2m.

From 1960 to 1973, the Industrial Bank advanced 4,837 loans totalling ID10.7m, or an average of ID2,212 per loan — obviously not a scale of operations which can be considered highly promotive. The Agricultural Bank advanced 64,361 loans, totalling ID23.94m, or an average of ID372 per loan. Despite the small scale of agricultural units, this average by itself is sufficient indication of the modesty of credit allotment to farmers on the average. Finally, the Estate Bank made 121,194 advances in the years 1960-73, a total amount of ID126.7m — an average of ID1,045 per loan.[58] All in all, over the fourteen years a total of ID161.3m has been advanced in industrial, agricultural and real estate loans by the three banks (apart from the loans by the Mortgage Bank which lent a total of ID110.2m against fixed and movable property combined). This is close to ID20m annually.

Probably what can be said in observation is that the resources of Iraq, properly mobilised and harnessed, could enable the specialised banks to play a distinctly more promotive role to the three sectors involved: industry, agriculture and construction. Nevertheless, the period covered witnessed an expansion in their operations, since the overall average of credit advanced per loan for the whole lifetime of each of these banks is much smaller than the average for this period alone — especially the years 1970-3.

The problems facing each of the three banks are the same in some respects, but differ in some other respects relevant to their nature. Thus, they all suffer from insufficient working capital, and they are all slow-moving organisations because, despite their autonomy, they have adopted some of the heavy routine associated with government organisations. In addition, the Agricultural Bank could have been more effective if its loans had been utilised for the purposes for which they had been advanced, not for consumption purposes as so often happened. Furthermore, only the large farmers can provide the type of security required by the Bank, which limits the comprehensiveness of the Bank's financing. Finally, the agricultural co-operative societies on the whole fail to receive adequate financing whether from the Agricultural Bank or the Cooperative Bank (before it was incorporated in the Estate Bank), while they could normally be well-equipped to reach and satisfy the needs of their individual members out of the credit coming to them from the banks. The Industrial Bank has been more influential in the promotion of industry than the data just presented would suggest. Its contribution came via the generation of entrepreneurial ideas, the setting up of industrial establishments jointly with private businessmen, and share capital participation, in addition to advancing credit. Various analysts have evaluated the work of the Bank and on the whole their findings are favourable, although there is a continuous thread of regret that the scale of operations has been small or at best medium.[59] As indicated earlier in this chapter, after the nationalisations of 1964, the role of the Bank, both as promoter and founder of industries, and as supplier of credit, shrank considerably.

If the expansion of the money supply has lagged behind that of the national product over the past two decades, the expansion of the state budget has far exceeded that of national product. Thus, while GNP for 1971 was 4.8 times that for 1950, money supply by the end of 1973 was 9 times that for the initial year. On the other hand, the budget expenditures were ID30m for the year 1949/50, including supplementary budgets and 'productive capital works' of ID3.3m, against a revenue of ID28.6m, including oil sector revenue of ID3.2m. The expenditure under the combined ordinary, capital and self-financing budgets rose to ID1,375m for 1973, while the revenue rose to ID1,290m (of which current budget revenue was ID379m).[60]

The supplementary budgets (which we designated as 'self-financing') are grouped into three sub-categories: administrations with supplementary budgets (comprising the ports administration, the railways, posts, telegraphs and telecommunications, tobacco monopoly administration, Higher Agrarian Reform Administration, Atomic Energy Commission, and several others); autonomous public administrations (including the municipalities, the electricity administration, the Industrial Management Development Center, Baghdad University, and a few others); and, finally, autonomous business administrations (like the National Iraqi Oil Company, state banks, Iraqi Airways, state industries and a few other administrations).

It can readily be seen that a public outlay of the size indicated for 1973 is much higher than that for 1949/50, and much more so than that for 1946 when total budget expenditure was slightly below ID24m, whether related to size of population, or whether it is related to national product, as it amounts to 86 per cent of GNP for 1973, while it represented 16.5 per cent of GNP for 1950. The rise in the size of the budget is steep, even if we take account of two factors which, other things equal, make the contemporary budget much larger than that for 1950.

The first is the depreciation in money over the years. But we have seen that price rises have been moderate in Iraq, and the wholesale price index for 1973 is 130.3 while that for 1953 is 90, with 1963 as base year. Between 1950 and 1953 the index could not have risen by more than, say, 5 points. Thus, in all, we can safely assume that the index rose from 85 to 130.3 between the two terminal years (1963=100). Population increases, where today's population is about twice as large as that for 1950, is not a qualifying factor to contend with since our comparison on a *per capita* basis already takes care of the increase. The second qualifying factor to take into account is the fact that the largest component of the consolidated budget is the supplementary budgets in their three categories, which represent activities and control resources and revenues (a contra-item to expenditures) which in 1950 had been mostly in private hands. Accordingly, in order to establish comparability, we will exclude the supplementary budgets and restrict the comparison to the ordinary budget and to the development budget.

The 1973 ordinary budget, by itself, amounts to an expenditure of ID36.4 *per capita*. In addition to this, the development budget amounts to ID28.4 *per capita*. Together they amount to ID64.8 *per capita* (in total, about 42 per cent of an estimated GNP of ID1,600m). Were the budgets to maintain the same proportion of GNP as in 1950, namely 16.5 per cent, they would now be ID264m, against their present size of ID675m. Thus it can be seen that the budget today represents a distinctly larger outlay than in 1950, even after population growth and the drop in the value of money are accounted for. It is over two and a half times the older budget as a percentage of GNP, and, because of the vast absolute increase in GNP, it amounts to about 22.5 times the older budget in absolute terms. Deflating for the change in the value of money, it would still be 14.7 times that for 1950.

The expansion is understandable, in view of the extension of government functions and services, the expansion in the civil service for various ideological and 'Parkinsonian' reasons, and the growing complexity of life generally. However, a close look at the sources of revenue reveals a much less healthy or defensible process or evolution. For, as I have already hinted, the oil revenue is the major contributor of state revenues under the ordinary and development budgets. Thus, oil revenue was ID276.3m for 1971, ID189.9m for 1972, and ID562.1m for 1973. The 1973 revenue represents 83.3 per cent of the combined ordinary and development budgets. True, the proportion of oil to total state revenue on the ordinary and development budgets is high. But nothing much can be read into this relationship by itself, since oil has been till June 1972 very much an exogenous factor to the extent that the determination of production and sales used largely to be effected not by the budget authority but by a non-Iraqi centre of decision. However, as oil has been growing in financial significance since 1972, and since decision-making with respect to volume of production is now in the hands of the government, it is only logical for oil to improve its relative position in spite of the growth of the size of the budget, to be more closely tied to the financial needs of the country, and to be better integrated into the whole economy.

What is serious and disturbing is the fact that Iraq has not developed, *pari passu*, its non-oil revenues.[61] Thus, according to one observer, 'One of the striking features of the fiscal system of Iraq during the past decade is the declining importance of taxes relative to the national income'.[62] (In the half decade 1965/6–1969/70 income tax collections *both* from public and private sector subjects have remained a tiny proportion of GNP — respectively: 1.4, 1.5, 1.7, 1.8 and 2.8 per cent. Even if oil revenue is excluded from GNP, the proportion remains a mere 2.3 per cent on the average.) While non-oil revenue and tax revenue as a proportion of national income have both been declining, current expenditure, also as a proportion of national income, has been rising. The widening gap has been filled by oil revenue. The findings of the writer just quoted relate to the years 1950-64, but a projection of the same type of analysis reveals and accentuates the same tendency. Furthermore, a comparison between the Arab countries also reveals that taxes on income and wealth raise a smaller relative revenue in Iraq than in Morocco, Algeria, Tunisia, Egypt, Lebanon or Syria, but more than Libya, Sudan or Jordan. Kuwait and Saudi Arabia do not levy direct taxes on their nationals. While the relative importance of taxes on income and wealth (excluding oil) in a major oil country is not expected to be as substantial as in a non-oil country, it is still worth underlining that in Iraq before the steep rise in oil revenues the country had been slowly building up sound fiscal traditions. Had this trend continued, the government would today have more resources at its disposal for recurrent and capital expenditures. On the other hand, criticism need not be very harsh, since in the other major oil countries (except Algeria, which is really a medium-sized oil country), direct taxes either play a minor role, as in Libya, or are not levied on nationals at all, as in Saudi Arabia and Kuwait.

Failing to mobilise enough resources via oil revenue and non-oil budget revenues, in order to meet its rising expenses, the government has had to resort to borrowing. Foreign loans have been resorted to before, but not on the same scale as currently. Thus, public indebtedness reached ID260.2m by the end of 1973, with internal loans amounting to ID107.9m and foreign loans to ID152.3m.[63] The situation in 1972 with regard to the petroleum industry, and the slow rate at which sales were being effected after June 1972 when the Iraq Petroleum Company (Kirkuk fields) was nationalised, coupled with the failure to establish tax discipline in the non-oil sectors and to develop direct taxes to a substantial degree, led, before October 1973, to expectations that foreign indebtedness would continue to increase for at least the next few years. However, redress was provided by the price increases of crude and the subsequent inflow of massive revenues.

With regard to expenditure on the ordinary budget, defence has always devoured the largest part of resources. As early as 1947/8, defence (including police departments) absorbed 37.1 per cent of the budget. Since then its share has ranged between 35 and 49 per cent over the past two decades. The next largest item is education, whose share has since the early 1950s ranged between 14 and 25 per cent of the ordinary budget, but has dropped noticeably in recent years. The latter outlay has borne fruit since the results of the educational effort, at least in quantitative terms, have been much better than average according to the region's standards. (The most recent *Annual Abstract of Statistics*, namely for 1973, does not indicate the outlay on defence. It is probably included under the main head, designated 'others', which amounted to ID161.2m for 1971/2, or 47 per cent of the total.)[64]

In conclusion, then, one can say that the Iraqi government has not developed its non-oil part of the revenues to the extent that would have been expected given the country's resources and their growth. Furthermore, defence and security under pressure of the Kurdish problem and the Arab-Israeli conflict have absorbed a very high percentage of the ordinary budget (an average of 45.3 per cent for the years 1966/7 – 1969/70) and of GNP (13 per cent on the average for these years). Considering the tendency for recurrent expenditures to move consistently upward, and considering the need for continued development expenditure if the course of growth is not to dip downwards, the country under the circumstances will find itself increasingly dependent on oil revenues for several years to come.

3. TRANSFORMATION OF THE SYSTEM

The fourteenth of July 1958 was a sharp line dividing two eras distinctly different with regard to socio-economic system and political structure. The significance of this date has already been underlined, though without much analysis or evaluation of the reasons.

The transformation of the system, designated as 'the socialist transformation' in many Iraqi circles, occurred in three phases. The first phase is July 1958 to July 1964, which was characterised by the initiation of agrarian reform and the restructuring of socio-political power as well as economic power and wealth attaching to and deriving from land ownership. The agrarian reform measures will be reported on in some detail presently, but for the moment it ought to be emphasised that this first phase, although it witnessed a redistribution of land, and therefore a widening of the base of land ownership, continued to maintain and underline the sanctity of private ownership of the means of production, and only moved in the direction of emphasising the promotion of co-operative societies in the agrarian reform lands. Other measures of social welfare were to follow and were to show concern for the well-being of the underprivileged and the poor, particularly the housing schemes which succeeded in moving thousands of *sarifa* dwellers around the Tigris in Baghdad out into newly constructed housing units of much better quality and supplied with basic amenities. But these measures could not in themselves be considered a manifestation of a socialist transformation but of social concern.

However, these qualifications ought not to be taken as a denial of the worth of the work done for the lower-income groups in the country, including the small farmers and tenants and the poorer urban dwellers — the last group benefiting in addition from the distinct amelioration of the amenities of life in the big cities, particularly Baghdad, in the years 1958-63. The improvement of conditions of a large segment of the poor is a fact which nobody can seriously deny.

The shift in the pattern of ownership of productive assets from the private to the public sector was initiated in the second phase of transformation, July 1964 to July 1968. The bulk of the shift was accomplished through the series of nationalisation decrees in the summer of 1964, to which reference has already been made. These decrees passed on to the public sector all insurance and re-insurance companies, all commercial banks and several large industrial and commercial companies. In addition, the 'Economic Organization' was formed for the purpose of running the companies nationalised as well as the management set-ups and companies originally in the government sector. The Organization was hailed as a 'socialist institution'. The nationalised banks were also placed under a newly formed institution, the 'General Organization of Banks'. (The re-allocation of the various companies and banks to larger, mother institutions was later rearranged, first in 1965 and later in 1968, 1969 and 1970.)[65]

The socialisation decrees of 1964 contain another element of social significance. This element, as already indicated in section 1 above, was the earmarking of 25 per cent of the profits of all corporations to the labourers and employees. In addition, these acquired power through the legislative clauses which stipulated that they should be represented on the boards of directors.

The third phase, July 1968 to the present, is characterised by three developments: broadening of the base of public ownership, through further nationalisations; reorganisation of the establishments in the public sector with a view to the strengthening of the control of this sector at the top level, and the regrouping of establishments on a functional basis at the lower level; and modification of the agrarian reform laws in 1970 in the light of the experience of the preceding twelve years. The second of these developments was meant to tighten the grip of government on the reins of top policy in economic establishments in its domain and, supposedly, to permit greater flexibility in operation. Thus, this measure *in itself* does not reflect some aspect of socialist transformation, but in effect was mainly an improvement at the operational level.

To the three developments one must add a fourth of a different nature but of equal significance, namely the promotion of planning to a higher level — in the sense that it became more serious, more comprehensive and more sophisticated. In fairness, it ought to be pointed out that planning witnessed a qualitative change in the 1965-9 plan, which was prepared in the two years following Qassim's overthrow. The authorities which took over in July 1968 can therefore claim full credit only for the 1970-4 plan, which is currently in operation.[66] (Further credit goes to the authorities in the period following July 1968 for the improvement in techniques and effectiveness in sectoral planning, in financial planning parallel to the economic planning, and in the establishing or evolution of ancillary or contributive agencies and services that enrich and add rationality to the planning, execution and follow-up processes.)[67]

The developments following the year 1958, but particularly those following 1968, have been incorporated into an ideological framework and plan of action, which is the Charter (or Covenant) of National Action of 15 November 1971, which was announced to the nation by President Bakr.[68] This important document relates in an integrated manner political independence to socio-economic independence, and with the socialist transformation. Essentially, the basic idea is that political democracy cannot be attained and preserved without an understructure of socio-economic democracy — or distributive justice within socialism. Although in a sense the Charter is an *ex post* justification or rationalisation of the policies formulated and implemented in the years 1958-71, it remains important in so far as it embodies and confirms the convictions and policies of the ruling group.

The steps followed in the transformation of the political and socio-economic system after July 1958 have also been placed within a theoretical framework by a former Secretary-General of the Ba'ath Party, Munif al-Razzaz.[69] In a pamphlet published in 1972, he describes the course which should be pursued in the transformation, and the course which is worded in general, aprioristic terms, follows step by step the actual unfolding of events in Iraq. Thus, beginning with the undoing of feudalist and capitalist control over government, the 'liberation' of government and the undoing of landed feudalism, the transformation proceeds to the setting up of the first stages of socialism, to comprehensive planning, and from there to the extension and deepening of these phases. The argument is not rigorous, in the sense that it does not prove that other possible courses of action are not 'maximising' or 'optimising' courses, or superior courses, but is simply assertive. One must admit, however, that this kind of presentation which is *ex post* theorising is comfortable only to the converts and believers. The open-minded critic can ask whether some other sequence of phases would not have been more effective in attaining the same objectives.

Agrarian Reform[70]

As in the case of Egypt and of Syria, agrarian reform in Iraq was defined to be more comprehensive and far-reaching than land reform. It was to encompass the limitation of land ownership, which is implied in land reform, but in addition to include the regulation of landlord-tenant relations in favour of the tenant, the improvement of the conditions of agricultural labour, and the promotion of co-operative societies in the reform areas. In this respect, the three pieces of reform legislation are almost identical in spirit for the three countries.

However, the background to reform was different, as the discussion of the situation preceding 1958 in Iraq and Syria, and preceding 1952 in Egypt, will show. One major area of difference is the pattern of land ownership between the private and the public sectors. The pattern was clearest in Egypt, as far as forms of tenure are concerned; furthermore private ownership was the predominating pattern in this country to an extent far exceeding that in either of the two other countries. While the failure to complete land settlement operations in Iraq and Syria made it impossible to pass final judgement on the forms of tenure and the pattern of state versus private ownership, it could still be said that tenure arrangements were much more complicated in Iraq than in Syria. In the latter country, state land, or *miri* land, was in considerable measure in private hands, but then under straightforward arrangements, comparatively speaking.

In contrast, in Iraq the disposition of *miri* land was complicated by the facts of tribal ownership, as well as by the multiplicity of forms under which *miri* land was under private control. Thus, out of an area of 120,000 sq. km. of cultivable land, some 80,387 sq.km. are accounted for in the following table. A little over 2 per cent of this latter area is genuine full-fledged private property *(mulk sirf)*, while about 72 per cent is in effect state land *(miri)* that was being exploited by private owners under either the *tapu* or *lazmah* forms or arrangements.

Table 2.14: Types and Areas of Tenure and Percentage of Totals

Type of Tenure	Area (ha)	Per Cent
Miri land: *Tapu*	3,120,397.0	38.82
Lazmah	2,646,919.0	32.92
Miri sirf	1,171,134.2	14.57
Miri land not yet declared	925,984.8	11.52
Total *Miri*	7,864,435.0	97.83
Waqf land	109,768.8	1.37
Sub-Total	7,974,203.8	99.20
Mulk Sirf land	64,499.5	0.80
Total	8,038,703.3	100.00

Notes: The definition of the various types of tenure was given earlier in this chapter.

'*Miri* land not yet declared' refers to land not yet covered by settlement operations and the identity of which has not therefore been determined finally.

Source: Abdul Wahab M. Al-Dahiri, *Economics of Agrarian Reform*, p. 166.

The table therefore shows that land reform, in its narrow sense, involved only a small fraction of the cultivable land, namely the relatively tiny area in full private ownership — *mulk sirf*. Redistribution of this area could not be expected to constitute a major measure of reform. However, the reform essentially aimed at the limitation of the size of ownership in the areas which are nominally at least state land (*miri* land) but which had been assigned to private owners either on *tapu* or *lazmah* terms. So, in effect, the reform to this extent constituted the reclamation by the state of its land for redistribution with the object of widening the base of ownership.

Agrarian reform was instituted through Law No. 30 of 30 September 1958, three days after Syria's first reform law. As indicated earlier, the reform legislation of Iraq aimed at, simultaneously, the elimination of feudalism and the preservation of private ownership. However, the latter was contained within specified limits. The principle of compensation was respected in law, while the principle of just distribution of land was also sought.

The decree contained four sections. The first relates to the setting of a ceiling for land ownership and the mechanisms and procedures involved. The second relates to the formation of co-operative societies in the agrarian reform lands. The third organises tenancy relations, while the fourth deals with the rights of agricultural labour. The highlights of this first piece of legislation will now be presented briefly, for the four sections together.

- A ceiling for private ownership was set at 250 ha of irrigated land (whether flow or pump irrigated) or at 500 ha of rain-fed land; in case the land was of both types, the area was determined in the ratio between the two.
- Companies and societies whose purpose was to develop or reclaim land were allowed to own land beyond the ceilings set.
- No further land allowance was made for wives and dependent children (as the Egyptian and Syrian laws had done) on the principle that the ceiling set in the Iraqi law was very high (compared with 80 ha in Egypt for irrigated land, there being no rain-fed agriculture which is not also irrigated there, and with 80 and 300 ha respectively in Syria).
- Excess areas were to be expropriated within 5 years of the coming into force of the law (later amended to 10 years as a result of the difficulties encountered in the establishment of ownership).
- Compensation was allowed to the landowner. The basis of compensation is the type of land and the amount of investment in it, as well as the extent and nature of relations between landlord, tenant enjoying usufruct, and farmer who merely plants trees in the land of others. The owner of title to the land was entitled to two-thirds and the beneficiary of the usufruct to one-third of the compensation. A further allowance was made to the landowner for machines or buildings on the land. The compensation for the land was to be estimated by special, widely representative committees.
- If the total compensation was ID1,000 or less, it was to be paid in cash; amounts in excess of ID1,000 and less than ID10,000 were to be paid for in bonds bearing annual interest at 3 per cent, and redeemable in 20 years. If compensation was still owed beyond ID10,000, then interest-bearing bonds redeemable in 40 years were given.
- Areas expropriated (plus *miri sirf* land earmarked for the purpose) were to pass to the control of the Agrarian Reform Authority for distribution. Eligibility for distributed land was determined according to a system of priority, under which landless farmers or farmers with holdings below the minimum of distributed plots were entitled to new land, provided they worked on the land in some capacity or other. Where two or more persons were equally eligible, priority was given to the one (or ones) with a larger family, in greater need, and closer to the land. Machines and equipment on the land may be passed on to co-operative societies that were to be formed under the agrarian reform law.
- The plots to be distributed were to be no less than 7.5 ha and no more than 15 ha of irrigated land, and no less than 15 ha and no more than 30 ha of rain-fed land (the minima were later made more flexible, if the quality of land was good and permitted a predetermined income considered adequate).
- Payment by the beneficiaries was to be effected in the following manner: half the value estimated for the land for compensation purposes, plus the full value of trees, plus 1 per cent interest, plus 10 per cent for administrative and distribution expenses were to be calculated and the total to be paid in 40 equal annual instalments.

— The beneficiary got the land free of all liens and ties, and was allowed to register title to it in his name without the payment of any fees. On the other hand, he was obligated to cultivate it, to join an agrarian reform co-operative society, and to facilitate the work of the society; he was liable to lose the land within five years if he failed in any of these obligations in the eyes of the Authority.
— The Agrarian Reform Authority was established in order to take over expropriated land and distribute it, to operate the land in the interim between expropriation and distribution, to form co-operatives and supervise them. The Authority was given considerable status through its composition; it was to be chaired by the Prime Minister and was to have 10 Ministers as members, one of whom was to be the Minister of Agrarian Reform (who was to run the business of the Authority).
— Agrarian reform co-operative societies were to be formed in villages and areas where the reform was applied; all beneficiaries were required to become members, as well as other farmers to whom agrarian reform land was leased. Other farmers were allowed membership if the area of their land-holding was within the size of the distributed plots.
— Tenancy relations between landowner and tenant or owner of irrigation facilities were regulated; these relations were to be recorded in a written, three-year contract. The contracts specified the respective shares of the produce for each of the parties, and protected the tenant against eviction except in the case of a major violation of the contract. (The tenant's share was to be 55 per cent of the produce of pump-irrigated land, 65 per cent in flow-irrigated land, and 75 per cent in rain-fed land).
— Finally, special committees were set up to determine the wages of agricultural labour, and labour was allowed to unionise.

The implementation of the first reform law met with many difficulties relating to expropriation and distribution. A brief listing of the main types of difficulties will suffice to indicate their nature.[71]

Expropriation moved faster than the capacity of the administration of the Authority warranted. Consequently, vast areas were expropriated and remained for years neither distributed, leased nor directly exploited. This resulted in a slowing down of total agricultural production. Delays in the land registration department were serious, owing to the insistence on documentary evidence of ownership which was often not available. Furthermore, land settlement operations had not covered all the areas involved in agrarian reform.

Another group of problems related to the delay in the selection by the former landlords of the areas they chose to keep, or in the many requests for substitution of certain plots of the former landlord's land for other plots, or in the take-over by the Authority of small parcels of land lying between the large expropriated holdings which had to be acquired for the purpose of consolidating land holdings with the Authority and effecting rational distribution and land use.

There was also the problem of multiplicity of types of land ownership and tenure in the country, and the lack of clarity and the overlapping of these types. This problem was compounded by the presence of pumps, buildings, trees and other forms of investment on a sizeable portion of the land affected by the reform law. Furthermore, when these problems were encountered in land that had not yet been covered by land settlement operations, or in land that had been sold but where the sales had not been registered in the registry offices, the establishment of legitimacy of ownership and the allocation of rightful claims became next to impossible.

Lastly, the shortage of engineers and surveyors, and of experienced land officers capable of serving on the various committees connected with expropriation, compensation and distribution (and willing to live or at least stay for extended periods in the countryside) was a further serious delaying factor. Even the means of transport for officials were grossly inadequate and added to the lengthy proceedings.

Another set of problems was related to the temporary administration and utilisation of the expropriated land by the Authority. I have already referred to this aspect, but it needs emphasis. Here the problem was, in addition to the problems already referred to under expropriation, one of shortage of personnel for administration and utilisation, shortage of equipment of all types and for all purposes, shortage of prior plans, but above all near-absence of a clear policy and guidelines. To all this must be added the overall, permeating inefficiency and weak motivation of the civil service, and its rigid bureaucratisation and heavy-handedness.

The distribution phase has proved more complicated and its problems more intractable than the earlier phase of expropriation and take-over by the Authority, if only because the organs charged with the task of distribution and choice of beneficiary had to deal with a much larger number of cases than the organs charged with effecting expropriation. Thus, in addition to the difficulties of establishing ownership rights and boundaries, there was the difficulty of distribution within a general context of administrative and technical inefficiency and personnel shortages, and of legal complications. The whole process was therefore painfully slow and tortured. Two specific problems merit separate mention here: the establishment of the *lot viable* in every case, or the area required to provide a reasonable income and level of living in the vast expanse of the country; and the selection of beneficiaries out of vast numbers of seemingly equally eligible candidates — without (overt) favouritism or corruption. To relate these problems is to indicate the near-impossibility of fairness and efficiency.

In summing up his evaluation of the first agrarian reform, Abdul Wahab M. Al-Dahiri, a leading expert on the subject, said: 'It can be concluded that agrarian reform had a legal and social content, but lacked a technological and production content.'[72] Behind this conclusion lie a number of findings and observations based on the experience of the years 1958-70. This experience showed that the mere mechanics of expropriation and distribution would consume many more years before these operations could be completed, judging by the slow achievement made in the twelve years preceding 1970 when Al-Dahiri was writing. The slowness is in turn inherent in the complicated nature of the operations of declaration of ownership of excess areas, establishment of boundaries and areas owned, actual expropriation, preparation for distribution, and finally distribution and registration of new title. The complicated nature of these tasks has been compounded by cumbersome procedures and shortage of personnel, within a confused legal framework and an incomplete land settlement-of-title situation.

By 1970 it became evident that the 1958 law had other defects with regard to concepts and principles relating to agrarian reform. Thus, on 21 May 1970, Law No. 117 put into effect the second agrarian reform and attempted to correct the procedural defects and to introduce certain amendments to the original law thought to provide greater social justice. The major changes in the law will now be recorded:

— The ceilings of ownership were lowered: thus, the ceiling for rain-fed land ranged now between 250 and 500 ha, and that for irrigated land between 10 and 150 ha (the first range including 4 steps, and the second 11 steps). The purpose of this amendment

was to further reduce the inequality in land distribution, and to take into account the various levels of rainfall, types of irrigation and crops.
— However, the law excluded from these limitations fruit and date tree-land where the trees were over 5 years in age and numbered at least 160 per hectare.
— Landowners were required to go on cultivating the excess areas that were to be expropriated, on contract with the government, until expropriation was effected. This measure was intended to avoid land lying idle, which had happened with the application of the original law.
— Evasions of the law through fictitious mortgages or through division of the land among heirs, even if these had pre-dated the new law, were considered null and void, and the new ownership limits applied as though the original landowner was still alive and no lien had been placed on his land.
— Compensation for the land was cancelled altogether, but remained effective for machines, pumps, buildings and trees. However, compensation was to be paid to owners of little parcels separating areas affected by the agrarian reform.
— Tenancy and cultivation rights, and the rights of *sirkals* (agents) were all clearly defined and expressed in terms of areas allowed or financial compensation.
— Distribution to beneficiaries continued to be governed by a system of priorities, but the areas allowed were altered. The plots of distribution ranged in area between 25 and 50 ha for rain–fed land, and 1 and 15 ha for irrigated land (or one-tenth the ceiling allowed in every case). The conditions of cultivation and non-sale, and of membership in co-operative societies, continued to operate as in the original law.
— Distribution could be extended to the citizens of other Arab countries.
— Distribution was not merely in individual plots of land, but could be in large areas to groups — a measure which was designed to lead to the setting up of collective farms.
— No payment was to be made for land thus distributed.
— Provisions were made for the regulation of tenancy relations in a more detailed and specific manner than in the original law.
— No provision was included regarding the wages of agricultural labour; presumably the old regulations continued to operate in this respect.
— Finally, land settlement-of-title operations were discontinued; the determination of rights in the land not yet covered by settlement was made to pass to agrarian reform committees in order both to avoid the irregularities that had accompanied the laws under which settlement had been conducted, and the legal and procedural delays that had been experienced. Under the new law the tenure system also was simplified: thus all land involved in the reform was considered *miri sirf*.

Another law had been issued at the same date (No. 116 for 1970) whose aim was to set up a Supreme Agricultural Council, under the chairmanship of the President of the Republic and the membership of the Ministers of Agrarian Reform, Agriculture and Irrigation, the President of the Federation of Agricultural Societies, plus five full-time members with high-level expertise in economics, irrigation and drainage and agrarian reform. The new agrarian reform law passed on to the Council all the rights and duties that the original law had entrusted to the Agrarian Reform Authority.

It is possible now to survey the country's performance in the field of agrarian reform from 1958 to the end of 1973, as data are available for the whole period. Three patterns can be distinguished: the first extending to 1964 and characterised by the active distribution of expropriated and of *miri* lands; the second covering the years 1965-8, characterised by a much slower process of distribution; and the third from 1969 to December 1973, again showing acceleration in land distribution, both of expropriated and *miri* lands.

The latter part of the sixties and the early seventies have also witnessed improvement in total agricultural production and in food production compared with the years 1961-5 as base. Likewise, the number of co-operative societies, their membership, their paid-up capital and the area of land operated by them have all shown notable expansion over the same period. In addition, by the end of 1973, 53 collective farms had been formed, reportedly with 75,000 ha of land in operation. These developments are no accident, but seem strongly to indicate that the government was becoming increasingly capable of coping with the problems which had been besetting the agrarian reform measures and slowing down their implementation. Table 2.15 will help in tracing developments since 1958 with respect mainly to the expropriation and distribution of land.[73] It ought to be explained here that the areas available for distribution comprised two categories: private lands and *miri* lands. The first category subject to agrarian reform has been estimated at 2.9m ha.[74] However, the tabulation takes into account the two categories and presents some information on the number of beneficiaries involved, and the co-operative societies formed and in operation.

Table 2.15: Expropriation and Distribution of Land, 1958-73

Areas expropriated From 1958 to 31 May 1970	1,047,377 ha
June 1970 to end 1973	1,366,714 ha
Total expropriated, 1958-73	2,414,091 ha
Areas distributed From 1958 to end 1970	839,503 ha
From 1971 to end 1973	466,379 ha
Total distributed, 1958-73 (of which 550,405 ha *miri*)	1,305,882 ha
Number of persons affected by expropriation From 1958 to end 1970	2,411 persons
From 1971 to end 1973	Not available
Number of beneficiaries of distribution From 1958 to end 1970	99,779 persons
From 1971 to end 1973	42,896 persons
Total beneficiaries	142,675 persons
Land temporarily under Ministry of Agrarian Reform leased to farmers in 1973	1,975,002 ha
Number of lessees in 1973	226,296 persons
Number of agricultural co-operatives formed by end of 1973	1,275 societies
Number of members	201,490
Paid-up capital	ID490,293
Reserve capital	ID330,880
Loans advanced to societies by Agricultural Bank in 1973	ID2,784,422
Cumulative area of land operated by societies, decade 1964-73	3,363,500 ha

Source: *Annual Abstract of Statistics*, 1970, Tables 45-48 and 52; *Annual Abstract of Statistics*, 1973.

In closing, it is appropriate to make two observations. First, that there is still a great deal to be done with respect to the completion of distribution, although the process has been accelerated since 1969; and second, that the relatively small number of beneficiaries suggests that what is basically needed is the large-scale reclamation and distribution of state *(miri)* land, along with the extension of irrigation and drainage works, extension services, much more adequate agricultural credit, and the availability of agricultural machinery and rural repair shops. There has been improvement in most of these areas of action, but a great deal more is called for.

4. DEVELOPMENT PLANNING

The planning experience of Iraq goes further back than that of any other Arab country. As early as 1927, when the government received its first oil royalties, these revenues were treated as a budgetary surplus and accordingly a three-year plan was drawn up for the years 1927-30. Two-thirds of these revenues were spent on roads, building and bridges. To set this procedure on firm ground, a capital works development law was passed in 1931 which governed the use of oil revenues; in addition to investment in public works, the revenues were also in part used as grants to industry.[75] 'The dual budgeting system, ordinary and capital, continued to be in effect until 1950. The "capital works" budget's expenditure ranged from ID0.43 million in 1933 to ID3.6 million in 1950.'[76]

The situation differed noticeably in 1950 in two ways, first, because in that year a Development Board was formed 'in anticipation of the pending change in the contractual arrangements between the government and the oil companies. . . [and] to serve as a vehicle for the utilization of the rising oil revenue';[77] and secondly because the size of the development plans was to become much larger from 1951 onwards. It remained true, however, that the 'planning' continued to be no more than programming in the public sector, that is, the compiling together of certain (usually large) capital projects that are normally executed by the public works ministry or department, or its equivalent.

The Board was entrusted with the task of formulating economic and financial plans for the development of the country's resources and the rise in the people's standards, as well as with the execution of these plans.[78] The combination is quite unusual, as the planning and the execution functions are normally undertaken by separate agencies for reasons of better control and avoidance of excessive concentration of power. The Board was initially allowed complete autonomy legally, financially and administratively. It was to receive all the oil revenues for development work; however, in 1952, owing to the steep rise in these revenues, and the obvious inability of the Board to invest all the allocations at its disposal, it was decided to reduce its share from 100 to 70 per cent of the revenues.[79]

The Board was heavily weighted in favour of engineers, and none of its five members (who had 5-year appointments) was an economist – the executive member being a retired British accountant with colonial experience. The engineering bias showed itself in the fact that the projects included in its plans were based on engineering, technical studies, but not on equally high-level economic studies of feasibility and general relevance to the whole economy. No system of priorities was laid down, and no development strategy was formulated.[80] Furthermore, the plans, inspired by the limited philosophy of the Board, had very little social content, and no concern for the destination of the flow of goods and services that were to result from the execution of the projects, and how this flow was to influence the level of living of the people. They merely had vague ideas that all would feel benefits as a result of development.

The Board's vast powers, resources and autonomy created jealousies in the circles of government, and by 1953 it was decided to curtail this 'extraterritoriality' of the Board by establishing a Ministry of Development, and changing the constitution of the Board. This body was now to be under the chairmanship of the Prime Minister, and to have the Ministers of Development and of Finance, and four other members. These four were to have expertise in economic, financial and other related areas, such as irrigation. Though enjoying less power now, the Board continued to have vast influence. It was during this period that Lord Salter, a British economist, was invited in 1954 to examine the whole field of development policy and the Board's role, and to submit recommendations.

Institutionally, the situation remained unchanged until after the July 1958 revolution. Thereupon the Board was abolished, and a ministerial committee in co-operation with the Ministry of Development was entrusted with the conduct of development planning and plan implementation. But in 1959 new machinery was designed. An Economic Planning Council was set up and the name of the ministry was changed to that of Ministry of Planning. The Prime Minister chaired the Council, and it included as members Ministers whose area of work was directly related to development. Another change, of even greater significance, was the further reduction of the share of the development agency from 70 to 50 per cent of oil revenues.

Later, in 1964, the composition of the Council was changed. It remained under the chairmanship of the Prime Minister, but only the Ministers of Planning, Economy and Finance remained as members. New additions to membership were made: the Governor of the Central Bank, and four full-time members with ministerial rank. Furthermore, a Steering Committee was established. This Committee (consisting of the Minister of Planning and the four full-time members) was to lay down planning policy and to formulate investment plans 'and to coordinate between economic, financial, and monetary policies, as well as follow up the plan in all the stages of its execution'.[81] The Council was to be the supreme authority at the top policy and decision level, while the Ministry was to examine the various suggestions and partial plans submitted by the ministries, to comment on them, and to submit its recommendations to the Council. Once the Council approves the plan in its final integrated form, it submits it to the Council of Ministers for final approval and the issue of the necessary decree for execution. This structure, with very minor alterations, has remained in effect to the present time. The changes that have occurred in the structure of the planning agencies since 1951 are not abnormally frequent, compared with other Arab countries. However, the plans formulated have been numerous, and the rate of 'plan turnover' has been high. The brief survey of the plans which follows confirms this judgement.

Seven plans have been formulated for the years 1951-69.[82] The eighth, which runs for the five years 1970-4, has just ended its life span. However, this plan itself was drastically amended in 1971, and again in 1974. The planned investment by the central government was raised in 1971 from ID536.9m to ID952.5m, as a result of the steep rise in the oil revenues expected for the years 1970-4, and further raised to ID1,169m in March 1974 for 1974/5 alone. The structure of the investment programme was also amended accordingly.[83] A summary of the first seven plans is presented in Tables 2.16 — 2.19, while the eighth plan is shown separately in Tables 2.20 and 2.21.

There are four magnitudes or dimensions to consider in connection with these plans: what might be called planned or 'theoretical' revenue allocations or revenues set for the plans in the plan documents and the laws instituting them, actual revenues allotted, planned or 'theoretical' expenditure allocations in the plans, and actual expenditures. The pattern

Table 2.16: Expenditures Outlined in the Various Iraqi Development Programmes and Plans 1951/2–1969/70 (millions of Iraqi dinars, except as indicated)

	The First Five-Year General Programme (1951/2–1955/6)		The Six-Year General Programme (1951/2–1956/7)		The Five-Year General Programme (1955/6–1959/60)		The Revised Six-Year General Programme (1955/6–1960/11)		The Provisional Economic Plan (1959/60–1962/3)		The Detailed Economic Plan (1961/2–1965/6)		The Five-Year Economic Plan (1965/6–1969/70)	
		Percentage		Percentage		Percentage		Percentage		Percentage		Percentage		Percentage
Agriculture	30.0	45.7	53.4	34.4	114.4	37.6	168.1	33.6	47.9	12.2	113.0	20.0	142.0	25.2
Industry	–	–	31.0	19.9	43.6	14.3	67.1	13.4	48.7	12.4	166.8	29.4	157.0	28.0
Transport and Communications	15.9	24.2	26.8	17.2	74.2	24.4	124.4	24.9	100.8	25.7	136.5	24.1	91.0	16.2
Building and housing	12.6	19.2	18.0	11.6	60.9	20.0	123.2	24.6	190.7	48.7	140.1	24.7	108.7	19.4
Other	7.2	10.9	26.2	16.9	11.1	3.7	17.3	3.5	4.0	1.0	10.0	1.8	62.5	11.2
Total	65.7	100.0	155.4	100.0	304.2	100.0	500.1	100.0	392.1	100.0	566.4	100.0	561.2	100.0

Source: Republic of Iraq, *Official Gazette*, Laws Nos. 35 of 1951, 25 of 1952, 43 of 1955, 54 of 1956, 181 of 1959, 70 of 1961 and 87 of 1965.

Table 2.17: Revenues Allocated in the Various Iraqi Development Programmes and Plans, 1951/2–1969/70 (millions of Iraqi dinars, except as indicated)

Sources of Revenues	The First Five-Year General Programme (1951/2–1955/6)	Percentage	The Six-Year General Programme (1951/2–1956/7)	Percentage	The Five-Year General Programme (1955/6–1959/60)	Percentage	The Revised Six-Year General Programme (1955/6–1960/1)	Percentage	The Detailed Economic Plan (1961/2–1965/6)	Percentage	The Five-Year Economic Plan (1965/6–1969/70)	Percentage
Oil	91.1	95.8	164.6	97.6	215.0	99.7	385.0	98.7	315.8	55.8	390.0	69.5
Foreign loans	4.0	4.2	4.0	2.4					77.2	13.6	95.0	16.9
Domestic loans											30.0	5.4
Interest payments					0.6	0.3	4.8	1.2				
Profits from government establishments and institutions									22.8	4.0	12.0	2.1
Cash balances									5.0[a]	0.9[a]	30.7[b]	5.5[b]
Revenues from other sources (deficit)									142.6	25.2		
Miscellaneous			0.1	0.1	0.1		0.2	0.1	3.0	0.5	3.5	0.6
Total	95.1	100.0	168.7	100.0	215.7	100.0	390.0	100.0	566.4	100.0	561.2	100.0

a. As of 31 March 1965.
b. As of 31 March 1968.
Source: As for Table 2.16.

of the relationship between these magnitudes is confused. Thus, from 1951/2 to 1955/6 the total of actual revenue exceeded that of planned, or theoretical, revenue by about ID24m.[84] Thereafter, actual revenue fell below planned revenue in every year. Another unusual feature is that in the First Five-Year General Programme 1951/2 — 1966/6 and in the Six-Year General Programme 1951/2 — 1956/7 (that is to say, the first plan and its amendment), planned revenue exceeded planned expenditure. (See Tables 2.16 and 2.17 above.) This feature was never to be repeated again.

There is greater uniformity with regard to the comparison between planned and actual expenditure, as in every plan except the Provisional Economic Plan 1959/60 — 1962/3 planned expenditure exceeded actual expenditure. For the whole period 1951/2 — 1969/70, planned allocations totalled ID1,947.5m, while actual expenditure totalled ID959.4m, or an overall rate of execution of 49.3 per cent. However, the rate varies from plan to plan, and from year to year, ranging from a low of 29.1 per cent for the year 1959/60 (when planning was virtually absent, and only a provisional plan was under way), to a high of 73 per cent for 1955/6. On the other hand, actual expenditure is a noticeably higher proportion of actual revenue (as against theoretical or planned revenue). Actual revenue totalled for the 19 years indicated ID1,093.7m, while actual expenditure totalled, as already stated, ID959.4m. The global performance here is as high as 87.7 per cent. However, this relationship is not very significant, since the fact that actual allocations are noticeably below planned allocations is in itself an indication that the economy is unable to absorb, and the planning authority unable to execute, a much larger volume of investment.

Table 2.19 presents a comparison between planned revenues or allocations, actual revenues, and actual expenditures year-by-year. However, looking at the performance plan-by-plan and sector-by-sector, in Table 2.18[85] we observe the total relationships for the seven plans for the years 1951-70.

Table 2.18: Total Planned and Actual Expenditure, 1951-70

Sector	Planned Expenditure	Actual Expenditure	Percentage Execution
Agriculture	483.1	187.4	36.9
Industry	412.9	189.0	45.8
Transport and communications	450.5	205.6	45.6
Building and services	513.9	290.4	56.5
Total or average	1,860.4	872.4	46.9

Two observations emerge from this brief summary. First, the highest rate of plan execution was in the years covered in those areas of investment least directly productive, namely in public buildings, housing and services, while the sector most obviously in need of investment and full of promise, namely agriculture, witnessed the slowest rate of execution. Industry, transport and communication fall in between with an almost identical performance. Second, the structure of investment allocation does not, *prima facie,* seem to reflect what one would presume to be the valid priority system in the economy. It would seem to me that a more defensible structure would give first priority to agriculture, equalled or closely followed by transport and communications, followed by industry, and finally by building, housing and services. The structure was obviously a question of deep concern for policy-makers and planners, as is evidenced by the frequent changes in the system of sector priorities from one plan to another, and even within some of the plans, as reflected in the amendments. (See Table 2.16.)

Table 2.19: Comparison of Planned Allocations, Actual Revenue and Actual Expenditure, 1951/2–1969/70 (ID million)

Year	Allocations	Actual Revenue	Actual Expenditure	Actual/Planned Expenditure (%)	Actual Expenditure/ Actual Revenue (%)
1951/2	9.4	7.5	3.1	33.4	41.9
1952/3	20.5	24.0	12.8	62.8	53.5
1953/4	28.4	35.3	12.3	43.2	34.7
1954/5	31.6	40.8	20.9	66.4	51.2
1955/6	46.6	60.8	34.0	73.0	56.0
1956/7	81.9	51.1	43.0	52.5	84.2
1957/8	101.6	35.9	57.4	56.5	160.1
1958/9	99.6	61.8	52.2	52.5	84.6
1959/60	171.7	43.4	49.9	29.1	115.0
1960/1	143.9	47.7	47.6	33.0	99.8
1961/2	196.9	66.7	66.9	34.0	100.4
1962/3	108.5	70.0	59.3	54.6	84.7
1963/4	118.3	67.6	54.3	45.9	80.3
1964/5	120.6	76.5	75.3	62.4	98.4
1965/6	126.0	75.0	59.8	47.5	79.7
1966/7	143.1	70.8	82.8	57.9	116.9
1967/8	142.3	81.8	68.9	48.4	84.3
1968/9	129.0	87.5	72.2	56.0	82.5
1969/70	127.6	89.5	86.7	67.9	96.5
Total or Average	1,947.5	1,093.7	959.4	49.3	87.7

Source: Ministry of Planning, *Summary of Results*, Tables 2 (p.9) and 9 (p.16).

How does one evaluate the overall performance of Iraq's experience in developmental planning until 1970? Here the picture can be both simple and complicated. It is simple inasmuch as the global performance in terms of ratio of execution is clear enough, both if considered as actual developmental expenditure related to planned expenditure (49.3 per cent), or related to actual revenue directed to the plans (87.7 per cent). It is obvious that what matters most for the purposes of the *practicability* of plan execution is actual revenues put at the disposal of the plan, and in this respect execution achieved a high level of 87.7 per cent over the two decades 1951-70. Equally clear is the performance in terms of the ratio of actual to planned expenditure. Here the verdict is much more severe, inasmuch as the performance fell to half the planned level.

What is more complicated is the picture of performance if this is examined year by year and sector by sector. It would occupy too much space to undertake this kind of detailed examination with a view to registering aberrations and discerning trends. We will therefore merely emphasise the wide divergence between planned and executed investment for all the sectors and for all the years. The reasons behind the divergence are many and fall in various areas, but we will defer their examination for the moment, dwelling instead on the conclusion that the planning experience of the country was wasteful in terms of resources and time, as well as expectations; and that in addition it resulted in a performance, in terms of growth, which was distinctly below the *prima facie* potential of the country.

The global assessment of the causes of relatively poor performance has already received some attention when the major cause was identified as lying in the realm of political management of the economy: a combination of violent political struggle, instability, change of policy and institutions, low level of popular political participation, and the resultant hesitation of the civil service on top of its inefficiency. It is time now to identify the major causes for the poor planning performance, both with regard to the methodology of plan formulation and to plan execution and follow-up. In this evaluation I rely both on the library material available and also on the view of close observers and their analyses and insights.[86] The picture that emerges reveals the following categories of shortcomings:

— absence of a global conception of the future society and economy desired, which would enable the planning policy-makers to conceptualise the future;
— insufficient clarity and firmness of development strategy embodied in the plans;
— non-comprehensiveness of planning prior to the 1965-9 plan;
— frequent changes of planning strategy and priorities and the consequent hesitation and slowness of investment activities;
— frequent and erratic policy changes;
— in many instances, lack of supporting policy measures to give body to plans, especially with regard to plan expectations of the private sector;
— contradiction between expectations of the private sector on the one hand, and the political and socio-economic framework on the other;
— weakness of planning units in the various ministries and autonomous agencies falling in the public sector broadly defined;
— the absence of a social content in the earlier plans, that is those preceding the 1958 revolution;
— inadequate concern for socio-cultural factors contributive to the success of planning, and poor mobilisation of the masses in support of the plans;
— until very recently, shortage of statistical information needed in the formulation of background studies and plans;
— general inefficiency, slowness and low motivation of the civil service; the fragmentation of its loyalty; and its relative unpreparedness for developmental tasks;
— weaknesses in execution; interruptions; insufficient co-ordination between executive agencies;
— inadequacy of plan follow-up and re-evaluation and adjustment processes;
— shortage of technical and economic research behind plan formulation;
— shortages of contracting services and failures of some contractors, as well as slowness to settle accounts for contractual work performed; and
— deficiencies in foreign aid utilisation.

Iraq has just implemented the latest of its plans, the Five Year Plan 1970-74. When passed in 1970 as Law No. 70 of 1970, the Plan was to have a total allocation of ID1,143.7m for the five years; this sum was to come from the public sector (including allocations by the central government; the public sector in the narrow sense, that is, the income-earning establishments in the hands of government as a result of nationalisation or established initially by the government; and local administrations) and the private sector. The pattern of allocations per agency or source of financing can be seen in Table 2.20.

Iraq

The objectives of the plan are summarised below:

— promoting national income with a view to achieving a growth rate of 7.1 per cent per annum on the average, in real terms;
— emphasising the development of 'productive' sectors (that is, commodity sectors — the distinction being made in the Plan between this category and each of the categories of distribution sectors including transport, communications and storage; trade; finance and insurance; and other service sectors including housing and other services). Special emphasis is placed on agriculture and industry;
— improving health, education and other social services;
— increasing employment opportunities and guaranteeing decent standards of living for low-income groups; and
— achieving better geographical distribution of projects, with special emphasis on the northern area in order to narrow the grounds of complaint by the Kurds there and by other communities which felt that the Baghdad area was being unduly favoured.

Financing of the Plan in so far as the private sector was concerned was to be effected out of the resources at the disposal of this sector. The same was true of the publicly owned, income-generating establishments and institutions. The central government was to rely heavily (to the extent of ID425m or 79.1 per cent of the central government's contribution) on oil revenues, whose ratio to the overall investment programme of ID1,143.7m was 37.2 per cent. The next largest source was to be foreign loans, to the tune of ID60m or 5.2 per cent of total allocations (equivalent to 11.2 per cent of allocations by the central government). None of the other sources exceeded 1 per cent of total allocations or 2.1 per cent of central government allocations. The distribution of investment allocations, both by sector and source, appears in Table 2.20. This table shows that if all sources of financing are considered together, agriculture comes out as the main beneficiary, followed by industry, transport, communications and storage and other services. The exact allocation pattern emerges from the table. It ought to be pointed out that there was a substantial allocation — ID27.3m — for foreign loans and other commitments, as well as ID44m as loans to various government agencies.[87]

It was not long before the Plan was subjected to major amendment in April 1971, in so far as the allocations by the central government were concerned.[88] These allocations were raised to ID952.5m, or an increase of 77.4 per cent over the original allocations of ID536.9m. The reason given in the enacting law was the steep rise in the expectations of oil revenues over the relevant period. The new pattern of allocation per sector of central government outlays is presented in Table 2.21.

Since the nationalisation of the Iraq Petroleum Company in June 1972 and the drastic drop in oil revenues, there has been serious speculation about the government's adherence to the more ambitious amended investment programme. It seemed then that this programme would have to be scaled down in practice (if not by legislation) to agree better with the financial realities of the new situation. This was but one illustration, if that was needed, of the rather spurious changes in plan strategies and investment programmes to which the country has been subjected throughout. Surely the steep rise in oil revenues did not provide adequate proof that the economy could *pari passu* absorb an equally steeply raised investment programme. The 1971 amendment was probably unwarranted in the first place.

Further evidence of this almost obvious observation has come much more recently — in March 1974, when the allocations made by the central government for 1974/5 were

Table 2.20: Sectoral Distribution of Investments in the 1970-4 Plan

Economic Sector	Central Government ID m	Central Government Per Cent	Public Establishments and Local Administrations ID m	Public Establishments and Local Administrations Per Cent	Private Sector ID m	Private Sector Per Cent	Total ID m	Total Per Cent
Agriculture	185.0	34.5	8.0	2.5	18.0	6.3	211.0	18.4
Industry	106.6	19.8	55.9	17.4	50.0	17.5	212.5	18.6
Mining and quarries	1.0	0.2	153.6	47.7	–	–	154.6	13.5
Electricity	24.4	4.5	2.5	0.8	–	–	26.9	2.4
Transport, communications and storage	60.0	11.2	54.3	16.9	35.0	12.3	149.3	13.1
Trade and finance	–	–	17.5	5.4	15.0	5.3	32.5	2.8
Housing	1.0	0.2	9.2	2.8	150.0	52.6	160.2	14.0
Other services	74.0	13.8	20.8	6.5	17.0	6.0	111.8	9.8
Miscellaneous other investments	13.6	2.5	–	–	–	–	13.6	1.2
Sub-total	465.6	86.7	321.8	100.0	285.0	100.0	1,072.4	93.8
Foreign commitments	27.3	5.1	–	–	–	–	27.3	2.4
Loans to government agencies	44.0	8.2	–	–	–	–	44.0	3.8
Sub-total	71.3	13.3	–	–	–	–	71.3	6.2
Total	536.9	100.0	321.8	100.0	285.0	100.0	1,143.7	100.0

Source: The Ministry of Planning.

very steeply increased, as the result of the much greater availability of financial resources after the October War of 1973 and the quadrupling of oil prices. As indicated earlier, the allocation was raised to ID1,169m, whereas it had stood at ID296m the year before. Table 2.22 shows the directions of the new allocation, compared with those for the year 1973/4.[89]

If one bears in mind the absorptive and project execution capacity of the country in the preceding 23 years 1951-73, one would realise that as large an allocation as that set for 1974/5 could not be justifiably used in one year. Here again, as in the past, the availability of financial resources has been confused with the ability to turn these resources into developmental projects within the same time-reference. It will probably prove possible (and wise) to expand investment considerably in 1974/5, but not at all close to the dimension of the newest allocations.

5. CONCLUDING REMARKS

The major conclusions which can be drawn from this analysis of Iraq's economic development over the past thirty years have already suggested themselves, and only a very brief highlighting of the one overriding observation need to be made at this point. This is that the economy's performance has been both good and poor. It can be considered good if it is viewed in itself — merely as a rate of growth of somewhat over 6.5 per cent on the average

Iraq

Table 2.21: Allocations after Amendment in 1971

	ID m	Per Cent
Agriculture	336.5	35.3
Industry	207.3	21.8
Transport and communications	96.6	10.1
Buildings, housing and services	120.1	12.6
Sub-total	760.5	79.8
Planning and follow-up agencies, statistical agencies, Special fund and other agencies	8.8	0.9
Loans to governmental agencies, including interest borne by the Plan	82.3	8.7
International commitments[a]	46.3	4.9
Miscellaneous investment expenditures[b]	54.6	5.7
Sub-total	192.0	20.2
Total	952.5	100.0

Notes: a. In original amendment, ID44m; later raised slightly.
b. In original amendment, ID56.7m; later reduced slightly.

Table 2.22: Allocations for 1973/4 and 1974/5

Sector	1973/4 ID m	1974/5 ID m
Agriculture	65	190
Industry	45	225
Transport and communications	35	120
Buildings and services	35	175
Major development projects	–	400
Other	116	59
Total	296	1,169

at constant prices for the period 1953-71 for which the statistical series is complete.

But the performance can be considered poor if this rate of growth is measured against the country's rich endowments and great potential which could have permitted a distinctly higher rate if certain conditions had been satisfied. The conditions relate mainly to the framework, institutions and processes of economic decision-making both in the public and private sectors; and it was and still is within the power of society to meet the conditions, foremost among which is political stability coupled with greater political participation and orderly, non-violent, change of government. The performance can also be considered poor in certain specific areas which lie behind the global rate of growth. We have already referred to a few of these, and we need only repeat here that much more can yet be achieved in the development of the oil sector, agriculture, non-oil state revenues and the capabilities of the public administration.

It is perhaps appropriate to end the chapter with a note of cheer that the present political management of the economy seems to be intent on and capable of bringing about those favourable changes in the economy which are necessary to turn a substantial part of its potential into actuality. The years 1968-74 amply justify such optimism on the several fronts of action in which the country has been engaged.

NOTES

1. Mohammad Salman Hassan, *Studies in the Iraqi Economy* (Beirut, 1966; Arabic), p. 308.

2. For an examination of the period preceding 14 July 1958, when a violent revolution overthrew the monarchy and radically changed the locus and structure of power, and of the subsequent years leading to 1968 (the landmark of relative political stability) see: (a) The Royal Institute of International Affairs, RIIA, *The Middle East: A Political and Economic Survey* (Oxford University Press, 1958, third edition), chapter on Iraq; (b) Peter Mansfield (ed.), *The Middle East: A Political and Economic Survey* (London, Oxford University Press, 1973); (c) Europa Publications, *The Middle East and North Africa: 1971-72, 1972-73, 1973-74 and 1974-75* (London, annual editions), chapter on Iraq; (d) Caractacus, pseud., *Revolution in Iraq: An Essay in Comparative Public Opinion* (London, 1959); and (e) Malcolm H. Kerr, *The Arab Cold War* (Oxford University Press, 1971).

3. The main references perused in the presentation of the general survey are: (a) F.H. Gamble, *Iraq* (Overseas Economic Survey Series, H.M. Stationery Office, London, June 1949, revised April 1950); (b) IBRD, *Economic Development of Iraq* (Baltimore, 1952); (c) RIIA, op. cit.; (d) FAO Mediterranean Development Project, *Iraq – Country Report* (Rome, 1959); (e) Mohammad S. Hassan, op. cit.; (f) General Union of Chambers of Commerce, Industry, and Agriculture in the Arab Countries (General Union. . .), *Economic Development in the Arab Countries 1950-1965* (Beirut, 1967; Arabic), Chapter on Iraq; (g) Jawad Hashem, Hussain Omar and Ali Al-Menoufi, *Evaluation of Economic Growth in Iraq 1950-1970*, Vol. I, 'The Experience of Planning', Vol. II, 'Evolution of Commodity Sectors'; and Vol. III, 'Appendices to Vol. II – Evolution of Commodity Sectors' (Baghdad, 1971; Arabic). This work has been most useful and I am especially indebted to it; (h) Albert Badre, 'Economic Development of Iraq', in Charles A. Cooper and Sidney S. Alexander (eds.), *Economic Development and Population Growth in the Middle East* (New York, 1972); and (i) Europa, op. cit. My examination of the national accounts of Iraq has benefited greatly from Khair id-Din Haseeb, *Estimation of National Income in Iraq 1953-1961* (Beirut, 1963; Arabic). Many other references have been consulted relating to specific areas of the economy, but credit will be attributed at the appropriate places in this chapter.

4. Gamble, op.cit.

5. FAO, op. cit., Appendix II – 1.

6. See, for instance, Abdul-Wahid Al-Makhzoumi, *Economic Survey of the Iraqi Republic* (Baghdad, 1969; Arabic), quoted in Hashem et al., op. cit., Vol. I, p. 14.

7. Hashem et al., op. cit. Vol. I, Table 8, p. 273, and Central Statistical Organization, *Annual Abstract of Statistics 1973*, pp. 55 and 58 for 1973. (See also Hassan, op. cit., Table 40, p. 172, relating to population distribution 1867-1947.)

8. UNESCO, *Comparative Statistical Data on Education in the Arab States, An Analysis 1960-61 – 1967-68* (prepared by the UNESCO Office of Statistics, Paris, and published by the Regional Center for Educational Planning and Administration, Beirut, 1970), p. 49.

9. *Annual Abstract of Statistics 1970*, pp. 58-9.

10. The potential labour force numbered 2.257m or 50 per cent of the settled population of 4.564m. Obviously this estimate is derived from the addition of all age groups capable of engaging in gainful employment. See Hassan, op. cit., pp. 176-82.

11. K.G. Fenelon, *Iraq: National Income and Expenditure 1950-1956* (Baghdad, 1958), pp. 9 and 10.

12. Table 248, p. 427.

13. Vol. I, Tables 11 and 12, pp. 276 and 277.

14. Doreen Warriner, *Land and Poverty in the Middle East* (London, 1948); Hashem et al., op. cit., Vol. II, Ch. 5; and IBRD, op. cit., Annex A, 'IV. Natural Resources'.

15. Quoted from IBRD, op. cit., pp. 138-9.

16. Published in 1970 in Baghdad; Arabic. For a study with a broad, regional (i.e. Arab) angle, see Abdul-Razzak al-Hilali, *The Story of Land, the Peasant and Agrarian Reform in the Arab Homeland* (Beirut, 1967; Arabic). This book is not as well organised as Al-Dahiri's, but it is well documented and useful for comparison between the various Arab countries that have initiated agrarian reform.

17. Doreen Warriner, *Land Reform and Development in the Middle East: A Study of Egypt, Syria and Iraq* (RIIA, second edition, 1962), p. 140.

18. Warriner, *Land and Poverty. . .*, pp. 106-7.

19. Warriner, *Land Reform*..., p. 136.
20. Warriner, *Land and Poverty*..., p. 113.
21. *Annual Abstract of Statistics 1970*, Table 3, p.8.
22. Europa, *1971-72*, pp. 279-80. However, estimates of irrigated area vary. Thus, FAO *Production Yearbook 1972* (p. 5) cites the irrigated area as being 3.675m ha in 1963 (no more recent estimate is given). The discrepancy probably arises from insufficient distinction between potentially and actually irrigated areas — to say nothing of confusion in the estimation of the latter category owing to the variation in the quantity of water available per hectare.
23. From an interview in March 1972 with a member of the Supreme Agricultural Council.
24. According to Hashem et al., (Vol. II, pp. sers are very sparingly used (about one sixth of current agricultural machines and pumps represents a mere 10 per cent of the needs of a modernised agriculture. Fertilizers are very sparingly used (about one-sixth of current needs being filled) and expansion would require a vast increase in the importation and/or local production of fertilisers. The use of pesticides and insecticides is also minimal, causing the loss of tens of millions of dinars worth of crops annually.
25. We must add to this part on agriculture that livestock is a rather important component of the sector. Although information on its specific contribution to national product is not available, the livestock population suggests its level of importance. The population and the number slaughtered in 1970 are detailed below:

	Population	Slaughtered
	(thousands)	
Sheep	13,831	2,410
Goats	2,412	624
Cattle	1,830	320
Buffaloes	288	27
Camels	253	15

(See *Annual Abstract of Statistics 1970*, Table 73, p. 121.) The *1973* Abstract records the numbers slaughtered in 1973, but not the total population (Table 76, p. 140).
26. The sources mostly consulted for the discussion on petroleum (in this as well as subsequent chapters) are: (a) David H. Finnie, *Desert Enterprise: The Middle East Oil Industry in Its Local Environment* (Cambridge, Mass., 1958); (b) George Lenczowski, *Oil and State in the Middle East* (Ithaca, New York, 1960); (c) Zuhayr Mikdashi, *A Financial Analysis of Middle Eastern Oil Concessions 1901-65* (New York, 1966); (d) Charles Issawi and Mohammed Yeganeh, *The Economics of Middle East Oil* (New York, 1962); (e) J.E. Hartshorn, *Oil Companies and Governments: An Account of the International Oil Industry in its Political Environment* (London, 1967); (f) Arabian American Oil Company, ARAMCO, *Aramco Handbook: Oil and the Middle East* (New York, 1968); (g) Stephen H. Longrigg, *Oil in the Middle East: Its Discovery and Development* (RIIA, Oxford University Press, 3rd edition, 1968); (h) Abbas Alnasrawi, *Financing Economic Development in Iraq: The Role of Oil in a Middle Eastern Economy* (New York, 1968); (i) Michael Tanzer, *The Political Economy of International Oil and the Underdeveloped Countries* (Boston, 1969); (j) George W. Stocking, *Middle East Oil: A Study in Political and Economic Controversy* (London, 1970); (k) Sam H. Schurr and Paul Homan, *Middle Eastern Oil and the Western World: Prospects and Problems* (New York, 1971); (l) Basim Itayim, *Iraqi Oil Policy 1961-1971* (M.A. thesis at American University of Beirut; unpublished; 1972); (m) Zuhayr Mikdashi, *The Community of Oil-Exporting Countries: A Study in Governmental Co-operation* (London, 1972); (n) Ragaei El Mallakh and Carl McGuire, *Energy and Development* (Boulder, Colorado, 1974); and (o) Nicolas Sarkis (ed.), *Arab Oil and Gas Directory 1974* (The Arab Petroleum Research Center, Beirut, October 1974).
27. Nicolas Sarkis, 'The Energy Crisis and the Challenge of Development in the Arab Countries', Paper No. 132 (A - 1) for the Ninth Arab Petroleum Congress, Dubai, 10 - 16 March 1975, p. 16.
28. Summed up in Itayim, op. cit., pp. 28-9, on the basis of the reporting of the *Middle East Economic Survey* (weekly, Beirut), especially 14 April 1961.
29. Itayim, op. cit., Ch. IV.
30. Ministry of Planning, Economics Department, *Summary of the Results of Follow-up of the Execution of Investment Targets for the Economic Programmes and Plans in Iraq 1951-1961* (Baghdad, May 1971; Arabic), various tables.
31. See Alnasrawi, op. cit., Ch. 3, and Badre, loc. cit., for a detailed examination of the significance of oil for Iraqi development.
32. I have relied in this section on several sources, particularly: (a) IBRD, chapter on 'Industry'; (b) Abdul Gani al Dally, 'Problems of Industrial Enterprises in Iraq', in *Middle East Economic Papers 1954* (Beirut, 1954); (c) Arthur D. Little, Inc., *A Plan for Industrial Development in Iraq* (2 vols., full report and summary report; Cambridge, Mass., May 1956); (d) Kathleen M. Langley, *The Industrialization of Iraq* (Cambridge, Mass., 1960); (e) UN, *Industrial Development in the Arab Countries* (New York, 1967), pp. 63-83; (f) Hashem et al., op. cit., Vol. II, Chs. 6 and 7; (g) General Union of Chambers of Commerce ..., *Arab Economic Report* (Arabic), annual editions including that of 1975; and (h) Europa, op. cit., the *1971-72, 1972-73, 1973-74* and *1974-75* editions.
33. Langley, op. cit., Table 5, pp. 58-9.
34. Ibid., Chs. III and IV.
35. Information for 1971 from *Annual Abstract of Statistics 1973*, Section VI, and from *Abstract 1970*, Section XXI for 1969. (*Abstract 1973* does not present an index number series for industrial production — hence the reference to 1969 in the text, but not to more recent years.)
36. The stock-taking for the years 1971-4 is based mainly on the *Arab Economic Report* (the relevant years down to the report for 1974) and Europa, op. cit., the *1973-74 and 1974-75* editions, chapter on Iraq in both sources.
37. Hashem et al., op. cit., Vol. II, pp. 447-55.
38. Thus, out of total allocations for industry of ID409.4m during the years 1951-69, only ID185m were actually invested, or 45.2 per cent of the total. Ibid., p. 509.
39. This discussion of problems encountered by industry follows the same pattern in ibid., pp. 499-523.

40. IBRD, op. cit., pp. 62-71 and Annex G.
41. *Annual Abstract of Statistics 1973*, Section XXII for 1972-3.
42. For 1949/50, see *Statistical Abstract 1959*, Table 246, p. 306; for 1972-3, see *Abstract 1973*, Table 180, p. 321.
43. IBRD, op. cit., p. 49.
44. Europa, op. cit., 1971-2 edition, p. 11.
45. The comparison is based on data in *Statistical Abstract 1951*, Ch. VI, and in *Annual Abstract of Statistics 1973*, Section XVIII.
46. Mud, reed or tin huts along the Tigris, clustered in the most unhygienic and unattractive way possible.
47. Only 2,900 housing units were constructed in 1972 by government (against 14,171 by the private sector). See *Abstract 1973*, p. 448.
48. K.G. Fenelon, *Iraq: National Income and Expenditure 1950-1956* (Baghdad, 1958), a pamphlet, pp. 3-29.
49. The 1953-6 estimates were initially made in a doctoral dissertation at Cambridge University. This work was later published under the title *The National Income of Iraq 1953-1961* (RIIA, Oxford University Press, 1964), and in Arabic under the same title (Beirut, 1963). Estimates for 1962 and 1963 appeared in a stencilled monograph for limited circulation entitled 'The National Income of Iraq 1962 and 1963'.
50. Other estimates were also made by Issam Ashour and Jan Ernest, but these were 'secondary source' estimates.
51. *Annual Statistical Abstract 1973*, Section IX. The UN *Statistical Yearbook 1973* (p. 544) quotes the consumer index for the whole country as being 121 for 1971 and 127 for 1972.
52. See Hashem et al., Vol. I, p. 14.
53. The discussion of investment, and the information contained, are based on: (a) Jawad M. Hashem, 'The Structure of Fixed Capital Formation by Foreign Oil Companies Operating in Iraq During 1957-1969 and its Contribution to the Iraqi Economy' (Stencilled paper; 15 pages); (b) Hashem et al., op. cit., Vol. I, Statistical Appendix Tables 23-39; and (c) Relevant issues of the *Abstract*.
54. Data from *Statistical Abstract 1951*, Section XXI; *Annual Abstract of Statistics 1973*, Section VIII; and *International Financial Statistics (IFS)*, December 1974.
55. See *Statistical Abstract 1951*, Section XXVIII, and *Annual Abstract of Statistics 1973*, Section XI.
56. This section draws on the general surveys cited in Note 3 above, as well as on Carl Inversen, *A Report on Monetary Policy in Iraq* (Copenhagen, 1954), Chs. 1 and 2; Lord Salter, *The Development of Iraq* (Iraq Development Board, 1955); and Alnasrawi, op. cit. For quantitative information, see *Statistical Abstract 1951*, Sections XXIX and XXXI; *Annual Abstract of Statistics 1973*, Sections X and XIII; and *IFS*, December 1974.
57. *IFS*, December 1974; data for July 1974 for all countries cited.
58. *Annual Abstract of Statistics 1970*, Section IX, and *Abstract 1973*, Section X.
59. Such as Inversen, Langley, Arthur D. Little, and Hashem et al. (Vol. II, Ch. 5).
60. *Arab Economic Report*, 1974 edition, pp. 372-5 for the 1973 budget. This report has a large discrepancy between the total allocations (and revenues) as registered, and the components once aggregated. On checking with the publishers, I ascertained that the aggregates are correct but that the supplementary budget estimates are wrong. They ought to read ID700m for expenditure (instead of ID1,375m), and ID615m for revenue (instead of ID1,290m).
61. This complaint has been voiced by several writers. But see especially Alnasrawi, op. cit. (Ch. 5 and 'Statistical Appendix') and Badre, loc. cit.
62. Alnasrawi, p. 125. For references to the ratio of income tax to GNP for the years 1965/6 – 1969/70, see *Annual Abstract of Statistics 1970*, Chs. VIII and XIII.
63. *Annual Abstract of Statistics 1973*, pp. 331 and 332.
64. These generalisations are based on *Statistical Abstract 1951*, Table 247, p. 307; Alnasrawi, op. cit., Table 24, p. 168; *Annual Abstract . . . 1970*, Table 113, p. 287; and *Annual Abstract . . . 1973*, Table 182, p. 324.
65. Hashem et al., Vol. I, pp. 2-5.
66. Ibid., Vol. I, Ch. I, for a thorough discussion of the developments in the planning techniques, mechanisms and institutions between 1951 and the end of 1969. More recent evaluations are contained in three papers (all in Arabic) presented at the Fourth Conference of the Federation of Arab Economists, held at Kuwait 17-20 March 1973: (a) Saqr Ahmad Saqr, 'Planning and Economic Development in Iraq 1959-1969'; (b) Taher Hamdi Kanaan, 'Planning Economic Development: The Iraqi Experience'; and (c) Jawad Hashem, 'Comment on Paper Presented by Dr. Taher Hamdi Kanaan on the Iraqi Experience in Planning Economic Development'.
67. Hashem et al., op. cit., Vol. I, Ch. II for a detailed examination of the areas benefiting from the improvements concerned. (See also Kanaan's paper cited in Note 66 above.)
68. 'The Charter of National Action' (announced by President Ahmad Hassan al-Bakr on 15 November 1971; a pamphlet published in Arabic in Baghdad, 1971, and distributed by the Ministry of Information); see also *Al-Thawra* (Arabic daily, Baghdad), Special Supplement to No. 987 of 16 November 1971.
69. Munif al-Razzaz, 'The First Stage in the Establishment of Socialism' (Culture-of-the-Masses Series, No. 1, Baghdad, 1972; Arabic).
70. This part of the chapter relies heavily for documentation (regarding laws – both original and amendments, statistics, institutions), for background, for policies, and for evaluation on the following sources: (a) Doreen Warriner, *Land and Poverty. . .* , Ch. VII; (b) FAO, *Iraq: Country Report*, Chs. I and II; (c) Doreen Warriner, *Land Reform . . .* , Ch. IV; (d) Sa'doun Hammadi, *Towards A Socialist Agrarian Reform* (Beirut, 1964; Arabic); (e) John L. Simmons, 'Agricultural Development in Iraq', in *The Middle East Journal*, Vol. 19, No. 2 (Spring 1965); (f) Sa'doun Hammadi, *Agrarian Reform in the Arab Countries: A Comparative Study* (Planning Institute for Economic and Social Development, Damascus, Research Paper, No. 2, 1967; Arabic); (g) Mohammad Salman Hassan, op. cit., Part II; (h) Ahmad Fuad Khalifah, *Agricultural Extension Services in the Arab Countries: A Comparative Study* (Community Development Center in the Arab World, Sers-il-Layyan, Egypt, 1967; Arabic), pp. 71-82; (i) Abdul-Razzak Al-Hilali, op. cit., Documentary Appendix for texts of laws and their amendments; (j) Riad el Ghoneimy, *Land Policy in the Near East* (Compilation

published by FAO, Rome, 1967, for the government of Libya), pp. 218-34; (k) Doreen Warriner, *Land Reform in Principle and Practice* (Oxford, 1969), Ch. IV. (l) Abdul Wahab M. Al-Dahiri, *Economics of Agrarian Reform* (Baghdad, 1970; Arabic), Chs. 17-29 and Appendices 3 and 4; and (m) Hashem et al., op. cit., Vol. II, Ch.V. I should here recognise a special debt to Dr Al-Dahiri not only for the help I have derived from his clear and careful research and has candid evaluation of agrarian reform measures, but also for the discussions I had with him in 1972 during an extensive interview.

71. See Al-Dahiri's relevant analysis, Chs. 18 and 19.
72. Ibid., p. 254.
73. Detailed quantitative information can be found in Parts Five and Six of Section V in *Annual Abstract of Statistics 1973*. However, area of land operated by the collective farms is reported in Europa, op. cit., *1973-74* edition, p. 339. The tabulation that follows draws on *Abstract 1973* for information to 31 December 1973, but on *Abstract 1970*, Tables 45-48 and 52 for information to 31 May 1970, when the new agrarian reform measures were taken.
74. This total is given by Al-Dahiri, op. cit., p. 295.
75. Langley, op. cit., p. 47.
76. Alnasrawi, op. cit., p. 35.
77. Ibid.
78. The only other Arab country where planning and execution functions were combined was Libya, in 1952 and again in 1960, for a very brief period in each instance.
79. Law No. 23 of 1950. For the historical narrative relating to planning machinery in Iraq, see Hashem et al., op. cit., Vol. I, pp. 41 ff.
80. Lord Salter was the first observer, as far as I know, who described the Board's planning as 'engineers' planning'. See Salter, op. cit., p. 49.
81. Hashem et al., op. cit., Vol. I, p. 50.
82. See 'Plan Implementation in Iraq, 1951-1967', paper by Dr Khair-al-Din Haseeb in UNESOB, *Studies on Selected Development Problems in Various Countries in the Middle East, 1969*, (New York, 1969), pp. 1-17, for a thorough examination and analysis of the structure of the plans, and the shortcomings of performance. (In this latter connection, see also Hashem et al., op. cit., Vol. I, pp. 81-91.) The fullest examination of plans and plan performance for the years 1951 through 1969/70 can be found in Ministry of Planning, *Summary of Results of Follow-up of the Execution of Investment Targets in the Economic Programme and Plans of Iraq 1951-1969* (Baghdad, 1971; Arabic). A summary of these results in this 'Summary' is to be found in Ministry of Planning, *Progress Under Planning* (Baghdad, 1972; Arabic). However, the most recent and thoughtful analysis is in Dr Taher H. Kanaan's paper already referred to (Note 66 above).
83. See Ministry of Planning, *Law of First Amendment to Law of National Development Plan for the Years 1970-74* (Baghdad, 1971; Arabic); text of law and appended tables; mimeographed. For 1974 amendment, see *Middle East Economic Survey* (Beirut weekly), Vol. XVII, No. 24, 5 April 1974, pp. 4-5.
84. See Table 3 in Haseeb's paper (p.8), referred to in Note 82 above.
85. Table 4 in Haseeb, loc. cit. (p. 9), and Tables 3-7 in *Results* . . ., op. cit., pp. 10-14.
86. Haseeb, loc. cit., pp. 81-91; Hashem et al., op. cit., Kanaan, op. cit., as well as interviews with several well qualified persons both formerly and currently involved in planning and development work.
87. The information presented with regard to the 1970-74 Plan comes from the Ministry of Planning, *Summary of Results*. . . , Tables 10 and 11, pp. 17 and 18.
88. Ministry of Planning, *Law of First Amendment. . . etc.*, especially p. 9 for the new global allocations by the central government.
89. MEES, op. cit., Vol. XVII, No. 24, 5 April 1974.

3 KUWAIT

The physical, social and financial contrast between the Kuwait of immediate post-war years and the Kuwait of today is so enormous as to defy brief description. Some of the accounts written of Kuwait's transformation might seem to a reader who is not acquainted with the country to dramatise the magnitude and directions of this transformation, but are in fact quite true to life. Even those surveys and analyses prepared by observers who cannot be accused of writing the 'public relations' kind of material devote sizeable portions to a recapturing of the change in the country's profile over the years.[1] To attempt to encapsulate the main features of the transformation in a few sentences would force us to use superlatives and would therefore sound both laboured and unconvincing. Consequently, we will try to introduce the analysis of this chapter by a brief highlighting of the main developments since 1946, in such a way as to suggest the major areas of progress and avenues of potential, without losing sight of the main shortcomings and weaknesses relating both to the past achievements and the directions the future seems likely to take.

Without anticipating the account to follow, it is relevant to emphasise here that the recent economic history of Kuwait brings out a point which sometimes fails to receive adequate recognition in the literature on development. This point is the simplicism implied in the identification between the level of *per capita* income and development. Thus Kuwait has come to enjoy 'super-affluence' before reaching a state of development in the sense most widely accepted today. A closely related point that emerges is the possibility for some countries under certain circumstances to jump one or more 'stages of growth'. Again, Kuwait seems to have been catapulted from the traditional phase, in the Rostovian sense, or at best from the stage of the preconditions to the take-off, right into the stage of high consumption, in less than one generation. The narrative of this sudden jump, and the dangers which have accompanied it, will occupy us in the first and last sections.

1. THREE PHASES OF TRANSFORMATION

The year 1946 is a clear dividing line between the pre-oil and the oil eras,[2] for it was in this year that the first shipment of oil was made from the country. Until then, the Kuwaiti economy depended mostly on pearl fishing, merchant shipping, shipbuilding, and import, export and re-export trade. The combination of these activities enabled the country to derive a relatively satisfactory income. Although this income did not exceed the equivalent of $21 per head, according to estimates made retroactively in the mid-sixties, it compared favourably with the level of well-being predominant then in the Gulf area.

The nature and exigencies of the economic activities which formed the sources of this income shaped the social structure of the community and its outlook and skills. Essentially the structure acquired strong elements of complementarity and co-operativeness. Thus, the shipbuilders built the boats that sailed the seas, and the boats carried the cargo which the import and export merchants dealt with. Likewise, the pearl divers who worked in teams for Kuwaiti captains and entrepreneurs in the summer became seamen on the boats during winter. It is estimated that thousands of men and hundreds of boats were occupied in this way between summer and winter, whether in pearl diving or in merchant shipping.

Apart from the obvious skills which the Kuwaitis acquired through their diving and seafaring activities, they also acquired more intangible but no less significant qualities and skills, such as daring and venturesomeness, shrewdness and calculativeness, dynamism, fluency in English, and the attributes of an open society — qualities and skills that even the casual observer cannot fail to see today.

However, even before the dramatic development of oil and gas resources at the end of World War Two, the pre-oil activities were being curtailed due to technological changes outside the control of the community. Thus, pearl fishing shrank considerably owing to the development of cultured pearls in Japan. Merchant shipping, which absorbed part of the shock and provided jobs for many divers, soon suffered in turn from the shift from sail to steamboats. The resilience of the Kuwaitis came to their rescue again, this time in the substantial promotion of trade in the precious metals with India and the Far East, along with the two-way trade in the exports and imports of the whole Gulf area.

It was probably the extreme frugality of nature that forced the Kuwaitis to become outward-looking. Going out to sea was hardly a matter of choice for a community which had desert and semi-desert land to live on, no agriculture, a rainfall of about 4 inches a year, flat land everywhere, an uncomfortably hot climate — and a sea adjoining its land. Drinking-water itself had to be brought by boat from Shatt-al-Arab, the meeting point of the Tigris and Euphrates in south Iraq. It is little wonder that the people turned to the sea and to trade for livelihood.

The first shipment of oil in 1946 had twelve years of preparation behind it, from 1934 when the Ruler granted a concession for exploration to the Kuwait Oil Company. It is interesting to note that the concession stipulated that the company should make a cash-down payment of £35,250 and in addition pay a royalty of 4 shillings and 6 pence per ton of production, provided the total royalty did not fall below £18,750 a year. From these very modest expectations, oil revenue rose for the first four years of production to reach a total of some KD^*5m, probably doubling the national income per year. While this was not opulence in absolute terms, considering the low income per head in 1945, it represented a sudden spurt in relative terms, which was to be followed by steep rises in revenue all through the period 1946-74 (except for 1968/9, when the revenue dropped by 6.3 per cent[3]).

The post-war period falls into three easily discernible sub-periods: (a) 1946-51, or the 'warming-up' phase, during which oil revenues, though rising fast, were still modest, being KD5m for the years 1946-9, KD4.9m for 1950, and KD6.7m for 1951; (b) 1952-61, or the building boom phase; and (c) 1962-75, or the independence and consolidation phase. Since oil occupies a central place in the post-war developments, it will be useful to present in Table 3.1 a tabulation of oil revenues from 1946 to 1974.

Phase One: 1946-51

We will briefly explain the marked difference between the oil revenue for 1951 and that for 1952. But it is necessary first to identify the years 1946-51. According to the First Five-Year Plan document, although these years had not witnessed the vast increase in oil revenues which came in later years, and although the society still lived within a political, social,

*Kuwaiti dinars.

Table 3.1: Kuwait's Revenues from Crude Oil Exports 1946 to 1974 [a]

Year	Receipts KDm	Annual Per Cent Change
1946-49	5.0	
1950	4.9	
1951	6.7	36.7
1952	20.7	209.0
1953	60.2	190.8
1954	69.3	15.1
1955	100.5	45.0
1956	104.3	3.8
1957	110.2	5.7
1958	128.5	16.6
1959[b]	159.8	16.0[c]
1960	158.6	6.4[d]
1961/2	167.1	5.4
1962/3	173.0	3.5
1963/4	190.6	10.2
1964/5	206.2	8.2
1965/6	216.2	4.8
1966/7	231.7	7.2
1967/8	263.1	13.6
1968/9	246.5	-6.3
1969/70	279.3	13.3
1970/1	279.7	6.6
1971	460.5[e]	64.5
1972	543.2	17.9
1973	992.9[f]	82.8
1974	2,588.2[f]	160.7

a. Starting 1960, years begin 1 April and end 31 March the following year.
b. Revenue from 1 January 1959 to 31 March 1960, or 15 months.
c. Since revenue indicated is for 15 months, the prorated annual revenue is KD149.1m, which shows the rate of increase indicated over the previous year.
d. The rate of change of 6.4 per cent relates to the prorated annual revenue of KD149.1m for the year before.
e. The dollar was devalued in 1971. The revenue in dollars, which was $1,399.8m, has been converted at the rate of $3.04 to one Kuwaiti dinar.
f. The conversion rate used for 1973 is $3.37, and for 1974 $3.40.

Sources: For 1946-9, Planning Board, *The First Plan for Economic and Social Development for the Five Years 1966/67-1970/71* (Kuwait, 1965; Arabic), Ch. 1; for 1950-1970/1, *Annual Statistical Bulletin 1970;* for 1971-4, for which calendar years are used, revenue is quoted from Nicolas Sarkis, 'The Energy Crisis and the Challenge of Development in the Arab Countries', Paper No. 132 (A-1) for the Ninth Arab Petroleum Congress held in Dubai, 10–16 March 1975, p. 17, Table 2. (Revenue for 1973 and 1974 is estimated by Dr Sarkis.)

economic, organisational and administrative system nearer to the traditional system characteristic of the pre-oil era than to the modern system whose features emerged in later years, 'yet the public authorities began to see the broad contours of the future, with its distinguishing features and its problems, its hopes and its misgivings, its abundance and its tensions',[4] This is manifest in the administrative reorganisation under which four boards were set up, for education, health, municipal affairs and *Waqf* (charitable endowments) affairs respectively. Furthermore, Kuwait was subjected to far-sighted town planning discipline; infrastructure received attention and funds, particularly in the areas of electricity, water, public works, public buildings and finance.

This first sub-period also witnessed the beginnings of the influx of thousands of skilled and semi-skilled labourers, and of professional men and executives, Arab and non-Arab, who were attracted by the promise of a building and reconstruction boom. The expectations were more than fulfilled in the years to come, but at a social cost which deserves, and will receive, special discussion at a later point.

The steep and sudden increase in oil revenues in 1952 over the year before arose partly from an increase in the volume of production, but predominantly from a drastic change in the formula for profit allocation between the concessionary companies (a second company, American Independent Oil Company, having in the meantime been granted a concession) and the country. According to this formula, which was first applied in Saudi Arabia between the country and the Arabian American Oil Company (ARAMCO) and was to become the general pattern for the whole Middle East, net profits were to be shared 'fifty-fifty', between Kuwait and the producing companies. The predominance of the profit-sharing factor over the production factor can be seen from the fact that production rose from 204.0m barrels in 1951 to 273.4m in 1952, an increase of 33.4 per cent, while revenue rose from KD6.7m to KD20.7m, an increase of about 209 per cent.

The sharing formula continued to improve in the interest of Kuwait over the years to come, with the result that the same discrepancy between increases in production and in revenue continued to appear. Thus, although production was to rise to an index of 390.5 for 1971 (1952=100), that is, to rise in absolute terms from 273.4m barrels to 1,067.6m, the revenue index was to rise to 2,225 for 1971 (1952=100), or in absolute terms from KD20.7m to KD460.5m.

The vast expansion in production itself relied on the existence of huge oil reserves in the country. The proven and published reserves stood at the beginning of 1974 at 10,540 million tons, second only to Saudi Arabia's reserves in the whole world. The ratio of total reserves to total production for 1974 is over 82 times — that is, at the 1974 rate of production, the recoverable reserves can last 82 years. These magnitudes are sufficient to give a clear indication of the significance of the country's oil wealth, particularly in the light of its small population and its relatively small land area. If reserves, production, revenue and exports are related to population *and* area, then Kuwait ranks second in the world after Abu Dhabi on the basis of *per capita* of population or square mile of land area. Put in a world context, and in absolute terms, Kuwait ranks second to Saudi Arabia in reserves, as already indicated, and sixth in production after the United States, USSR, Saudi Arabia, Iran and Venezuela — in that order.

It is relevant to add here that the country is 15,000 square kilometres in area, while the Neutral Zone, south of the country, and control of which it shares with Saudi Arabia, has a total of 5,700 square kilometres. The population at the start of the period under examination, 1946, could not have exceeded 90,000, since according to the census of 1957 it only numbered 206,473 inhabitants in that year, of whom 92,851 were non-Kuwaiti.[5] In addition to the need to eliminate the non-Kuwaiti elements and to account for natural increase in population between 1946 and 1957, there is need also to account for the several thousand tribesmen who came in the period in question from the Iraqi and Saudi Arabian deserts, settled in Kuwait and acquired citizenship. (The volume of settlement was to expand considerably in later years.)

It was thus this phenomenon of sudden super-affluence which made possible the leaps and bounds in terms of physical transformation and rise in *per capita* income to which repeated reference will be made in this chapter.

Phase Two: 1952-61

We indicated earlier that the second sub-period in the thirty years under examination stretches from 1952 to 1961. The choice of the first year has been explained; that of the last year is made mainly on political grounds. It was in June 1961 that Kuwait and the United Kingdom terminated an agreement dating back to 1899, according to which the latter controlled Kuwait's foreign policy. Formal independence was soon followed by entry into the League of Arab States and the exercise of other acts of sovereignty. The new political status imposed certain internal economic obligations on the new state, and inspired certain regional economic policies, all of which were made feasible thanks to the new wealth.

However, the ten years 1952-61 were already, even before independence, very busy years in the economic and organisational spheres, and they witnessed some important developments that were to leave their mark on the economy and society in the following period 1962-75, both at home and abroad. As the changes extended into many areas, it will be simpler to discuss them under appropriate headings.[6]

1. Government and Municipal Organisation: The government organised its structure to become more capable of handling the new and enlarged functions made possible by oil revenues and made necessary by the vast expansion in infrastructure. This manifested itself in the setting up of departments and staff, and in the strengthening of the municipality of the city of Kuwait. In the rush of construction it was not possible to set up a planning agency to deal with the allocation of resources; neither the experience nor the discipline required was available to make planning feasible. However, in 1952 the government set up a Development Board whose function was to co-ordinate construction activities, especially with respect to public utilities. The membership of the Board first included senior public officials only, but later (1960) representatives of the private sector as well. The Board continued to exist till 1962 when independence was obtained and the government was reorganised, and a new Planning Board was decreed. The programmes of the Board remained underfulfilled, mainly because it had no regulatory but merely co-ordinative and advisory power, and because pre-investment studies were, on the whole, slow and inadequate. Contractors were mostly non-Kuwaiti residents who employed engineers and skilled and semi-skilled labourers who also were expatriates drawn to the country by the construction and public works boom.

The city of Kuwait got its first town plan in 1954, which still comprises the broad lines of the city's expansion. Very large sums were spent on road-building, land expropriation, and the construction of business and public buildings and private housing (including 2,000 units of popular housing), in addition to schools, dispensaries, hospitals, a new airport and an agricultural experimental farm. Another aspect of governmental modernisation was the introduction for the first time of a general budget in 1956. This step was necessary, first, in view of the vast expansion in financial resources available and in government spending, both of a capital and a recurrent nature, and, second, in order to introduce modern fiscal methods.

One of the most significant developments within the framework of government action was the formation in December 1961 of the Kuwait Fund for Arab Economic Development. The Fund was to help finance development projects in capital-short Arab countries, and came in later years to be a major factor in the financing of projects of national significance in the whole region. This pioneering role and its dimensions will be dealt with later in this chapter.

2. *The Oil Industry:* The first and predominant feature of change was the new profit-sharing formula which came into effect in 1952. The formula was followed in 1955 by a new major amendment aiming at greater control by the government over its oil resources, and yet later in 1962 the Kuwait Oil Company was made to relinquish 60 per cent of the areas included in its concession, in favour of the Kuwait National Petroleum Company (KNPC), which had been formed in 1960 as a joint enterprise (owned 60 and 40 per cent by the public and the private sectors respectively).

In 1958 the government granted a concession to the Arabian Oil Company, a Japanese concessionaire of which the government owned 10 per cent. Greater share participation was stipulated in a subsequent agreement with the Shell (Kuwait) Company. Finally, in 1960 Kuwait joined OPEC (Organization of Petroleum Exporting Countries) as a founding member, with the object of unifying and co-ordinating the petroleum policies of the members and protecting their interests *vis-à-vis* the oil companies and the oil markets in general. (OPEC membership includes Abu Dhabi, Algeria, Dubai, Ecuador, Indonesia, Iran, Iraq, Kuwait, Libya, Nigeria, Qatar, Saudi Arabia and Venezuela, with Gabon as associate member. Presently, Abu Dhabi and Dubai will become one member under the United Arab Emirates of which they constitute a part.)

3. *Income, Population and Employment:* No national accounts series is available for the sub-period under consideration; the only series on hand being for the years 1962/3–1972/3 which fall into the third sub-period. However, there is one estimate which sets GNP at KD296m for 1959, and at KD370m for 1962/3. (The latter estimate disagrees with subsequently prepared estimates by the staff of the Planning Board, where GNP is set at KD460m for 1962/3.)[7]

The relationship between oil revenues and GNP in subsequent years, that is in the years 1962/3–1969/70, shows revenues as a rather declining proportion of GNP, dropping from 38 to 33 per cent. (According to one analyst, oil revenues constitute 40 per cent of GNP and 57 per cent of GDP as a broad generalisation.) It is tenable to suggest that oil revenues constituted a noticeably higher proportion of GNP for the very early years of the sub-period 1952-61, and slowly dropped in relative significance until 1971, when they rose again, reaching an estimated 75 per cent of GDP for 1974.[8] Probably for the first three or four years they were no less than 60 per cent, in view of the sudden rise in their size (and in the volume of oil production) after the adoption of the fifty-fifty sharing formula for net oil profits. Furthermore, the ratio must have been initially high for the added reason that oil revenue needed some time to make itself felt in the activation of other sectors, particularly construction and public works, and trade. Beginning with 1956, the rise in oil revenues became less dramatic while, on the other hand, the multiplier and accelerator effects became noticeably stronger. The combined result must have been the drop of the ratio of oil revenues to GNP, down to 40 per cent for the years 1960 and 1961. It is in accordance with these very crude and highly speculative but logically tenable estimates that we try to construct a GNP time series for the years 1952-61 in the following table.

Table 3.2: Estimates of Gross National Product, 1952–61[a]

Year	GNP KD Million	Percentage of Oil Revenue to GNP
1952	34.5	60
1953	100.3	60
1954	115.5	60
1955	182.7	55
1956	208.6	50
1957	220.4	50
1958	257.0	50
1959[b]	331.3	45
1960	396.5	40
1961	417.7	40

a. The column of percentages is our estimate of the relative importance of oil revenues in GNP, while the column of GNP is obtained by multiplying the oil revenue by the percentage for each year.
b. The oil revenue for 1959 in Table 3.1 above was, as indicated, for 15 months owing to the change in the accounting basis. We prorated this revenue for 12 months and used the lower figure in the calculations for this table.

It is difficult to relate the GNP data to population for two reasons: first, the fact that the first census taken relates to 1957 with no reasonably good estimates for earlier years available; and second, the disturbing effect of two types of influx which did not conform to any calculable rate — the influx of manpower for employment and business, and that of tribesmen to settle. We supposed earlier that the total population in 1946 could not have been in excess of 90,000, and by 1957, the total had risen to 206,473 inhabitants, Kuwaiti and expatriate together. By free-hand interpolation, manipulated in such a manner as to give much more weight to the years 1952 onwards, it can be suggested that the population in 1952 might have been around 125,000–130,000. With so much speculation with respect to both population and GNP, any calculation of GNP *per capita* becomes of minor value. Furthermore, the steep rise in GNP did not consistently ensure a rising GNP *per capita*, owing to the considerable waves of incoming expatriates. Consequently, it will only be meaningful to calculate GNP *per capita* beginning with 1957 when the first census was taken, and even then with reserve because my GNP estimate in Table 3.2 above is tentative. Be this as it may, GNP *per capita* for 1957 comes out at KD1,067, and for 1961 when the second census established the total population as 321,621 inhabitants, GNP *per capita* comes out at KD1,299. This constitutes a rise of 21.8 per cent in four years, or about 5 per cent per year.

From the moment it became obvious that the oil industry and its revenue were going to grow at a phenomenal rate, the government took three interrelated decisions which reflected a high level of development orientation, welfare-mindedness and practicality.

They decided to divert a very large part of the revenue to development work, beginning with investment in infrastructure, especially roads, electricity, desalination of sea water, schools and hospitals, public buildings and popular housing. Within the sphere of welfare, they decided that education and health services were to be free for everybody, and that electricity, water and housing were to be heavily subsidised to the user. Finally, they decided to attract expatriate manpower, in view of the virtual absence of the skills required for the implementation of the policies relating to development work and welfare services. To elaborate a permissive, even a promotive policy for the attraction and mobilisation of the required manpower revealed pragmatism. But the dimensions of this policy revealed generosity as well, in so far as the terms offered to expatriates in the public sector (and, by imitation and because of competition in the private sector too) are very liberal – indeed, in this writer's view go beyond the level called for by the type of functions performed and the hardships endured, which would put them beyond 'normal' rewards in the Marshallian sense of the term.

According to the 1957 census, the largest single foreign expatriate group was Iraqi, followed by Iranians, Palestinians, Trucial Coast citizens, Lebanese, Indians, Pakistanis, British, Syrians, Saudis and Egyptians, in that order, as well as over half a dozen other groups. The non-Kuwaiti population constituted 44.97 per cent of the total population whereas in 1946 probably no more than 10 per cent of the total were foreigners – Iraqis and Iranians and Trucial Coast citizens mainly. In the 1961 census, the non-Kuwaitis increased in proportion, reaching 49.66 per cent of the total, and in subsequent censuses in 1965 and 1970, the proportion rose to about 53 per cent. By 1973 it was 54.7 per cent.[9]

In absolute figures, the non-Kuwaitis numbered 159,712 in 1961, out of a total of 321,621. The leading six groups of non-Kuwaitis were, respectively, Jordanian, Iraqi, Iranian, Egyptian, Lebanese and Omani (together totalling 122,902 or three-quarters of the non-Kuwaitis). It is of significance that the males among the expatriates represented 78.5 per cent of the total in 1957 and 72.8 per cent in 1961. These very high proportions suggest that the bulk of the expatriate population was in the labour force, precisely as one would expect. The various censuses reveal an interesting development: the continuous decline in the proportion of males from 78.5 per cent for 1957, to 72.8 per cent for 1961, to 70.3 per cent for 1965, to 62.5 per cent for 1970, and to 58.5 for 1973. This drop suggests the tendency among the expatriates to settle and to think of themselves less as a transient community, although nothing in the legal-institutional framework has occurred to change the status of non-Kuwaitis with regard to residence rights, naturalisation, or the right to own real estate.

It remains to be said that the sex structure of the Kuwaitis is distinctly different. In the four censuses of 1957, 1961, 1965 and 1970, the Kuwaiti males represented respectively 52.1, 52.2, 51.1 and 50.5 per cent of the total Kuwaiti population. (The proportion continued at 50.5 per cent for 1973.)

Obviously, in a traditional or non-modern society the size of the labour force is closely related to the proportion of males in the community, and to its age structure. On both scores we see that the labour force constitutes a much higher proportion of the expatriate than of the Kuwaiti community. As far as age structure is concerned, the non-Kuwaitis in the six age groups 20-24, 25-29, 30-34, 35-39, 40-44, and 45-49 years, which are the years of peak economic activity, are almost twice as numerous, in relative terms (in the ratio of 1.8:1) as are the Kuwaitis in the same age groups. This is the ratio for the four censuses taken together, but it drops noticeably over the years. (By 1970, the non-Kuwaitis in the age groups specified constitute 51.9 per cent as against 31.6 per cent for the Kuwaitis, or a ratio of 1.6:1, while in 1957 the ratio was 1.9:1.) If it is recalled that a number of females among the non-Kuwaitis are in the labour force as teachers and nurses (as against a very small number of the Kuwaitis), it will be seen that the non-Kuwaitis constitute a very large proportion of the total labour force in the country.

In broad terms, about two-thirds of the total labour force consist of non-Kuwaitis, one-third of Kuwaitis. Official statistics contain a category in the force entitled 'not in need', which is explained as able to work but having no desire to work. If this category is excluded from the total labour force, then the Kuwaitis in the force constitute one-fourth, and the non-Kuwaitis three-fourths of the total. But this is not all. One additional factor qualifies the significance of the expatriate labour force upwards: this is the diffusion on a much wider scale among non-Kuwaitis than among Kuwaitis of professional, vocational and educational skills, and the inclusion among the non-Kuwaitis of people with much higher skills in cases where comparison is feasible. This advantage has resulted in the staffing of most posts requiring specialised knowledge by expatriates, while positions of top administration and policy level, and simple clerical jobs — or the two ends of the range — are filled by Kuwaitis.

This generalisation is true of the whole period under consideration, but there is a shift in the past half decade which suggests that Kuwaitis are filling more of the technical and professional posts, thanks to the spread of education and the acquisition of higher education by thousands of Kuwaitis in recent years. (However, the manpower problem is examined more thoroughly later on within the context of population policy. The role of expatriates in the civil service will be examined within the same context, as well as the reflection of population policy on labour commitment and productivity.)

4. *Physical Indicators of Achievement:* A large number of physical indicators can be used to establish the point that Kuwait has moved fast in all directions in the second phase under examination, 1952-61. These fall under the broad headings of infrastructure, public services, industry, trade and other areas. However, to present a number of these indicators here for part of the thirty-year period covered in this chapter would fragment the picture unnecessarily. Instead, such a presentation will be made later to cover the whole period, or as large a part of it as the availability of data would permit.

Phase Three: 1962-75

The third sub-period constitutes the independence and consolidation phase, with the consolidation stretching into the political and socio-economic fields and manifesting itself in both. Specifically, this can be seen in the country's movement in three directions: entry into regional and international organisations and participation there on a scale much larger than the size of the country would suggest; setting up representative democratic government and modernisation of the civil service; and, upon the completion of many basic investments in infrastructure and public services, greater concern with improvement and expansion of this infrastructure, and with the performance of the public sector and the diversification of the economy.

One aspect of the first avenue of action interests us specifically here. This is Kuwait's pioneering effort in the promotion of development in the Arab countries not endowed with large oil resources and blighted with balance of payments problems. This effort took several forms, as section 3 below will show.

The consolidation, streamlining and modernisation of government was necessitated by the achievement of independence, and the desire to improve performance in a manner consistent with the government's expanded functions and the country's increased wealth. (Developments in government machinery are closely related to the question of manpower development and manpower policies, and likewise to the broad question of education and motivation, both of which will also be discussed later.)

It is the third, economic aspect of consolidation which will be examined here. While the basic investments in economic and social infrastructure — roads, port, petroleum-loading ports, airport, water desalination, electricity, schools, hospitals, public buildings — were made and staffed, it could not at any one point be said that there was no more to be done. For several factors combined to make it necessary for more investments yet to be made: growth in population, both Kuwaiti and expatriate; growing expectations which meant that the more the appetite for public services was satisfied, the larger it grew for more and better services; growing liquid wealth which in itself created pressure for yet more public goods and services and for the assets that produce them; greater sophistication of the economy and community and rising levels of living which created pressures for an ever-changing pattern of consumption of public and private goods and services; greater elaboration of government organisation and administration, with what that involved in the setting up of new departments and expansion in building and equipment; emphasis on diversification of the economy and more particularly on industry; and promotion of the formula of joint public-private ventures in areas where large investments were called for.

The pressure for investment in satisfaction of these various factors became more acute in the third sub-period under consideration, partly spontaneously as a natural sequel to the construction and public works 'boom' characterising the second sub-period and partly deliberately as a safeguard against the dangers of a slackening in the intensity of investment.

2. INVENTORY OF ACHIEVEMENTS

It would be interesting to take stock of the achievements of the economy and society in each of the three sub-periods of the 1946-75 period separately, with relation to this third avenue of enquiry; but it is more defensible to perform the stock-taking for the whole period as one unit, or for the largest part of the period feasible. The moving picture of achievement will thus emerge whole and will accordingly be better appreciated. The achievement will now be considered under the heading of different sectors or categories. But first, a general evaluation of development will be attempted through the presentation of the national accounts for the years 1962/3–1972/3.

The eleven years covered by the series show a rise of 142 per cent in GDP, 177 per cent in GNP, and 174 per cent in NNP. The reason for the big discrepancy between rise in GDP and GNP is mainly the rise of net factor payments abroad more slowly than the rise in GDP over the years — in other words, the improvement in the profit-sharing formula between the government and the oil companies in favour of the government. Petroleum accounts for over half of the increase in GDP or GNP, as its predominance in the economy, which can be seen in Table 3.4, suggests.

On a *per capita* basis, GNP rose from KD1,265 for 1965/6 to KD1,486.3 for 1972/3. The calculation has been made on the basis of the 1965/6 GNP (KD591m) and the population census of April 1965, while for the end year GNP has been taken in conjunction with the population estimate at the end of 1972. However, not much significance should

Table 3.3: National Expenditure Estimates at Current Prices 1962/3–1972/3 (KD million)

Items	62/3	63/4	64/5	65/6	66/7	67/8	68/9	69/70	70/1	71/2	72/3
1. Consumption Expenditure	268	281	302	297	350	415	441	456	485	564	618
(a) Private	188	192	200	198	232	280	297	303	325	340	379
(b) Public	80	89	102	99	118	135	144	153	160	224	239
2. Gross Fixed Capital Formation	78	92	96	103	135	163	157	149	153	156	149
(a) Private and Semi-Private (Joint)	45	47	49	60	85	95	100	89	85	86	88
(b) Public	33	45	47	43	50	68	57	60	68	70	61
3. Increase in Stocks	7	3	3	15	16	23	14	21	13	–8	5
4. Total 1–3	353	376	401	415	501	601	612	626	651	712	772
5. Exports and Re-exports (Excl. Oil and Products)	8	10	12	21	20	21	28	33	39	52	64
6. Exports of Oil and Products	414	434	468	486	541	498	559	597	667	931	1,016
7. Expenditure on GDP and Imports	775	820	881	922	1,062	1,120	1,199	1,256	1,357	1,695	1,852
8. Less: Imports of Goods and Services	–122	–141	–141	–173	–208	–248	–248	–269	–273	–278	–271
9. Expenditure on GDP	653	679	740	749	854	872	951	987	1,084	1,417	1,581
10. Net Factor Income Transactions ROW	–193	–179	–198	–158	–172	–138	–158	–147	–175	–266	–307
11. Expenditure on GNP	460	500	542	591	682	734	793	840	909	1,151	1,274
12. Less: Depreciation	–19	–25	–28	–34	–40	–42	–45	–50	–55	–60	–65
13. NNP or National Income	441	475	514	557	642	692	748	790	854	1,091	1,209

Sources: For 1962/3–1964/5: *Statistical Abstract 1966*; for 1965/6: *Statistical Abstract 1969*; for 1966/7–1969/70: *Statistical Abstract 1971*; and for 1970/1–1972/3: *Statistical Abstract 1974*.

Table 3.4: Estimate of GDP at Factor Cost by Industrial Origin, Average for 1966/7–1972/3

Sector	Average Per Cent
Agriculture, forestry, hunting and fishing	0.4
Crude petroleum, natural gas and other mining and quarrying	59.9
Manufacturing	3.4
Construction	3.6
Electricity, gas, water and sanitary services	3.4
Transport, storage and communication	3.2
Wholesale and retail trade	7.9
Banking, insurance and other financial services	1.6
Ownership of dwellings	4.3
Public administration and defence	5.4
Services	6.9
Total	100.0

Source: Averaged from *Statistical Abstract 1974*, p. 137.

be attached to this modest change in GNP *per capita* (17.5 per cent in seven years), since it only means that the population rose less fast than the GNP during the five years in question, though both rose considerably — the rise for population being 83.4 per cent, while that for GNP was 115.6 per cent. (Developments behind the national accounts for the whole period 1946-73 will be examined in their broad features under the appropriate headings.)

Population and Manpower

1. *Population:* The population of Kuwait has risen over the years from 90,000 (our rough estimates) for 1946 to 206,473 in February 1957, 321,621 in May 1961, 467,339 in April 1965 and 738,662 in April 1970 — according to the censuses of the last four years indicated. (It was estimated at 907,240 for 31 December 1973.)[10] Obviously, a tenfold increase in 27 years could only occur because of the influx of a vast number of people who were not in the country before. The vast majority of these were expatriates who do not today hold Kuwaiti citizenship and who, now, constitute more than half the total population; the balance consists of tribesmen from neighbouring areas who have settled and been granted citizenship. The number of the Kuwaitis themselves has increased by 206 per cent between 1957 and 1970, or by 286 per cent from the estimate for 1946 to the census for 1970. The increase in the size of the Kuwaiti community, though not as high as that for the whole population, must also be explained through the naturalisation of tens of thousands of tribesmen. At best, the 113,622 Kuwaitis of 1957 (or the 90,000 of 1946) could not have risen in number to much more than 160,000–170,000 by 1970 through natural increase, while they numbered 347,396 in the actual count of that year.

2. *Education:* The change in the level of education of the Kuwaitis is the most remarkable aspect of change in population. It can be seen in a comparison between the size of the educated groups of Kuwaitis and non-Kuwaitis, in the last two censuses, and in the educational efforts in 1946 and 1970 respectively. The first comparison is presented in Table 3.5.

Table 3.5: Comparison of Certain Educated Categories of Kuwaitis and non-Kuwaitis, 1957 and 1970

	1957 Census				1970 Census			
	Kuwaiti		Non-Kuwaiti		Kuwaiti		Non-Kuwaiti	
Category or Level	No.	%	No.	%	No.	%	No.	%
Elementary and Intermediate	1,077	36.8	1,849	63.2	61,348	50.1	61,339	49.9
Secondary	197	5.1	3,700	94.9	7,094	19.9	28,585	80.1
University	51	3.8	1,309	96.2	1,347	3.3	13,023	96.7

Source: Calculated from data in the 1957 and 1970 censuses.

Before we draw some inferences from Table 3.5, it would be relevant to add that the number of illiterate Kuwaitis over ten years of age rose noticeably over the 13 years in question, from 41.0 to 47.2 per cent, while that of non-Kuwaitis dropped noticeably from 43.7 to 32.8 per cent. Read in conjunction with Table 3.5, this rise in illiteracy among Kuwaitis over ten years of age can only be explained by the influx of large numbers of illiterate tribesmen, as the educational effort of the state was remarkable during that period. On the other hand, the table shows a much faster rise in the number of Kuwaitis who have completed all three education cycles. In absolute terms, the improvement in educational levels is most conspicuous for the first cycle (elementary and intermediate), but in relative terms the expansion is largest in the second (secondary) cycle. For the non-relative terms the expansion is also high for the secondary and tertiary cycles. For the non-Kuwaitis, the pattern is different, the expansion being highest for the first cycle and second can only suggest a growing pressure by Kuwaitis for entry into the technical, professional and executive fields of work, as well as the merely clerical. The pressure, particularly at the higher levels of employment, is already felt and begins to constitute a serious two-pronged problem: between educated Kuwaitis and expatriates, and between newly educated, job-seeking Kuwaitis and established Kuwaitis. But the matter will receive further attention in the concluding section.

The second aspect of the comparison with regard to education between the immediate post-war period and the present relates to the educational effort in all its forms. One of these is the budget allocations assigned to education. Recurrent expenditure by government was a mere KD83,781 for the academic year 1946/7, but it rose to an estimated KD62.2m in 1974/5, plus KD9.1m for the University. This phenomenal increase reflects the vast expansion in population, the rise in costs per school or pupil, and the expansion in the educational system, but it also shows the vast absolute *and* relative increase in the number of children attending school. For instance, there were a mere 3,962 pupils in government schools (985 females) in 1946/7, or some 4.4 per cent of the population; by

1973/4 the number of pre-university students had risen to 169,417 (76,046 females), and the proportion of the population in schools had risen to 18.7 per cent. Another important indicator is the student-teacher ratio, which dropped from 24.3 to 13.4 over the years indicated, in spite of the vast rise in the number of pupils. (The data for 1973/4 must be adjusted upwards to account for pupils in private schools, who numbered 37,670 (17,453 females).) Total number of students both in government and in private institutions thus represented 22.8 per cent of the population — quite a high ratio.

Expenditure per pupil by government at the sub-university level amounts to KD321.6 for 1973/4, by far the highest for the world outside of some of the advanced industrial countries. (On the basis of *per capita* of total population it amounts to KD60.7 or $206.4.)[11] High as it is, this level of recurrent expenditure does not include the cost to the country of higher education, whose budget alone stood at KD7.2m for 1973/4, and KD9.1m for 1974/5. Apart from the University of Kuwait, the country had 19 institutions of higher or specialised education — teacher training colleges, a religious institute, special training institutes, an industrial college and commercial schools.

The University of Kuwait was established in 1966. Its total undergraduate student body was 3,836 in 1973/4, of whom 2,240 were female, a remarkable phenomenon of female education. The graduate students numbered 140. In addition, there were 2,228 students studying abroad, of whom 1,198 were supported by government, 751 self-financed, and 279 supported by other sources (such as the Crown Prince personally, the oil companies and scholarships from external agencies). Egypt and the United States drew over three-quarters of the total. Almost one-fourth of students abroad were in Lebanon and the United Kingdom. One significant indicator of the rush to university education is that, whereas the cumulative total of Kuwaiti holders of university degrees was 1,370 according to the census of 1970, 1,924 degrees were obtained by Kuwaitis in the four years 1969/70–1972/3.[12]

Finally, it is worth adding that public service in the field of education includes free midday meals, books, school uniforms, infirmary and clinic services and transport.

3. Health and Sanitation: The second aspect of public services to be discussed is the field of health and sanitation. Here too the record is outstanding. This can be seen from the comparisons presented in Table 3.6.

This table is restricted to government's effort in the field of health, mainly because private effort in 1949 was small in absolute terms, and it is not covered in official statistics. However, by 1973 private hospitals and physicians outside the government sector were an important component in the total health profile, and the addition of the private sector would greatly improve the population/physician and the population/hospital bed situation. (If physicians in the public and private sectors are taken together, there was one physician per 982 inhabitants in 1973. This is a very good ratio.) The extent of the private sector in 1973 is shown in Table 3.7.

We have no record available of the health budget at the start of the period under consideration. However, this budget was KD5.09m in the year 1957. By 1973/4 it had risen to KD26.7m or KD29.4 *per capita.* (The budget rose further to KD31.4m for 1974/5.) Kuwait has the highest *per capita* allocation for health in its budget in the world, except for the United Kingdom.[13] Public medical and dental services, including medicaments, hospitalisation, surgery and X-rays are offered completely free of charge. However, in terms of cost-effectiveness, Kuwait is only better off than the other Arab states with respect to population/hospital bed and population/physician ratios, but is surpassed on both scores

Table 3.6: Indicators of Development of Public Medical Services

	1949	1973
Hospitals and sanatoria	2	11
Hospital beds	n.a.[a]	3,731
Clinics	2	42
Dental clinics	–	47
Mother and child care centres	–	11
Preventive health centres	–	12
School health clinics	23	270
Clinics of medical specialists in School Health Department	–	9 (in 1970)
Physicians in government service	45	734
Inhabitants per physician	2,350	1,236
Dentists	–	66
Pharmacists	1	94
Assistant pharmacists	5	261
Qualified nurses	7	1,589
Assistant nurses	2	504
Male nurses	10	894
Dental technicians	–	51
Laboratory technicians	1	228
Radiographers	–	120
Public health officers	–	116
Quarantine officers	–	132
Therapists	–	48

a. There is no record of public hospital beds in 1949. In 1973 they numbered 3,731 against 2,724 for 1964.

Source: *Statistical Abstract* for *1965* and *1974*, Chapter on 'Public Health'.

by several dozen countries in the world outside the Arab region. Most of these better-served countries are in Europe, the Americas and Oceania.[14]

Health conditions have improved considerably, thanks to the government's efforts in preventive medicine, sanitation and hygiene, to the vast expansion and qualitative improvement in curative medicine both in the public and the private medical sectors, and to the vast improvement in diet. Widely spread diseases, especially tuberculosis, have been contained and their incidence narrowed. However, it is noticed that the incidence of diseases associated with high consumption and opulence, and with tension and strain, has risen, such as heart disease, high cholesterol level and nervous disorders.[15]

4. Welfare: There are no statistics capable of giving a comparative picture over the years of the government's efforts in the field of welfare. The most recent data in the *Statistical Abstract, 1974*, which only cover the years 1967-73 present the statistics of financial aid given by the Ministry of Social Affairs and Labour to needy families. Between eight and nine thousand families in each of the seven years received roughly KD328 per year per family in relief. In all during the years of independence, 1962/3–1973/4, a total of KD30m

Table 3.7: Private Sector Health Provision

	Number
Hospitals	8
Hospital beds	400
Physicians	190
Pharmacists	160
Opticians	15
Dental technicians	6
Tooth-makers	25
Physiotherapists	5
Midwives	60
Radiographers	18
Qualified nurses	193
Assistant nurses	22
Qualified male nurses	32
Aid nurses	79
Assistant aid nurses	44

Source: *Statistical Abstract 1974*, Table 185, p.282.

was paid in subsidies to the needy.[16]

But a wider definition of welfare to include free or heavily subsidised services would reveal that all the Kuwaitis benefit from the government's welfare policies and efforts. Thus, electricity and water are heavily subsidised to the consuming public, while public education and health services are completely free. If to these is added the vast sums paid out by the Ministry of Social Affairs and Labour to clubs, professional associations, religous groups and the like, as well as the government's liberal land-purchasing policy and cheap land sales and cheap credit for house-building by 'limited-income' and even higher-income government officials, then the overall picture which emerges is one of marked financial largesse by the government. This largesse is the most outstanding reflection of the government's desire to redistribute income and wealth and to let oil money seep down to the population.

5. *Labour:* It was only beginning with the 1965 population census that detailed information was obtained on the labour force, inside government and in the private sector, relating to various aspects such as educational level, sector of activity, nationality and so on. We need not go into the details of the 1965 census results, but a few observations are worth making.[17] The first is that the Kuwaiti labour force contains a category rarely encountered in labour statistics: that of people who are not in need of work — defined by the census report as those able to work but having no desire to work. Out of a total labour supply of Kuwaitis '12 years of age and above' of 126,521, this category numbered 76,574 (of whom 57,277 were males), or 60.5 per cent.

That three-fifths of the labour force of a community should declare themselves 'not in need of work' and presumably satisfy themselves with a *rentier* existence, often making

Kuwait 97

their money as 'sleeping partners' with expatriates in business who cannot have work licences in their own names but have to obtain them in those of Kuwaiti citizens, or making their money in the form of interest or dividends, is not utterly surprising in a society where fortunes are made easily and in large magnitude. However, it is more surprising that there should be 41,974 non-Kuwaitis (34,704 males) in the same category, constituting 22.7 per cent of the total non-Kuwaiti labour supply of 184,943. The expatriates are presumably in Kuwait for work, and the phenomenon is therefore baffling, even though the category of people 'not in need' can be partly explained in the fact that both for Kuwaitis and non-Kuwaitis a certain proportion of those in the category are school and university students, and a larger proportion consists of women who are presumably considered 'not in need' irrespective of their true income situation, simply because they do not seek gainful employment. However, for the two communities those in the age group 12-19 are about 23,000 and 16,000 respectively, together making about one-fifth of the total stated not in need. This explanation leaves the bulk of the category as constituting a *rentier* class.

The second observation relates to the distribution of the labour force actually working by sector of economic activity in 1965. Broadly speaking, the services sectors account for 83.4 per cent of the Kuwaitis and 59.7 per cent of the non-Kuwaitis in the labour force. The difference is indicative of the clustering of Kuwaitis in services — mainly government employment — and suggests a tendency for Kuwaitis to avoid more rigorous and/or more specialised activity in the commodity-producing sectors.

In the third place, the total Kuwaiti labour force actually in employment (whether self-employed or employed by others) numbers 40,166 or a mere 18.3 per cent of the community which numbered 220,059 in 1965. The non-Kuwaiti labour force in the same year numbered 139,118 or 56.3 per cent of the total, which was 247,280. The fact that thousands of Kuwaitis did not feel in need of work explains the very low proportion of Kuwaitis in the labour force, while the fact that expatriates are predominantly males who go to Kuwait for employment explains the inordinately high proportion of the labour force among them.

The fourth observation is the most startling. A total of 44,454 officials and employees were in government service according to the 1965 census. However, the total number on government payroll (except the army) was 60,820 according to the *Statistical Abstract, 1964*.[18] The difference between the two years is one of definition, since the number actually rose between 1964 and 1965. By 1973, a total of 104,794 officials and employees were in government service. This amounts to 11.5 per cent of the population, Kuwaiti and non-Kuwaiti together — a very high ratio indeed. But more surprising is the structure of government officials in 1964 according to educational status. These numbered 22,073, just over half of whom were Kuwaitis. No less than 25.8 per cent of the Kuwaiti officials were declared illiterate, probably mainly office boys of whom one sees large numbers in the corridors of ministries. The total distribution according to level of education is shown in Table 3.8.

Unfortunately, the most recent statistical picture relating to 1972 or 1973 does not have comparable detail with that of 1965. (The recent data are either estimates, or the results of a sample survey.) However, some demographic, educational and occupational characteristics can be compared.[19]

The proportion of non-Kuwaitis to total population has risen consistently. It stood at 44.97, 49.66, 52.91, and 52.97 per cent for each of the census years (1957, 1961, 1965 and 1970), and 55.1 per cent for the end of 1973 (official estimate). The ratio of illiterate to total population (10 years and over) is not available beyond the 1970 census, but

Table 3.8: Educational Level of Kuwaiti Civil Servants, 1964 (per cent)

College or university	1.6
Secondary	3.2
Intermediate	8.0
Less than intermediate	8.7
Literate	52.7
Illiterate	25.8
Total	100.0

Source: *Statistical Abstract 1964*, Table 37, pp. 42/3.

the drop between 1957 and 1970 for non-Kuwaitis (from 49.4 to 32.8 per cent) is larger than that for Kuwaitis (from 59.7 to 47.2 per cent), both in absolute and in relative terms, and for males as well as females. The startling observation made earlier concerning the large proportion of illiterate civil servants is now even more startling. By February 1972, this proportion had risen to 31.4 per cent for Kuwaitis, and to 31.1 per cent for non-Kuwaitis. The distribution of the 89,937 civil servants is shown in Table 3.9, for males and females combined.

In view of the fact that the non-Kuwaitis constituted 61.5 per cent of civil servants in February 1972, and that they had a clear 'edge' only with respect to university education, it can be inferred from the data recorded above that the expatriate civil service by and large does not possess vastly superior academic training. Competent observers conclude that the superiority or advantage of the expatriates derives mainly from their experience, technical skills (which are not reflected in the academic classification shown), and their greater work commitment. However, as indicated earlier, the Kuwaitis are becoming more numerous in professional, technical and teaching posts. This is true both of government service and of the private sector.

The *active* Kuwaiti labour force (the force defined as persons '12 years and over') has dropped from 38.5 to 31.7 and 29.9 per cent for the three census years 1957, 1965 and 1970 respectively. The active non-Kuwaiti labour force has likewise dropped, but from a much higher plateau: 77.5 to 75.2 and 66.9 per cent. The Kuwaiti group designated 'inactive' has thus risen both in absolute and in relative terms. This is only partly explainable in the rise in school and university enrolment by Kuwaitis. The phenomenon of 'dormant' partners and a *rentier* class must also have become more pronounced over the years. But essentially the explanation lies in the small female participation in active employment.

Examined with respect to distribution per division of economic activity, the active labour force has registered some very large changes, as Table 3.10 shows. The changes can be seen between sectors and inside sectors. The sectors marking the largest expansion are construction, trade, manufacturing and services. (This last includes government service.) It is also worth noting that though the active labour force in both communities has proportionately declined, it still constitutes a much larger percentage of non-Kuwaitis — over 2.2 times its counterpart for Kuwaitis for 1970. Kuwait participation is still very low: 29.9 per cent of those twelve years of age or older, but only 17.1 per cent of all Kuwaitis.

Table 3.9: Educational Levels of Civil Servants, 1972 (per cent)

	Kuwaiti	Non-Kuwaiti	Total
University level:			
Undergraduate	4.3	13.0	9.6
Graduate	0.3	1.4	1.0
Below university level	1.5	1.8	1.7
Secondary	10.4	14.7	13.0
Intermediate	10.1	6.5	7.9
Primary	8.0	4.4	5.8
Can read and write (below primary)	34.0	27.1	29.8
Illiterate	31.4	31.1	31.2
Total	100.0	100.0	100.0

Source: *Statistical Abstract 1974*, Table 41, p.72.

Land Purchases and Housing

We referred earlier to the largesse of government with respect to spending, and how this was in part a reflection of the government's desire to allow oil revenue to seep down to the population. The largest volume of such 'seepage', and the most notorious example at the same time, is embodied in the policy of land purchases or acquisitions. In brief, the policy involves the purchase by government or Kuwait municipality of land, mainly in the city of Kuwait but also in the band of land adjoining the city and in and around other residential centres, for the purpose of road and street-making, the construction of public buildings, industrial sites, public utilities and public squares and gardens, and for the setting up of housing projects for low and medium income groups.

The government and the municipality of the capital, and the evaluation committees which set up the purchase prices, have been generous in the prices assigned to the land sellers, partly because, as a matter of policy, the authorities are eager to allow a tangible part of oil revenues to go directly into private hands. In practice, the resultant transfer of income from the public to the private sector has not been remarkably even, owing to the fact that the influential members of society had much more land and property to sell in the first place than other citizens, and could also influence the price assigned for land transactions. Furthermore, many of them had the power and influence to claim land outside the confines of urban centres and establish ownership — often on flimsy evidence — and thus make fortunes. The dimension of riches made can be gauged from one statistic: that over the years 1952-71, some KD727m were disbursed for land acquisition. Another KD116.7m were allocated for the years 1971/2—1974/5,[20] bringing the total to KD844m.

Criticism of the land acquisition policy by Kuwaiti public-minded citizens and by foreign observers has been sharp. The issues mostly criticised have been the inflated prices set for land purchases, the rather arbitrary policy of land valuation, the flimsiness of evidence of land ownership in the areas outside urban centres, particularly in the environs of Kuwait city, and the resale of land thus purchased to individuals wanting to build houses or factories at quite nominal prices.[21] We find no better summary of the criticism of some of

Table 3.10: Population by Sex and Division of Economic Activity in Three Census Years

Economic Activity and Sex		1957 Kuwaiti	1957 non-Kuwaiti	1965 Kuwaiti	1965 non-Kuwaiti	1970 Kuwaiti	1970 non-Kuwaiti
Agriculture, hunting and fishing	M	603	446	566	1,408	798	3,253
	F	—	—	7	2	4	5
Mining and quarrying	M	1,211	4,088	1,337	5,241	1,627	4,828
	F	—	106	12	402	48	668
Manufacturing industries	M	1,009	5,539	1,823	16,103	6,100	25,876
	F	20	43	2	14	9	106
Construction	M	378	8,025	1,262	27,566	2,186	31,418
	F	—	—	2	18	2	66
Electricity, gas and water	M	—	—	1,645	5,341	2,130	5,106
	F	—	—	—	5	3	13
Wholesale and retail trade	M	4,107	4,058	5,115	17,769	7,261	25,181
	F	44	15	14	147	37	534
Transport and communication	M	1,513	2,053	2,612	7,336	2,357	9,640
	F	—	—	1	76	5	136
Services	M	14,365	27,697	24,571	50,123	34,919	54,401
	F	316	1,522	948	6,892	1,907	12,909
Activities not adequately defined	M	4,803	3,583	232	611	236	559
	F	4	7	17	64	5	21
Total active	M	27,989	55,489	39,163	131,498	57,614	160,262
	F	384	1,693	1,003	7,620	2,020	14,458
	Total	28,373	57,182	40,166	139,118	59,634	174,720
Inactive	M	10,472	6,180	25,583	10,240	43,123	17,341
	F	34,903	10,430	60,772	35,580	96,894	68,938
	Total	45,375	16,610	86,355	45,820	140,017	86,279
Population 12 years and over	M	38,461	61,669	64,746	141,738	100,737	177,603
	F	35,287	12,123	61,775	43,200	98,914	83,396
	Total	73,748	73,792	126,521	184,938	199,651	260,999

Source: *Statistical Abstract 1974,* Table 23, p. 44.

these aspects than that in the World Bank report which says:

> The Government buys land at highly inflated prices for development projects and for resale to private buyers... Whatever the political or developmental justifications for this practice, the prices fixed by the Government for these transactions and the small amount thus far collected on the resale of the land make the public land transactions a rather indiscriminate and inequitable way of distributing the oil revenues. In addition, probably the largest share of these funds are invested abroad, so that the land purchase

program fails to accomplish its main objective of invigorating the Kuwait economy.[22]

One bright side of the land acquisition policy is its promotive effect on housing. Thus, the land acquired has enabled the government to build and distribute 13,569 houses in the years 1953-73.[23] These houses have been distributed at subsidised prices to low-income Kuwaitis, often with very liberal credit and instalment facilities for repayment of the price. Housing projects are still actively pursued, though it will be long before every Kuwaiti becomes a house-owner. (A total of 18,872 applications for houses were still under consideration by the end of 1973.) House-building and owning has spread to include all income groups. The very rich have built villas and mansions on cheaply acquired land, and the medium-income groups, especially government officials in the higher echelons, have built elegant and expensive houses, mostly with cheap credit obtained from the Credit and Saving Bank and other sources. This bank alone extended a total of KD11.1m in loans to government officials between its formation and 31 March 1965, when it stopped this line of operations. Furthermore, the bank extended KD32.9m in real-estate loans, mostly for building purposes, between its formation and the end of 1970. However, its real-estate loans for the three years 1971-3 alone exceeded KD20.7m.[24]

Infrastructure

There has been occasion elsewhere in this chapter to refer to the Kuwaiti government's concern with the building of economic and social infrastructure. To deal again with infrastructure under a separate heading is merely to emphasise the significance of the achievement in this field of overhead capital and to add some greater specificity to the subject.

This will centre mainly around three components of infrastructure, apart from the roads and public buildings, the port (and the oil terminals at Ahmadi and Abdallah ports), and the airport — all of which are very adequate in terms of quantity and quality. These components are water desalination, electricity generation and the Shuaiba Industrial Area or Zone south of Kuwait city.

The country is very poorly supplied with subterranean sweet water, the total supply capacity of underground wells in two localities or fields developed being 4.1m gallons daily on the average. Consequently, Kuwait has had to desalinate sea water in large volume. For this purpose it has installed the largest units in the world, with a capacity of 52m gallons daily, consisting of three complexes: one at Shuweikh in Kuwait city, one at north Shuaiba, and the third at south Shuaiba. Total production of potable water averaged 25.5m gallons daily in 1973. *Per capita* consumption of both types of water has risen consistently over the years, from 9.1 gallons daily for 1957 to 29 gallons for 1973.[25]

In addition to potable water sources and consumption, there is brackish water in two main localities or fields. One of these fields already produced an average of 17.8m gallons daily in 1973 and the output is totally consumed. The second field is being developed, and is planned to give an output of 64m gallons daily by 1975 from 113 wells. Brackish water is partly used in mixture with desalinated water which is so pure as to be tasteless if drunk by itself. The bulk of the brackish water produced is put to municipal uses, gardening, industry and other non-domestic purposes.

The total water resources available are thus clearly in excess of the current needs of the country, even if projection is made for the next several years. However, such calculation is predicated on the absence or virtual absence of agricultural activity in the country. If such activity were to be envisaged on a sizeable scale, then, considering the cost-return relationship, there will be no answer to the problem of water shortage but the revival and implementation of a scheme of long standing, which is drawing water from Shat-al-Arab near Basrah in Iraq at very low cost. As of the time of writing, this scheme remains dormant.

The building of capacity in power generation has been equally far-sighted. Thus, by the end of 1973, total capacity in the three plants (also at Shuwaikh, north Shuaiba, and south Shuaiba) was 1,096 megawatts, while the total load was 860 megawatts. The users — households, offices, industrial plants and the like — exceed 175,000. Thus the whole country is supplied with electricity, since there are some 145,000 families in all, apart from non-domestic users. Consumption *per capita* averaged about 4,043 kwh per year in 1973. Again here, consumption has risen consistently from 1,200 kwh in 1957. (Domestic consumption alone averaged 3,675 kwh for 1973.)[26]

The capacity of the country's generating plants is well beyond current domestic and industrial consumption. There is no fear, for the few years to come, that industrial development will outstrip this capacity. However, according to the estimates of the Ministry of Electricity and Water, the load will exceed capacity after 1974. (In fact, the utilisation coefficient already was 78.5 per cent for 1973.) Consequently, plans are already under way to expand capacity well beyond the estimated needs of the middle of the present decade and to safeguard the country against possible power shortage. Finally, it is worth adding in connection with water desalination and power generation that all the producing plants use natural gas as fuel. It is furthermore planned to rely on gas for any future expansion in capacity.

The third component of infrastructure to receive separate discussion here is the Shuaiba Industrial Zone. The setting up of such a Zone was decided in 1961, and the site was selected in 1962. The impetus came when it was decided to set up a petrochemical industry and other allied industries, and it was realised that an industrial estate involving the bringing together of the supportive services (communications, water, electricity, housing, port facilities, laboratories, etc.) would be conducive to efficiency and a drop in unit costs. In 1964 an autonomous authority was established to supervise and run the Zone.

The Industrial Zone covers 8.4 square kilometres; 66 per cent of this area is devoted to industrial sites, 20 per cent to electric generation and water desalination plants, 10 per cent to roads, and 4 per cent to administrative and security offices. By the end of 1971, less than one-third of the area earmarked for industries had been utilised by seven industries which include the Kuwait National Petroleum Company (KNPC) refinery, the plants of the Kuwait Chemical Fertilizers Company, the plants of the Petrochemical Industries Company, the Kuwait Oxygen Company and the Kuwait Cement Company. The Industrial Zone is a large user of water; in 1970 it consumed about 683m cubic metres for cooling purposes plus 2.6m cubic metres of desalinated water. Natural gas is the basic source of power for electricity generation, water desalination and the other industries. Over 1,039m cubic metres of gas and 438m kwh of electricity were used in 1970. The Zone has excellent port facilities. In addition, it has a centre for the control of air and water pollution — an outstanding, far-sighted piece of planning. The centre has well-equipped laboratories, and researchers continuously on the alert. The research activities also include studies relating to the feasibility of certain industries that Kuwait could undertake.

While the infrastructural facilities of the Shuaiba Industrial Area are adequate and of high quality, the major industries operating there face serious problems. These however will be discussed below, when the major sectors of the economy will be surveyed.

Main Sectors and Diversification

Table 3.4 above presented the average GDP by industrial origin for the years 1966/7—

1972/3. The picture which emerges shows the petroleum sector to represent about 60 per cent of GDP, with the other commodity-producing sectors together contributing a mere 11.1 per cent. Agriculture, which normally is the backbone of every developing economy, represents only 0.4 per cent, while industry, despite its growth in recent years, represents only 3.4 per cent. (Construction accounts for 3.6 per cent, and electricity, gas, water and sanitary services account together for 3.4 per cent.)

Clearly this structure is heavily and unhealthily dependent on oil, which is a depleting resource. The chance of agriculture occupying a prominent place in the economy seems to be extremely remote if not non-existent, even assuming the inflow of substantial quantities of water from Shatt-al-Arab in southern Iraq. An agricultural census conducted in 1970 revealed that the country had a cultivable area of 27 square kilometres, of which 6.5 square kilometres were actually cultivated. The *Final Report of the Agricultural Census 1970*, a document of 190 pages, gives the visual impression of a much more important agricultural sector than the cultivated area of 6.5 square kilometres would seem to warrant. However, the country now produces 13 per cent of its requirements of vegetables, 6 per cent of milk, 45 per cent of poultry, and 20 per cent of eggs. Total employment was a mere 449.[27] Fishing and allied activities, though promising in the light of the availability of good-quality fish and shrimp in the Gulf area and the mounting effort to exploit the existing potential, remain of limited relative significance. Consequently the primary sectors together cannot seriously be expected to raise their contribution to GDP to more than a few percentage points during the present decade.

This leaves manufacturing industry as a hopeful sector if diversification is to be achieved effectively. However, the problems that beset this sector and narrow its scope are as substantial as the advantages which seem to favour its growth.[28] The advantages are few and readily discernible. There is, first, the abundance and cheapness of petroleum and natural gas (whether gas is used as source of energy — directly or indirectly via the generation of electricity which itself is used for the running of machinery — or as raw materials in some branch of petrochemical industry). Second, there is the abundance of funds and of foreign exchange, which makes the importation of machines and raw materials extremely easy. Third, the absence of taxes and the virtual absence of customs tariffs (which until 1971 ranged from zero to 4 per cent *ad valorem*, but which were raised to 15 per cent for protected products in 1971), plus the very low cost of industrial sites, combine to provide added attraction to the setting up of manufacturing industry. (Obviously, the low tariffs favour the importation of machinery and raw materials, but militate against the finished products.) And lastly, there is the Shuaiba Industrial Area which provides a wide range of facilities and permits the making of substantial external economies by the establishments located there. The impact of the various favourable factors has been felt and reflected mainly in the petrochemical industry — particularly the production of ammonia, urea and nitrogenous fertilisers — but also in the construction materials and the metal piping industries, all of which have witnessed considerable expansion.

Against these advantages, industry suffers from a number of handicaps. There is first the narrowness of the range of raw materials for industry available locally, and the necessity therefore to bear the transport costs of most materials that have to be imported. In the second place, the very abundance of funds has made for insufficiency of precision and carefulness in pre-investment studies, and a certain lavishness in the setting up of industry which has resulted in unduly high unit costs. Third, the Kuwaiti labour force is not adequate for the current needs of the industrial sector — let alone the growth of the sector beyond its present modest dimensions. While the expatriates include thousands of workers with advanced skills, they are not always in possession of the right skills needed, in addition to requiring high wages. The costliness of labour and of raw materials necessarily adds to the level of unit costs. One way of combating the cost problem is for industry to enjoy economies of scale, which cannot materialise owing to the narrowness of the local market. This is a fourth problem of significance. To solve it through exports would require subsidies or protective tariffs, especially at the early stages of manufacturing development. Yet the tariff structure is not protective. In theory, exposure to foreign competition can be healthy for industrial growth, but it can be fatal for infant industry.

Nor is Arab economic co-operation real enough and significant enough to widen the market. Such co-operation can take at least one of two forms in the present context: trade facilities for final products, or vertical integration whereby two or more countries would co-operate in the production of a product, each specialising in one or more stages or phases of production according to the dictates of comparative advantage. (The reality and limitations of Arab economic co-operation, and the problems with which it has been blighted since World War Two will receive adequate discussion in the last chapter of this volume.)

In the fifth place, much of industry seems to have received insufficient study and screening, and foreign consultants have not always proved immune to the dangerous mixture of technical advice with the commercial interests of machine suppliers abroad. Local technical knowledge has not been adequate enough to constitute an effective check against the errors of judgement — deliberate or unintended — of foreign consultants. A sixth handicap lay in the institutional field. According to many Kuwaiti observers, government industrial policy has neither been the product of profound and sustained study, nor has it been comprehensive and serious. There is even questioning whether industrialisation is indeed a serious official objective. Illustrations in support of this claim are not difficult to obtain. Until late in 1973, there was no industrial bank in the country, although the idea of its formation had been discussed for a few years at length. The industrial loans issued by the Savings and Credit Bank from its formation in 1963 to the end of 1973 total a mere KD3.1m.[29] The Industrial Law (Decree No. 6 of 1965) which defined the benefits that approved industries could enjoy under the Law also set up an Industrial Development Committee to supervise the implementation of the Law. The benefits did not constitute a new incentive, since they were mostly there anyway: cheap land sites, customs exemptions for machines and raw materials, absence of taxes, cheap credit and priority for consideration as supplier of government. The Law added tariff protection, with the proviso that 'local products shall be satisfactory from the points of quantity, type, quality and the consumer's interests'.[30] This latter clause has met with strong opposition by the merchants who argued that tariffs would damage trade which is already a strong and flourishing sector.

In addition to the fact that the benefits did not provide sufficient new attraction, the Industrial Development Committee has not been very energetic or noticeably promotive of industry. Its constitution was well balanced (with representatives both of the private and the public sectors). But its research activities have been very limited and its success in drawing forth industrial entrepreneurship has on the whole been clearly below expectations.

Another institutional problem has been encountered with respect to the Industrial Zone. In addition to the insufficiency of expertise and/or experience among its top personnel and the personnel of the individual establishments located there, and the conflicts of interest of many board members in the various companies, there has been a change in the pattern of relationship between the administration of the Zone and the government. Though the Zone started under an autonomous Authority, as already indicated, some of the facilities within its operational area remained administratively outside its control. Furthermore, the government has dissolved the board of the Authority and entrusted the management of the Zone to a department in the Ministry of Finance and Oil. What began as a very hopeful institution based on sound technical and economic ideas (including correct costing of overhead facilities and charging users on a cost-plus basis) shows signs of frustration today. This is all the more damaging because there seems to be no energetic search for the causes of industrial hesitation in the country and for appropriate remedies.

On balance, it can be said that industry is still hesitant in Kuwait. Some officials and businessmen who have given the matter sufficient thought seem to believe that the prospects of industrialisation are very limited, given the objective realities of the country's endowments and limitations, and of economic co-operation in the Arab world. The unsatisfactory financial results of the operations of some large companies, particularly the KNPC, the Kuwait Chemical Fertilizers Company and the refinery, have further slowed down the pace and lowered the expectations. To this must be added the continued predominance of mercantile attitudes in industrial entrepreneurship, owing to the long trading tradition of the community. Hence, quick returns are sought, and preference is often shown to investment in real estate or banking, which is less demanding than industrial investment.

At least three aspects of the picture have changed considerably in the years 1970-5. The first aspect is the setting up of many new industries, some of large size, and the expansion in industrial investment and employment. The second is the establishment in December 1973 of the Industrial Bank of Kuwait with a capital of KD10m, owned by the government (35 per cent), the Central Bank (14 per cent) and 13 other banks, insurance companies, and industries (51 per cent).[31] There are indications that the government is intent on giving the Bank its full support in order to enable it to have a clearly promotive effect on industrialisation.

The third propitious development has been the satisfactory financial results since 1973 of several industrial establishments, including the KNPC group of companies. This group made very large profits in 1973/4, thanks in part to improved management and market promotion, but mainly to the steep rise in the prices of oil and gas and their derivatives. Though not enough in themselves to suggest a major drive towards successful and profitable industrialisation, these three developments brighten the picture to a certain extent and suggest more cheerful prospects.

Against this general background, and notwithstanding the favourable evolution of the manufacturing sector, many persons in public life and in business still believe that diversification ought to be essentially based on certain service sectors, such as finance and banking, insurance, oil tankerage, shipping and air transport and trade. Together, these activities accounted for 12.7 per cent of GDP on the average over the years 1966/7–1972/3. One opinion, echoed in the original First Five-Year Plan, places considerable hope in a 'men-and-money' sector, whose activities would ultimately include investments abroad accompanied by Kuwaiti technicians, contractors and professional men. This expectation is based on confidence in the native talent of Kuwaitis and in their ability to acquire a high level of professional and technical expertise once the proper educational and training opportunities have been provided for them.

This approach to diversification and to a reduction of the high dependence on petroleum is based on the experience of the past decade, during which shipping, banking and investment activities have grown considerably. The Kuwait Shipping Company, now (1975) in its tenth year of life, has a relatively large fleet and tonnage. Oil tankerage has also attracted sizeable capital. The Kuwait Oil Tanker Company, which was formed in September 1962 with a capital of KD11.5m — all private — today has large capacity and several tankers, including 3 super-tankers. In addition, the Company also services all tankers berthing in Kuwaiti ports.[32] The commercial banks of Kuwait are all Kuwaiti now — the only non-Kuwaiti bank having been bought over at the beginning of 1972 by a new banking company jointly owned by government and the public. Banking operations have grown considerably, along with the financial resources of the country. Thus, the consolidated balance sheets of the banks showed a rise in assets from KD226.6m on 31 December 1962 to KD934.9m on 30 September 1974. Capital and reserves rose from KD11.8m to KD101.9m for the two dates respectively. However, it must be noted that the bulk of the assets are held abroad. The volume of foreign assets rose from KD148.7m to KD546.6m for the two dates, while advances and discounts (to residents) continued to constitute a modest portion of assets — 18.3 per cent for the initial year and 35.7 per cent for the terminal date.[33]

Obviously, the resources of the banks, considered by themselves, permit the banking sector to place substantial investments abroad as well as to open branches in Arab and other countries capable of attracting considerable business. Probably the major bottleneck which slows expansion outside the country is the shortage of banking experience and expertise among the Kuwaitis. But this need not be a permanent handicap, especially with the training begun by the Central Bank. (The Central Bank itself was established in 1968 and is beginning to assert its presence in monetary and credit policies.)

The government is reported to have had assets abroad worth about KD790m by the first quarter of 1973. According to one authoritative estimate, the country as a whole (including the private sector) had close to two billion Kuwaiti dinars invested abroad in securities, in bank accounts, in government-to-government loans, and in direct investment. Income on public and private foreign assets (including KFAED and the Central Bank) was estimated at KD125.5m for 1972/3,[34] in spite of some losses sustained as a result of foreign currency devaluations and depreciation, and the general instability in money markets and stock exchanges. This volume strongly suggests that the assets of the government, the banks and the general public add up to over two billion dinars, if we assume net returns at 6 per cent per annum.

However, these volumes of foreign assets have been dwarfed since the steep rise in oil prices in the last quarter of 1973, and Kuwait's rise of oil revenue in 1973 to an estimated KD992.9m, and in 1974 to KD2,588.2m. A very large proportion of these revenues is placed abroad, in one form or another. There are now three large Kuwaiti companies which specialise in foreign investment, the Kuwait Investment Company (capital KD7.5m), the Kuwait Foreign Trade, Contracting and Investment Company (capital KD20m), and the Kuwait International Investment Company (capital KD10m). The first two are owned jointly by the government and the private sector, while the third is fully private. Thanks to substantial loans by government, both mixed companies have operations well beyond the size of their share capital, and are active in floating foreign loans by issuing the necessary bonds and selling them to the Ministry of Finance and Oil. Since October 1973, Kuwait has formed and entered into several joint investment corporations in the Arab world, and further afield. The entry has been via the investment companies just listed, as well as banks and private businessmen. Kuwait stands ahead of all the oil-exporting countries in its dynamism and the initiative to invest abroad. Such investment takes the form of portfolio and direct investment, as well as bank deposits. There is a willingness to use new modalities and to enter new fields. The country can now boast a small but extremely capable reservoir of men and of adequate mechanisms to spearhead and manage the drive to substantial foreign investment.

The investment activities of Kuwait call for a discussion of the government's loans to other Arab governments out of its reserves, as well as the loans of KFAED. But owing to the importance of these loans, they will be discussed later under a separate heading. It should merely be added here that KFAED has participated to the extent of KD30m in the original share capital of KD100m of the Arab Fund for Economic and Social Development which was formally set up by the Arab Economic Unity Council (of the League of Arab States) in December 1971. Furthermore, Kuwait has been instrumental in the nurturing of the idea of an Arab agreement to guarantee the investment of Arab funds in Arab countries. Its efforts succeeded in the signing of this agreement by five countries in May 1971. The agreement stipulates for the establishment of an organisation to guarantee investment, with a capital of KD10m. This move is also expected to encourage Kuwaiti investment in the region.

The question of investment occupies a central part in the Kuwaiti concern for diversification in a manner capable, by the time petroleum resources are nearing depletion, to replace oil revenue fully. Whether or not such replacement is possible is a difficult matter to settle. It depends on the timing of the critical date when oil revenue begins to fall noticeably, on the identity and size of the sectors which are hoped to produce the compensating income, and on the magnitude of the country's income-earning assets abroad.

With regard to depletion of oil resources, a simple calculation would suggest that the proved and published recoverable reserves can last 76-82 years beginning with 1975, on the basis of production in 1974.[35] Recently, early in 1972, serious controversy raged in the Kuwaiti press and National Assembly with regard to an assertion made by a member of government that the oil reserves would last only 26 years. No explanation appeared indicating the basis of the assertion; it was probably based on a report by a foreign firm of consultants which stated that oil was expected to be depleted in about 30 years' time.[36] Another source of information, the Kuwait Chamber of Commerce and Industry *Journal*,[37] refers to estimates made during the spell of panic early in 1972, which placed the period of oil availability at 15 years only.

This last source argued cogently against such irresponsible and unfounded assertions. It maintained that the published reserves might not represent all that the country possesses in oil resources, since certain areas had not yet been surveyed. It further suggested that the oil companies which prepare the reserve estimates tend to underestimate the resources recoverable. It went on to suggest that the real danger was not from depletion in the next two or three decades, but from the change in energy technology. However, even if an alternative source of energy were to be developed and to replace oil as the predominant source, oil would still have a large variety of uses, whether as a heavy fuel, or as a raw material for 2,500 products that have petroleum as a base. Also according to the same source, the Minister of Finance and Oil, in full awareness of the question of depletion and diversification, indicated the government's intention to prepare a law according to which 12.5 per cent of the annual revenues of oil would be diverted to a general reserve account which would be guarded jealously, so that by the time the reserve had grown to KD6,000—8,000m, the income flow of this reserve, plus other income, would together assure the country a comfortable level of well-being and ward off serious financial worries.

The vast increase in oil revenues after the October war of 1973 has added a great deal of realism to such expectations, and has made them look modest and pale in the glow of current financial expectations. Indeed, Kuwait's present overriding concern is not to deplete its oil resources at the rate it had been doing until 1971. Hence the drop in the volume of production consistently in the four years 1972-5 as a firm policy of conservation. Such a policy has become possible *and* attractive since October 1973 and the subsequent quadrupling of the price of crude oil. Like the other oil countries members of OPEC, Kuwait is not worried about the future of oil as a source of energy, since the less oil is used as a fuel and the more (like gas) it is used as industrial feedstock, or for refined products, the longer this resource can last, and the greater the value added per unit of oil (or gas). Parallel with this relaxed attitude is the large volume of financial resources obtained from the export of oil. On the one hand, these resources far exceed the country's internal consumption and investment needs, plus what it directs to defence requirements. There is little point in piling up massive financial reserves in the Western money markets, only to see their value eroded by official devaluation of the major reserve currencies and by inflation and depreciation.[38]

The principle of building up huge reserves abroad remains the same for Kuwait, but the time it takes to do so has been drastically cut short. Yet another major departure from the avenue of thought characterising the years preceding 1973 has been registered. The country's political, intellectual and business leaders now prefer that their resources should as far as possible take the form of direct investment, in joint productive ventures or at least in equity, with lending and bank deposits taking quite a secondary position. Assuming no serious setbacks to the crude market and no substantial drop in the oil prices prevailing by the end of 1975, the country can build up a very impressive volume of investments outside its frontiers by the end of the seventies, along with the large investments already made and those envisaged in the home economy at the same time. The GNP expected from both masses of investment can assure the population of a very high level of living, even if the expected rates of return were estimated most cautiously. This could be achieved parallel with diversification in the economy. For, although oil will continue for many years to come to be available for export crude, it could be also used much more than at present as industrial feedstock, or for refined products.

We need not go any further into an exploration of possible avenues of action for the future; such an exercise will occupy us in the companion volume (Volume II), entitled *The Determinants of Arab Economic Development*. It is sufficient to indicate here that substantially more investment is going, and promises to continue doing so, into the other Arab countries, in concrete translation of the principle which the present writer has advocated for the consideration of the Planning Board. This principle is that the Arab world provides 'strategic economic depth' for Kuwait — in the sense that the relative scarcity or limitation of opportunities for rational and remunerative investment in Kuwait compared with the volume of savings available, should focus attention on the rest of the Arab region for substitute opportunities. This is being increasingly accepted, as well as becoming increasingly easy to implement, thanks to the fact that the bulk of the oil money is in public hands where policy formulation and decision-making are centralised and large-scale.

Until recently, the danger was real and great that Kuwait would turn more into a *rentier* society living mainly on the dividends and interest of its foreign reserves. The danger still exists, but can be substantially reduced if the population is made to participate more in the activities that precede, accompany and follow the act of investment. Only if Arab economic complementarity materialises very fast, and joint Arab projects cement the various Arab countries, with what that involves of free mobility of manpower and capital, will the danger become minimal. This danger has social and psychological implications to the extent that income and effort are estranged if not totally divorced in the case of Kuwait and other large oil producers with relatively small populations (like Abu Dhabi

Kuwait

and the rest of the United Arab Emirates, Qatar, Oman, Saudi Arabia and Libya).[39] Obviously, the Midas touch is not an unmixed blessing.

Before this section on the overall achievements in the post-war years is wound up, the performance of the economy and society ought to be examined from three other angles: budgetary development alongside the performance, external economic relations during the period — particularly trade and balance of international payments, and the pattern of relations between the public and the private sectors.

Public Finance[40]

The first proper budget was prepared for 1956. Between that year and the budget estimate for 1974/5, revenue has risen almost ninefold from KD113.1m to KD959.9m, while current expenditure has increased almost sixfold, from KD59.4m to KD394m. Three striking features of Kuwait's public finances over the years are worth noting. The first is the predominance of oil revenue among the government's total revenues, and the consistency of this predominance. Thus, oil accounted for 92.2 per cent of revenue for the initial year and 95.8 per cent in the last year. The consistently high proportion represented by oil revenue shows that no substantial effort has been made in the intervening two decades to raise the *relative* contribution of non-oil revenue, whether by way of direct or indirect taxation.

The second feature to note is the much faster rate of growth of expenditure than of revenue until 1971/2, owing mainly (a) to the vast expansion in the size of the civil service and the steep rise in the salary level, (b) to the vast expansion in the public services rendered by government and the increase in the cost of these services, and (c) to the slower rate of growth of oil revenue. Development expenditure, on the other hand, rose more moderately in the years 1960/1 to 1971/2 (from KD26.7m to an estimated KD60.6m). Indeed, even if the comparison is made between 1956 and 1971/2, the increase would still be moderate, considering that for the initial year development spending (which appeared under two headings: development projects and Public Works Department spending) totalled KD16.9m. Together these two prominent features carry serious implications for the state of health of the economy and even the society, as we will have occasion to demonstrate in the last section of this chapter. However, beginning with 1972/3, revenues increased at a higher rate than expenditures: by 1973/4 the ratio both of revenue and ordinary expenditure in the terminal to the initial year was almost the same. But 1974/5 marked the wide spurt of oil revenues that made budget revenue far outdistance budget expenditure.

The third feature relates to the land purchases and sales effected. Thus, while for the years 1962/3—1971/2 (the independence decade) land acquisitions absorbed KD386.3m of public funds, the government's receipts from land sales totalled KD25.7m and from land leases KD3.5m.[41] This shows clearly the vast discrepancy between the rates at which the government buys land and sells or leases it. Comparison for the whole period 1956—1971/2 is not possible because the data available for sales and leases only cover the decade 1962/3—1971/2.

This decade permits some very revealing analysis, thanks to a set of tables prepared in 1972 by the Planning Board to sum up the picture of the ten years of independence. The tables enable us to make a few more comments on the government's expenditure. Thus, it is found that Chapter One in the budget, 'Salaries and Wages', has over the ten years in question absorbed KD795m out of a total expenditure of KD1,720m — or 46.2 per cent. It ought to be pointed out that salaries and wages relating to the defence forces are not shown separately for the last five years of the decade. Judging by their level for the first five years, they would be no less than KD50m. Furthermore, while salaries and wages amounted to KD45.4m in the initial year of the decade, they reached KD110.5m for the last year.

Another comment is that actual expenditure on development projects invariably fell below allocations, but not by much, in contrast with the standards of many countries in the region. Thus, for nine years of the decade for which closed accounts were then available to the Planning Board (that is, excluding the year 1971/2), allocations totalled KD404.7m, while actual expenditure totalled KD336.7m, or 83.2 per cent. On the other hand, allocations and actual expenditures on land purchases have been nearly identical. (Actual expenditure on development projects for the years 1952–1970/1, also according to the Planning Board, totals KD502.3m.)

The distribution of development allocations among the various ministries and authorities over the past decade is shown in Table 3.11.

Table 3.11: Development Allocations, 1962-72

Recipient	Per Cent
Public works	11.7
Posts, telephones and telegraphs	10.7
Electricity and water	21.2
Desalination and electricity generation plants in Shuaiba	12.1
Salt, chlorine and caustic soda factories	0.7
Civil aviation	4.1
Ports and customs projects	2.9
Kuwait municipality projects	9.4
Education	12.6
Information	0.8
Health	2.0
Social affairs and labour (includes housing)	7.3
Waqf and Islamic affairs	0.6
Defence, foreign affairs, finance and oil, trade and industry, etc.	3.9
	100.0

This distribution shows that priority has been assigned to electricity and water (a total of 33.3 per cent), then to roads and other public works (if public works and municipality projects are added together), then to public services (education and health), and finally to posts and telecommunications — if recipients representing 10 per cent or more only are considered. Together, these priority items account for four-fifths of total expenditure.

It will be useful at this point to undertake a very rough estimation of the average capital-output ratio for the whole economy. To do so, we will have to add investment in the private and mixed (or joint) sectors to public investments. Information is available on the private and joint sectors for the years 1962/3–1969/70, though even then the information is not much better than enlightened estimation. (See Table 3.3 above.) Total invest-

Kuwait

ment for these eight years was KD570m. To carry the total forward to the end of the decade, we have to add investment for the two years 1970/1 and 1971/2, which amount to KD171m.[42] Thus total investment by the private and joint sectors for the decade was KD741m. Therefore total investment for the economy amounted to KD1,146m. Forgetting about the depreciation of capital, time lags and other refinements, we will now relate this volume of incremental investment to incremental GNP between 1962/3 and 1971/2, or KD691m. (See Table 3.3.) The capital-output ratio for the whole economy was accordingly 1.7:1. Such a low ratio, especially with considerable investment having been made in infrastructure which normally has a very high capital coefficient, is only possible because of the preponderance of oil income in GNP and the fact that this income flows into the economy without the economy itself having undertaken investment to permit the flow (the oil companies' investments are not included in the estimates presented here). If the share of oil in GNP were therefore excluded, the non-oil capital-output ratio would be about 5:1.

This much higher ratio befits a country towards which nature has been niggardly except in hydrocarbons, and one as deeply involved in the build-up of its social and capital overhead as Kuwait has been. It is necessary to point out that the government poured into the economy an additional KD441m against land purchases during the decade of independence, and this sum, in spite of the outflow to foreign countries of a large portion of it, must have augmented the income flow in the economy. (Spending for land acquisitions does not show in the budget account that has been presented.) Clearly, land acquisitions are not an investment in the economic sense of the term, but a transfer transaction. (The capital-output ratio for subsequent years is distinctly lower, owing to the rise in GNP mostly because of the increased intake by government of oil revenue. However, though information is available on this revenue, there is no information on investment by the private and mixed sectors after 1971/2.)

It has been stated that total spending under the general budget during the independence decade amounted to KD1,720m, and that salaries and wages accounted for KD795m and public development spending to KD404.7m. The balance of KD520.3m is accounted for by the items detailed in Table 3.12.

Table 3.12: Budget Expenditure excluding Salaries, Wages and Development Spending

	KD m
Chapter Two expenditure — current expenditure other than salaries and wages	411.4
Ministry of Social Affairs aid and assistance to the needy	23.2
Rent for government officials entitled to free housing	4.3
Allowances for the Head of State	81.4
Total	520.3

However, the KD1,720m only represents spending under the ordinary budget. There are other categories of public spending undertaken from the general reserves or from the overall revenue before the budget's share is allotted to it. The global account of overall public receipts and overall public spending appears in Table 3.13.

Table 3.13: Overall Public Receipts and Public Spending

	KD m	KD m	KD m
Total receipts by the state during the decade			2,706
Total spending (current and developmental) under the budget, as indicated above		1,720	
Add: Land acquisitions during the decade	441		
Miscellaneous expenditures: subscription to international bodies, internal commitments, etc.	107		
Foreign aid and loans	293		
Low-income housing, support to KFAED and to Savings and Credit Bank	20		
Loans to Shuaiba Industrial Area, support to companies	23		
Allotments to general reserve and foreign investments	103	987	2,707

(The difference of 1m is due to rounding.)

Trade and Balance of Payments

So far the examination has centred around the internal financial aspects of the economy's performance. Now the country's external economic relations will be discussed, under the two headings of foreign trade and balance of international payments.

Kuwait has the highest volume of trade *per capita* in the world, with imports worth KD310.6m for 1973, for a population of 907,200, or KD342 *per capita*. On the other hand, exports other than crude oil just exceeded KD91m for the same year. Between 1954, the first year for which complete data are available, and 1973, the last year, imports increased 10.4 times, while non-oil exports increased 21.2 times.[43] Though commendable, this performance still leaves a very wide gap between imports and non-oil exports. Furthermore, imports have amounted to about 27 per cent of GNP in recent years, the highest ratio in the world.

The increase in imports *per capita* over the years 1954-73 suggests a consistently high average propensity to import. All three main categories of imports were of significant volume: consumer goods, durables and capital goods, thanks to a high level of consumption, a strong desire by households and offices to equip themselves with refrigerators, washing machines and air-conditioners, and a strong drive towards capital formation for socio-economic development. This high level of imports created no foreign exchange strains for the economy, despite the fact that exports on the average paid only for one-eighth of imports. The relaxed exchange position was created by the abundant foreign exchange earnings from oil exports. As indicated earlier, not only has it been possible to finance the large imports of the country, but in addition to build up huge foreign exchange reserves abroad (in the form of loans, investments and bank accounts) and to make substantial grants and donations.

Probably because the country suffers no foreign exchange hardship, no balance of payments accounts were presented in official statistics before 1974. However, the Planning

Board has produced estimates for the years 1965/6 to 1971/2, and the *Statistical Abstract 1974* carries the picture one year further, to cover 1972/3. In each of the eight years covered a substantial surplus has materialised. The surplus on current account for the period totals KD1,617m.[44]

Economic System

Kuwait's socio-economic system is one of private enterprise successfully mixed with public enterprise within the framework of parliamentary democracy, a hereditary ruling family and a welfare state philosophy. The mixture of private and public enterprise produces joint enterprise, as a third sector. While the number of establishments owned jointly by the government and the private sector is not large, their role in the economy is significant, as is the ratio of their consolidated share capital to the total capital of shareholding companies. According to published information, by the end of 1970 there were 1,489 establishments in the country with the corporate or partnership form of organisation. Of this total, 42 were shareholding companies, 686 were companies with limited liability, and 761 were joint ventures. All but 50 establishments of the total have been formed since 1960. The total capital of the companies was KD158m.[45]

Nine out of the 42 companies were jointly owned, with a share capital of KD71m. The government's paid-up share is KD41.8m.[46] However, between the end of 1970 and 1974, many more companies have been formed, and seven of these fall in the 'mixed sector' with joint public and private ownership. It remains to be added that almost all the 16 joint companies are major establishments, as Table 3.14 suggests.[47]

The KNPC and the Kuwait Petrochemical Industries Company themselves own or have formed subsidiary companies, such as the refinery and the Kuwait Chemical Fertilizer Company. Together the establishments listed suggest the importance of joint enterprise and the breadth of its scope. In addition, the public share-holding companies include four operating banks, three insurance companies and one re-insurance company, the Kuwait Oil Tankers Company, the Kuwait Cement Company, and about two dozen other companies. A certain degree of interlocking characterises several of the companies listed. The KFTCIC leads the list in this respect, with 17 associated and affiliated companies and establishments by 31 December 1974 — 11 of them outside Kuwait.[48]

Great hopes had been pinned on the mixed sector. It was believed in the early sixties that the combination of government and the private sector would capitalise on the strength of both and avoid as much as possible the defects inherent in each. In particular, it was believed that the combination would mobilise enough funds for undertakings requiring large capital, would enrich the flow of entrepreneurial talent, and would provide a wide measure of security to private investors. In practice, however, the hopes have not all been vindicated. Thus, there has been excessive dependence on the government by the private sector partners, and insufficient concern for the costs-returns relationship by the government. Added to inadequacy of pre-investment studies in some instances, or to the prevalence of excessive optimism with regard to marketing prospects, or yet to the clash between political and economic considerations as in the case of the marketing of chemical fertilisers, the above-mentioned weaknesses threw a few of the joint companies (particularly the KNPC and the Petrochemical Industries Company with their subsidiaries) into serious financial difficulties, until 1973/4.

Thus today there is still some hesitation, even cynicism, with regard to joint enterprise, in spite of the fact that several of the companies in this sector are performing distinctly well. This performance in itself is used as an argument for private enterprise and against

Table 3.14: Jointly Owned Companies in Kuwait, 1974

Name of Company	Capital KD m	Government's Share (per cent)
Kuwait National Petroleum Company	15.0	60
Kuwait National Industries Company	1.5	51
Kuwait Flour Mills Company	2.0	50
Kuwait Investment Company	7.5	50
Kuwait Transport Company	2.0	50
Kuwait Hotels Company	2.0	50
Kuwait Petrochemical Industries Company	32.0	80
Kuwait Shipping Company	9.0	75
Kuwait Foreign Trading, Contracting and Investment Company	20.0	98
Kuwait and Middle East Bank	2.0	51
Kuwait International Market	0.6	35
Kuwait Fishing Company	10.0	48
Stores and Production Refrigeration Company [sic]	2.0	25
Kuwait Supplies Company	2.0	45
Marine Contracting Services Company	5.0	45
Industrial Bank of Kuwait	10.0	45
Total or Average	122.6	67.4

Source: *Statistical Abstract 1974*, Table 110, p.167.

state participation, on the grounds that the companies which are prosperous owe their prosperity to the enterprise of certain very able persons at the top executive and technical level, and that these persons would operate well in the totally private sector. Furthermore — the argument goes on — funds are not short, nor are entrepreneurial ideas, in the business sector and security, like over-protection of industry, tends to create less than healthy establishments. Consequently, the whole idea of joint enterprise is currently being subjected to a searching second look.

Despite the importance of the mixed sector, the economy is rightly characterised as adhering to private enterprise. Yet at the same time, Kuwait has one of the furthest-reaching welfare systems in the world, as has been indicated in the discussion of education, health, housing, and other services. This mixture of systems seems to raise neither ideological nor practical misgivings and problems. It is believed, rightly in our opinion, that a private enterprise system can run parallel with a system which provides extensive public services. The only incongruity in the situation is that the services are not made possible through the contributions of the economy via taxes, but through the bounty of nature. The problem here is sociological rather than economic, and we will turn to it shortly.

The economic role of the public sector is much larger than this brief discussion can suggest. Thus, in addition to public spending under the current and development budgets, and for land acquisition, the government has advanced large loans to several companies in the mixed sector, and has made vast investments in KFAED, the Savings and Credit Bank, the Kuwait Airways Corporation, and the Central Bank.

3. DEVELOPMENT PLANNING

Customarily, development planning is resorted to in order to ration, and introduce rationality into, the use of capital as the scarce factor in underdeveloped countries. This widespread, but erroneous (because narrow-focused) view of planning has its advocates in Kuwait. The error is multi-sided. First, the abundance of capital and of foreign exchange should not conceal the shortage of skilled manpower and organisational and institutional defects, nor should it disguise the fact that the mere abundance of capital can lead to its improper use, over-use, or use according to a wrong (therefore irrational) system of priorities. However, whether or not such notions of planning prevail in the circles of government and Parliament the fact remains that although a Planning Board was established in 1962, and a First Five-Year Plan for the years 1966/7–1970/1 was prepared and printed and put in the hands of government by November 1965, the Plan has not yet been examined by the National Assembly in either its original or amended and updated form, covering the years 1967/8–1971/2.

Some form of annual planning, or more precisely sectoral programming, had been in effect before 1962, under the Development (or Reconstruction) Board. The Planning Board itself was established soon after independence, upon the recommendation of a World Bank Mission which visited the country in 1961. The constitution of the Planning Board was sensible; it comprised the seven Ministers whose ministries' functions were related directly to socio-economic development, the mayor of Kuwait city, and four representatives of the private sector. The Board was chaired by the Prime Minister himself.

Kuwaiti planning has so far avoided highly sophisticated methodology, and has aimed at keeping the Plan within the grasp of the political decision-makers and their limited experience. In its revised version, it has also been careful not to raise controversy, rouse misgivings, or express harsh judgements, especially with regard to population policy and fiscal policy (the latter specifically in connection with direct taxation).

As neither the original Plan nor its revised version has been passed by the National Assembly, there is little to be gained in a detailed discussion of the targets of the Plan, of its strategy, its investment programme, and of the policies and procedures suggested in it. In very broad terms the Plan has the following targets:[49]

- achieving an overall rate of growth averaging 6.5 per cent per annum, or 37 per cent for the five years;
- achieving diversification and less relative dependence on the oil sector;
- development of manpower;
- completion of basic infrastructural projects;
- achieving social equilibrium on the basis of the principle of justice in income distribution, without damaging incentives;
- achieving balanced geographical distribution of development benefit; and
- strengthening of economic ties with the Arab countries.

Prominent emphasis is placed on the development of human resources. This is seen in the listing and discussion of the targets, as well as in the discussion of the policies called forth by the Plan.

These policies are grouped under four headings: general economic policy; population policy; the policy of general welfare; and fiscal and monetary policy. The population policy suggested emphasises reliance on Kuwaiti manpower to the utmost possible, including the encouragement of women's participation in the labour force. The guiding principle ought to be the absorption of all the Kuwaitis capable of gainful and productive employment. The employment of non-Kuwaitis ought to be accepted only to fill the gaps left open by the Kuwaitis while these are being prepared to take over; and such employment ought to be on the basis of a selective policy and in conformity with the country's cultural traditions and security considerations. The welfare policy recommended is based on the principle of the continuation of the welfare services currently offered, but with the insistence that the public ought to bear part of the costs, directly or through taxation, in order to safeguard society from the dangers of extreme dependence on the state, and to safeguard the state from extreme dependence on oil revenue as the source of financing of welfare.

The investment programme recommended is quite large. It totals KD912m for the five years, divided into KD507m by the public sector, KD345m by the private sector, and KD60m by the mixed sector. The largest single beneficiary is housing and public buildings (19.4 per cent), followed by transport and communications (16.7 per cent), industry (9.4 per cent), water and irrigation (7.9 per cent), petroleum and natural gas (7.7 per cent), power — electricity and gas (7.1 per cent), education (5.7 per cent), public utilities and municipal services (5 per cent), and so on along a descending scale. The allocation of investment by institutional sector reflects the structure of the economic system. Thus, investments in power, water and irrigation, information, public utilities and municipal services and security and justice are to be made solely by the public sector; investments in agriculture, transport and communications, research and training, education, social and religious services and health are to be predominantly made by the public sector. On the other hand it is the private sector alone that is expected to invest in the fishing industry, while the private sector is the predominant investor in petroleum and natural gas (with the mixed sector a minor investor), in housing, and in trade, finance and tourism. The mixed sector is the major investor in only one sector: industry.[50]

The rise in GNP expected to occur along with the investment programme of KD912m is KD238m. Assuming that increases in GNP in the initial part of the Plan which are attributable to investments made prior to the Plan are roughly equal to those that will fall outside the confines of the Plan at its later phase, we can relate the capital indicated to the output indicated. This produces a capital-output ratio of 3.83:1, which is much higher than that experienced in the first independence decade. (See discussion above relating to the years 1962/3–1971/2.)

In concluding this section, it should be noted that the attitude of hesitation towards planning, and of indifference to the rationale behind it at the decision-making level in the public and the private sector alike, has led to frustration among a small number of intellectuals and business leaders concerned over the hesitation, caused by the superabundance of capital. Furthermore, the concern extends to reach the population and manpower policies, and the welfare policies, now in force, which are believed to be harmful to national interest in the long run. This concern forms part of the background to the last section of this chapter.[51]

4. KUWAIT AND THE ARAB WORLD

Governments are not charitable institutions, but bodies seeking the interest of their countries. Nevertheless, certain acts undertaken can serve both self-interest and the interest of others. Kuwait is no doubt the most prominent Arab country which is pursuing economic self-interest through the pursuit of the economic interests of the Arab world. This it achieves through a multiplicity of courses: grants, loans, deposits in Arab banks and direct investments. The large volume of its economic contribution to Arab economic development broadly defined is made possible thanks to the combination of large oil revenues, a small population and the limited investment possibilities at home.

This contribution has taken six forms so far. The first is project loans to capital-needy Arab countries channelled through the Kuwait Fund for Arab Economic Development, KFAED. The second is non-project loans made by the government from the general reserves. The third is grants made by a special body called the General Authority for the South and the Arabian Gulf to the needy parts of the Gulf and to Yemen. The fourth is direct investments in real estate and other sectors, or portfolio investments, in certain Arab countries. The fifth is deposits in Arab banks. Lastly, the sixth is sizeable participation in the Arab Fund for Economic and Social Development.

KFAED was established at the end of 1961. It was the fruit of the thinking and promotion of a very small number of imaginative high officials in the Ministry of Finance and Oil, the support which the idea received from the World Bank mission of 1961, and the positive response of government. No doubt Kuwait was eager right after independence (and the brief challenge to that independence) to enhance its political position through sharing some of its new oil wealth. It is equally probable that it was also interested in promoting the development of sister Arab countries. Self-interest and public-spiritedness combined to produce KFAED.

The Fund's law and charter have been amended three times since its establishment. The most important amendment relates to the capital and borrowing powers of the Fund. Thus, the capital has been raised from an original KD50m to KD100m, then to KD200m, and finally to KD1,000m (the amendments occurring in April 1963, July 1966 and March 1974).[52] The capital is to be provided half out of the government savings (the general reserves), and half out of the current revenues through appropriations made in the annual budget, when such appropriations are made necessary. The amendment of 1966 stipulated that 'the amount so appropriated shall be transferred to the Fund's account in the fiscal year following the year when the Fund's obligations become equivalent to half its capital'. In addition to its capital, the Fund — according to the Amendment of 1963 — was empowered to 'borrow money and issue bonds within the limit of twice the amount of its capital plus its reserves'. Thus the Fund can now have a total working capital of KD3,000m, plus three times its reserves. It is important to add that the final amendment raising the capital to one billion dinars also empowers KFAED to extend loans to non-Arab, Third World countries as well.

The Fund pursues very sound lending policies and procedures, free of political pressures, thanks to an autonomy given to it and respected by the government. The conduct of the Fund's operations by its management has justified both the autonomy and the respect and has ensured their continuation. The borrowing countries equally respect the Fund's strictness in insisting that all loans should be based on adequate technical and economic studies which establish the ability of the projects financed to pay for themselves. The creditor-debtor relations are very good, and the experience of the fourteen years of operation has great promise for the Fund's future operations and its standards of work.

118 Kuwait

By the end of March 1975, the Fund had extended loans to twelve countries to the total of KD161m; they include all the countries covered by the present study except for Saudi Arabia and Libya, but with the addition of Bahrain, Yemen Arab Republic and People's Democratic Republic of Yemen.[53] (Loans to non-Arab Third World countries were only advanced in the following financial year, 1975/6.) The distribution of loans as of 31 March 1975 by country and by sector is shown in Table 3.15. It reveals that Egypt, Sudan, Tunisia, Syria and Jordan are the largest recipients of loans, in that order; together they account for over two-thirds of the total. Transport and storage together constitute the major recipient sector, followed by agriculture, electricity and industry (with the two last-named sectors receiving equal credit). It ought to be pointed out that the loans have been mostly, but not fully, drawn upon. Thus, by the end of March 1975, total disbursements were KD91.3m. Repayments under loan agreements totalled KD29.3m by the same date.

In addition to loans extended, the Fund also makes technical assistance grants. A total of KD1,176,000 was granted during the financial year 1974/5. The beneficiaries included one non-Arab country under the new extended mandate of the Fund. This was Afghanistan with a grant of KD400,000. (During the same year, loan requests were being examined for three Asian and seven African non-Arab countries.)[54]

Table 3.15: KFAED – Distribution of Loans up to 31 March 1975 (KDm and per cent)

Country	Agriculture	Transport and Storage	Electricity	Industry	Total	Per Cent
Jordan	6.48	–	3.26	4.48	14.22	8.83
Bahrain	–	0.50	7.35	1.49	9.34	5.80
Tunisia	5.20	3.75	8.35	2.00	19.30	11.98
Algeria	–	10.00	–	–	10.00	6.21
Sudan	9.11	7.00	–	6.17	22.28	13.83
Syria	–	7.00	9.90	2.00	18.90	11.73
Iraq	–	–	2.62	3.76	6.38	3.96
Lebanon	–	0.80	1.66	–	2.46	1.52
Egypt	–	27.80	–	7.00	34.80	21.61
Morocco	10.05	–	–	3.25	13.30	8.26
S. Yemen	4.53	–	–	–	4.53	2.81
N. Yemen	2.22	0.28	–	3.00	5.50	3.41
Total	37.59	57.13	33.14	33.15	161.01	100.00
Per Cent	23.34	35.48	20.58	20.58		100.00

Note: Percentages do not add up to 100 because of rounding.

Source: KFAED, *Annual Report 1974-1975*, Table C, p. 52.

Non-project loans made by the Kuwait government to Arab governments form the second type of economic help to the Arab world. Fifteen such loans were extended to ten Arab countries by the end of 1975, to the total of KD120.3m. (Some KD25m of this total was repaid by that date.) These loans are meant to be economic loans in general support of the recipient country's budget. The largest single recipient of loans has been Egypt (KD33.6m), followed by Iraq (KD30m), and Algeria (KD20m).[55] These loans, however, are apart from the much larger sums advanced, as grants or loans, to the 'front-line' countries, namely Egypt, Syria and Jordan, subsequent to the Arab-Israeli war of October 1973, to help them surmount their pressing economic problems and obligations.

The third form of economic help is grants made by Kuwait to the poorer parts of the Arabian Gulf and to the two Yemens, via the General Authority for South Arabia and the Arabian Gulf, which has a special budget. The cumulative total allocated down to March 1975 is KD19.4m. The grants in question are used mainly for education and health services. It is worth recording that although revenue from oil has become much larger in the Arabian Gulf since 1974, Kuwait government allocations for 1974/5 more than doubled compared with those for 1973/4; likewise, those for 1975/6 (which do not form part of the cumulative total indicated above) are more than double their counterpart in the preceding year.[56] The explanation of this recent trend is the desire of the Kuwait government to intensify its help to North and South Yemen and to those parts of the Gulf that produce no oil.

Detailed specific information is not available regarding the fourth and fifth forms of economic relations between Kuwait and other Arab countries, namely direct investments or portfolio investment, and deposits in Arab banks (notably in Lebanon). However, it has been officially stated that these two forms combined, together with the second form (government-to-government loans) constituted 28.3 per cent of the declared general reserves which stood at KD565m by the end of 1970. Since this proportion amounts to about KD160m, and since the government-to-government net loans amounted at that date to KD112.8m, then direct and portfolio investments and deposits in Arab banks together total about KD47.2m. However, the flow of Kuwaiti capital in the directions and forms indicated has since been considerably intensified. Furthermore, Kuwaiti participation in the capital of several joint undertakings has multiplied several-fold since the autumn of 1973. Kuwait occupies a leading position among the Arab oil countries with respect to its imaginative policy in supporting Arab developmental and financing efforts.

It has likewise played an outstanding part in the establishment and support of the newly formed Arab Fund for Economic and Social Development, AFESD. The capital of the Fund is KD100m (raised to KD400m in April 1975), and Kuwait's original subscription is KD30m. The seat of AFESD is in Kuwait, and this country's subscription has been made by KFAED, with which the new Fund works in harmony.

The account of Kuwait's financial support — whether in loans, grants or investments — to the various Arab countries would be incomplete if mention is not made of Kuwait's contributions, since 1967/8, to the support of Egypt and Jordan as the victims of the Arab-Israeli war of June 1967. Since the war of October 1973, Syria has also been the recipient of aid. Earlier support to Egypt and Jordan was in the amount of KD47.5m annually, and it was paid until late in 1970 when Jordan's share was suspended for political reasons relating to the latter country's major clash with Palestinian guerrillas on Jordanian soil. (Payments were resumed late in 1973.) In a sense, this support is economic in nature, as it aims at compensating part of the economic losses sustained by Egypt and Jordan. The payments made subsequent to October 1973 have been much more substantial, although the exact sums paid in 1973/4 have not been announced. However, as a result of the Rabat Arab Summit Conference in October 1974, Kuwait has undertaken to pay $391.5m annually in aid to the three front-line countries, as well as $5m to the

Palestine Liberation Organization.[57]

To sum up, one-third of Kuwait's declared general reserves in 1971 (i.e. about KD217m) was in the form of loans to the Arab countries. This is apart from the KD30m representing Kuwait's subscription to AFESD, and apart from all forms of grants which probably exceed KD220m in total.[58] This volume of aid has been vastly exceeded in absolute terms since 1973/4, though in relative terms it has probably declined, owing to the substantially increased volume of financial resources available.

Impressive as Kuwait's financial relations are with the Arab world, the scope for the future is much greater still. This is so considering the fact that investments within Kuwait during the past decade have been less than half total domestic savings, and can hardly reach 10 per cent at the present. (Indeed, the original version of the First Five Year Plan estimated that domestic investments for the five years would amount to just over 36 per cent of total domestic savings, the proportion being higher at the beginning and lower at the end of the period.)[59] This trend will scarcely be changed in the coming half-decade, with oil revenues being as high as they are. How Kuwait will allocate its oil revenue between 1975 and 1980 must largely remain a matter of speculation, but the indications are abundant that the Arab world will continue to receive some $1–1.5 billion a year unless the oil revenue drops substantially. The local opportunities, assuming the most optimistic rate of increase in absorptive capacity for investment, will remain unable to utilise gainfully more than a small part of the investible resources. This adds strength to the claim that the Arab world can provide major attraction to Kuwaiti savings, if the climate of investment were to be inviting and Arab economic co-operation were to be earnestly sought.

5. THE BURDEN OF FORTUNE

Enormous transformation has manifestly taken place in Kuwait, in the physical, economic and social realms. The dimensions of this transformation can be better appreciated if the original state of the economy and society in the early post-war years is remembered. The country today enjoys vast riches and a high level of well-being, and can claim greatly improved capabilities in the performance of its economic tasks. This record of achievement has been made possible not only because of the oil fortune enjoyed by Kuwait, but also of a happy combination of far-sightedness and development orientation in the circles of political leadership, political stability and participation among the population, a high level of economic motivation in the business community, and cultural adaptability in the community at large. In addition, the political leadership has adopted a liberal and pragmatic policy with regard to the attraction of skilled non-Kuwaitis for the undertaking of the many and varied tasks which fast and far-reaching development calls for.

However, the achievement has not been free of high social costs. For, in addition to the dislocations and tensions that normally accompany speedy development in its early phases, Kuwait has suffered a special type of ailment that can prove of long-lasting danger to society if not attended to carefully and speedily. This ailment has accompanied the ease and speed with which the country's fortune has gushed in the past two decades, in the midst of the niggardliness of the desert, the poverty of the economy and the backwardness of the society. Thus, the privilege of the Midas touch exacts an exorbitant price from those given the privilege, a price which we have called the burden of fortune.

This burden is not merely related to the jealousy of the 'have-nots' among the country's neighbours or to the precariousness of its existence — dangers which can relatively easily be warded off or guarded against in the modern world with its international system which is protective of sovereignty. It is more fundamentally related to the internal staying power of society itself and to its sense of responsibility. We will single out four among several aspects of this burden for examination and assessment in this concluding section of the chapter.

1. The first is lavishness with public money expressed in many ways. Thus, salaries are very high, probably higher than would be necessary either to attract expatriates into the country and to retain their services, or to induce nationals to work. This is particularly so given the fact that the policy governing the entry of expatriates has not been very exacting and discriminating with regard to qualifications and skills; and concern has rarely been exercised over the matching of the qualifications possessed with those claimed. The same applies, even more forcibly, to the salary level of the Kuwaitis themselves, where the functions performed by many of the civil servants often fall well below the remuneration received.

The argument is often advanced, in defence of the salary policy, that as far as the expatriates are concerned, salaries have to be high enough to attract non-Kuwaitis into the country and to create a satisfactory level of labour commitment; and, as far as Kuwaitis are concerned, salaries have to be high in order to constitute an effective and substantial transfer transaction or redistribution mechanism between the public sector (with its oil revenue) and the population of whom the Kuwait civil servants form an important component. The argument is sound in its relation to both communities, but the trouble arises with exaggeration in its application. For better service could be obtained with the level of salaries established; furthermore, a smaller salaries bill could procure the same total service if the civil service were not to be as numerically inflated as it is. The objective of better distribution of income would then have to be sought through other developmental policies. The lavishness is also manifest in the social services and other benefits enjoyed by the population, in the fields of education, health, housing, water and electricity. This is not to argue against the welfare state in principle, but to emphasise that the frontiers of this state have been extended far, to the point where some squandering of public funds has resulted. Thus, school buildings need not be as fancy and expensive as they are, the free distribution of medicaments and medical supplies need not be as wasteful as it is, and the resale by the government of purchased land for housing purposes need not be effected at as low a price as it is. Likewise, the bursaries and other benefits allowed to students abroad are so liberal as to invite luxurious living by the students and to militate against the hard work which 'financial discipline' would almost certainly impose.

Finally, the abundance of public funds has made for insufficient care in pre-investment studies of projects of which the state is owner or co-owner, with the result that the overall cost of these projects has been excessively high and the unit cost of products unnecessarily high. This has been a major factor in the troubles through which some of these projects are passing.

2. A second defect in the system of grave social implications is that the oil fortune has permitted the advancing of many economic and social benefits to the population without imposing even a partial counterpart responsibility in tax payment. This imbalance has resulted in two unhealthy developments. The first is the fast growth of the expenditures in the general budget, to the point where the annual allocations to the general reserves out of oil revenue have on average, until 1971/2, been smaller than desired and planned. This growth of expenditures has not outdistanced the growth in oil revenues only because increments in the earnings of the oil sector have been substantial. But the disturbing phenomenon has been that the excess of state revenue, including the oil sector, over state

expenditure, has (again until 1971/2) been uncomfortably small, which suggests that the urge to spend more public funds as soon as more funds are earned has been much stronger than the urge to be provident and to build up the general reserves.

The second unhealthy development derives from the fact that the population does not feel any responsibility towards financing the benefits it gets from the public sector. The bill for these benefits has been rising, both in the capital and recurrent components. Had it not been for the recent vast increases in the oil revenues, the expenditure of the state would have got uncomfortably close to the level of state revenues, given the size of the civil service and the level of salaries and wages, the regulatory annual increments in salaries, the continued pressure for more and better services extended to an expanding population, the 'natural' bureaucratic tendency for ministries and departments to grow in size, often without quality improvements, and the tendency for the defence bill to rise. A population not used to paying taxes to meet some of the financial burdens of government would find it extremely difficult suddenly to be asked to bear a tax burden, no matter how light. The rise in oil revenue came at the right time to act as a shock-absorber, but it is an unhealthy absorber because it delays the moment when it will be necessary for government to start imposing some direct and indirect taxes on the population. The discrepancy between the substantial benefits received and the absence of a tax burden thus still remains a serious social flaw in the system, and the longer the flaw stands uncorrected, the more difficult it will be in the future to train the population to bear its tax responsibility.

3. Not unrelated to the two negative aspects of Kuwait's fortune just discussed is the third which affects Kuwaitis both in the public and the private sectors. This is the divorce, or at least estrangement, in the minds or only the subconscious of most people, between income and effort. Thus, the ease with which income (and social benefits in kind) have been earned, or obtained, whether as salaries or dividends or interest, or with which capital gains have been made mainly through land sales to government, contrasted with the little effort expended to earn the income or make the capital gains, has already had serious social consequences. There is a general tendency, no less real because of the exceptions, for people to refuse to work hard or tolerate strict work discipline, or to learn and practise exacting skills.

Obviously not all Kuwaitis are millionaires. But precisely because of this fact, the Kuwaiti have-nots (relatively speaking) cannot fail to notice the ease with which fortunes have been made. If such feelings are still contained, this is because the building and development boom of the past two decades has padded the sharp edge of the feelings of the lower-income groups.

However, class or group discontent apart, the problem of continued dissociation between income and capital on the one hand, and effort on the other hand, remains serious for most people, and will certainly have serious implications for the work habits and income expectations of manpower in Kuwait. These implications, and the problems underlying them, will become more difficult to deal with, the longer the phenomenon of dissociation is allowed to continue.

4. The fourth aspect of the 'burden of fortune' relates to manpower. The problems encountered here, like those encountered in connection with the preceding three aspects, have been touched upon elsewhere in this chapter. But it is useful to focus here on the questions of heavy dependence on an expatriate labour force, population policy and the non-absorption of the expatriates, the size of the civil service and the allocation of functions between the Kuwaiti and non-Kuwaiti civil servants, work discipline in general, and the emergent competition between the more recently educated Kuwaitis seeking well-paying

and prestigious jobs and the earlier-educated Kuwaitis now entrenched in such jobs. These questions are all interconnected in one way or another and derive basically from the inadequacy of the Kuwaiti labour force for the tasks of a fast-developing, rich economy.

The inadequacy has necessitated the inflow of tens of thousands of foreigners to undertake the tasks of building up the economy at a speedy rate made possible by the oil fortune. While a sensible and necessary policy, the attraction of expatriates has sheltered the Kuwaiti labour force from the urgency of learning how to undertake the tasks. Yet the Kuwaitis have been extremely reluctant to allow citizenship to the more committed and more desirable expatriate elements. Furthermore, in its desire to find employment for as many Kuwaitis as possible, and given the shying away by Kuwaitis from jobs involving manual work or requiring specialised skills, the government has allowed the civil service to absorb many more Kuwaitis than necessary, at high salaries, to fill high policy-making and administrative jobs, or very low clerical and office-boy jobs. This has left the expatriates with unduly high concentration in the intermediate, particularly specialised, jobs. As a result of the inflated civil service and the relatively generous remuneration received, work discipline has slackened.

Finally, the newly trained Kuwaiti university graduates who see slightly older compatriots with no better qualifications in well-paid and prestigious jobs, who find that posts are not being created fast enough in government to absorb them, and who have been contaminated by the prevailing dissociation between income and effort in the public sector, tend to view the luckier compatriots in government with jealousy and to suffer the tensions of a competition that seems to have no immediate visible outlet.

The corrections of the situation should move along the same path that the problem has taken, namely beginning with the undertaking by the Kuwaitis of many more functions in the public and private sectors at all levels, whether technical, administrative or manual. This can be made to happen only if the largesse of the welfare state is curbed, and Kuwaitis begin to realise increasingly that income has to be worked for and earned. As more Kuwaitis become able and willing to handle the jobs which they now shun or are unable to handle, to that extent, at least, expatriates will become dispensable. Population policy should become operative here, with a view to allowing citizenship to the worthier expatriates, or at least allowing them longer-term contracts and the right to own property in Kuwait. This would enhance expatriate labour commitment, and would raise the propensity to save and invest in Kuwait rather than send the bulk of savings abroad. Gradually, the size of the civil service, job specifications, and the allocation of jobs between Kuwaitis and non-Kuwaitis should conform to the requirements of work and less to welfare considerations. Coupled with speedy development and with improved sectoral diversification making for the upgrading and expansion of now very minor sectors, there will be room for the Kuwaiti latecomers into the labour force.

As things stand today, the labour force is over-abundant for the country's current needs, and is only absorbed because a low level of work intensity is allowed, as well as a great deal of feather-bedding — in other words, it is only the substantial disguised unemployment which conceals the fact that the country can manage with a distinctly smaller labour force if manpower were to be employed more fully and effectively. The population policy in force is inadequate to cope with the situation, and the Five Year Plan does not provide the necessary guidelines for action based on the premiss of a reduced, but better trained and equipped, and more disciplined, labour force.[60] This must be considered an area of top priority for thought, planning and action.

6. CONCLUDING REMARKS

These are but a few pointers to certain aspects of the burden of fortune. The discussion preceding this last section clearly suggested that Kuwait has met much of the economic and technical challenge of a niggardly and harsh environment and a relatively backward population. But the pointers just examined suggest that the social challenge has yet to be met in some very critical areas. The issue acquires added urgency with the sudden improvement in the country's financial fortune after the new oil agreements entered into with the oil companies in 1971 and 1972, and more particularly after the application of new prices in the autumn of 1973, and the subsequent nationalisation of the oil industry in March 1975. This improvement may well conceal the need to face the social problems that we have focused upon from the sight of the general public. But it should not conceal them from the insight of the country's political and intellectual leaders.

NOTES

1. For a general survey of the first type, see David C. Cooke, *Kuwait: Miracle on the Desert* (New York, 1970). For more serious economic surveys, see: (a) Royal Institute of International Affairs, RIIA, *The Middle East: A Political and Economic Survey* (Oxford University Press, third edition, 1958), section on Kuwait; (b) Fakhri Shehab, 'Kuwait: A Super-Affluent Society', *Foreign Affairs*, April 1964; (c) IBRD, *The Economic Development of Kuwait* (Baltimore, 1965); (d) The General Union of Chambers of Commerce, Industry, and Agriculture in the Arab Countries, *Economic Development in the Arab Countries 1950-1965* (Beirut, 1967; Arabic), chapter on Kuwait; (e) Government of Kuwait, Planning Board, *The First Plan for Economic and Social Development for the Five Years 1966/67 – 1970/71* (Kuwait, 1965; Arabic), Ch. One; (f) Government of Kuwait, *The First Five-Year Plan for Economic and Social Development 1967/68-1971/72* (Kuwait, undated; Arabic), Ch. Two; (g) Ragaei El Mallakh, *Economic Development and Regional Cooperation: Kuwait* (Chicago, 1968); (h) Mohammad Al-Khoja, 'Distinguishing Features of the Kuwaiti Economy', lecture sponsored by the Kuwaiti Economic Association on 14 February, 1972; Arabic, stencilled monograph – a mainly technical examination of the growth potential of the economy; (i) Edmond Y. Asfour, 'Problems and Prospects of Economic Development of Saudi Arabia, Kuwait, and the Gulf Principalities', in Charles A. Cooper and Sidney S. Alexander (eds.), *Economic Development and Population Growth in the Middle East* (New York, 1972); and (j) Europa Publications, *The Middle East and North Africa 1971-72, 1972-73, 1973-74 and 1974-75* editions (London), chapter on Kuwait.

I served as Economic Adviser to the Planning Board of Kuwait from October 1964 to December 1965, and as Consultant to the Planning Board from April 1973 to March 1975. I have thus had the opportunity to examine a great deal of authoritative but unpublished material.

2. See items (e) and (f) in note 1 above in this connection.
3. Organization of Petroleum Exporting Countries, OPEC, *Annual Statistical Bulletin 1970*.
4. Planning Board, PB, *The First Plan...*, p. 10 (my translation).
5. PB, Central Statistical Office, *Statistical Abstract 1965*, Table 8. My estimate of 90,000 inhabitants in 1946 finds confirmation in an estimate that 'the population reached the first 100,000 by the beginning of the 1950s', in K.C. Zachariah, assisted by M. Ali Al-Khars and A. Al-Ayat, 'Trends and Components of Population Growth in Kuwait', in Cairo Demographic Centre, *Demographic Measures and Population Growth in the Arab Countries*, Research Monograph Series, No. 1 (Cairo, 1970), pp. 81-2.
6. I lean heavily in the immediately followed part of the chapter on PB, *Plan*... (in its original form – item (e) in note 1 – and its revised form, item (f) in note 1 above). However, the indicators listed in the text are amended or adjusted in accordance with the most recent data available in the *Statistical Abstract* for the years 1971, 1972, 1973, 1974 and 1975.
7. For the GNP estimates for 1959, and the lower estimate for 1962/3, see IBRD, pp. 167 and 168; for the higher 1962/3 estimate, see *Statistical Abstract 1966*, Table 78. (Ibid. for the years 1963/4 – 1965/6, and subsequent *Abstracts* for the years 1966/7 – 1972/3.)
8. Al-Khoja, op. cit., p. 3, for the proportion of GNP. According to an estimate made by the PB staff of GDP and GNP for 1970/1, the share of the oil sector rose to 60 per cent of GDP. This suggests a rise in the degree of dependence on oil by the economy. (See a sheet entitled 'Analysis of the Figures of National Product for the Financial Year 1970/1971', dated 21 February 1972.) The steep rise of oil revenue for 1971, 1972, 1973 and 1974 has caused the sector's share to mount still higher inasmuch as the oil-multiplier grows smaller owing to the enormous leakage abroad of the country's savings. The contribution of the sector to GDP seems to have risen from 60 per cent for 1970/1, to 63.7 for 1971/2, 63.3 for 1972/3, and an estimated 75 per cent for 1974. (Last estimate mine. Earlier proportions based on data in *Abstract 1974*, Table 88, p. 137.)
9. All references to census data relate to the census report for the relevant year: Department of Social

Affairs, *Population Census of Kuwait 1957: Some Detailed Tables* (Kuwait, June 1959; Arabic); Ministry of Social Affairs and Labour, *Population Census, May 21, 1961* (1 December 1961; Arabic); PB, Central Statistical Office, *General Population Census 1965* (6 May 1965, Preliminary Results; Arabic); and PB, Central Statistical Office, *Results of General Population Census April 1970* (1972; Arabic). Information for 1973 is based on sample surveys taken in February, and on estimates. See *Abstract 1974*, Table 8, p. 19.

10. *Abstract 1974*, Table 34, p. 61 for end-of-year estimate. The non-Kuwaitis were 55.1 per cent of the total according to the same source.

11. See UN *Statistical Abstract 1973*, pp. 783-8 for international comparisons. The preceding data on enrolment are obtained from *Abstract 1974*, Ch. XII, 'Education'. For budget estimates, see the Kuwait *Official Gazette*, issues between 22 April and 1 July 1973. It is worth noting that the budget allocations for recurrent expenditure on education for 1974/5 rose by 11.4 per cent to KD62.2m over 1973/4, and the allocation for the University rose to KD9.1m, or by 26.4 per cent. (See *Official Gazette*, issues between 31 March and 21 July 1974.)

12. The information comes from the censuses of 1957, 1965 and 1970 and the chapter 'Education' in the *Abstract 1965* and *1971*, while that on students studying abroad, and on degree-receivers in the years 1969/70 – 1972/3, comes from *Abstract 1974*, Tables 178 and 179, pp. 272 and 273.

13. IBRD, op. cit., p. 172 for 1957, and *Official Gazette*, op. cit., for budget information. For international comparison, see UN *Statistical Yearbook 1970*, pp. 633-704. The 1973 *Yearbook* does not provide information on budget allocations for health.

14. UN *Statistical Yearbook 1973*, pp. 719-22.

15. There is no official record to confirm these developments. However, knowledgeable practising physicians have emphatically confirmed the statement.

16. Information obtained from statements prepared by the PB staff down to 1971/2, and updated on the basis of *Abstract 1974*, Table 199, p. 303, and recent interviews in the autumn of 1974.

17. References to quantitative information relate to various tables of Section Two, 'Population and Vital Statistics' in *Abstract 1966*. For information on the labour force in government employment, see Section Five, 'Social Statistics', in ibid., and *Abstract 1964*, Tables 36 and 37. More recent information on employment (for 1970-3) comes from *Abstract 1974*, especially Tables 13-25, pp. 28-49, and Ch. III, 'Employment', Tables 36-46, pp. 65-81.

18. *Abstract 1964*, Table 37, pp. 42-3.

19. The characteristics compared are drawn from Tables 15 (p. 32), 16 (p. 33), 23 (p. 44), 24 (pp. 46-9), 38 (pp. 67-9), 39 (p. 70) and 41 (p. 72) in *Abstract 1974*.

20. For disbursements prior to 1959/60, see PB, *The Kuwait Economy 1969/1970*, p. 119. For the period 1959/60 – 1969/70, see ibid., and Ministry of Finance and Oil, *General State Budget and Independent and Appended Budgets for the Fiscal Year 1971/1972* (Kuwait, July 1971; Arabic), Statistical Appendix, p. 536. For 1971/2, see PB, *The Kuwait Economy 1970/1971 – 1971/1972* (Kuwait, undated; Arabic), p. 18. Finally, for 1972/3, 1973/4 and 1974/5, see budget data quoted from *Official Gazette* in *Middle East Economic Survey* (Beirut weekly), Vol. XVI, No. 42, 10 August 1973 for the first two years, and *MEES*, Vol. XVII, No. 41, 2 August 1974 for the third year.

21. Estimated by some at 4 per cent only of the purchase price. See Shehab, loc. cit.

22. IBRD, p. 4. The 'inflated prices' can be ascertained from a footnote on p. 79 which states that 'the price of land may be more than KD 8 per square foot'.

23. *Abstract 1974*, Table 198, p. 299. The same source provides information on 'applications still under consideration'.

24. Ministry of Finance and Oil, 'Statement by the Minister of Finance and Oil on the General Budget Project for the Financial Year 1971/1972' (Kuwait, undated), p. 36, for credit down to the end of 1970. For 1971-3, see *Abstract 1974*, Table 109, p. 166.

25. *Abstract 1974*, Table 64, p. 110. Production of brackish water is from ibid., information on the vast field being developed is from Ministry of Electricity and Water sources.

26. Ibid., Table 69, p. 114. *Per capita* consumption is calculated from data in the source. For future plans, see pamphlet prepared for official use by the Ministry of Electricity and Water entitled 'Summary on Electricity and Water in Kuwait' (Kuwait, 1972; Arabic).

27. PB, *Final Report of the Agricultural Census 1970* (Kuwait, 1970; Arabic), 'Summary' and p. 80. However, information for 1972 sets a much higher level of employment: 1,558 in government service, and 173 in the private agricultural and animal husbandry sector. See *Abstract 1974*, Table 46, p. 81. This same source (Table 77, p. 125) also shows considerable relative expansion in land utilisation for vegetables and crops: from 595 ha to 812 ha.

28. The focus of the discussion of industry has been sharpened by interviews held with several prominent men in government and the private sector between 1972 and 1974.

29. Ministry of Finance and Oil, 'Statement by the Minister . . .', p. 36 for 1963-70, and *Abstract 1974*, Table 109, p. 166, for 1971-3.

30. See the official text of the Law in English, Article 14 (C) – printed as a pamphlet by the Ministry of Commerce and Industry and entitled 'Decree No. 6 of 1965 to Promulgate the Industrial Law'.

31. See Industrial Bank of Kuwait, 'IBK General Policies' (November 1974); a pamphlet.

32. Information obtained from the two companies concerned.

33. Data from *Abstract 1964*, 'Banking' Chapter, and *IFS*, December 1974.

34. Ibid., for assets in the first quarter of 1973; and *Abstract 1974*, Table 97, p. 150, for investment income in 1972/3.

35. The lower estimate is quoted in *Arab Oil and Gas* (Beirut fortnightly), Vol. IV, No. 86, 16 April 1975, p. 28; the higher is calculated from Sarkis, loc. cit., Table 1, p. 16.

36. The Colin Associates *Report*, quoted in *Report of*

the *Kuwait Investment Company 1971*, p. 13.

37. Vol. XII, No. 15 (March 1972); editorial.

38. See Yusif A. Sayigh, 'Arab Oil Policies: Self-Interest versus International Responsibility', in *Journal of Palestine Studies*, Vol. IV, No. 3, April 1975.

39. This social danger is discussed at greater length in Yusif A. Sayigh, 'Problems and Prospects of Development in the Arabian Peninsula', in *International Journal of Middle East Studies*, No. 2 (1971), pp. 40-58. (Reprinted in Derek Hopwood (ed.), *The Arabian Peninsula: Society and Politics*, Studies on Modern Asia and Africa series, No. 8, London, 1972, pp. 286-309.)

40. Data relating to the years 1956 to 1970/1 come from the various *Statistical Abstracts*. For subsequent years, the relevant budget laws in the *Official Gazette* have been perused.

41. Information obtained from statements prepared by the PB for the first independence decade, as well as from Minister of Finance and Oil, 'Statement...'.

42. See PB, *The Kuwait Economy 1970/1971 – 1971/1972*, p. 12.

43. For 1954, see *Abstract 1972*, Table 144, p. 247; and for 1973, *IFS*, December 1974.

44. PB, *The Kuwait Economy*, various annual reports ending with 1971/2; and *Abstract 1974*, Table 97, p. 150 for 1972/3.

45. *Report of the Kuwait Investment Company, 1971*, p. 14.

46. Minister of Finance and Oil 'Statement...', p. 31.

47. In the text I have separated capital from reserves.

48. KFTCIC, *Ninth Annual Report for the Year 1974* (Kuwait, undated; Arabic), p. 22.

49. References will be to the revised Plan for the years 1967/8 – 1971/2, unless otherwise stated. No newer version has been prepared since the late sixties, and the Planning Board acts mainly as an economic advisory body, leaving aside its basic function.

50. Ibid., p. 58.

51. For a fuller discussion of some of the causes for concern see Shehab and El Mallakh (note 1), and Sayigh, 'Problems and Prospects...' (note 39).

52. See Law No. 35 of 1961 (31 December 1961), Law No. 9 of 1963 (April 1963), and Law No. 64 of 1966 (July 1966) for the basic law and amendments preceding 1974. The increase of capital from KD200m to KD1,000m was passed by the Council of Ministers in March 1974, but the law was approved by the National Assembly on 9 July 1974. Quotations are from KFAED's translation of Laws 35, 9 and 64.

53. Cumulative information on loans from KFAED, *Twelfth Annual Report 1973-1974*, Table 3, p. 26.

54. Ibid., p. 23.

55. Detailed information down to 31 March 1972 is available in Minister of Finance and Oil, 'Statement...', p. 34. However, the cumulative total down to June 1974 was announced by the Minister of Finance and Oil in a statement made in June. See *MEES*, Vol. XVII, No. 35, 21 June 1974, pp. i-vii.

56. Data for 1971/2 – 74/5 is collated from the relevant state budgets.

57. These details were revealed much later when the National Assembly approved the aid allocations for 1975. See *MEES*, Vol. XVIII, No. 25, 11 April 1975, p. 9.

58. Minister of Finance and Oil, 'Statement...', pp. 16-17.

59. Original version of the *First Five-Year Plan*, p. 82. The lower estimate for 1974 is based on my estimate of GNP as being around KD3,350m for the year, and of domestic investment falling below KD335m. Public sector allocations in the budget for 1974/5 are KD145m (apart from 35m set aside for acquisition of land). Investments by the private and mixed sectors could hardly reach 190m for the same year.

60. On this last point, see UN, *Studies on Selected Development Problems in Various Countries in the Middle East, 1968* (New York, 1968), 'Plan Implementation and Development Perspectives in Kuwait', especially 'Summary and Conclusions'. For a fuller examination of manpower issues, see the references to Kuwait in 'Some Aspects of the Development of Human Resources in Various Countries of the Middle East' in ibid.

4 SAUDI ARABIA

Saudi Arabia leads the list of oil producers among the twelve countries surveyed in this book. Since 1966 it has been the leading producer in the whole region (and the third in the world, after the USA and USSR), though in terms of revenue received, Libya led the list for the years 1968-70. With over $9.4 billion of oil revenue received by its government over the dozen years 1960-71, Saudi Arabia could already be considered a very rich country by regional standards at the beginning of the seventies. However, this substantial volume of income (which for 1971 alone reached $1.9 billion) had not by then produced the vast transformation that the $8.2 billion received by Kuwait over the same twelve years had produced, either in terms of a soaring income *per capita*, or — more fundamentally — in terms of socio-economic development.[1] The obvious reason is Saudi Arabia's much larger land area and population, and the less obvious reason is the lower amenability of its society to developmental effort and change. However, since 1972, but more particularly since the vast increase in oil prices (and revenues) of 16 October and 23 December 1973, the pace of industrialisation and physical development has accelerated most dramatically.

The land area of Saudi Arabia is about 2.2 million square kilometres, while population estimates range widely, between 5.6m and 8.9m for 1974. The lack of precision arises from the fact that the results of the only census taken have been officially repudiated for being thought too modest, and estimates have had to be based on conjecture.[2] The ambiguity of population data will no doubt handicap the quantitative *per capita* measurement of many variables; this is why we have opted for a population estimate of 5.75m, rounded to 6m, for 1974, in line with the judgement of several experts consulted, and with the assessment contained in a leading official Saudi publication.[3]

While the substantial oil revenue had not permitted a high income per head before 1973/4, or a very striking *general* physical transformation in infrastructure and in the non-oil sectors of the economy, it has made possible remarkable achievements none the less, particularly in certain areas. Sections 1 and 2 will report on these achievements, while the third section will discuss further potential in the light of the country's tangible and intangible endowments and the problems that block the way to the full development of these endowments.

1. FIVE PHASES OF TRANSFORMATION[4]

The years 1944-6 make a distinct starting-point for this analysis. For, although oil was first exported in 1938, and although its production rose several-fold in the war years 1939-43, it was only in 1944 that the oil exports surpassed the one million ton mark. Thus, production was just over 1m tons for 1944, over 2.8m tons for 1945, and about 7.9m tons for 1946, nearly tripling from one year to the next. It has gone on rising ever since in an unbroken trend, reaching more than 223m tons for 1971, 285.5m for 1972, 364.7m for 1973, and an estimated 420.9m for 1974.⁵ In view of the pre-eminence of the oil sector in the country as the major contributor to national product, government revenue, foreign exchange earnings, and national and regional development, the steep rise in the production and export of oil in the years 1944-6 fully justifies the choice of these years as starting-point.

However, a strong case can be made for the choice instead of the year 1950, because it was in this year that the government's oil revenues first rose very steeply — much more so than the rise in production — owing to the distinct improvement in December 1950 of the formula on which the government's revenue was calculated. In practice, neither year permits us enough source data and material to carry the analysis far back in time. For most practical purposes our analysis can only be satisfactory for the 1960s; only broad generalisations and spotty references are possible for the years before. Nevertheless, enough is known of the thirty years from 1946 to 1975 to enable us to divide this period into rather clear-cut phases. The basis of division relates essentially to the manner in which the real locus of political power during each of the periods influenced the economy and the course of development. Accordingly, five periods or phases can be identified.

First Phase: 1946-53

This phase begins with the end of World War Two, and ends with the death of King Abdul-Aziz al Saud, founder and unifier of the Kingdom. It can be divided into two sub-periods: 1946-50 and 1950-3, the latter division separating the years of very modest oil revenue from those when the new formula of profit-sharing on a 'fifty-fifty' basis was applied, namely 1950 onwards. (Saudi Arabia was the first Middle Eastern country to succeed in the imposition of this formula.) The first phase saw the beginnings of the modernisation of government and a modest concern with development and welfare. But the pace in both areas of action was slow. Indeed, the last three or four years reflected the King's failing health, since his style of government was marked by extreme centralisation in his person, and his health did not allow him to exercise the vigorous power of his earlier years. Upon his death his son Prince Saud was proclaimed King.

Two notable economic measures mark these years. The first was the setting up in April 1952 of the Saudi Arabian Monetary Agency which performs the functions of a central bank. SAMA has played a salutary role in consolidating the currency, guiding the steps of the banking system, and providing advice to the government on monetary, fiscal and general economic questions. The second measure was the announcement in 1949 of a four-year plan of development involving $270m. Communications were to receive the bulk of the allocations, and the most significant outcome of the plan has been the building of a railway linking Riyadh, the capital, with Dammam, the oil export port on the Arabian Gulf.

Second Phase: 1954-7

Saud's reign, which lasted till 1964 when he was deposed in favour of his next brother, the then Crown Price Faisal, witnessed extreme swings in economic performance and well-being. The downswings were largely due to Saud's behaviour, while the upswings were the work of Prince Faisal, when he was Prime Minister. The years 1954-7 were marked by grave financial irresponsibility by King Saud, although, ironically, the first state budget was prepared in 1954,⁶ and the first Council of Ministers was formed in the same year. Saud showed much less concern with expenditure for economic development than for the building of palaces and other personally gratifying purposes. Consequently, not only was the treasury emptied by the end of 1957, but a public debt of some $400m had been accumulated, half with SAMA and half with foreign creditors.[7]

A complex of inter-related setbacks occurred with financial irresponsibility and the accumulation of debt. With the vast and speedy rise in purchasing power, the foreign trade sector fell into serious imbalance when exaggerated permissiveness in consumption and the purchase of durables led to rash import practices. By 1957, SAMA's holdings of gold, silver and foreign currencies dropped to 14 per cent of the currency in circulation. And the value of the Saudi riyal (the unit of currency) dropped in the free markets from SR3.75* to SR6.25 to the US dollar.[8]

Third Phase: 1958-61

Crown Prince Faisal was made Prime Minister in March 1958 and was given wide powers in economic and financial as well as internal and foreign political matters. This was done in response to strong pressure exerted on the King by a few very influential members of the royal family, advisers and religious groups. The four years that followed were years of austerity, financial discipline and reform. The results were spectacular. Government spending was brought back into line with revenue, the riyal was stabilised, though at a lower level beginning with 1960 (SR4.50 to the US dollar), domestic and foreign debts were repaid, and the reckless spending which had caused the imbalance and dislocation in the first place was stopped.

Along with these achievements, the Crown Prince turned his attention to long-term development. Thus, towards the end of 1959, he formed the Committee for Economic Development, which without delay requested the World Bank to send a study mission to Saudi Arabia to investigate development potential in the country. The mission came and reported in 1960, but the report .. not been published.

Development effort received a boost during this period, thanks to a combination of factors. There was, first, Prince Faisal's serious concern with well-founded economic change; then the report of the World Bank mission which urged the adoption of a transitional two-year programme of development; and, finally, the increased allocations for development. To speed the process and give it continuity Prince Faisal set up in January 1961 a Supreme Council for Planning which was to operate under the chairmanship of the Prime Minister himself and to have several Ministers as members.

Fourth Phase: 1962-4

During these years Faisal's premiership was interrupted twice, owing to political tension between the King and his Prime Minister. Although allocations for development rose considerably, and an Economic Development Fund was established, the course of development wavered, mainly because the locus of political power shifted. The existence of 'a large, unwieldy, half-trained bureaucracy, a great deal of conflicting advice from a succession of foreign advisers, numerous false starts, and the continued absence of an effective planning agency'[9] were supplementary reasons for the faltering pace of development work.

King Saud had abdicated in practice by 1964 and was no longer active as monarch. Then, in November 1964, the *ulema* Council, the highest religious body, upon the decision of the members of the royal family, deposed the King and asked Prince Faisal to become King.[10] With Faisal's acceptance, the ambivalence and hesitancy in state affairs ended, and the course of political firmness and active economic progress has been set for the country ever since.

*Saudi riyals.

Fifth Phase: 1964-75

One of the first acts of King Faisal was to reorganise the planning authority by replacing the Planning Council with a Central Planning Organization at the end of 1964. The Organization has a President with ministerial rank and a technical staff. This reorganisation avoided the conflicts which characterised the era of the Council, and marked a slow but solid preparation for the formulation of a development plan. This plan appeared in 1970, after its guidelines had been set by the Council of Ministers in 1969 (embodied in a document entitled 'Guidelines for the Developmental Plan of the Kingdom of Saudi Arabia'). The achievements which mark the fifth phase, as well as the earlier achievements and the problems encountered in the course of development, will be examined in the section to follow.

The examination is easier for the decade 1964-75 than for the preceding decade, thanks to the considerable improvement in the sixties of the statistical services and the publication of many basic statistical time series for the first time. However, there is a time lag of one to two years between the year covered and the year of publication of material.

2. THE RECORD OF ACHIEVEMENT

The most relevant of these time series for our immediate purposes is the national product series which sums up the total economic performance of the country. The earliest published estimate of the gross national product related to the year 1960/1, and was prepared by Professor Edmond Asfour and a group of collaborators at the American University of Beirut. In addition to the estimate, an index of the growth of the GNP during the period 1950/1 — 1960/1 was constructed and formed the basis for projections reaching to 1975. On the basis of Asfour's estimates, official data and material in yet another source, the United Nations Economic and Social Office of Beirut (UNESOB) constructed a time series for the years 1954/5 — 1964/5. However, this series disagrees with Asfour's for the year of overlap 1960/1, and also disagrees with the official estimates for the years 1962/3, 1963/4, and 1964/5,[11] which are common between the two series. In both instances, the estimates of UNESOB are lower by 8 per cent than Asfour's estimate, and by 25 per cent than the official estimates for the three years indicated.

We lack the detailed information that would enable us to reconcile these three sets of data, or at least that of UNESOB for the eleven years 1954/5 — 1964/5, with the official series for the eleven years 1962/3 — 1972/3. Consequently, we will present both series separately first, then draw some inferences from them. The official time series for the eleven years 1962/3 — 1972/3 cannot be produced in form similar to the UNESOB series in order to make comparison readily feasible, owing to the absence of some relevant information. The official series appears in two versions: one at current prices, and the other at constant prices. In turn, the latter series is in two versions: one using 1386/87 (i.e. 1966/7) as a base and extending from 1962/3 to 1971/2; the other using 1969/70 as base year and extending from 1966/7 to 1972/3. As the former covers ten years, I have opted for it against the latter series with its smaller coverage. In order to extend the series by one year, namely 1972/3, I have deflated the current price magnitudes for this year by using the wholesale price index (1962/3 = 100, linked to the implicit index with 1966/7 = 100) which goes up to 1971/2, and by further accounting for the inflation factor between 1971/2 and 1972/3 as implicitly referred to by the Saudi Arabian Monetary Agency.[12] This is not a wholly satisfactory way of adjusting for price rises, but I deemed it adequate for my present purposes where the margin of error in the original data is probably much larger than the distortion likely to arise from my rule-of-thumb method.

Table 4.1: Gross National Product, Value Added, Gross Fixed Capital Formation and Consumption Expenditure for the Years 1954/5–1964/5 (in SR millions)

Year	GNP	Value Added Non-Oil Sector	Value Added Oil Sector [a]	Gross Fixed Capital Formation Total	Gross Fixed Capital Formation Non-Oil Sector	Private Consumption Expenditure
1954/5	2,535	1,452	1,083	487	261	1,338
1955/6	3,016	1,853	1,163	671	383	1,624
1956/7	3,269	2,162	1,107	904	594	1,819
1957/8	3,442	2,267	1,175	734	437	1,993
1958/9	3,491	2,187	1,304	591	...	2,007
1959/60	3,739	2,239	1,500	457	...	2,127
1960/1	3,927	2,325	1,602	575	...	2,165
1961/2	4,544	2,699	1,845	755	...	2,317
1962/3	4,847	2,797	2,050	681	...	2,652
1963/4	5,022	2,668	2,345	865	...	2,531
1964/5	6,068	3,107	2,961	1,094	...	3,187

a. I have added the column for value added in the oil sector to make comparison easier.
Source: UNESOB, *Studies on Selected Development Problems in Various Countries in the Middle East, 1968*, p.28.

Table 4.2: Estimates of the Gross Domestic Product by Industrial Origin 1962/3 to 1972/3 at Constant (1966/7) Factor Costs (in SR millions)

Industry Group	1962/3	1963/4	1964/5	1965/6	1966/7	1967/8	1968/9	1969/70	1970/1	1971/2	1972/3
1. Agriculture, forestry and fishing	879.2	894.7	887.4	877.4	862.4	897.4	923.9	952.7	986.6	1,021.8	889.6
2. Mining and quarrying:											
A. Crude petroleum and natural gas	3,843.1	4,115.5	4,678.4	5,501.4	6,052.2	6,572.7	6,957.6	7,964.5	9,747.9	12,204.5	21,078.8
B. Other mining and quarrying	17.5	20.1	26.6	32.6	35.4	38.6	39.5	38.5	39.6	45.4	55.3
3. Manufacturing:											
A. Petroleum refining	553.2	594.0	662.8	689.7	736.2	872.2	952.7	1,175.4	1,241.8	1,241.0	1,504.9
B. Other manufacturing	157.0	172.9	191.3	212.4	237.0	265.6	299.0	332.0	371.8	420.1	482.1
4. Construction	380.6	428.8	555.2	666.3	707.1	756.7	756.8	722.3	727.7	781.9	1,105.5
5. Electricity, gas, water and sanitary services	87.1	101.2	119.9	148.0	166.9	187.2	211.9	231.0	253.1	278.2	249.3
6. Transport, storage and communications	537.3	636.6	739.4	855.5	976.4	1,060.1	1,198.7	1,307.1	1,433.7	1,584.9	1,302.8
7. Wholesale and retail trade	559.0	638.6	766.3	858.5	876.3	987.3	1,157.3	1,177.7	1,212.1	1,311.6	1,029.5
8. Banking, insurance and real estate	47.3	52.0	63.1	70.6	81.9	89.9	95.7	98.3	101.3	121.2	572.0[a]
9. Ownership of dwellings	413.4	429.9	447.5	471.4	494.0	534.3	577.9	617.9	659.3	705.5	700.0
10. Public administration and defence	778.9	874.9	927.5	938.7	1,079.5	1,052.1	1,099.4	1,100.6	1,112.0	1,174.1	1,064.5
11. Services:											
A. Education	213.3	261.5	283.9	317.9	379.8	396.4	391.9	400.0	430.8	479.2	959.6[b]
B. Medical and health	91.9	105.1	112.3	120.2	136.0	129.9	129.0	128.5	129.2	141.2	
C. Other services	191.5	192.3	211.2	243.6	257.5	291.7	301.1	301.1	320.0	350.4	
Gross domestic product at factor cost	8,750.3	9,518.1	10,672.8	12,004.2	13,078.6	14,132.1	15,092.4	16,547.6	18,766.9	21,861.0	30,993.9[c]
Less: Net factor income payments to rest of world	2,154.8	2,014.0	2,289.2	2,894.1	2,961.0	3,132.1	3,266.2	3,772.4	4,714.8	5,833.5	6,515.5
Gross National Product	6,595.5	7,504.1	8,383.6	9,110.1	10,117.6	11,000.0	11,826.2	12,775.2	14,052.1	16,027.5	24,478.4
Less: Depreciation (estimated at 10 per cent of GNP)	659.6	750.4	838.4	911.0	1,011.8	1,100.0	1,182.6	1,277.5	1,405.2	1,602.7	2,447.8
National Income	5,935.9	6,753.7	7,545.2	8,199.1	9,105.8	9,900.0	10,643.6	11,497.7	12,646.9	14,424.8	22,030.6

a. Data for 1972/3 were compiled according to a revised System of National Accounts. Consequently, the item 'Banking, insurance and real estate' now also includes business services. Another new item that has been added above to 'Banking, insurance and real estate' is 'Community, social personal services' outside government. The two together contributed SR572.0m.
b. In the new SNA, all services by the government sector are combined, according to SAMA, *Annual Report 1392-93 A.H.*, pp.112-3.
c. GDP at constant (1969/70) prices amounts to SR27,716.3m, according to ibid., pp.114-15. The higher figure in the table is explained by the fact that the base year of the table, 1966/7, had a milder inflation. Therefore GDP for 1972/3 appears larger if deflated by the smaller (1966/7) deflator.

Sources: Department of Statistics, *The Gross Domestic Product of Saudi Arabia 1382/83 Through 1388/89 A.H.*, Table V, p.39 for the years 1962/3 and 1963/4; and Saudi Arabian Monetary Agency, *Statistical Summary*, 1st issue 1393/94 (1973/4), Table XXIX, p.69, for the years 1964/5–1971/2; and SAMA, *Annual Report 1392-93 A.H.*, (June 1974), Table XXVIII, p.112/13, for GDP for 1972/3 at current prices. (One very small error occurs in *Statistical Summary*, where the items do not add up to the total. I have assumed the individual items to be correct, and corrected the total.)

Saudi Arabia

The magnitude of change over the eleven years can be seen better from the presentation of the indices of change of the data in Table 4.2 above. Although the variations of the index from year to year are sometimes significant, only the index for the first and last years will be presented here. The discussion will underline the more important variations within.

Table 4.3: Indices of Change in Contribution to GDP by Industry Group, at Constant Factor Cost (percentages: 1962/3=100)

Industry Group	1972/3
1. Agriculture, forestry and fishing	101.2
2. Mining and quarrying: A. Crude petroleum and natural gas	548.5
B. Other mining and quarrying	316.0
3. Manufacturing: A. Petroleum refining	272.0
B. Other manufacturing	307.1
4. Construction	290.5
5. Electricity, gas, water and sanitary services	286.2
6. Transport, storage and communications	242.5
7. Wholesale and retail trade	184.2
8. Banking, insurance and real estate[a]	1,902.3
9. Ownership of dwellings	169.3
10. Public administration and defence	136.7
11. Public services	193.2
Gross domestic product at factor cost	354.2
Memo Item:	
Net factor income payments to the rest of the world	302.4
Gross national product	371.1
Depreciation	371.1
National Income	371.1

a. Item 8, 'banking, insurance and real estate' changed in content in 1972/3. It now includes private sector services not included in items 6, 7 and 9. This accounts for the enormous growth between 1962/3 and 1972/3.
Source: Calculated from Table 4.2 above.

The three preceding tables permit a number of important inferences on the growth and structure of the Saudi economy during the sixteen years 1954/5 to 1969/70. The length of the period can be increased by using the GNP estimates of Asfour for the years 1950 to 1953, which formed the launching pad for the UNESOB time series. GNP for these four years was 1,148, 1,316, 1,695 and 2,133 millions of Saudi riyals respectively.[13] This allows us a comparison of GNP over 23 years, but without enabling us to undertake any other more detailed comparisons.

1. The first overall observation to make is to note the spectacular rise in GNP over the years in question, from SR1,148m to SR24,478m (21 times). Even allowing for the low base from which the data start in 1950, the very limited comparability of the estimates on hand, and for the much more reliable quality of the more recent estimates, which is likely to have resulted in wider coverage than the earlier estimates, the fact still remains that the growth achieved is enormous by any standard. If the rate of growth in GNP for the years 1962/3 — 1972/3 alone is calculated, it amounts to 12 per cent per annum. This is

a remarkable rate, especially that the price level rose very gently for most of the period. The rate is about 9.5 — 10 per cent *per capita*, assuming population rose at 2 — 2.5 per cent per annum. Income per head probably rose from SR1,465 (or $326) for 1962/3 to SR4,184 ($1,089.7) for 1972/3 — assuming population was 4.5m in the earlier and 5.85m in the later year. (The rate of exchange dropped from 4.5 riyals to the dollar to 3.84 riyals; the latter is the average of the two rates applying for 1972 and 1973 respectively.)

2. However, this growth is not the product of the performance of the economy as a whole, but of the petroleum sector, which is largely a foreign island of technology, capital and management. More specifically, the contribution of the oil sector to GNP (Table 4.1) averaged over 41 per cent for the years 1954/5 — 1964/5, while its contribution to GDP averaged 52.6 per cent. (Natural gas and petroleum refining are included in these calculations.) The pre-eminence of the petroleum sector can further be seen from the fact that its revenues constituted until the early 1970s on average about 85 per cent of state revenues, and its exports about 90 per cent of total foreign exchange earnings in the current account of the balance of international payments. (The share of the oil sector in state revenue rose to 92.6 per cent in 1973/4, and its earnings of foreign exchange to 95 per cent of total exports.)[14] Furthermore, the sector accounted for 72 per cent of total growth achieved in GNP during the years 1962/3 — 1972/3.[15]

3. The difference between the contribution of petroleum to the GDP represents net factor payments to the rest of the world, or the remittances of the oil companies operating in Saudi Arabia. In this connection it is worth noting that the country's earnings from oil production and export have grown more rapidly than the companies' remittances, as can be seen from the difference in Table 4.3 in the growth indices of the oil sector on the one hand and the net factor payments on the other. This is because the government's net earnings per barrel of oil exported have risen over the period covered. (The same feature can be seen in the higher rate of growth of GNP than GDP.)

4. Careful examination of the relevant data reveals that all sectors except one underwent change in the relative size of their contribution between 1962/3 and 1972/3. (The exception is mining and quarrying excluding petroleum, whose contribution has remained stable at 0.2 per cent.) However, leaving aside the sector 'banking, insurance and real estate', whose content changed considerably, *all* sectors lost in relative importance, and the loss was made up by the gain of the sector of crude petroleum and gas whose share rose from 43.9 to 68 per cent. The most substantial absolute drop in sector shares has been in public administration and defence, followed by trade, public service and ownership of dwellings. If one general observation is to be made, it is that the rise in the share of oil and gas dwarfs all the individual changes in the shares of other sectors.

5. The overall achievement of the sectors as revealed in the indices (Table 4.3) is quite varied. While the slowest-moving sector — agriculture — reached an index of 101.2 only in the last year, the fastest-moving sector — 'crude petroleum and gas' — reached an index of 548.5, with 'other mining and quarrying' (the smallest in absolute terms) occupying a second, though distant, place. All the remaining sectors showed a rather poor record, for their index is far below the overall index of GDP or GNP. Indeed, only 'crude oil and gas' has a larger index than GDP and GNP. (All through we exclude the sector 'banking, insurance and real estate', the change in whose content and definition makes temporal comparisons unjustifiable.)

Further examination of Table 4.2 reveals the variation in the absolute size of the different sectors. However, the size is related to other aspects of the economy, like its degree of sophistication and monetisation, its population density and similarly important matters

Saudi Arabia

that deserve and will receive mention in other contexts later. Consequently no more than the comments made above on structure need be attempted here. The overall view of the non-oil sectors, both in terms of absolute and relative contribution to national product, suggests that despite its development efforts, the country failed in the eleven years covered to bring about marked transformation in the non-oil sectors, given the financial resources and the volume of investment made. (Investment will be presently examined by itself.)[16]

6. The performance of the sectors can be related to three factors, though this can be seen only in part from the tables presented. The first and by far the most influential factor is the growth of the oil sector, both in terms of increased production and of improved earnings per barrel of oil exported. This is a growth which essentially cannot be gauged from the investments made in the sector. The capital-output ratio of the sector is very low indeed over a long stretch of time. It would be very difficult, even if detailed information were available, to attribute to certain specific years their shares of past plus current investments which, by the technological nature of the oil industry, are very long-term. The second factor is rise in labour productivity. There is no information on the rise in average productivity for the economy as a whole, but sector by sector estimates place this rise for the years 1965-70 within a range of 2.0 per cent per annum for services and 7 per cent for petroleum. An unweighted average of all the sector rates gives an overall average of 4.4 per cent.[17]

Thirdly, there is fixed capital formation in the economy. Table 4.1 presents gross fixed capital formation for the eleven years 1954/5 — 1964/5. Information is also available, from official sources, for the years 1962/3 — 1972/3. However, the estimates for the three overlap years 1962/3 — 1964/5 vary considerably between the UNESOB table (Table 4.1) and the official sources. Furthermore, information obtained from the *Annual Reports* of the Saudi Arabian Monetary Agency (SAMA) on investment in projects made by the public sector differ from the official information just referred to. Finally, this information itself is presented in two versions: the first relates to the estimation of capital formation according to source (that is, in the public sector, in the private oil sector, and in the private non-oil sector); the second according to component (that is, capital formation in buildings and imported capital goods). The results are not far apart: indeed, over the years 1962/3 — 1968/9 aggregate capital formation totalled SR13,972.4m according to the first method, and SR14,076.7m according to the second. We will refer to the estimates according to source here, in view of their greater adequacy for our purposes of analysis.

Though rather tentative, the gross fixed capital formation data in the UNESOB time series (Table 4.1) clearly reflect the bad fiscal management of the third phase described in section 1 above, and the rigorous discipline made necessary as a result. However, there is a time lag between cause and effect. Thus, the years 1954/5 to 1956/7 showed a rise in capital formation in the non-oil sector as well as a rise in private consumption expenditure. A substantial part of the capital formation was effected through the building of a complex of palaces for the King and certain members of the royal family. The financial straits thus created resulted in a drop in fixed capital formation in the following year, while Crown Prince Faisal's strict control of the public purse in the three subsequent years resulted in a virtual freezing of fixed capital formation at a level distinctly lower than that for the year 1957/8. Indeed, during this period of austerity there were complaints that the reform policy of Prince Faisal was leading to a serious curtailment of employment.

As a ratio, capital formation averaged 17.8 per cent of GNP for the eleven-year period covered in Table 4.1 (1954/5 — 1964/5) ranging from a low of 12.2 per cent for the year 1959/60 to a high of 27.7 per cent for the year 1956/7. The years in the middle, 1958/9 —

Table 4.4: Gross Fixed Capital Formation, 1962/3–1972/3 (SR millions, at current prices)

Sector	1962/3	1963/4	1964/5	1965/6	1966/7	1967/8	1968/9	1969/70	1970/1	1971/2	1972/3
(A) Capital Formation According to Source (SR millions)											
Oil	261.2	252.8	412.9	589.9	451.0	398.3	383.2	327.4	577.4	670.1	2,039.5
Private non-oil	452.4	542.6	657.4	753.0	865.3	872.2	886.1	1,055.7	1,150.4	1,289.6	1,669.1
Public	462.0	414.0	640.9	986.7	1,010.7	1,273.8	1,406.0	1,213.9	1,203.9	1,442.6	1,985.2
Total	1,175.6	1,209.4	1,711.2	2,329.6	2,327.0	2,544.3	2,675.3	2,597.0	2,931.7	3,402.3	5,693.8
(B) Capital Formation According to Component (SR millions)											
Building and construction	690.6	818.4	1,114.8	1,407.4	1,571.2	1,768.9	1,853.6	1,968.7	2,195.4	2,594.6	4,706.4
Capital goods imports	308.8	411.1	604.9	757.2	826.4	900.8	1,042.6	628.3	736.3	808.0	987.4
Total	999.4	1,229.5	1,719.7	2,164.6	2,397.6	2,669.7	2,896.2	2,597.0	2,931.7	3,402.6	5,693.8
(C) Capital Formation as Percentage of GNP (Average of A and B Estimates)											
Per Cent	16.8	16.8	21.3	25.1	23.3	23.3	22.6	19.4	18.4	17.7	20.6 (est.)
(D) Capital Formation in Public and Private Sectors Percentage Contribution											
Government	37.1	31.6	35.1	39.3	38.8	43.2	46.7	n.a.	n.a.	n.a.	n.a.
Government projects and public institutions	2.2	2.6	2.4	3.1	4.6	6.9	5.9	n.a.	n.a.	n.a.	n.a.
Total public sector	39.3	34.2	37.5	42.4	43.4	50.1	52.6	46.7	41.1	42.4	34.9
Oil sector	22.2	20.9	24.1	25.3	19.4	15.6	14.3	12.6	19.7	19.7	35.8
Non-oil sector	38.5	44.9	38.4	32.3	37.2	34.3	33.1	40.7	39.2	37.9	29.3
Total private sector	60.7	65.8	62.5	57.6	56.6	49.9	47.4	53.3	58.9	57.6	65.1
Total economy	100.0	100.0	100.0	100.0	100.0	100.0	100.0	100.0	100.0	100.0	100.0
(E) Capital Formation in Private Sector by Destination (SR million)											
Agriculture	7.0	7.2	7.0	7.7	8.9	9.6	10.1				
Manufacturing (excluding oil refining)	31.6	34.7	38.6	42.9	47.7	53.6	61.6				
Electricity	8.4	12.6	30.5	51.5	117.0	49.8	50.3	Information not available			
Transport etc.	125.1	170.6	220.1	220.8	194.1	194.1	126.7				
Trade	17.4	20.2	24.4	28.1	29.9	33.6	40.0				
Ownership of dwellings	262.1	296.4	335.8	400.3	464.3	529.3	595.0				
Banks and other services	0.8	0.9	1.0	1.7	2.8	2.2	2.4				
Total	452.4	542.6	657.4	753.0	865.3	872.2	886.1				

Source: Privately obtained from Central Department of Statistics and Central Planning Organization, for the years 1962/3–1968/9, and the UN Economic Commission for Western Asia for the years 1969/70–1972/3.

Saudi Arabia

1962/3 show a depression in the trend, again reflecting the austerity and strict discipline in public investment to which reference has already been made.

Taking the eleven years together, and aggregating for the whole economy but without adjusting for time lags, we find that the average capital-output ratio is 2.2:1, which is very low. Considering that oil accounts for over 41 per cent of GNP during this period, and that its capital-output ratio is probably less than 1:1, then the capital-output ratio of the non-oil sectors combined must be about 3:1. This is quite low for a country involved heavily in investment in infrastructure and in directly productive projects of slow fruition.[18] An explanation has been suggested for the years in question to the effect that

> the country was starting from very low levels of production, while, simultaneously, the demand for goods and services was expanding rapidly in response to the rapid increase in oil revenues. Under such circumstances, opportunities to invest in activities bringing quick returns normally abound, particularly in the services sector...and in light manufacturing.[19]

If the same analysis is carried on to the year 1972/3 on the basis of data in Table 4.4, it is found that capital formation in the eleven years 1962/3 – 1972/3 averaged 20.5 per cent of GNP. The share of the private sector (including oil) dropped gradually from three-fifths to under half by the late 1960s, to rise again to about two-thirds by 1972/3. The early drop in private investment is the outcome mainly of a drop in the oil sector, which continued till 1969/70, but was reversed thereafter. However, the share of non-oil private sectors remained rather constant all through, but dropped to its lowest in the last year. Finally, the share of the public sector moved in the opposite direction to that of the private sector, being low in the early and late years, but distinctly higher in the middle years 1965/6 – 1969/70. In terms of destination of private non-oil sector investment, we find that ownership of dwellings predominates with a share which ranges from over one-half to two-thirds of investment for the years 1962/3 – 1968/9 for which detailed information is available. This sector is followed by transport and communications, in spite of the steep drop in the share of this sector from 1965/6 onwards. Together, these two sectors account for over 80 per cent of private-sector capital formation. It is worth noting that agriculture gets a mere 1.2 per cent of the total. The bulk of investment in agriculture comes from the government.

To appreciate government's investment in the various sectors, the student of the Saudi economy has to turn to SAMA's *Annual Reports*, where annual allocations are presented by sector. *Actual* expenditure on investment is available only in aggregated form, not sector by sector. Nevertheless, the sector distribution of allocations is indicative of the pattern of emphasis laid by government on the various sectors. The pattern shows that top priority has been given consistently to transport and communications, followed by municipalities (urban roads, electricity, sewerage works, municipal water) and finally by agriculture (including livestock, forestry and non-urban water). Education and civil aviation follow at a distance.[20] Actual expenditure on projects has recently risen as a proportion of allocations. For the last five years it averaged 70 per cent,[21] which suggests improved performance by execution agencies.

7. As a last comment, it remains to be said that private consumption expenditure represented just over half of GNP for the eleven years covered by Table 4.1; information for the seven subsequent years ending 1972/3 shows a decline in the proportion to about 40 per cent (about 27 per cent for the final year), despite a vast absolute increase in

consumption.[22] Obviously the rise in GNP has been much faster than that in private consumption. Public consumption continued all through to be much smaller than private consumption, with the absolute gap between the two widening, as they are both rising at about the same rate. In one sense, this is a healthy sign, for it means that the government machinery has not been excessively inflated in numbers and burdened with salaries. But in another sense the relative modesty of public consumption reflects a rather low salary level (compared with Kuwait) and rather restricted current expenditure on the various services undertaken by government.

Population and Manpower[23]

Saudi Arabia is no exception to the widespread phenomenon of inadequacy of information on manpower and employment disaggregated according to sex and age, level of education, sector of activity and occupation. Furthermore, qualitative indicators relating to productivity and level of efficiency are even scantier than merely quantitative data. Yet the Kingdom's problem is yet more serious, for the total population itself is still a matter of conjecture, as we have already indicated, and the size of the labour force can therefore only be more of a guess than that of the population.

In terms of very broad generalisation, the Saudi population, which we take here to be 6m by the end of 1974, had in 1962 the highest rate of illiteracy among persons aged 15-24 years among the twelve countries surveyed in this book: 95 per cent for both sexes, 91 per cent for males and 99 per cent for females.[24] Questionable as such data are under the best of circumstances, owing to difficulties of definition and counting, they serve to emphasise the low level of education in the country. Though no doubt considerable improvement has been marked since 1962, the year to which the data relate, no guess can be ventured as to the level of literacy prevailing today.

Yet some very rough appreciation of the size of the literacy gap can be obtained, to begin with, from a comparison of age groups in a few Arab countries where the structure is probably not very different from that of Saudi Arabia (for which no comparable data are available), for the purpose of establishing the size of Saudi school groups. Thus, for Iraq, Libya and Morocco the age groups 5-19 years constituted about 35-9 per cent; and we can suppose Saudi Arabia to fall in the middle at 37 per cent. This ratio of the population represents 2.2m persons. Total school population (excluding the third cycle), which it can be assumed falls between 5 and 19 years, numbered 727,974 for the year 1972/3.[25] Thus school population currently represents about 37.3 per cent of total population of school age in Saudi Arabia, or about 12.1 per cent of total population. If we further assume that many of the persons *today* in the age group 15-29 years must have gone through schooling when they were in the 5-19 age group (that is, a decade ago, which is the time to which the illiteracy data refer), and that many others today older than 29 had had at least primary education before 1962, then it becomes evident that illiteracy cannot be today higher than 80 per cent among the population, but slightly lower among persons aged 15-24. (This estimate takes into account the size of the school population and its growth during the preceding ten years.)

Obviously this exercise in rough estimation fails to show that literacy is anything but low. Yet it does not emphasise nearly enough other major deficiencies in the quality of Saudi manpower today. We particularly underline the much higher illiteracy among females than among males, the still largely inadequate content of education relative to the needs of a modernising society, and the inadequate level of vocational training, both in terms of numbers trained and quality of training. (Females in schools in 1972/3 constituted under

28 per cent of total pupils — a great improvement over the situation in 1960, but one still calling for considerably larger effort in women's education.) To all this must be added the fact, to which reference is frequently made by close observers and reports, that health conditions still allow for a great scope for improvement, in spite of the great strides already taken. Thus, malaria, tuberculosis, tetanus, eye diseases, dysentery and typhoid continue to be major diseases that have to be subdued.

The population is believed to include about 15 per cent of nomads, and another proportion of semi-settled inhabitants. (The rural population, including bedouin, is estimated to be 60·5 per cent of the total.) This ambiguity regarding the composition of the population adds to the difficulties of manpower estimation. However, there are enough statistics to serve as broad indicators of the manpower situation in the Kingdom. Thus, according to a survey conducted for the year 1965/6,[26] the total of employed persons 15 years of age and over for 1966 was just in excess of one million, as Table 4.5 below shows. This figure included nomads (the bedouin) which in itself should suggest the tentative nature of the survey, and its highly exaggerated results. Taken as a whole, the size of the labour force was slightly higher than the number employed: the former being 1,079,700 for 1966, as against 1,006,624 for the latter. This suggests a volume of unemployment of about 7 per cent — a modest proportion for a developing country with very small primary and secondary sectors, and with a large population component engaged in pastoral activities and animal-raising, where an excessive degree of under-employment usually prevails. The size of the 'active' labour force stated, taken at face value, which is about 25·7 per cent of population, betrays the marks of considerable overestimation, owing to the virtual absence of females from the active labour force. It is estimated that the female component constituted 1.1 per cent only of the labour force in 1966, and no more than 1.9 per cent of an estimated labour force of 1,249,400 in 1970.[27] (If the women in the age groups 15 years and over were added to the labour force, we would have a total force 50·5 per cent of the population, which is an absurdly high proportion.)

There are historical, social and cultural factors behind the low participation by females. Likewise, factors of non-economic nature also influence behaviour with regard to certain types of occupations which are considered 'shameful', 'unmanly' or 'indecent', and inhibit Saudis — either men or women, as the case may be — from taking them. The effect of such inhibition is to reduce the size of the Saudi active labour force.

The sectoral distribution of the labour force shows the predominance of the primary sector, with 46.2 per cent of the total. This is lower than the proportion usually encountered in developing, mainly agricultural countries, in spite of the fact that it is in effect inflated by the inclusion of bedouin whose activities are mainly associated with shepherding and livestock-raising and are characterised by considerable underemployment. On the other hand, in spite of the significance of the role of oil in the country's economy, mining and quarrying (where employment in oil is included) only account for 2.5 per cent of total employment. Together with manufacturing and construction, the first two sectors (which as a group represent the commodity-producing sectors) absorb 63.1 per cent of total employment, leaving 36.5 per cent to the services sectors broadly defined, and 0.4 per cent to 'activities not adequately defined'.

Some instructive comparisons can be made between the structure of GDP and that of employment for 1965/6, sector by sector, as seen in Tables 4.2 and 4.5. Thus, we find that although agriculture, fishing and livestock-tending account for 46.2 per cent of employment, they only contribute 7.3 per cent to GDP. This is enough indication of the low productivity of employment in the primary sector. The situation is more than reversed

Table 4.5: Employed Persons 15 Years of Age and Over Classified by Type of Economic Activity and Region, Kingdom of Saudi Arabia, 1966

Type of Activity	Central Region	Eastern Region	Western Region	Northern Region	Southern Region	Total	Per Cent of Total
Agriculture, fishing, livestock	83,312	33,782	78,196	55,547	213,937	464,774	46.2
Mining and quarrying	264	23,935	213	330	484	25,226	2.5
Manufacturing	7,226	7,265	18,685	990	6,853	41,019	4.1
Construction	32,149	11,197	46,459	3,458	10,765	104,028	10.3
Electricity, gas and water	858	1,369	3,391	147	2,586	8,351	0.8
Commerce	18,290	10,712	41,377	5,517	19,865	95,761	9.5
Transport, communication and storage	10,546	7,836	18,437	1,591	5,600	44,010	4.4
Services	60,710	24,852	87,949	18,359	27,073	218,943	21.8
Activities not adequately defined	2,158	823	978	44	469	4,472	0.4
Total	215,513	121,771	295,685	85,983	287,632	1,006,584	100.0

Notes:
(1) Above figures include bedouin population. The number of employed bedouins 15 years of age and over was estimated to be 151,220, of whom 150,376 were males and 844 females.
(2) Total number of employees in the oil industry in 1966 was about 14,000. These have been included in the figures for mining and quarrying.
Source: Central Department of Statistics, *Demographic Survey 1385/86 A.H.*

in the mining and quarrying sector, where 2.5 per cent of the employed contributed 46.1 per cent of GDP. This is indicative of the very low labour intensity of the petroleum sector, and its very high productivity. In fact, if the export of crude petroleum were to be taken in isolation from other mining and quarrying, then employment would be 1.4 per cent and contribution to GDP 45.8 per cent. In terms of value added per worker, this sector is by far the most productive. Manufacturing is another sector whose contribution to GDP in 1965/6 (7.7 per cent) was much higher than its share of employment (4.1 per cent).

Taken together, the commodity-producing sectors, whose share in employment was 63.1 per cent, contributed two-thirds of GDP, while the services sectors combined accounted for 36.5 per cent of employment and one-third of GDP. This apparent balance is misleading, for it conceals very wide sector by sector variations. The discrepancy between intensity of employment and value added reached its peak in agriculture, forestry, fishing and animal husbandry, where GDP per worker is extremely low, and in the sub-sector of crude petroleum and natural gas, where GDP per worker is extremely high. Construction and manufacturing are next in this context, with GDP per worker being low for the first and high for the second. The other sectors also show variation but it is generally mild.

So far the discussion has encompassed employment in the country as a whole. Again referring to data for 1966, the private sector absorbed 896,200 or 89 per cent of the total, while the public sector absorbed 110,400 or 11 per cent (including PETROMIN, the General Petroleum and Mining Organization). Estimates projected from the late sixties to 1975 predicted that employment in 1970 (out of a total labour force of 1,249,400) would rise to 1,180,700: with 1,040,600 in the private sector and 140,100

Saudi Arabia 141

in the public sector. It would rise to 1,376,200 in 1975 (out of a labour force of 1,474,700), with most of the employed — over 94 per cent — in the private sector. The active labour force would thus be 22.9 per cent of the population although, still according to the forecasts, female participation would only be 4 per cent. The growth in private employment between 1966 and 1970, and 1970 and 1975, is forecast to be higher than that of total active labour force, and therefore of the force employed by government.[28] However, this exercise in projection cannot be taken very seriously if the basis itself — namely total population — continues to be a matter of extreme conjecture. (Two censuses of establishments undertaken in 1967 and 1971 covered 25 and 61 cities or *urban* centres respectively, in the private sector. The more recent census found the number of workers to be 146,710. No overall breakdown of the employed by sector is available — though it is for establishments. Consequently, because of limited coverage and insufficient detail, this census cannot serve as a base for useful analysis.)

Population and labour data apart, government and foreign experts involved with manpower questions all agree that the major bottleneck of development work today is the inadequacy of the reservoir of Saudi trained manpower — now that government has been largely organised and many institutions established in line with the needs of development, the financial resources have risen to and maintained a·level of abundance — reaching a state of superabundance in 1974, and the existence has been established of enough water and other natural resources with exploitable potential, in addition to oil and gas as industrial feedstock. The manpower deficiencies are not just quantitative, namely shortages in many important skills and a low level of participation in the labour force, nor in addition merely qualitative, in terms of insufficient education and training, but also ones of insufficient motivation and social mobility — in short, socio-cultural deficiencies. The very low level of productivity which results has not been quantified, but knowledgeable observers are strongly aware of its existence, especially in the traditional sectors.

The situation is being improved through formal and adult education, and through training. The latter takes the form of on-the-job training, and until recently has been only of modest proportions. However, since 1970 and 1971, the government and PETROMIN have insisted on the training of nationals by foreign partners in all ventures entered into jointly. Hopefully, in a few years' time, this will provide the country with significant cadres of technicians and skilled workers, owing to the vast expansion in the number and scope of joint projects. Technical and vocational education is also performed through vocational training institutions. These can be divided into four broad categories: the Vocational Training Department of the Ministry of Labour and Social Affairs; other ministries, departments and agencies of government; the Institute of Public Administration for the training of civil servants; and private establishments. A listing of the ministries, departments and other autonomous agencies offering training facilities gives an indication of the spread of the effort undertaken. The list includes:

1. Ministry of Agriculture
2. Ministry of Health
3. Ministry of Communications
4. Ministry of the Interior and Municipalities Department
5. Ministry of Petroleum and Mineral Resources
6. Ministry of Education (schools for the handicapped)
7. Ministry of Commerce
8. Ministry of Labour and Social Affairs

142 Saudi Arabia

9. Department of Civil Aviation
10. Department of Meteorology
11. Customs Department
12. The Saudi Arabian Monetary Agency
13. Saudi Arabian Airlines
14. Industrial Studies and Development Centre
15. Petroleum and Mineral Organization (PETROMIN)

The effort is commendable. Nevertheless it still suffers from insufficient response by the workers, manifest in many instances in the existence of excess capacity in the programme offered. It also suffers from the low emphasis on practical training and case studies, and from the proliferation of agencies undertaking training and the resultant poor co-ordination and waste of resources.

Petroleum and Mineral Resources

1. Petroleum and Natural Gas: Another major factor of development is petroleum and natural gas resources which exist in great abundance. Indeed, Saudi Arabia has the largest proved and published reserves of this resource in the whole world (estimated at 17,600m tons on 1 January 1974), and the extraction and export of oil has been developed extensively, so that the country has reached the rank of the third producer and the first exporter in the world.[29]

Were petroleum to be merely a large sector with substantial value added and foreign exchange earnings it would still not deserve all the emphasis it has received in this chapter. The justification for this emphasis is the role petroleum plays as a *leading* sector, that is, as an engine which promotes development in the economy as a whole. This it succeeds in doing through the provision of huge revenue in the form of foreign exchange, and through the challenge it constitutes. This challenge is based essentially on the fact that petroleum is an exhaustible resource and that the economy has therefore to speedily develop alternative sources of income which are destined to replace petroleum in the near future as contributors to national product. Some such sources are already either in operation, or under active exploration. We refer specifically to large industries whether or not they use oil and natural gas as primary inputs, agriculture thanks to the discovery of huge underground reservoirs of water, and minerals other than petroleum — in addition to the development of supportive service sectors such as transport and communication, trade, finance and banking.

Exploration for oil began on a regular basis in the thirties, after the Arabian American Oil Company (ARAMCO) obtained a concession in 1933 (under another name, to start with) covering about 496,000 square miles of territory including Saudi Arabia's share in the offshore area and its share in the Neutral Zone between Saudi Arabia and Kuwait. Since then, the concession area has been substantially curtailed. Other concessionary companies have since taken up areas relinquished by ARAMCO, or areas not previously assigned. Two such companies took over exploration in the Neutral Zone: Getty Oil Company, as of 1948, obtained the concession for all of Saudi Arabia's undivided half-interest in the Zone, including territorial waters, and the Arabian Oil Co. Ltd. obtained a concession in 1958 covering the offshore area of the Neutral Zone extending beyond territorial waters. This latter company operates on behalf of both countries, Saudi Arabia and Kuwait, and they participate to the extent of 10 per cent each in its capital. The rest is owned by the Japan Petroleum Trading Company Limited.

Saudi Arabia

Elsewhere, three companies have obtained concessions. The first, Société Auxiliaire de L'Entreprise de Recherches et d'Activités Petrolières (AUXERAP), came in in 1965 and was permitted exploration in three blocks containing onshore and offshore acreage along the Red Sea coast (a total area of 10,348 miles). It is owned totally by a French group, but during the exploitation phase the government will come into partnership to the extent of 40 per cent of total capital. The second is Sinclair Arabian Oil Company, whose concession started in 1967 and covers half of the area along the Red Sea coast not held by AUXERAP.

Legal title to the concession resides with the Saudi Arabian Government agency the General Petroleum and Mineral Organization (Petromin) which has assigned its rights and obligations to the Sinclair-Natomas-Pakistan group. Sinclair Arabian is the operator. If commercial oil production is found, Petromin may participate 50 per cent in its development.[30]

Finally, the third concession is in the name of Petromin-AGIP; it starts from 1967 and covers about 30,000 square miles relinquished by Aramco, in the Rub' al-Khali (the Empty Quarter) area of Saudi Arabia.

Petromin retains legal title to the concession but has assigned its rights and obligations to AGIP Mineraria, S.p.A., a subsidiary of the Ente Nazionale Idrocarburi (ENI), an Italian state corporation. If commercial oil production is found, an operating company will be set up in which Petromin may own 30 to 50 percent, depending upon the level of production.[31]

Armaco is by far the largest-producing company: the combined production of Getty and Arabian Oil is less than 7 per cent of Aramco's, and the revenue paid by the companies follows the same pattern, more or less. Table 4.6 below traces the development of oil production and revenue from 1946 to 1974. It can be seen from the table that production has had a consistently upward movement, but that revenue has had setbacks in 1953 and 1956-60.

The steep rise in production and revenue is quite evident. However, the rise in revenue per barrel remained much more modest until 1974. Indeed, the average return has oscillated noticeably several times. The improvement in this return after the early fifties (that is, after the '50-50' sharing formula had been adopted in December 1950) is the result of the improvement in the terms of sharing of oil revenue and/or in the calculation of costs deductible from export revenue (such as expensing of royalties and exclusion of marketing expenses). The return per barrel to the government for 1971-3 rose considerably in relative (though not absolute) terms, thanks to the Teheran agreement of February 1971 and the Geneva agreement of January 1972. Both agreements are between OPEC (the Organization of Petroleum Exporting Countries) and the oil companies. According to the terms of these agreements, and on the basis of production projections which assume a rate of growth equal to the average rate for the years 1965-70, the revenues to Saudi Arabia were at the time expected to be $2,317m, $2,719m, $3,183m, and $3,720m for the years 1972, 1973, 1974 and 1975 respectively. This order of magnitude of oil revenue was expected to enable the country to put into effect, if the manpower and certain institutional constraints could be effectively relaxed, an ambitious development programme, and thus help the process of diversification in the economy.

Table 4.6: Oil Production and Revenues, 1946-74

Year	Production m barrels	Revenues $ m	Revenues per barrel, $
1946	59.9	10.4	0.17
1947	89.9		
1948	142.9		
1949	174.0		
1950	199.5	56.7	0.28
1951	278.0	110.0	0.40
1952	301.9	212.2	0.70
1953	308.3	169.8	0.55
1954	350.8	236.3	0.67
1955	356.6	340.8	0.96
1956	366.7	290.2	0.79
1957	373.7	296.3	0.79
1958	385.2	297.6	0.78
1959	421.0	313.1	0.74
1960	481.3	333.7	0.69
1961	540.7	377.6	0.70
1962	599.7	409.7	0.69
1963	651.8	455.2*	0.69
1964	694.3	523.2	0.75
1965	804.8	616.6*	0.77
1966	950.0	789.7*	0.83
1967	1,023.8	909.1*	0.89
1968	1,114.1	926.8	0.83
1969	1,173.8	949.0	0.81
1970	1,386.7	1,149.7	0.82
1971	1,675.5	1,884.9	1.13
1972	2,141.3	2,744.6	1.28
1973	2,735.3	4,340.0	1.59
1974	3,156.4	27,800.0	8.81

* Including special payments of $152.5 m in 1963, $46.0m in 1965, $29.4m in 1966, $29.3m in 1967.
Sources: For production in 1947-49, Aramco Handbook, op. cit. (1968), p. 135; for production and revenue for the years 1950-70, SAMA Annual Report 1389-90 A.H., pp.87 and 88; for production data for 1971-3, BP Statistical Review of the World Oil Industry 1972 and 1973; and for 1974 production, estimate in Nicolas Sarkis, 'The Energy Crisis and the Challenge of Development in the Arab Countries', Paper No.132 (A-1) for the Ninth Arab Petroleum Congress, Dubai, 10-16 March 1975, Table 1, p.16. Revenue data for 1971-4 from Sarkis, Table 2, p.17, based on SAMA, Annual Report 1392-93 A.H., p.27, and his estimate for 1974. Last column my calculations. In these calculations I did not take into account that the special payments made did not relate only to the years when they were received.

However, events since the historic measures taken in Kuwait and Teheran on 16 October and 23 December respectively (to which fuller reference has been made in the chapters on Kuwait and Iraq), have constituted a sharp and dramatic departure in the price course. By 1 January 1974 posted prices had reached a level four times as high as that prevailing in mid-October 1973. This change is so large as to be more rightly considered qualitative rather than quantitative. Along with improvements in the profit-sharing formula, the government's return per barrel for 1974 was over 5.5 times what it had been in 1973, and over 10 times the level of 1970.

This whole discussion is restricted to the production and export of crude petroleum. However, a vast volume of natural gas is also released from the wells, estimated for 1973 at about 2,688m cubic metres (of which 1,835m were utilised, and 853m flared).[32] Most of the total volume was pumped back into the wells in order to maintain pressure, while about one-third of the total was used for the generation of electricity and as feedstock in certain industries run by Petromin.

Finally, to complete the survey of petroleum activities, mention must be made of petroleum-refining. The country has four refineries: at Ras Tanura (started operation in 1945), Saud Port and Khafji (both in the Neutral Zone) and Jeddah (latest to start, in 1968). The Jeddah refinery is owned by Petromin. In total, some 222m barrels were refined in 1972, of which 208m were exported and 14m were sold locally. The whole of the production of the Neutral Zone refineries is exported, while part of Ras Tanura's and the whole of Jeddah's is for local use.[33]

The impact of the oil sector as an engine of development hardly needs elaboration. However, the course of exploitation of this resource is not free of dangers which inject uncertainty into the role of oil in development. These dangers are political and economic. Political uncertainty in the region has on a few occasions in the past curtailed the flow of oil, as in those instances when the flow through the pipeline of Tapline (the carrier company across Jordan, Syria and Lebanon to the outlet near Sidon in Lebanon) was interrupted, in the June 1967 war when an embargo was briefly placed on exports to certain Western countries, and in 1973/4 when considerable overall cutbacks in production as well as a selective embargo were ordered by government. The economic factors include fluctuations in the price which is used as a base for calculation of profit-sharing; this danger was more real in the past when 'posted prices' were used as base. The factors also include fluctuations in the world supply and demand, although the trend has been steadily favourable to exporting countries in view of the steady rise in demand. Devaluation of the currency of settlement for exports has been another danger, but the Geneva agreement of January 1972 adjusted for the devaluation of the United States dollar. Lastly, steep inflation since 1971 has been (and threatens to remain for a few more years at least) a serious corrosive factor, since inflation means the erosion of the purchasing power of the foreign currencies, however they are used.

Finally, there is the question of depletion of petroleum resources. In the case of Saudi Arabia, this danger is in the distant horizon, since at the current rate of production the country's reserves can last for well over half a century. Furthermore, Saudi Arabia is not only capable of accumulating financial reserves abroad more massive than those which any other producer is capable of accumulating, but is also better endowed in non-oil natural resources than any Arab producer except Iraq, and can therefore develop alternative sources of revenue more readily. (One important exception is Algeria, whose industrialisation is proceeding at a very fast rate; however, this country suffers from the fact that its oil reserves are much more modest than Saudi Arabia's, and its annual production is forced to remain relatively small for technical reasons.) Consequently, on balance the depletion problem will not be serious for decades to come — by which time the Kingdom will probably have significant other sources of income.

2. Mineral Resources: For many years it has been known that the country is in possession of a large variety of minerals, several of which are exploitable commercially. Some mining had been undertaken for centuries, especially in the area broadly known as the Arab Shield which roughly forms a crescent, with Mecca and Medina in the bulge, and the tips of the crescent lying about 1,200 km. from each other on the Red Sea, to the north-west and south-east. There are marks of mining cities having flourished in this area where gold, silver and other basic minerals had abounded.

Currently no minerals are being mined, although prospecting is undertaken. In fact, since 1963 more than SR200m have been spent (SR522m allocated) for the prospecting and the development of mineral wealth outside of oil.[34] The programme involved a general and specific geological survey of an area of about 1.2m square metres, an aerial survey of the whole Arab Shield area, an aerial magnetic survey of the Shield, experimental diggings in 42,000 square metres, the setting up of two laboratories for the examination of soil samples (so far, by the end of the early 1970s, a total of 79,000 samples had been tested), and the training of Saudi geologists to participate in the studies and surveys undertaken. The results so far achieved include several hopeful finds pointing to the abundance of many kinds of mineral deposits, ferrous and non-ferrous. Those finds relating to minerals already known and exploited in the past include gold, silver, copper, lead, tungsten, zinc, chrome, titanium, thorium, lithium, fluorite, pyrite, manganese and manganite, asbestos, barite, graphite, mica, sulphur, magnesium, phosphates. New finds, which are currently exploited but were not so exploited in the past include iron, marble, gypsum and salt.[35] Table 4.7 shows the main areas in which ore reserves exist.

The prospecting, which started between 1961 and 1964, is undertaken by several foreign companies, whose operations are governed by a mining code which was enacted in 1962. It stipulates that the ownership of all minerals is vested in the state, and that prospecting and exploitation can be undertaken by private groups only by concession and on certain rather rigorous terms. These terms, and some additional factors, are thought to handicap prospecting and exploitation. Among these factors is the lack of knowledge about the geological properties of the Arab Shield (but this deficiency is being overcome), the non-availability of promotive measures such as full studies that are usable by foreign groups, the absence of tax exemptions for mining operations, the insufficiency of the infrastructural facilities that are needed in the outlying regions where most of the mineral deposits exist (electric power and transport and port facilities are the most notorious examples of deficiency), the insufficiency of water resources necessary for exploitation, and the shortage of skilled manpower.

3. Petromin: It is appropriate to examine the General Petroleum and Mineral Organization, Petromin, at this point. Among other things, Petromin is the body charged with the practical steps of developing the minerals, including oil, found or expected to be in commercial quantities, and of building up petrochemical industry. These steps will be discussed in the context of Petromin's powers and activities. Although an important component of Petromin's work falls in the industrial sector, this component will be examined here rather than under 'industry' in order to preserve the integrity of the discussion of Petromin.

This organisation was established with the aim of undertaking a number of activities.

Table 4.7: Main Areas and Main Ore Reserves

Area	Minerals	Possible Reserves	Potential Reserves
Wadi Fatimah	Iron (hematite) 45%	–	50m tons
Wadi Sawawin	Iron (hematite, magnetite)	350m tons	–
Idsas	Iron (magnetite) 25%	80-110m tons	–
Samrah	Silver (3 kg./ton)	–	800,000 tons
Jabal Sayid	Copper 2.2%, zinc 1.4%	–	8m tons
Al Amar	Zinc, copper, gold, lead	–	5m tons
Wadi Wassat	Pyrite 80%	800m tons	300m tons
Jizan	Salt 96%	1000m tons	33.5m tons
Thaniyat Area and Turayf Area	Phosphate	1000m tons	–
Umm-Jarad	Barite	–	100,000 tons
Al-Doghm	Glass sand	Several m tons	–
Khashm Rida	Clay	56m tons	–
Al-Kharj	Gypsum	3m tons	–
Al Hith	Gypsum	10-15m tons	–

Note: 'Possible reserves' mean the quantitites of ore estimated to exist on the basis of geological and geophysical surveys, while 'Potential reserves' refer to the quantity of ore estimated to exist on the basis of drilling results. In other words, potential reserves are those that probably exist in the area covered by drilling operations.
Source: Petromin, *Annual Report 1969*, p.50. ARAMCO, *Aramco Handbook: Oil and the Middle East* (1968) contains a different evaluation of reserves.

These were, in the words of an official document of Petromin:[36]

1. The implementation and administration of public petroleum and mineral projects in the Kingdom.
2. The importation (directly or through agents) of the mineral needs of the country.
3. The preparation (on its own or through others) of both theoretical and practical oil and mineral research and studies, as well as actual operations entrusted to it by the Government, with regard to searching for, producing, refining, purchasing, selling, transporting, distributing and marketing petroleum and minerals at home and abroad.
4. Co-operation with private companies and organizations undertaking petroleum or mineral activities in order to facilitate prospecting, exploration, distribution and marketing.
5. The establishment of companies or enterprises at home or abroad. The Organization will participate in the capital of these companies with the purpose of engaging in all phases of the industry of petroleum and minerals and their derivatives and by-products including trade transactions, transportation, sales, distribution and marketing.

Broadly speaking, according to the Minister of Petroleum and Mineral Resources who is also Chairman of the Board of Directors of Petromin, the policies and aims of the organisation are as follows:[37]

1. Diversification of the sources of income to avoid the political and economic risks which may result from dependence on one source, namely petroleum, by establishing petroleum, mining, and petrochemical industries and undertaking such mineral exploitation operations as are commercially viable according to the studies of the Directorate General of Mineral Resources.
2. Encouragement of the private sector and mobilization of national capital to achieve the above-mentioned aim and to profit from the country's wealth and natural resources. Since our private sector has hardly got any experience of industrialization and since some of the industrial projects are too big, requiring huge finances and specialised know-how which cannot be provided by [the] private sector, the Organization (Petromin) has to play a leading role.
3. Establishment of connections throughout the world, particularly with business and engineering organizations, to seek assistance in meeting our technical, financial and business needs.
4. Acquisition of practical experience related to petroleum, mining and petrochemical industries and arrangements for the training of Saudis so that within [a] reasonable time they [may] become capable of participating effectively in all phases of these industries...
5. Provision of cheap energy for industry and related operations.

Petromin obtains the major part of its financing from the treasury, but it can also supplement these resources by loans from SAMA, private-sector (whether domestic or foreign) participation, and loans from international banks. Its assets include its participation in companies formed by it, alone or jointly, as well as the movable and immovable property under its administration.[38]

The activities and projects of the Organization, other than training, fall under three categories: the oil sector, the petrochemical sector, and the mineral and mining industries sector. Under the first fall Petromin's oil exploitation concessions via which it has entered into exploration agreements – as already indicated – with AGIP, the Natomas-Sinclair-Pakistan Group, and AUXERAP. All these agreements, it can be said without going into details, constitute an advanced step beyond the standing agreement with Aramco. Another feature of Petromin's activities in the oil sector has been the formation, in January 1966, of a company called the Arabian Geophysical and Surveying Company (ARGAS), jointly with the Compagnie Générale de Géophysique. The objectives of ARGAS are to carry out studies for the prospecting and exploration of natural resources (including oil, gas, minerals and underground water). Furthermore, it carries out surveys 'for engineering, military and construction purposes'. In addition to these aims, which have been translated into actual operations over wide areas of the country, ARGAS has completed a general geodetic map covering the whole of Saudi Arabia.

Petromin has also formed the Arabian Drilling Company jointly with two French firms for the purpose of undertaking drilling work on contract basis in exploration for minerals and underground water. The activities of this company have mainly centred around the offshore area beyond the Neutral Zone, the Red Sea area, and in the Aramco concession area. In the field of mineral prospecting, the company has been given a contract for drilling throughout the Kingdom.

In the field of refining and distribution of oil products, Petromin built the Jeddah refinery and completed it by the summer of 1968. The capacity of 12,000 barrels a day has just been expanded to 45,000 barrels a day. A second refinery, at Riyadh, with a capacity of 15,000 barrels a day, has been completed and trial runs on it were begun in August 1974. Two new refining projects are currently being undertaken, the first (for petrolube products) owned jointly with Mobil Company, will be located near the Jeddah refinery on the Red Sea coast; the second, owned jointly with Shell, will be located in the Eastern Province.[39] Finally, Petromin handles the distribution of all refined petroleum products in the Kingdom. In order to transport crude oil to the Jeddah refinery and achieve integration in its operations, Petromin established the Saudi Arabian Tanker Company. So far the company has purchased several tankers; it has plans for further expansion in tonnage capacity and has entered the international field of tankerage. Lastly, Petromin established two other companies which relate to the oil sector: the Petromin Lubricating Oils Company (in association with the Mobil Investments Company), and the Saudi Marine Petroleum Construction Company (in association with McDermott Company). The latter undertakes 'operations pertaining to marine installations, including onshore operations and other incidental construction operations'.

The second sector where Petromin is active is the petrochemical industry. The first area of activity here has been that of fertilisers, which had been under consideration since the late 1940s and under active study since the late 1950s. Large concerns from different countries have been involved with the project, owing to its size and the international implications of the fertiliser industry, particularly with regard to marketing. Finally, the Saudi Arabian Fertilizers Company (SAFCO) was formed in September 1965. The capital of SR100m was to be owned by Petromin to the extent of 51 per cent, and the Saudi public to the extent of 49 per cent.

SAFCO started with building a plant for the production of 1,100 tons of urea fertiliser and 35 tons of raw sulphur daily. The plant began operation in March 1969, but has met with technical difficulties. However, by the spring of 1971 it was functioning at 75 per cent of its capacity for ammonia and urea. Marketing does not constitute a problem for many years to come, as SAFCO entered into agreement with the International Ore and Fertilizers Company (INTERORE) to purchase, for 17 years, the entire production of SAFCO after local needs have been satisfied. The second company in the petrochemical field is the Petromin Sulfur Company, formed jointly with INTERORE and the Jefferson Lake Company, for the production of 150,000 tons per year of raw sulphur from natural gas, after a process of sweetening (desulphurising) the gas. Like SAFCO, this company has relied heavily on foreign firms for studies and for the building of its plant. The capital of the Sulfur Company is SR45m, two-thirds of which are owned by Petromin. Finally, the Petromin Sulfuric Acid Company (PETROCID) was formed for the purpose of building a plant at the industrial complex at Dammam to produce 50 tons of sulphuric acid daily. The major part of production, which has just started, is expected to be absorbed by the soap and fertiliser industries and the refineries in the country. PETROCID is wholly owned by Petromin.

The major industry undertaken by Petromin in the third sector, minerals and mining industries, is the iron and steel industry. The size and long-term nature of this industry have necessitated the setting up in 1968 of a special administration for the supervision of the complex of projects. The industry is to have three stages. The first, which involves 'the production of bars, angles and sheet iron for building purposes from imported steel billets', came into operation in October 1967, with a capacity of 30,000 tons annually for two shifts and 45,000 tons for three shifts. In the second phase it is envisaged to produce steel billets. And in the third phase Petromin expects to utilise iron ore from the rich deposits in the country by smelting the ore and producing steel ingots. Owing to the complexity and costliness of the industry, and the large number of ancillary plants required (water-treating unit, power supply and the like), Petromin has conducted extensive and thorough studies of all the aspects of the industry, including marketing. In April 1974 a joint venture contract for a steel mill to be set up in the Eastern Province (at Jubail) was signed with the Marcona Group, under the name of PETROMAR. The capital cost is $500m, owned on a 50-50 basis.

Other mining priorities include the mining of phosphate, which is a major source of fertiliser and an important input in several chemical industries. Studies for the recovery of the country's phosphate deposits, as well as deposits of magnesium, silver, copper, barite and other metallic and non-metallic minerals are under way currently. Two new agreements were signed in the spring of 1974 with Japanese and French concerns for survey and prospecting purposes in the Najd plateau, with possible extension to include mining subsequently.

In summing up this discussion of Petromin's activities and projects,[40] it is important to mention that the total manpower employed by the organisation was about 2,100 in 1970. The training of personnel forms an integral part of the agreements signed with Petromin's partners in the companies formed jointly, and part of Petromin's activities in the endeavours owned solely by it. This training covers administrative and technical skills, and is conducted both in the country and abroad.

It is evident that Petromin is a significant vehicle of development in the country, particularly with regard to the oil, petrochemical and mineral industries. (Its role has expanded considerably since October 1973, both with respect to wider coverage of projects and capital investment.) Its promotive power is drawn from the nature and size of the undertakings it has developed or intends to develop (undertakings which serve as foci of further development), from its ability to draw and mobilise local and foreign entrepreneurial talent and capital, from its policy of increasing the reservoir of managerial and technical skills in the country through a steady and firm process of training and participation in projects of manifest complexity, and from the flexibility which it enjoys through the autonomy allowed it in its statutes.

Industry

Manufacturing industry is discussed here instead of agriculture and water, or infrastructure, which are more basic, in order to provide continuity from Petromin's industrial activities.

Although several steps had been undertaken on the road to industrialisation in the 1950s, it was the year 1962 that witnessed an acceleration in industrialising efforts. This was mainly because of three institutional measures or acts taken: Royal Decree No. 50 of 23 May 1962 which enacted the Regulation for the Protection or Encouragement of National Industries;[41] the undertaking of an industrial survey during 1962 in the five main cities of Riyadh, Jeddah, Mecca, Medina and Taif; and the establishment on 22 November 1962 by Decree No. 25 of the General Petroleum and Mineral Organization, Petromin.[42] Three further steps were to follow in subsequent years: the enactment by Decree No. 35 of 24 February 1964 of the Foreign Capital Investments Regulations,[43] the enactment of a company law on 20 July 1965, and the establishment by Decree No. 41 on 5 March 1967 of the Industrial Studies and Development Centre.[44] The role of these measures has been examined by the institutions concerned.[45]

The impact of the various measures taken during the 1960s can be appreciated if the situation of industry in the early 1950s is compared with the situation in 1973 or 1974. Thus, in 1954 'there were only five industrial companies with a total invested capital of SR42million'.[46] By 1969/70, the value added in the manufacturing sector, including oil refining, was SR1,523.2m, or SR328.9m without refining (at current prices). In either case, this suggests a vast expansion in industrial investment — some $3,100–3,300m, assuming the incremental capital coefficient in manufacturing to be around 2.5 or 2.55, which is the average for non-oil sectors.[47]

However, the years 1970/1 to 1973/4 witnessed a marked acceleration in industrial investment and growth in value added, particularly the last-named year which was characterised by a vast expansion in national savings and in investment programmes, whether public, private or mixed. Thus, total gross investment in non-oil sectors was SR2,354.3m for 1970/1, SR2,832.2m for 1971/2, and SR3,554.3m for 1972/3. The year of 1973/4, for which no quantitative information is available, was marked by a very steep rise in industrial investment, judging by the reports of professional publications on new manufacturing projects launched and on existing ones expanded.[48] Nevertheless, taking the two decades covered as a whole, industrial investment has averaged distinctly less than one-sixth of total investment. Most of the gross investment made — indeed, about three-quarters — has been directed to construction in the public, private and mixed sectors. The long-term rise in industrial investment is the product of a general acceptance of industrialisation and the emergence of some industrial entrepreneurial talent, the facilities offered foreign enterprise, the availability of funds for investment, the various official promotional measures taken in the 1960s, and the general brightening of the whole economic outlook.

According to an official Saudi statement, 'The Government has adopted an industrial policy which is consistent with the economic and social conditions of the country. This policy aims at encouraging the expansion of the industrial sector as a means of accelerating economic development.'[49] More specifically, this policy stipulates that essentially the industrial sector should fall within the domain of private enterprise, but that public as well as joint public-private ventures (including foreign participation) should be established where necessary, in the case of

> strategic and vital industries in which the private sector alone is unlikely to invest in the short run either because of the huge size of the undertaking or because of the technical complexities involved. At a later stage, when these industries have been successfully launched, they will be handed over to the private sector.[50]

Some of the measures taken in order to give body to the policy have already been mentioned. Others include the building between 1968 and 1971 of three industrial zones or estates at Jeddah, Riyadh and Dammam (a measure which has encouraged some further industrial investment in these areas in direct response); the adoption of the metric system as part of a process of standardisation of measurements and specifications; the establishment of several vocational training centres; and the undertaking of complementary investments in transport and other communications and in electricity and municipal facilities. (With respect to electricity, the rates have been reduced in 1973 by 50-60 per cent, both for domestic and industrial use. This follows an earlier measure taken in 1972. The two measures together apply to 29 cities and towns.)[51]

The law for the protection and promotion of industry contains the standard stipulation for such incentives as duty and tax exemptions, the provision of cheap land sites and protective measures against foreign competitive products. It also prepared the ground for the establishment of the Industrial Studies and Development Centre. On the other hand, the law on foreign investments encourages the inflow of foreign capital to operate alone or in co-operation with private groups or with Petromin. This it aims at through extending to foreign capital all the facilities extended to domestic capital, and through allowing foreign capital tax exemptions and visa and residence facilities for foreign investors and their employees. According to SAMA's *Annual Report 1970*, the establishments set up in accordance with the Law on Foreign Investments by the spring of 1971 totalled 42 with an aggregate capital of SR71.8m, 30 per cent of which is foreign. A further 33 licences had been given for projects that were to be set up in the near future. (No such information is provided in SAMA's most recent report for 1973, published in June 1974.)

However, the authorities have not gone much beyond the level of generalities in their policy guidelines, nor has the institutional framework been complete or totally effective. With regard to the latter judgement, the Industrial Studies and Development Centre (ISDC) has not been very productive in its operations (mainly the preparation of studies that are usable by prospective investors); the industrial bank around which many studies have been prepared and which has been under consideration for several years was still a project on paper by the spring of 1972. However, an Industrial Development Fund with a capital of SR500m was set up by Decree No. M/3 on 20 March 1974, but it will take some time before its effectiveness can be assessed.[52] Visa and residence facilities remain very time-consuming to obtain and to renew; and the proliferation of agencies dealing with industrialisation (such as the Ministry of Commerce and Industry, Petromin, ISDC) acts as a deterrent to an industrial entrepreneurship which is still rather hesitant, and to foreign industrial entrepreneurs who are likely to be confused by this proliferation. (A new policy statement aimed at the promotion of industry was issued in February 1974. However, it is too early for the impact of the new policy to be felt.)

Manufacturing industry is taken in the present context to mean transformative industry and to exclude the production of crude petroleum and natural gas. It therefore includes petroleum refining, petrochemicals and steel. These three areas had been examined under 'Petromin' above, but only in so far as their institutional side is concerned. The statistics of their operations will be shown here. However, electricity generation will be surveyed elsewhere.

Manufacturing industry, in the aggregate, contributed a total of SR2,543m in 1972/3 (of which SR1,926.3m came from petroleum refining and SR617.1m from other manufacturing). This contribution represented a 254 per cent increase over that of 1962/3, when the total sector contributed SR685.6m — SR528.6m for refining and SR157.0m for the rest (all at current prices).[53] In relative terms, the significance of manufacturing industry as a whole has declined, despite its absolute increase, from 7.9 to 6.4 per cent of GDP. Refining apart, the relative size of the sector has declined more steeply, from about 1.8 to about 0.2 per cent, in spite of the fact that the contribution more than tripled in absolute terms. The reasons for the modesty of the absolute size of manufacturing industry (again apart from petroleum refining) are not difficult to imagine, but will be examined at the end of this section. For the moment, closer examination of the structure of manufacturing industry will be attempted.

Three broad surveys have been made of establishments, including manufacturing establishments, in the decade of the sixties, and one in 1971. The first was conducted in 1962 and was limited to five cities, as already indicated. The second was conducted in 1967

Saudi Arabia 153

and covered 25 cities and towns, and included all establishments, regardless of the size of labour force or capital invested.[54] The third was a sample survey conducted in 1969 among the establishments covered by the 1967 survey. The fourth was a census of all establishments engaged in economic activities in the private sector in 61 cities and towns.[55] In all instances, government-owned establishments as well as petroleum companies were excluded. (A sample survey covering 131 establishments and 156 workshops in eight industrial areas was conducted in 1966/7 by the Industrial Studies and Development Centre. However, owing to its narrow coverage, this survey will not be discussed here.)

The published results of the fourth study are the most revealing, and presumably the most comprehensive. Consequently a summary of these results is reproduced in Table 4.10. The difference between the findings in 1967 and 1971 is striking. Thus, in the earlier year there were 9,174 establishments with a total of 28,360 workers, but most of these were extremely small, as the summary in Table 4.8 shows.

Table 4.8: Employment in Private Sector in 25 Cities and Towns, 1967

	Establishments	Labourers	Per Cent
	8,168	1—4	89.0
	729	5—9	8.0
	169	10—19	1.8
	79	20—49	0.9
	12	50—99	0.1
	17	199 and over	0.2
Total	9,174		28,360	100.0

Source: *Statistical Yearbook 1390 A.H., 1970 A.D.*, Ch.V.

Two-thirds of the smallest establishments fell in the following three broad categories: machinery, electrical machines, apparatus and appliances; food, beverages and tobacco; and textiles, footwear, other weaving apparel and made-up textile goods. Also in 1967, as many as 2,399 establishments were owned by non-Saudis in the manufacturing sector, and 112 owned jointly by Saudis and non-Saudis. Over 93 per cent of the non-Saudis were individually owned business.

The census of 1971 found a total of 61,109 establishments, in all employing 146,710 persons, but including 51,949 unpaid family members and persons working on their own account. The distribution of establishments by size of employment is shown in Table 4.9.

The distribution of establishments by sector is available; so is that by size of employment. However, the actual number of workers per sector *and* per size of employment is not available. This serious gap notwithstanding, it will be interesting to examine the tabulation, and to focus on the place manufacturing occupies in the whole picture.

We need not dwell at length on the various differences between the number of establishments and the size of employment in the various sectors, as the landmarks stand out clearly, such as the preponderance of establishments in the group of trade, restaurants, hotels, etc., and the smallness of employment per establishment; the lead construction has in large establishments; the high percentage of manufacturing establishments employing 1-4 persons only (about 90 per cent) — exceeded only by those in the group trade, restaurants and hotels.

Probably the most interesting feature to identify is that of the *relative* increase in the number of establishments employing 1-4 persons, and the drop in that of establishments

Table 4.9: Employment in Private Sector, 1971 Census

Establishments	Labourers	Per Cent
57,716	1–4	94.5
2,305	5–9	3.8
597	10–19	1.0
312	20–49	0.5
91	50–99	0.1
88	100 and over	0.1
Total 61,109	146,710	100.0

Source: *Statistical Yearbook 1973*, Ch. XI.

employing 100 and over. In any case, there is no evidence that larger establishments on the whole are becoming more predominant in the structure. Taking the results in their entirety, we find that the average number of workers per establishment has dropped from 3.09 for 1967 to 2.4 for 1971. However this drop is most probably the result of the much wider coverage of cities and establishments in the 1971 census, which has weighted the results in favour of establishments with small employment.

A closer look at the manufacturing sector by itself is called for. Unfortunately, the most recent available breakdown by branch of industry relates to 1969. The branches are cross-tabulated with number of establishments and of workers, capital, wages and a few other variables. The results appear in Table 4.11.

Examination of Table 4.11 reveals some interesting aspects of Saudi industry. First, the average capital-output ratio is about 1:1, since fixed capital (in establishments with 10 or more workers) is SR234m, while value added (in all establishments regardless of the number of workers) is SR242m. In the second place, wages represent one-fifth of the total product, while raw materials represent 36 per cent of it. Thirdly, food and beverages and cement and non-ferrous metal products alone account for over half total product; together with transport equipment and wood and furniture the four branches account for just a little less than three-quarters of total product. In terms of employment too, these branches employ 73 per cent of all the workers in industry. However, the branch of cement and non-ferrous metal products has the largest size per average establishment in terms of capital invested, value of raw materials, wages, value added, and total product. Only in terms of workers per establishment does it fall behind the three other branches, but these are minor branches on any count.

In general, it is correct to say that industry in Saudi Arabia is still largely primitive and beset by a number of difficulties. One of these is the shortage of national industrial entrepreneurship as well as managerial, technical, supervisory and skilled manpower. Certain cultural influences pertaining to attitude to work, work intensity, incentives and the like tend to depress productivity, especially at the lower level of skills. Other difficulties include: insufficient clarity in industrial policy and insufficiency of legislation concerning incentives, commercial code and contractual relations; slowness in government departments and the proliferation of agencies dealing with industrial establishments; costliness of labour and the need to rely on expatriates whose visas and residence permits take an inordinately long time to obtain; costliness of imported raw materials and irregularity in their flow;

Saudi Arabia

Table 4.10: Distribution of Establishments by Main Kind of Economic Activity and Employment Size (1971 Census of Establishments)

Sector	Number of Establishments According to Size of Employment						
	1—4	5—9	10—19	20—49	50—99	100 and over	Total
1. Agriculture, forestry, livestock, hunting and fishing	74	8	1	1	1	—	85
2. Mining and quarrying	2	5	1	2	3	2	15
3. Manufacturing	8,559	746	194	105	16	18	9,638
4. Electricity, gas and water	68	19	16	8	2	9	122
5. Construction	533	51	40	29	13	30	696
6. Wholesale and retail trade, restaurants, hotels, etc.	39,445	925	153	66	23	8	40,620
7. Transport and storage	273	43	35	17	5	8	381
8. Financial institutions, insurance, real estate and business services	911	89	44	42	12	6	1,104
9. Community, social and personal services	7,851	419	113	42	16	7	8,448
Total	57,716	2,305	597	312	91	88	61,109

Note: The preponderance of establishments with very small employment is even greater than the table reveals, since we have combined two intervals appearing in the source: '1' and '2-4' employees. The number of establishments falling under the two categories are 39,161 and 18,555 respectively.
Source: *Statistical Yearbook 1972*, p.375.

the large volume of capital investment required generally, owing to the inability of most establishments to enjoy large-scale production, which is in turn at least partially due to the preference for imported goods in the market; and finally the inadequacy of certain public facilities like electricity, roads and means of communication, and studies by the competent government agencies.

Agriculture and Water

Although the sector of agriculture broadly defined (that is, including forestry, livestock and fishing) on the average contributed a mere 5.5 per cent of GDP during the eleven years 1962/3—1972/3, its contribution has declined sharply over the years, from 10 per cent in the first, to 2.8 per cent in the last year. Nevertheless, it has a significance well beyond these modest proportions. This is because it constitutes a traditional way of life and of making a living, the rural population engaged in it constitutes some 64 per cent of total population, and (according to estimates for 1970) it absorbs some 40.4 per cent of the active labour force — 12.3 nomadic and 28.1 settled workers. (In 1966, the proportion was 46.2 per cent, of whom some 15.1 per cent were nomads and 31.1 per cent settled workers.) But despite the drop in its share of the labour force, and its slow rate of growth as revealed in Table 4.2 above, it maintains a position of seniority among the

Table 4.11: Main Features of Selected Branches of Transformative Industries, 1969

Branch of Industry	No. of Establishments	No. of Workers	Fixed Capital[a] SR 1,000	Value of Raw Materials SR 1,000	Wages SR 1,000	Value Added SR 1,000	Total Product SR 1,000
1. Food and beverages	1,600	6,705	43,256	54,780	20,698	54,953	127,324
2. Textiles and apparel	1,219	2,156	2,899	10,857	3,547	12,826	24,750
3. Wood and furniture	1,074	3,938	10,825	17,367	12,736	24,915	45,196
4. Paper and printing	58	1,038	18,364	8,331	7,606	11,419	21,715
5. Leather goods and shoes	187	497	2,111	1,884	1,222	4,420	6,520
6. Rubber products	5	174	3,485	3,751	724	3,710	7,681
7. Chemical products	3	107	6,529	16,835	1,629	4,991	22,772
8. Basic metal industries	415	1,517	26,730	10,333	6,925	14,726	31,831
9. Cement and non-ferrous metal products	675	5,160	86,988	36,623	23,612	57,597	118,881
10. Equipment, apparatus and appliances	488	819	1,292	682	2,413	5,895	7,040
11. Transport equipment and appliances	2,574	6,378	29,536	11,206	19,063	41,014	64,005
12. Miscellaneous, not listed elsewhere	865	1,514	1,922	2,891	843	5,807	9,608
Total	9,163	30,003	233,937	175,540	101,018	242,273	487,323

a. Only establishments employing 10 or more workers. Other columns represent returns for establishments with one or more workers.
Source: Central Department of Statistics.

activities of the population and will become of greater significance if the promise of underground water, which extensive exploration has revealed, materialises.

Until recently, some Saudis complained that whenever they dug for water, they found petroleum instead. The restrictive scarcity of water counteracted in their minds the accommodating abundance of oil. But now the expectations are great, and seem to be well grounded, that the country will prove almost as rich with underground water as it is with oil. The examination of agriculture and water together is defensible under these circumstances, considering the extreme paucity of rainfall in all but the south-western part of the country.

The present underdevelopment of agriculture can be gauged from the fact that, even at the low dietary level prevailing, the country is a net importer of agricultural produce in general and of foodstuff in particular.[56] These imports have been rising over the decade of the sixties, and in the years 1970-3, at an average rate of 11.5 per cent per annum, to reach a total of SR1,097m in 1971 and SR1,222m in 1972. Nearly nine-tenths of the imports are foodstuffs, which gives an indication of the low performance of the agricultural sector.[57]

The basic resources for agriculture are land and water. The land area of the Kingdom is vast — about 2.2m square kilometres, or 220m hectares. Beyond this, all is confused. Thus, according to one estimate in a publication of the Food and Agriculture Organization, the total arable area in 1962 was 341,000 ha, expected to rise to 357,000 ha by 1985. Another, much more recent, publication estimates total arable land at 910,000 ha, but land under permanent crops at 95,000 ha. While the former source estimated irrigated area at 240,000 ha for 1962, the latter estimated it at 176,000 ha for 1971.[58] Yet a third source, a note by the Ministry of Agriculture and Water entitled 'Agriculture in the Kingdom of Saudi Arabia', estimated cultivable and cultivated land as being 400,000 ha.

The latter estimate, or something close to it, has been used by recent writers quoting Ministry of Agriculture and Water sources. One estimate of the area of agricultural holdings, broken down by region, puts the total at 451,310 ha (of which permanent crops constitute just under 10 per cent, and vegetables about 7 per cent; the balance is grown with field crops).[59] The irrigated area is estimated at about 135,000–140,000 ha.[60] We will subscribe to these estimates as representing cultivated area (rain-fed and irrigated), though actually cropped area varies considerably from year to year, especially in rain-fed regions.

The recent FAO estimate of cultivable land —an area of 910,000 ha — seems defensible. However, such global estimates of the country's agricultural potential must be only accepted with reserve. Much more needs to be known about specific regions with regard to soil, temperature, road facilities, farming population, technical level and — above all — water. Consequently, the country was divided into eight regions for the purpose of a thorough survey of agricultural resources. Contracts for this survey in six of the regions (totalling 1,273 sq. km. in area) have been awarded to three international firms, at a cost of SR105.6m. The survey work has been completed and the findings of these firms are now available. Broadly speaking, they are reassuring, in the sense that they indicate the possibility of horizontal expansion in agriculture through reclamation of new areas, and the availability of large reserves of underground water, in addition to possibilities of vertical expansion through intensification by utilising more capital, fertilisers and labour.[61] Although much more detailed information is still needed, the broad conclusions reached carry great hope.

Water scarcity is the main constraint to agriculture, with the average rainfall about

90 mm (3.5 inches) annually, and only 10 per cent of the country receiving 100 mm (4 inches) or over of rainfall. In addition, the rainfall varies sharply from year to year and from region to region. As this level is manifestly insufficient for sustained agriculture, recourse has to be had to alternative sources. The two available are underground water and sea-water. The country has for the past few decades relied to a certain extent on underground water, since it does not have substantial rivers flowing through the whole year, and since surface springs, where they exist, are already exploited by oasis dwellers. Underground water has been obtained through the digging of artesian wells, which generally have a small output. In recent years the Ministry of Agriculture and Water has dug up a total of 510 wells for drinking purposes (as water is generally insufficient for agriculture). (The cumulative number of wells in the country is around 62,500, 40 per cent of which or about 25,000 have engines and pumps.) The government also undertakes the operation and maintenance of the wells, and the building of distribution tanks. A large number of these wells have been entrusted to a big firm to operate and maintain.

However, in undertaking the survey of underground water the government has aimed at something much more substantial than the modest output so far obtained. Without going into great detail regarding the operation of exploration for water, it is enough to say that water was found under an area that may be as much as three-quarters of the country, at a depth reaching 5,500 metres in some instances. Of particular significance is one of the six regions under survey, in the north-west area of the country adjoining Jordan, where underground reserves have been estimated at 2×10^{13} cubic metres, while water currently available and consumed for all purposes in the same area is about 2.5×10^8 cubic metres. As the report of the firm undertaking the survey puts it,[62] even if only 1 per cent of these reserves were exploited, the water thus made available would be enough for several centuries at the current rate of utilisation. But the Kingdom is still far from the stage of execution of recovery of these resources, and it will be idle to dwell longer on the subject, particularly as the situation varies from one region to another. (The Development Plan of 1970 is totally silent regarding further exploration for and exploitation of underground water.) It is sufficient to stress in conclusion that Saudi Arabia is not only floating on oil, but — seemingly — also on water. It remains to be hoped that the country will be as successful in bringing the water to the surface as it has been with regard to the oil. No doubt this would entail considerable time and investment, and the government would have to surpass its current budget for agriculture and water by a very wide margin. (This sector budget rose from SR20m for 1958/9 to SR1,032m for 1973/4, of which 855m are for projects. However, though large, this sum cannot finance the development of underground water resources.)

1. Main Development Projects: There are five major agricultural and water projects worth reporting.[63] The first is the Al-Hasa irrigation and drainage project, which was initially designed to harness and benefit from flood water in the eastern area. It also aimed at protecting the soil from increasing salting and the reclamation of new land. So far this project has reclaimed 12,000 hectares, in addition to an original area of 8,000 hectares which now receives more water. Together the scheme has cost about SR250m, including the building of 1,521 km. of irrigation canals and 1,623 km. of drainage canals. The operation, administration and maintenance of the works are to be handled by a specialised firm until enough local experience has been gained to carry these responsibilities. Another project just completed is the Faisal Model Settlement Scheme at Harad, meant for the reclamation of 4,000 hectares and the settlement of 1,000 bedouin families. Work started in 1966 and has just ended, including the construction of 351 km. of main and secondary irrigation canals, and 305 km. of main and secondary drainage canals, 14 bridges and 52 wells. The total cost was initially set at SR100m, but has since risen considerably. The project is now in operation, with bedouin being trained in settled agricultural life, and hundreds of families already settled.

The third project to survey is the development of Wadi Jizan in the south, mainly through the building of a dam to hold flood waters and the reclamation of 8,000 ha of land. The capacity of the dam is 71m cubic metres. The dam and the irrigation and drainage networks were estimated to cost SR67m, and to be completed around 1974. A fourth project under planning is the construction of a dam at Abha in the south, where some fertile land exists. Not much is known about this project at the present moment. (Several other small dams have been constructed.) The improvement of about 5,000 ha of land in the Qutaif area by draining excess water which raises the level of salinity there is the fifth project. A drainage network has been constructed, and the land can now be cultivated.

Finally, a law was issued (Decree No. 26 of September 1968) whereby fallow land could be distributed to needy and worthy farmers. About 350,000—400,000 ha are involved in total; the area distributed was 34,238 ha by the end of 1973. The necessary services of extension, credit and education are also provided to enable the farmers to cultivate the new land efficiently. However, the implementation of the scheme of land distribution depends on the provision of agricultural water in sufficient quantities. Alongside these efforts, the government has set up a number of experimental farms for the improvement of crops and livestock and the provision of extension services. But, worthy as these efforts are, they still fall very short of the total needs of the country.

2. Water Desalination: The desalination of sea-water was mentioned earlier as a second major source of water, after underground water. Desalination serves urban needs mainly, and it would therefore be appropriate to include it in a discussion of municipal services, were it not for the desire to deal with water resources under one heading.

There are several desalination complexes in operation or under extension, as well as others under planning at present. A sea-water desalination and electric power complex was built at Jeddah, with a capacity of 5m gallons of water daily and 50,000 kilowatts of electricity an hour. The total cost of the project was SR95m, and it was completed for trial runs in the spring of 1971; it is operating fully now, but is already being expanded to double its capacity, or 10m gallons per day. The administration, operation and maintenance are undertaken by a foreign firm on contract while Saudis are being trained to take over in five years' time from the start of the contract. Two other towns on the Red Sea which have been supplied with desalination plants are Wajh and Deba, each with a capacity of 63,000 gallons a day. On the other hand, there are two other stations on the Arabian Gulf which have been expanded since construction. They are at al-Khobar and al-Khafji (7.5m and 120,000 gallons a day respectively). Two other plants are under construction at Jubail and Umluj, and others at Medina, Yanbou and Rabigh are in the planning stage. In all these cases, the same formula is adopted whereby a foreign management firm runs the plant and simultaneously trains Saudis to take over subsequently.

Alongside these developments, important work is being undertaken to develop the urban water supply systems. Expansion in the supply system of Riyadh and Jeddah has been completed, including pipe networks and large reservoirs. Other major works include extension of the present systems in Medina and Mecca (with the facilities taking into account the vast needs of the pilgrims during the pilgrimage season, which require an increase in the volume of water available and a vast increase in the accessibility to water). Finally, water projects for Hayil, al-Hafuf and Mubarraz are under work currently.

3. Livestock, Fishing and Forestry: According to estimates by the advisers of the Ministry of Agriculture and Water, the country has about 2.8m sheep, 1.4m goats, 0.6m camels and 0.27m cattle. The scarcity of water and the insufficiency of pasture land make the animal wealth of the country much less than it could be, given the area of the land and the sizeable component of bedouin, whose main activity is shepherding and animal tending. Furthermore, as the efforts for the settlement of nomads intensify, there is likely to be less attention to animal husbandry, unless the settlement takes the form of mixed farming. In this connection it should be added that the deliberate pace of settlement under government programmes is very slow; much of the settlement so far achieved has been spontaneously undertaken under the pressure of economic and social forces.

The Kingdom has a coast 1,000 miles long on the Red Sea, and a coast of 500 miles along the Arabian Gulf. This, plus the existence of many varieties of fish in the adjoining waters, suggests a reasonably good potential for the fishing and refrigeration industry. However, until now the efforts have been mainly small-scale and the methods on the whole primitive. The industry can only prosper if three conditions are satisfied: the utilisation of the fishermen now in the industry in any future modernisation, so that social tension may be avoided between the small fishermen and the big concerns that will look at fishing as a large-scale business; the setting up of enough refrigeration plants and the utilisation of refrigerated trucks for the transport of the fish to all parts of the country; and the development of canning and other industrial processes for fish which is not eaten fresh or deep-frozen. So far the plans to develop fishing along modern lines have clashed with the vested interests of the fishermen and the few small fishing concerns, but some modern establishments have come into existence.

Around 1.3 per cent of the land area of the country is designated as forest. These forests vary widely in thickness, and they are found mainly in the southern highlands where rainfall exceeds 200 mm (8 inches) a year. This is apart from palm and fruit trees elsewhere. Tree-planting is possible almost anywhere in the land if soil qualities alone are considered, but water acts as the limiting factor. Not only is afforestation limited, but the present forest wealth is continuously menaced by the cutting of trees for fuel. In turn this has a damaging effect on the cohesion of the soil and the moisture of the atmosphere.

4. Agricultural Activities: Only a small portion of the land in the country is privately owned — or some 0.8m hectares out of a total of 220m hectares. This already small area falls into over 188,000 ownerships where the average holding is about 4.1 ha. Information is not available on the pattern of ownership by size, but it is generally believed that the country does not have very large holdings. This is primarily because traditionally power was vested in two groups: the tribes, which were nomadic and did not care for settled agriculture and land ownership, or else owned the land collectively; and the city merchants, who concentrated on their earnings from trade and the pilgrimage season. There are wide variations in average size of holding from one region to another, and between one landowner and another. But on the whole it is the general inadequacy of the size of the holding that is subject to complaint, not the vastness of individual holdings.

Agricultural activities are handicapped further by the primitiveness of farming techniques, the very modest use of fertilisers (about SR2.7m worth annually), the low level of mechanisation (about 2,292 tractors for the whole country, though poor maintenance leaves the number actually in use an open question), and insufficient long-term credit. Furthermore, the high level of illiteracy and the generally low technological standards prevailing in the rural sector, plus traditionalism, all militate against a speedy renaissance in the countryside. On the other side of the account, it can be seen that where financial incentives become manifest, and where the government undertakes the necessary investments and overhead services, the farmers have not been unduly slow to learn new methods or to accept new crops and thus to raise productivity.

It remains to be added that the Agricultural Bank has been in existence since 1964; it has branches in eight towns, as well as 37 rural 'offices' connected either with the head office at Riyadh or with the branches. The cumulative total of its loans stood at SR121.3m by the end of the year 1972/3, divided as shown in Table 4.12.

Table 4.12: Total Loans from Agricultural Bank up to 1973

	Number[a]	Value (SR m)
Short-term	8,305	15.4
Medium-term	17,393	105.8
Long-term	6	0.1
Total	25,704	121.3

a. Not including 1972/3. The number for 1972/3 of short-, medium- and long-term combined was 4,477. This brings the grand total to 30,181 loans, or an average of SR4,719 per loan.

Sources: Data until 1971/2 collected from several issues of the *Statistical Yearbook* (including that for 1973); for 1972/3, from SAMA, *Annual Report 1392-1393 A.H. (1973)*, pp.35-6.

Finally, it is worth noting that agricultural production and food production, though they still fall very short of local needs, have made some advances since the early sixties. Thus the index of total agricultural production was 139 in 1973 (1961-5=100), with continuous growth since 1965; the index for food production for 1973 was, likewise, 139. (The index was a modest 106 for *per capita* production in both instances.)[64]

Infrastructure: Transport and Communications; Electricity and Public Utilities

1. Transport and Communications: The sector of transport, communications and storage contributed, in the decade beginning with 1962/3, on average 7 per cent to GDP, and now employs 65,000—70,000 workers (or 5-6 per cent of the employed labour force). But its significance for the economy far exceeds these indicators. The large land expanse of the Kingdom and its sparse population add emphasis to the need for good roads and other means of transport and communication if economic and socio-cultural contacts between the urban centres and rural areas are to be intensified. At the present moment, in spite of remarkable achievements in transport and communications, these services are still distinctly behind their optimum level and, of necessity, transport costs still feature importantly as an element in pricing, both of imported goods and of locally produced goods.

The importance of transport and communications, particularly roads, has been clearly appreciated by the government all along the last two decades. This is manifest in the large financial allocations directed to this sector in the past, which rose from SR209.9m for 1960/1 to SR2,051.7m for 1973/4.[65] If the actual performance has fallen behind allocations, it has not been for lack of concern but mainly for institutional deficiencies and manpower shortages. Aramco and Tapline have also attached great significance to road-building, and as a result have built a total of 1,615 km.[66] of road which serve their own purposes but also the general purposes of the country.

The examination of this sector necessitates an evaluation of the situation with regard to roads, ports, railroads, airports and air services, telecommunications and storage services. However, only the highlights of achievements and shortcomings or problems will be presented, in order to avoid excessive detail.

Roads: The road-building programme can be divided into two phases. The first stretched from 1951/2 to 1961/2 and witnessed the building of a total of 1,316 km. of road (with an average of 120 km. per year) at a total cost of about SR202m.[67] This total length included 250 km. previously asphalted that had to be re-asphalted. The quality of work in this phase was generally low and necessitated rebuilding and major repairs during the second phase. This second phase stretches from 1962/3 to the present. A total of 8,700 km. of new roads have been asphalted down to the end of 1972/3, bringing the grand total asphalted to over 10,000 km., in addition to about 5,800 km. of rural roads.[68] (These last connect some 500 villages with about 10 cities and towns.) Owing to the steep rise in the cost of road-building, and to recent inflationary pressures, there has been over the years a tenfold cost increase per kilometre. Average length built per year in this phase is about 790 km., if account is taken of the rebuilding of roads built in the first phase but subsequently found defective. The ministry hopes to raise its annual performance to 1,000 km. of asphalted roads. Upon the completion of the Tayif-Abha-Jizan road (715 km. in length) and the Barida-Hayil road (289 km.) the present network will have connected all urban centres with a population in excess of 10,000. The major task remaining would be the maintenance of this network and the expansion of the networks of rural and subsidiary (feeder) roads.

Partly because of the vastness of the country, and partly because there are not very many vehicles, there are no serious traffic problems except in the big cities, particularly Riyadh and Jeddah. Vehicles — private cars, taxis, transport vehicles and buses — registered in the 18 leading urban centres totalled 31,334 during 1972.[69] Though this is still a manageable annual increase, a 'car explosion' can be expected before the end of the decade, with the speedy rise in personal income. It ought to be added that there are no public bus services in Saudi cities and the inhabitants have to depend for transport on their private cars or on taxis, or on a cheaper taxi service charging passengers by the single seat.

Ports: The country has three major and several smaller ports. Four of these are on the Arabian Gulf, and three have facilities for loading crude petroleum: Ras Tanura, al-Khafji and Saud Port, which together had 4,087 ships call on them in 1972 to carry 2,198 million barrels of oil. These ports also handle ordinary cargo in addition to oil. Other non-oil loading ports are Jeddah, Yanbou and Jizan on the Red Sea and Dammam and al-Khobar on the Arabian Gulf. Four smaller ports are also in operation.

In spite of the fact that the ports handled about 2.2m tons of cargo other than oil in 1972, the last year for which data are available, they are still short of the current, and more so the growing, needs of the country. This is why major projects of expansion are under way in the three ports of Jeddah, Dammam and Yanbou to ultimately bring capacity to over 6m tons. In addition, expansion work has been completed on two smaller ports on the Arabian Gulf at Qatif and Jubail. Studies are also under consideration for the development of six new ports at different towns on the Red Sea, some of which have certain small facilities at present. Further expansion in the port of Jizan is under preparation. The administration of ports falls under several authorities, which complicates operations and delays development. Training for port personnel is undertaken at a special marine institute at Jeddah.

Railroads and Airways: The country is not well equipped with railroad lines, there being only two main lines: one linking Dammam with Riyadh (565 km.) and a much shorter line (17 km.) linking Dammam city with Dammam port. In addition there are subsidiary lines which total 125 km. in length. The engines and freight carriages are adequate for present use; however, passenger carriages are very old and in poor repair. According to the latest data available, 1,063,000 tons of cargo (or 68.4m ton-kilometres) and 133,000 passengers (48.3m passenger-kilometres) were transported during 1972.[70] It is believed that the service suffers from maintenance problems, which in turn are related to faulty construction to begin with, and to insufficient personnel training and a salary level lower than comparable services. Personnel deficiency seems to retard any suggestions for reform in the realm of operation or maintenance.

Because of the large land area and the insufficiency of road and railroad facilities, attention has been turned to internal aviation. Thus the country has established extensive domestic services in addition to the international services of the Saudi Arabian Airlines. A network of 23 airports and landing strips cover the country, but many of these have a very small movement of passengers, in two instances below 1,000 passengers during the year 1972, and in eight below 5,000. In all, total number of passengers transported was 482,727 for 1972. However, international services seem to be growing faster than internal services, judging by the operations of the decade 1963-72. (This is based on traffic in terms of seat/km. which quadrupled during this period.)[71]

Saudi Arabian Airlines is one of the more efficient companies in the Arab world, with a high rate of observance of schedules and a high rate of training for employees. The equipment is up to date but the airports vary widely in facilities. On the whole, however, maintenance is thought to be below the desired level of performance.

Telephones, Telecommunications and Posts: The country is in the process of establishing many types of facilities in a number of cities, towns and big rural centres by way of telephones and cable offices. Tens of thousands of telephone lines are being installed, and the next few years will witness more than a doubling of the cumulative total that had been installed until 1970. An automatic telephone network now connects the major cities. Thus the country has come a far way, with respect to the acceptance of telephones, the radio and television, 'since the Nineteen Twenties when King 'Abd al-'Aziz was said to have had verses from the Koran read over the radio in order to convince religious scholars that the instrument could be a means for moral betterment'.[72] Perhaps this and similar 'dramatic tales of the resistance of traditional communities to such "innovations" as the telephone, electricity or the radio, and the condemnation of these innovations as the work of the devil'[73] are apocryphal; if true, they are already recollections of the past.

But acceptance of the telephone and the radio and television does not mean that the country is well-equipped with these services. The size of the expansion programme is enough indication of the existing shortcomings, which are not only numerical but also qualitative. So, even when the planned 108,000 new telephone lines are installed, there will still be the problems of operation and maintenance, accounts and further expansion as demand is already outstripping the lines to be installed. (In any case, the cumulative total of automatic telephones in the Kingdom would then be a mere 198,700 lines.)[74] The level of personnel performance is so low that the government was reported in 1971 as being in the process of contracting with a foreign firm for the administration and operation of the automatic telephones network and the training of personnel. Training is now conducted at an institute in Jeddah for telecommunications. But the number under training in 1970 was a mere 21 officials.

Postal services are considered very inadequate by knowledgeable observers. An indication of the low level of confidence in the postal services is the resort to the registration of mail to the extent of half of all mail inside the Kingdom. The service is also slow, and formalities, especially where official mail is concerned, are cumbersome.

2. Electricity and Public Utilities: The sector of 'electricity, gas, water and sanitary services' is one of the smallest sectors in the economy. Its contribution to GDP was a mere SR319.1m in 1972/3, or less than 1 per cent of the total. Part of this sector has already been discussed, namely water, although it was then discussed in the context of water for agriculture. But in order not to fragment the subject, city water received some attention as well. We will not refer to it again here, except to emphasise that the administration of municipal water is quite confused, with different tariffs in different cities, and even in the same city depending on the object for which the water is purchased, with scarcities blighting the service, and finally with the influential often not settling their bills while the poorer members of the community are unable to escape payment.

The state of the electricity industry is rather complicated, with private companies having the concession of generating and selling power in the cities, the government (via one or more of four ministries: Interior, Agriculture and Water, Finance and Commerce and Industry) generating and selling electricity in the countryside, and large companies often having their private generating plants. Total power generated in the cities of Riyadh, Jeddah, Mecca, Medina, Taif, Dhahran, Al-Hasa and Rahima was over 640m kwh for 1969 and 1,186.2m kwh for 1973.[75] Electricity generated in some other cities for the same year totalled over 15.4m kwh. In both groups combined, industry's share of total consumption was about 7 per cent.[76] This is a reflection of the heavy dependence by industry on private generators. We have no data on electricity generated in smaller towns and in the countryside, or by private companies, and consequently cannot properly assess electricity generated by head of population. On the basis of information available, this would be about 200 kwh for 1969. Some observers believe that the addition of the production of the categories not included here would double the average per head, but this belief seems unwarranted, in view of the fact that the cities included in the published statistics no doubt predominate in power generation, and that industry is not a very significant sector, apart from petroleum-refining. However, if the observation were correct that electricity production per head is over 300 kwh a year (or, as one estimate has it, 370 kwh) then the country would not be poorly supplied with power by the standards of developing countries, and more specifically by the standards of the Arab countries covered in this study — though the pattern of distribution of the consumption would be extremely uneven.

Electricity generation has been rising fast over the past several years, and in spite of the inefficiency and insufficient far-sightedness of concessionary companies, expansion in the industry has taken place as well as some effort at improving the service. Where government plants are concerned, the problem is one mainly of failure by the influential to settle their bills, which skews the pattern of distribution of electricity cost still further against the poorer and less privileged members of the community. Other problems burden the industry, such as the multiplicity of authorities in charge, the failures and interruptions of the current, and above all the insufficiency of power. Regarding the last point, although in 1972 the capacity of the generators was well in excess of the power generated, yet there was not enough room for the expected increases in demand during the rest of the seventies. Furthermore, the industry should aim at supplying power in such quantity and at such quality and terms as to lure private businesses away from having their own generators. (The rates were lowered considerably in 1973, both for domestic and industrial use, as indicated earlier.) The government should also entrust the building of power plants to one authority only, which should also have the right to grant or withhold concessions. Finally, substantially more should be done to let the current reach the depths of the countryside. (It is only in 1973 and 1974 that preparation of a vast electrification programme began.)

Municipal services and municipal development are matters of grave concern in the Kingdom, in spite of the marked advances of the past decade or so. The cities and towns have had to contend with a number of challenging problems. The most notable of these are the rush and speed of development and construction; the fast growth of urban population, estimated at 8-10 per cent annually, mainly because of the exodus from the rural areas towards the city; the disorderliness of traffic in a culture which moved too suddenly to the car age; the initial primitiveness of such services as water, sewerage, roads, slaughterhouses and the like, which has created a wide gap between the needs and often demands of the city's population today and the facilities that it has been possible to install; and the minimal concern for the aesthetic aspect of the growth of urban centres.

In almost all of these respects the country is now at the stage of awareness, of being conscious of the nature of the problem and deciding to do something about it. The first step taken has been to make detailed aerial surveys of 41 cities and towns and to make a start with studies aiming at solving the many problems. These studies involve social and economic questions, as well as questions that it would be difficult to classify under any one label but had better be merely designated as 'urbanisation problems'. The internationally known firm Doxiadis Associates some years ago undertook a thorough study of the city of Riyadh,[77] and it is expected that other studies in depth will follow for other cities. In the meantime, the urban centres will have to improvise and probably accept a certain amount of waste because some of their investments will have to be discarded soon to make room for better thought-out and designed investments capable of coping with the requirements of growing urban centres.

Before this discussion is closed it is necessary to refer to the question of land acquisition by the government for public utilities. Unlike Kuwait, where the government bought private land at exorbitant prices only to sell parts of it later on at nominal prices, in Saudi Arabia the process has been reversed. In the early days of the building boom, the government, at the highest level of authority and further down to the level of Deputy Minister and Director-General, donated land to persons who were lucky enough to be in favour. (It is told that some of the donations were effected on the strength of a few lines scribbled on half a sheet of paper, without even clearly defining the boundaries of the land donated.) Later, when the government needed land for public utilities, it had to buy back land it had given free. In the absence of a law for expropriation, it had to pay the price charged by the new owners, which partly explains some of the problems associated with the construction of public utilities. However, this process of land donation has come to a complete stop and some of its adverse effects can now be countered.

Pilgrimage

The services sectors appear in the national accounts either under separate labels, such as trade, banking, transport and communication, ownership of dwellings, public administration, and education and health, or under a residual item marked 'other services'. This last item includes personal services (barbers, shoe-shines, auditors, to name a few categories), hotel and restaurant activities, pilgrimage and some other categories. This whole residual item constituted about 2 per cent of GDP.

Pilgrimage is the point of interest in the present discussion. It involves a very modest contribution to the economy, but an event of great cultural, social and administrative significance for the country. The pilgrimage season falls in the last month of the Hijra year, when the faithful from all parts of the world come to the most Holy Cities of Islam, namely Mecca and Medina, for worship and sacrifice-giving. In 1972, the last year for which information is available, an estimated 654,182 came from other countries, and about 353,000 from Saudi Arabia to the two cities also to perform the religious function.[78] (Over 600,000 sheep were slaughtered in sacrificial ritual.)

The contribution of pilgrimage to GDP is probably the smallest aspect of its total contribution, since the social and cultural contacts have been of great significance to Saudi Arabia over the centuries, providing cultural and social interaction and an occasion for the exchange of ideas. It must be admitted, however, that the exchanges are mainly of a purely religious nature; by definition, few if any pilgrims come to sow the seeds of social notions or to start social movements going, although recently the occasion of the *Hajj* (i.e. the pilgrimage) has been utilised for setting up some form of Islamic solidarity organisation.

The economic impact of the pilgrimage falls under 'other services' (via the spending of pilgrims on board and lodging), trade (via the substantial purchases made by pilgrims, particularly of such items as transistor radios, recorders and rugs, that are rather cheap and probably not available in the markets of the poorer of the countries of origin of many pilgrims), and transport and communications. The spending is effected through the sale of foreign currencies, usually 'hard currencies', and it is estimated that SR909m worth of such currencies was spent in the country in 1973. This constitutes about 2.5 per cent of the country's total earnings of foreign exchange, which places pilgrimage after oil (with 91 per cent of earnings) as exchange-earner. However, it must be remembered that quite a sizeable proportion of the earnings by the sector had already been sent out of the country for the import of the goods which the pilgrims buy on a noticeable scale.[79]

There is one aspect of the pilgrimage season which we must touch upon in connection with development. This is that work in government almost comes to a standstill for the period, with many officials performing the pilgrimage. If to this is added the month of fast, Ramadan, during which work hours (both in government and in private business) are short, and the intensity of work becomes distinctly low, then it is obvious that society must train its manpower to be able to bear the hardships of the fast without loss to work performance, and to make up for the time taken up with the pilgrimage. Otherwise a tangible part of the year, perhaps between 5 and 10 per cent, will be lost to productive work. In other words, the reconciliation of religious duty and work effort should be attempted by society, especially in view of the resolute developmental effort shown by the leaders of the country.

Money and Banking

The process of monetisation has been going on for a few decades in Saudi Arabia, mainly through the injection into the economy of monetary revenue from pilgrimage and oil.

This process can be said to have gone far, though its main advances are in the urban centres. The statistics of money in circulation and of bank deposits are the best way of gauging the degree of monetisation, especially when these magnitudes are related to the national product and to population.

The country passed through a spell of monetary confusion in the period 1953-7, as we have already indicated. This is reflected in the evolution of the volume of money supply. Likewise, the years of stabilisation and normality, when public spending was controlled and public debt repaid, also left their mark on this volume. The statistics show that money supply (including currency in circulation plus current and time deposits) has risen from SR1,045.1m at mid-1959 to 2,404m at the end of 1970, and 5,973m at the end of May 1974.[80] If we relate the growth of GNP for the years 1962/3 to 1972/3 to that of money supply for the same eleven years, we find that GNP has risen slightly more than money supply (by about 43 per cent) until 1972/3. But if we go back to 1958/9 and conduct the same comparison, we would find that GNP has risen by much more (691 versus 277 per cent), although here we are on less firm ground considering the lower level of confidence we have in GNP data for years preceding 1962/3. Be that as it may, there is still a wide gap between the expansion in money supply and that in GNP over the whole period, even after accounting for the possibility that the GNP may have been underestimated for the earlier years.

The conclusion is inescapable that the process of monetisation is not catching up with the growth of the national product plus that of population. Obviously, a large part of GNP which represents the contribution of the oil sector is government revenue, and a part of this revenue is not spent and is held by SAMA whose holdings do not show in the account of money supply, the latter only including private current and time deposits with commercial banks, in addition to money in circulation. Consequently part of the growth of GNP remains outside the growth of money supply. On balance, the money supply per head of the population is high by regional standards — only exceeded by Kuwait, Lebanon and Libya, and possibly Algeria.

The banking system only began seriously in the early fifties. Today the country has twelve commercial banks operating with 70 branches and pay-offices. Two of these banks are Saudi, three are other Arab, and seven are foreign non-Arab. The banks neither charge nor pay interest, as this is forbidden in Islam. Instead dividends are paid which are considered a reflection of the profitability of operations and are therefore justified. (Interest is considered sinful since it is fixed in amount and it reflects usury: money should not breed money; only the use of money in projects should do so.) However, this feature of the system does not seem to inhibit banking or business as a whole. The modesty of the size of banking operations is a reflection of the relative shallowness of banking habits and the hesitancy of businessmen to use banks more fully, and partly of the hesitancy or non-aggressiveness of the banks themselves.

As indicated earlier, no industrial bank existed in the Kingdom until March 1974, when the Industrial Development Fund was established with an initial capital of SR500m. There is an agricultural bank which was established and started operations in 1964. Its initial capital was SR10m, but it has been increased at different intervals and now stands at SR53m. (Its operations have already been referred to in Table 4.12, p. 161.) According to SAMA reports, over half of the medium-term loans have gone towards the financing of the purchase of pumps, engines and pipes, while one-eighth were for livestock and poultry. The balance is roughly divided between the purchase of trucks, tractors and their spare parts, and the drilling, deepening and casing of wells.

Another new bank has been set up recently — the Saudi Credit Bank, which was inaugurated in December 1973. Its main purpose is to provide credit to citizens of small means, in amounts not exceeding SR5,000 per loan. However, the capital of the bank is only SR5m, which would not enable it to be a very effective lending instrument.

Finally, mention must be made of SAMA, the Saudi Arabian Monetary Agency, which is in effect the bank of banks and of government, or the central bank of the Kingdom. SAMA was established by decree on 20 April 1952. In addition to its functions as the virtual central bank, it has been instrumental in the promotion of the Agricultural Bank, the new industrial fund, and the bank for people of small means. It was very active during the stabilisation period and its aftermath. And it conducts very valuable studies and publishes annual reports which compare favourably with anything that central banks in the Arab region produce.

Public Finance

The vast expansion in fiscal resources for the government, plus the increased awareness by government of the urgency of development work have resulted in a parallel expansion in public expenditure. Both the current expenditure (under Sections I and II of the general budget, which cover salaries and other recurrent expenses, and under Section III which comprises 'miscellaneous special expenses') and development expenditures (Section IV and a certain part of III) have risen noticeably over the years for which we have information, namely 1958/9 through 1973/4, yet the current allocations and expenditure (except for 1973/4) have risen faster, as Table 4.13 below shows. According to this table, the size of the general budget (both for revenue and expenditure, since the principle of a balanced budget is adopted all through) has risen from SR1,410m for 1958/9 to SR22,810m for 1973/4 — a net increase of 1,518 per cent over the base year. (This represents an annual compound rate of growth of 22 per cent on average. However, this high rate has been largely brought about by the vast increase in the allocations for the last three years, which rose steeply over the preceding plateau.)

Sections I and II of the budget combined rose from SR569.2m in 1958/9 to SR5,322.6m in 1973/4, while Section III rose from SR605.7m in 1964/5 to SR3,224.4m for 1973/4. Sections I and II represented 40.4 per cent in the base year, but 23.3 per cent in the last year, which reflects the faster acceleration in allocations for development. (Beginning with 1970/1, current expenditure included subsidy payments to Egypt and Jordan which, since 1967, when they were decided upon, had been paid out of the general reserves and not shown in the budget.) We cannot read much into the course of Section III because of the heterogeneity of the items included in it. By far the fastest-growing part of the general budget is Section IV, namely 'projects expenditures', which has risen from SR762m in 1964/5 to SR14,263m in 1973/4.[81] However, it is worth adding that allocations for salaries and wages (Section I) and for Section II are usually actually spent as envisaged, while development project allocations invariably prove to be larger than the actual expenditures subsequently made. None the less, even allowing for the fact that in recent years the allocations for development have far outdistanced the government's ability to execute projects (and this is even more true of the situation in 1974/5), it is still very significant that budget resources are being increasingly directed to development objectives.

The general budget for 1971/2 rose sharply over the budget of the previous year, from SR6,380m to SR10,782m — a rise of 69 per cent, which was made possible by the steep rise in oil revenues, and made necessary by the new Development Plan requirements in its first year of operation 1971/2. The two subsequent years witnessed further increases, especially 1973/4. These increases raise the question whether the mere availability of funds is justification enough for raising expenditure allocations so suddenly and enormously, in view of the country's inability to absorb the investment funds normally allocated. This budgeting largesse may well choke the economy with funds, since it is inconceivable that the public sector could expand its ability to use vastly increased development expenditure so soon, with technical and administrative skills growing much slower. While it is true that there is always a large backlog of projects which it is possible to develop, it is not equally true in the case of Saudi Arabia that the main bottleneck to implementation has been funds. (These observations are all the more pertinent to the further exaggerated increase in development allocations for 1974/5, to which we will refer later under 'Planning'.)

Table 4.13: Revenue and Expenditure, 1958/9–1973/4 (SR million)

Year	Estimated Revenue	Estimated Expenditure				Total
		Section I	II	III	IV	
1958/9	1,410.0	388.2	181.0		840.8	1,410.0
1959/60	1,405.0	410.9	196.1		798.0	1,405.0
1960/1	1,786.0	482.5	237.0		1,066.5	1,786.0
1961/2	2,166.0	577.5	299.3		1,289.2	2,166.0
1962/3	2,452.2	650.3	423.3		1,378.6	2,452.2
1963/4	2,686.0	1,016.8	556.8		1,112.4	2,686.0
1964/5	3,112.0	1,111.5	632.8	605.7	762.0	3,112.0
1965/6	3,961.0	1,254.7	621.4	682.4	1,402.4	3,961.0
1966/7	5,025.0	1,368.9	691.4	1,247.2	1,717.4	5,025.0
1967/8	4,937.0	1,432.9	624.6	732.7	2,146.8	4,937.0
1968/9	5,535.5	1,600.5	806.7	908.3	2,220.0	5,535.5
1969/70	5,966.0	1,688.0	711.5	884.5	2,682.0	5,966.0
1970/1	6,380.0	1,791.0	746.3	1,408.7	2,596.0	6,380.0
1971/2	10,782.0	2,537.1	1,015.8	2,193.4	5,035.7	10,782.0
1972/3	13,200.0	3,122.8	1,365.1	2,462.3	6,717.6	13,200.0
1973/4	22,810.0	3,583.4	1,739.2	3,224.4	14,263.0	22,810.0

Sources: *Statistical Yearbook 1385 A.H., 1965 A.D.*, Ch. VIII; *1390 A.H., 1970 A.D.*, Ch. X; and *1393 A.H., 1973 A.D.*, Ch. X for the various years. (Total Estimated Revenue and Estimated Expenditure for 1970/1 and 1972/3 disagrees with the addition of Sections I-IV.)

An item-by-item examination of the 1972/3 budget reveals some interesting features which will be highlighted here. Thus, the Private Treasury receives SR173.1m. This is only 1.3 per cent of the total for 1972/3, but a large sum in absolute terms. (In addition, the allocations for the Royal Cabinets and the National Guard, which is apart from the regular army and more of a Royal Guard, amount to over SR436m.) The Ministry of Defence and Aviation is by far the largest single beneficiary, with a budget exceeding SR3,545m, or over one-quarter of the total. The next largest recipients of allocations are, respectively, the Ministries of the Interior (including municipalities), Communications, Education (including the General Administration for Girls' Education, but excluding the universities and the College of Petroleum and Minerals), Finance and National Economy and Agriculture and Water. Naturally, the ranking varies if examined under each of the four budget sections.

In addition to allocations under the general budget, there are allocations to twelve special, independent budgets, as shown in Table 4.14.

Table 4.14: Special Budget Allocations, 1972/3

Special Budget	SR Million
Saudi Arabian Airlines	296.3
Saudi Red Crescent Society	11.1
College of Petroleum and Minerals	30.0
University of Riyadh	112.2
King Abdul-Aziz University	39.8
Industrial Studies and Development Centre	6.4
Pensions Department	75.8
Petroleum and Minerals Organization, PETROMIN	18.0
Saudi Railroads Organization	55.1
Public Administration Institute	9.5
Grain Silos Organization	7.0
S.A. Standards Organization	2.2
Total	663.4

Source: *Statistical Yearbook 1973*, p.367.

A grouping of the many heads of expenditure for recent years has been attempted by Hitti and Abed, to whose work reference has been made. They established five groups: agriculture and industry; infrastructure; education, health and social affairs; national defence and administration. Accordingly, it is found that over the last three years general administration and defence were the largest beneficiaries, their share a little over one-fourth of the total each. Infrastructure allocations account for one-fifth, social services for one-sixth, and agriculture and industry for the balance.[82]

If the development budget alone is examined for the last three years, it is found that transport and communications have received 23 per cent of the allocations, followed distantly by municipal affairs (urban amenities), agriculture and water. These groups together account for over 40 per cent of total project allocations.[83] (The projects considered here exclude those of a non-economic nature, such as investments in the defence sector.)

The External Sector

The very large size of the petroleum sector and the pilgrimage season together give the external sector its enormous dimensions. It was mentioned earlier that oil exports generally contribute 90 per cent of the country's foreign exchange earnings, and that pilgrimage, though a very small source of earnings in comparison, ranks second in size. As a result of the magnitude of these earnings, in normal periods the country experiences abundance and comfort in its balance of international payments, not hardship, like most developing countries. This abundance has permitted the inflow of a large volume of imports, both for the expanding consumption of the population and for the accelerated development of the environment. The growth of both imports and exports can be seen from the balance of payments accounts of the country.

Saudi Arabia

Balance of payments information shows that, exceptionally, the country had a deficit on the current account in the years 1968 and 1969, owing to the payments made in subsidy to Egypt and Jordan after the Arab-Israeli war of June 1967. The year 1970 escaped the same fate because oil revenue rose sharply from its 1969 level. The country's earnings in its current account have increased consistently over the years, rising sharply in 1971 and then in 1972, yet more steeply in 1973, and much more so in 1974. This is mainly attributable to the rise in government's take from the export of every oil barrel since 1971, but also to increased oil production.

Although payments have also risen steeply, they have fallen below earnings in all years except 1968 and 1969. This has made possible the accumulation of considerable reserves of gold and foreign currencies, and has permitted substantial foreign investments to be made. Foreign assets abroad stood at $788.6m by the end of December 1970, but had been higher in previous years. Thus they were $828.8m in 1968 and $990.2m in 1967.[84] The drop was mainly caused by the subsidies to Arab countries, foremost among which were Jordan and Egypt, though other countries have received Saudi aid from time to time. However, SAMA's holdings rose to $8,150m by May 1974,[85] and probably to $15 billion by the end of the year.

Until 1973, Saudi Arabia's situation with respect to the accumulation of foreign assets was not parallel with that of Kuwait, where larger sums could be added annually to the foreign reserves out of a smaller oil revenue. The size of Saudi Arabia's population, its area and non-oil resources, and the much wider opportunities (and pressures) for investment in the country together have – until recently – made the Kingdom's foreign exchange position very comfortable but not super-affluent. However, vast expansion in oil production and price increases since October 1973 have resulted in the widening of the flow of revenue to the point where sharply accelerated investment at home and asset accumulation abroad have become possible in combination.

The vast increase in domestic investment will not be examined here but will be reflected in the expansion in the plan allocations to which we will refer later. For the moment, the impact of the country's earnings from oil exports on the external sector will receive attention. The first striking feature in the picture is Saudi Arabia's relatively modest aid programmes – compared with Kuwait's, for instance. It was only in September 1974 that the Saudi Development Fund was established, with a capital of SR10,000m (about $2,817m). It will be some time before the Fund will formulate its rules and procedures, get its staff, and start operations.[86] Nevertheless, aid grants had been made since the late fifties, but they remained modest in size until 1967. Thus, only in 1967 did 'government expenditure abroad', which included aid to Arab countries, exceed $100m; by 1972 this expenditure had only reached $300m.

However, the picture has changed substantially since 1973. To begin with, the expenditure under reference exceeded $840m – most of it being aid to Arab countries. Then, in 1974, the government made substantial payments abroad. These included investments in various forms in advanced Western countries (direct investments, loans, public bonds, equity, bank deposits and credit facilities to the IMF Oil Facility and to the IBRD). Estimates of this group of items vary widely, but the outflow may well exceed $8,000m. In addition, some $2,500m was directed to the Arab countries, partly to finance military purchases and support the defence effort, partly in economic loans and grants. A further $500m was directed to non-Arab Third World countries, either through bilateral or multilateral arrangements.

These estimates are very tentative, but they suggest the broad order of magnitude of the loans, grants and investments undertaken in 1974. On this assumption, the country's foreign exchange earnings minus the non-recoverable payments made (grants, imports of consumer and capital goods and of arms), plus the foreign assets held by the end of 1973 would probably reach a cumulative total of $15,000m of foreign assets by the end of 1974.[87]

Such a volume of assets, held mostly in the industrial market economies, poses problems almost as much as it provides solace. This is for several reasons, including devaluation of foreign reserve currencies, steep inflation, and the danger of the use of foreign assets as an anti-Arab political pressure mechanism in case a new Arab-Western political and oil confrontation like that of 1973/4 were to recur. Above all, the accumulation of enormous foreign assets beyond the immediate or medium-term absorptive capacity of the Arab countries is itself an indication that oil production is undertaken at a scale beyond the needs of these countries. However, these and related issues will be examined on a regional basis in the companion volume. We will merely point to the issues here.

Education, Health and Social Affairs

1. Education:[88] An examination of the educational effort of the Kingdom raises mixed feelings. On the one hand there are the remarkable advances made in the post-war period and the breakthrough in the resistance to modern education (especially to girls' education) in certain powerful quarters. On the other hand, there are still very serious qualitative as well as quantitative shortcomings in the system and its achievement. What gives education its unique importance is not merely its own value as an end in itself, but also its function as a major factor in social change in a traditional country burdened by illiteracy, primitiveness of technology, and at best development-neutral attitudes of the mass of population. In the following discussion we will examine more the quantitative aspects, leaving the discussion of the qualitative aspects, such as purpose, content and methodology of education to the companion volume.

At the financial level, education has been receiving consistently rising allocations over the past decade and a half. Thus, in 1958/9 the total budget for education, including Riyadh University, was SR118m for all four sections, that is including salaries and wages, other recurrent payments and projects. The allocations have risen to SR1,677m by 1973/4, which represents a 14-fold rise. (These allocations include the special budgets of the universities and all other aspects of education administered by the ministry.) Other indicators confirm the same trend. Thus, an average of 158 new schools were built annually over the years 1966 through 1970, but the pace has quickened since then.[89] Student enrolment in government schools in 1954/5 totalled 64,667 at the primary, intermediate, intermediate-secondary, and secondary levels. These were all boys; girls' schools were started only in 1960, as we shall see later. By 1972/3, enrolment at the same levels had reached 527,500 boys and 200,474 girls, or a total of 727,974. This total includes 40,792 pupils in private schools; no information is available on private education in 1954/5, the first reference in official statistics to private schools being for the year 1960/1, although it is known that there were a few schools before. On the legitimate assumption that female education was minimal in 1954/5, if it existed at all, we can compare enrolment in the two end years 1954/5 and 1972/3, both for males and females and in both government and private schools combined.

The comparison reveals that enrolment in the later year is over eleven times that of the earlier year. Over the 18 intervening years enrolment grew by 1,026 per cent, at an annual compound rate of growth of 15 per cent on the average. Thanks to this growth, school enrolment (always referring to the primary, intermediate and secondary levels only) rose from an estimated 2.15 per cent of population (assuming a population of 3m in 1954/5) to an estimated 12.6 per cent of population in 1972/3 (assuming a population of 5.8m in this later year). Although the increase is considerable both in absolute and in relative terms, it falls far short of the achievement in a number of other countries in the region. Specifically, the situation is only better than that in Sudan, is about as good as that in Morocco, but is behind that in the nine other countries covered by this study. The enrolment of boys and girls between 5 and 19 years of age (who constitute about 33 per cent of total population), currently constitutes only about two-fifths of this school population.[90] The ratio reaches much higher levels in the nine Arab countries to which we have just referred.

The discussion so far has concentrated on the performance of the country in terms of education at the primary, intermediate and secondary levels. However, other levels exist, before and after, as well as alongside. There are kindergartens, which initially were all private, and universities, as well as vocational schools (commercial, industrial and technical), and religious 'colleges' and institutes. Table 4.15 below presents the course of advance made in education at the various levels. The initial year is 1954/5 wherever possible, or later years where certain forms or levels were started subsequently. The last year is mainly 1972/3.

This table is revealing with respect to the evolution of enrolment. Among the more noteworthy facts it brings out is the very steep rise in the education of girls, although the absolute numbers are still modest. Another feature of the profile of education in the Kingdom is the drop in interest among trainees in agricultural and commercial skills, judging by the serious decline in enrolment in schools teaching these skills. Then there is the noticeable popularity of training in religious institutions teaching *Shari'a* (Islamic statute), *Tawheed* (Tenets of Monotheism), and theological studies in general. But the most serious feature is the large drop-out rate, for boys and girls alike, between the elementary and intermediate cycles, and later in intermediate and secondary cycles. The 'survivors' in the last cycle constitute about 5 per cent of boys and 2 per cent of girls. These drop-outs are not picked by technical schools, so must obviously swell the ranks of the near-illiterate and the untrained.

There are other features that emerge both from official statistics and from reports on education and interviews with educators and officials in government. One of these is the insufficiency of Saudi teachers and professors, both in public and private institutions. Thus, in 1972/3 the proportion of Saudi to foreign-born teachers was low, as Table 4.16 shows.

Another feature is that notwithstanding the quantitative advances made with regard to enrolment, there is still some marked hesitation towards education in certain quarters, especially in the countryside, both among settled peasants and the bedouin. This reflects a traditional attitude which has not yet been reconciled to modern education. Even in the cities there is still a certain amount of conflict between traditional concepts embedded in the culture (as perceived and felt), and modern facts and notions. The physical sciences present one such area of conflict, where the pupils may find that their parents refuse to believe that man has reached the moon, or even that the earth is spherical in shape.[91] Conflict also arises in other areas of knowledge and around loyalties. In brief, there is a clash between the old and the new, the traditional and the modern. The society is in effect at the threshold of the transitional stage, in which the government is playing a decisive but quiet and sober role through education as well as through radio and television. Under the King's guidance, the transition may well be effected with a minimum of strain and

Table 4.15: Advances in Student Enrolment in Saudi Arabia

Type or Level of Education	Year	Number of Students	1972/3 Number of Students
Government Education (Males)			
1. Kindergarten	1965/6	60	971
2. Primary (elementary)	1954/5	57,841	332,352
3. Intermediate	1954/5	4,007	57,092
4. Intermediate-secondary (new intermediate)	1954/5	2,703 }	15,045
5. Secondary	1954/5	116 }	
6. Teacher training[a]			
— Elementary (primary)	1954/5	139	7,116
— Secondary	1961/2	67	
7. Agriculture schools[b]	1960/1	198	—
8. Commerce schools (intermediate)[c]	1959/60	214	321
9. Industry schools			
— Secondary	1954/5	174	977
— Higher (as from 1972/3)			58
10. Institutes of Theology[d]	1954/5	216	10,106
11. Technical education	1965/6	20	178
12. Physical Education Institute	1965/6	48	185
13. Complementary education	1966/7	940	995
14. Institutes for retarded children	1963/4	492	1,572
15. Night schools	1966/7	5,809	9,096
16. Adult education	1955/6	1,713	50,644
17. College of Petroleum and Minerals	1964/5	67	894
18. Islamic University (Medina)	1969/70	591	668
19. University of Riyadh (men students)	1957/8	(year started)	4,096
20. King Abdul-Aziz University[e]	1967/8	53	1,739
21. High Institute for Islamic Law	1966/7	67	68
22. College of Islamic Law and Language	1954/5	42	2,546
Total[f]			496,719
Government Education (Females)			
1. Primary	1960/1	5,180	169,739
2. Intermediate	1963/4	235	19,880
3. Secondary	1963/4	21	3,410
4. Teacher training			
— Intermediate	1960/1	20	3,954
— Secondary			1,675
— Technical			229
5. Girls' Training College	1970/1	80	312
6. Adult education (started 1972/3)			1,400
7. Nursing institutes	1970/1	114	187
8. Riyadh University (women students)			273
9. Abdul-Aziz University (women students)			741
Total[f]			201,800
Private Education (boys plus girls)			
1. Kindergarten[g]	1960/1	830	6,508
2. Primary (elementary)[h]	1960/1	5,626	19,031
3. Intermediate[i]	1960/1	97	7,097
4. Secondary[j]	1963/4	20	3,329
5. Adult education[k] (started 1972/3)			495
6. Other[l]	1970/1	2,814	4,332
Total			40,792
Grand Total			739,311

Notes:
a. From 1969/70, includes elementary training only.
b. Enrolment in agriculture schools rose till 1964/5 when it reached 844 students, then declined fast thereafter till 1970/1, after which it stopped.
c. Last year of operation was 1969/70. Since 1971/2, it has been given at the secondary level.
d. These institutions fall under a Directorate of Religious Colleges and Institutes.
e. This university was private until 1971/2, when it was taken over by government.
f. Totals vary from source, because I have separated male and female enrolment at Riyadh and Abdul-Aziz Universities, for the sake of consistency.
g. 3,808 male; 2,700 female.
h. 14,576 male; 4,455 female.
i. 6,459 male; 638 female.
j. 2,730 male; 599 female.
k. Sex distribution not available.
l. Includes schools for retarded children, the blind, etc.
Source: Collated from several tables in the chapter on 'Education' in *Statistical Yearbook 1393 A.H., 1973 A.D.* for 1972/3, and from *Statistical Yearbook 1390 A.H., 1970 A.D.* for earlier years.

Table 4.16: Proportion of Saudi to All Teachers (per cent)

Kindergarten	20.5
Primary (government)	54.8
Intermediate (government)	28.9
Secondary (government)	13.6
All cycles, private	9.7
University (Riyadh and Abdul-Aziz)	32.2

generational mistrust and estrangement. But to say that education is being used as an instrument of change is not to deny that the content of the curricula, especially in the case of girls' education, has too many very traditional courses in religion, language and history at the expense of science, mathematics and foreign languages, or that the methods of instruction still rely heavily on learning by rote and the 'imparting of knowledge by teachers' rather than analysis, experimentation, participation and dialogue. Thirdly, it must be emphasised that the university population is very small — indeed the smallest relative to population in the twelve countries surveyed. (Here we consider students at home and abroad combined.) It is worth noting that Saudis studying in universities abroad as government bursaries totalled 2,372 in 1972/3. There are probably as many, if not more, studying abroad at their own expense.

In closing this discussion of education, we should point out that there are modest indications that some questioning of the educational system — its methods, reach, content and quality in general — has begun to emerge. One expression of such questioning has been the convening by the Ministry of Education, in March 1974, of a conference to examine some issues relating to teacher training. Although the conference did not probe deep into the system of education and touched marginal matters in the main, and it came up with no radical findings or suggestions, yet it was encouraging as a first step in the right direction.

2. *Health:*[92] The country's advances in the fields of medicine, hygiene and health are probably not as substantial as those in education, but in any case it is difficult to measure them. Observers believe that the services available in the Kingdom fall somewhere between good and poor. Not much more has been achieved mainly because general awareness of the value of modern medical science and the observance of rules of hygiene has only recently begun. Growing awareness has exposed the insufficiency of the facilities, both curative and preventive. Thus there are still a number of diseases that debilitate the population and account for a number of deaths. These include malaria, tuberculosis, dysentery, typhoid, tetanus, intestinal diseases and eye diseases. It can probably be said, as a broad generalisation, that the city and town residents now understand what medicine and hygienic living can do to prevent and cure these diseases, and tend less to neglect themselves in a fatalistic way. The level of such understanding among the rural and bedouin population is probably lower.

Health services (and the term is used here generically to include all associated services) are offered mainly by the government, but also by the oil companies to their employees and their families and by certain large establishments. Within the structure of government, the services are administered by the Ministry of Health as well as by school health units and the Ministry of Defence and Aviation. The budget of the Ministry of Health has risen from SR59.6m for 1958/9 to SR499m for 1973/4. In addition, the health services offered by other agencies receive several million riyals more. Environmental sanitation has just begun to be studied seriously, and once some work is undertaken in this direction the budget is likely to expand much further. The country is poorly provided with medical personnel and hospital beds, as Table 4.17 shows.

Table 4.17: Health Personnel and Facilities, 1960 and 1972

Type of Personnel or Facility	Government Sector 1960	Government Sector 1972	Private Sector 1972
Physicians (and dentists)	280	1,081	192
Pharmacists	21	78	6
Male nurses	361	1,482	273
Nurses, midwives and assistants	388	1,480	422
Pharmacy assistants	80	513	22
Laboratory assistants	32	253	79
X-ray assistants	24	138	32
Hospitals	40	51	20
Beds in hospitals	3,668	8,132	1,004
Dispensaries	48	190	–
Health centres	59	343	–

Note: No information is available on the private sector for 1960.
Source: *Statistical Yearbook 1393 A.H., 1973 A.D.*, Chapter III, 'Health'.

A total of 1,273 physicians for a population of about 5.6m in 1972 provides one physician to every 4,000 inhabitants, which is a very inadequate ratio. Unsatisfactory as it is, the situation represents a marked improvement over the recent past, when in 1960, for instance, there were only 280 physicians and 21 pharmacists in government service for the whole Kingdom. It must further be pointed out that the country suffers from extreme dependence on non-Saudi physicians. Thus in 1972 there were only 153 Saudis among the 1,273 physicians in the country. Furthermore, the Saudis among the medical personnel in government service (other than physicians, but including pharmacists, nurses, technicians, laboratory assistants and the like) constitute about 58 per cent, but probably less in the private sector. The Saudis avoid certain types of service in hospitals, and there are only 94 Saudi midwives and female nurses out of 1,386 in ministry service. There are three health institutes in the country which train medical personnel. Between 1960/1 and 1972/3 a total of 1,145 people were trained. (A total of 531 Saudis were in 1972/3 receiving training abroad in medicine, public health and dentistry.)[93]

Until the end of the sixties, modest efforts were made in the field of preventive medicine, as can be seen through one indicator: the small number of vaccinations and inoculations against various diseases, such as cholera and smallpox. This was especially serious in a country which was highly vulnerable both because of its location rather close to regions in Asia where the two diseases have a high incidence, and of the vast numbers of pilgrims it receives annually. (Total vaccinations and inoculations given for the major ten diseases for the whole country were 1,114,811.) The preventive campaign gained considerable momentum in the following two or three years, as evidenced by the tripling of the total number of vaccinations and inoculations administered. Furthermore, it must be added that the oil companies provide adequate preventive coverage for their employees.

Finally, the most spectacular achievement in the field of health services has been the building of an extremely modern and well-equipped hospital in Riyadh, the King Faisal Model Hospital. This 250-bed hospital is expected to be completed in 1975. However, here as elsewhere in government health services, the facilities are largely concentrated in urban centres, especially where more sophisticated equipment and better-trained personnel are concerned. Furthermore, very little research related to health matters is conducted, and it will be many years before a research climate is created.

3. Social Affairs: Government's activities under this heading cover five areas: social security, social welfare, community development, co-operative societies and youth welfare. Some efforts have been expended to develop each of these fields, but nowhere is there an outstanding record worth dwelling upon. However, two comments are worth making with respect to two areas associated with social affairs: labour affairs and legislation, and housing.

The country first had a labour code in 1946, which remained in effect until 1969 when two decrees were issued: the first introducing a new labour code, and the second introducing social insurance. As a broad generalisation, it can be said that labour legislation and practices have moved from being harsh to being sternly paternalistic. Thus, unionisation and strikes are forbidden, but recent legislation provides more flexible machinery for the discussion and arbitration of disputes than older legislation, which relied on coercive methods, in effect if not in letter. It can perhaps be argued that labour legislation cannot be more advanced than, or outdistance, labour consciousness and industrialisation. This is a legitimate argument, except that the labour force must be prepared, in attitudes and outlook, to exercise the functions, enjoy the rights, and bear the responsibilities that it will be called upon ultimately to do. The code in force is not adequate for such preparation.

As to popular housing, the record here is very poor, as hardly any such housing has been provided. There has been a vast expansion in house-building activities, mostly in urban centres, but this has been undertaken virtually wholly by private individuals in the upper-middle and higher-income brackets.

3. DEVELOPMENT PLANNING[94]

Planning in Saudi Arabia has had a slow gestation period which has lasted a decade. This was understandable on two grounds: the unpreparedness for planning notions and planning discipline in the early years, and the near-absence of information necessary for a Plan. Around the mid-sixties the groundwork began to be prepared for a serious planning effort, with — among other things — the undertaking of a thorough stock-taking of the economic situation in hand. But it took another five years for the first plan to appear in August 1970. As reference has been made earlier in section 1 to the evolution of planning agencies and the political framework in which they found themselves, the discussion will now centre around the Plan and the main features will be summarised.

The Plan document does not at any point indicate the duration of the Plan or specify its initial and its last year. But it is understood that it is a five-year Plan, from 1971 to 1975. This silence in the document on this matter is deliberate: it is meant to allow for flexibility in implementation. However it causes embarrassment, since the calculation of rates of growth and other changes during the Plan period becomes a matter of conjecture. Where the rate of change makes the duration obvious, the silence becomes irrelevant. The Plan includes no models or integrated master-tables showing the expected availability and use of resources year by year; the presentation is fragmented and the approach more 'common-sense' than rigorous. No input-output or commodity balance tables are included. Nevertheless, or perhaps because of the approach and style adopted, the reader has the impression that the Plan is a practical, pragmatic, down-to-earth guideline for action which combines the use of financial magnitudes and indicators with real (physical) magnitudes and indicators, and which spells out the targets on a sector, subsector, and often project basis, as well as the policies and measures needed for attaining the targets. Finally, the Plan relates to the public sector only. The private sector and the oil companies are not included in it.

Three assumptions underline the expectations of the Plan:

1. Remaining within the defined limits of expenditures for Public Administration and Defense.
2. The oil companies' appreciation of the Kingdom's need for an exceptional financing capacity that dictates increasing their payments to the Government during the whole of the plan period.
3. The Government's seeking of new sources from which to increase its revenues by the amount required to finance the Plan . . .[95]

The objectives are broadly defined as follows:

1. Increasing the rate of growth of gross domestic product;
2. Developing human resources so that the several elements of society will be able to contribute more effectively to production and participate fully in the process of development; and
3. Diversifying sources of national income and reducing dependence on oil through increasing the share of other productive sectors in gross domestic product.[96]

There is no indication of the priorities, and it would seem to the observer that the first objective should come last, considering the high rate of growth already achieved and the grave urgency of human resource development and of diversification. However, it is obvious in the rest of the Plan document that manpower development is given high priority, and that the implicit strategy of development starts with manpower resources and their better education and training. Government administration is emphasised too as another area worthy of close attention and development; but it would seem to us that it ought to have received yet greater emphasis in the whole strategy of the Plan.

Table 4.18 presents the summary of the financial allocations for the Plan. The total of SR41.3 billion in (presumably) five years was certainly to lay a heavy strain on the economy, both with regard to the provision of this volume of finance averaging over SR8 billion a year, and with regard to the ability of the economy and particularly its manpower resources and public administration to cope with the programme of development involved and to efficiently absorb such a large volume of investment. Given the rate at which investment has been absorbed in the recent past, and at which manpower resources had grown numerically and improved in quality, one was at the time left with grave doubts as to the feasibility of the Plan. (We saw above in Table 4.13 that total budget allocations in the

Table 4.18: Summary of Financial Allocations for the Plan (SR million)

	Recurrent[a]	Project[b]	Total Amount	Total Per Cent
Administration	6,794.6	922.8	7,717.4	18.6
Defence	3,980.0	5,575.0	9,555.0	23.1
Education, vocational training and cultural affairs	6,150.2	1,227.5	7,377.7	17.8
Health and social affairs	1,612.9	308.2	1,921.1	4.7
Public utilities and urban development	1,246.9	3,325.4	4,572.3	11.1
Transport and communications	1,767.3	5,709.2	7,476.5	18.1
Industry	321.8	776.7	1,098.5	2.7
Agriculture	973.8	493.9	1,467.7	3.6
Trade and services	83.5	43.8	127.3	0.3
Total	22,931.0	18,382.5	41,313.5	100.0

Notes:
a. Covers expenditures under Chapters I, II and III of the annual budget.
b. Covers expenditures under Chapter IV of the annual budget.
Source: Central Planning Organisation, *Development Plan 1390 A.H.*, p.43.

whole decade preceding the first year of the Plan, that is the year 1970/1, were SR37.6 billion.) To this must be added the fact that actual expenditure had consistently been lower. It was difficult in 1971, for instance, to imagine that the economy could in the subsequent five years more than double its absorption of expenditure on projects both in terms of fixed investment and recurrent expenditures. To this must be added the wisdom of past experience, according to which actual expenditure had consistently fallen below allocations for projects. Thus, according to the *Annual Report* by SAMA, over the seven years 1963/4–1969/70 actual expenditure totalled SR7,875m while allocations totalled SR11,830m — that is, performance had been at the level of 79.9 per cent.[97] This level was quite high by regional standards, but it still left a serious question regarding the feasibility of Plan allocations and whether they were not over-ambitious. Such doubts may well have featured importantly in the minds of the planners and suggested to them the wisdom of not making the Plan period explicit, so that the phasing of implementation could be adjusted to the socio-economic and administrative realities as they unfolded during the process of implementation.

These early misgivings have been largely, though not wholly, swept away since then. With respect to financing available, there has been no problem whatsoever, as oil revenues have soared in the seventies. Indeed, the investment programme has been adjusted upwards in several places, and the whole Plan has been dwarfed by the new five-year plan which was announced around the end of August 1974. The new plan, which was to come into effect in January 1975, had an investment programme of SR213 billion[98] — five times the investment programme of the first plan.

We need not go into the details of the second plan. The point at issue is that there still seems to be some unwarranted association, indeed a parallelism, between the increase in the availability of financial resources and the investment programme which it is expected to undertake. Obviously, financing is not a bottleneck in Saudi Arabia, and unless the real bottlenecks (mainly skilled manpower and work attitudes) are widened, fast-expanding plans like the new one will remain underfulfilled. In fact, to be over-ambitious in planning, at the scale witnessed in the new Saudi plan, is as ineffective and ultimately frustrating as to be over-cautious. In addition, it can encourage wastefulness in financial resources and rashness in studies and execution. This is apart from the fact that excessive over-ambition, as in the present case, usually betrays insufficient identification and comprehension both of the promotive and the prohibitive factors in development.

4. CONCLUDING REMARKS

It would probably be right to say, at the same time, that the country has achieved a great deal, and very little, both with regard to physical transformation and to population progress. Thus, if the eye of the observer were to dwell on the islands of physical achievement and on the overall performance of the economy expressed in terms of national accounts, and his memory were to recapture the picture thirty or even twenty years ago, then the firm impression would be one of vast strides taken in the direction of building and equipping the economy and transforming important components of it. Likewise, if the observer were to compare the degree of spread, and the level of education, and even the change in the degree of acceptance of technological and cultural change, he would decide that part of the population observed has moved noticeably away from its position and level of two or three decades ago.

However, on closer examination it would appear that these are but islands of advancement and progress, even if large in some instances, and, as islands, they are not interconnecting or contiguous. Perhaps it would not be quite precise to say that they are not interconnecting, for social and economic change is a continuum in the sense that there is interaction and interdependence between the various components. Yet it would be true to maintain that the connections between the 'islands' are not very thick and strong, or that they are at times relationships of conflict and clash — the cultural conflict between the old and the new, the traditional and the modern, the socially conscious and the socially unconscious or indifferent, or even hostile — in brief the conflict between what is part of the twentieth century physically and culturally, and what is still part of the eighteenth.

This fragmentation of the picture is in large part due to the vastness of the country and sparsity of the population, which of necessity has meant that the population clusters in concentrations that are often far apart, with the socio-cultural and physical contacts in between, and the mutual impact naturally reduced. In strictly economic terms, this composite phenomenon of vastness and sparsity results in high unit costs of transport and communications facilities, and thus of production. Furthermore, because of the low levels of education and vocational and professional skill among the manpower at large, the situation cannot be considered as one of increasing returns to labour, because more labour employed at the present low level of qualification would not lead to greater product per labourer in the vast majority of instances.

The most outstanding of the islands to which reference has been made is the petroleum sector. Enough has been said about its primary and crucial role in the economy, and its central position as an engine of development to make it unnecessary to dwell on these aspects here again. It remains only to be emphasised that the drive towards sectoral diversification which is attempted now, for many years to come will have a chance of success only if the oil sector itself, dependence on which it is desired to reduce, will grow yet faster. This seeming contradiction is merely a matter of time, since it is only because the relative growth of other sectors and the materialisation of diversification is a function of the availability of various resources which the oil sector can provide, that the oil sector should grow further in relative terms for many years to come if it is to shrink in relative terms later on. What sounds like a paradox is natural and inevitable, given the factor endowments of Saudi Arabia and both the modest dimensions of the other sectors and their current low level of performance.

Two central factors must become operative if this whole process of transformation is to gain momentum and lead to its objectives. These are the modernisation of government and the vast improvement in its performance, and the spread of education and modernisation of its content. In turn, for these two processes to be possible, the condition of cultural change must be satisfied. This condition is indeed a whole basket of conditions, comprising values, motivation and incentives, system and locus of authority, attitude to time and to work, and so on. Intriguing as the discussion of these cultural components may be at this point, the temptation must be resisted, since the companion volume deals with them. For the moment it must be sufficient to confirm that there is room for vast changes in attitudes and outlook regarding all these matters, if far-reaching and deep-rooted change is to be sought – change which is consistent with development in the broad sense which is used in this study, involving liberation of the individual not merely from physical want but from social and cultural shackles as well.

However, four specific aspects of this liberation deserve to be mentioned, even if passingly here. The first is the need to draw women into the stream of modernisation through education and training, and particularly out of seclusion and into employment, on a par with men. The second is the faster sedentarisation of the bedouin through a complex programme involving not merely the provision of the economic and technical paraphernalia called for in the process of settlement, like water, cultivable land, credit and extension services, but also forward-looking education and the inculcation of new loyalties to replace those of nomadism. Thirdly, labour must be introduced into the new age as a partner, within a legislative framework which allows more participation and self-government and gives scope for self-expression and protest. And lastly, fiscal civic responsibility must be cultivated from now, despite the present abundance of revenues available to the state via petroleum exports. Today only the *Zakat* (a religious tax, similar to the Biblical tithe) is required of Saudi citizens. This is not enough. Those who earn income thanks to the circumstances and facilities that government and society make available must feel responsible, and be made to exercise such responsibility, towards the fiscal system and its resources. The *Zakat* embodies a noble principle, and it could well be preserved, but, in addition, progressive taxation ought to be instituted so that the lessons of fiscal responsibility and participation may be learned early when the availability of state revenue does not require taxpayer participation, for the time when such participation will be necessary but painfully difficult to obtain.

The concluding remarks ought not to convey the final impression that very little has been achieved very slowly. The opposite is true. But much more remains to be done. The weight of these remarks is to suggest that the present gaps and lags, and the conflicts and strains, have to be attended to profoundly, seriously and speedily before they become counter-forces that pull strongly in a direction opposite to that in which development efforts pull. Saudi society needs to mobilise the maximum forces at its disposal if it is to move firmly towards the objective of development in the full sense.

Saudi Arabia

NOTES

1. Organization of Petroleum Exporting Countries, OPEC, *Annual Statistical Bulletin*, for the relevant years.
2. The smaller estimate is a free-hand extrapolation of the census results and other estimates made in the early 1960s (including Asfour's estimate of 1963 – see the following notes). A small, more recent estimate by Asfour (published in 1972, noted further down) put the population range at between 4m and 6m. If 5m is adopted (as a mean) for 1971 and adjusted at 3 per cent annually to the end of 1974, the lower estimate would be about 5.6m. On the other hand, UN and IMF sources (see, for instance, UN *Statistical Yearbook 1973*, p. 70, and *IFS* December 1974) estimate the population at 8.2m for mid-1972. This would become about 8.9m by the end of 1974, again assuming a rate of net increase of 3 per cent per annum. (Reference in the text to the 'repudiation' of the census results is quoted from 'Notes' following the table on 'Population' in UN *Statistical Yearbook 1973*, p. 78.)
3. Central Planning Organization, *Economic Report, 1388-1389* (Riyadh). There is greater recognition today (1975) that the desire to assert that the country has a large population (close to 9m) is both political and economic in motivation. The latter motive is believed to support the argument that the Kingdom has to face heavy financial responsibilities at home and cannot therefore be very permissive in giving grants and loans.
4. I have mainly relied on the following surveys and studies for the 3-decade period 1944-75: (a) Royal Institute of International Affairs, RIIA, *The Middle East: A Political and Economic Survey* (Oxford University Press, third edition, 1958), section on Saudi Arabia; (b) IBRD, 'An Approach to the Economic Development of Saudi Arabia', a report made in 1961 and restricted to limited use; (c) Edmond Y. Asfour, *Saudi Arabia: Long-Term Projections of Supply of and Demand for Agricultural Products* (Beirut, 1965); (d) Arabian American Oil Company, ARAMCO, 'A Quarter Century of Economic Change in Saudi Arabia' (paper for Management Development Seminar, 6 March 1965); (e) Faysal Abdur-Rahman Al-Sudayri, *The Kingdom of Saudi Arabia and its Economic Development* (Riyadh, 1967; Arabic); (f) The General Union of Chambers of Commerce, Industry and Agriculture in the Arab Countries, *Economic Development in the Arab Countries 1950-1965* (Beirut, 1967; Arabic); (g) Arab Economic Bureau, *The Saudi Economy* (Beirut, 1967; Arabic); (h) UN Economic and Social Office in Beirut, UNESOB, 'Growth and Development Perspectives in Saudi Arabia' in *Studies in Development Problems in Selected Countries of the Middle East, 1969* (New York, 1969), pp. 25-34; (i) Ahmad Assah, *Miracle of the Desert Kingdom* (London, 1969); (j) Edmond Y. Asfour, 'Problems and Prospects of Economic Development of Saudi Arabia, Kuwait, and the Gulf Principalities', in Charles A. Cooper and Sidney S. Alexander (eds.), *Economic Development and Population Growth in the Middle East* (New York, 1972); (k) Saudi Arabian Monetary Agency, SAMA, *Annual Report* (series of annual issues, the most recent of which is for 1392-93 A. H. (1973), published in June 1974); (l) Europa Publications, *The Middle East and North Africa, 1971-72, 1972-73, 1973-74*, and *1974-75* (Annual edition, London); (m) The General Union of Chambers ... etc., *Arab Economic Report* (Beirut, various years ending with the 1974 issue; Arabic); and (n) Said H. Hitti and George T. Abed, 'The Economy and Finances of Saudi Arabia', in IMF, *Staff Papers*, Vol. XXI, No. 2, July 1974, pp. 247-306. Furthermore, I have greatly benefited from official reports not for public circulation that were put at my disposal by various government offices in the Kingdom. I have been allowed to peruse these documents but asked in a few instances not to make verbatim quotations from them. Where quotations or direct references are made, this is with explicit permission.
5. ARAMCO, *Aramco Handbook, 1960*, p. 171, for the early years; BP, *Statistical Review of the World Oil Industry 1972* and *1973* for 1971, 1972 and 1973; and Nicolas Sarkis, 'The Energy Crisis and the Challenge of Development in the Arab Countries', Paper No. 132 (A-1) submitted to the Ninth Arab Petroleum Congress, held at Dubai, 10-16 March 1975, for the estimate for 1974 (Table 1, p. 16).
6. In fact, the first budget was for the fiscal year 1947/8. However, only four annual budgets were published for the decade 1948-57. (See Hitti and Abed, loc. cit., p. 278). Consequently 1954 marks the meaningful start of budgeting, since the process has continued uninterrupted ever since.
7. Hitti and Abed (loc. cit., p. 287) estimate the debt at $480m by June 1958, 'the equivalent of one year's revenue'.
8. Arab Economic Bureau, op. cit., p. 242. The imbalance of the years 1954-7 and its outcome is discussed in the general surveys referred to in Note 4.
9. ARAMCO, 'A Quarter Century ...', p. 5.
10. See Assah, op. cit., pp. 75-8, for a narration of these events.
11. Asfour, op. cit. (*Saudi Arabia: Long-Term Projections ...*), pp. 17-18 and 129-35. The next estimate referred to is contained in Charles Issawi and Mohammad Yeganeh, *The Economics of Middle Eastern Oil* (New York, 1962). UNESOB's estimate appears in *Studies in Development Problems ... 1968*, p. 28. Finally the official estimates for 1962/3–1964/5 are recorded in Kingdom of Saudi Arabia, Ministry of Finance and National Economy, Central Department of Statistics, *The Gross Domestic Product of Saudi Arabia 1382/83 through 1388/89 A. H.* (Riyadh, 1390 A. H., September 1970 A. D.), Table III. It is worth noting at this point that I have adopted the years of the Gregorian Calendar all through, not the Hijri (Hejirah) years. The rough translation of the latter into the former is done by deducting '20' from the last two digits to the right. Anybody who is disturbed by the modest degree of imprecision involved in such a process ought to be sobered by the thought that the data themselves are very tentative and usually contain a large margin of error.
12. SAMA, *Annual Report 1392-93 A. H.* (1973), Table XXV, p. 109, for the wholesale price index, and pp. 13/14 for inflation between 1971/2 and 1972/3.

13. Asfour, op. cit., p. 43.
14. General Union of Chambers of Commerce..., *Arab Economic Report* (1974 issue), pp. 381 and 387.
15. Calculated from Table 4.2, where rise in factor payments abroad was all deducted from the contribution of the oil sector to GDP. This might press the contribution to GNP downwards slightly, but not seriously.
16. This judgement is more critical in tone than that expressed by Asfour, loc. cit., p. 375, or the implicit judgement in Hitti and Abed, loc. cit., pp. 264-8.
17. Central Planning Organization (CPO), *Development Plan 1390 A. H.* (August 1970), Table 13, p. 75.
18. See UNESOB, *Studies on Development Problems..., 1968* (pp.27/8), for reference to a lower set of capital-output ratios in the oil and the non-oil sectors respectively in the economy at large.
19. Ibid., p. 27.
20. SAMA, various issues of the *Annual Report*, ending with the 1972/3 issue.
21. SAMA, *Annual Report 1392-93 A. H.*, p. 47.
22. Information for 1966/7–1972/3 obtained from UN ECWA, Beirut, based on recent tables prepared by the Central Department of Statistics (CDS).
23. The fullest and most recent discussion of manpower exists in an International Labour Office report prepared in 1971, entitled *Report to the Government of the Kingdom of Saudi Arabia on Manpower Assessment and Planning* (Geneva, 1971), and in the *Economic Report 1970* (Ch. IV). However, both these documents are confidential and may not be quoted from directly. (The ILO had prepared and presented other reports earlier.)
24. UNESCO, *Comparative Statistical Data on Education in the Arab States, An Analysis: 1960-61–1967-68* (published by the Regional Center for Educational Planning and Administration, Beirut, 1969), p. 49.
25. *Statistical Yearbook 1973*, p. 36. For an informative source, see Ministry of Education, *Education Diary for the Year 1391-1392 A. H.* (Riyadh, 1392; Arabic).
26. CDS, *Demographic Survey 1385/86 A. H.*
27. *Development Plan 1390 A. H.*, Table 13, p. 75, and Table 16, p. 78 give the size of employment which is smaller than the labour force estimate by 68.7 thousand — presumably representing the unemployment gap.
28. Information (based on ILO, op. cit.) obtained from authoritative persons interviewed. See also Asfour, loc. cit., p. 374; Hitti and Abed, loc. cit., pp. 270-3; and 'Census of Establishments 1971' reported on in *Statistical Yearbook 1972*.
29. For reserves, and production in 1974, see Nicolas Sarkis, 'The Energy Crisis and the Challenge of Development in the Arab Countries', Paper No. 132 (A-1) submitted to the Ninth Arab Petroleum Congress, Dubai, 10-16 March 1975, Table 1, p. 16. For production in earlier years, see BP, *Statistical Review of the World Oil Industry*, various annual issues.
30. ARAMCO, *Aramco Handbook: Oil and the Middle East* (1968), p. 92.
31. Ibid.
32. Sarkis, op. cit., Table 1, p. 16.
33. *Statistical Yearbook 1973*, pp. 239 and 242. However, refining capacity is stated as being 21m tons annually (157.5m barrels) in BP, *Statistical Review... 1973*, p. 12.

34. Information from the Directorate-General of Mineral Resources, up to 1972. More recent information has been collected from SAMA, *Annual Report 1392-1393 A. H.* (1973) and from General Union..., *Arab Economic Report*, 1974 issue. Allocations are collated from annual budgets and the *Development Plan 1390 A.H.* (hereafter the *Plan*), Chs. II and IX.
35. Directorate-General of Mineral Resources, *Mineral Resources of the Kingdom of Saudi Arabia – A Handbook of Investment and Development*, Bulletin No. 1, 1968.
36. Petromin, *Progress Report 1968*, p. 9.
37. Ibid., p. 5.
38. Ibid., p. 9.
39. General Union..., *Arab Economic Report* (1974 issue), Chapter on Saudi Arabia, as well as *Middle East Economic Survey* (a Beirut weekly), Vol. XVII, Nos. 26, 30, 31 and 39, and *Arab Oil and Gas* (Beirut fortnightly) for the same period. These sources cover developments till the end of 1974.
40. Information and quotations relating to the years preceding 1968 are from Petromin, *Progress Report 1968*. Information for 1968 to end of 1974 is from SAMA, *Annual Report* for various years, *Arab Economic Report*, the issues from 1971 through 1974, and a careful scrutinising of the weekly issues of *MEES* down to 31 December 1974, and the fortnightly issues of *AOG*.
41. Text published in English as a stencilled pamphlet by the Industrial Studies and Development Centre, ISDC.
42. Petromin, 'The General Petroleum and Mineral Organization', including the text of the Decree (undated pamphlet).
43. Text published in English as a stencilled pamphlet by ISDC.
44. Kingdom of Saudi Arabia, 'The Industrial Studies and Development Centre in the Service of Industry' (Pamphlet; 1st issue 1969; English and Arabic).
45. See for instance the Petromin and ISDC pamphlets referred to above, as well as: (a) Abdulhady Hassan Taher, 'Petromin and its Role in the International Industry', lecture delivered at the joint Harvard-MIT Seminar on Eastern Hemisphere Petroleum, at Boston on 26 April 1966; and (b) Ahamd Zaki Yamani, 'Foreign Investment Atmosphere in Saudi Arabia', lecture delivered at the Symposium of the International and Comparative Law Foundation, Dallas, Texas on 22 June 1966. It is worth noting that the policies and atmosphere of foreign investment in the Kingdom, in partnership with Saudi citizens or institutions, has remained virtually unchanged since the early and mid-1960s, except for the great expansion in opportunities.
46. United Nations, *Industrial Development in the Arab Countries* (Selected documents presented to the Symposium on Industrial Development of the Arab Countries, Kuwait, 1-10 March 1966), 'The Industrial Situation in Saudi Arabia', pp. 112-16. The quotation is from p. 112. For value added in manufacturing, see sources of Table 4.2 above (which record the value added at current prices as well).
47. Based on Tables XXVIII and XXIX (pp. 112-15) in SAMA, *Annual Report 1392-1393 A. H.* (1973), and information obtained from ECWA (referred to earlier).
48. *MEES* and *AOG*, down to the end of 1974.
49. UN, *Industrial Development...*, p. 113. We rely

heavily on this source for the discussion of industry up to the mid-1960s.

50. Ibid.
51. *Arab Economic Report*, 1974 issue, pp. 392/3.
52. SAMA, *Annual Report 1392-1393 A. H.* (1973), p. 36.
53. See the sources for Table 4.2 for GDP at current prices.
54. All data relating to the 1967 Survey come from *Statistical Yearbook 1390 A. H., 1970 A. D.*, Ch. V.
55. Reported on in *Statistical Yearbook 1393 A. H., 1973 A. D.*, Ch. XI, 'Census of Establishments'.
56. See Edmond Y. Asfour, op. cit., for a discussion of the situation in the early sixties, and for projections of supply of and demand for agricultural products in the Kingdom.
57. SAMA, *Annual Report 1392-1393 A. H.* (1973), Table XX, pp. 102-3 for a breakdown of imports.
58. FAO, *Indicative World Plan for Agricultural Development 1965 – 85, Near East*, Subregional Study No. 1, Vol. II, p. 101, for the earlier estimate; and FAO, *Production Yearbook, 1973*, p. 5 for the more recent. The note referred to was supplied to the writer in the spring of 1972.
59. Hitti and Abed, loc. cit., p. 269, in a table quoting Ministry of Agriculture and based on 'data collected over the period 1961-67'.
60. Ibid., p. 268, and Asfour, loc. cit., pp. 380-1. This estimate is not irreconcilably far from that in FAO, *Production Yearbook 1973* referred to above.
61. This is the summary contained in a report on agriculture and water to whose substance I have been allowed to refer, though not with direct quotation. See also: Ministry of Agriculture and Water, 'Basic Information on the Two Sectors of Agriculture and Water with a Memorandum on the Most Important Projects that are being Executed' (September 1969, updated to spring 1972; stencilled; Arabic); the memorandum 'Agriculture in the Kingdom' already referred to; and finally SAMA, *Annual Report 1389-90 A. H.*, pp. 48-54.
62. Parsons-Bazil Report, Vol. III, *Water Resources* (Riyadh, September 1968), p. 125. Earlier exploration efforts had been undertaken by FAO in 1950/1, and a French company in 1956. See RIIA, pp. 88-9.
63. Discussion of these projects relies on SAMA, *Annual Report 1392-1393 A. H. (1973)*, Asfour, loc. cit., and Europa Publications, *1973-74* edition, p. 551, as well as on the less recent note 'Agriculture in the Kingdom'.
64. FAO, *Production Yearbook 1973*, pp. 26-32.
65. For 1960/1, See *Statistical Yearbook 1388 A. H., 1968 A. D.*, p. 263; for 1973-4, see SAMA, *Annual Report 1392-1393 A. H. (1973)*, p. 46.
66. Information from the Ministry of Communications.
67. The source of information is largely pamphlets and reports by the Ministry of Communications. Of particular value is the report entitled *Roads and Ports in Saudi Arabia* (Riyadh, 1391 A. H., 1971 A. D.). SAMA reports and Statistical Yearbooks are also source material of importance. Finally, I have also benefited from interviews. It ought to be indicated that data sometimes vary from one source to another, in which case I choose what seems to me the more authoritative source.
68. SAMA, *Annual Report 1392-1393 A. H. (1973)*, p. 48.
69. *Statistical Yearbook 1973*, p. 271.
70. Ibid., p. 282.
71. Ibid., pp. 292 and 286.
72. Aramco, *Aramco Handbook, 1968*, p. 184.
73. Yusif A. Sayigh, 'Problems and Prospects of Development in the Arabian Peninsula', in *International Journal of Middle East Studies*, No. 2 (1971), p. 43. (Article reprinted in Derek Hopwood (ed.), *The Arabian Peninsula: Society and Politics*, London, 1972.)
74. SAMA, *Annual Report 1392-1393 A. H. (1973)*, p. 50.
75. Ibid., p. 65 and Table XXVI, p. 110.
76. *Statistical Yearbook 1973*, pp. 251 and 254.
77. Doxiadis Associates, *Riyadh, Existing Conditions* (July 1968).
78. *Statistical Yearbook 1973*, pp. 168 and 171. The estimate of sheep slaughtered was obtained in an interview.
79. See SAMA, *Annual Report 1392-1393 A. H. (1973)*, Table XIX, pp. 100-1, for the balance of payments from 1963 through 1973. The receipts from pilgrimage rose from SR180m to SR909m in eleven years.
80. For the money supply in mid-1959, see *Statistical Yearbook 1385 A. H., 1965 A. D.*, Ch. VIII, 'Financial Statistics'; for 1974, see *IFS*, December 1974. The calculations which follow, relating growth of money supply to that of GNP, are based on data in the various issues of the *Yearbook* and of *IFS*, for money supply, and the sources of Table 4.2 above, for GNP at current prices.
81. Before 1964/5, Sections III and IV were presented together. Their combined total for 1958/9 was SR840.8m. For sources of information, see Table 4.13.
82. Hitti and Abed, loc. cit., pp. 283-7; for the grouping, see Table 17, p. 284.
83. SAMA, *Annual Report 1392-1393 A. H. (1973)*, Table IX (b), p. 90.
84. SAMA, *Annual Report 1389-90 A. H.*, pp. 36-7.
85. *IFS*, December 1974.
86. The Statutes of the Fund appeared in the Official Gazette, *Umm al-Qura*, on 20 September 1974.
87. The latest issue of the *IFS* available at the time of writing is that of December 1974. According to it, the net foreign assets of SAMA by the end of May were $8,340m. They had been rising by $1,000m a month over the three preceding months. So it could legitimately be expected that the assets would be at least $15,000m by the end of December 1974. This approach to estimation reaches the same results as the approach in the text.
88. I have relied heavily for information on education and social affairs on the following sources: (a) Ministry of Education, *Report on Education in the Kingdom of Saudi Arabia for the Year 70/71 A. D.* (prepared for the 33rd Session of the International Education Conference in Geneva; stencilled; Arabic); (b) Ministry of Education, *Education Diary for the Year 1391-1392 A. H.* (1392; Arabic); (c) Ministry of Social Affairs, *Report Presented to the First Conference of Arab Ministries of Social Affairs* (held at the Arab League, Cairo, October 1970; stencilled; Arabic); (d) Recent issues of SAMA, *Annual Report*,

the relevant sections; and (e) Recent issues of *Statistical Yearbook*, the relevant chapters on education and social affairs. (Specific references will be made when it is necessary.) Furthermore, I have had extensive interviews related to education, health and social conditions and efforts.

89. See SAMA, *Annual Report 1389-90 A. H.*, pp. 58-63 and *Annual Report 1392-1393*, pp. 59-62.

90. Comparison of enrolment as a percentage of total population in the twelve countries covered by this study has been undertaken on the basis of data in UNESCO, op. cit., Tables 1.2, 2.2 and 2.3. Table 1.3 was used for the calculation of the number of Saudis in the age groups 5-19 years, which are approximately the years of pre-university schooling.

91. Indeed, a series of articles appeared in May 1966 in the leading paper in which the Head of the Council of 'Ulema (Theologians) claimed — among other things — that he had repudiated the contention by the infidels that the earth was spherical.

92. Quantitative information from *Statistical Yearbook 1973*, Ch. III, 'Health'.

93. Ibid., pp. 72-3.

94. I rely mainly on three sources: (a) Interviews with the President of the CPO (who is the Minister of State for Planning), and his senior assistants; (b) CPO, *Development Plan 1390 A. H.;* and (c) *SAMA*, various issues of the *Annual Report* for allocations for, and expenditure on, development projects.

95. *Plan*, p. 21.

96. Ibid., p. 23.

97. SAMA, *Annual Report 1389-1390 A. H. (1970)*, p. 39.

98. *MEES*, Vol. XVII, No. 46, 6 September 1974.

5 JORDAN

A little over two decades ago, a perceptive and able Western economist, then serving in the Arab world, could see nothing ahead of the Jordanian economy but stagnation at a low level of income per head.[1] In addition to a dearth of natural resources and of local skills, and the continuous struggle with the desert whose onslaught against the settled areas was physical, cultural, sociological and technological, there was the further imposition on the original society of the Palestinian expellees who had to flee their homes and country in their hundreds of thousands after the Zionist take-over of Palestine, to seek refuge in a country incapable of coping with its own population.

Against this background, the energetic movement forward of the Jordanian economy is as remarkable as it was unexpected. Even compared with the oil-producing Arab countries (except such cases as Libya at the outset of the fantastically steep rise in its oil production and revenue, and except the major oil producers since October 1973) the growth rate of the Jordanian economy, in the decade and a half preceding the catastrophic war of June 1967 between Israel and three of its neighbours, has been uniquely high. Iraq, as a case for comparison, registered a higher rate, but that was only for a brief period which began with the very early fifties and ended in the middle of 1958.

The Jordanian case is of special interest to the development economist because it forces him to widen the angle of his vision and look for explanations and determinants of development beyond the conventional factors of land, capital, labour and entrepreneurship narrowly defined. True enough, all these factors were altered favourably as a result of the influx of the Palestinian expellees and the merger, in April 1950, between what was then known as Transjordan (today's East Bank of the Hashemite Kingdom of Jordan) with eastern Palestine, specifically the area not occupied by the Zionists in the fighting of 1948/9, which after the merger became known as the West Bank of the Hashemite Kingdom of Jordan. The influx brought into Transjordan more highly skilled administrators, craftsmen and agriculturists, as well as capitalists, entrepreneurs, industrialists, physicians, engineers, lawyers, teachers, nurses — in short, a large body of men and women much better equipped for handling a more sophisticated economy than was remotely available at the time to the original community. Furthermore, the newcomers, while including many destitute people who carried nothing with them but their misery and the clothes on their backs, also brought in funds estimated at 20 million Palestinian pounds[2] (the £P had been legal tender in Transjordan and was equal to one pound sterling). This sum was probably greater than the total money supply in Transjordan at the time. Furthermore, the land which was renamed the West Bank was much more productive than Transjordan in fruit and vegetables, and initially better equipped with manufacturing industry and trading establishments.

But this windfall also represented a huge burden. The population of Transjordan tripled within a matter of weeks, without the resources available undergoing comparable increase or expansion. Public administration, public services, housing and community facilities, foodstuffs and all the other goods needed — all had to expand in order to cope with the demographic elephantine growth, without adequate means being available and while a state of war with Israel still existed, albeit in low key.

Without fully anticipating the discussion that will follow in this chapter, and the assessment of the determinants of development in Volume Two of the book, it can be said here that at least three accommodating factors combined to help overcome the disadvantages attaching to the new burdens, to capitalise on the advantages that formed the other side of the burden, and to give the economy the push which it badly needed to bring about the commendable rates of growth of the past two decades. These factors were: foreign aid which, though modest in absolute terms, constituted a high percentage of GNP and made possible otherwise impossible investment; a relatively efficient and development-minded government and civil service; and a high level of achievement motivation among the skilled Palestinians, stemming from their desire to compensate for the loss of homeland and career.

Two handicaps stand in the way of a complete examination of developments in the Jordanian economy in the post-war period. The first refers to the definition of the subject examined. The Kingdom was established in 1946, at which time it included only the lands east of the river Jordan. In 1950, the size of the country and of the population changed upon the formal merger with Transjordan of the eastern hilly parts of Palestine which had not been occupied by the Zionists in 1948. For the sake of comparison we will therefore largely ignore the four years between 1946 and 1950 about which information is scanty anyway, and treat 1950 as our starting point. References to the earlier period will only be made in order to bring into relief certain points of the background to the period which is our main interest. The second handicap arises from the loss of the West Bank as a result of the war with Israel in June 1967. In a way this is the reverse process of the first handicap. As the 1967 occupation has been the result of war, and has been denied legality by almost all countries of the world and in many United Nations resolutions, particularly Security Council Resolution No. 242 of 22 November 1967, and on the basis of moral and nationalistic considerations, we will continue to consider Jordan as it was constituted, in territory and population, prior to the occupation. Official statistics, wherever possible, follow the same practice. Where necessary, explanatory notes are added to indicate what information in fact relates to the occupied territory.

1. THE BACKGROUND[3]

Transjordan, on the eve of the merger, was a large country, with some 91,000 square kilometres (about half the area of Syria), and a population estimated for the end of 1947 at 375,000. The land was mostly uncultivable, considering the scantiness of rainfall in general and the poverty of river, *wadi* (little river of great seasonal variation) and spring resources. (The thirty-year average of rainfall for 1931-60 records the highest rainfall in Ajloun, at a mere 628 mm per year, and the lowest at Ma'an at 39 mm.[4] The overall annual average for more than 86 per cent of the country is below 200 mm,[5] so most of the country falls within the sub-cultivation level of rainfall. As to the Jordan and Yarmouk rivers, their water is only available in limited degree, owing to the other claims by Israel and Syria, respectively, to the two rivers.)

The area cultivated in the East Bank was roughly 5.5 to 6 million dunoms, or 550,000 to 600,000 hectares, in the early fifties. According to the *1953 Census of Agriculture*, total cultivated area was 575,500 ha; out of this total, about 43,700 ha were irrigated, including 10,100 ha of orchards and vineyards. Against these areas, the West Bank had, for the same year, a total cultivated area of 243,500 ha or about 30 per cent of the whole area for the Kingdom. Out of this figure, the irrigated area was 32,200 ha while the area devoted to fruit trees and vineyards was 58,300 ha. (The tree-planted area was not all irrigated.) In other words, the West Bank was disproportionately fortunate with regard to cultivated area out of its total area (which is some 600,000 ha), and with regard to irrigated and tree-planted area. It is interesting to note, in this connection, that the official *Report on Agriculture Census 1965*[6] shows a slight drop in the area of unirrigated crops compared with the 1953 census, but a considerable drop (from 75,900 ha to 44,300 ha) in irrigated area. Considering the fact that twelve years of development had intervened between the two censuses, and the assumption that water resources were better harnessed and more fully utilised in 1965 than in 1953, the drop in irrigated area is surprising, all the more since the 1953 census did not include ownerships below one hectare in size. The phenomenon can only be adduced to poor quality of data in the earlier census. Lastly, with regard to this account, the total cultivable area in the East Bank must have been (and remains) around 700,000 ha, while that of the West Bank was (and remains) around 300,000 ha. In other words, given the present level of technology and available resources, the room for expansion is quite limited.[7]

The population, estimated at 375,000 in 1947, included tent-dwelling nomads (bedouin), whose number according to the 1961 census was over 80,000.[8] Probably the number in 1947 or 1948 was not less, if not definitely more, on the assumption that the increase in population is probably smaller than the rate of sedentarisation. But in any case, the impact of nomadic tradition is even now of much greater significance than the figures quoted would suggest, in view of the tenacity of 'desert culture' and the cohesive social organisation of nomadic tribes. It is still common practice even for urbanised groups (and more so for villagers) to identify themselves as tribes and clans, more or less as they did when still in tribal nomadic state.

This population was very poor in 1947 or 1948. Income per head was probably no more than £P15 in Transjordan, as against £P53 for Palestinian Arabs for the same year.[9] It was very poorly equipped in terms of education and managerial and technical skills. A large proportion of the big businesses, stores selling cars and household equipment and manufactured consumer goods, as well as of manufacturing establishments, were either branches of Palestinian firms or partnerships between Transjordanians and Palestinians or Syrians. Many of the country's high-school pupils were schooled in Palestine. This latter country was the market for any excess cereals that Transjordan could afford to export, and the supplier of a large volume of the fruit, vegetables and manufactured products imported into Transjordan. Furthermore, Haifa in Palestine was almost the sole port for the handling of Transjordan's imports.

Data are not available on money supply, public finance or balance of payments for the years 1946-9. The first sets of data apply to 1950, and are mostly intelligent guesses, or official statistics with a rather high margin of error. Yet even in 1950, after the influx of hundreds of thousands of Palestinian expellees and the merger between the two Banks of the Jordan, the magnitudes of money supply and other national aggregates suggest a very low level of development.

At this point, we must, because of sheer dearth of data, stop referring to the background between 1946 and 1948, and use the period 1948-50 as our reference point. From 1950 onwards, statistical material becomes more abundant, even if its quality and coverage still leave a great deal to be desired.

It was stated earlier that the impact of the take-over by the Zionists of a large part of Palestine in 1948/9 (78 per cent of the country seized and declared the State of Israel) had very serious territorial and demographic effects on Transjordan. The most immediate of these effects was the tripling of the population. According to various tenable estimates,[10] the original population of Transjordan as at the end of 1947, namely 375,000, was increased within a matter of weeks by another 350,000 Palestinian Arab expellees who crossed the river for safety. Furthermore, upon the merger with the West Bank, the population of the new State of Jordan grew by another 460,000 persons, bringing the total to 1,185,000 — almost 3.2 times the original population of Transjordan. In terms of territory, the merger added a mere 7 per cent to total area but some 30 per cent to arable area.

As already stated, housing and community facilities, foodstuffs and other necessities were all dangerously short of the dramatically increasing needs. Many of the facilities literally broke down under the pressure, and had it not been for Arab and international aid — in the form of tents, essential foodstuffs, clothing, medicaments and later clinics, there would have been starvation and death on a very large scale. Even years later, there were still expellees living in caves, makeshift tin huts, or crowding already crowded relatives in the cities and towns whose hospitality was being tried to dangerous extremes. The demographic problem was more serious because of two additional complicating factors. Some 120,000 Palestinians living in the West Bank, who were not considered by UNRWA (United Nations Relief and Works Agency for Palestine Refugees in the Near East) as refugees, because they had not lost both homes *and* means of support, suddenly became destitute upon the signing of the Armistice Agreement between Jordan and Israel on 3 April 1949, because although their houses were on the Arab side of the line, their land was on the Israeli side. The second problem arose from the fact that many thousands of West Bank residents, before the establishment of Israel, worked in factories, businesses and farms in the Arab area which fell into Zionist hands in 1948/9. They too were not technically 'refugees' according to UNRWA's definition of the term, and were therefore not eligible for relief. In any case, the relief — whether in terms of food or services — was minimal. The food rations provided between 1,500 and 1,800 calories a day per person; and in terms of overall services, the budget of UNRWA over the years (including such supplementing aid from WHO, UNICEF and UNESCO) has provided between 7 or 8 cents' worth for the early years and 22 cents' worth for 1973/4, of services per relief-recipient per day. (The rise is solely due to the inflationary course of prices between 1951/2 and 1973/4.) This miserably small allotment includes the cost of administration as well.[11]

The focus of this chapter is neither the Palestine problem (in so far as part of Palestine became in 1950 part of Jordan), nor even the problem of the Palestine 'refugees' in Jordan. But the fact that two-thirds of Jordan's population is Palestinian in origin makes it imperative that, from time to time and as it becomes necessary, specific reference be made to the expellees and their problems and activities, or to the impact of the problem on Jordan. It is with this qualification in mind that some other aspects of the expellee problem will be examined in their relevance to the Jordanian economy.

Two major aspects come readily to mind. The first is the unduly high level of unemployment which has continuously beset Jordan, but with special vehemence in the early years after the influx of Palestinian expellees. As it is, job opportunities were not enough to absorb all Transjordanians into full employment even before the influx; the problem was compounded thereafter. No economy, no matter how developed and well-equipped in terms of capital goods, dynamic technology and fast-growing national income could in a matter of weeks receive and find employment for an influx of newcomers twice the size of the original population. Understandably Jordan, a country at a very low level of development, with backward technology and inadequate capital goods, at a very low level of income *per capita*, was simply overwhelmed with the influx, and suffered massive outright unemployment, amounting on average perhaps to a third, but initially to over half, of the total labour force, as well as a large measure of disguised unemployment.[12] Of those employed, many could only obtain seasonal and precarious employment. The development programme which the IBRD mission suggested could not but admit that, even in the best of circumstances, at the close of the ten years of the programme the labour force would have grown in size by more than the new jobs created.

The second aspect resulting from the Palestine problem, and Jordan's special involvement owing to the demographic structure arising from the Arab-Israeli war, was the need to form, equip and maintain an army much larger than otherwise would have been necessary. All along, under the British Mandate over Transjordan and before the establishment of Israel, the British fully subsidised this army — obviously not as an act of charity but because it served their imperial interests in the region to have a British-financed and — officered efficient army which could be used within and outside Transjordan. (It was actually used in Palestine against the Arab revolt of 1936-9, and later in 1941 to counter the nationalist anti-British and anti-Palace *coup d'état* in Iraq led by Rashid 'Aali al Kaylani.) The situation required expanding the army considerably after 1948, with the British again subsidising it heavily but with the Americans, less than a decade later, replacing the British as the major source of general aid to the budget (apart from aid for specific development purposes). Furthermore, the government began to receive financial support from three Arab states (Syria, Egypt and Saudi Arabia) in the late fifties. Much later, after the 'Khartoum Arab Summit Conference' of September 1967 — aid to the tune of JD40 million* annually was pledged by the three oil-rich countries: Kuwait, Saudi Arabia and Libya. Jordan's strained relations with the Palestinian resistance movement and its anti-Communist, pro-Western stance have resulted in the inflow of substantial aid from the United States, while its hardship because of Israeli occupation of the West Bank has brought in significant aid from Arab sources. The convergence, seemingly paradoxical, is thus easily explained.[13]

It has been stated that the relatively extensive *per capita* economic aid received by Jordan has been a factor in its remarkable growth rate. It is worth noting that the IBRD mission, which reported on the economy in 1957, in looking at the early fifties and projecting ten years ahead, remained pessimistic with regard to prospects, in spite of the improvement it could envisage as a result of the expenditure programme it then suggested. Its pessimism centred mainly around two points: the ability of Jordan to develop its agricultural and mining resources beyond a certain level, and the restricted demand capacity in the neighbouring countries for Jordan's foreseeably expanded production of vegetables and fruit. The pessimism has proved faulty in both instances, as we will have occasion to see in the next section. Nevertheless, as a careful researcher writing much more recently has concluded, the remarkable performance of the years since 1950 should not be mechanistically and optimistically projected into the late 1970s, the 1980s and beyond. This applies to growth rates in general and to agricultural expansion in particular. Mazur, the researcher in question, treats the modest area of cultivable but still uncultivated land, and the water available or potentially available for irrigation, as the major constraints facing such expansion.[14]

It remains to be said, finally, that the background of the economy was mainly primitive

*Jordanian dinars.

agricultural, with very few small, unsophisticated industries (the types conventionally initiated — food processing, soft drinks and beer, cigarettes and matches, furniture, biscuits and the like). Advanced professional and business services — consulting firms, insurance, advanced local banking, aviation, refrigeration, etc. did not then exist. With regard to agriculture specifically, many vegetables were not grown in Transjordan up to 1947/8, but were introduced later. Furthermore, owing to the harshness of nature and the scarcity of rainfall and river water readily available for irrigation, the farmers were on the whole very hard up, with a high level of debt.[15] The problem was so serious, and the individual debts growing so fast owing to the usurious rates of interest applied, that the IBRD mission suggested a moratorium on debt settlement until a Royal Commission could be formed in order to assess the debts on the basis of fair rates of interest.

2. ECONOMIC DEVELOPMENT AND STRUCTURAL CHANGE 1950-74

Overall and Sectoral Economic Growth

The starting point for an examination of development and structural change cannot go back much beyond 1952, the first year for which national income estimates were produced. These were prepared for the Jordanian government by the Economic Research Institute at the American University of Beirut, but were never published or given wide circulation.[16] Right after that, R. S. Porter, formerly with the British Middle East Office but later with the Middle East Development Division at the British Embassy in Beirut, produced a new set of estimates covering the years 1954-9.[17] From 1959 on, the Department of Statistics has produced its own estimates, up to the year 1973. It is to be observed that the first set of estimates was restricted to national income, while later estimates provided data on gross domestic product and gross national product.

Fortunately, it is possible to link the different series and undertake comparisons over the years, since the first series prepared by the Economic Research Institute estimated national income at JD50 million, while Porter's estimates are only slightly lower for the same year. Porter's estimates for the years 1954-8 are here linked to those of the Department of Statistics for the years 1959-73. This is legitimate because the same methods were generally used. However, estimates by the Department of Statistics are believed to be of wider coverage. (Porter's estimates for 1959 are discarded in favour of the official estimates for that year.) Tables 5.1 and 5.2 below present first national income for the three years 1952-4, and then GDP and GNP for the years 1954-73.

Table 5.2, as already indicated, is a composite table originally prepared by two different sources. It presents GDP, GNP, and for the last nine years, NNP as well.

It would be rash to compare national income for 1952 with that for 1973, owing to the difference in the coverage and quality of data for the two years, and the different methodology used. None the less, as a simple rule-of-thumb comparison, we can set the two figures side by side as a first approximation at an examination of the growth of the economy in the intervening years. The result is overall net growth of 430 per cent (1952 = 100), or an average annual growth (cumulative) of about 8.5 per cent at current prices. If we take 1954 as base year, and compare GDP and GNP at market prices in 1973 with 1954, we find that the average cumulative annual rate of growth for GDP has still hovered around 8.5 per cent (overall total net growth of 400 per cent for GDP, and 420 per cent for GNP).

There is no adequate price index series for Jordan with which to deflate the market-price series and to find out growth at constant prices. For the earlier period 1954-9, Porter accepts the available wholesale price index which showed a rise for these years of 22 per

Table 5.1: National Income 1952-4 (JD million)

Sector	1952	1953	1954
Agriculture	17.6	11.6	19.7
Mining and quarries	0.1	0.1	0.2
Industry	1.8	2.1	2.7
Construction	0.6	0.4	0.6
Real estate	4.8	4.8	4.9
Public utilities	0.2	0.1	0.1
Transport and communications	2.7	2.9	3.2
Government	7.6	7.9	8.8
Trade	7.4	7.1	7.9
Services	1.4	1.5	1.6
Finance	0.3	0.3	0.3
Total	44.5	38.8	50.0

Source: Economic Research Institute, American University of Beirut. Mimeographed. 1956.

cent, thus leaving a rate of growth in real terms of 34 per cent, or 5.5 per cent per annum.[18] The FAO's *Jordan: Country Report,* while again regretting the absence of a reliable index, affirms that 'it is safe to say, on the basis of available data, that Jordan has enjoyed a degree of long-run price stability which is not often encountered in a developing country whose money income rises at a fast pace'[19] — thanks to the development of productive resources simultaneously with the presence of large unemployed and underemployed manpower resources, and to the monetary and import policies applied, the combination of which made available goods and services fast enough to counter inflationary pressures. Various attempts have been made to establish a usable and defensible index, but these vary widely from each other. The FAO *Country Report* seems to suggest a price rise on the average for the years 1954-66 of just under 2 per cent per annum. This would indicate that growth in real terms has been about 6.5 per cent per annum on average for GDP and GNP. (It was only beginning with 1970 that the price stability began to be upset. Between 1970 and the end of 1973 prices rose by 49.4 per cent, according to *International Financial Statistics.*)

The series in Table 5.2 betrays wide variations from year to year in the total, owing in the main to the wide fluctuations in the contribution of the sector of agriculture. While it is true that there are fluctuations in other sectors, they are less frequent and less extreme. On the whole, the sudden spurts in the other sectors have been upwards. If these spurts happen to coincide with a good agricultural harvest, the net effect is a more than matching rise in total GDP at factor cost than in the share of the agricultural sector; if they happen not to coincide but to move in the opposite direction, then their effect is to cushion the impact of the drop in the harvest and therefore in the contribution of the agricultural sector. Broadly speaking, the combined sector 'trade and banking' seems generally to move in greater harmony with the size of the contribution of agriculture than any other sector. This is understandable because the size of the harvest in a predominantly agricul-

Table 5.2: Gross Domestic Product by Sector and Gross National Product at Current Prices 1954-73[a] (JD million)

Sector	1954	1955	1956	1957	1958	1959	1960	1961	1962	1963	1964	1965	1966	1967	1968	1969	1970	1971	1972	1973
Agriculture	14.2	6.2	19.0	12.8	12.9	15.1	14.6	25.3	20.9	22.1	34.1	34.1	27.7	38.7	27.6	36.3	28.7	37.8	39.0	28.5
Manufacturing, mining, electricity and water supply	4.2	5.2	6.3	6.8	7.6	6.9	7.6	9.5	8.8	11.5	13.8	17.9	19.2	19.6	22.3	25.2	22.1	23.3	26.9	30.5
Construction	1.2	1.5	1.7	1.9	2.4	4.7	4.5	4.5	6.1	6.1	5.4	7.9	9.3	8.7	9.8	10.9	7.8	7.5	11.5	18.0
Transport	4.4	5.5	6.8	8.3	9.0	10.7	11.1	12.6	12.5	12.8	12.0	12.6	14.4	14.6	14.6	16.0	15.9	16.2	17.0	20.0
Trade and banking	9.3	9.3	10.5	12.0	14.4	18.9	20.5	25.6	25.1	27.7	29.5	33.5	31.7	41.9	32.0	42.6	42.2	42.4	45.2	49.5
Ownership of dwellings	2.3	2.3	2.9	3.1	3.3	6.3	7.1	8.0	8.6	9.4	9.9	10.7	11.2	11.9	12.3	12.8	13.6	14.4	14.8	15.5
Public administration and defence	9.1	9.7	11.5	13.5	15.6	14.9	15.8	16.7	17.1	17.6	19.7	21.4	22.0	26.0	33.3	36.3	37.9	39.0	39.5	42.5
Services	3.0	3.3	2.7	3.7	3.9	7.8	8.3	8.6	9.5	10.4	11.2	12.8	14.1	15.2	16.6	18.3	21.3	22.0	23.1	25.5
GDP at factor cost	47.7	43.0	61.4	62.1	69.1	85.3	89.5	110.8	108.6	117.6	135.6	150.9	149.6	176.6	168.5	198.4	189.5	202.6	217.0	230.0
Plus: Indirect taxes	3.6	4.4	5.0	5.6	6.3	8.4	8.9	9.3	10.3	11.4	13.4	16.7	20.9	17.6	18.4	21.3	20.3	20.8	22.5	27.0
GDP at market prices	51.3	47.4	66.4	67.7	75.4	93.7	98.4	120.1	118.9	129.0	149.0	167.6	170.5	194.2	186.9	219.7	209.8	223.4	239.5	257.0
Net factor income from abroad	1.1	2.5	1.9	2.7	1.9	5.6	7.4	7.0	11.9	8.6	11.7	12.9	15.1	11.2	10.4	14.0	12.6	13.2	12.9	15.0
GNP at market prices	52.4	49.9	68.3	70.4	77.3	99.3	105.8	127.1	130.8	137.6	160.7	180.5	185.6	205.4	197.3	233.7	222.4	236.6	252.4	272.0
Less: depreciation allowances	—	—[b]	—	—	—	—	—	—	—	—	—	6.0	7.2	6.7	8.2	8.7	8.3	8.5	9.0	9.0
Less: indirect taxes	3.6	4.4	5.0	5.6	6.3	8.4	8.9	9.3	10.3	11.4	13.4	16.7	20.9	17.6	18.4	21.4	20.3	20.8	22.5	27.0
= NNP at factor cost (= national income at factor cost)[c]	—	—	—	—	—	—	—	—	—	—	—	141.3	157.1	157.5	181.1	170.7	203.6	193.8	207.1	220.9	236.0

a. We have followed the arrangement of Table 9, p.15, of FAO, *Country Report: Jordan* up to 1965. For the years 1966-8 we have used the *Statistical Yearbook 1969*, p.218; for the years 1969-72, Central Bank of Jordan, *Monthly Statistical Bulletin*, Vol.9, No.12, December 1973, Table 33; and for 1973, Central Bank of Jordan, *Tenth Annual Report, 1973* (Amman, 1974; Arabic), p.6. The 1973 estimates are provisional, and they do not include the estimates for depreciation. However, this writer has estimated depreciation at JD 9m and arrived at an NNP of JD236m.
b. — indicates non-availability of information.
c. A JD0.1m discrepancy appears in the years 1964 and 1965 for national income estimates between the table above and the *Statistical Yearbook 1969*, owing to rounding.

Jordan

tural country largely determines the volume of internal commerce, imports, exports and banking activities to finance the operations associated with the handling of the harvest.

Owing to the wide fluctuations in year-by-year contributions by agriculture, we have deemed it advisable in our examination of structural change to take a three-year average of the contributions of each of the sectors. This applies to data in Table 5.1 and to the first three and last three years in Table 5.2. Although the examination of the structure would not be overly influenced by the fact that the 1952-4 data relate to national income, while the data for 1954-73 relate to GDP, we will compare three sets of data: the sectoral distribution for national income for the average of the years 1952-4, that for the average GDP for the years 1954-6, and that for the average GDP for the years 1971-3. The results appear below in Table 5.3.

Table 5.3: Comparative Sectoral Structure Averaged for 1952-4, 1954-6 and 1971-3 (per cent)

Sector	1952-4	1954-6	1971-3
Agriculture	36.7	25.8	16.2
Manufacturing, mining, quarrying, water and electricity	5.6	10.3	12.4
Construction	1.2	2.9	5.7
Transport and communication	6.5	11.0	8.2
Trade and finance	17.5	19.1	21.1
Real estate	10.9	4.9	6.9
Government and defence	18.2	19.9	18.5
Services	3.4	5.9	10.9
Total	100.0	100.0[a]	100.0[a]

a. The figures do not add up to 100.0 because of rounding.

The sectors which have shown a consistent trend are agriculture, manufacturing, construction, trade and finance, and services. The first has lost consistently in importance, in relative terms, while the others have gained consistently. Furthermore, in absolute terms, agriculture has grown most slowly over the years — so slowly indeed, that its percentage contribution has dropped by more than half between 1952-4 and 1971-3, or by more than one-third between 1954-6 and 1971-3. All the other sectors listed have made gains, the fastest in relative terms being construction, followed by services, and then by manufacturing, mining and public utilities. It is worth noting that the commodity-producing sectors have suffered a drop in their contribution vis-à-vis the service sectors, from 43.5 per cent for 1952-4 and 39 per cent for 1954-6, to 34.3 per cent for 1971-3. The explanation is to be found in the considerable drop in the share of agriculture, without a compensating rise in manufacturing and construction, on the one hand, and in the large size of the share of the contributions of trade and finance, and of government and defence.

The contribution of the commodity sectors as a group is very small in Jordan. Only Lebanon among the countries included in this study has a slightly smaller contribution. But the case of Lebanon is less surprising, considering its much higher level of average GNP *per capita*, and the greater positive association that exists generally between higher *per capita* product and services share in national product, as the studies of Kuznets and others have demonstrated amply.[20] The sectors most responsible for this pattern in Jordan are agriculture with its 'abnormally' low relative contribution, manufacturing industry with a rather small share, and trade and government with their large relative contribution. We need not go into the reasons behind this pattern here; it is sufficient to mention that the government sector has a large share in national product in the majority of the Arab countries, owing to the vast expansion in the civil service and the security forces after independence (for reasons that do not always derive from need or efficiency). In the case of Jordan the army has become disproportionately large for a country with Jordan's population and domestic resources.

A discussion of the subject of structure calls for the examination of the economy from two other angles. The first relates to the comparison of the sectors' shares in GNP or GDP with the sectoral distribution of the labour force. However, this discussion will be deferred until we reach the subsection 'Population, Labour Force and Social Conditions' further down. The second angle is that of growth of national product and of individual sectors as between the West Bank and the East Bank.

When the Hashemite Kingdom of Jordan was formed in 1950 after the merger of the Palestinian enclave (later designated 'the West Bank') with Transjordan (designated 'the East Bank'), the West Bank had clear advantages over the East Bank in almost every respect — physical and human, economic and social. The arable land per inhabitant was less meagre in the West than in the East Bank, while industry (though not at a very commanding height) was more advanced, skilled manpower resources more abundant relatively and absolutely, and transport and communication, banking, insurance and construction better developed. By the time the two Banks were separated in the June war of 1967, the pattern had been reversed. Today in the mid-seventies, the discrepancy is even larger and more in favour of the East Bank, as the West Bank has lost more of its skilled cadres to the East Bank, and ceded more in the fields of manufacturing, banking and the professions. The contribution of the East Bank to the national product has become much larger than that of the West Bank, as has its share in national capital. Though the quantitative evidence of these statements regarding the reversal of the pattern is not abundant, it exists in adequate measure. Nevertheless, the marshalling of the evidence will not be attempted here.[21] Instead, the causes for the reversal will be explored, on the assumption of the tenability of the statements.

One of the main causes has been the relative backwardness itself of the East Bank in 1950, which made it necessary to devote more resources and effort to it than its population and area by themselves warranted, to enable it to catch up quickly with the West Bank. The East Bank was the centre of political gravity in the Kingdom, and that in itself required the construction and expansion of government buildings and facilities, and of the civil service. To this must be added the fact of the large influx of Palestinian refugees which necessitated and gave incentive to expansion in residential building, social services, shops, restaurants, transport, commercial activity and all that goes with demographic expansion. Many of the businesses, including banks, that had had their headquarters and centres in the West Bank reversed the arrangement and chose Amman instead of Jerusalem as home to their main offices. Much of the fast-growing army was recruited from the East Bank and located there, which meant that a larger share of the wage bill was paid in the East Bank, and that more army equipment, roads and barracks were also located there. With the severance of the ties between the West Bank and the rest of Palestine upon the establishment of Israel, the West Bank (and Transjordan, for that matter) lost the use of the close and convenient port of Haifa on the Mediterranean. As a result, the port of

Aqaba had to be developed, along with the road system connected with it. Likewise, land connections with Syria had to be improved in order to facilitate the use of the port of Beirut. Obviously, all this favoured the sector of transport in the East Bank, with all that goes with the sector with respect to equipment, import trade, financing, insurance and employment. Finally, the agricultural sector expanded thanks to the search for and harnessing of water resources in the East Bank, as well as the development of rain-fed agriculture. The largest irrigation scheme in the whole Kingdom, the East Ghor Canal project on the east side of the River Jordan, and several smaller projects on *wadis*, are located in the East Bank. In conclusion, even without invoking the accusation of favouritism to the advantage of the East Bank that is often made, there are enough objective causes for the faster growth that has been witnessed in the East Bank since 1950, to the point that this Bank ended by outdistancing the West Bank and acquiring a much heavier weight in the economic scales.

The Role of the External Sector

The importance of the service sectors is itself in part a function of the special circumstances of Jordan as a country which has always received foreign economic aid representing an unusually high proportion of its GNP. This is essentially the result of certain political factors, which differ with the difference in the angle of vision. From the standpoint of the United Kingdom and the USA, the large foreign (non-Arab) donors and/or creditors, Jordan is a reliable friend in an Arab world that has been largely disenchanted with and hostile to the West because of its support for Israel. To the Arab states that on three occasions — briefly in the late fifties, again beginning in 1964 and, more recently, beginning in 1967 — pledged (and fully or partly gave) financial support, Jordan was the Arab country with the longest armistice lines with Israel and therefore the country in greatest need of financial support in order to maintain a large defence army to provide some protection for itself against Israel.

The non-Arab aid received has flowed in without break, though with wide fluctuations, while Arab aid was soon discontinued in the late fifties when inter-Arab politics changed their pattern. The aid pledged and started in 1964 has also been erratic. The much larger volume of aid, which began flowing in the autumn of 1967 from three countries, has continued to flow without interruption from only one country — Saudi Arabia. Libya, the second contributor, stopped its payments totally late in 1970 as a result of the Jordanian army's attack of September 1970 on Palestinian guerrillas operating against Israel from Jordan, and has not resumed them since. The third country, Kuwait, also suspended its contribution, but resumed it a little after the Arab-Israeli war of October 1973.

The foreign aid — non-Arab and Arab alike — has permitted the government to expand, both in its civilian and its military branches, current and developmental alike, and has enabled the country to finance an import surplus of relatively large size. However, as Table 5.4 below reveals, the import surplus is very large in relation to GDP and GNP, but not as impressive in absolute terms on a *per capita* basis. Thus, although in percentage points of GNP or GDP, or total resources available, it is as high and occasionally higher than the import surplus of Israel, which is inordinately large, on a *per capita* basis it is of considerably more modest size.[22] Per Jordanian, on the average the import surplus has been about $49 per year for the period 1950 to 1974, whereas it has been $346 per Israeli for the same period.

Foreign official bilateral aid allocated to Jordan from Arab and non-Arab sources has totalled $2,085m from June 1945 to the end of 1973. (The largest Western donors and creditors are the United States, the United Kingdom and West Germany.) The balance of payments records however show an inflow of transfers to government (preponderantly grants) totalling $1,576m for the years 1950 to 1973. The difference is probably in part due to the discrepancy between allocations and actual disbursements, in part to some duplication in the method of calculation of the larger sum.[23] It ought to be noted that Jordan has further received substantial aid from multilateral agencies, particularly the IDA of the World Bank, but probably more substantial remittances over the years from Jordanians working in the Arab oil countries and sending financial help to their relatives back home. It is the convergence of all these streams of unrequited transfers and capital movements that has added up into a substantial inflow and permitted the financing of the import surplus plus the building up of reserves (in gold, foreign currencies, etc.) totalling $349.7m by the end of 1974. The relatively large inflow of aid has not imposed a heavy debt-servicing load on the economy since the grant component is very much larger than the loan component. The foreign public debt outstanding by the end of 1974 was merely JD79.72m. Most of the loans are owed to Britain, West Germany, the United States, Kuwait, Saudi Arabia and the IDA, in that order.[24]

According to Table 5.4, the average import surplus (i.e. deficit on current account) has been JD31.4 million per year, while the average aid received has been JD29.5 million. Jordan has received a certain amount of private aid — from charitable institutions and remittances from Jordanians abroad. This last item is the next most important one after official aid. Together, the inflow from private sources has more than closed the gap between average import surplus and average official aid. It is already apparent that foreign aid plays a vital role in the country's economy. Table 5.5 below reflects this role in another way, namely through presenting the import surplus in relation to GNP and total resources available.

The country's dependence on foreign financing of its import surplus was definitely becoming less marked after 1963, but rose again in 1966 and continued to be high except in 1967. After 1960, and until 1968, with the exception of 1963, the trend of the ratio of the import surplus to GNP was clearly downwards. Yet even the years 1968-73 have a lower import surplus, relative to GNP, than the years 1954-60, though slightly higher than the average for the whole period 1954-73. The table shows indications that Jordan again entered a phase of hardship in its external sector after 1967. The year 1968 began to reflect this, with a rise in its import surplus larger than the rise in the foreign aid received. The year 1969 has accentuated the deterioration, with a much larger import surplus than 1968 and an absolutely lower volume of foreign aid. The excess of import surplus over official and UN aid has continued through 1973.

The volume of foreign aid has reflected itself in yet two other important ways: in enabling the government to maintain a large recurrent expenditure budget, and to achieve a much higher level of investment than would otherwise have been possible. The main elements of revenue and expenditure in relation to national accounting aggregates will be presented in Table 5.6.

The first part of Table 5.6, which shows how total government revenue is apportioned between domestic sources and foreign aid, is the most significant part of the table for our purposes, though the remaining parts serve to underline the role of foreign aid in making possible a large defence and internal security outlay, a large share for government in total expenditure out of GNP, and also a large share in total fixed capital formation.

This last point was mentioned earlier as another reflection of foreign aid. Strictly speaking, it is not a separate point, but one derived from the first, namely that foreign aid makes government's outlay (including investment) as large as it is. However, it is worth

Jordan

Table 5.4: Balance of Payments Current Account and Foreign Official Grants and Loans (JD million)

Year	Current Account (Goods and Services)		Import Surplus (Deficit on Current Account)	Official Grants and Loans (including UN Agencies)
	Credit	Debit		
1950	4.4	14.8	10.4	6.0
1951	4.5	17.6	13.1	6.7
1952	5.4	18.5	13.1	10.1
1953	6.2	20.0	13.8	12.7
1954	7.7	20.4	12.7	13.8
1955	8.0	27.0	19.0	17.9
1956	10.2	26.7	16.5	16.7
1957	13.6	32.6	19.0	15.7
1958	11.9	36.8	24.9	24.9
1959	9.9	42.8	32.9	25.6
1960	11.1	45.9	34.8	27.0
1961	20.6	46.1	25.5	25.6
1962	23.9	50.8	26.9	25.3
1963	25.2	61.3	36.1	22.5
1964	32.7	57.1	24.4	32.5
1965	37.3	64.1	26.8	29.0
1966	41.6	77.1	35.5	36.2
1967	36.8	64.6	27.8	53.3
1968	37.2	81.6	44.4	58.1
1969	46.1	109.5	63.4	48.3
1970	32.3	79.9	47.6	39.1
1971	40.4	98.3	57.9	35.5
1972	51.9	118.9	67.0	66.0
1973	76.8	137.6	60.8	60.0
Total	595.7	1,350.0	754.3	708.5

Source: For years 1950-4, IBRD, *The Economy of Jordan* (Baltimore, 1957), pp.461-2; for 1955-69, *Statistical Yearbook* for various years; for 1970-2, Central Bank of Jordan, *Monthly Statistical Bulletin*, December 1973, Table 15; and for 1973, Central Bank of Jordan, *Tenth Annual Report 1973*, p.41. (Data for 1973 are provisional.)

referring to investment separately owing to its great significance for the development of the country simultaneously with a large outlay on defence. Capital formation related to GNP has moved up from 9.2 per cent for 1954, our base year, to 15.6 per cent for 1972. It has averaged 14.3 per cent for the whole period.[25]

This average rate of fixed capital formation is not very high, and could not by itself explain the high rate of growth. The explanation ought to be supplemented by another fact relevant to growth of output: rise in productivity, thanks not only to investment in capital goods, but mainly in training, research, administrative reorganisation, extension services and generally to a more scientific and rational approach to production and distribution problems.[26] The civil service, especially its technical cadres, has benefited exten-

Table 5.5: The Ratio of Import Surplus to GNP and Total Resources Available 1954-73 (JD million and per cent)

Year	GNP at Market Prices	Import Surplus	Total Resources Available	Import Surplus as Per Cent of: GNP	TRA
1954	52.4	12.7	65.1	24.2	19.5
1955	49.9	19.0	68.9	38.1	27.6
1956	68.3	16.5	84.8	24.2	19.5
1957	70.4	19.0	89.4	27.0	21.3
1958	77.3	24.9	102.2	32.2	24.4
1959	99.3	32.9	132.2	33.1	24.9
1960	105.8	34.8	140.6	32.9	24.8
1961	127.1	25.5	152.6	20.1	16.7
1962	130.8	26.9	157.7	20.6	17.1
1963	137.6	36.1	173.7	26.2	20.8
1964	160.7	24.4	185.1	15.2	13.2
1965	180.5	26.8	207.3	14.8	12.9
1966	185.6	35.5	221.1	19.1	16.1
1967	205.4	27.8	233.2	13.5	11.9
1968	197.3	44.4	241.7	22.5	18.4
1969	233.7	63.4	297.1	27.1	21.3
1970	222.4	46.6	269.0	20.9	17.3
1971	236.6	57.9	294.5	24.5	19.7
1972	252.4	67.0	319.4	26.5	21.0
1973	272.0	60.8	332.8	22.4	18.3
Total or Average	3,065.5	702.9	3,768.4	23.0	18.7

Source: Tables 5.2 and 5.4, plus calculation of ratios.

sively from technical assistance programmes provided by various UN agencies and by US aid missions. Jordan is one of the few Arab countries where the relations with the members of such UN (and US) missions have been smooth, and where the counterparts to the advisers are well chosen on the whole, take their tasks seriously, and benefit from the association. The 'management' of the public sector of the economy and the advisory services to the private sector have reflected this phenomenon, and the net result has been a rate of growth higher than the rate of investment *by itself* would warrant.

Population, Labour Force and Social Conditions

The latest official estimate of the population at mid-1973 is 2.54m, including the residents of the West Bank which has since June 1967 been under Israeli occupation, and including the Arab population of Jerusalem which has been unilaterally (and contrary to repeated UN resolutions)[27] annexed by Israel and placed under full Israeli sovereignty. (The population of the East Bank alone is estimated at least at 1.7m.) Population estimates are always recorded with the warning that the 'figures should be used with

Table 5.6: Main Elements of Government Revenue, Domestic Revenue and Expenditures and their Relation to National Accounting Aggregates, 1954/5–1973 (per cent of sub-total)

	1954/5	1955/6	1956/7	1957/8	1958/9	1959/60	1960/1	1961/2	1962/3	1963/4	1964/5	1965/6[a]	1966	1967	1968	1969	1970	1971	1972	1973
Total Government Revenue																				
Domestic revenue	42	42	41	40	46	42	43	44	54	53	52	60	66	36	37	48	42	46	42	44
Total foreign aid	58	58	59	60	54	58	57	56	46	47	48	40	34	64	63	52	58	54	58	56
Domestic Government Revenues																				
Indirect taxes[b]	63	63	67	69	58	68	63	61	46	56	52	62	65	60	64	50	58	57	66	66
Direct taxes	12	12	13	12	14	10	15	17	15	18	15	15	9	9	8	6	13	8	8	8
Other	25	25	20	19	28	22	22	22	39	26	33	23	26	31	28	44	29	35	26	26
Total Government Expenditures																				
Defence and internal security	61	60	63	56	57	56	56	57	51	53	48	46	43	40	48	51	46	46	42	40
Education, health and welfare	9	10	9	10	10	10	12	12	12	12	12	13	13	10	9	9	11	27	25	26
Other non-development	14	14	14	16	13	12	14	16	17	19	19	17	18	15	14	14	7			
Government development expenditure	16	16	14	18	20	22	18	15	20	16	21	24	26	35	29	26	36	27	33	34
Gross National Product																				
Total government expenditure	32	35	31	34	38	38	31	26	29	29	27	26	21	23	28	29	27	26	27	n.a.
Private sector expenditure	68	65	69	66	62	62	69	74	71	71	73	74	79	77	72	71	73	74	73	n.a.
Gross Fixed Capital Formation																				
Government development expenditure	52	34	34	37	37	28	26	33	37	36	32	43	57	56	53	42	35	34	44	n.a.
Private sector development expenditure	48	66	66	63	63	72	74	67	63	64	68	57	43	44	47	58	65	66	56	n.a.

a. Fiscal years run from 1 April to 31 March until 31 March 1966, while national accounts are for calendar years. Budget years relate to the calendar year in which most of the fiscal year falls; thus, 1964/5 relates to 1964. Budget year 1966 covers 9 months only, namely 1 April to 31 December. From 1967 onwards, the fiscal years, like the national account years, are full calendar years.
b. Indirect taxes include customs duties, excise, licences and fees.

Sources: Budgets: For 1954/5 to 1965/6, FAO, *Country Report: Jordan*, p.31, with minor adjustments or deletions; for 1966-70, *Statistical Yearbook 1972*, pp.138-9; and for 1971-3, Central Bank of Jordan, *Tenth Annual Report, 1973*, p.91. (The calculations are made to conform to FAO, op. cit.) National accounts: 1966-72, *Statistical Yearbook 1972*, p.175, and Central Bank of Jordan, *Monthly Statistical Bulletin*, December 1973, Table 34.

caution'.[28] Among other things, the data do not provide adequate and reliable coverage on emigration, and presumably death is to a certain extent under-reported, especially among the Palestinian refugees. However, considering that the net natural increase in population (births minus deaths) is *at least* 3 per cent per annum, a population of some 1,220,000 by the end of 1948 could easily have reached nearly 2.6 million by the middle of 1973. Thanks to the high percentage of Palestinians among the population, to UNRWA's educational efforts among these refugees, and to the government's own efforts, the literacy rate was in 1966 the highest in the Arab world except for Lebanon. (The rate for Jordan was 62 per cent for both sexes aged 15-24, 80 per cent for males and 43 per cent for females.)[29]

The government's effort, expressed in terms of the ratio of public expenditure on public education, has not been remarkable by Arab standards. For the sixties it has exceeded only the effort of Kuwait, South Yemen and North Yemen. The comparison with Kuwait is misleading, owing to the fact that the Kuwaiti budget is about five times that of Jordan, although the Kuwaiti population is less than a third of that of Jordan. Consequently a comparison of crude percentage points is misleading. Comparison on a *per capita* basis of absolute expenditure would also be misleading, unless to the government's expenditure were added that of UNRWA and of private institutions. Once this is done, then Jordan's rank rises to the level of Syria's and exceeds that of Egypt and Sudan, but falls short of that of Kuwait, Saudi Arabia, Lebanon and Libya — just to cite a few cases.

Related to the size of population, Jordan has by far the highest ratio in the Arab world of students at university level at home and studying abroad. The number for 1966 was 18,326, of whom a large proportion are of Palestinian origin. (In addition there were 9,720 Palestinians, as a separate category, in universities abroad.) Thus the number of university students recorded as 'Jordanian' per million of population would be 8,145 for Jordan — apart from the category of Palestinians, many of whom have their families in Jordan — against 5,900 for Egypt, the country with the next highest ratio. Over 83 per cent of Jordan's university population of 47,144 in 1973/4 were in universities in the Arab world, including that of Jordan. The rest were mainly in Europe. Almost 73 per cent of the total were in the humanities, education, social sciences and fine arts. Total enrolment at the University of Jordan for 1973/4 was 8,186, including 2,649 women (32 per cent of the total). The courses offered were in the fields of arts, education, economics and commerce (the largest faculty), science, agriculture, medicine, nursing and *shari'a* or religious law.[30] (The size of enrolment was smaller in 1971/2 than it had been in 1966 or 1967, probably because the number of West Bank students dropped after Israeli occupation.)

There is no reliable information regarding the student body in the West Bank under Israeli occupation. The enrolment of Palestinian Arabs in universities in Israeli-occupied territories is minimal, as there is open and covert discrimination against them aimed at blocking as many applicants as possible from the opportunity of higher education.[31] As to the Palestinians in general, it is estimated by knowledgeable and careful researchers that they include some 55,000—60,000 university degree-holders. (This is about one in every sixty Palestinians.)

Total student population has risen considerably in Jordan from the early 1950s to the early 1970s. The earliest full and detailed information for all levels of education and for all categories of schools (public, UNRWA and private) relates to 1954/5. In that year total enrolment stood at 202,014 pupils (including 57,778 girls or 28.6 per cent of the total, but excluding 11,500 boys and girls in kindergartens). The largest component of this aggregate was in government schools (57.6 per cent); the balance was divided almost equally between UNRWA schools and private schools.[32] It is noteworthy that, like Lebanon but unlike the other Arab countries, Jordan had and continues to have a relatively large number of pupils in private schools.

In contrast with the enrolment in the pre-university cycles in 1954/5 which constituted about 50 per cent of the school-age population then, enrolment stood at 492,885 in 1973/4 in the East Bank alone,[33] or approximately 91 per cent of school-age population. Information is not available on enrolment in Arab schools in the West Bank after 1967, but it is believed that enrolment has continued to be high since Israeli occupation, as the Jordanian government still shoulders the financial responsibilities as it did before the occupation. Indeed, in 1966/7 the ratio of West Bank pupils to population was 10 per cent higher than in the East Bank. If this pattern persisted, the enrolment in West Bank schools in 1973/4 would have been about 175,000.[34] (It ought to be recalled that the population dropped after the 1967 war, as about 300,000 had to flee the West Bank into safety in the East Bank.) Thus total enrolment in Jordan would be about 668,000 by 1973/4. This represents a vast expansion beyond the situation as it stood in 1954/5, not only absolutely but also relatively.

Apart from formal scholastic education, Jordan provides vocational training at the secondary level. In all, there were in 1971/2 ten vocational schools for agricultural, industrial, commercial and nursing trainees, as well as six institutions that provide higher-level training in nursing, midwifery, social work, statistics and industry. All these facilities are in the East Bank; those in the West Bank do not appear in the official publications.[35] However, in 1965/6 there were several schools for vocational training in the West Bank, and enrolment there was well over half total enrolment for the whole country.[36]

As indicated in section 1 above, the population of Transjordan (the original population of the East Bank) was generally less well-educated and sophisticated and skilled than the Palestinians who later formed part of Jordan. Tribal attitudes, habits and social structure are still visible among the East Jordanians, or, if not visible, then only thinly disguised. But, as the army's experience and that of the schooling system has proved, the learning aptitude of East Jordanians, including the bedouin, is high. Mechanical gadgets and machines (especially tanks and armoured cars) have a special appeal to the bedouin. The general aptitude and readiness to learn has enabled the population to perform well and to achieve a creditable rise in national product.

The 1973 GNP *per capita* at current prices was JD105.8 or $329, and national income *per capita* was JD91.9 or $285.8. Despite the country's commendable performance this average is still below that for any of the countries covered in this study except Sudan, Egypt and Morocco.

The distribution of the GNP or national income *per capita* is very uneven, considering the destitution of a large mass of the Palestinians who are on UNRWA's records as eligible for relief of some sort or another. This very poor majority, to whom must be added a high proportion of the bedouin population, live at or near subsistence level. The inadequacy of the level is seen in the malnutrition and undernourishment of these people, and the very low standard of housing and of such community facilities as sewerage and sanitation. UNRWA tries to do the utmost possible with the very small budget available to it; nevertheless this leaves hundreds of thousands of the population, especially in the Eastern Bank, at a deplorable level of living, with respect to food, clothing, housing and degree of crowding, life-style and conditions in general.[37] The relatively large-scale investment in private housing over the past two decades has mainly been aimed at middle- and higher-income groups, and has failed therefore to alleviate the crisis of the lower-income groups. The very restricted employment opportunities accentuate the gravity of the situation because rations and services are only minimally supplemented, and then irregularly and not for everybody.

The health services have shown tangible improvement over the years. This improvement goes back to the early fifties, and it enabled the IBRD mission in their report (published 1957) to state that progress had been achieved. But seen against the vastly expanded need under the impact of the influx of Palestinian refugees, the mission also noted the inadequacy of curative as well as preventive medicine, and of housing and community services for the lower-income groups who formed the vast majority of the population. Specifically with respect to health services there has been marked improvement in some fields, as Table 5.7 shows, but not as much improvement on a *per capita* basis.

Table 5.7: Number of Hospitals, Hospital Beds and Medical Staff 1953, 1966 and 1974[a]

	1953	1966	1974[a]
Hospitals[b]	29	57	28
Hospital beds	1,994	3,447	2,170
Hospital beds per 1,000 population	1.5	1.6	1.3
Physicians	185	505	763
Thousand people per physician	7.4	4.2	2.1
Dentists	41	75	123
Pharmacists	86	196	344
Professional nurses[c]		312	318
Bacteriologists[c]		23	33

a. Data for 1974 cover East Bank only.
b. Hospitals exclude military and UNRWA hospitals.
c. Beginning with 1966 for nurses and bacteriologists, who were not included in earlier statistical reporting.
Source: *Statistical Yearbook 1966*, pp.61-2, and *Yearbook 1974*, pp.81-5, for 1972.

Lastly, the availability of electricity and piped water for household use is still limited compared with Syria and Lebanon, though vast improvement has taken place over the past two decades. In 1954, only 0.5 million out of about 1.4 million inhabitants lived in towns and villages which then had electricity. So at best only a small fraction of the population had electricity installed in their houses. (Production figures are not available.) In 1965, production was 75 kwh per person for the Kingdom on the average (compared with Syria at 116, Turkey at 159, and Lebanon at 318). Data for 1974 include East Bank only; here production per year per person averaged about 192 kwh.[38] (Production per head was initially much higher in the West Bank, partly because that region had had electric installations for much longer and on a much wider scale than the East Bank, and partly because the refugee and bedouin populations in the East Bank were much less adequately supplied with facilities than any other group in the West, or even the East, Bank. However,

Jordan

installed capacity and production have risen considerably in the East Bank since the mid-1960s.) With respect to piped water, the lack of empirical information forbids us from providing any specific assessment of progress achieved in quantitative terms. But knowledgeable and responsible officials affirm that 'vast progress has occurred in the past two decades'.

The size of the active labour force of Jordan is difficult to assess. This is mainly due to the phenomenon of the existence of a large community of relief-receiving Palestinian refugees who have never formed an active part of manpower resources. Furthermore, the inability of the economy to provide employment for a substantial proportion of the manpower requires some qualifications in definitions. To these complications must be added the irregularity and seasonality of employment of those who are neither fully employed nor totally unemployed. Estimates appearing in the IBRD mission report placed the active labour force (among men and women between 15 and 65 years of age) at about 25 per cent of the population — 23.8 male and 1.2 female. There is also an estimate of refugees working in 1953. This estimate places the number at between 71,000 and 80,000 (at most 13—15 per cent of the total number). By far the largest proportion of those employed — some 60 per cent — have seasonal agricultural employment; another 20 per cent have part-time employment (excluding agriculture), and the rest are full-time employees and self-employed. Lastly, an overall estimate for total work-force and employment in 1955 (excluding women in agriculture) divides the total as shown in Table 5.8.

Table 5.8: Total Work-force in Employment, 1955

Public sector	59,000
Urban enterprises	55,000
Total urban	114,000
Agriculture	195,000
Refugees without occupation	61,000
Total	370,000

Source: IBRD, *The Economy of Jordan*, Annex II, pp.441-4.

This distribution is too broad and vague to be adequate or useful as a starting reference point. The first population census was undertaken in November 1961, and produced some reliable information on the labour force. According to this census, the active labour force was about 390,000, of whom some 57 per cent were in commodity-producing and 43 per cent in service-producing sectors.[39] (The distribution included 27,300 or 7 per cent 'seeking work'.) *The 7-Year Development Program for Economic Development of Jordan 1964-1970*, which was prepared in 1962, contains only the sketchiest references to manpower and the labour force. Owing to the confusion with regard to unemployment and underemployment estimates in existence, there is no more than a shy attempt in this Plan to estimate employment increases. These are projected at about 5 per cent per year (after allowing for rises in productivity), or 20,000—24,000 jobs created per year. Against this, there is an estimated rise of 4 per cent in the labour force, which would leave very little net increase in employment.

We have no official evaluation of the economy's performance in this respect during the Plan years 1964-70. Indeed, owing to the severe rupture in the continuity of this time span and in the geographical unity of the country caused by the Israeli occupation of the West Bank in June 1967, it would be meaningless as well as extremely difficult to attempt such an evaluation. However, there are in hand a few attempts at an examination of the size and structure of the labour force which are more recent than the 1961 census or the estimates of the Plan to which reference has been made. Two of these were studies undertaken by the Department of Statistics before the June war, 1967. The first was a sample survey conducted in 1966 which covered all sectors except agriculture. The second was a census conducted in the first quarter of 1967, but which was restricted to agriculture.[40] The latter study came out with the conclusion that the 1961 census had underestimated employment in agriculture, especially with respect to the partial or seasonal employment of women and children. The two studies together tend to correct the widespread impression that unemployment was very high in Jordan.

An estimate reached independently by Mazur, on the strength of official surveys and of his own analysis of the growth trends of national product and labour, confirms the need for such correction. Mazur estimates that the part of the labour force seeking work in 1966 was only 3.5 per cent of the total. According to his estimates, the labour force grew on the average by 3.3 per cent per annum between 1961 and 1966, while employment grew by 4 per cent. The faster rate accounts, in his view, for the drop in unemployment from 7 per cent in 1961 to 3.5 per cent in 1966.[41] The present writer believes that the picture emerging from the studies and Mazur's estimate is probably excessively rosy, and that unemployment was and still is considerably higher. The estimate could only be considered a true representation of the situation if the refugee camp-dwellers and the poor urban refugees were to be counted as employed even if they had extremely low-paid jobs for very brief periods in the year, and if full employment were defined very liberally — that is, if the number of days worked per year was less than half the total work-days which are usually taken as the dividing line between partial and full employment.

Since the June 1967 war there has been one other large manpower study. This was conducted in the East Bank late in 1970 and early in 1971 and included all sectors except agriculture. Only establishments employing five or more persons were surveyed.[42] However, it is not possible to make detailed comparisons between 1961 and 1970/1 because the last survey, like that conducted in 1966, was a sample survey, and while generalisations can be made with regard to certain characteristics of the labour force, no quantitative comparisons can be made relating to growth and distribution of the total labour force between the first and last year in the decade separating the two. To this handicap must be added the difference in geographical coverage, as the 1961 census covered both Banks of the Kingdom, while the 1970 survey was confined to the East Bank. However, the 1970 survey is useful in that it sums up and evaluates all the preceding studies, which include one full population census, one agricultural census and several sample surveys (in 1957, 1959, 1963, 1966 and 1969).

In view of all the complications and limitations cited, in conclusion one can only venture a guess — and a limited one at that, as it relates to the East Bank only — that the degree of fullness of employment is today roughly what it had been in 1961. This means that there is still a large measure of unemployment. This assessment is authoritatively supported by the National Planning Council. The NPC says in the 1973-5 Plan: 'Manpower studies indicated that the labour-force participation rate is 20 percent. The total labour force amounts to 370,000, of whom 150,000 are in the non-farm civilian sectors.'[43] (These figures relate to the East Bank only.) However, the NPC attributes the low participation to the youthfulness of the population, the high school enrolment, and the low female participation in active employment. Obviously, this analysis leaves out one major factor: the inability of the economy to absorb all those who are of work age and are seeking employment. This can be proved from the fact that the industrial countries normally have a higher school enrolment, and at the same time about twice as large a rate of participation.

Finally, it ought to be remembered that many thousands of Jordanians work outside Jordan, mainly in the oil-producing countries around the Arabian Gulf. This factor reduces the size and pressure of unemployment. The emigration of skilled Jordanians also reduces the intensity of the imbalance manifest in the inordinately high unemployment of well-educated men in the cities, which coincides with shortages in the rural areas. This phenomenon of structural unemployment, associated with disharmony between the supply of and demand for specific skills, is one with which many Third World countries are familiar.

Two points remain to be raised regarding the imbalance under reference, despite the fact that our information is frugal. First, that in terms of occupation, the labour force in 1961 showed a shortage of professional and technical, administrative, executive and managerial, and clerical skills, the supply of which stood at 4.1, 0.6 and 4.1 per cent of the total need respectively. The gravity of the situation was made more serious by the 'skill drain', as 16.8, 10.1 and 19.4 per cent of these groups respectively worked abroad, mostly in the oil-producing Arabian Gulf region.[44] (This evaluation leaves out of account the serious 'brain drain' into Lebanon and the United States of highly trained physicians, scientists and social scientists, particularly Jordanians of Palestinian origin. For instance, the second-largest Arab group of professors and technicians at the American University of Beirut is of Palestinian origin.) Furthermore, most of the 50,000—60,000 university degree-holders among the Palestinians are outside Jordan, spread in the other parts of the Arab world and in the USA and Western Europe. Although today the proportion of the technical and administrative categories of manpower is larger than in 1961, the outflow is also larger. On balance, the shortages in key manpower categories are less serious, while the skilled Jordanians (and Palestinians) abroad are more numerous.

The second point is a comparison between sector shares in GDP compared with sector shares in the labour force, or the 'relative sectoral product per worker'. This will be done for 1961, the only year for which it is possible. The comparison is presented below in Table 5.9.

This table shows the low level of productivity of the labour force in the various commodity-producing sectors (both primary and secondary) and the high productivity of the labour force in the various service-producing sectors. Grouped together, the commodity sectors have a relative sectoral product per worker of 0.62, against 1.50 for the group of service sectors. The phenomenon is not unique to Jordan but is generally encountered elsewhere in the countries covered by this study. Usually, however, the agricultural sector makes a large contribution to national product but employs a larger component of the labour force, while the manufacturing sector achieves a state of welfare balance, in the sense that the relative size of the labour force in it is nearer to the relative size of the sector's contribution to GDP or GNP.

Progress in Main Sectors, Economic Institutions and Major Projects
Although it is severely limited in its growth prospects by the area of cultivable land —

Table 5.9: Sector Shares in GDP and in Labour Force for 1961

Sector	Per Cent Share in GDP (1)	Per Cent Share in Labour Force (2)	Relative Sectoral Product per Worker (3)
Agriculture	22.8	35.3	0.65
Manufacturing, mining, quarrying, electricity and water	8.6	11.2	0.77
Construction	4.1	10.3	0.40
Transport, storage and communication	11.4	3.1	3.7
Trade and finance	23.1	8.0	2.9
Services	30.0	13.7	0.93
Activities not adequately described		18.4	
	100.0	100.0	

Source: For columns (1) and (2), Table 5.2 and information already cited regarding labour distribution; column (3) is column (1) divided by column (2).

given present technology and feasibly available financial resources, and by limitations of rainfall and river and spring water — agriculture still represents a major sector in its contribution to national product (exceeded only by the combination of trade *and* finance, and by public administration and defence). But it derives yet further importance from the fact that the majority of the population is rural and is still associated or identified with agricultural activities or those related to them.

The limitations we have listed, and others arising from social organisation, motivation, financing and institutions, have not meant the stagnation of the sector. The manner of assessment should indeed be reversed: over the past two decades agriculture has progressed *in spite* of the limitations imposed on it, thanks to the combination of a group of technical, institutional and financial reform measures taken. It is to these that we will now turn. In the process of discussion, we will have occasion to refer to the major projects and reforms undertaken in agriculture (as in the other sectors discussed later), rather than deal with the sectors, the institutions and the projects as separate sub-headings — a method which would make for fragmented presentation and unnecessary repetitiveness.

Perhaps the first important condition in the progress of agriculture is the understanding of the role, and the assessment, of the various factors related to it: underground water, soil classification, pattern of land ownership, rural indebtedness, patterns of cultivation, marketing possibilities and projects capable of profitable development. Numerous studies have been undertaken by the various government agencies in association with or under the guidance of UN, US and UK technical aid missions,[45] and a relatively large degree of information is now available on agricultural conditions and further development prospects. Such assessment shows that the results of research, experimentation, use of fertilisers and insecticides, and mechanisation have not been very marked or consistent, owing mainly to the inadequacy of water resources and the extreme untrustworthiness and scantiness of rainfall.

The use of modern aids to agriculture, and of mechanisation, was largely restricted in the early part of the period under consideration by the severe poverty of the landowners of medium- and small-sized plots; on the other hand, the large landlords were nowhere, in terms of affluence, comparable to their counterparts in Egypt, Iraq or Syria. Hence in 1952, for instance, a total of 175 tractors of all sizes were in the country (23 in the West Bank), and agricultural loans for the whole Kingdom totalled only JD330,668 and JD342,676 for 1951 and 1952 respectively. As late as 1958, a total of only 2,707 tons of all kinds of fertilisers were sold in the country (apart from the use of natural manure). Against this modest quantity, the IBRD mission in its Report 'conservatively' estimated the needs for 1955 or 1956 at 52,700 tons of superphosphates and 38,100 tons of ammonium sulphate. The comparison in Table 5.10 shows the progress achieved with regard to the use of inputs, mechanisation and other indicators of change. The starting year is not the same throughout, owing to the nonconformity in statistical reporting.

It can be concluded from the comparisons just made that progress had been achieved by 1966 with regard to mechanisation, fertilisers and insecticides, co-operative societies and nurseries, and agricultural credit facilities. However, the data for 1972 and 1974 are restricted to the East Bank only, and conclusions cannot be drawn with respect to the indicators between 1966 and 1974. Yet the perusal in detail of the sources from which the data have been collected leads to the conclusion that for the East Bank alone progress has been achieved in most of the indicators. The main exceptions are the co-operative movement and the use of fertilisers.

With respect to the question of loans and indebtedness, it is worth mentioning that the volume of outstanding debt recorded officially as JD6.245 million by the end of 1966 is true only of debt against mortgage. This kind of debt hardly witnesses any diminution, owing to the existence of a moratorium on loans, first imposed in 1947, then renewed in 1953 for ten years, and twice renewed since then. On the other hand, the debt shown as outstanding by the end of 1972 includes *all* institutional sources. Other kinds of debt, however, weigh down the agricultural sector. By the end of 1966, the aggregate was JD14.3 million, and it is *this* sum which should be compared with the total indebtedness of JD19.4m as at the end of 1972, shown in the tabulation of indicators. (Only debt against mortgage is reported for 1974.) The composition of total debt for 1966 is detailed in Table 5.11.

This volume of indebtedness no doubt constitutes a heavy burden, since it mostly falls on the rural sector of East Jordan (that is, the original Transjordanian peasants, who probably numbered in 1966 no more than 80,000—90,000 families — after excluding the refugees and most of the nomads). The debt burden thus would constitute something between JD158 and JD168 per family. This burden is much heavier for 1972 owing to the increase in indebtedness by about 36 per cent above the 1966 level. Rural indebtedness is particularly disturbing beyond what the figures suggest, in view of the fact that not all debts are contracted for bona fide productive purposes, but also for social purposes (consumption, pilgrimage, a second marriage, expanding the family's house), even if these purposes may have been disguised initially. (Furthermore, there are debts owing to commercial banks, and to private 'loan sharks', where the volume of loans could not be ascertained, but it is believed to be rather modest.)

There are five institutions which have debt records: the Agricultural Credit Corporation (ACC), the Jordan Central Co-operative Union (JCCU) representing co-operative societies,

Table 5.10: Indicators of Agricultural Progress

Indicator and Unit	Year	Quantity
Inorganic fertilisers (tons)	1958	2,707
	1966	10,232
	1972[a]	3,807
Chemicals (insecticides and for treatment) (tons)	1960	63
	1966	107
	1972[a]	209
Tractors (cumulative) (units)	1952	175
	1966	2,068
	1972[a]	2,954
Loans outstanding (JD m)	1960	3.7
	1967	6.2
	1972[a]	19.4
Loans advanced during year (JD m)	1951	0.3
	1966	1.6
(from ACC alone)	1974[a]	2.1
Number of borrowers	1951	n.a.
	1966	6,723
	1974[a]	2,122
Agricultural co-operatives by end of year	1954	53
	1966	337
	1974[a]	124
Number of members	1954	2,071
	1966	15,755
	1974[a]	4,494
Paid-up capital (JD '000)	1954	21.8
	1966	158.2
	1974[a]	565.8
Reserves (JD '000)	1954	1.1
	1966	141.8
	1974[a]	82.5
Government nurseries	1958	13
	1966	17
	1972[a]	n.a.
Workers in nurseries (technical staff and employees)	1958	119
	1966	156
	1972[a]	n.a.
Labourers in nurseries	1958	324
	1966	659
	1972[a]	n.a.

a. Only in East Bank.
Source: Data collected from *Statistical Yearbook 1952, 1960, 1966* and *1972;* chapter on 'Agriculture'; FAO, Mediterranean Development Project, *Jordan: Country Study* (Rome, 1967), p.103 for loans outstanding 1960. Information for 1974 is very spotty, so it has been recorded here only occasionally. (See *Yearbook 1974,* pp. 148-52.)

Table 5.11: Total Agricultural Debt, 1966 (JD '000)

Loans by Agricultural Credit Corporation	5,270
Less: Loans by Jordan Central Co-operative Union (from fund originating in ACC)	482
	4,788
Loans by co-operative societies to members	1,202
Loans secured by land mortgages	5,902
Land taxes overdue	17
Loans due to East Ghor Canal Authority (later National Resources Authority, see below)	2,350
	14,259

Source: FAO, Mediterranean Development Project, *Jordan: Country Study* (Rome, 1967), p. 101.

the Department of Lands and Surveys which records mortgages against debt, the Department of Taxes and the Natural Resources Authority (with respect to debts owing after the redistribution of the East Ghor Canal lands to beneficiaries). It is from the records of these five agencies that the detailed account of indebtedness shown above was drawn.

The ACC was established in 1959 in order to centralise and consolidate, as far as possible, the credit-granting activities of several fragmented agencies. The board of directors of the ACC is composed of representatives of the private and the public sector, and the ACC is run efficiently. It advances credit for various lengths of time, up to ten years. But besides lending directly, it also allows the JCCU a certain fund from which this institution lends to individual co-operative societies, which in turn advance loans to their members. The ACC is flexible in its operations. Thus, 'as security, the ACC accepts real estate, crops, stocks and shares, evidence of deposit in banks, proper guarantee documents, joint security and promissory notes carrying two or more signatures issued by banks and other lending institutions acceptable to the ACC Board.'[46] The allocation of loans among various uses follows a policy of priorities. According to this policy, the direct lending operations of the ACC since its establishment have emphasised, respectively: livestock, poultry and bee-raising; irrigation work; terracing and land reclamation; agricultural machinery and equipment; tree planting; and constructions on farms.

The co-operative movement grew in the decade and a half after 1952. By mid-1966, there were 702 societies in Jordan, of which 337 were agricultural for various purposes. The largest other group is school saving co-operatives. The societies are bound together through the Jordan Central Co-operative Union (JCUU), which is run by a board consisting of government officials and society representatives. In addition, there is a Co-operative Institute (CI) which since its establishment in 1964 has been active in training officials for co-operatives (accountants, managers, organisers, board members).

Agricultural co-operative societies undertake credit, supply of inputs and grading and marketing. Despite enthusiasm (especially in the East Ghor Canal area), the movement suffers from inadequacy of funds, shortage of qualified management, inconsistency of enthusiasm (alternation between outbursts and general slackening of interest), and insufficient co-ordination between government departments associated with the movement and the societies in the field.

In addition to marketing via co-operatives, there is a special Department of Agricultural Marketing which undertakes research, demonstration, training and general advice. It also keeps an eye on the operations of wholesale exporters and importers of agricultural produce and their special markets, the *hisbis,* and on price movements. To this effect, it has a good price-recording section.

Jordan has not had a major land reform, because it has not had the serious problem of large landholdings which Syria, Iraq and Egypt had. The agricultural census of 1965 (the most recent) records the distribution by size of 93,492 holdings. However, the general census results were deemed unsatisfactory by the Department of Statistics through being probably understated, but the pattern of ownership distribution by size of holding was thought satisfactory, after a post-enumeration sample survey was undertaken. The summary results of the census are shown in Table 5.12.

Table 5.12: Distribution of Land Holdings

Size Group (hectares)	No. of Holdings	Per Cent of Total
Less than 1 ha	33,986	36.3
1 and less than 5	32,573	34.9
5 and less than 10	14,221	15.2
10 and less than 50	11,748	12.6
50 and less than 100	688	0.7
100 and less than 200	198	0.2
200 and less than 500	60	0.1
500 and less than 1,000	16	–
1,000 and over	2	–
	93,492	100.0

Source: Department of Statistics, *Report on Agricultural Census 1965* (Amman, 1967), table on p.86.

The distribution shown in this table (and in more detailed tables in the census report) reveals excessive fragmentation in land ownership — the curse which accompanies land ownership in the Arab world in general. Considering the poverty of land and water resources in Jordan, we can say that anybody with an area of 10 ha or below is severely handicapped, except if this ownership falls in the very tiny proportion of irrigated and tree-planted land. This means that over 85 per cent of ownerships range from extremely small to small. On the other hand, large ownerships, say in excess of 100 ha, are only one-third of 1 per cent of the total. The medium-sized holdings are one-eighth of the total.

It is usually the phenomenon of a very tiny proportion of all landowners holding a substantial proportion of the land which creates dissatisfaction with the pattern of distribution and paves the way for land reform. According to an earlier census conducted in 1953, the *1953 Census of Agriculture,* holdings in excess of 100 ha in area totalled only some 208,600 ha.[47] Most of this area was inadequately rain-fed, and only partly exploited, and therefore one can only speculate that the situation did not, and does not today, constitute a serious socio-economic problem of massive land ownership.

However, beginning with Law 14 of 1959, and through a series of amendments and laws down to Law 37 of 1966, legislation aiming at limiting ownership and redistributing excess holdings was enacted, to be applicable to land benefiting from large public irrigation works. The region which inspired the policy and made it necessary was the East Ghor area in the Jordan Valley. The pattern of distribution of ownership in the Valley had been established through a study conducted by UNRWA, and reported in *Jordan Valley Land Tenure Survey*, published in February 1956. According to this survey, the total area involved was 43,439 ha.[48] The pattern is no different, in general outline, from that relating to the whole country. A subsequent survey conducted by the Department of Statistics was reported in *The East Jordan Valley, A Social and Economic Survey* in 1961 on the type of tenure in the area. According to the *Survey*, one-fourth of the total area of 20,794 ha was entirely owned by the operator, while 56 per cent was entirely sharecropped. The remaining 20 per cent were mainly mixed owned and not owned, or entirely leased out for short or long term, or occupied free of rent. This last *Survey* defined the backdrop of the land reform that was to follow in the East Ghor Canal area. But before we describe this reform, which despite the small area it involves is important as a successful experiment in more than one sense, we must place the irrigation of the East Ghor area in the context of the utilisation by Jordan of its river resources.

It is estimated that some 1,250 million cubic metres of water flow into the Dead Sea — which is more than the Jordan Valley needs for irrigation. However, Jordan does not have uncontested right to the use of the Jordan water, with Israel on the other side. But it can, uncontested, use some 475m cubic metres of water from the Yarmouk, plus 123m cubic metres of East Bank *wadis*, plus 78m cubic metres from West Bank *wadis* flowing towards the Jordan river. The total of 676m cubic metres is not all available, since 71m cubic metres are not usable. The irrigation needs are estimated at 760m cubic metres, which leaves a shortage between needs and availability of 155m cubic metres.

The Jordan government decided in the mid-fifties that it had to plan its own irrigation work on the basis of water to which its right was uncontested and within the area of its sovereignty — namely part of the Yarmouk and all of *wadi* flows. The decision was crowned in 1957 with an agreement between the Jordanian government and the US aid mission in Jordan for the building of a 69-km. canal in the East Ghor, which would irrigate some 15,000 ha, at a cost of $18 million. The US government was to donate $13 million of the total. The project constituted an expandable part of a project of larger scope for the use of Yarmouk waters, the broad lines of which had been agreed between Syria and Jordan in 1953. This larger project agreement involved the construction of two dams at Maqarin and Wadi Khalid, along the course of the Yarmouk, for the storage of enough water to irrigate more than 52,000 ha on both sides of the river Jordan and to generate 200 million kwh annually. The project was to be executed in five phases within a maximum period of twenty years, at a total cost of JD54 million.

If this broad Syrian-Jordanian agreement was the context for the more modest East Ghor canal project, the decision to implement the latter project in turn came after a background of failure to harness and utilise the waters flowing into the watershed on a global, inter-state basis. Years of negotiation had taken place, in the first half of the fifties, involving Jordan, Syria, Israel and later the League of Arab States, with the USA as intermediary. Many proposals and counterproposals were put forth, over the few years of negotiation, but in the end all attempts at a regional utilisation of the waters failed because of the basic stumbling block: the inability to reach economic agreement within the context of an unsolved political conflict which not only made the emergence of mutual confidence impossible, but was always fraught with the danger of a military flare-up.[49] Specifically, it was impossible to reach agreement on a technico-economic question in a vacuum — or rather within the framework of political *dis*agreement. Such questions as location of storage of water, control of flow of dammed or other water, location of electricity generating plants, and allocation of the water available constitute insurmountable problems in the absence of political understanding and normal treaty arrangements; they are difficult to regulate and settle even within the framework of normal political relations — let alone within the framework of a legal state of war or belligerency, and occasional wars.

Work on the first part of the Canal and the network of irrigation and drainage canals and on land reclamation was finished in the mid-sixties. Alongside the construction work, the government, through the East Ghor Canal Authority, undertook the expropriation of land holdings in excess of the ceiling of 20 ha. The redistribution was made along the scale shown in Table 5.13.

Table 5.13: Redistribution of Land Holdings

Area Previously Held	Area Allotted to Holders
3–5 ha	Allotted in full
5.1–10 ha	5 ha allotted plus 25 per cent of area in excess of 5 ha
10.1–50 ha	6.2 ha allotted plus 17 per cent of area in excess of 10 ha
50.1–100 ha	13 ha allotted plus 12 per cent of area in excess of 50 ha
100.1 ha and over	20 ha allotted

Source: FAO, Mediterranean Development Project, *Jordan: Country Study*, p.95. Data on compensation obtained from East Ghor Canal Authority.

The beneficiaries were defined according to a scale of priorities, beginning with owner-operator, professional farmer from the area, down to tenants in the project area and, finally, absentee owners. In case of holdings being below 3 ha in size, the Authority was empowered to sell or lease additional land to bring the area up to 3 ha of Class I or II, or to 5 ha of Class III land. (The classes rank the land according to quality, Class I being the best.) In the size scale, consideration was given to expectations of an income capable of assuring a certain pre-set level of living.

Compensation for expropriated land was to be undertaken by special assessment committees, along clear-cut guidelines. The accounts between the Authority and land-holders as of the end of June 1967 are shown in Table 5.14.

The Authority was to compensate old holders within ten years, whereas beneficiaries were to pay for the land within twenty years. Water was to be rationed and paid for, in order to avoid wasteful water-use habits. Along with the redistribution and water allotment, the government provided technical services aiming at optimising crop rotation, use of fertilizers and introduction of new crops, as well as making the new co-operative societies responsible and active institutions. The distribution process covered 6,360 ha by the middle of 1967, as can be seen from Table 5.15.

Owing to the activities of the Palestinian guerrillas across the River Jordan and Israeli 'punitive' raids, the East Ghor Canal area has witnessed a severe drop in land utilisation since the middle of June 1967, and indeed the main canal and the network have been damaged seriously in several places by Israeli shelling. Thus by far the main agricultural project in Jordan, and the one which was beginning to fulfil its promise in socio-economic

Jordan

Table 5.14: Accounts between East Ghor Canal Authority and Land-holders

	JD million
Value of capital assets and water rights taken over by EGCA	8.75
Value of land and water rights remaining with original owners	6.40
Capital value owed by new holders	2.35
Capital value owed by Authority to old holders	2.28
Instalments paid by new holders	0.21
Instalments paid by Authority to old holders	1.25

improvement of the conditions of new holder-operators, has had to turn from a green prosperous field to mostly dry wasteland.

But there have been some compensatory developments since the mid-1960s. Jordan has proceeded with work on certain smaller water schemes or *wadis*, as the following recapitulation shows:[50]

- Wadi Ziqlan (completed 1967),
- Wadi Kafrein and Wadi Shuaib (completed early 1969),
- sides of the East Ghor Canal raised,
- Wadi Zarqa (work begun in 1971; now under work and irrigation canals near completion),
- Yarmouk River dam (work begun in May 1966, but stopped because of the June 1967 war).

However, the East Ghor Canal extension southwards, for which the plans are ready, cannot be undertaken before the completion of the Yarmouk project. The West Ghor Canal scheme, which is to be located on the western banks of the Jordan River, cannot be initiated as the site of the scheme is now under Israeli occupation. The Yarmouk project is expected, once completed, to irrigate over 51,000 ha (80 per cent of which would be by gravity). Beyond this, and apart from the *wadis* now being harnessed, there is very little scope for expansion in irrigation. Most of the remaining prospects lie in underground water and *wadis* south of the Jordan Valley. Together, these are estimated to provide irrigation water for some 12,500 ha. The potential is obviously very modest, except in the Jordan River watershed. But even here the benefits would be localised; the rest of the country has very little to expect by way of irrigation prospects.

Discussion will now very briefly cover the sectors of mining, manufacturing industry, electricity, transport and tourism, the development of which will be assessed. Jordan has relatively large potential in the field of minerals, including potassium chloride in the Dead Sea (estimated at 2,000 million tons), magnesium bromide (980 million tons), sodium chloride — table salt (11,000 million tons), magnesium chloride (22,000 tons), and calcium chloride (6,000 tons). In addition, the country has vast deposits of phosphates, especially at Ruseifah (with 72 per cent content), Hasa, Ma'an and Ras an-Naqb. In all, these deposits

Table 5.15: Distribution of Land Ownership in East Ghor Canal Project Area After the Reallocation of land[a]

Size of Ownership (ha)	Number of Landowners		Area Owned	
	Number	Per Cent of Total	Area (ha)	Per Cent of Total
3.0–5.0	1,046	74.9	3,485	54.8
5.1–6.2	128	9.1	748	11.8
6.3–13.0	195	14.0	1,623	25.5
13.1–20.0	19	1.4	307	4.8
Over 20[b]	8	0.6	197	3.1
Total	1,396	100.0	6,360	100.0

a. This land ownership covers 22 out of 24 'development areas', having a total area of 6,360 ha or 52 per cent of 12,000 ha of the total project area. The remaining part of the project was in mid-1967 almost completely allotted to new farmers but the final ownership classification records are not available.

b. 2,158 holders had owned farm units smaller than the minimum holding allowed under the law in the form of joint ownership through inheritance or additions. Due to the shortage of lands and to the great number of original holders involved, and in order to avoid displacement of these holders, the original law was modified to reduce the maximum limit of ownership from 50 to 20 ha. The priority scale in the selection of farmers was likewise changed, so that professional farmers in the project area were given priority over absentee owners or those who utilise their land by lease or share-cropping. As such, a total area of 1,973.5 ha of the project area was allotted in the form of farm units shared by more than one holder.

Source: FAO, *Mediterranean Development Project, Jordan: Country Study*, p.98, attributed originally to Sweilem M. Haddad, 'Principles and Procedures Used in Planning and Executing the East Ghor Irrigation Project', paper presented to the International Conference on Water for Peace, Washington, 21-31 May 1967; Schedule No.2.

are estimated at 400 million tons.[51] Phosphates are now being developed and exported via Aqaba and Beirut ports. Production reached 1,088,955 tons in 1969 and rose to 1,674.808 tons in 1974.[52] The significance of phosphates covers employment, a relatively high percentage of export earnings, and a noticeable contribution to GDP. A large company was formed in 1956 for the extraction and export of potash, with contributions to the capital by some Arab countries. The initial, pilot stage called for a capital of JD4.5 million, which is not yet fully paid up, but in any case the works cannot be established because the pilot works were to be near Jericho, now under Israeli occupation, and the final works are to be near the Dead Sea, which is in danger of destruction so long as military clashes with Israel remain real and menacing. In its final form, the project envisages the production of 1.2 million tons annually with an expected value of $29 million. The capital cost has been estimated at $100 million. A road from the Dead Sea to Aqaba is necessary, at a cost of JD9 million. Finally, marble quarrying and export is also of importance in Jordan.

The country has attractive plain and coloured marble which it exports to neighbouring and some European countries. However, in relative terms, this activity is not very significant.

The sector of manufacturing (including mining, electricity and water supply) has grown only modestly in significance between 1954-6 and 1971-3, from a contribution to GDP of 9.4 per cent to 12.5 per cent. In absolute terms, it registered the largest jump for any sector, except for trade and banking and public administration and defence. (Construction expanded most dramatically, in relative terms, by raising its contribution from 1.2 to 5.7 per cent, but in absolute terms the rise was smaller, as Table 5.3 reveals.) But manufacturing industry by itself remains on the whole of modest dimensions in Jordan, and it comprises the very simple and conventional 'initiation' industries that accompany early development, like food processing, soft drinks, soap, flour milling, cement, matches, shoes, clothing apparel, textiles, furniture and cigarettes. (The studies of Kuznets, already referred to, suggest that countries at Jordan's income level have a more substantial manufacturing sector.) However, there is a petroleum refinery which has been in operation since 1960 and uses crude oil from the pipeline that carries Aramco's crude from Saudi Arabia to the Mediterranean at Zahrani in South Lebanon.

The industrial census of 1959 revealed that there were 6,887 industrial establishments in the country, employing 23,068 labourers — which reflects the very small scale of establishments on the average, especially if it is remembered that some 50 per cent of labourers are owners working in their own factories. Some 63 per cent of the establishments and 53 per cent of the workers were located in the West Bank. However, a survey undertaken in 1965 showed a smaller number of establishments and a larger labour force — 6,630 and 33,132 respectively — and total fixed capital assets of JD18.38 million for 1965 against JD6.21 million for 1959.[53] To this change in major magnitudes must be added the fact that there has been expansion in existing industries, such as tobacco, and the introduction of new industries such as porcelain products, canning, plastics, kitchen utensils, batteries and pharmaceuticals.

Electricity generation still provides the country with very low *per capita* energy. However, it has risen considerably from the early fifties. The IBRD mission reported an installed capacity of 10,315 kw in 1955,[54] which has since risen to about 50,000 kw at the present moment. Total energy generated in 1966 (the last year for which data are available for both Banks) was 178.8 million kwh or about 90 kwh per person during the year. However, energy generated in the East Bank alone was 310.2 million kwh in 1974, which suggests the installation of sizeable new capacity between 1966 and 1972.

The sector of transport and communication witnessed a moderate retreat in its share in GDP in relative terms, from 11 to 8.1 per cent between 1954-6 and 1971-3; in absolute terms its share rose from an average of JD5.6 million to JD17.7 million. This expansion has occurred thanks mainly to the transformation of Aqaba from a very modest port, with hardly any modern facilities, into a large port which is very well equipped and active, and to the growth of the road network. Total goods handled at Aqaba rose from 92,351 tons in 1954 to 1,483,597 tons in 1974. (The tonnage dropped from 1.2m tons for 1966 to 743,549 tons for 1969, owing to the initial severance of trade ties between the West Bank and the rest of the country subsequent to Israeli occupation.)[55]

Other important components in the expansion of the sector are the development of ALIA, the national airline, and of Amman and Jerusalem airports. Generally speaking, the country is now well equipped with good roads, especially after the construction of three or four major highways leading to Aqaba, to Syria and to Jerusalem, and the development of linkage networks between towns, and between the countryside and urban centres.

The railroads are of comparatively minor importance in the movement of goods and passengers. On the other hand, bus services have improved considerably in the past two decades. Lastly, the transit fees received from the Tapline (JD3.39m for 1973, but JD1.16m for 1974), the petroleum carrier from Saudi Arabia to Lebanon, fall under the earnings of the sector of transport and communications.[56]

Finally, tourism. This sector was making vast strides and earning income beyond expectations when the war broke out in 1967. It is the best single earner of foreign exchange. The FAO *Country Report* states that in 1966 its contribution in foreign exchange totalled JD12.3 million,[57] a very significant contribution, foreign aid apart. The tourist facilities and attractions were being increased, improved or made more accessible and better advertised when the 1967 war started. Group arrangements were becoming large-scale and extending to cover sight-seeing in Lebanon, Syria and Egypt, in addition to Jordan. Such integrated tours were of special appeal to tourists, because of the reduction in unit cost they represented. The contribution of the sector to GDP is not shown separately in the national accounts. However, some indicators show its significance. Receipts from travel rose tenfold from JD1.2 million in 1958 to JD12.3 million in 1966, while the number of visitors rose from 104,000 to 938,000.

Reference has been made to the Agricultural Credit Corporation as one source of sectoral financing. It must be pointed out that the country has several other financing institutions for the promotion of agriculture, industry, tourism, trade and other activities. The oldest of these is the Agricultural Bank, which was inherited from Ottoman days. Next to it comes the Arab Land Bank, formed in 1947 with a capital of £P1 million, to which the League of Arab States subscribed. To these two institutions must be added the Development Board, all three of which provided agricultural credit. The last named institution, however, extended its financing activities into other sectors as well. A Municipal Loan Fund specialises in advancing loans to municipalities for the development of public utilities and community facilities. A Housing Agency was established in 1966, also for community development with emphasis on housing, but its operations are small-scale.

In 1952 UNRWA, in collaboration with the government, established a Development Bank, with a capital of JD500,000. The Bank gave its support to agricultural and industrial development. Almost simultaneously, an Industrial Development Fund was established and attached to the Development Board. But the Fund was incorporated into a new Industrial Development Bank which was formed in 1965 with a capital of JD3 million, with private and public participation (two-thirds and one-third respectively). The Industrial Bank has been active in promoting manufacturing industry and tourism, in the ratio, roughly, of 85 and 15 per cent of total loans respectively. In 1966 the government set up the Jordan Electricity Authority, with private participation of 49 per cent, for the purpose of consolidating the ownership of electric generating and transmitting establishments in the settled north of the country. Municipalities and private companies were to continue to distribute power. Finally, the Central Bank was formed in October 1964, and took over from the Currency Board which had been established in 1949 and which had its offices in London.

However, government support and promotion of the various sectors are not restricted to credit via the institutions enumerated, but extend to direct participation, out of the general budget, in the capital of certain large establishments — mainly in the sectors of industry, public utilities, mining and transport.

It will be useful at this point to recapitulate the operations of the specialised financial

Jordan

institutions. The unified balance sheet of these institutions shows that their total assets (and liabilities) averaged JD16.91m for the three years 1968-70, and rose to JD19.14m, JD20.61m, and JD23.06m for 1971, 1972 and 1973 respectively. The combined paid-up capital was JD10.05m, 11.25m, 11.82m, and 12.49m for the same years. On the other hand, their loans to the private and public sectors combined, again for the same reference years, totalled JD13.62m, 14.87m, 16.24m and 17.52m, with the share of the private sector slightly more than double that of the public sector.

The combined cumulative loans outstanding at the end of 1973 just cited, namely JD17.52m, are shown in Table 5.16.

Table 5.16: Loans Outstanding, 1973 (JDm)

Municipal and Village Loans Fund	5.22
Industrial Development Bank	3.04
Housing Agency	1.16
Agricultural Credit Corporation	7.27
Jordan Co-operative Organization	0.83
Total	17.52

Source: FAO, Mediterranean Development Project, *Jordan: Country Study*, pp.75 and 77.

The private commercial banks do not limit their operations to commercial credit, though it represents the largest single beneficiary (with about 41.5 per cent for the three years 1971-3 on average). Industry and mining have received roughly one-tenth of total credit advanced, with construction, agriculture, real estate, tourism and transport also benefiting in varying degrees.[58] In effect, though these commercial banks are supposed to extend short-term credit only, they allow their loans to stretch to medium- and even long-term periods, through renewal of loans.

3. PLANS AND PLANNING[59]

As early as 1952, Jordan established a Development Board, with the object of preparing development plans and programmes and supervising the expenditure of development loans which Jordan used to obtain from the United Kingdom. The old Board was reconstituted and became better equipped in terms of skilled professionals and technicians. It remained in existence until 1972, when it was replaced by a National Planning Council. The first Board had worked on a much more modest scale than the second, as the total expenditure it had handled was some JD6.5 million, including projects in the transport and communications, agriculture (forests, experimental and research institutions) and storage sectors.[60]

In the meantime, the IBRD mission had recommended a programme of public capital expenditure for the years 1955/6–1964/5 totalling JD42.35 million, to be divided as shown in Table 5.17.

This programme was restricted to the public sector, including the municipalities in certain respects, and did not take into account either total resources available or total uses of resources. Per year, the programme stipulated an expenditure of JD4.24 million on average. Until 1962, the government was actually spending more than this average,

Table 5.17: IBRD Recommendations on Public Capital Expenditure, 1955/6–1964/5

	JD million	Per Cent of Total
Land use (agricultural credit, Jordan Valley Pilot Project, hill fruit programme, minor irrigation and rural water supplies, research, agricultural education, etc.)	17.16	40.5
Mines and minerals (phosphate and potash)	2.39	5.6
Industry (industrial credit and tourism)	1.04	2.4
Transport (roads, railway, port, civil aviation)	10.28	24.3
Communications	1.17	2.8
Education (general and vocational, including 1m municipal expenditure)	3.00	7.1
Health	0.64	1.5
Housing	1.00	2.4
Administrative buildings	0.60	1.4
Urban development (municipal expenditure)	2.00	4.7
Electric power (municipal expenditure)	1.56	3.7
Other	1.50	3.5
Total (rounded)	42.35	100.0

Source: IBRD, *The Economy of Jordan*, p.6.

thanks to the rise in aid received and the emergence of the United States as another major donor or creditor, which had soon replaced the United Kingdom as the top-ranking donor.

Late in 1961 the government asked the Development Board to prepare a development plan for the years 1962-7, which would project private as well as public investment. The Board formulated a plan totalling JD127.3 million (an average of 25.5 million per year), which was to be divided as shown in Table 5.18. The contribution of the private sector was to be JD47 million, or 36.9 per cent. The priorities of this programme were in this order: (a) increase in national income; (b) reduction of unemployment; and (c) improvement in the balance of payments.

However, late in 1962, the government asked the Development Board to revise the plan in order to make it a seven-year plan; so to shape it as to make it compatible with the objectives of Arabic economic unity; and to rearrange the priorities to be as follows in the order indicated: (a) reduction in the deficit in the current account of the balance of payments, thus reducing the dependence on foreign aid, (b) raising *per capita* income fast and in consistency with the first priority, and (c) increasing job opportunities. The strategy of the plan was to be based on the basic sectors of agriculture (especially the development of water resources and irrigation); mining; tourism; manufacturing industry; and on supporting services, such as education, health, transport, communications and popular housing. In rearranging the priorities and laying a clear strategy, the Development Board benefited from the arrival to its leadership of new, competent and dynamic young men who worked

Table 5.18: Development Board Plan for Public and Private Investment, 1962-7

	JD million	Per Cent of Total
Agriculture	40.3	31.7
Industry	22.8	17.9
Tourism	6.4	5.0
Construction and public buildings	19.9	15.6
Transport	13.2	10.4
Communication	4.2	3.3
Public services (education, health, social affairs)	10.3	8.1
Municipalities	7.3	5.7
Trade and services	2.0	1.6
Other (government administration, statistics, fiscal programme)	0.8	0.6
Total (rounded)	127.3	100.0

Source: H.K.J., *The 5-Year Program for Economic Development 1962-1967*, p.361.

in harmony with an equally dynamic new cabinet.

The combination of the level of professionalism attained, the benefit of accumulated experience in planning, and the better knowledge of the economy thanks to improved statistical services reflected itself in the formulation of a plan which was more comprehensive than any programme or plan previously formulated, one which took into account total resource availability and use, and, tenably, a more defensible order of priorities for the economy, given its problems and its potential likewise. *Ex post*, it can be seen that the projections of expenditure on GNP at market prices for the years of the Seven-Year Plan, interestingly enough, run very close to actual GNP generated. The investment programme as projected stood as shown in Table 5.19.

The assertion can be defended, even in the absence of performance data with regard to the Plan, that this performance, in global terms, conformed remarkably to the projections between 1964 and mid-1967, and that the country could legitimately have been expected to overfulfil the Plan had it not been for the war of 1967 and the occupation of the West Bank. This dislocated the economy seriously and caused it losses of grave dimensions, and no doubt slowed down the pace of development. It also meant the diversion of more resources than ever before towards defence. The overall performance of the Jordanian economy in the post-war years can only be described as clearly beyond what a mechanistic view of the natural resources and financial availabilities of the country would suggest, thanks to the factors referred to early in this chapter. The 1964-70 Plan seems to have been sound in the priorities pattern adopted, and was moving in the direction of achieving its objectives as set, mainly with respect to the reduction in the deficit on current account and the rise in income *per capita*. Its weakest performance was in the area of reducing unemployment. This was and still is the most intractable of the country's problems, and has if anything become more serious, with the aggravation of the refugee problem, after the rise in the number of refugees by about 300,000 in the wake of the 1967 war.

The life of the 1964-70 Plan was cut short by this war. Economic life in general slackened

Table 5.19: Planned Sectoral Distribution of Investment 1964-1970 (JD million and percentages)

Sector	Private	Public	Total	Per Cent of Total
Agriculture and water resources	16.3	54.3	70.6	25.6
Mining	22.7	7.6	30.3	11.0
Manufacturing	8.1	–	8.1	2.9
Electricity	2.8	5.7	8.5	3.1
Transport and communications	12.3	40.9	53.2	19.2
Tourism	9.7	2.5	12.2	4.4
Trade and services	7.1	–	7.1	2.6
Education, health and social services	3.9	6.7	10.6	3.8
Housing and building	31.7	5.3	37.0	13.4
Public administration	–	9.0	9.0	3.3
Local government	–	14.8	14.8	5.4
Unallocated	14.6	–	14.6	5.3
Total	129.2	146.8	276.0	100.0

Source: Arrangement follows table on p.21 of UNESOB, *Studies on Selected Development Problems in Various Countries in the Middle East,* 1969.

and was dislocated. Expenditure on defence had to be increased. Phosphate exports had to change route with the closure of the Suez Canal, and their competitiveness weakened for a time. Tourism lost its momentum, and its earnings dropped. The financial burden was not reduced as a result of the occupation of the West Bank, owing to the continued shouldering by the government of the responsibility to pay the salaries of government officials and to advance loans to municipalities in the West Bank. With the closure of Arab banks in the occupied territory, the banks in the East Bank had to honour the drawings by depositors in the branches in the West Bank. The private investment climate became less inviting in general, and some flight of capital — at least initially — occurred. This was coupled with a certain volume of brain drain. Finally, dependence on foreign sources for budget support (both for recurrent and development expenditure) intensified.[61]

Many of the emerging economic problems had distinct security aspects, and the government established the Economic Security Committee to cope with the situation. The disruption of normal planning and execution activities, coupled with the new economic-cum-security problems resulted in the relative eclipsing of the Development Board. Projects began to be completed slowly, and new ones initiated, but on an *ad hoc* basis, or on a selective basis out of the docket of projects in the 1964-70 Plan. The priorities had to be varied in order to cope with the new situation, particularly with those aspects relating to foreign exchange availability, keeping the morale of the West Bankers, recapturing and then maintaining economic and financial stability, and redressing the hardships befalling large groups of the population as a result of the dislocations.

However, the economy recovered remarkably fast, considering its structural shortages, shortcomings and handicaps. The turn of the 1970s saw a serious concern for renewed planning and development work. In 1972 the National Planning Council was established and took over from the Development Board, as already indicated. The NPC nominally had very much the same powers, but the policy directives under which it was to operate asked it to view its main functions as planning, the allocation of foreign aid received for development purposes, and the supervision and evaluation of the execution of development programmes and projects. Less emphasis was to be placed on actual execution, which the Board had been authorised to undertake, at least theoretically.

It was under the NPC that the latest plan was finally produced, for the years 1973-5. This three-year Plan was launched, with energy, during a conference which brought together representatives from donor countries, leading journals dealing with economic matters, and international organisations. It was realised by the authorities that the Plan was formulated in the midst of uncertainty, with the West Bank still under occupation, and no assurance as to the date of its liberation. However, although the initial chapters in the Plan document speak of the Kingdom as a whole as the geographical frame of the Plan, in practice the chapters dealing with specific sectors include projects in the East Bank only. All through, the document starts with an evaluation of the situation inherited, an analysis of the problems besetting progress, and then moves on to a presentation of the objectives and projects to be pursued and implemented. A common-sense, pragmatic approach (as against an over-ambitious and abstract approach) characterises the Plan document. Furthermore, it takes full cognisance of the many social, political and public administration factors associated with plan execution, and suggests how these can be moulded in order to serve the objectives and policies of the Plan.

The objectives as formulated in the opening chapter of the document are:

(a) Achievement of the highest possible level of employment, the improvement of the labour force and the upgrading of manpower potential for serving development.
(b) Realisation of the highest possible growth in GNP with the maintenance of relative price stability. (An average growth of GDP by 8 per cent per annum is quoted in the following chapter on 'The Framework of the Three Year Plan'.)
(c) Redistribution of public services and ensuring gains more properly among the different regions and population groups.
(d) Gradual reduction of the trade deficit, together with bringing the balance of payments in equilibrium.
(e) Enhancement of the general budget's dependence on domestic financial sources for the purpose of achieving equilibrium in the long run.

We will not detail the objectives any further, but will concentrate on the investment programme envisaged. This investment is to come from the private as well as the public sector. For the three years taken together, the contribution of the private sector is projected as 44.4 per cent, that of the public sector as 55.6 per cent. However, it is expected that the share of the public sector will drop gradually between the first and last year. Total investment is projected as JD179m. The distribution between public and private sources, and among economic sectors, is shown in Table 5.20.

The financing of the investment programme was considered feasible, given the flow of domestic resources into the treasury and the expectations of foreign aid. For instance, the budget estimates for 1973 included JD47.56m of aid expected from the two Arab countries that had frozen their assistance since late in 1970, namely Libya and Kuwait. The preliminary closed accounts for 1973 show that no part of this sum actually

Table 5.20: Three-Year Plan Investment by Sector, 1973-5 (JD '000)

Sector	Total Investment	Per Cent	Public Sector Investment	Private Sector Investment
Agriculture	13,020	7.3	8,937	4,083
Irrigation	14,636	8.2	14,636	–
Industry and mining	26,120	14.6	5,810	20,310
Tourism and antiquities	7,170	4.0	2,105	5,065
Electricity	9,781	5.5	5,700	4,081
Transportation	35,812	20.0	27,812	8,000
Communication	6,712	3.7	6,712	–
Trade	775	0.4	125	650
Total, Economic Sectors	114,026	63.7	71,837	42,189
Education and youth care	10,914	6.1	7,673	3,241
Health	1,480	0.8	880	600
Social affairs and labour	1,455	0.8	1,395	60
Housing and government buildings	34,890	19.5	3,420	31,470
Municipal and rural affairs	14,758	8.2	14,108	650
Awqaf	1,214	0.7	–	1,214
Statistics	263	0.2	263	–
Total, Social Sectors	64,974	36.3	27,739	37,235
Total Investment	179,000	100.0	99,576	79,424

Source: *Jordan Development Plan 1973-1975*, pp.2-19.

materialised. On the other hand, the budget support for ordinary expenditures, estimated at JD40m, was exceeded in fact by JD4.69m.[62]

Mainly because of this shortfall, but also because of the bad harvest in 1973, as well as some chronic problems associated with the design and execution of projects (inadequate studies, insufficient skilled manpower, delays by contractors, etc.), actual development expenditure fell well below planned expenditure. This reflected itself in a drop in the performance of the economy in 1973 well below expectations. Thus, while 1972 showed a growth of 11.3 per cent over 1971, 1973 showed only 6.1 per cent at current prices. However, the performance was much poorer, as the price index rose from 129.4 for 1972 to 142.9 for 1973 (1970=100).[63] In other words, in real terms, GDP in 1973 fell below that for 1972. Examined separately, the various sectors fared differently. Thus, while the contribution of agriculture dropped by JD10.5m, that of the remaining sectors combined rose by a total of JD23.5m, leaving a net absolute rise of JD13m at current prices. Yet this rise was less significant than that in the price index, which was 10.5 per cent.

4. CONCLUDING REMARKS

Speculation on the future course of development in the Jordan of today is more difficult than ever, with the very size of the country being in question. If the break between the West and the East Bank continues much longer, there will have to be many structural and basic adjustments, many deeper far-reaching dislocations than have occurred so far, and the country's leadership will have to steer a totally new course of action to suit the new conditions. The very foundations on which the creditable performance of the past two decades has been based will probably be put into serious question, and nobody can foretell what the answer will be.

In one sense, the last eight years since June 1967 resemble the earliest years surveyed — 1946-8. Jordan today comprises nothing but the territory it had in 1946, when Transjordan was merely the land east of the River Jordan. Like yesterday, this land is today largely bereft of the territory, the resources, the agriculture and manufacturing, and of the professional and other activities conducted by the people of the West Bank. But in one important sense the situation is worse today than it was just after the establishment of Israel in May 1948. Then, Jordan suffered the disruption of its trade routes, lost the use of Haifa port and the passage of Iraqi petroleum on to Palestine. However, it continued to have normal trade relations and free movement of persons and capital between the unoccupied part of Palestine and itself. Today, even this last advantage is lost. It is true that the country is today in command of much more impressive financial resources, more effective productive capacity, a better-educated population, and the valuable experience of the civil service and the private sector that have been a rather successful 'going concern' for a quarter of a century. None the less, the dislocations after 1967 in trade patterns, the limitations on the passage of persons and capital between the two Banks, and above all the political uncertainty and the very territorial integrity of the country itself together impose yet more severe hardships owing to the integration of the economies of the two Banks that has been achieved since 1967. The cycle has moved full circle, but at a higher level of suffering and hardship. Yet if the political and economic leadership of the country can repeat the commendable economic performance of the past two decades, then the country in its trimmed area may still be able to find some economic consolation for its territorial and political loss.

NOTES

1. James Baster, then Economic Adviser to the United Nations Relief and Works Agency for Palestine Refugees in the Near East (UNRWA) in Beirut, Lebanon, in a paper for limited circulation entitled 'Economic Prospects of Jordan', Spring 1951. See also his article 'The Economic Problems of Jordan', in *International Affairs*, January 1955.

2. R.S. Porter, *Economic Survey of Jordan* (British Middle East Office, 1953), Appendix II. According to Porter £P10m were in bank deposits transferred to the East Bank, and £P10m in banknotes, which were converted into Jordanian dinars.

3. Much of the material in this section on background draws on the IBRD, *The Economy of Jordan* (Baltimore, 1957), 'The Summary Report', and Ch. 1 in the Main Report, as well as on tables in the Annexes. Other references include in particular: (a) Doreen Warriner, *Land and Poverty in the Middle East* (London, 1948), chapter on Transjordan; (b) Burhan Dajani, *Lectures on Jordan's Economic Development* (Arab League Center for Graduate Studies, Cairo; Arabic), especially Ch.1; (c) Royal Institute for International Affairs, *The Middle East: A Political and Economic Survey* (third edition, 1958, London), chapter on Jordan; (d) FAO, Mediterranean Development Project, *Jordan: Country Study* (Rome, 1967), background chapter; (e) General Union of Chambers of Commerce, Industry, and Agriculture in the Arab Countries, *Economic Development in the Arab Countries, 1950-1965* (Beirut, 1967; Arabic), chapter on Jordan; (f) Ministry

of Culture and Information, Hashemite Kingdom of Jordan, *Economic Development* (prepared by Hanna S. Odeh, Amman, 1971), the relevant parts; (g) Michael P. Mazur, 'Economic Development of Jordan', in Charles A. Cooper and Sidney S. Alexander (eds.), *Economic Development and Population Growth in the Middle East* (New York, 1972); and (h) Europa Publications, *The Middle East and North Africa 1971-72, 1972-73, 1973-74,* and *1974-75* (yearly editions, London), chapter on Jordan.

4. Hashemite Kingdom of Jordan (HKJ), Department of Statistics, *Statistical Yearbook 1966*, p.112.

5. IBRD, p.42.

6. HKJ, Department of Statistics, *Report on Agriculture Census 1965* (Amman, 1967), table on p. 84.

7. For a thorough discussion of land use in Jordan, see FAO, *Jordan* (cited under note 3 above), especially pp. 41-5. It ought to be stated here that areas quoted in FAO *Production Yearbook 1972* (Rome, 1973), Table 1, p. 5, vary considerably from those appearing in the text above. According to FAO's *Yearbook*, Jordan has 1,132,000 ha of arable land, 168,000 ha of land under permanent crops, and another 100,000 ha of permanent meadows and pastures. If arable land and land under permanent crops are combined, they would add up to 1.3m ha of cultivable land, or 13.3 per cent of the total area of the country. This seems to be a liberal estimate, if compared with official Jordanian estimates, and with Mazur's careful research (see the reference to Mazur in note 3 above).

8. *Statistical Yearbook 1966*, pp.2-3. According to another source, the number is currently 120,000. See The League of Arab States, *Sedentarization of Bedouins in the Arab World* (Cairo, 1965), Vol. 5, p. 112, quoted in UN Economic and Social Office in Beirut, UNESOB, *Studies on Selected Development Problems in Various Countries in the Middle East, 1970* (New York, 1970), p. 106.

9. The earliest estimate of national income was made by the Economic Research Institute at the American University of Beirut for the years 1952-4. National income according to this estimate was JD44.5m for 1952, or some 32.4 dinars per head. However, as the IBRD (especially p. 5) emphasises, the years 1948-55 were years of very fast growth, possibly averaging more than 8 per cent a year. The estimate for Palestine is projected from the data for 1945 as in Government of Palestine, *National Income of Palestine, 1945* (report by the Government Statistician P.J. Loftus, Jerusalem, 1947).

10. See IBRD; various issues of UNRWA *Quarterly Bulletin*, Nos. 1-14; Dajani; etc. The population data have been the subject of controversy between Zionist groups attempting to show that the estimates of refugees entering Jordan and moving from Israeli-occupied territories to the West Bank were grossly overestimated, and UNRWA and Arab authorities insisting on the correctness of their estimates. The evidence is overwhelmingly on the side of UNRWA and Arab estimates. See: (a) Government of Palestine, *Village Statistics* (Jerusalem, 1945) for population data by district, sub-district, urban centre, and individual village; (b) UN, *Final Report of the United National Economic Survey Mission for the Middle East* (New York, 1949), p. 22; and (c) UNRWA, *Quarterly Bulletin*, No. 3, May 1952, Appendix, p. 51.

11. These data are based on the various issues of the *Annual Report* submitted by the Director (later the Commissioner-General) of UNRWA to the United Nations.

12. Hamad al-Farhan, 'Development Projects in Jordan', in *Al-Abhath* (journal published by the American University of Beirut, in Arabic), Vol. 8, No. 3. Al-Farhan was the first Director of the Department of Statistics in the Kingdom. He estimates the labour force at 270,000 in 1949, of whom 110,000 (41 per cent) were employed. His calculations suggest an almost 100 per cent unemployment among Palestinian refugees in the East Bank, 60 per cent among West Bank residents, and 30 per cent among the original citizens of the East Bank. Though Mazur (see note 3 above) does not discuss this early phase at length, he leaves his reader with the impression that the level of unemployment was much lower than that suggested by Al-Farhan. In fact, his estimates of unemployment for the whole period covered (say, till 1970) seem to the present writer to be distinctly on the low side.

13. Michael Getler in *International Herald Tribune*, 28 September 1970.

14. Mazur, loc. cit., especially Section V, pp. 225-66.

15. Indebtedness is discussed further below, in Section 2, sub-section on 'Progress in Main Sectors, Economic Institutions and Major Projects'.

16. The writer, as member of the Economic Research Institute, has had access to the estimates.

17. R.S. Porter, 'Economic Trends in Jordan 1954-1959' (Beirut, July 1961; mimeographed).

18. Porter, p. 2. Mazur in several places in his chapter assumes a lower rate, something in the neighbourhood of 2 per cent per annum.

19. FAO, *Jordan*, p. 17. For price movements from 1967 to the end of 1973, see *IFS*, September 1974.

20. See Simon Kuznets, 'Quantitative Aspects of the Economic Growth of Nations: II. Industrial Distribution of National Product and Labour Force', in *Economic Development and Cultural Change*, Supplement to Volume V, No. 4, July 1957, especially pp. 5-16. P.T. Bauer and B . S. Yamey had observed and recorded the same phenomenon in two articles in *Economic Journal*, December 1951 and March 1954. Likewise, Colin Clark in *The Conditions of Economic Progress* (London, 1951) and A.G.B. Fisher, 'The Economic Implications of Material Progress' in *International Labour Review*, July 1935, and in *Economic Progress and Social Security* (London, 1945) discussed the association between income levels and sectoral distribution – though no writer has gone into this question with as much careful empirical research as Kuznets.

21. The reader who is interested in the matter can find an interesting discussion of it in Odeh (see note 3 above), but more particularly and fully in Mazur, to whom I am indebted for some of the points in the examination of the course of development in each of the Banks.

22. Data on Israel's import surplus have been compiled as follows: For 1950-8, from Don Patinkin, *The*

Israeli Economy: The First Decade (The Falk Project for Economic Research in Israel, Report for 1958 and 1959; Jerusalem, 1959); for subsequent years to 1974, from Bank of Israel, *Annual Report* for 1959-1974 (Jerusalem, 1960-75). It ought to be added that Israel has received a total of economic aid (grants plus loans) in excess of the aggregate import surplus. Hence a total exceeding $18,500 million of *recorded and published* aid was received from 1950 to the end of 1974. There is reason to believe that certain amounts of aid do not appear in the official statistics. By the end of 1974, the Bank of Israel revenues amounted to $1,201.6m (including $1,151.4m in foreign exchange), according to *IFS*, June 1975.

23. The larger total has been compiled from several sources, as follows: (a) *Time* magazine, 29 March 1963, for a listing of US aid from July 1945 through June 1962, quoting official US sources; (b) OECD, *The Flow of Financial Resources to Less-Developed Countries 1961-1965* (Paris, 1967), p. 155, for 1961-5; (c) OECD, *Development Assistance: 1969 Review* (Paris, 1969), pp. 170-1 for 1966-8; (d) OECD, *Development Co-Operation: 1973 Review* (Paris, 1973), for 1969-72; (e) IMF, *IFS*, September 1974 for 1973; (f) Central Bank of Jordan, *Monthly Statistical Bulletin*, various issues between 1967 and June 1974, tables on balance of payments; and (g) Kuwait Fund for Arab Economic Development, *Annual Report 1973-74*, p. 24. The data included in these sources all relate to OECD and Arab countries only. Jordan has received no aid from any socialist country.

The smaller total has been compiled from: (a) IMF, *IFS Supplement to 1967/68 Issues* for 1950-60; (b) *IFS*, September 1968 for 1961-7; and (c) *IFS*, September 1974 for 1968-73.

24. *IFS*, February 1976 with respect to the reserves, and Central Bank of Jordan, *Tenth Annual Report 1973*, p. 96, for foreign debt. For the ranking of the creditors by size of loan, see Europa, *1973-74*, op. cit., p. 415.

25. Average for the years 1954-65 is 14.1 per cent, as FAO, op. cit., p. 15, shows. The slight rise in the whole period 1954-72 suggests only a moderate rise in the level of investment in the period 1966-72. The calculations are based on data in FAO, op. cit., p. 21 (for 1954-65); *Statistical Yearbook 1972*, p. 175, for 1966-71; and CBJ, *Monthly Statistical Bulletin*, December 1973, Table 34, for 1972.

26. See Mazur, loc. cit., p. 225 and table on p. 226 for a thorough examination of growth of labour productivity. According to him, this accounted for 30-40 per cent of growth in NDP over the years 1960-6 at current prices, or for 20-30 per cent at constant prices.

27. Such as: (a) General Assembly Resolution No. 2253 (ES-V) of 4 July 1967; (b) General Assembly Resolution No. 2254 (ES-V) of 14 July 1967; (c) General Assembly Resolution No. 2851 (XXVI) of 20 December 1971; (d) Security Council Resolution No. 252 (1968) of 21 May 1968; (e) Security Council Resolution No. 267 (1969) of 3 July 1969; (f) Security Council Resolution No. 271 (1969) of 15 September 1969.

28. See, for instance, the first and the most recent issues of *Statistical Yearbook*, for 1950 and 1972 respectively, in the chapter on 'Population'.

29. UNESCO, *Comparative Statistical Data on Education in the Arab States, An Analysis 1960-61 – 1967-68* (prepared by the UNESCO Office of Statistics, Paris, and published by the Regional Center for Educational Planning and Administration, Beirut, 1970), p. 48.

30. Ibid., pp. 58-61, for 1966, and *Statistical Yearbook 1974*, pp. 84, 92-3, and 104-5 for 1973-4.

31. For data on students in 1971/2 see *Statistical Yearbook 1972*, pp. 74-8. For 1973/4 see *Statistical Yearbook 1974*, p. 88. The estimate regarding Palestinians with university degrees is based on a research project undertaken by the Palestine Planning Center, Beirut, and on two articles: (a) Nabeel Shaath, 'High Level Palestinian Manpower', in *Journal of Palestine Studies*, Vol. I, No. 2 (Winter 1972), pp. 80-95; and (b) Antoine Zahlan and Edward Hagopian, 'Palestine's Arab Population: The Demography of the Palestinians', in *Journal of Palestine Studies*, Vol. III, No. 4 (Summer 1974), pp. 32-73. The references to the education of Palestinian Arabs under Israeli occupation come mostly from: Fayez Sayegh, *Discrimination in Education Against Arabs in Israel* (Palestine Research Center, PRC, Beirut, 1965); Munir Bashshur and Khaled M. El-Shaykh Youssuf, *Education in Israel* (PRC, 1969; in Arabic), especially Chapter 9, and Saleh Abdallah Sirriah, *Educating the Arabs in Israel* (PRC, 1973; in Arabic).

32. IBRD, op. cit., pp. 301, 305.

33. *Statistical Yearbook 1974*, p. 88.

34. Calculations based on data in Ministry of Education, *Yearbook of Educational Statistics in the Hashemite Kingdom of Jordan for the Scholastic Year 1965-1966* (Amman, undated), Ch. 2.

35. *Statistical Yearbook 1972*, pp. 72-3. No information appears in *Yearbook 1974* with respect to technical training.

36. See Ch. 3 in *Yearbook of Educational Statistics... 1965-1966*.

37. With regard to the sub-standard calorie intake *per capita* (especially in the form of Vitamin A, riboflavin, animal protein and fats) see two studies: *The Hashemite Kingdom of Jordan, Nutritional Survey, April-June 1962*, A Report by the Interdepartmental Committee on Nutrition for National Defence (Washington, 1963), pp. 2, 3, 64, 65, 68, quoted in FAO, *Jordan: Country Study*, pp. 8 and 9. See also Usama Khalidi, 'The Diet of Arab Refugees Receiving UNRWA Rations, up to 31st May 1967' (Institute for Palestine Studies, April 1970), pp. 1-18. For housing conditions, see *First Census of Population and Housing 1961*, Vols. 1 and 2 (Amman, 1964); and IBRD, op. cit., Ch. 7.

38. IBRD, op. cit., Ch. 7 for 1954; FAO, op. cit., p. 11 for 1965, and *Statistical Yearbook 1974*, p. 206 for 1974.

39. Department of Statistics, *First Census of Population and Housing 1961*, Vol. 2 (Amman, 1964), p. 10.

40. See Department of Statistics, *Labour Force Study, 1966, in the Sectors of Mining, Manufacturing, Wholesale and Retail Trade, Electricity, Finance and Services* (Amman, July 1968; Arabic); and *Population and Labour Force in the Agricultural Sector 1967* (Amman, 1968, Arabic).

41. See Mazur, loc. cit., pp. 230-7.

42. Department of Statistics, *Manpower 1970* (Amman, 1972; Arabic).

43. The National Planning Council, *Jordan Develop-*

ment Plan 1973-1975 (undated), Ch. 18, especially p. 323.
44. FAO, op. cit., p. 7.
45. For the fullest and clearest summing up, see the relevant chapters in FAO, op. cit.
46. Ibid., p. 102. Most of the material on agricultural conditions, produce grading, packing and marketing; credit and co-operative societies; research; land tenure and land reform; and the East Ghor Canal Authority and project, as well as technical assistance and training is based on the relevant parts of FAO, *Jordan: Country Report*, which had been originally written by the present writer, as co-author of that *Report*.
47. Department of Statistics, *1953 Census of Agriculture* (Amman, undated), pp. 3 and 7.
48. UNRWA, *Jordan Valley Land Tenure Survey* (Amman, 1956), p. 23.
49. For a full description of the schemes relating to the Jordan Valley waters and their regional utilisation (that is, the utilisation of all water resources flowing into the watershed) see: (a) UNRWA, *Quarterly Bulletin of Economic Development* (Beirut, July 1954), No. 11, pp. 99-112, 'Comparison of Various Plans for Development of Jordan Valley'; (b) UNRWA, *Quarterly Bulletin* (Beirut, July 1956), No. 14, pp. 8-118, 'Comparison of Recent Plans to Utilize Waters of the Jordan River and its Tributaries', report prepared by Norman Burns. This is the most thorough and comprehensive treatment available; (c) Georgina Stevens, 'The Jordan River Valley', in *International Conciliation*, January 1956; (d) Victor Khoury, 'The River Jordan: Its Promise and its Menace' in *Ar-Ra'id* (Arabic monthly, Beirut): a series of 4 articles in February, March, April and May 1962; and a fifth updating article in the issue of April 1963; (e) Victor Khoury, 'Plans to Divert the Jordan River Waters', in *Middle East Forum* (Beirut), Vol. XL, No. 6, Summer 1964, pp. 18-21; and (f) Kathlyn B. Doherty, 'Jordan Water Conflict', in *International Conciliation*, May 1965.

For technical reports on the subject, refer to: (a) M.G. Ionides, 'Jordan Valley Irrigation in Transjordan', in *Engineering*, Vol. 162 (13 September 1946); (b) M.G. Ionides, 'The Disputed Waters of the Jordan', in *Middle East Journal*, Vol. 7, No. 2, Spring 1953, pp. 153-64; (c) Walter Clay Lowdermilk, *Palestine: Land of Promise* (New York, 1944), pp. 201-18; (d) James B. Hayes, *T.V.A. on the Jordan* (Washington, 1948), report prepared under the auspices of the Commission on Palestine Surveys; (e) Sir M. MacDonald and Partners, *Report on the Proposed Extension of Irrigation in the Jordan Valley*, March 1951; (f) Chas. T. Main, Inc., *The Unified Development of the Water Resources of the Jordan Valley Region* (Boston 1953, prepared at the request of the T.V.A.); (g) American Friends of the Middle East, *The Jordan Water Problem, An Analysis and Survey of Available Documents* (Washington, December 1964; Conference Proceedings); (h) Joseph Cotton, *The Cotton Plan for the Development and Utilization of the Water Resources of the Jordan and Litani Waters* (New York, February 1964, Israeli Office of Information. Report prepared for the Israeli Government); (i) *The Arabs' Plan for Development of Water Resources in the Jordan Valley*, prepared by the Arab League Technical Committee (March 1954), translated from Arabic in *Egyptian Economic and Political Science Review* (October 1955); and (j) *Yarmouk – Jordan Valley Project, Master Plan Report* (prepared by Michael Baker, Jr., Inc., and Harza Engineering Co., 1955, for the Jordanian Government. 8 vols.)
50. Information and estimation of potential are based on Mazur, loc. cit., pp. 260 and 264, FAO, op. cit., p. 148, and interview with the President of Dar al-Handasah. the major Arab engineering consulting firm which is deeply involved with the irrigation schemes of Jordan.
51. General Union of Chambers of Commerce, Industry, and Agriculture in the Arab Countries, *Economic Development in the Arab Countries 1950-1965*, pp. 28 ff.
52. *Statistical Yearbook 1969*, p. 208 for 1969, and *Yearbook 1974*, p. 201 for 1974.
53. Comparisons based on data in *Manufacturing Industry in Jordan, Report on the Industrial Census of 1959* (Amman, undated), and the *1965 Survey* results.
54. IBRD, op. cit., p. 354.
55. See the relevant issues of *Statistical Yearbook*.
56. Central Bank of Jordan, *Monthly Statistical Bulletin*, January 1976, Table 15.
57. FAO, op. cit., p. 26.
58. Central Bank of Jordan, *Tenth Annual Report 1973*, p. 73.
59. This section relies mainly on: (a) General Union of Chambers of Commerce, Industry and Agriculture in the Arab Countries, op. cit.; (b) HKJ, *The 5-Year Program for Economic Development 1962-1967;* (c) HKJ, *7-Year Program for Economic Development of Jordan 1964-1970;* (d) Edmond Asfour, 'Problems of Development Planning in Jordan', in *Middle East Economic Papers 1963;* (e) UNESOB, 'An Analysis of Development Plans in Various Countries in the Middle East', *Studies of Selected Development Problems in Various Countries in the Middle East*, 1967 issue, pp. 1-12; (f) UNESOB, 'Plan Formulation and Development Perspectives in Jordan', in *Studies of Selected. . . , 1969*, pp. 19-32; and (g) HKJ, *Jordan Development Plan 1973-1975*.
60. General Union of Chambers of Commerce..., op. cit., pp. 61-2.
61. See *Jordan Development Plan 1973-1975*, Ch. 1, for a discussion of the economic impact of the war in 1967.
62. For the 1973 budget estimates and preliminary closed account, see Central Bank of Jordan, *Tenth Annual Report 1973*, p. 88.
63. *IFS*, September 1974.

6 SYRIA

Many more outsiders probably associate Syria with political instability and *coups d'état* than with a basic economic stability and solidity. Yet Syria is one of the very few Arab economies which managed, on the whole, to achieve a reasonable rate of growth without the benefit of large petroleum resources and without the inflow of substantial foreign aid. The fact that in the past few years the country became an oil exporter — albeit a modest one — and the recipient of foreign economic aid does not invalidate our statement, which refers to the post-war period as a whole.

The first estimate of national product available — a private one — relates to 1950.[1] According to it, the national income totalled £S1,250 million,* and derived in large part (44.3 per cent) from agriculture. By 1973, net domestic product at factor cost had risen to £S5,574.6 million at constant (1963) prices while NDP at market prices had risen to £S6,452.1m.[2] Unfortunately, the series is not complete from 1950 to 1973; furthermore, the 1973 estimate is official while that for 1950 is not. We can safely assume wider coverage and better quality of data in the later than in the earlier estimate. The official, recently revised series stretches over 21 years, from 1953 to 1973.[3] According to this revised series, net domestic product at factor cost was £S2,264.3 million for 1953. Thus growth in real terms over this period is 146.2 per cent, or a cumulative rate of about 4.5 per cent per annum on the average. (If NDP at market prices is considered, then growth amounts to 170.6 per cent, or 5 per cent per annum on average.)

With a population of some 6.9 million in the middle of 1973, the income per head amounts to £S809 or $187 at the free rate of exchange for 1973 (212 at the official rate).[4] Against this, at mid-1953 the population numbered about 3.61 million and income per head amounted to £S627.[5] Thus, on the basis of these estimates, income per head in real terms in Syrian pounds rose by 29 per cent over 21 years, or by 1.3 per cent per annum. Population increased by 90 per cent, or by 3.3 per cent per annum over the same period. (Comparison of income in dollars is rather misleading, owing to the movement of the rate against the Syrian pound over the years.)

Obviously, the assessment of growth in the Syrian economy requires much more examination than these few figures are capable of providing, and such assessment will be attempted later. For the moment, we will simply add that in terms of socio-economic development, Syria ranks high in the Arab world. Thus its literacy rate is next only to the rate for Lebanon and nearest to that of Jordan. (The rate was 44 per cent in 1960 for both sexes aged 15-24, 65 per cent for males and 23 per cent for females; but probably the current overall rate of literacy is around 60 per cent.)[6] According to the Harbison, Maruhnic and Resnick index of cultural development (which takes into account newspaper circulation, radios owned, telephones installed, cinema attendance, vehicles in use and literacy rate), Syria ranks second after Lebanon. However, the index of health development (using doctors, dentists, pharmacists, nurses and hospital beds per population unit, protein, cereal

*Syrian pounds.

Table 6.1: Net Domestic Product at Factor Cost by Sectors, for the Years 1953–73

Sectors	1953	1954	1955	1956	1957	1958	1959	1960	1961	1962	1963	1964	1965	1966	1967	1968	1969	1970	1971	1972	1973
Agriculture, forestry and fisheries	873.1	1,048.5	817.3	1,046.8	1,109.1	827.0	693.0	564.9	766.8	1,226.7	1,126.9	1,291.8	1,226.9	1,006.1	1,202.0	1,025.0	1,336.5	1,086.0	1,117.8	1,442.4	1,012.8
Mining and manufacturing[a]	285.1	327.5	368.0	364.2	386.1	432.2	455.1	469.5	475.2	501.0	532.3	573.6	570.8	576.9	616.2	692.9	832.4	919.9	984.9	1,004.8	896.7
Building and construction	69.0	73.0	87.0	96.0	71.0	94.0	69.0	105.0	106.0	99.0	104.0	104.0	101.0	121.0	104.0	142.0	147.0	141.2	183.5	178.3	160.3
Transport and communication	200.0	206.0	231.0	247.0	198.0	245.0	268.0	278.0	295.0	351.0	295.0	323.0	346.0	339.0	363.0	451.0	482.0	556.1	702.6	564.8	812.0
Wholesale and retail trade	386.1	489.1	499.1	484.6	468.2	528.7	475.5	464.9	415.0	516.2	541.2	534.6	520.7	543.6	560.7	621.1	646.2	672.3	700.2	694.0	601.5
Finance and insurance	40.0	46.2	46.4	46.8	51.7	51.0	56.7	66.1	69.5	74.6	79.5	78.6	106.6	80.2	72.7	89.1	103.7	116.6	128.0	151.8	158.7
Ownership of dwellings	206.0	210.0	216.0	222.0	228.0	233.0	240.0	247.0	254.0	258.0	268.0	275.0	283.0	289.0	297.0	303.0	311.0	322.2	330.6	337.9	346.5
Government	76.0	78.0	99.0	103.0	129.0	147.0	183.0	202.0	260.0	319.0	368.0	429.0	436.0	474.0	482.0	571.0	592.0	700.3	809.5	912.3	1,102.0
Services	130.0	146.0	132.0	159.0	160.0	168.0	171.0	178.0	190.0	197.0	204.0	223.0	282.0	288.0	300.0	327.0	339.0	378.2	420.3	456.4	484.1
Total	2,264.3	2,624.3	2,495.8	2,769.4	2,801.1	2,725.9	2,611.3	2,575.4	2,831.5	3,542.5	3,508.9	3,832.6	3,873.0	3,719.8	3,997.6	4,222.1	4,789.8	4,892.8	5,377.4	5,742.7	5,574.6

Note: a. Including electricity, gas and water.
Source: Statistical Abstract 1971, pp. 484-5 for 1953-69; and Statistical Abstract 1974, p. 865 for 1970-3.

Syria

and starch intake in food, and life expectancy at birth as indicators) places Syria at the bottom of the list of Arab countries.[7] (It ought to be pointed out, in this connection, that the index in question leaves out Kuwait, Saudi Arabia and Sudan, but includes the other countries covered in the present study.)

1. CHANGES IN STRUCTURE IN THE POST-WAR PERIOD

The average rate of economic growth of 4.5–5 per cent per annum in real terms over the years 1953-73 has behind it an erratic course, with wide fluctuations from year to year. This is mainly explained by the fact that agriculture is at the same time the largest contributor to national product and the sector most exposed to fluctuations owing to its heavy dependence on generally poor rainfall and erratic climatic conditions. (The contribution of agriculture, as Table 6.3 shows, has on average been 29.6 per cent – about twice as high as that of manufacturing at 15.7 per cent or trade at 15.4 per cent.)

However, broadly speaking, the contribution of agriculture has tended to decline in relative terms. Thus it averaged 35.1 per cent during the seven years 1953-9, but dropped to 26.6 per cent for the fourteen years 1960-73. Taking all the sectors and their respective contribution into account, we find that by 1973 agriculture had made the lowest gain, while the largest gains were made by public administration (understandably, in view of the socialist transformation in the 1960s), transport and communication, finance and insurance, services, mining and manufacturing, building and construction, ownership of dwellings and trade – in that order. With 1953 as base year (= 100), the various sectors, and the NDP, stood at the indices indicated in Table 6.2 by the end of 1973.

Table 6.2: Comparison of Economic Sectors and NDP in 1973 (1953=100)

Agriculture	116.0
Mining and manufacturing	314.5
Building and construction	232.3
Transport and communication	406.0
Trade	155.8
Finance and insurance	396.7
Ownership of dwellings	168.2
Government	1,469.3
Services	372.4
NDP	246.0

Some observations can be made relating to Table 6.3. First, that agriculture continues to occupy first place in the structure of the economy, although in 1973 'government' ranked ahead of agriculture owing to the very poor performance of the latter. If an average for the last three years is taken, the contributions of agriculture and government stand at 21.3 and 16.9 per cent respectively. (In absolute terms, there has been no worse crop year than 1973 since 1962, except 1966.) However, judging by the experience of the past two decades, and because of its slow progress, agriculture might lose its position of predominance to mining and manufacturing considered together before 1980, thanks to the energetic programmes of industrial development and prospecting for more petroleum reserves, and to the steep rise in the price of crude petroleum, and despite the expectation

Table 6.3: The Structure of Net Domestic Product at Factor Cost by Sectors for the Years 1953–73 (at constant prices of 1963)

Sectors	1953	1954	1955	1956	1957	1958	1959	1960	1961	1962	1963	1964	1965	1966	1967	1968	1969	1970	1971	1972	1973
Agriculture, forestry and fisheries	38.6	40.0	32.7	37.8	39.6	30.3	26.5	21.9	27.1	34.6	32.1	33.7	31.7	27.1	30.1	24.3	27.9	22.2	20.8	25.1	18.1
Mining and manufacturing[a]	12.6	12.4	14.7	13.2	13.8	15.8	17.4	18.2	16.8	14.1	15.2	15.0	14.7	15.5	15.4	16.4	17.4	18.8	18.3	17.5	16.1
Building and construction	3.0	2.8	3.5	3.5	2.5	3.4	2.6	4.1	3.7	2.8	3.0	2.7	2.6	3.3	2.6	3.4	3.0	2.9	3.4	3.1	2.9
Transport and communication	8.8	7.8	9.3	8.9	7.2	9.0	10.3	10.8	10.4	9.9	8.4	8.4	8.9	9.1	9.1	10.7	10.0	11.4	13.1	9.8	14.6
Wholesale and retail trade	17.1	18.6	20.0	17.5	16.7	19.4	18.2	18.1	14.6	14.6	15.4	13.9	13.4	14.6	14.0	14.7	13.5	13.7	13.0	12.1	10.8
Finance and insurance	1.8	1.8	1.9	1.7	1.8	2.0	2.2	2.6	2.5	2.1	2.3	2.1	2.8	2.2	1.8	2.1	2.2	2.4	2.4	2.6	2.8
Ownership of dwellings	9.1	8.0	8.6	8.0	8.1	8.5	9.2	9.6	9.0	7.3	7.6	7.2	7.3	7.7	7.4	7.2	6.5	6.6	6.1	5.9	6.2
Government	3.3	3.0	4.0	3.7	4.6	5.4	7.1	7.8	9.2	9.0	10.2	11.2	11.3	12.8	12.1	13.5	12.4	14.3	15.1	15.9	19.8
Services	5.7	5.6	5.3	5.7	5.7	6.2	6.5	6.9	6.7	5.6	5.8	5.8	7.3	7.7	7.5	7.7	7.1	7.7	7.8	8.0	8.7
Total	100.0	100.0	100.0	100.0	100.0	100.0	100.0	100.0	100.0	100.0	100.0	100.0	100.0	100.0	100.0	100.0	100.0	100.0	100.0	100.0	100.0

a. Including electricity, gas and water.
Source: *Statistical Abstract 1971*, pp.484-5 for 1953–69; and *Statistical Abstract 1974*, p.865 for 1970–73.

that agriculture too will be increasing its contribution in absolute terms. This increase will probably be distinctly slower than that in manufacturing and mining, notwithstanding the development of irrigation projects crowned by the Euphrates Dam, and the increased efficiency to be expected from institutional and technological changes introduced during the past decade. These favourable changes in agriculture will probably not make their full impact before the passage of several years.

Again looking at the 21 years as a whole, we notice that the wholesale and retail trade lost its rank as second-largest contributor to NDP at the turn of the sixties. The winner has been mining and manufacturing which kept its position consistently except for two years. It would seem that this shift is now final, given the nature of the economic system and its priorities. The government sector has made much more substantial advances over the years, with its rate of growth being the highest. But apart from the nature of the sector and the service it renders to the economy, with all the misgivings that attach to such fast growth, its contribution averaged for the last three years in the series remains just below that of mining and manufacturing. And, in any case, the growth of this latter sector has been steady. In this respect, mining and manufacturing is the most solid sector and the least subject to violent fluctuation and/or variation, and therefore the most reassuring.

Some further comment is called for in relation to the government sector. The phenomenal expansion in the contribution of this sector is related to the change in the socio-economic system and the expanded economic role of the government, which we will come back to later. To a much lesser extent, however, the increase in the contribution of the sector is attributable to the natural growth of government services which are not inherently oriented to or arising from the new socio-economic system. However, it is only fair to say that the 'Parkinsonian Law' of administrative inflation has not seriously afflicted Syria. Indeed, the civil servants who are subject to Basic Law merely doubled between 1955 and the beginning of 1973 — a very modest increase by comparative standards. But this category of public employees comprises only 23 per cent of the total labour force employed by the government plus the public sector and its establishments and institutions, or 44,868 men and women out of a total of 193,738 (of whom 31,460 are females).[8]

Another observation worth making is that with one or two exceptions, the other sectors have not undergone drastic change in the contribution to NDP. One of the exceptions is transport and communications. Indeed, this sector was the fastest-growing after government, but currently it only occupies fourth place in the ranking. Finance and insurance has registered a rate of average annual growth almost as high as transport and communication, but its contribution was, and remains, very small (being 1.8 per cent for 1953, rising to 2.8 per cent for 1973). On the other hand, ownership of dwellings has been a declining sector, with its share dropping from 9.1 to 6.2 per cent over the 21 years of the series.

The final conclusion to be drawn from an examination of all the sectors examined together is that the structure has undergone enormous change in its broad contours over the 21 years 1953-73. Thus, the commodity sectors as a group now account for 37.1 per cent of NDP (or for 41.8 per cent if the last three years are averaged), against 54.2 per cent in 1953 (or 50.1 if the first three years are averaged). This is a substantial drop over the years, and conversely a substantial gain by the group of service sectors. The two sectors most responsible for this structural shift are agriculture, with its fast declining contribution, and government, with its even faster rising contribution.

Another aspect of structure is the distribution of the labour force among sectors (and among occupations), and the change over time in this distribution. Unfortunately, information is not available for the period under consideration in sufficient detail and with enough reliability to permit meaningful comparisons and inferences. In fact, as recently as 1960, it was only possible to produce the roughest estimate in global aggregates for the distribution of the labour force. This estimate which was used for the first year of the First Five-Year Plan 1960/1–1964/5 was presented with serious reservations in the Plan document itself. According to this document, the labour force was expected to total 1.53m in 1960/1, distributed as shown in Table 6.4.

Table 6.4: Labour Force Expected in 1960/1

		Per Cent
Agriculture	820,000	53.6
Industry and construction	110,000	7.2
Services	600,000	39.2
Total	1,530,000	100.0

Source: *Draft Plan for Economic and Social Development for the Five Years 1960/61–1964/65* (Damascus; Arabic; the literal Arabic title is 'Project of . . . Plan . . .'), p.25.

A more reliable estimate is available for November 1969. According to it, the labour force was 1,970,940, of whom 85,305 were unemployed. The females constituted 34.4 per cent of the total, over 94 per cent of employed women were in 'agriculture, forests, hunting, and fishing'. The distribution by activity is shown in Table 6.5.

Table 6.5: Breakdown of Labour Force by Sector, 1969

		Per Cent
Agriculture and hunting	1,322,636	67.1
Mining and quarrying; manufacturing	149,976	7.6
Building and construction	74,288	3.8
Electricity, gas, water and sanitary services	7,000	0.4
Commerce, restaurants and hotels	132,911	6.7
Transport, communication and storage	44,805	2.3
Insurance and services	189,990	9.6
Activities not adequately described	49,334	2.5
Total	1,970,940	100.0

Source: *Statistical Abstract 1971*, Ch. XII, 'Social Statistics', Tables 224 and 228.

The degree of reliability of the first estimate is so low that it would be reckless to compare it with the second and draw conclusions from the comparison. This is all the more obvious if we look at the labour force as a ratio of total population, and at the sectoral distribution of the labour force. We would find exactly the opposite of what we would expect in a situation where the level of education, physical fitness and female participation in extra-mural activities have increased over time. Thus, in the 1960/1 estimate the labour force was 33.6 per cent of an estimated population (according to the Plan document) of 4.55 million; while in November 1969 the labour force constituted 31.4 per cent.

Syria

Furthermore, the relative size of the labour force in agriculture seems to have increased instead of decreased over the nine-year period, a phenomenon which can only be attributed to inaccuracy of the earlier, less scientific estimate. This attribution is tenable because, in its absence, it would be difficult to explain why the absolute and the relative size of the agricultural labour force should have increased by much more than the expansion in area cultivated, particularly when mechanisation has consistently followed an upward (though flattening) course during the years in question.

An earlier estimate than that for 1960 is available, but it is also very rough and rather contrived. It appears in the FAO Mediterranean Development Project *Country Report* on *United Arab Republic — Syrian Region*, and relates to the year 1957. The distribution according to this estimate is given in Table 6.6.

Table 6.6: FAO Estimate of Sectoral Distribution of Labour Force, 1957

		Per Cent
Agriculture	1,270,000	75.4
Manufacturing	70,000	4.2
Crafts	30,000	1.8
Construction	20,000	1.2
General government	22,000	1.2
Transport, trade, services and other	273,000	16.2
Total	1,685,000	100.0

Source: FAO, Mediterranean Development Project, *United Arab Republic — Syrian Region: Country Report*, (Rome, 1959), Ch II, pp. II—11 and 12.

Here again, meaningful conclusions cannot be drawn from this distribution through comparison with that of 1969. For, although on the one hand it shows a much higher proportion in the agricultural sector, as one might expect, on the other hand the total labour force estimated for 1957 is 40.7 per cent of the population, which is much higher than the ratio of the labour force for 1969. Consequently, one is forced to leave the labour size and distribution aspect of the structure of the economy without venturing any conclusions based on the comparison of data over time.

Nevertheless, beginning with 1970, labour data have become more reliable in quality, adequate in volume, and sufficiently detailed to permit examination. The process began with a census in 1970, followed by sample surveys in 1971, 1972 and 1973. Table 6.7 presents the more important components of the labour picture for the four years 1970-3.

The census and subsequent sample surveys provide the researcher with abundant material in addition to what Table 6.7 contains. This includes a breakdown by occupation, age group, sex, marital status, employment status, educational status, district and area of residence (rural v. urban). Cross-tabulations are also provided. However, in spite of these improvements over the past in terms of the availability of statistical information, the data still suffer several shortcomings. One of these is that the labour force has been taken to include every person ten years of age and over. This inflates the results. Nevertheless, in spite of such inflation, the labour force (employed and unemployed combined) amounted to 1,688,564 for 1973, or only one-fourth of the population. If persons below 15 years and above 65 years of age were to be excluded, the proportion would drop to 21.2 per

236 Syria

Table 6.7: Labour Force by Sector [a] 1970–3

Sector	1970	1971[b]	1972[b]	1973
Agriculture, forestry, etc.	752,404	926,196	925,345	857,643
(Females)	(107,237)			(280,031)
Mining and quarrying	8,949	2,155	3,291	14,921
(Females)	(237)			(–)
Manufacturing	190,345	181,886	185,307	166,098
(Females)	(20,452)			(20,520)
Electricity, gas and water	7,565	7,244	19,348	7,601
(Females)	(218)			(183)
Construction and building	114,890	77,692	105,719	95,758
(Females)	(640)			(276)
Trade, restaurants, hotels	144,854	148,382	140,431	159,215
(Females)	(2,052)			(1,613)
Transport, storage and communications	63,934	47,943	65,403	66,607
(Females)	(856)			(947)
Finance, insurance, real estate and business services	9,978	10,062	9,114	10,423
(Females)	(1,073)			(578)
Community, social and personal services	214,161	190,027	218,950	269,471
(Females)	(27,909)			(34,222)
Not stated	5,043	1,023	– –	– –
(Females)	(176)			(–)
Seeking work for the first time	58,653	53,111	42,164	40,827
(Females)	(7,027)			(5,586)
Total	1,570,776	1,645,721	1,715,072	1,688,564
(Females)	(167,877)			(343,956)

a. The sectoral data include those actively engaged in work, and those unemployed.
b. Breakdown by sex is not available for 1971 and 1972.
Source: *Statistical Abstract 1974*, pp.142-3 for 1970 and pp.158-9 and 170-1 for 1971–3.

cent. The smallness of this proportion suggests that the labour force (including the unemployed) is grossly underestimated. A second shortcoming of the data is the severe fluctuation of the number of persons engaged in almost all the sectors, from year to year. No explanation is offered in the introductory notes of the *Statistical Abstract,* and none can be ventured by the present writer. For, while it is to be expected that the results of the sample surveys will (or may) deviate from those of the census of 1970, the absence of consistency or trend makes it difficult to suggest an explanation.

Finally, it remains to be said that Syria can absorb many more workers in its economy once adequate employment opportunities and proper training have been provided. There is no overwhelming problem of unemployment and underemployment, like that suffered, for instance, by Jordan, Egypt or Morocco. A not inconsiderable part of unemployment is probably structural in nature and related to low geographical and occupational mobility. The economy is capable of coping with this and other aspects of the problem without much delay.

2. PHASES OF DEVELOPMENT 1946-75

1946-55

World War Two created economic pressures on Syria that proved decisive in the country's subsequent growth. Thus, the rise in the expenditure by French (and later British) troops and the resulting rise in effective demand, coupled with shipping restrictions and shortages in importable goods, combined to promote local agricultural and industrial production. Private enterprise, endowed with dynamism and energy, given to a high propensity to save, and operating in an accommodating political and social system, rose to the challenge and registered remarkable growth.

Furthermore, the first few years of independence, or until the first military *coup d'état* in the spring of 1949, witnessed a permissive and not very imaginative or perceptive phase of political rule, but one which was capable of enforcing a large measure of law and order and of attending to certain basic forms of social and economic infrastructural investments. Indeed, without fully anticipating the discussion which follows, we can say that the many Syrian governments in the thirty years since independence have, despite political ups and downs in a series of *coups d'état*, and a total change of system, succeeded in going their economic way, steadily investing and consolidating the economy in a manner which has enabled Syria to escape many of the hardships and frustrations that have befallen countries going through a similarly chequered political career.

A point of caution is in order here. The reader might find this generalisation with respect to economic performance rather baffling, in view of the modesty of the rate of growth for the period 1953-73, namely 4.5 per cent as we have indicated. However, three things ought to be borne in mind in explanation. First, that the years between 1945 and 1953, which are not included in the calculation of this rate of growth, probably witnessed a higher rate. Thus, according to a report by the mission sent by the IBRD to Syria early in 1954, 'rapid growth' had been one of 'the most noteworthy features of the Syrian economy' over the two decades preceding the mission's visit.[9]

Some indicators are used to substantiate this judgement. For instance, the 'area under cultivation, including fallow land, rose from about 1.75 million hectares in 1938 to 2.3 million in 1945 and has since continued to expand, reaching a total of around 3.65 million in 1953'. More is supplied as evidence with regard to the reclamation of previously unploughed land, the rise in output, the twofold increase in area irrigated between 1946 and 1953, and most significantly, the dramatic expansion in the cultivation of cotton thanks to 'the stimulus originally imparted by the Korean war boom'. Manufacturing industry also registered vast advances, particularly in the fields of textiles, food-processing, soap, sugar, glass, vegetable oils, cement, cigarettes and matches. Transport, commerce and construction paralleled agriculture and manufacturing in their growth. The overall indicator, namely national income, seemed to the IBRD mission to have risen between 1949 and 1953 by about 28 per cent in real terms — which would suggest that growth per annum averaged 5 to 6 per cent. The findings of other competent researchers confirm this general trend.[10]

The second explanation why Syria's record of growth in the immediate post-war period was remarkable is that the average overall rate of growth of 4.5 per cent was achieved despite the country's heavy dependence on agriculture, which is at the mercy of rainfall that is subject to shortages and severe fluctuations, and with neither especially lucrative natural resources nor with foreign aid. (Indeed, aid began to flow in only in 1957.) Thirdly, not many developing countries could claim a comparable rate of growth for the earlier part of the post-war period; and even today, with the first 'development decade' over, a 5 per cent rate is still considered a respectable and challenging target.

There is near-consensus in the studies to which reference has been made in the preceding paragraph that the post-war growth in the Syrian economy was the product of the co-operation of several factors, with relatively heavy investment the one factor consistently receiving strongest emphasis. Other factors receive credit, such as the dynamism of private enterprise, the accommodating circumstances created by rising demand in the war and post-war periods as well as in the Korean war boom, and the compatibility of the socio-political system. To these must be added the fact of the low base from which the economy started, a fact which in itself made expansion easy to achieve in relative terms. Likewise, Syria had (and still has) noticeable — though not dramatic — potential for expansion, particularly in terms of unexploited or underexploited land and to a lesser extent water. In the immediate post-war period this point applied with special relevance to the Jezirah area, in the north-east of the country, and to a lesser extent to the central northern area in general. In the manufacturing sector, easily discernible potential presented itself in those industries which conventionally first catch the eye at the pre-industrial stage: textiles, food processing, sugar, cement, tobacco and the like. Neither the capital funds nor the technical and managerial skills required were far beyond the capabilities of the Syrian economy at the time.

The story of this first phase would be incomplete and unnecessarily stripped of drama if mention is not made of the role of what Doreen Warriner has aptly called the 'merchant-tractorists',[11] in the expansion in the northern-north-eastern arc, both through extensive rain-fed and privately irrigated agriculture, on vast new areas of land in the Deir-ez-Zor and Hasakeh *Mohafazat* (districts). This expansion materialised at the hands of merchants from the northern cities, notably Aleppo, who shifted huge investments from earlier-accumulated fortunes earned in trade into mechanised agriculture. Hence the phrase 'merchant-tractorists'. A numerically disproportionate percentage of this group belonged to religious minority communities in the country. Their innovations went beyond 'opening-up of the northeastern frontier' to include the introduction on a very large scale of machines (called for both because of the vastness of the land area involved and the sparsity of the resident population), to include the building of roads, the installation of irrigation pumps and the creation of irrigation networks, the financing or arranging of finance needs, and finally to include new tenure arrangements totally different from those in existence elsewhere.

The end result of the activities of the merchant-tractorists has manifested itself in multiple facets: the settlement of a number of bedouin tribes; the attraction of Syrians from other less favoured and/or more crowded districts; the use outside trade of funds originating in trade; the use of unused or underused land and water resources; the vindication of the dynamism, entrepreneurial talent, and far-sight of the private sector once basic conditions (particularly law and order) are satisfied; and — above all — the expansion of agricultural production and income and consequently of exportable produce. Government's direct contribution to this whole process was minimal.

Most students of the Syrian economy agree that the first post-war decade marked the end of the notable expansion achieved, rather painlessly and easily, at the hands of the private sector, and that by the mid-fifties it had become evident that the state had to play a more active promotive role than had been the case until then. The various factors making for expansion, to which reference has been made, had mainly exhausted themselves by 1955 or 1956, including the impetus gained by the break of the customs union with Lebanon (in March 1950) which allowed Syria a freer hand in the protection of its agriculture and industry, and by Decree No. 151 enacted in 1952, which restricted the business and investment freedom of Lebanese (and other non-Syrian) traders, middlemen and investors and prescribed for much greater Syrian participation. This first phase was by no means uniform in political ideology and style of action. It witnessed the first military *coup d'état* in 1949, which was to open the Pandora's Box for a few more. The young, relatively reform- and development-minded officers who (overtly or behind the scenes) ran the affairs of the country between 1949 and 1956 took certain important economic measures during this period.

In addition to the measures already mentioned, there was the start of the building of Lattakia port, destined to become the main outlet for the exports of the northern and north-eastern agricultural regions, and to draw to itself much of Syria's imports coming in previously via Beirut port. Likewise, the Ghab project, a multi-purpose project involving the draining of marshes, the creation of an artificial lake, irrigation and the introduction of new crops, was put into the first phase of execution in 1950, after years of preparation going back to the last years of the French Mandate. Finally, the pipeline destined to carry the petroleum of Aramco Company in Saudi Arabia across Jordan, Syria and into its terminal outlet in South Lebanon, was built in 1950-1.

But perhaps above all, the subsequent vast expansion in cotton cultivation had its foundation laid in 1951, with the establishment of a cotton bureau, which was to undertake or advise on research, greater use of fertilisers, seed selection, pest control, grading, packing, marketing and allied functions. (An indication of the expansion of cotton-growing can be seen in the fact that the unginned crop amounted to 6,000 tons in 1939, and 100,000 tons in 1950, but rose to 404,300 tons for 1973,[12] and is now the most important single product in terms of value of production and of export.) Other significant developments, mainly of an institutional nature, characterised the greater activity and involvement of the public sector in the years 1949-56 of the first post-war decade. (In terms of investment the public sector provided only something like 16 per cent of the total at most, but the trend was upward.) We will list the developments chronologically. The first was the decision in the middle of 1950 to refuse economic aid from the United States (under President Truman's then new 'Point Four' programme). The Syrian government preferred to rely on its own resources for investment, and on United Nations and IBRD services for technical assistance.

The second development was the passing of three decrees in January-November 1952 by the military strong man at that time, General Adib Shishakli, who was known to be favourably influenced by the reformist ideas of certain political parties and individuals. The decrees aimed at instituting land reform, through limiting the area of state domain and private land which any one individual could hold (in a situation characterised by individuals holding vast areas of state land, which constituted a high percentage of total land area in the country), and providing for the distribution of excess area in small plots. However, nothing came out of these decrees, which remained a dead letter owing to the strength of propertied politicians and their resistance to the reform envisaged. The third, fourth and fifth developments fell in the monetary field. They were the establishment in 1953 of a Money and Credit Board, and in 1956 of a Central Bank, and the conclusion in 1956 of an agreement with the USSR for economic (and military) assistance.

If the first post-war decade is to be described in overall summary terms, it would be characterised as a period in which law and order were established firmly (particularly with regard to the control of relatively small marauding bedouin tribes in the semi-desert separating Syria from Iraq); the social and economic infrastructure received a big push compared with the tightly rationed efforts of the French Mandatory power; change occurred in social structure, with tribal chiefs in the Jezirah becoming landowners — albeit non-operating, land-leasing ones — and the 'merchant-tractorists' transferring capital and effort from the cities of Aleppo, Homs and Hama to land reclamation, irrigation, road-building, large-scale mechanisation and cereal- and cotton-growing in the Jezirah; new middle-class elements emerged with the expansion in the number of professional men and technicians and of army officers moving out of their barracks into the 'corridors of power', and with many more politically articulate and active groups participating in political decision-making at different levels.

The economic end result was expansion in existing crops and the development of new crops, rise in the activity of breeding sheep and goats, and rise in the level of industrialisation, so that the industrial sector which contributed probably no more than 7 or 8 per cent of GNP immediately after World War Two moved up to about 14 per cent in the mid-fifties.

1956-8

Yet another crop had grown and was ready for harvest by the end of the first phase: political divisiveness, hesitation and contradictory influences on the socio-political system. A political tug-of-war characterised the years 1956-8, during which period various groups in the political arena in Syria (and some groups and currents beyond Syria's frontiers) were competing for supremacy. By late 1957 it became evident to the main actors on the stage, the military and the Ba'ath Party, that national security lay in a merger between President Gamal Abdul-Nasser's (very popular and prestigious) Egypt and Syria into the United Arab Republic. This merger was achieved in February 1958, and it lasted until 28 September 1961.

The 1956-8 period was as devoid of important economic achievements as it was productive of political manoeuvring. No significant economic landmarks characterise it.

1958-61

On the other hand, the third phase, that of union with Egypt, represented drastic institutional and economic change which has marked the life of the economy and the society ever since, in spite of the break-up of the merger in the autumn of 1961. But the transformation did not pass without resistance. This resistance was fundamentally conceived within the ranks of Syrian capitalists, who had, until 1958, been extremely enthusiastic about the union but became gradually disenchanted because of the *étatiste* economic policy applied in Egypt and projected into Syria. They allied with the Ba'ath Party, who were equally disenchanted because of becoming a very junior partner in power, and used army officers smarting under the predominance of Egyptian officers, administrators and policy-makers. The resistance finally erupted on 28 September 1961 in an army separatist *coup* which President Nasser at the last moment refused to challenge.[13]

The most decisive event during the process of resistance-building and planning for secession was the vast and far-reaching nationalisation programme legislated in Egypt in July 1961 and in part paralleled in Syria. However, these measures will be discussed at greater length in the chapter on Egypt. None the less, the three-and-a-half year merger laid the foundation for, or brought about, several lasting changes which need singling out, although some of them will receive separate treatment elsewhere. Five such changes or processes will be pointed out.

The first, and the one to which attention was given earliest, was agrarian reform. The term, by common current usage, comprises a wide range of actions, such as the limitation of size of ownership, the establishment of credit and marketing co-operative societies, the spread of extension services, and so on. Most emphasis was first laid on requisitioning of land in excess of the ceiling allowed by the new law and the redistribution of the areas seized according to a scale envisaged to create a wide base of small ownerships. The total area of land expected thus to be available for redistribution was 5.3 million hectares: 1.5 million of private lands consisting of 3,240 ownerships (including 94,109 hectares of irrigated land), and 3.8 million hectares of state domain. The law was made retroactive in operation to the beginning of 1950 — a measure which was presumed to penalise certain politicians of the old régime who had sold land between 1950 and 1958.

The second important measure was the formulation of a development plan for the five years 1960/1–1964/5, to replace the plan then in force though not very seriously pursued, and to fall in step with Egypt's planning experience where a five-year plan for the same years had just been formulated. The Syrian plan, which was the fourth to be suggested or even formulated since 1955 (the first having been recommended by the IBRD mission in 1955), had a broader ten-year framework, exactly like its Egyptian counterpart, and had the same overall target of doubling GNP in ten years and of achieving a 40 per cent growth in the first five years. But, unlike the Egyptian plan, it left to the private sector a larger role to play, envisaging an investment of £S1,000 million in five years by private businessmen and £S1,720 million by the public sector, or 37 per cent versus 63 per cent respectively.

The calibre of the investment plan, which was much larger than that of earlier plans, and the relatively good record of implementation have resulted in the launching of a larger number of projects in the fields of irrigation and land reclamation, transport and communications, industry, electricity, mining and prospecting for petroleum, agriculture proper, housing and education — to list the more important fields in the order in which they were allotted funds. However, the national accounts for the years 1960/1 and 1961/2 do not show the results of the stepped-up process of investment and capital formation. This is because the period of 1958-61 turned out to form a cycle of poor rainfall and very poor harvests, with the result that the contribution of agriculture to national product for these four years was the lowest in the whole 21-year period 1953-73. Naturally, the Syrian elements dissatisfied or disenchanted with the union with Egypt blamed the setback reflected in the national product on the union itself.[14]

But as a matter of fact, all the other sectors (except trade) showed a marked expansion for the four years in question, as the indices for net domestic product for the years 1953-73 show.[15] There is supportive evidence of the expansion during the years of union. The index number of major mechanised industries in Syria (1956=100) shows a marked rise for the years 1958-61, but particularly for 1960 and 1961, the two years during which the development plan began to be implemented. But it is also significant that the three years 1962-4 witnessed further tangible rises beyond the level of 1961.[16] It can rightly be assumed that the fruition of investments made in the early years of the plan needed two or three years to appear in the form of increases in output. Yet the foundations for an expanded industrialisation process were laid in this third phase, and industrialisation can therefore be rightly listed as the third important development of the phase. (Another indicator of the process is the marked increase, beginning with 1958 and more markedly with 1959, in the number and paid-up capital investment of industrial and commercial joint-stock companies, and in the volume of trade between the two 'Regions' as compared with the three preceding years 1955-7.[17])

The fourth important development within this third phase was the large measure of nationalisation of banks, insurance companies, large industrial concerns and large import and export houses. These nationalisations, which duplicated their counterpart in Egypt, were less far-reaching. However, they hit 'national capitalism', that is, Syrian capitalists who had been no less sincere and active in resisting the French Mandate and striving for independence than any other group, unlike the capitalists affected by the Egyptian measures, many of whom were of non-Egyptian origin, even non-Arabs, who had reputedly identified with the British and other foreign interests in Egypt. But the scale notwithstanding, the Syrian nationalisations prefaced the socialist transformation which was to be further consolidated in the years 1963-73. (Whether or not the transformation in Syria, and even in Egypt, was really socialist, is a point disputed by some writers. We will not examine the issue here, but will discuss it in the chapter on Egypt and in the companion volume (Volume II).

The fifth development, which is a result and a projection of land reform and nationalisation, was the achievement of a larger measure of distributive justice than before. This was made possible both through the widening of the base of land ownership through land redistribution, and through the changes instituted in the fields of taxation (and tax collection), and of the expansion of social services thanks to the availability of a larger volume of resources in the hands of government.

1961-3

The fourth phase, which covers the period September 1961 to March 1963, was — like the phase between 1956 and 1958, one of hesitation and indecision, and of immense political vacillation. The *coup d'état* which broke the union between Syria and Egypt had meant to most property-owners, the 'national bourgeoisie', and to most other citizens the undoing of the land reform and nationalisation measures initiated in the period 1958-61. Indeed, certain steps were taken to return some establishments to their original owners, and in 1962 there was a reconsideration of the structure of land reform measures — involving such things as the areas to be allowed to the original landowners, the compensation to be paid and the manner and terms of repayment, and so on. However, at no time was there a complete undoing of the measures of land reform and socialist transformation. The resistance to such a step was enormous, among the vast masses — essentially the beneficiaries of the measures — and among the rank and file of the army. The resistance built up momentum until, in March 1963, it brought an end to the fourth phase and put the country back on the same socio-economic, though not political, path of the 1958-61 period.

Statistical evidence is not plentiful and detailed enough to enable us to examine the effect of the secession and the shift away from the 'left' which resulted from the *coup* of September 1961, but there is enough material to suggest that private investment in joint-stock companies rose very slightly (by less than 3 per cent) in 1962 over 1961,[18] but private-sector investment as a whole rose considerably — by 69 per cent — over 1961, though it dropped from that elevated level by about 3 per cent in 1963 and by about 16 per cent in 1964 compared with 1963. The significant rise between 1961 and 1962 can legitimately be attributed in the main to two factors: the substantial rise in GNP in 1962 over 1961 (by some £S736 million, or 25 per cent), thanks to the vast improvement in the agricultural season after the years of drought 1958-61; and the return of confidence to private businessmen as a result of the change in the socio-economic system. Thus, private investment constituted 9.4 per cent of GNP in 1961, but 12.6 per cent for 1962, 11.9 per cent for 1963, though only 9 per cent for 1964 and less than 6 per cent for 1965. This course is quite significant, and 'makes sense' in the light of the effects of the changes in the socio-economic and political system on the mood of investors after September 1961, when this mood brightened, and again after March 1963, when yet another *coup d'état* reinstated the trend towards socialist transformation and dampened the mood of private investors. The other side of the coin, namely public investment, shows movement along a declining course through 1964, dropping by 11.4 per cent in 1962, by 4.2 per cent in 1963 below 1962, and by 8.7 per cent in 1964. However, in 1965 it rose by about 60 per cent over 1964.

Contrary to the expectations in the First Five-Year Plan 1960/1–1964/5, public investment was considerably less than private investment in each of the four years 1961-4, the former constituting about one-third of total investment on the average. (Understandably, it was lowest in 1962, when it represented only 26 per cent of the total.) It was only in 1965 that public exceeded private investment, being 52.7 per cent of total investment. For the five-year period as a whole, actual investment was roughly equal to planned investment as in the First Five-Year Plan, but there was very wide divergence between the planned and the actual share of the private (versus the public) sector, and between the planned and actual relative shares of the various economic sectors.[19]

1963-75

The fifth and last phase stretches from March 1963 to the present moment. (In November 1970, a minor *coup* within the Ba'ath Party which had been in power since 1963 brought into predominance one wing in the Party reputed to be of milder socialist leanings than the one hitherto in power, and also possessing a more liberal attitude on internal affairs and a more open attitude towards the other Arab régimes, regardless of their system and ideology.[20]) This phase, enjoying on the whole the longest stretch of political stability, has witnessed both an intensification in the socialist transformation begun in the 1958-61 phase during the union with Egypt, and the consolidation and extension of the economic base, made concrete in the expansion or initiation of a large number of projects in almost all sectors of economic activity. (It ought to be remembered that the First Five-Year Development Plan, 1960/1–1964/5, ran partly in phase four and partly in phase five.) However, in the aggregate, the expansion and initiation do not reflect themselves clearly in the index of net domestic product at factor cost for the years 1953-73 (at constant prices of 1963). The index for 1963 (1953=100) is 155. Against the rise of 55 points in the index between 1953 and 1963, there is a rise of 58.9 points between 1963 and 1973.[21] The difference between the two equally long periods is very small, and the greater stability of the second period has not resulted in a distinctly better economic performance as measured in national accounts.

The picture becomes clearer, and the performance more striking, when examined in disaggregated form. In the sector of industry, all the industries registered expansion in their output in the period 1965-73, with an overall growth of 77 per cent in 1973 over 1965. For the group of ten major industries, the index of output rose from 166 for 1963 (1956=100) to 411 for 1970. The most significant expansion since 1965 has been in mining and quarrying, followed distantly by mineral products and equipment, paper and printing, chemicals, mineral industries, wood and furniture and electric power. The remaining industries expanded more slowly than the whole sector did.[22]

In the field of extractive industries, petroleum has gained status, with production in the Karatchouk and Sweidieh fields begun in June 1968, and in the Rmeilan field begun in the spring of 1969. The three fields produced a total of 5.9 million tons in 1972, rising from 1m for 1968, 2.6m for 1969, and 4.2m for 1970. However, production dropped to 5.5m tons for 1973, owing to the outbreak of the Arab-Israeli war in October of that year. It had been expected that 1974 would witness a substantial expansion, to some 8m tons, but actually it stood at 5.8m tons only.[23] It ought to be added that petroleum reserves so far established are some 547 million tons.[24]

Three important projects are associated with the production of petroleum:

(a) The laying of a pipeline to carry oil exports to Tartous — with an 18-20-22 inch capacity for a length of 650 kilometres. The value of exports of crude petroleum for 1973 was £S291.6 million.
(b) The building of a refinery at Homs (the contract for which was awarded to a Czech group in 1957), whose initial capacity was 1.5 million tons a year, now expanded to 2.75 million tons.
(c) The construction and completion of a nitrogenous fertiliser plant with a capacity of 148,000 tons a year.

Also in the field of extractive industry, there is the exploitation and industrialisation of phosphates, the reserves of which are estimated at 155 million tons. The target capacity of the present works which had been set originally at 175,000 tons a year, has already been surpassed. Production was 300,000 tons in 1973, and it is expected to reach 1.2m tons for 1974.[25] Two other major industries involve the construction of a fine steel rolling plant with a capacity of 105,000 tons a year, and of a tractor and diesel engines compound with a capacity of 2,000 tractors a year. Work on both projects was started in 1968; the former is now complete, but not the latter.[26]

In all, capital invested in major industries (including those not referred to specifically here, such as electricity generation, spinning and weaving, plastic products, and many others in the chemical and engineering group), and likewise invested in the petroleum fields, pipeline and refinery, adds up to £S2,880m at current prices (or £S2,227m at constant 1963 prices) for the eleven years 1963-73. (Total gross fixed capital formation for this period was £S9,725m at current prices, and £S7,453m at constant prices. Thus the overall share of the sector of industry has been about 29 per cent.) For the period as a whole, only the dwellings (building and construction) sector has attracted slightly larger investments, though the lead of industry has been unchallenged since 1971.[27]

The next area of action of major importance to be discussed is irrigation. Syria's record here is remarkable in relative (though not absolute) terms, again remembering the limitations in funds and in easily exploitable water, and also that the first large pioneering steps in the immediate post-war period were taken by private businessmen. To begin with, Syria's rivers only include one major river, the Euphrates, whose average flow in 1973 was 476 cubic metres per second, four intermediate rivers (Khabour, Al-Assi or Orontes, Yarmouk and Sinn) whose joint average flow was 75 cubic metres per second, and several much smaller rivulets totalling 23.4 cubic metres per second in 1973.[28] However, the Euphrates originates in Turkey and flows on into Iraq, and Syria can use only a part of its waters. Likewise, the Yarmouk joins the Jordan river and both flow into the Dead Sea in Jordan.

Whatever river (and minor spring) water remains available for use in the land has to satisfy a vast demand. Syria has an area of 184,480 square kilometres, of which (according to the earliest official record available) the cultivable part amounts to 84,140 sq. km. Out of this part, 20,330 sq. km. are uncultivated, and one can presume that they include some marginal land, or land where the cost-return relationship is less favourable than in the other areas actually cultivated. Thus the area cultivated in 1961 was 63,810 sq. km., some 40 per cent of which lay fallow. Finally, the area under crops was 38,140 sq. km., of which only 5,580 sq. km. (558,000 hectares) were irrigated. The balance of the country's area is divided thus: 4,020 sq. km. of forests, 64,630 of pastures, and 31,690 'miscellaneous' — presumably semi-desert and rocky on the whole.[29]

It is worth noting that the area irrigated was no more than 324,000 hectares in 1945. It rose to 558,000 hectares in 1961. The most recent data in the *Statistical Abstract 1974* suggest only a small expansion over the years 1961-73. Irrigation thus spreads over 619,000 ha (or a gain of about 11 per cent in twelve years). Cultivated land has remained almost unchanged since 1968, but has declined since 1961, from 63,810 sq. km. to 58,780 sq. km. Furthermore, the estimate of cultivable but uncultivated land has also declined between 1968 and 1973 by about 29 per cent. However, the components of the total under cultivation are more erratic than the total. The largest variation appears in the area irrigated, which dropped from 546,000 to 451,000 hectares between 1969 and 1970, then rose to 619,000 for 1973. The area left fallow amounts roughly to one-third of the 8m ha of cultivable land.[30] (This is apart from the impact of the Euphrates project, to which reference will be made later.) Expansion in irrigated area in recent years came mainly through the completion of, or advances made in, the Ghab, Rouj, Yarmouk, Sinn, Barada, Upper Orontes and Khabour projects. These projects have over the years expanded the area irrigated by some 185,000 hectares. (The Ghab accounts for 72,000, and the Khabour for 60,000 new hectares.)

The most important single project, and the one which will double the present area under irrigation, is the Euphrates High Dam, which is being constructed with financial and technical aid from the USSR. The project involves the elevation of the water level by a dam 60 metres high, to store 11.9 billion cubic metres and to irrigate a total of 600,000 ha, and to generate 1 million kilowatts of electricity. The total cost is estimated at some £S2.4 billion, of which some £S600 million will be in foreign exchange (from the USSR). The cost attributable to irrigation alone will be some £S640 million. Work so far completed includes the building of the residential and social facilities to cope with the labour force that was to be engaged, the construction of the protection dams, central electric station and connection lines, and the transformation station. Completion of the whole project had been scheduled for 1975, but work proceeded faster than scheduled, and both the dam and the hydro-electric station were completed and inaugurated in the spring of 1974.

The impact of the dam will go beyond irrigation and power generation. It will include the transformation of agriculture in a vast area of land, the promotion of tourism and fishing thanks to the new lake that will fill up behind the dam (estimated at 670 sq. km.), the speeding up of the electrification of the country with what this implies in social and economic terms, and the greater availability of exportable goods such as cotton, vegetables, poultry, livestock and dairy products.[31]

Finally, 50 small dams were built during the years 1966-9 in the Syrian desert and near it, with a total storage capacity of 81 million cubic metres. The favourable results of this scheme have urged the government to decide to construct 38 more dams whose total capacity — probably over-optimistically — is to irrigate 300,000 hectares.[32]

Agriculture as such has received less attention and less investment than irrigation works.

Rain-fed agriculture, as we have indicated, suffers severe fluctuations because of the irregularity of rainfall over the years. The overall index of net domestic product at factor cost attributed to agriculture (at 1963 constant prices) has risen from 100 for 1953 to 153.1 for 1969, but dropped to 124.3 for 1970, and up to 116 for 1973.[33] As stated earlier, agriculture has the lowest record of growth among all the sectors. However, the record of expansion in agriculture will be incomplete if no reference is made to the vast expansion in mechanisation and to the less spectacular expansion in the use of fertilisers and insecticides and pesticides, in addition to the extension of the area brought under the plough since World War Two. Mechanisation was started on a large scale in the late forties and early fifties, and it kept its pace until 1959, after which there was a steep rise in the purchase of tractors until 1964 (when the number of tractors sold during the period 1962-4 was approximately three times the number in the fifties). But sales dropped suddenly by about 60 per cent in 1965, and slid steeply down in 1966. In absolute terms, the average for the fifties was in excess of 525 tractors a year; in the peak years 1962-4 the annual average was 1,638 tractors. For the years 1965-73 the annual average stood at 521. The course of sales since the early fifties has been very erratic. The cumulative total of tractors registered by the end of 1973 was 16,858.[34]

Thousands of other agricultural machines were also bought in Syria: harvesters, combined harvester-threshers, threshers, seed drills, fertiliser distributors and so on.

Irrigation works by private businessmen necessitated also the purchase of many thousands of pumps. But the purchase of pumps, which averaged about 2,500 a year in the early fifties, dropped to 1,600 in the second part of the decade, and further to 520 a year for the period 1960-73.[35]

The use of fertilisers expanded between 1952 and 1969, the years for which data are available. But the rate of expansion was very modest. The peak year of 1970 witnessed the importation of no more than 155,584 tons of all kinds of fertilisers. Likewise, the importation of insecticides, although rising, averaged 1,165 tons annually for the period 1952-69.[36]

Examined in its overall dimensions, Syrian agriculture can be said to have expanded much more modestly than its physical potential suggests. Indeed, considering the horizontal extension of the early fifties, and the less far-reaching but nevertheless significant vertical expansion (that is to say, the increase in area of cultivation and the greater resort to irrigation and mechanisation), it is surprising that agricultural output and contribution to national product have made very slow, if any, progress over the years. Specifically, the index of total agricultural production, and of food production, averaged a mere 101 for the three years 1970-2, with 1961-5 as base. On a *per capita* basis, the index was considerably lower for 1970-2: it stood at 78.3 for food, and 79.3 for total agricultural production. Against this poor performance, the period 1964-6 stood at 140 for total agricultural production with the years 1952-6 as base, and at 116 for food production. *Per capita* food production dropped from 100 in the base years 1952-6 to 83.3 for 1964-6.[37] These figures are eloquent enough and do not need further elaboration to emphasise the decline of Syrian agriculture since its dramatic upsurge in the early fifties.

The judgement that agriculture has not served as the engine of development that it could have been is saddening, though not perplexing. The causes for the setbacks suffered by agriculture are not far to seek. They can be found mainly in the areas of political instability, landowner insecurity, institutional and attitudinal problems associated with a land reform which proved to have been too sudden and inadequately prepared for, and the disappearance of the class of agricultural entrepreneurs which had proved very enterprising and successful in 'extending the frontiers' of agriculture coupled with the slow emergence of a substitute to this class. The shortage of capital and technical skills has compounded the problems cited earlier.

Before this section is wound up, mention must be made of other economic and social aspects of infrastructure which received particular attention in Syria's post-war development. Like many of the projects in the fields of industry, irrigation and agricultural mechanisation to which reference has been made, the aspects to be discussed at this point relate to the whole post-war period, and are not the sole achievement of the last phase under discussion, namely the years 1963-75. None the less, they received greater emphasis during this phase, and/or came to fruition during it. Three aspects will be listed: transport and communications; power generation; and education, public health and housing.

Transport and communications, as a sector, increased its contribution to net domestic product considerably during the years 1953-73. Thus its index of growth in 1973 was 406, with 1953 as the base year. (In absolute terms, its contribution was £S200m in 1953, but rose to £S812m in 1973.) The sector is only outdistanced by government, whose expansion is not necessarily an indication of healthy growth.

The transport and communications sector is known generally to have a high average and incremental capital-output ratio. However, in Syria's instance, this sector's contribution to NDP related to net investments made suggests a low ratio. This is probably explainable in the nature of investments made, being mainly in roads, not in sophisticated and costly transport and communications facilities. The indices of net capital formation for the years 1963-73 at current prices show transport and communication as lagging behind mining and manufacturing, agriculture and construction, although its rank was higher in the middle of the period. (It ought to be recalled that mining and manufacturing include investments made in electricity, gas and water, as well as petroleum, in addition to manufacturing industry proper.) The cause of the drop is that, beginning with 1970, investment in agriculture, mining and manufacturing and construction rose very steeply, while investment in transport and communications did not.[38] Evidence of the emphasis placed on transport and communications can be seen in the various development plans formulated, from 1955 onwards, through the Third Five-Year Plan 1971-5. This emphasis it has shared with irrigation and reclamation, mining and manufacturing (including power), and to a lesser extent construction and public utilities, and social services. The pattern of ranking has varied from plan to plan, but always with these four sectors heading the whole list.

The priority that these sectors have consistently enjoyed in the planning of investment and development over the past decade and a half is legitimate and understandable. Syria is a predominantly agricultural country, and — specifically — it has achieved most of the horizontal expansion in agriculture of which it is capable in the rain-fed areas. Hence the supreme significance of the intensification of efforts to expand irrigation facilities and networks and to move to irrigated, more lucrative crops, and furthermore to promote industry energetically and to develop the electricity and petroleum sectors considerably.

But Syria is also a vast country for its population, and transport and communication are bound to receive appropriate investments to link the various production areas together, as well as with the centres of population and of government, and with their internal marketing and exporting outlets. Furthermore, Syria has two petroleum pipelines crossing it from Iraq and Saudi Arabia. Transit fees reached about £S350m in 1973 (in spite of the oil embargo implemented as a result of the October war), and were budgeted to reach £S608m in 1974.[39] This important source of revenue adds further significance to the improvement of transport and communication services and networks. It is important to add that during the last phase (1963-75) 5,068 kilometres of asphalted road were built, in addition to thousands of kilometres repaired, paved or levelled.[40] Furthermore, a 750-kilometre railway linking Lattakia with Aleppo and Kamishli was begun with USSR help. By 1973 some 527 km. had been built, along with many other parts and facilities of the project. Completion was originally set for 1971, but now seems probable only in 1975. (Total cost of the project is estimated at £S450 million.) Finally, a new Damascus International Airport has been built and equipped at a cost of over £S30 million to become a Class I airport.

Another significant aspect of the creation of economic infrastructure is electricity generation. As indicated above, the sector of 'mining and manufacturing' includes electricity, gas and petroleum. Hence separate analysis of investments in power generation cannot be made consistently for the whole post-war period. But it is sufficient to repeat here that the sector as a whole has always ranked second or third among the top-ranking sectors in investment and development plans. Electricity ranks third among the ten major divisions of industry with regard to increase in production during the period 1963-70 (base year is 1956). However, its pace slackened slightly recently and it occupied sixth place in 1973.[41] But 1974 witnessed a vast jump with the completion of the power station at the Euphrates Barrage.

The government and municipal authorities had turned their attention to the construction of generating capacity as soon as possible after independence. Thus, the IBRD mission could say in 1955 in this connection that public utilities were 'increasing their capacity over the last years at a mean annual rate of about 17 per cent', but that 'total installed capacity at the end of 1953 amounted to only 34,350 KW or 44,776 KVA'.[42] Power generated in 1949 totalled 70.34 million kwh.[43] Against this situation, installed capacity for 1973 had risen to 476,902 kva, while energy generated had risen to 1,145 million kwh.[44] (This equals 167 kwh *per capita* for 1973.) Evidently, the installation of new capacity of 1 million kw upon the completion of the Euphrates High Dam vastly expands the availability of electricity for household and industrial uses, and at much lower rates than exist today.

In the context of social infrastructure, education and public health (along with housing as a junior partner) have made large strides during the post-war period. This has been the result both of determined and consistent efforts on the part of independent Syria, and of substantial allocations for facilities and recurrent expenditures. The IBRD mission in their plan proposals assigned to education the largest single share of expenditure. Indeed, the combined proposed allocations for education, public health and housing exceed 30 per cent of total allocations. But subsequent plans did not approach this high allocation, and indeed could be said to have neglected these social services in their investment-allocating process, though they allotted adequate funds for recurrent expenditure. (Taking education alone, we see that the state budgets have since 1925 allotted a noticeable and rising allocation to this sector. Thus the ratio was 7.8 per cent for 1925, rising gradually to an average of 13.4 per cent for the four years 1946-9, and to 14.5 for 1959-60.)

It was the First Five-Year Plan, 1960/1—1964/5, that raised the *investment* allocations again, which then exceeded 15 per cent of the total (£S416 million). The Second Five-Year Plan, 1966-70, allocated some 3 per cent (£S146 million) for education, public health and housing, apart from vast amounts to municipalities and urban water systems.[45] On the other hand, the Third Five-Year Plan 1971-5 allotted over £S550m (or 6.7 per cent of the whole investment programme) for these areas and in addition vast sums for munici-

Syria   249

palities and utilities.[46] The scale of recurrent expenditure allocations can be appreciated from an examination of the consolidated budgets for 1973 and 1974 which allot about £S484m and £S682m respectively for education and culture, social welfare, public health and housing. The calculation of the proportion that these allotments represent of the whole budget is misleading, since the budget includes the allocations to self-financing institutions and funds. If these are deducted, the allocations stand at 17.9 and 15.3 per cent of the 1973 and 1974 budgets respectively.[47]

But the effort expended in the field of social development can better be seen in physical results than in the fragments of statistics which we have presented. Thus, between 1945 and 1973, pre-university education has grown, as Table 6.8 indicates.

Table 6.8: Comparative Statistics on Pre-University Education 1944/5 and 1972/3

	1944/5	(Of which governmental)[a]	1972/3	(Of which governmental)[a]
Number of schools:				
Primary	1,072	658	6,446	6,218
Preparatory and Secondary	64	17	967	849
Professional, Intermediate Institutes, and Teachers' Colleges[b]	13		55	All
Number of pupils:				
Primary	148,428	85,540	1,102,652	1,044,086
Preparatory and Secondary	11,592	n.a.	388,473	358,071
Professional Institutes and Teachers' Colleges[b]	1,304	n.a.	18,415	All
Number of graduates:				
Primary	4,011	n.a.	104,130	n.a.
Preparatory and Secondary	1,180	n.a.	69,677	n.a.
Professional Institutes and Teachers' Colleges[b]	170	n.a.	5,049	All
Funds for Education (including Higher)		£S9.9m		£S368.3m

a. The balance consists of private schools and schools run by UNRWA.
b. Excluding religious institutes.

Source: *Statistical Abstract, 1974*, Ch. 10, several tables.

Higher education has expanded at an even higher rate. Thus the number of universities has risen from one to three between 1945 and 1973; the number of faculties from 2 to 23; and the number of students from 736 to 49,255 (19 per cent of whom are women). In addition, a total of 1,432 students were studying outside Syria on government scholarships by the end of 1972-3. The largest single group (about 31 per cent) was made up of engineering students, followed by science and medicine. The geographical distribution of these bursary students reflects Syria's new orientation: the largest group is in the USSR, followed by East Germany, Bulgaria, Hungary, Czechoslovakia, Poland, Algeria, etc. However, 28,476 students study abroad at their own expense. About 60 per cent are training in medicine and engineering, while about 33 per cent are in literature, law and commerce.

The geographical distribution of these students is given in Table 6.9.

Table 6.9: Distribution of Students Studying Abroad

Western countries	12,505
USA and Canada	1,541
Arab countries	10,451
Socialist countries	3,624
Others	355
Total	28,476

Source: *Statistical Abstract 1974*, p. 638.

One noticeable shortcoming in Syria's education effort must, however, be indicated. This is in the field of adult literacy courses, where progress has been slower than in Jordan, Kuwait, Libya, Saudi Arabia, Sudan or Tunisia. Only 9,723 participants made use of the programmes for adult education in the year 1972-3. This is a very small proportion of the illiterate population.[48]

After the IBRD mission visited Syria in 1954, it reported that the progress in public health had been 'much less spectacular and less steady than that in education'.[49] This judgement, which relates to the years 1946-54, can equally be extended to the period 1955-73, as can be seen from the comparative statistics recorded in Table 6.10.

The comparative data indicate that although in absolute terms progress has been made in hospital building and equipping, in the training of larger numbers of physicians, and in the ratio of inhabitants to hospital beds and to physicians, there is still vast scope for further improvement.

In addition, marked improvement has occurred in preventive medicine, sanitation and general hygiene. This is visible not only in the urban centres, but also in the countryside. Coupled with these improvements is the concrete progress in the supply of piped water to many villages that lacked it two decades ago, the extension of electric power for household use, the laying of sewerage systems in urban centres, and the efficient and large-scale immunisation campaigns.

Not much can be said about housing, owing to the scarcity of information. The IBRD mission reported in 1955 a house construction boom in the period 1946-54. The period 1963-73 shows some modest progress in residential buildings, both with regard to number of permits granted, floor space involved, and average floor space per permit. However, the increase in floor space has merely been equal to that of population, with the result that the average area per person has risen only minimally from 8.2 to 8.4 square metres, for residential floor area for the two years 1963 and 1973 respectively.[50] (Similar data are not available for the years between 1955 and 1963.) Of course, another indicator is gross fixed capital formation in residential housing, which rose by about 210 per cent at current prices between 1963 and 1973 (50 per cent at constant 1963 prices). Finally, the visitor who is familiar with Syria can see the vast improvement in housing conditions that has taken place during the post-war period, even in the outlying villages of Hauran, Aleppo or Lattakia areas. The improvement is evidenced both by the structure of houses and by the furniture and household equipment inside. But the scale of performance notwithstanding, one must remember that Syria does not suffer from a severe housing problem,

Table 6.10: Progress in Public Health Provision

	Year	Number
Government hospitals	1949	16
	1973	30
Government hospital beds	1949	1,290
	1973	4,618
Private hospitals	1949	–
	1973	60
Private hospital beds	1973	1,280
Sanatoria	1949	3
	1973	4
Sanatoria beds	1949	175
	1973	780
Persons per bed	1949	2,137
	1973	1,032
Clinics and health centres	1955	107
	1973	288
Physicians	1945	616
	1973	2,371
Persons per physician	1945	4,545
	1973	2,906
Dentists	1945	241
	1973	561
Pharmacists	1945	147
	1973	1,016
Midwives	1945	245
	1973	932
Female nurses	1962	685
	1973	2,632

Source: *Statistical Abstract 1974*, Ch. XI, 'Health'.

nor do its cities have, on the same scale, the slums and *bidonvilles* which are a painful eyesore in so many other cities of the Arab world. Indeed, town planning in post-Mandate Syria has been much better than average in the Arab world.

A few final observations are called for at the close of this whole section. It is worth noting that Syria's economic performance has been achieved with remarkable price stability. Thus the wholesale prices index number dropped from 99 for 1956 (base period: 1952-4 = 100) to 97 for 1964. A new chain has been made with 1962 as base year. According to this chain, the wholesale prices index number for 1973 stood at 171. Year-by-year examination reveals that it was the period 1967-70 that witnessed a sudden spurt upwards (1965 stood at 100). (However, the year 1973 showed the steepest price increase with a rise of 32.6 per cent over 1972.) The explanation may well be the steeply accelerated investment programme in the Second Five-Year Plan 1966-70, whose fruition has been relatively slow in appearing. Most of the rise in the years under reference has been in the prices of foodstuffs, owing to bad crops in the years under question as a whole and a drop in the contribution of agriculture to NDP for the years 1966-70 taken together, in comparison with the few preceding years. Another factor has been building materials. However, this category accounts for 8 per cent of the weights, against about 56 per cent for foodstuffs.[51]

Understandably, state spending has increased considerably during the post-war period. Thus, from 1948 to 1969 the ordinary expenditure budget rose from £S136.3 million to £S1,199 million — or by more than eight times. On the other hand, the development budget rose from £S25.8 million for 1950, to £S146.5 million in 1960, to £S980.8 million for 1969. (As from 1969, the ordinary and development budgets have been combined into a unified or consolidated general budget. This last stood at £S3,413m for 1973, and at £S6,480m for 1974, including £S1,743m and £S3,598.4m for development.) The consolidated budget takes into account the revenue and expenditure of self-financing enterprises in the public sector. Municipal budgets stand separate. Total budget expenditure for 1973 was £S144.5m.[52]

Alongside, there has been considerable expansion in the money supply, from £S295 million at the end of 1951, to £S2,087.7 million at the end of 1969 and £S3,819m at the end of 1973. However, substantial as this increase is, it still reveals a low level of monetisation in the economy, considering the size of population and of the national product. Looked at more closely, the data reveal a very slow growth in the habit of banking, as is evidenced by the fact that in 1973 currency in circulation represented 72.9 per cent of money supply. (In 1951, private deposits stood at £S60.5m and public deposits at £S111.9m, while they totalled £S1,055.2m in 1973 — or only a six-fold rise.) Another way of gauging the extent to which banking has developed is to look at the consolidated statement of specialised banks (indeed, this includes all the banking groups operating in Syria, except the Central Bank). The total assets (and liabilities) amounted to £S3,057.8m at the end of 1973. The largest single user of banking services is the government, whether directly for its own uses, or for lending to the public. Thus 75 per cent of all the loans made in 1973 by the 'specialised banks' went to the public sector. The private sector received 22 per cent, and the small balance went to the mixed and co-operative sectors. To these loans must be added the claims of the Central Bank on government, which amounted to £S2,621.6m by the end of 1973, against £S358.9m for 1958. It will be recalled that the years 1958-73 witnessed a vast expansion in government borrowing. Again here we see the very limited extent to which the private sector uses banking services. Total credits extended by the specialised banks amounted for 1973 to £S2,494.6m, out of which trade received the lion's share (£S1,782.1m), followed distantly by agriculture (£S272.5m), industry (£S165.2m), construction (£S92.2m), services (£S1.2m) and miscellaneous (£S8.8m).[53]

Syria's account with the rest of the world normally shows balance or a very small surplus or deficit. Thus, the current account in the balance of payments, including transit fees received from oil companies whose pipelines cross Syria, plus private donations and emigrant remittances, leaves a very small balance to account for through compensatory financing. In absolute terms, the earnings and payments sides of the current account each ranged roughly between £S400m and £S500m for the years 1951-3, and between £S1,325m and £S1,600m for earnings and £S1,500m and £S1,900m for payments for the three years 1969-71, netting an unfavourable balance which rose from £S158.8m to £S225.2m, to £S288.1m for these years respectively. The balance for 1972 was adverse likewise, and stood at £S209m.[54] In brief, it can be said that Syria, in spite of its accelerated investment programme and, necessarily, rising capital imports, does not suffer a 'balance of payments hardship' to an appreciable extent.

Finally, Syria's overall economic performance in the post-war period can be said to be on the average satisfactory, in spite of the fact that the major sector — agriculture — has not been allowed to fulfil its great promise, and that the global rate of growth has ranged between 4.5 and 5 per cent on the average. One special merit of Syria's record is that it has been achieved without considerable foreign aid, almost with exclusive dependence on Syrian skilled manpower, and in spite of the political instability that characterised much of the thirty years under examination.

3. THE SOCIALIST TRANSFORMATION

The process described here, and in official pronouncements and commentaries, as 'the socialist transformation' must be described and understood as a transformation involving a mixture of ingredients. Some relate to the widening of the base of land ownership and the destruction of the privilege and power — social, economic and political — of large landowners and other capitalists. Others relate to the emergence of the state as a major owner of the means of production and a sole or major owner of title to capital in some service sectors, and to the state's resort to central planning. Yet others relate to the pursuit of egalitarian distributive policy with regard to the application of progressive taxation and the provision of free or subsidised social services.

It would be an unrewarding exercise to find or coin a universally accepted definition of socialism, and to test the transformation process in Syria against this definition. It is sufficient for our purposes to cede the point that the decision-makers in Syria, the ideologists behind them and the publicists talking for them all refer to the process which we will be examining in this section as one of socialist transformation. This process is no less one of legislation, control of economic power, and state management of large parts of the economy than a conviction, a mood and an outlook. The socialist stance expresses itself beyond the purely social and economic realms to reach the field of international relations: identification, diplomatic and political attitudes and alignments, orientation of foreign trade and aid, support of causes believed to be liberationist or anti-imperialist, empathy.

For our purposes, the socialist transformation will be examined under four headings, as indicated earlier in section 2 above (in the phase covering the period 1958-61). These are agrarian reform; the formulation of the First Five-Year Plan 1960/1–1964/5, the Second Five-Year Plan 1966-70, and the Third Five-Year Plan 1971-5; the nationalisation of most large concerns in the fields of industry, banking, insurance and foreign trade; and the formulation and implementation of measures designed to bring about a larger measure of social justice and egalitarianism. The four areas of legislation and action, taken together, had the combined effect of drastically changing the power structure of society in the economic, social and political fields. While the army as an institution today in effect controls the affairs of Syria — within the ideological framework of the Ba'ath Party — it is neither the same institution nor the same party group that launched the socialist transformation beginning with the merger with Egypt in February 1958. And certainly both army and party are very unlike their counterparts in power, on and off, between 1949 and early 1958.

The four areas of action marking together the socialist transformation of Syria between 1958 and the present will be examined here as representing structural changes of significant impact on the economic (and socio-political) life of the country. In the present section, these areas of action will receive general description and examination. However, their more thorough examination as determinants of development will be postponed to Volume II (the companion volume). The present discussion will prepare the ground for the more questioning analysis to follow.

Agrarian Reform

The abortive attempt by Shishakli in 1952 to institute agrarian reform was not the first attempt in the country's history. Earlier, and equally unsuccessful, efforts, relating both to state domain and large private holdings, had been tried in 1926 and 1929 under the French Mandate. Shishakli's own attempt, which was in fact a trial of strength between him and the strong propertied class, came through a series of three Legislative Decrees between 30 January and 3 November 1952. These decrees were based on the Constitution of 5 September 1950, Article 22 of which provided for the limitation of the ownership of agricultural land and the encouragement of the emergence of small and medium holdings, and lastly the redistribution of state domain.[55]

Between January and November, the provisions of the first Legislative Decree were amended in favour of the landlords. This whole effort came to very little, if anything, owing to the resistance of landlords, 'political instability, the weakness of the administrative machinery and the fact that the rural lands belonging to the state were not surveyed'.[56] However, the failure did not deter the Shishakli régime from incorporating similar reform provisions in Article 35 of the Constitution of 11 July 1953.

It was six years later that agrarian reform was at last instituted in Syria as the 'Northern Province' of the United Arab Republic, through three Decree Laws issued in 1958. Thus, on 27 September 1958, Law No. 161 relating to agrarian reform was promulgated. Its main features were the following:

— Limitation of the ceiling of ownership and requisitioning of excess area. The limits were 80 hectares of irrigated land or land planted with trees, or 300 hectares of rain-fed land; in addition a further 10 ha of irrigated or 40 ha of rain-fed land could be transferred to the spouse and each child, provided the total transfer did not exceed 40 ha or 160 ha of the two types of land respectively.
— Compensation for land requisitioned was to be ten times the average rent (calculated on the basis of the preceding 3-year rotation), payable in bonds carrying 1.5 per cent interest and redeemable in 40 years. The bonds were to be nominal, and negotiable only in settlement of the price of any land bought from the state, of agricultural taxes, or of inheritance taxes.
— Redistribution of excess land seized by the Agrarian Reform Agency to landless farmers or small owners in plots not exceeding 8 ha or 30 ha of irrigated or rain-fed land respectively (except in the north-eastern areas where the ceiling was 45 ha of rain-fed land, owing to the scarcity of rainfall there.) The distribution pattern was to follow a system of priorities based on size of family, degree of poverty, and actual ownership of land prior to the reform law.
— Payment by redistribution beneficiaries was to be effected on the basis of the following calculation: price was fixed at ten times the average rent of the land plus interest at 1.5 per cent per annum, plus an extra 10 per cent of the price to cover the expenses

Syria

of requisitioning and redistribution. Repayment of the total was to be effected over forty years in equal instalments.
— Finally, the beneficiaries, as well as other landowners in the village owning land less than the area allotted under land reform, were required by law to join co-operative societies which were to provide supplies, credit and marketing facilities, as well as advise on planning operations.

An earlier law, No. 134 of 4 September 1958, had attempted to regulate and organise the relationships between landlords, tenants and agricultural workers. And a subsequent law, No. 252 of 19 October 1959, was issued to regulate the distribution of state domain. Under this last law the Agrarian Reform Agency could distribute such domain free of charge, but subject to the same area stipulations of Law No. 161. As mentioned earlier in section 2 above, the total area believed then to be affected by the reform measure was some 5.3 million ha, of which 1.5 million were privately owned and 3.8 million state domain.

The background to land reform needs to be described for the relevance of the reform to be understood. Three aspects of this background have special significance. *First*, the pattern of distribution of land by size of holdings. This pattern showed 'a preponderance of small and medium-sized properties in the provinces of the Hauran, Jebel Druze, and Lattakia',[57] but many large land holdings also existed, mainly in the Aleppo, Euphrates, Jezira and Hama provinces. Land ownership by size of holdings is summarised in Table 6.11.

Table 6.11: Land Ownership by Size of Holdings, 1948

	Hectares	Per Cent
Small (under 10 ha)	1,097,491	13.5
Medium (10-100)	2,892,414	36.5
Large (over 100)	2,348,783	30.0
Sub-total	6,338,688	80.0
State domain	1,593,000	20.0
Total	7,931,688	100.0

Source: Doreen Warriner, *Land Reform and Development in the Middle East* (London, 1948), p. 83, quoted from Bureau de Documentations Syriennes et Arabes, *Etude sur l'agriculture syrienne* (Damascus, 1955), p. 24.

Another pattern of distribution by owner and size of holding is available; it is summarised in Table 6.12.

Unfortunately, information is not also available as to the average area for each category of size of holding; consequently it is not possible to calculate the area owned by each category of owners. But it is certain that the figures just cited, which add up to a total of 292,273 owners, can only represent partial coverage in a country where some 60-65 per cent of the population is rural, that is, some 800,000 families live on the land and make a living out of it. Recent information which has much wider coverage indicates clearly that landless families constitute 55 per cent of the total number of Syrian families, both

Table 6.12: Distribution of Holdings by Size Before Agrarian Reform

Size of Holding	No. of Owners		Per Cent of Total	
	Rain-fed	Irrigated	Rain-fed	Irrigated
1–50 ha	225,525	42,752	91.0	96.3
50–100	15,189	780	6.1	1.8
100–500	5,297	552	2.1	1.2
500–1,000	1,581	209	0.7	0.5
Over 1,000	293	95	0.1	0.2
Total	247,885	44,388	100.0	100.0

Source: Salah Dabbagh, 'Agrarian Reform in Syria', *MEEP 1962*, p. 7, quoting Centre d'Etudes ... etc., *L'Economie et les Finances de la Syrie et des Pays Arabes* (Damascus, May 1962), Vol. V, No. 53, p. 42.

rural and urban, which stood at 1,064,486 in 1970. The average holding of land-holding families (which numbered 476,636) was 102.7 *dunoms*, or 10.27 ha, consisting of 97 *dunoms* of cultivable and 5.7 *dunoms* of uncultivable land. As the rural families averaged 5.9 persons per family according to the 1970 population census, the total of rural families numbered 600,000. Therefore roughly 80 per cent of these had land, and 20 per cent were landless.[58]

Associated with the question of size of holdings was the serious problem of fragmentation in the more crowded areas of the country where the old *masha'a* (communal) form of tenure still prevailed. Fragmentation was wasteful in the extreme and aggravated the problem of ownership of very small tracts by many farmers.

The second aspect in the background is the unfavourable tenancy conditions, particularly in the crowded provinces. These conditions worked against the tenant who usually did not have security of tenure, a written contract, access to reasonably cheap credit, or a fair share in the produce. The situation was detrimental to investment by the tenant and therefore to increases in productivity.

In the third place, the large landlords enjoyed a disproportionately strong position politically and socially, and thus controlled the affairs of the country to an extent much beyond what their numbers would justify.

The kind of generalisation made regarding the background is rather similar to generalisations usually made in connection with Egypt and Iraq before the introduction of agrarian reform. But it is necessary to introduce certain qualifications here, as the true picture was rather differentiated. Syrian landlords on the whole were more patriotic and anti-colonialist than their counterparts in the two other countries, in the sense of identifying themselves more sincerely with the issues of independence (when foreign rule still existed) and with more nationalistic objectives after independence. Furthermore, they showed more interest in their land and in the 'extension of the agricultural frontier' than their Iraqi counterparts. (One ought here to remember the remarkable role of the 'merchant-tractorists' discussed earlier.) Tenancy conditions, though bad, were not as bad as those in Iraq. On the other hand, the Egyptian pattern of land distribution, though characterised by the highest ratio for the three countries in very small land holdings, did not suffer from the existence of large land holdings to the same extent as in Iraq and Syria. On this last point, Iraq had larger holdings than either of the two other countries. Lastly, Egyptian landlords on the whole were attentive to their land if only because the return per hectare was very high on the average (clearly higher than in Iraq or Syria).

After the break-up of the union between Egypt and Syria, Law 161 of September 1958 was amended by Law No. 3 of 20 February 1962. The latter law did not undo the reform altogether, but raised the ownership limits to a range of 80–200 ha of irrigated land, and 300–600 ha of rain-fed land, depending on volume of rainfall and of irrigation water available, quality of land and similar criteria. Likewise, it reduced the maturity of bonds given to former landlords from forty to ten years, and removed the upper limit on the number of wives and children to whom the landlord could transfer specified areas of his land.

However, restiveness in the countryside and in the army, and certainly among reform-minded radical elements, made the new government amend the February law on 2 May 1962. According to this latest amendment, the ceiling in irrigated land was set at 80 ha, in rain-fed land at 300 ha, except in the Hasaka, Deir-ez-Zor and Rasheed districts where the ceiling was set at 450 ha. The parcels of redistributed land were to be set at a maximum of 10 irrigated ha or 40 rain-fed ha (60 ha in the eastern districts excepted above). Compensation to landlords was to be in bonds bearing an interest at 1.5 per cent and redeemable in ten years if the value involved did not exceed £S100,000 or in fifteen years for larger values.

Lastly, subsequent to the *coup* of 8 March 1963 which pushed out the secessionist army and civilian elements that had brought off the *coup* of 28 September 1961 and broke the union, the law of agrarian reform was again amended. Two amendments were incorporated in Decree Law 88 of 23 June 1963 and Decree Law No. 125 of 12 June 1964. The main provisions were the following:

— Ownership limits were set at a scale, depending on the type of irrigation (flow, pump, well) and the abundance of water and on the amount of rainfall in the area concerned, as well as on the existence of trees. The scale ranged from 15 ha per owner in the best endowed land up to 55 ha of irrigated land, and between 80 ha and 200 ha of rain-fed land.
— Dependants could each receive up to 8 per cent of the area allowed the head of the family.
— Compensation was to be calculated as stipulated in the original reform law, and to be paid in interest-bearing bonds redeemable in forty years, and only transferable in settlement of agricultural taxes, inheritance taxes, or the purchase prices of any land bought from government.
— Area allowed to beneficiaries was to be 8 ha of irrigated or tree-planted land, 30 ha in rain-fed land if average rainfall was above 350 mm per year, and 45 ha if below.
— Settlement by beneficiaries for the value of the land received was to be on the basis of one-fourth the expropriation value, payable in twenty equal annual instalments to co-operative societies for use in development and social purposes.
— The laws of 1963 and 1964 were, like Law 161 of 1958, retroactive to 1 January 1950, with regard to sales within the family effected since that date.

All the laws enacted, beginning with September 1958 and ending with June 1964, had provisions for the creation of co-operative societies in reform areas, where membership was obligatory for beneficiaries as well as for other small landowners whose area of ownership was equivalent to or smaller than that of the new beneficiaries. Likewise, tenancy arrangements purporting to protect the tenant and to give him greater security and a larger share of the produce than in pre-reform days were also part of the laws.

Expropriation moved much faster than redistribution. In the first years of uncertainty, between the beginning of 1959 and the middle of 1964 — the period characterised by legislation, abrogation, amendment and so on — expropriation was by far fastest in 1959, but dropped considerably in 1960. It went on dropping for 1961 and 1962, stabilised in 1963, and rose moderately in 1964. Redistribution was even more erratic, as the following table indicates. However, total redistribution amounted to 23.3 per cent of expropriation in the period covered, namely 1959-64, or 232,060 ha (of which 11,437 ha were irrigated and/or planted with trees) out of a total of 994,058 ha expropriated (of which 44,003 ha were irrigated).[59]

Table 6.13: Expropriated and Distributed Land in the Period 1959—64 (hectares)

Year	Expropriated		Distributed		Individual Beneficiaries
	Irrigated	Rain-fed	Irrigated	Rain-fed	
1959	11,577	505,253	3,504	33,230	14,319
1960	8,680	158,888	2,445	20,903	8,897
1961	9,219	123,979	7	3,523	1,355
1962	2,347	47,481	4,379	88,006	34,921
1963	3,970	46,475	840	64,170	20,096
1964	8,210	67,979	262	10,791	4,921
Total	44,003	950,055	11,437	220,623	84,509
Total Expropriated: 994,058					
Total Distributed:			232,060		
Total Families Benefiting:					15,392

Note: Total rain-fed area expropriated includes an area of 206,018 ha designated as 'uncultivated'.

The cumulative total of expropriated, and of distributed, land as on 31 December 1969 is shown in Table 6.14.

In addition to land distributed, there is land expropriated which is leased out while arrangements are being made for distribution. This category of land totalled 1,080,736 ha in area by the end of 1970, and is divided as shown in Table 6.15.

There are several reasons for non-distribution, including the time-consuming process of selecting beneficiaries according to the priority system set in the reform law and the regulations based on it. However, one other reason is the slow process of land survey and settlement of title. Syria's 185,179 sq. km. have by the end of 1970 only been partly surveyed. The situation with regard to land survey and settlement of title stood at the

Syria

Table 6.14: Total Expropriated Land, 1969 (hectares)

Irrigated and tree-planted area	85,554
Non-irrigated area	1,139,695
Non-cultivated area	288,315
Total area expropriated	1,513,564
Irrigated and tree area distributed	60,125
Non-irrigated area distributed	382,510
Area set apart for distribution	145,833
Area excluded (not fit for distribution)	192,296
Sub-total	780,764
Area not yet prepared for distribution	732,800
Total involved (expropriated)	1,513,564
Number of families benefiting (new landowners)	52,504
Number of villages involved	1,386

Source: *Statistical Abstract 1969-1970*, pp. 130-5, *S.A. 1971*, Ch III, Tables 81 and 82, and *S.A. 1974*, p. 221, for the data on expropriation, distribution and land survey.

end of 1969 as shown in Table 6.16.

The discussion so far has concentrated on privately owned land. State domain, which was presumed to reach an area of 3.8 million ha available for distribution, has been reassessed. It now seems to appear that more than half this area is not fit for distribution, or is too costly to prepare for remunerative cultivation, or otherwise inaccessible. In any case, a decree issued on 18 December 1968 made 600,000 ha[60] of state land available for purchase by peasants, on the same terms as those applicable to land expropriated from private landlords. Out of this total, 30,010 ha were sold in the five years 1969-73. On the other hand, a total of 222,875 ha have been leased out. Here again, land survey operations are far from complete, which is a delaying factor in the distribution of state domain.

Lastly, a word about co-operative societies. The number of societies formed in connection with agrarian reform law totalled 1,725 by the end of 1973, with 134,562 members, and a land area of 929,000 ha. (The official sources do not distinguish between agrarian reform and other societies.)[61] A quick comparison between these numbers and those recorded earlier with regard to number of beneficiaries and land area involved shows that there are still many farmers and substantial areas which have not yet been included in the co-operative movement in accordance with the reform law. The lag is explained partly through administrative delays in government and the insufficiency of advisers and supervisors, and partly through the lukewarm reaction among villagers to the idea of co-operation in a culture highly characterised by individualism. But agrarian reform in general has suffered from other shortcomings, which will receive consideration later.

Table 6.15: Expropriated Land under Temporary Leasing by End of 1970

Irrigated	54,348
Planted with trees	6,562
Non-irrigated	1,019,826
Total	1,080,736

(The total area stood at 799,536 ha at the end of 1969.)

Note: The *Statistical Abstract 1974* records *smaller* areas for 1970 than for 1969 with respect to expropriation and some other categories. Furthermore, no information is available beyond 1970.

Table 6.16: Progress of Land Survey, 1969

	Sq. Km.
Area surveyed	63,079
Area not yet surveyed	56,892
Area not included in the survey programme	65,208
Total	185,179

Central Comprehensive Planning[62]

Syria has had development plans since 1947, when Sir Alexander Gibb and Partners, a firm that had been commissioned by the government to report on development, suggested a ten-year investment programme totalling £S477 million, the bulk of which was to be for infrastructure. This figure proved not out of line with the public investments made outside the scope of the ordinary budget which totalled £S427.5 million for the years 1945-55.[63]

In 1955, the IBRD mission suggested a public expenditure programme for six years totalling £S1,903.5 million. Although this recommendation was not implemented, some institutional steps followed, such as the formation in 1955 of a Permanent Economic Council and an Economic Development Authority (or Institution), as well as the formulation by the government of a seven-year programme dated 29 August 1955. This programme was much more modest than that suggested by the (traditionally conservative) IBRD mission: it involved total development expenditure of £S659.9 million for irrigation and agriculture, transport and communications, and industry — in that order, and much further down, several other areas.

The seven-year programme was discarded in 1956, after some £S136 million had been expended. In 1957 an economic aid agreement was reached with the USSR, and in 1958 a new ten-year programme was formulated. The main objectives of this latest programme were to free agriculture from excessive dependence on rainfall, improve agriculture, produce fertilisers, provide a network of roads between centres of production and of distribution, build an oil refinery, and set up an industrial base. Total allocations were £S2,139.4 million — a much larger programme than hitherto ever envisaged. Of this total, £S1,461.5 million were for agriculture, irrigation and hydraulic power; £S350 million for transport and communications; £S160 million for industry and petroleum; £S30 million for tourism; £S10 million for training; £S15 million for administration; and £S98.4 million for interest on loans. In order to strengthen the industrial base of the country, the government further

Syria

formulated an industrialisation programme involving the spending of another £S560 million, mainly for petroleum (£S266.2 million) and transformative industry (£S216.9 million).

But these programmes were not comprehensive; both were restricted to the public sector and failed to take into account the total availability and uses of resources in the whole economy. Furthermore, in order for Syria to co-ordinate its planning process and methodology with Egypt, with which it united in February 1958, the earlier ten-year programme was discarded, and a new plan for five years was formulated within a wider ten-year framework. The new plan, the First Five-Year Plan 1960/1–1964/5 (FFYP) was the first comprehensive plan which encompassed the private along with the public sector, and projected the total availability and total uses of resources for the five years ahead.

The ten-year framework, like its Egyptian counterpart, envisaged a doubling of GNP in ten years, or a cumulative average growth rate of 7.2 per cent per annum. The FFYP had several objectives: raising national and personal income, and level of living; changing the sectoral structure of the economy in such a way that agriculture, though growing in absolute terms (and faster than population growth) would become less important in the structure in relative terms; widening the range of production and diversifying the economy; increasing job opportunities slightly faster than the natural increase in population (the labour force was to rise by 12.4 per cent, from 1,530,000 in 1960 to 1,720,000 in 1965); achieving a wider measure of equity in the distribution of income; strengthening the base of the economy as a protection against fluctuations; achieving price stability in spite of the accelerated investment programme; and self-sufficiency in certain industries for military or political reasons. There is in the Plan document no rigorous examination of the degree of consistency between this long list of objectives, and to that extent the Plan fell somewhere between a sophisticated instrument utilising refined methodology, and a rule-of-thumb exercise.[64] The overall 'master table' which represented the vision of the planned change in the various components of the FFYP is given in Table 6.17.

Table 6.17: Estimated Change in Population, Income and its Uses Between the Base Year and the Five Years 1960/1–1964/5

Year	Population '000	National Income (£S m)	Saving (£S m)	Public Consumption (£S m)	Private Consumption (£S m)	Per Capita Income £S	Per Capita Consumption £S
Base Year	4,550	2,400	275	400	1,725	527	379
1960/1	4,660	2,566	310	420	1,836	551	394
1961/2	4,770	2,743	345	450	1,948	575	408
1962/3	4,885	2,932	385	480	2,067	600	423
1963/4	5,000	3,134	430	520	2,184	627	437
1964/5	5,120	3,360	480	560	2,320	656	453

It can be seen from Table 6.17 that income was expected to rise by 40 per cent over the base year, while consumption was to grow by 34.5 per cent, which suggests a slowly decreasing marginal propensity to consume. Local saving was to rise from 11.5 per cent to some 14 per cent in the target year. Total saving was to add up to £S1,950 million; thus it would fall short of planned investment by £S770 million. This gap was to be filled in part by internal loans (£S130 million), but mainly by foreign grants and loans (£S640 million).

Until the FFYP was formulated, a sizeable portion of public investment had gone into infrastructure. The FFYP, on the other hand, in cognisance of the fact that large investments had already been made in infrastructure, and consistently with the predominance of agriculture in Syria's economy, devoted the largest single allocation to irrigation and land reclamation, and the fourth to agriculture proper. Together, these two areas of activity were allotted over 40 per cent of total planned investment. The second and third places, respectively, were occupied by transport and communications, and by industry, electricity, mining and petroleum. The planned investment programme is given in Table 6.18.

Table 6.18: Investment Programme 1960-5 (£S m)

Economic Sector	Public Sector	Private Sector	Total Investment	Per Cent of Total
Irrigation and land reclamation	780	50	830	30.5
Agriculture	95	175	270	9.9
Industry, electricity, mining, petroleum	–	509	509	18.7
Transport and communications	387	150	537	19.7
Education	100	–	100	3.7
Health	46	10	56	2.1
Public utilities and tourism	32	–	32	1.2
Housing	255	5	260	9.5
Social affairs	18	–	18	0.7
Recreation	–	11	11	0.4
Laboratories, training, research	7	–	7	0.3
Change in stocks	–	90	90	3.3
Total	1,720	1,000	2,720	100.0

The year-by-year planned investment was as follows in £S millions: 420, 574, 626, 578, 522. The hump-shaped curve must have reflected the conviction that early in the Plan, the absorptive capacity would be low owing, *inter alia*, to the slowness in pre-investment studies, and that in the last two years there would be mild saturation. It is difficult to venture another explanation for the decline of investment after the third year.

The sources of financing were to be those shown in Table 6.19. Thus, foreign aid apart, investment forecasts suggested roughly a 50-50 distribution between the private and the public sectors. *A priori,* the rosy expectation of such active participation by private businessmen is puzzling and would suggest insufficient realism. After 1958 and the institution of agrarian reform, the private sector began to show considerable caution and hesitation in investment, owing to its fear of 'creeping socialism' — both in legislation and

Table 6.19: Planned Sources of Finance for Investment Programme

	£S
State and municipal budgets, surpluses of public institutions, internal loans	1,080,000
Private sector	1,000,000
Foreign grants and loans	640,000
Total	2,720,000

measures taken, and in public slogans and pronouncements diffused on a large scale. While it was true that the private sector had more reason for concern in the Egyptian Province, its counterpart in the Syrian Province could not wait until the shadow of socialist decrees (or nationalisations, in any case) covered its customary terrain.

However, as we saw earlier, and contrary to *a priori* expectations, fixed capital formation in the private sector continued to be far greater than in the public sector until 1965. Part of the explanation might be the indomitable entrepreneurial spirit of Syrian businessmen, who restructured their investments among the sectors but continued to invest heavily. But in part, the unexpected performance of the private sector is explainable in the fact that the union between Egypt and Syria broke soon after the end of the first year of the FFYP, thus promoting private investment considerably in the following two years, 1962 and 1963, and continuing to bring about more private than public investment in the year 1964. (It will be recalled that in March 1963 a new *coup d'état* returned the Ba'ath Party to predominance in political life, where it has since stayed.) Obviously the secession of 1961 revived the hopes of the private sector that the Syrian political establishment was not going to imitate its Egyptian counterpart in its accelerated trend towards nationalisation and socialist transformation, in spite of the clear Syrian shift 'leftwards'. However, by 1965 these hopes were dashed irrevocably.

The Plan years, until 1965, ran from 1 July to the next 30 June (for 1965 the plan ended on 31 December 1965), while the national accounts cover calender years (see Table 6.1). Comparison between the forecasts for national income according to the FFYP and the estimates of Net Domestic Product is revealing, the variation in concept (between NNP and NDP) notwithstanding. With these qualifications in mind, we list, side by side, the two sets of figures in Table 6.20.

It can readily be seen that NDP was higher than NNP right from the first year, but that by the second year the NDP had risen by more than the initial difference between the two aggregates. Indeed, a sector-by-sector comparison reveals wide divergence on the whole. Likewise, a year-by-year and sector-by-sector comparison between planned and actual investment reveals equally wide divergence. Yet, considering that this was the first experience in comprehensive planning, that the institutions involved with planning and execution were trying their first steps, and that the political course of events was far from even, the performance can be considered satisfactory.

The Second Five-Year Plan 1966-70 (SFYP) ran from January 1966 to 31 December 1970, or on a calender year basis. The highlights of this Plan will now be presented.[65] Eleven objectives or targets were listed:

1. Achieving self-sustained growth conducive to greater economic and social welfare.
2. Directing society towards evolving socialism based on the encouragement and promotion of socialist labour and production, the elimination of human exploitation, and

264 Syria

Table 6.20: Comparison of Planned NNP and Actual NDP

Year	FFYP NNP Forecasts £Sm	Year	Actual NDP £Sm
1960/1	2,566	1961	2,831
1961/2	2,743	1962	3,542
1962/3	2,932	1963	3,509
1963/4	3,134	1964	3,833
1964/5	3,360	1965	3,873

the provision of equal opportunities for all citizens.
3. Increasing GDP by 7.2 per cent per annum on the average.
4. Raising agricultural productivity, mechanisation, and as full a utilisation of water for irrigation as possible.
5. Establishing an industrial base in harmony with the country's agricultural and natural endowments, with a view to import substitution and raising export possibilities.
6. Raising labour productivity and the training of new technical skills in order to overcome unemployment and disguised unemployment.
7. Improving the level and conditions of the rural areas in all districts, through increasing social services, elimination of illiteracy, and increasing job opportunities.
8. Laying the foundations capable of achieving a comprehensive scientific renaissance.
9. Improving spatial distribution of the factors of production.
10. Consolidating the security of the state against colonialism and Zionism.
11. Contributing to the achievement of economic complementarity between Arab countries, as a first step towards achieving full Arab unity.

It was from these broad objectives that the detailed targets of the Plan were derived.

Unlike the FFYP, the SFYP did not contain a master table that recorded the major magnitudes and their projections. Consequently we will try to combine several tables from the official text of the SFYP into one master table somewhat similar to Table 6.17 above, and then we will present a comparison between the investment programmes of the two Five-Year Plans.

Comparison of this table with actual achievements suggests a very high level of fulfilment with regard to NDP, where actual NDP at market prices was £S5,425.9 million, against planned NDP of £S5,230 million. Gross fixed capital formation, however, contrasted with planned investment, reveals a consistent under-fulfilment for the years 1966-70 at constant (1963) prices. The discrepancy began with the year 1966, when planned investment was £S807 million, while the base year showed £S640 million. (Actually, gross fixed capital formation for 1965 was £S457 million at constant prices of 1963, and £S484 million at current prices. The discrepancy for base year is not explained. The shortfall for the five years amounts to £S1,389m.)[66]

Population estimates in the SFYP were low; by the middle of 1970 the actual population was 6.247m against Plan forecasts of 5.6m. The labour force according to the count of November 1969 was 1,970,940 (of whom 85,305 were unemployed). Here too the SFYP has underestimated, since it forecast the size of the labour force to be only 1.44

Table 6.21: Estimated Change in Population, NDP at Market Prices, Consumption and Investment Between the Base Year (1965) and the Target Year (1970)

Year	Population '000	NDP £S m	Private Consumption £S m	Public Consumption £S m	Investment £S m	Labour Force '000	New Jobs
Base Year	5,062	3,695	2,570	660	640	1,295	34,681
1966	5,173	3,923	2,719	693	807	1,323	42,685
1967	5,287	4,215	2,913	728	887	1,352	44,712
1968	5,402	4,529	3,096	764	987	1,381	46,260
1969	5,522	4,867	3,299	802	1,095	1,412	47,594
1970	5,643	5,230	3,517	842	1,179	1,443	48,767

Note: The base year data differ from the actual data for 1965. According to a footnote in the official text in Arabic (p. 13), NDP for the base year as shown above is the mean for the years 1960-4, plus 4 per cent increase for 1965 over 1964.

million for 1970. The underestimation arises from two factors: the underestimation of the population itself, and the underestimation of the ratio of labour force to total population. According to the SFYP, the ratio is some 25.6 per cent; in fact it was 31.4 per cent. However, these discrepancies apart, the overall performance under the SFYP was satisfactory. But looked at more closely, it reveals wide divergences at the sector level between planned investment and planned value added, on the one hand, and actual investment and value added, on the other hand. One major factor ought to be offered as part explanation: the Arab-Israeli war of June 1967, and its extensive disruptive effect. The shadow of this war continues to retard development until today and right into the Third Five-Year Plan 1971-5, if only because of the enormous diversion of human and physical resources into defence.

Finally, a comparison between the two investment programmes of the FFYP and SFYP is in order. Such comparison reflects the change in emphasis, which in turn is the result of change of rationale and in the rate of development of various sectors.

Table 6.22 is quite clear with regard to the different patterns of emphasis. It remains to be added that the private sector was assigned £S1,500.6 million, or 30.3 per cent of total investment. In fact, its contribution amounted to 33.5 per cent for the five years 1966-70. For the economy as a whole, net savings were to rise from 13.6 to 17 per cent (from base to target year). Table 6.23 sets out clearly the major expectations with regard to the 'expenditure on GDP, 1965-1970'.

Syria's current development plan is the 'Third Five-Year Plan for Economic and Social Development in the Syrian Arab Province, 1971-1975'. This Plan became law on 31 January 1971, upon the signature of the President of the Federal State which then comprised Syria, Egypt and Libya. (Hence the reference in the title of the Plan to the Syrian 'Province' rather than 'Republic'.)

A total of fourteen broad objectives are set for this Plan, as follows:

Syria

Table 6.22: Comparison of Investment Programmes in the FFYP and the SFYP

Sector	First Plan £S m	Plan Per Cent	Second Plan £S m	Plan Per Cent	Per Cent Difference	£S m Difference
Irrigation and land reclamation	830	30.5	955.8	19.3	-11.2	+125.8
Agriculture	270	9.9	436.3	8.8	-1.1	+166.3
Industry and mining	235	8.6	398.5	8.0	-0.6	+163.5
Electricity and petroleum	274	10.1	612.0	12.4	+2.3	+338.0
Transport and communications	537	19.7	894.3	18.0	-1.7	+357.3
Public utilities, debt servicing	484	17.9	1,278.2	25.8	+7.9	+794.2
Services, etc.	90	3.3	379.9	7.7	+4.4	+289.9
Total	2,720	100.0	4,955.0	100.0	0.0	+2,235.0

1. Consolidation of the material foundations for economic and social evolution, via the comprehensive mobilisation of all production capabilities in the service of the struggle for liberation.
2. Intensification of the drive towards comprehensive Arab unity through the evolution of Arab economic complementarity, the co-ordination of economic and petroleum policies, the encouragement of joint Arab investment projects, and the development of the Arab economy and its liberation from subservience to foreign economic interests.
3. Realisation of economic and social evolution within the framework of a unified socialist Arab society..., the realisation of the principle of equality of opportunities among all citizens, and of justice in the distribution of income, and the elimination of monopoly and exploitation...
4. Adjustment of the structure of the national economy in the direction of the establishment of an agricultural-industrial advanced economy that can form a strong basis for the drive towards a continuous self-sustained development, and the achievement of a rate of growth in the Net Domestic Product of 8.2 per cent annually, with the object of the doubling of 'national income' within a maximum of nine years.
5. Deriving optimum benefit from water resources, agricultural land, and manpower...
6. Speeding up the execution of the Euphrates Project and the preparation, in the physical, human and organisational fields, for the exploitation and development of the lands that will be irrigated by the project.
7. Completion of the establishment of the industrial base...
8. Deriving optimum benefit from the potential made available by the country's geographic location...
9. Marching alongside the scientific advances and technological revolution, especially in the basic branches of production,...
10. Diverting great attention to the rural parts of the country, especially in the distant provinces...
11. Diversification and increase of the manufactured commodity exports via the direction of investments towards such commodities and import substitutes...
12. Development of internal trade with a view to guaranteeing balance and harmony

Syria

Table 6.23: Expenditure on Gross Domestic Product, 1965-1970
(£S million except as otherwise indicated)

Item	Base Year 1965	Total Plan	Index of Growth	Annual Rate of Growth
Private consumption expenditure	2,570	15,544	136.9	6.5
Public consumption expenditure	660	3,829	127.6	5.0
Gross domestic fixed capital formation	640	4,880	–	–
Changes in stocks	10	75	–	–
Export of goods and services	880	4,812[a]	120.9	3.9
Less: import of goods and services	910	5,421[a]	126.5	4.8
Expenditure on GDP (at market prices)	3,850	23,719	141.5	7.2

a. Financing the trade gap:
Net factor income from abroad	120
Net current transfers from abroad (from Syrians abroad and UNRWA expenditures)	328
Deficit of the nation on current account	161
	609

Source: UNESOB, *Studies on Selected Development Problems in Various Countries in the Middle East, 1969* (New York, 1969), Table 2, p. 35.

between this trade and the branches of the national economy, and harmony between consumption and production on the one hand, and consumption and foreign trade on the other hand. This is to be achieved through gradual control of wholesale trade and the allocation of a large role to co-operative trade as a supplement to the public sector, and through the evolution of the price system to be used as incentive and promotive force — all of this with the object of supplying the masses with the quantities of goods at specifications, timing and appropriate prices suited to the level of living of these masses . . .
13. Raising the level of services in the educational, health, cultural, social and housing fields, and the evolution of public administration procedures . . .
14. Development and support of the popular organisations and of creative initiatives, and providing the means necessary for the undertaking by these organisations of socio-economic construction.

The major economic variables are projected to move in the following manner:

1. Net Domestic Product is planned to grow at 8.2 per cent per annum, so that NDP in 1975 may reach an index of 148.3 compared with the base year. The rate of growth in the commodity sectors is projected to be:

Agriculture: 5.1 per cent
Industry: 15.8
Construction: 11.5

2. Public consumption is to grow by no more than 8 per cent per annum (to reach an index of 147 for 1975).

3. Private consumption is to increase by no more than 6.8 per cent per annum, to reach an index of 138.8 for 1975.

4. Total consumption is to represent no more than 82.6 per cent of total product in 1975, against 87.1 per cent in the base year.

5. Domestic saving is therefore to rise from 12.9 to 17.4 per cent of total product during Plan years, that is, to grow at a rate not below 14.8 per cent per annum.

6. The increase in imports of goods and services is not to exceed 5 per cent per annum, that is, to reach an index of 127.6 for 1975.

7. The increase in the export of goods and services is to be no less than 6.5 per cent per annum, such that exports may reach an index of 137 for 1975 and thus reduce the deficit on current account and ensure the requirements of development and defence.

8. In order to achieve a rate of growth of 8.2 per cent in NDP, investments are to grow by 10.7 per cent per annum and to reach an index of 166.5 for 1975.

9. Measures will be taken for the absorption of manpower in production and service activities, such that the number of those actively engaged will rise by 4.7 per cent per annum, and productivity will increase by 3.3 per cent per annum.

These quantified targets are further detailed by sector and subsector, but we will not go into this degree of detail here. It is sufficient to indicate that strong emphasis is placed on physical targets. This is a healthy development in the form of planning used, as in the final analysis what matters is not some rather abstract monetary values, percentages and indices, but additions to the number of teachers trained, kilowatt-hours of electricity generated, hectares irrigated and tractors produced.

The investment programme totals £S8,000m for the five years. The share of the public sector of this total is £S6,447.1m; the balance of £S1,552.9m is expected to be invested by the co-operative and private sectors. However, to this investment programme which represents the 'first priority' programme is added a supplement representing 'second priority' investments totalling £S1,673.2m. The supplementary programme is listed as a contingency plan, and projects falling under it can only be implemented after the approval of the President of the Council of Ministers who is also the President of the Supreme Planning Council (and the President of Syria), after recommendation by the SPC and the Planning Authority. (The investment projections shown include credit facilities to be made available in connection with the programme.) Table 6.24 presents the investment programme in summary form, showing the sectors and their allocations, as well as the source of investment or the authority performing the investment.

The investment programme as it appears in the Plan document is not presented in an annual breakdown, though this breakdown is available separately. Averaged, it amounts to £S1,600m per year. If this volume of investment is compared with the NDP for 1972 or 1973, which fall about the middle of the Plan years, it will be found to represent a very high percentage of the NDP — over one-quarter of it. Considering the ambition of the Plan to raise domestic savings from 12.9 to 17.4 per cent of NDP between the base and terminal years (or roughly an average of 15 per cent per annum), it can be seen that Plan execution will have to depend heavily on foreign resources, even without the supple-

Table 6.24: Investment Programme and Projections in the Third Five-Year Plan 1971-5 (LS million)

		Public Sector									Programmed and Projected Investment (Public, Co-operative, and Private Sectors)	
		First Priority			Second Priority							
Sector	Projects in Progress	New Projects	Total Investments	Of which Credit Facilities	Investments	Of which Credit Facilities	Private and Co-operative Sectors	Total Public Sector Investments	Of which Credit Facilities	Less Second Priority	With Second Investment
1. Euphrates	1,593.0	—	1,593.0	355.0	—	—	—	1,593.0	355.0	1,593.0	1,593.0
2. Irrigation and land reclamation	56.9	154.8	211.7	33.5	138.1	—	140.0	349.8	33.5	351.7	489.8
3. Agriculture	176.9	259.2	436.1	48.2	81.6	—	140.0	517.7	48.2	576.1	657.7
4. Mining and industry	616.4	556.6	1,173.0	231.6	669.9	167.7	150.0	1,842.9	399.3	1,323.0	1,992.9
5. Electricity and fuel	299.0	714.8	1,013.8	294.2	414.0	111.7	—	1,427.8	405.9	1,013.8	1,427.8
6. Transport and communications	577.5	205.5	783.0	226.3	85.6	15.0	100.0	868.6	241.3	883.0	968.6
7. Public utilities and popular action	63.9	522.0	585.9	11.0	18.6	—	902.9	604.5	11.0	1,488.8	1,507.4
8. Services	109.3	416.4	525.7	31.6	259.7	10.6	100.0	785.4	42.2	625.7	885.4
9. Internal trade	3.5	121.2	124.7	5.9	5.8	—	20.0	130.5	5.9	144.7	150.5
Total	3,496.4	2,950.5	6,446.9	1,237.3	1,673.3	305.0	1,552.9	8,120.2	1,542.3	8,000.0[a]	9,673.3[a]

a. Total rounded.

Source: Office of the Prime Minister, State Planning Authority, *Legislative Decree No. 8 Dated 31/1/1971 Comprising the Adoption of the Third Five-Year Plan for Economic and Social Development in the Syrian Arab Province 1971–1975*, pp. 31 and 34.

mentary investment programme being implemented at all. The Plan projections are silent about the manner and sources of financing. Although 'Annex 3' in the Plan document is supposed to specify these sources, this Annex is not included in the document, and no explanation is provided for its 'disappearance'. (No printing error is involved, as the pagination between Annex 2 and Annex 4 is continuous.) It is this writer's estimate that some £S2,000m will have to be financed through the import surplus and capital inflow. Plan requirements in foreign currencies are estimated in the document at about £S3,944m. This would mean that about half these requirements would be provided by the country's earnings of foreign exchange, and about half will have to be received as loans and grants.

There is no indication in the Plan document as to whether the investment programme is calculated at current or constant prices. If the former is applicable, then the investment programme has been largely met during the three years 1971-3, inasmuch as investments undertaken total £S4,707m at current prices and average £S1,569m per year, which is very close to Plan projections. (However, at constant prices they totalled £S2,905m and averaged £S968m per year.) Investment allocations for 1974 for the public sector alone are estimated at £S3,598.4m, which would suggest very heavy dependence on foreign aid.[67]

At this point it is appropriate, in connection with foreign financing, to assess Syria's receipts of economic foreign aid between the end of World War Two and 1973, although the country was very hesitant to accept aid for the first dozen years after the war and aid began to feature somewhat importantly only much later. Total economic aid received (under bilateral and multilateral arrangements) during the 28 years covered amounts to the equivalent of $1,302m, of which $180m came from Western sources, $587m from the socialist countries, and an estimated $535m from Arab sources, including $35m from the Kuwait Fund for Arab Economic Development down to 31 March 1974.[68] One favourable aspect of this otherwise disadvantageous reality (namely, the modesty of the aid received by Syria) is that the country has been made essentially to rely on itself and its resources, and today has a light foreign debt to face. (Another aspect of Syria's policy is that the country has as a result not had to accommodate Western donors in terms of political alignments — which has not pleased foreign political decision-makers.) According to the most recent information contained in the *International Financial Statistics*, foreign liabilities of the Central Bank amounted to $374m by December 1974. This sum is certainly an underestimation, as it probably excludes the country's financial obligations towards the socialist countries and the debts owed to donor Arab countries.

A few broad generalisations can be made here at the close of this discussion of central comprehensive planning. They will centre around the series of three five-year plans which stretch from 1960 to the end of 1975, as earlier plans did not qualify as being comprehensive, and were quite inferior in quality, form and methodology. The first generalisation is that the Syrian socio-economic system, using planning and control of means of production as instrument, is taking steady steps towards what we have decided to call the 'socialist transformation', although since 1971 there has been some revival of private entrepreneurial spirit and activity. This revival has not resulted in a substantial intensification of private investment, but it promises a larger absolute role for the private sector. In this connection it is interesting to note that private enterprise does not restrict its investment activity to agriculture, hotel-keeping, restaurants and such services, but is moving into industry as well, though hesitantly and in small doses. Another noteworthy feature is that the new entrepreneurs are by and large not the old class or group of entrepreneurs, but a 'new class', the members of which were not affected by the nationalisations of the sixties. (Indeed, the old entrepreneurial class has largely left the country.)

The second generalisation is that the planning process is becoming more sophisticated and refined, and that valuable experience has been gained, not only in the formulation of technically satisfactory plans, but also in the execution, follow-up and readjustment of the annual plans in the light of experience. In this respect Syria has proven far-sighted in having built up rather efficient statistical services, though the process has been slow and constrained by the shortage of skilled professionals and funds. These services place the country at an advantage in comparison with some of the Asian Arab countries.

Thirdly, the three plans under reference have all run through their full course. This is a unique experience in the Asian Arab countries, where the plans have either not been implemented, or changed in mid-course. In the African Arab countries there has been less interruption than in the first group, though Egypt has failed to draw a second plan after 1965, and remains today without a comprehensive published plan in effect, with the seven-year plan 1973-80 still subject to amendment. The three Maghreb countries, Tunisia, Algeria and Morocco, stand out favourably in this comparison, as they have a long tradition of planning and their plans are allowed their full span. However, in the case of Syria, the favourable judgement made here does not mean that the plan projections have been adhered to closely. Deviations, and wide ones at that, exist, as the fifth observation further down will show. None the less, the 'integrity' of the plans has been kept, broadly speaking.

A fourth observation relates to the allocation of emphasis among the various sectors in the investment programmes. The three plans under review have different patterns of allocation of investment, which reflect different outlooks on priority and different strategies of development. This is both legitimate and reprehensible. For the broad strategy of development should be carefully thought out and laid down once the future image of the economy has been drawn, even if in broad strokes. This kind of strategy ought to remain largely unchanged over the years, unless serious error is discovered in it. Frequent changes will betray insufficient prior thinking and also possibly insufficient stability in the decision-making process. In addition, such changes are disruptive of the course of development and wasteful of time and resources. What remains legitimate and acceptable with a widely varying pattern of investment are those changes that are reasonable in magnitude, that occur not too frequently, and that reflect the changed realities and new objective conditions. What has taken place in Syria (as indeed in the planning experience of the other Arab countries covered in this study, to varying degrees) belongs to the category of extreme, unwarranted variations from plan to plan, and also between projections and execution. Table 6.25 illustrates the point.

The fifth, and final, generalisation to make is that, notwithstanding the sector-by-sector and year-by-year variations between planned and actual investment, the overall performance under planning has been quite commendable. The NDP achieved has not varied considerably from that projected, except when the agricultural harvest has been extremely good or extremely bad. This may be said to reflect good projection, not necessarily the successful implementation of the plans. In other words, it can be argued that the economy would have achieved the growth it turned out to achieve, planning or no planning. There is certainly an element of truth in this kind of argument, especially if the sectoral and annual variations are borne in mind. However, the husbanding of the resources globally available and the direction of that volume desired towards investment, and the adoption of a system of priorities in investment, together influence the resultant rate of growth. These operations

Table 6.25: Pattern of Investment by Sector in the Three Five-Year Plans, 1960-5, 1966-70 and 1971-5 (percentage)

Sector	Plan I	Plan II	Plan III
Irrigation and land reclamation	30.5	19.3	4.4
Euphrates Dam	–	–	20.0
Agriculture	9.9	8.8	7.2
Industry and mining	8.6	8.0	16.5
Electricity and petroleum	10.1	12.4	12.7
Transport and communications	19.7	18.0	11.0
Public utilities	17.9	25.8	18.6
Services	3.3	7.7	7.8
Internal trade	–	–	1.8
Total	100.0	100.0	100.0

Source: Tables 6.22 and 6.24.

of husbanding and direction are functions of planning, and to that extent planning can be said to be responsible for the results to a not inconsiderable extent. However, in closing, it can also legitimately be said that to the extent that planned and executed investments vary considerably, as they do, planning remains of limited impact on the course of development — more of an intellectual and professional exercise than a discipline and an instrument for action. On balance, one is left with mixed feelings about results.

Nationalisation of Large Concerns

This is the third instrument and indicator of the socialist transformation in Syria. It is the indicator that raises (for Syria as for Iraq, Algeria and Egypt) a great deal of controversy among radical writers concerned with social thought in the local press. The controversy centres around the question whether the nationalisation of large privately owned establishments in the various sectors (especially industry, banking, insurance and import-export trade) represents socialist transformation or mere state capitalism, or *étatisme*. The supporters of the first claim maintain that in our age and time, when the state has not 'withered' and seems to be far from withering, it is the state that naturally should own the major means of production on behalf of society. Thus, according to such apologists, nationalisation is an instrument and an indicator of socialist transformation. The adversaries to this position maintain that socialism means more than the mechanistic passage of title deeds from private to public hands, that it involves an attitude to man, to social organisation, to participation by the masses, and so on — matters that are far from having materialised in the Arab countries claiming socialist transformation. At this point we shall keep clear of the controversy and use the definitions current in the countries of socialist transformation themselves. Hence the inclusion of the discussion on nationalisation in this section of the present chapter.

Between Syria's merger with Egypt in February 1958 and July 1961, when at the latter date President Abdul-Nasser declared his now-famous long series of decrees of nationalisation, there was hardly any nationalisation of establishments in Syria. Even the July 1961 decrees did not apply in their full coverage and intensity to the Syrian Province. In what follows, we will briefly survey the nationalisation measures taken beginning with July 1961, and ending with 1965. Since then there have been no major nationalisations — merely reorganisational measures, or ones dealing with extension of coverage of the substance of measures already in force.

Some 13 Decree Laws stand out as the great avalanche of nationalisation that surged forward in July 1961. Not all extended in effect to include the Syrian Province. The more important ones which applied to Syria were the following: Law No. 117 which fully nationalised all banks and insurance companies in both Provinces of the UAR, as well as 51 large Syrian (and 42 Egyptian) industrial, commercial, financial, transport and land reclamation and development companies. The banking, financial and insurance establishments in Egypt had earlier (since the Suez war in 1956) gone through an Egyptianisation process. Partial nationalisation of 11 Syrian (and 82 Egyptian) concerns was decreed by Law No. 118, in the sense that these concerns were to transform themselves into Arab (i.e. UAR) share companies and the state was to own at least 50 per cent of their share capital. Furthermore, under Law No. 119 no citizen or corporation (share company) was to own shares worth more than £E10,000 (or its equivalent in Syrian currency) in eleven companies in Syria (and 148 in Egypt). Compensation was to be paid in these cases by 15-year negotiable government bonds, which bore interest at 4 per cent and were redeemable in ten years. Several more decrees were enacted which affected both regions, but they relate to the area of 'social justice' to which we will devote the next subsection of this chapter. The Egyptian Province was to see several more nationalisation decrees. But Syria was to wait until after the next *coup d'état*, carried out on 8 March 1963, before it was to experience the second wave of nationalisation and socialisation measures.

In the meantime, the effect of most of the 1961 decrees was reversed, either through outright abrogation or drastic amendment, after the 'rightist' *coup* of 28 September 1961. Consequently, the Syrian decrees that started being enacted as of 2 May 1963 were to reinstate, and extend, earlier nationalisation measures. The more important of the Syrian decrees, all of which fall in the fifth phase that was discussed above in section 2, and were enacted in the years 1963-5, will now be listed:[69]

— Decree No. 37 of 2 May 1963 nationalised all banks operating in Syria.
— Decision No. 46, stemming from Decree 37, merged all nationalised banks upon the recommendation of the Economic Organization, the body which supervised the operation of state-owned establishments. (This merger which simply reduced the number of banks in operation from fifteen to five was later amended so that the banks were regrouped on a functional basis, depending on the type of credit they extended; thus today Syria has — in addition to the Central Bank — four bank groups: The Industrial Bank, the Cooperative Agricultural Bank, the Real Estate Bank and the Commercial Bank.)
— After a long explanatory note justifying the measures (including the purpose of encouraging auto-management), seven decrees nationalised wholly or partly 106 establishments (21 fully, 24 at 90 per cent and 61 at 75 per cent of their capital). In the explanatory note, the 21 companies were reported as having a combined capital of £S111.7 million; the 24 companies £S426.3 million, though in the overall summing-up of the capital value of nationalised establishments, a capital of £S109.1 million

seems to be attributed to this group of 24 establishments; and the last group of 61 establishments had a combined capital of £S22.5 million. In view of the lack of clarity in the account presented, it seems tenable that the total capital of £S243.3 million (of which the explanatory note speaks) is the actual paid-up capital, not the registered capital; this would explain the discrepancy with regard to the 24 establishments. The combined labour force of the 106 establishments was 11,780 labourers. The operations fell in the fields of cement, sugar, glass, vegetable oils, pressed wood, textiles, cables, wools, cloth, sulphur and other products.

Compensation, according to Legislative Decree No. 3 issued on 2 January 1965, was to be paid to 'small shareholders who, prior to nationalization, supported themselves from income derived from their shares'. They were to receive 'the stated nominal value of these shares'. No definition is supplied as to the limits involved in the term 'small shareholders' or as to the manner of payment.

— Legislative Decree No. 5 of 4 January 1965 and No. 25 of 26 January 1965 added a total of 19 establishments to the list of 106 affected earlier; 11 were to fall in the category of 75 per cent and 8 in that of 90 per cent nationalisation.
— Legislative Decree No. 35 (later supplemented by Decree No. 36) of 18 February 1965 fully nationalised 46 import establishments that dealt with the most important import items (particular emphasis being placed on medicaments).
— Legislative Decree No. 133 of 22 December 1964 forbade the granting of any concession 'to utilize mining or petroleum wealth in the territories' of Syria to any natural or legal person. Furthermore, Decree No. 57 of 4 March 1965 fully nationalised all fuel and petroleum distribution companies. This involved nine establishments. The net assets of these companies were to 'be converted into negotiable State bonds, redeemable within a period of 15 years and carrying an interest of 3 percent'. A subsequent decree, No. 65 of 17 March 1965, added another company (under the same provisions of nationalisation and compensation); however, there is no reference to the field of activity of this last company.
— Decree No. 77 of 24 April 1964 nationalised the cotton-ginning industry of Syria. This involved 57 establishments, the owners of which were to be compensated by bonds bearing 3 per cent interest and redeemable in 10 years. Subsequently, Decree No. 106 of 8 June 1965 set up the General Organization for Cotton Ginning and Marketing to replace private establishments previously engaged in this kind of activity.
— Decree No. 8 of 1 October 1965 took over 21 municipal electricity companies and placed them under a newly established General Electricity Organization of Syria.
— Decree No. 168 of 21 September 1963 nationalised all university books, in the sense that no book was to 'be prescribed as a textbook for the students ... until a decision has been issued to this effect by the University Board upon the recommendation of the faculty or department concerned'. Members of the teaching staff (except with regard to courses given in a foreign language) were required 'to provide their students with mimeographed notes or regular textbooks specifically compiled by them to serve as the students' principal reference alongside with any other general references'. Finally, 'members of the teaching staff shall have the right to choose between dictating notes or compiling regular textbooks for the use of their students although it shall be left to the University Board to decide when it would be more advisable to request qualified members of the teaching staff to compile within a set period of time whatever textbooks are required for a university course.'[70]

— Decree No. 76 of 24 April 1965 restricted the right of exporting wheat, barley and cotton to the state through special Boards.

Social Justice

There is, in fact, no separate group of laws and measures that ought to be singled out as being undertaken for the sake of social justice, in isolation from the other areas of socialist transformation to which we have devoted space so far. These areas — agrarian reform, central comprehensive planning and nationalisation — were *all* areas of action aiming in the final analysis at improving the use of resources, dividing these resources among the population with greater equality, and transferring the ownership of a large part of non-agricultural resources to the state so that the services and products resulting from the use of the resources might be more equitably distributed among the citizens.

Yet there is, on the other hand, justification for separate treatment of the subject, for two reasons: first, that a number of decrees were enacted dealing specifically with social justice in the sense of improving the returns to labour, reducing rents, etc.; secondly, that certain measures fall under the category of social justice but have not been discussed in this section so far. The most important decrees of relevance will now be enumerated and briefly described:

— Law No. 134 of 4 September 1958, amended and extended later by Law No. 218 of 20 October 1963, which organised and regulated agrarian (tenure) relations, raised the share of the tenant, and gave him much greater security of tenure.
— Law No. 91 of 1959, which covered both Provinces of the UAR, set the maximum number of work hours a day for labour at 8, and a maximum working week of 48 hours.
— Law No. 111 of 19 July 1961 set aside 25 per cent of the profits of a company (after certain reserve deductions had been made) for employees. Of this portion, 10 per cent was to be distributed directly, 5 per cent to be directed to social services and housing, and the remaining 10 per cent to be set aside as a fund for central social services.
— Law No. 113, of the same date, prohibited the receipt by any director, manager or employee of total remuneration in excess of £E5,000 per annum (or its equivalent in Syrian currency).
— Law No. 114 of the same date stipulated that the board of directors of every company should include a representative of the employees and another of the workers.
— Law No. 125 of 21 July prohibited the holding of more than one post or job in government or the private sector. The idea was to spread employment among more people.
— Law 133 of 28 July fixed the working week in industry at 42 hours, and prohibited overtime work or the holding of more than one job with different establishments. Later, on November 4, a new decree stipulated that the overtime pay previously obtained should be added to the basic pay.
— After the March 1963 *coup*, Syria introduced a few additional measures in this field. The first, Decree No. 24 of 25 January 1965, reduced the rent of residential and business premises (whether the lessee was a private citizen, a business, a government or a municipal body) by 25 per cent, effective immediately. Furnished apartments were made subject to a 30 per cent reduction.
— Decree No. 40 of 28 February 1965 set up a General Consumers Organization with the aim of making available, and of distributing, 'consumer goods at reasonable prices

and with suitable conditions'.

A second manifestation of the concern with social justice is the promotion of public services — education, health, recreation, cultural institutions, housing and urban development especially with regard to sewerage and sanitation services — at subsidised prices to the public, or altogether free of charge. Reference to this area of activity by the government has already been made.

Yet another way of looking at the concern with social justice is the share of progressive direct taxes out of total government revenue. In 1953, direct taxes amounted to £S34.9 million out of total revenues of £S217.7 million, or 15.6 per cent. For 1974, direct taxes imposed on income, rent, production and capital gains (excluding petroleum transit fees) were estimated to amount together to £S429.3 million, or 7 per cent of the total *consolidated* budget (less the revenues of self-financing sectors and institutions totalling £S2,083m).[71] In itself, this comparison, in spite of the twelve-fold expansion in absolute terms, reveals a drop in relative terms. However, a very serious qualification ought to be taken into account here. This is the presence of huge surpluses accruing to government from the ownership and operation of many establishments previously in private hands. These establishments do not *now* pay direct taxes on their profits, but leave behind surpluses. And the surpluses ought to be added to the income and capital taxes if a fair picture is to emerge of the availability to the government of funds for use in public services and for other purposes. (The surpluses were estimated at £S2,083 million for 1974, or 32.1 per cent of the total estimated revenue of the consolidated budget for the year. Together, the two percentages add up to 39.1 per cent.)[72]

4. CONCLUDING REMARKS

The account of post-war developments in Syria, whether with regard to structural changes; actual expansion in social and economic infrastructure and the development of a wide range of establishments in the various fields (especially industry, petroleum and mining, and irrigation); socialist transformation; and the spread of social justice and implementation of a more egalitarian policy with respect to income, ownership and public services — this account, as it stands, is almost naively optimistic and overly rosy. The reader is urged to free himself of any such impression.

Many qualifications ought to accompany the account. In effect, the rest of the 'balance sheet' will appear in Volume II of the book, when the credibility of these post-war developments as an engine for, or determinants of, development, will be examined more critically. Yet it is necessary, at this early stage and without anticipating the forthcoming examination, to list some of the qualifications.

One of these is the risk of reading published official statistics 'at face value'. Another is to look at aggregates and register expansion in them on balance, without looking at the components of these aggregates and seeing the failures that stand side by side with the successes. A third is the inadequacy of the examination presented of the effect of the agrarian reform, planning and socialist measures on productivity and production. A fourth is the absence of an examination of the efficiency of operation of establishments in the hands of government, as well as of the efficiency of the provision of the services which are now financed in part out of the surpluses arising from the means of production whose ownership has passed to government hands. A fifth is the net effect on private entrepreneurship, or more precisely, a comparison between the experience gained in the field of public entrepreneurship and the loss of private entrepreneurship. And lastly, the loss by Syria of thousands upon thousands of capitalists, entrepreneurs, professionals, technicians and skilled labourers, many of whom seem to have settled outside (mainly in Lebanon and Kuwait[73]) because of the socialist transformation and their disapproval of the system now established in the country. The merits or demerits of the system notwithstanding, the loss of such a component of skilled manpower in a developing country seriously short of skills at almost every level and in every field cannot but be a serious drain on the economy and society. This drain must be set against the gains — real as they are — that have characterised the post-war development of the country.

NOTES

1. Sami Wafa Dajani, 'The National Income of Syria of 1950', in *Al-Abhath* (Beirut, Arabic), December 1953, pp. 437-46. According to the International Bank for Reconstruction and Development, IBRD, *The Economic Development of Syria* (Baltimore, 1955), p. 19, income was £S1,380m for 1950 and £S1,600m for 1953.

2. Syrian Arab Republic, Office of the Prime Minister, Central Bureau of Statistics, *Statistical Abstract 1974*, Tables 1/17, pp. 840-1, and 23/17 and 24/17, pp. 860-1.

3. *Statistical Abstract 1974*, Ch. Seventeen, 'National Accounts'.

4. Ibid., Table 31/17, pp. 868-9 for population and NDP at factor cost for 1973; *International Financial Statistics*, November 1974, for rate of exchange in 1972. The official rate varied slightly for 1973, but there is no record of the free rate.

5. *Statistical Abstract 1974*, Table 31/17, pp. 868-9.

6. UNESCO, Office of Statistics, Paris, *Comparative Statistical Data on Education in the Arab States, An Analysis: 1960-61 – 1967-68* (published by the Regional Center for Educational Planning and Administration, Beirut, 1970), p. 49. According to the IBRD, p. 149, the literacy rate for the population was 'probably around 40%' in the early fifties. This figure is clearly inconsistent with a rate of 44 per cent for the age group 15-24 for 1960. Likewise, both these estimates diverge widely from the level of 27.5 per cent for 1950 for persons aged 15 years and over, as quoted in Bruce M. Russett *et al.*, *World Handbook of Political and Social Indicators* (Yale University Press, 1964), p. 223.

7. Frederick H. Harbison, Joan Maruhnic and James R. Resnick, *Quantitative Analyses of Modernization and Development* (Princeton, 1970), Appendix II. However, it ought to be pointed out that the findings of this study are based on data that seem to be seriously questionable at times. Likewise, the weights allotted to the variable can also be debated. In connection with performance in social areas, see also UNESOB, *Studies on Selected Development Problems in Various Countries in the Middle East, 1971* (New York, 1971), article on 'Development Planning and Social Objectives in Syria', especially p. 2.

8. *Statistical Abstract 1974*, Table 31/3, p. 187, and Table 25/3, p. 178. B. Hansen (pp. 358-9) also observes that the civil service is not inflated in Syria – indeed, that it is still small as a group compared with the population and the tasks called forth by modern administration. (See note 10 below for full bibliographical notation.)

9. IBRD, *The Economic Development of Syria* (Baltimore, 1955), p. 18 ff. See also Samir Makdisi, 'Syria: Rate of Economic Growth and Fixed Capital Formation, 1936-1968', in *Middle East Journal*, Spring 1971.

10. See the following sources in this connection, and with respect to the overall evaluation of the economy: (a) Doreen Warriner, *Land and Poverty in the Middle East* (London, 1948), chapter on Syria; (b) IBRD, *The Economic Development of Syria* (Baltimore, 1955), Part I, Ch.1; (c) Awad Barakat, 'Recent Economic Development in Syria', in *Middle East Economic Papers 1954 (MEEP)* (Beirut), pp. 1-25; (d) Royal Institute of International Affairs, *The Middle East: A Political and Economic Survey* (Oxford University Press, 1958, third edition), chapter on Syria; (e) Doreen Warriner, *Land Reform and Development in the Middle East – A Study of Egypt, Syria and Iraq* (London, 1962), chapter on Syria; (f) FAO Mediterranean Development Project, *United Arab Republic, Syrian Region: Country Report* (Rome, 1959), especially Ch. I. According to this source (p. I-1), GNP increased 'at an annual average of 8 percent in the decade'; (g) Edmond Y. Asfour, *Syria: Development and Monetary Policy* (Harvard Middle Eastern Monograph Series, Harvard University Press, 1959), especially pp. 6 and 16; (h) Samir Makdisi, 'Some Aspects of Syrian Economic Growth, 1945-1957', in *MEEP 1961*, pp. 45-63; (i) Samir Makdisi, 'Fixed Capital Formation in Syria, 1936-1957', in *MEEP 1963*, pp. 95-112; (j) General Union of Chambers of Commerce, Industry, and Agriculture in the Arab Countries, *Economic Development in the Arab Countries, 1950-1965* (Beirut, 1967; Arabic); chapter on Syria; (k) Bent Hansen, 'Economic Development of Syria', in Charles A. Cooper and Sidney S. Alexander (eds.), *Economic Development and Population Growth in the Middle East* (New York, 1972); and (l) Europa Publications, *The Middle East and North Africa 1971-72, 1972-73, 1973-74, and 1974-75* (yearly editions, London); chapter on Syria.

11. Doreen Warriner, *Land Reform and Economic Development in the Middle East* . . . for the coinage of the term 'merchant-tractorists' and the discussion of the emergence and role and functioning of this group. (Especially Chs. II, III, 'Conclusion' and 'Postcript'.)

12. *Statistical Abstract 1960*, p. 288, for 1950 and

278 Syria

Statistical Abstract 1974, p. 241, for 1974.

13. For a careful examination of events leading up to the merger between Egypt and Syria, see Patrick Seale, *The Struggle for Syria* (London, 1965), and Malcolm Kerr, *The Arab Cold War 1958-1967: A Study of Ideology in Politics* (New York, 1967).

14. See Table 6.1 for the contributions to NDP by sector.

15. Ibid.

16. *Statistical Abstract 1964*, p. 252.

17. Ibid., p. 381.

18. Ibid.

19. Ibid., p. 388, for data for 1961-4; *Statistical Abstract 1969-1970* for 1965.

20. This was not the only *coup* within the Party in the decade 1963-73. In 1966 a *coup* occurred which ousted the founders of the Party and brought in a more radical group.

21. Calculations based on data in *Statistical Abstract 1974*, pp. 840-1.

22. Ibid., p. 282 for data relating to 1965-73, and *Statistical Abstract 1971*, p. 144, for the years 1956, 1963 and 1970.

23. General Union of Arab Chambers of Commerce ..., *Arab Economic Report* (Beirut; Arabic; for 1973 dated January 1974), p. 398. See Nicolas Sarkis, 'The Energy Crisis and the Challenge of Development in the Arab Countries', Paper No. 132 (A-1) submitted to the Ninth Arab Petroleum Congress, held at Dubai, 10-16 March 1975, for the estimate for 1974 (Table 1, p. 16).

24. *Statistical Abstract 1969-1970*, pp. 485, 144-145, and *Statistical Abstract 1974*, p. 287, for production data.

25. General Union ..., *Arab Economic Report* (1974), p. 403.

26. For a careful and objective survey and analysis of Syrian industry, see Abdallah Sallouta, *Industrial Development Strategy and Policies, The Experience of the Syrian Arab Republic* (paper prepared for UNIDO, undated, but known on its author's assurance to have been prepared in 1974); and Abdallah Sallouta, *Highlights of Industrial Development in the Syrian Arab Republic* (conference paper, July 1974). For reports on individual large projects, the reader is advised to refer, among others, to: (a) General Union of Chambers of Commerce ..., *Economic Development in the Arab Countries 1950-1965*, and the *Arab Economic Report*, published annually; (b) *Middle East Economic Survey* (weekly, published in Beirut); and (c) *Monthly Survey of Arab Economies* (published in Beirut).

27. See *Statistical Abstract 1974*, p. 889 for information regarding GCF.

28. Ibid., p. 66. 1973 was a year of poor rainfall, and other years show a much larger flow of water.

29. *Statistical Abstract 1961*, p. 255.

30. *Statistical Abstract 1974*, p. 216, for 1968-73, and *S.A. 1971*, p. 66 for earlier years.

31. Information obtained from field trip by the writer in April 1974, as well as from documentation produced by the ministry. The most detailed document is *Among the Achievements of the March Revolution: The Euphrates Barrage* (published by the Ministry of Culture for the Ministry of the Euphrates Barrage, in Arabic, in 1974). For a collection of background material on the project, see Centre d'Etudes et de Documentations Economiques, Financières, et Sociales, 'The Syrian Economy in 1971 (1)', Supplement to *The Arab Economist*, No. 47, December 1972.

32. Centre d'Etudes ..., *Etudes*, Special issue on economic developments in Syria during 1969 (undated), section on 'The Agricultural Sector in 1969'.

33. *Statistical Abstract 1974*, pp. 864-5.

34. Ibid., pp. 270-1. For information relating to the sixties, see *S.A. 1969-1970*, p. 484.

35. *Statistical Abstract 1971*, pp. 123 and 127, and *S.A. 1974*, p. 271.

36. Data collected from various annual editions of the *Statistical Abstract*.

37. FAO, *Production Yearbook 1967* (Vol. 21), pp. 27-9 for the period 1952-66; and *Production Yearbook 1972* (Vol. 26), pp. 28, 30, 32 and 34 for the period 1961-72.

38. *Statistical Abstract 1974*, p. 892.

39. *Arab Economic Report*, January 1974, p. 409.

40. *Statistical Abstract 1974*, p. 342.

41. *Statistical Abstract 1969-1970*, p. 142 for years before 1970, and *S.A. 1974*, p. 282, for 1970-4.

42. IBRD, op. cit., p. 122.

43. Ibid., p. 411.

44. *Statistical Abstract 1974*, p. 288.

45. Data collated from details in *Le Second Plan Quinquennal de La République Arabe Syrienne 1966-1970: Texte et Commentaire* as published by the Centre d'Etudes ..., op. cit. (undated). Other information relating to the share of education in ordinary state budgets has been collated from the issue of the *Statistical Abstract* for the years 1960 to 1969-70.

46. Office of the Prime Minister, State Planning Authority, *Legislative Decree No. 8 Dated 31/1/1971 Comprising the Adoption of the Third Five-Year Plan for Economic and Social Development in the Syrian Arabic Province 1971-1975* (Damascus; Arabic; January 1971), data collated from the detailed master table No. 1/A, pp. 36-51.

47. Calculation based on budget data for 1973 and 1974 in *Statistical Abstract 1974*, pp. 772-7.

48. Ibid., p. 642.

49. IBRD, op. cit., p. 158.

50. Ibid., p. 313.

51. For the years 1952-64, see *Statistical Abstract 1964*, p. 208; for the period 1965-9, see *S.A. 1969-1970*, p. 246; and for the period 1969-73, see *S.A. 1974*, p. 464.

52. *Statistical Abstract 1974*, pp. 786-7, for the more recent years; *S.A. 1969-1970*, pp. 297 and 302 for the sixties, and IBRD, p. 21 for 1950.

53. *Statistical Abstract 1969-70*, and *1974*, Chapter on 'Finance'.

54. For the years 1951-3, see IBRD, p. 251; for 1968 and 1969, *S.A. 1969-1970*, p. 197. (For 1969, the data are adjusted for receipts from oil transit fees, emigrant remittances, and invisible exports.) For 1970 and 1971, see Centre d'Etudes ... etc., *Supplement, L'Economie Syrienne en 1971*, p. 44. For 1972, *IFS*, November 1974.

55. Much of this information and the material that follows relating to events up to the break-up of the

union between Syria and Egypt draws on Salah Dabbagh, 'Agrarian Reform in Syria', in *MEEP 1962*, pp. 1-15. This article itself is the product of much more extensive research which the present writer has had the opportunity to examine and supervise as adviser to Dr Dabbagh while the latter undertook graduate work. For provisions of the law of September 1958 and subsequent amendments, the original text of the law has been consulted. (See also Abdul-Razzak al-Hilali, *The Story of the Land, the Peasant, and Agrarian Reform in the Arab Homeland* (Beirut, 1967; Arabic), relevant parts on Syria.) For background information in general, Doreen Warriner's remains the classic work.

56. Dabbagh, loc. cit., p. 8.
57. Doreen Warriner, *Land Reform and Development in the Middle East*, p. 82.
58. Data from *Statistical Abstract 1973*, p. 152. For size of family, see *S.A. 1974*, p. 93.
59. *Statistical Abstract 1964*, pp. 332 and 333.
60. *Arab Economic Report, 1970*, pp. 235-6. For information on areas of state land sold or leased, see *S.A. 1971*, p. 135, for 1969 and 1970; *S.A. 1972*, p. 113, for 1971; *S.A. 1973*, p. 160, for 1972; and *S.A. 1974*, p. 222, for 1973.
61. *Statistical Abstract 1974*, p. 257.
62. Except where otherwise indicated, this subsection on 'Central Planning' is based on: (a) Official plan documents (in Arabic) ending with the Five-Year Plan 1971-5; (b) other special studies by the Centre d'Etudes ... etc., especially the collection on Syria for 1969 entitled *Etudes*, and *Le Second Plan Quinquennal de la République Arabe Syrienne 1966-1970: Texte et Commentaire* (No. 19); (c) UNESOB, *Studies on Selected Development Problems in Various Countries in the Middle East, 1967*, 'An Analysis of Development Plans in Various Countries in the Middle East', pp. 1-12, and UNESOB, *Studies... 1968*, 'Plan Formulation and Development Perspectives in Syria', pp. 33-45. Other sources have been consulted in connection with the evaluation of Syria's planning experience. They will be referred to specifically later.
63. Mohammad al Imadi, *Development and Planning in the Syrian Arab Republic* (1966; Arabic); pp. 4-5.
64. For an analysis of the First Five-Year Plan, see Muhammad Diab, 'The First Five-Year Plan of Syria — An Appraisal', in *MEEP 1960*, pp. 13-23. See also, for an analysis of planning experience after the FFYP, *Planning in the Syrian Arab Republic: Its Status and Evolution* (Proceedings of a Seminar held in Damascus in October 1966. Damascus, 1967; Arabic). A study that covers all three 5-year plans, from 1960-75, is Sayyid Abdul-Aziz Dahiyyeh, *Appraisal of Planning Experience in the Syrian Arab Republic* (paper submitted to the 4th Conference of the Federation of Arab Economists held in Kuwait, 17-20 March 1973; undated; mimeographed; Arabic). This last study devotes much more space to the first and second plans (FFYP and SFYP) than to the third.
65. Mainly based on Syrian Arab Republic, Ministry of Planning, *Basic Trends in the Second Five-Year Plan for Economic and Social Development 1966-1970* (Damascus, August 1966; Arabic); especially pp. 11-30.
66. *Statistical Abstract 1971*, Ch. XIV, Tables 283 and 296.

67. Investment data for 1971-3 are taken from *Statistical Abstract 1974*, p. 889. Budget allocations for development for 1974 are from ibid., p. 771.
68. The calculation of foreign economic aid is based on several sources listed below: (a) *Time* Magazine, Vol. LXXXI, No. 13, 29 March 1963, for the period July 1945 to end June 1962, quoting official US sources; (b) OECD, *The Flow of Financial Resources to Less-Developed Countries 1961-1965*, p. 155, for the years 1960-5; (c) OECD, *Development Assistance: Efforts and Policies of the Members of the Development Assistance Committee, 1969 Review*, p. 170, for 1966-8; (d) OECD, *Development Cooperation: Efforts and Policies of the Members of the Development Assistance Committee, 1973 Review*, p. 208, for 1969-72; (e) UN *Statistical Yearbook, 1973*, p. 715, for aid from socialist countries 1955-70, checked against *Arab Economist*, No. 53, June 1973, quoting US Department of State, *Communist States and Developing Countries: Aid and Trade in 1970* (Washington, 1971). The UN source shows the aid from the socialist countries to total $546m from 1955 to 1970 (or $587m to 1972), whereas the US source records $233m. Probably the larger estimate relates to commitments, not actual flows; (f) KFAED, *Annual Report 1973-1974*, p. 24, for KFAED loans; (g) For the estimation of other Arab aid, *Middle East Economic Survey*, weekly issues, and the authoritative dailies *Al-Ahram* of Cairo and *An-Nahar* of Beirut (especially their reporting of official statements by donor countries).
69. For information on these decrees (including full text in English), see: (a) *New Laws to Implement and Consolidate the Socialist, Democratic, Cooperative Society in the UAR* (Cairo; no other particulars indicated); (b) Central Bank of Egypt, *Economic Review*, No. 2 of 1961; (c) Charles Issawi, *Egypt in Revolution*, especially pp. 56 ff; and (d) Syrian Arab Republic, *Documents Relating to Socialist Conversion in the Syrian Arab Republic* (Damascus, 1966).
70. Long quotations of this Decree on textbooks have been inserted in order to emphasise the suffocating effect of the Decree. Other articles, like Article 8, aggravate the situation by prescribing that textbooks should continue to be assigned for a three-year period 'which may however be extended year by year upon the recommendation of the University Board'. It remains to be added that according to Article 4, the professors' dictated (mimeographed) notes were to be sold to the students.
71. Data for 1953 come from General Union of Chambers of Commerce ..., *Economic Development in the Arab Countries 1950-1965*, p. 287; for 1974, calculated from *Statistical Abstract 1974*, pp. 778-81.
72. See ibid. for the details of these surpluses.
73. For the number of Syrians in Lebanon, *Recueil de Statistiques Libanaises 1969*, p. 57. For those in Kuwait, who numbered 27,217 in 1970, see *Statistical Yearbook of Kuwait, 1974*, p. 23. It is worth noting that the most recent *Recueil*, for the year 1973 (p. 84) records a total of 159,885 Arab non-Lebanese residents (excluding camp-dwelling Palestinian refugees). This figure was derived from a sample survey of 'active population' conducted in November 1970.

7 LEBANON

The Lebanese economy is not a typical Arab economy. On the one hand, it differs from the majority of the Arab economies, which are predominantly agricultural in character in the sense that agriculture is the major contributor to their national product, since agriculture in Lebanon occupies third place among the individual sectors. On the other hand, it differs from those economies which are mainly oil-producing and -exporting, where the main income-generator is petroleum, as there is no petroleum extraction in Lebanon. Thus Lebanon is the only country in the region where the largest single contribution to national product is made neither by agriculture nor by petroleum, but by a non-commodity sector: trade. Furthermore, though a non-oil producer, Lebanon in 1974, with an estimated GNP *per capita* of $1,189, enjoyed the highest income in the countries covered by this study except for Saudi Arabia, Kuwait and Libya. GNP *per capita* in Iraq was probably as large as that in Lebanon, while that in Algeria was lower. There is another area of difference. Lebanon has a wider range of agricultural products, and more so of agricultural exports, than any country in the region. Furthermore, it also has a wider range of manufactured products than any country except Egypt and Algeria. (In the case of Algeria, the whole composition of industry is different, with much greater emphasis on intermediary and capital goods. On the other hand, Egypt excels both with respect to consumer and producer goods.)

At the social level, the rate of literacy is high by Arab standards. According to the only statistical regional study on education,[1] the rate for the adult population of both sexes between the ages of 15 and 24 was as high as 89 per cent for the year 1962 (93 per cent for males and 86 per cent for females). The country nearest to this level was Jordan, where literacy for the same age group, but for 1966, was 62 per cent for both sexes (80 per cent for males and 43 per cent for females). Along with literacy go other social indicators of modernisation and sophistication to which reference will be made later in this chapter. A final distinguishing characteristic is the country's adherence to a system of private enterprise far exceeding its counterpart anywhere else in the Arab world in liberalism, and enjoying far more permissiveness from government. The effect and implications of such a system reach into every aspect of social life, as the forthcoming discussion will show.

1. THE POST-WAR EVOLUTION OF THE LEBANESE ECONOMY

The National Accounts in the Context of Political Developments

Lebanon, though formally independent since 1943, became totally free of foreign troops by the first day of 1946. An important landmark in the country's economic history since independence is the break-up in March 1950 of the customs union with Syria. Until that date, the meagre data available for Lebanon were mostly aggregated into Syro-Lebanese combined statistics. It was a convenient coincidence, from the standpoint of the observer of economic development, that the first complete estimates of national income for the country should have been made for the year 1950, which marks the first year of the separate existence of the Lebanese economy. This makes comparison more feasible, since the data for 1950 and for more recent years relate to the same economic and political entity. However, such comparisons are dangerous to the extent that the estimates for 1950 were made according to a different method from those for the years 1964-72 (the recent years for which the estimates are relatively reliable), and the coverage of the last nine years is almost certainly wider than that for the year 1950. Wider coverage and better quality of data together make for the plausible proposition that a non-negligible part of the rise in national income between 1950 and 1972 is attributable to improved statistics. Another part is attributable to the rise in the price level; and the balance, which is satisfactory in itself, derives from genuine growth in real terms.

National income at factor cost accruing to residents for 1948-50 was estimated by Albert Badre and his associates at the Economic Research Institute of the American University of Beirut. Their studies placed income at £L1,026.3* million for 1950,[2] the year for which the data were considered most satisfactory. Current estimates are made by the Directorate of Statistics at the Ministry of Planning. The estimate for 1972 for national income at factor cost accruing to residents is £L5,796 million.[3] (We do not compare gross national product or gross domestic product, both of which are estimated currently, because the estimate for 1950 was limited to the national income.)

Income *per capita* is rather difficult to calculate, because population statistics leave a great deal to be desired. The last population census was conducted in 1932, and the results were checked and updated in 1942. Since then there have been partial surveys, and adjustments have been made of the 1932 figures to take into account net change in population. According to the latest sample survey, the population was 2,179,634 at the end of 1964, with a margin of error of 'at least' 8 per cent.[4] This figure excluded foreigners resident in Lebanon (of whom there were 536,797 at the end of 1969,[5] a number which included people who happened to be in Lebanon when the survey was made and not necessarily the holders of residence permits). It also excluded some 100,000 Palestinian refugees living in the camps of UNRWA, the United Nations Relief and Works Agency for Palestine Refugees (but included non-camp Palestinians). However, it included hundreds of thousands of Lebanese emigrants who had not forfeited their original citizenship although they have settled abroad and have acquired the citizenship of their adopted countries of residence, as well as many thousands of dead Lebanese whose death had not been recorded.

The most recent, and possibly the most reliable estimate, was derived from a sample manpower (and housing) survey undertaken in November 1970. According to this estimate, the total number of *residents* was 2,126,325, including 184,065 non-Lebanese. This total excludes camp-dwelling Palestinian refugees and other possible omissions. Thus the adjusted figure for the end of 1970 is quoted at somewhere between 2.3 and 2.4 million.[6] However, there is widespread non-acceptance of these estimates, on the grounds that they underestimate the size of the resident population. For our purposes, we consider the population as being 2.75m by the end of 1974 — Lebanese and foreigners residing in the country combined.[7] Under the circumstances, it is not easy to establish the rate of population increase; however, the Directorate of Statistics is of the opinion that it is at least 2.7 per cent per annum.[8] Considering the confusion surrounding the population estimate as of 31 December 1964, there is little point in calculating the natural increase between this date and the end of 1973 or 1974, in order to attempt a more precise determination of the total size of the population. The adjustments that will have to be intro-

*Lebanese pounds.

duced — with regard to the emigrants, the dead but still registered Lebanese, the Palestinians, and those others registered as non-Lebanese residents but who in reality are temporary visitors — are so many and contain such a large element of doubt that it would be futile to undertake elaborate accounting.

The ambiguity, coupled with the large margin of error, make the calculation of national income (NNP) *per capita* of dubious usefulness, except as a broad order of magnitude. Be that as it may, we will venture this calculation. Thus, NNP was £L5,796m for 1972,[9] projected by this writer for 1974 on the assumption of 5 per cent *real* growth per annum, or 11 per cent for 1973 and 16 per cent for 1974 at current prices (taking into account the rise in the consumers' price index).[10] This adds up to an NNP of £L7,361m for 1974 at current prices. *Per capita* NNP would thus be £L2,677, or $1,180 at the free rate of exchange (which is the operative rate in the case of Lebanon). On the other hand, GNP *per capita* at market prices amounts to £L3,046 or $1,342.

According to the two end estimates of national income at current prices, namely £L1,026 million and £L7,361 million, income has risen by 617 per cent in 24 years, or at an average compound rate of growth of 8.5 per cent per annum. The only price deflator available for much of the period under consideration is the wholesale price index for Beirut. According to this index, prices rose by a mere 27 per cent between 1950 and end of 1971 (1950=100).[11] It is widely believed that this index is most inadequate, and that the price rise over the 21 years interval is probably three times as high. Furthermore, the index does not cover enough commodities, and no services, to make it a plausible deflator. Widening the coverage would bring into the index prices that have risen much more than those relating to commodities currently encompassed. Alternatively, the consumer price index could be used to advantage, as it includes services as well. However, this index was constructed only beginning with 1966. Therefore it cannot be used alone as deflator. Fully aware of the imprecision involved, I have chosen a rule-of-thumb course of action. This is to use the wholesale price index from 1950 to 1965, then the consumer price index from 1966 through 1974, and finally to adjust the result upwards in the light of discussions with well-placed officials in the Ministry of Planning. Prior to adjustment, the rise was 42.8 per cent. However, after adjustment, it exceeded 103 per cent (1950=100), or a compound price rise of 3 per cent per annum on the average.

If a doubling of the level of prices in 24 years is tenable — and in the view of very knowledgeable economists on the spot it even represents an understatement — then the growth of NNP at constant (1950) prices averaged 5.5 per cent per annum between 1950 and 1974. We can assume that a tiny part of this growth in real terms is attributable to improved coverage in national income estimation, and that it mostly reflects actual growth achieved. This performance compares favourably with that of the countries covered, except the major oil-producers in the phases of accelerated increase in their oil exports.

Further support of these findings can be seen in the improvement in the level of living in Lebanon. This is a matter of general observation, in addition to what the statistics and estimates suggest. *Per capita* improvement of some 2.8–3 per cent per annum can be accepted without difficulty, on the assumption that population increase ranged between 2.5 and 2.7 per cent during the years 1950-74. Such tangible indicators as food consumption, electricity consumption, purchase of household durables, educational levels, and housing and clothing in the cities and the countryside provide ample substantiation to the naked statistics of growth.

The course of growth behind this overall picture will not be followed in an unbroken way, owing to the existence of a large gap in reliable national income statistics. Some

284 Lebanon

estimates have been made privately,[12] but they cannot be accepted as sufficiently reliable for detailed analysis. On the whole they were projections of the 1950 data, made in a rather unwarranted fashion. This reservation notwithstanding, we will present the series 1950-63 in Table 7.1 below, and present the 1964-72 series later.

Table 7.1: Net National Product at Factor Cost, 1950-64 (£L million at current prices)

Year	NNP
1950	1,042
1951	1,086
1952	1,115
1953	1,168
1954	1,256
1955	1,374
1956	1,417
1957	1,503
1958	1,325
1959	1,570
1960	1,671
1961	1,789
1962	1,877
1963	1,951
1964 (UN)	(2,038)
1964 (Revised)	2,861

Sources: For the years 1950-58, A. Y. Badre, as published in the UN, *Economic Development in the Middle East 1953-1954* (p. 153) and *1956-1957* (p. 69), later revised and published in FAO, Mediterranean Development Project, *Lebanon: Country Report* (Rome, 1959), p. II-13; for 1959 and 1960, from a study obtained privately from the US Embassy in Beirut by Nadim G. Khalaf, as quoted in his book *Economic Implications of the Size of Nations, with Special Reference to Lebanon* (Leiden, 1971), Table 2 in Appendix. Finally, for 1961-4, *IFS*, November 1968. However, Albert Y. Badre, in Cooper and Alexander (eds.) (see footnote 14 at end of chapter, p. 179) records an NNP series for 1950-65 which omits the years 1959 and 1960, and which differs from Khalaf's data for 1956. Furthermore, while Khalaf records GDP for 1964, Badre first states an NNP estimate by the UN Statistical Office and reported in *IFS*, then reports a revised estimate which was officially made by the Direction Centrale de la Statistique of Lebanon in *Les comptes économiques 1965*. The revised estimate links the series in Table 7.1 with that in Table 7.2 below. To complete the record of growth for the period 1950-72 for which NNP data are available (even if heavily qualified), we present in Table 7.2 below the GDP, GNP and NNP for 1964-72 at current prices.

We can identify several phases in the history of the Lebanese economy, and some of its features, through an examination of the quarter-century covered, 1950-74. This is in part possible to achieve on the basis of a scrutiny of the national accounts presented, in part on the basis of careful observation of developments in the social and administrative framework of the economy and how these on the one hand reflected certain political events and changes, and on the other were reflected in economic performance.

The year 1950 was preceded by an event of serious consequences: the establishment in 1948 of the state of Israel and the expulsion of 750,000 Palestinian Arabs, of whom an estimated 150,000 sought refuge in Lebanon.[13] This event naturally severed the circuit of life between Lebanon and Palestine, thus depriving an estimated 20,000—30,000 Lebanese of their businesses and employment in Palestine, and bringing to an end all commercial

Table 7.2: Gross Domestic Product, Gross National Product and National Income at Factor Cost, 1964-72 (in £L million, at current prices)

Year	GDP	Per Cent Change	GNP	Per Cent Change	NNP (National Income)	Per Cent Change
1964	3,200.0		3,309.5		2,861.4	
		10.1		10.0		10.2
1965	3,523.4		3,639.9		3,154.2	
		9.7		9.7		9.7
1966	3,866.7		3,994.7		3,460.0	
		−1.2		−0.8		−0.5
1967	3,820.1		3,960.9		3,442.9	
		11.9		11.8		12.2
1968	4,273.2		4,428.0		3,861.7	
		6.8		6.7		6.5
1969	4,564.6		4,725.0		4,112.2	
		6.6		6.5		7.3
1970	4,866.0		5,031.0		4,411.0	
		10.9		11.2		11.2
1971	5,399.0		5,595.0		4,903.0	
		17.9		17.9		18.2
1972	6,365.0		6,595.0		5,796.0	
1964-72		98.9		99.3		102.6

Sources: For 1964, Direction Centrale de la Statistique, *Les comptes économiques de l'annee 1968*, p. 11; for subsequent years, *Recueil . . . 1973*, pp. 326-7.

transactions with occupied Palestine. In addition, the influx of refugees imposed on Lebanon certain hardships, with regard to housing, education and health facilities and with regard to pressures on price levels.

On the other hand, the Arab boycott of Israel gave a boost to Beirut port, and subsequently to the Beirut International Airport, as well as added appeal to Lebanese schools and hospitals for Palestinian and Transjordanian students and patients. Furthermore, the pressure on housing and on the price level led to intensified construction and trade activity. Since that time, UNRWA has relied heavily on the Lebanese money market for the sale of foreign currencies to finance its local purchases of goods and services. Finally, the Iraq Petroleum Company, which until May 1948 had used Haifa in Palestine as an outlet for part of its petroleum exports, now chose Tripoli in Lebanon as its new outlet, upon the stoppage of the flow of oil through Israel. Likewise, ARAMCO (Arabian American Oil Company) used south Lebanon as an outlet for part of its Saudi oil exports, by building a pipeline in 1951 from Saudi Arabia to Lebanon, via Jordan and Syria.

The interval 1950-8 can be described as a period of accelerated economic activity in Lebanon.[14] This assertion cannot be substantiated by national income data, but can be adequately confirmed by such indicators as registration of new firms in the fields of industry, trade, transport, contracting and finance. For those years, as for the whole period under study, the Lebanese socio-economic system can be described as one of private enterprise, conforming to one of the most extreme laissez-faire outlooks of the contemporary world. But the sub-period 1950-8 was an interval of minimum governmental interference and maximum direct encouragement. The break-up of the customs union with Syria in March 1950 allowed the Lebanese more and freer room for independent action, and seems to have let loose new, or constrained, stores of private enterprise. Although manufacturing establishments grew tangibly in number and in total capital invested during the years

1950-8, and although legislation encouraged the entry of foreign capital into partnership with Lebanese industrial capital, this interval carried the supremacy of merchants and the trade sector to new heights and endorsed the predominance of the services sectors in general over the commodity-producing sectors.

It is true that entrepreneurship was already beginning to show signs of greater sophistication and rationality, and marked social valuation was being already accorded to financial and industrial activities.[15] But basically, trade still constituted the main reservoir of entrepreneurial talent, and the requirements of trade still largely determined government economy policy. The overall public orientation, whether in government or in parliament, was one inclined to serve commercial interests and to give priority to the merchant community. The basic philosophy underlying this orientation was not only the superfluity of government interference in the economic realm, beyond the provision of (some but not all) infrastructural facilities, but the outright *danger* of such interference. Thus such public utilities as the port, the railways, urban transport, electricity generation and drinking water installations and services were all in foreign or in local concessionary private hands, and this was believed to be right and proper.

Nor was government well-equipped by and large to provide guidance or direction, or even to collect and process information on the conduct of the economy as a prerequisite for new policies aiming at gently helping the drive for development shouldered by the private sector. To provide such a technical and administrative framework was thought to be unwarranted interference which dangerously bordered on state capitalism or even socialism, and which was both dangerous to the economy's performance and wrong in terms of society's ideology. Consequently, the first plan for development, which was submitted to the Cabinet on 25 February 1958, that is, at the end of the sub-period under examination, was a shy attempt which was restricted to a cataloguing of the major projects envisaged by the government, and was subsequently shelved as quietly as it had been formulated.[16] It was neither heralded at birth nor mourned at death.

The next period is that of the six years 1958-64. It is clearly discernible because it coincides with the tenure of office of a new president who espoused a different set of ideas relating to development and its philosophy and objectives from his predecessor.[17] The new head of state, though fundamentally a believer in private enterprise, had great faith in dedicated and 'clean' technocrats coupled with a mistrust of professional politicians. He believed that the government had to act in the economic field in four directions not contemplated before. First, the economy had to be subjected to thorough socio-economic study. Secondly, its growth had to be planned. Thirdly, it had to be equipped with certain essential public institutions capable of introducing rationality and modernity to the operation of the system. And lastly, the strong drive for economic growth and prosperity had to be injected with social content and a sense of social responsibility, so that the accumulation of private fortunes may not proceed unheeding of the welfare of people in the lower-income brackets.

These four new concerns coloured the six years 1958-64, but in addition this sub-period saw two parallel processes. The first was the continuation of the build-up of economic infrastructure, in the form of roads, water and electricity systems, and the like. The second was a marked expansion in the banking and industrial sectors, both thanks to energetic private enterprise.[18] The banking system, however, continued to be virtually solely designed for and oriented towards the financing of commercial operations, although the abundance of deposits seeking investment outlets enabled the banks to finance agricultural and industrial projects (but mainly the latter) under one guise or another. Within the limitation that the system was predominantly a commercial banking system, it was highly developed and expansionary, and the finance sector indeed marked the fastest rate of growth among all the sectors in the post-war period.

Industry also expanded considerably, in terms of the setting up of new establishments, capital outlay, employment and exports. The overall growth of industry enabled it to overtake agriculture as the second-ranking sector in the economy during the six years 1958-64. Indeed, by 1964 the contribution of industry had risen to 15 per cent of gross domestic product, as against 12 per cent for agriculture, compared with 13.4 per cent for industry and 20.2 per cent for agriculture in 1950. (The structure of the economy will be examined more fully later.)

We stated earlier that four new concerns or themes characterised the six years under survey and determined certain directions of action. The first direction was symbolised in the hiring in 1959 of the services of a well-known French research outfit headed by Père L. J. Lebret, the Institut de Recherches et de Formation en Vue de Développement, IRFED. The contract was for three years, but was subsequently extended to five years. The Mission conducted the most thorough-going and far-reaching study of socio-economic conditions, and finally incorporated its findings and conclusions in a report of three volumes and in a project for a development plan.[19]

The study is rather verbose and contains conclusions often based on methodologically unsatisfactory sample surveys and on unwarranted and facile generalisations. Nevertheless, it merits credit for being the first comprehensive diagnosis of the Lebanese economy and for the first massive argument and appeal for social concern on the part of government. Some of the Mission's findings and its injunctions regarding the maldistribution of income, the housing and other social conditions of the lower-income groups, and the avenues for corrective action have since become popular quotes by radical politicians and reformist intellectuals and groups.[20]

Planning, though nominally in existence in the previous sub-period, received a boost between 1958 and 1964, both because of the studies and the data accumulated by IRFED, and because of the greater attention it received under the new president. This attention took the form of a strengthening of the Ministry of Planning and the Planning Board, and the establishment of a Central Directorate of Statistics in May 1962, attached to the Ministry of Planning. But more importantly, the new conception of the role of government, which was characterised by the belief in the need for order in the economy and by recognition of the legitimacy — indeed, necessity — of the government performing a positive role in the guidance of the economy, all created a climate more clement for development planning than had ever previously existed. IRFED's plan project was — after some adjustment — incorporated in 1961 in a five-year plan centring around public-sector projects such as roads, power, water and popular housing. This plan was for 1964-8 and involved total investment of £L450 million. Subsequently in 1965 the plan period was extended to 1969.[21] However, this Plan, like its predecessor for the years 1958-62, was a mere listing of projects in the public sector, and not a comprehensive plan.

The third new direction took the form of the establishment of a number of public institutions basic to the rationalisation and modernisation of government machinery. The most conspicuous of these institutions were:

Civil Service Commission
Institute for Administration and Development (attached to the Commission)
Central Inspection Office

Social Rehabilitation Service
Council for Execution of Major Projects
Council for Beirut Projects
Green Project, 'Plan Vert' (Authority for Land Reclamation)
National Council for Development of Tourism
Central Bank (Banque du Liban, established in 1964, subsequent to the promulgation in 1963 of Currency and Credit Law)

In addition, at the suggestion of IRFED, special training was provided to development workers in such a manner that it was possible to form multi-purpose teams possessing training in the economic, sociological, administrative and technical aspects of development. Credit also goes to the President and governments of this six-year period for three other measures: (a) laying the foundation for and the drafting of the law of social insurance (however, actual implementation was carried out in two stages, one under the next president whose term ran from 1964 to September 1970, and the other under the current president who took office in September 1970); (b) the formulation in 1963 of a new, more progressive labour code to replace the code of 1946; and (c) the expansion and reorganisation of the directorate of vocational training.

The fourth direction of action was less tangible: it involved sharpening the awareness of the administration and the public of the need for the introduction of notions of social justice into the content of development. This meant a better distribution of income and a better geographical spread of investments and public services. To this end the government devoted funds and efforts to the expansion and improvement of education and health services, the reclamation of marginal land for the benefit of small landowners, and better supervision of the prices of essential commodities and prevention of exploitative abuse by shopkeepers.

However, it is safe to say that official concern at the top level with distributive justice did not translate itself into concrete measures that can be reported. Indeed, it is fair to maintain that the government on the whole underwent no profound change in orientation and intentions which could be felt in public policy and subsequently in the behaviour of the business community. Rather, government concern was merely an echo of the President's *personal* concern. In Lebanon, as in other countries of the Arab world, it takes more than the personal predilections and convictions of a president, no matter how powerful, to bring about during one term of office change of vast dimensions involving the business community and the largely immobile civil service.

A number of factors combined to make the next sub-period, namely 1964-70, rather sterile of major developments, whether in the economic, administrative or social field. The President who took office in 1964 was of a more contemplative and less decisive temperament than either of his two predecessors; the predominantly strong business community had begun to be actively dissatisfied with the mild regulatory attitude and measures characterising the previous term of office; the major Lebanese bank, Intra Bank, with shareholdings in the largest and nationally most important corporations collapsed in October 1966, which brought about serious shrinkage in credit and investment, and in national income in the following year; and the Arab-Israeli war of June 1967 had disruptive effects far wider in reach than the countries that had actually participated in the war, thus adding further to the atmosphere of hesitation in the economy and to sluggishness in general. Consequently, while additional income (and gross national product) rose in 1966 by 9.7 per cent over 1965, it *fell* by 0.5 per cent from 1966 to 1967 (0.8 per cent for GNP) — all at current prices.

Behind the broad picture of change in the national accounts between 1950 and 1972 there were a number of forces in operation. We have already referred to the influx in 1948 of some 150,000 Palestinian Arab refugees into Lebanon as one such factor. However, this was less significant than a series of external factors that have activated various aspects of the economy. To begin with, there was in the early fifties the introduction of the '50-50 formula' for the equal sharing of net profit from the production and sale of crude petroleum between producing countries in Iraq and the Arabian Peninsula and the concessionary companies operating there. This formula led to a vast increase in the revenue of the oil-producing countries, a process which in 1974 brought into the treasuries of these 'Gulf' countries (to say nothing of Libya and Algeria, which are not relevant to the point at issue) an estimated total of $50,900 million.[22] (The countries concerned include Abu Dhabi, Dubai, Qatar and Oman, which are not encompassed in this study, as well as Iraq, Kuwait and Saudi Arabia.)

This huge inflow of foreign currencies, which has grown in volume since the early fifties, poured in at a time when the Arabian Peninsula had neither the financial institutions, nor the immediate investment opportunities, nor the skills necessary for and capable of absorbing or otherwise handling the large sums involved. Lebanon, in contrast, was well-known in the region for its more advanced financial structure and its shrewd and enterprising financiers. And, as Lebanon is an Arab country, both the governments and the newly-enriched citizens of the oil-producing countries felt a trust in and an affinity with the Lebanese, paralleled initially with some ignorance and fear of the European and American money markets, which resulted in the direction of vast sums into Beirut's money market. This process was epitomised in the rise in bank deposits (demand and fixed) from £L215 million at the end of 1950 to £L9,106 million by the end of 1974.[23] It is currently estimated by knowledgeable bankers and economists in Lebanon that about one-third to one-half of these deposits belong to non-Lebanese — mainly residents and governments of the Arabian Peninsula.[24] It is worth noting that the volume of deposits (and savings) at the end of 1972 represented about 92 per cent of GNP for that year — a proportion unrivalled by any country.[25] (The unduly large 'external sector' of Lebanon will be examined further below.)

Another external event, or indeed process, which has had major impact on the Lebanese economy has been the series of *coups d'état* that have occurred in neighbouring Syria, Egypt and Iraq. (Jordan had an attempted *coup* in 1957.) These *coups* have resulted in the movement of a substantial — though undetermined — volume of flight capital from the three countries into Lebanon. This inflow has supplemented the steadier economically motivated inflow from the oil region.

The impact of the *coups* was intensified by the growth of nationalist feelings accompanied by an increase in restrictive economic measures; by a tendency towards autarky in the three countries listed; and by socialist transformation in the socio-economic system, again in all three countries. This process had contradictory effects on the Lebanese economy. On the one hand it tended to reduce the size of Lebanon's role as a country of services, particularly in the field of transit trade destined to Syria, Jordan and Iraq, and in the field of transport as a country whose main port, Beirut, used to serve Jordan and Syria and to a lesser extent Iraq, but now had to face competition from the development of national port facilities in each of the three countries. On the other hand, liquid capital, always sensitive to the change of political climate, was fast in its flight in the direction of Lebanon.

The tone of this narrative probably exaggerates the passive role of Lebanon in the flow of flight capital (and indeed an almost equally important flight of skilled and economically active manpower — technicians, capitalists and even politicians who for one reason or another decided to take residence in Lebanon as a result of political and social developments in their countries) away from Syria, Iraq or Egypt, and into Lebanon. In fairness, Lebanon also provided a pull effect on its own, which actively attracted both capital and skills. The freedom which it provided — whether with respect to investment, employment or living conditions, to the establishment of business by non-Lebanese, or to speech and publication — was a marked attraction. Furthermore, the intense drive and energetic entrepreneurship of the Lebanese provided a challenge which appealed to a number of the many capitalists, entrepreneurs, technicians and intellectuals who chose this country for their new abode. The freedom, to which credit is being given now, stretched far. It encompassed also a permissiveness with regard to the application of economic rules and regulations and the scope for their circumvention which could not but have been as welcome to guest capital as it is to native capital. (However, the inhibiting side of the permissiveness will be examined further down.)

We reached the conclusion earlier that income *per capita* has been rising at the average (simple) rate of about 3 per cent annually.[26] This is a satisfactory but not sensational rate. However, it would be wrong to base judgement on the performance of the Lebanese economy solely on growth in income as indicator. Again, as stated earlier, other indicators, no less significant, are available to establish the reality of substantial development — indicators that relate to different aspects of the standard of living and of modernisation in general.

A number of quantitative studies which have attempted ranking developing countries in accordance with socio-economic criteria of development and modernisation agree in placing Lebanon in the top category of developing countries. Thus, Harbison and Myers put Lebanon in their composite index of human resource development in what they call 'Level III — Semi-Advanced Countries'.[27] (We are not now commenting on the content of education in the country and the extent of its appropriateness for the country's needs.) Elsewhere, and more recently, Harbison has found that Lebanon (with Iraq and Peru) has made 'the greatest upward movement in rank' with regard to level of human resource development. In the same study, Harbison and his associates give Lebanon first rank in the indices of economic development, cultural development, health development and life expectancy, high-level manpower, demographic indicators, and (along with Iraq and Egypt) educational effort. Lebanon also occupies first place in the composite index of development.[28] An earlier study had made the same findings over a much wider range of social, economic and political indicators.[29]

However, in a study which in this writer's view embodies the most searching enquiry of its kind, Irma Adelman and Cynthia Taft Morris have come up with a more differentiated picture. Thus, they have found Lebanon more advanced than any of the other Arab countries with regard to economic performance and socio-cultural development. The latter relates to modernisation of outlook, role of the middle class, social organisation, democratic institutions and freedom of the press and of political parties, urbanisation, acceptance of technological change in agriculture and industry, literacy, weakness of the traditional élite, and insignificance of socio-economic dualism. The score is not as high, however, with a respect to commitment of political leadership to economic development and efficiency of the civil service.[30]

On balance, it can safely be said that Lebanon stands now at the highest level among the Arab countries with regard to its economic, technological and socio-cultural development. The evidence can be found in the level of income per head, as in a large number of other indicators. It is also to be found in the various individual sectors: their size, facilities, growth and general performance. Hence the brief examination that follows of the sectoral developments in the post-war period.

This examination is all the more necessary as we do not propose in this chapter to reproduce the structure which has been adopted, even if flexibly, for the other chapters in the present volume. The reason for the departure from the broad pattern so far established, whereby a rather thorough examination is undertaken of the growth pattern in the several aspects of the economic life of the countries concerned, is essentially because Lebanon is different in one important aspect. This is that the country, in this writer's view, seems now capable of achieving self-sustained growth, its take-off being based on the satisfactory performance of the economy as a whole, and the high level of income *per capita* this economy can generate. This income is the end result of activity on a broad front, not of any one rich resource like petroleum or phosphates that permits substantial exports and the earning of huge revenues, which 'produce' a very high income per head.

Once the examination of the leading sectors is completed, the emphasis in the rest of the chapter will be placed on the potential of, and impediments to, growth. To that end, the peculiar structure of the economy will be examined, and its implications for development will be explored. Likewise, the great discrepancy between the efficiency and performance of the public and private sectors and the serious threat that this discrepancy represents for continued development will be probed, in the hope that better understanding of the various factors at issue will lead to better visualisation of those corrective policies and measures which can leave the option open for continued development.

Sectoral Developments, 1946-75

That the various commodity and service sectors have marked considerable progress during the independence years 1946-75 is amply in evidence. This can be seen through the physical manifestations of development, the improvement in the level of living of the population at large, and the substantial growth rates of individual sectors. It might be most appropriate to start with the last source of evidence, by presenting the progress achieved by the sectors between 1950 and 1972, with the former year taken as base year.

The ranking of the sectors, which reflects the disparity in the magnitude of their individual contributions to national product, has a clear message at the surface. This ranking shows which sectors have advanced most, and which least, since 1950. Likewise, if the individual indices are compared with the average index for all sectors, the sectors can be classified as sluggish or fast-growing, depending on whether individual indices are below or above the average index. (On this last basis, agriculture, finance and insurance, and housing are sluggish, the others dynamic.) However, the ranking on the basis of magnitude of contribution to national product must not be considered as the only, or even the most important, inference to be drawn. For, on the one hand, there might be statistical causes why some sectors have increased their contribution tremendously, such as a very small base in absolute terms, which permits a modest absolute advance to loom large in relative terms. Alternatively, sectors that started with a large base would not be able to register a substantial expansion in index points beyond the base year.

On the other hand, significant as the indices are, they do not necessarily reflect in full the advances made in the various sectors, in terms of investments made, improvement

Table 7.3: Percentage Growth of Sectors between 1950 and 1972 (1950=100)[a]

Sector	Index for 1972
Agriculture, livestock, fisheries	305.6
Electricity and water[b] } Industry and crafts	737.3
Construction	695.4
Transport and communications	1,320.4
Housing and real estate	581.3
Finance and insurance	495.8
Trade	703.0
Professional and other services	674.7
Government	664.3
Average all sectors[c]	622.4

a. The data for 1950 relate to NNP, while those for 1972 relate to GDP. The two sets are not strictly comparable; however, the internal structure in 1972 could not have been vastly different if GDP rather than NNP is considered, though the indices recorded above must be higher than those relating to NNP. What matters for present purposes is the *ranking* of the sectors, and this cannot be very different in the two cases.
b. Included under 'industry' in 1950, and combined here for the sake of comparability.
c. If NNP were taken for 1972, its index would be 578.0.

Source: Calculated from data in Tables 7.2 and 7.5.

in quality of performance, and increased capability to serve developmental purposes. Consequently, in reporting on the progress achieved in the various sectors, we will bear in mind, simultaneously, the growth in the size of the contribution of each, and the advances made in the intrinsic worth of each: its size, facilities, quality of performance, and how these have changed over time.

It is appropriate to say at the outset that almost all the sectors have marked considerable progress, including agriculture, whose index betrays a poor performance. Probably the major exception among the sectors named in Table 7.3 is 'government', whose actual progress over time has distinctly fallen behind that of the other sectors. (But more on this later.) Another exception is the 'communications' part of the sector 'transport and communications'. There has been little progress, if not outright deterioration, in the services rendered by this subsector, probably because it is handled by government, while the transport subsector, which has on the whole made satisfactory progress in size and quality of performance, falls mainly in the private sector.

Agriculture: As there will be occasion to see later, agriculture lost its rank in the sectoral structure between 1950 and 1972, by ceding the second place it used to occupy to industry. (In fact, 'other services' now occupies third place, ahead of agriculture, but 'other services' is a bundle of sectors grouped together and ought not therefore to be compared with agriculture.) In spite of this decline in rank, agriculture has undergone radical changes over the years. It has become much more mechanised, and consequently has released a substantial part of its manpower for work in industry and other sectors. The use by agriculture of fertilisers and insecticides and pesticides has also risen considerably; terracing continues to be made and to be very effective; new crops have been introduced and existing ones expanded or improved; and generally technology and organisation have become more modern and scientific. Dairy farming and poultry raising have become very successful agricultural industries, and provide the economy with significant export earnings.

The country is well-endowed with two agricultural resources, arable land and water. The arable land is estimated at 240,000 ha (out of a total land area of 10,400 square kilometres, or 1.04m ha), while 68,000 ha are reported as being irrigated. (The arable land was reported at 273,000 ha, of which 48,000 were irrigated in 1958.)[31] Although irrigation seems to have expanded by about 42 per cent in one decade, it still falls below the country's potential. This is essentially because of the extreme slowness of irrigation schemes undertaken by government. The crowning example of slowness, indecision and wastefulness is the Litani Project.

This project had been under study for many years before the government in 1955 finally applied for and obtained a loan of $24m from the World Bank to start work. The Litani river, whose water was to be harnessed for irrigation and electricity generation, rises in the central eastern plateau, the Beqa', and flows southwards, then westwards to the Mediterranean close to the city of Tyre. The volume of water flowing in the river is about 900m cubic metres per annum. The work on the project has suffered from many setbacks, including insufficiency of background studies, such as cadastral and aerial surveys, soil analyses, research on farmer attitudes and the like; false starts; change in priorities; defective work performance (resulting in the collapse of tunnels and other serious and costly results); and disagreement (among the large landlords and political pressure groups allied with them) as to the course of irrigation canals and the altitude which irrigation water is to reach. Indeed, when the National Authority of the Litani River in May 1974 took over the management of the small Qasmiyyeh irrigation scheme which uses Litani water (involving 6,000 ha in the coastal area) and which had been completed under the French Mandate, it found that operational expenses exceeded income from water sales, that many of the files of subscribers were missing, the works were short of technicians and in great need of maintenance and repairs, individual incursions into the property of the scheme were prevalent, and the irrigation technology used was very primitive and water use very wasteful.

Several years ago, electricity generation was given priority over irrigation in the Litani Project. To this end, a dam was built in southern Beqa' (forming an artificial lake capable of holding 225m cubic metres), as well as a tunnel higher up in the mountain range west of the new lake, into which the water was to be pumped thanks to the electricity that was to be generated at the dam site. After long delays, project execution setbacks, and considerably larger financial outlays than earlier expected, three power plants were completed which produce 500m kwh per annum. Their capacity exceeds half the hydro-electrical capacity installed in the country, and over one-fourth of total capacity, hydro-electric and thermal combined.[32]

The irrigation aspect of the project, which is expected to provide water for 26,000 ha, has moved much more slowly than the generation of electric power. The problems are mainly economic in the Beqa' area, but socio-political as well as economic in south Lebanon. Financing is presently a serious overall problem, for, although the World Bank has agreed in principle to provide $50m of credits, and Abu Dhabi has promised to advance (or possibly grant) £L150m for the project, the budgetary constraints that have become increasingly handicapping in recent years will force the pace of execution to be slow, in so far as local financing is concerned. As of late 1974, it was expected that most of the basic irrigation works in the Beqa' and the south would be completed by the end of 1980, and that the subsidiary works would be completed by the end of 1982. Judging by past experience, and the indecision, corruption and political mismanagement that have played havoc with timetables, it can be said that these time forecasts are probably no better than well-intentioned hopes.

We have dwelt at some length on the Litani project because it provides one illustration of how the public sector in Lebanon, through faulty decision-making or, indeed, through indecision, has in effect wasted valuable time and financial resources, and has frustrated expectations. Many other illustrations can be provided; however, the general phenomenon itself will be examined in a later section of this chapter. In the field of agriculture itself, one other major institution has emerged in the past decade: the Green Project (Le Plan Vert), which was set up in order to help land-holders, especially those with rather small holdings and limited means, clear their properties of stones, undertake terracing, obtain cheap tractor services, intensify tree-planting from nurseries run by the Project, and dig wells or otherwise obtain and utilise water for irrigation. The impact of the Green Project on agriculture in general has been small, in spite of the dedication and earnestness of its executives. This essentially reflects the coolness of the politicians (who ultimately have the power to vote for or withhold funds) and the general cynicism and individualism of the farmers. The project has not succeeded in generating a mood of dynamism and co-operation, but has continued to be considered a convenient source of certain facilities, not the instrument of a rural revival.

Though Lebanon is still a net importer of agricultural products, particularly foodstuffs, its exports of fruits and vegetables and of dairy and poultry products have increased considerably over the years. Agricultural production has marked some positive growth since the early sixties; the index of total agricultural production stood at 136 for 1973, with the years 1961-5 as base, but the index for *per capita* production was only 102. The parallel index numbers for food production were 135 and 101 respectively.[33] The main weakness in the performance of the sector is in cereals, and this weakness has almost neutralised the healthy growth in fruit, vegetable, dairy and poultry production.

Industry: In some sense, industry occupies pride of place in the economy of the early seventies, although the contribution of the sector to national product is surpassed by that of trade, and its growth index is bettered by transport and communications. The significance assigned to industry arises from two factors: first, that it has moved ahead from modest beginnings in 1950, both with respect to absolute contribution to national product and to share in the labour force, to its present very satisfactory position on both scores. The second factor is the hardships which industrialists have had to overcome in an economy and society in which mercantile attitudes prevail and trade and commerce still command more sympathy, resources and power within a structure that continues to be service-dominated.

Lebanon stands today among the three or four major industrial countries in the Arab world. Obviously, this is a relative achievement, since no Arab country is advanced industrially. Nevertheless, within the confines of relativity, Lebanon has advanced with great strides. Unfortunately, statistical reporting in Lebanon is spotty, slow and half-hearted. The most recent records available early in 1975 have no more recent information than that relating to 1964, which is based on the industrial census of that year. No index numbers are prepared which permit the assessment of the growth in the various branches of industry, or in the sector as a whole, between, say, 1955, when the first industrial census was undertaken, and 1973 or 1974. Nevertheless, occasional studies in the local press strongly confirm the impressions of government authorities and industrialists that manufacturing industry has acquired considerable momentum and is becoming increasingly competitive in the domestic and export markets. (Export figures provide further proof of this.) Many new industries have been introduced, and design of products and technology used are becoming increasingly advanced. Indeed, as far as consumer goods are concerned, the variety and 'finish' of these goods place Lebanon ahead of any other Arab country.

Construction: As the last commodity sector, this also deserves special, if brief, mention. Apart from its growth, this sector has achieved qualitative transformation. Thus office and apartment buildings currently include a large component of very well-designed and well-equipped constructions. While it can be complained quite legitimately that the cities, and even the countryside, are becoming crowded, and the natural beauty of the country is spoiled by insufficient or faulty town planning (or by the disregard of the constraints of town planning), as well as by the increasing height of buildings and the increasing use of concrete, it can also justly be said that many architects are attempting to compensate for these 'sores of modernisation' by making a more judicial use of building materials, reflecting greater sensitivity to the aesthetics of design, and paying better attention to the installation of comforts and facilities. Nowhere else in the Arab world are buildings equally equipped, or the population as abundantly provided with housing facilities.

However, on the whole these facilities are available to those who can afford them. With the level of rent becoming extremely high and constituting an unduly onerous proportion of disposable income, and in the virtual absence of housing schemes by the government for the middle- and lower-income groups, adequate housing has become very expensive. This is particularly true in the context of the drive towards luxury apartments on the part of landlords and tenants alike. Luxury apartments are a forceful status symbol in a society where conspicuous consumption is prevalent and exerts strong pressure towards social emulation. Once again, the observer here comes across the discrepancy between what the private sector actually provides for those who have the means and the failure of the public sector to provide adequate amenities at low cost to those who are at the lower range of income distribution.

Transport and Communications: The transport and communications sector calls for mixed comments. On the one hand, there is the very poor quality of telephone, telegram and postal services. Indeed, these 'services' had by the end of 1974 become so unreliable and their facilities so inadequate and expensive that many foreign firms left the country and installed their regional offices in other countries, such as Greece, Bahrain and Iran, and many more were considering a similar move. (The expenses go much beyond the 'visible' items. To acquire a telephone line, for instance, may cost two to three times the official dues for those who do not have the 'right' contacts.) Another reaction has been the search for alternatives; reportedly, a foreign company has been asked by some businessmen to consider the anachronistic assignment of handling the incoming and outgoing mail of a number of large corporations for an annual fee.

At the other extreme, there is the brilliant performance of the air industry, both passenger and freight. The growth record of the two companies involved is enviable by any standard. The causes for this record are more to be sought in true entrepreneurial talent, good planning, organisation and administration than in good fortune or luck.

That the air industry is privately owned largely explains its dynamism. But for a utility or service to fall in the private sector is no guarantee of dynamism and responsiveness to the pressure of demand. The best illustration of this qualification is the port, which is privately owned. In spite of the increase in the demand for the services of the Beirut port over the past two decades, and the abundance of indications that these services will continue to be increasingly sought, the expansion in facilities (piers, loading and unloading space and storage space) and in equipment has fallen way behind the needs. Thus, of late it has become usual to see between 60 and 90 freighters anchored in open sea for weeks, awaiting their turn to load and unload, incurring heavy expenses in the process.

Apart from inadequate urban bus services and antiquated railways, there is no public transport system in the country. The private transport system provides the facilities that the economy needs. However, the road system is generally satisfactory, and it connects the vast majority of villages with the towns and cities, and with each other. This can be affirmed, in spite of the very long delays in the completion of highways and roads, and in road repairs. The shortcomings of road-building and maintenance partly derive from the heavy dependence on private contractors (who find it in their interest to produce work which it will be their pleasure to be called to repair after a few years) and from the temptations the relationship between civil servants and contractors constitutes for the former. To another extent, these shortcomings derive from the manner in which part of the budget of public works is allocated. This part, which has recently ranged between £L50m and £L70m, is allotted to the members of parliament (except those representing the capital) for use, within the confines of their constituencies, for 'internal' roads (that is, excluding international and main highways). This does not mean that they have direct access to the funds, which continue to be disbursed by the Ministry of Finance according to its rules and procedures, but that the members of parliament submit their decision as to how the allocations are to be spent, after which the funds become disposable accordingly. Obviously, this does not necessarily lead to the optimisation of resource allocation for road-making and -maintaining.

Banking: The banking sector deserves to be assigned much more importance than its contribution to national product and its share in the labour force suggest. Its fast growth and its dynamism have enabled it to attract a large volume of non-resident deposits, and have turned Beirut into the most important financial centre in the region. However, the strong points of the banking system have also spelled danger, and for some individual banks, collapse and ruin.

As in the case of the transport and communications sector, here too there is call for mixed reactions. The banking sector has expanded considerably in the independence era in number of banks and branches operating, and in scale and total size of operations. After a slow start, modernisation moved fast in such matters as mechanised account-keeping, communications with almost all parts of the world, and prompt service. The capabilities of the banking system and its familiarity with its counterparts in the industrial world, which have made the system attract foreign capital in large volume, have also resulted in easing the balance of payments difficulties. These difficulties arise essentially from the continuous and large balance of trade deficit. This deficit is in part counteracted through the surplus in the services part of the current account, but more so thanks to capital inflow. Thus the country suffers no shortage in foreign exchange. Indeed, the reverse is true, to the point where the excess supply has resulted in the overpricing of the Lebanese pound.

On the other hand, the banking system suffers from some serious structural weaknesses. With two exceptions, all the banks are essentially commercial and deal in short-term credit. If they undertake medium-term lending, this is camouflaged as short-term loans that are repeatedly renewed. Obviously, the banking mentality and methods characterising medium and long-term lending for investment purposes are not the same as for mercantile credit. If to this is added the virtual absence of research services in the banks to enable them to better assess investment opportunities and priorities, the dangers involved in the current practices will be better appreciated.

The large number of the operating banks, which in one sense shows drive and dynamism, also reflects individualism, fragmentation and vulnerability. Thus, apart from the failure of several banks since 1966, control over several others has been effected by large foreign banking concerns, to the point where no more than a few banks have remained truly Lebanese in capital ownership out of the almost 80 banks in operation by the end of 1974. Equally seriously, the banking system by and large acts as a 'transit station' for the funds deposited, prior to the placing of the funds in the Western money markets. The process is understandable, given the volume of deposits which far exceed the opportunities for profitable use in the country. However, the special function which the banking system performed ten or fifteen years ago when the petroleum-exporting countries of the Gulf were still insufficiently acquainted with the world money market and its mechanisms and routes is no more so special. These countries can now handle it themselves. To that extent, unless the Lebanese banking system has something unique to offer in the field of investment, the flow of oil funds will drop further than it already has.

From the regional viewpoint, there is the added desire in the capital-needy countries that more of the oil funds should find their way to productive investment in the Arab world, not in the industrial countries. Unless the banking system undertakes those structural and technical changes which enable it to play an active role in the regional flow of funds for investment purposes, Lebanon would miss a very lucrative opportunity, and fail to play a most meaningful role. There are some signs of the realisation of this issue, but these are manifest in the establishment of some new finance corporations, owned jointly by Arab and foreign (mainly European) interests. It is yet to be seen whether these constitute another mechanism to syphon more Arab funds away to the Western money markets, or to draw funds into productive investment in the Arab world. The writer is sceptical on this score.

It was indicated earlier that the country has only two investment banks. The first, Banque de Crédit Agricole, Industriel et Foncier, BCAIF, was founded in 1954 jointly by the public and private sectors (40 and 60 per cent of capital respectively) for the purpose of providing medium- and long-term credit to agricultural, industrial and real estate (essentially hotel) development. However, neither the size of capital, nor the rules and procedures adopted permitted BCAIF to play an important role. In fact, the larger establishments (and the more influential applicants) continued to get the greater part of credit, and the collateral requirements continued to operate against the small farmers who constituted the neediest group. (Declared capital is only £L5m, but a loan of £L52m from the Central Bank, and another of £L15m from local banks, have enabled BCAIF to have a much larger working capital.)

The other institution is the National Bank for Industrial and Touristic Development, established in 1973 with a capital of £L60m (51 per cent of which is owned by the government, and 49 per cent by several banks operating in Lebanon). This bank has started operations and committed the bulk of its paid-up capital of £L45m. Judging by its far superior staffing compared with BCAIF's, its clearly developmental philosophy and its energetic style, it can be expected to have a clear promotive developmental effect, given the availability of adequate investible funds.

Trade: Reference has to be made to trade, considering the fact that it constitutes the most important contributor to national product. Yet there are other reasons why the development of trade ought to be assessed. For one thing, the volume of imports and exports, and of transit trade and re-exports, is substantial, as the figures for 1973, shown in Table 7.4, indicate.

Table 7.4: Breakdown of Trade Figures, 1973 (£L million)

Imports	3,786.8
Exports	1,599.5
Re-exports	265.1
Transit	1,345.3

Source: *Recueil de Statistiques Libanaises 1973*, p. 381. For revenue from customs duties, p. 315.

Apart from the factor income generated in the conduct of operations of this size, the economy makes other important direct gains, such as the activation of the transport and finance and insurance sectors, the earning by the treasury of large revenues through import duties (£L305m in 1973, the largest single heading), and the attraction which the availability of a large variety of consumer goods constitutes for visitors and tourists. However, there is another aspect which merits particular emphasis in the context of development. This is that exposure to attractive and appealing imported consumer goods, which begins by being a drain on resources to some extent and a factor for excessive 'consumerism', often ends as an incentive to industry. This occurs via the process of import substitution by Lebanese industry, and ends, given the right conditions, by generating a drive towards export expansion. The industrial and technological implications of this process hardly need any elaboration.

It was mentioned earlier that the large balance of trade deficit which recurs every year is financed partly through the export of invisibles, and partly through net capital inflow. The most important foreign exchange earning services are tourism, air travel and air freight on national airlines, and contract work undertaken abroad by a number of large contracting firms which are active in many countries and areas of specialisation. Of smaller significance are educational and medical services to non-residents who come for the purpose of education or treatment. A further item is more appropriately a form of 'unrequited transfer': this is remittances by emigrants settled abroad who, thanks to strong family ties, continue to remit money to their poorer relations at home. On the other hand, the remittances of the thousands of Lebanese professionals, technicians and labourers who work mainly in the Gulf area, Saudi Arabia and Libya and send their savings back home is one form of service export. The size of this last item is substantial.

The net capital inflow, which amounted to £L919m and £L876m for 1971 and 1972 respectively,[34] more than balances the accounts. It permits a substantial increase in monetary holdings, both official and private. The inflow of capital originates mainly in deposits made by institutions and nationals of the Gulf countries (but whose accounts in many instances are considered 'resident' accounts either in order to be able to earn interest, or simply because the owners of the deposits have a mailing address in Lebanon). A smaller stream of capital inflow comes from emigrants who send funds for investment and deposit purposes. This should be distinguished from remittances aimed as gifts to relatives for use by these.[35]

This method or process of financing of the import surplus is a feature of long standing in the balance of payments. The process has two aspects. The first, with which we will deal in the sections below, relates to the development of the external sector as a whole, and the implications of the structure and size of the sector for development. The second, to which attention is directed presently, is the notable growth of the major services exported, namely tourism, contracting, aviation and remittances by Lebanese manpower abroad. These are so well established that they have become a dependable feature of the economy. Although it is true that tourism is a delicate service which is very sensitive to political turmoil in Lebanon and the neighbouring countries,[36] and although the work of Lebanese nationals and contracting firms is influenced by the development climate in the countries concerned and by the relations these countries have with Lebanon, it is none the less equally true that the Lebanese are very resilient and resourceful. These qualities enable them to compensate for one slackening activity by activating another, or by shifting emphasis from one country to another, or finally (in the case of tourism) by bending to the wind of political unrest until it passes and then re-activating their tourist attractions.

Education and Health Services: This will be the last sector to be commented upon.[37] Lebanon enjoys advantages in both. Its educational institutions and services rank among the very best in the Arab world, though this should not be taken as an endorsement of the educational system and its content and methods. Indeed, it merely means that the system is less objectionable in most respects than that in most other countries of the region. The medical facilities available, including medical personnel and equipment, are definitely unsurpassed in the Arab world. The general educational and health levels enjoyed by the population reflect the advantages the country has in the services available.

There are a few features of education and health services that are special to Lebanon. First, nowhere else in the Arab world does the private sector play as important a role on either score as in Lebanon. Thus, pupils in pre-university private schooling exceed 55 per cent of the total. Furthermore, the best kindergarten, elementary, intermediate and secondary schools are privately owned. Secondly, girls constitute roughly 45 per cent of the total, private and public, and all cycles combined. Finally, the school population ranges between 80 and 85 per cent of children of school age. If it is recalled that the countryside in the districts of the South, the North and the Beqa' is much less adequately supplied with schools, it will be seen that in the cities and the district of Mount Lebanon the school population must be well in excess of 90 per cent of school-age children. (The proportion acquires more significance once it is realised that not all private schools report their statistics regularly to the Ministry of Education.)

The university student body is large in Lebanon — some 46,000 in 1972-3.[38] More than half the student body is in the Beirut Arab University, which is affiliated with Alexandria University of Egypt. To this number must be added about 5,000 who attend university-level teacher training colleges, specialised faculties attached to universities, and Beirut University College. About 46 per cent of the total student body of 51,000 are Lebanese. The largest single component among the non-Lebanese is Palestinian/Jordanian. The oldest of the universities is the American University of Beirut, established in 1866. Indeed, with the exception of al-Azhar of Cairo (which is essentially an institution for religious studies and Islamic jurisprudence, and which is over 1,000 years old), this is the oldest university in the whole Arab world, and probably the best equipped and staffed. Indeed, the faculty-student ratio in this university is the most favourable (less than 9 students per member of faculty), and research opportunities and facilities the most encouraging. Elsewhere in the national universities in the Arab region, which account for about 97 per cent of Arab students in the whole region, the old French system (that is before the reforms of 1958-9 in France) still prevails by and large. Under this system, professors lecture to very large audiences, often numbering several hundred students at a time, before the 'classes' are broken into smaller groups to meet with junior members of faculty. Because pay is rather low, the faculty undertake much heavier lecturing assignments than the nominal maximum allowed to obtain extra income. Under the circumstances, research becomes a luxury few can afford. The Lebanese (national) University is still young, and will need tremendous efforts and financial outlays before it can have the personnel, buildings and laboratory and library facilities that satisfy the ambitions of the country. Finally, Université St Joseph (a Jesuit French institution) is the second-oldest in Lebanon. Like the American University of Beirut, it has a wide range of faculties and a small student body.

Very much the same can be said of health as of education services, with respect to public and private sector roles. The private sector attracts many more doctors than the public; the discrepancy is equally glaring in hospitals and hospital beds, with 20 government hospitals and 1,401 hospital beds, against 123 hospitals and 9,969 beds in the private health sector, by the end of 1972. The population as a whole in 1972 had one physician for 1,090 inhabitants, and one hospital bed for 229 inhabitants. These ratios, especially the latter, are very satisfactory by regional standards. As far as quality of service, facilities and equipment, and laboratory and other research are concerned, the public health sector is far inferior to the private. The fact that the American University Hospital and the Hôtel Dieu Hospital are attached to medical schools in the American University of Beirut and the Université St Joseph respectively provides these hospitals with the services of very well-trained medical faculty and very well-equipped laboratory and research facilities. (This is particularly true of the new Medical Center of the American University of Beirut, which is professionally ahead of any comparable institution in the Arab world.)

There is a particularly dark side to the otherwise bright coin of education and health. There is, first, the high cost of services provided by private institutions, which makes them prohibitively expensive for people of small means — a feature of social inequality of grave dimensions. In the second place, there is a very heavy concentration of schools and health facilities in Beirut. This concentration, bad as it is in quantitative terms, is even more serious owing to the distinctly better quality of the facilities available in Beirut. The implications of the maldistribution (in its two aspects) for social harmony are becoming increasingly grave.[39]

2. STRUCTURE OF THE LEBANESE ECONOMY

Mention has been made that the freedom of enterprise in Lebanon has reached the level of permissiveness, and we can add here that there is confusion in the country, even among some social thinkers, between the services-biased structure on the one hand and the extreme freedom and weakness of regulatory measures on the other. It is a moot point whether the predominance of the services sectors has led to the permissiveness and to the creation

Lebanon

of the accommodating socio-economic and political system now in existence, or whether it is the permissiveness and the system that have favoured the rise into predominance of the services sectors, or indeed whether it is another set of independent variables altogether that has brought about the predominance and the permissiveness. The question can be the starting point for a fascinating cultural and socio-psychological study, for which, however, this book is not the right place and which the present writer is not qualified to undertake.

What is none the less relevant here is the fact itself that in Lebanon at the beginning of the fifties the services sectors contributed about two-thirds of the national product against one-third for the commodity sectors, and that this structure has been confirmed or even strengthened, since 1950, as Table 7.5 below shows.

Table 7.5: National Income 1950 and Gross Domestic Product 1972 by Sector[a]

Sector	1950 £L m	Per cent of Total	1972 £L m	Per cent of Total
Agriculture, livestock and fisheries	207	20.2	631	9.9
Electricity and water[b]			129	2.0
Industry and crafts	137	13.4	884	13.9
Construction	42	4.1	290	4.6
Transport and communications	36	3.5	478	7.5
Housing and real estate	96	9.4	558	8.8
Finance and insurance	47	4.6	235	3.7
Trade	286	27.9	2,007	31.5
Professional and other services	100	9.8	676	10.6
Government	72	7.0	477	7.5
Total	1,023[c]	100.0[d]	6,365	100.0

a. Although the data for the two years refer to different concepts, no serious violation is committed in undertaking the comparison, as the internal structure would be almost identical for NNP and GDP for the same year.
b. Electricity and water were included under 'industry' in 1950.
c. Net of adjustment for rest of the world — i.e. national income at factor cost.
d. Items do not add to 100.0 because of rounding.

Sources: For 1950, Albert Y. Badre, 'The National Income of Lebanon', *Middle East Economic Papers, 1956* (Beirut, 1956); for 1972, *Recueil de Statistiques Libanaise 1973*, p.329.

Four major observations can be made on this table. First, that the services sectors make an unusually high contribution to national product. Second, that this structure has not only continued over the two decades covered, but that the share of services has risen: precisely, from 62.3 per cent in 1950 to 69.6 per cent in 1972. Third, that within this structure, an important change has occurred in the ranking of agriculture and industry. The former has dropped from second place in 1950, with a contribution of 20.2 per cent to third place with as small a contribution as 9.9 per cent; while industry has moved up from third to second place, with a contribution of 15.9 per cent for 1972, versus 13.4 for 1950. (We combined electricity and water with industry for 1972, so that the contribution can be compared with that for 1950.) Fourth, that trade makes by far the major single contribution, amounting to 27.8 per cent in 1950 and 31.5 per cent in 1972. The welfare aspect of this structure carries special significance for the development and sense of participation of the economy and society. This aspect can be seen through the parallel examination of the manpower structure, that is the distribution of the labour force among the sectors and the industrial origin of the domestic product which was presented in Table 7.5 above.

Table 7.6: Distribution of the Active Labour Force by Sector

Sector	1950		1970	
	'000	Per Cent	'000	Per Cent
Agriculture	200	50.0	101.8	18.9
Industry	42	10.5	95.5	17.8
Electricity and water			5.6	1.0
Construction			35.1	6.5
Trade and finance[a]	106	26.5	91.6	17.0
Transport and communication	16	4.0	38.2	7.1
Other services, administration, armed forces[b]	36	9.0	168.2	31.2
Undefined			2.4	0.4
Total	400	100.0	538.4	100.0[c]
Add: unemployed			33.6	
			572.0	

a. This item changed composition in 1970, where it grouped 'trade and hotel-keeping'.
b. This item was designated 'administration' in 1950; 'armed forces' was a separate item. There was no record of 'other services'. I have grouped these together for both years, although the grouping does damage to detail. (For 1970, trade and hotels accounted for 91,620 workers or 17 per cent, finance and business services for 18,420 or 3.4 per cent, and other services 149,790 or 27.8 per cent).
c. Items do not add up to 100.0 because of rounding.
Sources: For 1950, Royal Institute for International Affairs, *The Middle East: A Political and Economic Survey* (London, 1958, third edition), p.357-8. The information is attributed in this source to Charles Churchill, *City of Beirut — A Socio-Economic Survey* (Beirut, 1954); however, the information does not appear anywehre in Churchill. For 1970, information is from Direction Centrale de la Statistique, *L'Enquête par sondage sur la population active au Liban, Novembre 1970* (Beirut, July 1972), vol.1, 'Méthodes, analyse et présentation des résultats', p.114. This is the only reliable study of manpower in Lebanon.

Judging by the sources as they appear above, the earlier information cannot claim a high degree of reliability. Furthermore, sector-by-sector comparisons are not possible in a few cases because of changes in nomenclature and content. In any case, the 1950 data are unsatisfactory not only because they are essentially estimates, but also because they ignore employment in some service sectors. These qualifications notwithstanding, the table can help us draw some tentative inferences with regard to the structure of employment, and, if seen in conjunction with data in Table 7.5, to the relationship between each sector's contribution to national product and the proportion of the labour force engaged in it. (This is known as the 'relative national product per worker', RNPW.) The most striking inference is the large discrepancy between the contribution of agriculture to domestic product (one-fifth in 1950, but one-tenth in 1972), and the sector's absorption of labour force (one-half in 1950, one-fifth in 1972). This finding contains a harsh verdict on the low productivity of labour, particularly as the statistics for 1972 exclude Syrian labour engaged in agriculture, which is thought to be far from negligible. The finding thus shows that agricultural workers are badly off in terms of welfare. However, there has been a slight improvement in their position over time, judging by the change in RNPW.[40]

Industry and construction, which were grouped together in 1950 (and which also included electricity and water), and which we will combine for 1972 in the present context for the sake of easier comparison, together contributed 17.5 per cent of domestic product and engaged 10.5 per cent of the labour force in 1950, but 20.5 per cent and 25.2 per cent respectively for 1972. The situation encountered in the case of agriculture is reversed here, that is, there is a considerable drop in the RNPW, from 1.66 to 0.81. Together, the commodity-producing sectors contributed 37.7 per cent in 1950 and 30.4 per cent in 1972, but engaged 60.5 per cent and 44.1 per cent of the labour force for the two years respectively. Thus RNPW rose from 0.62 to 0.70. Against this, the services-producing sectors contributed 62.3 per cent and 69.6 per cent but engaged 39.5 per cent and 55.9 per cent respectively. (RNPW dropped from 1.58 to 1.25.) This suggests a higher productivity of labour in the services sectors than in the commodity sectors, but that this advantage in productivity has declined over time. The last observation is of significance, since it shows some evening out of distribution of national product between the commodity and service sector groups. However, the change is small and the process very slow. (The reader ought to be warned that the data on labour distribution for 1950 are very tentative, and the conclusions based on them are of necessity equally tentative.)

The predominance of the services sectors in the structure of the economy is not an isolated phenomenon, or a matter of accident. It is closely tied, within an intricate system of interaction, with attitudes, human skills, legal framework, institutions, values and group perception of role in society, as well as with cultural heritage, geographical location and natural endowments.

3. THE STRUCTURE, THE SYSTEM AND ACCELERATED DEVELOPMENT

Neither undue pride nor undue shame should attach to this structure. Essentially, the question of structure should raise one basic question: is this structure compatible with accelerated development? — this last term defined in a broad sense to incorporate a high rate of growth plus modernisation in social institutions and technology, and a rather equitable distribution of national product, in reality not in statistical records. And if the answer is in the negative, then what is the course that the economy and society should pursue for the correction of the structure?

Cool analysis of this issue is often beclouded by four factors or arguments. The first relates to the climate of feeling and/or thinking around the question. Here one encounters writers who, with obvious obscurantism, equate the present structure with Lebanon's 'vocation', and express their views as an act of faith. To these, the structure and the vocation are both part of mountainous Lebanon and of its Phoenician heritage, its world view, its enterprising genius, its sea-faring tradition. Holders of these views usually refuse to enter into systematic argument, having reached aprioristic positions. This attitude has for about a quarter-century drawn support from a statement attributed, perhaps apocryphally, to Paul Van Zeeland, the Belgian politician and financial expert, who was invited by the government in 1948 to examine the French-Lebanese currency agreement. He is reputed to have said, 'I don't know what makes the economy work, but it seems to do pretty well. I suggest therefore that you leave it alone.'[41]

A second argument for permissiveness and maximum freedom of enterprise and the preservation of the present structure of the economy has been the low level of efficiency in public administration and of dedication to public welfare and public responsibility among politicians. This is used to argue in favour of minimum official 'interference' aimed at varying the structure, *not* on grounds of principle but of pragmatism and realism. Writers and thinkers who take this position draw attention to the disparity in levels of efficiency between government and private business, and conclude from this that an inefficient government cannot order and discipline a business sector which, in any case, is prosperous.

The third argument is even stronger than the second. It centres around the record of development of Lebanon, and asks why, given this record, there should be any attempt at 'correction' of the present structure. The argument is often knowledgeable and specific enough to marshall evidence from the high rate of real income per head, the high level of socio-cultural achievements and institutions, modernisation in outlook and in technological methods — all superimposed on a niggardliness of natural resources. There cannot be much which is wrong with the economic structure and with its socio-economic framework, the argument proceeds, if these are capable of producing such a performance.

Lastly, there is the power argument, namely that to attempt to change the structure — if this were to be necessary — would mean to clash with the very powerful community of businessmen that controls and benefits from the services sectors. The merchants are the most involved and most outspoken in this connection. They strongly maintain that the preferential development of agriculture and industry would presumably involve, among other things, the formulation and implementation of a highly protective and regulatory policy which not only would do violence to their established rights but also would undermine the 'system' and alter its free character. The merchant community further maintains that the Lebanese are eminently qualified to play the role of intermediary and thus enjoy a position of comparative advantage in the services sectors where mediation is a basic function of entrepreneurial activity. The combined force of their established power position and their argument gives to the merchants a formidable economic leverage in internal politics.

The cumulative effect of these four arguments has been to insist on the preservation of the present structure and of the socio-economic and political system which serves as framework for it. As a necessary corollary, businessmen, writers and politicians who are of this conviction have all been apologists for permissiveness on the part of government and for maximum freedom of enterprise, on the grounds not only that the government cannot by guiding or directing the economy or even by putting more order into it improve its performance, but that such action would be outright harmful to the economy.

The evaluation of these arguments with a view to answering the question which set off the present enquiry cannot be undertaken directly. One important aspect of the services-biased structure has first to be examined — namely, the nature, size and implications of the 'external sector' or the external aspect of services.[42] By external sector we mean services produced for the purposes of an external market, that is for the use or consumption of non-residents, whether the consumption takes place inside Lebanon or outside.[43]

Reference has already been made to the impact of several factors originating outside Lebanon on the Lebanese economy — particularly on the finance sector. These factors have been of varied nature: influx of Palestinian refugees in 1948; military *coups* in neighbouring countries; vast increase in the revenue of the oil-producing areas in the Arabian Peninsula; and socialist transformation in Egypt, Syria and Iraq. Their combined result has been the inflow of a large volume of flight capital into Lebanese banks (and the influx of thousand of capitalists, intellectuals, technicians and politicians).

The growth of the external sector has manifested itself in other spheres of the economy as well. Thus the volume of trade is very high for a country of Lebanon's population and level of income. (Imports constitute about half of national income.) If it is recalled that a sizeable part of the imports is cleared off the market by visitors who come to Lebanon in very large numbers as tourists or for a somewhat longer stay in the country's summer resorts (but who do not become residents), and if it is further recalled that the whole of the transit, export and re-export services are for foreign users, then it becomes clear that an important part of the trade service is for the purposes of the external sector. This sector also includes a large part of the services of tourism and resorts, and of contracting, as well as a small but not insignificant part of the activities of the transport and communications sector, and of the real estate sector (to the extent that there are many non-resident visitors — tourists and summer resorters — who lease residential facilities for short periods in the cities and the countryside).[44]

As we have seen, about 70 per cent of the gross domestic product is contributed by the services. The activities destined for the external sector are all service activities. It has been estimated[45] that the equivalent of 36 per cent of the contribution of the services is destined for the external sector, or approximately 25 per cent of the GDP (i.e. 36 × 70 per cent). This is a high ratio indeed, and it raises the question of the dependence of the Lebanese economy on non-resident users of its services, and its vulnerability in a region characterised by political instability and political feuds, where economic relations often serve as 'whipping boy' for political disagreements.

A second more fundamental question arises in this connection. While it is granted that the bias in favour of services in the structure of the economy is to a considerable extent the product of the economy's and the society's skills, endowments, tradition and other inherent factors, it is also true that to another considerable extent the development of the services sectors in the post-war years has been favourably influenced by events and socio-political and economic trends originating in neighbouring Arab countries. There is no reason to believe that these events or trends can or will be repeated or continued, nor, if they were to continue, will they produce an influence with the same intensity and volume. Therefore they cannot be relied on as an engine for future growth to the same extent that they have so far served. This is particularly true in the light of recent autarkic tendencies, and tendencies for increased self-dependence in the countries that have been good clients for Lebanon's services in the fields of transit trade, estivage, contracting or banking.

The vulnerability of the services sectors can be seen from yet another angle on the demand side.[46] So far Lebanon has been in command of certain service skills that have created an advantage for the country. However, these skills are not a natural monopoly — even the resorts of the country can be challenged in scenery in certain parts of Syria, Iraq, Tunisia, Algeria or Morocco. Furthermore, price incentives aimed at promoting local resorts elsewhere can counterbalance the advantages of Lebanese resorts. Other services, such as contracting and transit trade, relate to skills that can be acquired, although — it ought to be admitted — Lebanon also has the advantage of location with respect to transit trade. Finally, certain services — finance features importantly here, as well as tourism and estivage — are receiving tough competition from their counterparts in Europe and the United States. Rich Kuwaitis and Saudis are familiar enough now with the money markets and the resorts of Europe and the United States not to have to reach these markets via Beirut.

Studies are not available on the comparative profitability of one unit of investment in the various sectors. Consequently it cannot be claimed with certainty that the country has reached the most productive (or the optimising) allocation of its resources. Indeed, it can be argued that Lebanon is equipped, in terms of natural endowments, for certain lines of agricultural development which are not yet adequately explored; and that it is equipped, thanks to the good taste, adaptability and dexterity of its artisans, for certain industries that are also insufficiently developed. A thorough investigation of this question would probably suggest new avenues for investment and development in the commodity sectors. This would lead to diversification *with* improvement in the pattern of resource allocation.

There is in Lebanon an unwarranted belief in many private and official circles that the prosperity of the country and the relatively high level of income it has achieved are due to the absence of government regulation or interference. This belief has found support in the special nature of services which do not seem to render themselves liable to ordering and organisation as readily as agriculture and (more so) industry. Indeed, one can venture the proposition that the present level of performance has been achieved in spite of, rather than because of, the absence of order in the economy. In other words, the great enterprising drive of the Lebanese has covered up for the weakness of order and for the government's inefficiency and permissiveness. But this should neither suggest a viable situation nor an immunity to the long-run danger of the low level of public services, the inefficiency of the civil service, or the disregard by businessmen of discipline even when it is in their interest. A good illustration of such disregard is the practice of agriculturists to pack fruit and vegetables of uneven quality but to put the better-quality pieces on top and to charge on the basis of the top layer. Many lucrative contracts have been lost as a result of such practices, and because of the general lack of co-operation in the implementation of regulatory measures relating to grading and packing.[47]

There is a broader principle involved here. It is the necessity, for development, of qualifying freedom with order when such order is demonstrably beneficial to the business community itself. The concept of freedom of enterprise has become so confused and overstretched that even such a limited resort to regulatory order is suspected and evaded. The proposition that is being suggested is precisely that freedom of enterprise, in the sense in which it is understood and practised, shelters behind two defence lines. The first is the insistence on the preservation of the present services-biased structure, on the grounds that the maximum freedom enjoyed is necessary for the structure which has proved lucrative to the country. The second defence line is the claim that the regulation of freedom, even if it takes the mild form of 'putting order into freedom', would lead the country into socialism, for, after all, the long road to socialism begins with one step — as the advocates of permissiveness contend. And socialism would violate society's political philosophy and its system of values.

It is maintained here that both defence lines are tenuous. It is further maintained that regulation and order are becoming absolutely essential if the economy is to move beyond the plateau which it has reached. This is necessitated by the growing complexity of production and distribution, of business association, of audit and cost-accounting methods, of specifications and quality control, of technical, economic and business research, but above all of the web of social relations necessitating certain state functions connected with public services, taxation and social justice which cannot be ignored in the latter part of the twentieth century. Finally, it is here maintained that attending to the logical implications and requirements of this complexity calls for a clearly wider regulatory role for government, and that this role is a necessary condition for promoting economic growth to the level of which the society and economy are intrinsically capable.

Lastly, the predominance of services in the economic structure points to a danger outside economics — in the national character. Thus:

while it is true that the prosperity of . . . (services) sectors reflects a brisk and refined business sense, a sensitivity to world markets and to price fluctuations, mental alertness, skill in trading and in the performance of services, and an ability to cater to clients' tastes — while this is all true, it is equally true that the activities involved carry with them certain disagreeable and unfavourable qualities. Thus, cleverness and smartness acquire a premium over material creativity; the emphasis on gains through clever bargaining becomes larger than that on steady business relations and on deals based on the respective merits of the goods exchanged; and the search for quick turnover and easy, large profits accentuates an inclination to speculative enterprise and militates against sustained hard work and against long-term investment promising long-term, though low-level, profit rates. 'Catering' which is a major feature in a services-biased economy is also an attitude and a frame of mind.[48]

We ought to go back to a question posed above which has still to be answered directly: is the present structure compatible with future accelerated development? In attempting an answer, we should first indicate that the fundamental *malaise* with the present structure is not caused by the failure of its performance to produce economic growth. The rate of growth is satisfactory by regional standards. The *malaise* is caused rather by the belief that Lebanon could show a much better record of growth and development on the basis of the skills and endowments of its society. It is further contended here that the fortuitous operation of a number of factors in large part accounts for the growth witnessed in the post-war era. But these factors are not inherent in the economy and are not under society's control. Furthermore, even if economic analysis were to prove the advisability of preserving the present structure, which is an option that is left open for the moment, the question still remains valid and relevant whether the socio-economic system should not be adjusted in the direction of greater order, better public services, more efficient administration, greater willingness to accept government's authority, and the introduction into the values of the business community of greater regard for social responsibility.

The fundamental question, then, is not whether the commodity sectors should predominate over the services sectors in the structure, or the reverse, but whether true wide-reaching development calls for change in the present structure and in the socio-economic framework or system, and if so, in what directions. The question will receive more attention further on, in the companion volume (Volume II), where the determinants of development will be formulated and examined. For the moment, the analysis, in so far as it relates to the external sector, will focus on the question of the availability and use of total resources, with a view to the assessment of the possibility, under present circumstances, not only of maintaining the present rate of growth, but of raising it.

The defence of the present structure finds added strength in the fact that the balance of trade, which is consistently against Lebanon, equally consistently relies heavily on the export of services and the net inflow of capital as sufficient corrective. Thus, during the fourteen years for which there is a rather reliable series of balance of payments statistics, namely 1960-73, the deficit on the balance of trade has ranged from a low of £L662.7m for 1963 to a high of £L2,187.3m in 1973, while the surplus on invisible trade has ranged from a low of £L482.3m for 1960 to a high of £L926.7m for 1972, with net capital inflows reaching a peak of £L902.6m in 1971.[49] (Balance of payments data are not available beyond 1972, except for commodity trade.) Indeed, the net capital inflow has permitted the country to build up an international liquidity of $1,674m by the end of December 1974.[50]

The relevant question at this point is whether the country can continue to finance a large volume of imports if the net inflow of capital is threatened. Indeed, the volume of imports rose consistently from 1960 to 1966 and, despite its fall for 1967 and 1968, it picked up again in 1969 and rose consistently thereafter. This suggests a consistent tendency to rise in normal years. While this trend has been counteracted in large part by the upward trend of visible and invisible exports, the trade pattern must be examined not in isolation but with respect to the availability and uses of total resources.

Table 7.7: Total Availability and Use of Resources (in £L million, and at current prices)

Resources	1964	1965	1966	1967	1968	1969	1970	1971	1972
Gross domestic product at market prices	3,200.0	3,523.4	3,866.7	3,820.1	4,273.2	4,564.6	4,866	5,399	6,365
Imports minus exports	670.2	734.4	860.6	668.6	607.3	729.3	748	867	1,046
Total resources	3,870.2	4,257.8	4,727.3	4,488.7	4,880.5	5,293.9	5,614	6,266	7,411
Uses of Resources									
Consumption									
Households	2,856.4	3,110.7	3,393.4	3,299.4	3,666.6	3,934.2	4,197	4,656	5,543
Administration	309.3	354.6	401.1	418.9	438.7	478.0	512	541	571
Gross fixed capital formation									
Business sector	563.3	649.4	761.3	627.0	640.6	703.7	766	846	1,086
Administration	133.8	129.8	127.8	131.8	146.1	173.2	172	175	182
Change in stocks	7.4	13.3	43.7	11.6	−11.5	4.8	−33	48	29
Total uses	3,870.2	4,257.8	4,727.3	4,488.7	4,880.5	5,293.9	5,614	6,266	7,411

Sources: Direction Centrale de la Statistique, *Les comptes économiques de l'année 1969*, p.1, until 1968, and *Recueil...1973*, pp.324-6, thereafter.

It can be seen from Table 7.7 that consumption constitutes a very high percentage of gross domestic product, its ratio hovering around 97 per cent of GDP. Measured against total resources available (and therefore against total resource use), consumption is around 83 per cent for the nine-year period, which is still a very high ratio. Furthermore, the relationship is quite steady and almost unfluctuating in either measurement.

Relating consumption to GDP is quite revealing, since it shows that the economy does not domestically produce enough resources to satisfy simultaneously a high average propensity to consume plus a level of investment capable of assuring it of a rate of growth compatible with its developmental ambitions.[51] Investment of this calibre would only be possible if the import surplus (that is, the excess of imports over exports) permitted it. But a large import surplus is, in turn, possible only if the country continues to receive a sufficiently large volume of donations and unilateral transfers and/or a sufficiently large inflow of capital — given the present pattern of visible and invisible trade. As things stand, only 1 per cent of real growth (out of 5.5 which is the average for the period 1950-72) is brought about by domestic investment financed by domestic savings (on the assumption of an incremental capital coefficient of 3). To aim at a rise in the growth rate by another, say, two percentage points, would require the foreign financing of an increment of £L381m in the import surplus. This might not be impossible, but the crux of the problem is the *precariousness* of such a form of financing. A society cannot hope to achieve *and* maintain a high rate of growth predominantly on the basis of a large net inflow of capital. A time of reckoning will come when the owners of the inflowing capital assets will claim them, or will deposit less capital funds in Lebanon. In this eventuality, either consumption or growth or (most probably) the two in combination will have to be compressed. The social and economic, and possibly the political, implications are then likely to be serious.

An increment in investment of the dimension just suggested cannot be assumed easy to achieve under the circumstances, even were it to be desirable. Indeed, considering the nature and sources of remittances and other capital flows it would be more reasonable to warn against the precariousness of the present form of compensatory financing in the balance of payments. Private donations mainly come from Lebanese emigrants. Net donations have shown a downward tendency over the past two decades. For the years 1955-9 the average was £L86m per year, but the average dropped to £L65m for the period 1960-72.[52] Capital movements, on the other hand, have shown no tendency to drop but have until 1969 hovered on the average around £L306m (the average would be lower but for the year 1965 when capital movements were twice the ordinary volume). However, these movements have averaged £L766.9m for the three years 1970-2. It is significant in this connection that about 70 per cent of these capital inflows is short-term capital, a fact which adds a further note of precariousness. Perhaps the period surveyed (1960-72 in the present context) is not long enough to permit far-reaching conclusions. However, the analysis of factors behind the development of financial and other services in the post-war era, added to the observations made on the balance of payments for the years 1960-72, together indicate the need for serious examination of the prospects of faster development in Lebanon. As this analysis is not designed to lead to the formulation of development policy, only the directions of change needed to cope with the situation will be suggested.

Given the present volume of resources available, the first point to raise is the necessity of restricting growth of consumption. The marginal propensity to consume has kept its level over the years 1964-72, at around 97 per cent of GDP. The most obvious remedy of this high level is taxation. In view of the multiple problem of evasion, under-assessment and refusal to pay taxes by many of the taxable residents[53] — and these are not merely the rich and influential — it is evident that a sizeable shift of resources can be made, via the public sector, from consumption to investment. However, such a shift is not easy to perform, in view of the present socio-political and economic power structure in the country. Hence the need to focus on the social framework while dealing with economic reform.

The next area to look into is the development potential in agriculture and industry, the sectors which have not moved ahead as speedily as most services sectors. The principle underlying attention to these commodity sectors should not be to retard the services sectors in favour of commodity sectors, but to devote more relative attention to agriculture and industry in the expectation of raising their percentage contribution to national product. Here again the pursuit of economic policy is likely to clash with the vested interests of the leaders of the services sectors. And, since the economic structure has been translated into a socio-political (and even a cultural) structure accommodating to the services sectors, strong resistance to policy is most likely to arise. The last direction to suggest itself is the introduction of greater rationality and order into the operation of the current activities and relations in the economy. Here too the reform needed calls for a drastic change in attitude to the government's regulatory role and in the conception and exercise of economic freedom.

Consequently, the avenues of reform aiming at accelerating development, placing it on less precarious ground, and giving it a longer time-horizon, all suggest concrete changes in the socio-political framework. The question then imposes itself as to how the framework can be altered in consistency with the requirements of development, at a time when the framework has an understandable tendency to perpetuate itself. Although an attempt to show how this vicious circle can be broken is beyond the frame of this study, we will put into sharper focus in the concluding section the major issues that have to be contended with urgently.

4. CONCLUDING REMARKS

To say that it is imperative for Lebanon to undertake serious examination of those political, social and economic matters relating directly to its continued development is not at all an over-dramatised judgement. The justification of the insistent tone of this chapter, at least in its last section, will, it is trusted, become clear from the identity and content of the major issues identified in the concluding remarks to the chapter.

If there is one feature that is common to almost all the issues, it is that they have closely intertwined and interacting political, social and economic aspects. One illustration may put the point into relief, particularly that this illustration falls outwardly inside the economic framework. This is the financing of development. The inability of the treasury to bear from its own resources the burden of financing of projects in the public sector has been becoming increasingly obvious and alarming. In fact, since the early sixties when the budget surplus disappeared, the state began to solve its financing problem either through the use of funds in its custody that in fact belong to the municipalities, or through the accommodating slowness in project execution. Though outwardly economic in nature, this problem is also social and political, to the extent that the effective answer ought to have come via increased taxation (better assessment and collection of taxes, even without raising tax rates). But to do so would have run counter to the established interests of the middle and upper classes, whose interests are translated into, or aligned with, political power. Furthermore, tax evasion has become part of the 'social ethic' in general, a popular topic of conversation not untinged with envy by those who are incapable of evading taxes — mainly the salaried in the private and public sectors. This social attitude has also been strengthened by a high propensity to consume in a culture characterised by a strong desire to emulate the consumption patterns of the better-off. It is no wonder, under the circumstances, that the income and related taxes imposed on profits, professional earnings and interest and dividend receipts bring into the treasury hardly 2 per cent of GDP, in spite of some improvements in recent years in assessment and collection. Direct taxes as a group, including income and related taxes, the real estate tax, the tax on the transfer of property and car licences are estimated to provide the treasury with less than 5 per cent of the GDP estimated for 1975.[54]

The other issues are more clearly of mixed nature. We will merely list them and explain their nature where necessary, in order to preserve the conciseness of this conclusion.

1. At the political level the country suffers from indecisiveness and procrastination by government. It is rare for decisive positions to be taken, no matter how important, pressing and even vital the economic issues involved. There are multiple reasons for the defect in decision-making, or — worse still — the inability to take decisions. One of these is the 'political confessionalism' prevailing,[55] whose dictates have to be observed in every decision, even if it is not of major significance. The interests of the various sects and

communities have to be weighed and compared in the process, not only with respect to the economic impact on the communities, but also to the distribution of office-holders connected with the decision at issue among the various communities. Another reason for indecisiveness is the exposure of the executive and the legislature to, and permissiveness toward, the vested interests of the leading groups in the business communities: merchants, industrialists, bankers and the like. Pressure by such groups is experienced in all countries, but in Lebanon it is particularly strong. The 'community of interests' between politicians and businessmen is specially potent and determining in Lebanon.

Lastly, the country lacks the institutions (such as a central economic and social council) which are capable of examining the economic issues that call for a decision and submitting reasoned views and suggestions. This hiatus is exacerbated by the extreme shortage of technicians and economists who can be trusted to provide the decision-makers with advice after serious analysis and objective consideration.

The sum total of these and related factors is extremely damaging socially and economically. Thus, the country now finds itself face to face with a large number of major crises that could have been avoided had they been dealt with as they began to emerge (or, better still, in anticipation). Some of the crises are: water shortages, especially in the capital, the threat of serious shortage in refined petroleum products, serious inadequacy in port facilities, unhygienic slaughter-house facilities, food impurity because of ineffectiveness of sanitary control, scandalously inadequate and inefficient communications — to name only a few.

2. Rising political unrest and instability, especially since 1969,[56] have seriously harmed the economy, inhibited investment, and caused long stoppages in work. The factors behind the unrest and the instability are numerous. In the present writer's view, one of the most damaging is political fragmentation and the near-absence of consensus, even around the most vital issues. This in turn is caused by sectarian and ideological factionalism, the inability to reconcile narrow and short-sighted group interests, and excessive individualism which aborts co-operation among politicians, making them focus on their own particularist interests and political fortunes. Permissiveness by the general public permits the politicians to continue on their course unconcerned with public interest.

3. Inefficiency, corruption and particularist loyalties in the civil service. Again, the causes are multiple and have cumulative effects. To begin with, appointment is influenced (even determined in many instances) by confessional affiliation, not considerations of merit. Furthermore, there is insufficient concern with specialisation and technical aptitude. Relatively low salaries are used in rationalisation of the acceptance of 'presents' from people who have transactions to be concluded — these transactions range from building permits or registration of purchase of property to renewal of car licences, having a telephone installed, or obtaining work permits for non-Lebanese technicians or teachers. Finally, most civil servants owe allegiance to the influential politicians or religious leaders who found them their posts in the first place. The end result of all this is non-concern and slowness of grave dimensions.

4. Social unrest has in recent years become a serious reality inhibiting investment and production. Obviously, strikes are not particular to Lebanon. However, the socio-economic gap between the rich and the poor has become wide and increasingly menacing. The *malaise* has been exacerbated by the very expensive health and education services and the prohibitive rent of decent housing. The working classes feel the burden of the high cost of living (which is often translated into outright deprivation in food, schooling, housing and medical treatment) more painfully because of the opulence which they see around, plus the weak-

ness of social concern in the governing circles. It is true that social and health insurance measures have been introduced, and the government provides free education. Nevertheless, the adequacy and quality of these public services leave a great deal to be desired, while the physical availability of more adequate and better services that the income of the mass of the population makes unobtainable sharpens the sense of bitterness of the poor. (Socio-economic differentiation is all the more explosive since it is tangential in many instances to political differentiation which is in turn associated with sectarian factionalism.)

5. The last issue to be highlighted — and a few more could be added — is the defective approach to development. The sound approach calls for a clear conception of the economic image desired for the country's future, the formulation of a development strategy capable of directing and shaping development efforts, planning in consistency with the image and the strategy, and finally the drawing up of policies and implementation of measures capable of translating development intentions into concrete results.

The country's record in this whole area is very poor. The planning experience to which we referred earlier is minimal.[57] The current plan for the six years 1972-7 is still in fact no more than a listing, with costing estimates, of public sector projects.[58] Though better in quality and of wider coverage than earlier plans, this last plan still falls short even of being an 'indicative plan'. (However, it must be stressed that there is now better co-ordination between the various ministries and the Ministry of Planning in the preparation of projects, and between the Ministry of Planning and the Ministry of Finance with regard to the incorporation in the 'capital budget' part of the general budget of those projects approved by the Ministry of Planning.)

At the root of the present state of affairs lie the basic suspicion and dislike of planning in political decision-making circles, and in the business community at large. The attitude, as we indicated earlier, ranges from disbelief in the developmental value of planning to the belief that it indeed represents 'creeping socialism'. This results in the untypical reaction that even lip-service is denied to planning. It is ironical that a loud outcry against confusion, chaos and failure to provide the basic social and economic amenities to the country at large should run parallel to and coexist with abhorrence of effective planning. The indoctrination (whether suggested or auto-suggested) against planning must be quite deep, and only a radical change in the convictions of the political management of the economy and of the business community can bring about a meaningful shift in the reaction to, and therefore the role of, planning. The present writer can only see the embryonic beginnings of such a change.

These concluding remarks are admittedly gloomy. However, one must not overlook an underlying streak of hope. This is that the intelligence, resilience and resourcefulness of the Lebanese, plus sheer self-interest, may yet before long and before the economy begins a downward dip, make the Lebanese undertake that arduous and lengthy process of radical reform in the political, social and economic realms. Only then can development plus social justice be assured.

NOTES

1. Report prepared by the Office of Statistics of UNESCO, Paris (published by the Regional Center for Educational Planning and Administration, Beirut, Lebanon, 1970), *Comparative Statistical Data on Education in the Arab States: An Analysis: 1960-61 – 1967-68*, Table 1.4, p. 49. A more recent survey of the 'active population in Lebanon' showed that the rate of literacy among those aged 15-24 years was 80.7 per cent for men and 47.1 per cent for women, or some 64 per cent for both sexes. See Republique Libanaise, Direction Centrale de la Statistique, *L'Enquête par Sondage sur la Population Active au Liban Novembre 1970* (Beirut, July 1972), Table 43, p. 88.

2. Albert Y. Badre, 'The National Income of Lebanon', *Middle East Economic Papers, 1956 (MEEP)*, (Beirut, 1956), p. 13.

3. Republique Libanaise, Ministère du Plan, Direction Centrale de la Statistique, *Recueil de Statistiques Libanaise, 1968* for the years 1964-68, and *Recueil... 1973*, for the latter years through 1972.

4. *Recueil... 1969*, p. 52. However, the same source lists the 'registered population' at the end of 1964 as 2,367, 141 (p. 56).

5. Ibid., p. 59.

6. The results of the survey were published by the Direction Centrale de la Statistique under the title *L'Enquête par Sondage sur la Population Active au Liban, Novembre 1970* (Beirut, July 1972), in two volumes. (See Vol. 1, pp. 59-60). The main results are reproduced in *Recueil... 1973*, pp. 72-103.

7. For yet another estimate of population, see UN Economic and Social Office in Beirut, UNESOB, 'Demographic Characteristics of Youth in the Arab Countries of the Middle East: Present Situation and Growth Prospects, 1970-1990', in *Studies on Selected Development Problems in Various Countries of the Middle East, 1970*, (Beirut, 1970), p. 73. UNESOB's estimate is 2.6m on 1 January 1970.

8. *Recueil... 1969*, p. 54. Elsewhere, the rate is stated as 2.3 per cent. See Institut de Recherches et du Formation en Vue de Développement Harmonisé (IRFED), 'Etude et Documents' series *Le Liban face à son développement* (condensation of first study by IRFED on the economy of Lebanon 1960-1), p. 209. The discrepancy is all the more puzzling since the original study under reference quotes a rate of 2.7 per cent. See Mission IRFED, *Besoins et possibilités de développement du Liban, 1960-1961*, which is the study condensed, as indicated above. (However, Albert Badre supports a rate of population increase of 2.4 per cent in his essay 'Economic Development of Lebanon' in Charles A. Cooper and Sidney S. Alexander (eds.), *Economic Development and Population Growth in the Middle East* (New York, 1972), pp. 184-5.)

9. *Recueil... 1973*, p. 327. For the conversion rate of Lebanese pounds to US dollars, see *IFS*, December 1974. We must add here that the rate of exchange improved considerably in favour of the Lebanese pound: from £L3.02 to one dollar in 1972, to £L2.27 in 1974. This accounts for the much higher rate in *per capita* NNP in dollars than in pounds over the period under examination, 1950-74. (In 1950 the rate was £L3.47 to the dollar.)

10. Ibid., p. 247, for consumers' price index for Beirut. According to this index, prices rose by 6 per cent between 1972 and 1973. According to the Direction Centrale de la Statistique, *Bulletin Statistique Mensuel*, December 1974 (pp. 78-79), average rise in the index was 11 per cent in 1974 over 1973 (from 121.7 to 135.2 points). Thus, total price rise for 1973 and 1974 was 17 per cent, plus an assumed real growth of 10 per cent, add up to an increase in NNP of 27 per cent at current prices. (It must be pointed out that the price rise is overestimated to the extent that it reflects conditions in the capital where life is much more expensive than in the countryside. On the other hand, it is authoritatively believed that the composition and weighting system of the index number tend to underestimate price rises. These two opposing factors have been assumed here to cancel each other out.)

11. *Recueil... 1973*, p. 245.

12. Projections were made by Albert Y. Badre, the Economic Division of the US Embassy in Beirut, and the IRFED Mission. See Emile Ghattas, *The Monetary System in Lebanon* (Beirut, 1968; Arabic), p. 39.

13. Those receiving relief from the United Nations relief agencies were recorded as numbering 131,100 on 1 January 1949. However, the number was reduced to 106,753 by June 1951, after re-checking and removal of duplications was achieved. See UN, *Assistance to Palestine Refugees: Report of the Director of the United Nations Relief and Works Agency for Palestine Refugees in the Near East* (General Assembly, Official Records: Sixth Session, Supplement No. 16 (A/1905), Paris, 1951), p. 3.

14. This survey of the economy's performance from 1946 (or, more appropriately, 1950) onwards suffers from the paucity of serious studies of wide spread. Being a resident in Lebanon since 1949 has helped the writer obtain a great deal of information, and reach a number of assessments, on the basis of direct experience. In addition, recourse has been had to the following studies: (a) Sir Alexander Gibb and Partners, *The Development of Lebanon* (London, 1948); (b) Doreen Warriner, *Land and Poverty in the Middle East* (London, 1948); (c) Royal Institute for International Affairs, *The Middle East: A Political and Economic Survey* (Oxford University Press, 1958, third edition), chapter on Lebanon; (d) FAO Mediterranean Development Project, *Lebanon: Country Report* (Rome, 1959, Report prepared by Albert Y. Badre for FAO); (e) Development Studies Association, *Modern Concepts of Development in Lebanon* (Beirut, 1966; Arabic; a collection of essays); (f) Development Studies Association, *Financial Resources and Development in Lebanon* (Beirut, 1967; Arabic; a collection of essays); (g) General Union of Chambers of Commerce, Industry, and Agriculture in the Arab Countries, *Economic Development in the Arab Countries, 1950-1965* (Beirut, 1967; Arabic); (h) General Union..., *Arab Economic Report*, an annual publication, the most recent of which was published in 1974; (i) Nadim G. Khalaf, *Economic Implications of the Size of Nations, with Special Reference to Lebanon* (Leiden, 1971), especially Part Two, Chs. VI-X; (j) Albert Y. Badre, 'Economic

Development of Lebanon', in Cooper and Alexander (eds.), op. cit.; and (k) Europa Publications, *The Middle East and North Africa 1971-72*, as well as subsequent issues for *1972-73, 1973-74*, and *1974-75* (London, respectively 1971, 1972, 1973 and 1974), chapter on Lebanon.

15. See Yusif A. Sayigh, *Entrepreneurs of Lebanon: The Role of the Business Leader in a Developing Economy* (Harvard University Press, Cambridge, 1962), Ch. 4.

16. Republic of Lebanon, Ministry of Planning, Planning and Development Board, *Five-Year Programme for Economic Development in Lebanon* (Beirut, 1958; Arabic).

17. President Fouad Chéhab, former Commander-in-Chief of the Army, took over in September 1958 from President Camille Chamoun, who in turn had succeeded President Bechara al Khouri — Lebanon's first President since independence in 1943.

18. Regarding the speedy growth of the banking sector, see Ghattas, op. cit., especially Ch. 3. See also Lebanese Republic, Currency and Credit Board, 'Currency and Credit Law-Explanatory Note', published in *An-Nahar* (Beirut daily), Special Issue on Banks in Lebanon, 1 July 1963 (Arabic). Growth in industry is best brought out by a comparison of the results of two industrial censuses conducted in 1955 and 1964: Ministry of National Economy, *Industrial Census 1955* (Beirut, 1957); and Direction Centrale de la Statistique, *Recensement de l'Industrie au Liban: Résultats pour 1964* (Beirut, 1967).

See also Mustapha Nsouli, *Towards a Better Future for Lebanese Industry* (Beirut, 1968; Arabic), chapter dealing with 'Industrial Situation in Lebanon', pp. 3-32. Nsouli quotes data obtained from the Industry Department of the Ministry of National Economy indicating that there were 1,412 industrial establishments in 1950 with a declared capital of £L161m, against 6,138 establishments in 1965, with a declared capital of £L869m (p. 33). (Aggregate industrial capital in 1973 has been estimated at £L2,000m. See General Union of Chambers of Commerce, Industry..., *Arab Economic Report*, 1974 issue; Arabic; p. 473.)

19. IRFED, *Besoins et possibilités de développement du Liban* (Beirut, 1961), 3 vols, I II and Annex.

20. Particularly Kamal Jumblatt, respected deputy and many times minister, and his Progressive Socialist Party; the '22 November Club', a group of 'Young Turks' eager for socio-economic reform who formed themselves into an intellectual pressure group and who supported President Chéhab's reformist ideas and measures; as well as a number of reformist individuals.

21. The Plan was first decreed by Law 7277 of 7 August 1961, and later extended by Law 14/65 of 17 February 1965. For final version, see Ministry of Planning, *Five-Years Development Plan for the Years 1965-1969*, approved by the Council of Ministries on 21 April 1965 (Beirut, n.d.; Arabic).

22. Nicolas Sarkis, 'The Energy Crisis and the Challenge of Development in the Arab Countries', Paper No. 132 (A-1) submitted to the Ninth Arab Petroleum Congress held at Dubai, 10-16 March 1975, Table 2, p. 17.

23. *Bulletin Statistique Mensuel*, December 1974, p. 51, for end of 1974; and *Recueil*... *1963*, p. 198, for end of 1950.

24. The proportion of deposits owned by non-residents by the end of 1966 was estimated as ranging between 50 and 66 per cent of the total. See Yusif A. Sayigh and Mohammad Atallah, *A Second Look at the Lebanese Economy* (Beirut, 1966; Arabic), pp. 83-4.

25. Ibid., pp. 21-2 for the proportion in 1965. The proportion for the following 13 countries averaged 36 per cent for 1965: United States, Canada, Britain, Holland, Switzerland, France, Federal Germany, Italy, Greece, Turkey, Kuwait, India and Thailand. (These were selected as a fair sample of countries representing different levels of economic and banking activities.)

26. The discussion of aggregate and *per capita* real growth in Badre, loc. cit., pp. 178 ff, would leave the reader with the impression that I underestimate the rate of real growth. Indeed, physical indications of prosperity in Lebanon suggest that Badre's higher estimate is more warranted. However, to cede the point is to contend that the price level did not rise by 3 per cent per annum on the average, as I estimate it, but by 2 per cent, between 1950 and 1972. However, I cannot accept such a contention, nor is it accepted by those officials of the Ministry of Planning who work on the preparation of price indices (wholesale and consumer).

27. F. H. Harbison and C. A. Myers, *Education, Manpower and Economic Growth* (New York, 1964). The top category among developing countries is Level III, Level IV being reserved for 'Advanced Countries'.

28. Frederick H. Harbison, Joan Maruhnick, and James R. Resnick, *Quantitative Analyses of Modernization and Development* (Princeton, 1970), various tables (quotation from p. 61).

29. See Bruce M. Russett and H. R. Alker, K. W. Deutsch and H. D. Lasswell, *World Handbook of Political and Social Indicators* (New Haven, 1964), for ranking of countries with respect to a very large number of indicators.

30. Irma Adelman and Cynthia Taft Morris, *Society, Politics and Economic Development: A Quantitative Approach* (Baltimore, 1967), Ch. II.

31. For the estimate for 1958, see General Union of Chambers of Commerce..., *Economic Development in the Arab Countries, 1950-1965*, pp. 439-40. The more recent estimate relates to 1968 and is recorded in FAO, *Production Yearbook 1973*, p. 5.

32. *Recueil de Statistiques Libanaises 1973*, p. 161. The information on the Litani project is obtained mostly from the Litani Authority itself, in interviews late in 1974.

33. FAO, *Production Yearbook 1973*, pp. 26-32.

34. *Recueil*... *1973*, p. 337.

35. For many years, balance-of-payments estimates and analysis were undertaken by the Economic Research Institute of the American University of Beirut, on contract with the Ministry of Planning. However, this task has been taken over since 1968 by the Directorate of Statistics.

36. See Badre, loc. cit. (pp. 170-3) for his interesting differentiation between the degrees of 'sensitivity' of Arab and non-Arab tourists to political instability.

37. Data obtained from *Recueil*... *1973*, 'Health' and 'Education', pp. 340-75.

38. The *Recueil... 1973* only has information on the Lebanese (state) university. Data on the other universities have been obtained from their respective authorities.

39. This general review of sectoral developments and issues has benefited from interviews with several authoritative persons in government and in the private sector, as well as the perusal of relevant source material (other than items listed in note 14 above) such as: (a) Fawzi M. Al-Haj and Salah M. Yacoub, 'Factors Affecting Adoption of New Agricultural Techniques in Lebanese Agriculture', in Cooper and Alexander (eds.)., op. cit.; (b) Mustapha Nsouli, op. cit.; (c) Elias S. Saba, *The Foreign Exchange Systems of Lebanon and Syria 1939-1957* (Beirut, 1961); (d) Elias S. Saba, 'Lebanon's Banking Problems: I', *The Bankers' Magazine*, June 1967, and 'Lebanon's Banking Problems: II', in ibid., July 1967; (e) Ghattas, op. cit.; (f) Samir Khalaf, 'Adaptive Modernization: the Case for Lebanon', in Cooper and Alexander (eds.), op. cit.; and (g) Elie Salem, *Modernization Without Revolution: Lebanon's Experience* (Bloomington, Ind., 1973).

40. For a discussion of the 'relative national product per worker', RNPW, see Simon Kuznets, 'Quantitative Aspects of the Economic Growth of Nations: II. Industrial Distribution of National Product and Labour Force', in *Economic Development and Cultural Change*, Supplement to Vol. V, No. 4, July 1957, especially pp. 5-16, 36, 41 and 44. (See note 20 in 'Jordan' chapter for other references to writings on the same subject by B. S. Yamey, Colin Clark and A. G. B. Fisher.) (The RNPW is obtained by dividing a sector's share in GDP by its share in the labour force. The higher the ratio thus obtained, the greater the welfare of workers in the sector, other things being equal.)

41. Quoted by A. J. Meyer, 'Economic Thought and its Applications and Methodology in the Middle East', in *Middle East Economic Papers 1956*, p. 74.

42. The question, and implications, of the external sector have received attention from a few writers who all based themselves on the initial findings of Albert Badre (in *MEEP 1956*) regarding the predominance of services in the economic structure. For various aspects of the structure, see: (a) Yusif A. Sayigh, 'Lebanon: Special Economic Problems Arising from a Special Structure', in *MEEP 1957*, pp. 60-88; (b) Yusif A. Sayigh, *Entrepreneurs of Lebanon: The Role of the Business Leader in A Developing Economy* (1962), Ch. 1; (c) Elias S. Saba, 'The Implications of the Foreign Sector in the Lebanese Economy', in *MEEP 1962*, pp. 140-54; (d) Yusif A. Sayigh and Mohammad Atallah, *A Second Look at the Lebanese Economy* (Beirut, 1966; Arabic), Chs. 1 and 2; (e) Emile Ghattas, *The Monetary System of Lebanon*, ... (1968), Ch. 2; (f) 'Prospective Growth and Development of the Lebanese Economy', in UNESOB, *Studies of Selected Development Problems ..., 1970*, pp. 1-32. (M. A. Diab served as consultant for the preparation of the study, which provides a rigorous quantitative examination of the problem of structure and its implications for development); and (g) Albert Y. Badre, in Cooper and Alexander (eds.), op. cit., Ch. 4.

43. Sayigh and Atallah, op. cit., pp. 16-17.

44. The number of casual visitors who came for brief visits (i.e. not as residents) was 1.9m in 1973. *(Recueil... 1973*, p. 69). Obviously, only a small fraction of these spent three days and over in the country. Those who qualify as tourists either stay in hotels or rent furnished apartments. (Hotel beds numbered 28,835 in 1973. Ibid., p. 237.) It is estimated that some 600,000 non-Lebanese reside in the country, although many of these do not hold residence permits. The number includes some 350,000 Palestinian refugees, at least 100,000 Syrians, and some 60,000 non-Arabs. However, the manpower survey of November 1970, to which we have referred more than once, records only 286,350 non-Lebanese residents, excluding Palestinian refugees in camps who number about 100,000. (Ibid., p. 85.)

45. Sayigh and Atallah, op. cit., pp. 16-27.

46. Ibid., pp. 41-52, for an examination of the weaknesses of the structure of the Lebanese economy.

47. This last instance was reported in *An-Nahar* (Beirut Arabic daily) on 26 April 1971.

48. Sayigh, *MEEP 1957*, pp. 86-7.

49. See *Recueil... 1973*, pp. 337 and 381, for trade and balance-of-payments data.

50. *IFS*, October 1975.

51. See UNESOB, *Studies on Development Problems ... 1970*, pp. 1-32, for a thorough examination of this point in its broad context.

52. For the years 1955-59, see Ghattas, p. 52; for 1960-72, see *Recueil ...*, several issues ending with that for 1973, under 'Comptabilité nationale', tables on 'Compte de l'extérieur'.

53. See *The Daily Star* (Beirut daily), Sunday Supplement on 25 April 1971, for an interview with the Minister of Finance in which he emphasised the problem. According to him the many millions of income tax arrears, though a serious matter, pose less serious a problem than continued under-assessment of taxable income.

54. It is useful to review the annual report introducing the budget, issued by the Ministry of Finance under the title *Preamble to the Draft Budget for the Year ...* This publication comprises a brief survey of economic developments in the country, and ends with data on past budget performance and the budget estimates for the year ahead. (The *Preamble* for 1975 has many major printing errors in the tables. However, the calculations referred to in the text are based on corrected budget data.)

55. In this connection, see Sayigh in *MEEP 1957*.

56. See Albert Y. Badre in Cooper and Alexander (eds.), op. cit., with respect to political strains.

57. See George G. Corm, *Politique économique et planification au Liban 1953-1963* (Beirut, 1964).

58. Ministry of Planning, *The Six-Years Development Plan for the Years 1972-1977* (Beirut, 1970; Arabic).

8 EGYPT

The period 1952-75 has witnessed the most far-reaching transformation in Egypt's economy and society. In spite of the fact that a few countries, such as Kuwait, have seen immense economic and social change over the same period, Egypt's case, like that of only one other Arab country — Algeria — is specially noteworthy in the sense that the change has not only been considerable, but it has also occurred on several fronts: from the technological and economic to the social and political. It has been qualitative on each of these fronts, not merely quantitative. This is true in spite of some major political setbacks that have seriously slowed down the pace of progress.

Most writers on the development of the post-war Egyptian economy have emphasised the decade preceding the *coup d'état* as the backdrop to the *coup*. This *coup*, which on 23 July 1952 swept the monarch away from power and brought in the strong man of the *coup*, Gamal Abdul-Nasser, has irreversibly changed the course of Egypt's socio-political and economic evolution and structures. On the other hand, the conditions characterising the period between the end of the war and the *coup* condense in themselves the economic, social and political grievances which inevitably led to the eruption of 1952. And most writers agree that in few other Arab countries — indeed in few other Third World countries — has a *coup d'état* approached being a revolution as in Egypt.

This chapter will not attempt to describe the transformation sector by sector and institution by institution; that would be not only tedious reading but tedious writing as well. So much indeed has happened, particularly in the first fifteen years, that the chapter would grow out of proportion in size if the approach were to be chronological and descriptive. Although there will be some history and some description, basically what is being sought is a comprehensive understanding of the nature and directions of, and reasons for transformation in the structure of the economy, the social system, and in development broadly defined. As such, the chapter will not even try to compete in coverage or in the detailed and thorough examination of the Egyptian economy with what the better-known works on Egypt have attempted and achieved.

1. THE BACKDROP TO THE REVOLUTION

Charles Issawi, in his book *Egypt in Revolution,* aptly entitles the chapter dealing with the background to the revolution 'Accumulating Difficulties, 1920-1952'.[1] This period saw the gathering clouds thicken with ominous and almost inescapable inevitability until the storm broke out. The bare and simple elements of the process of accumulation of difficulties need only brief recording and explanation.

By the middle of the century, the country was getting gradually but relentlessly overcrowded, given the level of technology at the close of the war and the usable resources available to society. With its population of 19 million in 1974, Egypt had at its disposal 5.8 million *feddans* of land, or 2.436 million hectares,[2] which represented just 2.4 per cent of the total area of 1m sq. km. (100m ha). Admittedly, this area of cultivable *and* cultivated land was fertile and all irrigated, and annually received the Nile's generous gift of silt during the flood period. Yet the rate at which the land was being exhausted through continuous cropping, mostly twice a year and to a certain extent three times a year, almost cancelled out the effect of the Nile's gift and that of the increasing recourse to chemical fertilisers. Though the population was not all rural, the proportion which was — some 60-65 per cent, depending on the definition of urban centres adopted — meant that between 11.4 and 12.4 million rural inhabitants relied most heavily, if not solely, on agricultural activities and income for their living. In addition, there were all those in the urban centres who worked in sectors and activities directly related to the trade in and storage and financing of cotton, Egypt's main crop and source of income of government revenue, and of foreign exchange. Thus, if we were to take an intermediate figure of 12 million inhabitants as representing the direct pressure on land resources, there would only be 0.203 hectares per person, or one hectare per family of five.

Compared with the period preceding World War One, when a population of 12 million (of whom some 8.5 million were rural) shared 5.3 million *feddans* or 2.226 million ha, and the land ratio was therefore 0.262 ha per person or 1.310 ha per family, the ratio in 1952 showed a clearly greater pressure of population on land resources. Specifically, the ownership situation worsened by 23 per cent in 35 years. The process has continued, so that in 1971, despite the extension of the area irrigated by over 33 per cent (let alone the transfer of more land from basin to perennial irrigation, which is not strictly relevant to the argument) the ratio of land to rural inhabitant was no more than 0.168 ha or 0.840 ha per family of five. In turn, this represents a further worsening of the situation between 1947 and 1971 by 18 per cent in 25 years. (If account were not to be taken of the expansion in irrigated land, then a family's share would be a mere 0.63 ha or 38 per cent below the area in 1947.)

However, such statements must be qualified in two ways. First, with respect to the fact that the area actually cropped is more than double the area irrigated and cultivated, thanks to the ability of the land to grow two, and in some cases, three crops a year. Second, with respect to the use of inputs and to technical advances. Thus over the decades, between the turn of the century and the end of World War Two, the land gained in productivity, thanks to the availability of more water and the acquisition of more rational practices in water use, to the intensification of the use of pesticides, fertilisers and improved seeds, to greater mechanisation, and to the availability of more advanced technical and extension services.

On the other side of the account, there has been growing fragmentation of ownerships, which meant that many thousands of owners had (and still have) less than the average ratio, and many thousands of peasants owned no land at all. Furthermore, productivity per labourer was not rising noticeably before the revolution, because of labour pressure on land on the one hand, and on the other because the peasants had reached the peak of their capability, given their training and methods of cultivation. Thus, the relentlessness of Malthusian and Ricardian realities meant a stagnation or even a decline in real wages, while rents and profits were getting larger. Many indicators substantiate these statements, which are now so well established that there is no further need for repeating the empirical evidence here.

To this must be added the extreme and dangerous dependence on one crop: cotton. Cotton accounted for about half of agricultural production, for a quarter to a third of cropped area, and for 75-80 per cent of exports.

Egypt

This was not all. Other sectors outside agriculture, though making good progress, were not moving fast enough to make up for the population pressure, and to counteract the unusually large volume of unemployment and disguised unemployment in the economy as a whole. Industry — which had received increased attention and capital funds after World War One, further support subsequent to the founding in 1920 of Bank Misr which made serious efforts to promote manufacturing industry, and much greater impetus upon the cancellation of the 'capitulations' system in 1930 after which the government could impose protective tariffs for the benefit of infant industries — was still of modest dimensions both as an employer of labour and a contributor to national product. (Industry in 1950 absorbed 250,000 labourers, had a capital estimated at £E66 million*, and contributed 12 per cent of GDP.) The other sectors — trade, finance, professional services, tourism, construction — all registered tangible growth, but again remained in the aggregate incapable of solving the massive problems of the countryside or of seriously changing the structure of the economy away from excessive dependence on agriculture for employment and contribution to national product.

The one indicator which sums up these various, and sometimes clashing, trends is national income. There is not a single very reliable series of national accounts among the several attempted. As Issawi says, 'Post-war estimates range from 504 million and 600 million in 1945 to 860 million in 1950.' Furthermore,

> a series prepared by the National Planning Committee put gross domestic product at market prices at £E193 million in 1938, 660 million in 1945 and 858 million in 1950; at 1950 prices, the figures were £E634 million, 688 million and 858 million respectively.[3]

Indeed, Hansen and Marzouk estimate national income at current market prices at £E183 million for 1939 and 528 million for 1945. (At constant 1939 prices, the figure is £E183 million for both years respectively, which suggests no change at all between 1939 and 1945, or a declining national income *per capita* of about 2.5 per cent per annum — probably a conservative estimate since it is now thought that population was growing after the war at 2.8 or 2.9 per cent compound rate.) For better comparison, we will take Hansen and Marzouk's[4] estimates of real gross domestic product at 1954 prices for the years 1945 to 1952 and set them against those of the NPC. The set of estimates by Hansen and Marzouk is £E719 million for 1945, 956 for 1950, and 1,004 for 1952. If we forget about the difference of the base year (1950 in the NPC set; 1954 in the latter set), and look at the change between 1945 and 1950, and compare that change with change in population, we would come out with the results shown in Table 8.1. These figures show a reasonably high rate of growth *per capita* between 1945 and 1950, though the latter set of data shows a substantially higher rate than the NPC set.

However, the situation changed considerably from 1950 to 1954. Again according to Hansen and Marzouk, whose authoritative work commands respect for its thoroughness and responsibility, GDP at 1954 prices rose as already indicated, from £E956 million for 1950 to 1,004 million for 1952 and 1,023 million for 1954. With 1950 as base year (= 100), 1952 and 1954 would be 105 and 107 respectively. Against this 7 per cent rise in GDP in real terms between 1950 and 1954, the population rose by at least 7.5 per cent, which clearly suggests a decline in *per capita* GDP. This trend finds support in the references in Issawi to the estimates by El Sherbini and Sherif, who put *per capita* annual income, at

*Egyptian pounds.

Table 8.1: Two Estimates of Indicators of Growth, 1945-50 (per cent)

Growth in GDP between 1945 and 1950, NPC data	24.7
Compound annual rate of growth over period	4.5
Compound annual rate of population increase over period, at least	2.5
Per capita annual rate of growth in GDP 1945-50, about	2.0
Growth in GDP 1945-50, Hansen and Marzouk data	33.0
Compound annual rate of growth over period, almost	6.0
Per capita annual rate of growth 1945-50	3.4

1913 prices, at £E9.6 on the average for 1935-9 and £E9.4 on the average for the years 1940-9. Elsewhere, Issawi attributes to a third Eygptian economist, A. Hosni, the finding that *per capita* income at constant 1954 prices moved from £E34.8 for the average of the years 1937-9 to 34.5 for the years 1951-3, to 38.8 for the years 1954-6.[5]

The discrepancy for the decade preceding 1950 between Hansen and Marzouk's data and NPC data quoted by Issawi is considerable, the results ranging as they do from a reasonably appreciable rate of increase of 2–3.4 per cent *per capita* to a decline of a fraction of 1 per cent per annum. However, closer scrutiny would reveal that the discrepancy relates essentially to the half decade immediately following the war, or the years 1945-50. Between 1950 and 1952 there is no disagreement with regard to the trend or to the volume of decline in *per capita* income of GDP. There seems to be near unanimity among careful students of the Egyptian economy that the two or three years preceding the July 1952 revolution had witnessed a drop in *per capita* income and level of living of the Egyptian masses — an income and a level that had already been extremely low.

Thus, on the eve of the revolution, the claim that Egypt was weighed down by its three enemies: 'poverty, illiteracy and disease' was as real and crippling as it was rhetorical in the mouths of popular orators. These 'enemies' were stronger and more firmly entrenched than British occupation, which was to end in 1955. As many underdeveloped countries were to discover in the post-war period, occupation by a foreign colonialist was much easier to remove than socio-cultural and economic ills, and political liberation much simpler to achieve than socio-cultural and economic liberation. In the specific case of Egypt, the colonialist rulers and foreign interests that were jealously and effectively guarded by British and other European and Levantine nationals, had allied themselves in a cohesive web of relations (sanctioned and protected by certain powerful Egyptian politicians and some privileged groups — naturally partners in the lucrative benefits) in a manner worthy of the clearest Marxist analysis and its harshest condemnation.

The alliance was a long-standing one, coming down at least from the second half of the nineteenth century. It reached far to cover almost all sectors, including in its coverage land ownership, operation, reclamation and development; the hotel business; trade and banking; insurance; the financing, ginning and export of the cotton crop; public utilities; and even the press. Nowhere in the eastern Arab world (the Mashreq) — indeed nowhere in the whole Arab world — was such an alliance as strong and penetrating, or the foreign interests as powerful and firmly supported by equally highly placed nationals.

'National capitalism' on the whole, especially outside the field of industry — that is, in the services sectors — was a junior partner in most of the big enterprises. The present writer examined the Companies' *Directory* for 1945 in 1946, scrutinised the names of company directors, and found that the identifiably Egyptian Arab names were no more than 15 per cent of the total. Issawi did the same for 1951 and found the Egyptian (Moslem and Copt) component to be 35 per cent, while 65 per cent were Europeans, Greeks, Armenians, Syrians or Lebanese, and religious minorities.[6] (Many of these presumably had Egyptian passports.) This phenomenon could not have continued for many generations without the protection and shelter of the political system. And the system would not have provided its protection without receiving its share in the exploitative profits made. Last, the political system, or its leading architects, supporters, or spokesmen and representatives could not disguise the association and as a result roused the anger and often the violence of the masses and of certain opposition politicians and parties.

The national resistance to this process often became a 'new class' itself, and ultimately built up its vested interests and got its due share of the spoils. The Palace was neither slow nor inept in helping this process of corrupting initially clean politicians, with honours, land or money — or with power, which would in turn translate itself into the first three instruments of corruption. Admittedly, there were many politicians who were not corrupt, but they were either few in number at any one time, or divided among themselves, or else they had corrupt secretaries or friends or sons-in-law who smeared them in due course. But the phenomenon of a powerful politician who was not also wealthy was very rare indeed.

The privileged groups, as we have indicated, had their economic wealth spread over several sectors and types of wealth. But the largest common form was land ownership. As we will have occasion to see in quantitative terms when we come to discuss land reform, on the eve of this reform a very small number of landowners, about 5,300, representing one-fifth of 1 per cent of the total number of landowners, owned over 25 per cent of the land. What is more significant at this point is to indicate the counterpoint to this fact, namely that 94 per cent of landowners, with an average ownership of 0.824 of an acre or 0.35 of a hectare, among themselves owned just over one-third of the land — 35.5 per cent, to be exact. This contrast is too eloquent to need to be elaborated on, and it typified the lopsidedness in socio-economic and political structure.[7]

The lopsidedness was manifest in the existence of a tiny numerical minority holding a disproportionately massive slice of power and of wealth, and a huge majority with a fraction of land and very little wealth outside of land, as well as very little effective power, and of a rather large middle class which was much less powerful than its numbers would normally suggest. For the situation in the rural community was not reversed or corrected in the urban centres, where the industrial proletariat was small, weak and poor. The army of small government officials was so poorly paid (though probably not so in view of their low average productivity), and so insecure and dependent on their jobs because of the ferocious competition for jobs in a labour-surplus economy that they could not be counted upon as a pressure mechanism for reform. The rest of the urban workers, no matter in what sector they were, stood equally at the mercy of the employers' political and/or material power, and were compliant to the point of obsequiousness.

This explains the reason why economic power in the hands of the privileged groups translated itself into political power. How it was translated was through the mechanism of outward democracy — a parliamentary system where the large mass of electors, especially in the countryside, voted the way the Bey or Pasha wanted them to and put him in or returned him to power, thus consolidating and perpetuating his grip over them via his withholding or granting of employment and income. As President Nasser was to say in many speeches later on,[8] and as was to be argued in *The Charter* of June 1962,[9] true political democracy could not come about without true economic and social democracy. That is, the man in the street could not participate adequately in political life and decision-making through his vote unless his economic conditions were better and more secure, his share in the national product was more equitable, his standard of literacy was reasonably high, and his social status was more respectable and dignified as a human being. This, obviously, the privileged classes were not eager to bring about: they could not be expected to themselves pull the rug from under their own feet by introducing anything more than tightly rationed measures of economic and social reform.

To the combination of the interests of the British, and the vested interests of strong foreign communities, and those of the Egyptian bourgeoisie, was thus added the poverty and powerlessness of the masses of Egyptians, in turn reinforced and perpetuated by their illiteracy and dependence on the privileged classes. The pattern and structure were not unique to Egypt, but rather appeared there in exaggerated form. The process was cumulative and forged a vicious circle which could not be broken by very mild and very slow reform from *within* the system. The sledge-hammer of a *coup d'état* was necessary.

Three indicators ought to be mentioned to provide substance to the claim of the helplessness of Egyptian masses. The GDP, as we have indicated in quoting the figures of Hansen and Marzouk, was some £E1,004 million for 1952. On the assumption of a population of 21.6 million[10] at the end of 1952, GDP *per capita* would be in the neighbourhood of £E46.7 at 1954 prices. Hosni's estimates, also already referred to, placed national income per head for the years 1951-3 at an average of £E34.5. Whichever series is adopted, the fact remains that the average Egyptian was very poor. For the average in itself is very misleading, considering the wide disparity in income distribution in Egypt before the revolution. Thus, with a very large slice of the national product in the hands of the privileged classes, and with the land ownership pattern being what we have indicated, the bulk of the population which lived in the countryside, and the millions of poor urban Egyptians, could not have approximated the average income and must have lived on a much lower income per head at a near-subsistence level.

Second, there were severe diseases which beset and debilitated the poor Egyptian masses; these diseases were caused both because of malnutrition and because of the conditions of work and living. Contagion was (and is, but less so) very easy owing to the crowded living facilities, and because of the sheer inadequacy of sanitary facilities. Thus, the most serious of the endemic diseases, bilharziasis, was caused by the disease-carrying snail which penetrated the skin and entered the bodies of millions of Egyptians who spent long hours in the irrigation canals for performing their agricultural work, and who in turn sent the worms back into the canals, because whether there was sewerage or not, human refuse found its way back to the canals, completing the transmission cycle of the disease. Trachoma was another serious widespread disease, as well as tuberculosis and malaria.

Third, illiteracy. According to a study by UNESCO, illiteracy stayed at practically the same level between 1947 and 1960 — some 74 or 75 per cent for the adult population aged 15-24 (65 per cent for males and 83-4 per cent for females). It would probably be wrong to compare 1947 with 1960, if only because the earlier estimate was most probably less reliable than the latter estimate. As a rough estimate, therefore, it can be said that illiteracy prevailed among three-quarters of those aged 15-24 in the year 1952 — a very high level indeed. (This was exceeded for 1952 in Algeria, Libya, Morocco, Saudi Arabia, Sudan, Tunisia and Yemen[11] — all countries which represent 'special cases', either because of their more marked backwardness or late independence.) The illiteracy rates in Egypt again constituted a sharp contrast with the relatively large reservoir of highly educated persons side by side with the illiterates. Some 7 per cent of the labour force, or 750,000

Egypt

persons, had intermediate — second-level — diplomas and university degrees. Diploma and degree-holders in 1952 constituted a social problem arising from the ambition of their expectations for jobs which they considered commensurate with their education and their search for status, their insistence on desk 'white-collar' jobs, and the relative modesty of opportunities and of the remuneration attaching to job opportunities available.

As a last component of the background to the revolution, we will record three tables, the first of which sets down gross national product and income for the years 1945-54, as presented by Hansen and Marzouk, the second the industrial origin of GDP for 1947 and 1952, and the third the occupational distribution of Egyptians and foreigners in 1947, according to the *Population Census, 1947*.[12]

The structure of GDP which emerges from this table will now be described. The years 1947 and 1952 will be singled out, the first because there is a parallel occupational distribution for that year, and the second because it was the year of the revolution. The GDP according to industrial origin is shown in Table 8.3 in percentages.

This structure shows that the commodity-producing sectors accounted in 1952 for half the GDP, and that agriculture alone accounted for one-third of GDP. A more interesting observation is that industry, even as far back as the end of World War Two, contributed over one-eighth of GDP, which is a ratio unparalleled anywhere else in the Arab world. The second place in the whole structure was occupied in the post-war period by the combined sector of commerce and finance, but if this sector were to be disaggregated, then industry would occupy that position. It would be interesting to compare the distribution of GDP according to industrial origin with the distribution of the labour force among the sectors, as it appears in Table 8.4. This comparison reveals the 'relative sectoral product per worker', which is obtained by dividing the sector's contribution to national product by the proportion of the labour force engaged in that sector. The results of such a calculation appear in the last column of Table 8.4.

This table should not be accorded great significance, since it includes all residents in Egypt above five years of age. Consequently the 16.4 million shown above are by no means the labour force, or manpower, as it is conventionally defined. None the less, there is a clear if rough indication of the general structure of the labour force, and of the relative sectoral product per worker. In other words, the commodity-producing sectors employed just over one-half of manpower, and they contributed a little over half GDP for the same year (54.4 per cent to be exact). Agriculture alone accounted for 46 per cent of employed manpower; it certainly also comprised the largest component of the items designated 'ill-defined and unproductive' and 'unoccupied persons'.

A comparison between Tables 8.3 and 8.4 reveals that persons engaged in commerce and finance had the highest return per person as a group, inasmuch as the discrepancy between their share in manpower employed and contribution to GDP was the widest. Other sectors where the returns were comparatively high (i.e. share of GDP was higher than share in employment) were transport and communication, construction and manufacturing. The other items are not easily comparable because of difference in nomenclature and presumably in definition.

To bring some of the darker features of the background of the revolution into relief is not to deny that the government had made some efforts, before 1952, even if slowly and modestly, to develop the country and to equip it with certain important institutions. Indeed, on the eve of the revolution, Egypt was better equipped in many respects relevant to development than most if not all the other Arab countries. Some illustrations before

Table 8.2: Gross National Product and Income 1945-54 (£E million at constant 1954 prices, unless otherwise stated)[a]

Sector	1945	1946	1947	1948	1949	1950	1951	1952	1953	1954	Average annual rate of change compound per cent		
											1945-51	1951-4	1945-54
Agriculture	303	302	299	328	325	303	304	334	315	312	0.0	0.9	0.3
Industry and electricity	91	92	101	113	126	133	132	132	134	146	6.4	3.4	5.4
Construction	19	22	25	31	25	22	36	30	37	33	11.3	−2.9	6.3
Transportation and communication (incl. Suez Canal)	38	43	46	61	72	78	81	81	86	88	13.5	2.8	9.8
Housing (ownership of real estate)	50	51	53	56	59	62	65	68	73	77	4.5	5.8	4.9
Commerce and finance	122	142	147	169	190	210	209	193	181	188	9.4	−3.5	4.9
Other services, including government	96	101	110	122	139	148	157	166	166	179	8.5	4.5	7.2
Total: GDP at 1954 market prices	719	753	781	880	936	956	984	1,004	992	1,023	5.4	0.7	3.8
+ net factor income from abroad	−8	−9	−5	−3	−9	−11	−13	−12	−11	−13			
GNP at 1954 market prices	711	744	776	877	927	945	971	992	981	1,010	5.3	1.4	4.0
GNP at current market prices[b]	552	535	578	718	829	916	1,016	920	888	936			

a. This is not a full reproduction of the table in the source. We have deleted several columns not necessary for our presentation, and rearranged the table.
b. The estimate for GNP at current market prices is attributed in the source to E.H. Abdel Rahman. (See source for full attribution.)

Source: Bent Hansen and G.A. Marzouk, *Development and Economic Policy in the UAR (Egypt)* (Amsterdam, 1965), p.319.

Table 8.3: Industrial Origin of GDP for 1947 and 1952 (percentages)

Sector	1947	1952
Agriculture	38.3	33.3
Industry and electricity	12.9	13.1
Construction	3.2	3.0
Transportation and communication	5.9	8.1
Housing (ownership of real estate)	6.8	6.8
Commerce and finance	18.8	19.2
Other services including government	14.1	16.5
Total	100.0	100.0

Source: Hansen and Marzouk, *Development and Economic Policy.*

we turn to the next section will establish the point:

— the agricultural Bank was established in 1902, and, though it collapsed in 1937, it was established again after reorganisation;
— Misr Bank was established in 1920 and was later to be very active in financing industry;
— the Agricultural Credit Bank was established in 1931;
— the Agricultural Mortgage Bank was established in 1932;
— the National Bank of Egypt was established in 1898; it was to be given power to act like a central bank in 1950 (the Central Bank itself was established a decade later, in 1960); and
— the Industrial Bank was established in 1949.

In the field of education, the four leading universities had been established before the revolution: Al-Azhar — the oldest university in the world — now over 1,000 years old, its curricula were modernised and expanded in 1961; Cairo (previously Fouad First) University in 1925; Alexandria University in 1942; Ain Shams University in 1950. Only Assiut University was established later — in 1957. The country also had several learned societies in operation for many years before 1952.

Community facilities and rural services had also made some strides before the revolution. Thus, while in 1936 pure drinking-water was not available in the villages, and only to 3.5 million city-dwellers, by 1952 it was available to 5 million city-dwellers and to 2 million villagers. Rural combined units (later to be called combined social centres) were started in 1939; by 1952 some 150 of them were already in operation. In the field of health services, over 500 health centres were established by 1952, and the country had 5,200 physicians. However, there was concentration of hospitals and doctors in the cities and towns. Finally, the co-operative movement had started in 1913, and by 1952 there were 2,071 societies in various states of activity.

The finances of the country in the early post-war period were rather relaxed, with some £E400 million of accumulated foreign exchange balances, thanks to the wartime spending of the British forces and the severe limitations on imports and shipping which led to forced

Table 8.4: Number and Percentage of Persons in Different Sectors, 1947

Sector	Number (thousand)[a]	Per Cent	Relative Sectoral Product per Worker for 1947[b]
Agriculture and fisheries	7,555	46.1	0.83
Mining	13	0.1	2.93
Manufacturing and handicrafts	709	4.3	
Construction	113	0.7	4.57
Transport and communication	203	1.2	4.92
Commerce and finance	620	3.8	5.05
Personal services (hotels, restaurants, bars, cleaning establishments, mortuaries, domestic servants, etc.)	2,856	17.4	
Professions and non-industrial public services	515	3.1	
Ill-defined and unproductive	1,570	9.6	
Unoccupied persons	2,227	13.6	
Total	16,381	100.0 (rounded)	

a. The distribution excludes children under 5 years.
b. The ratio is the result of dividing the percentages for 1947 in Table 8.3 by the percentages above, wherever the nomenclature is similar.

Source: Hansen and Marzouk, *Development and Economic Policy*, calculation of RSPW added.

savings on the part of the country during the war. On the eve of the revolution, the budget constituted about 20 per cent of GNP, which is not a modest proportion for that period under similar circumstances.

2. THE REVOLUTION

On 23 July a military group, calling itself 'The Free Officers' took over power in a bloodless *coup d'état;* a few days later it deposed and deported King Farouk; on 18 June 1953 the Revolutionary Command Council (RCC) proclaimed the end of the Egyptian monarchy and the establishment instead of a Republic with the titular head of the RCC, General Mohammed Neguib, as President, and with Colonel Gamal Abdul-Nasser, the strong man of the RCC, as Minister of the Interior and later as Prime Minister. On 12 February 1953 the RCC reached agreement with Britain over the Sudan, which was nominally ruled jointly by Britain and Egypt. On 19 October 1954 Egypt signed an agreement with Britain ending the latter's political presence in Egypt and its military presence in the Canal Zone, but permitting the continued existence of civilians to operate and maintain the Canal for a limited period.

This is not a complete history of events; it leaves out inter-Arab relations and activities, especially Egypt's reaction to the Baghdad Pact, which was being promoted openly by Britain, and less so by the USA. It also leaves out of account the situation on the armistice lines between Israel and Egypt, which was to play a decisive role in 1955, when Israeli raids into the Egyptian-controlled 'Gaza Strip' made Nasser, then the open ruler of Egypt, seek arms from the Eastern bloc. But for our purposes of economic analysis, it is sufficient to note that with Egypt's success in ending British presence in the country, the officers of the RCC had their hands freer to face their problem-burdened heritage.

The Free Officers, it is now evident from several autobiographies and biographies, and from interviews, books and articles, did not come on to the stage of power with an ideology; they instead came with a set of simple ideals and objectives.[13] As Maxime Rodinson has summed it up, 'The motivating ideas they had in common can be related to two main aims: national independence and modernization.'[14] Nasser, in his *Philosophy of the Revolution*, makes his conviction clear that 'every people must undergo two revolutions: a political revolution defined in terms of emancipation from foreign rule and a social revolution.' *The Charter* itself states the following:

> The Egyptian people's revolutionary will, appears in its great and proper perspective if we recall that those valiant people began their revolutionary march with no political organization to face the problems of the battle. Moreover, this revolutionary march started without a complete theory for the revolutionary change (p. 4).
> In those eventful circumstances, the sole basis of work was the famous six principles carved out of the demands and needs of the people's struggle (p. 5).

These principles, as reworded in *The Charter* almost a decade after the *coup* of 1952, were:

1. Facing the lurking British occupation troops in the Suez Canal Zone, the first principle was: Destruction of imperialism and its stooges among Egyptian traitors.
2. Facing the despotism of feudalism which dominated the land and those on it, the second principle was: Ending of feudalism.
3. Facing the exploitation of wealth resources to serve the interests of a group of capitalists, the third principle was: Ending monopoly and the domination of capital over the Government.
4. Facing the exploitation and despotism which were an inevitable consequence to all that, the fourth principle was: Establishment of social justice.
5. Facing conspiracies to weaken the army and use the remaining part of its strength to threaten the internal front eager for revolution, the fifth aim was: Building a powerful national army.
6. Facing political forgery which tried to veil the landmarks of true nationalism, the sixth aim was: Establishment of a sound democratic system (p. 5).

The government, under President Nasser's continued and uncontested leadership, attempted to make concrete all these principles, with varying degrees of success. What is most worth noting, especially because of its absence among the six principles, is the drive for economic development. Emphasis on military strength, sound democracy, political independence and social justice is explicit and strong. But development of the economy, the foundation upon which the social justice was to be built and without which political independence would in effect remain incomplete, does not feature among the six principles. This hiatus was to be filled cogently in *The Charter*.[15]

Later, but gradually and through a process of trial and error and pragmatic discovery, President Nasser and to a lesser extent his associates (with notable contribution from the journalist Mohammed Hassanein Haikal and a small group of economists) built a rather coherent theory embracing the interrelationships between economic and socio-political change and development. The purist might refuse to call it an integrated and complete ideology, or a system of thought, or social theory; yet it is the nearest to what practising politicians normally achieve. The process, which stretched from 1952 to 1962, thus saw the gradual movement from ideals to ideology, and from social objectives to socialism. Again here, the contention that the Egyptian system became socialist after 1961 has been challenged by a few writers who looked at the question from different angles of vision.[16] The question will receive further consideration later. But for the moment, we will examine the highlights of the achievements of the revolution in the years 1952-60.

3. THE LANDMARKS, 1952-60

Admittedly, development is a continuous process. Any slicing of the period 1952-75 is merely a matter of convenience in order to mark out the more important turning-points in the continuum. Thus, we can recognise the following major events and turning-points in the 24-year period: agrarian reform; nationalisation of the Suez Canal Company and the Egyptianisation process immediately following; the industrialisation plan of 1957, and subsequent industrialisation efforts; the 5-year plan 1960-5 and post-Plan developments; the High Dam; and the nationalisation decrees of 1961 (including the second set of agrarian reform measures), which constitute the decisive turning-point in the process of socialist transformation (vocalised and formalised in *The Charter*). As an overall review, we will attempt to draw into relief the contours of structural change in the economy, the transformation in the productive capacity of the country, and the measures of social justice taken. The present section will only cover agrarian reform (which will be discussed in its various phases, including those of 1961-9), nationalisation of the Suez Canal Company and Egyptianisation, and the initiation and subsequent phases of the energetic industrialisation process.

Agrarian Reform — The First Measure and Subsequent Amendments[17]

Agrarian reform was one of the major six objectives of the Free Officers on taking over power. This reform had multiple objectives: to abolish 'feudalism'; to break the landowners' tendency to hold wealth in the form of land and to encourage them to divert investments into industry; to redistribute the land more equitably by placing a ceiling on the size of ownership, expropriating excess areas, and selling them to landless peasants or tenants, or peasants with tiny holdings; to alter tenancy relations in favour of the tenant by giving him more security and a larger share of the produce; to develop technical and extension services in the agricultural sector and to make available more credit and selected seeds and other inputs through co-operative societies and other means and institutions; and generally to improve the lot of the vast mass of peasants. Before these measures receive further consideration, the picture of land holdings on the eve of the reform will be studied in Table 8.5.

This table shows very clearly the polarisation in the pattern of ownership, with 94.2 per cent of owners owning 35.5 per cent of the land, and one-tenth of 1 per cent of owners owning 19.8 per cent of the land. The remaining 44.7 per cent of the land was owned by 5.7 per cent of landowners. The other side of the coin, the average size of ownership, betrays the degree of hardship of the majority of owners even more clearly. The average ownership for 94.2 per cent of owners was less than one-third ha (indeed, for 72 per cent of owners, the average holding was one-sixth of a hectare), while the average size of holding

Table 8.5: Agricultural Land by Size of Holdings, 1952

Size-Group		Owners		Area '000		Average Area	
Feddans	Hectares	'000	Per Cent	Feddan	ha	Per Cent	Fed	Ha

Feddans	Hectares	'000	Per Cent	Feddan	ha	Per Cent	Fed	Ha
1 and under	0.42 and under	2,018.1	72.0	778	326.8	13.0	0.4	0.168
Over 1 under 5	Over 0.42 under 2.1	623.8	22.2	1,344	560.5	22.5	2.1	0.882
Over 5 under 10	Over 2.1 under 4.2	79.3	2.8	526	220.9	8.8	6.6	2.772
Over 10 under 20	Over 4.2 under 8.4	46.8	1.8	638	268.0	10.7	13.6	5.712
Over 20 under 30	Over 8.4 under 12.6	13.1	0.5	309	129.8	5.0	23.6	9.912
Over 30 under 50	Over 12.6 under 21.0	9.2	0.3	344	144.5	5.7	37.4	15.704
Over 50 under 100	Over 21.0 under 42.0	6.4	0.2	429	180.2	7.2	67.3	28.266
Over 100 under 200	Over 42.0 under 84.0	3.2	0.1	437	183.5	7.3	137.2	57.624
Over 200	Over 84.0	2.1	0.1	1,177	494.3	19.8	550.9	231.378
Total		2,802.0	100.0	5,982	2,508.5	100.0	2.135	0.895

Note: Conversion of *feddans* into hectares calculated at 1 *fed* = 0.42 ha. Total area in *feddans* differs slightly from hectares because of rounding.

Source: *Statistical Pocket Yearbook, 1953*, p.33.

for the very large landlords (who owned one-fifth of total land) was 231.4 ha. If it is recalled that irrigated agriculture in Egypt was very remunerative, and that a hectare gave a net income of some £E100 (or £E40 per *feddan*), then it will be seen that the average holding of 231 ha provided the owner with a net income from land of £E23,100 (over $92,000) a year — a very large income indeed.

The first measure of agrarian reform was incorporated in Decree No. 178 of 9 September 1952, which included six sections dealing with the following broad subjects:

1. limitation of agricultural ownership, expropriation of excess areas held, and distribution of excess areas to small peasants;
2. the requirement of the establishment of agricultural co-operative societies in land reform areas;
3. restriction of further fragmentation of land;
4. imposition of surtaxes on areas held in excess of 200 *fed.* (84 ha) which was the ceiling set for ownership — areas that would be held until expropriation was effected;
5. definition of relationship between tenant and owner; and
6. definition of the rights of agricultural labour.

This law had several amendments down to August 1969. We will refer to the amendments and then point out the landmarks of agrarian reform measures considered in their entirety, rather than measure by measure. Some of the amendments will be elaborated on while the landmarks are being identified.

One major amendment needs to be mentioned here — Law 127 of 25 July 1961, whose main import was to lower the ceiling by half, as we shall see. A subsequent less important law, No. 15 of 14 January 1963, prohibited land ownership by foreigners, no matter what the type of land (even desert land was prohibited). Prior to that, ownership was permitted for reclamation purposes. Law No. 138 of 24 March 1964 reduced the burden of repayment by the beneficiaries of redistribution, as will be mentioned later. Law No. 150 of 1964, which placed some 600 persons under sequestration (as 'elements hostile to the system') also expropriated their lands. Finally, Law No. 50 of 16 August 1969 set yet a new ceiling, again halving that set in July 1961. However, the present writer has found only brief reference to this last-mentioned law. According to this reference, the 1969 measure involved the expropriation and subsequent redistribution of 1.13m *feddans* (0.479m ha), owned by 16,000 owners.[18] If these magnitudes are correct, then they underline the great significance of this last measure. However, both the area and the number of owners cited seem to clash with the data existing just before the 1969 measure. The main features of the body of legislation on land reform will now be listed:

— A ceiling of 200 *fed.* (84 ha) was set per owner, plus 50 *fed* (21 ha) per dependant, the total allowable per family not to exceed 300 *fed.* (126 ha). (Exemptions were made for land reclamation companies and co-operative societies.) This ceiling was, however, lowered in July 1961 to 100 *fed.* (42 ha) per owner, but the total allowable per family remained unchanged. Law No. 50 of August 1969 lowered the ceiling further to 50 *fed.* (21 ha) and lowered the family's total allowance to 100 *fed.* (42 ha), regardless of the type of land — irrigated, fallow or desert.
— The owners of land in excess of the ceiling were allowed five years to dispose of this land by sale, which was the period set for the General Authority for Agrarian Reform to expropriate excess holdings. However, evasion ensued, and many fictitious sales to

loyal retainers and reliable distant relatives were effected. The law had initially defined the priorities to apply in such sales. They were: workers on the land, tenants on the land, land-holders with holdings below 10 *fed.* (4.2 ha) including original plus new ownership, and graduates of agricultural schools (allowed 20 *fed.* – 8.4 ha). An amendment tightening the rules of sale was enforced in 1958.

— Initially, no ceiling was set on land operated on lease. However, Law No. 24 of 29 April 1958 set the same ceiling on tenancy as an ownership. The excess land was to be released. Law No. 127 of July 1961 further reduced the area on lease to 50 *fed.* (21 ha). These limitations on area leased to tenants were occasioned by the phenomenon of large leaseholds. Thus, in 1956, 1 per cent of operators held 18.2 per cent of cultivated land, at an average of 602 *fed.* (252.8 ha).

— All the land owned by the former Royal Family was expropriated without compensation, under Law No. 598 of 1953.

— *Waqf Ahli* (family endowment) land was expropriated under Law No. 178 of September 1952, upon the abolition of the institution. Then, *Waqf Khairi* (charitable endowment) land was expropriated under Law No. 152 of 1957 and Law No. 44 of 1962.

— Compensation to be paid to landlords was to be ten times the rental value, which was to be not the going market rate, but seven times the basic land tax. In other words, land value was to be 70 times the tax. This measure penalised landlords who had earlier had their land assessed at low value for tax evasion purposes; indeed it was estimated that the compensation would come to about half the market value of land on the average. (Average tax was some £E2.3 per *feddan;* value therefore was £E161 per *feddan* or some £E300 per ha.) Trees, buildings, machines, etc. on the land were assessed and their value added. Total compensation for 462,663 *fed.* (194,318 ha) amounted to about £E73.2 million, plus £E3.85m for trees, buildings, etc.

— Settlement was to be in the form of non-transferable bonds in 30 annual instalments; bonds bore interest at 3 per cent per annum. However, in 1958 this was amended and settlement was to be over 40 years with interest reduced to 1.5 per cent. Settlement for *Waqf Khairi* land was to be effected over ten years and interest on bonds was 3 per cent. Settlement proved slower than expropriation, with a lag of almost two or three years. (Bonds were not negotiable, but acceptable in settlement of death duties, of surtax on land in excess of ceiling still held by landlord pending expropriation, or for buying land for reclamation.)

— The 1961 measure (Law No. 127 of 25 July) did not allow landlords to dispose of their excess land by sale as Law No. 178 of September 1952 had done; nor were landlords allowed to move tenants to less fertile land while holding on themselves to better land.

— Compensation terms for land expropriated in 1961 were more favourable: 15 instalments, 4 per cent interest, redeemable bonds that were transferable at the stock exchange by sale. However, the process of compensation remained slow. By 1964, for instance, settlement for roughly one-third of land till then expropriated had been effected, to the amount of some £E50 million.

— Land expropriated was to be redistributed, according to a system of priorities favouring workers and tenants on the land or neighbouring families with very tiny holdings (below the range of areas allowable). The plots were to range from 2-5 *fed.* (0.84–2.1 ha).

— Payment by beneficiaries was to be at the price of expropriation (later in July 1961 the price was halved, and still later under Law No. 138 of 24 March 1964 the price was

reduced to a quarter the value as assessed for compensation purposes. The reduction in both instances was made retroactive to beneficiaries of the 1952 reform). Settlement was to be effected in 40 instalments with 1.5 per cent added to the value payable.
- The beneficiaries of agrarian reform were required to join co-operative societies. These were to provide credit (obtained from the Agricultural Bank), selected seeds, fertilisers, advice and management help. The societies had officials from the Ministry of Agrarian Reform delegated to them to help in technical, administrative, managerial and accounting matters. The co-operative movement has come to prove more successful in land reform than in other areas, although it has not been spontaneous but imposed by decree.
- Rents paid by tenants were fixed by the original 1952 Law at seven times the land tax (i.e. one-tenth the land value assessed at 70 times the tax). In effect, this meant a reduction by at least 35 per cent on the average from market rates prevailing. In the case of share-cropping, the share of the landlords was made 50 per cent of the produce at the highest; all expenses were to be shared equally.
- Tenancy contracts were made for a minimum of 3 years, and were automatically renewable. Eviction of tenants and share-croppers was prohibited, which meant greater security and encouragement for investment in the land, in addition to protection against the greed of absentee landlords who had been in a favoured bargaining position compared with the fiercely competing tenants. (For the indolent tenant, it must have also meant less effort in the absence of the menace of eviction.)
- The Reform Law of July 1961 made all loans extended by the Agricultural Bank free of interest.
- Agricultural labour, the most miserable party in the rural sector owing to the massive pressure of population on land and job opportunities, was the least favoured in the various reform measures. This is probably a reflection of the legislator's realisation of the economic realities of the situation. The law set a minimum age limit for work: 14 years. It also set a minimum daily wage: £E0.180 for men and £E0.100 for women and children. Neither stipulation could be enforced, owing to the pressure of supply.

There have been slightly conflicting estimates of the area of land involved in land reform and expropriation of excess holdings. But the net estimates, excluding the area involved in the 1969 amendment, generally hover around one million *feddans* (420,000 ha), that is one-sixth of the area cultivated in 1952 or one-eighth of the area presently under cultivation. (If the 1.13m *fed.*, or 0.479m ha reportedly expropriated as a result of the 1969 measure are included, the picture changes drastically. There would be 2.13m *fed.* or some 900,000 ha affected by reform. This area would then constitute over one-fifth of the total cultivated area at the present moment, estimated at 10.7m *fed.* or 4.5m ha.)[19] Some 297,678 *fed.* or 125,025 ha were considered not fit for redistribution — either because they were poor and unproductive, or because they contained orchards, or yet because their ownership was subject to judicial disputes. We present in Table 8.6 a summary of areas expropriated which seems to us the most tenable among the few estimates available.

In addition to this area, the Ministry of Agrarian Reform in May 1959 took over 135,000 *fed.* (56,700 ha) of state lands and broke them into 54,000 holdings of 2.5 *fed.* (1.05 ha) each for redistribution. A further 192,903 *fed.* (81,019 ha) of newly reclaimed land has been made available for redistribution. Thus a little over 1.27 million *fed.* (533,400 ha) were over the years ready to change hands. As just indicated, this total does not take into

Table 8.6: Areas Acquired for Redistribution 1952-64

	Feddans	=	Hectares
Under original Land Reform Law No. 178 of 1952 and Law 598 of 1953 confiscating Royal Family estates	450,305		189,128
Under Law No. 152 of 1957 and Law No. 44 of 1962 for transfer to land reform of Waqf lands	148,787		62,491
Under second Land Reform Law No. 127 of 1961 for reducing maximum holdings to 100 *feddans* (42 ha)	214,132		89,935
Purchase of lands sequestrated in 1956, including those of the Kom Ombo Land Company	25,807		10,839
Under Law No. 15 of 1963 excluding foreigners from land ownership	61,910		26,002
Under Law No. 150 of 1964 for the confiscation of land owned by persons placed under sequestration	43,516		18,277
Total	944,457	=	396,672

Source: Riad el Ghonemy, 'Economic and Institutional Organization of Egyptian Agriculture since 1952', in P. J. Vatikiotis (ed.), *Egypt Since the Revolution* (London, 1968), p. 72. Calculation of hectares added.

account areas expropriated and made available for redistribution as the result of Law No. 50 of 1969, which reduced the ceiling to 50 *fed.* (21 ha). The estimate of 1.13m *fed.* (0.479m ha) is suspiciously exaggerated, since after the 1961 Second Reform Law, there remained roughly 5,000 owners with 100 *fed.* each, or a total of 500,000 *fed.* (210,000 ha). Not all this area would have been expropriated, since many of the owners must have been married and therefore entitled to a further 50 *fed.* for their dependants, aside from the 50 *fed.* allowed them. We do not therefore suppose that more than 100,000–150,000 *fed.* (42,000–63,000 ha) could have become available for redistribution after the 1969 measure. If so, then the total area involved in land reform would not exceed — indeed, could hardly reach — the 1.25m *fed.* mark, or 525,000 ha, which constitutes about 11.6 per cent of total area currently cultivated.

Data on actual redistribution are available only till the end of 1971, and are shown in the summary in Table 8.7. This summary shows that very little land remained for redistribution beyond the end of 1971, except for the small balance on hand, and the land not fit for redistribution. It has recently been stated that reclamation efforts will be increased, and indeed a new financial and technical agreement was signed in the summer of 1971 with the USSR for help in expediting the process of land reclamation. Probably between 100,000 and 150,000 *fed.* (42,000 and 63,000 ha) are being reclaimed annually. The completion of the High Dam itself has meant the reclamation of a vast area of additional land, as well as providing perennial instead of basin irrigation for another million *feddans*. Thus reclamation in general over the years 1952-72 has totalled about 1.2m *fed.* (0.504m ha). This has brought the area under cultivation to the total of 10.7m *fed.* (4.5m ha) to which reference has been made. To all this must be added the conversion of some 700,000 *fed.* (294,000 ha) from basin to perennial irrigation, which means a shift from one crop to two or three a year.[20]

Table 8.7: Land Redistribution up to 1971

Agrarian reform lands	822,923 *fed.*
Land belonging to organisations	184,411
Nile deposit	29,755
Total	1,037,089 *fed.* or 435,577 ha

Source: Central Agency for Public Mobilisation and Statistics (CAPMS), *Statistical Abstract of Arab Republic of Egypt 1951/52 — 1970/71* (June 1972), p. 55. Virtually the same areas are reported in CAPMS, *Statistical Abstract of the Arab Republic of Egypt, 1952-1974* (October 1975; Arabic), p. 59. Obviously no redistribution occurred between the end of 1971 and the end of 1974.

Before an evaluation can be made of the effects of agrarian reform, the new structure of land-holding must be described. Table 8.8 presents this structure.

Unfortunately there is no breakdown of ownership by size of holding and number of owners for subsequent years to take account of redistribution of land expropriated or reclaimed after the 1969 reform. None the less, enough emerges from Table 8.8, when compared with data in Table 8.5, to reveal the drastic change in four ways: the increase by 74 per cent of total area owned by those owners whose holdings are under 5 *feddans* against an increase of 15 per cent in the number of owners; the increase in the area of holdings in the middle range by about 13 per cent while the number of owners remained unchanged; the disappearance altogether of holdings in excess of 100 *fed.* (42 ha), which used to account for over one-fourth of total area (but only of 0.2 per cent of all owners); and finally the rise in the average size of holding in the category 'under 5 *feddans*' from 0.8 in 1952 before the first reform, to 1.2 after the reform measures of 1952-64. Though the improvement is small in absolute terms, it is significant in relative terms, especially if we remember the rise in the number of owners in the meantime by some 911,000. (However, this overall positive development may well have been accompanied by greater fragmentation of holdings, under the pressures of population increase and the application of inheritance laws which entitle *all* heirs to land.) With the disappearance of holdings beyond 100 *feddans*, the range of average size of holding for the various size categories has also become much narrower. Before the 1952 reform, the range was from 0.8—550.9 *fed.* (0.336—231.38 ha); after the 1961 reform it narrowed to 1.2—100 *fed.* (0.5—42 ha). The new range is less than one-fifth the size of the old.

What has the outcome of reform been with respect to its other aspects? El Ghonemy, an FAO specialist in the field of reform, presents a well-reasoned assessment which we accept; it can be summarised as follows:[21]

— Agrarian reform rearranged the ownership structure and narrowed the range of ownership.
— It led to the control of the land market and reformed the traditional land tenure system.
— It led to a reorganisation of the crop rotation system (through the dual policy of widening the base of ownership while at the same time consolidating fragmented holdings into large operational units).
— It led to the establishment of multipurpose co-operative societies throughout the

Table 8.8: Structure of Land Ownership in 1965 (after reform)

Holdings		Owners	Area Owned ('000)		Per Cent of		Average Size of Holding	
Feddans	Hectares	'000	Feddans	Hectares	Owners	Area	Feddans	Hectares
Under 5	Under 2.1	3,033	3,693	1,551	95.05	57.1	1.2	0.53
5 and less than 10	2.1 – 4.2	78	614	258	2.44	9.5	7.9	3.48
10 and less than 50	4.2 – 21.0	90	1,342	564	2.19	20.8	19.1	8.40
50 and less than 100	21.0 – 42.0	6	392	165	0.19	6.1	65.3	28.73
100 and less than 200	42.0 – 84.0	4	421	177	0.13	6.5	100.0 (max.)	42.00
200 and over	Over 84.0	–	–	–	–	–	–	–
Total		3,211	6,462	2,715	100.00	100.00		

Note: Data exclude government desert land, fallow land, and land under redistribution.
Source: CAPMS, *Statistical Abstract . . . 1952–1974*, p.62. (Coversion to hectares added.)

country.
- It enabled the state to better control credit and trading in the main farm products for facilitating vertical integration between production, marketing and industrialisation.

More specifically, always according to El Ghonemy, generally so according to Issawi though in less affirmative terms, and in accordance with our own findings, the reform measure led to the following results:

- It transformed the power structure in the country, by eliminating the base of power of most traditional politicians.
- It found room for private ownership in land, albeit in relatively small-size holdings, within the socialist framework.
- It removed the possibility of exploitation by landlords of tenants and other peasants.
- It enabled the *fellahin* (farmers, peasants) to participate more actively in political life, and to turn in no less than 25 per cent of the members of the National Assembly.
- It led to notable improvements in levels of production, especially in the case of tenants-turned-owners, thanks to the reform.
- It encouraged investment and better maintenance by the former tenants who now became owners, or by those tenants whose status has not changed but who now have greater security and a larger slice of the produce.
- It led to greater use of fertilisers, insecticides and improved seeds and brands, and it has led to fuller utilisation of the skills of persons trained in agricultural sciences and techniques.
- It led to a more equitable distribution of income, not only via the more equitable distribution of land, but also via the improvement in tenancy and share-cropping arrangements in favour of the tenant and share-cropper. This is probably the most notable achievement of the Egyptian agrarian reform.
- However, it had very little, if any, effect in improving the lot of agricultural labour.
- As stated above, it led to the consolidation of ownerships in many villages for operational purposes, where the land was divided into three large areas for three different crops, which would be rotated. Each landowner would then receive a share in the total produce proportional to his share in total land area. This measure combined the advantages of a large base of ownership with large-scale operation, and minimised the bad effects of fragmentation.
- Again as mentioned earlier, the requirement that reform beneficiaries should join agrarian reform co-operatives made available to the farmers a wide range of services and inputs, free or at low prices, which otherwise would hardly have been available in the quantity, with the quality, or at the price now prevailing.

As an overall evaluation, El Ghonemy observes that the achievement has been noteworthy and striking, especially if it is compared with the experience of other countries. Even Issawi's less rosy overall evaluation is, on careful scrutiny, still favourable, especially if one looks more at his empirical data and less at his reading of these data.[22]

Agricultural co-operatives play a role important enough to deserve separate mention. A few co-operatives had been established in 1913, and the number grew slowly until there were 539 societies in 1931, with 53,000 members. The *Annuaire Statistique 1951-1952, 1952-1953, et 1953-1954*[23] gives the number of societies as 2,071 by the end of 1951, with 757,111 members, and an aggregate of about £E2.25 million for paid-up capital and accumulated reserves. By the end of 1967, the situation was as shown in Table 8.9.

Table 8.9: Agricultural Co-operatives, 1967

Type of Society	Number of Societies	Membership	Capital (£E)
The General Authority for Agrarian Reform	625	418,884	793,116
The General Egyptian Agricultural Co-operative Organisation	4,113	2,264,517	1,905,169
The General Egyptian Organisation for Desert Rehabilitation	91	30,916	69,631
The General Egyptian Organisation for the Exploitation and Development of Reclaimed Lands	36	11,080	78,860
Total	4,865	2,725,397	2,846,776

Source: CAPMS, *Annual Bulletin for Cooperative Activity in the Agricultural Sector* (Cairo, May 1969; Arabic).

This tabulated summary shows a vast expansion in the number of societies and in membership, but very little in paid-up capital. The discrepancy is puzzling and the source does not explain it. As far as membership is concerned, it shows that most land-holders in Egypt are co-operative members. This reflects the benefits which accrue from membership, in the form of cheaper credit and agricultural inputs, the availability free of charge of extension and technical services, and in addition in the case of co-operatives under the General Authority for Agrarian Reform, it reflects the fact that membership is required by law.

A more recent source of information contains data down to the end of 1973, though not in equal detail. According to this source, slow growth continued after the late sixties as far as the number of societies was concerned, but remarkable expansion in paid-up capital occurred. By the end of 1973, there were 5,075 co-operatives with 3.24m members. However, the six years intervening witnessed a vast increase in capital, which reached £E8.124m.[24]

Several observers have found fault with the development of the co-operative movement, both because it is not spontaneous from the base, but has always been energetically urged from above, and because in the case of agrarian reform co-operative membership is compulsory. Be that as it may, the fact remains that people learn through experience and joint action, and what may have started as a government-initiated or even government-enforced movement may well become a deeply ingrained force in the countryside.

Finally, brief reference is necessary to another process which, though not an aspect of agrarian reform strictly speaking, aims like it at serving agricultural development and the improvement of the conditions of the rural community. This is land reclamation, which has received some mention already. What is relevant at this point is to say that there are three major projects in this field, in addition to many small scattered schemes. The oldest of the three is the Tahrir (i.e. Liberation) Province, which was a huge experiment involving at least 125,000 *fed.* (52,500 ha) and which was meant to embody integrated revival: the reclamation of land, as well as the establishment of new model villages, the selection of trained farmers, the adoption of Western dress by the inhabitants of the new land, and the growing of new crops.

The idea generated a great deal of excitement and enthusiasm among the actors and the observers alike, as a symbol of the regeneration of rural Egypt. Because of the enthusiasm of the managers and the authorities, strict economic controls were relaxed to the point where the project became uneconomic. We need not go into the financial details here, but we will merely add that now there is stricter control of the running of the Province, the ambitious expectations have been curtailed, and the economic results are not as out of line with the agronomic-technical results, which were more favourable than the financial-economic.

Two other main projects are in the stage of study and exploration. One is the New Valley in the Western Desert comprising 5 oases, in which it is believed 3 million *fed.* (1.26 million ha) could be irrigated by underground water. Tied to this project is the conviction by engineers that water could be pumped by electricity, which could be generated through the development of the Qattara project. This project involves an area west of the Nile Delta by 200 km., which lies 50 metres below sea level. The scheme envisages drawing in sea water across 70 km. of desert and generating electricity at low cost, which would be used in pumping underground water for the New Valley. As neither project is now under execution, the discussion will be restricted to this brief introduction.

In general it can be said that the scope for further low-cost, uncomplicated reclamation is very limited — and this, in spite of the energetic efforts of the Ministry of Land Reclamation and the associated bodies: the General Authority for Land Development, the General Authority for Desert Development, the General Organisation for Land Reclamation, and the General Organisation for Utilisation and Development of Reclaimed Land. A few hundred thousand *feddans* more will not change the rural landscape considerably — if at all, given the large rural population and the overall meagre land resources.[25]

Egyptianisation, 1956/7

The most notable act of 'Egyptianisation', and the one which led the series of acts that characterised the year 1956/7, was the nationalisation on 26 July 1956 of the Suez Canal Company, a French concessionary company which operated the Suez Canal. The background to this act does not concern us, and anyway is well covered in books dealing with the contemporary Egyptian political scene. The nationalisation led to violent reaction by Western European countries, especially France and Britain. These two countries, as has been established beyond doubt, in collusion with Israel,[26] attacked Egypt on 31 October 1956, two days after Israeli forces invaded Sinai. Egypt reacted by Egyptianising (i.e. nationalising) the vast French and English property, as well as much Jewish property.

The contribution to the country's balance of payments by the Suez Canal Company (in dues paid to government and in salaries and wages paid to residents in Egypt) amounted to £E31.8 million for 1955.[27] By 1966, the year before the Canal was closed again during the Arab-Israeli war of June 1967, the revenue to government had risen to some £E95 million. (It remained closed until late in 1975.)

After the massive Egyptianisation measures in the year following the take-over of the Suez Canal Company (which has since been compensated fully, at the value of the Company's shares on the closing of the Paris Stock Exchange the day before nationalisation), the most important single act of Egyptianisation has been that of the immense Belgian

Egypt

interests, in December 1960 subsequent to the Congo conflict and the assassination of Prime Minister Lumumba.

The Drive for Fast Industrialisation: The Pre-Plan Phase[28]

Industrialisation had from the outset occupied high priority in the list of objectives of the Free Officers. In 1956 this concern for industrial transformation and for sectoral diversification was given expression through the establishment of a separate Ministry of Industry. Between 1952 and 1957 there was some expansion in industry manifest in the formation of 75 new companies and in the investment of a total of £E33.4 million of capital, both in new ventures and in expanding already existing ones. (In 1953, there were 184 industrial share companies whose paid-up capital was £E66.3 million; the number rose to 259 and £E99.7 million respectively.)

In 1957, a five-year industrial plan was launched, with the following objectives:[29]

— achieving self-sufficiency in manufactured products that could be produced locally, thus saving foreign exchange,
— promotion of export industries, wherever possible, thus earning foreign exchange; and
— equipping the country with basic industries more advanced than those then existing.

The total investment projected under the 1957-62 industrial plan was initially £E250 million, divided as shown in Table 8.10.

Table 8.10: Initial Projected Industrial Investment, 1957-62

	5-Year Total £E m	Reserve £E m
Manufacturing	162.0	19.2
Vocational training	2.3	—
Productive efficiency	0.3	—
New mining projects	4.8	5.5
General mining projects	12.5	—
Reserve for research	3.8	—
Petroleum	35.0	5.0
Sub-totals	220.7	29.7
Total		250.4

Source: Ministry of Industry, *The Industrial Revolution in Eleven Years 1952-1963* (Cairo, Arabic).

Gradually, ambition rose, as did the investment plan, to a point where a total of about £E330 million was allotted (an extra 80 million) for 502 new projects, divided as shown in Table 8.11.

Financing was to be in large part external. Towards the end of 1959, credit facilities of about £E165 million had been extended to Egypt from the USSR, West Germany, Japan

Table 8.11: Revised Projected Industrial Investment, 1957-62

	Number of Projects	Estimated Cost £E m	Number of Projects	Estimated Cost £E m
Manufacturing			456	258.1
Chemical industries	118	103.8		
Food industries	105	77.1		
Engineering industries	160	27.0		
Weaving and spinning	73	50.2		
Petroleum industries			14	55.7
Mining			14	15.1
Training centres			18	1.7
Total			502	330.6

Source: Minister of Industry, *The Industrial Revolution*.

East Germany (in that order) and a few other countries. Within two years of its initiation, the Plan had been translated into implementation; 105 projects were established at a total cost of £E88.5 million.[30] But by the end of 1961, according to budgeting authorities, foreign loan and credit facilities had reached £E443.8 million (206.5 million from Western countries, 217.6 million from the Soviet bloc, and 19.7 million from IBRD). Only £E174.6 million had been contracted or utilised out of the 443.8 million by March 1961.[31]

However, the plan was not pursued, owing to the government's decision to formulate a 5-year comprehensive plan for economic and social development, to run from July 1960 through June 1965. Thus, the unfulfilled part of the 5-year industrial plan was incorporated into the comprehensive plan (to which hereafter we will refer as the Plan). Total investments in industry under the Plan were to be £E434 million, covering 230 projects, distributed as shown in Table 8.12.

We will not here examine the industrialisation drive as it materialised under the Plan and in later years, deferring this examination till later. But it will be useful to make some provisional comparisons between 1952 (or earlier years, where data are available) and the year 1960, the year in which the Plan started. Between 1952 and the end of 1959, the index of industrial production rose from 68 for 1946 and 95 for 1952, to 142 for 1959.[32] Another global indicator is contribution to GDP. In 1945 this was £E91 million, of 12.7 per cent of GDP. In 1952, it was £E132 million, or 12.1 per cent. In 1960 it rose to £E256.3 million or 20 per cent of GDP. Behind this increase in value added between 1952 and 1960 was a similar increase in value of output, from £E314 million to £E661 million. A few other indicators of growth are shown in Table 8.13.

This record of achievement, impressive as it is, falls far short of the advances that were in fact to be made in the years after 1960. Indeed, the strides made were so large and fast, that they were to create problems that can best be described as 'fast-growing pains'. Industrialisation under the Plan and in subsequent years will now be surveyed.

Egypt

Table 8.12: Projected Industrial Investment in 1960-5 Plan

Petroleum	£E 82.5 million
Mining	36.7
Chemical and pharmaceutical	83.2
Food	30.1
Spinning and weaving	43.8
Metal	46.8
Engineering	57.5
Rural industries	1.9
Vocational training	3.5
Complementary projects	16.0
Replacement and renewal	30.0
Central laboratory for testing material	2.0
Total	434.0

Table 8.13: Indicators of Growth, 1952-60

	1952	1960
Number of establishments (employing 10 or over)	3,445	3,336
Number of persons employed	273,136	344,830
Wages and salaries (£E thousand)	31,864	50,380
Exports of industrial products (£E thousand)	13,578	45,200*

* For the year 1959/60.

Source: Al-Barawy, General Union of Chambers of Commerce, Industry and Agriculture in the Arab Countries, *Economic Development in the Arab Countries, 1950-1965* (Beirut, 1967; Arabic), chapter on Egypt. Data obtained from CAPMS. According to *CAPMS... 1952-1974* (pp. 70, 202), industrial production doubled in the first decade of the Revolution.

The Drive for Fast Industrialisation: The Plan and After[33]

Industry (including mining and electricity, but excluding petroleum) was allotted the place of honour in the 5-Year Plan, which will be examined immediately after. Its share in investment was the largest among the sectors (36.7 per cent, as Table 8.17 below will show); the expected rise in income accruing in the industrial sector was the largest in absolute terms and in rate of growth, by far outdistancing the sector next to it; it was to be the only sector whose contribution to national product was to rise at the target year compared with the base year: the contribution of all the other sectors was to drop in relative terms. As the Plan was implemented, industry emerged as the largest sector in relative *and* absolute terms, although its rate of growth was not the highest among the sectors as had been envisaged. (Construction achieved a higher rate. This sector was the greatest surprise of all: instead of a planned decline in its contribution of 0.4 per cent, it achieved a rise of 10.4 per cent.)

Actual investments in industry (including mining and electricity) during the Plan totalled

£E516.5 million, three-quarters of which were made in the last three years. Output grew considerably, from £E1,105.1m in the base year to £E1,662.7m in the end year. Employment likewise rose, from 613,700 in the base year to 843,000 in the target year. A remarkable increase also occurred in exports, where industrial exports rose from £E45.4m in the base year (equal to 23.6 per cent of all commodity exports) to £E78.3m in the target year (29.5 per cent of all exports).[34] It is worth adding that industrial exports had been £E13.6m, or 9.3 per cent of exports in 1952.

However, since the end of the First 5-Year Plan, the pace of growth has slackened, mainly because too much had been attempted during the Plan and it was later thought more advisable to improve the huge industrial base established and to achieve better internal consistency and co-ordination among the hundreds of existing industries, than to go on setting up new industries at the rate of the years 1959/60—1964/5. In any case, foreign exchange constraints would have made the continuation of the pace next to impossible.

Investment in industry (again including mining and electricity, but excluding petroleum) since June 1965 will now be presented in tabular form. As Table 8.14 shows, the Arab-Israeli war of June 1967 caused a dip in the volume of industrial (and of total) investment. Indeed, it was only in 1972 that total investment and industrial investment exceeded the level attained in 1966/7. The years 1974 and 1975 have witnessed a steep increase from the preceding level, the former marking a rise of 19.1 per cent, and the latter of 42.9 per cent, over the preceding year in each instance.

Table 8.14: Total Investment and Investment in Industry (Including Mining, Petroleum and Electricity), 1965/6—1975 (at current prices)

Year	Investment in Industry £E m	Total Investment £E m	Industry as Percentage of Total
1965/6	161.7	377.4	42.8
1966/7	167.7	358.8	46.7
1967/8	138.7	292.2	47.5
1968/9	133.0	343.5	38.7
1969/70	150.4	355.5	42.3
1970/1	148.8	361.0	41.2
1972	178.7	410.1	43.6
1973	184.6	465.2	39.7
1974	219.9	645.1	34.1
1975	314.2	1,201.0	26.2

Note: As of 1972, the various national accounts (and their components) are presented for calendar, rather than financial year.

Sources: For the years 1965/6—1967/8, CAPMS, *Evolution . . . 1960/61—1969/70* (see note 25), p. 45; for the years 1968/9—1973, CAPMS, *Statistical Abstract . . . 1952—1974*, p. 204 (this source was quoted for the years 1968/9 and 1969/70, rather than the previous one, because the *Abstract* incorporated adjustments to the data in *Evolution . . .*); and for 1974 and 1975, Ministry of Planning, *Preliminary Report on the Follow-Up of the General Plan of the State for the Year 1975*, Memo No. 19 (March 1976, Cairo; Arabic), p. 16.

Industrial output continued to rise in the early post-Plan period, but more slowly in relative terms, especially for manufacturing. None the less, the index of the value of industrial output (excluding mining and electricity) for 1973 stood at 391 (1951/2 = 100). Value of output rose by 70 per cent from the last Plan year to 1974, from £E1,662.7m to £E2,824.9m (and to £E3,227.7m for 1975), while employment rose from 843,000 to 1,117,500 workers in 1974.[35] (Employment data for 1975 are not available.)

In all, the progress of the sector of industry can only be described as marked for the whole period 1952-75 (or as dramatic if the period 1952-65 alone is considered). This is true whether we take manufacturing industry or electricity. In the case of manufacturing, it is not merely the huge number of factories established (which has variously been reported as ranging from 760 to 900) but also the variety of the types of industries set up which is worth noting. Egypt has virtually taken off in this field, with its products covering a very wide range. The following are the leading categories of industries in existence: food processing, textiles, furniture, cement and other building materials, soft drinks (all of which are conventional or 'initiation' industries which the country had in existence before the Revolution), as well as engineering, metallurgical, electrical, chemical and petrochemical, pharmaceutical, household durables, railway carriages, tractors, cars and lorries, plastics, synthetics, steel and several other categories of industries. It is important to add that the country's capability in design and technological adaptation has also increased considerably.

The wide range of products has enabled the country to expand its industrial exports considerably by 1964/5, as has already been indicated, and to expand them further to 49 per cent of all commodity exports by 1975. The factor share of industrial labour in total factor receipts rose from £E91.2m in 1959/60 (the base year for the Plan) to £E343.8m in 1974. This is almost a fourfold increase, much larger than the relative rise in industrial output or in the sector's contribution to GDP, and it reflects on the one hand the steep rise in *per capita* remuneration, thanks mainly to the measures of income equalisation taken and to a certain extent to rises in productivity, and, on the other hand, the vast expansion in the size of the industrial labour force. The rate of growth of the total share of industrial labour over the 15 years 1959/60-1974 is the highest for the economy, except in the case of labour in housing. However, in the latter case, the base in absolute terms was a mere £E0.1m in 1959/60, consequently the subsequent absolute increases (to £E11m in 1974) appear considerably larger in relative terms.[36]

The growth of the petroleum sector has also been beyond expectations, and this has more than compensated for the production of the wells of Sinai which fell into Israeli hands during the June War of 1967 (some 5 million tons a year). Vigorous prospecting started during the latter part of the Plan, and production has risen in the last dozen years from a few million tons a year to around 16 million tons in 1972, but to 11.7m in 1975. The (abortive) 1973-82 Plan projected production at 60m tons of crude by 1982. Already Egypt has been transformed from a net importer into a net, though very small, exporter. Most of the discoveries have been in the Western Desert and in the Gulf of Suez, and gas has been found in the Nile Delta area.

The closure of the Suez Canal in 1967 (the second in eleven years) has given impetus to the idea of building a 42-inch, 330-km. pipeline connecting Suez and the Mediterranean at Alexandria (SUMED), with an initial capacity of 40 million tons a year, to be raised after seven months of operation to 60 million tons. (The construction period is in two phases – 19 and 7 months.) The estimated cost was initially set at £E76 million, mostly in foreign currencies expected to be loaned by the contractors, who were reported to have got the contract in July 1969. However, there have been serious delays arising from a substantial rise in estimated costs owing to inflation in the early seventies, and from slowness in making financing arrangements. A financing agreement was finally made in mid-1973, with several European and Arab countries undertaking to provide the foreign-exchange component of the capital cost.

This pipeline would make up in part for the loss of revenue sustained owing to the closure of the Canal, and would attract petroleum — then going to Europe from the Arabian Gulf via the Cape of Good Hope — back to the shorter route. It will also compete with Israel's Eilat-Eshkelon pipeline already in operation. A smaller Egyptian pipeline was constructed and put into operation in the middle of 1969; its capacity is about 1.5 million tons a year.

The sector of electricity (included in 'industry' in much of the preceding discussion) has expanded considerably thanks to two factors: expansion in already existing capacity and generators, and — by far the more important of the two — the construction of the High Dam with its very high-capacity turbines. The 12 turbines in the High Dam alone now generate 10,000m kwh, as against 6,012m kwh generated in 1967 in the whole country — mainly from thermal stations but also at the old Aswan Dam. It ought to be added that the scheme for the complete electrification of Egypt was under way by 1975, but it has so far made only very slow progress in the countryside — with only a few hundred villages out of a total of about 10,000 involved.

The very fast pace of industrialisation, and here we refer specifically to manufacturing industry, has not been free of social cost. Indeed, the pace itself has revealed built-in problems. These must be understood apart from those problems associated with exogenous factors, particularly the war of June 1967, which had a serious retarding effect on the economy as a whole, and naturally on industry, resulting in a shrinkage in investment owing in part to the accelerated defence effort and a stricter control over the import of industrial raw materials and spare parts; the building up of unsold stocks; and idle capacity in general. However, what is more relevant here is the inherent problems of the industrial sector, which are mostly a function of the fast pace, as already indicated, and therefore a function of insufficient experience at the executive, managerial, supervisory and technical levels. It would be more realistic than optimistic to say that the problems are surmountable and will be overcome once sufficient industrial experience has been gained and enough time has passed for industries to come to full fruition. Already there are signs of improvement, and the eight years after 1967 have mostly reflected a desire to 'absorb and digest' the fast growth in the decade before, and to correct the maladjustments that had bedevilled the sector. (That this desire has not shown very tangible positive results is not to deny that it has been presented as an explanation for the slower pace of industrial growth after 1967.) Nevertheless, it is useful to draw an inventory of the difficulties so far encountered by the manufacturing sector:

1. Industries were established in large numbers — some 800 or more factories in 18 years, but most clustered in the years 1962-8. The rate for the years 1957-70 during which the drive for industrialisation was marked with energy (the last year being the final year in Nasser's era), was too high for the available skilled labour and technical, supervisory, managerial and top executive cadres to maintain efficiently.
2. Complementarities and linkages, backward and forward, were not carefully observed and well-timed.
3. Co-ordination was not always properly established between the flow of raw materials, intermediate goods, spare parts and the stream of production demanded.

Egypt 345

4. Import needs were not always well co-ordinated with the availability of foreign exchange resources.
5. Adequate cost and return studies, taking into account technical, economic and marketing factors, were not thoroughly undertaken before projects were selected for construction.
6. Staffing at the supervisory and managerial levels was at times influenced by political factors and by social policy, in the sense that padding or feather-bedding (in industry as in the civil service) was allowed in order to find employment for all the graduates of certain technical schools and institutes, or to find room for some former army officers, without insistence on work qualifications germane to efficiency and directly dictated by it.
7. Although profit continued to feature as a criterion of efficiency, it was overshadowed by quantitative criteria: that is, by the fulfilment of predetermined physical production targets, in some disregard of the cost-return calculus.
8. Production and market demand were not sensitive to each other and adjustment of production to the pressure, or the slackening of, demand was slow — both as to quantity and to quality of product.
9. The newness of many of the industries established created unavoidable problems which necessarily needed time to be overcome.
10. Maintenance and repair services were not given the attention they deserved.
11. A priority system was not clearly established, and where established, it was not closely adhered to.

4. PLANNING AND THE PLAN[37]

The First Five-Year Plan

Egypt was one of the late starters in planning in the Arab world, if we ignore the two early attempts (1935-9 and 1946/7—1950/1), which were no more than the listing of public works projects. But having decided on planning in the proper sense of the term, Egypt took it seriously. The planning machinery changed over time, and several institutions participated in the process, foremost among which in the early years were the Permanent Council for the Development of National Production and the Permanent Council for Services, and in later years the Supreme Council of National Planning (under the President himself), the National Planning Committee (or Commission), the Institute for National Planning, the Ministry of Planning, and local organisations as well as planning units in the various ministries. For many years there was one Vice-President in charge of planning, broadly speaking, but President Nasser himself continuously showed active interest in planning and Plan results, very much the way Nehru did in India.

The Plan (short for *General Frame of the Five-Year Plan for Economic and Social Development, July 1960—June 1965*) had for its base the year 1959/60. It had a broad framework of ten years, during which GDP at constant prices was expected to double, that is growth was projected at a compound rate of 7.2 per cent per annum on the average. But the detailed Plan was drawn for the five years indicated. Parallel with the ten-year framework and the detailed five-year Plan for Egypt ran a similar framework and Plan for Syria, then the Northern Province of the United Arab Republic of which Egypt was the Southern Province.

Before we present the main features of the Plan and its expectations, we will record the growth of national product in the years preceding the Plan, in order to define the background.

Table 8.2 had presented the national accounts for calender years; Table 8.15 does so for financial years, which makes comparison of data slightly difficult. However, the difference between GNP for 1952 (in Table 8.2) which is £E992 million, and GNP for 1952/3 in Table 8.15) which is £E990 million, is insignificant. Consequently we can consider the series continuously from 1945 to 1959/60, since both tables show GNP at constant 1954 market prices.

The year 1959/60 shows total growth of 80.6 per cent over the year 1945. This represents an average compound rate of growth of about 4 per cent per annum, which is slightly over the natural increase in population, assumed for the whole period as being 2.6 per cent on the average (a little less for the earlier years, a little more for the later years). Table 8.2 shows the average compound rate of change for the period 1945-51 as 5.3 per cent, while Table 8.15 shows the rate for the years 1952/3–1959/60 to be 3.8. The slight dip in the fifties, compared to the half-decade immediately following the war, was reversed in the sixties, as we shall see.

The Plan was preceded by a two-year transitional plan for the years 1958 and 1959, which, though not implemented, served as trial ground for the economists and statisticians who were later to contribute greatly to the formulation of the Plan. In addition to the experience gained, the planners produced 'an 83 x 83 input-output table and commodity balance data showing sources and uses of approximately three hundred specific commodities'.[38] Indeed, the last few years preceding the Plan, and the two or three following its inception, were years of intense intellectual probing and professional activity at the National Committee of Planning and the Institute of National Planning, where scores of very capable Egyptian professionals, in association with a few foreign specialists, were producing, in many cases *de novo*, material, supportive studies on propensities, and models that were to lead ultimately to the formulation of the Plan, and after 1960 to the follow-up and scrutiny of the Plan.[39]

However, probably the most important decision in the Plan, the average target rate of growth, was not left to the planners, and to the economic realities and potential of the country, to decide. According to the planners, the rate would have been in the range of 3-4 per cent; instead it was handed down as a political decision from the President, who insisted on the doubling of GNP in ten years – which involved a compound rate of 7.2 per cent per annum on the average. Another political constraint was the choice of projects to be included in the Plan. These were not always the ones most clearly dictated by economic logic; many industrial projects were included because the pressure for speedy industrialisation – itself in part a function of political and prestige considerations – dictated their adoption. This upset the system of priorities which the planners favoured on purely technical and economic grounds. Finally, two unforeseen political factors caused major economic dislocation: the break-up of the Egyptian-Syrian union in September 1961, and the despatch of a large expeditionary force to North Yemen – in September 1962 – to bolster the new revolutionary republican régime there.

The Plan will now be presented, with emphasis on three main features: the sectoral distribution of aggregate output; the investment programme, also distributed by sector; and the method of financing.

There are divergences between all sector shares in the base year 1959/60 as they appear in Table 8.15 and Table 8.16, but total GNP is practically the same. The rise by 40 per cent in 1964/5 over 1959/60 was expected to be achieved thanks to an energetic investment programme, totalling £E1,697m (excluding land but including change in stocks). This total

Table 8.15: Gross National Product 1952/3 – 1959/60 (£E million, constant 1954 prices)

Sector or Magnitude	1952/3	1953/4	1954/5	1955/6	1956/7	1957/8	1958/9	1959/60	Average Annual Compound Growth Rate 1952/3–1959/60
Agriculture	325	315	318	329	339	355	376	392	2.7
Industry and electricity	140	143	152	163	174	190	202	213	6.2
Construction	25	27	26	25	28	33	38	42	7.7
Transport and communication	54	55	58	62	58	62	69	88	7.2
Housing	59	56	62	65	67	68	70	73	3.1
Commerce and finance	170	161	164	174	175	193	209	217	3.5
Other services	217	232	235	237	236	240	245	259	2.5
Gross National Product	990	989	1,015	1,055	1,077	1,141	1,209	1,284	3.8

Note: The table in Mead has two variants for commerce and finance, and for GNP. We have opted for Variant I which is more in line with GNP data appearing in the Plan. We have also stopped the series at 1959/60, which is the base year for the Plan, and excluded the series for 'Gains from Terms-of-Trade Change' and 'Gross National Income'.

Source: Donald C. Mead, *Growth and Structural Change in the Egyptian Economy* (Illinois, 1967), Table I-A-8 in Appendix, where it is attributed to B. Hansen and D. Mead, *The National Income of the U.A.R. (Egypt), 1939-62*, Memo No.355 (Cairo, Institute of National Planning, July 1963), Table 8, except that it is expressed in 1954 prices rather than in terms of 1953-54 prices, as that table is.

348 Egypt

Table 8.16: Actual (1959/60) and Target Income Levels by Sector (£E million, constant prices)

Sector	Base Year 1959/60	1964/5	1969/70	Implied Annual Compound Growth Rate 1959/60-64/5	1964/5-69/70
Agriculture	400	512	627	5.1	4.1
Industry	273	540	802	14.6	8.2
Construction	52	51	75	−0.5	8.0
Sub-total, commodity sectors	725	1,103	1,504	8.7	6.4
Trade and finance	127	162	265	5.0	10.4
Basic development sectors:					
Transport and communications	97	117		3.8	
Housing	73	84		2.9	
Public utilities	7	9		5.2	
Security, justice, defence	51	61		3.6	
Public administration	33	45		6.4	
Basic development	261	316	435	3.9	6.6
Other services:					
Education	52	67		5.2	
Health	11	15		6.4	
Social and religious	4	6		8.4	
Culture and recreation	13	18		6.7	
Personal services	89	108		3.9	
Sub-total, other services	169	214	360	4.8	11.0
Sub-total, all services	557	692	1,060	4.4	8.9
Grand total	1,282	1,795	2,564	7.0	7.4

Note: The total refers to gross national product at market price but excluding customs duties. The rather odd breakdown, calling public administration a 'basic development sector' while education is in 'other services', for example, is taken from the Plan.

Source: Mead, *Growth and Structural Change*, Table 10-1, p. 240 (last column in source deleted above), from *General Frame* etc.

is slightly above 20 per cent of the combined income for the five years, but it includes foreign loans as well as domestic savings. The expected growth rate during the Plan of 7 per cent was far from even for the various sectors and widely differentiated. The differences depended on the investments directed to each sector and to their incremental capital-output ratios, and the amount of investment was in turn determined by policy considerations regarding each sector and the growth rate projected for it. The following detailed expectations will help define the contours of the Plan more clearly:

— Expected sectoral rates of growth: See Table 8.16

Egypt

- Implied incremental capital-output ratios:[40]
  - Agriculture 3.00
  - Industry, total 1.57
    - Mining and manufacturing 1.30
    - Electricity 11.84
  - Total economy 2.95

- Expected population growth over 5 years ..... 14.8 per cent

- Expected total rise in level of living *per capita* ..... 22.0 per cent

- Expected increase in employment ..... 1,026,000 jobs = 17 per cent

- Expected rise in consumption ..... 24 per cent

- Expected change in sectoral structure (i.e. change in relative sectoral contribution to GNP):

	1959/60	1964/5
Agriculture	31.2	28.5
Industry	21.3	30.1
Construction	4.1	2.8
Sub-total, commodity sectors	56.6	61.4
Transport and communication	7.6	6.5
Trade and finance	9.9	9.0
Personal services	6.9	6.0
Other services	19.0	17.1
Sub-total, services sectors	43.4	38.6
Total	100.0	100.0

- Exports expected to rise by ..... 35.4 per cent
  (share of cotton expected to drop from 66.6 to 54.2 per cent)

Although agriculture was to have less relative significance in 1964/5, it still remained the basic foundation in the strategy of the Plan, especially as the construction of the High Dam has to be considered a major component of agricultural development. In relative terms, industry was to receive the greatest emphasis, and it was to absorb *all* the decreases in the percentage contributions of the other sectors. Thus its contribution was to rise by 41 per cent, from 21.3 to 30.1 per cent. Every other sector was to contribute relatively less by the target year. This reflects the second point in the Plan strategy: speedy industrialisation. Understandably, this second point was predicated on a third element in the Plan strategy: raising the degree of economic rationality; introducing radical technological change; sectoral diversification and, relatively, lessening of dependence on agriculture and, within this latter sector, on cotton; absorption of much more agricultural produce and surplus agricultural labour into industry. Lastly, emphasis was to be placed on 'supporting sectors': social overheads, transport and communications, housing services, public services and organisational and technical government services.

350 Egypt

The investment pattern, both according to sector and to internal source of financing (private vs. public) is summarised in Table 8.17.

Table 8.17: Investment by Sector and by Source 1960/1–1964/5

Sector	Private £E m	Per Cent of Total	Public £E m	Per Cent of Total	Total £E m	Per Cent
Agriculture, irrigation, and High Dam	78.9	12.2	313.1	33.6	392.0	24.9
Mining and industry	375.0	58.0	203.7	21.9	578.7	36.7
Trade, housing, public utilities	159.3	24.7	335.9	36.1	495.2	31.4
Services	32.8	5.1	78.2	8.4	111.0	7.0
Total	646.0	100.0	930.9	100.0	1,576.9	100.0
Add: Change in stocks					120.0	
Grand Total					1,696.9	

Source: *Five Year Plan, 1960-65.*

Combining internal and external financing, investment was to rise from 14 per cent of GNP in the base year to 22 per cent in the target year. Planned external financing was £E646 million, against domestic savings of £E931 million. To the latter volume is to be added the change in stocks of £E120 million, which brings total domestic savings to £E1,050 million.

A broad evaluation of the results of the Plan is now in order. The assessment that follows takes official data and data adjusted or qualified in an essay by Hansen, whose analysis seems to us to reflect scholarly responsibility without loss of sympathy.[41] As the two sets of results recorded below reveal, official data indicate an overall increase in GDP at factor cost (at constant base-year prices) of 37.1 per cent, or an annual average combined rate of 6.5 per cent, while Hansen's indicate an overall increase of 31 per cent and an annual rate of 5.5 per cent. The two sets of figures year by year are set out in Table 8.18.

It is clear from these figures that the divergence grows year by year. However, if *actual* official GDP for 1964/5 is set against *planned* GDP for the same year (see Table 8.16) some divergence between the two sets will appear. Both comparisons (actual official with actual according to Hansen, and actual official with planned official) show moderate divergence, especially the latter, since actual falls below planned GDP by a mere 2 per cent. However, what is more significant and what reveals wider divergence is the comparison between planned and actual value added *sector by sector*. Hansen has attempted such comparison, as well as a comparison between planned and actual investment, also sector by sector. The latter comparison appears separately in Hansen's analysis, but we have consolidated both comparisons, as well as actual with planned employment. The results appear in Table 8.19.

The divergence between planned and actual investment on the one hand, and planned and

Egypt 351

Table 8.18: Official and Hansen's Data (£E million)

Base Year	1960/1	1961/2	1962/3	1963/4	1964/5	Total Increase (per cent)	Average Compound Increase (per cent)
1,285.2	1,363.5	1,411.1	1,536.7	1,669.7	1,762.2	37.1	6.5
Hansen's Data							
1,285.2	1,356.3	1,397.6	1,509.0	1,605.9	1,684.2	31.0	5.5

actual GDP on the other, is quite clear from this table. Admittedly, within reasonable limits the magnitude of the divergence is not very meaningful, since in the absence of a mention of the absolute size of GDP and of investment sector by sector, the divergence between planned and actual rates of growth in itself is not very revealing, except if it is of large magnitude or if the *direction* of divergence is such that it moves in the case of GDP away from the divergence in the case of investment. Thus, actual investment in agriculture was larger in relative terms than planned investment, while actual growth in the sector was smaller than planned growth. Here and in similar instances the divergence is meaningful and significant. Likewise it is meaningful and significant if, although it happens to be in the same direction for investment and GDP, its size is widely different. A case in point is construction.

We will not enter into a detailed analysis of these divergences and seek explanations for them. In any case that would require much more detailed information than we possess. What is worth recording here is the fact of wide divergence and of divergence in opposite directions in several of the sectors, a phenomenon which qualifies the sense of achievement which is felt if examination is restricted to total — not sectoral — GDP, planned and actual. The sector-by-sector examination is a sobering experience, in the sense that it underlines the deviation of fulfilment from expectations.

Several factors underlie these deviations, and certain comments relating to the general planning performance of Egypt for Plan years are now in order. We will try to present the more salient among them.

1. The Plan was formulated under great pressure of time, in the absence of certain 'understructure' studies; of adequate knowledge of propensities, elasticities and capital coefficients; of facts on the economy; and of verification tests;
2. The planners had to operate within a political frame not of their choosing — indeed, the Plan was formulated under one socio-economic system, but implemented under a vastly different system, which influenced expectations and achievements in various ways. Furthermore, the planners set global growth targets not suggested by their findings and professional convictions, but politically dictated from above.
3. The pace of development, especially with regard to industrialisation, was too fast for the economy and for the reservoir of skilled manpower and of resources and experience to be digested fully without serious troubles and problems. (An inventory of the main problems and defects of the drive for industrialisation has already been drawn.)

Table 8.19: Average Annual Growth Rates 1959/60–1964/5 (per cent)

Sector	GDP Actual	GDP Planned	Employment Actual	Employment Planned	Investment Actual	Investment Planned
Agriculture (including irrigation, drainage, High Dam)	3.3	5.1	3.3	3.2	23.4	22.0
Industry	8.5	14.6	6.5	6.0	26.7	28.2
Electricity	19.1	14.7	6.5	6.0	7.4	9.1
Construction	10.4	−0.4	13.3	−1.4	0.9	0.3
Transport, etc. (including Suez Canal)	11.1	3.9	4.9	0.7	19.6	17.7
Trade and finance	3.3	5.0	2.8	3.0	1.3	0.3
Dwellings	1.9	2.8	5.5	4.6	10.7	12.6
Public utilities	2.8	5.2	3.8	4.2	3.3	3.2
Other services (including government)	4.1	4.8	4.1	2.8	6.8	6.5
Total or average	5.5	7.0	4.1	3.2	100.0	100.0

Hansen's Notes: From Table 8:' ... A problem arose in calculating the planned growth rates because the statistics for the base year 1959-60 have been revised since the plan was drawn up, while no corresponding revision of the plan has been made. Here I have measured the planned growth rate on the unrevised statistics for 1959-60. This gives the most correct impression of the intentions of the planners. The differences are small, however, and would, if at all, show up in the first decimal of the growth rates.'
From Table 9: 'The figures given in the sources for planned investments do not coincide with plan figures of the "comprehensive" plan, see *General Frame*, etc., p. 23. For most sectors the difference between the two sources is small, but for agriculture, irrigation and drainage, it is great. The total of planned investments of the first source is, however, equal to the source of all fixed investments planned according to the *General Frame*. I take it, therefore, that the planned figures according to Table 8 pertain to fixed investments only, and that the plan figures have been reclassified in order to fit with the sector classification for actual investments. The exclusion of stocks from the plan figures implies, however, that the last two columns are not fully comparable.'

Present Writer's Note: 'Table 8' in the preceding note relates to GDP and employment data. The immediately preceding reference to 'the last two columns' relates to the two columns above dealing with investment.

Source: Bent Hansen, 'Economic Development of Egypt', in Charles A. Cooper and Sidney S. Aledander (eds.), *Economic Development and Population Growth in the Middle East* (New York, 1972), Table 8, p. 31 and Table 9, p. 35, attributed to the *General Frame*, etc. and *Statistical Indicators for the UAR*. Only the last two columns of Table 9 are reproduced above; they are the last two columns here relating to 'investment'.

4. The planning process took into account, but inadequately, the opinions and criticism of local authorities and ministerial planning units. The give-and-take process was not enriched by continuous dialogue between 'the centre and the periphery'.
5. The private sector, to which a large share of the investment programme was assigned, was not made as full a partner in the planning process as its share demanded. Furthermore, a contradictory policy was pursued since, on the one hand, this sector was asked to behave with confidence and to invest according to Plan expectations, while on the other hand nationalisation was resorted to increasingly, especially in 1961. The slackening of the process of nationalisation beyond this year could not recapture the confidence lost. And in any case, with respect to the respective roles of the public, private and mixed sectors, it was only in mid-1962, when *The Charter* was proclaimed as embodying policy, that the frontiers of these sectors were broadly defined — by

which time it was too late for the recapture of confidence with regard to industry and other economic sectors into which nationalisation had already made serious incursions. Investment by the private sector for the years 1967/8–1969/70 averaged 7.4 per cent of total investment, whereas it had been assigned a share of 41 per cent in the investment programmes for these years. The gap between the expected or planned investment by the private sector and that effected continued to be serious until the end of 1975, but the size of this gap has shrunk. Yet even a smaller gap remains in itself an indication of the extent to which the private sector has been alienated. Taking the post-Plan decade 1965 to 1975, the share of the private sector in total investment has ranged between a low of 4 per cent and a high of 15 per cent, according to the official reports on the performance of the economy and its evaluation, year by year, to which we have referred on several occasions.

6. Important changes in the parameters were forced on the planners and executors, owing to unforeseen political events, such as the break-up of the union with Syria in September 1961, and the Yemen expedition subsequent to the republican *coup d'état* there in September 1962.
7. Underestimation of lags and delays in delivery of machines and spare parts, coupled with overestimation of own performance, constituted a dangerous combination that resulted in divergences between Plan and achievement.
8. Underestimation of foreign exchange needs deriving from the very ambitious Plan led to wide divergence between the foreign exchange plan, which projected that in the target year there would be a surplus on current account in the balance of payments to the tune of £E40.4 million, which would be used for repayment of foreign debt, and the fact that there was actually a deficit in that year of £E75.9 million.
9. Underestimation of the rise in the rate of natural increase in population[42] — a rise to at least 2.8 per cent — thanks to the improvement in health conditions and in sanitation and preventive medicine, led to the rise in total consumption. Added to the rise in the marginal propensity to consume beyond expectation, the dual process squeezed domestic savings, and necessitated heavier reliance on foreign financing. (Domestic savings were 12.8 per cent of GNP in the base year, and ran as follows for the five years of the Plan: 14.4, 10.9, 11.6, 12.6 and 14.0 per cent respectively. The average 12.8 was well below expectation.) This reliance on external finance led in turn to the deviation from the projections with regard to the foreign exchange situation and the sobering of earlier optimistic expectations with regard to the balance of payments. Mention should be made here of policy inconsistency in two areas with regard to consumption. First, official pronouncements and the mass media combined to make lavish promises with respect to the improvement in disposable income and the availability of more money for the purchase of more food, clothing and household durables by the masses. Second, legislation in July 1961 assigning a certain portion of company profits to labour as cash payments further enhanced the natural tendency to consume more. These forces combined led to a serious rise in consumption beginning with 1962/3. It was only in 1965 that full realisation of this economically dangerous trend dawned on the political decision-makers to the point where measures (albeit gently proclaimed and diffused) were taken to curb the excesses, through pricing and other policies.[43]
10. Vast expansion in the civil service, through the absorption of whole graduating classes in total disregard of job requirements, was inefficient and cumbersome. Appointment was no more a response to employment needs, but a welfare measure

taken indiscriminately. Such large-scale absorption inflated an already grossly inflated civil service, led to more proliferation of departments and jobs (created for the newcomers), to more diffusion of responsibility, and hence to less efficiency and more bureaucratic heavy-handedness. Every new appointee has to justify his desk; therefore he becomes more inventive in paper-work. This is a 'classical' Parkinsonian pattern. And it is all the more regrettable in view of the vast improvement in technical and administrative standards at the top and next to the top, from Cabinet Ministers down several rungs in the ladder. This phenomenon resulted in rationalisation and better standards at the decision-*making* level, and civil service inflation and overcrowding at the decision-*executing* level.[44]

This long inventory of criticisms should in no way detract from the basic favourable assessment of the results of planning and the Plan — indeed of the country's whole drive for industrialisation and development in general. The inventory merely qualifies the achievement; it does not deny its reality and its dimensions. Thus, in global terms, while it is true that a planned combined average rate of growth of 7 per cent annually (at constant prices) for the five years of the Plan was rather ambitious and could not therefore be fulfilled, given (a) the experience, the reservoir of skills and the physical and financial resources available; (b) the innovations involved in the introduction of hundreds of new industries and other unfamiliar activities; (c) the low rate of growth of the half-decade before; and (d) the unforeseeable non-economic setbacks, it is still worth remembering that the performance, even according to Hansen's estimate, was better than the expectations of the planning experts. (It will be recalled that the experts believed a 3-4 per cent rate to be the limit of feasibility, while Hansen's finding is 5.5 per cent.) This performance, after the dip in the average rate of growth for the years 1952–1959/60 to 3.8 per cent, is creditworthy, and it speaks well of the determination and sense of purpose of Egypt's political and economic leadership in the sixties, with special tribute to President Nasser's tireless efforts and unshakeable faith in the country's and the people's potential.

Developments in the Post-Plan Years
However, before we move on to the next section, it is relevant at this point to refer briefly to planning and growth in the ten years since the middle of 1965. Towards the end of the Plan period, vastly rising consumption, coupled with growing foreign exchange difficulties and the inability of increases in production and imports to catch up with consumption and population increases without damaging investment, together led to inflationary pressures. Until somewhere in 1964 Egypt had experienced notable price stability on the whole, with average price increases ranging between 1 and 2 per cent per annum. But the index for 1965 rose to 112, whereas it was 104 for 1964 (1963 = 100). Thus the government began in 1965 to take restrictive measures: freezing of wage and salary increases, curtailment of instalment sales, reduction or cancellation of subsidies to certain basic consumption goods, physical rationing of a few commodities, and the introduction of compulsory saving schemes.

Nevertheless, the combined effect of these measures fell short of consumption pressure. Thus, while growth in national product was 4.8 per cent in 1965/6 over the preceding year, consumption rose by 5.7 per cent.[45] Consequently, the wholesale price index rose to 121.5 for 1966, and to 130.1 for 1967. The process was checked and reversed in 1968 and remained under control until 1974. (The index reading dropped to 126.8 for 1968 and to 126.2 for 1969. With 1970 as base year, the wholesale price index stood at 101.5 for 1972 and 108.4 for 1973, but rose to 123.9 for 1974, while the consumer price index

Egypt

stood at 105.3 for 1972, 109.8 for 1973, 121.7 for 1974, and 132.3 for the second quarter of 1975.[46])

Preliminary thinking preceding the formulation of a second five-year plan concentrated on measures capable of correcting the demand-supply disequilibrium. Thus, the Prime Minister late in 1965 indicated that while industry was to continue to receive vigorous promotive support, emphasis must be placed on projects capable of meeting domestic demand at economic prices, or of raising exports and earning badly needed foreign exchange, and that accurate and careful studies should precede the establishment of new projects. In the meantime, existing establishments were to be improved, idle capacity was to be activated whenever possible, management and productivity were to be examined and improved, incomplete projects were to be completed, the public sector was to be reorganised with a view to increased efficiency, and an incentives system was to be widely applied.[47]

Initially, it was thought advisable to relax the pace of development during the second plan, owing to the large investments made in the first plan, and the need to 'digest' these properly before launching the new plan. It was thus estimated that the next plan should stretch for seven instead of five years, if the original target of doubling GNP was to be at all possible. However, the seven-year plan was not formulated. Instead, year-by-year plans have so far been announced and budgeted for. Recourse to available sources enables us to construct the picture for the years 1965-75 with regard to investment, growth, foreign trade and balance of payments. This picture will appear in the few tables to follow. These record the actual performance of the economy, rather than the planned performance. Because no rigorous plans were formulated, it was felt preferable to set down the results of the economy's activities without comparing them to a plan that was never laid down formally after 1965. What were actually laid down, and which are often referred to as the annual plans in official documents, are investment programmes incorporated in the annual budgets. These programmes invariably went through wide alterations during the year. This is an added reason why this writer felt that not much could be gained by the reconstruction of the annual projected or allocated investments.

Table 8.20 singles out investment, as this is the economic factor most relevant to growth in product. Furthermore, changes in productivity, another important (though lesser) factor, are subject to milder fluctuation and, anyway, are not recorded consistently in official documents; consequently, their impact cannot be assessed. Though significant and meaningful in themselves, and permitting a number of inferences, these investment data will not now be commented on. It would be more advisable to defer commentary till after Table 8.21, which records GDP, change in GDP, and fixed capital formation as a proportion of GDP. These relationships are interesting to examine. To give the examination deeper perspective, the data will stretch back to the beginning of the sixties (that is, will cover the First Five-Year Plan). This will permit comparisons between the Plan and the post-Plan years.

The year 1959/60 is recorded in Table 8.21 because it was the base year to the Five Year Plan 1960/1–1964/5. The Plan years that follow mark a distinct rise from the base year as far as investment is concerned. Indeed, the five Plan years stand out as a group among the 16 years included in the table, with the exception of 1975. This last year continued, but much more steeply, the rise in investment that started in 1974. The very high level of investment in 1975 is not an indication of a sudden, severe discipline in private and public consumption in Egypt which permitted a sharply rising saving out of domestic resources, although these resources had risen considerably at current prices over the preceding years. Indeed, consumption rose considerably, both public and private. The near-doubling of investment in 1975 is mostly the result of a large increase in the availability of foreign

Table 8.20: Fixed Public Investment by Sector at Current Prices 1965/6 – 1975

	1965/6		1966/7		1967/8		1968/9		1969/70		1970/1		1972		1973		1974		1975	
	£E m	Per Cent	£E m	Per Cent	£E m	Per Cent	£E m	Per Cent	£E m	Per Cent	£E m	Per Cent	£E m	Per Cent	£E m	Per Cent	£E m	Per Cent	£E m	Per Cent
Agriculture	30.7	8.0	31.3	8.6	24.9	8.4	25.6	7.4	27.0	7.6	27.9	7.7	27.8	6.8	35.2	7.6	32.7	5.1	42.4	3.5
Irrigation and drainage	32.6	8.5	34.4	9.4	25.1	8.4	32.5	9.5	29.1	8.2	22.0	7.0	27.3	6.7	22.4	4.8	21.5	3.3	40.9	3.4
High Dam	19.0	4.9	16.5	4.5	12.5	4.2	9.5	2.8	5.2	1.5	3.4									
Electricity	61.1	26.2	69.3	26.9	52.9	17.6	31.9	9.3	27.3	7.7	23.1	6.4	25.8	6.3	30.3	6.5	30.0	4.7	49.3	4.1
Industry	100.6	15.9	98.4	18.9	85.8	28.9	101.1	29.4	123.1	34.6	125.7	34.8	152.9	37.3	154.3	33.2	234.0	36.3	382.3	31.8
Construction	6.8	1.8	3.9	1.1	1.0	0.3	2.6	0.8	3.4	0.9	8.9	2.5	5.5	1.3	5.0	1.1	10.6	1.6	22.8	1.9
Commodity Sectors	250.8	65.3	253.8	69.4	202.2	67.8	203.2	59.2	215.1	60.5	211.0	58.4	239.3	58.4	247.2	53.2	328.8	51.0	537.7	44.7
Transport and communication	49.4	12.9	42.6	11.6	38.3	12.9	69.5	20.2	71.4	20.1	81.2	22.6	75.6	18.4	123.0	26.3	187.0	29.0	373.7	31.1
Suez Canal	3.7	1.0	3.5	1.0																
Finance and trade	2.7	0.7	2.6	0.7	0.7	0.2	2.7	0.8	3.6	1.0	9.5	2.6	2.9	0.7	2.7	0.6	5.2	0.8	9.3	0.8
Housing	47.5	12.4	42.3	11.6	41.7	14.0	46.9	13.6	36.5	10.3	26.5	7.3	41.9	10.2	40.3	8.7	51.5	8.0	169.3	14.1
Public utilities	12.4	3.2	8.6	2.3	4.2	1.4	5.8	1.7	10.9	3.1	16.8	4.7	15.9	3.9	22.8	4.9	28.7	4.4	39.2	3.3
Other services	17.3	4.5	12.4	3.4	10.9	3.7	15.4	4.5	18.0	5.0	16.0	4.4	34.5	8.4	29.2	6.3	43.9	6.8	71.8	6.0
Service Sectors	133.0	34.7	112.0	30.6	95.8	32.2	140.3	40.8	140.4	39.5	150.0	41.6	170.8	41.6	218.0	46.8	316.3	49.0	663.3	55.3
Grand Total	383.8	100.0	365.8	100.0	298.0	100.0	343.5	100.0	355.5	100.0	361.0	100.0	410.1	100.0	465.2	100.0	645.1	100.0	1,201.0	100.0

Notes: 1970/1 stretches till 31 December; beginning with 1972, years quoted are calendar years.
'Industry' includes petroleum and mining.
Percentages added.

Sources: For 1965/6-1960/70, CAPMS, *1951/52-1970/71*, p.168; for 1970/1, 1972 and 1973, CAPMS, *Statistical Abstract...1952-1974*, p.204; for 1974, *Evaluation...1974*, p.63; and for 1975, *Follow-Up...1975*, p.17.

Egypt

Table 8.21: Gross Domestic Product at Market Prices and Gross Fixed Capital Formation 1959/60–1975 at Current Prices

Year	GDP £E m	Change in GDP Per Cent	GFCF £E m	GFCF as Per Cent of GDP
1959/60	1,375.6		171.4	12.5
1960/1	1,459.3	6.1	225.6	15.5
1961/2	1,513.3	3.7	251.1	16.6
1962/3	1,684.6	11.3	299.6	17.8
1963/4	1,887.9	12.1	372.4	19.7
1964/5	2,213.5	17.2	358.4	16.2
1965/6	2,402.9	8.6	377.4	15.7
1966/7	2,480.7	3.2	358.8	14.5
1967/8	2,533.0	2.1	292.2	11.5
1968/9	2,696.4	6.4	343.5	12.7
1969/70	2,971.3	10.2	355.5	12.0
1970/1	3,145.5	5.9	361.0	11.5
1972	3,417.0	8.6	410.1	12.0
1973	3,661.0	7.1	465.2	12.7
1974	4,063.0	11.0	645.1	15.9
1975	4,602.0	13.3	1,201.0	26.1

Sources: For GDP, *Evolution... 1960/61–1969/70*, p. 7 for 1959/60 to 1969/70; Ministry of Planning, *Follow-up and Evaluation of Economic and Social Growth in the Arab Republic of Egypt 1971/1972*, (Cairo, December 1973; Arabic), p. 187, for 1970/1; and *Follow-up... 1975*, p. 3, for 1972-5 (GDP calculated from data in this reference). For GFCF, see Sources in Table 8.14 above for the years 1965/6–1975; for the years 1959/60–1964/5, *Evolution... 1960/61–1969/70*, p. 7. Change in GDP and GFCF as percentage of GDP both calculated.

resources, thanks mainly to aid (in grants and loans) from the oil-producing countries — specifically, Kuwait, the United Arab Emirates, Qatar and Saudi Arabia. In this connection, it is useful to point out that domestic saving constituted about three-quarters of investment on average in the sixties, but this proportion fell in the first half of the decade of the seventies. (Data are not available on savings for all the years covered in Table 8.21.)

As the column showing change in GDP reveals, the course of GDP over the years has been very erratic. In addition to wide fluctuations, the performance has been distinctly poor for some years, if price increases are taken into account. Three of the years included, namely 1961/2, 1966/7 and 1967/8 did not mark enough real growth to permit any improvement in the level of living *per capita*, but rather a deterioration. The two last-named years were adversely affected by the Arab-Israeli war of June 1967, whereas the first year was affected by the disruptive nationalization decrees of July 1961 which passed massive assets to an inexperienced public sector, inhibited private sector investment, and generally lowered the level of national product; and later by the break-up of the Egyptian-Syrian union in 1961 with its dampening effect on economic activity.

The last three years of the Plan period marked notable growth, though, admittedly, the last two years began to register clear inflationary pressures. Likewise, the years 1973-5, but particularly the last two of these three years, have suffered heavily from the strain of the new inflationary wave that has characterised the seventies. Inflation, rising consumption, but above all a low national product to start with and a heavy military burden have combined to squeeze the volume of domestic savings consistently. Even investment, which is larger than domestic savings thanks to the inflow of foreign aid, is a small proportion of national product, for a country desirous of marking fast growth and development.

In addition, the economy has suffered from overstaffing in many sectors coupled with low productivity except in agriculture, badly co-ordinated expansion, and — above all — a shortage of foreign exchange resources. Together, these ills accounted, before the June war of 1967, for resource dislocations, unduly high costs, and insufficiency of raw materials and spare parts needed by the expanded industrial complex as well as by the tourist and hotel facilities, the transport and communications system, and other important areas of economic activity.

The 1967 war only helped to bring about further deterioration in the state of the productive assets of the country, extreme slowing down in many areas of activity, the closing of the Suez Canal, the accentuated neglect of maintenance of capital assets, and deterioration of morale and direction in the circles of the general public and the leadership. Furthermore, huge resources continued to be diverted away from development work into armaments and the maintenance of a large army. This diversion is larger than the budget and balance of payments data suggest, since certain important arms imports were contracted for without publicity and do not leave their trace in the relevant national accounts. It is probable that, on average, Egypt has been diverting the equivalent of 15-20 per cent of its GNP to defence.

The reduced availability of resources for development coincided with distinctly increased burdens. Thus, in addition to the closure of the Suez Canal and the loss of direct revenues from passage fees, and of indirect income from activities associated with Canal operations, Egypt lost the Sinai oil-wells and copper mines. (The wells accounted for 60 per cent of all oil production in 1966.) Furthermore, the very extensive shelling by the Israelis of the Canal cities — Port Said, Port Tewfiq, Ismailia and Suez — resulted in almost total destruction of buildings and utilities: the extent of the destruction has to be seen to be believed. In consequence, around 750,000 inhabitants had to flee their cities and overcrowd and overburden Cairo and other cities where relative safety was possible. Vital economic targets, such as refineries, the petrochemical complex at Suez, and electricity and water installations were seriously damaged, high-power transmission lines were hit in the heart of the country, and the war of attrition which spread between the full-scale war of 1967 and the summer of 1970 exacted a heavy human toll in addition to material damage.

The most recent half-decade, ending with the year 1975, has witnessed some important changes in economic orientation and policy, as we will have occasion to indicate further down. The greater liberalisation that has characterised these years and the wider scope for private sector activity have not, in themselves, helped the economy. The tangible increase in investment is not a reflection of more disciplined consumption, a drop in the military burden, or so much an increase in the availability of domestic resources thanks to the increase in national product (although this has occurred), but rather to the marked growth in the inflow of Arab funds. This is truest of 1974 and 1975, and it can particularly be seen in the rise in gross fixed capital formation at a much higher rate than that of GDP. (GFCF in 1975 rose by 38.7 per cent, as against 13.3 per cent for GDP.)

The terminal picture of the economy is one of great distress, shortages, misallocations, inadequacy and deterioration of public utilities and other capital assets, and a general sense of loss of direction. The larger inflow of foreign resources has failed to leave a strong impact

Egypt

on the performance of the economy and the well-being of the population. The heavy cumulative burden of defence which has built up into an enormous strain on the economy and its resources over the past two decades (as military expenditure accelerated in 1955, and has continued to be high) is the primary cause for the present serious crisis of the Egyptian economy. But it is not the only cause. Economic policy ought to receive its due share of blame as well. The two causes, operating within a context of shortage of resources, have constrained the economic growth of the country while the pressures for more and better consumption continue to be heavy and to increase their weight.

These pressures have been compounded for most of the period under consideration with fast population increase. However, demographic developments have tended to show favourable tendencies in recent years, with a drop in the live births rate much larger than that in the mortality rate. (In the decade 1961-70, the birth rate dropped from 44.1 to 35.1 per thousand, and the death rate from 15.8 to 15.1, thus reducing the rate of natural increase from 28.3 to 20.0 per thousand.[48]) Nevertheless, notwithstanding this development, the population problems remain largely intractable. The level of redundancy in the labour force is still very high. (The work-force is recorded as a little over 9m for 1974, or just under 25 per cent of a total population of 36.4m. This suggests a substantial unemployment, in addition to underemployment.[49]) Emigration to Arab and other countries, though substantial now, remains a very minor numerical corrective; furthermore, the emigrants include a high proportion of well-trained Egyptians.

Table 8.22: The Distribution of Employment by Sector, 1974 (thousand employees)

Sector	Number	Per Cent of Total
Agriculture	4,212.4	46.6
Extractive industries	32.0	0.3
Manufacturing industry	1,117.5	12.4
Construction	315.2	3.5
Electricity	38.3	0.4
Total, commodity sectors	5,715.4	63.2
Transport, communications and storage	405.0	4.5
Trade and finance	883.2	9.8
Total, distribution sectors	1,288.2	14.3
Housing	139.1	1.5
Public utilities	43.0	0.5
Services	1,853.1	20.5
Total, service sectors	2,035.2	22.5
Grand total	9,038.8	100.0

Source: *Evaluation... 1974*, p. 6 in Appendix.

The picture of employment as presented in Table 8.22 — even if qualified as wanting in precision, like all employment data in developing countries with a large agricultural sector and inadequate statistical services — is clear enough to indicate the seriously pressing need for job creation in Egypt. As the rural sector is already well-manned, even superfluously manned outside the peak of certain seasons, the solution to the problems of unemployment and underemployment must necessarily reside in the other sectors. The creation of job opportunities in the economy to absorb, say, another 3 million workers, in order to bring the employed to about one-third of the population would require investments of such enormity that they are beyond the capability of Egypt for the foreseeable future. On the other hand, to pad the economy with more labourers than needed by the tasks and the technology at economic levels, would raise unit cost in production, make the products non-competitive, and generally reduce the marginal productivity of labour. The national product would scarcely become abler to sustain the extra cost of such work-creation policy. The solution must remain, as it always does in countries where the population pressure on resources is very high (given the level and quality of these resources, the capital availability, and the level of technology), on the dual approach of development and containment of population growth. It seems now possible to say that the latter is being gradually achieved, but the former will have to be accelerated for tangible results in employment to be attained.

Another aspect of population is agricultural production, since 'overpopulation' cannot be said to exist without reference to foodstuff availability and employment opportunities. According to FAO sources, agricultural food production rose to an index of 152 in 1966 (1952-6 = 100), against an index of 149 for the whole Near East. With 1961-5 as base, the index rose to 132 in 1972, against 125 for all developing countries, but 136 for the Near East.[50] This suggests a drop in the rate of growth over the past ten or fifteen years. Although the rate of growth of production is above that of population increase for the period covered, it is still uncomfortably low. The recent drop in the rate of natural increase of population, though of significance, cannot provide enough reassurance unless it goes further and the new low rates are sustained. It would seem at this juncture that more emphasis should be laid on the expansion of agricultural (especially food) production, through the introduction of the necessary economic, technical and institutional reforms.

This chapter has pointed up three of the four major economic issues with which Egyptian society has had to contend if it is to witness accelerated and sustained development. We refer here to the large absolute size of population (given the other production factors available), and the (until recently) very high rate of natural population increase; the scarcity of cultivable and of cultivated land, and the disturbingly close race between population increase and food production; and the shortage of foreign exchange earnings. In none of these problem areas can substantial redress be envisaged in the short or even medium time range. Before the situation with respect to foreign exchange availability is discussed somewhat more fully, what we consider to be the fourth problem area must be mentioned. This is the civil service, which is overly large and heavy-handed, slow and bureaucratic, in spite of marked improvements at the higher rungs of authority since the Revolution. This last area will be dealt with at greater length in the second, companion volume of this book, but we will refer to it briefly further down in the context of the recent developments in the economic system.

Egypt's chronic shortage of foreign exchange can best be seen in the fact that in the twenty years 1956-75, not once were the goods and services exported able to pay for those imported. The shortfall has become more serious since 1969, and in 1974 and 1975 widened considerably, as Table 8.23 shows. Indeed, even if unrequited transfers to the government and the private sector are added to the account, the overall balance remains deficitary in all but two of the twenty years. The problem is compounded by the obvious fact that if Egypt were to head towards balance or near-balance between its earnings and its expenditure of foreign exchange, it will have first, and for many years to come, to receive enormous aid from external sources. Such aid will, in turn, impose a heavy servicing burden to be added to the one already suffered. Furthermore, no comforting answer can be found in the country's foreign exchange resources and reserves, as these have been seriously depleted, as we will see shortly. In brief, a massive aid operation is needed, preferably consisting mainly of grants, if the economy is to expect reprieve in the present context, in the decade to come.

Table 8.23: Current Account of Egypt's Balance of Payments, 1956-75 ($ million)

Year	Goods and Services (net)	Unrequited Private	Transfers Government	Overall Balance
1956	−142	6	24	−112
1957	−96	1	10	−85
1958	−61	1	−1	−61
1959	−132	11	3	−118
1960	−92	14	−2	−80
1961	−176	20	−8	−164
1962	−380	41	−4	−343
1963	−292	7	−8	−293
1964	−294	8	5	−281
1965	−262	10	10	−242
1966	−174	6	6	−162
1967	−298	12	122	−164
1968	−248	3	251	6
1969	−304	8	288	−8
1970	−462	4	304	−154
1971	−486	11	268	−207
1972	−465	5	290	−170
1973	−564	6	635	77
1974	−1,364	42	993	−329
1975	−2,476	90	987	−1,399

Sources: *IFS, Supplement to 1967/68 Issues; IFS,* September 1967; *IFS,* March 1974 and *IFS,* November 1976.

Apart from presenting the basic data of Egypt's balance of payments in order to show the degree of the country's dependence on foreign aid (whether as grants and other unrequited transfers, or as capital inflows representing loans contracted), we have to examine the country's foreign liquidity. However, a look at the account of the aid received is in order here.

The task of ascertaining the volume of aid and indebtedness is especially difficult in the case of Egypt, owing to the fact that the economic relations with the Soviet Union and other socialist countries are not always publicised in detailed and specific terms, particularly when the transactions have a military aspect. Even loans from Arab sources are difficult to assess, in so far as some transactions are reported in the press but do not get finalised, or alternatively, are consummated, but not reported. Consequently, the estimate to be presented here must be considered tentative; it is further thought to include only loans avowedly for economic purposes.

According to data available, Egypt has received about $9.1 billion over the period mid-1945 to 1974, detailed in Table 8.24.

Table 8.24: Estimated Aid Received by Egypt, 1945—74

	$ million
Net official flows from OECD countries and from multilateral agencies, from mid-1945 to the end of 1974	2,088
Aid committed by centrally-planned countries	3,016
Arab aid:	
Kuwait Fund for Arab Economic Development (to end 1975)	163
Arab Fund for Economic and Social Development (to end 1975)	105
Other Arab aid, from national development funds and from governments, about	3,270
Aid from other sources (mainly Iran)	500
Total aid (grants and loans)	9.142

Source: For aid from Western sources, see *Time* Magazine, Vol. LXXXI, No. 13, 29 March 1963, for the period July 1945 to end June 1962, quoting official US sources; OECD, *The Flow of Financial Resources to Less-Developed Countries 1961-1965*, p. 155, for the years 1960-5; OECD, *Development Assistance: Efforts and Policies of the Members of the Development Assistance Committee, 1969 Review*, p. 170, for 1966-8; OECD, *Development Cooperation: Efforts and Policies of the Members of the Development Assistance Committee, 1973 Review*, p. 208, for 1969-72; UN, *Statistical Yearbook 1975*, p. 829, for 1972 to 1974. For aid from socialist sources, 1954-1974, see UN, *Statistical Yearbook 1975*, p. 827. For aid from Arab sources, see Table 14.6 in Chapter 14 below and for aid from specific aid funds, see Kuwait Fund for Arab Economic Development, *Annual Report 1975/76* (various pages) and Arab Fund for Economic and Social Development, *Annual Report 1975* (various pages).

It ought to be pointed out here that aid from the socialist countries is recorded as $1,011 — for the years 1955-70 in US Department of State, *Communist States and Developing Countries: Aid and Trade in 1970* (Washington, DC, 1971), as against $1,844m for the same period in UN, *Statistical Yearbook 1975* quoted above. Presumably the difference between the two estimates is that between commitments and actual flows.

There is no clear indication of the distribution of this total of $9.1 billion between grants and loans, and therefore of the extent of the burden foreign aid has imposed on the economy. But it is reliably thought that loans by far exceed grants. However, the economy's debt burden goes well beyond the loans it has contracted, whatever the volume of these is. This is because of the substantial debt transacted with the USSR and other socialist countries for arms deliveries, as well as Arab loans for the purpose of financing arms imports. One source has estimated total indebtedness by the end of 1971 at $5,600m, while another source quotes total military aid from the socialist countries for the period 1955-70 as being some $2,700m.[51] The two estimates are too far apart for reconciliation. Furthermore, neither takes into account any loans incurred during the four years 1971-4. What makes the matter yet more confused is the publication in the Arab press of widely divergent estimates of Egypt's *net* foreign indebtedness. One of these which seems to this writer to be plausible runs in the neighbourhood of $8-9 billion down to the end of 1974. While loans from Arab sources are generally on easy terms and are not expected to involve exacting repayment schedules, those from the socialist countries are becoming pressing, owing to the recent refusal by the USSR to reschedule them subsequent to the serious rift between the two states after Egypt's signature of the second Sinai accord with Israel in the spring of 1975.

Against the external financial obligations of the country, there is very little cushioning. Thus, international reserves were a mere $294m by the end of 1975; indeed, these had reached a low level of $41m by the end of 1972. The foreign liabilities of the Central Bank were $2,751m by the end of 1975. In addition, the Central Bank's claims on the government totalled £E1,590m at the same date.[52] The government's extensive recourse to deficit financing has led to the build-up of a considerable internal debt.

The large and heavy-handed civil service has been cited as one of the major millstones around the neck of the Egyptian economy. The retarding effect of the bureaucracy has been all the more pronounced with the vast expansion in the domain of the public sector and, later, the 'socialist transformation' of the economy. It is useful to pause briefly here and to examine the contours and features of the socio-economic system as it has come to be under President Sadat, who took office upon President Nasser's death in September 1970.

Egypt approved a new permanent Constitution on 11 September 1971. Like the old (Interim) Constitution, the new one stated that Egypt was a republic with '. . . a democratic, socialist system based on the alliance of the working people and derived from the country's historical heritage and the spirit of Islam'. Further on, in Chapter 1, 'The State', it is stated that the Arab Socialist Union (the one party allowed to exist) 'is the political organization of the State which represents the alliance of the working forces of the people: the farmers, workers, soldiers, the intelligentsia and national capitalism'. Chapters 2, 5 and 6 present practically no change, but Chapters 3 and 4 incorporate some features of liberalisation in the areas of public liberties, citizens' rights and duties, and judiciary processes.[53]

Though formally the system seems to have kept the broad content and characteristics which it came to have under Nasser, in practice the new leadership has permitted (if not encouraged) the criticism of certain hitherto untouchable matters, such as the size and performance — and even the very existence — of the public sector, the agrarian reform measures, sequestration measures, economic policy, and the High Dam (built in close co-operation with the Soviet Union). The President has had to steer a safe course delicately, between the outward desire to preserve the socialist system which many people (especially industrial workers, landless peasants and small land-holders and tenants) felt had brought them concrete gains, and the desire, in practice, to allow much more scope for private enterprise, to return sequestrated property to its owners and to free property under trusteeship, to ease import controls, to attract foreign private investments, and generally to liberalise the economy.

Like all balancing games, this one has bordered on danger, and has drawn criticism both from those who welcomed the new measures (who feel too little is being done, too slowly) and those who have reacted with anxiety to the measures (feeling that too much is being ceded to the bourgeoisie, whether old or new). However, the authorities are moving gradually in the direction of liberalisation, irrespective of the outward preservation of the socialist stance and credo. The policy option taken has been influenced by pressure from two sources: the extreme hardship and deprivation suffered by the population for many long years and the need to ease the living conditions of the masses, and the ebb of socialist influence in the region as a whole. The latter phenomenon has been influenced considerably by the acceleration of enrichment in the oil region and the expectation in the capital-hungry countries that the inflow of capital aid from the capital-surplus countries could not be substantial if socialist leanings remained strong in recipient societies and economies.

The economy is rather unsettled, hesitant, and without clear direction, in the midst of these contradictory pulls. Basic long-term guidelines which ought to be formulated and day-to-day decisions which should be made remain in the twilight area of indecision, partly because of the struggle between ideological and pragmatic exigencies, partly because of the difficulty of determining the pattern of resource allocation between defence and development in a protracted state of no-war-no-peace, and partly because of the divergent pulls of interest groups which differ on intellectual as well as on concrete material grounds.

5. THE HIGH DAM

The construction of the High Dam at Aswan, just south of the old Aswan Dam, is the prize single economic-engineering achievement of the revolution. While it is true that the Dam was constructed with vast technical and some financial help from the USSR, it is equally true that the Dam personified in very concrete terms President Nasser's and Egypt's determination and reply to challenge.

The challenge came in the spring of 1956, when aid from the IBRD, the USA and Britain, pledged in support for the project, was brusquely withdrawn at the instigation and upon the initiative of the then US Secretary of State John Foster Dulles, who had been angered first because of Egypt's refusal to join any regional defence pacts against the USSR, secondly by President Nasser's pursuit of a policy of neutrality or non-alignment, and thirdly because Nasser broke the arms monopoly enjoyed by the West by successfully making a large arms deal with the Eastern bloc. Upon withdrawal of the support pledge, President Nasser nationalised the Suez Canal Company in order to use the revenues from Canal dues for the construction of the Dam. Much later, on 27 December 1958 and on 27 August 1960, Egypt signed two agreements with the USSR, according to which this country was to supply technical and financial assistance totalling 1,300 million roubles (some £E113.2 million) out of total costs estimated at £E415 million. The balance was to be borne totally by Egypt.

The idea of a second major dam on the Nile had acquired wide acceptance, in order to control floods, enable the country to have more water for irrigation, and avoid silting, which used to occur owing to the free passage of flood water through the old Aswan Dam into the sea and consequently to lead to the loss of 'some 30 milliard of the total river flow of 84 milliard cubic meters'.[54] The project had been considered under the monarchy, but it was the new government which, in 1954, began to examine the question of implementation seriously and to prepare plans to that end. The idea and the site of the High Dam took precedence over alternative ideas that involved dams outside Egyptian territory, with all that that would have meant in loss of political control and other complications.

Agreement with the Sudan was necessary in order to regulate the apportioning of Nile water, and this agreement was reached before work started. The agreement covered the question of water allocation, as well as the compensation for Sudanese territory to be flooded upon completion of the project. The entire amount of compensation, a total of £E15m, has now been paid.

The plans submitted by Egyptian experts were amended, after discussions with international and USSR consultants. The main idea of the Dam was to block the Nile waters for 'century storage', thus forming an artificial lake behind and raising the water level. This lake, with an average length of 500 km. and an average width of 10 km., was to be the second-largest lake in the world, with an area of 5,000 sq. km. The capacity of the reservoir was to be 151 billion cubic metres, assigned as follows:

— 30 billion cubic metres (bcm) for silt collection over the next 500 years;
— 37 bcm reserve for exceptionally high floods; and
— 84 bcm of steady accumulation in the year, of which 55.5 bcm would be for Egypt, 18.5 bcm for Sudan, and 10 bcm for evaporation and leakage.

The Dam has 6 main tunnels which branch off into 12 smaller tunnels leading to 12 hydro-electric generators with 175,000 kw capacity each, or a total capacity of 2.1m kw, capable of generating 10 billion kwh a year.

The economic implications of the High Dam can be summarised as follows:

— irrigation of 1.3m *feddans* (546,000 hectares) of new land, and transformation of 0.7m *fed.* (294,000 ha) from basin to perennial irrigation;
— protection against floods and against dry years;
— lowering of water level in land north of the Dam thanks to regular irrigation;
— expansion of rice production and consequently promotion of rice exports;
— improvement of navigation in the Nile all the year round;
— doubling the electric-generating capacity of the country, and lowering the cost to users;
— apart from direct benefits (initially estimated at raising national product by some £E234m a year), generation of indirect benfits, including tourism and fishing in the new lake; and
— in Sudan, tripling of area cultivated and assuring all irrigation needs, extension of area for long-staple cotton, and increase in government revenue and value added in agriculture by some 30 per cent.

An original cost-benefit estimate had been prepared, according to which the total cost of the project was to be £E415m. However, the National Bank of Egypt revised this estimate later in view of rise in prices, and estimated the cost to reach £E618 million.[55] The NBE made its calculations on the basis of a 75-year span of time — a very conservative estimate. Taking interest into account, the study shows an annual expected return of £E197 million, and a cost of £E63.2 million. Thus, the benefit-cost ratio is 3.1:1.

Work on the Dam started in January 1960, and was to be completed late in 1970 or early in 1971. It is to the credit of Egypt, and of the USSR technicians, that the project was completed, and the turbines installed, several months ahead of time. President Nasser was able to attend the completion ceremonies before his death on 28 September 1970. Furthermore, the USSR credit was not all used: there has been a saving of £E4 million, which reflects careful calculation and planning. Total cost remained very close to the original estimate; it amounted to £E450 million, instead of £E415 million envisaged before the start of work.[56] The benefit/cost ratio is now re-assessed at 3.9:1. The improvement is due both to the materialisation of total cost at £E450 million, instead of the NBE estimate of £E618 million, and of annual revenue at £E235 million instead of the NBE estimate of £E197 million.

Criticism has recently been levelled against the project.[57] In fact, this criticism echoes objections that had been levelled at the original idea in the late forties. In summary, it is maintained that the Dam will make the country lose the very fertile silt that the flood water carried; it will increase the spread of bilharziasis because of the extension of perennial irrigation; and it will upset the balance of sea life north of the Delta. These objections, and a few more, had been foreseen by the technicians who had planned the project. Thus, to the extent that silt will be lost, fertilisers can be used to compensate for the loss in fertility. Furthermore, the government will save the millions of pounds that used to be spent on clearing the canals from silting. While it is true that the area of perennial irrigation will expand and therefore exposure to bilharziasis will increase, this is only an incremental problem and the core of the problem — which is to eradicate the endemic disease — has anyway to be faced and solved, and is being tackled seriously. The balance of sea life can be reconstituted, and in any case account will have to be taken of the compensatory factor represented by the new vast lake to be formed.

On balance therefore, and taking into account the net benefit of some £E174 million (235 less annual cost of 60.7), it can be claimed that the High Dam represents a great net benefit and a monument to the determination of the country and its leadership, and to Egyptian-USSR co-operation in the face of the challenge posed by the withdrawal in 1956 of the Western and IBRD pledge to help finance the project. Likewise, the Dam is a successful response to the challenge of nature, which is niggardly in rainfall.

Yet it should be indicated that the easing of the pressure of population on land resources, which the Dam will help on the side of extension of the supply of irrigated land, ought to be met from the population end too, through limitation of the demand for land — that is, through family planning and a tangible drop in the rate of natural increase in population to something more manageable in the very near future. This is necessary because the extension in land area irrigated by about one-third has almost all been counteracted by the increase in population by about one-third since 1960. This does not negate the value of the Dam on this score, as some critics have wrongly maintained, because, in the absence of the Dam the population would still have increased by one-third and the imbalance in the relationship between population and land would have become all that more serious, and pauperisation, *pari passu*, would have increased by about that much.

6. THE SOCIALIST TRANSFORMATION

The first nine years of the revolution were characterised by four main processes or currents: achievement of full political independence and consolidation of this independence; agrarian reform in order to break the power of the very influential class of landlords and improve the lot of the owners of tiny land holdings and of cash- and share-tenants and agricultural labourers; Egyptianisation of English, French, and later Belgian and other non-Egyptian establishments; and initiation of the drive for fast industrialisation. All four processes unfolded within a framework of private enterprise, where emphasis was on production rather than on distribution, in spite of the increasing involvement of the public sector in the economic life of the country and the direct ownership by the state of a certain volume of productive assets. These assets mainly comprised the Egyptianised properties of non-Egyptians.

The ninth anniversary of the revolution, in July 1961, was the occasion for the announcement by President Nasser of vast measures of nationalisation which, literally overnight, changed the character of the socio-economic system. These measures fall into three categories. The first category involved nationalisation of scores of big establishments in the finance, insurance, industry, transport, foreign trade, and distribution sectors. The second category constituted the 'second agrarian reform', which involved reducing the ceiling of land ownership; the measures falling in this category (as well as amendments in 1963, 1964 and 1969) have already been discussed in section 3 above. The third category comprised measures aimed at equalisation of income and the promotion of greater social justice broadly defined. More decrees were yet to follow later in the years 1961-4, the last decree on record being in March 1964.

It ought to be mentioned, however, that a few measures for the nationalisation of mixed or purely Egyptian establishments had occurred before this 'avalanche' of decrees — for instance those relating to the Cairo Water Company and the National Bank of Egypt on 1 July 1957, and Misr Bank on 11 February 1960. Before that, between March 1956 and July 1957 the government entered into mixed ownership with companies prospecting for or exploiting the mineral wealth of the country, with petroleum producing, refining and distributing companies, and with transport companies. The government's share in the capital of these concerns as well as the control of the totally nationalised (formerly British, French and other non-Egyptian) companies was centred in the Economic Organization which was established in January 1957 for the purpose.

These were little streams flowing in the direction of the general current of nationalisation, but they were not *the* socialist transformation. None the less, it is now clear that President Nasser's thinking and that of his close associates was groping gradually for some version of socialism — one which would not violate the cultural sensitivity of the people and yet satisfy the leaders' concern with a speedy achievement both of development and of egalitarian distribution. It must be admitted that there was a great deal of experimentation with ideas and with institutions. If this were to be condemned as a sign of inexperience, or of indecision, or of insufficient concern with the advantages of continuity of system and policy, it could still be argued that the groping for suitable ideas and institutions was a sign of flexibility and pragmatism. Indeed, it is questionable if it would have been preferable — less wasteful and more productive because more resolute — to have 'imported' wholesale one version of socialism as it prevailed in some country. (If this had been done, Yugoslavia would have probably been the exporter, because it is known that there always was a great deal of personal, political and ideological affinity between the Egyptian and the Yugoslav leaders.) In the end, the contours of a system became clear, and the body of thinking on the system was incorporated into *The Charter*, which was discussed by the Congress of National Forces in May and made final in June 1962.

Patrick O'Brien, who has written the most thorough book on the change of system in Egypt,[58] divides the period covered into the following phases: the free-enterprise phase 1952-6; guided capitalism 1957-60, which marked the 'demise of private enterprise'; and the socialist system from 1961 onwards. However, O'Brien argues and concludes that the system is not truly socialist, and that the arbitrariness of power in it as well as the existence of disparities in wealth and income not called for by social purpose or by the dictates of efficiency, and the still large share of productive assets in private hands together raise doubts about the eligibility of the system to be called socialist.[59]

In fact, strictly speaking, the Egyptian leaders refer to their society in *The Charter* and elsewhere as 'socialist, democratic, and cooperative'. The controversy is largely a question of definition and the nature of the 'ideal type' that the critic sets as standard of measurement. O'Brien does not make explicit his 'ideal type', although he clearly sets some criteria against which he examines the system in Egypt after 1961. However, here we prefer to confine ourselves to drawing attention to this question that O'Brien and some Arab writers have raised, without entering the debate.[60] We will instead now present the measures that are believed by the authorities in Egypt to have brought about the socialist transformation and which, along with other economic and political measures, have presumably made society socialist, democratic and co-operative.[61]

Nationalisation
— Law 117 decreed that all banks and insurance companies be fully nationalised, as well as 42 large industrial, transport, commercial, financial and land reclamation companies.
— Law 118 decreed partial nationalisation of 82 companies and establishments.
— Law 119 limited ownership by any one person or company to £E10,000 worth of shares in a list of 148 companies.
— Law 120 amending Law No. 71 of 22 June of the same year decreed that all establishments engaged in cotton export trade must take the form of an Arab (i.e. United Arab Republic) joint-stock company, at least 50 per cent of the capital of which must be owned by a public organisation;
— Law 107 decreed that only government-owned companies or companies affiliated with public organisations and at least 25 per cent of the capital of which belonged to the government could act as commercial agenices.
— Law 108 decreed that all imports should be made by government-owned companies.
— Presidential Decree No. 1203 required that all public works on behalf of government departments or organisations must be undertaken by companies at least 50 per cent of whose capital is government-owned, provided contracts were for £E30,000 or over. (In the four months subsequent to the break-up of the union with Syria on 28 September 1961, some 850 persons — deemed dangerous to the system and likely to attempt to overthrow the government, were sequestrated and control of their property passed to an administrator. Further, by August 1963 a series of new nationalisations were decreed, mainly to achieve vertical integration of business. And in March 1964, 119 contracting companies which had earlier been partly nationalised were now fully nationalised.)

Second Agrarian Reform
— Law 127 reduced the maximum size of individual ownership of land to 100 *fed.* (42 ha), and maximum family ownership to 300 *fed.* (126 ha).
— Law 128 decreed that instalments due to the government by beneficiaries of agrarian reform (both old and new) be reduced by half. (Other decrees in 1963, 1964 and 1969 amending agrarian reform further have already been mentioned.)

Distribution and Equalisation
— Law 111 set aside 25 per cent of the net profits of companies for labour, as cash payments and allocations for social services.
— Laws 115, 129 and 153 raised taxes on persons and property and made them very steep (income tax up to 90 per cent on the highest slice of income), while making generous (indeed, *very* generous) allowances and exemptions for the lower-income groups.
— Law 113 prohibited company directors or employees from obtaining more than a total of £E5,000 annually in remuneration and other benefits.

Egypt

- Law 125 limited the holding of office to one post (in order to break the control by individuals over many establishments, and to spread the benefits).
- Law 133 reduced the working week to 42 hours without loss of pay.

The number of persons involved in the nationalisation measures (the first category) has been estimated at 7,000. It is also believed that many of the landlords affected by the 1961 agrarian reform decrees (the second category) were among the 7,000 persons, while the number of landlords dispossessed as a result of the 1969 agrarian reform amendment has been reported to be as high as 16,000.[62] (This estimate seems extravagantly high, in the light of data contained in Table 8.8 above relating to number of land-holders.) Various estimates have been made of the value of property nationalised (including a figure of £E500 million quoted by President Nasser in a speech). Official quotations put the total market value of the shares of the companies affected by Laws 117, 118 and 119 to £E258 million. The value of the shares of the companies fully nationalised was £E52 million; the other companies covered by Laws 118 and 119 were only partly nationalised. In total, it is calculated that

> the Government took over, in all, £E124 million of shares, and acquired control of over 70 percent of Egyptian company capital. The amount of shares remaining in private hands was put at £E194 million, ... plus £E66 million of securities of companies not affected by the nationalization decrees.[63]

It is this kind of pattern of ownership that partly spurred O'Brien to maintain that the system had not become socialist, with a large slice of capital still in private hands. In addition, land was mainly privately owned, as well as small industry, internal retail trade, residential buildings, small contracting business, entertainment establishments (cafés, restaurants), taxis, and many other types of small business. The overall pattern seems to have frozen along the main lines mentioned in *The Charter* ever since, although — as indicated earlier — since Nasser's death and the election of Anwar Sadat to the Presidency there has been an extensive debate around the efficiency and integrity of the public sector, and a good deal of arguing in favour of the liberalisation of the economy. But so far the pattern has not changed tangibly.

However, the socialist transformation ought not to be understood in the narrow sense of public versus private ownership, but as a composite process involving the broadening of the base of ownership — as in the case of land, the limitation of large ownership of capital in most sectors, the total ownership by the state of certain sectors (finance and insurance), and the equalisation, as far as possible, of income both through the broadening of the base of ownership and through a taxation-and-transfer policy.

Other aspects of the efforts of the public sector have also been described as part of socialism, such as the immense drive to build, equip and staff schools; the opening of the gates of the universities to scores of thousands and the relaxation of entrance requirements (often at the expense of quality); the provision of many thousands of units of cheap housing; the expansion both in terms of variety and geographical diffusion of health and sanitation services; the promotion of the co-operative movement; the carriage of pure drinking-water to all villages; and the acceleration in the setting up and staffing of rural combined units (or combined social welfare centres) offering economic, social and health services.[64]

Obviously, to describe such services as part of the socialist transformation is to stretch the definition of socialism very far. They are public services that can be found in the most capitalistic country as well. However, in the minds of many Egyptians and other Arabs, these services are associated with the system that brought about the transformation; the association has often been turned into identification.

Brief description was made in section 1 of the status of some of these services. Although statistics are not available for recent years for some of the services, it is still possible to underline some of the highlights of the achievements in this area as well as related areas.

Education, which in the early fifties absorbed only 43 per cent of children eligible for school, has expanded to the point where today over 60 per cent are in school. School population (first and second cycles) was 6.3m in 1975, against 1.9m in 1951. Enrolment in universities and other institutions of higher learning totalled 329,300 in 1975.[65] Over 36 per cent of all pupils and students are now females. Furthermore, while foreign education dominated high-level schooling in the early fifties, it has relinquished its position to the national system. Education is virtually free for all, at all levels, whereas it used to be prohibitive for most Egyptians in the second and third cycles. In addition, some 3.5m schoolchildren now receive a free midday meal. Finally, the education budget hovers around 18 per cent of total ordinary expenditures.

It must be emphasised that Egypt's achievement has a deep perspective, since serious educational efforts (including the despatch of bursary students abroad for training) began with Mohammed Ali in the early part of the nineteenth century. The revolutionary government thus accelerated a process that had been in motion for generations. Thanks to this process, Egypt finds itself today with a very large body of educated men and women, including many with university, professional and technical training. Indeed, because of this availability, Egypt is capable of permitting many thousands of teachers, doctors, engineers, lawyers and other professionals, as well as technicians and skilled workers in large numbers, to serve in other Arab countries.

However, it must also be emphasised that the opening wide of the doors of schools and universities has, at least during the years 1956-67, resulted in the lowering of educational standards. The student body grew much faster than the teaching force; less scope was provided for true exchange between teachers and students; laboratory and library facilities came under serious pressure; the teaching of foreign languages suffered; and in general quantitative gains were made at the expense of the quality of education. It is refreshing to observe, though, that since 1967, there has been greater awareness of the ills of the system of education, and several corrective measures have been taken, with respect to curricula, methods, and foreign language instruction. Nevertheless, the sheer weight of numbers, the excessively heavy bureaucracy and the shortage of financial resources have forced the pace of improvement to be very slow. The question of the large size of university enrolment, given the physical facilities, is yet to find a solution.

With regard to health care, there is today a serious confrontation of bilharziasis, malaria, tuberculosis and eye diseases, and concrete improvement has taken place. Over 2,400 hospitals, health units and centres were established by the end of 1974 to serve in towns and cities. In addition, 2,228 rural units were established, reportedly to serve 5,000 inhabitants each. The number of hospitals, hospital beds, and doctors and nurses has risen steeply, although it is still glaringly inadequate for the population if a reasonably satisfactory standard of service is to be provided. Hospital beds totalled 76,254 in 1974, or about one bed per 477 inhabitants.[66] The number of physicians has increased five-fold since 1950. However, supporting staff is still in very short supply. The number of nurses was reported as being only 22,528 in 1971, just slightly over the total number of physicians for the same year, namely 18,802.[67] (Roughly speaking, there is one physician for every 1,650 inhabitants, which is a very low ratio by the standards of some Arab countries like Lebanon and Kuwait.)

Family planning has become an established effort, and a great deal of experimentation is done, and several pilot projects are now trying to popularise family planning and to diffuse it. This area has registered remarkable success, judging by the tangible drop in the rate of natural increase in population, down to about 20 per thousand for 1971. This is reported as being mainly due to the drop in the birth rate. The success has encouraged the government to become rather overly ambitious and to aim at substantial further lowering of the rate of natural increase in a very short period of time. The expectation to bring this rate down to 13.2 per thousand in 1978 is wholly unrealistic in the present writer's view.[68]

The final area of social concern to mention here is cheap urban housing. This housing activity has helped provide accommodation for many in the lower and intermediate rungs in the civil service, with hundreds of thousands of units built and sold at moderate prices on instalment, both in urban and rural areas. The pace of construction slackened after the war of June 1967. Nevertheless, 183,476 units were built in 1969-74, including 33,375 in rural areas (in the last instance, between 1969 and mid-1973.)[69] However, the facilities available still fall very short of the needs, and urban overcrowding still chàracterises the big cities, in spite of the effort made.

It has been possible for Egypt to divert a large volume of resources to development work, to public services, and to the defence effort as well, because of the centralisation in government hands of a large portion of the productive assets of the country and the mobilisation of resources with more vigour than ever before. The expansion of the public sector reflects itself in the budget, which is now unified, and which reached a total of £E5,626m for expenditure in 1975. Although this is an estimate, it indicates the vast expansion since the early fifties. In contrast, in 1951/2 the budget totalled £E194.8m for revenue and £E233.6m for expenditure.[70] The expansion reflects that in the security, economic and social functions of the state, the large increase in population, the expansion in resources, inflation, but also the change in the economic system. Owing to the transfer of many productive assets to the government, the income and expenditure of the establishments operated by the public sector now appear in the unified budget (whereas these were private budgets in the business sector before nationalisation and the socialist transformation). The public sector is currently reported to account for about 44 per cent of national income.[71]

But domestic resources, mobilised through savings, taxation and the surplus obtained by public sector establishments are not sufficient to meet investment requirements. The government has been resorting to the import surplus, financed by foreign loans and grants, to attain the level of investment recorded. Thus, in 1975, foreign financing accounted for over 35 per cent of total investment.[72]

But, as indicated earlier, the aid coin has another, unpleasant side: the accumulation of foreign debts, and the strain which the balance of payments suffers in consequence, in addition to political implications which are frequently embarrassing and constraining. The strain is understandable, and should not be used as an excuse for criticising Egypt's borrowing policy unduly harshly — assuming an economically sound and defensible use of the resources borrowed. Indeed, Egypt could have avoided this strain by pursuing a much more relaxed investment and development policy. But the country would have thus bought some immediate comfort in its balance of payments at the expense of long-term comfort. This is the kind of hard choice that most developing countries face and have to make, unless they have a lucrative exportable resource in large quantities. (The burden of arms purchases is presumed here not to be reflected in the balance of payments. The arms agreements are secret, and they are believed to involve barter arrangements with the USSR.)

Foreign exchange problems led to very strict exchange controls through almost the entire period 1952-74, and, understandably, to very active efforts at evasion and black market operations. (Recently, after the Arab-Israeli war of October 1973, there has been some relaxation in the regulations.) The value of the Egyptian pound in terms of the dollar has suffered, and although this value until 1973 and the setting in of steep inflation was not a true reflection of the pound's purchasing power at home, it is still probably true that officially the pound has been for many years overvalued.

7. CONCLUSION

Many things can be said in conclusion to this chapter. But I prefer to leave its sections to speak for themselves; each, it is hoped, has pointed to the inferences to be drawn from the discussion. Instead, two observations will serve to wind the chapter up.

The first is that the Egyptian economy and society have undergone vast and radical changes within a very short span of time. These have spread into the political, social, economic, structural and technological fields. Against severe hardships, in the face of external and internal opposition, against the niggardliness of nature and the irresponsibility of over-procreating men and women, Gamal Abdul-Nasser has inspired the country into a record of achievement which, in spite of its many shortcomings, is remarkable — not only by Arab, but also by Third World standards. Purely in terms of growth, the performance has been good, with GDP rising between 1952 and the end of 1975 at about 8 per cent at current prices on the average, or about 5 per cent at constant prices.[73] GDP *per capita* seems to have doubled in 24 years in real terms, with a distinct improvement in the pattern of distribution in the meantime, in spite of some departure from the socialist stance and policies since 1972 or 1973.

The effort of Nasser and his associates has been a strong response to the many harsh challenges facing the country. The response often was unjustified by cold economic arithmetic. But the leadership of revolutionary Egypt rightly realised that more was at stake than this arithmetic: what was involved was stirring society's awareness of its potential and mobilising and using this potential. If the leadership is to be blamed, this must be more with respect to its political style than its political options, its economic measures than the economic and social desiderata that it set as objectives.

The achievement just described quantitatively is the rather bright side of the coin. But there is a dark side too. For, it is equally true that development is primarily a change in attitudes involving a socio-cultural as well as an economic revolution, and that the Egyptian bureaucracy, technocrats and masses have not been stirred and 'revolutionised' to the extent that the official media would want us to believe, although radical change has actually occurred. It is also true that the legal framework for the socialist transformation was laid down, while the mental framework remained deep down and on the whole less than fully prepared for the transformation. Nevertheless, enough political, socio-cultural, economic and technological change has been effected that Egypt will never be the same as in its pre-revolutionary days. There might, and probably will be many setbacks, but basically certain social and economic, as well as political, forces have been liberated or generated that cannot now be contained for long.

Our second final observation extrapolates the recent past and the present into the future. Will Egypt be capable of overcoming its basic economic difficulties and constraints in the relatively near future? These difficulties, it will be recalled, relate to a large population with very limited resources; severe foreign exchange constraints which cannot be relaxed in the short term or even medium term if fast economic development is sought and therefore a large import surplus is to be financed; a substantial public sector which is inefficient alongside a private sector which has been subdued and whose more recent burgeoning is still insecure and largely ill-directed; erratic and seemingly hesitant and confused economic policy; and very heavy bureaucracy making for extreme slowness in the design, execution and correction of projects, as well as burdening economic policy and forcing it to be much less dynamic than it could otherwise be.

To overcome these difficulties calls for bold and sound policies and measures, both internal and external, that are not likely to be formulated and implemented at an even pace. The internal measures which fall within the decision-making capability of the leadership cannot be brought into being in a relatively short time, without far-reaching participation by the population and a sense of involvement born of effective mobilisation, and supported by heightened motivation based on credible policies and measures. These conditions do not seem to be presently satisfied.

Those difficulties relating to investible resources constitute less intractable problems. With the vastly increased financial resources of the large oil-exporting countries, Arab economic aid has risen and promises to rise still further. Yet the expansion in the volume of the inflow of Arab capital into Egypt cannot be set apart from this country's success in solving, or at least containing its purely internal problems. Furthermore, the easing of the external constraints (that is, the inflow of a larger volume of aid) does not seem to be directly instrumental in either improving economic policies or in activating the slow bureaucracy. Such interaction is conceivably possible, but it will take time. Therefore, the unhappy conclusion seems to be inescapable that a solution to the major difficulties involving satisfactory growth along with an easing of foreign exchange problems and a substantial reduction of foreign debt, cannot be envisaged within, say, the next five or seven years. And even if relief is to be obtained in the next decade, this will be so not only because substantial aid flows in, but essentially because the society and economy acquire purposefulness and succeed in formulating and implementing sound policies and measures, through the joint effort of a motivated private sector and an activated public sector.

NOTES

1. Charles Issawi's *Egypt in Revolution* (Oxford University Press, 1963) stands out among books dealing with the same subject and period, in thoroughness of research and coverage of material. (Of course, there are very good more recent books, as the list further down will show.)

This writer felt it was not necessary, in this brief background section, to research the years preceding the revolution *de novo*, with Issawi's wealth of carefully accumulated and scrutinised material on hand. (Hence my reliance on his examination of the background in Ch. III.) However, I find myself in disagreement with some of the concluding remarks in his last chapter, Ch. XIII, where I consider the harsh remarks against the system unwarranted, to say the least, even on the basis of his own earlier analysis of the years 1952-61.

I have used and benefited from several sources and reference works, both for the examination of the background and of later developments. Foremost among these are: (a) Doreen Warriner, *Land and Poverty in the Middle East* (London, 1948), chapter on Egypt; (b) Charles Issawi, *Egypt at Mid-Century* (OUP, 1954), especially Chs. IV, XII and XIII; (c) Royal Institute of International Affairs, RIIA, *The Middle East: A Political and Economic Survey* (OUP, 1958, third edition), chapter on Egypt; (d) Abdul-Aziz Mar'i and Issa Abdu Ibrahim, *Contemporary Economic Problems in the Egyptian Province* (Cairo, 1961; Arabic); Part II, Chs. 4 and 5; (e) Doreen Warriner, *Land Reform and Development in the Middle East – A Study of Egypt, Syria and Iraq* (London, 1962), chapter on Egypt; (f) Hussain Khallaf, *Renovation in the Modern Egyptian Economy* (Cairo, 1962; Arabic. A more liberal translation of the title would be 'Modernization in the Contemporary Egyptian Economy'); (g) Charles Issawi, *Egypt in Revolution* (London, 1963); (h) Bent Hansen and G. A. Marzouk, *Development and Economic Policy in the UAR (Egypt)* (Amsterdam, 1965), Chs. 1-9; (i) Peter Mansfield, *Nasser's Egypt* (Penguin Books, London, 1965), the relevant parts; (j) Patrick O'Brien, *The Revolution in Egypt's Economic System* (Oxford University Press, 1966), Chs. 1 and 2; (k) Donald C. Mead, *Growth and Structural Change in the Egyptian Economy* (Illinois, 1967), Chs. 1-3; (l) George K. Kardouche, *The U.A.R. in Development: A Study in Expansionary Finance* (New York, second printing, 1967), especially Chapter 1, 'Introduction and Summary', and Part I, Ch. 1; (m) General Union of Chambers of Commerce, Industry, and Agriculture in the Arab Countries, *Economic Development in the Arab Countries, 1950-1965* (Beirut, 1967; Arabic), chapter on Egypt; (n) Magdi M. El-Kammash, *Economic Development and Planning in Egypt* (New York, 1968); (o) Bent Hansen, 'Economic Development of Egypt', in Charles A. Cooper and Sidney S. Alexander (eds.), *Economic Development and Population Growth in the Middle East* (New York, 1972); (p) Europa Publications, *The Middle East and North Africa 1971-72, 1972-73, 1973-74*, and *1974-75* (yearly editions, London), chapters on Egypt; (q) National Bank of Egypt, and Central Bank of Egypt, various annual reports and issues of *Economic Bulletin* relating to different years. The most recent of these is Central Bank of Egypt, *Report by the Board of Directors on the Year 1973* (Cairo, June 1974; Arabic); and (r) Robert Mabro, *The Egyptian Economy 1952-1972* (Oxford, 1974). More specialised source material will be referred to in the appropriate places.

2. An acre is 0.42 of a hectare. We will uniformly use the hectare (ha), which is 10,000 square metres in area, as the unit of measurement, as we have done elsewhere in the book. For a larger estimate of 'arable land', see FAO, *Production Yearbook 1972* (Rome, 1973), Vol. 26, p. 6.

3. Issawi, *Egypt in Revolution*, p. 34. All subsequent references to Issawi relate to this book.

4. Hansen and Marzouk, 'Statistical Appendix', pp. 318-19.

5. Issawi, op. cit., pp. 34 and 111.

6. Ibid., p. 89.

7. To the best of this writer's knowledge, it was Issawi who first used the term 'lopsidedness' in reference to Egypt's economic structure. The usage of this term is here extended to social and political spheres.

8. All references to Nasser's speeches are to the collection of volumes, *Speeches and Statements of President Gamal Abdul-Nasser*, the series *1952-1959* (nine parts; 'Ikhtarnalaka' Series, Cairo; Arabic); and from later collections for the years 1960-6.

9. UAR, Information Department, *The Charter* (June 1962; Arabic, English and French editions).

10. Central Committee for Statistics, *Collection of Basic Statistics* (Cairo, 1962; Arabic).

11. UNESCO, *Comparative Statistical Data on Education in the Arab States, An Analysis 1960-61–1967-68* (prepared by the UNESCO Office of Statistics, Paris, and published by the Regional Center for Educational Planning and Administration, Beirut, 1970), p. 49.

12. UAR, *General Frame of the 5-Year Plan for Economic and Social Development, July 1960–June 1965* (Cairo, 1960).

13. See, in particular: (a) Gamal Abdul-Nasser, *The Philosophy of the Revolution* (Cairo, 1954); (b) Mohammad Najib, *Egypt's Destiny* (London, 1955); (c) Anwar Sadat, *Revolt on the Nile* (London, 1957); (d) P. J. Vatikiotis, *The Egyptian Army in Politics: Pattern for New Nations?* (Bloomington, Ind., 1961); (e) Peter Mansfield, *Nasser's Egypt* (Penguin Books, London, 1965); (f) Malcolm Kerr, 'The Emergence of A Socialist Ideology in Egypt', in *The Middle East Journal*, Spring 1962; (g) Fayez Sayegh, 'The Theoretical Structure of Nasser's Socialism', in *St. Antony's Papers*, No. 17, Middle Eastern Affairs, No. 4, 1965; (h) Maxime Rodinson, 'The Political System', in P. J. Vatikiotis (ed.), *Egypt Since the Revolution* (London, 1968).

14. Rodinson, loc. cit., pp. 87-8.

15. For a careful and candid analysis of *The Charter*, see Burhan Dajani, 'The National Charter and Socio-Economic Organization in the United Arab Republic', in *Middle East Economic Papers, 1963*, pp. 33-54.

16. Anwar Abdel-Malek, *Egypte, société militaire* (Paris, 1963) who takes a Marxist position, and Patrick O'Brien in *The Revolution in Egypt's Economic System: From Private Enterprise to Socialism 1952-1965* (Oxford, 1966).

17. To avoid frequent interruptions with notes, we will cite here the main reference works used for the discussion: (a) Doreen Warriner, *Land Reform and Development in the Middle East* (cited earlier), Ch. I and 'Postscript'; (b) Abdul-Razzak Al-Hilali, *The Story of Land, The Peasant, and Agrarian Reform in the Arab Homeland* (Beirut, 1967; Arabic); Documentary Appendix, pp. 447-522, for texts of reform laws and amendments; (c) Gabriel S. Saab, *The Egyptian Agrarian Reform 1952-1962* (Oxford, 1967); (d) Riad el Ghonemy, 'Economic and Institutional Organization of Egyptian Agriculture Since 1952', in Vatikiotis, *Egypt Since the Revolution*, pp. 66-83; (e) General Union of Chambers of Commerce, Industry and Agriculture in the Arab Countries, op, cit., chapter on Egypt; (f) Sa'ad Hagras, *Agrarian Reform in the United Arab Republic* (Cairo, 1968; Arabic); (g) Ali Wassal, *Agrarian Reform in the United Arab Republic* (Cairo, 1969; Arabic); (h) Ministry of Land Reclamation, *Land Reclamation Development in U.A.R.* (Cairo, 1970); (i) Sa'ad Hagras, *The March of Agrarian Reform in 18 Years* (Cairo, 1970; Arabic); (j) Sa'ad Hagras, *Agrarian Reform: History, Philosophy, Method* (Cairo, 1970; Arabic).

18. The 1969 Law is mentioned in Rashed Al-Barawy, *Economic Development in the United Arab Republic* (Cairo, 1970), p. 81, as well as in Robert Mabro, op. cit., pp. 65-6. However, the only reference to the significance of the Law is in Europa Publications, op. cit., the 1973-4 edition, p. 262. Mabro (table, p. 68) does not include data on the 1969 measure.

19. Central Agency for Public Mobilisation and Statistics, CAPMS, *Statistical Abstract of Arab Republic of Egypt 1951/52–1970/71.* (June 1972), p. 26. (Hereafter referred to as *CAPMS... 1951/52–1970/71.*)

20. Ministry of Land Reclamation, op, cit., pp. 4-5, quotes an area of 895,000 *fed.* by the end of 1969/70. Europa Publications, 1973-4 edition (p. 263) quotes the

total expected to be reached by the end of 1972 as 1.2m fed. The expectation has been fulfilled, though with a little over one year's lag.

There is some ambiguity with respect to the area reclaimed. Thus, it is not clear from the perusal of the various references (including Al-Barawy, Ch. IV, General Union of Chambers..., chapter on Egypt) whether the 1m fed. reclaimed during the period 1952-69 is the same that was to be reclaimed upon the completion of the High Dam project. As the detailed data show the process of reclamation to have started before the construction of the High Dam was begun, we have considered each of the one million *feddans* to be separate: one due to the Dam, the other to the use of existing water resources and better use of water. (The Tahrir Province, with 148,000 fed. reclaimed, is a case in point.) Furthermore, Mabro (table, p. 99) shows a total of 805,500 fed. reclaimed from 1960/1 to 1969/70, of which 630,000 fed. are due to the High Dam (p. 100).

21. El-Ghonemy, loc. cit., pp. 70-80.
22. Issawi, op. cit., especially Chs. IV and XIII.
23. *Annuaire Statistique 1951-1952, 1952-1953, et 1953-1954*, p. 130-1.
24. CAPMS... *1952-1974*, p. 58.
25. See especially Mabro, op. cit., Ch. 5.
26. The collusion is now beyond doubt, as careful research and analysis have established since then. The reader who is interested in this 'episode' is referred to Erskine Childers, *The Road to Suez*; Anthony Nutting, *No End of A Lesson*; Kenneth Love, *The Twice-Fought War*, as well as to other sources cited in Love.
27. Balance of payments data and report on Suez Canal in National Bank of Egypt, *Economic Bulletin*, Vol. IX, No. 3, especially pp. 223-7.
28. For a thorough examination of Egypt's industry outside the reference works already cited, see UN, Department of Economic and Social Affairs, *The Development of Manufacturing Industry in Egypt, Israel, and Turkey* (New York, 1958).
29. Ministry of Industry, *The Industrial Revolution in Eleven Years 1952-1963* (Cairo; Arabic); pp. 15 ff.
30. The General Authority for the Implementation of the Five-Year Plan for Industry, *Annual Report 1958-1959* (Cairo; Arabic), p. 145.
31. Issawi, op. cit., p. 240, from *Exposé on Budget Project for First Year July 1961–June 1962*.
32. Ibid., p. 173 (in table), from various sources (UN, op. cit.; Federation of Industries in Egyptian Region, *Yearbook 1961*; and Central Bank of Egypt, *Economic Review*, No. 3, 1962).
33. Reference will be made in this subsection to CAPMS, various Yearbooks; Ministry of Planning, *Follow-Up and Appraisal Report for the First Five-Year Plan* (Cairo; Arabic); General Union of Chambers..., various annual issues ending with the 1974 issue of *Arab Economic Report* (Arabic and English editions); NBE, *Economic Bulletin*, various issues; and *Annual Reports* of the Central Bank of Egypt.
34. CAPMS, *Evolution of National Economic Variables During the Sixties, 1960/61–1969/70*, Reference No. 05-110 (Cairo, 1972; Arabic), hereafter referred to as *Evolution...*, pp. 45, 33 and 30 for the various items reported relative to the Plan years.
35. CAPMS... *1952-1974*, p. 70 for index numbers;

Ministry of Planning, *Preliminary Report on Follow-Up and Evaluation of Economic and Social Growth in the Arab Republic of Egypt 1974* (hereafter referred to as *Evaluation... 1974*), p. 6 of Appendix; and Ministry of Planning, *Preliminary Follow-Up Report on The National Plan for the Year 1975* (hereafter referred to as *Follow-Up... 1975*), p. 29.
36. *Follow-Up... 1975*, p. 44, for share of industrial exports in total commodity exports. For the wages received by labour in the various sectors, see *Evolution...*, p. 50 for 1959/60, and *Evaluation... 1974*, p. 51 for 1974. (No such information is available for 1975.)
37. Except where specific reference is made, this section is based on the coverage of the subject of planning in: Issawi, O'Brien, Hansen and Marzouk, Mead, Hansen, loc. cit., and Mabro – in addition to the Plan document itself *(General Frame of the 5-Year Plan for Economic and Social Development July 1960–June 1965)*. Of more direct relevance to planning are: Kardouche, El-Kammash and Hansen, 'Planning and Economic Growth in the U.A.R. 1960-5', in Vatikiotis (ed.), *Egypt Since the Revolution*. For evaluation of Plan performance, we have relied heavily on tables in *Evolution...*, Ministry of Planning, *Follow-Up and Evaluation of Economic and Social Growth in the Arab Republic of Egypt 1971/1972* (Cairo; Arabic); *Follow-Up and Evaluation of Economic and Social Growth in the Arab Republic of Egypt 1973; Evaluation... 1974;* and *Follow-Up ... 1975.*
38. Mead, op. cit., p. 234.
39. For an evaluation of the strong points as well as the limitations and shortcomings of the process and institutions of planning in Egypt, see the relevant parts in Hansen and Marzouk, Mead, Mabro, El-Kammash and Albert Waterston, *Development Planning: Lessons of Experience* (London, 1966).
40. Mead, op. cit., p. 241.
41. In this writer's view, the most thorough (and non-emotional, non-partisan) evaluation of Plan results is to be found in Hansen's essay in Vatikiotis (ed.), *Egypt Since the Revolution*. I rely on Hansen's findings which are based on careful scrutiny and take into account several adjustments of official data. To a lesser extent I rely also on Hansen's more recent essay on Egypt in Cooper and Alexander (eds.), op. cit. However, all through I have compared Hansen's data with those in *Evolution...*
42. See CAPMS, *Population Increase in the UAR and Its Challenges to Development* (Cairo, 1966; Arabic).
43. President Nasser himself, in 'Statement to the National Assembly' on 20 January 1965, emphasised the need to check consumption if savings and investment were not to suffer. The Prime Minister did so too on more than one occasion during 1965 and 1966. But these invocations came too late and were too inadequate for the dimensions of the problem.
44. For a general official appraisal of the Plan, see Ali Sabri, once Prime Minister, *The Years of Socialist Transformation and Appraisal of the First Five-Years Plan* (Information Department, Cairo, 1967; Arabic). See also Information Department, *Responsibilities of the Second Five-Years Plan*, Government Statement to the National Assembly in its Third Session, 4 December 1965 (Cairo, 1965; Arabic), where Premier Ali Sabri stated that

when the First Five-Years Plan was drawn 'there was no adequate scientific study of interrelationships between the different sectors of the national economy, nor of changes in these relationships following the changes in the rates of growth in the sectors. There was also no sufficient coordination on either the planning or implementation level between the sectors of the national economy as a whole or between the projects included in each separate sector, with the result that certain bottlenecks arose in the transport and communication sectors for example.' (Al-Barawy's translation, p. 304.)

45. The Ministry of Planning, *Report for 1965/66* (Cairo; Arabic), p. 80.
46. For the more recent index quotations, see *International Financial Statistics (IFS)*, October 1974 and *IFS*, November 1976.
47. In 'Statement to the National Assembly' on 4 December 1965, already cited.
48. *CAPMS... 1951/52−1970/71*, p. 19.
49. *Evaluation... 1974*, p. 6 in Appendix for labour force, and *CAPMS... 1952-74*, p. 8 for population for 1974. For a thorough examination of the question of labour and employment in Egypt, see Mostafa H. Nagi, *Labor Force and Employment in Egypt: A Demographic and Socio-economic Analysis* (Praeger, 1971).
50. See FAO, *Production Yearbook, 1967*, Vol. 21, pp. 26 and 27, and FAO, *Production Yearbook, 1972*, Vol. 26, pp. 27 and 28.
51. Europa Publications, 1973-4 edition, p. 265 for the larger estimate. See *Arab Economist* (Beirut monthly), No. 53, June 1973, for the smaller estimate.
52. *IFS*, November 1976.
53. For text of the Permanent Constitution in English, see Europa Publications, 1973-74 edition, pp. 273 and 274.
54. Issawi, op. cit., p. 129.
55. NBE, *Economic Bulletin*, Vol. XVIII, No. 4, 1965, pp. 66-77.
56. General Union of Chambers..., *Arab Economic Report, 1970*, pp. 260-70.
57. One widely circulated critique was made by Claire Sterling and publicised by the Associated Press (reproduced in the *Daily Star*, Beirut, on 26 February 1971). For a general examination of the project, see T. Little, *High Dam at Aswan* (London, 1965), though this book was written much before the Dam was completed. However, Y. Shibl, *The Aswan High Dam* (Beirut, 1971) has a more recent and careful analysis of the cost-benefit relationships of the project broadly defined. (The present writer feels that Shibl's rather stern conclusions are not warranted.)

58. O'Brien, op. cit. With regard to the system, see also note 13 above, Dajani in note 15, and Abdel-Malek in note 16.
59. O'Brien, op. cit., Ch. X.
60. Aside from Abdel-Malek, there are the Marxist-Leninist writers of *Dirasat Arabiyya* (Arab Studies), a periodical published by Dar al-Tali'a, Beirut.
61. See Central Bank of Egypt, *Economic Review*, No. 2, 1961, for a list of the Decrees. Issawi has a brief description of these, pp. 58-61.
62. We have already referred to this estimate before in note 18, based on Europa Publications, 1973-4 edition, p. 262.
63. Issawi, op. cit., p. 60, quoting *Al-Ahram* (daily Cairo paper), 24 December 1961, for Nasser's speech, and of 9 February 1962 and 3 March 1962, as his source for the valuations presented.
64. It is not possible to provide recent quantification of all these indicators, as the information is mostly not available.
65. *Follow-Up... 1975*, pp. 36-8.
66. *CAPMS... 1952-1974*, pp. 118-27.
67. UN *Statistical Yearbook 1973*, p. 719, for the number of physicians and nurses in 1971.
68. General Union of Chambers..., *Arab Economic Report* (October 1973), p. 89.
69. *CAPMS... 1951/52−1971/72*, p. 126, and *CAPMS... 1952-74*, p. 146.
70. *Follow-Up... 1975*, p. 59 for 1975, and NBE, *Economic Bulletin*, Vol. 23, No. 2, 1970 for the earlier year.
71. *Evaluation... 1974*, pp. e and f in 'Resumé' chapter.
72. *Follow-Up... 1975*, p. 21.
73. See Tables 8.2 and 8.21. Deflation of current prices has been done on the basis of price indices reported in *IFS, Supplement to 1967/68 Issues*, for 1952-66, *IFS* November 1974 and November 1976, for 1967-75.

9 SUDAN

With an area of 2.5 million square kilometres, Sudan is the largest Arab state; but it has the lowest income *per capita* among the twelve countries covered in this book. It is a land of contrasts in other respects too, for it has enormous potential in the fields of agriculture, forestry and livestock, but equally enormous problems blocking the way to translating this potential into achievement; it runs one of the most efficient and successful experiments in agriculture in the region, along with some of the most primitive primary activities; and it contains communities more dissimilar in terms of race, religion, language and culture than any other Arab country.

The state is twenty years old, having acquired its independence on the first day of 1956. The examination of development and structural and institutional change is thus handicapped by the relative brevity of the period covered, but it is more seriously compounded with the dearth and non-reliability of material on socio-economic development. The small number of reference works which contain somewhat reliable surveys often repeat each other, with very little originality in any of them.

Unlike chapters on such countries as Egypt, Jordan or Iraq, the present one will contain more of the survey type of material, though with as much analysis as is possible under the circumstances. It will largely describe the features, the performance and the structure of the economy at the present moment and describe post-independence changes, small as they are, relatively speaking. It will also point to the potential of the economy, and the main problems which slow down the process of development.

1. BROAD SOCIO-ECONOMIC FEATURES

A brief sketch of the broad physical features like the one attempted here cannot do justice to a country as vast in area as the Sudan, but it can give the reader a feel of these features. However, most of the reference works on Sudan[1] contain good descriptions of the economic geography of the land and can be used for a fuller acquaintance with its main features.

For our purposes, it is sufficient to state that in terms of type of terrain, climate and rainfall, the country is divided into clearly differentiated regions. There is a low rain area in the northern and north-western plains, and in the central plateau. This plateau is bounded by mountains and hills in the south and west. The climate is desert and semi-desert in the centre and the western part of the country, but is characterised by tropical rains and savannah cultivation and woods in the south. The land, considered as a whole, is well endowed with water resources, though certain regions are very poorly endowed. The main rivers are the White Nile, originating in Uganda, the Blue Nile, originating in Ethiopia, and the Atbara, also originating in Ethiopia, and there are other smaller rivers, such as Gash, Rahad and Baraka. The meeting of the Blue and White Niles at Khartoum creates the main Nile. The availability of river water is recorded in Table 9.1.

Table 9.1: The Volume of the Flow of the Nile (billion cubic metres)

River	Total Annual Flow Volume	Per Cent	Flow July-December Volume	Per Cent	Flow January-June Volume	Per Cent
White Nile	27.0	30.2	17.0	23.1	10.0	62.5
Blue Nile	50.5	56.4	45.0	61.2	5.5	34.4
Atbara	12.0	13.4	11.5	15.7	0.5	3.1
Main Nile	89.5	100.0	73.5	100.0	16.0	100.0
Main Nile at Aswan (after evaporation)	84.0		69.0		15.0	

Source: KFAED, *Report on the Sudanese Economy* (mimeo, 1969; Arabic) p. 17; percentages have been corrected slightly.

The table reveals very extreme variation between the thaw-and-flood season (July-December) and the dry season (January-June). No doubt variation of this calibre constitutes a serious limiting factor on year-round irrigation. None the less, thanks to dams and reservoirs on the rivers (to be discussed later), it is possible to undertake substantial irrigated agriculture.

In terms of source of water for agriculture, the land is divided into rain land in the south, flood irrigation in the east, mostly through the use of the flow of the Gash, Atbara and Baraka streams in Eastern Sudan, and irrigation — through gravity, pumps, or traditional lifting devices — in the central belt and the north. The western and lower central parts are mostly pastoral, owing to the scarcity of rainfall and the absence of irrigation facilities there.

By far the most important crop is cotton, which came into prominence in the 1920s. Other important crops include gum arabic from the country's forests, sesame, timber, *dhurra (sorghum vulgare)*, groundnuts, wheat rice and *lubia* (beans). Livestock is plentiful and is a significant source of wealth, but the fishing industry is very small, and commercially exploitable minerals are negligible.

The population numbered some 16.9 million by the end of 1973, and it grows at a high net rate of increase estimated to range between 2.8 and 3 per cent per annum. Just over a quarter of the population lives in Southern Sudan and are both non-Arab and non-Moslem, consisting of Hamitic groups, both pagan and Christian. The rest of the population contains communities that are non-Arab *or* non-Moslem, estimated at some 20-30 per cent of the population. Thus about 39 per cent of the population (according to the 1956 census) are declared Arab in race *and* Moslem in religion, though Arabic is the language of slightly over half the population.

The economy is agricultural and pastoral in character, and operates at a low level of performance, except for the modern sector (mainly irrigated agriculture, with a nascent industry). In 1970 it produced £S40* of gross domestic product at market price *per capita*, (equivalent to $114.9 at the official rate of exchange of $2.872 to the Sudanese pound).[2] This low level of income is attributable to general underdevelopment, compounded with economic dualism characterised by the presence of a very substantial traditional sector

*Sudanese pounds.

Sudan

alongside the more modern sector.

The process of development, which is handicapped by this structure and the poverty it generates, is further delayed because the economy is incapable of earning as much foreign exchange as speedy development would require. This necessitates heavy dependence on foreign loans of a volume which would constitute too onerous a strain on the economy if it were to be forthcoming, but which it has proved very difficult to attract, given the present status of aid and lending stringency in the world today. Underlying all this there is the basic problem of a backward society which does not enjoy homogeneity and in which excessive effort has had to be diverted to the resolving of community conflict and to the establishing of one circuit of economic life for the country as a whole.

2. POPULATION, LAND AND WATER

The population is tradition-bound on the whole, particularly so in the retarded south. It has a very high rate of illiteracy, estimated at 85 per cent. For those aged 15-24, the rate of illiteracy was the highest for the twelve countries covered and stood at 80 per cent for 1961 (69 per cent for males, 91 for females), according to the UNESCO study quoted frequently in this book.[3] However, here as elsewhere literacy statistics must be taken with a great deal of caution and reserve. At best they are well-meaning guesstimates. The rate must have dropped noticeably since 1961, owing to the strong efforts that are being made to expand education, particularly in the districts outside the south, where law and order permit sustained effort. The Khartoum University, formerly Gordon College of pre-independence days, has high standards which it attempts to maintain.

The country is divided into nine *mudiriyyas* or provinces: three in the south with 26 per cent of the population, two in the west with 37 per cent, and four in the north and east with 37 per cent. The population distribution runs very closely to that of land area of provinces. Population data relate to the only census so far taken — that of 1955/6. More recent figures derive from extrapolations and sample surveys and incorporate adjustments of the original figures.

The population is highly concentrated in the rural sector. According to the FAO *Indicative World Plan for Agricultural Development 1965-1985 — Near East*, the rural population was as high as 85 per cent of the total in 1965, and was projected to stay high at 78 per cent by 1975.[4] Likewise, the agricultural population (i.e. that part of the rural population engaged in agricultural and directly related activities) was 77 per cent of the total in 1965 and is projected to be 70 per cent by 1975. In both instances and for both years, Sudan stands at the top of the list of twelve countries surveyed in this book. The results of the census of 1955/6 showed the settled rural population to be 78 per cent of the total, while the urban population was 8 per cent; the balance of 14 per cent consisted of nomads.[5] The FAO data do not agree with the census data, and the trend between 1955/6 and 1965 moves in an unexpected direction, in the sense that the rural population seems to have risen proportionately. We believe the explanation of this discrepancy to lie in the aggregation in the FAO study of the settled rural and nomadic components of the population, or the adoption of a definition of 'urban centres' different from that adopted in the census.

The division of the population in one of the tables in the FAO study into 'agricultural' and 'non-agricultural' is based on economic activity. This division, which as already indicated set the agricultural population at 77 per cent of the total for the year 1965, is not noticeably out of line with the distribution of the Sudanese labour force by economic sector as it emerges from the census of 1955/6, and from a subsequent family budget

380 Sudan

survey in 1968. The first sets the labour force engaged in primary activities in the census year at 86 per cent, while the survey sets it at 71.4 per cent. The proportion in 1965, if data for these end years are nearly correct, must have been close to the figure given in the FAO study, namely 77 per cent. The total distribution of the labour force is presented in Table 9.2.

Table 9.2: Sectoral Distribution of the Labour Force (thousands)

	1955/6 Number	Census Per Cent	1967/8 Sample Survey Per Cent
Total population	10,365	100.0	
Labour force	4,844	47.0	
Primary activities[a]	4,155	85.8	71.4
Industry	241	5.0	4.5
Construction	31	0.6	1.5
Trade	100	2.1	3.6
Transport and communications	31	0.6	1.8
Services[b]	223	4.6	14.8
Others[c]	64	1.3	2.3
Total[d]	4,844	100.0	100.0

a. Includes agriculture, livestock, forestry and fishing.
b. Includes education, health, public security and administration in census data, and services both of the public and the private sectors in the sample survey data.
c. Unskilled labour engaged neither in agriculture nor in construction, as well as unclassified labourers in the census data, and labourers seeking employment in the sample data.
d. Figures do not add up to total, owing to rounding. In a more recent reference work, the 'total economically active population' is set at '5,016,000, including 4,007,000 in agriculture'. See Europa, *1974-75*, p. 634, where these data are described as 'ILO and FAO estimates'.

Source: KFAED, *Report on the Sudanese Economy,* p. 35; attribution to original sources in this work. Percentages in census data show some very minor differences from the source.

It should be first pointed out that the sample survey excluded the three provinces of the south, and that its coverage of the six remaining provinces was limited to the point where generalisations referring to the whole population can be drawn only tentatively and with qualifications. However, a comparison of the census and sample results can lead to some preliminary observations. To begin with, the drop in the proportion of labour engaged in primary activities is understandable, but not so in the proportion of labour engaged in industry. The latter phenomenon must be attributable to a change in definition of industry between the data of the census and that of the sample survey twelve years later. The more strict the definition becomes, the less inclusive the category 'industry' becomes, which means dropping handicrafts and very small mechanised workshops from the count. This explanation is necessary in view of the actual tangible rise in the number of workers in manufacturing industry over the twelve years in question.

A second observation is the rise in the proportion of labourers in trade — always assuming a high level of reliability for the sample survey. This would suggest a large relative (though small absolute) shift from a barter and subsistence economy, to one of monetised exchange. The same kind of reasoning applies to the rise in the share of transport and communications. On the other hand, the vast expansion in employment in the services sectors is primarily due to a widening of the definition of services, whereby the more recent study took into account services in the private sector as well as those in the public sector. It is also very likely that the urbanisation movement has led to an expansion in the demand for (and supply of) personal services.

A final but general observation refers to the size of the labour force as a whole in the 1955/6 census. This is set at 47 per cent of the population, a very high proportion indeed. The explanation lies in the definition used, which was 'economically active' rather than 'gainfully employed'. This permitted the inclusion of the children of nomads and semi-nomads, 'whose children become economically active, as shepherds, at a very early age'.[6] The fact that almost 20 per cent of the labour force according to the census were below 15 years of age, and nearly 50 per cent below 20, further explains the high proportion of the population in the labour force.

The other side of the coin in this respect, if the size of the GDP is recalled, is the very low productivity of this over-sized labour force, as well as the volume of underemployment that the economy suffers. This low productivity, and the resulting low product, lead to a very low level of living and help to explain the very large size of the subsistence sector in Sudan.

The availability of cultivable land is of direct relevance to the question of the economic performance and production of the labour force, all the more so in view of the heavy dependence of the population on agriculture and the large contribution of this sector to the national product. Consequently, the subject of land (and subsequently water) will receive some attention here.

The land area of Sudan is divided into the categories shown in Table 9.3.[7] Serious discrepancies exist between the two breakdowns in almost every category of land. While the greater detail and obvious precision of the second (Lebon) breakdown makes it preferable to the first (FAO), the FAO breakdown is essentially based on official data and is therefore more authoritative. According to an official Sudanese report, cultivated land is divided into rain-fed and irrigated areas as shown in Table 9.4.

The FAO data agree closely with this quotation as far as irrigated land is concerned, but contain a much more liberal estimate with regard to rain-fed cultivated land. (The difference is probably one of definition: the FAO estimate referring to cultivated *including* fallow, while the official source just cited probably refers to *cropped* land.) On the other hand, Lebon's data locate under the heading 'cultivated' vast areas which are grazing land, or areas which are cultivated only once every three years.[8]

Lebon's estimate of cultivated land is of significance in our appraisal of the man-land ratio in the Sudan. Such evaluation obviously ought to take into account the various categories of cultivated land, and the assumptions underlying cultivable potential with regard to water and capital investment needs. However, a crude relation of 2.3 hectares of cultivated land per inhabitant emerges which, on face value, is quite high by the standards of the Arab world. (The ratio for Egypt is roughly 0.1 ha per person.) This shows the land-man ratio as very favourable, particularly in view of the fact that much of the cultivated land is not exhausted and, once prepared properly for cultivation, can be very fertile if the necessary inputs are available.

Table 9.3: Land Area and Land Use

(i) Type of Land	Thousand ha	Per Cent
Agricultural area		
Cultivated area	7,100	2.8
(of which irrigated)	(711)	(.3)
Pastures	24,000	9.6
Forests	91,500	36.5
Unexploited (but potentially productive) land	38,016	15.2
Deserts etc.	89,965	35.9
Total	250,581	100.0
(ii) Land Use	Thousand ha	Per Cent
Built-up area (towns and villages)	14.5	—
Permanent irrigation	601.7	0.2
Temporary irrigation (flood)	358.7	0.1
Rain-fed cultivated land	35,875.8	14.3
Utilised pastures	129,881.2	51.6
Unutilised pastures	9,875.5	3.9
Forests	24,395.7	9.7
Swamps	2,666.3	1.1
Deserts	47,856.0	19.0
Rivers	258.5	0.1
Total	251,783.9	100.0

Sources: (i) FAO, *Production Yearbook 1973* (Rome, 1974), p. 3; (ii) J. H. G. Lebon, *Land Use in Sudan* (Geographical Publications Ltd., Bude, U.K., 1965), Table XXII, pp. 174-5. The nomenclature in the source differs slightly from that in the text.

But it is precisely this last condition that is both operative and restrictive in the case of Sudan, with the very limited resources available to it from its GDP and its import surplus. According to one Sudanese scholar, the late Dr Sa'ad ed Din Fawzi,[9] the *lot viable* for a family is about 3 *feddans* (1.26 ha), given present technology and level of agricultural skills. If so, then the land-man ratio of 2.3 ha per person suggests great potential, since this area would allow the family of 5 some 11.5 ha or nine times as much land as is needed for the provision of bare necessities. However, the land-man ratio of *actually cultivated* land (taking the FAO area into account) is only 0.45 ha per person or 2.25 ha per family. Though this area is much smaller than that based on Lebon's data, it is still almost twice the *lot viable* of 1.26 ha per family.

Fawzi also suggests that it is arguable that Sudan, even given the primitive technology prevailing, is short of population, and that it is now in the phase of increasing returns to population. This seems tenable at face value, particularly if it is borne in mind that in many underdeveloped countries there is scope both for a rise in productivity of labour and in yields of land, upon the improvement of methods of cultivation or upon institutional and organisational reform.[10] It would seem in the particular case of Sudan that the extension of the irrigated area, coupled with intensified motivation and better organisa-

Table 9.4: Division of Cultivated Land

	1967/8 (thousand ha)	1968/9* (thousand ha)
Rain-fed land	3,305.6	2,471.9
Irrigated land (perennial and flood)	787.8	786.1
Total cultivated	4,093.4	3,258.0

*Tentative figures

Source: Research and Statistics Division, Ministry of Planning, *Economic Survey 1968* (Khartoum, August 1969), p. 14 and Appendix Table (1), p. 102.

tion — all of which are witnessed in and around the irrigated zone — would bring about the dual improvement in labour productivity *and* in land yields. (Obviously, it would be facile to talk with greater precision and definiteness of labour shortages, even if labour-intensive agriculture were to predominate, before the possibilities of absorbing the large mass of the underemployed, and of training the labour force in general, were substantially explored and exploited.)

Such extension seems to be imminent now, after the completion of the High Dam in Egypt. Work on the Dam was begun only after Egypt and Sudan had entered agreement late in 1959 on the allocation of the water of the Main Nile. This agreement superseded an earlier one entered into in 1929, according to which Sudan was entitled to 4 billion cubic metres of Nile water annually for its own use. The 1959 agreement raised this entitlement to 18.5 billion at the Dam, or the equivalent of 20.5 billion cubic metres within Sudan. (The difference is lost largely in evaporation and seepage.) The agreement also stipulated for the compensation of Sudan for the evacuation of Halfa town and Nuba lands that were to be flooded as a result of the formation of the lake that would fill behind the Dam over the years; the sum involved was £E15m, which has all been paid. The vast increase in water availability makes it possible to expand — almost double — the area irrigated in the Sudan, and thus to translate substantially more of its potential into reality.

The development of water resources began seriously and on a large scale in 1924, with the completion of the Sennar Dam in 1924 on the Blue Nile, in order to irrigate the flat land between the Blue and White Niles known as the Gezira (i.e. the island). The capacity of this dam was 0.9 billion cubic metres annually. The dam with the largest capacity is Jabal al Awlia on the White Nile, not very far south of Khartoum; it stores 3.5 billion cubic metres of water. The Roseires dam on the Blue Nile, with a capacity of 3 billion cubic metres, was completed in the 1960s, as was the Khashm al Girba dam on Atbara with 0.3 billion cubic metres capacity. The total volume stored in the whole country is 9.7 billion cubic metres. This volume provides irrigation on a perennial basis, while flood water provides flood or basin irrigation. The Roseires dam is now set for serving the Rahad project, which is expected to need 4 billion cubic metres of water a year and to cover about 210,000 ha. The financing of the project, which was estimated to cost £S102m, was assured by the end of 1974, with participation by the Kuwait Fund for Arab Economic Development (KFAED), the IDA, West Germany and the World Bank. Sudan will provide the local currency component of about £S35m. The works to be undertaken include large pumping installations, irrigation canals, drainage facilities, land reclamation and roads. Upon its completion, the Rahad project will greatly improve the income of some 14,000 families and also provide seasonal work for about 9,000 labourers.

The Gezira scheme remains the pride and glory of Sudanese agriculture. The idea of the irrigation of the vast area (5 million *feddans,* or 2.1m ha) enclosed between the Blue and the White Nile south of Khartoum dates as far back as 1904. This region had been relatively prosperous in terms of agricultural production in times past, but at the turn of the century the British decided to develop perennial irrigation in it. The first step undertaken was the conduct of land survey operations there, which was achieved between 1907 and 1910. However, it was only in 1925 that the project was completed, the intervening years having been used not only for the building of the Sennar Dam and the irrigation network attached to it, and for the settlement-of-title operations, but also for research, experimentation and the trial of pilot projects, and for the formulation of the organisational structure of the scheme that was envisaged. Thus, right from the start the scheme was conceived as an economic and a social experiment, involving tenure, management, financing, agricultural advice (what is now placed under the heading 'extension services'), marketing and social welfare.

The government at the time had to weigh between expropriating the land and paying fair compensation, and taking the risk of anxiety and loss of incentive among the future operators on the scheme; and allowing private ownership, with its prevailing inegalitarian pattern, to continue; or of finding another formula which would combine the advantages of private ownership, egalitarianism, and large-scale rationalised operation all at once. Such a formula was found: it was to recognise private ownership but to make participation in the scheme obligatory, and to introduce large-scale management. The owners had to lease their land to the government for forty years (which meant till 1961; since then the leases have been renewed) against a rental of £S0.100 per *feddan* per annum which was considered liberal at the time. The next step was to assign a parcel of land to each owner, with the permission for owners to take on partners in case they had more land than the statutory size permitted. The operation was not to continue automatically, but was subject to cancellation if deemed unsatisfactory or contrary to the terms of management. In the meantime, the government stood ready to buy whatever plots fell for sale, with the object of ultimately becoming the largest if not the only proprietor.

At the start the area assigned to each operator was 30 *feddans* (12.6 ha), which was quite 'comfortable', given the costs and returns relationships and the prevailing level of living. The rotation system in force was then a three-year system. But the area was raised in the 1933/4 season to 40 *feddans* (16.8 ha) and the system of crop rotation was altered such that a quarter of the land was to be grown with cotton, a quarter with *dhurra* and *lubia,* and about half to be left fallow to 'rest'. (Previously the division into cotton, *dhurra* and *lubia,* and fallow was one-third each.)

As time passed, the unit size dropped on the average and ranged between 20 and 40 *feddans* (8.4 and 16.8 ha), owing to several reasons: death of operators, which in practice resulted in parcellation, although the unit of land was not legally to be passed on as inheritance; the break-up of many partnerships into units operated by farmers singly; the desire by farmers to give pieces of land to relatives whom it was desired to keep in the village; and the desire to avoid hiring labour and therefore the relinquishing of part of the land.

The question of optimum area of land unit has received a great deal of attention and has roused some controversy among observers, analysts, policy-makers and administrators.

The idea that has prevailed has been to lean towards a reduction in the area. Hence, when the original scheme which had covered one million *feddans* (420,000 ha) was enlarged by adding the Managil Extension to the part already developed, some changes were introduced. The Extension covered an area of 800,000 *feddans* (336,000 ha) and was completed during the years 1957-60. The rotation system in the Managil Extension was to involve dividing the land into three parts: one-third cotton, one-third food and fodder, and one-third fallow. The total unit-area was to be 15 *feddans* (6.3 ha). Considering the actual drop in the average size of tenancy in the old part of the Gezira scheme, the difference between it and the size in the new Extension is not all that large. The new, reduced size encourages operation by the tenant rather than the employment of cash or share labour.

The scheme involves three parties: the government, the management and the tenants, who operate in a unique form of association. As one observer says, this form is not a partnership in the strict legal sense of the term, nor is it a typical co-operative society or state farm. It would be easier to describe rather than label the pattern of association, and the distribution of functions and of returns under this association.[11] The government's function has been to construct dams and build irrigation canals, and to undertake research. The tenants provide the labour involved in sowing and harvesting. The management, while it formed one of the three parties, was in charge of preparation of land, supervision, marketing, and the provision of economic, technical and social services such as the putting up of agricultural buildings like housing and storage facilities, the provision of credit and inputs, ginning of the cotton, and so on. Until 1950, management was entrusted to a British company. Then it was replaced by a government-controlled Board, or Authority.

The division of the product was as follows between the years 1924 and 1950: the farmers got the whole crop of food and fodder (*dhurra, lubia,* and the like); the net proceeds of the cotton crop were to be divided into 40, 40 and 20 per cent to the government, the tenants and the Company respectively. However, this pattern of distribution of net cotton proceeds underwent two alterations in the sixties: according to the first, the government received 42 per cent, the Board 12 per cent, and the tenants 46 per cent. The current allocation allows the tenants 50 per cent, the government 38 per cent, the Board 10 per cent, and social services 2 per cent. The share of the Board goes to meet its administrative expenses; anything remaining after that goes to government, either in the form of interest on the loan advanced by government to the Board on the non-renewal of the concession of the Company (£S4 million), or as contribution towards research conducted by government. The tenants' 50 per cent includes 2 per cent for the purpose of building a price-equalisation fund. The balance is distributed among the tenants in proportion to their deliveries of cotton. The 2 per cent assigned for social services goes into a fund for education, the provision of piped drinking water, housing, entertainment, and improvement of livestock.

It is obvious from the area of the Gezira scheme and its extension, and from the description given of the formula governing the relations of the Government, the Authority and the tenants, and from the pattern of distribution of the produce of the scheme, that the scheme has great economic and social significance. In particular, this significance derives from the 'example effect' of such a large and central scheme. This effect is felt all over the northern and north-eastern parts of the country, where irrigation and irrigation potential exist, and it manifests itself in the several projects in operation or in design that involve repetition or modification of some aspect or aspects of the Gezira scheme. (Reference will be made later to the leading projects.) In brief, the Gezira scheme may well turn out to be the 'leading sector' in Rostow's terms, thanks to its economic, social and technological impact. (However, it must be recognised that fluctuations in the value of crops create some instability in the disposable income of the tenants and in the government's programmes.)

All authors and reports dealing with the scheme have assessed its significance for the economy. According to a study by the IBRD made in 1966,[12] it is estimated that 66 per cent of long staple cotton, 47 per cent of wheat, 14 per cent of beans *(fool)* and 12 per cent of maize *(dhurra)* in the country are grown on Gezira land. The scheme also provides some 30 per cent of government revenue (if export fees are included), and 35 per cent of export earnings. Other important features will now be summed up:

— About 7 per cent of net domestic product is directly imputable to the scheme, while indirectly imputable contribution amounts to about 30 per cent. Furthermore, direct contribution to net domestic product arising in the modern sector (that is, excluding the traditional sector) is approximately 15 per cent.
— About 80 per cent of Nile water utilised in irrigation (in 1966) was used in the scheme; its share of the country's enlarged share of Nile water (18.5 billion cubic metres per annum, according to the 1959 agreement) is estimated at about 30 per cent, or some 5.5 billion cubic metres, once the present extension work is completed.
— The area cultivated (some 756,000 ha) constitutes about 11 per cent of total area cultivated in normal years; the significance of the 756,000 ha is in effect much greater than appears at first glance, since it represents *irrigated* land.
— Employment is very high; according to the IBRD study around 600,000 persons are involved, distributed thus:

> 80,000 tenants;
> 200,000 dependants of these tenants who are capable of working;
> 300,000 wage labourers, and
> 15,000 employees of the Gezira Authority or the Ministry of Irrigation.

As indicated earlier, the Gezira scheme is the largest, the oldest, and the most prestigious agricultural project, but not the only one of importance. In the field of irrigated agriculture, a number of projects exist, in which some of the ideas and practices tried in the Gezira are put into effect.[13] The most important relate to the dams of Khashm el Girba (on the Atbara river) and Roseires (on the Blue Nile), the first of which is designed to irrigate 210,000 ha and the latter to make further expansion and intensification of irrigation possible in the southern reaches of the Gezira scheme. Also, south of the Gezira, the New Dam is expected to provide water for the irrigation of some 750,000 ha in the Kenana area. The Rahad project to the south (around the river Rahad) is designed to irrigate 210,000 ha and to utilise some 4 billion cubic metres of water annually, while the Sukki project is designed to irrigate some 70,000 ha.

All the projects so far referred to rely on gravity irrigation. Another important type of irrigation is by pump. This type has gained considerable significance in the post-war period, after an early start in the twentieth century. From a few hundred pump schemes in the early thirties, the number has risen to almost 4,000 currently (including just over 100 public schemes). 'In size they vary considerably from 10 feddans to 18,000 feddans.'[14] The total area irrigated by pump was roughly 1.6m *feddans* (672,000 ha) in 1969. A more detailed breakdown for 1967 provides the information in Table 9.5.

Table 9.5: Use of Pump Irrigation

	Number	Area Covered (m ha)
Private pumps	3,594	0.557
Public pumps	101	0.060
Total	3,695	0.617

Source: IBRD, 'Current Economic Position and Prospects of the Republic of the Sudan' (January 1969), Table 4. The *feddans* in the original have been converted into hectares.

Two-thirds of the area thus irrigated, and over two-fifths of the number of pumps, are in the Blue Nile Province, while just under one-fifth of the area and over two-fifths of the pumps are in the Northern Province. The rest of the area and of the pumps are in Khartoum, Upper Nile and Kassala provinces which together account for about 14 per cent of the area and 13 per cent of the number of pumps.

All private pump schemes have to be authorised by government, the pump-owner obtaining a sort of concession which specifies the amount of water allowed and the area of land involved. The concessionaire is required to prepare the land for cultivation, maintain the irrigation canals and roads, provide certain inputs (principally water), and manage the project. The farmer provides the labour required. Together they usually provide fertilisers, seeds, insecticides and pesticides, as well as ploughing, transport, ginning and marketing services. The distribution of the net proceeds is 56 per cent to the concessionaire, and 44 per cent to the farmer. In addition, the concessionaire pays a tax of 5 per cent of the proceeds to the government, as well as business profits tax.[15]

Lastly, there are large mechanised agricultural projects on rain land. The most prominent of these is in the Gedaref area in Kassala Province, and in Dali and Mazmoum regions in the Blue Nile Province. All together, this category covers about half a million acres (210,000 ha).[16] It will be recalled that rain-fed agriculture covers a total area about ten times that of irrigated agriculture.

The multiplicity of types of agriculture and of projects, and the better supervision of the terms which govern the relations of the various parties in the hundreds of irrigation (gravity and pump), and mechanised rain-fed agriculture projects, have necessitated close observation and study by the government. This was particularly necessary in view of the need to use water resources most rationally, co-ordinate the use by various sectors of the scarce skilled labour force, and achieve as much equity as possible in the apportioning of the net produce. As a result the government formed in 1967 an Agricultural Reform Corporation[17] to attend to these issues, as well as to take over private pump schemes as soon as the concessions came to an end, and in certain instances to take over unexpired concessions against compensation.

Emphasis is necessary, before this section is wound up, on the importance of cotton production and export to the economy. A few brief indicators will be sufficient: cotton accounts for one million acres (420,000 ha) or 50 per cent of the area irrigated (if account is taken of rain-fed cotton as well, then total cotton acreage accounts for 15 per cent of total area under cultivation); it also accounts for 17-20 per cent of government revenue through taxes and the government's share in the returns of the Gezira scheme, for about 60 per cent of exports and 40-50 per cent of foreign exchange earnings, and for some 12 per cent of gross domestic product.

These indicators in themselves suggest scope for future growth, but also carry within themselves the danger of over-concentration on one major crop. Another serious question arises, if expansion in cotton cultivation is to be opted for, namely the ability to draw into the new cotton areas enough workers with the adequate skills without disturbing the existing pattern of labour distribution in the country. This last question touches on the whole issue of the density of population to which reference has already been made and will be made again later. (To emphasise the predominant place of cotton in the agricultural sector and in the whole economy is not to ignore the other important products to which reference has already been made. Furthermore, the potential of Sudanese agriculture not only for Sudan but the Arab world as a whole will be brought out in the Concluding Remarks further down.)

3. THE STRUCTURE AND PERFORMANCE OF THE ECONOMY

A Sectoral Appraisal

The description of the broad features of the economy touched upon the economy's structure in very general terms. A closer look is now called for. This will be done first through an examination of the series of national accounts for the years 1955/6 to 1971/2, then through a very brief examination of the various economic sectors, and lastly through the identification of the traditional versus the modern sector of the economy. The level of performance of the economy will emerge during the description and analysis of the structure from the various angles suggested.

The first official document of independent Sudan on national accounts contains data for the year 1955/6.[18] It is a thorough and competent document, with an introduction including definition of concepts and description of methodology, as well as the identification of conceptual areas where terms coined and used for the national accounts of developed countries are not as appropriate for underdeveloped countries, both with regard to content and context, and to methodology and measurement. Nevertheless, despite the care taken and effort made, these first estimates were very rough and tentative, by the admission of official sources in a relatively recent document for the years 1966 and 1967,[19] and according to the appraisal of the IBRD and other users of Sudanese national accounts. The data for 1967 are considered of greater reliability, but still suffer from serious defects, to the point where they become doubtful as the basis for policy considerations and precise analysis.[20] (Drastic revision of the method of national accounts estimation has been recently undertaken with the aid of UN specialists. However, it is not known to what extent the improvement is reflected in the estimates for the years 1968-72. One thing is certain, though: that the preparation and publication of national income – and other statistical – data is still a very slow process. By early 1976, the most 'recent' estimates related to 1971/2.)

Be that as it may, we feel it of some considerable use to record the evolution of national income over the years 1955-72, as a broad indicator, even if one which suffers from a large margin of error. The data between the two terminal years are to a certain extent interpolations, particularly between 1961 and 1966, since the early work continued up to 1961/2 on the basis of small surveys, which were meant to provide material for adjustments in data on

Table 9.6: Gross Domestic Product at Factor Cost, 1955–1972[a] (£Sm and percentages)

Sector	1955/6 £Sm	Per Cent	1956/7	1957/8	1958/9	1959/60	1960/1	1961/2	1962/3	1963/4	1964/5	1965/6	1966	1967	1968	1969	1969/70	1970/1	1971/2	Per Cent Average 1969/70 – 1971/2
Agriculture	105.6	37.1					124.5	148.7	133.5	125.9	146.6	151.4	111.0	126.1	131.6	118.7				
Livestock	32.3	11.4					39.2	39.0	40.9	42.8	44.9	46.5	44.7	46.0	47.4	49.1				
Forestry	28.3	10.0					33.2	33.2	34.7	36.4	37.7	38.9	14.4	15.3	16.9	17.2				
Fishing	6.5	2.3					7.9	7.8	8.2	8.5	9.0	9.3	2.9	2.9	4.0	4.9				
Sub-total	172.7	60.8					204.8	228.7	217.3	213.7	238.2	246.1	173.0	190.3	199.9	189.9	207.6	217.3	241.4	39.7
Mining	0.2	–					0.3	0.2	0.3	0.3	0.3	0.3	1.9	2.0	2.3	1.7				
Manufacturing	2.8	1.0					5.7	6.4	8.0	9.2	11.0	13.0	22.6	24.0	25.7	35.3				
Crafts	9.8	3.4					11.9	11.8	12.4	12.9	13.5	13.9	14.1	16.0	15.8	15.7				
Sub-total	12.8	4.4					17.9	18.4	20.7	22.4	24.8	27.2	38.6	42.0	43.8	52.7	52.5	51.5	52.6	9.3
Construction	16.2	5.7					25.0	21.6	25.8	33.0	25.4	25.7	23.9[b]	21.7	24.3	28.6	23.3	22.3	25.7	4.2
Transport, Distribution and Services	54.9	19.2					73.9					88.2	149.8[c]	157.0	172.7	163.6	116.4	116.9	163.5	23.6
Government	17.2	6.1					33.2					54.5	40.6	46.3	51.5	73.9	77.1	84.5	91.8	15.1
Public Utilities	1.0	0.4					1.5					2.6	16.8[d]	16.3	16.7	16.3	16.5	16.5	16.8	3.0
Finance and Real Estate	9.5	3.4					12.8					15.6	14.5	16.2	18.1	24.7	23.2	22.5	40.6	5.1
Sub-total	82.6	29.1					121.4	129.0[e]	137.9[e]	148.0[e]	150.2[e]	160.9	221.5	236.8	259.0	278.5	233.2	240.4	312.7	46.8
Total	284.3	100.0	314.6[g]	311.4[g]	321.7[g]	347.8[g]	369.1	397.7	401.7	417.1	438.6	459.9	456.9[f]	489.9[f]	527.0[f]	549.7	516.6[g]	531.5[g]	632.4[g]	100.0

a. 1955/6–1959/60 at constant 1955/6 prices; 1960/1–1972 at current prices.
b. For 1966–70, the item 'construction' includes public works also.
c. As from 1966, the 'services' sector has come to include 'restaurants, hotels and bars', 'business services', and 'other services', as these appear in the statistical table entitled 'Economic Indicators of the Sudan'.
d. The item 'public utilities' does not appear as such in 1966–70, but a new item, 'electricity and water', appears. We have listed the latter item in the row of public utilities. Electricity and water probably appeared under 'government' in previous years.
e. Sector-by-sector details for the four years 1956/7–1959/60 are not available in comparable form.
f. The total above is larger by £S0.1m than that in the source, because of rounding.
g. The accounting year was altered as of 1969 to run parallel with the financial year. Hence the two series for 1969 and 1969/70 shown side by side.

Sources: For 1955/6, *The National Income of Sudan 1955/56*, for 1956/7 to 1959/60, Ministry of Finance and Economics, Department of Research and Statistics, *Economic Survey 1961* (Arabic; Khartoum, 1962); Tables 2 and 3, pp.14-16; for 1960/1, same source with later adjustments (as in KFAED, *Report on the Sudanese Economy*, p.46); for 1952/3–1964/5, Omar Osman and A.A. Suleiman, *The Economy of Sudan*, in P. Robson and D.A. Lury (eds.), *The Economies of Africa* (London, 1969), pp.440-1, quoting Ministry of Finance and Economics, Dept. of Economic Planning; for 1965/6, KFAED, *Report on the Sudanese Economy*, quoting IBRD, *Gezira Study Mission, The Importance of the Gezira Scheme in the Economy of Sudan* (1966); for 1966-9, Dept. of Statistics, Ministry of Planning, The Democratic Republic of the Sudan, *The National Accounts and Supporting Tables 1966, 1967* (Khartoum, July 1970), table entitled 'Economic Indicators of the Sudan' for 1966–9. For 1969/70 and 1970/1, *Economic Survey 1972*, p.21; and for 1971/2, *Economic Survey 1974*, p.42.

GDP and capital formation to the 1955/6 estimates.

There is very little difference between the series expressed in terms of current or constant prices, except possibly for 1970/1 and certainly for 1971/2. The GDP at current prices and the GDP at constant prices run as shown in Table 9.7.

Table 9.7: Gross Domestic Product at Current and Constant Prices, 1960/1–1967/8

Year	Current Prices	Constant Prices
	(£S million, 1964/5=100)	
1960/1	347	369
1961/2	398	419
1962/3	402	419
1963/4	417	425
1964/5	442	442
1965/6	455	455
1966/7	465	461
1967/8	498	491

Source: *Economic Survey 1967.*

As will be indicated presently, remarkable price stability lasted till 1971. Consequently, the GDP at current prices for the years 1968/9, 1969/70 and 1970/1 could not have varied considerably from that at constant prices, inasmuch as in 1971 the price index rose only by 1.4 points over 1970, the base year. However, prices rose by 11.1 per cent in 1972 over 1971 (and by 14.4 per cent in 1973 over 1972). As the accounting year since 1969 begins on the first of July, the price rise can only partly be related to 1972 in the accounting year 1971/2. We estimate the share of 1972 of the 11.1 per cent to be no more than 5 per cent, as the trend from then onwards was upwards.[21]

We can now draw some conclusions for the period 1960/1 to 1971/2. This is that the margin of error in the price index used for deflation of current prices is most probably larger than the resultant difference in the two sets of figures tabulated above. Furthermore, prices — both wholesale and consumer — were quite stable between 1967 and the end of 1971, the former in fact dropping by 0.4 per cent, and the latter rising by only 6.8 per cent (1970=100). It was 1972 that witnessed the first sharp rise in the whole period. Consequently, if we were to deflate GDP for 1971/2 by 5 per cent (as suggested in the preceding paragraph) we can safely make comparisons in aggregate and *per capita* GDP for the initial and terminal years of the series without serious concern over the difference between constant and current prices.

The series 1955/6 to 1971/2 shows reasonably small fluctuations in total GDP (except between the two initial years and the two terminal years), but considerable fluctuation in some of the individual sectors. Calculation of the rates of growth over the 17-year period will now be undertaken, but with the adjustment of the GDP for the terminal year (as indicated above) to make it acceptable and in line with the constant price estimates. Thus, overall growth between the initial and the final year is about 112 per cent, or 4.8 per cent per annum as a compound rate. On a *per capita* basis, GDP rose from £S27 to £S36.5, or by 35.2 per cent. This represents an annual compound rate of growth of just under 1.2 per cent on the average.

Evidently, the rates of growth just mentioned should be accepted with considerable caution, owing to the fact that GDP for 1955/6 was very low compared with 1956/7, and that for 1971/2 was very high compared with that for the preceding year. Furthermore, although price increases over the seventeen years have been very modest, they are still a factor to contend with. Finally, the system of accounting differed substantially between the initial and the terminal years. It might, therefore, for all these reasons, be more advisable to average the first two and the last two years and then to examine the rate of growth emerging. Once that is done, and a certain very mild price increase is allowed for (say about 1 per cent per annum on the average), we are left with about zero growth *per capita* in real terms between 1955/6 and 1971/2. Alternatively, it might be more appropriate to measure growth for the twelve years 1960/1 through 1971/2 (the latter adjusted as indicated earlier). This would again result in an average annual rate of 4.5 per cent, or about 1.12 *per capita* growth. Once we account for price increases, we would arrive at a zero, or even a negative, rate of *per capita* growth in real terms.[22]

The investment behind this grim picture is quite low. Thus, for the years 1955/6 to 1959/60, it amounted on the average to about 9 per cent of GDP, while it rose to about 12 per cent for the years 1960/1 to 1967/8, and to 15.5 per cent on the average for the three years 1969/70 to 1971/2. But if domestic savings alone are considered then investment would be only 7 per cent on the average. (Savings dropped steeply over these three years, from the equivalent of 12.9 to 6.4, and finally to a mere 2.8 per cent.)[23]

As indicated in the notes to Table 9.6, the definition of certain sectors varies in the national accounts for 1966-72 from that for the earlier years. The sectors in question are construction (which now includes public works), public utilities (which does not now appear; instead there is an item 'electricity and water', which we have taken to belong under the heading of 'public utilities'), transport and distribution, which now appears as transport and communications, while distribution (trade) is now a separate item, and services as a broad item which is now more detailed. In all these cases, comparisons over time will be unsound, in the absence of the necessary detailed breakdown on a comparable basis. Lastly, the contribution of 'government' to GDP, which – understandably – rose consistently between 1955/6 and 1965/6, dropped considerably in 1966 and 1967, but rose considerably from 1969 onwards. In the *National Income of Sudan 1955/56*, public utilities are explicitly said to include, *inter alia*, the public electricity companies. However, in the same volume, 'Government' is defined to include 'Public Corporations', which in turn explicitly include at least one of the electricity companies already referred to. On the other hand, *The National Accounts and Supporting Tables 1966, 1967* explain that public departments and corporations which were paid for their services were listed as 'industries' independently and not under 'government' where only services not paid for by the public were included. This would explain the drop in contribution of government for the years 1966 and 1967, since electricity and water and other public 'industries' were not included.

However, comparison over time is possible for the commodity-producing sectors. Agriculture, construction, forestry and fishing show vast variation. This is most true of agriculture and then of construction. For forestry and fishing the movement is consistently upwards, except for the years 1966-9, when the contribution dropped from £S38.9m in the year 1965, to £S14.4m for 1966 and 17.2m for 1969 for forestry, and from £S9.3m for 1965 to 2.9m and 4.9m for each of the two years 1966 and 1969, for fishing. This is a very baffling phenomenon, in view of the trend in the preceding ten years for each of these two sectors. Livestock also suffered some fluctuation, but it has been of minor magnitude. If the four sectors within the field of primary activities are taken together, they show a considerable drop in their combined contribution for the last five years in the series (for which sufficient detail is available) from the preceding years in the 1960s, both in absolute terms and in relative terms. (Their percentage contribution in 1955/6 was 60.8 per cent; it dropped to 55.5 per cent in 1960/1, to 38.8 per cent in 1967, and to 40.2 per cent in 1969/70.)

Mining, manufacturing and crafts (except for a few minor aberrations in the case of mining and even less significant drops in the case of crafts) showed no relapse. Indeed, crafts showed a rise of some 33 per cent in the decade 1960/1–70, but manufacturing a steep rise of 520 per cent for 1969 over 1960/1. This last sector has made the second-largest gain in the whole economy (after finance and insurance) even though here again the years 1966 and 1967 show a sudden and very large rise over the preceding trend, which might suggest some change in definition or coverage in addition to bona fide growth. But even if we made allowance for the possibility of change in definition and coverage, and assumed instead a continuation of the trend preceding 1966, the growth would still be considerable. (We exclude 'public utilities' from this comparison as their coverage changed drastically beginning with 1966.)

As far as overall structure is concerned, it can be concluded from the examination of Table 9.6, qualified by the comments made with regard to the comparability of data over time, that the internal relationships among groups of sectors have not changed drastically (nor could they legitimately be expected to change substantially, given the low level of the economy's performance, and the social structure underlying it, and also the brief span of time involved). This does not mean of course that there have not been sharp movements in some instances, as in the case of the secondary sectors (mining, manufacturing, crafts) whose relative importance doubled by 1971/2, and reportedly more than tripled by 1973.[24] Likewise, the importance of the primary sectors dropped from about 60 per cent of GDP in 1955/6 to about 55 per cent in 1960/1 — mainly because of a seasonal drop in the contribution of agriculture, coupled with the severe but unexplained drop in that of forestry and fisheries — to 50 per cent in 1971/2. It would, however, be difficult to draw conclusions from the change in the relative contribution of transport and distribution, government, or other services, owing to the misgivings we have regarding the definition of these sectors. Finance has witnessed a large expansion in relative terms and a more striking expansion in absolute terms. But, as in the case of manufacturing industry, the base had been very small in absolute terms in 1955/6. The expansion in the finance sector is largely a reflection of the overall expansion in the modern sector and the increase in monetisation. (Money in circulation was £S2 *per capita* in 1956, but £S12.7 in December 1974. Likewise, private savings and deposits in banks rose from £S0.9 to £S7.8 *per capita*.)[25]

Agriculture, narrowly defined, will not be included in the following brief survey of individual sectors, because in one way or another it has received repeated reference so far. The survey will include livestock, manufacturing, transport and power.

The livestock wealth of the country is enormous, but underexploited as well as primitively exploited. The main types of livestock are cattle, sheep, goats and camels, whose numbers since 1944 have developed as shown in Table 9.8.

The unsatisfactory performance of the livestock sector can be quantitatively demonstra-

Table 9.8: Number of Livestock in the Sudan 1944 and 1955/6–1970 (millions of head)

	1944	1955/6	1964/5	1965/6	1966/7	1967/8	1968/9*	1973/4
Cattle	3.2	6.9	9.1	10.0	11.0	12.1	13.3	14.1
Sheep	4.8	6.9	8.7	9.5	10.5	11.5	12.7	13.4
Goats	4.0	5.8	6.8	7.5	8.3	9.1	10.0	10.5
Camels	1.1	1.5	2.0	2.2	2.4	2.7	2.9	2.7

*Estimates

Sources: For 1944, KFAED, *Report on the Sudanese Economy*, p. 136; for the other years except 1973/4, *Economic Survey 1968*, p. 31; for 1973/4, *Economic Survey 1974*, p. 56.

ted, both from Table 9.8 and from statistics on livestock slaughtered, which show a modest activity. It is worth noting in this connection that exports of livestock are always on the hoof.[26] This is because the country does not have the facilities to deep-freeze meat and export it in properly equipped railway carriages and trucks on to refrigerated ships. Furthermore, importers prefer live animals owing to their greater confidence in their ability to exercise better sanitary control than over meat. The absence of a meat-freezing and exporting industry is, however, not merely the result of importers' distrust of sanitary regulations imposed and Arab consumers' general preference for 'fresh' (that is, not deep-frozen) meat, but also of the cost factor on the supply side. The areas where livestock are abundant are far from the exporting points on the northern and eastern frontiers, and the equipment and transportation costs required for frozen meat still seem prohibitive. Two other problems which beset this sector are the high mortality rates and the low meat component per head of livestock. The livestock wealth of the country clearly reveals the great potential both for the exportation of live animals and that of frozen meat, once the markets have been duly assured of quality and sanitary specifications.

Care for and breeding of livestock are largely part of the traditional sector in the economy. The manpower involved in these functions is large in size, and comprises a considerable proportion of very youthful members of the labour force (boys and girls below 15). Likewise, it comprises a large proportion of the disguised unemployment or underemployment in the country.

Manufacturing industry was of extremely modest proportions on the eve of independence, and was restricted to the processing of agricultural exports, chiefly cotton-ginning and the extraction of cotton-seed oil. Between 1955 and 1959 there was some expansion in the area of import substitution by local manufacture, but still on a very modest scale, and with capital coming in totally from the private sector. In 1959 the government invested in industry for the first time, and since then there has been relatively extensive investment, both by the private and the public sectors. During the sixties, this investment is estimated to have totalled £S59.6m (23.7m by the public sector and 35.9m by the private sector — of the latter £S16.1m being from Sudanese investors, and £S19.8m from foreigners resident in Sudan). Since then, the pace has accelerated, with a larger inflow of capital for industrial investment. Unfortunately, however, detailed information is not available with respect to the new projects initiated. But the following industrial projects are reported as being developed since 1970: a second tannery completed and a third under construction, factories for the processing of agricultural and dairy products, a foundry, a textile mill, a dairy products factory, and expansion in the existing sugar factories.[27]

The sixties and early seventies also witnessed a number of legislative and institutional measures for the promotion of industry. These included the founding in 1962 of the Industrial Bank (capital £S2m), the sponsoring by the government of an Industrial Institute for the undertaking of technical and economic research for possible industrial projects, the setting up in 1965 of an Industrial Development Corporation for the establishment of new enterprises and the management of government-owned enterprises already in existence, and the enactment in 1967 (to be operative on 15 March 1968) of the Organization and Promotion of Industrial Investment Act No. 55 of 1967 (which repealed and replaced an older act, the Approved Enterprises (Concessions) Act, 1956 which had a much narrower scope). A new act for the Promotion of Industrial Investment was put into effect in 1972, with the objective of extending the effectiveness of the Act of 1967 to include smaller-size enterprises. Finally, the capital of the Industrial Bank has been doubled (from the original £S2m) under the new Five-Year Plan 1970/1–1974/5. This Plan allots £S49.2m for industry and power.

The IDC was founded in order to speed up the industrialisation process, particularly in view of the weakness of private industrial enterprise; the provision of certain products deemed necessary for the country; the desire to spread out industrial establishments instead of allowing the process of concentration around Khartoum to continue; the desire to use local raw materials more intensively; and the desire to provide more employment opportunities and to combat excessive population movement into the urban centres. The Acts of 1967 and 1972 are designed to supplement government's promotive measures by allowing tax and duty exemptions, and to provide cheap land sites for industry and cheap electricity and railway freight rates. Though well-intentioned, all these promotive measures taken together still constitute a modest effort. This effort has been basically constrained by the shortage of investment resources. However, beginning with 1973, these resources have become markedly more abundant, as we shall see later during the examination of Sudan's development in the context of Arab economic co-operation.

Finally, it remains to be added that oil and gas were discovered in commercial quantities in the territorial waters of the Red Sea. A Romanian-Sudanese joint company is in charge of exploration. Furthermore, Saudi Arabia entered into agreement with Sudan in May 1974 for the developing of the resources of the Red Sea basin.

According to data already supplied in this chapter, the share of the industrial sector in the distribution of the labour force is about 5 per cent, but slightly less than 1 per cent relates to modern industry; the balance relates to crafts (traditional industry). Indeed, a relatively recent industrial survey[28] undertaken late in 1969 gives the number of workers in industry as merely 34,042, as Table 9.9 shows.

The Industrial Development Corporation controlled nine industrial establishments by the early 1970s, four of which belonged to one group as they were financed out of a loan of £S7.6m from the USSR for industrial development.[29] The modern industries under the IDC have suffered from many shortcomings. Foremost among these are: insufficient or faulty pre-investment studies; bad co-ordination between design of capacity and availability of inputs (whether with regard to quantity or quality); insufficient co-ordination between capacity installed and the combined needs of the country and the export market; insufficient concern for distance and transportation problems, both with respect to incoming inputs and outgoing final products; insufficient storage and transport facilities; inade-

Table 9.9: Summary Results of Industrial Survey, 1969

Type of Establishment (by size of labour force)	Number of Establishments	Output (£S thousands)	Value Added (£S thousands)	Number of Workers
Less than 30 workers	413	5,194.8	1,733.7	3,622
30-100 workers	89	18,190.7	3,321.1	5,569
100-500 workers	44	23,564.9	5,597.8	10,214
500 and over	9	16,706.8	5,113.0	14,637
Total	555	63,657.2	15,765.6	34,042

Note: The categories of type of establishment are given in the source as quoted above, although there is overlapping at the end of intervals. (Addition mistake in 'Value Added' total has been corrected.).

Source: Division of Industry, Ministry of Industry and Mining, *Summary of Industrial Survey Report and Its Recommendations* (Khartoum, 25 May 1970; Arabic).

quate specifications with regard to the quality of machinery installed and date of arrival of such machinery; underestimation of costs of installation; and insufficient skilled manpower at the managerial, supervisory and labour levels. In a country where the shortage of foreign exchange is serious and the heavy dependence on foreign loans is necessary and burdensome, and where skilled manpower is extremely scarce, bad planning is a very serious problem, and a very costly one to the economy and society.

The most important means of transport in the country is the railway. The railway system was built in the latter part of the last century and in the first two decades of the present. Extension of the network, which brought it to a total rail length of 4,756 km., was undertaken in the independence era. The inadequacy of the railways in relation to the population and total land area is best seen when it is remembered that the former is about 17m, and the latter about 2.5m sq. km.[30] The seriousness of the situation in the transport sector becomes all the more visible when it is remembered that the other means of transport are all less developed and less adequate than the railways. Recent data provide the information given in Table 9.10 regarding roads and river transport.

It is obvious from this limited set of data that the country is grossly under-equipped with transport facilities. Furthermore, the picture which emerges from these data is one which has undergone improvement in the independence years. The inadequacy of facilities makes transport difficulties and bottlenecks specially harsh and handicapping, and transport unit costs specially burdensome. The situation is all the more serious since there is concentration of facilities in and around the cities, particularly with respect to vehicles and good, all-weather roads. The problem and its seriousness are closely related to the sparseness of the population, which in its turn makes the unit cost of social services, as of economic overheads, inordinately high.

Dissatisfaction with the services offered by the railways has in recent years been specially pointed. Consequently efforts have been exerted to obtain financing facilities for renovation (including dieselisation), extension and improvement of the railways. These have been 7

Table 9.10: Transport by Road and River

All-weather asphalted roads (of which in Khartoum Province 178 miles)	208 miles
Cleared gravel tracks	3,210 miles
Just cleared tracks (no gravel, usually not passable after rain)	7,810 miles
Number of vessels in river fleet (old, low-speed steamers)	386
Distance covered (less than half of which is navigable all the year round)	2,545 miles
Number of Sudanese dry cargo ships, 5,000 tons capacity	7
Part of imports and exports carried by Sudanese ships in recent years, about	6 per cent
Passengers carried by railways 1973/4	2.81 million
Freight carried by railways 1973/4	2.58m tons
Number of passenger vehicles in country 1972	29,407
Number of goods vehicles 1972	20,768
Number of ships calling at Port Sudan (the country's only port) in 1972/3	818
Total incoming tonnage 1972/3	1.168m tons
Total outgoing tonnage 1972/3	1.913m tons
Number of passengers carried by Sudan Airways 1973/4	227,000

Source: Data collected from Europa, *1974-75*, pp. 633 and 641, *1971-72*, p. 549; and *Economic Survey 1973* and *1974*, Ch. V.

million Kuwaiti dinars from the Kuwait Fund for Arab Economic Development, 12.4m from the Arab Fund for Economic and Social Development, and two loans totalling $70m from the IBRD. In addition, expansion of the national shipping line, the development of river transport, and the building of the Khartoum-Port Sudan highway (including bridges on the Blue Nile and the Rahad rivers), and further 'consolidation' of the railways, telecommunications and television — have all received foreign financial assistance in the years 1970-4. (Total allocations for the sector in the 1970/1–1974/5 Plan amount to £S29.6m.)

It ought to be pointed out that there are some inherent difficulties in the transport situation not directly related to the performance of the railways (or the road system, for that matter). One of these is the seasonality of many of the crops which provide transport activity. This bunches the income, and also bunches the loss over a few months in the year, thus forcing the facilities to operate below capacity on an annual basis. Another is the incompatibility relative to many lines or roads, or river routes, between the volume of goods passing one way and that passing the opposite way. Again, under-capacity and high costs result. Obviously, better development of the country's vast agricultural wealth would itself provide more goods to transport and would enable the means of transport to operate nearer to capacity, and would even necessitate the provision of more means, including longer road and railway mileage. All this, however, does not negate the fact that the railways are not operated with enough efficiency to maximise their returns, given the type of external problems to which we have alluded.

The Sudan has a very low electricity output and consumption. Indeed, consumption per head is the lowest among the twelve countries surveyed in this book, and less than half the next country in the ranking.[31] Capacity installed was 118,353 kw in 1972, and output generated 503.9m kwh, of which 308.9m kwh was sold. The output produced averaged

30.5 kwh per head for that year; consumption only 18.7 kwh. In fact, household consumption was much less, since part of the output was used in industry and for other business uses. The consumers were in the large towns and cities, and numbered 68,529 households and businesses, in addition to 558 agricultural and 844 industrial users.[32] It ought to be pointed out, however, that certain projects, including many ginning factories, oil mills, grain silos and the sugar factories at Guneid and Khashm el Girba, have their own private generating capacity.

The country has immense potential in the field of hydro-electricity, considering its many rivers and its dams, and the fact that the level of terrain varies considerably in the south, thus permitting the utilisation of the drop of water for the generation of electricity. There is a *prima facie* case for the development of energy sources, both for household and business uses. But here again, as in the case of transport and the development of the vast agricultural potential of the country, the sparseness of the population compared with the vastness of the land constitutes a limiting economic factor. To this factor must be added the stringency of financial means, particularly with respect to foreign exchange.

July 1971 was a turning point for Sudan in a political and economic sense. An abortive *coup d'état* took place on 17 July and ended in extreme, but brief, bloodshed. Since then the country has had relatively greater calm. This, plus some extraneous factors, has helped the government concentrate more on development work.[33]

Internally, an attempt has been made at reorganising institutions engaged in developmental efforts, putting promotive legislation into effect, mobilising somewhat more domestic resources for investment, taking stock of projects that had already been studied and were essentially in need of financing to be initiated, and general implementation of the second Five-Year Plan 1970/1–1974/5. In other words, after putting its 'political house' into order, the government was capable of turning with more energy and effectiveness to economic matters.

The internal effort met with a favourable external response, both from the oil-rich Arab countries (especially Kuwait, Saudi Arabia, Libya and Abu Dhabi) and from Western industrial countries. The result was a more substantial inflow of capital in the period July 1971–December 1974 than optimistically expected before. (See the summary account of foreign aid further down for an estimate of aid received.) To encourage the inflow further, particularly where private capital flows are concerned, the government in May 1973 enacted the Organization and Promotion of Investments in Economic Services Act of 1973. The Act was designed to benefit the tourism, transport and storage sectors, and any other sectors or utilities deemed by the Minister of National Economy as likely to serve and develop the national economy. Later in the year, the Organization of Banking and Savings Act of 1973 was enacted. These two acts, together with the Organization and Promotion of Industrial Investment Act of 1972, strengthened the legislative framework of development and investment.

The soaring oil revenues received by the members of OPEC subsequent to the corrective pricing measures taken on 16 October and 23 December 1973 have also been a major external factor in the improved prospects for development financing. The year 1974 (and the early months of 1975) have witnessed large transfers and/or commitments of capital from some of the Arab oil countries to Sudan. Support, both financial and in terms of studies and the design of 'aid formulas' for the development of whole programmes (instead of individual projects) has also come from KFAED and from the Arab Fund for Economic and Social Development, AFESD.

The AFESD is to be credited with vision and a correct sense of priorities and strategy. It has advocated, promoted, and finally succeeded in initiating a comprehensive view of agricultural development in Sudan. This view involves, *inter alia,* the development of all the sectors, subsectors, or activities and facilities conducive or contributive to agricultural production. The comprehensive approach thus involves efforts and investment in roads, transport equipment, trucks and railroads; storage and refrigeration facilities; irrigation, drainage and land reclamation; power generation; rural education, extension services and experimental stations; agricultural industries; livestock breeding and meat industry; and dairy farming.

Initial recognition of the soundness of this comprehensive approach has been expressed by the Sudanese and (potential) donor Arab countries, and the AFESD proceeded to undertake a study aiming ultimately at the promotion of an ambitious and very large integrated programme of agricultural development in Sudan, one which could turn the country into the basic supplier of foodstuff (including meat) to the Arab world. The study involves two parts: project identification, stock-taking of projects already studied, and preliminary financial estimation of the cost involved; and the more far-reaching search for areas of development of priority within the integrated approach. The study was initiated in the summer of 1974 and completed in the spring of 1975. It is understood that aid commitments in the range of 2-3 billion dollars have been made, subject to the completion of the feasibility and investment studies. This may mark the start of the most significant development in Sudan's recent history, with far-reaching implications for the future of the whole economy. The work of AFESD has been crowned by the establishment of the Arab Authority for Agricultural Investment and Development, which will undertake work in Sudan as well as other Arab countries with significant agricultural potential. Its initial capital is about $510m.[34]

The increased inflow of capital after 1971 has permitted an investment programme larger and more dynamic than that initially designed in the second Five-Year Plan 1970/1–1974/5. Thus, while the (revised) investment programme for the public sector totalled £S215m, allocations over the four years 1970/1–1973/4 exceeded by a third the combined five-year allocations of the Plan. However, actual expenditure is reported to be smaller, in relative terms, than in the few years before. Understandably, the basic bottlenecks to execution are not widened by the mere increase in budgetary allocations, and the road to substantially greater absorptive capacity of investment is long and uphill.

Dualism in the Economy

The concept of a 'dual economy', which has relevance to economic structure, acquired wide circulation after Boeke's use of the term in connection with the Indonesian economy. It has sociological as well as economic connotations. Although it is not our purpose here to analyse the concept and to examine its relevance and meaningfulness, it is appropriate to say — as most of Boeke's critics have done[35] — that there is no economy or society which is uniformly homogeneous, and that in every single underdeveloped country there are some more advanced and some more retarded sectors where the 'actors' within the sector have different world views, different degrees of contact with the world market economy, and different degrees of technological openness.

With this qualification in mind, we will indicate that most surveys of the Sudan emphasise that the Sudanese economy is dual: it has a traditional and a modern sector. The present writer knows of no other Arab country, Morocco and Algeria notwithstanding, to which this distinction has been applied as aptly and consistently, although every other Arab country can be said to have a dual economy.

As Table 9.11 demonstrates — and again with the qualification that the division between the two sectors is somewhat arbitrary and the resulting data are necessarily approximate — the two sectors are about equal in performance in terms of GDP. The table also points in specific terms to the share of the traditional and the modern sector in each economic sector individually.

Several comments are called for with regard to Table 9.11. First, the determination of the size of the contribution of the traditional sector to GDP is not the result of a year-by-year estimate based on field-work or other relevant statistical material, but on an aprioristic determination or assumption of the share of the sector, plus an assumption that the sector grows evenly at a certain rate. The trend, in fact, has been established on the basis of a rate of growth of 3.3 per cent annually, regardless of the variation in the determining factors behind the economic sector concerned, such as rainfall and climatic conditions in the case of agriculture. As Table 9.11 shows, the traditional sector grows evenly, while the modern sector suffers narrow or wide fluctuations, depending on the case concerned.

In the second place, and again with the qualification regarding the calculation of the share of the traditional sector in mind, it is evident that this sector's share in GDP has slightly dropped in the sixties, as compared with the fifties, although on a year-to-year basis the share fluctuates upward and downward. This would suggest a rise in the share of the modern sector by more than the 3.3 per cent growth assumed for the traditional sector. Furthermore, the fluctuations must be the result of fluctuations in the modern sector, as the assumption of an even rate of growth for the traditional sector constitutes built-in evenness in it.

The third comment centres around the identity of traditional and modern activities (or economic sectors), since so far the discussion has treated all these activities together. Within the primary activities, agriculture proper has both a modern and a traditional sector. The former comprises irrigated agriculture and rain-fed cash crops. Its size is a little over two-fifths of the total contribution by agriculture. It ought to be pointed out here that subsistence agriculture has been included in the national accounts, and rightly so, as the authors of the first report, *The National Income of Sudan 1955/56*,[36] have argued. It is subsistence agriculture which constitutes the bulk of the traditional part of the sector. Furthermore, forestry falls almost totally within the traditional sector, while about 90 per cent of livestock-breeding and all of fishing activities fall in the traditional sector.

In the secondary activities, mining is all placed in the modern sector, while crafts, which constitute part of the sector of industry, fall in the traditional sector. Modern manufacturing using power-operated machines naturally falls in the modern sector. Construction is divided roughly equally between the modern and the traditional sector, the first referring to construction in towns and cities and the second to what is termed 'African style' building.

The service, or tertiary activities, vary from service to service. Thus, transport and distribution, government and ownership of dwellings fall totally in the modern sector. 'Other services', which include banking and finance, catering services, education and health services, and professional services are divided as a group into three-quarters modern and one-quarter traditional.[37]

The distinction between a modern and a traditional sector is based mainly on differences in the methods of production. It is equally tenable on the basis of the average income accruing per earner in each of the two sectors. The classification of the working population according to income levels is not possible, since the income tax was introduced only after

Table 9.11: Distribution of GDP at Constant Prices between the Traditional and the Modern Sector, 1955/6–1967/8

	1955/6	1956/7	1957/8	1958/9	1959/60	1960/1[a]	1961/2	1962/3	1963/4	1964/5[b]	1965/6	1966/7	1967/8[c]
Traditional (£S m)[d]	160.7	164.9	170.5	174.8	181.6	191.6	197.7	204.2	211.1	218.2	225.4	232.8	240.5
Modern (£S m)	123.5	149.7	140.9	146.9	166.2	177.9	221.6	214.5	214.0	224.0	229.4	228.5	250.4
Total (£S m)	284.2	314.6	311.4	321.7	347.8	369.5	419.3	418.7	425.1	442.2	454.8	461.3	490.9
Traditional (per cent)	56.5	52.4	54.7	54.3	52.2	51.8	47.2	48.8	49.7	49.3	49.6	50.5	49.0
Modern (per cent)	43.5	47.6	45.3	45.7	47.8	48.2	52.8	51.2	50.3	50.7	50.4	49.5	51.0
Total[e,f] (per cent)	100.0	100.0	100.0	100.0	100.0	100.0	100.0	100.0	100.0	100.0	100.0	100.0	100.0

a. The year 1960/1 appears in the first series in the *Economic Survey 1961*, but it makes the first year of the second series. We have adopted the more recent estimate.
b. The modern sector series was revised as from 1964/5.
c. Rough estimate for 1967/8.
d. Trend estimates for the traditional sector are based on a rough annual growth rate of 3.3 per cent.
e. For the whole period, for the whole economy, the traditional sector averages 50.8 per cent and the modern sector 49.2 per cent.
f. Sector-by-sector breakdown for the traditional and the modern sectors is available for the years 1960/1–1969, but for GDP at current prices. The above series was preferred because it renders itself more amenable to comparison over time.

Sources: For 1955/6–1959/60, *Economic Survey 1961*; for 1960/1–1967/8, *Economic Survey 1967*.

independence, and the vast majority of the members of the labour force remain outside the reach of this tax. However, it is generally believed that income per earner in the traditional sector is roughly half its counterpart in the modern sector.

So far we have implied that a large part of the traditional sector coincides with the subsistence sector, particularly in the fields of agriculture, fisheries and construction. However, the conceptual distinction between the two must be kept clear, since a large part of the output of the traditional sector is market-oriented, such as gum arabic, timber for railway beams, pulses, milk, fruit and so on. Likewise, a certain part of the agricultural output of the modern market is for the consumption within the productive unit or household, such as food grains grown on that part of the area of land held by tenants on the Gezira and similar schemes. One researcher has attempted to find the share of subsistence transactions in the country for the year 1955/6. According to him this share varied from region to region, being lowest in northern provinces (Kassala, Khartoum and Northern Province), where these transactions constituted 11 per cent of total consumption and 10 per cent of GDP. In the Blue Nile Province, the ratios were 31 and 21 per cent respectively; in the Darfur and Kordofan Provinces they were 46 and 45 per cent; and in the southern three provinces they were 82 and 78 per cent respectively.[38] For the whole country the ratios were 38 and 33 per cent respectively. However, these calculations refer to the first year of independence, and it can be safely assumed that the market economy has grown noticeably since then, although information on this point is not available.

The relatively large size of the subsistence economy reflects itself in the relatively small volume of money in circulation, and in the small size of the banking sector. The money supply per head is the lowest among the twelve countries surveyed in this book, and was £S12.7 or $36.5 by December 1974. Another indicator is the ratio of currency in circulation to GDP, which was 11.4 per cent for 1971/2. Were the degree of monetisation to be much higher (that is, were the subsistence economy to be insignificant) the money in circulation would have been of much larger volume, given the backwardness of commercial banking and the narrow spread of banking habits. (The ratio had been 5.5 per cent in 1960.) Thus in Lebanon, where the banking system is very well advanced, and where the market economy reigns virtually unchallenged, none the less the money in circulation stood at 17 per cent of GDP by the end of 1971, or £L363 per head, equivalent to $112. The explanation of the discrepancy between the two countries lies in the relatively large size of the subsistence economy in the Sudan compared with Lebanon. However, because of the very low level of *per capita* national product in the Sudan, compared with Lebanon, the discrepancy is not even larger. Thus, the ratio of money in circulation *per capita* in Lebanon to that in Sudan is 3.1 to one, and the ratio of GDP *per capita* in Lebanon ($659) to that in Sudan ($110), is 6 to one – all figures relating to the year 1971.[39] (The calculation, instead, of the bank deposits and savings *per capita* reveals a much sharper contrast than money in circulation *per capita* does.)

It is relevant at this point to describe the banking system. The Central Bank, the Bank of Sudan, was established by decree in December 1959. The Bank issues the currency and performs the usual functions of a central bank. Beginning with 1968 and until early 1972, the gold and foreign exchange cover behind the currency dropped considerably. It stood at 26.7 per cent in 1968, which is close to the absolute minimum of 25 per cent permitted by law. The consolidated account of the seven commercial banks in operation shows claims on the private sector to have been £S123.2m by the end of December 1974. The largest part of the credits advanced was for the financing of import and export operations, about a quarter went to industry, and the balance financed miscellaneous operations.

It remains to be said that all banks were nationalised in May 1970. In addition, there are three 'development banks' owned by the state: Agricultural Bank of Sudan, Estate Bank of Sudan, and Industrial Bank of Sudan.

The first of these was established in 1957, with an authorised capital of £S7m. The Estate Bank was established in 1966, with a capital of £S7m (shared by the state and the Bank of Sudan), for the purpose of helping in the financing of housing. The Industrial Bank was established in 1962, with a capital of £S2m. (Another £S2m were advanced to its working capital in 1972.) Most of the loans of the Agricultural Bank are seasonal or for short term, an insignificant part has in recent years been for medium term, and virtually none for long term. This distribution is indicative enough of the very limited developmental effect of the loans of the Bank. In addition the working capital of the Bank is very small, faced as it is with the colossal agricultural needs of the country. The Industrial Bank, as its capital suggests, also has very limited means at its disposal. Its operations have been further handicapped by losses on investment and by failure of some debtors to repay the loans.[40]

This section set out to discuss the structure and performance of the economy. Two more subjects which reflect the level of performance need to be brought in now: the balance of payments (including foreign trade and aid) and the state budget.

The largest item in the balance of payments is trade. Sudan's commodity imports have risen from £S27.3m in 1950 to £S207.7m in 1974; its exports from £S33.1m to £S137.4m. Between 1958 and 1974, the current account with two exceptions, in 1959 and 1973, has shown a deficit, and this deficit has varied between a minimum of £S1m in 1960, and a maximum of £S99.4m in 1974. (In fact, 1973 showed a surplus on current account of £S6.4m.)[41]

The main burden of meeting the chronic deficits in the balance of current account has fallen on foreign loans and grants advanced to the Sudan, the country's holdings of gold and foreign currencies, and the building up of foreign liabilities. Thus, while foreign reserves dropped from the equivalent of £S58.2m in 1960 to £S38.7m in December 1974, foreign debt outstanding reached a level of £S254.3m by the end of December 1974, apart from short-term borrowing and loans contracted under the United States Aid Programme. This is a very heavy debt burden, considering the country's national product and its strained balance of payments position. The latter makes debt servicing particularly difficult. (The net foreign assets position worsened considerably over the decade 1965-74, dropping from £S15.5m to −46.1m.)

Total aid received — grants, long-term and medium-term loans in cash and in kind — during the period 1960-9 reached £S140.9m; out of this total grants reached £S23.2m, and advances in kind £S28.5m, the balance of £S89.2m being credits. (Loans from the IBRD head the list in size, followed by those from Kuwait, Saudi Arabia, USSR, Libya and West Germany. Together these account for £S71.2m out of total credits of £S89.2m.) The volume of debt involved was perhaps moderate in size by the end of the decade, compared with GDP, but heavy compared with annual earnings of foreign exchange if annual servicing is considered. Thus, servicing constituted 12.5 per cent of export proceeds for 1969 — quite a high proportion.[42]

However, it will be more useful to reconstruct the picture of economic aid (loans and grants) for a much longer period of time: specifically from the end of World War Two to the end of 1973. As in the case of the other countries for which this global account has been made, the data are collected from several sources, and are subject to a not inconsiderable margin of error. This arises mainly from two causes: non-availability of data on

Table 9.12: Summary of Balance of Payments 1964-74 (£S million)[a]

	1964	1965	1966	1967	1968	1969	1970	1971	1972	1973	1974
Balance of Trade	−17.7	−1.4	−8.2	−5.6	−9.0	+2.6	−2.8	−3.7	−5.9	+27.5	−70.3
Balance of Invisibles	−15.1	−13.6	−11.2	−11.9	−9.8	−12.9	−12.1	−11.1	−15.9	−21.1	−29.1
Balance on Current Account	−32.8	−15.0	−19.4	−17.5	−18.8	−10.3	−14.9	−14.8	−21.8	+6.4	−99.4
Balance on Capital Account[b]	+15.5	+8.3	+16.5	+9.3	+5.4	+11.6	+0.8	−6.5	+8.1	+1.3	+91.1
Overall Balance of Payments[c]	−17.2	−7.0	−3.0	−8.4	−12.7	+1.6	−11.5	−20.1	−9.6	+9.0	−9.5

a. Plus (+) denotes a surplus, minus (−) denotes a deficit.
b. Excluding monetary movements.
c. After allowing for 'errors and omissions'.

Source: *Economic Survey 1974*, Table 6-1, p. 107.

aid for the years 1945-56 except in so far as the United States is concerned; and possible duplications or omissions in the published source material. These reservations notwithstanding, we find that the equivalent of $1,000m of net capital inflow has been received by Sudan from the governments of industrial market economies and of centrally planned economies, multilateral agencies, the World Bank group and the Arab countries. (The flow of private capital, though not included here, is not insignificant.) In addition, the sources consulted also indicate commitments and/or actual aid amounting to $480 from the Arab oil-exporting countries and from AFESD, between October 1973 and December 1974.[43] The grand total of $1,480m is not considerable, if full account is taken of the size of the country and its population, its enormous needs, its great potential, and the length of the period covered. The inflow is merely $5 *per capita* per year.

Finally, the general budget. Apart from the recurrent revenue and expenditure budget of the central government, there are the budgets of local councils, public institutions, economic projects and development. The current budget will be discussed presently, while development expenditure will fall under the next section. The other budgets will not form part of this discussion; their net revenue is extremely small in comparison with the general budget, and they are either financially self-sufficient or moderately surplus-creating.

The closed accounts for the years 1957/8 to 1973/4, and the estimates for 1974/5, except for the year 1966/7, show a surplus in the current budget. This surplus has ranged from a mere £S0.57m in 1958/9 to a high of £S22.54 in the following year. The single deficit in the series was £S0.6m. In gross terms, the budget has risen from £S47.38m for revenues, and £S41.33m for expenditures in 1957/8, to £S222.8m for revenues, and £S217.1m for expenditures in 1973/4, and to £S277.5m and £S268.3m respectively, for 1974/5.[44] Considering the remarkable price stability of the country until the end of 1971, the sixfold increase is explained by the expansion in the civil service, the army, and in the operations of the various ministries and departments — especially education, health and social welfare. (Public services account for about half the current budget for 1973/4.) Only beginning with 1972 did inflation begin to make itself felt as a tangible factor in the rise in budget estimates.

Indirect taxation has all through been the main source of revenue. It comes in the form of customs duties on imports, excise duties, fees and charges (mainly on production and consumption), reimbursements, inter-departmental services, and revenue from government enterprises and property. Revenue from direct taxation (personal income and business profit taxes) was smaller than any of these categories until 1967/8. Only beginning with the estimates for 1968/9 does direct taxation rise slightly in rank. Thus, the maximum receipts from direct taxes in the 17 years ending 1973/4 were £S23.6m. It was in 1969/70 that these receipts went above the £S10m mark. It is not surprising that the liquidity of government has for several years been strained, owing to the lag between accrual of expenditures and collection of revenues. In recent years the government has resorted to borrowing from the Bank of Sudan, and has used up all the credit allowed by law (which is a determined ratio of the expected revenues). It must be pointed out that in general deficit financing has reached serious proportions in Sudan (it stood at £S56.48m at the end of 1968, but at £S196.9m at the end of December 1974, mainly credits by the Bank of Sudan). The recent (end 1974) net claims on government amount to about 70 per cent of budget revenue estimates. The situation is all the more serious in view of the fact that most of the funds borrowed by government are used for non-developmental purposes.

4. DEVELOPMENT PLANS[45]

Planning, in the narrow sense of programming in the public sector, began right after World War Two in Sudan. Two five-year plans were formulated and more or less implemented before independence, the 1946-51 and 1951-6 plans, involving a total investment of 14.55m and 49m Egyptian pounds (then legal tender) respectively. A third plan followed independence, for the years 1956-61 for a total investment of 120m pounds. The investments in all three plans were to go mainly to productive schemes (irrigation, dams), and to communications, social services and public utilities. Total investment projected was thus over 183m pounds, but actual investment seems to have fallen behind and to have been around 100m only.

A ten-year plan was formulated to stretch over the decade of the sixties, for the years 1961/2–1970/1. This plan was comprehensive, in the sense that it accounted for the private as well as the public sector. As Table 9.13 indicates, the plan set out to achieve a noticeable increase in GDP, both global and *per capita* (63.6 per cent and 23.7 per cent respectively). Its other major objective was to achieve diversification, both in the sectoral distribution and geographically. With regard to sectors, it was hoped that the modern sector would raise its share of GDP from 47.6 per cent in year 1 to 55.7 per cent in year 10. This was to happen through the expansion and/or intensification of irrigation and rain-fed agriculture, the expansion of the market economy, and the modernisation of agricultural methods, as well as the vast expansion – relatively speaking – of industry, the railways, communications and modern (non-traditional) housing.

Three objectives other than growth of GDP ranked high. One was the increase in exports and the achievement of a notable measure of import substitution. The second was the improvement in the levels and conditions of education, training and health, and the expansion in job opportunities. And the third was the maintenance of price stability.

The GDP was planned to rise from £S357.2m in 1960/1, the base year (£S29.9 per head), to £S584.5m in the year 1970/1 (£S37.0 per head). This rise was to be achieved through rise in labour productivity and a total gross investment of £S565.4m (a net investment of £S472m). The public sector was to provide 59.6 per cent and the private sector 40.4 per cent of total investment. As far as economic sectors are concerned, the distribution was rather even among four clusters: primary activities; secondary activities; transport and distribution (including railways); and social services, including housing, health care, education and general administration, etc. The detailed breakdown appears in Table 9.14.

From Tables 9.13 and 9.14 it can be seen that the incremental capital-output ratio for the whole economy was about 2.5. This is probably low, considering the fact that the investment includes large sums for infrastructure whose returns are normally small per unit of investment.

The financing of the Plan was to rely heavily on external sources, in addition to domestic savings, as the summary in Table 9.15, based on the Plan document, shows. Thus, a total of £S149.5m was expected from external sources for both sectors, in the form of grants and loans. In actual fact, this expectation proved to be rather realistic, as we have seen in discussing foreign aid and the foreign debt. Grants and loans flowing in during the decade 1960-9 totalled £S140.9m, which fell short by a small amount of the projected foreign aid.

The economy's performance in general seems also to have varied reasonably little from the Plan expectations. Thus GDP for the terminal year 1970/1 was projected in the Plan to reach £S584.5m at factor cost. This was in fact £S524m instead, or a shortfall of about

Table 9.13: Proposed Growth of GDP and Population 1960/1–1970/1

	Base Year 1960/1	1 1961/2	2 1962/3	3 1963/4	4 1964/5	5 1965/6	6 1966/7	7 1967/8	8 1968/9	9 1969/70	10 1970/1
GDP (factor cost) £S m											
Traditional	187.2	193.3	199.7	206.3	213.1	220.1	227.4	234.9	242.7	250.7	259.0
Modern	170.0	191.8	190.6	200.7	213.6	227.3	241.9	260.5	280.6	302.2	325.5
Whole economy	357.2	385.1	390.3	407.0	426.7	447.4	469.3	495.4	523.3	552.9	584.5
Population (thousands)	11,928	12,264	12,610	12,966	13,332	13,733	14,120	14,518	14,927	15,348	15,781
GDP per capita (whole economy) £S	29.9	31.4	30.9	31.4	32.0	32.6	33.2	34.1	35.1	36.6	37.0

Source: *Ten-Year Plan of Economic and Social Development 1961/62–1970/71*, p. 42.

Table 9.14: Summary of Investment in the Development Plan 1961/2–1970/1

Sectors	Private £S m	Public £S m	Total £S m	Per Cent of Total
Agriculture, livestock, forestry and fishing	30.0	90.1	120.1	21
Industry, including public utilities, building, civil engineering and mining	65.0	41.9	106.9	19
Transport and distribution	32.0	63.0	95.0	17
Social services, including housing, health care, education, general administration and other	60.0	90.0	150.0	27
Total Net Investment	187.0	285.0	472.0	84
Replacement Investment	41.4	52.0	93.4	16
Total Gross Fixed Investment	228.4	337.0	565.4	100

Source: *The Ten-Year Plan of Economic and Social Development 1961/62–1970/71*, p. 65.

10 per cent. (It ought to be mentioned, however, that GDP dropped in 1970, from its level of £S549.7m for 1969.)

However, these overall indicators of virtual agreement between the planned and the actual inflow of foreign aid and planned and actual growth are misleading by themselves. They hide wide variation if the data are examined on a year-by-year, or a sector-by-sector, basis. Furthermore, while foreign financing actually conformed with Plan expectations, domestic savings did not. As a result, actual investment (both public and private) began to lag behind planned investment after 1963/4. For the first seven years performance in this sense seems to have been 70 per cent, a level below expectations, but not bad if compared with the experience of most of the twelve countries included in this study. However, by the terminal year 1970/1, the proportion was 72.3 per cent for investment from domestic sources, but 65.3 per cent from foreign sources.[46]

The investment programme, both from domestic and from external sources, represented an average of 11.2 per cent of GDP for the whole ten-year period. Domestic savings were to account for 8.3 per cent, and external financing for 2.8 per cent. Both the private and the public sector failed to save the resources expected of each of them under the Plan, especially after the year 1963/4. In the case of the private sector, the cause was possibly hesitation arising from the instability which began to loom large on the political horizon. The public sector, on the other hand, saw its economic projects and revenue-earning public enterprises (the Gezira and similar schemes, the railways, White Nile projects, public corporations for power and water) provide smaller and smaller surpluses over the years. The combined effect of the factors affecting the savings of both sectors was to depress aggregate domestic savings even below the already low level of 8.3 per cent of GDP. It was fortunate, under the circumstances, that external grants and loans did not prove to be much lower than had been expected. Otherwise, the implementation of the Plan would

Table 9.15: Financing Sources for the Ten-Year Plan, 1961/2—1970/1

	£Sm	£Sm
Public Sector		
Planned Investment		337.0
Domestic Savings	219.7	
External Sources	117.3	
Private Sector		
Planned Investment		228.4
Domestic Savings	196.2	
External Sources	32.2	

Source: *The Ten-Year Plan* . . ., p. 75.

have been further handicapped.

The Plan suffered two other types of handicap. The first, as we have seen in connection with the projects of the Industrial Development Corporation, was associated with the design, phasing, construction and conduct of projects, as well as with the co-ordination and linkages between projects, or between projects and their inputs on the one hand and markets on the other. The second was institutional. Thus, the planning machinery which was set up in 1961 was cumbersome and inefficient, in addition to being handicapped by meagre experience. The machinery comprised an Economic Council as the supreme body overseeing the whole process. The Council consisted of the Prime Minister as chairman with a number of Ministers as members. Next came a Development Committee, under the chairmanship of the Minister of Finance and Economics and composed of the Ministers who were not members of the Council. The third organ was a National Technical Planning Committee, under the chairmanship of the Governor of the Bank of Sudan, which had for members most of the heads of government and semi-government departments. Subsequently, a Planning Secretariat was established and placed in the Ministry of Finance and Economics under the Under-Secretary for Economic Planning. Finally, currently the responsibility is in the hands of a Ministry of Planning. (The last reorganisation measure was taken in 1972.)[47]

The powers and functions of each of these bodies were defined, as was the web of relations between them. However, the structure was cumbersome; the membership, especially in the Council, the ministerial Development Committee, and the Technical Planning Committee, was determined on the basis of political considerations to some extent and lacked clear justification on grounds of functionality; the number of members of the Technical Planning Committee was large; technical and professional talent in the Secretariat was insufficient for the size of the task; and all round the experience with comprehensive planning was inadequate and work had to proceed within a political context that was not conducive to successful planning and implementation.

Three issues of political significance had to be contended with. The first was the sudden change of political leadership that occurred a few times in the decade in question. Naturally this undermined the smooth unfolding of the Plan and its implementation. The second was the unrest in Southern Sudan which diverted attention and resources away from development work, first into armed action and later into pacification efforts. The third was the controversy over the question of geographical diversification, which called for spreading development investment and works to reach the extreme west and the south, as against concentrating investment in the central area and adjoining regions where the net returns would be optimised owing to the more appropriate infrastructure already in existence there. In essence, this was not merely an economic issue but a political one as well. So far, it seems concentration still prevails. Hence the emphasis on a relatively small number of very large projects, mostly falling in the fields of irrigation and manufacturing industry.

The Sudan is now, in 1976, towards the end of another planning phase, namely the second Five-Year Plan for the period 1970/1–1974/5. The phrase 'towards the end' is justified because the Plan was extended to 1977 in 1974. The year 1970/1 overlaps with the last year of the Ten-Year Plan and incorporates important changes. Total investment forecast in the original version of the Plan is £S372m for the five years — £S200m by the public sector (as against 137m in the last five years of the Ten-Year Plan), and £S172m by the private sector (as against £S125m in the Ten-Year Plan). Domestic savings are expected to provide £S277m, while foreign grants and loans are expected to provide the balance of £S95m. All capital flows into the country are expected to go to the public sector. (Soon after its formulation, the Plan was revised in 1970 so as to include another £S15m in public-sector allocations, bringing this sector's total to £S215m. The increase was designed to take care of the compensation made necessary by the nationalisations made earlier. Other revisions of the allocations by the public sector followed, resulting in more than a tripling of the original allocation. The vast expansion was meant to take care of the increase in the number of projects included in the Plan, the enlargement of some that had been there already, and the steep rise in costs under the inflationary pressures that began operating in 1972.)

Table 9.16: Initial and Revised 5 Year Plan Investment Allocations (£S million and per cent)

| Sector | Initial Plan | | | | | | Revised Plan | |
| | Private Sector | | Public Sector | | Total | | Public Sector Only | |
	£S m	Per Cent	£S m	Per Cent	£S m	Per Cent	£S m	Per Cent
Agriculture	26.5	15.6	80.0	37.2	106.5	27.6	155.8	23.6
Industry	24.0	14.1	36.4	16.9	60.4	15.7	117.8	17.9
Transport and communications	31.0	18.2	29.6	13.8	60.6	15.7	228.7	34.7
Power	–	–	12.8	5.9	12.8	3.4	37.2	5.6
Services and construction	88.5	52.1	44.1	20.5	132.6	34.4	92.4	14.0
Technical assistance	–	–	9.8	4.6	9.8	2.5	–	–
General reserves and Southern Region	–	–	2.3	1.1	2.3	0.7	28.0	4.2
Total	170.0	100.0	215.0	100.0	385.0	100.0	659.9	100.0

Sources: For the Initial Plan, General Planning and Economic Studies Administration, *Economic Survey 1973*, p. 111; for the Revised Plan, National Planning Commission, *Economic Survey 1974*, p. 172.

The main objectives of the Revised Plan are the following:

- Raising the rate of growth from 4.9 per cent, the level believed to have been achieved on the average during the five years preceding the Plan, to 7.6 per cent, thus bringing GDP in the target year 1974/5 to £S816m.
- Increasing government revenue at an annual average rate of 11.9 per cent.
- Raising the contribution of primary and secondary sectors from 61.1 per cent — the level for 1969/70 — to 65 per cent for 1974/5. (This involves raising agricultural production by 60.8 per cent, livestock production by 75.5 per cent, and industrial production by 57.4 per cent.)
- Expanding the network of electricity in urban centres and in the countryside.
- Achieving a surplus in the current account of the balance of payments.
- Promotion of the co-operative movement with a view to raising agricultural productivity and consolidating 'the socialist foundations for the development of the economy'.
- Increasing GDP *per capita* to £S46.6 for the target year — an increase of 31 per cent over the first year.
- Increasing the well-being of the people through raising productivity, achieving full employment, increasing the technical capability of labour, and expanding public services.

In the initial plan, the grand total of £S385m of private and public investment was expected to create an incremental GDP of £S249m (£S816m for 1974/5 minus £S567.4m for 1969/70). Thus the incremental capital-output ratio foreseen was 1.54:1. Obviously, this is unrealistically low, considering the large proportion of infrastructural investment involved, and the low productivity of labour.

According to the latest data available, which appear in the *Economic Survey 1974* (published in the summer of 1975), the performance under the Plan, measured by the actual investment as a proportion of planned investment, started satisfactorily but dropped considerably. Thus, for the four years 1970/1 through 1973/4, the proportions were 71, 43, 45 and 45 per cent respectively. The slowness of the rate of execution of projects was the main factor behind the extension of the operation of the investment Plan till 1977. In fact, the pace was even slower than these proportions suggest, as the execution performance outwardly rose because of the rise in the costs of materials, machines, labour and other inputs; this naturally was reflected in a rise in the 'accounting' results which were not fully matched by better performance in real terms.

Allocations for 1974/5 were raised once more in the development budget for that year. Early indications suggest that the financial constraints, which had been one factor forcing the pace of implementation to be slowed down, had been loosened through accelerated aid, mainly from Arab sources. However, the other constraints, particularly institutional and manpower, remain tight and retarding.

5. CONCLUDING REMARKS: DEVELOPMENT POTENTIAL AND PROBLEMS

Potential and problems in the main represent two sides of the same development coin in the case of Sudan. The juxtaposition is best represented by the country's vast endowment in land and water, on the one hand, and the inadequate size and proficiency of its population, on the other hand. Thus, while development can proceed faster if the population

Sudan

were less sparse and contacts between population centres were more feasible and less costly, the acceleration of the pace of development requires change in the quality of the population (in terms of education and training) to make it capable of better exploiting the natural resources and of better benefiting from the economic infrastructure.

Likewise, the dualism of the economy and the existence of a large traditional sector, which constitutes a challenge and an opportunity for development, on the grounds that the low base makes a relatively high rate of growth feasible, on the other hand constitutes a handicap because the low base in itself implies the inability of the economy's performance to foster substantial progress.

A detailed stock-taking of the country's economic potential (and of its problems) is not called for at this point, since the discussion in this chapter has pointed to both. It will be sufficient here merely to underline the main areas of potential. These are agriculture, both irrigated and rain-fed, but particularly a fuller and more optimal utilisation of water resources; forestry; livestock; and industries based on or associated with these primary activities. The country is well endowed with arable land and water, forests and livestock wealth. Indeed, this combined sector can well become the granary, and the supplier of meats and hides, timber and other agricultural produce to the Arab countries which have a deficit in all these outputs, as well as a notable exporter to non-Arab countries. The dimensions of growth possibilities entitle the sector to become the 'leading sector' of development in Rostow's terminology — given the satisfaction of the other necessary conditions. In this connection, the country is not forced to start from scratch, thanks to the development of irrigated agriculture (notably in the Gezira scheme) and to the awareness of the significance, and the partial exploitation, of the forestry and livestock wealth.

These statements need not remain at the level of generality, thanks to two recent studies, which are without doubt the most comprehensive in their field. The first was undertaken by the Food and Agriculture Organization (Policy Analysis Division), and appeared in April 1973, in 25 monographs, under the Country Perspective Studies Programme. However, because the second study appeared more recently and made full use of the FAO study, we will not use the latter in emphasising the agricultural perspectives of Sudan. The more recent study was undertaken by the Arab Fund for Economic and Social Development, between the spring of 1974 and that of 1975, and explored the possibility of launching a whole programme for the development of the agricultural sector along with all supportive activities in other sectors. The results of the AFESD study appeared in five volumes in October 1975. A further volume appeared later in February 1976 under the title *The Arab Authority for Agricultural Investment and Development — Invitation to Founders*. This Authority, which is to undertake much of the development work, and to which we have already referred earlier, has since been founded and is now being capitalised.[48]

The AFESD study results, showing the average annual imports of the major food commodities by the 20 Arab states during the 1970-3 period, are given in Table 9.17. Demand and supply projections made on the basis of the past recent trends suggested that the gap would widen considerably by 1985, and the estimates are given in Table 9.18. Against this increasingly deficitary situation, Sudan has the scope for a vast expansion in production of agricultural foodstuffs and produce for industrial purposes. The country has a potential for a threefold expansion in irrigated area (presently 1.22m ha according to the study), an even vaster potential for rain-fed agriculture (from the present 5m ha to an estimated minimum of 29.8m ha), the yet vaster possibility to exploit its forest wealth which is merely scratched at the present moment, and a considerable potential for fishing,

Table 9.17: Average Annual Food Imports of the 20 Arab States 1970-73 (million tons)

Wheat	6.00
Sugar	1.00
Vegetable oil	0.40
Meats (red)	0.13

Table 9.18: Estimated Increase in Imported Foodstuffs by 1985 (per cent)

Wheat	40
Sugar	100
Vegetable oil	150
Meats (red)	600

thanks to the 2.6m ha of fresh-water surfaces and 750 km. of Red Sea coast that the country possesses. Instead of the present 23,000 tons of fish caught annually, the potential annual catch is estimated in the study at about 200,000 tons.

Considered globally, the AFESD programme envisaged increases in production between 1976 and 1985 ranging between 100 and 150 per cent compared with the base year 1972/3 for most major crop and livestock commodities, except for sugar production, which was estimated to increase by 700 per cent, and wheat production, which would increase by 500 per cent. These targets would not represent the limit according to the programme. Yet, according to the *Résumé*,

> they would achieve sulf-sufficiency for the Sudan in all major commodities. In addition, considerable expansion and diversification of agricultural export commodities would take place. Export surpluses would be available for the first time for sugar, rice, wheat, fruits and vegetables... Projections of agricultural imports by other Arab states in 1985 indicate that these markets are potentially capable of absorbing all the Sudan major agricultural exports except cotton and gum-Arabic.

The emphasis placed on production in respect of crops, forestry products, livestock and fisheries, should not conceal the further emphasis placed by the programme on other areas of development. These include agro-allied industries, transport, water resources, electric power, and supporting infrastructures and services. As far as agro-industries are concerned, certain steps have been taken by the government, and although these had not received adequate pre-investment studies and preparation in earlier years, the authorities have not been slow in recognising the areas of weakness and the need for correction. But what is at issue is much more than the limited number of factories for food processing already in existence, both in terms of scale and range.

The country's potential is indisputably vast. However, there are many obstacles that block the road from potential to achievement, notwithstanding the fact that the authorities are development-oriented and serious in their desire to improve the performance of the economy, and the civil service is disciplined — factors which should in themselves be listed as a distinct potential for development. (To describe the civil service in this manner is not to deny the demoralising effects of political instability on government officials.)

Against this potential, the list of major problems is formidable. The first of these relates to the population, which suffers from a very high rate of illiteracy and from a very low level of vocational and professional training. Thus, according to the most recent publication available — the *Economic Survey 1974* — the illiterate constituted 87 per cent of the whole population as late as 1970. Admittedly, this rate, like its counterparts in Third World countries, should be accepted with great reserve; yet it is significantly high even if it is considered broadly imprecise. Educational efforts have been remarkable, as Table 9.19 suggests, but even with the vast expansion in enrolment over the decade covered, total enrolment in the public and private systems of education represented no more than 33 per cent of school-age children in 1974/5, or 1.61m out of 4.85m. Yet this proportion in itself represents a vast increase over its counterpart in 1965/6. With this latter year as base, enrolment in 1974/5 is an index of 307, which represents a compound rate of growth of 13.3 per cent per annum over the ten years in question.

One encouraging aspect is the very fast rate of increase in the enrolment in technical training; the index for 1974/5 is 601, compared with 1965/6 as base. Yet not much should be read in this satisfactory phenomenon, in so far as the absolute size of enrolment in technical training is very small. The total number of trainees in the higher secondary cycle stood at 5,993 or 10.85 per cent of total enrolment in the cycle, against 997 or 3.54 respectively for 1965/6. Finally, it must be pointed out that enrolment in universities has moved up satisfactorily in the decade in question, from 7,884 to 22,828 men and women, or an increase of 189.5 per cent, which amounts to about 12.5 per cent per annum on the average. This is a very high rate which compares favourably with the rates of the remaining countries.

One serious aspect of education is the problem of drop-out, which is very high in Sudan. Thus, in 1965/6, enrolment in intermediate and preparatory schools was a mere one-sixth of that in elementary schools, and those who went further on, to post-intermediate and secondary education, were only two-fifths of those in the cycle before. The division into cycles changed by 1974/5, but the drop-out rate became more alarming. Thus, enrolment in general secondary schools was a mere 14 per cent of enrolment in primary schools, while enrolment in higher secondary was only 30 per cent of that in general secondary schools. Likewise, the education of girls in the public school system has made no progress during the decade under examination. In fact, enrolment dropped from 33 to 31.6 per cent of the total.

The data in Table 9.19, in addition to information obtained through interviewing in Sudan, combine to indicate that the cadres necessary for development, from managerial and executive level down to skilled manual labour, are in seriously short supply. (Vocational training, for instance, in terms of size of enrolment, constitutes only 7 per cent of enrolment in Egypt, 15 per cent of that in Algeria, 31 per cent of that in Morocco, but 120 per cent of that in Saudi Arabia for 1970/1 — the size of population being adjusted for the sake of comparability.) Teacher training also reveals the same general trend: 12 per cent its counterpart in Egypt, 40 per cent that in Algeria, 15 per cent that in Saudi Arabia, but about twice that in Morocco.[49] Furthermore, attitude to work is not very conducive to developmental effort, but it is a moot point whether the cause of slackness is climatic, cultural, economic or a combination of these.

Associated with the population is the added problem of ethnic, religious and linguistic heterogeneity. This is not equal to pluralism, which is a useful quality, inasmuch as pluralism can be enriching in cultural and social terms, and in terms of motivation and perform-

Table 9.19: Enrolment in Educational Institutions 1965/6 and 1974/5

Educational Level (Public)		1965/6	1974/5
Sub-grade, elementary and primary	Male	276,032	851,191
	Female	150,702	406,148
	Total	426,734	1,257,339
Intermediate and preparatory (general secondary)	Male	54,479	133,269
	Female	16,734	52,896
	Total	71,213	186,165
Post-intermediate and secondary (higher secondary)	Male	22,539	41,235
	Female	5,623	13,983
	Total	28,162	55,218
University (in Sudan)	Male	7,246	18,890
	Female	638	3,938
	Total	7,884	22,828
All levels (private)	Male	n.a.	65,270
	Female	n.a.	43,534
	Total	n.a.	108,804

Sources: For 1965/6, *Economic Survey 1970*, Appendix, Table 2.3, p. 126; for 1974/5, *Economic Survey 1974*, Table 2.2, p. 23, Table 2.3, p. 25, and Appendix, Table 2.8, p. 189.

ance, once certain basic features are shared by the whole population. This condition is largely missing in the case of Sudan.

The divisiveness is reflected most strongly in the north-south schism and conflict. The problem of the south, with what it involves in terms of political unrest, blockage of social homogenisation and of the build-up of social and economic infrastructure in the south, and the warping of socio-economic priorities, is too obvious to need elaboration. This is all the more regrettable in view of the growing serious concern with the development of the underprivileged south. One manifestation of this concern has been the Erkowit conferences at Juba, of which five have so far been held (the last on 2-8 January 1970).[50] Earlier, on 9 June 1969, self-rule had been decided on for the south, soon after the takeover of power on 25 May by General Ja'far Numeiry. However, political life became eventful again in July 1971, when an abortive (but bloody) *coup d'état* occurred. Although quiet has largely reigned after this *coup*, the cumulative effect of past unrest, protracted civil war and economic shortages has made political, administrative and socio-economic development less than needed and desired.

The dualism in the economy poses very grave limitations on development. These arise from the two main features underlying dualism: a low level of technology in the traditional sector, and a subsistence non-monetised economy in much of the country, even in parts where economic activity is at a high level of performance (as in Gezira). As was stated earlier, these features do not overlap, but they fortify each other and make the disappearance of dualism necessarily slow.

Entrepreneurship constitutes another issue to be faced. To begin with, entrepreneurial resources are not abundant, and the socio-economic setting has not been very conducive to entrepreneurship. In addition, the public sector entered the field of entrepreneurial activity probably too soon, thus inhibiting private investors and setting a rather poor example owing to the failure of some government projects or at least their poor performance. Planning has been undertaken in part as an attempt to introduce rationality into the allocation and use of resources. However, as we have already seen, the planning process is handicapped both by very meagre experience and by the cumbersomeness of planning machinery.

But the basic problem that constitutes a drag on planning and execution of projects is the serious shortage of foreign exchange. The shortage is due to the modesty of exports and their inability to generate a large surplus over imports. Resort to an import surplus has until recently been handicapped both by the current stringency of foreign aid and by political instability. Here lies a major problem which can probably only be met through the inflow of Arab economic aid. Only by breaking the vicious circle of underdevelopment, poverty, low investment, development hunger and insufficiency of external resources through Arab economic aid can the country accelerate its progress without paying the political price which attaches to the receipt of substantial foreign aid from non-Arab sources. As things stand now in 1975 or 1976, the vicious circle seems to be loosening, and the development prospects begin to look brighter for Sudan than ever before.

NOTES

1. I have relied heavily in this section on the relevant parts of the following works: (a) RIIA, *The Middle East* (London, 1958), 'The Sudan'; (b) *The Sudan – A Record of Progress 1898-1947* (no author indicated, designated as 'Printed by the authority of the Sudan government'; not dated); (c) Dr Sa'ad ed Din Fawzi, *Lectures on Aspects of the Sudanese Economy* (Center for Higher Arab Studies of the League of Arab States, Cairo, 1958; Arabic); (d) Dr Sa'ad Maher Hamza, *The Economy of Sudan* (Supplement to *The Economic Ahram*, issue of 1 September 1965, Cairo; Arabic); (e) Research and Statistics Division, Ministry of Planning, Sudan Republic, various annual issues entitled *Economic Survey*; (f) KFAED, *Report on the Sudanese Economy* (mimeographed, for limited circulation, 1969; Arabic); (g) Omar Osman and A. A. Suleiman, 'The Economy of Sudan', in P. Robson and D. A. Lury (eds.), *The Economies of Africa* (London, 1969); (h) General Union of Chambers of Commerce, Industry, and Agriculture in the Arab Countries, 'Economic Development in the Democratic Republic of Sudan 1950-1969', study submitted to the 16th Conference of the General Union held 16-20 January 1971 at Khartoum (Beirut, 1971; Arabic); (i) General Union . . ., *Arab Economic Report* (Beirut; annual issues ending with the issue of January 1974; Arabic); and (j) Europa Publications. *The Middle East and North Africa 1971-72, 1972-73, 1973-74* and *1974-75* (London, yearly issues).

2. The most recent full information on national accounts reaches to 1969. The source is Department of Statistics, Ministry of Planning, The Democratic Republic of the Sudan, *The National Accounts and Supporting Tables 1966, 1967* (Khartoum, July 1970), p. 7; and typed table obtained from the same source entitled 'Economic Indicators of the Sudan' for 1966-9. For 1970, global data come from *IFS*, December 1974, and FAO, *Perspective Study of Agricultural Development for the Democratic Republic of the Sudan*, Monograph 2, *The Macro-Economic Framework* (a study for restricted use consisting of 25 monographs, dated April 1973); hereafter referred to as FAO, *Perspective Study;* and for 1971, from *IFS*, June 1975. Data on GDP differ for the same year as between *IFS* and FAO, *Perspective Study*, being £S637.6m in the former, and £S620m in the latter.

3. UNESCO, *Comparative Statistical Data on Education in the Arab States, An Analysis: 1960-61 – 1967-68* (prepared for the Office of Statistics of UNESCO, Paris, and published by the Regional Center for Educational Planning and Administration, Beirut; 1969), p. 49.

4. FAO, *Indicative World Plan . . .*, Subregional Study No. 1, Vol. II: Explanatory Notes and Statistical Tables (Rome,1966), Tables 1.2 and 1.3, pp. 2 and 3.

5. Department of Statistics, *First Population Census of Sudan 1955/1956;* 1961/62 Final Report, in 3 volumes.

6. Osman and Suleiman, loc. cit., p. 461.

7. See also FAO, *Production Yearbook 1967*, p. 7,

for category of 'unexploited but potentially productive land'.

8. J. H. G. Lebon, *Land Use in Sudan* (Geographical Publications Ltd., Bude, U.K., 1965). For an even more liberal estimate of cultivable land than Lebon's, where the area of such land is given as 200m *feddans* or 84 million hectares (= 33 per cent of the total area of Sudan) see Europa in the various issues used, including the *1974-75* issue, p. 626. This estimate is 2.4 times as large as Lebon's. On the other hand, Fawzi (op. cit., p. 42) estimates cultivable land as being 120m *feddans* or 50.4m ha. According to this latter estimate, the land-man ratio would be 3.2 ha per person.

9. Fawzi, op. cit., p. 45.

10. See Gunnar Myrdal, *The Challenge of World Poverty: A World Anti-Poverty Programme in Outline* (Penguin, 1970), Ch. 4.

11. Fawzi, op. cit., pp. 64-5.

12. IBRD, Gezira Study Mission, *The Importance of the Gezira Scheme in the Economy of Sudan* (1966), Annex 1; quoted in KFAED, op. cit., pp. 89-91.

13. Information is collated from Europa, various annual issues, chapter on Sudan; Osman and Suleiman, loc. cit., pp. 455-61; and KFAED, op. cit., pp. 85-6.

14. Osman and Suleiman, loc. cit., p. 457, quoting O. M. Osman, 'Some Aspects of Private Pump Schemes', *Sudan Notes and Records*, Vol. XXVII, 1956.

15. KFAED, op. cit., pp. 99 and 100.

16. Ministry of Planning, Research and Statistics Division, *Economic Survey 1968*, Appendix, Table 5.

17. KFAED, op. cit., p. 85, refers to an 'autonomous authority called The Public Institution (or Authority) for Agricultural Production', which is a slightly different name for the same body.

18. The Republic of the Sudan, Department of Statistics, *The National Income of Sudan 1955/56*, by C. H. Harvie and G. J. Kleve (Khartoum, March 1959).

19. Ministry of Planning, Department of Statistics, *The National Accounts and Supporting Tables 1966, 1967* (Khartoum, July 1970).

20. IBRD, op. cit., p. 39.

21. See *IFS*, December 1974 and February 1976, for price movements 1967-73.

22. See *IFS*, September 1967, for price movements 1960-6.

23. *Economic Survey 1973*, p. 23 for the last three years.

24. For 1973, see *Arab Economic Report*, January 1974, chapter on Sudan.

25. For 1956, *IFS* Supplement to 1967/8 issues; for December 1974, *IFS*, February 1976.

26. For such exports in the 1960s, see *Economic Survey 1968*, Appendix, Table 20; for exports in 1974, see *Economic Survey 1974*, p. 139.

27. Europa, *1971-72*, op. cit., p. 545. The *1974-75* issue and the *Arab Economic Report* of January 1974 contain some particulars with regard to new industries, and speak of relatively considerable expansion in industrial investment and production.

28. Division of Industry, Ministry of Industry and Mining, *Summary of Industrial Survey Report and Its Recommendations* (Khartoum, 25 May 1970; Arabic).

29. Europa, *1971-72*, p. 545; and KFAED, op. cit., pp. 148-55.

30. The discussion on transport relies on Europa and on KFAED, op. cit., pp. 160 ff, on other survey sources (see note 1) to a lesser extent, and on more recent annual issues of Europa, op. cit.

31. United Nations, *Statistical Yearbook 1973*, Table 139 for international comparisons; Europa, *1974-75*, p. 633, for capacity and production of power.

32. Europa, *1974-75*, pp. 633 and 637.

33. For the brief reference to recent developmental measures, see Europa, *1974-75*, chapter on Sudan; *Arab Economic Report* of January 1974; and the annual *Progress Report on Results of Execution on the Five Year Plan Targets* (published by the Ministry of Planning), the most recent issue of which by early 1975 was for the year 1971/2.

34. AFESD, *Basic Programme for Agricultural Development in the Democratic Republic of the Sudan, 1976-1985; Résumé* (Kuwait, 1976); especially pp. 12 and 13.

35. J. H. Boeke, *Economics and Economic Policy of Dual Societies* (New York, 1953), and other writings in journals. For a thorough argument in reply to Boeke, see Benjamin Higgins, *Economic Development: Problems, Principles, and Policies* (New York, 1959), especially Ch. 12.

36. Pages 8 and 11.

37. This division is based on Osman and Suleiman, loc. cit., pp. 440-1.

38. G. J. Kleve, 'The Share of Subsistence Transactions in the Economy of Sudan', *Sudan Economic and Financial Review* (Ministry of Finance and Economics, Khartoum, not dated) quoted in KFAED, op. cit., p. 181.

39. *IFS*, February 1976 for 1971, and *IFS*, Supplement to 1967/8 issues, for 1960.

40. The information on commercial banks comes from *IFS*, February 1976.

41. Data relating to trade and balance of payments have been collected from the (already cited) sources: *Economic Survey 1961 and 1974*; KFAED, op. cit.; UN, *Statistical Yearbook 1970* to *1973*; Europa, *1971-72* to *1974-75*; and *Arab Economic Report*, January 1971 to January 1974. Data following subsequently on foreign reserves and indebtedness come from *Economic Survey 1974*, pp. 120 and 121.

42. KFAED, op. cit., p. 220; Europa, *1971-72*, p. 555; *Arab Economic Report 1971*, pp. 436-7 and table in Appendix; and *IFS*, December 1974.

43. The data on capital inflow have been collected from the following sources: (a) *Time* Magazine, Vol. LXXXI, No. 13, 29 March 1963, for US aid from July 1945 to June 1962, quoting official US sources; (b) OECD, *The Flow of Financial Resources to Less-Developed Countries 1961-1965*, p. 155 for 1962-5; (c) OECD, *Development Assistance: Efforts and Policies of the Members of the Development Assistance Committee, 1969 Review*, pp. 170-1, for 1966-8; (d) OECD, *Development Co-operation: Efforts and Policies of the Members of the Development Assistance Committee, 1973 Review*, pp. 208-9, for 1969-72; (e) OECD, *Development Co-operation: Efforts and Policies . . . 1974 Review*, pp. 262-7, for 1973; (f) UN, *Statistical Yearbook 1973*, p. 715, for aid from centrally planned economies, 1954-72; (g) KFAED, *Annual Report 1973-1974*, Table 3, p. 24, for cumulative aid from KFAED, 1962 – end of March 1974; (h) *Middle East Economic Survey* (Beirut

weekly), survey of all issues between 15 October 1973 and 31 December 1974, for aid by Arab countries (except KFAED) during this period; and (i) AFESD, *Annual Report 1973*, and *Annual Report 1974* (Arabic).

44. Europa *1971-72*, p. 553; Europa *1974-75*, pp. 631-2; *Arab Economic Report* of January 1974, p. 226; and *Economic Survey 1974*, p. 157. For a discussion of the taxation system in general, or some special aspects of it, see: (a) Ali Abdel Hamid, *The Evaluation of the Sudan Personal Income Tax*, Occasional Papers, No. 19, published by the Institute of Public Administration, which is a joint undertaking by the Sudan government and the United Nations (Khartoum, May 1967); (b) Ali Abdel Hamid Ali, *Structure of Indirect Taxation in the Sudan*, Occasional Papers, No. 18, published by the IPA (Khartoum, April 1969); and (c) Ali Ahmed Suliman, *Taxes in the Sudan* (University of Khartoum, 1970; Arabic).

45. Regarding planning prior to independence, see Fawzi, op. cit., Osman and Suleiman, loc. cit. For subsequent planning, see Europa, issues from *1971-72* to *1974-75;* Ministry of Planning, *The Ten-Year Plan of Economic and Social Development 1961/62–1970/71;* and Ministry of Planning, *The Five-Year Plan of Economic and Social Development in the Democratic Republic of the Sudan, 1970/1971 – 1974/75*, vols. I and II. See also Selma M. Suliman, *An Analytical Evaluation of the Sudan Ten Year Plan 1961/62 – 1970/71* (published by the Institute of Public Administration, Khartoum, 1970); and Zafir al-Bishri, *The Experience of the Democratic Republic of the Sudan in Development Planning*, paper submitted to the Fourth Conference of the Federation of Arab Economists held in Kuwait, 17-20 March 1973 (undated; Arabic).

46. Ministry of Planning, *Progress Report on Results of Execution of the Five Year Plan Targets During 1970/71* (Khartoum, December 1971), pp. 1-4.

47. Al-Bishri, op. cit., pp. 38-40.

48. See FAO, *Perspective Study of Agricultural Development for the Democratic Republic of the Sudan*, monographs ESP/PS/SUD/73/1 - 25; the first of which being the *Central Policy Paper* and the last the *Statistical Annex*. The AFESD study was entitled *Basic Programme for Agricultural Development in the Democratic Republic of the Sudan 1976-1985*. We refer to the last volume, *Résumé* (this last was in Arabic). Quotations are from section 5 in *Résumé*.

49. UNESCO, op. cit., pp. 54-5.

50. See *Economic and Social Development in the South, Final Report and Recommendations*, School of Extra-Mural Studies, University of Khartoum (5th Erkowit Conference held at Juba, 2-8 June 1970).

10 LIBYA

Several years after Libya's independence and the initiation of some measures of economic and social development, Benjamin Higgins, an economist who was closely familiar with the country's conditions, could still say:

> Libya combines within the borders of one country virtually all the obstacles that can be found anywhere: geographic, economic, political, sociological, technological. If Libya can be brought to a stage of sustained growth, there is hope for every country in the world.[1]

These words may seem to contain an overdose of cynicism, coming as they do from a scholar who knew what these obstacles had been on the eve of independence, and the magnitude and directions of change in the intervening years.[2]

This impression is strengthened if it is realised that by the time Higgins wrote in the late fifties, Libya was already marked as a potential oil-producer, with a large number of concessionary companies already actively prospecting for oil and, in the process, contributing relatively handsomely to the state budget and to the domestic product. The country had also by then had more than half a decade of (relatively) substantial financial and technical support from various United Nations agencies as well as from Britain and the United States. Furthermore, the harsh and self-centred Italian colonialism that had sat heavily on the chest of the people for some three decades was a matter of the past, and the country had its own national government to steer its course towards development.

The observations just quoted were not alone in the class of gloomy predictions. They had been preceded a few years before by another evaluation by the same writer, and another a year earlier by an expert commissioned for a study of the economy by the United Nations.[3] These evaluations all moved roughly along the same lines, based more or less on the same premises, though more implicitly. But what is more interesting is that a survey mission sent to Libya early in 1959 by the International Bank for Reconstruction and Development, reporting in 1960, advised cautious optimism with regard to potential oil revenues in the forthcoming four or five years,[4] although vastly expanded crude petroleum exports and revenues were to materialise in 1962, less than three years later. No complicated explanation is needed for this expectational discrepancy: petroleum emerged on the scene with a dramatic suddenness which probably surprised everybody concerned except perhaps the oil companies themselves.

The analyst writing in the early seventies has the advantage of hindsight and is likely therefore to be impatient with the judgements and evaluations made before the turn of the sixties. However, any serious student of the phenomenon of underdevelopment (both with regard to its manifestations and causes) would then have believed that Libya 'qualified' to rank among the most handicapped of the underdeveloped countries of the world. Notwithstanding the development-oriented efforts and the financial and technical assistance of the fifties, the country had a long and arduous march ahead of it before it could enter the stage of self-sustained growth, with all that this achievement implies in the economic and non-economic fields. This position tends to underline the well-founded conviction that development is not synonymous with financial sufficiency (or even affluence), and that development can only go ahead after successful breakthroughs have been achieved not only in the economic but also the equally important socio-cultural, political and technological blocks in the path of progress.

Though rich in petroleum resources like Kuwait and Saudi Arabia in the Mashreq, and Algeria in the Maghreb,[5] Libya differs from all three in important respects. For instance, Kuwait, during the comparable period of the development of its oil sector, adopted a much more liberal policy with regard to the attraction of expatriates to work both in the public and the private sectors and to compensate for manpower shortages in the country; Saudi Arabia, on the other hand, has all along been much stricter than Kuwait in this respect. Furthermore, Saudi Arabia did not suffer from foreign domination and the settlement of colonisers, as Libya or Algeria did. On the other hand, Algeria, which has oil resources of the same magnitude as Libya (but much more natural gas), and which suffered a much longer and more brutal colonisation, has in the first decade of its independence more definitely succeeded in building up a solid base for accelerated development than Libya in the comparable decade (apart from the fact that Algeria had a much more significant and efficient physical infrastructure bequeathed from the days of French presence). These variations reflect themselves in marked differences in the courses of development, and in turn are a reflection of internal (subjective) and exogenous differences, as the analysis of the experience of the four countries concerned shows. The first step in this analysis, with regard to Libya, starts with an examination of the background to independence. Thus, those conditions of relevance to socio-economic development on the eve of independence will be identified and their significance underlined.

1. THE COLONIALIST 'LEGACY'[6]

The Italian colonisation of Libya, which had started with aggression against Tripolitania in October 1911, ended in effect at the close of 1942, with the defeat of Italian (and German) forces in the Western desert. The brunt of the fighting during World War Two was mostly felt in Cyrenaica, the province east of Tripolitania, which was the stage for advances and retreats by the Allied and Axis armies. As can be expected, much of the infrastructure which had been built by the Italians during their thirty-year presence was destroyed, particularly port installations and other transport and communications facilities and public buildings. Furthermore, agriculture suffered heavily, as it fell mainly in the northern littoral of the country, which witnessed virtually all the fighting.

The Italians had not built anything nearly as extensive and efficient as the infrastructure built by the French in Algeria. Libya was smaller in area (having 1,759,000 square kilometres of area against Algeria's 2.4m sq. km.) and much smaller in population (on independence, the two countries had approximately 1 and 10m inhabitants respectively). More significantly, the Italians did not have the grandiose and fantastic idea of turning their colony into an extension of Metropolitan Italy, as the French did with respect to Algeria. And, in any case, Algeria had more resources to develop, and an earlier start. Furthermore, settler colonisation was restricted in absolute size in Libya — the Italian community settling there had reached at its peak some 110,000, though this constituted roughly 10 per cent of the population, or the same *proportion* as the French constituted of the Algerian population on the eve of independence.

The comparative picture is rather less to the disadvantage of the Libyans with respect to colonisation of agricultural land. Here we find that the French *colons* took over — in one way or another — some 2.8m hectares of the best agricultural land, which was roughly about 28 per cent of the cultivable land of Algeria. On the other hand, the Italian settlers took into their possession — through the same combination of means as the French did in Algeria — some 225,000 hectares of the best land, out of a total of 1.8 to 2.0m hectares suitable for *settled* cultivation, or roughly one-eighth of the total. Furthermore, in addition to the slightly more limited scope of the dispossession of Libyans, the total cultivable area allowed the Libyan approximately twice as much land as the counterpart land allowed the Algerian on the average — namely two hectares versus one hectare.

There is one area where both colonialist groups acted the same way. This was to keep the nationals at an extremely low level of education and training, and therefore incapable of performing the functions that an advancing economy and society requires, and equally incapable of manning anything but the meanest posts in the civil service. However, Algeria suffered more than any of the other three Maghreb countries in the fact that Arabic, the country's language, was not only *de facto*, but officially, considered a foreign language. This the French did in order to give further credence, over the years, to their claim that Algeria was really an extension of France across the sea.

The burdensome legacy of Italian colonialism was made more painful and economically retarding for Libya because of the country's tenacious and often heroic resistance to the colonialists — a resistance which brought forth harsh repression and economic disruption and destruction. It was only in the late thirties that Italy's hold was secure enough to permit it to turn to the economic consolidation of its colonisation of the north of the country. (The north consisted of the two provinces, Tripolitania and Cyrenaica, where resistance had been toughest, and where ultimately the presence of the Italian authorities was most evident — the southern province, Fezzan, being mainly desert and very sparsely inhabited.) This consolidation took the form of first extending the economic infrastructure in the directions most useful from the standpoint of Italy (transport and communications, public buildings for the use of the administration), and subsequently settler colonisation of agricultural land. In this respect too, the Italian farms concentrated on those products most in demand by the Italians and with the production of which the Italians were most familiar. Thus fruits and vegetables were of primary significance and permitted the Italian farms to obtain remunerative returns. Altogether, Italy is estimated in total to have spent no more than the equivalent of 150 million pre-war US dollars on 'public works, utilities and agricultural development during the 30 years of its administration'.[7] It is obvious that an average of $5m a year did not reflect colonialist largesse.

When Britain and France cleared Libya of the Axis armies in 1942 and took the country over at the beginning of 1943, with Britain administering Tripolitania and Cyrenaica, and France the Fezzan province, they found on their hands a war-ravaged country that had not been equipped and prepared for self-government. The poverty was appalling, and estimates of income per head during the late forties range between 15 and 20 pounds sterling a year. Nevertheless, as one reference work puts it, during this British and French military administration, '... the country was administered with the greatest economy *on a care and maintenance basis.*'[8] While one does not expect colonialist powers to behave like charitable institutions, this economy in administration reflects extreme callousness, considering the enormity of the economic disruption and outright destruction brought about by the former colonising power, Italy, and the new ruling powers, Britain and France, in turning the country into a battlefield at the mercy of fierce modern warfare. Thus, the period 1943-51, which preceded independence, can be said to have kept the country as unready for efficient self-government as it had been under the Italians, with only marginal improvements in the services of education and health, but no major programmes of social and economic development.

2. A GENERATION OF INDEPENDENCE: 1951-75

The United Nations resolved in 1949 that Libya become independent by 1952, and that the two administering powers prepare it for that end. A constitution was drafted in readiness for independence, and in October 1951 this constitution was promulgated. Full independence followed in December of that year, and the Kingdom of Libya thus emerged. It took federal form, with the three Provinces of Tripolitania, Cyrenaica and Fezzan enjoying a large measure of self-government.

While the loose political structure chosen may have reflected realism and tried to satisfy at the same time the dictates of geography and the sense of regionalism, in so far as the three provinces formed separate entities and had their own clusters of population, and their distinct outlooks and loyalties, it was none the less cumbersome, costly, and hardly conducive to serious developmental efforts. The costliness did not reflect itself in monetary terms only, but also, and more importantly, in the frictions between the federal and the provincial governments and in the wasteful (because repetitive) deployment of the country's most scarce of resources: qualified civil servants at almost all levels of skill and responsibility. The federal structure, unsuitable in itself for Libya, was superimposed on a political base which on the whole suffered from a large measure of inefficiency, corruption, reaction and general ineptitude with respect to the vision, planning and decision-making required in the process of social and economic development. There is no better evidence of these shortcomings of the government and civil service than that contained in the IBRD mission report to which reference has already been made;[9] the assessments made by this mission must be considered a polite understatement, since IBRD missions are not known for exaggeration and harshness when referring to the governments of the countries surveyed. In fairness, it ought to be pointed out that Libya could not have had a distinctly more efficient and more public-minded political system and civil service with the background of colonialism which had failed to prepare the people for self-government. Furthermore, the socio-cultural traits of a country like Libya — illiteracy of at least 90 per cent of the population, tribalism, nomadism, exclusion of women from the urban work-force, traditionalism, primitive technology, low esteem for manual labour — could not produce a political and administrative machinery very different from the one that existed at independence.

Other problems made the development tasks very hard to fulfil. The country was poor in natural endowments; oil had not then been discovered, and only 5-10 per cent of the land was considered at all cultivable, the remainder being desert or semi-desert. A mere 1 per cent of land area was considered fit for *settled* cultivation, the balance of the cultivable area being merely adequate for pastures, nomadic or semi-nomadic cultivation, and oases in the south. Rainfall was very meagre, only satisfying the requirements of agriculture in the littoral. Here, it will be recalled, the best tracts of land had been taken by Italian settlers, and in the instances where these had left the country after the defeat of Italy and Libya's independence several years later, the farms had been left untended and had become derelict.

Libya

The distribution of holdings by size in the early sixties reveals only a few of the gross inequalities that characterised land-holding in Egypt, Syria or Iraq before agrarian reform. Thus, as Table 10.1 shows, half the holdings fall in the category 5-10, 10-20 and 20-50 hectares, and together these three groups constitute 35 per cent of land area. However, in the group of large holdings, a mere 2.2 per cent of the holdings account for almost 31 per cent of land area. This is the most glaring manifestation of inequality in the Libyan pattern of distribution. In other words, inequalities exist and are quite enormous, but distinctly less so than in the early fifties in the three countries cited.

Table 10.1: Distribution of Holdings by Size

Size of Holdings (hectares)	Total Land Area (hectares)	Per Cent of Total Area	Number of Holdings	Per Cent of Total Number of Holdings	Average Area of Holdings (ha)
Without land	–	–	6,153	4.2	–
Under 0.5	1,447	0.03	6,118	4.2	0.23
0.5 – under 1	3,041	0.08	5,146	3.5	0.59
1–2	10,620	0.27	9,295	6.4	1.14
2–3	17,059	0.44	8,218	5.6	2.07
3–4	24,096	0.62	7,896	5.4	3.05
4–5	25,532	0.65	5,814	3.9	4.39
5–10	149,358	3.86	22,358	15.3	6.68
10–20	355,642	9.19	27,097	18.6	13.12
20–50	841,421	21.74	29,282	20.1	28.73
50–100	636,101	16.44	10,020	6.9	63.48
100–200	613,829	15.86	4,890	3.7	125.52
200 and over	1,192,556	30.82	3,231	2.2	369.09
Total	3,868,728 [sic.]	100.00	145,518	100.0	26.6

Source: Ministry of Agriculture, *Agricultural Statistics in Libya, 1963*, p. 60.

Note: The statistics shown above relate to holdings in the private (individual and corporate) sector, in the 'communal' (tribal) sector, and in the government sector. However, by far most of the holdings and of the area are in the lands of private individuals (or of joint owners), as the following breakdown shows:

Tribes (communal holdings)	418 holdings	47,811 hectares
Government	247	3,298
Corporations	73	12,026
Sub-total	738	63,135
Civil persons	144,780	3,805,593
Total	145,518	3,868,728

(Source for information in the note: *Statistical Abstract 1963*, p. 153.)

The Libyan population was very small upon independence in a country with a vast land area. The 1.1 million inhabitants which the census of 1954 recorded were very unevenly distributed, with 738,000 in Tripolitania, 291,000 in Cyrenaica, and 59,000 in the Fezzan. Hundreds of miles of desert separated each of the three groups from the others, apart from socio-cultural differences. The sparsity of the population in itself constituted a serious handicap, since the cost of linking population centres with each other necessitated very high investment per head for transport and communication. Yet the neglect of such investment spelled marketing and storage problems and retarded development. In addition to the unsuitable geographical distribution of the population, there was the high level of semi-nomads and nomads, and of illiteracy to act as barriers to progress. Estimates vary, but it is generally believed that the urban centres claimed only 30 per cent of the population, while 30 per cent were rural inhabitants, and the rest semi-nomads and nomads. The level of illiteracy, to which reference has been made, was higher among females — reaching some 99 per cent. (According to a UNESCO study, illiteracy was as high as 82 per cent among those aged 15-24 years in 1954, 69 per cent for males and 97 per cent for females.[10]) In the year 1950-1, a total of 32,115 pupils (including 3,664 girls) were in elementary schools, and a mere 626 in preparatory, secondary and vocational schools. The holders of university degrees are estimated to have numbered ten persons when independence was achieved. Thus school-goers represented about 15 per cent of school-age population, and a mere 3.7 per cent of the total population. The quality of the education made the picture gloomier still.[11]

None of the sectors was advanced enough to be, or was capable of being, the engine of development, and no separate treatment for any sector is called for here. However, it is worth noting that establishments in Italian hands — enjoying as they did advantages in entrepreneurship and management, capital, technology and organisation — were distinctly more efficient, modern and successful than their counterparts in Libyan hands. Yet this dualism must not lead one to the conclusion that the Italian businesses were very large-scale, or together formed a very important group. The general economic and manpower limitations made even the Italian 'sector' of the economy rather modest.

Finally, the monetary and financial institutions of the country were generally underdeveloped. Monetisation was at a very low level, with currency in circulation in Tripolitania and Cyrenaica together hovering around the equivalent of 3.5m pounds sterling, or £3.5 per head, while total money supply was about £5m for the whole country. The total state revenue for 1949/50 was about £1.8m, but it rose to £2.5m for 1951-2. The level of public expenditure was slightly higher, which resulted in a deficit that the British and French governments made good. The financial outlook for development spending looked as distinctly bleak at independence as the outlook for manpower and public administration.[12]

The 24 years of independence surveyed here fall in fact into two distinct political periods: 1952 to 1969, or the era of the monarchy, and 1969 to the present or the era of the republic. The dividing line was the overthrow of the monarchy and the declaration of the republic by a group of army officers, the 'Free Officers', headed by Colonel Muammar al-Ghaddafi. Likewise, the two and a half decades can be divided into two periods with regard to the predominant economic features: the period preceding the export of oil and the inflow of substantial oil revenues, stretching roughly from 1952 to 1961; and the period when oil became the source of considerable income, from 1961 to the present. However, the discussion which follows will not proceed strictly along rigid lines determined by clear-cut dates, but will overlap somewhat for reasons which will become clear as we analyse the economic evolution of the country. The exception to this procedure is the survey of the years 1969-75, since this period is characterised by a distinct political, social and economic flavour, and it represents a qualitative as well as a quantitative departure from the earlier years.

The Pre-Oil Decade: Development Through Foreign Support

The government's immediate and long-term task upon assuming responsibility for the running of the independent country was to find adequate finance to lubricate any development programmes to be embarked on, and to have enough trained personnel in government and in the private sector to carry on these programmes and be the engine of development. Although both bottlenecks were widened in the years that were to follow, it was easier to increase the volume of investment funds than the reservoir of skilled manpower. The second problem continues to impede speedy development until today, although financial resources have become unlimited for all practical purposes.[13]

Oddly enough, the flow of foreign financial assistance was distinctly greater in the first independence decade than during the trusteeship of Britain and France. This is all the more surprising since Great Britain, which administered most of Libya's land, population and economy itself, subsequently became a substantial source of financial support. The paradox becomes clearer when it is remembered that as an occupying power, Britain could use the military facilities without financial cost to itself, which it could only have against compensation once the country became independent.

But a second factor operated to make several countries extend assistance to Libya. This was intervention by the United Nations which set into motion arrangements for aid to Libya and actively organised technical and financial assistance from the various UN specialised agencies. Bilateral support came mainly from the United Kingdom and the United States, but also from France, Egypt, Italy, Pakistan and Turkey. The first two countries, but more the United States, provided the bulk of assistance flowing into Libya. However, UK and US support came not as 'unrequited' aid, like that from the other countries cited, but in payment for services rendered by Libya. These services consisted of facilities put at the disposal of the two powers — certain airfields, roads, public buildings, air space, ports — under treaties permitting the two governments to have bases in Libya. Receipts from Britain and the United States against these military facilities usually appear under aid, or unrequited transfers. But the matter is not that simple, and some conceptual and terminological questioning has accompanied it, inasmuch as there is a strong argument in favour of considering the flows as invisible exports, since they were payments against services rendered.[14] However, the matter will not be pursued further here.

Capital flows from Britain and the United States come under different forms: as grants for development projects or broader programmes, as loans for this purpose, and as budget support to meet current expenditures. Aid from United Nations agencies came mainly in the form of technical assistance in the fields of health, education, labour, agriculture and other specialised areas. The period 1952-61 witnessed significant increases in these various flows, and this largely permitted the expansion of public expenditures from the equivalent of 5.9 million Libyan pounds (later to be designated as dinars) for 1951-2, to about LD28.3m* for 1960-1 and LD34.5m for 1961-2. Internal sources of revenue accounted only for a small part of the increased financing facilities. Another small part was accounted for by fees and other payments made to the government by oil companies seeking concessions and undertaking reconnaissance work, prospecting, or, having struck oil, building the facilities needed for its flow, storage and transport. (More will be said later about this source of capital inflow.) Not only did these various forms of capital inflow

*Libyan dinars.

permit an expansion in current and capital public expenditure, but also an expansion in imports distinctly beyond that of exports. In other words, foreign 'grants' and loans and receipts from oil companies together succeeded in meeting both the budget deficit and the deficit (the import surplus) in the current account of the balance of payments.

Allocations made by foreign governments and the United Nations during the first decade of independence total around LD104m, all but 4.2m of which came from the British and American governments, and all in grants except for LD1.8m of United States loans. The balance is divided approximately half and half between United Nations technical assistance and grants from five countries: France, Italy, Egypt, Turkey and Pakistan. However, funds *actually* received add up to LD58.3m, or to 56 per cent of allocations. The total inflow of foreign funds amounted to 43 per cent of the government's total revenue for the years in question. This is a significant enough indicator of the country's heavy dependence on foreign financial support. Just over 44 per cent of the aid received was directed to capital investments and expenditures associated with them.[15]

A volume of aid as large as that allocated for or flowing into Libya in the first decade of independence necessitated the setting up of machinery for the receipt and handling of the financial and technical aspects of this aid. Two agencies were therefore set up for the purpose: the Libyan Public Development and Stabilization Agency (LPDSA), created in 1952, whose function was to make plans and programmes for the use of funds received from the United Kingdom and other countries, and the Libyan-American Reconstruction Commission (LARC), created in 1955 to fulfil the same function as LPDSA but with respect to funds coming from the United States. Technical assistance was handled by the US Operations Mission in Libya (USOM), the Libyan-American Joint Services (LAJS), and the UN Technical Assistance Mission, through which assistance from FAO, ILO, WHO and UNESCO was channelled. However, in July 1960 the Libyan Development Council was empowered to take over the functions of the LPDSA and the LARC and to replace these two agencies with regard to rights, powers and duties.

The second major flow of foreign exchange derived from the local expenditure of the oil companies. Although this source of finance did not directly influence the state revenue, in the sense that it did not flow into the treasury, it was of great significance to the economy and its activity, and indirectly to the treasury, since it raised the taxability of the recipients. Oil company expenditure was in the form of salaries and wages, rents, and payments for other services such as transport, hotels and restaurants, as well as local purchases. The company imports were on the whole effected directly by them, but a certain volume was brought in by local merchants. In any case, these imports created a certain income for local transport and porterage services. Local expenditure by the oil companies through the year 1961 totals LD73m.[16] This is a large sum, but its effect must have been rather less widespread than its size suggests, inasmuch as a relatively small proportion of the labour force, and of service establishments, was involved.

However, the one single sector which felt the strong impact of company spending was that of construction, owing to the immense pressure that was created by the entry of many expatriate labourers and technicians, all requiring accommodation, in addition to the pressure created by Libyans eager to improve their housing conditions under the impetus of increased incomes. During the same period, revenue to the government originating in oil company payments remained very modest. In all, such receipts totalled just under half a million Libyan dinars. Thus, in the financial year 1960-1 oil company payments to the treasury formed one-half of one per cent of total state revenue.[17]

The increased economic activity arising from expanded public spending (in turn made possible largely because of foreign financial support) and rising oil company spending reflected itself, among other things, in the increase in money supply, from LD9.8m in 1955 to LD26.1m in 1961. Just under half of this supply was in the form of currency in circulation.[18] However, imports rose faster during the same period, from LD14.4m to LD53.3m, while exports rose very modestly from LD4.3m to LD6.5m.[19] Consequently prices did not rise except by about 8 per cent per annum — a steep rise, but one which remains below the rate of increase of money supply.

The combined effect of foreign aid and oil company spending and the increased taxability of the population together put in the hands of the government and the private sector increased resources for investment. Roughly speaking, the rate of investment has been estimated at 15-20 per cent of gross national product for the 1952-61 period. Libya would certainly have had a much smaller GNP during this decade, and a much smaller ratio of investment, had it not been for the conjuncture of the two factors of aid and oil company spending. Statistics are not available regarding the evolution of national product for the ten years under study, and what is available beginning with the year 1957 contains a large margin of error and must be treated with considerable reserve. None the less, the gross domestic product for the years 1957-61 is presented in Table 10.2.

Table 10.2: Gross Domestic Product, 1957-61

Year	GDP in LDm	Percentage Rate of Growth
1957	43	
1958	52	20.9
1959	56	7.7
1960	61	8.9
1961	70	14.7

Source: Information obtained from the Census and Statistical Department in an interview in February 1973.

The overall increase between 1957 and 1961 is 62.8 per cent or 12.5 per cent per annum (compound rate) at current prices. This means a rate of growth in real terms of 4.5 per cent on the average, if we accept the estimate referred to earlier of an average price rise of 8 per cent per annum. A 4.5 per cent growth in real terms is a considerable rate in view of the country's physical and human endowments in what we have called the pre-oil decade. However, the picture is less satisfactory when it is examined from year to year, where the progress was very erratic. Indeed, the two years 1959 and 1960 marked very small real progress, if the inflation factor is accounted for. In these two years, the *per capita* growth at constant prices was negative, even considering that the rate of natural increase of population was very low — an estimated 1.25 per cent at the time.

Tentative as the national accounts for the late fifties are, it is still useful to use them for an examination of the broad contours of the structure of the economy in terms of sector contribution. According to the GDP estimates for 1958 or 1959, agriculture accounted for about one-fourth of national income, but this sector presumably experienced wide fluctuations owing to the vagaries of the climate and of rainfall. It is interesting to note that although oil was still not exported in 1959, prospecting accounted for 7.7 per cent of GDP. Trade, plus other services, accounted for just over half, and the commodity sectors (including petroleum prospecting) for just under half of the GDP.

Reference has been made to the inflow of funds from foreign sources, and to the direction of about LD25.8m, or 44 per cent of these funds, to development expenditure. The balance must have gone towards current expenditure. Information is not available on the proportion of the LD25.8m that went into the restoration, repair or replacement of assets damaged or destroyed by war, and how much to net capital formation. But it is significant to note that during the nine years 1952/3 to 1960/1 to which these data apply, all development expenditure except for the year 1960/1 came from foreign sources. In this latter year, the newly formed Development Council is marked as the source of LD6.7m for development expenditure; but as this body was created in order to take over from the LPDSA and the LARC, it can be safely assumed that even the funds spent on development in 1960/1 came from foreign sources. If adjustment is made along these lines, then development expenditure out of foreign funds for the nine years in question totals LD32.5m, or 56 per cent of all receipts from foreign sources. The largest investment – about LD13m – was directed to agriculture.[20] (This figure includes not only federal but also provincial capital expenditure.)

Obviously an investment of this size, under the best conditions and assumptions, could only bring about a very modest increase in the national product – an increase which would certainly have been far from sufficient even to cope with the natural increase in population. The increase of national product from about LD15m in 1952 to about LD70m in 1961 is to a large degree the result of rising oil company spending in the country, and also to a large extent of the government's rising current expenditure (which rose from LD6.3m in 1952/3 to LD18.6m in 1960/1). Increases in government current spending, as has been mentioned, were made possible by the combination of three factors: foreign aid directed to budget support, increased economic activity and increased direct taxes as a result (which includes modest payments made to the government by the oil companies), and increased indirect taxes – predominantly tariff duties – thanks to the expanded volume of imports.

However, the country's performance during the first decade of independence must not be seen only from the narrow angle of changes in the state budget in its two branches: current and capital, or of the growth in money supply, or yet of the growth of national product – important as all these indicators are. Although the scale of the performance must not be exaggerated, and – foreign aid and oil activities apart – the country remained economically viable only at a very low standard of living and well-being, yet the sharp edge of its extreme underdevelopment and poverty was smoothed slightly in the first decade. Government organisation improved, and the political decision-makers and the civil service started to learn the arts of governing and administering the country. While it was true that the federal system remained cumbersome, wasteful, irresolute and inefficient, by the end of the decade the awareness had considerably grown that the system of government was in need of drastic change. (The constitutional change was to come in 1963.) Manpower training and education made steady progress in the period under discussion. Thus, the number of students at the elementary level rose by a net 252 per cent in the years 1951/2–1960/1, or from about 14 per cent of the school-age population to about 38 per cent. This is a remarkable increase, but what is more significant is the increase in the number of pupils in preparatory and secondary schools, which was from 402 to 12,320, or a net increase of 2,965 per cent. This in itself suggests that before independence, not only a very small proportion of school-age children went to elementary schools, but that only a tiny proportion of these upon independence (just 1 per cent) went further to preparatory and secondary education. Conversely, by the year 1960/1, a higher proportion went to elementary schools, and a much higher proportion of those in elementary schools went on to preparatory and secondary education (9.5 per cent). A notable, though not as spectacular expansion in attendance at vocational schools was registered. In 1951/2, there were 568 students in 10 such schools, but the number rose to 4,328 in 24 schools in 1960/1, which represents a rise of 662 per cent.[21]

In addition to these remarkable strides in the field of formal education at the sub-university level, important achievements were made in higher and more professional education. Thus, the University of Libya was opened in 1958 in Benghazi, with faculties of arts and commerce, soon to be followed by faculties of science, law, agriculture, engineering and teacher training. Some of these are in Tripoli, while the others are in Benghazi. Professional training was also boosted by an ILO-sponsored Technical and Clerical Training Centre in Tripoli, teacher training schools for men and women, agricultural training centres, commerce and industry centres, a mechanical engineering school, a handicraft institute, and one legal studies centre. In addition to all this, one must remember the on-the-job training obtained by thousands of Libyans engaged in the oil industry, light industrial work (including repair works), the building industry, and hotel and restaurant services. This training was on the whole not formal and deliberate, but none the less real inasmuch as it was a form of 'learning by doing'. The intensified economic activity with the resultant rise in salaries and wages was a pull factor for young Libyans, while the rise in the cost of living which necessitated rising earnings to ensure at least the preservation of one's level of living constituted a push factor.

The gains in education and training just described were not quite adequate for the country's growing needs, particularly as these needs included intermediate and high executive, managerial, technical and financial skills in the various sectors. In order to loosen this manpower bottleneck, the government was rather permissive with regard to the entry of expatriate workers — though not as permissive and encouraging as Kuwait was in its comparable phase of development, when expatriates were attracted by high salaries and tempting employment terms in general, and were given important posts in the civil service as well as in the private sector. Thus by 1961 the total number of expatriates in the active labour force was rather small. Unfortunately, information is not available for the period under study, but later data published in 1965 (based on the 1964 census of population) show that the total number of expatriates (designated 'aliens') was 48,868. Presumably the majority of these were Italians who had stayed on after the disappearance of Italian colonialism. Those engaged in the active labour force numbered 17,559, mostly craftsmen and labourers, clerical workers, and professional and technical personnel — in that order of magnitude. A certain number were in agriculture and fisheries, and they were presumably mostly Italians. (This last category was the fourth in size, with 1,250 workers.)[22] One can only deduce, with this material in mind, that — even including the Italians — expatriate workers by 1961 were a tiny community.

Marked progress was also achieved in the fields of health, transport and communication, power generation, construction and housing, and services in general. However, in none of these areas did Libya qualify as advanced or well-equipped. (For instance, electric power generated rose from about 55m kwh in 1955 — excluding the production of small stations outside Tripoli and Benghazi, and of private stations whose total does not exceed one-third of the figure quoted above — to about 79m kwh in 1958. Even as late as 1965, power generated stood at 152m kwh, or about 101 kwh *per capita*. Likewise, the provision of water to urban dwellers progressed but slowly. Thus, while 7.4m cubic metres were supplied to Tripoli city in 1958, and 9.1m in 1961, less important cities and towns fared much less well.[23]) In addition, progress was achieved in the setting up of institutions in a number of fields, the creation of which is essential for modernisation. The National Bank of Libya was established in 1956 to replace the Currency Board of earlier days and become in the full sense of the term a central bank. Likewise, commercial banks grew in number and operations, and banking statistics reveal expanded activity with regard to deposits and loans. A National Agricultural Bank was formed in 1955 with a capital of half a million pounds (later raised to one million). But no industrial bank was formed, and industrial loan applicants, like others seeking credit for construction and other developmental financing, were forced to obtain loans from commercial banks at high rates of interest. These loans were short-term, but renewed in order to get round the injunction that commercial credit has to be for a matter of months only.

The most spectacular and significant development of the first decade of independence was the discovery of oil in large quantities in Libya. (It is worthwhile mentioning also that a code governing reconnaissance and exploration work by oil companies was also prepared in this period — a measure in which Libya moved ahead of the other oil countries.) However, the export of crude was still on a small scale by the end of 1961. And, in any case, it will be more appropriate to discuss the dramatic growth of the oil sector and the significant changes that have overtaken company–government relations in an integrated, not fragmented, fashion. Thus oil will be examined in a separate section further down.

Although modest in terms of the experience of Iraq, Kuwait or Saudi Arabia at comparable phases of their development, the development effort of Libya had to be organised and disciplined during the years 1952-61. This was done through the setting up of development and planning agencies, appropriate departments in ministries, and through the unfolding of planning work. The country's experience in this respect has to be analysed and evaluated. But here again, as with the case of the oil sector, it would be advisable to refer the discussion to a later stage rather than fragment it by including a part under developments in the first decade, and a second part under the second decade. Notwithstanding these two qualifications with respect to oil and planning, it should be possible and it is probably useful at this stage to make an overall evaluation of development in the decade of foreign aid. The main characteristics of this decade differ so sharply from those of the decade of development through self-financing that separate evaluations are warranted.

An observer who has made a detailed study of the country's development and planning efforts for the period from independence to 1971 sums up the experience of the first decade by saying that these efforts proved to be

> ... far from being the orderly, complementary, carefully coordinated evolution envisaged by the committee of experts (that is, the committee under Benjamin Higgins), or by the foreign powers associated in the planning initiatives. It was, all in all an untidy state of uncertainty, the only persistent factor being foreign-aid support for the persistent Libyan deficitary gaps.[24]

However, the same observer, like others before him, notes that significant achievements marked this period, mainly in transport and communications, urban water supply, power generation, public buildings, certain agricultural crops, experimental farms, a few fields of industry, and education and health.

Yet the overall prospect remained dim. This was because of a number of basic adverse factors, which fall into the political, social, technical, as well as economic fields. Politically, the federal system was condemned by all sensitive and knowledgeable observers. The civil service to some extent reflected the shortcomings of federalism, plus its own weaknesses, short experience, non-professionalism, and low motivation. Social attitudes in general did not express a release from the fetters of subjugation to underdevelopment, and the joy of participation in a national movement of rejuvenation and development. Most people felt uninvolved in, and did not identify with, the development effort, and this factor was compounded by the fact that what prosperity had materialised in the first decade only affected a very small proportion of the population, leaving the large masses, especially the majority who constituted the rural population, largely untouched. This bleak situation was not the result solely of human, institutional, and governmental shortcomings, but also of the niggardliness of nature. Technology was primitive on the whole, and the capability for the absorption of technological improvements was bound to be limited, in view of the low levels of education and training, and of work experience. Entrepreneurial talent was short, as were managerial and supervisory skills, and even at the level of labourers the shortages were serious.

Foreign aid, on which the bulk of development work depended, was uncertain. It was determined on a year-by-year basis, and often firm commitments came too late for the year in question to benefit from them. These lags were superimposed on lags in execution of projects owing to shortages in planning and execution personnel and institutional and bureaucratic factors. Co-ordination among the aid-givers left much to be desired, and as the years went by only Britain and the United States continued with their aid programmes, Italy, France, Turkey, Egypt and Pakistan having stopped their contributions. Yet even in the case of British- and American-financed programmes, not enough consideration was given to the priorities and strategies of development within an overall view of the objectives of modernisation. And correction was not forthcoming from the circles of government or the thinking public. Planning itself remained ineffective, because of insufficient and qualitatively inadequate staffing, lack of experience, internal conflicts, duplication of work and inadequate consultation with government.[25]

The overall evaluation of the World Bank mission, made in 1960, sums up the situation near the end of the first independence decade in clear and forthright terms:

> These observations [that is, relating to the results achieved by the various aid and development agencies] are not to be taken as a criticism of what the Libyan Government and the foreign aid agencies have been trying to do. They reflect rather the inherent difficulties of promoting balanced economic development in the circumstances in which Libya found itself at the time of Independence. Much of the initial effort had to be directed toward making good the neglect of education and training under the pre-war administration and to repairing the physical damage to harbors, roads and other installations caused by the war and by lack of proper maintenance during and after the war. On top of this, the very size of the country in relation to the paucity of its population and the poverty of its natural resources (oil apart) makes heavy expenditure on internal transport and communications a political and administrative necessity ... Finally, as already noted, there are the peculiar difficulties associated with agricultural development.[26]

The Second Independence Decade: Self-Financed Development

The year 1962 is an appropriate starting point for the era of self-financed development, although the government's *current* receipts from the export of oil were still about half its receipts from foreign aid. (However, if accruals are added, these receipts exceed transfers from abroad by LD3m.[27]) The year is significant on a number of counts. Most essentially, it marks the point in time when the realisation became firm that the country could count on substantial oil reserves, production and revenue. This realisation was soon to be translated into hard cash. The local expenditures of oil companies also rose substantially in 1962 over the level of 1961, by 50 per cent to be exact, and were never to rise as fast in later years. Likewise, government spending out of its general budget in 1962/3 witnessed a rise higher in absolute and relative terms than anything preceding it in the decade before (except between the years 1954/5 and 1955/6 when the relative but not the absolute rise was higher).[28] Furthermore, it was in this year that the LAJS (the Libyan-American Joint Services) ceased to operate, following the transfer of the functions and assets of the LARC and the LPDSA earlier to the Development Council. Libyan development agencies took over fully from there on.

It is not as easy to agree on the terminal point of this era. It can be the time of writing, since Libya is today even more rightly in the era of self-financed development. However, for various reasons it may be appropriate to divide this era into two parts: 1962-9, and 1969 to the present. The change in the political system and all that has accompanied it in the economic field are so significant that they ought to be brought out independently.

Nevertheless, development is a continuum. Our attempt at setting temporal frontiers and dividing the post-war period into sub-periods is mainly meant to underline certain basic distinguishing features between one sub-period or era and another. Thus, our subsequent examination of the growth of national product, education and matters of this nature will be uninterrupted, while in the examination of the oil sector the sharp new departures in oil policy under the republican régime will be portrayed in their fullness. Likewise, the new delineation of the frontiers of the private and the public sectors in the economic life of the country will be set out as clearly as the data available permit.

The record of development during the decade under review (or the 13 years 1962 to 1974, in so far as the information on hand allows) is largely the record of the dramatic expansion and increase in unit profitability of oil production and export. To this extent, a certain part of the development is no more than an 'optical illusion', since the increase in the statistical national product is not by any means matched by development in the broad sense in which we understand the term. For, although the performance of the economy has improved, its capital equipment and manpower capabilities have been considerably expanded, and its government and administrative machines have gained in effectiveness and efficiency, these positive developments by themselves would have only resulted in a marginal increase in national product.

Yet, be that as it may, there is no good reason to think less of the gains made in terms of national product and growth, much greater availability of financial resources, and the widening of the frontiers of development opportunities that these factors now make possible for the society and economy. The hard blocks to development that remain in the way, and the manpower and attitudinal problems which most probably will stay intractable for many years to come, will be examined further down, when we become in a position to make broad overall evaluations.

Two important changes occurred in the political framework of the economy in the second decade of independence. The first came in April 1963, when federalism was cancelled and replaced by a unitary state, as a result of the conviction that the federal state was uneconomical and inefficient, and the feeling that the separatist (or at least particularist) feelings of the provinces had faded out and had been replaced by a stronger sense of national unity — a sense which had been fortified by the exercise of the monarchy's power over the whole country during the preceding years 1952-63, the closer contacts provided by better means of transport and communication, the spread of education, and the emergence of a major national resource which had the power (via the use of its financial blessings) to develop the country as a whole.

This constitutional change made economic sense, especially in view of the small size of the population and the absurdity of having three provincial governments and one federal government to administer its affairs. However, in view of the vastness of the country, and the spread of the population clusters, movement to the other extreme through an insistence on excessive centralisation would have been almost as costly administratively and economically as federalism had been. The new formula provided for a compromise, through the delegation of some powers in the fields of education, health, labour, communications and agriculture to the administrators who were to represent the central government in the administrative areas. (The country was divided into ten such areas, to replace the former three provinces.) Each administrator was to be aided by a local advisory council.

The second, but by far the more significant political change, was the overthrow of the monarchy on 1 September 1969 by a group of young officers, and the announcement of the republic, under the name of the Libyan Arab Republic. The new ruling group declared itself intensely Arab nationalist, determined to follow the Nasserist line in international affairs and internal politics, and on social justice, development and the liberation of national resources from foreign control. The background to the military *coup* was a troubled political life, and a distinct orientation towards the Western powers and those Arab governments who did not identify themselves as radical. Complaints against misgovernment and corruption added strength to the motivation of the young officers. In this writer's view, economic factors were of minor importance, although the new ruling group declared itself interested in changing the economic system and paying greater attention to distribution and the provision of much wider opportunity to the bulk of the population. Indeed, by the late sixties, the economy was much better organised and development planning had become more rational, orderly and efficient. Only in the sector of oil has the new group proved itself noticeably different from the monarchy in the *economic* field, although it has in addition undertaken a number of measures such as nationalisation and government controls.

The revolutionary group headed by the Revolutionary Command Council (RCC) annulled the old constitution and later, on 11 December 1969, made a 'Constitutional Proclamation' which was in effect a provisional constitution.[29] The permanent constitution has not yet been declared. Political participation was provided for (along the lines set years earlier by Nasser in Egypt) by establishing a one-party system, in June 1971, under the Arab Socialist Union. (However, it is emphatically denied that the Union is a party, and parties are condemned for being a divisive force in society. The Union, instead, is a broad stream that brings together all those who want to serve within the framework of a set of general ideas and principles.) The RCC announced the adoption of socialism as a system — qualified alternatively as 'Arab' or 'Islamic'. (The latter designation merely means that Libyan socialism draws on the tenets of Islam and on Islamic culture.)

The republican government was eager to undo the agreements with the United Kingdom and the United States, under which these powers had military bases and were allowed a number of facilities with regard to the use of transport and means of communication, air space, and the like. Libya was successful in the cancellation of the agreements and the evacuation of the British and American bases in March and June 1970, respectively. In line with its strongly Arab nationalist tendencies, Libya asked most of the Italians who still remained in the country to leave it. Their property was taken over without compensation, in view of the heavy debt that Italy owed the country because of the sufferings of the Libyans under colonialism and their losses in the fight against it. Most of the European and American professionals, technicians and teachers who were in the country found their contracts not renewed or were otherwise discouraged from staying on. Arab replacements with equal qualifications (especially Egyptians, with whom the strong man of the new government, Colonel Ghaddafi, has particular affinity) were brought in to man the vacated posts, and many more as well under the impetus of accelerated development.

Earnest and honest, and dedicated to development and serious in its pursuit as the new government is, its major distinctive and spectacular contribution has really been in the field of oil relations and the terms of its exploitation, as we shall see further down. But, first, a brief characterisation of the new socio-economic system is in order.

The Free Officers, in their preparation for their take-over of September 1969, were in part influenced by the historical fact that the country had known monarchy only since independence in 1951. The monarchy, 'reinforced and supported by élitism — a small group of ruling families traditionally accustomed to power as a natural right'[30] — roused the resentment of intellectuals and of most of the educated, especially when the government's policy moved dramatically away from that of the leading radical Arab country, Egypt. But in addition, and again as in the case of the Egyptian Free Officers seventeen years before, the Libyan Free Officers were moved by a number of simple ideals rather than an integrated and sophisticated ideology. They wanted the vastly expanded oil revenue to seep through to the masses in larger volume; to see agriculture improve and recover the ground it lost owing to the preoccupation by the rural labour force with employment in oil or oil-related and oil-promoted activities; to rid the country of provincialism or regionalism; to clean the system of government of patronage and the civil service of corruption and waste; to combat inflation; to achieve diversification and balance in the economy in the sense of promoting the non-oil sectors; to provide the administrative and technical cadres which a modernising economy like Libya badly needed.

Like the ruling groups in Egypt, Syria and Iraq, the new rulers of Libya set as their targets and slogans the three desiderata: Freedom, Socialism and Arab Unity. By freedom they meant not only political liberation, but also social and economic liberation of the masses through development, better distribution and expansion and equality of opportunities. Freedom of the individual in belief, thought and expression also received assurances both in the Constitutional Proclamation and in later statements. As far as Arab unity is concerned, the RCC, and especially its Chairman, Colonel Ghaddafi, has pursued this objective with a great deal of dynamism and steadfastness.

It is the Libyan brand of socialism that raises some questions. Apart from the matter of its lineage, drawing as it is supposed to do on the Arab and Islamic cultural heritage, this socialism dissociates itself from the socialist models as known in the contemporary world. It recognises the role of the private sector in the economy and sanctifies private ownership. It does not lean on the proletariat, but instead preaches a distinctly nationalist line and system of values. While it is true that the government has nationalised all banks and insurance companies (in two steps which began with Libyanisation through acquiring a controlling proportion of capital and then ended with full nationalisation); and that it has nationalised public transport and a part of the construction and manufacturing sectors, it has left the rest of the economic system largely unchanged.

However, the government has been very active in promoting agricultural development, in order to make up for the relative neglect of agriculture in the years preceding 1969, when the oil exploration rush, and later the vast production activities, resulted in the syphoning away from agriculture of thousands of energetic labourers, and in depriving this sector of badly needed attention and investments (particularly before 1965). The revolutionary régime has started several land reclamation and irrigation projects. The area now under irrigation, thanks both to efforts expended before and after 1969, is some 515,000 hectares — as against 121,000 hectares in 1960, according to the agricultural census of that year. The allocations for agriculture in the 1971/2 budget total LD70m in the ordinary (current) budget, and LD50m in the capital (development) budget. (See section 4 below for more recent allocations under the Three-Year Plan, 1972/3–1974/5.) The provision of credit is vastly expanded, as are the facilities for the supply of select seeds, fertilisers, agricultural machinery and technical skills. The beneficiaries most fortunate in this respect have been the poor peasants to whom was distributed what remained of the lands in Italian hands by 1969. But the limited area involved could not have provided redress to a large number of peasants.

Another aspect of serious concern with, and effort for agriculture and the rural community is the energetic rural road-building programme which involves 2,400 km. of new roads — now either built or being built. In addition, 1,200 km. of highways are also in the phase of construction.[31] Finally, the oases, whose total population was a mere 79,000 in the 1964 census[32] (and is probably much less today owing to rising urbanisation) are the recipients of considerable investment, technical help, education effort, and other support to make life richer and more acceptable. Exploration for water in the southern part of the country, and the development of the water resources already available, is another area of serious endeavour. This applies to other regions in the country as well, where water resources are being developed and the supply of water is being expanded.

This brief record of some of the main interests of the RCC and the government would be incomplete if it did not include a reference to the strong emphasis placed on industrialisation. The industrial base in the country was very modest and weak, and achievements will have to be understood with this background in mind. Nevertheless, the few years since 1969 have demonstrated that notable results can be achieved in a short time if a country is fortunate enough in having the resources as well as the will and direction to develop industrially. But this aspect of development, as well as the other aspects, will receive some attention further down when we undertake a complete evaluation of the generation of independence.

3. LIBYAN OIL: A DRAMATIC RECORD

Before proceeding with the evaluation of the process of development, we will trace the record of the oil sector during its meteoric progress. This is essential because of the enormous impact of oil discoveries on the country in all aspects of its economic as well as social life.

Relations with the Oil Companies

As has been rightly observed by a leading Libyan economist,[33] Libya was fortunate that oil was discovered in the late fifties, and not a decade or more earlier. Had it been discovered before independence, the European countries then controlling the destiny of Libya would have manoeuvred to block independence and would have clung to the resource by all kinds of delaying tactics. Furthermore, the lesson of Iran's nationalisation of the Anglo-Iranian Oil Company in 1951, and how the company succeeded — with the political support of Britain — in bringing the oil industry to a standstill, and thus penalising Iran while the controversy lasted, was of great value to the Libyan authorities. This made them decide on a policy under which no one company would be able to 'blackmail' the country or immobilise its oil industry.

The exploratory studies and tests undertaken in the forties and the first few years of the fifties were not very encouraging or conclusive. Yet there were hopes that the picture could change significantly with further exploration. In anticipation, the government passed legislation to control exploration (and subsequently production) activities, under Mineral Law No. 9 of 1953.[34] This law provided for the coexistence of a large number of companies at the same time, by allowing relatively small concession areas to each. The first effect of the Mineral Law was that nine companies started reconnaissance work. This activity expanded fast, so that by early 1955 it was necessary to have a new law specifically relating to petroleum and capable of coping with the new situation. This was Petroleum Law No. 25 of 1955 (later amended on 21 April 1955, and on 21 May 1955, and enacted in July 1955). Within one year of the enactment of Law 25, 40 teams were already busy conducting surveys and tests, and by the middle of 1958, the year when the first discovery was made near the Libyan-Algerian frontier, 80 teams were operating. Drilling was started soon afterwards, with dozens of rigs probing deep in the earth for the black gold. The first production year was 1961, but the volume produced (and exported) was small — under one million tons. (The level rose tenfold in the year after.)

Among other things, Law 25 of 1955 set up an autonomous Petroleum Commission, whose membership consisted of three representatives of the three provinces of Libya, under a chairman who was to represent the federal government, that is, the interests of the country as a whole. This law contained provisions relating to the distribution of Libya's territory into zones for reconnaissance and exploration purposes. A reconnaissance permit did not automatically imply the extension of an exploitation concession to the company. Other provisions stipulated the relinquishment, under a phased schedule, of proportions of the concession area; for the start of exploration within a number of months from the granting of the concession, and the spending of certain minimum sums by the concessionary; for the payment of rent, fees and royalties, and, upon production and export, for the sharing of net profits in half between the government and the company; and for other matters of relevance.

The federal system of government led to certain delays and friction within the Petroleum Commission, and between it and some of the federal ministries. The friction was caused by disagreement with regard to authority over concession areas, manner of execution of federal decisions, and other matters where the frontiers between federal and provincial powers were not clearly drawn. But essentially the friction was between the Ministry of Petroleum Affairs and the Commission, each being jealous of what it considered its prerogatives. In the end, the tension was released by the cancellation of the Commission, just on the eve of the production of petroleum. The ministry took over all matters relating to the oil sector.

At the time, and afterwards, both in Libya and in other Arab countries, criticism has been levelled at the 1955 and 1961 laws for being too permissive and generous with the oil companies. This was most probably true. But the true motivation behind the generosity, once understood, can justify this feature. It was to encourage as many companies as possible to obtain reconnaissance and exploration permits and concessions in a situation where the risks of failure were still high. As amendments soon corrected some of the earlier excesses of the Laws of 1955 and 1961, the damage could not have been great.

The oil sector was at the peak of its activity at the time. This was so not merely because of the very large number of companies operating at various levels from reconnaissance to production and export, or because of the even larger number of concessions, but also because the dates for the relinquishment of concession areas were close, which made for continuous changes and follow-ups, and because the duration of concessions as a whole was generally shorter than its counterpart in the Mashreq oil countries. By 1961, it was realised that the law needed amendments, particularly with respect to the financial terms of concessions. The new law was issued as a Royal Decree on 3 July 1961. Its main provisions were the reduction of the depletion and amortisation allowances to the companies; the introduction of bidding for concessions; a better definition of the concessionaire's income and expenditures for the calculation of net profits; and other matters.

Other minor amendments followed in the same year. But a major amendment came on 20 November 1965. Its main provision related to the use of the posted price (rather than the actual price, or the posted price minus discounts, as had been the practice then) as reference or base price for profit calculation. This Law became operative at the beginning of 1966, and it brought to the treasury vastly increased revenues. For instance, it produced an extra revenue of LD43m for 1965 alone.

The improvements embodied in it notwithstanding, the Law of 1965 also came under criticism. The main objection was against the manner in which the law was formulated. For, after preparing the draft, the government invited the oil companies to examine it and to suggest alterations. This procedure was unprecedented. It resulted in the companies smuggling in certain changes and clauses favourable to themselves and at the expense of Libya, which it took the government a good deal of time and effort to correct.[35] The critics saw in this procedure another instance of the government's excessive permissiveness and neglect of the country's interests in its desire to curry favour with the Western countries with whose general policies and political stance it was aligned.

The year 1967 marked the beginnings of Libya's direct participation, in one way or another, in the activities of the oil sector. Thus, in July the Ministry of Petroleum declared its intention to undertake the following measures:

— The establishment of a Libyan petroleum institute for research and training.
— The organisation of a training programme in oil matters (technical, economic, accounting, administrative) for Libyan nationals.
— The construction of pipelines in the western area.
— The setting up of a number of projects directly connected with the hydrocarbons sector, with the help of oil concessionary companies. These projects were to include an ammonia-producing plant, refining and petrochemical industries, as well as the initiation of training programmes with the help of the companies as part of their contribution to the country against the benefits they were reaping from Libyan oil production and export.

This initial stance, which embodied a firmer official position with regard to the concessionary companies, was followed by other measures relating to increased revenues (or the abolition of selling discounts), the avoidance of waste of gas in production, the application of economical and technically sounder practices in the extraction of oil and the operation of the wells, and the submission of production plans acceptable to the government. Finally, two institutional measures were taken. The first was the setting up by Royal Decree on 20 April 1967 of the Libyan Petroleum General Authority whose functions were reported to be to:

> support the Libyan economy through development, administration and utilization of petroleum resources in various stages, to establish national petroleum industries, to market local and imported petroleum products and to participate with departments concerned in the planning and implementation of the state's general petroleum policy and in the fixing of crude oil and petroleum products prices and in maintaining the standard of these prices.[36]

The second measure was the setting up in 1968 of the Libyan General Petroleum Company (LIPETCO), to act on behalf of the government in the assigning of areas for prospecting and exploration and generally to undertake operations related to the industry. (However, this body was replaced in 1970 by the Libyan Oil Corporation, LINOCO, which was assigned very wide powers.) Some measures followed which reflected the growing self-confidence of the government, but the more significant changes in the structure of the oil industry were to come after the *coup* of September 1969.

The first such change occurred on 4 July 1970, when the government nationalised all foreign distribution companies, with their equipment and networks. This step was in line with the new government's avowed socialist orientation and its desire to put the public sector in control of strategic activities or commodities. However, steps more expressive of such a desire have followed, beginning with December 1971, down to the autumn of 1974. These have involved the nationalisation of majority shares (at least 51 per cent) of capital of all foreign oil companies in Libya. This has been done for politico-economic reasons, the political factor predominating in some instances (as in the partial nationalisation of British Petroleum on 7 December 1971, in protest against the British government's acquiescence in Iran's occupation of three Arab islands in the Arabian Gulf before British withdrawal from the Gulf), and the economic factor predominating in some others. In all instances there has been disagreement over the question of the legitimacy of nationalisation measures, and beyond this largely academic matter, over the terms of compensation which have frequently been considered unacceptable because 'unilaterally determined and arbitrary'.

Equally important as this sustained policy of growing control over the production side has been that of price determination. Libya has been a leader in obtaining substantially increased prices for oil. The Mashreq oil-producing countries have been more patient in their negotiations with the companies, and more modest in their demands. Indeed on more than one occasion, the first of which was the agreement of September 1970, while the oil countries of the Mashreq had negotiated certain price increases, Tripoli forced the hands of the companies by insisting on, and obtaining, substantially better prices and different terms. Obviously, in doing this Libya was relying confidently on its two advantages: the low sulphur content of its oil and its greater proximity to European markets. But the differential in terms was larger than these advantages by themselves warranted. This no doubt was the outcome of the determination and steadfastness of the revolutionary government and its skill in negotiation, as well as its self-confidence and its belief in the rightness of its position.

Libya

Growth of the Oil Sector

The dynamism and speedy growth which characterise the Libyan oil sector reflect themselves in the statistics of production and revenue to government, as well as in the local expenditures of the oil companies. As these expenditures predated production, we will present them first, in Table 10.3.

Table 10.3: Local Expenditure by Oil Companies (LD m)

Year	
1957	4.3
1958	9.6
1959	10.3
1960	21.3
1961	27.5
1962	40.0
1963	42.2
1964	47.6
1965	50.7
1966	47.7
1967	43.3
1968	60.1
1969	78.8
1970	73.0
1971	55.5
1972 (4 months)	14.0
Total	625.9

Sources: Ahmad Ali Attiga, *The Impact of Petroleum on the Libyan Economy, 1956-1969* (Dar at-Tali'a, Beirut, 1972; Arabic), p. 44 for figures up to 1969. The data appear in much greater detail in Census and Statistical Department's annual reports entitled *Report of the Annual Survey of Petroleum Mining Industry*, of which the latest report available in 1973 was for 1970. The expenditure for 1970, 1971 and the first four months of 1972 came from Bank of Libya, *National Bulletin*, Vol. 12, No. 3 (May-June 1972), Table 33 in Appendix.

These expenditures have had a strong impact on the economy, via the recipients of the income — labourers, merchants, contractors, caterers and owners of houses and means of transport, and via the multiplier effect of the income received. The impact was much greater in the first half of the fifteen-year period, since these local expenditures constituted a major income injection into the economy — in fact, one which until 1964 was larger than the government's share in the profits from oil export operations.

The production of oil rose steeply from about 0.9m tons in 1961 to 8.7m tons in 1962, and to 108.2m in 1972, 105.1m in 1973, and to 77m in 1974.[37] (Production in 1972 and 1973 dropped below the level of the years 1968-71. The drop has been deliberately engineered since 1971 by the government, under its policy of preservation of the oil resources. However, the level of production in 1974 was further influenced by the cut agreed on by all the Arab members of OPEC in connection with the Arab-Israeli war of October

1973.) Parallel with the general rise in production there is the rise in revenues to government, from LD14.2m for 1962, to LD514m for 1972, and an estimated LD651m for 1973, and LD1,746m for 1974.[38] The rise in revenues is much steeper than that in production, thanks to the vastly improved terms obtained recently by Libya, and to the steep shift upwards of prices for all OPEC countries since the Arab-Israeli war. The last column in Table 10.4 shows the revenue to government per ton of production. This is not a very precise measurement, since the revenue consists of a few components which do not all vary at the same rate, and since the revenue in fact accrues for exports, not production. However, these qualifications remain minor and the general trend seen from the table is meaningful enough for our purposes.

Table 10.4: Oil Production and Government Revenue, 1962-74 (production in million tons; revenue in million dinars)

Year	Production	Revenue	Revenue/Ton (LD)
1962	8.7	14.2	1.632
1963	22.4	38.5	1.718
1964	41.4	75.2	1.816
1965	58.9	125.4	2.129
1966	72.3	186.7	2.582
1967	84.0	223.3	2.658
1968	125.7	357.8	2.850
1969	149.8	419.7	2.810
1970	159.8	482.6	3.020
1971	133.1	593.7	4.460
1972	108.2	514.0	5.750
1973[a]	105.1	651.0	6.194
1974[a]	77.0	1,746.0	22.675

a. Estimates.

Source: For production, The British Petroleum Company Limited, *BP Statistical Review of the World Oil Industry – 1973*, p. 18. For revenue, OPEC, *Annual Statistical Bulletin 1972*, p. 134, to 1972; for estimates for 1973 and 1974, see Dr Nicolas Sarkis, 'The Energy Crisis and the Challenge of Development in the Arab Countries', Paper No. 132 (A-1) for the Ninth Arab Petroleum Congress) held in Dubai, 10-16 March 1975.

The revenue per ton has risen consistently except in 1969, when it dropped slightly from the level for 1968. The upward trend shows two sharp increases in the government's intake per ton or barrel: the first in 1966, because of the implementation of the new fiscal terms set by government to apply as from the beginning of 1966, and the second, much larger, improvement in 1971, thanks to the success of the Libyans in making the oil companies accept a much higher reference price for crude in agreements entered into in September 1970 and April 1971. The year 1972 witnessed another improvement, but not as large as that of 1971. But the most dramatic improvement of all came in 1974. Libya can thus be said to have capitalised handsomely on the quality of its crude which has a low sulphur content, and on its advantageous geographical proximity to the European markets. This it has done with remarkable adroitness, especially under its new régime. While it is true that the revolutionary government has had the experience of the Mashreq oil countries to learn from, it is equally true that it has acted ably and firmly, considering Libya's short learning period. Indeed, its intake per unit of export is much better than that of the more experienced Mashreq oil-producing countries. However, the most dramatic changes in the structure of oil prices occurred on 16 October and 23 December 1973. The cumulative effect of the adjustment involved was to make the prices on 1 January 1974 roughly four times what they had been on 15 October 1973.

Another interesting aspect of Libya's oil policy is the government's early awareness of the need for poise with respect to the volume of production. Thus Libya has turned its back on the temptation to increase production as fast as possible and to accumulate as large a financial reserve as possible, by capitalising on the growing world energy crisis and the advantageous position of oil sellers vis-à-vis buyers. In reversing the policy prevailing until the end of 1970, the new government has taken many considerations into account. The first is the size of the country's published proven reserves, which at the end of 1970 stood at 29.3 billion barrels.[39] They ranked fifth in the Arab world, after Saudi Arabia, Kuwait, Iraq and Algeria, in that order. At the scale of production of 1970, these reserves could last for only 24 years.

The second consideration was the policy-makers' disenchantment with foreign reserves, which were vulnerable to devaluation, and whose purchasing power was being eroded year after year by inflation. In the third place, the country's absorptive capacity for investment was (and would probably remain so for a number of years) well below the resources at its disposal — which reduced the pressure for expansion in production.

In reaching its policy decision with regard to the limitation of production, Libya stood in sharp contrast with Saudi Arabia which, since 1971, has made it clear that it was eager to increase production considerably, even though the revenue was to pile up in dimensions well beyond the capability of the Kingdom to dispose of. The huge monetary reserves that were to be accumulated were to find a large outlet in investment in the United States. (This policy stance became considerably more pronounced for Saudi Arabia after the quadrupling of prices in the last quarter of 1973 and the more than fourfold increase in revenues to the government — as a combined result of price increases, participation by the government in company operations, and improvement in the profit-sharing formula.) If there have been occasional deviations from this stance, this has reflected short-term political restraints or tactics and has been of marginal quantitative effect. (In practice, billions of dollars of 'surplus funds' found their way to the United Stated in 1974 alone.)

As can be expected, Libya's revenue from oil exports has resulted in a very steep rise in national product (as well as the accumulation of enormous financial reserves). Thus, from an estimated national product of 15 million pounds (dinars) upon independence, the country has moved up to a GNP of LD1,257.7m for 1971, LD1,356m for 1972, LD1,423m for 1973, and LD2,700m for 1974.[40] (The population was one million in 1961 but rose to 2.3m in 1973. Thus, national product *per capita* rose from 15 dinars in 1961 to about 1,174 dinars in 1974.) Even taking into account the considerable inflation, these data (which are at current prices) still show an increase which would be impossible to achieve under normal circumstances. (The price and cost-of-living indices are not very satisfactory, especially for the period preceding 1964. However, the first cost-of-living series, with 1955 as base year, rose to 146 for 1963. The second series, with 1964 as base year, rose to 165 for 1971. The index stood at 113.6 for 1973, with 1970 as base year. If 1964 is retained as base year, then the index for 1973 would be 163.9 according to the *International Financial Statistics*. Even allowing for underestimation of inflation, this factor could only account for a very small part of the very substantial growth.)[41] It is pointless to attempt the calculation of the annual rate of real growth under these circumstances.

The contribution of the oil sector to national product is very high. The latest (and most reliable) series on hand relates this contribution to gross domestic product at factor cost.[42] According to this series, the share of oil in GDP has risen from 24.4 per cent in 1962 to 62.7 per cent in 1972. The increase of this share has been continuous, except in 1967 when oil exports rose, but at a much lower rate than that applying for 1966 compared with 1965, or 1968 compared with 1967; and except in 1971 when oil production was deliberately compressed. The contribution of the sector is very close to that of Kuwait's oil sector. (The series for the years 1957-72 is presented below in section 5.)

Two qualifications are in order here. First, that the ratio of oil revenue to GNP is higher than that to GDP, and is more meaningful as an indicator of the economy's performance. Second, that the very steep rise in oil revenue for 1974 makes the oil multiplier smaller and the ratio of oil revenue to GNP (and GDP) noticeably higher (about 65 per cent). As can be expected, the large revenues from oil have activated the whole economy, although not through the same channels as in the case of Kuwait. Libya has been more cautious with its oil income than the average Mashreq oil-producing country. Furthermore, the oil money has not seeped through to the bulk of the population through a policy of land acquisitions like that adopted in Kuwait, according to which the government spent hundreds of millions of dinars buying land from private owners, in order to use the plots for public buildings and housing schemes, or for resale (at nominal prices) for private house building.

The oil income of Libya found its way to the population at large via government spending, mainly in investment projects, but also through salaries and wages and certain cash transfers, as well as via the many contracting firms undertaking projects for the government and the oil companies. However, the impact of oil income on the various sectors will occupy us further down. It is sufficient to indicate here that the super-affluence created by oil has brought with it a number of problems, which will receive some consideration in the concluding section of this chapter. Fortunately for Libya, the authorities are now aware of these problems and are concerned about them and their solution. Such awareness was beginning to be felt in the last two or three years before the *coup* of 1969, but the successive governments that came to power before 1965 or 1966 were dangerously permissive in this respect.

4. LIBYAN PLANNING

Both the negative approach, involving the awareness of the adverse effects of oil on the economy and society, and the positive approach, involving the awareness of how best to use oil resources for developing the economy and the society, show that planning coincided with awareness. The periods characterised by improved planning were the periods when the authorities understood both the adverse aspects of oil resources and their great potential. This phase of greater maturity and vision stretches roughly from the mid-sixties down to the present. But it can probably be said with safety that the RCC and the governments under it combine clearer vision with firmer activism than the governments preceding them in dealing with both sides of the coin of oil resources and affluence.

The country experienced some form of programming or project planning under the Italian administration, but right after the war and before independence, that is, between 1946 and the end of 1951, there were no signs of planning that can be discerned. Likewise, the years characterised by foreign economic support, or 1952-61, were managed financially on a hand-to-mouth basis, which was not appropriate for planning. However, this period began with a plan proposal and ended with another. The first was drawn by the UN Mission sent to Libya in 1951. The second was the plan proposal of the IBRD survey mission. The UN mission came up with a very long-term plan which had three phases, each with special areas of emphasis and a strategy particular to itself. Phase one which was to be of six years' duration stressed training and education; agricultural promotion (through research and other activities); the repair of war damage to public transport, public works and public utilities; and the absorption of inactive manpower into the economy. This phase was to depend heavily on foreign financing, and net investment in it was to be of the order of 5-10 per cent of national product.

The second phase embraced two six-year plans. These were to aim at further improvement in agriculture, the setting up of certain light industries, and the reduction of the deficit in the current account of the balance of payments. Investment in this phase was to range between 10 and 15 per cent of national product. Phase three consisted of the fourth six-year plan and of a series of plans that were to follow. Here development was to move further in the fields of agriculture and industry, mechanisation and balance in the external sector. Investment was to be at least 15 per cent of the national product.[43]

This rather grandiose vision stretching decades ahead was predicated on the assumption that the country was not only poor, but had no prospects of significant exploitable resources. Its land was exhausted and its manpower was far from being able to compensate for the niggardliness of nature. The vision had a tangible impact on the government, because it adopted, in one form or another, many of the institutional recommendations as well as the assumptions and the strategies contained in the report. The LPDSA, the LAJS, the LARC and the Libyan Finance Corporation came into being as an embodiment of some of the recommendations. Finally, the Development Council was established in 1956, and it was later in 1960 to take over the functions of the organs just cited.

As the first decade of independence, despite the emergence of the institutions purportedly created for the undertaking of planning functions, did not witness planning in the sense in which the term is accepted today, we will not survey its experience here. The development work undertaken during this period reflected some system of priorities, and a certain view of the overall picture of the economy as it was desired to evolve. But it did not reflect rigorous or comprehensive planning. At best, there was programming; at worst poor co-ordination between the various agencies supposedly working for the same ends, within the same framework.

In 1960, the IBRD survey mission came up with a suggested plan in their report.[44] This was to be a five-year plan beginning with 1 April 1960. Total allocations for public expenditure were LD25m, with additional allocations for recurrent expenditures on development totalling LD11.9m for the five years. The largest beneficiary of investment allocations was the primary sector (water resources, agriculture, forestry and dune fixation) which was to receive 32 per cent of the total. Transport and communications ranked second with 23 per cent, followed closely (21 per cent) by the social services of education, health, housing and sanitation. Electric power and town and village water together were allotted 17 per cent, and the balance of 7 per cent went to industry, handicrafts and fisheries (3 per cent), public buildings, capitalisation of the National Bank, and antiquities and tourism. This pattern in its general contours agreed with the pattern of public investments in the period 1955/6–1957/8, except for social services, which were to receive increased allocations under the IBRD proposal, and public buildings that were to receive much less.

The five years during which the plan was to be implemented witnessed far-reaching changes in the financial picture, with the emergence of oil revenues as the major source of public revenue. Thus, actual development expenditures rose well above the planned LD5m on an annual average, and this in spite of the limited effectiveness of planning and of planning institutions; the disappearance of the various institutions that used to handle development work as the Development Council was empowered in July 1960 to take their place, while the Council itself lacked the experience and was short on technical staff; and the very limited degree of mobilisation of public opinion behind the development effort. The process of accelerated public expenditure not only left the proposed plan expenditure well behind, but it also distorted the pattern of expenditure suggested by the IBRD mission. Inflation added to the distortion of the allocation of resources.

The new facts forced certain actions on the government. One of these was the preparation, soon after the IBRD plan proposals were supposed to go into implementation, of a new plan which could reflect the new financial availabilities. The new plan was to run for five years, 1963-8. Other institutional changes occurred that were to be of extreme importance for development work. The first was the establishment in May 1961 of two new ministries: the Ministry of Industry and the Ministry of Petroleum Affairs. The second was the constitutional amendment of April 1963, according to which Libya became a unitary state and gave up federalism, along with the diffuseness of authority and decision-making between the federal government and the three provincial governments.

Finally, under Law No. 5 of 16 July 1963, the Development Council was replaced by a National Planning Council. The change was not merely one of form. It embodied a different attitude to planning and outlook on development. For one thing, the NPC had much more power assigned to it in this law. This power comprised planning proper after a thorough examination of the economy's needs, potential and problems; the recommendations of legislation called for by the plan; the formulation of regulations and instructions to govern plan implementation; the supervision, follow-up and evaluation of the execution of the plan; and the recommendation of alterations in plans and execution and follow-up procedures. Another important change related to the new status given to the NPC. This was reflected in the composition of the NPC, which consisted of the Prime Minister as chairman, and the Ministers of planning and development, finance, national economy, petroleum affairs, agriculture and animal wealth, and industry. The old Development Council had under-secretaries as members. The new composition was meant to reduce the authority gap between the planning agency and the political leadership of the country, and to assure the plan fuller support by this leadership.

As a well-informed expert observed, the stage was set for the 1963-8 Plan.[45] But, more importantly, as the same expert believes, the political and attitudinal framework was by then ready for the country's first real experiment and experience in planning. This framework he describes as 'quiet nationalism'. This feature helped the country proceed with development work, despite its acknowledged serious physical and manpower problems. According to him:[46]

> As the first Libyan five year plan swung into the second year of implementation, it was remarkable that Libya, in the face of... frustrations and in contrast to many another developing country, faced with some success the formidable array of drags with an apparently enviable calm, eschewing ideological semantics, blaming neither imperialism nor colonialism, blaming neither the past nor the present, and certainly betraying none of the fatalism that Higgins so simplistically ascribed to the Libyan character.

The First Five-Year Plan 1963-68 was to start with the financial year 1963/4. Its aims, broadly defined, were to ensure speedy improvement in the level of living of the people, particularly low-income groups; to give strong emphasis to agriculture, as the rural sector was where most of the population lived and worked; to enable the government to continue with its drive for improvement and expansion in education, health, housing, communications and those sectors that serve as infrastructure; to formulate and pursue those commercial, monetary and fiscal policies required for the success of the investment programme; and finally to develop the organs responsible for the accumulation and processing of statistical information and for research and studies connected with developmental planning.[47]

The Plan envisaged a total public expenditure of LD169m. However, allocations for the five years totalled LD324.9m (at current prices). The sums actually spent were not very far from the allocations: LD298.2m in five years,[48] or a rate of execution of 91.8 per cent. Normally, this would be considered an excellent performance, but in the context of Libyan circumstances and its windfall revenue, the high rate might be understood rather as a sign of permissiveness in public expenditure in a situation where resources were no longer a bottleneck. (It should be noted that gross domestic capital formation by the public sector is reported as LD262.6m for the five years 1963-8. However, in this latter calculation, calendar rather than financial years are taken into consideration.[49])

The Plan document itself sets investment and project targets, but is silent with regard to expected changes in national product, private and public consumption, and private fixed capital formation. Perhaps this silence was advisable, considering the great fluidity of the situation and the extreme difficulty, if not impossibility, of making estimates with regard to national product and its uses, while the oil sector and its growth were in effect matters well outside the determination of government.

The planning authorities started in 1967 to prepare the Second Five-Year Plan 1969-74, and the Plan was approved by government on 27 March 1969 — that is, a full year after the lapse of the First Plan. This delay was the result of the decision to extend the First Plan by one year in order to complete certain projects in it. The Second Plan reflected, once again, the improved financial fortunes of the country, as well as the system of priorities opted for by the authorities at the time. Thus, allocations for investment totalled LD1,149m. Public works, communications, agriculture, housing, education, municipalities, industry and health (in that order) together accounted for LD980m or 85 per cent of the total. (Their respective shares were: 15.4, 14.1, 13.1, 11.1, 10.1, 8.9, 7.9 and 4.9 per cent.[50]) However, the Second Plan only had five months of life, instead of five years. On the takeover of power by the Free Officers on 1 September 1969, the fate of the Plan was decided. The operation of the Plan was suspended, although many of the projects in the pipeline were continued. (The allocations for the year 1969/70, or the first year of the Second Plan, had been set at LD145m.[51])

For the two years following, independent annual allocations were made while a new plan was being prepared. The first annual development budget for the year beginning 1 April 1970 totalled LD200m, divided among the various sectors. The largest allocation, 25 per cent of the total, went to agriculture and agrarian reform. The next-largest allocation went to housing and public utilities, followed by transport and communications, municipalities, industry, public works, and education and national guidance — to list the sectors with allocations in excess of LD10m each (or 5 per cent or more of the budget). Together, these sectors received LD185.8m, or 92.9 per cent of the total.[52] The year 1971/2 received a total allocation of LD300m. Agriculture was allotted about the same absolute sum as in the year before (LD50.4m, against LD50m). Five other sectors received at least 10 per cent of the budget each (that is, at least LD30m), and they were: housing and public utilities; transport and communications; industry and mineral wealth; the Ministry of Interior and Local Government; and education and national guidance. All together, the six sectors (including agriculture) received LD224.2m, or some 75 per cent of the total.[53] (More recent allocations for the period 1 April 1972 to 31 December 1975 fall under the current Three-Year Plan, and will be examined further down where this plan will be presented.)

Actual gross domestic capital formation by the government has varied from planned capital formation (and from budget allocations) in every planning year, that is from 1963 to 1971, even after allowing for the difference between the calendar years (for which data on capital formation are presented) and financial years (in terms of which planning programmes are presented down to 1972/3). The next 'period' was nine months, 1 April to 31 December 1973; thereafter calendar years have been in use. But what is more serious than the divergence between total allocations and total capital formation is the divergence for each sector between planned and executed capital formation. This latter divergence is of much larger relative size. Table 10.5 sets out for comparison purposes the annual totals, first as planned, and then as actually executed. In this table we compare financial years, where allocations are concerned, with calendar years, where actual capital formation is concerned. Each financial year will fall where most of its months fall — for instance 1963/4 will be considered 1963, and 1971/2 will be considered 1971. This is not legitimate if we are to be very strict, in which case pro-rating would be required, but it is good enough for the purpose of this analysis, namely to provide some indication of the level of performance — defined as actual related to planned capital formation.

It would seem from Table 10.5 that a certain degree of execution saturation had been reached by 1970, in the sense that the greater availability of investment allocations brought about larger absolute actual investment, but not larger relative investment (that is, actual as a proportion of planned investment or allocation). Consequently, the index of performance for the two years 1970 and 1971 was lower than in any of the previous years, while the planned investments were much higher. This is all the more true with respect to 1971.

Reference has been made to the fact that divergence, sector by sector, between planned and actual investment was wider than divergence beteen annual aggregates as they appear in Table 10.5. We will now present a comparison, sector by sector, for seven major sectors for the four years 1968-71. As information is not available for each of the nine years 1963-71 broken down by sector, the results are bound to be partial and incomplete. Furthermore, here we are comparing planned investment, not allocations, with actual investment, owing to the non-availability of detailed allocation data. In spite of these limitations, the findings are instructive, as Table 10.6 shows. (Here again, we will use calendar years to represent actual annual investment, although budgeted or planned investment is presented in terms of financial years.)

The fluctuation between planned and actual investment for each of the sectors is wide. First, the lowest performance has been in industry, where only in 1971 did actual investment reach a reasonably high level. Next in poor performance is agriculture, with an average performance of 34 per cent. (It must be noted that the percentage calculation for several years can be misleading, since a large actual investment for one year may greatly outbalance small investments in the other years. This is the case of agriculture, with an average of 34 per cent, against the distinctly poor performance of industry, with an average of 39 per cent — all because in 1971 investment in industry was large enough absolutely and relatively to conceal the very low performance of the three preceding years.)

The second observation is that there has been 'overfulfilment' of the plan in the case

Table 10.5: Comparison between Planned and Actual Gross Domestic Investment 1963-71 (LD million, at current prices)

Year	Planned Investment (or Allocations)[a]	Actual Investment[b]	Percentage Performance
1963	21.7	16.7	76.9
1964	38.3	24.5	64.0
1965	58.0	44.5	76.7
1966	92.3	69.3	75.1
1967	119.7	107.4	89.7
1968	193.9	122.5	63.2
1969	145.0	111.4	76.8
1970	200.0	122.6	61.3
1971	300.0	165.9	55.3
Average performance for the years 1963-71			67.1

a. Planned investment for the year 1963/4 (according to the Plan) was LD21.7m, while allocations were LD16.7m. The Plan did not contain annual budgets for the three last years 1965/6—1967/8, and allocations have had to be used. Plan allocations from 1968/9 onwards have been used.

b. An earlier official source (the first source cited below) has (on p.124) a different series entitled 'Expenditure on Five-Year Plan'. This expenditure is listed as 12.5, 23.0, 52.4, 82.3, and 128.1m for the five years respectively. The divergence adds up to LD35.9m. The difference is probably caused by the divergences in definition.

Sources: For 'Planned investment or allocations', Technical Planning Authority, Directorate-General, Economic and Social Planning, *Survey of the National Economy of the Libyan Arab Republic 1964-1968* (Tripoli, not dated), p.123, for the years 1963-8; *Details of the Development Budget for the Financial Year 1969/70, 1970/71*, and *1971/72* for the years 1969-71 inclusive. (The *Details ...* is published annually, and the citation just made refers to three sources for the three years respectively.) For actual gross domestic capital formation, data have been obtained from Ministry of Planning, *National Accounts of the Libyan Arab Republic 1962-1971* (October 1972), Table 12, pp. 67-9.

of the sectors of electricity, water supplies, sewerage and housing. This phenomenon reflects the great emphasis placed on these sectors, as well as the abundance of resources which permits actual investment to outdistance planned investment. (Obviously, this 'overfulfilment', parallel with that of the drastic 'underfulfilment' in other sectors, suggests a certain measure of inadequacy of planning and its distance from realism, and a certain measure of arbitrariness and aversion to discipline in plan formulation and execution circles.)

Finally, as in the case of annual aggregates presented in Table 10.5, here again at the sectoral level we observe greater 'resistance' in some sectors than in others to investment injections. This can be traced back to a number of reasons, which can be grouped together under the rubric of 'low absorptive capacity' for investment. Furthermore, time lags vary from sector to sector, and the execution of projects is not of uniform ease (or difficulty) in various sectors.

Libya is presently in the process of implementing its latest Plan: the Three-Year Plan 1972-75. This Plan was issued by Law No. 56 of 27 April 1972,[54] while the budget for

Table 10.6: Comparison between Planned and Actual Investment by Government in Major Sectors for the Years 1968-71, at Current Prices (amounts in million dinars, performance in percentage)

Sector	1968 Planned	(1968/9) Actual	Per Cent	1969 Planned	(1969/70) Actual	Per Cent	1970 Planned	(1970/1) Actual	Per Cent	1971 Planned	(1971/2) Actual	Per Cent
Agriculture	11.1	5.7	51.4	16.4	5.2	31.7	50.0	10.7	21.4	50.4	21.3	42.3
Industry	7.7	1.2	15.6	7.9	0.7	8.9	20.5	4.4	21.5	32.0	20.1	62.8
Transport and communications	23.7	23.3	98.3	22.7	19.4	85.5	27.1	15.8	58.3	39.8	25.3	63.6
Electricity	n.a.	16.0		13.0	18.4	156.8	9.5	14.9	156.8	21.5	22.6	105.1
Water supply and sewerage	n.a.	9.7		5.7	7.7	135.1	18.1	21.6	119.3	18.3	22.1	120.8
Education	13.8	11.5	83.3	14.6	9.4	64.4	11.4	8.1	71.1	30.2	11.3	37.4
Housing and state property	12.0	26.5	220.8	22.2	31.2	140.5	32.8	30.2	92.1	40.0	26.5	66.3

Note: Information is not available on planned investment in electric power and in water supply and sewerage for 1968/9. These two subsectors were grouped under other broad headings for that year. Performance cannot therefore be calculated.

Sources: Annual Reports entitled *Details of the Development Budget for the Financial Year ...*, for each of the years indicated, for planned investment; and *National Accounts of the Libyan Arab Republic 1962-1971*, p.73, for actual investment.

the first year 1972/3 was issued by Law No. 57 of the same date.[55] The Three-Year Plan is the most sophisticated and comprehensive planning document that has so far appeared in Libya. It includes investment projections for the public sector, and expectations for the private sector, including the private oil sector, as well as projections of the availability and use of resources for Plan years. Although it does not contain a model in the same document, presumably one had been prepared as part of the background or infrastructural studies prior to the preparation of the Plan.

The underlying 'analytical infrastructure' is explicitly stated, via an examination of the directions in which the economy had moved in the oil era, particularly the years 1967-9, when the rise in oil revenue, though still substantial, had stopped being as steep as in the few years before and had become more predictable. This analytical infrastructure also comprised an examination of the dislocations of which the economy had been victim — with regard to inflation; the divergence in growth rates between oil, the other commodity sectors, the distribution sectors, and the service sectors in a manner which resulted in excessive and growing dependence on one commodity alone; the growing inequalities and disparities of income distribution alongside the rise in the general income level; the geographical inequalities between the regions; and the unhealthy dependence on an ever-increasing volume of imports at the expense of local production.

The Plan document moves on to a statement of broad aims and more precise targets, which are designed to correct the dislocations and imbalances, and to further healthy development. This latter aspect lays particular emphasis on the better integration of the oil sector into the economy in the sense of developing sectors and industries linked backward and forward to oil, and in the sense that oil can and should become the engine of development of all productive sectors. The non-oil sectors should thus grow in relative size, in addition to growth in absolute terms, and should correct the present situation where much of the growth in oil leaks out to finance huge imports, and as capital outflows. (The very steep rise in oil revenues since the last quarter of 1973 has thrown this policy into disarray, despite the more energetic efforts to develop non-oil sectors.)

The strategy of the Plan is also articulated, though in brief terms, with emphasis on the need for the duration of the Plan to resort to capital-intensive investment in order to prepare the machinery for productive and supportive sectors, and the need to speed up the education and training programmes of the country. This strategy is considered necessary in the short term within the framework of a much longer-term view of development.

Initially, the investment programme contained in the Plan totalled LD1,165m for the three years for the public sector. This includes LD1,007m for gross fixed capital formation (designated as 'gross fixed invesement'), LD88m for financial investment (investment credits, increase in the capital of lending agencies, and like items), and LD70m for 'other investment expenditures'.[56] (Gross domestic fixed investment by the public sector is planned as LD995m.[57]) The expected gross fixed domestic investment by the private sector totals LD527m. This amounts to 34.6 per cent of the total of LD1,522m. (All these figures are set at 1971/2 market prices.) The distribution of the investment among the various economic sectors, and institutionally between the private and the public sectors, is presented in Table 10.7.

Table 10.7 shows that the largest share of public investment goes to transport, communications and storage, closely followed by transformation industry, while the largest share of private-sector investment goes to the petroleum sector which receives twice as much investment in absolute terms as transport, communications and storage. (Development of the oil sector involves sound exploitation along with expansion of reserves through

Table 10.7: Gross Fixed Domestic Investment in the National Economy in the Three-Year Plan 1972/73–1974/75, by the Public Sector and the Private Sector (at 1971/2 market prices, and in LD millions)

Economic Sector	Public Sector	Private Sector	Total	Percentage Distribution		
				Public Sector	Private Sector	Total
Agriculture, forestry and fishing	111.6	24.0	135.6	7.3	1.6	8.9
Petroleum	40.6	377.0	417.6	2.7	24.7	27.4
Mining and quarrying	2.6	3.0	5.6	0.2	0.2	0.4
Transformation industry	183.2	24.0	207.2	12.0	1.6	13.6
Construction	9.7	12.0	21.7	0.6	0.8	1.4
Electricity	101.5	–	101.5	6.7	–	6.7
Total commodity sectors	449.2	440.0	889.2	29.5	28.9	58.4
Transport, communication and storage	187.3	24.0	211.3	12.3	1.6	13.9
Wholesale and retail trade	2.1	7.0	9.1	0.2	0.4	0.6
Total distribution sectors	189.4	31.0	220.4	12.5	2.0	14.5
Banks and insurance	1.0	–	1.0	0.1	–	0.1
Housing	84.5	48.0	132.5	5.5	3.2	8.7
Public services (excluding education and health)	144.4	–	144.4	9.5	–	9.5
Education services	95.4	0.5	95.9	6.3	–	6.3
Health services	48.1	0.5	48.6	3.1	–	3.1
Other services	–	10.0	10.0	–	0.7	0.7
Total service sectors	373.4	59.0	432.4	24.5	3.9	28.4
Grand total (including land value)	1,012.0	530.0	1,542.0	66.5	34.8	101.3
(excluding land value)	17.0	3.0	20.0	1.1	0.2	1.3
Grand total	995.0	527.0	1,522.0	65.4	34.6	100.0

Source: *The Three-Year Plan for Economic and Social Development 1392-95 A.H.–1972-75 A.D.* (published by the Technical Planning Authority; Arabic), p.67.

exploration, utilisation of natural gas, setting up advanced petrochemical industries, the storage of oil derivatives for 'sufficient periods', finding new markets, and placing emphasis on tankerage of oil.[58])

Capital-output ratios have been calculated for the Plan. The overall capital coefficient for the three years is 3, but there is wide variation behind this coefficient. The coefficients are given in Table 10.8.

Table 10.8: Sectoral Breakdown of Overall Capital Coefficients, 1972-5 Plan

Sector	Capital Coefficient
Agriculture, forestry and fishing	8.5
Petroleum (private companies)	1.6
Transformation industry	10.5
Electric power	17.5
Transport, communications and storage	7.0
Housing	10.0
The national economy (excluding oil)	4.3
The national economy (including oil)	3.0

Source: Technical Planning Authority, *The Three-Year Plan for Development 1392/95 A.H.–1972/75 A.D.*, p.78.

The investment budget for the first year of the Plan amounts to LD367m. The pattern of distribution of investment by economic sector differs from that for the three years aggregated. For the first year, it is agriculture that receives the largest share of allocations, followed by housing, industry and mineral wealth, then transport and communication. Together these four sectors account for about 55 per cent of the investment planned. The sectoral structure is expected to change, but very slightly, between the base year, 1971/2, and the terminal year, 1974/5. This is understandable, considering the briefness of the intervening period. However, the most notable shift in the structure is the expected drop in the share of the oil sector from 56.4 per cent to 51.6 per cent — the largest shift in absolute terms. (Every other sector will gain except 'ownership of dwellings', which will lose 0.5 per cent.[59]) These structural change expectations are not sensational, but they are probably all that can realistically be expected.

Manpower development receives major emphasis and attention in the Three-Year Plan. This expresses itself in the programmes for education and training in order to raise the productivity of the work-force and its capability to absorb a modern technology. It also expresses itself in the energetic housing schemes that have been and are still to be undertaken, in health and other social services and benefits apart from education, and in the attempt to create as many new jobs as possible — a problem made all the more difficult by the large volume of underemployment and the high rate of population increase which is estimated at 3.7 per cent annually.

It is worth mentioning here that the revolutionary régime preaches the ethic of work very earnestly and is concerned about the strong tendency for a large part of the labour force to work in the petroleum sector or activities closely related to it. The fact that employment in the oil sector is very small compared with the size of the active labour force does not seem to have totally exploded the false hopes and expectations of many young Libyans. When frustrated, many go into government service, where they swell the ranks of the underemployed, rather than into productive employment in other sectors where a salary can only be earned through commensurate effort.

The investment programme of the public sector of the Three-Year Plan has undergone three increases since its formulation. The first was in the spring of 1973, when it was raised by about 70 per cent — from LD1,165m to LD1,965m. The main beneficiaries of the increase were agriculture (whose allocations almost quadrupled, rising to LD416m), industry (with a gain of LD235m), housing and utilities (up by LD193m), petroleum (up by LD124m), education and health (up by LD117m), and electricity (up by LD89m).[60] The second increase in allocations was made in January 1974, when the programme was revised upwards: from LD1,965m to LD2,115m (of which LD740m were earmarked for 1974, the second year of the Plan).[61] Finally, a third additional allocation of LD40.8m was made in September 1974, bringing the total investment programme in the Three-Year Plan to LD2,115.8m. An internal reallocation was also effected, whereby 1974, the second year, received an additional LD119.4m — presumably at the expense of the first year when the Plan was underfulfilled.[62]

As a final evaluation of the planning experience of Libya, it can be said that although the first efforts were not very determined and steadfast, and did not produce results that could be directly attributable to developmental planning, there are some attenuating circumstances for the shortfall. Foremost among these is the hectic activity of the sixties, as a result of the swift expansion in oil activities. On the one hand the abundance of financial resources masked the need for planning and spending discipline, and on the other the planning and execution agencies were not yet ready for higher-quality planning and plan implementation. Furthermore, these agencies operated within a political framework that lacked stability and participation — indeed, one which often exemplified divided loyalties, in the sense that the population felt alienated from its government because political leadership opted for political values, alignments and affinities distinctly different from those of much of the population. This applied to the intellectuals, the articulate semi-educated, and to a large proportion of what is designated as the 'masses'.

The latest plan, which went into implementation in 1972, corrects many of the shortcomings of earlier plans. Experience has been gained with regard to planning techniques, project studies, plan execution and follow-up. But, in addition, it would seem that the political framework is more amenable to planning discipline and to better execution. Alienation has by and large disappeared, motivation is growing, the civil service is more strongly aware of government's authority and more given to abide by professional, universalistic rules and norms. It would probably not be rash to say that planning and plan implementation are today bound to be less frustrating than in the sixties to the planners and to those who execute the plans alike, and even that planning is positively more efficient and effective.

However, on the negative side, government is conducted with outbursts of arbitrariness from time to time; a 'cultural revolution' unleashed in 1973 has created an atmosphere of insecurity and some disregard for professionalism; and — declarations and some measures to the contrary notwithstanding — excessive centralisation in the administration is a retarding factor to efficient plan execution. Finally, given the tight manpower bottlenecks, it is most unlikely that the very ambitious current investment programme could be put into effect on schedule.

5. LIBYA'S POST-WAR ECONOMY: DEVELOPMENTAL PARADOXES[63]

'From rags to riches' sums up Libya's economic fortunes of the past two decades. From a national product reputedly of LD15m in 1951 or 1952, upon independence, to a GNP of LD1,356m by the end of 1972 (and an estimated LD1,746m in 1974) is a quantified rephrasing of the shift in fortunes.[64] Yet behind this picture, which is simple in its contours and clear in its message, lie a number of qualifications, divergences and dislocations — and of paradoxes — that need to be examined in the context of and along with an examination of the record of achievement.

Earlier in this chapter the gross domestic product estimates for the years 1957-61 were reported, with the admission that the quality and reliability of these estimates were not high. The national accounts for the years 1962-71 are now available, at current prices and at constant (1964) prices.[65] If it is desired to have a long series stretching from 1957 to 1971, then this can be done for GDP estimates, with reservations regarding the quality of earlier data, as well as regarding the legitimacy of making a continuous series. In this case, the GDP at factor cost will be seen to have risen from LD43m to LD1,468.6m. The year-by-year figures are given in Table 10.9[66]

Table 10.9: Gross Domestic Product at Factor Cost, 1957-71 (LD million)

Year		Change (Per Cent)
1957	43.0	
1958	52.0	20.9
1959	56.0	7.7
1960	61.0	8.9
1961	70.0	14.7
1962	155.5	122.1
1963	235.3	51.3
1964	364.6	54.9
1965	492.1	35.0
1966	634.9	29.0
1967	747.8	17.8
1968	1,072.6	43.4
1969	1,223.0	14.0
1970	1,288.3	5.3
1971	1,468.6	14.0

Note: GDP at market prices for 1972 is recorded as LD1,599m in *International Financial Statistics*, December 1974.

The increase from 1961 to 1962 was the largest of all in relative terms, but all the subsequent years except 1963 and 1970 showed a larger absolute increase. However, the vast growth reflected in the data from 1962 onwards is misleading, since it incorporates the enormous rise in prices during that period.

Normally, a national accounts series at constant prices is more useful and meaningful for analysis purposes than one at current prices. However, in the case of Libya, the reverse is true. According to the official source from which these data have been taken '...the reliability of the estimates at constant prices must be lower than that of the estimates at current prices.'[67] This is attributable to the difficulty of establishing the correct price index deflators for each of the sectors. If the series at current prices is deflated by the price index, the result would be a series which is distinctly higher for every year than the series at constant prices as given in official sources. Thus, a comparison of the growth between 1962 and 1971 shows that this growth is 427 per cent higher when current prices are considered than when constant (1964) prices are considered. This difference of 427 per cent must presumably represent the rise in the price index between 1962 and 1971. However, the price index shows a rise of about 200 points only. (The index rose by 150 points between 1964, which is the base year of the new price index series, and the end of 1971; and it could not have risen by another 50 points between 1962 and 1964.)[68] The huge difference between the real growth as given in official sources, and that derived if the current price series is deflated by the reported price increase of 200 per cent must relate to the method of calculation of the price index. Bearing the size of the discrepancy in mind, we record in Table 10.10 the GDP at constant (1964) prices for the decade 1962-71.

Table 10.10: Gross Domestic Product at Constant (1964) Prices, 1962-71 (LD million)

Year		Growth (Per Cent)
1962	177.2	
1963	250.3	41.2
1964	364.2	45.6
1965	468.0	28.6
1966	557.2	19.0
1967	619.1	11.1
1968	835.3	35.0
1969	947.2	13.4
1970	993.3	4.9
1971	916.5	−7.7

Source: Calculations based on data in Table 10.9.

The compound growth rate per annum has been about 20 per cent on the average, with actual wide variations from year to year, as the calculation of the growth rate in the last column shows. Indeed, between 1970 and 1971 GDP in real terms dropped, owing to the reduction in oil production and export during 1971. Yet, the variations notwithstanding, the growth rate is high for all years except the last two. Even assuming as high a rate of population increase as 3.7 per cent per annum for the whole period, which is the rate presumed to be prevailing now in the early seventies, this would still leave the unusual rate of growth *per capita* of 15.7 per cent annually.

The fact that this high rate of growth owes its origin to the vast expansion in the country's earnings from the oil sector also explains the far-reaching changes in the structure of the economy between 1962 (or, more significantly, 1958, when oil was struck), and 1971. This change in structure can be seen in Table 10.11 where we present the contributions by sector, at current prices, for the three years 1958, 1962 and 1971.

Table 10.11: Distribution of Gross Domestic Product at Current Prices by Sector, for 1958, 1962 and 1971

Sector	1958		1962		1971	
	LD m	Per Cent	LD m	Per Cent	LD m	Per Cent
Agriculture, forestry and fishing	13.6	26.1	14.9	9.6	32.9	2.2
Petroleum mining	3.6[a]	6.9	38.0	24.4	920.5	62.7
Other mining and quarrying	3.6	6.9	0.6	0.4	2.2	0.1
Manufacturing	6.0	11.5	9.0	5.8	25.0	1.7
Construction	1.8	3.4	10.3	6.6	100.1	6.8
Electricity and gas	0.8	1.5	0.9	0.6	7.3	0.5
Transport and communications	2.9	5.6	8.6	5.5	63.7	4.3
Wholesale and retail trade	7.3	14.0	14.2	9.1	60.8	4.1
Banking and insurance	—[b]	—	1.7	1.1	11.6	0.8
Ownership of dwellings	5.9	11.3	29.4	18.9	66.9	4.6
Educational services	c		5.0	3.2	43.4	3.0
Health services	c		2.1	1.4	19.1	1.3
Public administration and defence	6.7	12.8	15.5	10.0	100.8	6.9
Other services	c		5.3	3.4	14.3	1.0
GDP at factor cost	52.2	100.0	155.5	100.0	1,468.6	100.0

a. For 1958, this item means 'petroleum prospecting'.
b. This item was insignificant for 1958. The sector as a whole contributes extremely little to GDP, mainly because it is underdeveloped and, until the revolution of 1969, most of the banks operating were foreign or branches of foreign institutions.
c. Education, health and other services were included under 'banking and insurance' and 'ownership of dwellings' in the accounts of 1958.
Sources: For 1958, *Statistical Abstract of Libya 1958-62;* for 1962 and 1971, *National Accounts of the Libyan Arab Republic 1962-1971,* pp.23 and 24.

Table 10.11 reveals that, with the exception of 'other mining and quarrying', whose contribution even in absolute terms dropped, and of 'electricity and gas' and 'banking and insurance', whose contribution in absolute terms rose by very little over the thirteen years in question, the other sectors have all registered vast expansion in their contribution. Ranked according to the size of increase in this contribution in absolute terms, the sectors are: petroleum, construction, public administration and defence, ownership of dwellings, transport and communications, education, agriculture, manufacturing and health services.

However, the structure expressed in percentage tells a different story. For, in spite of the vast expansion in absolute terms of the contribution of several sectors, in relative terms these sectors have dropped in importance. The most dramatic shift in relative terms has been the rise of the share of petroleum by 55.8 points. The balancing drop has been sustained mostly by agriculture (23.9 per cent), trade (9.9 per cent) and manufacturing (9.8 per cent), which together lost ground by 43.6 per cent. The remaining sectors account for the balance.

Though understandable and unavoidable, the extreme preponderance of the oil sector is none the less disturbing. Excessive dependence on one predominant source of income (and a depleting one at that) is a cause for anxiety to all oil-producing countries, even though now in the seventies it has become manifestly evident that they are in a favoured strong and competitive position versus the industrial, oil-importing countries. However, the anxiety stems from long-term economic considerations associated with the danger of a sluggish growth in non-oil sectors which may fail, when oil resources are depleted, to generate enough income to compensate for the drop of oil income at that future time. Socially, too, there is ground for anxiety, since the dependence on the oil sector, whose income flows into the treasury almost independently of the quality and intensity of the community's performance, tends to encourage the emergence of a *rentier* class and the transformation of the mass of the people into beneficiaries of liberal social and welfare services whose flow is adverse to productive effort to the extent that it remains unrelated to this effort.

Such thinking has guided the new leaders of the country into urging the people to work in non-oil, productive sectors. And, although the essential public services are made available free or at subsidised prices, largesse is avoided in order to immunise the population against over-dependence on the welfare state. In fact, the work ethic is given prominent place in the statements, speeches and exhortations of the present leaders, especially the Chairman of the Revolutionary Command Council. The attitude of the authorities has been made necessary by the tendency, which was first seen to emerge during the frenzied, large-scale operations of reconnaissance and exploration for oil, of a substantial part of the workforce to seek employment in the oil sector. When the activities in this sector became more stabilised, and the absorption of new labourers became extremely limited, many workers (including large numbers that had left the countryside for the cities) flocked into government service. They thus congested the civil service, particularly at the low levels of skill and responsibility. Understandably, this development causes great concern to the government.

Nevertheless, in spite of the awareness by the authorities of the implications of the present sectoral structure of the economy, the planners have reined in their expectations for dramatic corrective change in the near future. Indeed, the Plan document for the years 1972-5, in its projections of the relative shares of individual sectors and groups of sectors, only envisages a drop of 4.8 per cent in the contribution of oil between 1971/2, the base year, and 1974/5, the last year. The projections by sector and group are shown in Table 10.12.

It seems legitimate to assume that the drop in the share of petroleum from 56.4 to 51.6 per cent can only be the result of deliberate policy decisions purporting to curtail oil production, rather than of an increase in the share of the other sectors enough to raise their significance in the structure and thus reduce that of the oil sector by the percentage points indicated. Indeed, in a sense it must be frustrating for planners and economic decision-makers keen on diversifying the economy and on pushing the contribution of the non-oil sectors upwards to see the very sectors that they want primarily promoted reduced to insignificance, as in the case of agriculture, or restricted to a very minor place, as in the case of manufacturing industry.

The only commodity sector which escapes this predicament is construction, if we are to

Libya

Table 10.12: Change in the Structure of Gross Production between the Base Year 1971/2 and the Last Plan Year 1974/5 (percentages)

Economic Activity	Base Year 1971/2	Last Year 1974/5
Agriculture, forestry and fishing	2.3	2.5
Petroleum mining	56.4	51.6
Other mining	0.2	0.2
Transformation industries	2.7	3.6
Construction	10.2	12.5
Electricity	0.8	1.0
Total commodity sectors	72.6	71.4
Transport, communication and storage	4.2	4.8
Wholesale and retail trade	3.2	3.3
Total distribution sectors	7.4	8.1
Banking and insurance	0.9	1.0
Ownership of dwellings	3.8	3.3
Public services (excluding education and health)	10.4	10.8
Education services	2.6	3.0
Health services	1.4	1.5
Other services	0.9	0.9
Total service sectors	20.0	20.5
Total all sectors	100.0	100.0
of which petroleum	56.4	51.6
other sectors	43.6	48.4

Note: The table shows the structure of 'gross production', as the original in Arabic states. This explains the difference between the structure in this table and that in tables presenting GDP, whether at constant or at current prices.

Source: *The Three-Year Plan for Economic and Social Development 1392-1395 A. H. — 1972-1975 A. D.*, p. 22.

take the Three-Year Plan projections as an indication. But if we take what has happened between 1962 and 1971 as our guide, then this sector too has lost ground in relative terms. (The other two groups of sectors, distribution sectors and service sectors, remain largely unchanged in their relative significance.) The implications of the present situation, and even of the expected changes in the structure which Table 10.12 presents, are clear and far-reaching for a policy of diversification that is earnestly sought.

This discrepancy between what is desired and what is attained or even what is likely to be attained in the coming few years as a result of determined effort is but one of the dislocations that have been caused by oil — the very source of the country's prosperity.

458 Libya

We have had occasion to refer to one or two other dislocations, namely inflation and the enormous expansion of imports, for consumption as for investment. The inflationary pressure seems (according to official statistics) to have raised the price level by about 300 points between 1955 and the end of 1971, and by 13.6 points between 1970 and 1973. (The consumer price index rose by about 146 points by the end of 1963, and by 151 points between January 1964, when a new series was started, and the end of 1971.[69] We think that the price rises are understated, if only because of the limited representativeness of the consumption items included in the index and the official reluctance to admit the existence of a galloping inflation.)

The inflationary rise in prices represents a cumulative average increase by about 7 per cent per annum, which has occurred in spite of the fast growth in imports. The value of imports rose from LD14.4m in 1955 to LD235.4m in 1971 (or, if the imports of oil companies are included, to LD253.7m, fob). On the other hand, exports have dropped from LD4.3m in 1955 (when oil was not yet being produced and exported), to LD1.9m of exports plus re-exports, if oil is excluded.[70] However, the effectiveness of imports as a counter-inflationary measure has been limited by the oligopolistic structure of the wholesale import market. This structure was maintained and controlled before 1967 by Italian and Jewish traders, to the point where the government had to intervene. The intervention came in the form of a Libyanisation law in August 1967 which provided for the transfer of agencies to Libyans within two years, the setting of a ceiling of ten general agencies per importer, and other matters relating to mark-ups. The oligopolistic structure had already been a source of concern for several years. Thus, in a study prepared by the National Bank of Libya in 1961, it was emphasised that a small number of importers controlled a wide range of imports, and imposed prices which were high to an unwarranted degree. In 1965 a study prepared for the government by the Economist Intelligence Unit confirmed the earlier finding.[71] We can presume that the situation was largely the same in 1967 when the Law of August was passed.

The large expansion in imports has not led to a stringency in foreign exchange resources, because these had been rising by more than the rise in imports. Thus, the current account of the Libyan balance of payments which showed a deficit of about LD5m in 1954, and of LD11.5m in 1960, showed a surplus of LD4.5m for 1962. This surplus has been on the rise until it reached LD292.5m for 1971.[72] The picture improved considerably during 1974, although no data on the balance of payments are available to provide details. The cumulative surpluses have enabled the country to build up huge foreign assets. These assets amounted to LD14.9m at the end of 1956, but rose to LD1,200m by December 1974 (after foreign liabilities have been deducted).[73] Furthermore, it ought to be pointed out that not all the imports have been for consumption purposes. Indeed, consumer goods imports, which during most of the fifties constituted more than half total commodity imports, have fallen in relative significance since then. If the period 1954-71 is taken together, then the capital goods imported are found to be more than three-fifths of total imports. This is a commendable feature of the country's import activity, and it reflects the emphasis placed on the provision for investment projects of the capital goods they need. (The proportion of capital goods imports has dropped for 1973 owing to the faster expansion in consumer goods imports.)[74]

No doubt local production has risen — slowly and erratically for agricultural produce as a whole, whose index rose to 184 for 1972, with 1963 as base year, and for industry where value added rose by 66 per cent for 1970 over 1966.[75] Industry, which does not include petroleum and other mining, shows some stagnation for 1968-70. However, since

1971 there has been a marked expansion in industrial production, though this is not recorded in official publications. (These are slow in appearing. Thus, by the end of 1974, the most recent *Statistical Abstract* was that for 1971. Information in generally, non-quantified terms has had to be obtained through interviews.)

The growth of value added in the national accounts for the decade 1962-71 testifies to the expansion in agricultural and industrial production, and in construction, within the group of commodity sectors. Yet it must be pointed out that even in the case of manufacturing industry the growth rate is not substantial, while for agriculture it is very modest. Thus, to take the change in value added for each of these two sectors, agriculture has witnessed an expansion by 120.8 per cent at current prices, but only 15.6 per cent at constant (1964) prices between 1962 and 1971, while for manufacturing industry the total growth over the decade indicated has been 142.7 per cent and 121.0 per cent respectively. Apart from the better overall performance for industry, there is the added advantage of a steady, though not spectacular, growth from year to year, while in the case of agriculture there have been some sharp ups and downs along the slightly rising trend.[76]

One special aspect has to be focused upon here: the 'race between population and agricultural production' and the desire for the country to make production beat reproduction. The FAO records show that the index number *per capita* total agricultural production was 121 for 1972, compared with 1961-5 as base (and 114 for 1966 with 1952-6 as base), while the index number *per capita* for food production was 123 for 1972 compared with the base years 1961-5 (and 116 for 1966 with 1952-6 as base).[77] This record is not dramatically good, but certainly favourable in comparison with several other Arab countries. Nevertheless, the government is very eager to considerably promote agricultural (horizontal) expansion and (vertical) improvement: witness the large appropriations for the sector of agriculture in the Three-Year Plan, and the increase in appropriations in the amendments of 1973 to which reference has been made here. The emphasis on agriculture derives from a combination of long-term economic and social considerations that are high in the list of the preoccupations of the new leaders of Libya.[78]

The expansion in the production of goods and services domestically has been far from adequate for the vast expansion in effective demand for consumption and investment, both in the private and the public sectors. This expansion created increasing pressure for imports. Alongside this factor, there has been a clear shift from lower- to higher-quality consumer goods, as well as a demand for a larger range and variety of goods. (Likewise, the demand for foreign services, such as travel, education and medical treatment, has resulted in a faster growth of invisible imports than of invisible exports.)

The fact that imports absorbed a vastly increasing portion of the growing effective demand does not simply reflect the paucity of local resources other than oil, but also, and more seriously, the paucity of entrepreneurial resources and talent. This latter factor explains why more of the opportunities created simultaneously by the vast expansion of economic infrastructure, of credit facilities, and of effective demand remain inadequately exploited locally by entrepreneurial activity in the agricultural and industrial fields. However, the state is playing a role that is growing in scope and importance, in the developing of many agricultural projects, of which six are large, centring mainly on irrigation and land reclamation, as well as in building a number of industries related to oil as a raw material, and also in other areas of manufacturing.

Another aspect of government's promotive effort is its liberal financing policy for development projects in the private sector. Thus, loans outstanding by the National Agricultural Bank of Libya stood at LD18.2m by the end of March 1972. (Another indicator with respect to agriculture is the rise in the number of tractors and pumps, and in the use of insecticides, fertilisers, feed and equipment.) In addition, the commercial banks have been active in the extension of credit in the various sectors. Credit outstanding by the end of March 1972 totalled LD113.6m, spread over 21,360 individual loans. Industry, construction, transport and communications, agriculture, hotels and restaurants, and public utilities together account for LD43.6m or 38.4 per cent of the total. Trade receives the largest single share of credit.[79] (By May 1974, the claims of commercial banks on the private sector totalled LD306.6m, while those of the Development Bank reached LD25.3m by the fourth quarter of 1973.)[80]

The public developmental effort in general (whether in the provision of infrastructural investment or in other promotive measures) as well as the execution of many projects in the fields of agriculture, industry and housing are likely to have different effects. On the one hand, they may help to create a climate more conducive to the encouragement of private entrepreneurs, as a result of the earnestness and seriousness of the government's efforts manifest in many areas of action. But they might also inhibit private entrepreneurs who may suspect that the public sector might make arbitrary and unpredictable incursions into the areas of activity which they think had been assigned to them. With the ideological stance of the RCC rather vague in this respect, and with the decisions of this all-important body tending to be sudden, it is our feeling that the inhibiting effect of government activity on the private sector might well outweigh the promotive effect.

Another dislocation to which reference is made by some students of the Libyan economy is the growing inequality in income distribution. Here we feel on less secure ground, not being in possession of the statistical information that would make generalisation sufficiently warranted. Furthermore, it would seem to us that Libya did not witness the accumulation of huge private fortunes as a result of the oil gush as had Kuwait, Saudi Arabia and the other small Gulf oil areas. In the midst of these qualifying statements, it is probably safe only to note that the pattern of income distribution may have remained skewed, or may even have become more so, although an upward shift of the whole 'curve' has occurred, that is, the poor have become less poor and the rich richer. But it ought to be added that, unlike any major oil-producing country in the Mashreq, Libya is at present particularly careful not to allow the gross inequalities in income distribution to go uncorrected.

Two major correctives are direct taxation whose impact is real though not back-breaking, and strictness in the award of contracts and the supervision of large businessmen in order to safeguard against the accumulation of immense individual fortunes. No doubt this leaves the question of how much oil money is to seep through to the masses unsolved — a question to which we will address ourselves in the concluding section, and which is all the more relevant in the context of the austerity and puritanism of the ruling group currently in power.

Many Libyans, particularly in the business community, ask why they should be subjected to income and other direct taxes, considering the vast oil revenue and the relatively small population. The argument proceeds to state that government revenue from domestic sources has risen from LD4.9m for 1952/3 to LD200.7m for 1971/2, and LD231.9m for 1972/3.[81] (These data relate to the current revenue, apart from the allocations directed to the development budget.) Finally, it is added that in spite of the vast rise in government's current and development expenditures combined, huge foreign assets have been built up, all of which goes to prove that the government is not seriously in need of taxpayers' money which, for 1972/3, is estimated at LD17.2m only.

The government, on the other hand, has two main considerations in mind in imposing direct taxes on citizens. The first is that petroleum is a depleting resource, and that sooner or later the country will have to rely to an increasing extent on sources of revenue other than oil. This consideration is based on a long time horizon, which businessmen usually ignore in favour of the present. The second point raised by responsible government officials is that the population ought not to get accustomed to the receipt of welfare services and to the provision of a vast economic and social infrastructure without a feeling of personal financial responsibility and participation, no matter how modest, and that it is important for the social and psychological health of the nation for the citizens to recognise that they have to shoulder some tax duties against the rights and privileges which they enjoy.

The last area of achievement relates to population. Thanks to improved health and sanitation conditions, and to advances in preventive and curative medicine, the natural rate of population increase has risen substantially since independence to about 3.7 per cent, and subsequently to 4.2 per cent per annum.[82] This rate is not disturbing at the present moment if attention is focused on the small absolute size of population as such. Related to this is the fact that the land-man ratio is not very unfavourable in spite of the paucity of rainfall (over 1 ha of arable land per inhabitant, or 3.5 ha per rural inhabitant).[83]

However, a number of problems are associated with the growth, movements, education and training of the population. The rising rate of growth itself ought to be a cause for concern and a heavy burden inasmuch as it will for many years raise the ratio of dependants to earners in the population, and require a large outlay for schooling, medical care and housing. All three areas are now the beneficiaries of concentrated attention and large investment funds, as we will see shortly. Another area of concern is the high degree of urbanisation that has accompanied the oil era. Thus, although precise information is not available, it is believed that the urban population has increased from 25 per cent in the fifties to about 70 per cent by the end of the sixties. The speed of this process of urbanisation has caught the towns and cities utterly unprepared in terms of houses, schools, health centres, water, electricity, sewerage and other amenities. But investment has been energetically directed to the satisfaction of the new needs, as the investment pattern over the past half-decade shows. Many of the projects in the new Three-Year Plan also aim at repairing the dislocations caused by the very fast urbanisation. The projects are of two types: preventive and curative, if the designation is permissible.

The preventive projects are ones which aim at developing the countryside, and making it more comfortable and rewarding for the rural community to avoid urbanisation, and even making it attractive for many peasants who have moved to urban centres, and whose exaggerated rosy expectations have not been satisfied, to move back. This group of projects includes the provision of water and electricity, schools and hospitals, roads and, essentially, more work opportunities in agriculture and other activities. The curative projects purport to expand the amenities and facilities which are under strain and pressure in the cities. Furthermore, this category of projects includes the expansion in job opportunities in the commodity sectors in or near the urban centres.

The provision of water for urban use is among the large beneficiaries of investment allocations. The major work in this field has been a desalination plant in Benghazi with a capacity of 4.3m gallons a day, the construction of which was started in 1969 — apart from a number of other projects all over the country, in urban as well as rural centres. Likewise the building of electricity-generating plants is actively pursued. The investment programme of the Three-Year Plan reflects the emphasis on power along with other infrastructural investments. (Several new projects in the area of public utilities have been contracted for or initiated in 1973 and 1974.)[84]

Housing began receiving attention and investment allocations in the early years of independence. Thus, in the years 1954-7, a few hundred housing units were constructed to replace very old ones that had crumbled or been destroyed, while in the years 1958-63 the pace of construction did not accelerate, but emphasis shifted to the building of houses for government officials. The years 1963-8, which coincided with the First Five-Year Plan, witnessed an acceleration in housing efforts, and some 2,000 units were built annually for lower-income groups under Plan allocations. Then in the years 1969-72 the performance rose to about 6,000 units annually. Finally, reports published in 1974 point to a more ambitious programme, but to a slower performance. Thus, while 10,933 units were contracted for (for 1971), only 4,212 were completed. (A further 18,353 units were contracted for in 1972, plus an additional 10,000 units of prefabricated housing for Tripoli and Benghazi. However, the report is silent on performance.)[85]

The future plans are based on the expectation of the construction annually of 12,000 units during the Three-Year Plan, and of 20,000 units thereafter, until the point is reached when adequate housing is available for the increase in population as well as for the growing demand for independent living by newly married couples and for better-quality housing by the lower-income groups. (In 1970 the government issued a law setting rental levels, and in 1972 another piece of legislation was issued permitting the government to buy land in order to forestall speculation in land and to acquire the necessary areas for housing and public building purposes.)[86] In the light of recent experience, it seems doubtful that the physical targets indicated can be met on time.

Finally, education. Here again, as in almost all the countries included in this study, we see the large strides taken in the field of education, not only in quantitative but also in qualitative terms. Thus, in the year preceding World War Two, when the country was under Italian occupation, there were in all 15,726 pupils at all levels of schooling. The number rose to 36,887 (including 4,995 girls) by the first year of independence, 1951/2. The expansion in numbers between 1951/2 and 1972/3 represents an enormous jump indeed, for the number of elementary pupils alone in the latter year was 461,962 (of whom 3,674 were in private schools), while that of pupils in the intermediate and secondary cycle (including technical education, but excluding 6,056 in teachers' institutes) totalled 70,491 (of whom only 733 were in private schools). The total school population numbers 542,422 pupils, including first stage (kindergarten) and teachers' institutes. Regrettably, there is no breakdown by sex for 1972/3, but girls represented 37 per cent of the total for 1971/2.[87] These statistics indicate that around 86 per cent of the children of school age were in school in the academic year 1972/3, but, considering the smaller percentage of girls than of boys in school, it would seem that almost all the boys who are 'schoolable' are actually in school, whereas about three-fifths of the 'schoolable' girls are in school. This is a remarkable achievement of which Libya can be rightly proud.

Where curricula and methods of education are concerned, the performance is less satisfactory. But here again, what should be considered is *not* how Libya stands *vis-à-vis* the Scandinavian countries, or some very advanced schooling system around the Harvard or Princeton community, but *vis-à-vis* the rest of the Arab world and its own immediate past. Here we find that the country has made great progress in terms of the quality of education, compared with the level and content of education just before, and just after, independence. However, the education system must move further ahead fast if it is to compare favourably with some of the Arab countries, and more specifically with its Maghreb neighbours.

Outside the two first cycles of general education, Libya now provides professional and vocational training, teacher training, and higher (third-cycle) education. In each of these areas the development has been speedy. Thus, in order to train the teachers who would be able to expand schooling opportunities, teachers' training institutes were established as far back as 1947/8, when one institute with 4 teachers and 20 male trainees was founded. Since then, the number has risen considerably, to reach 701 teachers and 6,056 trainees.[88]

Technical training consists of three parts: industrial, commercial and agricultural. All three branches had 3,202 students (at the intermediate and secondary levels) and 376 teachers during 1971/2. (The number of trainees dropped to 2,360 while that of teachers rose to 437 for 1972/3.) Evidently, the level of the training provided is rather low, preparing workers in the three areas mentioned, but not skilled overseers and technicians in the proper sense of the term.

Higher education started modestly in the year 1955/6 by the establishment of a college of letters, which was followed two years later by a college of commerce and economics and a college of science. In 1961 a faculty of engineering was established, and in 1965/6 a faculty of education. All these colleges (or faculties) were grouped to form the Libyan University in its two locations at Benghazi and Tripoli. The university now also has a new faculty of medicine, a faculty of law, and a faculty of agriculture, while the names of some of the older colleges have changed. Numerically, the student body increased from 31 in the year 1955/6 to 8,220 in the year 1972/3. This number, however, includes regular students in attendance as well as external students. The Libyan component of the faculty consisted of 83 members in 1971/2, or 19.3 per cent of the total teaching force. With few exceptions in some of the faculties, university education suffers from the same shortcomings common to the national universities in the Mashreq, though to a much larger degree. What is even more disturbing is that 'corrective measures' seem to be slow, inadequate and undertaken in an inappropriate setting. Thus, the recent 'cultural revolution' which extended to the universities weakened discipline, damaged the image of faculty, watered down curricula, set student committees up as judges of what books ought to be used and what books ought to be discarded in the libraries, and demoted academic excellence as a standard of measurement.

Finally, adult education. Here it is found that the effort expended is not reflected in the number of adult students. Thus, these totalled 37,170 in the year 1970/1, and it is believed that the drop-out rate among them is high. The hope of the nation in further lowering the level of illiteracy must therefore essentially rest with the spread of education among school-age children.

There is one other aspect of population which ought to be examined here — manpower. Estimates of the labour force, both total and active, were at best estimates of varying degrees of reliability and credibility before the population census of 1964 and 1973. According to the 1964 census, the total population was 1,564,369, out of which those citizens six years of age and over numbered 1,182,194. More than half of this latter figure, or 794,495 (67.2 per cent) are designated 'not in labour force' — a category which consists essentially of women, plus all those whose age or state of health disqualifies them from work capability. The category designated labour force (excluding expatriates) numbered 387,699 — 32.8 per cent of the population six years of age and over, or 24.8 per cent of total population. But only 30 per cent of the labour force were actually employed. The balance of 2.8 per cent, numbering 33,596 persons, was designated as seeking work. But in fact, if those below 15 years of age and those above 65 years of age are excluded from the labour force, which is legitimate, we would be left with a total labour force of 349,748 persons, representing 22.6 per cent of total population. This is understandably a very low proportion.

Observers agree that the level of unemployment and of underemployment among this already small labour force is high. The main cause for this phenomenon is the initially excessive portion of the labour force in agricultural activities. At the time of independence the agricultural labour force (whether as owners, tenants or wage labourers) was believed to be as high as 70 per cent. Obviously underemployment, and outright unemployment, accounted for this high percentage in a country with limited land resources like Libya. The subsequent shift to non-agricultural activities as a result of the oil and construction boom led to a significant restructuring in the labour force. Already in 1964 the labour force in agriculture had dropped to 37 per cent of the total — to present just one illustration of the shift. By 1968, the last year for which we have some tentative estimates, the pattern had more or less stabilised along the lines of the pattern of 1964, with a few shifts of minor significance, as Table 10.13 shows. (The published preliminary results of the 1973 census do not include data on the labour force.)

Table 10.13: The Distribution of the Active Libyan Labour Force by Sector (in percentages)

Sector	1964	1968
Agriculture, forestry and fishing	37.0	32.5
Mining and quarrying (including petroleum)	3.0	4.3
Manufacturing industry	6.8	8.4
Building and construction	7.7	11.7
Electricity, gas, water and sanitary services	1.5	1.8
Trade	6.4	7.4
Transport, communication and storage	5.6	8.3
Other services and activities not adequately described	31.9	25.6
Total (rounded)	100.0	100.0

Note: For 1964, 'other services' account for 20 per cent, while 'activities not adequately described' account for 11.9 per cent. But in the 1968 data the latter category does not appear, and 'other services' account for 25.6 per cent.

Sources: For 1964, *Statistical Abstract 1969*, p. 48; for 1968, Ali Ahmed Attiga, *The Impact of Petroleum on the Libyan Economy, 1956-1969* (Dar at-Tali'a, Beirut, 1972; Arabic), p. 120, quoting the Census and Statistical Department without further specification.

In addition to the Libyan labour force, Libya also had in 1964 a small-sized 'alien' labour force numbering 17,559. Over one-fourth of the latter group were in service sectors outside of trade and transport and communications — probably in professional and technical services, as doctors, engineers, teachers, nurses, and the like. The next-largest group was in manufacturing, and the one after in mining and quarrying — mainly in the petroleum sector. The female members of the expatriate labour force constituted 17.2 per cent of the total, while among the Libyans the females constituted no more than 5.1 per cent. Most Libyan women actively employed and included in census figures were in manufacturing industry (39.2 per cent), while services accounted for 23.3 per cent and agriculture for 15.3 per cent.[89] The high concentration in industry probably means employment in crafts and cottage industry, or else in very unskilled work in mechanised industry.

What is most significant with regard to the expatriate labour force, though it is small in absolute size, is that most of its members fall in the categories of craftsmen and production process workers; professional, technical and related skills; and clerical workers. Together these account for about two-thirds of the total. If the distribution of citizens and aliens in the various occupations is considered, it is found that the aliens do not constitute a substantial proportion in any occupation, not even the high-level professional, technical or administrative occupations. This situation is quite different from that in Kuwait and — to a lesser extent — in Saudi Arabia. But it must be remembered that the total expatriate labour force in Libya is tiny in comparison with that in Kuwait. This seemingly healthy situation hides a factor which acts as a deterrent to development, to the extent that Libya has not yet developed the varied and numerous skills in the volume which a modernising economy requires, yet it has not been very encouraging to the inflow of expatriate skills.

Now, by 1976, the country is known to have a much larger expatriate labour force than it did in 1964. But this force is predominantly Arab (mostly Egyptian). Its contribution to economic life is considerable. This factor notwithstanding, in Libya one meets with the paradox of abundance and scarcity of labour at the same time. This is true not only in the sense that skilled manpower is in short supply simultaneously with the abundance of unskilled manpower, but also in another serious sense. This is that even given the skills available, imperfection in the labour market, insufficient job information, or other rigidities related to cultural blocks against certain types of work or insistence on certain fields or locations of work, mean that some jobs go unfilled although they can be filled from the labour reservoir avilable. Although this is but one small impediment to development, it supplements the overall evaluation that unless manpower skills and attitudes change appropriately and speedily, and civil service and government adjust to the needs of a modernising society, the development of Libya is bound to remain slow no matter how fast and dramatically its financial opulence proceeds.

6. CONCLUDING REMARKS

At the risk of oversimplification, one can sum up Libya's economic experience in the 30 years since the end of World War Two as one of paradoxes and surprises. In 1946 Libya was still licking the deep wounds cut into its economy and manpower by a cruel, self-centred colonialism which had neglected the real interests of the national population, present and long-term, and had savagely repressed the people's brave and determined struggle for independence. The economy's deeper wounds were suffered during the war between the Axis powers and the Allies. In both experiences, it was Cyrenaica's misfortune to be hurt much more than the two other provinces, first during the war of liberation, the bulk of the burden and sacrifices of which it bore, and then during World War Two, the fiercest and most destructive battles of which took place on its territory.

Not endowed with any natural resources of great value and extent — as far as was visible in 1946 — Libya emerged from colonialism and war as a very poor country, but more seriously as one over the health and viability of which very gloomy judgements were passed. Into this setting came a United Nations trusteeship delegated to Britain and France, two colonial powers which, in the typical tradition of colonialism, were not known to take much fancy to international developmental responsibility unless it happened first to serve their military, political and/or economic interests. Consequently the country was run only on 'a care and maintenance basis' (a judgement which we quoted earlier), and, although the dual administration of the two Western European powers did not run in the grooves set by

Italian colonialism before, the new 'heirs' merely behaved like a tenant who knows that his tenure is very brief and therefore not worth the investment of much effort.

The economy was a little better off in this period, which lasted from the beginning of 1943 to the end of 1951, but only with respect to the availability of slightly higher income thanks to the assistance made by the two powers. On the other hand, the economy was slightly worse off owing to the destruction during wartime of much of its infrastructure and the damage caused to its agriculture through neglect and destruction. On balance, Libya may have been very marginally better off — probably the improvement could best be expressed in saying that the economy shifted from being 'not viable' to 'possibly viable'.

Then came independence, and with it came, in the fifties, two new factors: foreign 'support' — or more correctly foreign payments by the United Kingdom and the United States against their infringement of national sovereignty (with the government's acquiescence) through the maintenance of military bases there; and the widespread and frenzied search for oil by a legion of oil companies, major and small alike. In both instances, the income injected into the economic system was substantial, in the context of Libya's scale of financial resources. Thus the equilibrium at a low level of income and resources was disturbed, first gently and then with great force.

The government and the political system at large, and the civil service, were totally unprepared for the new tasks, whether these were the routine management of the economy or the handling of the new problems such as inflation and dislocation of resources, and fast-growing imports at the expense of local production, or the charting of a sound course of development. Inevitably the authorities had to co-operate with agencies representing Britain and the United States, and with United Nations agencies. This was a period when growth did occur, but largely *in spite* of the style of economic management by government and private entrepreneurs alike, rather than because of it.

Libya continued to witness fast transformation in the sixties and down to the present, except that this was at a much higher rate. But the most sensational and dramatic difference from the fifties was that the transformation was now supported by a major national resource, oil, and its steeply growing revenues to government. Growth rates rose to dizzying heights. But again, the government, in spite of certain improvements, continued to be incapable of coping with the new situation with all its opportunities and challenges — at least during the first half of the sixties. It was only later in the decade that the political system became capable of controlling the situation to a reasonable extent and of managing the economy with more efficiency and effectiveness. But it was in late 1969, and from then onwards, that the control and the management became firmer, more clearly focused and oriented, and better based, if only because it enjoyed wider popular support thanks to the government's greater effort to widen the socio-economic opportunities open to the people.

This summary repeats some of the statements and judgements made earlier in the chapter. But this is necessary for a better understanding of the great contrast between the situation at the end of 1942, when the Italians disappeared as rulers, and as it stood in 1975. Taking the economic and the political indicators together, we can assert that Libya has moved a considerable distance ahead in the direction of social and economic development. Its rate of progress is remarkable, given the disadvantages with which it had to contend upon independence.

However, the right contrast to make is not simply one between 1942, or 1951, and the present, but also between Libya's endowments on the one hand and its problems on the other. The critical factor which will decide how well the endowments will be used in solving the problems and facing the challenges, and positively in expediting the social and economic progress of the country towards productive efficiency and high performance, social justice, satisfactory levels of living for the large masses and cultural fulfilment — the crucial and critical factor is manpower and government. All revolves on the quality of manpower, of government, and of the civil service in the several years to come.

Several questions are related, directly or indirectly, to this central question of manpower and of government. For instance, recognising the long-term significance for the country of developing its own skilled cadres and becoming self-sufficient with regard to manpower, what policy should Libya in the meantime devise and pursue with regard to the entry of skilled manpower, so that the developmental tasks may not go unperformed? In the second place, how is the government to reconcile its understandable desire to provide maximum employment in the civil service in order to combat urban unemployment, even if in part, with its legitimate desire to encourage employment outside government in the productive sectors, while these sectors still have a very low absorptive capacity for more labour?

A major question relating to the population at large revolves around the clash between the official desire to enable the Libyans to benefit from generous welfare benefits, and the simultaneous desire to emphasise effort and the connection between benefits and work. Then there is the additional question as to how more of the oil money is to seep through to the broad masses, without turning them into the beneficiaries of financial largesse, which would entail the risk of their becoming heavily dependent and flabby. The policy-maker faces the two horns of a painful dilemma here, being eager on the one hand to reduce poverty and being unable, on the other hand, to do so through the provision of remunerative jobs to all or most able-bodied Libyans. For it is quite obvious that the increase in the national product moves leaps and bounds ahead of the increase in employment. It is true that the labour force has been inclined to eschew work in agriculture, or in jobs involving physical hardship. But even if this tendency were reversed, it remains true that work opportunities are not capable of meeting the supply of labour, and with the fast expansion of secondary and higher education, the problem is likely to become more acute and pressing, at least for some time.

The listing of such issues is enough to suggest that there is no clear and quick answer. But then Libya is much more favoured than many other developing countries which have the problems but not the means to face them. Thus, given Libya's financial resources, and its development-oriented government, and given the soundness of the directions in which public thinking and policy are moving, Libya will be able in a decade or two to expand its productive capacity outside the oil sector enough to face its serious manpower problem. To achieve this, care must be taken not to allow the feeling of dependence on government and its social services to become more pronounced. Simultaneously, education and training should be restructured to produce the manpower attitudes and skills which the pattern of development requires. And, since an enormous responsibility in this respect rests on the shoulders of the government and the civil service, here, too, these two institutions should prepare themselves to cope with their developmental tasks at all levels — from conception to planning, execution, follow-up and re-evaluation. Finally, government must draw the frontiers of a clear economic policy within which the private sector can see its place and role and, thus seeing, can feel confident enough to apply its entrepreneurial abilities within its field of activity. This naturally implies the avoidance of abrupt, half-studied and arbitrary decisions, and an option for pragmatism and flexibility within the ideological framework which the revolutionary government has formulated for the society.

The tasks are enormous. But it would seem to be that Libya is showing its capability of coping with them. There is more in this assertion than a statement of faith. There are enough objective indicators to suggest that Libya stands a good chance of turning its oil wealth into a sound process of development where the non-oil sectors will soon be able to reach a satisfactory level of performance — though this performance may be preceded by an arduous experience of 'trial and error'.

NOTES

1. Benjamin Higgins, *Economic Development Principles, Problems, and Policies* (New York, 1959), p. 37.

2. Professor Higgins led a UN economic survey mission to Libya, which visited the country in 1951-2, that is, upon independence. The findings and suggestions of the mission were incorporated into a United Nations report entitled *The Economic and Social Development of Libya* (New York, October 1953).

3. This was John Lindberg, who reported to the UN slightly earlier than Higgins did. See United Nations, *A General Economic Appraisal of Libya* (New York, 1952).

4. IBRD, *The Economic Development of Libya* (Baltimore, 1960).

5. Egypt and other Arab countries east of it are grouped in common usage as 'Mashreq' countries, while Libya and countries west of it are grouped as 'Maghreb' countries. However, Libya is often excluded from the latter group by writers who understand the 'Maghreb' group to consist of the three countries formerly under French rule: Tunisia, Algeria and Morocco, without necessarily being included in the 'Mashreq' group. It thus is often left in an indeterminate category.

6. The discussion of the background to the independence era, as of the independence era itself, draws on the two UN reports and the IBRD survey to which reference has already been made. Four newer books have been of great help to this writer: (a) Abdul-Amir Q. Kubbah, *Libya: Its Oil Policy and Economic System* (Baghdad, 1964); (b) Rawle Farley, *Planning for Development in Libya: The Exceptional Economy in the Developing World* (Praeger, New York, 1971); (c) Ahmad Ali Attiga, *The Impact of Petroleum on the Libyan Economy, 1956-1969* (Dar at-Tali'a, Beirut, 1972; Arabic); and (d) Europa, *The Middle East and North Africa 1971-72: A Survey and Reference Book* (London, 1972); *1972-73* (1973); *1973-74* (1974); and *1974-75* (1975), chapter on 'Libya'. Unfortunately, the economic literature on Libya is very scanty.

7. IBRD, op. cit., p. 27.

8. Europa, *1971-72*, p. 451 (emphasis mine).

9. IBRD, op. cit., in several parts of Chs. 1 and 3, but especially Ch. 6.

10. *Comparative Statistical Data on Education in the Arab States — An Analysis: 1960-61 — 1967-68* (Prepared by the Office of Statistics of UNESCO, Paris, for the Conference of Ministers of Education and Ministers Responsible for Economic Planning in the Arab States, Marrakesh, 12-22 January 1970. Published by the Regional Center for Educational Planning and Administration, Beirut; 1969), p. 49.

11. Ministry of National Economy, Census and Statistical Department, *Statistical Abstract of Libya 1958-1962*, pp. 145-6.

12. See Attiga, op. cit., Ch. 2, and IBRD, op. cit., Chs. 1 and 2.

13. The situation in Libya (as in such countries like Kuwait, Abu Dhabi and Saudi Arabia) conforms to a model of development with 'unlimited supplies of finance', which is the reverse of Arthur Lewis's famous model in his article 'Economic Development with Unlimited Supplies of Labour', in *The Manchester School of Economic and Social Studies*, May 1954, pp. 139-91. See in this connection, Farley, op. cit., Ch. 10, and his reference to Libya's case as that of the 'super-affluent poor society' (Ch. 4).

14. See IBRD, op. cit., pp. 44-5, in this connection.

15. The total was arrived at by perusal of IBRD, op. cit., Table S. 1, p. 347, Table 1, p. 48, and pp. 38-9, as well as Europa, op. cit., 'Libya'. For actual receipts (as against allocated funds) and for development expenditure by the various agencies, see Bank of Libya, *The Development of Public Finance in Libya, 1944-1963* (Tripoli, August 1965), quoted in Farley, op. cit., p. 177.

16. Attiga, op. cit., p. 44 (quoting the Oil Ministry and the Bank of Libya).

17. Ibid., p. 52.

18. Bank of Libya, *Economic Bulletin*, Vol. X, No. 2 (quoted in ibid., p. 65).

19. Ministry of National Economy, Census and Statistical Department, *Statistical Abstract 1963*, p. 16.

20. Bank of Libya, *The Development of Public Finance in Libya, 1944-1963*, p. 43.

21. *Statistical Abstract of Libya 1958-1962*, pp. 145-6.

22. *Statistical Abstract 1965*, pp. 4 and 11.

23. See IBRD, op. cit., Annex XVI, p. 478, for electric power generation in 1958; Farley, op. cit., pp. 155-6 for generation in 1965. It should be noted that power sold was distinctly less than power generated. For information on water supply, IBRD, op. cit., Annex XXIII; and for data on water supply in Tripoli city for 1958 and 1961 see *Statistical Abstract 1969*, p. 195.

24. Farley, op. cit., p. 172.

25. Ibid., pp. 176-8, regarding the planning experience of the country during the first independence decade.

26. IBRD, op. cit., p. 56.

27. See Ministry of Planning, *National Accounts of the Libyan Arab Republic 1962-1971* (October 1972), Table 3a, p. 28.

28. For local company spending, see Attiga, op. cit., p. 44; for budget comparisons, see Bank of Libya, *The Development of Public Finances in Libya 1944-1963*, p. 43.

29. Revolutionary Command Council, 'The Constitutional Announcement', 11 December 1969, pamphlet

issued by the Libyan Cultural Center.

30. Farley, op. cit., p. 267.
31. Europa, *1971-72*, p. 457.
32. *Statistical Abstract 1969*, p. 6. The details of the new census (undertaken on 31 July–1 August 1973) are not yet available.
33. Observation made by Dr Ali A. Attiga, in Attiga, op. cit., pp. 29-30.
34. Apart from official documents relating to the legislation governing activities in the oil sector, see Kubbah, op. cit., Ch. 3; Farley, op. cit., Ch. 6; and Attiga, op. cit., Ch. 3.
35. For a detailed discussion of the controversy around the law of 1965 and the role of the companies in its shaping, see Farley, op. cit., Ch. 9.
36. Farley, op. cit., pp. 220-1, quoting *News from Libya*, IV, 12 (May 1958), pp. 15-16.
37. The estimates vary between one source and another, such as British Petroleum, *BP Statistical Review of the World Oil Industry 1972* and *1973* (from which the estimates for 1972 and 1973 are reproduced); *Arab Oil and Gas (AOG)* (Vol. IV, No. 81, 1 February 1975), p. 32; and *Middle East Economic Survey (MEES)*, Vol. XVIII, No. 18, 21 February 1975, p. vi. We adopted the estimate of *AOG* for 1974, as it appears in tons per year rather than as barrels per day.
38. Revenue for 1973 and 1974 is an estimate. See Dr Nicolas Sarkis, 'The Energy Crisis and the Challenge of Development in the Arab Countries', Paper No. 132 (A-1) for the Ninth Arab Petroleum Congress held in Dubai, 10-16 March 1975.
39. *Oil and Gas Journal*, 28 December 1970.
40. Ministry of Planning, *National Accounts of the Libyan Arab Republic 1962-1971* (October 1972), pp. 23-4. For a slightly higher estimate for 1971, see *International Financial Statistics (IFS)*, December 1974, under 'Libya'. The estimate for 1973 is quoted from Sarkis, loc. cit., Table 4, p. 19 (in turn quoting IBRD, *Annual Report 1974*; UN, *Monthly Bulletin of Statistics*, December 1974; and *IFS*, November 1974, for the table). The estimate for 1974 is made by the present writer.
41. For the period ending 1963, see the National Bank of Libya (later the Bank of Libya), *Economic Bulletin*. For 1964-72 and 1973, see *IFS*, July 1973 and December 1974, under 'Libya'.
42. *National Accounts . . . 1962-1971*, pp. 23-4, and *IFS*, December 1974.
43. I have followed the description of this UN plan by Farley, op. cit., pp. 164-5. Throughout the examination of Libya's planning experience, from 1951 through the 1963-68 Plan, I have relied heavily on Farley's discussion in Ch. 8. For planning since 1969, other sources have been perused and will be indicated as the occasion arises.
44. See IBRD, op. cit., Ch. 5.
45. Farley (op. cit., p. 195) served in Libya in the period 1964-6 as UN Development and Planning Expert and Senior Economist at the Ministry of Planning and Development.
46. Farley, op. cit., pp. 197-8. The criticism of Higgins refers to the latter's very pessimistic outlook in the report he prepared as Chief Economist of the UN mission of 1951.

47. Ministry of Planning and Development, *Five-Year Economic and Social Development Plan 1963-1968* (Tripoli, undated), pp. 10-11.
48. Technical Planning Authority, Directorate-General, Economic and Social Planning, *Survey of the National Economy of the Libyan Arab Republic 1964-1968* (undated), pp. 121, 123.
49. Ibid., p. 51.
50. Ministry of Planning and Development, *Second Five-Year Economic and Social Development Plan 1969-1974*.
51. Kingdom of Libya, Ministry of Planning and Development, *Second Five-Year Plan, Details of the Development Budget for the Financial Year 1969/1970* (Tripoli; Arabic), pp. 2-6.
52. Libyan Arab Republic, *Details of the Development Budget for the Financial Year 1390/1391 (1 April 1970–31 March 1971)*, (Tripoli; Arabic), p. 2.
53. Libyan Arab Republic, *Details of the Development Budget for the Financial Year 1391/1392 AH, 1971/1972 AD* (1 April 1971–31 March 1972), (Tripoli, Arabic), p. 2.
54. Law Published in *Official Gazette*, Volume 10, No. 28 of 26 June 1972. The detailed Plan document is entitled *The Three-Year Plan for Economic and Social Development 1392-95 A. H.–1972-75 A. D.* (published by the Technical Planning Authority; Arabic). The discussion of the Plan draws on this document, except for recent adjustments undertaken in the spring of 1973 and reflected in the Plan which include a change in its coverage (from 1 April–31 December 1973, through 1974 and 1975) as well as size of the investment programme (raised from LD1,165m to LD1,965m for the public sector.) For the revised plan, see Ministry of Information and Culture, The General Administration for Information, *The Revolution of 1st September: The Fourth Anniversary* (undated), p. 8.
55. This allocation was decreed by Law No. 57 of 27 April 1972, published in *Official Gazette*, op. cit. The detailed plan for 1972/3 appears in Technical Planning Authority, *The Three-Year Plan for Development 1392/95 A. H.–1972/75 A. D.; The Development Budget for the First Year 1392-93 A. H.–1972-73 A. D.* (Tripoli; Arabic). Since then, allocations for 1974 and 1975 have been increased substantially even beyond the revised figures (see note 54 above). But we will not pursue the frequent upward adjustments.
56. *The Three-Year Plan . . . 1392-95 A. H.–1972-75 A. D.*, p. 88.
57. Ibid., p. 67.
58. The pattern of planned public investment for the first year differs from the aggregated three-year pattern. Agriculture receives the largest share in the first-year projections, followed by industry and mineral wealth, and transport and communications. (See *The Development Budget for the First Year . . .*, p. 2.)
59. *The Three-Year Plan . . .*, p. 22.
60. See The Arab Libyan Republic, *The Revolution of 1st September: The Fourth Anniversary*, p. 8.
61. See *MEES*, Vol. XVII, No. 14, 25 January 1974, pp. 10 and 12.
62. Ibid., Vol. XVII, No. 47, 13 September, p. 1.
63. See in this connection Farley, op. cit., Chs. 9 and 10. Dr Farley puts his finger on some of the most serious

dislocations and contradictions that have burdened Libya in its march towards development. His particular emphasis is on the unusual coexistence of affluence and poverty, very fast growth of resources and underdevelopment.

64. The GNP at factor cost for 1971 is at current prices. It is reported at LD716m at constant (1964) prices. Even the latter is about 48 times the national product for 1951. See *National Accounts for the Libyan Arab Republic 1962-1971*, pp. 24 and 93. *IFS*, December 1974, quotes GNP for 1972 at current prices. My estimate for 1974.

65. *National Accounts... 1962-1971*, pp. 23-4 for the accounts at current prices, and pp. 92-3 at constant 1964 prices. (The 1971 estimates are stated to be provisional.)

66. *IFS*, July 1973, reports the GDP at current prices slightly differently – on the whole higher by about 3-4 per cent. The *IFS* data follow the UN System of National Accounts.

67. *National Accounts... 1962-1971*, p. 9.

68. See *IFS*, July 1973, under 'Libya'.

69. See Table 23 in the Statistical Appendix of the *Economic Bulletin* of the Bank of Libya, Vol. 12, No. 3 (May-June 1972) for the index number average for 1963. This index number measures the movement in the prices of foodstuffs in Tripoli city. For 1964-71, see *IFS*, July 1973, 'Libya', and for 1970-3, see *IFS*, December 1974. There is no indication here whether the index number relates to the whole of Libya, or to Tripoli alone.

70. For 1955, see Attiga, op. cit., p. 190; for 1971, see Table 24 in *Economic Bulletin*, op. cit.

71. National Bank of Libya, *Inflation in Libya* (March, 1961; Arabic), pp. 32-3, 58 ff. The reference to the Economist Intelligence Unit comes from Attiga, op. cit., Ch. 5.

72. For 1954, see Attiga, op. cit., p. 211; for 1962, see Bank of Libya, *Eighth Annual Report of the Board of Directors, Financial Year Ended the 31st of March, 1964*, pp. 34-5; and for 1971, see Bank of Libya, *Balance of Payments for 1971 A. D., 1390-1391 A. H.* (September 1972; Arabic), p. 7. The trade balance for 1973 was LD536m (or $1,778m), as recorded in *IFS*, October 1975.

73. Attiga, op. cit., p. 218 for 1956 (quoting the *Economic Bulletin* for the National Bank of Libya). *IFS*, October 1975 for December, 1974.

74. For 1973, see *Arab Economic Report* (published by the General Union of Arab Chambers of Commerce, Industry, and Agriculture; Arabic; 1974), pp. 425-6.

75. UN *Statistical Yearbook 1973*, p. 95 for agriculture and p. 199 for industry. (See also Section VIII, on Agriculture, and Section IX on industry in *Statistical Abstract 1969*.)

76. See *National Accounts... 1962-1971*, pp. 23-4 and 92-3.

77. FAO, *Production Yearbook 1972*, pp. 31 and 33, and *1967*, pp. 29 and 30 respectively.

78. In this connection, see Europa, op. cit., 1973-4, pp. 488-9, and *Arab Economic Report* (1974), pp. 426-7.

79. Central Bank of Libya, *Economic Bulletin*, Vol. 12, No. 3 (May-June 1972; Arabic), Tables 12 and 18 in Appendix for data on credit, and pp. 83-92 for information on the use of agricultural imports.

80. *IFS*, December 1974.

81. Bank of Libya, *The Development of Public Finance in Libya 1944-1963* (August 1965; Arabic), p. 64 for 1952/3, and Bank of Libya, *Economic Bulletin*, Vol. 12, No. 3 (May-June 1972; Arabic), p. 82 for 1971/2 and 1972/3.

82. According to the 1973 census, net population increase averaged 3.7 per cent per annum for 1954-64, but 4.2 per cent for 1964-73. See Ministry of Planning, Census and Statistical Department, *Preliminary Results of the General Population Census, 1393 A. H., 1973 A. D.* (25 August 1973). Table 1, p. 1, states that total population in mid-1973 was 2,257,037.

83. See FAO, *Production Yearbook 1972*, p. 6, for area of arable land (which is estimated at 2,377,000 ha).

84. For details, see the issues of *Middle East Economic Survey* and *Arab Oil and Gas* for the two years 1973 and 1974.

85. See *The Revolution of 1st September: The Fourth Anniversary*, p. 158.

86. Information from an interview in February 1973 with a senior officer in the Public Housing Corporation

87. Ministry of Education, *Historical Study [Survey] of the Evolution of Education in the Libyan Arab Republic* (Tripoli, November 1972; Arabic), pp. 3, 8, 10, 13 and 17 up to 1971/2, and ibid., p. 130, for 1972/3.

88. Same sources as for note above, regarding teacher training and the subsequent information on technical training.

89. Manpower data come from *Statistical Abstract 1971*, Part 2, especially pp. 25-8.

11 TUNISIA

Tunisia is the easternmost of the three Maghreb countries formerly under French rule, and the most thoroughly Arabised among them. It is also the smallest in area and population, and the one with the most homogeneous and cohesive society. As a result of these features, it suffers least from the strains of linguistic and social estrangement which are felt more deeply in Algeria and Morocco *vis-à-vis* the rest of the Arab world, but suffers more from the relative niggardliness of nature, especially when compared with Algeria. The country was invaded by the French in 1881, after a period of financial strain which led to extreme dependence on France, and was declared a French protectorate in 1883, but was actually governed as a colony. It was on 20 March 1956 that the slow easing up of the colonial status and the growing autonomy of Tunisia ended in its full independence — but with a continued French military presence embodied in a few bases and the right to use certain military and communication facilities.

The colonial heritage of the country subjected it to harshness, usurpation of land and *colon* settlement, and the imposition of an extreme economic dependence on France, which was very much like the pattern witnessed in Tunisia's sister Maghreb countries to the west, and Libya to the east. But Tunisia was spared the very harsh forms and overwhelming magnitude of French military suppression to which the three other countries were subjected during their struggle for independence.

Simultaneously, the colonial heritage of Tunisia enabled it to have some French investment in physical infrastructure, mainly in the sector of transport and communications (and to some extent in the subsector of European agriculture) — an investment which was meant primarily to serve French economic and military interests, but which could not fail somewhat to benefit the national economy as well. However, the *social* infrastructure — education and health services — was as grossly neglected in Tunisia as in Algeria, Morocco and Libya. Yet Tunisia was fortunate in maintaining a few prestigious and influential centres of learning which not only preserved Islamic *shari'a* (law) and Koranic interpretation but Arabic language and culture as well, and in two outstanding instances — those of the Sadiquiyya College founded in 1875, and the Khalduniyya College founded in 1896 — attempted some form of reconciliation between traditional Arabic learning and modern French education. Furthermore, a relatively modern press made its appearance in the early 1880s. Finally, the relative nearness of Tunisia to Egypt, the centre of gravity of all the Arab countries in traditional and later modern education, and in journalism, enabled Tunisia to remain more Arabised and culturally less isolated and deprived than Morocco, Algeria and Libya.

Tunisia was in addition fortunate in the acquisition of some valuable political experience through the emergence in the years before World War One of a reformist national movement, the 'Young Tunisians', which asked for the institution of democratic life, and later in 1920 in the emergence of a much more influential movement embodied in the Destour (Constitution) Party. The Destour had greater thrust and political acumen and was later to lead the country into independence, and indeed controls its political affairs to this day. The Destour, and its subsequent version named the Neo-Destour which took over the leadership in 1934 under Habib Bourguiba, have both struggled for a two-pronged platform: political independence, and social reform and modernisation.

The Neo-Destour, under Bourguiba, has been a formidable asset for the country's overall development. This leader's political maturity, far-sightedness and flexibility, and his concern with modernisation in society have assured him the virtually unchallenged leadership of the country from its pre-independence days to the present. No other country in the whole Arab world has enjoyed a politically and socially stabilising factor of this magnitude, a factor which has assured the country of continuity for over half a century under the leadership of the same party, and for four decades under the same leader. The region's experience with political continuity has more often than not been characterised by autocracy and/or stagnation, while Tunisia's experience has been marked with dynamism and a large measure of broad-based participation, even though considerable paternalism has been present since independence. Finally, these advantages of political leadership and continuity have operated within the framework of a cohesive society and have therefore largely spared the country the ills of factionalism and divisiveness that bedevil many of the other countries surveyed in this study.

1. THE ECONOMY IN THE PRE-INDEPENDENCE DECADE[1]

The economic performance of the country in the ten or eleven years between the end of World War Two and independence was a function not merely of the coexistence side by side of a modern sector owned and/or controlled by the European (mainly French) community, with adequate capital funds and advanced management, and of a poor, capital- and management-hungry traditional sector, but was also a function of the basic limitations in the country's natural resources, capital stock and capital funds, and skilled manpower. Furthermore, the overall modest performance was rendered less conducive to general welfare owing to the very uneven distribution of wealth and income. The unevenness prevailed not only between the *colons* and the nationals as groups, but also among the Tunisians themselves. Thus, according to one author, about 1,000 Europeans and Tunisians 'in the modern sector owned one-third as much land as the half million small farmers in the traditional sector'.[2] If the two groups were compared from the standpoint of land ownership and share in agricultural output, the discrepancy would emerge more pointedly. Thus, out of a total cultivable area of 3.8—4m hectares (excluding pasture land),[3] the colons owned about 600,000 ha or a little over 15 per cent, but contributed 40 per cent of agricultural output.[4] On the other hand, the ratio of Europeans to total population in 1946 was 7.4 per cent (239,549 out of 3,230,952 inhabitants).[5] Thus, 7.4 per cent of the population owned 15 per cent of cultivable land which, because of its better quality and of the greater capital outlay and better technology it enjoyed, accounted for 40 per cent of agricultural output. The pattern, though the magnitudes may differ, was also to be encountered in Morocco, Algeria and Libya during the colonialist days.

Discrimination between the two communities, national and alien, though never reaching the gross and glaring dimensions it reached in the other Maghreb countries, expressed itself in other social and economic forms. Thus, the growth of school enrolment was extremely sluggish in the pre-war and war period, and it was only in the twelve years following 1944 that enrolment witnessed an upsurge, when the number of school-going children tripled. This was a remarkable performance in absolute terms and viewed by itself, but more so if

Tunisia

it is recalled that in 1943 enrolment was merely at the level reached in 1934.[6] The upsurge was not a reflection of a sudden interest in education among the Tunisians, but of the relaxation in restrictive colonial measures tending to impede schooling, and the larger measure of autonomy enjoyed by the nation in the immediate post-war period. Another social-economic-administrative expression of discrimination was to be seen on the eve of independence in the comparative social classification of the urban Tunisian and urban European working population, and in the average income of each of the two groups. The structure of the working population and the average income per category of work-force for each of the groups in 1955 is given in Table 11.1.

Table 11.1: Structure and Income of Working Population, 1955

	Moslems		Non-Moslems	
	Per Cent	Thousand fr	Per Cent	Thousand fr
Workers	56	160	21	400
White-collar workers	17	300	27	530
Middle classes	25	300	40	1,150
Upper class (upper-income group)	1	1,000–1,500	11	3,000
Total or average	100[a]	210	100[a]	950

a. Total rounded.

Source: Samir Amin, *The Maghreb in the Modern World* (Penguin African Library, 1970), pp. 73-4. As in the case of Algeria and Morocco, colonial statistics categorised the population on the basis of religion. The non-Moslem category consisted of Europeans and native Jews. However, it is known that many of these had 'double citizenship'.

It can be seen from Table 11.1 that the average income per earner of the Moslem (Tunisian) population was a mere 22 per cent of its counterpart for non-Moslems (Europeans). What does not appear in the table, but can be calculated from population data, is that the Tunisian urban labour force constituted about 16 per cent of the urban population, whereas its European counterpart was more than twice as large. Thus, in the first case there was a high level of urban unemployment, representing about one-third of the labour supply (in itself lower than that for Europeans, largely because of the withdrawal of most women from the supply), whereas in the second case there was virtual full employment. Another feature which the tabulation does not reveal is that of the occupation by Europeans of virtually all positions of real authority in the civil service, and of positions involving professional and technical competence. As far as the civil service was concerned, this feature might merely indicate the near-absence of Tunisians fully qualified for upper-echelon responsibility. But more profoundly, the situation represented the deliberate failure by the colonial power to prepare the population for the shouldering of this responsibility, both through the insufficient education and training provided and the exclusion of Tunisians from the important posts in the administration and thus from 'learning through doing'.

So far we have been concentrating on the urban population, both because the statistical information relating to the agricultural population is less adequate, and because this latter group habitually suffers from greater disguised unemployment. However, the data available show that for the population as a whole, the discrepancy in income distribution is very glaring, as the Moslems constituted over 90 per cent of the total, but had 50 per cent of the income, while the other half went to the non-Moslems who constituted under 10 per cent of the total.[7]

The case of Tunisia reveals a milder form of maldistribution of income than that of Algeria. None the less it clearly shows the symptoms of colonialism. Behind these symptoms was the political factor which the French manoeuvred in the interests of the European community, and the economic factor. This latter was embodied in the ownership of assets: the better agricultural land, as we have already indicated, and the means of production in the fields of mining, industry, transport and communication, and external trade. Thus, the Tunisians performed the more arduous and less remunerative tasks in these sectors, usually in the earlier phases of production in the case of multi-tier activities, while the Europeans were engaged in the higher (forward) phases with better pay and greater profits. In many instances in the fields of mining, industry, power, transport, and even agricultural colonisation, the corporations operating in Tunisia were European-owned ones based in Algeria where their major work was centred.[8]

The more readily available and reliable information regarding the performance of the economy in the pre-independence decade starts with 1950. According to one careful estimate, average production *per capita* in the years 1950-4 was only slightly higher than in 1920-4.[9] Taken as a whole, the post-war decade witnessed positive growth, but the rate was modest. Thus gross domestic product at constant 1957 prices for the nine years 1950-8 rose from an index of 100 in the initial year to 130 in the last year.[10] This represents a cumulative rate of growth of 3.3 per cent per annum. Modest as it is, this rate is to be further adjusted downwards owing to the exceptionally good harvest in 1958, a fact which pushed the GDP for that year upward altogether beyond the trend in the preceding years.

Furthermore, the economic performance in the post-war decade was to a large extent compensatory for the 'destruction and deprivation' of the war years. The accelerated investment by the French community in the building materials industry and in construction, and less so in manufacturing industry, was of limited value in the overall expansion of the economy, in the transformation of the traditional sector which continued to have more or less the same contours and dimensions, or in the mitigation of the sizeable unemployment problem from which the Tunisian population suffered. One major agricultural and irrigation project, in the Medjerda Valley in the north-east of the country, was only to be of beneficial effect after the decade in question, and then mainly in its immediate neighbourhood.[11]

Also with regard to land and agriculture, the decade failed to witness vast expansion in the area under cultivation. This area stood at about 3.1m hectares during the years 1954-7, divided almost in halves between the north (1.6m ha) and the centre and south (1.5m ha). The area actually cropped was between one-fourth and one-third less than the cultivable area. However, agriculture in general suffered – as it does in the present day – from extreme dependence on rainfall, a factor which, along with the near-absence of important all-season rivers, makes the chances of extension in the cropped area extremely slim. The irrigated area for the years under reference was no more than 20,000 ha in the north, and 100,000 ha in the centre and south.[12] The latter region accounted for a substantially larger measure of irrigation thanks to the oases and artesian wells that predominate in the south.

This brief survey will be incomplete if it does not stress three other handicaps to agricultural prosperity: fragmentation of land ownerships, traditionalism of techniques and methods, and the near-sterilisation of about 1.6m ha[13] in *habous* (*waqf*, or endowment) institutions or arrangements — a fact which resulted in poor exploitation of this vast area. The combined effect of these handicaps was to make agricultural operations costly and/or wasteful, as well as less productive — even given the other factors and institutions.

As Table 11.2 shows, agriculture leads among the sectors, followed by trade, manufacturing industry, transport, construction and public works, mining, and electricity, gas and water — in that order. Together, these sectors account for about seven-eighths of GDP. The balance is 'other services' combined, which together account for slightly less than manufacturing industry by itself.

The structure of the economy conforms to what can be expected in a state of underdevelopment: an agricultural sector which contributes roughly one-fourth of national product (except for 1958, when the ratio was almost one-third), a manufacturing sector which falls below one-tenth of national product, and a rather high share for trade, roughly around one-fifth. The commodity sectors together account on the average for 45.7 per cent, the service sectors for the balance of 54.3 per cent.

If the former group adds up to slightly less than expected, it is because agriculture is somewhat less contributive than in other underdeveloped economies in the Arab world as a whole (except for the desert and semi-desert countries). Furthermore, mining, which occupies an important place in the Tunisian economy, is distinctly more significant as an export sector and an earner of foreign exchange than as a contributor to national product. As Table 11.2 shows, the relative share of mining averages slightly over 3 per cent. In this connection, it ought to be stated that Tunisia is a large producer/exporter of phosphates. In fact, it had the first phosphates industry in the world, and in the years 1945-54 it produced one-sixth of the world total, or an average of 1.5m tons per year. (However, in 1930 production was 3m tons.) Next to phosphates in importance comes iron ore. Over one million tons were produced in 1953.[14] Lead is the third important mineral in the country. All three have had their ups and downs since production was started in 1900, 1905 and 1915 respectively, but have neither singly nor together constituted a solid bulwark for the post-war economy — except, as already stated, as earners of foreign exchange.

Two further observations on the overall performance of the economy are in order. The first relates to the course of GDP seen in the table. This course is marked by wide fluctuations which do not always reflect the changes in the contribution of the agricultural sector. Indeed, there are some instances of wide divergences between the two courses. The second observation emphasises the consistent downward trend in gross investment as a proportion of GDP. The only exception appears in 1958, when the proportion rose by two percentage points over that for 1957. The three independence years in the table average 10 per cent, whereas the earlier six years average 16.7 per cent. This substantial drop largely records the shying away from investment by the European community as soon as independence was obtained, and the drop in official French aid. But even before that, European investment began to fall as awareness grew that independence was not far off into the future.

2. THE ERA OF INDEPENDENCE

The era of independence began in March 1956. Thus at the time of updating this chapter in the spring of 1975, there were 18 years to survey, which is a long enough period to mark changes in the economy and its performance. However, there is only a limited amount of information that goes beyond 1970: in fact the most recent statistical yearbook relates to 1969. (But the full national accounts reproduced in the *International Financial Statistics*

Table 11.2: Gross Domestic Product and Gross Investment by Sector, 1950-8 (in million dinars, at 1957 prices)

		1950	1951	1952	1953	1954	1955	1956	1957	1958
1.	Agriculture	59.2	50.9	67.8	71.9	68.9	53.3	74.3	67.4	89.2
2.	Mining	6.5	7.5	9.2	7.9	8.2	9.0	8.7	8.6	8.8
3.	Industry	20.6	20.3	20.7	22.2	22.7	23.0	25.0	25.4	28.1
4.	Construction and public works	12.3	13.9	12.4	13.0	12.0	12.2	9.6	7.1	9.3
5.	Electricity, gas and water	1.9	2.1	2.2	2.4	2.8	3.0	3.1	3.2	3.2
6.	Transport	12.4	14.4	12.3	11.7	13.5	14.1	13.8	13.8	14.4
7.	Trade	41.6	41.5	43.7	43.8	43.6	42.1	47.8	43.3	46.6
8.	Other services (including communications)	14.6	16.5	19.1	20.1	22.4	23.3	21.4	21.7	22.7
9.	Value added at factor cost (1–8)	169.1	167.1	187.4	193.0	194.1	180.0	203.7	190.5	222.3
10.	Indirect taxes less subsidies	27.0	28.4	28.8	32.9	34.2	35.6	32.0	33.2	32.1
11.	Gross domestic production (9+10)[a]	196.1	195.5	216.2	225.9	228.3	215.6	235.7	223.7	254.4
12.	Salaries of Tunisian civil servants	18.3	22.0	26.2	26.4	29.2	30.3	22.6	23.8	23.9
13.	Gross domestic product (GDP)	214.4	217.5	242.4	252.3	257.5	245.9	258.3	247.5	278.3
14.	Index of GDP (1950 = 100)	100	101	113	118	120	115	120	115	130
15.	Gross investment (fixed capital)	42.0	44.3	39.9	40.3	36.0	35.3	28.5	23.1	27.8
16.	Ratio of investment to GDP (per cent)	20	20	16	16	14	14	11	9	10

a. This designation conforms to the French system of national accounting, according to which GDP included the salaries of civil servants, but gross domestic production excluded them.

Source: FAO, Projet FAO de Développement Méditerranéan, *Tunisie: Rapport national* (Rome, 1959).

of the IMF in the October 1975 issue relate to the year 1973.) Nevertheless, in spite of the spottiness of data for the four years 1970-3, an attempt will be made to trace the developments in the economy over the years of independence whose performance has been recorded.[15]

The legacy of colonial days has been sketched, even if the brush has been broad. Expressed through one indicator, the performance of the economy in 1956, the base year for our present discussion, is reported to have produced a *per capita* GDP of 68 Tunisian dinars in 1956, or some $170. (The rate of exchange then was 2.5 dollars to the dinar. It is currently, in June 1975, $2.629 to the dinar.) While the equivalent of $170 is not opulence, it stands clearly above the *per capita* GDP for several of the Mashreq countries for the same year. The comparison is more in favour of Tunisia if a higher estimate is used: one made by the FAO put the figure at about $200.[16]

Normally, history does not move in leaps and bounds. But for countries like Tunisia, whose political status altered from that of protectorate to that of sovereign state, the event of achieving independence represents a decisive turning-point and carries with it immense and immediate changes, challenges and, at times, responses involving the whole society and economy. Yet although the new leadership of the state was faced with pressing needs in all areas of action, not least the economic, their most spectacular and decisive action fell essentially in the political and social areas.[17] What preoccupied the new government in the former area was the take-over of the functions of political decision-making at the top of the pyramid of authority, as well as the manning and running of the administration further down. (In the few years following independence, about 12,000 French civil servants were withdrawn by France and returned home.)[18] In addition, the political transformation involved the setting up of legislative machinery as well as the meshing of the Neo-Destour party into the political machine.

Social modernisation received as much attention and scored at least as much success as political modernisation. Indeed, in many ways Tunisia has been ahead of the rest of the Arab countries in taking daring measures of modernisation. These included steps towards a fuller emancipation of women (including abolition of polygamy, submission of demands for divorce to civil instead of *shari'a*, that is religious, courts); elimination of *shari'a* courts; elimination of the system of *habous*, that is endowment, which was very wasteful (and which involved about 1.6m ha, or about one-fourth of arable land, according to one author);[19] application of common law; emphasis on co-operation and other social aspects of agrarian reform; and the vast extension of education and the improvement of its quality. Furthermore, advanced social legislation was enacted soon after independence. This covered the setting of minimal salaries and wages, of maximum working hours, of paid leaves, seniority rules, accident indemnity, and allowances for children (the last being of dubious relevance for the country's state of poverty coupled with a fast increase in population).

Concern with economic reform and with development was to come a few years after independence. To start with, the leaders contented themselves with 'economic liberalism' and eschewed interventionism. It was only after the Sixth Conference of the Neo-Destour in March 1959 that the leadership moved on to the adoption of an active role in economic affairs and to the formulation of development plans. This has been described as motion 'From Pragmatism to Plan'.[20] We need not go very far in attempting to understand and interpret the delayed reaction to the pressing economic needs, in contrast with the quicker reaction to the political and social needs. For one thing, the course adopted was the easier of the two, since action for economic reform is more demanding in resources and skills.

For another, political and social reform can show quicker results, and the achievements are less exposed to the possibility of critical evaluation and assessment by the masses. And finally, this seems to be the course taken by almost all the Arab countries upon achieving independence, where — understandably — there was invariably a near-obsession with political sovereignty and a desire first to consolidate independence, coupled with much less understanding of economic matters and confidence in the ability to deal with them.

The Colonial Economic Legacy in a Setting of Independence

The new economic setting continued to be characterised by dualism, where a small but relatively productive modern sector existed side by side with a much larger but less productive traditional sector. But with one major difference. The modern sector was to witness in the few years immediately following independence a serious drain of European manpower: entrepreneurs, administrators and managers, technicians, foremen, skilled workers, as well as civil servants. The drain hit the sectors of industry, transport and communications, government service and other services as hard as it hit agriculture where many *colons* left the land. The departing thousands were not all European in origin, but included a number of Tunisian Jews who went to Europe as well. Thus Tunisia was left with the dualistic structure in its economy, but not with the manpower capable of efficiently running the modern sector.

The problem was not as serious and intense in this instance as it was to be in Algeria six years later, both because the European community was much larger in the latter country, and its exodus was much more abrupt and complete. None the less it was real and did not lend itself to immediate solution. It is true that outwardly the economy witnessed certain adjustments meant to correct the situation, or to fill the gap created by the exodus of Europeans. These included the re-allocation of manpower, whereby Tunisians filled the empty jobs. But this was mostly an optical illusion, because what was needed was the filling of the functions rather than the posts — a task for which the poorly trained Tunisian work-force had not been prepared. None the less substantial reallocation did occur, as Samir Amin's data show. Thus, the number of 'Moslems' (that is, Tunisians) in permanent non-agricultural employment more than doubled between 1955 and 1960. It is most interesting that the increase was more noticeable in the categories of white-collar workers (180 per cent), master craftsmen, small traders, etc. (120 per cent), business executives (200 per cent), and Tunisian public servants (567 per cent), than in the lowest-income and most numerous category of manual workers (27 per cent).[21] The overall increase was 102 per cent — from 210,000 to 425,000.

The demographic and manpower problem was not merely to replace the departing workforce adequately and speedily. It was indeed a two-faceted problem: how to pull the economy out of the stagnation into which it had plummetted upon independence and the European exodus, and thus how to provide work and jobs in the re-activated economy, and in the second place how to fill the jobs with persons capable of performing the functions involved. Both aspects of the problem were near-intractable in the short term. Yet the government attempted to provide relief for the suffering population, if not to find full-fledged solutions.

As far as the urban population is concerned, the swift rise in urbanisation was counteracted by the expansion in urban employment, as we have seen. If the productivity per labourer did not rise but in fact fell, at least many able-bodied men found jobs and income and some personal welfare through employment. Indeed, much of the expansion in urban employment, particularly in the public service, had a definite welfare motivation. In addition to the absorption of over 200,000 Tunisians into non-agricultural sectors, there was the programme entitled 'workshops for the unemployed' which the government instituted, and which employed some 180,000 adults by 1960. But this programme catered essentially to the needs of the unemployed in rural areas.[22] It fell into the category of 'work-relief' facilities which aim at creating the impression that income is earned via work, rather than given out in charity. However, the programme could not cope with the large volume of rural unemployment and underemployment.

To sum up this brief discussion of employment and economic activity, it can be said that the Tunisian population did not suffer as a result of the departure of the Europeans who left, since this provided the opportunity for work to scores of thousands of nationals. However, most of the newly acquired employment was in the service sectors and included a large element of 'padding', and the expansion in employment was not matched by a commensurate increase in national product. In fact, as Table 11.2 shows, GDP dropped in 1957 by some 11 million Tunisian dinars below 1956.

If the departure of the Europeans did not happen suddenly and fully — having stretched over a few years, and if the transfer of some 600,000 hectares of better-quality and better-developed land from the *colons* to private Tunisian hands or to the public sector took some eight years to be consummated, French aid became erratic with occasional stoppage. Likewise, the drying-up of private French investment — which had started a few years before the formalisation of independence — was complete immediately after. (The aid constituted the equivalent of 15 per cent of GDP upon independence, or slightly over the proportion of GDP then assigned to gross investment.) The resultant drop in resources available placed an added burden on the shoulders of the new *dirigeants* of the economy. It is commendable that these succeeded by about 1959 or 1960 to recapture their breath, to put their economic house again in some order, and to mobilise just enough resources to attend to the economy's basic consumption and investment needs. The mobilisation was not just one of resources, but of public will as well. Thus, President Bourguiba said on 10 December 1959:

> We want all citizens to be imbued with the will to conquer misery and resignation, to uproot the belief in blind determinism ... The greatest problem is to engage the vast numbers of unemployed in the struggle against underdevelopment. The unemployed are capital that is asleep. This manpower can create wealth ... and contribute to the national income.[23]

Two factors beyond the internal measures taken helped bring about the recovery. The first was the fortuitous but timely occurrence of two very good harvests in 1958 and 1959, which brought immense relief to the strained food situation that had caused extended hardship and some starvation in 1957. The second was the conclusion of an aid agreement between the United States and Tunisia, according to which the former was to provide relatively substantial financial and technical assistance. (During the 1957 drought, the United States provided 45,000 tons of wheat which had an immense and immediate beneficial effect on the food balance.)

These two factors, plus the determination by the government at almost all levels to steer the economy towards recovery, ended by creating a situation that was noticeably less bad in 1960 than could have been foreseen in 1956 or 1957. Thus, the deficit in the balance of payments actually dropped considerably in the last three years of the decade — and this in spite of the stoppage in 1957 of French aid, and the disappearance of new French investments. The aid was resumed a couple of years later and, coupled with increased agricultural exports (thanks to the bumper crops) and the expanded American aid, resulted in the building up of the country's foreign exchange assets.

That the situation was brought under control in a few years was no doubt thanks to the existence of a rational and enlightened leadership, a devoted civil service, the energy of the new politico-economic and intellectual élite, the building up of some of the institutions of a modern economy (including the Central Bank which was founded in 1958) — in addition to what may be considered 'exogenous' factors, particularly the excellent harvests of 1958 and 1959, and foreign aid by the United States and France. Yet, as the following discussion will try to show, although the country was and may continue to be able to solve many of its pressing economic problems, it does so and will probably continue for many years to do so at a 'low level of equilibrium'. In other words, neither its domestic resources nor the level of its activity will permit in the immediate future the absorption of the vast body of the unemployed and underemployed into gainful employment. The achieving of growth and development at a rate high enough to considerably improve the level of living of the Tunisians, which has been witnessed in 1971 and 1972, remains predicated on substantial foreign aid, and — domestically — on the success in further modernising agriculture and rendering the mining and modest petroleum sectors much more remunerative.

The Performance of the Economy

A well-balanced understanding of the performance of the economy between 1956 and the end of 1972 or 1973 cannot be achieved through a restricted examination of the course of progress of the national product by itself. To begin with, the growth registered in the 18-year period does not do justice to the determined efforts exerted to develop the economy, constrained as this economy is by a fast-growing population with a large proportion of dependants, limited natural and man-made resources, a rather low level of national product *per capita* to begin with, and a volume of foreign aid not capable — though not modest — of permitting investments substantial enough to speedily break the 'vicious circle of poverty'. In the second place, there is more to development than growth in national product. Thus it is noteworthy that in the field of social work the country has marked considerable progress, particularly with respect to education and the creation of cadres in the civil service — ones which combine competence with conscientiousness, and which justify the claim that Tunisia has largely compensated for the exodus of trained Europeans.

But first, the economic performance. Here it is to be observed that no continuous and *uniform* GDP or GNP series exists for the years 1950-73, or even for the years since independence. There are estimates for the 24 years beginning with 1950, but these are not strictly comparable, either because the methods of calculation and/or presentation are different, or because of the absence of a continuous cost-of-living series for the 24 years (or even for the 18 years 1956-73, for that matter) good enough to serve as a deflator in translating the data from current to constant prices.

Nevertheless, by accepting a reasonable amount of patching and connection of data, as well as the use of the cost-of-living index for Tunis city as deflator — an exercise which is unavoidable for much of the Third World where statistical information suffers from various gaps and shortcomings — we can end up with a measurement of the performance of the economy which is satisfactory and can be accepted as having a reasonable degree of credibility. This exercise results in a series stretching for 24 years, from 1950 through 1973. Gross domestic product rose from TD214.4m* for 1950 to TD279.9m for 1961

*Tunisian dinars.

(during which period the data are calculated at constant 1957 prices), to TD753.5m for 1971 at current prices, or to TD556.5m at constant (1963) prices, and finally to TD1,109.9m for 1973 at current prices (TD768.8m at constant, 1963, prices.)[24] With the reservations stated earlier in this paragraph in mind, we find that the total real growth achieved in 1973 over 1950 is 258.6 per cent, that is, at an annual compound rate averaging 6.0 per cent. (However, growth by the end of 1971 was merely 159.6 representing a cumulative rate averaging just over 4.5 per cent per annum. Thus the years 1972 and 1973 achieved considerable progress over 1971, and account for the marked difference in the two annual averages.)

If the GDP for 1973 is related to that for 1956, that is TD258.3m, both at constant prices, the rise is found to be 198 per cent.[25] The average cumulative rate of growth is thus 6.5 per cent per annum. As the population rose from 3.44m to 5.51m during the same period, or by 60 per cent, representing an average cumulative rate of increase of about 2.9 per annum, growth in real GDP *per capita* during the period 1956-73 must have averaged 3.5 per cent per annum. Although this rate is satisfactory, it has an element of precariousness because actual year-to-year growth was far from even. Likewise, the course of the various sectors was uneven over the years, with the rates of growth in several instances (agriculture, mining, transport and communication, real estate, commerce and other services) oscillating between positive and negative magnitudes, and elsewhere with consistently positive but uneven magnitudes. This can be easily seen in Table 11.3. (This table does not go beyond 1971 because the sectoral distribution of GDP is available only until then. Only global estimates of GDP are available for 1972 and 1973.)

The range of the fluctuations was quite wide. Thus, the growth marked (at current prices) was as low as 2.3 per cent between 1965 and 1966, and as high as 13.1 per cent between 1970 and 1971, and 13.9 per cent between 1964 and 1965. However, the highest rate achieved was 18.6 per cent between 1971 and 1972, according to the latest estimate available.[26] The year 1971, but particularly 1972 and 1973, have started a new leap in the performance of the economy — an observation which is strengthened by preliminary sectoral impressions and by estimates of GDP. It is tenable to suppose that the economy has entered the seventies with a solid foundation and can now be counted upon to keep on an even course.

Tunisia provides an interesting case where long-term expectations put on record a dozen years ago can be measured against recorded achievements. Two documents make this measurement possible. The first is entitled *Perspectives Décennales de Développement 1962-1971*,[27] and it was designed not only as a chart for the future (as described in the words of President Bourguiba in the Introduction), but also as a broad and flexible frame for the development plans that were to follow (as stated in 'Avant-Propos' of the *Plan Triennal 1962-1964* which was to follow six months after the *Perspectives*).[28] The second document, published in January 1972 and entitled *Retrospectives Décennales 1962-71*,[29] examines the degree of the realisation of the *Perspectives*. The exercise of putting on record the *Perspectives* and later the *Retrospectives* is unique in the countries under survey in this book, since nowhere else has an evaluation been undertaken for the performance of more than one or two, or at most three years against the expectations earlier expressed in the plan. Furthermore, the Tunisian precedent is candid and self-critical, neither understating the failings nor exaggerating the achievements.

To review the detailed projections in the *Perspectives* for the years 1961-71, and the actual performance recorded in the *Retrospectives* during the same ten years, would involve a degree of detail too excessive for our present purposes, particularly as we plan to under-

Table 11.3: Gross Domestic Product by Sector, and Gross Investment 1956-71 (in million dinars)

	1956	1957	1958	1959	1960	1961	1962	1963	1964	1965	1966	1967	1968	1969	1970	1971
Agriculture	74.3	67.4	89.2	77.4	84.6	57.7	75.5	84.7	86.8	98.0	74.5	70.0	86.6	80.6	91.9	115.7
Mining	8.7	8.6	8.8	8.5	8.7	7.8	5.3	5.9	6.9	10.7	11.5	10.8	11.2	9.8	9.8	10.1
Energy: Electricity, gas, water	3.1	3.2	3.2	3.9	4.3	4.5	6.3	6.7	6.9	7.4	8.2	8.8	11.0	12.0	12.7	13.8
Petroleum	—	—	—	—	—	—	—	—	3.2	3.0	6.7	15.1	20.1	25.5	30.3	36.8
Industry	25.0	25.4	28.1	24.3	30.4	33.3	43.0	45.7	51.3	56.8	61.2	64.5	69.9	79.5	82.1	92.2
Construction and public works	9.6	7.1	9.3	10.4	13.9	16.8	32.5	34.4	33.4	40.0	41.5	42.0	42.0	48.5	48.5	56.2
Tourism	—	—	—	—	—	—	—	—	—	4.8	7.0	9.1	11.1	13.6	16.4	21.8
Transport and communications	13.8	13.8	14.4	17.8	19.7	19.3	24.2	27.5	29.7	37.0	41.3	43.0	40.9	40.6	46.0	43.2
Trade and other services	69.2	65.0	69.3	76.9	89.2	97.2	93.0	93.8	103.2	111.5	106.2	112.2	122.2	126.2	130.0	146.7
Value added at factor cost	203.7	190.5	222.3	219.2	250.8	236.6	279.8	298.7	321.4	369.2	358.1	375.7	415.0	436.3	467.7	536.5
Add: Indirect taxes less subsidies	32.0	33.2	32.1	21.5	21.7	24.7	46.3	52.0	60.9	67.9	77.6	77.7	80.4	94.8	95.9	104.0
Gross domestic production	235.7	223.7	254.4	240.7	272.5	261.3	326.1	350.7	382.3	437.1	435.7	453.4	495.4	531.1	563.6	640.5
Add: Administrative services	22.6	23.8	23.9	17.3	17.5	18.6	47.7	50.9	52.9	58.8	71.8	77.8	87.2	93.4	102.4	113.0
Gross domestic product at market prices																
1956-61 at 1957 prices	258.3	247.5	278.3	258.0	290.0	279.9										
1962-71 at current prices							373.8	401.6	435.2	495.9	507.5	531.2	582.6	624.5	666.0	753.5
1962-71 at 1963 prices							385.4	401.6	418.5	446.8	441.3	447.1	478.7	492.5	519.9	556.5
Index of GDP at constant prices	100.0	95.8	107.8	99.5	99.9	108.4	149.2	155.5	162.0	173.0	170.8	173.1	185.3	190.7	201.3	215.4
Gross investment (at constant prices)	28.5	23.1	27.8	31.6	62.6	69.7	91.3	105.2	127.2	116.1	112.1	106.7	104.6	110.4	114.6	128.2
Ratio of gross investment to GDP (at constant prices)	11	9	10	12	23	29	24	26	30	26	25	24	24	22	22	23

Source: Data for 1956-61 from Duwaji, pp.27-8 converted from percentages into absolute values. (Duwaji quotes the Secrétariat du Plan, *L'économie de la Tunisie en Chiffres* (Tunis, 1962), p. 15, while data for 1962-71 are from *Statistiques Financières*, May-June 1974 (Nos. 21 and 22), p. 58. For the conversion of data at current to constant prices, see note 25 at end of chapter.

take an assessment of the performance of the major sectors later in this section. Furthermore, the overall judgement of the ten years in question has been provided in succinct form in a much more recent document, entitled *IVe Plan de Développement Economique et Social 1973-1976*.[30] (This Plan is the first within the frame of the second decennial 1972-81.) According to this official publication, although the record of the decennial is not brilliant if measured in terms of the rate of growth achieved, it is remarkable since the country was placed during this period 'solidly and irrevocably' on the development course.[31] (The rate of growth at current prices was 7.2 per cent per annum on the average, or just over 4 per cent at constant prices, whereas the *Perspectives* had assumed a rate of 6 per cent at constant prices.)

The assertion that the economy performed well seems to run counter to the admission, in the same document,[32] that the rate of growth of national product was only 4 per cent per annum on the average, or a mere 2.4 per cent if national income is considered — a rate which 'amounts to semi-stagnation' once average growth per head of population is taken into account. Nevertheless, the paradox can be explained away easily, once clear differentiation is made between three indicators or components of development. First, it is necessary to differentiate between economic performance expressed in terms of the rate of growth, which was low, and the strengthening of the underpinnings of the economy and the improvement of its income-generating capacity, both of which moved more satisfactorily than the rate of growth by itself suggests. Furthermore, whereas the rate of growth is an indicator which is measurable, and relates to a specific span of time, raising the productive capacity of the economy is less measurable, takes longer to achieve, and has its effect felt over many years. Thus Tunisia's main achievement in the decade in question was precisely in that area which was bound not to show the imprint of growth immediately or with a short lag.

Another differentiation ought to be made between economic and social indicators of progress. Thus the country's performance was remarkable in the fields of education, training and generally the preparation of Tunisian manpower to shoulder the responsibilities called for in a developing economy and society. Again, this investment in human capital is bound to have its effect felt in years and decades to come, but not immediately while the investment was being made. Evidence of the awareness of these important differentiations by Tunisian decision-makers, beginning with the President, can be found in Chapter Four, entitled 'Fundamental Objectives', in the *Perspectives*. The objectives are: decolonisation, the development of man ('la promotion de l'homme'); structural reform (the reform of economic, democratic, administrative and popular institutions and structures); and self-sustained growth ('l'auto-développement'). The analysis in this chapter, and the general tone of the *Perspectives*, together suggest that the order in which the objectives are listed is deliberate and reflects a system of ranking based on significance and causality. Hence, self-sustained growth becomes the end result of developments along the other fronts enumerated earlier.

Again without going into excessive detail, we can measure the expectations of the course of GDP and investment over the years against actual achievements. Unfortunately, the comparison cannot be rigorous, since the GDP projections in the *Perspectives*[33] for the decade 1962-71 are expressed in 1957 prices, while the series of GDP actually achieved appears in current prices, and, if translated into constant prices, this will have to be done on the basis of a new deflator with 1963, and later 1970, as base. Nevertheless, by allowing for price increases during the decade we can obtain a fair enough view of the true dimension of growth achieved. The comparison appears in Table 11.4.

Table 11.4: Comparison between Projected and Achieved Gross Domestic Product 1962-71 (TD million)

Year	Projected GDP[a]	Achieved GDP[a]	Projected Investment	Achieved Investment
1962	287.0	385.4	56.0	91.3
1963	304.0	401.6	68.0	105.2
1964	322.0	418.5	76.0	127.2
1965	341.0	446.8	84.0	116.1
1966	362.0	441.3	88.0	112.1
1967	384.0	447.1	92.0	106.7
1968	407.0	478.7	100.0	104.6
1969	432.0	492.5	104.0	110.4
1970	458.0	519.9	112.0	114.6
1971[b]	486.0	556.5	116.0	128.2

a. The projections are expressed at constant (1957) prices, while the series of achieved GDP and investment is in constant (1963) prices.
b. The terminal year represents an increase of 69 per cent over the initial year in the projected GDP, and 107 per cent in the projected investment. On the other hand, the terminal year for GDP was higher by 44.4 per cent than the initial year, and the increase in investment between the two years was by 40.4 per cent.

Source: The projections are obtained from *Perspectives...*, p. 44, while the achieved GDP and investment are obtained from Table 11.3 above.

The method used for comparison is not wholly satisfactory, since in the one instance the data are measured against dinars of 1957, and in the second against those of 1963. The difference in the base year has quantitative implications, yet the difference between the initial and the terminal years in the two series is of a size that leaves no doubt that the expectations of growth of GDP did not materialise. In other words, the lag of the performance behind the projections could not be avoided, in spite of the efforts made to improve the income-generating capacity of the economy both through its economic and social infrastructure.[34]

One fundamental part of this effort is gross investment. The performance here seems to be good, since investment at constant prices ranged between a 'low' of 22 per cent of GDP for 1969 and 1970 and a 'high' of 30 per cent for 1964. The incremental capital-output ratio for the whole period 1962-71 amounts to 5.8 — assuming a time lag of one year and therefore disregarding the investment made in 1971, whose impact is assumed to be felt after 1971.

Considering the total resources available to the country, including foreign aid, the volume and proportion of investment could not be substantially bettered. But account must be taken of the composition of investment. This shows that about 51 per cent of total investment made in the decade 1962-71 was directed to 'non-administrative services', namely to transport and communications, housing, tourism, trade and other services, and 'collective equipment'. To have achieved the rate of real growth projected in the *Perspectives*, namely 6 per cent per annum, would have required an average annual investment of about 35 per cent of GDP, as against the actual 24.6 per cent, given the high capital-output ratio experienced. Obviously, such a proportion was beyond the means available to the country. (Of course, in relating investment to GDP we are not insisting that it should all come from domestic sources, but from foreign sources as well. To refer to a proportion of GDP is merely a way of measuring the size of investment.)

Finally, through recourse to Table 11.3, two broad observations can be made with respect to the structure of the economy over the 22-year period 1950-71, and more specifically over the two sub-periods 1950-61, and 1962-71 (the latter being the decade covered in the *Perspectives*). The first is that the distribution between the commodity and the service sectors remained more or less unchanged, with the share of the former, rising from 45.6 to 47.7 per cent from the first to the second sub-period. The second major observation to be made relates to the share in GDP of specific sectors. Here we find that agriculture dropped in significance from an average of 26.9 per cent to 16.8 per cent in passing from one sub-period to another. Most of the drop was gained by industry, mining and construction, whose combined contribution rose from 17.6 to 25.5 per cent. The balance of 2.2 per cent was accounted for by a rise in the share of the service sectors combined.

Leading Economic and Social Sectors

So far the appraisal of the performance of the economy in its decade and a half of independence has been restricted to global magnitudes. In what follows this performance will be examined more closely, through specific sectors. The sectors selected for further scrutiny are agriculture, industry (with special emphasis on the extractive branches, namely mining and petroleum), and the external sector (which is not one sector strictly speaking, but a composite of tourism and trade, both of which have a major impact on the balance of payments). In the social field, the country's advances in education will be examined, since they probably are the most outstanding achievement and hold the greatest promise for development.

Agriculture: Land, water and agricultural activity will be discussed under the general rubric of 'agriculture', owing to their interconnection, and to the fact that the sector of agriculture by itself represents the largest single contributor to national product. The land resources of Tunisia are moderately good, in the sense that the cultivable area is estimated variously at between 3.1m ha and 4.8m ha.[35] An official statistical note prepared early in 1972 for limited circulation entitled 'Superficie des Exploitations Agricoles' spoke in its introductory note of Tunisia as having 321,350 agricultural farming units ('exploitants agricoles') cultivating more than 4.5m ha. This latter estimate will be used here, since it is the most recent on hand and is accepted officially. However, the 4.5m hectares, as the note takes pains to emphasise, is not the only cultivable area. Another 700,000 ha are said to be exploited directly by the Office of State Domain (L'Office des Terres Domaniales), 1,240,000 ha are covered by forests and are managed by a special government service, and 2,550,000 ha are natural pasture land belonging to the state or to collective ownership. All these components add to 9m ha of what the note refers to as 'useful agricultural land' ('terres agricoles utiles'). Relating land to population, even assuming the estimate of 4.5m ha, allows about 0.83 of a hectare to every Tunisian, or about 4.2 ha per family. This represents a land/man ratio which is not unsatisfactory.

A quick survey of the shift in ownership in land since independence is called for before we turn to an examination of the structure of land ownership as it stands today. Reference in this connection has already been made to the cancellation of public and private *habous* in 1956 and 1957 respectively. Public *habous* land was incorporated in public domain, while the right of ownership of private *habous* land was awarded to those groups which were occupying the land or else were the beneficiaries of its returns at the moment. The two categories totalled some 1.2 or 1.3m ha in 1957.[36] It can be presumed that virtually the whole of this area was cultivable land. (Another estimate puts the total area at 1,750,000 ha, of which private *habous* accounts for 1,600,000 ha and public *habous* for the balance.[37])

The settlers owned somewhere between 600,000 and 700,000 hectares, but this land had an economic significance much beyond its area, owing to its superior quality. About 20 per cent of the settlers' land passed from the colonists to the Tunisian government subsequent to an agreement reached with the French in 1958 regarding the question of land. Some land had changed hands before upon the departure of a number of Europeans soon after Tunisia's independence. Later in 1960 another 25 per cent of the colonists' land was confiscated by the Tunisian government (though compensation was paid for buildings and machinery on the farms). Finally, under a law passed on 12 May 1964, all land was Tunisised, in the sense that only nationals could own land in the country. The government was to take over itself all land owned by foreigners. The National Office for the Development of State Land was to take over and operate the land acquired under the new law, as well as state domain in general. Presumably all colonist land passed over to Tunisian hands as of May 1964. According to the official sources, 505,000 ha were taken over under the Law of 12 May 1964. (This would suggest that the Europeans held at least 775,000 ha, apart from the land that was surrendered right after independence and before the 1958 agreement.) Of equal significance to the total area recovered is the distribution by size of holdings of the area recovered. Thus, while 2,630 holdings (or 59.7 per cent of the total) were less than 20 ha in area each and together represented 17,500 ha or 3.3 per cent of total area, and while 850 holdings ranged between 20 ha and 100 ha each (18.5 per cent of the total) and added up to 38,000 ha or 7.6 per cent of total area, 970 holdings were above 100 ha each (21.8 per cent) and totalled 448,700 ha, thus constituting 89.1 per cent of total area. The average holding in this last group had over 462 ha — of good quality land.[38]

The structure of land ownership in Tunisia reflects the customary pattern encountered elsewhere, especially in Egypt and in the Mashreq countries, but without the excesses encountered there. Thus, as the following table shows, small holdings represented the largest single group, but their combined area represented the smallest group but one. On the other hand, the group of very large holdings was the smallest both with regard to number of holdings and of total area, but whereas the group of privileged operators or owners represented only one-fifth of one per cent of all operators or owners, they owned 6.3 per cent of the total area of all private holdings, or only slightly less than the largest single group (40.9 per cent) who all have small holdings. The group of holdings representing the largest area had an area interval of 20—50 hectares. In summary, it can be said that the group distribution by area was close to a 'normal distribution', but with regard to number of operators or owners per each size interval, the group size declined consistently as the size interval rose.

The structure of private land ownership suggests the need for land reform, if the quantitative picture is looked at by itself. However, a few qualifications have to be made in this respect. First, the large ownerships are not scandalously large, as they were in Egypt, Syria or Iraq before land reform and redistribution. Second, most of the land involved is rainfed, where the net return per hectare is much below the return in the countries of the Mashreq which have undertaken land reform. Third, a decree issued on 28 September

Tunisia

Table 11.5: Distribution of Holdings by Number and Area (as of 1972)

Size Interval (ha)	Number	Per Cent of Total Number	Area (ha)	Per Cent of Total Area
0—less than 5	131,600	40.9	304,000	6.7
5—less than 10	72,300	22.5	507,000	11.2
10—less than 20	63,800	19.8	879,000	19.4
20—less than 50	41,500	12.9	1,287,000	28.4
50—less than 100	8,000	2.5	541,000	11.9
100—less than 200	2,600	0.8	372,000	8.2
200—less than 500	1,150	0.4	356,000	7.9
500 and over	400	0.2	271,000	6.3
Total	321,350	100.0	4,517,000	100.0

Source: 'Superficie des Exploitations Agricole' — note prepared by the Ministry of Agriculture in 1972; stencilled.

1957 provided for the distribution of collective or jointly owned land (designated in Arabic as 'socialised' land) which until then had been in the hands of tribes. (Exception was made for threshing grounds, built-on land, and pastures and similar areas for communal use.) The areas affected were mainly in the centre and the south. The decree aimed at activating agriculture in the areas subject to the new law through the institution of private instead of collective ownership, thereby raising the level of motivation.[39] The 1957 law notwithstanding, only limited distribution of collective land was effected in 1971, where the beneficiaries were the old *de facto* users of the land. No information is as yet available of the area distributed.

A fourth qualification relates to the distribution of irrigated land. Measures had been taken already by 1958, 1960 and 1963 (Laws 63/58, 6/60 and 18/63 respectively) with regard to the development of land through irrigation, the participation in the costs of this development by the private beneficiaries, and the limitation of private ownership in publicly irrigated lands.[40] Again in 1970, new legislation was issued relating to the distribution of publicly irrigated land, in which all the earlier measures were amended and/or unified. The net result with respect to the limitation of ownership and the distribution of land in excess of the ceiling permitted has by the time of writing been extremely small and unimportant. No factual information is available beyond this. The order of magnitude of the areas involved in total can be realised from the modesty of irrigation. In all, by the spring of 1972 no more than 53,000 ha were irrigated, of which 23,000 ha were irrigated from wells, and 30,000 ha from dams. To these must be added some 8,500 ha of oases, mainly served by artesian wells and cultivated by primitive methods. Without anticipating the discussion of irrigation to follow, it can be said that the most optimistic estimates refer to no more than a total of 100,000 ha of irrigable land, including the areas currently irrigated.[41] As much of the area already under irrigation does not consist of large-scale ownership, the scope for redistribution of irrigated land is very limited.

The net result of all four qualifications is that land reform, in the limited sense of setting a ceiling to ownership and distributing the excess areas, is not a pressing issue in Tunisia. Thus, instead of placing emphasis on land reform, the government has directed its attention — beyond the Tunisisation of land ownership and the reforms involving *habous* and collective land — to the reorganisation of agricultural structures. The most conspicuous modality of such reorganisation has been the promotion of agricultural co-operative societies, which will come under examination further down.

Another aspect of agriculture other than land is water. It has already been said that river water is scarce in Tunisia. Much of the underground water is in the centre and some parts of the south. To compound the problem of scarcity, there is the high level of salinity. At present, the large, medium and small dams in operation together have a capacity below 300,000 million cubic metres. At best, as the *Perspectives* foresaw, 10 new dams are expected to add about 252,000 million cubic yards (184,000 million cubic metres) of capacity. Once the plans are implemented, irrigation capacity will be about 484,000 million cubic metres — obviously not a very impressive volume of water for a country with some 4.5m ha of cultivable land. The long-term, expected near-doubling of irrigated land (from 55,000 to 100,000 ha) is tenable in the light of the increase by 61 per cent of stored water for irrigation. But these magnitudes define the limits of the feasible and economical, given present technology, financial resources, and knowledge about underground water.

The land situation by itself, as already indicated, is not as serious as in most countries in the region. Thus, the pressure of population (or of rural working population) on cultivable land is lighter than in the other African Arab countries except Sudan, and lighter than in Lebanon, Jordan, Kuwait and Saudi Arabia in the Asian part of the Arab world.[42] Whatever serious pressure exists is therefore attributable to the scarcity of water, as well as to the 'quality and conditions of agricultural exploitation'.[43]

To face the various problems and retarding factors, the *Perspectives,* and the plans falling within the decade covered by the *Perspectives,* comprised several corrective policies and measures, which were hoped to help the agricultural sector attain its objectives. These objectives included raising the rate of agricultural production from 2.2 to 5.5 per cent at constant prices annually, the diversification of produce, the improvement of organisation and services, and of the quality of produce, the co-ordination of agricultural with industrial development, and the reduction of underemployment and unemployment plus the increase of employment.

The success in achieving these objectives has been mixed. Thus, the growth rate of the sector's share in GDP averaged 5 per cent for the decade 1962-71 at current prices, but only 1. per cent at constant prices.[44] (According to *Retrospectives,* the former rate for the 11 years 1961-71 was 2 per cent, and the latter −1.8 per cent,[45] on the basis of an average rise in the price index of 3.8 per cent per annum. However, this is based on a calculation mistake, since the overall growth during the 11 years was 47 per cent, or a compound average annual rate of about 3.8 per cent. In other words, there was stagnation — neither growth nor decline in real terms.) This is explained in the *Retrospectives* as being the result not only of sluggishness in the sector, but also of the fact that much of the investment had been of a long-gestation nature. It must be added here that the independence period has not witnessed any noteworthy extension of the area under cultivation — the difference between the 3.1m ha reported for 1957 and the 4.5m ha reported for 1972 being merely one of definition. The smaller area relates to land *actually* cropped.

Another objective that was not achieved was the increase of employment. Again the *Retrospectives* states that in spite of the absence of a thorough and reliable examination of the employment situation in the agricultural sector, it can safely be said that no noticeable improvement had occurred. Indeed, it is stated that the general situation had remained more or less unchanged, with unemployment ranging between 18 and 24 per cent for the whole economy. The intractability of the problem was caused by the unexpected rise in the size of the population. This rise would have ended in a large volume of unemployment, had it not been for the absorption of many thousands of those in the active age groups in emigration to Europe, and in the school system through extended schooling.

It remains to be added, as a final observation, that the other objectives proved more feasible to reach. However, taken together, the objectives can be said to have been beyond the sector's reach. This sector has been the slowest-growing in the whole economy and today fails to satisfy even as large a part of the country's internal and trade needs as it did at independence.

How has agricultural production fared in the two decades 1952-72? The answer is not easy to provide, since the fluctuations from year to year have been severe. Thus, with 1952-6 taken as base (=100), total agricultural production in 1964 registered 137 points, fell to 112 in 1965, and further to 95 in 1966, while food production registered 138, 111 and 93 respectively. The record continued to be bad till 1970, but suddenly improved for 1971 and 1972. With 1961-5 as base, the index for 1966-70 ranged between a low of 95 and a high of 108; however, it was 137 for 1971 and 131 for 1972. Food production was even less spectacular, with the index for 1966 being 74 (1952-6 = 100). However, beginning with 1967, and down to 1972, the indices for food production were almost identical year for year with those for total agricultural production. On a *per capita* basis, the situation was not at all cheerful between 1952 and 1966, with the index being as low as 76 for total agricultural production and 74 for food production, both in 1966. However, later years witnessed an improvement, in the sense that stagnation rather than decline occurred between 1961 and 1972. Thus the index for 1972 was 100 for total agricultural production, and 101 for food production. (The base was unchanged in all calculations.)[46] Only Algeria showed a poorer performance among the African Arab countries.

Industry: The secondary group of sectors, broadly defined to include mining and petroleum as well as manufacturing industry, construction and public works (all of which appear under 'Industry' in Tunisian national accounting) represented around 28 per cent of GDP in 1971, against 23 per cent in 1962 and 16.6 per cent in 1957. Compared with the contribution of agriculture and services – the primary and tertiary sectors – that of the secondary sectors rose from a position where it had been 15.3 per cent higher than that of agriculture but 25.7 per cent lower than that of services, to one which by the end of the decade under examination stood 80.7 per cent higher than agriculture and 11.1 per cent higher than services. The increase in absolute and relative importance is owed essentially to the vast increase in the contribution of the energy sector: from TD3.2m in 1957 to TD6.3m in 1962, and finally to TD50.6m in 1971 and TD54.4m in 1972.[47] (Earnings from oil exports rose considerably after October 1973–January 1974, when the posted price of crude quadrupled. However, considering the small volume of oil exports, the 'windfall' remains of limited size.) It ought to be emphasised that about three-fourths of this upsurge in the contribution of the energy sector was in the petroleum subsector specifically. In fact, this subsector made its first contribution to GDP in the year 1964. In 1974, petroleum was by far the largest single contributor to national product, despite the fact that Tunisia is a modest oil producer in the Arab world.

The next-largest single branch of industry is that of agricultural and foodstuff industries, which in 1957, as in 1962, was by far the largest single branch of the secondary group of sectors, but dropped to second place in 1971. More specifically, its index rose to 140 in 1971, with 1962 as base year, while the index of energy rose to 803 over the same period. The wide divergence is explainable in the large absolute difference in the base year. The third branch is currently that of textiles, clothing and leather manufactures. (Construction and public works is actually the largest branch in the secondary group — even a larger contributor than energy — but to consider it as a branch of *industry* is rather misleading, hence our preference for its isolation in the ranking just made.)

It is not intended to undertake a thorough examination of the industrial sector, because it does not embody a dramatic achievement for Tunisia, in spite of the vast expansion in the value added in the energy, mining and manufacturing components of industry. Suffice it to say here that manufacturing industry is invested with a great deal of hope as both an engine of development and an expression of development; as an instrument for teaching the work-force not only the habits and skills required in industry, but also the attitudes and values of industrialism; as a substantial contributor to national product and therefore as an instrument of further increasing this product; and as the provider of new opportunities for employment in an unemployment-ridden economy.

These objectives and hopes have in various degrees been satisfied, though the last has been achieved least. But it can still be said that much of the country's hope must remain pinned on agriculture, not only because it is a well-established sector, parts of which are already advanced and highly remunerative, but also because its prosperity means welfare for the rural half of the population. Fortunately, Tunisia does not have a starry-eyed attitude to industry and industrialisation, nor does it have a compartmentalised approach to development, but an integrated one which enables it to realise that the promotion of agriculture and industry is closely and organically intertwined and that the two are truly interdependent. The three development plans which stretched across the eleven years 1962-72 testify to these assertions, and more so the most recent plan, the Fourth Plan of Economic and Social Development 1973-6.

The dualism inherited from colonial days reflected itself in 1956 in industry, as in agriculture and other sectors, and in social and educational structure. This dualism was manifest in the presence of a small but efficient and remunerative modern manufacturing subsector, where the units were rather large, and a large traditional subsector, characterised by smaller, less efficient units, as well as by a widely spread handicraft industry. The pattern remains today, although the dividing lines have shifted location and become rather blurred. Furthermore, it is the Tunisians who today own the industrial means of production in both subsectors.

The shifting and blurring of the dividing lines have come about to some extent thanks to the shifting in the pattern of ownership of industrial establishments. Thus, as the modern subsector used to be owned by Europeans (mainly Frenchmen), the dividing lines remained largely fixed. But as the Europeans moved out of the country and Tunisisation was pursued, and as the nationals gained experience and self-confidence, more of the establishments in the traditional sector became medium- or large-sized, and more linkage and integration began to take place among establishments of various sizes and at different technological levels. The dualism is distinctly less pronounced today, though still existent. But even though its features can still be discerned, they are economic and not social (and also definitely not political), as in colonial days.

The handicraft sector also has undergone considerable modernisation. Textiles, rugs, blankets, copper utensils, leather goods, metal decorative trinkets — that is, the main handicraft products — have undergone considerable redesigning. Though realising the modest contribution of handicrafts to national product — estimated at some 3 per cent on the average[48] — the government attaches some considerable significance to this subsector. This arises from the employment aspect of handicrafts, as they absorb currently some 50,000—60,000 (as against some 100,000 upon independence), as well as from the social significance of keeping skilled persons in the countryside and giving them an enjoyable and remunerative occupation as well.[49]

Whatever the exact number of those actively engaged in handicraft industries, they represent a large figure compared with those employed in all branches of mechanised industry. Thus, according to census results for the years 1957, 1958 and 1959, the number averaged 25,722 of permanently employed persons and 795,165 man/days for seasonally employed persons.[50] (In defining a seasonal worker, this category was designed to include those employed for less than 300 days a year. In the most recent census available, namely that of 1969, it is stated in the 'Notes Explicatives' that man/days of seasonal work are convertible to permanent work at the rate of 250 man/days for one year of employment. If this rate is applied to 1957, 1958 and 1959, then the three-year average number of permanent workers would rise by 3,180, bringing the combined average to a total of just under 29,000.) As against this total the number of permanent workers and seasonal workers (duly converted from total man/days worked) stood at 100,391 in 1969.[51] Consequently, it can readily be seen that the handicraft industry was and continues to be a larger employer than the mechanised industry.

In addition to modernisation in design and techniques, some institutional reorganisation has also been introduced to the subsector of handicrafts. Thus, side by side with the family workshop, which predominated overwhelmingly in pre-independence days, there are today many collective workshops that probably employ half of those actively engaged in handicrafts. The government also established a National Bureau for Handicrafts in 1959 with the purpose of setting standards of quality and improving quality, training workers, encouragement of co-operatives, provision of reasonably priced inputs, and help in marketing of products with a view to the reduction of middlemen's share in the sales returns. The Bureau has set up dozens of production centres in the main areas of traditional industries, as well as a few exhibition and selling centres abroad.[52]

Before we move on to examine the very important subsectors of mining and energy, it is appropriate to mention here the steep rise in the volume of investment in industry, both in absolute and in relative terms. Thus, whereas the investment declared by establishments according to the census for the years 1957, 1958 and 1959 amounted to TD2.8m (after the deduction of investments in transport) out of a total for all sectors of TD42m, or a mere 6.7 per cent, it rose for 1971 to TD52.7m out of a total of TD173.6m for the economy, or 30.4 per cent. Energy receives the largest share, of TD30m.[53]

Extractive Industry: Attention will be focused here on Tunisia's underground wealth of phosphates and petroleum, which constitute its major natural wealth after land and scenery. The two components of natural resources mentioned pose a paradox, since they have in the independence period been only a modest contributor to national product, but have always claimed a place of eminence in every examination of the country's potential for development. This seeming paradox can be explained through the presentation of the various related facts together. Thus, while it is true that the mining and petroleum industries have for the whole period 1950-71 accounted for just under 4 per cent of combined value added, they have none the less accounted for a much larger share in exports. In the years 1962-72, minerals, ores and petroleum have together represented 44.5 per cent of the value of the exports of the 11 years combined. (Crude petroleum exports started only in 1966; if the calculation is made for the 7 years 1966-72, then the share would rise to 49 per cent.)[54]

Parallel with this comparison runs another which is equally, but superficially, puzzling. This is that the size of the reserves of these natural resources (with the exception of petroleum) is enormously large — much larger than the share in national product or even that in exports would suggest. This is mainly because the proportion of the reserves exploited annually is relatively very small, and again because in all instances, including petroleum but excluding phosphates, what is exported is exclusively the mineral in its crude form, therefore in a form where the unit of export is not highly remunerative. The exception relates to the more recent production of superphosphates where the return per ton is roughly six times that for phosphates that have not been processed.

The major mineral resources of Tunisia are phosphates; iron, cast iron and steel; iron ore; and lead. Also in existence, but of lesser significance are zinc, potash and salt. Phosphates are by far the most important. This resource, whose presence was first established in 1885, has been estimated '... at one billion tons for the present, with a total reserve of probably eleven billion tons'.[55] (Most of the known and exploited reserves lie in the Gafsa area — in the centre and west of centre of the country.) Obviously, even the more conservative estimate — presumably one of established reserves — can allow production and export for several generations even at a distinctly higher level than the present. However, the fact that the quality of the mineral is inferior to that in Morocco, and that this latter country is a much larger producer, have placed serious limits on Tunisia's gains from the export of phosphates. The determination to switch increasingly to the production of hyperphosphate, superphosphate and triple phosphate can boost the returns considerably beyond what the mineral obtains now as it is largely exported in its raw state. (The exports have been recently hovering around the 2.5m ton mark.) As things stand today, Tunisia is the fourth-largest exporter of phosphates, after the United States, the Soviet Union and Morocco.

Iron ore is mainly found in the northern part of the country, north and south of the river Madjerda. The reserves are estimated variously: one estimate puts them at 30m tons of high-quality ore, though the exploitation is mainly restricted to the Djerissa area. Average production over the past decade has hovered around three-quarters of a million tons a year, but with a slight downward trend. It is now believed that the reserves that are commercially recoverable are nearing exhaustion.[56] Likewise lead seems to have a gloomy prospect, and in addition its reserves and production are at a much lower level than those of iron ore.

The Office National des Mines is responsible for the mining sector. This generally entails the planning and conduct of the search for new supplies, the modernisation of mining methods, the exploitation of mines assigned to the Office by the government, trade in minerals, handling the government's share in mining enterprises, and generally the promotion of mining. It is also entrusted with the promotion of exploration for oil.[57] However, actual production and export is conducted by three companies: one for phosphates, the second for iron, and the third for non-ferrous metals. These companies are mixed private and public, the private share being in part foreign-owned. A flexible and pragmatic approach to the subject of ownership has been adopted. Thus, the companies had been private French before independence, but since then the government has become the major share-owner, without excluding the French altogether.

Petroleum production is a newcomer among the economic activities of the country. Though exploration began soon after it had been initiated in Algeria in the mid-fifties, production only began in 1966. Since then it has risen fast to attain precedence over the other aspects of mining, both as a contributor to national product and as an export item. By 1968 it was leading on both scores. However, and in spite of the spectacular earnings made out of crude oil exports in 1972, 1973 and 1974, and to be expected for a number of years to come, the petroleum resource is highly unreliable, owing to the modesty of the reserves so far established. These stand at about 40m tons, or no more than enough to permit production till the middle of the eighties at the present rate of production. Hence the active search for new reservoirs of oil. In 1972 the government established a state company to take charge of the activities of planning and controlling the search for oil, and to handle the government's share in the operating oil companies. Government participation amounts to 50 per cent of the total. The production and exports of petroleum are shown in Table 11.6.

Table 11.6: Volume of Production and Value of Petroleum Exports

Year	Volume (in thousand tons)	Value (in TD million)
1966	771	4.2
1967	2,241	10.5
1968	3,191	14.1
1969	3,707	21.2
1970	4,151	23.5
1971	4,096	28.7
1972	3,975	38.8
1973	3,878	52.1

Sources: Banque Centrale de Tunisie, *Statistiques Financières*, Nos. 15, 16 and 17, p. 45 for production and p. 54 for value of exports, all till end of 1972. For 1973, see *Arab Economic Report* (1974), pp. 302 and 307.

It is worth adding a final word on the vast expansion in the generation of electricity, both thermal and hydraulic. The expansion was made possible thanks to the rise in installed capacity. Thus, whereas this capacity remained constant at about 67,000 kw in the post-war period until 1954, it rose from 85,000 kw to 103,000 kw from 1955 to 1956, and up to 252,000 kw by the end of 1972. Likewise, production rose from 141m kwh for 1950 to 228m kwh for 1956, and finally to 1,000m kwh for 1972 (including 140m kwh of private generators).[58] However, though the production increase is spectacular, it still fails to permit a consumption *per capita* of more than 192 kwh for 1972.

No doubt marked progress has been registered in the industrial sector, broadly defined to include manufacturing, electricity and extractive industries and petroleum. The quantity and quality of industrial production have made advances after the period of retrenchment immediately following independence. Likewise, the variety of industries established has expanded to include totally new lines of production (such as chemical industry, petroleum refining, glass, fertilisers and many new products in already established industries), as the sophistication of techniques of production has improved and the skills of the labour force have risen. All these transformations have reflected themselves in measurable indicators, such as share in national product and in exports, and indices of production, as well as in intangible manifestations such as the deeper acceptance of industrialism, factory discipline, improved organisation and a higher level of managerial and labour skills. Given the erratic nature of agricultural production (manifest in areas annually under the plough and in volume of crops), the country will have to rely increasingly on the industrial sector. This is all the more convincing now that the sector (in its broad definition) has for the decade 1962-71 acquired precedence over the agricultural sector in contribution to national product.

Doubtless there are other aspects which will continue to make agriculture maintain its pre-eminence, such as the nature of its produce and the dependence of the population on this produce, and the close relevance of agricultural activity to a large proportion of the population. Yet, as more and more time passes and the country becomes more industrialised, the promotion of the industrial sector will be not only an end in itself, and not only an indicator of higher and more solid development, but also an instrument for the promotion of other sectors — pre-eminently agriculture.

The External Sector: There is, strictly speaking, no such thing as an 'external sector' which stands on a par with agriculture and industry. But we have opted for this nomenclature in order to discuss under the same heading tourism, which is the largest single contributor to the earnings of foreign exchange, and the other components of the balance of international payments. The country's situation with regard to foreign exchange availability is a major factor in its drive to develop and to finance the import needs of development.

Endowed with attractive tourist natural assets, such as sunshine and scenery, and with appealing though still insufficient man-made facilities, Tunisia places considerable hope on the tourism sector. This sector has only recently begun to acquire significance. Thus in 1958

> there existed in Tunisia only a small number of hotels essentially located in Tunis and in the large cities. After some hesitation with regard to the impetus which touristic activity could derive from the Algerian war, the public authorities finally opted in favour of the development of this sector. It was in 1960 that the first touristic units were put under construction, and it was the government which took charge.[59]

Tourist facilities and activities have gone far in the years since 1960, considering their modest beginnings. (The most prominent centres of tourism are Hammamet, Sousse, Djerba and Tunis.) The *Perspectives* and the three plans drawn within its framework had stipulated the tripling of the number of hotels, the doubling of the number of rooms (to reach 5,500) and of the number of beds (to reach 9,406), and for the reception of an estimated 300,000 tourists in 1971 (as against 60,000 in 1960). The investment allocated for the purpose of providing the necessary facilities was TD13.3m. Against this total investment, the earnings of the sector in the year 1971 alone were expected to reach TD14.6m. It is enough to place these expectations against the realisations as they stood in 1971 and 1972 to see that the sector has blossomed beyond the rosiest hopes of the planners. Thus, the investments actually made amounted to a total of TD96.6m during the decade 1962-71 (with the year 1971 alone witnessing a larger investment than the total projected for the ten years in the *Perspectives*). The beds in service rose to 42,996 by the end of 1971

Tunisia   495

(and to 48,824 in 1972). The number of tourists rose to 608,206 in 1971, and to 780,350 in 1972, but dropped to 710,000 in 1973, while the tourist/nights spent in the country rose to 5.8m for 1971 and to 6.8m for 1972. The receipts of the sector reached TD53.8m for 1971 (and to a reported TD70m for 1972, and TD72m for 1973.)[60] Yet, in spite of these very bright achievements, the sector needs substantial investment and expansion, and considerable qualitative improvement, if it is to capitalise adequately on the country's attractiveness to tourists and to appropriate to itself a larger slice of the tourist business which the Mediterranean region has been increasingly drawing to itself. Tunisia, like Morocco and Algeria, has yet very far to go before it can be as important as Spain, Italy or Yugoslavia are in the field of tourism. Yet with the active interest of private investors, including sizeable foreign financing (mainly French, West German and British), the sector seems to have no worry regarding its ability to expand. There is a dynamic National Tourism Office, along with the Compagnie Financière et Touristique, and the two are very busy building new facilities and modernising those in existence.

When Tunisia was under French rule, any shortfall in the earnings of the current account of its balance of payments used to be compensated for through grants, the expenditure of the French army in the country, and investment funds going into the European sector of the economy. The situation worsened in the few years following independence because much of this inflow dried up. Furthermore, in the decade that was to follow independence, the vicissitudes in Tunisian-French relations reflected themselves in a tide-and-ebb pattern of French aid and, to some extent, of trade with France.

However, taking the independence era as a whole into account, it can be said that though the shortage of foreign exchange is a major bottleneck which slows down the importation of capital goods and technical assistance called for by the drive for development, the country has largely been spared serious deterioration in its balance of payments. This has been mainly due to the inflow of grants and loans from various sources. These inflows have been directed to different purposes, from general budget support, to sectoral development programmes, to specific project financing. The form has also varied from direct grants, to short-term loans, and to long-term loans. The following account sets out to sum up the receipts over the years.[61]

The years covered in this account stretch from July 1945 to the end of March 1974. However, the data have to be accepted with caution and reserve. This is because the sources of information are diverse and do not use uniform methods of reporting. Furthermore, in some instances adjustments and interpolations have had to be made in order to fill in some gaps. In all instances, only official (bilateral) flows have been included, as information on the inflow of grants and loans from multilateral and private resources is not available consistently for the whole period. In total, the account shows that the equivalent of $1,178m of bilateral aid came in from OECD in the twenty-two and a half years covered, plus the equivalent of $58.8m (from 1963 to March 1974) from the Kuwait Fund for Arab Economic Development, plus the equivalent of $143m (from 1954 to 1972) from the socialist countries. Thus total inflow amounts to $1,379.8m.

Obviously, this sum is not impressive when contrasted with the needs if substantial growth is envisaged. Yet it ought to be seen against the volume of international aid prevailing in the long period covered, which was modest. The future promises to be brighter, with the major Arab oil-producing countries intent on directing a large volume of the vast financial resources at their disposal since October 1973 to the aid of their sister countries that are not as generously endowed with oil riches.

The course of the balance of payments has been erratic owing to two factors: the erratic nature of agricultural harvests and therefore of the exportation and importation of agricultural produce (where fluctuations from year to year have been violent and very large); and the rather erratic course of the production and exportation, as of the prices, of phosphates and mineral ores. Tourism, on the other hand, which is the largest single item among the services exported, has followed an upward path almost continuously over the past dozen years — the share of tourism in the earnings of services has risen steadily to reach 45 per cent of the total in 1972. (Over the decade 1962-71 the importance of traditional commodity exports — olive oil, wine and phosphates — declined, and that of new commodities — petroleum, processed phosphates, fertilisers and processed iron ores — rose.)

It is noteworthy that the receipts from invisible (services) exports have on the whole been in recent years equal to those from commodity exports. This unusual phenomenon is explainable first in the relative modesty of commodity exports, and secondly in the relative significance of services exports. The latter include, in addition to the earnings of tourism, one other very large item: the remittances made by Tunisian workers mainly in France and Federal Germany. (However, these remittances are to a certain extent offset by remittances made abroad by non-Tunisians, mainly French citizens, working in the country.) Table 11.7 contains in condensed form the balance of payments series for the years 1969-72. (Details are not available for 1973, but — according to the *International Financial Statistics* of December 1974 — the current account balance was deficitary. It amounted to $38m, or TD16.72m. The deficit for 1972 is very close in size, or TD16.2m, as Table 11.7 shows.)

The discussion of the external sector calls for emphasis on the 'popularity' of Tunisia among Western governments and multilateral organisations. Although the country has opted for socialism, and for about a decade witnessed a highly centralised system of economic decision-making with one Minister virtually the final authority on the directions and behaviour of the economy, and although planning is taken very seriously both at the level of plan formulation and plan execution, Western donors and the World Bank group have been very helpful and co-operative financially. This has been, and continues to be, mainly due to the general Western political orientation of the country and its leadership, and the relatively moderate political style of this leadership, coupled with the serious-mindedness of the leaders and the conscientiousness of the civil service. (If a cynical factor is to be added, it would be that the West has never taken the pronouncements regarding socialism seriously.) Reference has already been made to the flow of grants and loans. That part of the flow designated for development work has largely gone into the SND and the COFITOUR — respectively Société Nationale d'Investissement and Compagnie Financière et Touristique.

Tunisia, like the other Maghreb countries, has asked for and obtained partial association with the European Economic Community, thanks to long-standing economic connections with Europe when the Maghreb countries were under French rule and their economies were closely tied with that of France. The association, agreed on in 1969 for a period of five years, allows all industrial exports into EEC countries without tariffs (with the exception of petroleum products where a restricted free quota is allowed), subjects olive oil and fish to reduced duties, and admits some types of agricultural produce under preferential treatment. These facilities notwithstanding, the balance of trade is turning against Tunisia, and efforts are being made to renegotiate the agreement to make it more equitable.

The four Maghreb countries (Libya, Tunisia, Algeria and Morocco) have, since 1964, attempted to establish a pattern of close economic co-operation among themselves. Indeed,

Table 11.7: Balance of Payments Summary 1969-72 (TD millions)

	1969		1970		1971		1972	
	Receipts	Payments	Receipts	Payments	Receipts	Payments	Receipts	Payments
A. Goods and services	166.0	212.3	186.5	238.7	241.7	257.2	299.4	318.2
Merchandise	87.0	135.0	95.8	154.5	111.9	174.6	148.9	216.1
Trade balance	−48.0		−58.7		−62.7		−67.2	
Services								
Transport	10.7	23.4	13.3	25.0	15.4	21.2	18.7	28.5
Travel (including tourism)	28.3	12.6	34.3	12.0	56.5	15.3	71.5	18.4
Revenue on capital	1.2	13.9	1.5	15.5	2.9	12.8	3.6	21.7
Revenue on labour	11.5	13.6	15.3	14.5	22.9	12.7	29.7	10.2
Other services	27.3	13.7	26.3	17.2	32.1	20.6	27.0	23.2
B. Current transfers	3.9	1.7	4.7	1.9	8.1	1.9	5.7	3.1
Total current account	169.9	214.0	191.2	240.7	249.8	259.2	305.1	321.3
Balance of current account	−44.1		−49.5		−9.4		−16.2	
C. Capital movements								
Long-term capital	75.5	23.9	73.5	28.4	86.9	25.7	90.2	33.3
Grants	19.2	–	17.8	0.1	13.0	–	13.5	–
Direct investments	33.5	8.3	22.6	10.5	30.4	9.1	31.3	20.2
Private sector capital	19.2	14.9	23.6	17.0	30.9	16.4	29.4	12.0
Short-term capital	25.6	24.4	32.6	22.9	25.4	31.5	22.6	30.8
Total capital movements	101.1	48.3	106.1	51.3	112.3	57.2	112.8	64.1
Balance of capital account	+52.8		+55.8		+55.1		+48.7	
D. Deposit money	3.1	3.0	0.9	–	0.9	–	1.8	–
E. Allocations of SDRs	–	–	3.0	–	2.0	–	2.6	–
Total A+B+C+D+E	274.1	265.3	301.3	292.0	364.9	316.4	422.3	385.4
Overall balance	+8.8		+9.3		+48.5		+36.9	
F. Changes in exchange revenues	0.2	9.0	7.9	17.2	3.8	52.3	3.0	39.9
Grand Total	274.3	274.3	309.2	309.2	368.7	368.7	425.3	425.3

Note: Totals do not always tally because of rounding.
Source: *Statistiques Financières*, Nos. 15, 16 and 17, p.60.

498 Tunisia

it was President Bourguiba who, as early as 1957, advocated economic unification from Libya east to Morocco west. However, the Ministers of national economy of the four countries in their initial meetings between 1964 and 1967 decided on more modest and realistic goals, particularly:

— Co-ordination of commercial policy with a view to the promotion of transactions among the Maghreb countries.
— Co-ordination of the industrial aspects of activity.
— Formulation of common policy with regard to economic relations with Europe, particularly with the Common Market.
— Co-ordination of the development plans in force in the countries.
— Co-ordination of policies applied in the various sectors of the national economies.[62]

However, the success in achieving these goals has been modest and quite mixed. Thus, certain institutional and organisational measures have been taken, and some preparatory studies undertaken, but neither the institutions nor the studies have led to specific, concrete co-ordination and co-operation which is the core and substance of the whole effort. (A Maghreb Permanent Consultative Committee, then an Industrial Studies Center, have been formed, and a number of bilateral and multilateral agreements for specific objectives have been signed since 1968 among the Maghreb countries.)[63] At the time of writing, the Maghreb is only slightly nearer readiness for co-operation, and is still very far from economic unity. Consequently, the individual economies have not felt the impact of the drive for co-operation on their external (or internal) sectors, and this impact remains therefore a matter of faith and hope for the future.

On balance, the external sector of Tunisia is critical for development and yet insufficiently endowed for the task. It can be said that the human factor is now ready to exert a developmental effort beyond the capability of the external sector to generate the volume of foreign resources called for by the effort. However, very recent developments since the vast increase in the earnings of the petroleum sector in October 1973, and since the emergence of huge oil revenues in the large Arab petroleum-exporting countries, together make the prospect of accelerated development much brighter, given the quality of government, of the civil service, and of manpower in the private sector.

The Leading Socio-Economic Sector, Manpower and Education: The country's achievements in the field of manpower in general, and education in particular, can be appraised properly only if the basic problem of unemployment and underemployment and the long-term nature of investment in the population are given full account. Superficially, the picture looks confusing. For, side by side with a very serious and successful effort in the field of education and training (and in health services), the result of which is a distinctly better-educated and trained (and a healthier) generation of young people, there runs an unsatisfactory record with regard to the effort to absorb a sizeable proportion of the unemployed and underemployed in gainful occupations.

Observations made right after independence with regard to the superabundance of shoeshines, flower vendors, newsboys and pavement fruit vendors can equally be made today — and with the same degree of emphasis.[64] In a sense, the judgement is quite pertinent that, with regard to employment, Tunisia has so far had to run hard in order to remain more or less in the same place. What makes the situation even worse is the combination of accelerated training and education with minimally increased employment opportunities.

The net result has been frustration, a measure of cynicism among the young, and a serious brain drain in search of jobs and steady incomes abroad.

The Tunisian population has a high percentage of youthful and dependent persons. This is the usual pattern in the Arab world, owing to both the high birth rate and the sharp drop in the death rate in the post-war period. The number of persons actively employed is recorded as having been 1,424,000 by the end of 1971 — or some 27.4 per cent of total population. Those permanently employed in the active work-force total only 764,000 (or just under 54 per cent of the work-force), and those seasonally employed add up to the equivalent of 660,000 (just over 46 per cent).[65] These figures must be taken with considerable caution, first, because an estimate was initially made for the total, and then from this total the number of the employed in all the sectors except agriculture was deducted leaving the number of agricultural workers as a residual. The second cause for reserve is that the number of the seasonally employed is largely a matter of estimation, and the conversion of man/days worked into man/year equivalents is a matter of definition, the result of which depends on the assumption made with respect to the number of man/days to be included in a man/year.

The size of the labour force indicated — assuming it is accepted as the best-informed guess — is small, but no smaller than in most other Arab countries, where the same intractable problems of unemployment and underemployment are encountered. The very limited participation of women in non-agricultural work (8.8 per cent) is one factor making for the small size. Another factor is the high rate of dependency. But these are factors of marginal effect. The major determinant of the small overall size of the labour force in active employment is the weak absorptive capacity of the economy for employment, handicapped as the economy is with a predominantly extensive agriculture and an industry which is not as yet very labour-absorptive.

A truer appreciation of the slow growth of employment opportunities can be acquired if the size of the work-force in 1971 is compared with that in 1956.[66] In the latter year, a total of 1,328,000 persons were employed (including 106,000 non-Tunisians). The work-force in 1971 represents an increase of 7 per cent over 15 years, a period during which the population rose by about 38 per cent. If the comparison is restricted to the Tunisian population, then the increase in employment would amount to 16.5 per cent, and that in population to 53 per cent. The gap becomes larger, although the increase in employment is now larger. The many thousands who are designated by this gap have been partly 'absorbed' in unemployment and underemployment, partly in emigration. (According to the *Retrospectives,* net emigration of Tunisians in the decade concerned added up to 158,000. Virtually all belong to the work age groups. However, a more recent estimate places the number at 212,000.[67])

Table 11.8 shows the structure of the labour force in 1956 and in 1971, despite the tentativeness of the data. If the distribution of the labour force by sector is compared with the distribution of GDP also by sector (as seen in Table 11.3 above), the same inference can be drawn as in the case of the other Arab countries (with few exceptions, such as Lebanon and the oil-producing countries, which have an unduly small agricultural sector). This is that the labour force engaged in agriculture is much larger than its relative contribution to national product, while the reverse (with greater emphasis) is true of the force engaged in services. Industry broadly defined, or the secondary sectors, fall somewhere in between, but even here the contribution of the industrial labour force to GDP is slightly larger than its relative size in total labour force. The welfare implications of these observations cannot be overstated, particularly with respect to the rural sector which accounts

500 Tunisia

for 59 per cent of employment (but where over 60 per cent of this employment is seasonal).

Table 11.8: Distribution of the Labour Force by Sector, 1956 and 1971

Sector Group	1956 Number (thousand)	Per Cent	1971 Number (thousand)	Per Cent
Primary	1,000	75	839	59
Secondary	139	11	259	18
Tertiary	188	14	326	23
Total	1,327[a]	100	1,424	100

a. The labour force for 1956 includes non-Tunisians. This inclusion is justified on the grounds that the volume of employment for the whole economy in the first and last year is being compared.

Source: For 1956, FAO, Project FAO de Développement Mediterranéen, *Tunisie: Rapport nationale* (Rome, 1959), Table II-4 (sectors grouped in the source, but percentages calculated here); for 1971, *Retrospectives...*, p. 108 (sectors grouped by the writer).

Comparison of the distribution of the labour force by sector between the two years brings out some findings which are not surprising: a drop in the agricultural labour force both in absolute and relative terms (which normally goes with greater mechanisation in agriculture and other improvements in methods); a rise in the labour force in the secondary sectors, also in absolute and in relative terms (owing to the expansion in the manufacturing sector and in the emergence of a petroleum sector); and finally a rise in the labour force in the tertiary groups both in absolute and in relative terms (to be accounted for in the expansion in certain service sectors, in the 'padding' that usually accompanies early development, and in the expansion in the civil service and the army).

What adds irony to the bitterness in the situation with regard to unemployment and underemployment in the case of Tunisia is that in spite of the shortages in cadres (especially the middle level — supervisory and technician — categories) the country is believed to be ahead by some 10—15 years of Algeria and Morocco in this respect. The overall negligence of education by the French authorities notwithstanding, an accident (which history produces occasionally) enabled Tunisia to have an advantage over its western Maghreb neighbours. The coming into power in France of the Socialists under Léon Blum in the mid-thirties, and the coincidence of there being at the same time in Tunisia a Resident-General of strong reformist leanings, resulted in heavy emphasis on education for several years. In addition, despite the difference in size of population among the three Maghreb countries, Tunisia at the time had twice as many students in France as Morocco and Algeria combined. Likewise, local government was then active in the field of education and training, partly as a result of a reformist attitude and partly to make up for the scarcity of resources. The combined effect of these factors, and of the strong emphasis the Destour Party has always placed on modernisation and education, was to enable Tunisia to be less seriously handicapped upon independence, with respect to educated and trained manpower, than the two Maghreb countries to the west and the third to the east.

The determined effort in the independence era to accelerate social development has built upon but considerably gone beyond the limited advantage of 1956. One aspect of this social development needs special mention. It is the improvement in the social status of women, which probably places Tunisia ahead of all the Arab countries in this respect. Legislation favourable to women has been enacted in several areas, such as divorce, polygamy, inheritance and political rights. This is in addition to gains made by women in the field of education.[68]

Reference has already been made to the short supply in cadres, especially at the supervisory and technical levels. The picture with respect to entrepreneurial resources is not as clear. However, it can be stated in summary form that, in the view of businessmen, these resources are not in serious short supply though they may be inhibited for various reasons from coming forth. On the other hand, government officials, party leaders and economic analysts seem to think differently and to conclude that the public sector – in some form or another – is called upon to make up for the shortage in certain key areas of entrepreneurship.

Wherever the truth lies, it seems certain that the Tunisian entrepreneurs have been rather inhibited, in spite of sporadic indications to the contrary. The inhibition has its roots in the era of the protectorate as in the sixties, after independence. When the French ruled the country, French businessmen in the various sectors had distinct advantages in the form of greater experience, readier finance and promotive cultural factors – in addition to a favourable political atmosphere. No wonder that their Tunisian counterparts – or potential counterparts – felt inhibited and outshone and allowed their entrepreneurial tendencies to be suppressed.

Independence created rosy expectations. But before these could be translated into investment and brisk expansion, the socio-economic system changed again, and the climate became generally unfavourable for entrepreneurial activity. This refers to the decade beginning in 1959 when the system became associated with socialism, collectivisation, and 'co-operative organisation'. We will not dwell here on the transformation, since this will occupy us further down. It is sufficient for our present purposes to state here that it was in 1969 that the business community began to regain confidence, when the Law of 22 September of that year undid much of the restructuring of the economic system which Ahmad Ben Saleh had been engaged in during his long tenure of office in the key economic ministries. Today the entrepreneurs of Tunisia, particularly the industrialists, seem to be capable of launching into new avenues of activity in more than one direction, within an organised society and the framework of a strong government. The major bottleneck seems to be financing and foreign exchange.

The place of education in national life and in social and economic transformation had been recognised long before independence. The Destour party and independent intellectuals consistently pressed for a greater educational effort on the part of protectorate and local authorities. This concern has continued into the era of independence, but with greater force and with the advantage of sovereignty and the ability of the political system and its institutions to set the objectives, choose the strategies, lay down the policies and take the steps capable of leading to the objectives. The tone and the direction for the national effort in education were set by Bourguiba who, in 1957, stated:

> Education is one of the most urgent tasks of the state. It is the fundamental foundation on which the structure of the state reposes firmly. In fact, education is the factor which guarantees the conditions of progress and of general well-being and which ensures a decent level for everybody.[69]

The national effort — and it is predominantly undertaken by the public sector — has been enormous and growing since then. In fact, in a study on the costs of education in Tunis it is stated that the financial burden has been growing at about 14 per cent per annum on average since 1960, so that by 1968 this burden reached 8.2 per cent of GDP or 10.5 per cent of national income. (It rose from 17 to 26.4 per cent of the state budget between 1960 and 1968, reached 30 per cent in 1970, and dropped slightly to 26 per cent in 1971.)[70] This outlay has reflected itself in the growth of school population, from an index of 100 in 1956, to 412 for primary, 559 for secondary, and 514 for higher education in 1970/1. Another significant indicator is the proportion of school-age population actually in schools. This proportion reached 85.2 per cent for boys, 58.5 per cent for girls, and 72.4 per cent for both sexes in the academic year 1971-2 at the primary level. Finally, participation of females has risen consistently from 1956. Thus, from 34 per cent, 20.7 per cent and 17 per cent it rose to 38.7 per cent, 28.4 per cent and 23 per cent for primary, secondary and higher education respectively.[71]

The data so far presented have all related to public education. Private education exists, but it constitutes a very small proportion of the total picture today. Thus in 1971/2, the number of primary school pupils was 8,196, or under 1 per cent of total primary school population in the country. The private secondary (non-vocational) schools accounted for 5,566 pupils, or under 3 per cent of the total. However, private education was much more important upon independence, and even more so in the late forties. Thus, in 1948, private education at all levels accounted for 19.3 per cent of total school population. It is noteworthy with regard to this year that the Tunisian 'Moslems' in all represented only 60.7 per cent of total school population at all levels. This proportion included students in private Moslem (designated as 'Modern Koranic') schools, who constituted over one-fifth of the total. It is also significant that there were *fewer* Tunisians than French in the secondary schools run by the state in 1948![72]

The expectations of the *Perspectives* had been brighter with respect to the spread of education than the actual performance. Thus it had been expected that the number of school-age children in 1971 would be 1,182,000, and that *all* these would be in school by that year. In fact, it had been expected that beginning with October 1966, *all* school-age children would be admitted to schools.[73] While it is true that the rate of population increase proved higher than expected, the shortfall in admission to school is none the less real and substantial.

The quantitative indicators of the expansion of education in the independence era are only a partial manifestation of the deep concern with education. There is also the equally significant concern with the substance, methodology, quality and aims of education. The concern with quality has had to find its expression within a framework of fast change, crisis and uncertainty. For the end of French rule and the subsequent clashes with the French led to the withdrawal of hundreds of French teachers on whom the system had depended rather heavily, especially as the language of instruction in general was French. Not only did the government have to replace the departing staff, but also to add considerably to the teaching force in order to cope with the fast-increasing student body. There were also the burning issues of the use of French as the language of instruction as against the shift to Arabic or the resort to a dual system;[74] the purposes and methods of education; the relevance of education to the developmental needs of the economy; and the building up of a national university system.

The educational system comprises three cycles, with horizontal branching off into vocational training within the second (secondary) cycle. Promotion from the first (elementary) cycle to the second is made on the basis of examinations in Arabic, French and arithmetic. After passing, the pupil may either go to the second cycle of general education or to vocational training, or drop out. The first cycle has a light load of school hours: 15 weekly for the first year, and 25 for each of the remaining five years. The pupils get some 'travaux pratiques' in addition to conventional class-work. Elementary instruction does not provide the child with any substantial preparation for life if he fails to continue with secondary or vocational training. The system suffers from a number of problems and shortcomings, such as short hours of instruction, insufficient housing facilities for schools, shortage of teachers, especially in Arabic, too great haste in training of teachers, and the need to collect teachers from different countries with different backgrounds to meet all the requirements of the schools.

The second cycle also provides insufficient preparation for life and practical applied work. This question is being looked into and corrected, but the feeling in the country is that more emphasis would still have to be placed on the encouragement both of practical (usable) training and of creativeness.[75] This writer's evaluation is that notwithstanding such criticism, Tunisia (like Algeria) leads the Arab world in what its educational system offers.

The University of Tunis was established in 1960, but already in 1957 three university-level institutions existed. Today, higher education comprises five faculties (arts, sciences, law, medicine and theology), four institutes (agronomy, business administration, commerce and journalism), and four schools (engineering, law,[76] teacher training and assistant-teacher training[77]). The total student body registered in 1971/2 was 10,992 (excluding 524 students in journalism and teacher training).

Except for theology and Islamic studies, Arabic literature and law at the school of law, where Arabic is the language of instruction, French is in exclusive use. This does not constitute as much of a problem as it would if a foreign language were used in, say, Egypt or Iraq. The difference arises from the fact that French is actually widely used in the country — in the cities, among the young, in business and in much of government. Nevertheless, the wider use of Arabic is a burning issue — one of several that have been and still are under live and serious examination since the spring of 1972. They relate essentially to the question of the degree of faithfulness of education to society's cultural heritage and its relatedness to its future needs. The issues also include the methods of education, and the proper balance between theory and application, lectures and workshops; as well as the scope and substance of education with specific emphasis on the question of generality versus specialisation.

Behind some of the issues is the concern with the matching of supply of university graduates in the various categories of skill with demand for them. It is felt that quantitatively, and disregarding quality and skill differentiation, there is no serious gap between global supply and demand. In fact, some observers contend that there is an over-supply, and that this is creating a serious problem of unemployment among university graduates, frustration and manpower waste. This phenomenon, coupled with serious shortages in certain key fields of training, has been taken into close consideration in the most recent development plan for the years 1973-6. Reconsideration has also been made of the ease with which secondary school graduates are admitted to university. Thus, 95 per cent of the holders of the *baccalauréat* enter the university. This, plus the inadequate training at the secondary level, accounts for the very high proportion of failure among university men and women — stated as 80 per cent for the whole student body. Although there are university fees, some 60 per cent of students are state bursaries. To these factors must be added the fact that many entrants do not have a clear notion of what they really want to train for, and whether they are suited by temperament and mental aptitude for the field of their choice. This last question has led the Minister of Education in a statement made to the National Assembly in 1972[78] to suggest that a year be inserted between the *baccalauréat* and admission to the university, during which the student would be trained and observed to help him and the system determine what he is best suited for.

In addition to institutions of formal higher education, there are a number of research institutes in the country which are concerned with the social sciences, medical science, agronomy, arid zone technology, and the like. These are generally active and conduct studies of relevance to the country's problems. Some of these research outfits are autonomous or loosely connected with the university; some fall under ministries.

A second area of achievement in the social field is that of health and sanitation. Here the country's first concern upon achieving independence was to replace the foreign medical personnel who left the country or were to leave. Subsequently, it was aimed to re-establish the level of services of pre-independence days, and then to improve on it. Since it is difficult to assess what happened to the standards of health and hygiene, we will concentrate here on a comparison of the medical personnel (in the public and private sectors) available at the close of World War Two, in 1956 and in 1971 (the last year for which data are available) as shown in Table 11.9.

Table 11.9: Medical Personnel, 1946, 1956 and 1971

	1946	1956	1971
Doctors	434 (about 30 per cent Tunisians)	548	1,004 (mostly Tunisians)
Dentists	57	81	76
Pharmacists	144 (including wholesale distributors)	186	163
Veterinary surgeons	25	33	n.a.
Diploma midwives	94	134	225 (public sector only)

Sources: For 1946 and 1956, *Annuaire Statistique de la Tunisie 1956*, p. 27; for 1971, UN *Statistical Yearbook 1973*, p. 719.

Though fragmentary, these figures suggest a tangible improvement in the absolute numbers of medical personnel. However, the achievement is not remarkable if it is remembered that the population increased by 60 per cent between 1946 and 1971.

Transformation of the Socio-Economic System

Tunisia is the only Arab country where transformation in the socio-economic system has occurred *within* the political system in existence and by the group effectively in power. This is essentially because effective power resides in the President personally, and it is he who accepted and blessed, if not altogether initiated, the change in the socio-economic ideology of the country.

However, this change must not be overestimated. Tunisia was and remains a country that espouses liberalism and democracy in the forms known to the West, though with a strong flavour of personal power which is made possible through the prestige and unchallenged standing of Bourguiba, his charisma, and his firm grasp of the strings of power. But within these limitations — which are not minor — the people, the press and the politicians can discuss controversial issues and disagree over them, particularly when the President has not said 'the final word' on the issues under discussion.

Change has not at any one point come abruptly and in very painful doses, but gradually and within the framework of legality. In Amin's words, 'In Tunisia, the modern national movement gradually moved from a moderate position towards more radical attitudes, without a real break at any given time.'[79] The attitude with regard to socio-economic change can be summed up as always having been 'evolutionist but not revolutionist'. This was true of the shift from the Liberal Constitutional Party, or the Destour, to the Neo-Destour in 1934, as well as of the shift in attitude to independence and modernisation. It was also true of the shift from economic liberalism, in which the political leaders of independence days believed, to 'socialism' — or, more correctly, state capitalism or state interventionism — towards the end of the fifties, mainly under the pressure of harsh economic realities. It was finally true of the change in the name of the party from Neo-Destour, to the Destourian Socialist Party, DSP, in November 1964. This new 'baptism' put the seal on the transformation, and it occurred when the wave of 'socialism' under the dynamic and powerful hegemony of Ahmad Ben Saleh was at its peak. No doubt it found help in the ranks of the technocrats and civil servants, and blessing in party circles, and final approval from the President. Again, as Amin puts it, this transformation, and its later consolidation in structural measures in 1967-8, brought about a closer 'fusion between the state and the party'.[80]

The predominant specific form which Tunisian socialism took, apart from general *étatiste* tendencies, the extension of the public sector, foreign exchange controls and the like, was the large-scale adoption of the co-operative form of business organisation, first in agriculture and later in other sectors. The chief engineer and builder of the new system, Ben Saleh, supported by a strong civil service, the party apparatus and many intellectuals, and echoed by the press, described the new trend of co-operation or collectivisation as a step towards socialism. The approach to the new system was well-integrated and coherent, and in order to establish consistency among the various components of economic and social policy, Ben Saleh accepted to carry the ministries of finance, national economy and planning, and in 1968 that of education as well. By 1969, the system was seen to be very costly, overly centralised, unproductive and wasteful. It also probaby gave the political image of Ben Saleh a suspiciously large boost which was not very pleasing to the party and the President. Consequently, abruptly and decisively, Ben Saleh was dismissed in September 1969, and he was later arrested for being responsible for the excesses in co-operation and for the failure of the movement. His subsequent trial and long prison sentence (which he managed to cut short by escaping from prison in 1973) provided a useful alibi for the political leadership, and has also marked a turning-point back towards economic liberalism but within greater state economic control and participation (or state capitalism). However, the system claims to be still under the socialist flag.

It is instructive to examine a little more closely the background to the Ben Saleh era, and then the experience of collectivisation itself.[81] The national private sector was weak before 1956, and was restricted to agriculture. But even in this sector, the best plots were in the hands of the *colons*. In industry, the imposition of the protectorate meant that Tunisia had to have enforced on it a customs union with France, which hampered the emergence of national industries. The activity of Tunisian industrialists was thus restricted to the simple transformation of grains, grape and other agricultural produce. Foreign trade and internal wholesale commerce were also in the hands of foreigners, as was banking. Tourism had not yet come on to the stage.

Beginning with 1956, and until 1962, opportunities opened up for Tunisians thanks to the disappearance of economic discrimination and pressure, and the emergence of some national banks which provided credit facilities to Tunisian businessmen. However, industry remained rather paralysed, because the customs union with France remained in force until 1959. (The Central Bank was established in 1958 but started operations in 1959, and the country acquired an independent currency in the latter year.) The private sector tried in the years 1956-9 to recapture some institutions, assets and utilities, such as *colon* land, and part of trade and of banking; it also became somewhat active in industry in spite of the customs union. However, it was in the years 1959-62 that the Tunisisation of trade was completed by smooth non-confiscatory methods, and Tunisian industry became active in the field of import substitution.

The movement began to slacken in the year 1962-3, owing to the initiation of collectivisation. A new pressure, Tunisian this time, began to operate downwards on business — in favour of co-operatives and government enterprises, at the expense of the private sector. This sector was slowly pushed aside to make room for the expansion of the public sector (as for example in textiles, a typically private enterprise area). In agriculture, co-operatives were forced 'from above', instead of being formed in response to a genuine desire among the farmers at the grass-roots level. In trade too co-operatives were forced, for large and small businesses, at district, sub-district and local levels. (The pyramid, as far as trade went, was headed by the Bureau of Tunisian Trade, whose powers included price-setting and choice of commodities to be traded in.) The same thing also happened in industry.

A 'white revolution' occurred in September 1969, when Bourguiba admitted error in letting Ben Saleh act freely. He then revised policy courageously and to the satisfaction of the business community and the landlords, but probably not of the technocrats and bureaucrats and the ideologically oriented young intellectuals. The years 1969-72 have represented a recapture of breath for the economy and a pause for reconsideration of its directions. Manifestations of the revision of policy have included the undoing of land co-operatives except when voluntarily wanted, the undoing of state trade institutions, and the easing or release of pressure and controls on industrialists. As things stand today in 1975 the public sector restricts its activities to the fields of air and sea transport and the railways; the water, gas and electricity sector (the last-named branch of industry had been taken over from foreign ownership gradually); underground wealth in the form of mines and petroleum; some large manufacturing industries still in public-sector hands from the 1962-9 period; the car assembly industry and part of the textile industry. However, there is now greater flexibility in operation though the government is in possession of productive capital. The rest of the economy is in the hands of, or is open to, the private sector.

A quick evaluation of the collectivisation and socialist period reveals that the new drive was probably less oriented towards the welfare of the masses than it was inspired and guided by the ideas of élitist groups interested in the restructuring of economic and political power and in ideological formulae. The down-to-earth questions of increased production, greater economic efficiency and greater distributive justice and welfare, though matters of serious concern, received less thought and attention than abstract ideological questions. It is currently contended that behind the condemnation of collectivisation by the business community and the landlords lies a deeper satisfaction at collectivisation because it enabled them to have a stronger say in their branches of economic activity inside the frame of co-operation. However, it is also contended that the business community began to feel restless when it found that the *dirigiste* tendencies of the government were depriving the businessmen of their freedom of action *vis-à-vis* the small establishments, be these small farms or small retail shops and groceries. At this point the collectivisation drive began to damage Tunisian entrepreneurship and to dampen its expectations and its dynamism.

Parallel with this, it seems easily demonstrable that the collectivisation hurt the weaker, poorer groups of the population whom it had presumably set out to benefit. Hence the disenchantment, even among the poor, with collectivism or co-operation. Behind the disenchantment lie several factors such as the drop in overall production in several areas of activity; change in familiar economic relations between groups, from the 'personal and brotherly', especially in agriculture, to the formal and harsh; the drop in the benefits obtained by tenants and agricultural workers; the rise in the number of beneficiaries out of a given area of land; the disappearance of the old landlord in his role of provider of certain basic functions such as credit, management, and the continuity of decision-making — the last giving way to arbitrariness and variability;[82] the over-reach of the co-operative or collective measures, both in that they included far too many sectors, and subsectors, and too many units within the sectors; the excessive interference by bureaucrats in small decisions; the entry of politicians and opportunists into the decision-making process with motivation often alien to the objectives of the economic units concerned; and finally the weakness of the cadres in charge.

It is obvious that the previous paragraph echoes the tone of the business community. A balanced appraisal of the Ben Saleh era calls for the introduction of some qualifications to the statements just recorded. With regard to the background to collectivisation, several things ought to be kept in mind. One of these is that the party had been committed to socialism since about 1962, on the basis of a loose social philosophy designed just before independence. More specifically, the sixth congress of the Neo-Destour Party, held in 1959, had designed an approach to progress through the three avenues of the public sector, the private sector and the co-operative sector. Soon after, preparations were initiated for the first plan of development within the framework of the 1962-71 decade, and this has since been considered as a step within the framework of socialism.[83] The conceptualisation of the system included the delineation of the frontiers of each of the sectors.

In addition to this conceptualisation, there were some strong arguments underlying the expansion of the role of the public sector and the initiation of socialism (as seen by the architects of the system). One of these was the slow and weak initiative of the private sector in taking over the functions vacated by French entrepreneurs upon independence, and in launching into new areas of enterprise. Another was the relative weakness and defencelessness of the small farmers and agricultural workers in the face of the strong landlords with their economic and financial power and their political influence. A third was the urgency of the problem of disposal of lands vacated by or expropriated from the French. These lands, plus the excess areas to be expropriated from large land holdings under agrarian reform, were to be dealt with in a new fashion. This was the setting up of collective farms, each of 500 hectares at least. These collective farms, as well as the conventional co-operative societies, were to be the recipients of state financial and technical aid and of such inputs as select seeds, water and cheap electricity. Towards the end of Ben Saleh's tenure, some 220 state collective farms existed, and many more were being established. (Later, it was revealed in Ben Saleh's trial that many of these were wasteful and had been making losses that the Ministry of Finance bore out of its own resources. Since then, the farmers have been allowed to leave the collective farms, and agrarian reform involving an estimated area of 750,000 ha has been legislated. Emphasis now is on voluntary co-operation.)

On balance, therefore, the period 1962-9 can be said to have represented a serious confusion between ideology and practical issues, idealism and political favouritism and power hunger, technocratic and bureaucratic zeal and insufficient readiness for the tasks involved, and a basic espousal of liberalism and private enterprise parallel with declarations of socialism — whether or not the latter was really state capitalism. When the final dismantling of the structures built by Ben Saleh was completed, it could be said that the country had strayed into a different system for the best part of a decade, but had by 1971 'gone back to base'.

3. PLANNING AND PLANS

Planning in the true sense of the term started only with the first plan in Tunisia, which ran for three years beginning 1962. However, right after World War Two a systematic approach to investment by the public sector took form in the formulation in 1947 of what was called the 'Plan de Modernisation et d'Equippement'. This plan depended mainly on the inflow of foreign resources.[84]

Planning preparations started formally in 1958, or two years after independence. The preparatory work accelerated in tempo and grew in extent and reach, at the same time as it became more refined in quality. Nevertheless, it took about four years before the first attempt at planning was published, namely the *Perspectives Décennales de Développement 1962-1971*. This document, which we have had occasion several times to quote or to peruse, is in a sense a planning document, inasmuch as it projected an investment programme for the decade 1962-71, for the purpose of achieving a number of quantitative and qualitative objectives. To this extent, therefore, we have already appraised the planning experience of Tunisia since we have identified the expectations indicated in the *Perspectives* and later examined the performance as it has been reported in the *Retrospectives Decennales 1962-71*, in the preceding section of this chapter.

In another, more rigorous sense, the *Perspectives* is not a plan but only a broad framework — as its authors assert in several places — within which two plans were to be prepared. The first, itself also called a 'pre-plan' because of its tentative nature, ran for the three years 1962-4, and the second was to have run for seven years, 1965-71, but was later split into two four-year plans, 1965-8, and 1969-72.[85] Thus, in fact, the decade covered by the *Perspectives* came to spread into eleven years in the three plans formulated within the framework of the *Perspectives*.

About six months after the preparation of the *Perspectives*, the *Plan Triennal 1962-1964* was published by the Secrétariat d'Etat au Plan et aux Finances, and it became law in May 1962. The examination of this Three-Year Plan reveals that it was comprehensive in more than one sense. Thus, it concerned itself with the whole economy, its private and public sectors. It also concerned itself with structural change, growth and the development of manpower resources. The Three-Year Plan is much more detailed than the *Perspectives*, going down to specific projects, policies and measures.

The objectives of the *Perspectives*, already recorded in section 2 above, were adopted for the three plans that were to be formulated subsequently. However, each of these plans concentrated on one or more different objectives. Thus, the first of the three emphasises certain objectives 'which it is urgent to attain in order to make all the easier the realization of other objectives in the *Perspectives*. In fact, this involves effecting decolonization,

Tunisia

implementing the structural reforms, and finally preparing the second plan (1965-1971).'86 The second aim of the plan is related to the first, in so far as structural reforms involve the reduction in the degree of dualism through the spread of the modern and the shrinkage of the traditional sector, injecting rationality into the economy, promoting and rendering more efficient the handicrafts sector, achieving a better distribution of income, and modernising and raising productivity in the civil service.

The silence in the first plan with regard to the rate of growth projected for the three years is more than compensated for in the quantification and detail that fill the 505 pages and the 23 annexed tables of the document. Understandably, only the global expectations under the plan will be presented here, first, because the sectors, subsectors, programmes and projects which receive minute examination in the document will require much more space than we have available if they are to be surveyed here, and secondly because the implementation, and the results, have in fact moved far from the expectations and the projections. It is enough for our purposes, therefore, to record in Table 11.10 the aggregates foreseen with regard to the availability and the use of resources for the last year 1964.

Table 11.10: Planned Availability and Uses of Resources, 1964 (TDm, 1957 prices)

Resources	
Production	616.1
Imports	110.4
Total	726.5
Uses of Resources	
Intermediate consumption	261.0
Final consumption	277.3
Exports	63.1
Gross capital formation	125.1
Total	726.5
Gross Capital Formation (GCF)	
GCF by the administration	55.1
GCF by business	68.0
GCF by households	2.0
Total	125.1

Source: Secrétariat d'Etat au Plan et aux Finances, *Plan Triennal 1962-64*, pp. 11-12.

Against this volume of capital formation we have domestic savings (gross production less intermediate and final consumption) amounting to TD77.8m. The difference between

510 Tunisia

capital formation and domestic savings, which amounts to TD47.3m, constitutes a deficit which was expected to be financed through the import surplus, that is from external sources.

We cannot calculate the average annual rate of growth as no estimates of national product are given for the years 1962 and 1963, and those for 1964 relate to 'gross production' rather than 'domestic production', or gross domestic product.[87] It can only be assumed that the rate of growth expected was on the average in the neighbourhood of 6 per cent, which had been the rate projected in the *Perspectives*. Domestic savings were to amount to about one-fifth of domestic production (therefore to a smaller proportion of GDP). The expectation was that growth would be slow in the three years under examination, owing to the heavy investments to be made in economic and social infrastructure, and in tree-planting and irrigation works, all of which require a long gestation period.

The Four-Year Plan 1965-8 which was to follow was enacted by law on 29 May 1965. Even more than the one before it, the second plan related the expectations and investments recorded and programmed to the overall transformation of the society and economy and to society's objectives. It set out to examine the degree of success in the achievement of those objectives, and showed that decolonisation was largely wiped out, while dualism was greatly reduced, and structural reform was moving ahead very satisfactorily, particularly with respect to education and training. However, the document is not very articulate with regard to achievements in terms of growth of national product during the three years of the First Plan.

The Four-Year Plan concentrated on the promotion of industry — in fact this Plan is characterised as 'the plan of Tunisian industrialization'.[88] However, no less than the first plan, the present one emphasises manpower development and likewise devotes to it a very large part of the plan document: in fact, the whole of Volume III is taken up by the subject of manpower development in its various aspects (including housing and public utilities).

Total investment for the four years is programmed at TD380m at 1960 prices, or TD455m at current prices. Industry (including handicrafts), energy and tourism were due to receive the largest allocations, or a little over one-third of the total, followed by agriculture with just under one-third. The balance goes to the rest of the sectors, with more than half of it directed to collective equipment. Again as in the Three-Year Plan, more than half of the investment was expected to be made by the private sector. The distribution by source of investment is shown in Table 11.11.

Table 11.11: Planned Sources of Investment, 1965-8 (TDm)

The administration	149.3
Business	205.5
Households	25.2
Total	380.0

Taking the year 1968 by itself, the Plan document expects domestic saving to be TD88.3m. Gross investment for that year, again at 1960 prices, is estimated at TD110m. This leaves a deficit of about TD22m to be financed through the import surplus. It can be observed

Tunisia

here that although the deficit in the current account of the balance of payments for 1968 was expected to drop below the level expected for 1964 in the Three-Year Plan, which is a healthy sign in itself, gross investment itself was also to decline. It is likely that more sober expectations of foreign aid and loans for 1968 than for 1964 led to a smaller estimate both for the deficit on the external sector and for gross investment. This is manifest in a table in the Four-Year Plan document, where a slight improvement in the rate of growth of GDP between the period 1960-4 and 1964-8 (from 5.8 to 6.5 per cent) is contrasted with a substantial decline in the annual rate of growth of gross capital formation, from 11.7 to 4.3 per cent for the two periods respectively.[89]

The rise in domestic production between 1960 and 1968 is estimated at 6 per cent, or from TD290.2m to TD472.3m (at 1960 prices), while the rise in GDP averages 6.1 per cent, from TD335.3m to 539.5m. The rosiest expectation of growth is to be found in the energy sector (14.5 per cent), and the lowest is in the agricultural sector (2.8 per cent), with the other sectors ranging between 6.4 per cent for transport, commerce and services, and 9 per cent for buildings and public works.[90]

With remarkable punctuality, the Second Four-Year Plan, entitled Plan de Développement Economique et Social 1969-1972, became law on 30 May 1969, the two earlier plan laws having been enacted on 30 May and 29 May respectively. The change in the official name of the Plan does not reflect greater emphasis being placed on the social aspects of development and the promotion of manpower broadly defined, since these aspects had already received the maximum attention and resources possible under the circumstances, thanks to a correct understanding of the enormous significance for society and economy alike of such promotion.

The Second Four-Year Plan sets a number of objectives which are grouped under qualitative and quantitative objectives. The first group emphasises reform in the sectors of agriculture, commerce and industry, while the second emphasises reform in what is called 'economic agents', particularly non-financial enterprises, financial enterprises and the administration. Finally, the quantitative objectives are three: a rate of growth in GDP averaging 6.5 per cent per annum; improvement in the balance of payments position with a view to increasing the reserves of foreign exchanges by TD31m for the four years, so that the net reserves available in 1972 should be sufficient for one month's imports; and establishing equilibrium in the public finances of the country and achieving a rate of increase of monetary supply not exceeding 6.5 per cent per annum, which is equal to the growth rate envisaged for GDP.

This performance is expected to be achieved thanks to an investment programme totalling TD617m for the four years, contrasted with an actual investment of TD505.8m for the preceding four years — both figures at current prices. The pattern of investment is not radically changed between the two four-year plans. Thus agriculture received almost one-fifth of total investment over the years 1965-8, and was scheduled to receive very much the same proportion in the years 1969-72. Likewise, industry, energy and tourism together received 40 per cent of the total and were scheduled to receive over 36 per cent. The overall picture of expectations, including data for 1968, both at current prices and at constant (1966) prices, is presented in Table 11.12.

It remains to be added that once again the gross investment envisaged exceeded domestic savings, and the deficit was to be made good through foreign loans and grants. This can be seen in Table 11.13.

Table 11.12: Resources and their Uses 1968 and 1969-72

Resources	A. In TD million at Constant (1966) Prices					Growth Rate (Per Cent) 1972/68
	1968	1969	1970	1971	1972	
GDP (at market prices)	547.3	593.7	621.0	660.3	703.3	6.5
Imports	161.1	181.5	201.0	208.1	218.0	7.8[a]
Total	708.4	775.2	822.0	868.4	921.3	6.9
Uses						
Private consumption	358.9	386.9	400.6	423.0	451.9	6.0
Public consumption	105.8	110.2	117.5	124.0	132.5	5.8
Gross capital formation	112.2	133.6	145.0	151.5	157.5	8.6[b]
Changes in stock	2.5	−4.0	2.9	3.9	1.4	−
Exports	129.0	148.5	156.0	166.0	178.0	8.4
Total	708.4	775.2 [sic]	822.0	868.4	921.3	6.9
	B. In TD million at Current Prices					
Resources						
GDP	572.2	626.2	656.5	696.5	746.2	6.8
Imports	156.3	175.9	194.7	202.0	207.8	7.2
Total	728.5	802.1	851.2	895.5 [sic]	952.0 [sic]	6.9
Uses						
Private consumption	371.1	405.4	419.9	443.5	471.2	6.2
Public consumption	110.7	115.8	123.8	130.9	139.4	6.2
Gross capital formation	117.9	140.2	152.3	159.0	165.5	8.6
Changes in stock	2.6	−4.5	3.1	4.2	1.5	−
Exports	126.2	145.2	152.1	160.9	174.4	8.4
Total	728.5	802.1	851.2	898.5	952.0	6.9

a. The rate is relatively high because imports were abnormally low in 1968. If the calculation were based on 1967, the rate would only be in the order of 4 per cent per annum.
b. The same observation applies here as that relating to the imports of 1968. Investment in 1968 was lower than in any of the four years 1965-8, which results in a rate of growth which is relatively high. The average rate that would result if investment in the four years 1969-72 were related to that in the four years 1965-8 is merely 5.9 per cent.

Source: *Plan de Développement Economique et Social 1969-1972*, 1e Volume, p.25.

Table 11.13: Financing of the 1965-8 Plan and the 1969-72 Plan (TD million at current prices)

	Actual Performance 1965-8	Plan Projections 1969-72
Domestic Savings	256.8	403.6
Administration	(66.7)	(104.7)
Business	(160.6)	(268.9)
Households	(29.5)	(30.0)
Net External Aid	250.0	248.7
Gross aid	(328.0)	(360.3)
Less: Repayments	(78.0)	(111.6)
Change in Foreign Exchange Reserves	−10.9	+31.0
Investment	517.7	621.3
Gross capital formation	(505.9)	(617.0)
Change in stocks	(11.8)	(4.3)

Source: *Plan de Développement Economique et Social 1969-1972*, 1e Volume, p.26.

We need not go into an examination of the performance of the economy under planning during the eleven years covered by the three plans. Enough examination for our purposes has been undertaken in section 2 above, particularly in the context of the spotty comparisons made between expectations incorporated in the *Perspectives* and the actual results recorded in the *Retrospectives*.

However, a better and more systematic evaluation of the planning experience of the country, and therefore of the performance of the economy, is possible through the perusal of the long introductory chapter of the Fourth Plan of the *IVe Plan de Développement Economique et Social 1973-1976*,[91] which is currently in operation. This introduction, in addition to data presented at many points in the Plan document dealing with the preceding decade, enables the analyst to draw some important conclusions regarding the economy and the society over the years 1962-72. Furthermore, the broad features of the future image can be discerned, inasmuch as this plan document is not restricted to the four years 1973-6, but also attempts, as the *Perspectives* did over a decade before, to project the important economic and social variables into 1981. Such projection will not occupy us at length here as we present the very broad outline of the contents of the Fourth Plan.

The Plan is part of a new decade, the Décennale 1972-81. However, the Plan itself starts in 1973. This lag is due to the fact that the authorities allowed themselves one year between the lapse of the Third Plan (1969-72) and the start of the Fourth Plan. (The latter plan was enacted by law on 3 August 1973.) Side by side with the projections for the four years 1973-6, several longer projections are made to reach into 1981. The major quantitative objectives are the achievement of a real rate of growth of 6.6 per cent annually on the average, over the base year 1972; the raising of gross investment by 72 per cent over that achieved for the preceding four years (the tripling of investment if the decade 1962-71 is compared with expectations for the following decade); the financing of three-quarters of investment from domestic savings; and the creation of about three times as many new jobs as were created during the preceding decade.

A statement made by the Prime Minister in which he introduced the Plan to the National Assembly set the broad political, social and intellectual — in addition to the economic — framework within which the objectives, strategies and mechanisms of the Plan had been formulated. The long statement constitutes one of the ablest, most penetrating, and comprehensive of its kind in the Arab world. Without summarising it, or presenting its main features or points, we would like to stress here that it examines the nature, functions and limits of the political forces that manage the economy or else prepare the stage for the decision-makers in the private sector, and it lays down the principles and operational rules for the organic fusion and the performance of the state and the party, at the central as well as the regional and local levels. Likewise, it delineates the boundaries of the three sectors — the public, the private and the mixed, and the powers and duties of management, labour and the state. In doing all this, and much more, the statement examines the performance of the country in the decade before, dwelling particularly on the major error committed under the Ben Saleh era when economic power was unduly centralised and concentrated, and collectivisation was forced and extended beyond reason or logic, and contrary to the interests of all the parties concerned. Education and its role occupy a large part of the Prime Minister's statement. The emphasis here is on the new tasks ahead: those relating to the improvement in quality and emphasis on relevance, after the success in the quantitative expansion witnessed since independence.

The General Introduction to the Plan document goes into the analysis of the past and the projection of the present into the future in more specific terms. The central theme here is the need in the decade 1972-81 to concentrate on directly productive sectors and activities, as the preceding decade had concentrated on the development of the social and economic infrastructure. The new focus of concentration was to take body through the redirection of effort, investment and organisation in the service of the new overall objectives.

These objectives are expressed in quantitative and qualitative terms. How the Plan is hoped to serve these objectives can be seen in a few tables presented in the first chapter of the first part, which deals with global estimates. It might be useful to recapitulate here the main ideas and expectations and, parallel with that, to draw comparisons with the preceding decade. Thus, we find that average annual investment tripled during 1962-71, compared with the average for the five years 1957-61. The fact that the rate of growth in real terms remained very modest at 4 per cent per annum on the average, despite the commendable achievement in investment, has already been stated and explained. The explanation, it will be recalled, is to be found in the emphasis on infrastructural investment. Furthermore, where investment was in directly productive activities, it went into very slow-gestating projects.

The gross investment made averaged about 24.6 per cent of GDP during the first decade of planned development. (See Table 11.3.) This is a high proportion. However, less than 60 per cent of it was financed from domestic sources, or about 14 per cent of GDP; the rest came in the form of foreign aid. But there was marked progression during the decade, from a domestic financing effort reaching only 40 per cent at the start, to one reaching 80 per cent of total investment during the Third Plan 1969-72. Another characteristic of the investment during 1962-71 was that two-thirds of it went into activities not directly productive, and 72 per cent of it was undertaken by the public sector broadly defined. But here again, the share of the private sector rose, even if modestly, during the decade. In absolute terms, the average annual investment, which was TD124.5m during 1962-71, is projected to be TD364m during 1972-81. (The average for the four years of the Plan 1973-6 is about TD299m.) Domestic savings are expected to account for 21.8 per cent of GDP in the decade 1972-81. This would enable the economy to provide 80 per cent of the resources for investment and to reduce dependence on the external sector to 20 per cent of these resources.

The rate of growth of GDP will reflect the changes expected to be undertaken. Thus, a rate of 7.6 per cent is expected for the decade, against 4 per cent for the decade before. Table 11.14 shows the level of the expected balance between the availability and the use of resources. Finally, employment will make notable gains, although the problems of unemployment and underemployment will remain substantial. The decade 1962-71 witnessed the creation of 132,500 new jobs outside agriculture (but most of these were in the civil service, where 'new employment' was to a certain considerable extent a form of padding and did not reflect an equivalent degree of increase in production or productivity). Emigration 'solved' the problem of unemployment in the active age groups for 212,000 persons, 161,000 of whom were males. Against these modest results, the new decade is expected to witness the creation of 50,000 new jobs every year on the average.[92]

Table 11.14: Resources and their Uses in 1971, 1976 and 1981 (at 1966 prices)

Resources	1971 TD m	1976 TD m	1981 TD m	1981/72 Per Cent Average
GDP (at market prices)	729.0	1,127.7	1,703.2	7.6
Imports	234.4	453.9	611.7	8.3
Total	963.4	1,581.6	2,314.9	7.9
Uses				
Private consumption	483.9	754.6	1,071.1	7.7
Public consumption	120.5	172.5	208.1	5.5
Gross capital formation	172.1	324.9	511.0	11.9
Change in stocks	7.4	18.0	27.3	–
Exports	179.5	311.6	497.4	7.9
Total	963.4	1,581.6	2,314.9	7.9

Source: *IVe Plan de Développement Economique et Social 1973-1976*, p.50.

One last word is due regarding planning agencies and methods. Right from the outset interest in planning was expressed concretely by the authorities at the highest level. Thus, the President is the president of the National Planning Council, which is the highest planning authority. Further below, there is an Inter-Ministerial Council, a Permanent Committee for Planning, as well as three 'Commissions de Synthèse', in addition to sectoral committees and subcommittees, as well as regional and local committees. There is a considerable measure of consultation and dialogue between the centre and periphery of power, and between the public and the private sector.[93] We need not pursue here the institutional development of planning over the years, except to say that the excessive centralisation of power and functions that accompanied the Ben Saleh era was changed in October 1971, when the planning ministry was normalised through being made independent (it had formerly been attached directly to the Prime Minister).

An overall evaluation of the planning experience would show that the country has moved very far in elaborating well-balanced plans, with adequate studies supporting them and a keen public and private interest in planning and in the plans. However, the various advisory committees seem not to have contributed much to the enrichment of the planning process. Nor have the various committees of businessmen and trade unions.[94] Nevertheless it can be said in conclusion that although there is scope for great improvement at the levels of conception, plan formulation and plan execution,Tunisia can rightly claim to be one of the few Arab countries where planning and plans are taken seriously, where there is a large measure of national mobilisation behind the plans, and where the development orientation of the party and the government, combined, promise to make planning an effective and efficient instrument in the social and economic development of the country.

CONCLUDING REMARKS

The broad generalisations with which this chapter can be concluded have already suggested themselves during the analysis of the experience of the economy in the post-war years. If the lessons drawn from the analysis are to be summed up in a few sentences, then four concluding remarks can be stated.

The first is that Tunisia's record of development expressed simply in average growth rates (in real terms) has so far ranged from poor to moderate, but that it has shown a marked upward tendency in the early seventies. Second, the social and political development of the country has been more pronounced. This is manifest in its performance in the fields of education; the formation of skilled cadres; the building up and Tunisisation of the civil service and the achievement of a high level of proficiency and motivation in its ranks; and the provision of a strong, development-oriented, stable and determined political leadership. These factors, in turn, will prove of immeasurable benefit (as they already have begun to prove) to the economic development of the country and its growth rates specifically defined.

The third concluding remark is that whatever development has been or will be achieved will come about in spite rather than because of the country's physical endowments, though these include remarkable components as far as the scenery, beaches, the climate — and the deposits of phosphates — are concerned. In other words, the achievement must be marked as largely to the credit of the determined and intelligent will of the economic *dirigeants* applied to the endowments.

The projection of this inference leads to the final conclusion, namely that once the major bottleneck of foreign exchange availability (and therefore of the ability to obtain resources and skills from abroad for the needs of the development effort) has been widened — and this promises to be a matter of high probability in view of the abundance and the increased availability of financial resources in the Arab region as a whole — then the development of the country will proceed at a distinctly higher speed, since the physical and (mainly) the organisational, institutional, attitudinal and manpower aspects of the infrastructure have been provided adequately. Indeed, the country's experience since 1969 gives strong credence to this conclusion and makes it even more credible for the years to come. Planning as a modality and an instrument of development occupies a central position in the determination of development presently and in the foreseeable future.

NOTES

1. As general references, see: (a) Jules Lapidi, *L'économie tunisienne depuis la fin de la guerre* (1955); (b) Jean Vibert, *Tableaux de l'économie tunisienne* (Tunis, 1956); (c) Secrétariat d'Etat à l'Information, *Aspects de l'économie tunisienne* (Tunis, 1957); (d) FAO, Project FAO de Développement Méditerranéen, *Tunisie: Rapport national* (Rome, 1959); (e) Moncef Guen, *La Tunisie indépendante face à son économie* (Tunis, 1961); (f) F. Perroux and R. Barre (eds.), *Développement, croissance, progrès: Maroc-Tunisie* (Paris, 1961); (g) Charles A. Micaud (with Leon Carl Brown and Clement Henry Moore), *Tunisia: The Politics of Modernization* (London, 1963); (h) Ghazi Duwaji, *Economic Development in Tunisia* (New York, 1967); (i) Samir Amin, *The Maghreb in the Modern World* (Penguin African Library, 1970); (j) Europa Publications, *The Middle East and North Africa 1971-72, 1972-73, 1973-74, and 1974-75* (London), chapter on 'Tunisia'; (k) various issues of *Economie, Revue Tunisienne de l'Economie* (Publication trimestrielle du Ministère de l'Economie Nationale); and (l) Banque Centrale de Tunisie, *Rapport Annuel* (various reports).

2. Micaud, op. cit., p. 168.

3. FAO, op. cit., Ch. II, p. 15. (Other estimates exist. See note 35 below.)

4. Micaud, op. cit., p. 182. However, another source (Europa, *1973-74*, op. cit., chapter on Tunisia (especially p. 640) implies that the area was smaller by about one-third. A third source, Amin, op. cit. (p. 147) also refers to 600,000 ha as *colon*-owned.

5. Royaume de Tunisie, Présidence de Conseil, Service Tunisien des Statistiques, *Annuaire Statistique de la Tunisie 1953*, p. 8.

6. FAO, op. cit., Ch. II, p. 20.

7. Amin, op. cit., p. 89. However, elsewhere (p. 61) Amin shows that the non-Moslems (about 8 per cent of population) had 43 per cent of the income.

8. Ibid., p. 102.

9. FAO, op. cit., p. II-15.

10. Ibid., Table I-5.

11. For a summary of developments in the decade, see ibid., pp. 25-8.

12. Ibid., Table VII-4.

13. Micaud, op. cit., pp. 15-17, and 159.

14. Ibid., pp. II 15-20; and Amin, op. cit., pp. 40-1.

15. The examination of the post-independence economy has drawn on some publications in addition to those cited in note 1 above. They will be referred to as the analysis proceeds and as the occasion arises.

16. Duwaji, op. cit., Table 6, p. 26, where the calculation results in the lower estimate. However, FAO, op. cit., p. II-14, which is the source of the higher estimate, betrays a contradiction between the $200 estimate for 1957 (when GDP was lower than for 1956 though the population was larger) and the result of the calculation of GDP *per capita* from Table II-5 in the same source.

17. See, in this connection, Micaud, op. cit., Part I, Ch. 1, and p. 174; Amin, op. cit., pp. 145-55; and the Proceedings of the Fifth Conference of the Neo-Destour Party held on 15 November 1955 at Sfax, and of the Sixth Conference held at Sousse on 2 March 1959.

18. Amin, op. cit., p. 147.

19. Micaud, op. cit., p. 159.

20. This is the title of Part III, Ch. 3, in Micaud, op. cit.

21. Amin, op. cit., p. 150.

22. Ibid.

23. Quoted in Micaud, op. cit., p. 174.

24. For 1950 and 1951, see source of Table 11.2; for 1971, see Banque Centrale de Tunisie, *Statistiques Financières*, Nos. 21 and 22 (May-June 1974), p. 58. The GDP estimate for 1973 is from *International Financial Statistics (IFS)*, December 1974. The price index in *IFS* has 1970 as base, but we have calculated GDP at 1963 prices by linking the relevant index series.

25. See *Statistiques Financières*, op. cit., p. 41 and FAO, op. cit., Ch. II, section on 'Policy on Prices and Salaries', for price increases.

26. Banque Centrale de Tunisie, *Rapport Annuel 1972*, Introduction in the Letter of Transmittal from the Governor of the Banque to the President of the Republic.

27. Published by the Secrétariat d'Etat au Plan et aux Finances, probably in 1961 as the document is undated.

28. Secrétariat d'Etat au Plan et aux Finances, 'Avant-Propos' and p. 1 of 'the Objectives of the Pre-Plan'.

29. Ministry of Planning (which was to follow the Secrétariat d'Etat au Plan), January 1972. (Arabic version, to which all references are made here.)

30. The *IVe Plan*... appeared in two volumes, one containing the general plan report, and the other the Annexes. The Plan was approved in September 1972.

31. The *IVe Plan*..., Vol. I, p. 5, states: '... la Tunisie s'est engagée définitivement et sans retour dans la voie du développement: on peut dire que le principal résultat des trois premiers plans de développement économique et social est que ce pays a véritablement tourné le dos au sous-développement' (p. 5).

32. Ibid., p. 43.

33. *Perspectives*..., p. 44.

34. Duwaji (op. cit., p. 179) writing in the first half of the decade 1962-71, foresaw the difficulty of achieving an annual rate of real growth of 6 per cent on the average and allowed the prospect of such a rate a very low probability.

35. FAO, op. cit., Table VII-4 for the lower estimate, and Duwaji, op. cit., p. 91, for the higher estimate. (The former refers to 'terres labourables', and the latter to 'arable land').

36. See Neville Barbour (ed.), *A Survey of Northwest Africa (The Maghreb)* (London, 1959), p. 328, for data regarding *habous* and other land categories.

37. Moncef Guen, *La Tunisie indépendante face à son économie* (Paris, 1961), in his discussion of Decree of 2 March 1956 and 18 July 1957.

38. Note on 'Superficie des Exploitations Agricoles' already referred to. This note was obtained from the Ministry of Agriculture by the author during an interview there.

39. Guen, op. cit., Partie Première, Titre Premier, Ch. III, 'Les structures mentales et sociales'.

40. All legislation relating to land has been compiled in one volume. The volume, however, has no title whatsoever. (Copy obtained by the writer from the Ministry of Agriculture; French.)

41. Data obtained from an interview with a highly placed official in the Ministry of Agriculture during June 1972. For a discussion of land categories and related matters, see: Guen, op. cit.; Ezzedine Makhlouf, *Structures agraires et modernisation de l'agriculture dans les plaines du Kef — Les unités coopératives de production* (Cahiers du CERES, Paris, 1968); Ministère de l'Agriculture, *Organisation de la Production Agricole*, Deuxième Partie (March 1972); *Bilan...*, op. cit.; as well as general references listed in note 1 above, items (h) and beyond.

42. This judgement is based on calculations of land and population ratios, in turn based on data in FAO, *Production Yearbook 1972* (Vol. 26), Tables I/1, II/3 and II/5.

43. As expressed in KFAED's *Report on the Tunisian Economy* (Kuwait, 1968; Arabic; stencilled, for internal use), p. 80.

44. Calculated from data in *Statistiques Financières*, Nos. 15, 16 and 17, op. cit., pp. 58 and 41.

45. *Retrospectives*, op. cit., pp. 27-8 and 79-80 (all references are to the Arabic version).

46. For the years 1952-66, see FAO, *Production Yearbook 1967*, pp. 27-30; for the years 1961-72, FAO *Production Yearbook 1972*, pp. 27, 29, 31 and 33.

47. See Tables 11.2 and 11.3 except for 1972; information for 1972 is derived from Banque Centrale de Tunisie, *Rapport Annuel 1972*, p. 52, where the energy sector is reported to have made a growth of 7.6 per cent at current prices.

48. KFAED, op. cit., p. 186.

49. Duwaji, op. cit., p. 140, quotes a labour force of some 100,000 in the mid-sixties, whereas KFAED (note 48) has a more modest quotation.

50. Data calculated from Table 1, 'Effectif du Personnel Permanent et Saisonnier', in Secrétariat d'Etat au Plan et aux Finances, Service des Statistiques, *Recensement des Activités Industrielles 1957-1958-1959*, Publications Spéciales, Etude No. 1 (March 1961). This census also includes data for transport, but these have been deducted from the total by me before reaching the figures shown in the text.

51. For 1969, See Institut National de la Statistiques, *Recensement des Activités Industrielles — Résultats 1969*, Tableaux Statistiques (August 1971), pp. 238 and 239. Again here, the number of workers in the transport 'industry' has been deducted.

52. See KFAED, op. cit., p. 188. In interviews in June 1972 with officials of the planning and national economy ministries I gained the impression that the efforts for the promotion of handicrafts occupy a minor place in the official overall concern for modern industry.

53. For 1957, see *Recensement;... 1957-1958-1959*, Tableau IV; for 1971, *Statistiques Financières*, Nos. 15, 16 and 17, op. cit., p. 59.

54. The share in combined value added for the years 1950-71 is calculated from Tables 11.2 and 11.3 in the text. That of the share in exports for the period 1962-72 from *Statistiques Financières*, op. cit., pp. 52 and 54.

55. Leon Laitman, *Tunisia Today: Crisis in North Africa* (New York, 1954), p. 60, quoted in Duwaji, op. cit., p. 52.

56. From an interview with a responsible official in June 1972.

57. In the words of Europa, op. cit., *1973-74*, chapter on 'Tunisia', p. 645.

58. For capacity and production in 1950-6, see Service des Statistiques, *Annuaire Statistique de la Tunisie, 1959*, p. 85, for 1972 see Ministère de l'Economie Nationale, *Economie* (Revue Tunisienne de l'Economie), No. 4, Vol. II — No. 1, Vol. III, October—December 1972 — January—March 1973, p.33.

59. Commission Sectorielle, Tourisme et Thermalisme, *Rapport de Synthèse, L'Evolution du Tourisme en Tunisie — Retrospective 1961-1971* (May 1972), p. 5.

60. See *Rapport de Synthèse...*, p. 4, for number of beds and receipts by the sector in 1971; and see *Statistiques Financières*, op. cit., pp. 47 and 49 for data on nights spent, and number of tourists, and p. 59 for investments made in tourism. The estimate of tourist earnings for 1972 comes from Europa, op. cit., *1973-74*, p. 649, while that for 1973 comes from *Arab Economic Report, 1974*, p. 294.

61. The sources from which information on aid has been compiled are detailed below: (a) for US aid 1 July 1945 — 30 June 1962, a table in *Time Magazine*, 29 March 1963, quoting official US sources; (b) for OECD aid for the four years 1960-4, and for 1965, OECD, *The Flow of Financial Resources to Less-Developed Countries 1956-1963*, Table II-12, pp. 44-5, and *1961-1965*, p. 155; (c) for 1966-8, OECD, *Development Assistance 1969 Review*, p. 170; (d) for 1969-71, OECD, *Development Cooperation 1973 Review*, Table 26, p. 216-17; (e) for 1972 (and average 1970-2), UN, *Statistical Yearbook 1973*, p. 716; (f) for KFAED aid, KFAED *Annual Report 1973-1974*, p. 26; and (g) for aid from the socialist countries, UN, *Statistical Yearbook 1973*, p. 715.

62. As stated in KFAED, op. cit., pp. 295-6 (verbatim). This source has been used in tracing the steps actually taken by the Maghreb countries; I have also relied heavily on an interview with the Secretary-General of the Maghreb Industrial Studies Centre held in Tunis, June 1972. For a fuller survey of the measures taken in the field of economic co-operation and co-ordination see Volume II of this study (the companion volume).

63. Reported in Europa, op. cit., *1973-74*, op. cit., p. 649, and pp. 121-3, for recent developments.

64. For 1957, see FAO, *Tunisie*, op. cit., Chs. II and

III. The writer has been struck by the same phenomenon in recent years.

65. *Retrospectives*, pp. 107-8, regarding employment in 1971 (both methods of calculation and data).

66. As recorded in FAO, *Tunisie*, op. cit., Table II-IV.

67. *Retrospectives*..., p. 102. For the larger estimate, see *IVe Plan* ... *1973-1976*, Ch. I in Part I.

68. I have relied heavily here, and in the discussion on entrepreneurship to follow, on interviews with a number of well-informed Tunisians. They belong to the worlds of government, business, labour, research and education.

69. Quoted in Abdeljabbar Bsais and Christian Morrisson, *Les Coûts de l'éducation en Tunisie* (Centre d'Etudes et de Recherches Economiques et Sociales, Tunis, Cahiers du CERES, Série Economique No. 3, June 1970), p. 34.

70. Ibid., p. 35 for 1960 and 1968; Europa, op. cit., *1973-74* for 1970; and *Retrospectives*.... p. 114, for 1971.

71. For all the information regarding numbers of students from 1956-7 to 1971-2, see Ministère de l'Education Nationale, Direction des Statistiques et de la Planification, *Statistiques essentielles de l'éducation nationale pour l'année 1971-1972* (December 1971), pp. 11, 12 and 15.

72. For private education in 1971-2, see ibid., pp. 146 and 148; for 1948, see *Annuaire Statistique de la Tunisie 1953*, pp. 19 and 20.

73. *Perspectives*..., p. 248.

74. Bilingualism and the place of French in general have received a great deal of attention in the three Maghreb countries formerly under French rule. But for Tunisia the question has been less problematic, owing to the wider familiarity with Arabic than in the two countries to the west, particularly in Algeria. For a comprehensive examination of bilingualism and Arabisation, see Rachad Hamzaoui, Zohra Riahi and Habib Ounali, *Quelques aspects de bilinguisme en Tunisie* (CERES, Tunis, Série Linguistique No. 3, November 1970).

75. In what follows, I have relied on several interviews with educators, party leaders and very senior officials in the Ministry of Education.

76. The law school is the Arabic branch of the faculty of law where instruction is in French.

77. The assistant-teacher training school has since been discontinued in order to make teacher training more rigorous.

78. The speech of the Minister was made on 20 June 1972, and published in *As-Sabah* (daily Arabic newspaper), 21 June 1972. The same issue published the text of a law passed on 20 June regarding the modalities of the reform of the university – in its structure, functions and methods, and its relevance to the nation's needs.

79. Amin, op. cit., p. 112.

80. Ibid., p. 201.

81. I owe this examination of the background and of the experience of the years of collectivisation to interviews with several leading businessmen, economists and party leaders.

82. See Ezzedine Makhlouf, 'Les coopératives agricoles en Tunisie: structures et difficultés', and Lilia Ben Salem, 'L'encadrement des unités de production agricole', in *Revue Tuniessienne de Sciences Sociales* (Publication de CERES), Vol. 8, No. 26, September 1971.

83. See the proceedings of the 5th congress in Sfax in November 1955, the 6th congress ('The Congress of Victory') in Sousse in March 1959, the 7th congress ('The Congress of Destiny') in Bizerte in October 1964, and the 8th congress in Sousse in October 1971 (all in Arabic).

84. FAO, *Tunisie*, op. cit., p. II-12.

85. The official titles of the 3 plan documents are (a) Secrétariat d'Etat au Plan et aux Finances, *Plan Triennal 1962-64;* (b) Secrétariat d'Etat au Plan et à l'Economie Nationale, *Plan Quadriennal 1965-1968*, 3 volumes; (c) Secrétariat d'Etat au Plan et à L'Economie Nationale, *Plan de Développement Economique et Social 1969-1972*.

86. *Plan Triennal*..., p. 4.

87. For a review of 1962, see Secrétariat d'Etat au Plan et aux Finances, *Plan Triennal 1962-1964, 1962* (special issue, September 1963), p. 22. Gross production at current prices, as reported in *Statistiques Financières*, op. cit., (p. 58) stood at about TD280m for 1962.

88. *Plan Quadriennal 1965-1968*, Vol. I, p. 18.

89. Ibid., p. 129.

90. Ibid., p. 131.

91. *IVe Plan de Développement Economique et Social 1973-1976* (two volumes). The evaluation depends largely on the chapter entitled 'Introduction Générale', as well as on the Arabic version of the *Fourth Plan* which contains, in addition, a long statement by the Prime Minister (made on 27 July 1973 in Parliament), which evaluates economic and other developments in the decade 1962-72.

92. All the data are obtained from Part One, Chapter One, in the *Fourth Plan*... *1973-1976*.

93. For a lucid presentation of the Tunisian planning experience with regard to agencies, methods, techniques and execution, see Sadok Bahroun, *La Planification Tunisienne* (Tunis, 1968). Marked improvement has been registered since the publication of this book.

94. This judgement was obtained from interviews with high-ranking planning officials.

12 ALGERIA

Algeria's experience in the field of social and economic development is unique in the Arab world. This uniqueness derives much more from the country's colonial perspective — with its heritage and its challenges, and Algeria's pungent response to the challenges — than from the country's physical endowments.

Alone among the regions colonised in the nineteenth century, Algeria was pressurised to become part of the metropolitan colonising country — France in this instance. Geographical closeness nurtured the fantasy of the French that Algeria was merely an extension of France. Economic and social policy, including dense settlement by the French in Algeria, was designed to give substance to the determination to make Algeria part of France. Military policy and the exercise of harsh military and administrative coercion were liberally applied to supplement economic and cultural measures when these seemed to fall short of their objectives.

This is not a political history of Algeria. Yet it is essential for a proper understanding of the country's process of development in the dozen years since independence in mid-1962 to relate — even if very briefly and graphically — this process, both with its faltering and its acceleration, to the decisive years before independence. The pre-independence years 1946-62 will therefore receive attention in the section to follow. However, in these introductory observations it is useful to underline the special flavour of Algeria's experience.

Paradoxically, the country was provided with a distinctly adequate physical infrastructure under French rule — a phenomenon which defies the norms and experience of colonialism as they unfold elsewhere. The exception must be understood in the context of the Frenchification of Algeria attempted by Metropolitan France. Yet the infrastructure, as well as other areas of emphasis, was mainly designed to serve the interests of the *colons*, the European settlers. Furthermore, against this physical infrastructure and material equipment (which included the modernisation of certain sectors or subsectors) the country was deliberately and tragically denied and barred from the development of its human resources, and of its own political life and institutions.

The war of liberation, which lasted for almost eight years, played havoc with the economy and inflicted casualties and demographic dislocations on a massive scale. Here again the cruel experience of the war was later to serve as an invaluable lesson in discipline, activism and social mobilisation. In this writer's view, it can safely be said that Algeria today is consolidating the ground for its social and economic development more effectively and hopefully than any other Arab country.[1]

1. THE PRE-INDEPENDENCE ERA

Algeria shares several features with the three other Maghreb countries, Morocco, Tunisia and Libya, such as settler colonisation, usurpation by the European settlers (mainly Frenchmen and Italians) of much of the best land, the dualistic shaping of the economy, particularly with regard to industry, mining and trade, in such a way as to serve the interests of the metropolitan power, and a polarisation of political, social and economic power with the settlers or *colons* exercising power and enjoying privileges and high incomes, and the nationals suffering loss of status, subservience and poverty. Yet although these features were common to all four Maghreb countries, and although they constitute standard characterisations of pre-independence conditions as they are described in most books on the political, social and economic history of the Maghreb, they remain differentiated between one country and another among the four. However, the differentiation is greatest between Algeria on the one hand, and the three other countries on the other.

The sixteen years preceding Algerian independence, but particularly the period 1 November 1954, when the final phase of the war of liberation was launched, to 1 July 1962, when a referendum resulted in a 91 per cent vote for independence (to be followed two days later by President de Gaulle's proclamation of the country's independence) were decisive years. These years witnessed hectic activity on the economic front, along with bloody war — the latter between the French army and the Algerian army and guerrillas, and towards the end of the period between the large European urban community and the Algerian urban population. In both areas — war and economics — matters were coming to a climax. This looks paradoxical superficially, as there seems to be an inherent conflict between intensified economic developmental activity and military activity. Yet deeper down one can discern the internal logic of this strange parallelism: the continued fantasy that with improved economic conditions the Algerians might accept integration within France and the European community would have a greater stake in the country; and that the exercise of harsh military action would give credibility to France's determination to stay put and to proceed with the absorption of Algeria into the French political and economic framework.

These theses were flatly refused, and intellectually as well as physically resisted, by the more activist elements among the nationalists. What on 1 November 1954 became the Front de Libération Nationale, the FLN, and later in August 1958 the Provisional Government of the Algerian Republic (the GPRA), went beyond rejection. They built up a body of thought over the war years, which culminated in the Tripoli Programme and later, soon after independence, in the Charte d'Alger (of April 1964). The Programme drawn up at the end of May 1961 defined Algerian leaders' vision of the future of their country in the political, social and economic fields. Specifically, the Programme defined the main objectives as being radical agrarian reform, the setting up of state and co-operative farms, nationalisation of large businesses in all sectors, and socialism. Furthermore, it emphasised the independence of the country economically as well as politically. Thus, the umbilical cord with France was to be neatly and decisively severed and economic sovereignty, in the form of Algerian control of Algerian resources and economic life was to be asserted as an integral part of political independence. The Algeria Charter (La Charte d'Alger — Ensemble des Textes Adoptés par le Premier Congrès du Parti du Front de Libération Nationale du 16 au 21 Avril 1964) went much further in detail and elaboration than the Programme. It attempted to set the thinking behind the image desired for the Algeria of the future in the political, social and economic realms.

It is necessary at this point to define the countours and substance of the European presence in Algeria. (By 'European' is meant mainly French, but also Italian, presence, as well as the solidarity of the bulk of the Algerian Jewish community with the Europeans and the inclusion of this community in the category of Europeans, as most of its members had acquired French citizenship and identified with the French.) This presence manifested itself in the demographic structure of the country, as well as in land ownership and the ownership and administration of economic activities outside the agricultural sector — obviously in addition to the exercise of political and administrative power through the firm grip of the French on the army and the civil service.

By 1960 the Europeans numbered 1,059,581 out of a population of 10,784,309, or 10 per cent of the total. (Hence the 91 per cent vote for independence — that is, virtually a unanimous vote by the Algerians.) Even as far back as the 1856 census, the Europeans represented 7.2 per cent of the total, and were to rise to 12 per cent by 1875.[2] This underlines the special interest the colonialists had in acquiring a strong foothold in Algeria. The major part of these Europeans had always lived in urban centres — 81 per cent of the European community, or between 29 and 36 per cent of the urban population in the years between the end of World War Two and independence. On the other hand, the European component of the rural population hovered around a mere 2.5 per cent. The opposite pattern is true of the Algerian population (designated in pre-independence documents as the 'Moslem Population'). Thus, about 20-23 per cent of the Algerians lived in urban centres, and 77-80 per cent in rural centres, during the post-war and pre-independence years. The proportion of Europeans in urban centres to total population was 9-10 per cent, while it was 17-21 per cent for the Algerians.[3]

In addition to their presence in numerical strength in urban centres, the Europeans enjoyed advantages of much higher educational, technical and organisational levels than the Algerians. Their control of non-agricultural activities can be seen from the fact that in 1957, over 44 per cent of salaried employment was taken by 'non-Moslems', and — more strikingly — over 70 per cent of the civil service consisted of non-Moslems, that is, Europeans. It is worth adding that out of a total non-agricultural 'theoretical' (i.e. potential) labour force of 1,033,000 there were 224,000 'unemployed and underemployed',[4] mainly urban Algerians. On the other hand, the vast majority of the 'active population' in agricultural professions — over 98 per cent — were Algerians.[5] However the fact that only some 2 per cent were Europeans must in no way conceal the fact that this tiny group of Europeans owned and operated the choice lands of Algeria along the Mediterranean littoral, as the discussion will show.

Cultural and educational colonialism manifested itself in two ways, mainly in the 'rationing' of education manifest in the provision of very inadequate opportunities for the education of Algerian youth at all three levels of instruction, and the promotion of French as the primary language, along with the demotion of Arabic to become not only a secondary, but a 'foreign', language. On the eve of the war of liberation in 1954, European children in primary schools were over 30 per cent of the total, though by the school year 1959/60, the ratio had dropped to 19 per cent.[6] Algerian boys and girls in primary schools were 8 per cent of the children of school age in 1944 (as against 90 per cent for Europeans) but rose to about 22 per cent in 1954 and to about 37 per cent on the eve of independence. The rise was mostly under the pressure of demand by parents, rather than purely spontaneous by the French authorities.[7]

The discrepancy was much greater in primary technical education and in secondary and higher education. There is no need for the presentation of ratios in this respect as there was with regard to primary education; it is enough to say that Algerian secondary school pupils numbered about 4,000 in 1950 (against over 22,000 Europeans). This pattern was to continue with only marginal improvement until independence. Thus, in 1954, the numbers were about 7,000 versus 29,000, and in 1959 (the last year for which we have pre-independence data that permit of comparison) the numbers were 11,000 versus 34,000 for Algerians and Europeans respectively.

However, the situation was most discriminatory at the university level. Shortly before independence, there were about 5,000 students at Algiers University, only about 14 per cent of whom were Algerians.[8] The social or political background of many of these privileged Algerians suggested that their parents generally formed part of the national bourgeoisie which was not particularly active in the struggle for independence. Furthermore, technical training was practically barred to Algerians. It is today stressed by leaders in the field of education that the country claimed only two Algerian engineers on the eve of independence. Considering the very thin participation by Algerian workers in industrial and other non-agricultural activity, it can be realised that the Algerians acquired only the most elementary technical skills. Even at this low level, there were some 4,900 Algerians against 3,800 Europeans in elementary technical schools in 1954, and, in spite of the relative improvement in the situation, the numbers were 10,900 and 5,300 for the two groups respectively in 1959.[9]

To sum up, it can safely be stated that the French notion of Algeria's integration with France was a very selective one, since it did not seem to envisage the raising of the educational and training levels of the Algerians to meet those of the French. The opposite is demonstrably true: that official policy was aimed at the preservation of a wide gap between the two communities. Thus the Algerians were to be kept in a virtual state of dependency on the French for the performance of the functions of a modernising state and economy.

Another major aspect of the dualism in the Algerian economy, and one which receives distinct attention in the economic literature of or on the pre-independence era, is land ownership and agriculture. It is suggestive in this respect to state that the Europeans owned about 28 per cent of the cultivable land, but it is more significant to emphasise that in addition to the fact that this proportion was higher than that of the European to the Moslem population, the land owned by foreigners was the best in the country, falling almost totally in the north littoral which receives the highest rainfall, and is the most fertile and the nearest to urban population concentrations. This proximity conferred the advantages of markets and savings in transportation costs, as well as the convenience of exportation of agricultural produce. Furthermore, European agriculture comprised a large proportion of vegetable- and fruit-growing, in addition to cereal-growing in large, mechanised operations. One dominant feature of the modern, European agriculture was vine-growing and the manufacture of wines, mostly for the French market. Against this modern agricultural sector, the Moslem sector was predominantly traditional, consisted mostly of small holdings, and placed a larger emphasis on cereals. The technology of the European sector was distinctly more advanced, the capital investment was heavier, and mechanisation was at a much higher level.

The distribution of agricultural holdings by size between the two communities equally revealed dualism, with greater fragmentation and a smaller average size of holding for the Moslem than the European community. This comes out in Table 12.1.

A closer look at the part pertaining to the north in Table 12.1 reveals that the two communities are almost equally disadvantaged with respect to holdings less than one hectare in area, with average size of holding being about 0.35 ha for Moslem and 0.33 ha for non-Moslem holdings, although Moslem owners in this size bracket constituted a higher ratio than non-Moslems: 16.8 versus 10.8 per cent. More than half the Moslem holdings cluster in the 1–10 ha bracket, although the bracket which leads as a ratio of total area for Moslem holdings is that of 10–50 ha. On the other hand, the largest concentration of non-Moslem holdings is in the bracket 100 ha and over, with 29 per cent of holdings falling

Algeria

Table 12.1: Land Holdings by Size and Ethnic Category

Categories of Size (ha)	Number of Holdings			Area of Holdings (thousand hectares)		
	Moslems	Non-Moslems	Total	Moslems	Non-Moslems	Total
Less than 1	105,954	2,393	108,347	37.2	0.8	38.0
1—less than 10	332,529	5,039	337,568	1,341.2	21.8	1,363.0
10—less than 50	167,170	5,585	172,755	3,185.8	135.3	3,321.1
50—less than 100	16,580	2,635	19,215	1,096.1	186.9	1,283.0
100 and above	8,499	6,385	14,884	1,688.8	2,381.9	4,070.7
Total	630,732	22,037	652,769	7,349.1	2,726.7	10,075.8
of which: North	543,310	21,674	564,984	7,131.2	2,706.1	9,837.3
South (mainly desert)	87,422	363	87,785	217.9	20.6	238.5

Source: Statistique Générale de l'Algérie, *Tableaux de l'Economie Algérienne, 1960*, p.129.

here and representing 87.3 per cent of the area held by non-Moslems.

This is the most telling part of the comparison, where concentration appears most glaring. Finally, the Moslem holdings in this largest size bracket, which number 8,499, represent about 23 per cent of the area held by Moslems. This shows that there was a rather large number of Moslem landowners of substance, although their average holding was only 198.7 ha in area — a fact that suggests that drastic land reform was not a compelling need of the country. Against this, the average non-Moslem holding in the highest size bracket had 373 ha of area. Finally, the overall average size of Moslem holdings (always excluding the Sahara) was 11.6 ha, against 123.7 ha for non-Moslem holdings. The enormity of the difference calls for no comment. This numerical picture does not fully bring out the discriminatory features of land-holding in Algeria. There is need to stress that the *colons* largely obtained their holdings through extortion, forced sales imposed on the Algerians, foreclosure and other forms of legal or economic pressure, or outright dispossession.

The total area of private holdings, which as Table 12.1 shows is about 10.1m ha (or 100,758 sq. km.) constitutes a small proportion of the total area of Algeria which, according to the same official source as that of the table, is 238.2m ha, or 2.38m sq.km. (According to the most recent official publication, the country's area is 2,293,190 sq. km.[10]) This proportion is a mere 4.2 per cent of the country's area, but, if the Sahara which swallows most of the country is excluded, it rises to 34.1 per cent. However, the proportion of cultivated land is smaller than these ratios suggest, as a certain part of private holdings consists of uncultivable land. The overall picture of land use in 1958 emerges in Table 12.2.

The conjuncture of several factors gave the land operated by Europeans a distinct advantage in production. Thus, the 28 per cent of land in non-Moslem hands accounted on average for 60 per cent of agricultural production and income in the period preceding independence. As suggested above, these factors included greater mechanisation and heavier investment, improved inputs including skilled labour and fertilisers,[11] larger-scale operation, and better-organised and more efficient administration — in addition to superiority

Table 12.2: Land Use, 1958

Designation	Non-Sahara (thousand ha)	Sahara (thousand ha)
Land utilised for agriculture		
Cultivable land	6,176	17
Natural meadows	32	–
Vineyards	367	–
Tree and fruit land	199	25
Pasture land and bushland	9,606	29,133
Unproductive land	314	1
Sub-total	16,694	29,176
Esparto-grass zones	3,976	–
Forests	3,045	5
Miscellaneous [a]	5,788	179,490
Total	29,503	208,671

a. Includes state or communal land.

Source: Statistique Générale de l'Algérie, *Tableaux de l'Economie Algérienne, 1960*, p.128.

of land quality and better choice of cash crops. A much larger portion of the produce of non-Moslem farms was sold than of Moslem farms — 71.5 versus 28.5 per cent — which underlines the greater market orientation of the non-Moslem farms. The predominant single item of output here is grapes and wine. In the second half of the 1950s, the production of wine averaged 16.6m hectolitres a year, while exports averaged 14.3m hectolitres.[12] By far, most of this production was carried out in non-Moslem farms and distilleries.

Another phenomenon worth noting with respect to the agricultural sector of the two communities is the large discrepancy between the relative size of the labour force to which credit must go for the sector's activities. Thus, only 9.2 per cent of the non-Moslem labour force were engaged in agricultural professions, while the proportion for the Moslem force reached 81.5 per cent (in both instances, female workers and helpers are included.)[13]

Finally, the favoured position of non-Moslem agriculture reflected itself in the very uneven distribution of income between members of the two communities. According to one estimate relating to the pre-independence period, income per head in agriculture was quoted as being £20.5* ($57.40) for Moslems, and £735 ($2,058) for Europeans. It is worth adding here that the income gap in agriculture was much larger than in non-agricultural activities, the income range in these being £47 ($131.60) per head for Moslems, and £330 ($924) per head for Europeans.[14] This is a very clear indication of the enormous privileges, and much greater productivity, of European agriculture.

Examination of the structure of the Algerian economy in pre-independence days shows that agriculture made the largest single contribution to the gross domestic product. However, its relative contribution dropped between 1954 and 1959, from one-third to about one-fourth of GDP (if the government sector is excluded), as the GDP itself moved consistently upwards in absolute terms. The percentage *structure* of the economy for these two

*Pounds sterling.

Algeria

terminal years is shown in Table 12.3. In absolute terms the GDP at current prices rose from 6.788 to an estimated 14,000 million Algerian dinars (each dinar being equal to 100 old French francs, or one new franc).

Table 12.3: Industrial Origin of Gross Domestic Product (per cent)

Sector	Including Administration[a]		Excluding Administration	
	1954	1959	1954	1959
Agriculture, forestry and fishing	30	19	34	24
Mining, energy	5	4	5	5
Manufacturing and Construction	19	18	22	23
Manufacturing	(n.a.)	(11)[b]	(n.a.)	(14)[b]
Construction	(n.a.)	(7)[b]	(n.a.)	(9)[b]
Services	34	39	39	48
Algerian and French administration	13	21	–	–
Total (rounded)	100	100	100	100

a. According to the source in which data on administration are calculated, 'The French national accounts system which was used in Algeria does not include a figure for government product (i.e. government salaries etc.) in their figure for Gross Domestic Production.'
b. Figures in brackets are crude estimates.
Sources: For 1954, Statistique Générale de l'Algérie, *Tableaux de l'Economie Algérienne, 1960*, pp.61 and 65; for 1959, ibid., p.61 and République Française, Délégation Generale du Gouvernement en Algérie, Direction du Plan et des Etudes Economiques, *Plan de Constantine 1959-63, Rapport Général* (Imprimerie Officielle, Algérie, 1960), p.429. The estimation of data on administration and their inclusion within the structure of GDP in the table was made by O. Norbye in 'The Economy of Algeria', in P. Robson and D.A. Lury (eds.), *The Economies of Africa* (London, 1969), p.484. The table in its present integrated form is taken from the last-named source.

Table 12.3 portrays the structure of the whole economy, Moslem and European together. But for our present purposes it is necessary to show the social structure within the economic structure, or the shares of each of the two communities in various major magnitudes. In doing this I draw mainly on Samir Amin's study.[15] This study is probably the most careful and valuable in its category, not only for Algeria but for the three French-ruled Maghreb countries, both in thoroughness and in breadth of vision. According to Amin, the discrepancy between the size of each community and its share in the rewards of the economy is enormous.[16] Thus, the income of Moslems in 1955 totalled 223 billion *old* French francs, while 'other incomes', that is non-Moslem and corporate profits, totalled 414 billion. It would seem, from the perusal of Amin's data, that the corporate profits and the incomes of public companies, which presumably were mixed in ownership, totalled 116 billion. Agricultural income constituted about 70 per cent of this last sum. Most of these companies were European-owned. The discrepancy further showed itself in the relatively much larger scale of European business establishments, whether these were in the agricultural sector or in non-agricultural sectors. The income per head differed considerably in 1955, at every level of authority and within every group. Thus, it averaged 150,000 old francs for Moslem workers, 270,000 for white-collar workers, 270,000 for members of the middle class, and 1,000,000 – 1,500,000 for senior executives and company directors – as against 400,000 old francs, 530,000, 1,150,000 and 3,000,000 respectively for the non-Moslem counterparts. The overall average for Moslems was 230,000 per earner, compared with 950,000 for non-Moslem earners. Judging by the trend for the 70—80 years preceding 1955, these discrepancies must have remained at least as significant in the seven pre-independence years to follow.

Reference was made earlier to accelerated efforts by the French administration during the latter part of the war of liberation to develop the economy, and the rationale behind this move was suggested. This effort was embodied in the so-called Plan de Constantine (after the city in north-east Algeria), which was to run for five years, from 1959 to 1964, within a ten-year framework.[17] Prior to the announcement of the Plan there had been in 1955 an attempt to make a ten-year projection. Gross investment in the five years preceding the Plan rose consistently from 1954 to 1958, totalling 10 billion old francs for these years.[18] This level of investment was to be raised very steeply in the Plan.

General de Gaulle, then President of France, gave the tone of the Plan in a speech in the city of Constantine on 3 October 1958, when he defined the central theme of the effort as follows: 'The whole of Algeria ought to have its share of what modern civilisation can offer to people in terms of well-being and dignity.'[19] It is interesting to follow the trend of de Gaulle's thought in a speech that followed almost a year later in the same city, when he stated that 'France wanted to and could pursue with the Algerians the task which she had undertaken and of which she was capable — that Algeria will become a prosperous and productive country in 15 years.'[20] That is what Algeria has become in effect in 12 years, but thanks to its own efforts since independence.

The Plan committed an investment of public funds totalling 29,900m old francs, over five years, or a sum which was 'about 215 per cent of the GDP in 1959'.[21] The breakdown of this sum into its major components is given in Table 12.4.

Table 12.4: Projected Investment under Plan de Constantine, 1959-64 (billion francs)

Net investment in the Plan itself	19,400
Investment by the oil industry	5,520
Replacements against depreciation	2,700
Investments outside the Plan	2,280
Total	29,900

The net investment within the Plan was to be divided among the various sectors in the proportions shown in Table 12.5.

In physical terms, the objectives included the creation of 400,000 new jobs (in addition to the absorption of 60 per cent of the urban unemployment), the housing of one million persons, agrarian reform on 250,000 hectares, and the schooling of two-thirds of school-age children. The Plan also aimed at the 'renaissance of the *bled*' (the countryside), land reclamation and improvement of half a million hectares, afforestation, dam-building, the training of agricultural technicians and extension officers, as well as the expansion of modern Algeria in the non-agricultural sectors, such as industry (which was hoped to grow by 88 per cent), transport and communications, power, and small-scale crafts industries. The most impressive works were to be in the petroleum sector (two gas pipelines and one oil pipeline), in the power sector (a central hydroelectric station in the Kabylie and a

Table 12.5: Breakdown of Investment by Sector in Constantine Plan (per cent)

Agriculture, water development, rural programme	29
Housing, urban development	25
Infrastructure, transport, public utilities	18
Education	10
Industry	9
Public administration	5
Health	3
Total (rounded)	100

thermal station in Algiers); and three industrial complexes (metallurgy in Bône, chemical works in Arzew, and a refinery in Algiers).

The projected cumulative rate of growth of GDP was to average 12 per cent per annum or a total growth of 76 per cent over the five years; the rate was to be 9.7 per cent on the average annually (or 58 per cent for the period) if oil expansion were to be isolated. Gross domestic product, excluding the government sector, was to rise from 11.1 to 19.6 billion old francs between 1959 and 1964. This outstanding expected performance was to be made possible through the injection of vast investments. From an estimated average of 2 billion old francs per year during the period 1954-9, gross investment was to rise to an average of 6 billion old francs in the subsequent five years of the Plan. Roughly half this investment was to be financed by France, the other half out of domestic savings.[22] The actual performance fell short by about one-third of the expectations.

However, what is more serious is not the numerical shortfall, since this was moderate, but the misconceptions surrounding the planning exercise of the technocrats, as Amin suggests eloquently.[23] A plan of the present magnitude could not be implemented in conditions of severe warfare. The rural rejuvenation was disfigured in practice and became a vast process of *regroupement* which forced between one and two million Algerians to change their places of residence and forced several hundreds of thousands of them to become landless peasants after being gainfully self-employed on their own land. Quarter of a million people had to flee the country altogether into Tunisia and Morocco. The agrarian reform at best was to touch no more than a tiny fraction of the total cultivable area but was not to touch the land owned by the *colons* anyway (which was eleven times larger in area than the land to benefit from reform). And, instead of the problem of unemployment being largely solved by economic absorption, it was largely 'solved' by non-economic means: the death in battle or under torture of hundreds of thousands of urban and rural young men, and the absorption of scores of thousands into the ranks of the National Liberation Army and the guerrillas.[24] Furthermore, the intention of raising the living standards in Algeria to those of Europe within a generation was as fanciful as it was meaningless, considering the very uneven distribution of income prevailing in Algeria where arithmetic averages were so unrepresentative as to be deceitful, and where real economic power was to remain overwhelmingly in European hands. The country as a whole was to remain part of France and to accommodate the French economy against which it was in no way sheltered. Finally, to have expected French-Algerian economic co-operation within the context of bitter warfare was nothing short of a fantasy.

The main push to the economy during the eight years of the war of liberation came from military expenditures, which rose from 14 to 220 billion old francs between 1954 and 1961; the oil industry, which was witnessing a (relatively) very steep expansion; and expenditure on basic capital projects — to follow the presentation of Amin.[25] The two major areas that were to be the beneficiary of vast investments and expansion — agriculture and industry — were deprived by the atmosphere of war of their due share of investment. What happened to the rural sector by way of uprooting of large masses of peasants and the destruction of thousands of villages has already been referred to. Industry, which was to receive substantial private investment from France, witnessed a reversal in the process, with disinvestment, again owing to the atmosphere of political uncertainty. A substantial flight of capital characterised the last few years before independence, which could only be tolerated by the economy because of the movement into the country of funds to finance the war and to build up the oil and gas industry and its facilities, from wells to pipelines and refineries.

Thus the unfolding of the Plan was grossly distorted. Investments fell by about one-third below expectations. And the Plan was not allowed to run its normal course of life. In July 1962 Algeria obtained its independence and started on its own path of development.

2. 1962-75: AN ERA OF FUNDAMENTAL TRANSFORMATION[26]

The twelve years following independence day in July 1962 have been no less full and intense than the almost eight years of the war of independence preceding July 1962. The society and the economy have marched at a fast pace in many directions towards development, and have achieved notable results already. The performance is all the more praiseworthy inasmuch as it has basically depended on the clear vision and determination of the Algerians themselves. This is not to say that there has not been substantial foreign aid in the initial years of the independence era, or that Algeria has not had a windfall in its well-endowed oil, gas and mining sectors. It is merely to underline the qualities of discipline, sense of priority, and strong belief in mobilisation and participation by the people in the economic and social spheres, qualities which have been revealed in good measure by leadership and cadres alike.

However, this admittedly rosy picture did not emerge immediately after independence. Indeed, at least on the surface, the rush of events after the Evian Agreement of March 1962, and for about a year thereafter, was ominous and foreboding. The war years, especially the last two or three, had witnessed truly alarming economic and demographic dislocation, and the disruption of planning, investment and actual activity in a number of sectors. Yet the first year of independence witnessed dislocations and disruptions of even greater magnitude in the sense that these did not merely force a slower rate of growth on the economy, but actually forced a sharp drop (by about one-third) in the national product, and this not because of some seasonal adversity like a drought, or some political misfortune like civil war, but because of the physical exit and loss of the bulk of the country's skills in the various economic occupations and sectors, and the resulting loss of the advantages of advanced technology and organisation which this skilled body of manpower possessed. In brief, in spite of the assurances contained in the Evian Agreement with regard to the status, assets and work of the European community, perhaps 80-90 per cent of this community left the country in panic, leaving behind farms, factories, houses and service establishments either idle or outright sabotaged.[27] They could not conceive of an honest implementation of the Agreement, after the bitterness and bloodshed of the war years between Algerians and Europeans.

A closer look at the fortunes of the economy in the first year after independence will spell out with greater clarity the economic hardships and setbacks caused by the exodus of over four-fifths of the *colons*, many of whom were skilled men, but will also help the reader ascertain the extent of the recovery subsequently made in the twelve years of independence, that is through the year 1974. The details which emerge from this closer scrutiny of the first year of independence are recorded by Amin in his praiseworthy work,[28] and will be recapitulated briefly in Table 12.6.

Table 12.6: Indices of Change in Selected Areas

	Base Year = 100	1963
Real value of production	1960	65.0
Wine production	1960	68.5
Fresh vegetable production	1960	75.0
Industrial crops production	1960	67.0
Sheep and goats (stock)	1959	75.0
Cereal production	1959	148.0[a]
Citrus fruit production	1959	109.0[b]
Production of manufacturing industry (at current prices)	1959	79.6
Mining and oil extraction:		
Iron ore and phosphates	1959	97.0[c]
Oil production	1958	5,568.1[d]
Electricity and water supplies	1959	88.0
Investments (at current prices)	1959	22.7
of which the oil industry	1959	10.7
Transport	1959	77.0
Other services	1959	51.0

a. According to Amin, cereal production registered a notable increase, first, because it depended vastly on climatic conditions which were much more clement in 1963 than in 1959, and secondly (in my own view), probably because the skills involved in this type of production were easily within the grasp of Algerian peasants.
b. Again in my view, citrus fruit production did not suffer from the exodus of the *colons* because the citrus tree is not influenced by year-to-year activity, as the vines or vegetables are, and because much of the labour employed in the citrus groves had been Algerian.
c. According to Amin, phosphate mining had been showing some decline even before independence.
d. It is misleading to compare the production of oil between the late fifties and 1963 because production and export only started in 1958 and was bound to show a very steep rise in a short number of years. (The calculation of the index number for 1963 is based on production data given in *Annuaire Statistique de l'Algérie 1970*, p. 130, while the production figure for 1958 is taken from the General Union of Chambers of Commerce, Industry, and Agriculture in the Arab Countries, *Arab Economic Report* (Beirut, 1971-4, annual issues; Arabic), p. 31.) The transport of commercial gas by pipeline only began in 1961, and the export of liquefied gas was first effected in 1964 (my note).

In addition to the enormous setbacks sustained by the economy as a result mainly of the exodus of most of the *colons* — but also as a result of the enforced re-allocation of the Algerian population under the policy of *regroupement* which distorted the pattern of manpower allocation — the exodus also paralysed the administration, most of whose sensitive, skilled and responsible posts had been occupied by Frenchmen.

The economic plight of the country can be demonstrated in a few sentences taken from a recent reference work. According to this source,

> Some 90 percent (one million) of the European settlers, representing all the entrepreneurs, technicians, administrators, teachers, doctors and skilled workers had left the country; factories, farms and shops had closed down leaving 70 percent of the population unemployed. The eight years' war had left over one million dead, two million in concentration camps and 500,000 refugees in Tunisia and Morocco; as well as the destruction of public buildings and records by the O.A.S.[29]

(The OAS*, or Secret Army Organisation, consisted of the hard-core French army units that were fanatically determined on inflicting as much human and economic suffering on the Algerians as possible, because of their resistance to the OAS insistence that Algeria be a province of France.)

The act of massive exodus whose proportions and impact must by now have become obvious (despite some marginal disagreement between writers and sources as to the degree of unemployment suffered), constituted at one and the same time a serious blow to the economy and the public administration, and a challenge and an opportunity to the Algerians. As the years to follow have since amply proved, the damage has been largely made good because the country's response has come with energy and firmness. And yet, strict objectivity requires the admission that the proper and effective response did not materialise without foreign technical and financial assistance and, more importantly, without first the passage through the purgatory of some anarchy, demagoguery, arbitrariness and emotional outbursts,[30] into a state of quiet serious work, planning, a proper definition of priorities, more genuine participation in the process of economic decision-making, and greater discipline in the work-force at all levels of responsibility.

Yet, also in the interest of objectivity, one can assert that the seeds or beginnings of the great landmarks that were to characterise the Algerian economy and society from the midsixties onwards had been sown in the first three years of independence, which were marked by President Ben Bella's rule and bore the stamp of his political style. And, if the years to follow were to witness the growth and expansion of the original acts and policies, they also bore the stamp of President Boumedienne's political style.

The two styles could hardly be more different — the first flamboyant, explicitly image-making, emphasising political ideas and desiderata, and given to showmanship to a considerable extent; the second silent and retreating to the point of introversion, pragmatic and emphasising economic and social issues, and given to isolation from the public eye. There is no doubt in the writer's mind, from a reading of the indicators of socio-economic development of the twelve years of independence, that after the deliberate generation — or spontaneous eruption — of the main events and policies of the first three years (such as 'autogestion' or self-management in agriculture and other sectors, among other things) rewarding fruit could only be borne under a climate like the one provided by the rulers in the nine remaining years of the period.[31]

The predominant trends and policies that characterised the early years of independence, and that have in effect been consolidated and extended in later years, had their beginnings in the Tripoli Programme of May 1962, to which reference has already been made. The

* Organisation de l'Armée Secrète.

reader is reminded that this Programme set as major objectives radical agrarian reform, the establishment of state and co-operative farms, nationalisation of large establishments in all sectors, and the adoption of socialism as ideology and system. (In addition, the Programme provided for anti-colonialism and the political neutrality of the country, and the struggle for Maghrebian unity and Arab solidarity.) However, events marched faster than legislation and institutional arrangements. Thus, while many thousands of farmers and labourers in non-agricultural sectors and establishments had in the summer and autumn of 1962 taken over the management of deserted farms and factories and other businesses in order to prevent the idleness of these productive units and the drop in production, it was in March of 1963 that the necessary legislation was to appear for the legalisation of these measures of self-management, or what is known in Algeria as *autogestion*. More will be said on *autogestion* later, but it will be immediately evident that lack of managerial and advanced technical skill resulted in confusion and damage to production, which were not compensated for by revolutionary zeal or the joys of self-management or ownership. Later on, in October of the same year, other decrees were promulgated which also endowed ownership on the labourers working the French farms and estates. The whole process of *de facto* take-over and self-management, legislation and theorising about these events was finally embodied in the *Charte d'Alger* of April 1964, to which reference has been made.

The March and October 1963 decrees had, however, not affected French interests in the mining and oil and gas sectors. An attempt had been made before the signing of the Evian Agreement in March 1962 for the partitioning of Algeria so that the Sahara would remain 'French' and French interests would continue to exploit Algeria's mineral wealth. This wealth consisted of rich resources of high-grade iron ore, phosphates, lead, zinc and antimony. Exploration had also, before independence, revealed large reserves of oil and gas, in both of which Algeria now ranks among the leading countries of the world. The French finally removed the pressure to partition Algeria in exchange for the renewal of the rights awarded earlier by the French government to French companies.[32] In all cases except for oil and gas, the pre-independence level of production fell in the few years immediately following independence, partly because of the general disruption in the political and economic life of the country in the phase of transition, but also partly because French investments shied away from the sector of mining in spite of the reassuring stipulations of the Evian Agreement. (The production of the leading mineral, iron ore, declined considerably: from 3,444,000 tons in 1960 to 1,976,900 tons in 1963.[33] The decline in the case of phosphates, the mineral next in importance, was much less marked and represented a longer-term trend.)

It has been stated here that the rate of progress of the economy in general, and of certain trends in the realms of agrarian reform, hydrocarbons and industry was rather sluggish in the first three years of independence, but that it accelerated in the rest of the independence era. Likewise, the reasons for the initial sluggishness have been suggested. It remains to be added that, notwithstanding the limitations on growth in the initial three years of independence, this transitional period witnessed significant transformation in socio-economic (and obviously political) structures. The composition of the labour force underwent far-reaching change, as did the distribution of earnings per category of labour. Likewise, the socio-economic system became socialist-oriented and, through the mechanism of *autogestion*, became a pioneer in the Arab world in the transfer of *real* economic power to large groups of farmers and workers.

Understandably, the shift in the pattern of ownership and/or control of the productive assets in a few important sectors led to a redistribution of income and therefore of consumption and savings patterns. Thus, while income per head dropped suddenly on the achievement of independence, the identity of the income-groups varied substantially from that of pre-independence days, and many thousands of Algerians as a result moved up the wage and salary ladder upon their assumption of responsibilities previously held by the French. In spite of the limited degree of reliability of income estimates for the few years covering the last phase of colonialism and the first phase of independence, and in spite of the existence of three or four such estimates for the years 1962 and 1963 (as for the rest of the sixties), it is still possible to draw some indicative conclusions with regard both to the change in national income and to its distribution.

According to some estimates, shortly before independence income per head averaged about 201 Algerian dinars (at the rate of conversion between the new French franc and the dinar that was to follow in 1964) per Algerian in rural areas, but 7,203 dinars per European.[34] The averages for the non-agricultural population were, respectively, 461 dinars and 3,234 dinars. For 1963/4, the data relate only to Algerians, as the income earned by Europeans (the oil companies excepted) had dropped to a tiny fraction of its earlier magnitude. The average income per head of the Algerian agricultural population rose to 380 dinars (on the assumption that the rural population represented two-thirds of the total), while that of the urban population rose from its pre-independence level to 1,133 dinars. The overall average for Algerians in all types of economic activity rose from 289 dinars to 630 dinars between the two points of time (according to Amin's conservative estimate, but after adjustment of his data to deduct transfer payments[35]).

It must be underlined that this average for Algerians rose from the first to the second reference point, while the country's overall average dropped owing to the inclusion in the earlier estimate of the huge income of the European community. Even if we accept an estimate for 1963 less conservative than Amin's, we will still encounter a drop of about 29 per cent between 1959 or 1960 and 1963 (i.e. from about $285 to about $205).[36] But whatever the true magnitude of the income per head, especially in 1963, two important facts emerge clearly: first, that though *total* income for the country dropped sharply upon independence, *average* income per Algerian earner rose substantially, and the income structure between groups of earners varied considerably; and secondly, that the drop in total income coupled with the rise in the average income, thanks mainly to the extensively improved position of a relatively small part of manpower (both in the private and the public sectors), meant that the pattern of income distribution for Algerians had suddenly become noticeably less equitable and much more skewed than before. If to this is added the chronic problems of unemployment, underemployment and landlessness with which hundreds of thousands of Algerians of working age were afflicted, it will be seen that the bright side of the income coin had its gloomier side too, which needed, and seems to have received, serious attention in the latter part of the independence era (but with insufficiently satisfactory results).

It has been stated earlier that the first three years of independence were characterised by a measure of political strife and showmanship at the level of leadership which resulted in some economic confusion and in some diffusion of focus in the governmental economic decision-making apparatus. To a certain extent the confusion was to be expected, considering the turbulent background to independence and the exodus of most of the country's skilled and affluent manpower. Yet these same years witnessed the emergence of a number of socio-economic currents and policies, and of institutions, that were to play vital roles in the true development and independence of the economy. Apart from the promotion (and glorification) of the spontaneous acts of *autogestion* into a philosophy which was *ex post* institutionalised and legalised, the government created the Central Bank of Algeria at the beginning of 1963, as well as a development bank a few months later (La Caisse Algérienne de Développement). More significantly, it created SONATRACH (short for Société Nationale pour la Recherche, la Production, le Transport, la Transformation, et la Commercialisation des Hydrocarbures) on 31 December 1963. This organism was not only a pioneer in its own right, but proved later (i.e. after 1965) to be capable of putting Algeria at the head of all Arab oil-producing countries in the mastery over its oil and gas resources and in the handling of operations involved in the oil industry. Finally, the government formed ONRA (Office National de la Réforme Agraire) in July 1963 to look after this important area of activity. (This body was dissolved in February 1968.)

Another commendable achievement relating to the first three years of independence was the crash programme launched for the replacement, as far as was possible, of the teachers, civil servants, technicians and skilled labourers who had left during the sudden French exodus. (The replacement came predominantly from French and Arab sources, but also marginally from some other East European countries.) Lastly, as the combined result of good fortune with respect to cereal harvests, hard work and dynamism in the self-managed and the traditional subsectors, and speedy expansion in the production and export of oil and gas, the country managed to earn an increasing sum of foreign exchange each year and thus to raise its cumulative reserves. These stood at over 832 million dinars ($169m) by the end of 1965.[37]

In what remains of this section an examination will be attempted for the independence era as a whole, of the leading landmarks of socio-economic change, and how the course of change has tended to reflect the broad lines of the system's ideas and ideology, and to embody the country's response to the harsh challenge of its hard-won independence and the hardships and sufferings that were the price of this independence.

Rural Development: An Integrated Approach[38]

In much of the Third World, agrarian reform (which is part of the much wider concept of rural development), has come to mean substantially more than land reform, the latter centring mainly around the limitation of the size of individual holdings in order to widen the base of land ownership, while the former has a much wider focus that comprises, among other things, the improvement of extension services, credit facilities and technical help, as well as tenancy arrangements. Wherever the more comprehensive usage has prevailed, it has generally been associated with the achievement of economic as well as social objectives, and in a number of cases the restructuring of political life has also been a major objective. When the concept has all these far-reaching dimensions, it effectively denotes rural development in general.

Nowhere in the Third World, to this writer's knowledge, has agrarian reform and the restructuring of the countryside under the aegis of agrarian reform (or of the 'agrarian revolution', as it is now referred to in Algeria) gone as far and as profoundly as in Algeria. In my view, the Algerian agrarian revolution since late 1966, but especially since the adoption of the Charter of the Agrarian Revolution (and the promulgation of Ordinance No. 71-73 of 8 November 1971 embodying the Charter), is unique in philosophy, ideas, content, reach and structure, and will have far-reaching significance for the socio-economic and political life of Algeria. If studied carefully in other Third World countries, and if endowed with the appropriate objective conditions in the environment, it could well be an experiment of world-wide import.

This is not the right place for a step-by-step description of the course of evolution of agrarian reform (or revolution) in Algeria. It is enough to emphasise that what is involved has gone very far beyond the simple modalities of *autogestion* with which the government found itself faced in 1962 and which it soon codified into law. From these simple beginnings, and through a series of decrees and ordinances the agrarian reform legislation and institutions, as well as its content, have all become more complex and far-reaching, and justly explain the change in nomenclature from 'reform' to 'revolution'. It is to the end product that we will now turn, with some background information, as the analysis requires.

The agrarian revolution, in the state it has reached, is built around a few basic ideas:

— That the rural society is of primary importance and should be developed and rejuvenated economically, socio-culturally, and politically.
— That this development and rejuvenation should form an integral part of the same process for the whole society and should be in harmony with it; therefore, the spread of education and training is a basic pillar of rural rejuvenation, and — as a forward linkage — this rejuvenation serves in turn as one pillar for industrialisation.
— That putting agrarian reform of revolutionary dimensions into effect is a time-consuming process — not one that can be brought about overnight through demagoguery and the propagation of slogans.
— That the basic simple principle in reform is that the land should only be in the hands and for the benefit of those who work it and live on it and from it.
— That although reform takes into account the better distribution of land ownership in the case of the private sector, other modalities ought to be sought, such as collective farms (in the case of self-managed land that had been vacated by the *colons*), and co-operatives of various farms; and that pragmatism and flexibility ought to be allowed adequate scope within the general principles of the agrarian revolution.
— That reform also involves, as an integral part of its content, financial, technical, marketing, organisational and structural changes in the countryside.
— That in all the operations involved (such as the limitation of the size of land ownership, the size of the *lot viable* (plots distributed to the landless and other beneficiaries), the decisions ought to be taken at the village or *commune*, not the ministerial, level, always within the general principles laid down by law; this obviously embodies administrative decentralisation and self-government and, therefore, true democracy (the implementation of local projects which form part of the Plan for development is another reflection of this democracy).
— That the exercise of such powers requires the organisation of each of the *communes* and larger groupings of the population into an organism called Assemblée Populaire Communale (APC) within the *wilaya* (district), as well as the formation of an Assemblée Populaire for each *wilaya*.
— That this convergence of ideas, principles and institutions constitutes 'Algeria's path to socialism', as Algerian leaders like to emphasise.[39]

Deep concern with the rural society among Algerian political leaders, economic planners and intellectuals in general is unparalleled in the Arab world in its volume and seriousness. Elsewhere, where a large measure of agrarian reform has been instituted, as in Egypt, Syria and Iraq, the 'operation' has largely remained centralised, emanating from the Cabinet and

Algeria

radiating outwards, and becoming in the process weaker and weaker the further away from the capital it reached. It has been largely done *for* the villagers, rather than *by* the villagers; and it has not been accompanied with socio-cultural changes and political organisation without which the rural community could not radically change its attitudes, nor could it acquire the political awareness and power to which it is entitled. In Algeria, the content and style of agrarian reform, along with the institutional restructing involved, have succeeded in mobilising the villagers, and this mobilisation, being based on demonstrable benefits to the countryside and endowing power on the peasantry, seems to have a very good chance of surviving. In the Mashreq (i.e. in the Arab countries east of Libya) mobilisation is often a short-lived affair, whipped up by slogans and short-term excitement.

The Algerians are not unique among the Arabs only because of the quality of their concern for agrarian reform, but also because this concern has been with them for many years and has been an integral part of their national awareness for generations. It always made part of the thinking and deliberations of groups struggling for national liberation and independence, and more clearly of the FLN, and – as already indicated – featured importantly and explicitly in the Tripoli Programme, and by implication earlier in the Proclamation of 1 November 1954, which constituted the call to arms in the war of liberation.

It has become clear that the agrarian revolution is inseparable in the Algerian context from the socio-economic mobilisation of the nation and its organisation in a manner that enables even its smallest hamlet or village to exercise a measure of self-government and decision-making. This is what we meant by qualifying the title to this discussion of rural development by the phrase 'an integrated approach'. It is necessary therefore to discuss agrarian reform along with the APC with respect to content, institutions and manner of implementation.

In its crudest and earliest form, agrarian reform involved the take-over by agricultural workers of the farms vacated or abandoned by the French, and the setting up of 'management committees' to operate these farms. Furthermore, it involved the take-over by government action of whatever *colon* land that had not been vacated upon independence, as well as the nationalisation of the land of Algerian collaborators (though there are no statistics of the area of the latter category) and of large holdings. Parallel with this process ran another whereby the *moudjahidine* (i.e. the combatants or fighters for independence) were also given large tracts of land to operate collectively. (The limitation of the size of holdings of large Algerian landlords, and the distribution of expropriated land, constitute the second phase of the reform, after the distribution of state domain. Both phases have been under implementation since June 1972, as we shall see below.)

In its present form and after its evolution over the years of independence, agrarian reform has come to mean much more, as the discussion will now show in concrete terms. To begin with, the self-managed sector *(secteur autogéré)*, or socialist sector as it is also called, in effect comprises the modern sector of agriculture, inasmuch as French agriculture was modern, in contradistinction with Algerian, traditional agriculture. This sector includes some 2.3–2.5 million hectares (the estimates of area vary), or roughly 30 per cent of the cultivable area, but it accounts for 60 per cent of agricultural production by value. It is preponderantly in large farm units and in the littoral along the Mediterranean, with better rainfall on the average than the rest of the country. It is also better equipped with machinery, farm buildings, terracing and irrigation facilities.

The sector is now organised as collective farms, with the ownership of the land vested in the state and not in the names of its operators. The workers on the land are essentially those who were on it before the *colons* left, and they are in permanent employment. Estimates of their numbers vary, but hover around 135,000, while in addition there are 100,000 –124,000 seasonal workers. Together they work about 56m days a year, or an average of 215 days a year per worker. (The 1966 census reported 65.5m days a year.) The seasonal or temporary workers account for much fewer working days per year per man than the permanent workers. The two groups together account for about one-fifth of the total agricultural labour force which numbers 1.3 million men and women.[40] (Parenthetically, this last figure suggests a high level of unemployment and of underemployment, inasmuch as the rural population is estimated at about 8m, within which those of working age, both male and female, should number at least 2.5m.) All workers on self-managed farms receive cash wages — the permanent on a monthly basis; the temporary on a daily basis. But permanent workers, in addition, are allowed a small family plot each (not to exceed 5 ares or 500 sq. metres) on which to grow vegetables for their own use, and to own some cattle and fowl for the family's dairy and poultry needs.

The organs stipulated for (and now actually in existence) in the laws governing the agrarian revolution are the following:

The workers' general assembly which is the sovereign body entrusted with the overall decision and control of the 'enterprise' and which adopts the production plan in its broad lines.

The workers' council which exercises direct control over management and lays down general management standards.

The self-management committee which prepares the production plan and exercises direct control over the plan and enjoys direct decision-making power. This committee is presided over by a Chairman who exercises a day-to-day follow-up of the Committee's orders.

The Director who is appointed by the Minister of Agriculture and Agrarian Reform and is responsible for real execution of plan details. He is supposed to be technically qualified for the job and is empowered to submit a draft plan for the consideration of the Committee and the Assembly.

The Assembly consists of all the workers, and the other bodies are all elected, as is the Chairman. Where the views of the Director clash with those of the Chairman and Committee, the difference will be examined by the APC (or the expanded APC known as the Assemblée Populaire Communale Elargie), but finally, the issue can be sent to the Minister for final decision.

The remaining 70 per cent of the cultivable land outside the socialist sector in principle belongs to the private sector. According to a survey of the northern part of the country by the Ministry of Agriculture and Agrarian Reform, the pattern of distribution of holdings by size is distinctly uneven. Thus:

— 16,500 'exploitations' or holdings are in excess of 50 hectares in area each, and represent 25 per cent of the area of the private sector;
— 147,000 are between 10 and 50 ha, and represent 50 per cent;
— 114,000 are between 5 and 10 ha and represent 15 per cent;
— 310,000 are less than 5 ha in area and represent 10 per cent.

This means that some 3 per cent of the total number of holdings dispose of 25 per cent of the area, while about 53 per cent dispose of 10 per cent of the area.[41]

This situation led the government to opt for the limitation of land ownership and for the distribution of expropriated land as another aspect of agrarian reform. This aspect is incorporated into the Charter of Agrarian Revolution and Ordinance 71-73 of 8 November 1971. However, the law does not set one rigid ceiling to areas held, or one size for plots to be distributed to landless peasants or peasants with tiny holdings. In both instances the law prefers pragmatism within general principles. The guiding principle relative to the ceiling is that the size should be such as to be cultivable solely through the effort of the farmer and his family, without need for hired labour; and in all cases no absentee landlordship is allowed, no matter what the size of the holding is. (Legitimate cases of temporary absenteeship are excluded.) Likewise, the size of the plots distributed out of expropriated land is in principle to permit an income roughly equal to that obtained by a permanent worker in the socialist (the self-managed) sector working a total of 250 days a year; but in no case should the area exceed that size which is estimated to provide the equivalent of three years' work in one year. The exact determination of area in either case is to be left to the APC or the APC Elargie, owing to the sensitivity of this body to the local conditions of the soil, water and type of cultivation and to its ability, much better than some official or committee in the capital, to decide on area. Compensation is payable for the excess land expropriated from landlords (except when the land had been acquired during the war of liberation − on the presumption that the acquisition had been effected through extortion or the exploitation of the poverty and need of the peasants). The size of the compensation is determined as a certain multiple of the land tax, and it is paid in interest-bearing bonds of 15 years maturity.

Mechanisms of protest and appeal are provided for in the law at the local, *wilaya* and national level. But the procedures in this eventuality are simplified and the time limits allowed are very brief. Thus decisions can be finalised without much loss of time, unlike the situation in the Mashreq where the complexity and length of proceedings, and their extreme centralisation, have blighted reform and slowed it considerably.[42]

Land expropriated (i.e. 'nationalised') in the case of excessively large holdings, as well as land expropriated in the case of unjustified absentee ownership, public domain, communal land, land whose ownership is not established, and land newly reclaimed − are all passed on for disposal to the National Fund (or Estate) of the Agrarian Revolution (Fonds National de la Révolution Agraire). Part of such land is distributed to landless peasants with very small holdings, preference being given to those already working on the land, to *moudjahidine*, and to beneficiaries with large families where other qualifications are equal. The rest of the land goes to the establishment of collective farms (in the case of newly reclaimed land) or to distribution to individuals.

In all instances, the beneficiaries have to join co-operative societies. These societies, which follow the common pattern with regard to structure and functions, are also open to other farmers (i.e. those who are not recipient of FNRA land) if they so choose. Multi-purpose co-operatives (Coopératives Polyvalentes Communales de Services) which are broader in scope than producers' co-operatives, are also formed in every 'commune'. They bring together individual and collective operators, where again membership by the beneficiaries of the agrarian revolution is mandatory. These societies offer a wide variety of services aimed at improving not only production and the level of technical and marketing services, but living levels as well.

A wide-ranging look at the structure of the agrarian revolution shows the interrelationships between the various institutions and functions. The basic unit is the commune. The organs of implementation at the commune level are the APC and the APC Elargie (i.e. including local representatives of the FLN, the labour union, and other technical, economic or political groupings), the Communal Technical Committee, a body which is designed to help the APCE in technical matters relating to the agrarian revolution; and the multi-purpose co-operative. The APCE and the CTC are temporary: they only exist for the period when nationalisation and distribution of agrarian revolution land are undertaken. It is the ordinary APC and the co-operative which will remain thereafter to co-operate in implementing the objectives of the agrarian revolution and to bring about rural development.

At the *wilaya* level, there is the Assemblée Populaire de *wilaya*, and the *wilaya* executive (including the representative of the FLN and other national bodies). The two together are entrusted with the task of co-ordinating production and related operations within the *wilaya*, and in general the smooth and efficient functioning of the agrarian revolution. (The *wilaya* too has an enlarged Assembly and executive for the duration of the operations of nationalisation and redistribution of land. Thereafter, the ordinary structure — that is, minus the 'extensions' or enlargements — remains in operation.)

Finally, at the national level there is the Commission Nationale de la Révolution Agraire. This is a ministerial committee headed by the Minister of Agriculture and Agrarian Reform. It has a general supervisory function with a view to the proper implementing of the objectives and laws of the agrarian revolution.

The development of the rural society involves, in addition to what has been said, the extension of education and training, with emphasis on the modernisation of education with regard to content and methods, and on the relevance of training to agricultural activities. Furthermore, this development has called for a decentralisation of manufacturing industry, with the object of spreading industrial establishments for the purpose of spreading the various benefits of industrial activity (such as skills, employment, organisation and income). Finally, rural development means the implementation of many local projects, and the democratisation of development has meant — as it has already been stated — the participation of the APC (at the commune and the *wilaya* levels) in the planning dialogue and in decision-making, and ultimately the implementation of local projects under the control of local bodies. All these aspects of rural development, plus those related directly to agrarian reform, tend to make the peasants more attached to the countryside and tend to reduce the volume of emigration to large urban centres. Obviously, if life in the countryside becomes rewarding economically and satisfying socially, and if conditions improve visibly, fewer people will want to leave.

So far, the discussion could be said to have emphasised the rosy side of rural development and the agrarian revolution. Yet there is another side which is less rosy: actual performance and implementation. There are some serious evaluations of the agrarian revolution, with suggestions for improvement or correction in one or two of them.[43] In general, most of the criticism refers to the earlier phases of legislation and implementation, although some criticism persists. Broadly speaking, the following main points are emphasised:

> The election of the various bodies in the APC has not been as free as claimed at the start, which weakens the claim to democracy.
> The control by the Ministry of Agriculture and Agrarian Reform was heavy-handed, though it is less so now, which narrows the scope for local initiative and subjects the communes to unnecessarily heavy bureaucracy.

Algeria 541

The functions of the Director of the self-managed enterprise often clash with those of the Management Committee and its Chairman, and the dividing lines are not as clear as they should be.

The general guidelines for the determination of the upper limit of the size of land holdings, and of the plots distributed to the beneficiaries of the agrarian revolution, impose a heavy responsibility on the APC inasmuch as this body may not have the experience or technical or other knowledge of conditions in the country in general to set the sizes in question equitably.

Employment in the socialist sector is superfluous and control over expenditure is not very strict. As a result, the net returns (both in total and per worker) have been inordinately small, and in many instances net losses persist.

The functions of marketing and export, which are supposedly assured by agencies at the national level, are not efficiently performed, with heavy cost and wastage ensuing.

The country is still grossly short of agricultural technicians (in the fields of financing, production, grading, marketing, extension and audit) to cope with the needs. Some 12,000 persons are estimated to be needed while approximately only one-seventh to one-eighth of this number are available.

While admitting the validity of most of these points, responsible Algerians point out that the current situation is much healthier and functions much better than when the legislation for the agrarian revolution was first issued. The present writer, who attended the debate of the national conference of the Assemblées Populaires Communales (about 700 of them) in Algiers in February 1973 could see first-hand the frankness and seriousness with which the representatives examined their experience and performance, the self-criticism made, and the constructive suggestions offered for correction and improvement. This is a healthy phenomenon which is a reflection of a well-working and valuable social experiment.

The fact that not much nationalisation of large estates has yet taken place, and therefore that redistribution has to wait, does not negate this conclusion. First, the nationalisation operations cannot take place before the completion of a thorough survey of existing land holdings and title to them — an operation which is also conducted by the local bodies. In the second place, the revolution involves much else, as has been indicated, in the fields of education and training, planning and the building of projects by local authorities. These are moving satisfactorily. In any case, the agrarian revolution has all through been emphatically claimed as a long operation. And it is much better to allow it to take its legitimate time through the mechanisms of local self-rule than to subject it to pressure-cooker speed through the application of central authority at ministry level — and risk an even worse performance.

It will be useful at this point to record the developments ascertained by the end of 1974. According to information available early in 1975, the first phase of the Agrarian Revolution had as its objective the distribution of state domain formerly leased to farmers. This phase was initiated in June 1972, and has so far involved the distribution of some 800,000 ha and the formation of 2,919 co-operative societies. The beneficiaries total some 54,000 co-operative members, plus 2,316 individuals not yet associated. No payment is required for the plots distributed, and the land has to be worked by the beneficiaries under co-operative arrangements. Another 1.5m ha are yet to be distributed, but this area will first have to be reclaimed and made cultivable.

The second phase involves the undertaking of cadastral survey and determination of ownership, with a view to the expropriation of the areas in excess of what is allowed under the regulations emanating from the Charter. Understandably, this phase has brought out some resistance from the large landowners and their influential friends, and therefore the government has had to tread carefully. Furthermore, the operations involved are rather difficult to perform technically and legally. On the other hand, there has been spontaneous positive response by a large number of public-spirited absentee landowners who have voluntarily surrendered all their land, because they do not exploit it themselves but draw their income from non-agricultural activities. (These landowners include many civil servants and all army officers.)

Parallel with this development, share-tenancy has legally come to an end, since it meant absentee land ownership in most instances and, in those cases where the landowners lived in the countryside, it meant that their ownerships were larger than they could personally cope with. Thus, the application of the principle that the land should belong to those who work it, in plots that they can exploit without hired labour (except, of course, in collective farms as a transitory phase), will eventually mean the end, *de facto*, of share-tenancy and absentee land ownership.

The area expropriated by the end of 1974 has been 494,101 ha, divided among some 80,000 farmers who have formed 2,331 co-operative societies. An additional total of 3,907 individuals are temporarily allowed to work plots without forming co-operative societies.

A third phase in the Agrarian Revolution is being prepared. It has the objective of developing the pastoral sector. This phase, however, is still at an early stage of preparation.

It would be less than candid to pretend that the implementation of these aspects of the Agrarian Revolution has been occurring smoothly and without impediments. On the contrary. There have been delaying tactics, resistance and even counter-manoeuvres within government circles. However, the top leadership is steering its course with a mixture of firmness and patience. This leadership has opted for a slower performance with a larger probability of success, rather than impulsiveness and seeming speed, but in effect with a small probability of success in the longer run.

Lastly, the performance of agriculture must be examined via the productivity of agricultural labour and land in the socialist sector. The test shows a distinct deterioration both with regard to one unit of labour and of land, and for almost all crops, between the days when the French colonialists ran the farms and the end of the sixties.

But this need not be taken necessarily as a sign that the system is condemned to chronic inefficiency and cannot be improved. It is to be expected that the drop in the level of the managerial function, superimposed on political conditions still in the process of transition, was bound to result in a drop in productivity. The final test cannot be applied before a decade of the agrarian revolution has passed, since the socio-cultural, technical, organisational and managerial factors essential for success need several years to be reshaped before they become promotive of improved performance.

If these observations are borne in mind, one can even say that the socialist sector — given its short experience and the disadvantages it has had to contend with — has done rather well. From the social point of view it ought also to be remembered that under colonialism some 22,000 European farmers owned all the land now in the socialist sector and retained the lion's share of the net returns. Now it is over 250,000 Algerian earners who are receiving the net returns and reaping the fruits of their efforts. The net profits are divided between the state and local bodies on the one hand, and the 'exploitation', or the farm, on the other. The relative shares are defined annually by decree, upon the recommendation of the Minister of Agriculture and Agrarian Reform. The share of the farm is divided into (1) allocations for the operation such as reserves, working capital and investments, and (2) income for the workers. This second category is in turn divided into a fund for distribution, a fund for bonuses, and a fund for social services.

Until the mid-sixties, the agricultural sector was the largest single contributor to national product, an honour which passed in 1966 to the petroleum and gas sector. Notwithstanding the agrarian revolution, which has injected dynamism in society and in the economy, the sector as a whole, viewed from the angle of production and use of modern inputs (such as farm machinery and fertilisers) has not moved forward noticeably under independence. Thus, in absolute terms, value added in agriculture has more or less remained at the same absolute level, except for years of particularly good or particularly poor harvests. On the other hand, in relative terms, value added has dropped noticeably, with the petroleum and gas sector moving upwards and with consumer, basic and extractive industries slightly improving their combined position within a rising national product.

The large-scale exodus of European farmers, the unsettled political events of the mid-sixties, and the new legislation affecting agriculture in the later sixties and further in 1971 have together adversely affected decision-making in agriculture with regard to the various factors contributive to production. Thus the volume of production as a whole fell (except for livestock, whose numbers increased substantially). The area of cultivated land, which is about 552,000 ha, has not varied considerably between 1958 and 1969. (The area of irrigated land, some 270,000 hectares, has expanded little also.) Total agricultural production stood at an index of 68 in 1966, with 1952-6 as base, while it stood at 105 with 1961-5 as base. The *per capita* index was even less satisfactory: 54 and 77 respectively. Food production fared slightly worse, with the indices for total production being 66 and 103, and for *per capita* production being 53 and 76 respectively. With respect to modernisation, it is observed that the stock of tractors in the years 1953-9 rose much faster than in the parallel years 1963-9. Nevertheless the years 1967-70 witnessed an acceleration in the sale of equipment compared with the earlier years of the sixties.[44] It remains to be seen, in conclusion, whether the efforts deployed under the 1970-3 Plan, and in the 1974-7 Plan, which is now being implemented, will change the picture drastically in favour of the sector as a whole.

Industrialisation

The speedy development of manufacturing industry is the second pillar of the general development of the economy, within an integrated structure also involving rural development in its broad sense, and the development of and control over the country's petroleum and gas reserves and its other metallic and non-metallic minerals. It is noteworthy that Algeria's approach towards these three objectives is balanced. Furthermore, it is underlined by the firm conviction that national liberation cannot have full meaning and substance unless it is based on the achievement of the three objectives (with respect to agriculture, industry and underground wealth) alongside social and political development.

It can even be argued, on the basis of a large body of evidence, that socio-political development (including the proper education of the population, and the mobilisation of the masses through firm organisation and not emotional slogans) interacts with the three areas of economic development and serves as a *sine qua non* for this latter development. This whole outlook, and the systemic relations between the component ideas underlying it, may be said to form an ideology on its own. Algerian political leaders and intellectuals call the ideology Algeria's path towards socialism. Yet it ought to be emphasised that the style of socialism adopted, or the particular flavour of the ideology, is that of pragmatism and flexibility. It is an ideology applied by men who are essentially activists and 'doers' (whether as political leaders, top administrators, civil servants, managers, executives, planners or technocrats) and not essentially the coiners of phrases and verbalisms. Therefore, if the results do not justify the ideology in some of its aspects, it is the ideology that will be adjusted to become more translatable into concrete action capable of success.

Unfortunately, the publication of the national accounts for Algeria is not made in enough detail to permit the examination of the pace of progress of industry, since the sector is combined with construction and public works. (However, there are indications that make possible the assessment of the relative importance of industry by itself.) Another problem relating to the national accounts is the slowness of their publication. Thus, in the spring of 1975, the only sectoral data available in published form relate to 1969, though global information is available for 1973. Finally, the series for the years 1963-8 is not presented in a form that allows comparison, even for this limited number of years: the data for 1963, 1964 and 1965 are given in terms of current prices, while those for 1966, 1967 and 1968 are in 1965 prices. (There is also an estimate for 1969, as we shall see later.) Nevertheless, for our purposes this last problem is not of significance, inasmuch as we are presently concerned with the change in the relative importance of industry in national product.

In this respect we see that the share of industry has risen only slightly from the immediate pre-independence years to 1968, namely from about 10.5 to about 12 per cent of national product. In absolute terms, the contribution of industry (i.e. value added in it) has doubled between 1955 and 1968. While this record may not look very impressive, its significance will become clearer if compared with that of agriculture for the same period. The absolute contribution of agricultural activity (both modern and traditional) has remained rather the same, and therefore the relative share of this sector has dropped from around 25 per cent for the late fifties, to 13 per cent for 1967 and 1968.[45] (This suggests that much more structural and institutional change has taken place in agriculture than change in the volume and value of production.)

There is another angle from which the significance of the course of development of industry will become clear: this is the examination of a cross-section of industry before independence and towards the end of the independence decade. Such examination will reveal telling differences. The first major difference is obvious: it relates to the ownership of industrial establishments. Thus, whereas virtually all of these were European-owned before 1962, they are now Algerian-owned. The transfer, as in the case of French farms, was *de facto* to begin with: the take-over by management committees of abandoned (and often sabotaged) factories. This was subsequently in 1962 and later in 1963 legalised by decree, and formerly French-owned industry fell into the 'secteur autogéré'. This change in ownership is but one aspect of the overall change in the structure of the sector, but the structure will be examined further down.

For the time being, we are interested in the other major difference revealed by the comparison of the composition of industry before and after independence. This is the vast change in the types of industries prevailing then and now. Under the French, these were mostly consumer goods industries, designed to remain of limited importance in order to allow wide scope for French industry to sell substantial quantities of its products in Algeria. Today, Algeria, in addition to expanding the industries taken over, has built many more import-substituting industries, and has also gone into basic industries such as petrochemicals, iron-smelting, automotives, construction materials, engineering and electrical and mechanical industries.

The extractive industries are, on the whole, part of the colonial heritage. French concessionaires continued to control this group of industries for the first few years of independence, as stipulated for in the Evian Agreement of 1962. However, in May 1966 the government nationalised the eleven largest companies active in the mining of iron ore, lead, copper and zinc. Today all mining enterprises are in the public sector. Only quarrying is in private ownership. As stated earlier, iron ore is by far the most important branch of this group. Production in the group as a whole dropped in the first couple of independence years, but picked up again, though the course varies from mineral to mineral. In the case of iron ore, production has averaged over 3 million tons for the seven years 1967-73, reaching about 3.7m tons for 1973. The same trend can be seen in the production of phosphates — a non-metallic mineral. It was only in 1969 that production reached its pre-independence high of 420,000 tons; it surpassed this level in subsequent years, and reached 1.13m tons for 1973.[46]

Finally, the sector of industry broadly defined includes the generation of electricity. Here too we find that power generation dropped considerably between 1961 and 1962 (by about one-sixth), stabilised at the lower level for the years 1962-6, then began to rise until in 1971 it exceeded the level of 1966 by 75 per cent, and in 1972 it grew further by 6 per cent, reaching 2,019m kwh.[47] However, even the production of 1972 provides an average of 130 kwh per head, which is a very low level, especially if it is recalled that industrial uses and domestic uses together result in this average. (The 1970-73 Plan provides for the increase by 25 per cent of power consumption in Algeria. Gas consumption — both industrial and domestic — is rising fast and has the effect of adjusting upwards the average use of energy in the country.)

The examination of the production trends of the major two dozen products shows that in all but a few cases production in 1970 and/or 1971 is distinctly higher than in the previous years, although it also appears that the trend suffered a dip in the mid-sixties. The output of what has been referred to as 'basic industries', which are all in the public sector, shows a disquieting tendency to level off (or even to drop) in 1971, compared with 1970. This is true of such products as cast iron, tubes, tip-lorries, trailers, buses and mini-buses, cisterns, insulated electric cables, telephone cables, boilers, framing material and many items in the construction industry whose volume for 1970 dropped from its 1969 level (but regarding which no data are in hand for more recent years). Several items in the consumer industry (such as textiles, women's and men's clothing, leather, paint and varnish, detergents) suffered the same drop in 1971 compared with the one or two years preceding it.[48]

A tendency involving a group of products this wide and varied cannot but call for a pause. It would seem that many industries are unable yet to sustain a steady rate of growth. This is the result of a combination of factors including managerial and technical shortcomings and high unit costs, and therefore reduced marketability. Most of the products involved fall in industries owned and run by the public sector, although many others are in the private sector as well. This suggests that the 'managerial function' broadly defined is still at an early stage of efficiency.

While disturbing, this problem is understandable. Experience will have to be gained the hard way over a number of years. And Algeria's experience is still too brief to permit of a distinctly better performance, although this explanation must not conceal the legitimate presumption that the managerial function in the public sector suffers, as it does universally, from bureaucracy, slow decision-making, and an insufficient concern with profitability.[49]

Furthermore, the intensified emphasis on industrialisation (and more particularly on the basic industries in the fields of electrical equipment, petrochemicals, metallurgy, engineering, mechanical equipment and construction materials) seems all the more justifiable since already one can see a tendency towards greater balance among the major activities of agriculture, industry, mining and hydrocarbons. This diversification will guard the country against the dangers of lopsidedness or excessive dependence on one major activity, such as the production and export of crude petroleum, from which the major Arab petroleum-exporting countries are trying to escape with very limited success so far.

In addition to diversification, Algeria's determined efforts to industrialise do not constitute an independent streak of policy, but form part of an integrated strategy of development which has been crystallising over the past five or six years, but particularly in the context of the First Four-Year Plan of Development for the years 1970-3, and the Second Four-Year Plan 1974-77. To this extent industrialisation is one major thread in the fabric of Algeria's economic future as its leaders want it to be. If we use the qualifying word 'economic' here, this is not to ignore the social, and even political, implications of the Algerian approach to development which is predicated on the convergence of the major fields of activity already mentioned.[50]

An inventory of the industrial projects undertaken by Algeria would be a long one. In this summary we will attempt to enumerate the major projects initiated or under expansion during the three years 1972-4. This period reversed the position in 1971, which was marked by strained Algerian-French relations in the oil field, and the interruption of oil production. Furthermore, 1974 is the year when the full impact of the steep rise in oil prices decided upon by the Organization of Petroleum Exporting Countries (OPEC) in October and December 1973 was felt, and when the vastly expanded revenues permitted substantially larger investment in industry. The major projects, which reflect the emphasis placed on basic and heavy industry, included:

— Expansion in the iron and steel industry in the El Hadjar complex, particularly the addition of two new converters which are designed to increase steel production from 800,000 tons to 1.5m tons by 1975.
— The completion in 1973 of a new refinery at Arzew.
— The construction of a new gas liquefaction plant, to be completed in 1976.
— The construction of a vast petrochemical complex at Skikda, to produce polyethylene, PVC, caustic soda and chlorine, as well as the preparation for the construction of factories to produce nitric acid and ammonium nitrate at Arzew.
— The completion in September 1972 of one paint and two plastics factories at Setif.
— The expansion of the existing vehicle industry and construction of a heavy vehicle assembly plant at Rouiba.
— The construction of two factories at Constantine for the production of 4,000 tractors, 10,000 diesel engines and 1,500 public works vehicles annually.
— The completion of a plant at Guelma for the production annually of 30,000 motorcycles, 15,000 bicycles and 5,000 small motors.
— The construction of a farm machinery factory at Sidi Bel Abbès, to be completed in 1976.
— The virtual completion at Médéa of a factory for pumps and irrigation equipment.
— The completion of a metal works plant in 1972 at Meftah.
— The preparation for the construction of a large shipyard at Oran.
— The construction of an electrical goods factory at Tizi Ouzou.
— The establishment of a large printing complex.

— Miscellaneous large factories (either completed, expanded or under construction) in the electrical, paper, textiles, tobacco and building materials industries.

Two final comments are in order. First, the government attempts, as far as advisable, to disperse the industrial complexes, taking into account simultaneously the desire to provide employment and experience on as wide a geographical basis as possible, and the desire to locate industries in such a manner as to satisfy the requirements of raw materials and fuel (or gas) transport and of access to marketing outlets. Second, that the forward and backward linkages between agriculture and industry, and between industry and hydrocarbons, are taken as fully as possible into account in the determination of what industries to establish. This complementarity makes economic sense and is conducive to a better integration of the economy. But it also carries the dangers of the establishment of some industries that the economic logic does not justify only because the raw materials are locally available, or energy is very cheap.

Most of Algeria's industry is organised in the form of public companies ('Sociétés Nationales'). Each of these embraces a number of industrial establishments. There were 30 of them in 1969, including SONATRACH (which deals with petroleum and natural gas, from prospecting and production to processing, transport and commercialisation). In addition to these public companies there is a category, designated 'Other Public Enterprises', which includes 36 enterprises. A third group of 172 enterprises falls in the self-managed, socialist sector ('Entreprises Autogérées'). Finally, in 1969 there were also 1,816 enterprises in the private sector. (More recent information is not available; nevertheless it can safely be assumed that many more establishments and groupings have emerged, in view of the vast expansion in industrialisation in the years 1970-4.) The Sociétés Nationales have by far the largest number of establishments per Société while in the other categories the 'entreprise' and the establishment nearly overlap.

In the matter of employment, the Sociétés Nationales account for 49.6 per cent of total employment, followed by private enterprises with 41.2 per cent, self-managed enterprises with 6.5 per cent, and other public enterprises with the balance of 2.7 per cent.[51] (These data do not include SONATRACH.) A comparison for enterprises with 20 employees or more, between the Sociétés Nationales on the one hand, and the three other categories combined on the other, with respect to a few indicators for the two years 1968 and 1969, produces a mixed picture, as the summary of the comparison in Table 12.7 reveals.

According to this tabulation, no one group has a consistent superiority with regard to the indicators chosen. Thus the explanation of the performance must be sought in the operation of several factors, not all of which necessarily pull in the same direction. Taking all manufacturing and extractive industries with 5 or more employees per enterprise, and comparing sales, purchases and wages shows that the volume of sales exceeds the total of purchases and wages for the two groups (i.e. Sociétés Nationales and the three other categories combined) for the years 1968, 1969 and 1970. (The data available for 1970 only relate to Sociétés Nationales.) However, the surplus drops in relative terms between 1968 and 1969 for both groups.[52]

Finally, a comparison for 1969 for the major groups of industry (including mining, electricity and petroleum and gas in addition to manufacturing) shows that while enterprises in the public sector account for exactly two-thirds of the industrial labour force, they account for 61.7 per cent of wages, 41.8 per cent of sales, and 40.7 per cent of purchases.[53] These results suggest greater padding in the labour force in the public than in the private

Table 12.7: Comparison of Enterprises of More than 20 Employees, 1968-9

	Sociétés Nationales		Other Enterprises	
	1968	1969	1968	1969
Sales per employee (dinars)	47,693	57,160	48,192	51,309
Value added per employee (dinars)	24,600	27,035	20,619	19,360
Value added per 1,000 dinars of sales	517	472	306	377
Sales per enterprise (dinars)	97,236	117,471	3,549	3,450
Employees per enterprise	2,038	2,055	74	67

Source: Chambre de Commerce et d'Industrie d'Alger, *Situation Economique de l'Algérie 1970/71* (Algiers, 1972), Part I. Unfortunately, the pages in this volume are not numbered.

sector, considering the respective shares of the two sectors in labour and wages on the one hand, and sales and purchases on the other. Furthermore, the ratio of the surplus for each group (i.e. sales less the total of wages and purchases) is about 50 per cent higher in the private than the public sector. While admitting that profitability is not the only (or perhaps the major) concern of public-sector enterprises, these findings must nevertheless serve as a spur for greater efficiency and sales in these enterprises. Again here, as in the case of the agricultural socialist sector, more time must be allowed before a more definitive judgement can be passed on public sector performance. This is particularly true of the major industrial complexes that were built in the late sixties and early seventies (such as the steel, motor, tractor, chemical, engineering and canning industries).

A word concerning the mode of application of socialism to the sector of industry is in order here, since the structure and functioning of the agricultural socialist structure has been described. The socialist organisation of enterprises in all sectors outside agriculture is governed by a document entitled 'Charte de l'Organisation Socialiste des Entreprises' (Charter of the Socialist Organisation of Enterprises) and by two Ordinances: No. 71-74 and No. 71-75, all dated 16 November 1971.[54] They apply to all enterprises and units or establishments within the enterprises where the state owns the assets of the enterprise or unit. In these instances the collectivity of workers enjoys the use of the assets, but their ownership is vested in the state. The enterprises fall under the competence of ministries or other central bodies, the nature of the product determining the ministry to which the enterprise is attached. Beyond this, the collectivity of workers is autonomous, within the spirit of the Charter and the content of the two Ordinances.

This collectivity elects a Workers' Assembly consisting of 7—25 members, depending on the total number of workers. The Assembly can have permanent committees composed of its own members, with participation by other workers, for various functions relating to production, finances, training and personnel, discipline, hygiene and security. (The list of candidates to Assembly membership is prepared by a special nominations committee that includes representatives of the labour union, the party (the FLN), and the governing body or ministry.) As in the case of the Assembly in an agricultural 'exploitation', the Assembly in the present context serves for three years.

The functions of the Assembly include the overall planning and control of operations. But the closer responsibility of management falls on a Board of Directors or Management

Board (Conseil de Direction) which consists of a Director-General at enterprise level (or Director at unit or establishment level) with his deputy and assistants, plus one or two workers elected by the Assembly. The Board serves for three years and is eligible for extended periods of service. The Director-General is appointed by decree upon the recommendation of the governing body, under whose authority he operates. It is the Director-General who recommends to the governing body the name of a unit Director for appointment.

Unionisation is allowed and membership is open to all workers. The net returns, when positive, are divided between the State, the enterprise (for further investment), and a workers' supplementary fund. The shares are determined by decree.

It is appropriate to emphasise here that the workers in the private sector also enjoy a certain measure of authority, under Ordinance 71-75. Every establishment has to have a trade union and the union elects its secretary. The union is entitled to receive copies of the production plans, the general regulations governing the operation of the establishment, and the balance sheet and profit and loss account. It is empowered to comment on these, and to strike when it feels that the management violates its members' rights or contravenes the provisions of the appropriate laws. The workers in the private establishment receive a certain portion of the net profits, and they are assured the basic social, cultural and hygienic amenities. With regard to this last point, all workers in Algeria, whether in agricultural or non-agricultural establishments, enjoy social and medical security, in addition to the educational facilities assured for their children.

The Petroleum and Gas Sector[55]

The hydrocarbons sector (petroleum and gas) was already under development in Algeria before independence. All the concessions for exploration, production, distribution and export were awarded by the French colonial authorities to French companies. But the scale of operations was very modest until 1958, when a little under half a million tons of oil were produced. Since then, but particularly since the mid-sixties, oil production has accelerated, reaching 50.1m tons for 1972, 51m for 1973, and an estimated 49.9m for 1974. Likewise, the revenue of the sector has risen considerably from its level in 1958, which was just under one million US dollars, to reach $613m for 1972, $1,050m for 1973, and an estimated $4,100m for 1974.[56]

If looked at from the narrow focus of volume of production and earnings, the Algerian hydrocarbons sector is not sensational: its growth is less dramatic than that of its counterpart in Libya or some of the oil-producing Gulf countries, notwithstanding the fact that the country's proven reserves of oil by January 1974 stood at 1,341m tons, and those of natural gas were estimated at 3.99 trillion (or 3.99 million million) cubic metres, constituting some 10 per cent of total world reserves.[57] Algeria ranks after Saudi Arabia, Kuwait, Iraq, Libya and United Arab Emirates.[58] However, what is significant about the oil and gas sector of Algeria is the speed, the thoroughness and the efficiency with which the state acquired control of its oil and gas resources at all levels of operation. Algeria's experience is so unlike that of any other Arab country, and so educative, that it deserves some space to be recounted.

The sector's operations were governed in 1958 by the Sahara Oil Code of 1958, which stipulated for a 50-50 profit-sharing between the companies and the Algerian government (administration). The Evian Agreement of 1962 affirmed the concessions and the companies' rights under them (and equally affirmed the mining companies' concessions). Prior to this, the French had attempted to separate the Sahara from the north to keep control of the mineral wealth of the south in French hands in the face of the impending independence of the country. The attempts were foiled, and the Algerians paid in human lives on 5 July 1961 in order to bring about the failure of the partition policy. The Evian Agreement gave the Algerians the satisfaction that the integrity of their homeland was kept intact, and the French the control of Algeria's oil and other mineral wealth.

It is now obvious, from evidence accumulated over the years, that the leadership of the country had from the start meant to gain control over its natural resources and to supplement political with economic sovereignty, but had adopted a phased, pragmatic policy within the general principle of sovereignty. The first step towards the acquisition of the technical and managerial skills necessary for such control was the setting up on 31 December 1963 of SONATRACH, for the purpose initially of transporting and marketing oil and gas, but gradually for incursion into the fields of exploration, production and export; and finally for entry into the fields of refining and petrochemicals. Subsequently, the government set up several institutions that were designed to better enable SONATRACH to carry on its functions. Thus, nine subsidiaries have been established (with majority shares for SONATRACH) for undertaking geophysical surveys, drilling, sub-oil testing, electric diagraphs, reservoir engineering, construction, and so on.

Likewise, the training of Algerians for managerial, technical, accounting and supervisory skills was undertaken with great energy, both inside the country and abroad. In Algeria itself, the task was undertaken at the University of Algiers (where special programmes were designed) as well as at the African Centre for Hydrocarbons and Textiles, the Algerian Petroleum Institute, and other technical institutions that were set up for the purpose. (By the end of 1970, 2,000 Algerians were enrolled in the various institutes, where training takes between four and six years. At the present moment the country has virtual self-sufficiency in almost all fields and types of expertise related to hydrocarbons.) Finally, all agreements with foreign oil companies include arrangements for the training of Algerians. It is estimated that by the end of 1973 the country had over 10,700 trained personnel, over 30 per cent of whom fell in the managerial, technical and supervisory categories, while the remainder were skilled workers.

The framework of French-Algerian oil relations underwent its first major change upon the signature, on 29 July 1965, of a new agreement which, *inter alia*, provided for:

— The abolition of the old system of concessions and its replacement by a system of co-operation within an 'Association Coopérative' (ASCOOP), which stipulated for the allocation of plots to prospectors for exploration and exploitation; the periods involved were to be much shorter than in the old concessions. SONATRACH was empowered to pay for the recovery of oil concessions.
— The companies were allowed to expatriate only their post-tax profits and any mandatory payments (such as social security dues to the French government); any amount in excess of this was to be retained and invested in Algeria.
— Take-over of all the operations of treatment and domestic distribution of the gas produced jointly with oil, and the take-over of all gas export operations except those destined for the French market which were left in the hands of a joint Algerian-French company.
— The profit-sharing formula was amended in two ways: the setting of a base price for profit calculation purposes, and the increase of Algeria's share to 55 per cent.

Algeria took further steps which enabled it to obtain effective control over its oil and gas in the span of about six years, between the agreement of 29 July 1965 and the nationali-

Algeria

sation decrees of 24 February 1971 and the subsequent legislation of 12 April 1971, which created a new oil code. In order to avoid tedious detail but still to trace these important and considered steps, a brief outline of the measures taken after July 1965 will now be given:

- The government decided that land transportation of the oil constituted a bottleneck, and built a pipeline (from Haoud El Hamra fields to Arzew just east of Oran on the western part of the coastline — a distance of over 800 km.); this pipeline, the third in the country, was inaugurated on 19 March 1966, and it allowed the increased flow of oil by some 7m tons. A fourth pipeline, built and operated by SONATRACH, links Mesdar fields and Skikda, on the eastern coastline.
- The sales network of British Petroleum, and later the refining and distribution facilities of Esso and Mobil, came under the control of the state by the summer of 1967.
- Upon the issue of Ordinances on 13 May 1968 the nationalisation was effected of companies in the fields of storage, transport and marketing of oil products and of the derivatives of liquid or gaseous hydrocarbons; this measure was extended soon after to include the production, distribution and marketing of fertilisers.
- Feeling that the consolidation of its control over the oil and gas sector was moving slowly, the government appealed to the non-French companies to surrender (voluntarily and against equitable compensation) 51 per cent of their shares to SONATRACH. The exclusion of the French companies did not reflect satisfaction with the Algerian-French relationship — indeed, Algeria was unhappy as a result of the conviction that the French were being slow in exploration and exploitation operations and in the training of Algerian cadres and technicians under the terms of ASCOOP. Yet the French companies were left alone, though under a cloud of suspicion and discontent, for the time being. The only foreign company that responded positively was Getty Petroleum, which surrendered 51 per cent of its shares and entered into a co-operation agreement with SONATRACH, under which SONATRACH became a joint operator and manager with full rights.
- By the end of 1969, the government's control over production was still very limited (25 per cent, versus 57.5 per cent in transport, 56 per cent in exploration and refining, and 100 per cent in domestic distribution). Furthermore, it was soon to embark on the ambitious 1970-73 Plan, and it thus needed increased revenues for investment. So it entered into negotiations with France for the revision of the 1965 agreement and, in June 1970, it nationalised the non-French companies, with the result that it expanded its control over production by about 10 per cent and over refining by 24 per cent — bringing the latter to a total of 80 per cent control.
- Negotiations with France stretched over 1970, but without reaching agreement. In fact the French asked for a temporary suspension of the talks. However, with the world energy crisis becoming more deeply felt, and with the market increasingly becoming a seller's market, Algeria acted firmly on 24 February 1971, days after the Teheran agreement between OPEC and the oil companies which improved the terms for OPEC members considerably. The action consisted of four decrees (Nos. 71-8 to 71-11) which brought into effect the raising of Algeria's participation in all French oil companies to 51 per cent, the nationalisation of all natural gas fields, and the nationalisation of all transport facilities in the country (i.e. the foreign-owned pipelines).
- Partly to counter French (government and company) claims that the measures were in certain respects unacceptable (because of being unilateral, because the Sahara Oil

Code of 1958 had not been annulled and was therefore claimed to be in effect, and because the compensation offer was considered both inequitable and arbitrarily fixed), the Algerian government issued a new code on 12 April 1971. This code, which replaced that of 1958, eliminated concessions and defined the new framework within which relations could be set, namely that the government would always own no less than 51 per cent of the share capital of any company in the oil sector and would be a full partner in all aspects of the company's operations. In addition to this basic code, the government decreed that the fiscal arrangements with foreign companies should conform to those practised by OPEC members, and it finally set the reference prices applicable for 1969 and 1970, and those to apply for the years 1971-5 along the lines taken earlier in February in the Tripoli agreement between the Libyan government and the companies operating in Libya.

— The French (government and companies) reacted angrily: the government attempted an economic boycott in addition to diplomatic frostiness; the companies published notices that Algeria's action was unacceptable and that the oil offered from nationalised fields was 'red' and buyers would be open to law suits.[59] Nevertheless, the resentment of the companies did not last long. Beginning with 30 June 1971, agreements were signed with all the French companies and a settlement was reached, according to which the tax dues claimed by the government were set against the compensation claimed by the companies. In the case of the ERAP group, the back taxes exceeded the compensation, and the group had to relinquish a large part of their shares in final settlement. Another group relinquished all their remaining shares in final settlement of claims and counter-claims.

It will be useful to present at this point in tabulated form the evolution of Algeria's control over its resources and the various operations related to them. Table 12.8 shows that by 1972, Algeria had very high, though less than full, control of oil production, but full control of every other aspect. The table also shows the pattern of evolution from 1966 onwards, with SONATRACH's role expanding as its experience and power to conduct operations increased. Behind the picture that emerges there is not only the flow of laws and measures, which has just been outlined, but an arduous and sustained process of disciplined thinking and conception, planning, legal and administrative preparation, personnel training, and finally legislation, take-over and operation.

Furthermore, in physical terms, the process has meant the construction of major works at all stages of the industry. Thus Algeria is no more 'a spectator and tax collector'[60] in the field of hydrocarbons, but a fully-fledged operator. It took steps which have proved more daring, quicker and more successful than any other oil country in the Arab world has taken. These include the vast expansion of gas transport and liquefaction facilities (to cope with large export agreements with the United States and England, in addition to increased exports to other countries); entry into the field of oil and gas tankerage; the expansion of existing refining capacity plus the building of new refineries; and the setting up of plastics and other petrochemical complexes.

Continuing the practice so far adopted in this study, we will now present the series of oil production and revenue data available in Table 12.9. Unfortunately, data are not available in series form for the quantities of gas produced for export. However, one official source states that the production of gas for commercialisation rose from 221m cubic metres in 1961, the first year when such production was started, to 2.9 billion cubic metres in 1971.[61] No gas revenue estimates are available.

Algeria

Table 12.8: The Evolution of SONATRACH's Control over the Hydrocarbon Sector in Algeria (percentages)

Aspect of Control	1966	1967	1968	1969	1970	1971	1972
Exploitation areas (where SONATRACH executes works)	12.0	21.0	51.0	65.0	92.0	100.0	100.0
Oil production	11.5	11.8	13.7	17.75	35.0	56.0	77.0
Natural gas reserves under SONATRACH control	18.0	19.5	19.5	23.5	29.0	100.0	100.0
Pipeline transport	38.0	38.0	39.0	40.0	50.0	98.0	100.0
Refining	20.4	44.0	66.0	66.0	90.0	100.0	100.0
Distribution in Algeria	0.0	48.6	100.0	100.0	100.0	100.0	100.0

Source: Sonatrach, *SONATRACH* (?1972; Arabic), p. 12.

It is not possible to measure the evolution of the relative importance of the hydrocarbons sector in the structure of the economy, via its contribution to national product, because no continuous series of national accounts exists for the years 1958-72 or 1973. We are in possession of two brief series: 1955-8, and 1963-8, but even with this shortcoming, the two series suffer from insufficiency of detail. None the less, enough is known to show the vast rise in the significance of the oil and gas sector. The contribution of this sector rose from a negligible figure in 1958, when the export of oil began on a very modest scale, to 21.6 per cent of national product in 1968, but it fell to 14.7 per cent of GDP for 1973. Even in this last year, the share of the sector was the largest single share.[62]

Nevertheless, in spite of the predominance of the oil sector, it is not expected that the continued expansion in it will result, as it has done in Libya and the large Mashreq oil-producing countries, in excessive dependence on oil. Indeed, other sectors were already gaining ground, as the data for 1973 suggest. However, the steep rise in oil prices and revenues in 1974 will re-establish the vast lead of oil as a contributor to GDP. Yet ultimately, as other sectors (particularly industry) grow fast, the relative structural importance of oil will decline. This is for two reasons. First, despite the large oil reserves, Algerian production is not as easy as in the Mashreq owing to the relative smallness of individual oil wells and certain geological difficulties. Second, that development strategy and policies are so designed as to keep as much inter-sectoral balance as possible, and that development efforts are deployed in such a fashion as to promote the achieving of this objective. The stabilisation of oil revenue at a certain level (that associated with about 50m tons of crude production) already means that Algeria is domestically absorbing all its oil revenues. No other OPEC country is in the same position; all the other OPEC members, though in varying degrees, are building up large reserves abroad. Iraq stands next to Algeria in this respect, and will probably be absorbing all its oil revenue domestically in a few years' time.

For Algeria to have started its independence era with an already remunerative oil sector was a piece of good luck. That it has developed the sector as far as it has done is a matter of sound planning and action. One of the aspects of the good luck was that the country did not have to go through the balance of payments hardships which are part of the normal experience of most developing countries. Thus, foreign exchange earnings from the export of petroleum and, later, gas, from the export of minerals (especially iron ore and phosphates),

Table 12.9: Production of Crude Oil, and Oil Revenue

Year	Oil Production (million tons)	Oil Revenue ($ million)
1958	0.4	n.a.
1959	1.2	n.a.
1960	8.6	n.a.
1961	15.8	n.a.
1962	20.7	n.a.
1963	23.9	54.1
1964	26.5	61.2
1965	26.5	91.8
1966	33.9	128.6
1967	39.0	199.1
1968	43.0	261.8
1969	45.0	266.7
1970	48.2	271.9
1971	36.5	324.0
1972	50.1	613.3
1973	51.0	1,050.0
1974	49.9	4,100.0

Sources: For oil production 1958-71, Sonatrach, *SONATRACH* (?1972; Arabic), p. 26; for 1972 and 1973, *BP Statistical Review... 1973;* and for 1974, Nicolas Sarkis, 'The Energy Crisis and the Challenge of Development in the Arab Countries', Paper No. 132 (A-1), submitted to the Ninth Arab Petroleum Congress, Dubai, 10-16 March 1975, Table 1, p. 16. For oil revenues, Ministry of Information and Culture, *1962-1972: Algeria in Numbers* (Madrid, 1972), p. 24, for 1963-6, and Sarkis, Table 2, p. 17, for 1967-74.

from the large military expenditures of the French and, after independence, from French aid, combined to give the country a surplus on current account and on capital account in the balance of international payments. (Indeed, it was only beginning with 1969 that the commodity imports began to exceed commodity exports noticeably, and 1970 was the first year with a large trade deficit arising mainly from the increase in the importation of industrial equipment and, to a lesser extent, of semi-finished products.) This general convergence of factors has enabled the country to accumulate relatively large reserves of gold and foreign exchange, which began appearing in the first full year after independence, namely 1963.[63] These reserves grew in the manner shown in Table 12.10.

It remains to be added, finally, that Algeria has sought, and succeeded in, establishing greater balance in the geographical distribution of its foreign trade. This has reduced her excessive dependence on the French market and assured her of greater security inasmuch as trade between the two countries has tended to reflect the political climate prevailing, as France's decision to cut down on her substantial wine imports from Algeria in protest against the latter's oil policy has clearly shown.

Education, Training, Public Health and Other Services[64]

The insistence by Algerian leaders on social and economic balance must have become clear by now. This balance reflects itself in the deep concern with the welfare of the rural

Algeria

Table 12.10: Foreign Assets, 1965-74

	Million Dinars	Million US $
End of 1965	832.3	
End of 1966	1,270.4	
End of 1967	2,040.4	
End of 1968	2,350.0	
End of 1969	1,843.0	
End of 1970	1,337.2	
End of 1971	2,490.7	507
End of 1972	2,210.5	493
End of 1973	4,525.5	1,143
End of 1974	7,061.4	1,689

Sources: For data on trade and gold and foreign exchange reserves till end of 1970, see Ministry of Information and Culture, *1962-1972: Algeria in Numbers* (Madrid, 1972), pp. 88 and 19 respectively. For more recent data, see *International Financial Statistics*, October 1975.

community (a concern to which only lip-service is paid in many developing countries) along with that of the urban community; in the allocation of emphasis and human and material resources for the healthy progress of all sectors; and the multi-course approach to development via political, social and economic mobilisation and participation. This balance can also be seen in the simultaneous concern with and emphasis on physical as well as human capital and infrastructure.

On various occasions reference has been made to physical (economic) infrastructure in areas such as electricity, energy or basic industry. To this must be added that the country is investing serious effort and large sums in the expansion and improvement of the networks of transport and communication (which, admittedly, were well-developed on the eve of independence, but need continued attention and expansion); in housing schemes, including the completion of 42,000 units started but not finished by the French, the building of about 48,000 urban and about 12,000 new rural units between 1962 and 1971, and, finally, the ambitious target of building 1,000 new villages by 1980, each with 100–300 houses. These villages are meant partly to replace the 8,000 destroyed by the French during the war of liberation, and to ease the housing situation. The villages will be supplied with the necessary economic and social amenities. Finally, there is considerable investment in the building of dams and barrages to conserve and better utilise the very scarce water resources (18 such dams are now in existence for holding 1 billion cubic metres out of a total of 65 billion of rainfall, only one-sixth of which goes into streams).

We must now focus on human (social) infrastructure. The work done in this field can be seen in the building up of cultural facilities and opportunities; in social welfare, in public health; but above all in education and training. In the field of public health, preventive medicine is receiving relatively larger resources than curative medicine, in an effort to treat the main health problems at the source. These are listed by official sources as the incidence of tuberculosis, trachoma, malaria and malnutrition. The campaigns to fight these social ailments are gaining in momentum, and they are spread to include infant care and nutrition, school hygiene, free school canteens (meals for 800,000 school-children in

1972/3), medical-social assistance, and a social security system (which combines social insurance, industrial injuries and family allowances) which, by fighting the shortcomings of income, also directly help in the fight against poor health. The ministry is building up the stock of facilities and the reservoir of medical personnel at all levels, in the universities, at hospitals, and in the National Institute for Public Health. However, the sudden exodus of most of the European community, which supplied the majority of the professionals in the field of medicine, has meant that Algeria has acted fast and hard mainly to make up the loss. Thus, between 1959 and 1963, the number of doctors, dental surgeons and pharmacists dropped from 1,870, 449 and 611 to 1,278, 147 and 240 respectively. By the end of 1969, these three categories numbered 1,700, 222 and 265 respectively.[65] However, the training of paramedical personnel and technicians is progressing energetically, as the statistics for the second half of the first independence decade show.

The determining objectives of the policy of education and training have been the expansion (i.e. democratisation) of education; the introduction of more options into curricula with emphasis on scientific and technical orientation; the improvement of the quality of education through better studied and more suited content and methodology; and Arabisation, which is part of the decolonisation of education. Algeria can pride herself on all these scores.

A limited number of statistics will underline the quantitative advances made. To begin with, the budget allocation for national education rose consistently from 1963 to 1973 except in 1966, the first year after the change in political leadership. The largest increases in allocations, both in absolute and in relative terms, occurred between 1963 and 1964, and 1968 and 1969. Over the nine-year period, the current education budget rose from DA322.7m* to DA1,825.6m, or from 11 per cent to 23.5 per cent out of a fast-expanding state budget. (It stood at about 26 per cent for 1973.) It is worth noting that the proportion directed to investment in equipment (as against operating, recurrent expenditure) rose noticeably, beginning with 1969. The advances in the number of pupils, and of students at the level of higher education, can be seen from Table 12.11.

Coupled with gains made in the number of children schooled, which were at a much higher rate than the net increase of population, and which raised the proportion of school-age children actually in schools from about one-third to over one-half of the total, an energetic campaign against adult illiteracy has been deployed. It was estimated that the rate of illiteracy for Algerians between 15 and 24 years of age was as high as 92 per cent in 1954 (88 per cent for males, 96 for females). The rate is reported to have dropped to 67 per cent by 1966 (52 per cent for males, 82 for females).[66] Tentative as such estimates always are, they nevertheless serve to broadly suggest the scale of progress made. Today, in the early seventies, the situation must be distinctly better than in the mid-sixties.

There are several other numerical indicators of this progress. The teaching force has kept pace with the growth in the student body, and the student-teacher ratio has not suffered except marginally. (But against this must be placed the distinct increase and improvement in equipment, textbooks and other teaching aids.) Furthermore, whereas in 1962/3 there were 12,696 Algerian and 7,212 foreign (i.e. European) teachers (of whom 3,452 taught in Arabic and 16,456 in French), the composition changed into 38,162 Algerian and 5,494 foreign (European and Arab) teachers (of whom 26,338 taught in Arabic and 17,318 in French) in 1970/1. The use of Arabic as a language of instruction made further progress in 1971/2, with 32,018 teachers using Arabic, and 17,861 using

*Algerian dinars.

Algeria

Table 12.11: Number of Students in the Public School System by Category 1962/3–1972/3

Category	1962/3	1970/1	1971/2	1972/3
Elementary				
Girls	282,842	700,924	771,516	855,031
Boys	494,794	1,150,492	1,246,575	1,351,862
Total	777,636	1,851,416	2,018,091	2,206,893
Secondary-General				
Girls	8,896	51,288	n.a.	n.a.
Boys	23,027	129,522	n.a.	n.a.
Total	31,923	180,810	n.a.	269,572
Secondary-Technical				
Girls	5,093	12,156	n.a.	n.a.
Boys	13,475	35,585	n.a.	n.a.
Total	18,568	47,741	50,283	55,618
Secondary-Teacher Training				
Girls	257	2,926	n.a.	n.a.
Boys	366	5,407	n.a.	n.a.
Total	623	8,333	7,845	7,128
Secondary-Total				
Girls	14,246	66,370	83,084	102,237
Boys	36,868	170,514	204,617	230,081
Total	51,114	236,884	287,701	332,318
Higher Education				
Women	579	4,838	5,540	6,039
Men	2,230	14,375	18,794	20,493
Total	2,809	19,213	24,334	26,532

Note: The private sector of education provides training at the elementary and secondary (both general and technical) levels, but the number of students in private institutions is very small, as the following data for 1970/1 reveal:

	Boys	Girls	Total
Elementary level	17,037	19,900	36,937
Secondary (general)	5,385	4,053	9,438
Secondary (technical)	1,332	1,067	2,399

The totals in private schools amount to less than 2 per cent of all elementary students, but to about 5 per cent of all secondary students (in the 'general' and 'technical' categories).

Sources: *1962-1972: Algeria in Numbers*, Table 10.2.1, pp. 102-3 for data on the public system of education; *Tableaux de l'Economie Algérienne 1971* (pp. 100 and 102 for data on private education); *Tableaux... 1973*, pp. 96-109; and *The Algerian Revolution: Facts and Prospects* (second edition, 1974), Ch. 7.

French as their medium. University faculties grew from 365 (of whom 262 were foreigners) in 1962/3 to 1,224 (of whom 103 were foreigners) in 1971/2.[67] State scholarships at the secondary level have also risen considerably from 18,000 in 1962 to 205,000 in 1972/3 (totalling DA77m); university scholarships have also risen, from 1,769 to 12,400 for the two years respectively.

Whereas university education facilities were very restricted to Algerians before independence — some 700 of whom attended Algiers University then — they are now open to all deserving men and women. And, whereas the country inherited one university, that of Algiers, it now has three: a second at Oran and a third at Constantine. In addition to a wide range of fields in which training is now possible at the universities (humanities, arts — including economics, sciences, law, medicine, pharmacy), a number of specialised professional and technical institutes and schools of higher education provide training in business administration, journalism, engineering and technology, architecture, town planning, agriculture, political science, applied psychology — in addition to the petroleum institutes to which reference has already been made, and to other technical institutions falling under various ministries. The government has also promoted the setting up, and expansion, of libraries — in the institutions of higher education as well as public libraries. It ought to be recalled, in this connection, that the country suffered a serious setback when the OAS, in a mood of frustration and destructiveness towards the end of the war of liberation, burnt the library at Algiers University, destroying hundreds of thousands of books and manuscripts.

Furthermore, a dozen other institutes *below* university level provide technical and vocational training in subjects which range from agriculture to finance and accounting, hotel management and topography — to list a few areas only. Most of these have been set up to operate under the Four-Year Plan, 1970-73, and the record for 1970 and 1971 suggests a satisfactory performance in terms of number of trainees projected and number actually enrolled.

The decolonisation and democratisation of education take predominantly two forms: Arabisation and expansion of the system to reach substantially more, and ultimately all, school-age children, and to cease being within reach only of the privileged few, as it used to be under colonialism. The former aspect of decolonisation has two facets: the transformation of Arabic from a foreign language in the education system, as it used to be under the French, to the national language, in which instruction is given; and the Algerianisation of teaching and inspection staffs.

With regard to Arabic, the government is moving cautiously but not too slowly. It has opted for realism within the general principle of Arabisation. This applies to the use of Arabic as a language of instruction, the preparation and printing of books and manuals in Arabic, and the use of Arabic in government correspondence, reports and records. The process has been slowed down and complicated by the fact that Algerianisation of cadres does not mean Arabisation. Far from it, since even today a number of Algerian teachers are unable to use Arabic. (Arabisation in government departments is distinctly slower than in the public system of education.) However, very serious efforts are being expended to make Arabisation almost parallel with Algerianisation through the insistence on the fluent use of Arabic as a qualification for all government posts — albeit a qualification which is to be met gradually, as time and facilities permit. At the student level, the first two years of elementary schooling are now given in Arabic, with French introduced thereafter.

Insistence on Arabisation is not being made at the expense of the knowledge of foreign languages. Indeed, foreign language requirements are among the highest in the Arab world (particularly with regards to French), and the political leaders and intellectuals are determined not to cut themselves off from the stream of foreign languages, culture and technology. But this is not taken to mean the demotion of the national culture of which Arabic is a pillar, or the admission that Arabic is incapable of being the medium of thinking, research, writing and teaching, both in the humanities and in the sciences. The universities, in compliance with the dictates of realism, are introducing Arabic into the various schools and departments gradually. Often there are parallel programmes in French and in Arabic. Understandably, the more technical the field of training, the slower the shift to Arabic.

Finally, the commendable educational effort of the country is directed towards greater emphasis on science and technology — an emphasis which reflects not only concern with the functions of education and its relevance to modern life, but also a belief in the value of intellectual discipline brought about by a scientific approach. It is also directed towards the improvement of the methodology of education, with greater use of laboratory and audio-visual facilities, greater concern with analysis and dialogue (as against the traditional reliance on education by rote), and generally greater concern with self-dependence among the students. (A large measure of reform was introduced into the system of education in July 1971, after a thorough study of the country's educational problems and needs that lasted over two years.) Combined, these shifts add up to a distinct improvement in the quality of education. Furthermore, the idea is being inculcated in the students' minds that though education has the function of preparing the country's youth for job opportunities in the various fields and sectors of activity, it also has a very significant mobilisation function at the level of the whole society, and it is insistently referred to as a process which will enable the population to undertake more participation — economically, socially and politically. This three-pronged participation is essentially the mainstream of Algeria's style of socialism.

All Algeria's efforts notwithstanding, it cannot yet be said that what was the country's most serious problem upon independence, namely the tragic shortage of cadres and skills in absolutely every sphere and sector, has been overcome. The dimensions of the problem were such that a dozen years of intelligent and determined work are still unable to make good the shortages. However, the problem is being contained, and the rate of progress towards its solution is unquestionably satisfactory. At this rate, Algeria's manpower which was a decade ago the strangling bottleneck for development, may well become in the forthcoming decade the country's most dynamic engine of true development.

One of the major beneficiaries of the spread of education has been the civil service. The Algerian government is run today by Algerians at all levels. The accuracy of this statement is not reduced by the fact that the country has a number of foreign experts, consultants, teachers and technicians, since the *bulk* of the civil service is Algerian. This is a vast improvement on the situation when independence was proclaimed. It remains to be added that the civil service, though somewhat inflated in numbers, shows remarkable signs of discipline and devotion in addition to competence. Corruption is much below the levels prevailing in Mashreq countries.

3. PLANNING AND DEVELOPMENT

It is common knowledge that it is grossly misleading to assess the process of development on the basis of changes in income (or national product) per head, as simple averages hide a legion of sins behind them. Yet merely to look at national income data — meagre though they be — and to see that after only twelve years of independence the Algerians have managed to end the first decade with an average income per head one-third higher than that with which they started it (namely, about 1,800 dinars, or $400 at the then prevailing rate of exchange) is to say that the development effort has had remarkable results. (Indeed, GDP *per capita* for 1973 was about 1,900 dinars, or some $450 at the new rate of exchange for 1973, which was more in favour of the dinar.) However, this improvement notwithstanding, so many things have happened during the ten years in question that a mere quotation of an income per head is not meaningful enough.

First, there is the fact that the pre-independence income derived mainly from two sources that represented an encroachment on the national entity and a serious menace to its character: a community of settler-colonialists and a large army in action against the national community. For the Algerians to have managed to push their national product upwards from the low level of $200 per head to which it dropped after the European exodus to $400, which is one-third higher than the level at which it stood just before independence, is an indication that they relied on their own manpower — inadequate as it was — and on other sources than foreign military spending. In the second place, the beneficiaries today are the Algerians, whereas it was the *colons* who formerly obtained an inordinately large share.

Third, the country today has a much more dynamic and prosperous hydrocarbons sector, a manufacturing and basic industry sector, and — although in terms of production it has not made notable gains — a much better-mobilised and much more promising agricultural sector, if only because the rural community has recovered its dignity as well as a large measure of initiative through self-management in the economic (as in the social and political) sense. But above all, the human capital of the country — which before independence was forcibly dwarfed and impeded from the growth to which its dynamism, innate intelligence and discipline entitled it — is now growing fast in terms of education, capabilities, organisation and motivation. And finally, much greater balance has been established in the society and economy, as between sectors (though not in a mechanistic sense implying equal status, but in the sense of interdependence, interaction and complementarity), between regions, and between socio-economic groups. Only with these qualifications in mind does the income per head reached, say, by the end of 1972 or 1973, become more fully meaningful and better appreciated.

The national accounts from which the income per head under independence is derived are not of very satisfactory quality. The tentativeness of the official estimates has led to the appearance of at least two private estimates. There is also the series published by the International Monetary Fund, which differs from the ones cited before.[68] The differences between the four series involved are substantial for some of the years, and the coverage varies from one series to another. We have here adopted the estimates quoted by Farrel, which stretch from 1963 to 1968, extended forwards by the addition of the estimate of gross domestic product for 1969-73 as it is quoted in *IFS*, and backwards for 1962 through the incorporation of one official estimate available for this year. Admittedly, the extensions at both ends are not totally justified because the estimates for the terminal years are made by different bodies, and the methodology and/or concepts may vary. But in view of the general tentativeness of all the estimates on hand, a slight methodological impurity need not disturb us unduly. The end result, with full reservations, is presented in Table 12.12.

The growth achieved between 1963 and 1973 is 124 per cent. (1962 is discarded, as it measures gross domestic production, not gross domestic product.) Though the data are subject to substantial questioning, the average annual rate of cumulative growth is found to be 8.5 per cent. Behind this rate lies some oscillation, which is essentially related to exogenous (political) factors. Thus 1963, which was the first full year of independence that followed the massive exodus of skilled Frenchmen, marked a negative growth in GDP. Likewise, 1966, which followed the political instability of 1965, showed a sharp decline in GDP. Finally, 1970, but more so 1971, reflected the strained Franco-Algerian relations and

Table 12.12: Gross Domestic Product, 1962-73

Year	GDP (DA billion)[a]	Annual Growth (per cent)
1962	13.5	
1963	13.3	−1.5
1964	14.5	9.0
1965	16.2	11.2
1966	16.0	−0.1
1967	17.8	11.1
1968	18.7	10.5
1969	20.5	9.6
1970	22.9	6.8
1971	23.5	2.6
1972	27.4	16.6
1973	29.7	8.8

a. The estimate for 1962 relates to domestic production rather than GDP — the former being a concept which, in French usage, refers to GDP less the government sector. GDP is at current prices for 1963-65, but at constant (1965) prices for 1966-68. The estimates for 1969 to 1973 are again at current prices. In the absence of a price index series, it is not possible to put the whole GDP series in terms of constant prices.

Sources: For 1962, Caisse Centrale de Coopération Economique, *Eléments d'Information Economique sur l'Algérie* (January 1970); for 1963-8, R. E. Farrel, 'L'Algérie sept ans après', *Expansion* (April 1969); for 1969-73, *International Financial Statistics*, October 1975.

the drop in oil production, owing to disagreement over the Algerian desire for capital participation in the oil industry.

Certain reservations notwithstanding, it can be said that Algeria has by and large been capable of marking good progress in its national product, even if it is recollected that the data for the years 1963-5 are not strictly comparable with those for subsequent years, as the former are at current prices and the latter at constant prices.[69] This progress has been achieved in the face of two factors pulling in opposite directions: unsettled conditions subsequent to the drastic economic dislocations arising from the exodus of the Europeans and the abandoning of their productive assets idle and/or sabotaged; and the expansion of the oil and gas sector, and to a lesser extent the group consisting of industry, construction and public works, which are quoted together.

Changes in the structure of the economy cannot be measured with greater precision than the reliability of the overall estimates of GDP themselves would permit. And in any case, six years do not provide a long enough span of time to justify the expectation of important structural changes. Nevertheless, the six-year period 1963-8 for which the GDP by industrial origin is available suggests a few observations which are worth noting. First, the primary sector broadly defined (agriculture, forests, fishing) which has remained largely stable in terms of its absolute contribution to GDP, has lost ground by about one-third in relative terms. On the other hand and even more pointedly, the mining and energy sector, which already made a respectable relative contribution in 1963, increased its share by about 50 per cent by 1968, to reach about one-fourth of GDP and thus occupy the first place among the sectors. (Oil and gas combined account for over one-fifth of GDP for 1968.) The group 'industry, construction and public works' (of which industry alone constituted more than 63 per cent in 1963, but more than 72 per cent in 1968) also grew faster than GDP as a whole did, with industry alone raising its contribution by 58 per cent. The place of industry in the whole structure has improved, from the contributor of one-tenth of GDP, to just under one-eighth. Another group of sectors shown together, namely transport, trade and services, increased its contribution in absolute terms by 50 per cent, but only by 2 per cent in relative terms. And finally, and most surprisingly, public administration has kept its contribution in absolute terms, and has therefore lost in relative terms by dropping from 17.3 per cent to 11.8 per cent, contrary to the trends prevailing in newly-independent developing countries where the government machinery tends to become larger, more cumbersome and more expensive, especially in cases where the public sector grows fast.[70] Recent data for 1972 and 1973 confirm and intensify the structural trends of the late 1960s. Thus, the share of agriculture was about 12-13 per cent of GDP, that of hydrocarbons about 22 per cent, mining and industry about 18 per cent, trade and non-government services about 31 per cent, and the balance of some 16 per cent was contributed by economic and social infrastructure and public administration.

Judging by recent observations made in 1973, and by a number of physical indicators and (admittedly fragmentary) statistical evidence, the structure by the end of the first independence decade almost certainly emphasised these trends: a further improvement in the relative position of mining and energy, and of industry, at the expense of agriculture and the service sectors (including public administration). Within the service sectors, the trends marking individual sectors probably vary considerably, but as a group they most certainly have grown in absolute size but not in relative importance. The only disturbing element in this estimation is the sluggishness of agriculture — a sluggishness which is predominantly dictated by the scarcity of water and therefore the severe limitations on expansion in the area of cultivable land.

It is relevant at this point to relate the shares of the various sectors (or groups of sectors) in GDP to their shares in the labour force. The comparison is shown in Table 12.13 for 1966, the year in which a population census was undertaken.

Table 12.13: Sectoral Shares in GDP Compared with Shares in Labour Force

Sector(s)	Share in Value Added (per cent)	Share in Labour Force (per cent)
Agriculture	9.5	56.2
Industry and energy (including construction, public works and mining)	35.5	7.2
Transport, commerce and services	42.0	22.6
Administration	13.0	14.0
Total	100.0	100.0

Source: J. F. Laulaine,'La Croissance de l'Economie Algérienne (1963-1968)', *Revue Algérienne des Sciences Juridiques Economiques et Politiques,* Vol. VIII, No. 1, March 1971, p. 91.

Algeria

The most striking feature of this tabulation is the wide discrepancy between the primary sectors and the secondary sectors. In the former a very large labour force contributes very little, while in the latter the reverse is true. This evidently reflects a disturbingly high level of underemployment in the primary sectors, and therefore very low productivity, and a much fuller level of employment in the secondary sectors and very high productivity. The service or tertiary sectors share the same feature as the secondary sectors, but to a distinctly smaller degree. The primary significance of this whole comparison is, in my view, that it forcibly underlines the urgency of development and social policies capable of injecting more dynamism into the sector of agriculture and extracting much more production out of it, and capable also of absorbing a substantial portion of the rural labour force in gainful employment.

The fact that the table relates to 1966 does not reduce the significance of the picture it portrays. Thus, to begin with, the labour force in 1973, which is estimated at some 3.3m in the First Four-Year Plan 1970-73, includes about 1.5m of unemployed and underemployed men and women (mostly in rural areas). The problem's seriousness becomes more menacing if it is realised that the labour force of 3.3m constitutes no more than 22 per cent of the population. If the proportion considered were 30 per cent, which is rather moderate, the labour force would be 4.5m, and the wastage in unemployment and underemployment would be even greater. Indeed, this wastage has been officially estimated at 50 per cent of the 4.5m. The performance of the economy and its expansion in the years 1967-73 has created only 500,000 new jobs, which is less than the increase in the number of new job-seekers by about 250,000. Expansion in the number of workers in France over the same period has been roughly equal to the shortfall of job creation. The tentative nature of these data notwithstanding, it is clear that the enormity of unemployment and underemployment has remained unchanged over the period 1967-73.[71]

The second aspect of the tabulation just presented relates to the 'relative national product per worker' (which is the result of the division of a sector's share in GDP by its share in the labour force).[72] The RNPW in agriculture was very low in 1966; that in industry and energy very high, which revealed low labour productivity in the former and high productivity in the latter activity. The situation remains largely the same today, with minor change only, owing to the stability of the pattern of sectoral distribution both of GDP and of labour.

The rather satisfactory growth achieved in the sixties and early seventies (particularly in 1967-73) has been possible through two energetic processes: that of investment and that of improving labour productivity. Reference has already been made to the country's efforts in the fields of education and training, and to these must be added the experience gained by the labour force at the various levels of skill and responsibility, as factors making for higher productivity.

Investment can be more easily measured in quantitative terms. Total gross domestic investment for the seven years 1963-73, by the public and private sectors together, amounts to DA62.5 billion,[73] but the flow is not even over the years. The volume of investment dropped considerably from 1963 to 1964, and it largely remained at the same low level for 1965 and 1966. Finally it rose considerably in 1967 and continued its upward trend in the subsequent years. The ratio of gross domestic investment to GDP follows the same general pattern, and was as shown in Table 12.14 for the eleven years covered.

The drop between 1963 and 1964, then 1965, is mainly due to the general economic climate created by the *autogestion* legislation of 1963 which was not inviting to investment. Thus, in spite of the assurances in the Evian Agreement, the French mining and oil compan-

Table 12.14: Ratio of Gross Domestic Investment to Gross Domestic Product (per cent)

1963	21.8
1964	11.7
1965	9.9
1966	11.2
1967	19.8
1968	25.1
1969	29.8
1970	36.2
1971	36.2
1972	40.1
1973	42.6

Sources: J. F. de Laulanie, 'La Croissance de l'Economie Algérienne (1963-1968)', *Revue Algérienne des Sciences Juridiques Economiques et Politiques,* Vol. VIII, No. 1, March 1971, p. 95, for 1963-6; *IFS,* December 1974, for 1967-73.

ies became very hesitant — indeed, there was some capital flight in the two or three years to follow, and failure to maintain capital was marked in several instances.

Another major explanation for the trend in its early part is to be found in capital flows from France. Before independence, these consisted of outright grants-in-aid to the Algerian administration, and subscriptions by the French government to loans sought by the Caisse de l'Equipement de l'Algérie (later to become Caisse Algérienne de Développement). The flow was to continue under the terms of the Evian Agreement. Thus, grants amounting to DA950m and DA997m were made for supporting the capital budget in 1963 and 1964. The 1965 agreement between the two countries stipulated reduced help: DA1,000m to be advanced over five years but only one-fifth of this sum was to be a grant and the rest a loan. Thus, although French aid increased slightly in 1964 over 1963, it failed to compensate for the retreat of private French investment for that year. The years 1965 and 1966 witnessed continued hesitation on the part of French firms, as well as a substantial drop in official French aid. From 1967 onwards, domestic savings and a number of important foreign credits enabled the economy to make substantially increased investments.

The expansion of the hydrocarbons sector in the latter part of the decade and the early seventies has been the major contributory factor to the vast increase in investment. However, official (net) foreign loans and grants have also accounted for a large proportion of investment finance. Total economic aid from independence until the end of 1973 was about $3,454m. Most of this came from OECD countries ($2,809m); loans from the 'centrally planned' economies totalled $611m; and the balance of $34m came from the Kuwait Fund for Arab Economic Development.[74] Thus foreign aid accounted for about one-fourth of total investment effected. (This is based on the assumption that the inflow of capital was all invested.) The indebtedness resulting from the inflow is not disturbing, since the country had *net* foreign assets amounting to DA7,061m by the end of December 1974, as already indicated. Nevertheless, the ambitiousness of the revised investment programme in the Second Four-Year Plan 1974-77 can create financing problems of some magnitude.

In the few years immediately preceding independence, investment expenditure was phased and incorporated into the Constantine Plan (for the decade 1959-69), to which reference

Algeria

has already been made. The Plan was discontinued when the French left the country, and for the first few years investment spending, albeit reduced, continued on a year-by-year basis, with priority given to projects already being executed. Serious preparation for a new plan only came afterwards, preceded first by the laying down of a broad development strategy in 1966, and then by the definition of a set of perspectives for the seven years 1967-73 (Perspectives Septennales 1967-1973) within which a three-year plan 1967-9 was formulated.[75]

The development strategy was in effect a development charter, whose 'main political commitments . . . quantified and projected in time, are included in the preamble of the general report of the Four-Year Plan' (which was to follow, for the years 1970-3).[76] Briefly, this charter emphasised the 'basic options and priorities' of the country, essential among which was firm industrialisation, the provision of new job opportunities, development of the economic and human basic structure of the society and economy, the development of the country's mineral wealth, rural rejuvenation, and complementarity and balance as between sectors, regions and social groups. Translated into more concrete terms, the global strategy was subsequently expressed in terms of the seven-year prospects.

The document 'Perspective Septennales 1967-1973' listed five major goals:

— the initiation of economic integration;
— increase of the process of capital accumulation;
— full employment;
— adjustment of the training facilities to suit the requirements of the country; and
— a more equitable redistribution of income.

Then it went on to elaborate on each of these, with background data and assessment of future needs in various fields. The seven-year prospects defined the contours of the Three-Year Plan 1967-69. This Plan was largely treated as a training and preparation phase, during which the authorities would improve their planning methodology and techniques, and would learn more about execution and follow-up, as well as the organisation and management of planning organs. Finally, the first plan would suggest corrections and adjustments in the structure of investments. Because of this general tentativeness, the Plan only had a minimum of quantified objectives. Emphasis was placed on the policies and measures, the structures and agencies, and the time needed for the achievement of the objectives broadly defined.

An average rate of growth of 7 per cent per annum was envisaged for the seven years, and a total gross investment of DA21.3 billion was to be directed to that end. The Three-Year Plan 1967-69 itself received allocations totalling DA5.4 billion. The largest slice of this total, or DA2.7 billion, went to petroleum and gas, followed by the iron and steel industry (DA1.2 billion), transformation industries (DA1.05 billion), energy (DA280m), and mining (DA180m). It was under this Plan that Algeria succeeded in implementing its programmes for building

the first stages of heavy industry, the speedy developing of the petroleum and gas sector, the construction of the iron and steel complex at Annaba and the ammonia and fertilizer plant at Arzew, and the initiation of the exploitation of iron-ore mines.[77]

The Four-Year Plan 1970-73, which was to follow, was a more comprehensive, more carefully prepared and more ambitious plan than anything before it. This was not merely a reflection of the experience gained by Algeria in the decade of the sixties, nor of the greater financial resources at the disposal of the country, nor yet of the improved methodological capability of the planners. Two important factors significantly contributed to the distinguishing attributes of the new plan. The first was the establishment of the foundations and legal and organisational structure for much fuller participation by the population and its local bodies in the processes of thinking, dialogue, determination and final execution of the projects that were to be included in the plan. This is what we called earlier greater mobilisation and participation in the political as well as the social and economic fields. The second factor was the maturing of an integrated, well-perceived view by political and intellectual leaderships of the desired future image as well as the objectives, priorities and options of the society and economy.

It is within this integrated, whole view that the phasing and substance of broad developmental policies can be understood. As one analyst put it:

> Algeria moved in stages. Indeed, the features of each of these is marked by the concrete circumstances of its materialisation, inasmuch as Algeria makes use of the circumstances available. But, if we consider the whole period 1962-70, we observe marked coherence: none of the groups of decisions makes sense except in relation to those preceding and following it; none of the phases in the conquest of economic control is crossed before progress had been made in the development of the forces of material production already under the control of the state.[78]

The significant observation in this quotation is the reference to the whole, integrated view of the broad development of the economy. No doubt it made the Four-Year Plan an instrument of development with more imagination and vision behind it, and more feasibility and operational usefulness ahead of it.

This Plan was to involve a total public investment of DA26.4 billion over four years, but allocations totalling DA27.7 billion were set aside for it; the surplus was designed 'to permit the effective realization of [the Plan's] programmes' — as Ordinance No. 70-10 of 20 January 1970 concerning the Plan stated. In addition, private investment totalling DA2.6 billion was envisaged during the Plan. Most of this sum, or DA2.2 billion, was expected to be in the sector of industry broadly defined (hydrocarbons alone were to get DA1.7 billion); the balance was to go into agriculture.[79] Since the private establishments operating in the oil and gas sector were all foreign, it was obvious that over three-fifths of private investment was to be externally financed.

The total volume of investment was hoped to bring about a cumulative growth averaging 9 per cent annually. Detailed physical objectives (or objectives in kind) were listed, in preference to monetary objectives. One of the most significant objectives, considering its urgency, was the provision of 100,000 new jobs every year to absorb the incremental labour force. The Ordinance also stipulated that beginning with 1971, the government would assign two sessions annually for an examination of progress under the Plan and for corrections in allocations, execution and follow-up that might prove necessary.

The Plan will now be presented in somewhat greater detail, in view of its marked impact on economic behaviour in the country and the discipline with which the authorities and decision-makers at the central, regional and local levels have applied the provisions of the Plan. Table 12.15 sets the structure of public investments.

The Plan document goes on to present a breakdown of these global, sectoral investments into subsectors, programmes and projects (where the projects will have a significant enough

Algeria

Table 12.15: Investments under the Four-Year Plan 1970-3

Type of Investment	Sector		Allocations (DA million)	Per Cent
Directly productive investment	Agriculture	3,360	13,478	49.0
	Industry	10,118		
Research	Hydrocarbons	1,310		
	Mining	267	1,777	6.4
	Hydraulics	200		
Renewals, major reparations	Agriculture	780		
	Communications	455		
	Transport	250	1,535	5.5
	Telecommunications	50		
Cultural and economic infrastructure	Education, training	3,307		
	Communications	557		
	Telecommunications	315		
	Barrages	600	6,164	22.0
	Electricity	735		
	Industrial Zones	100		
	Transport	550		
Tourist and thermal equipment	Tourism	700	700	2.5
Social and collective equipment	Housing	1,520		
	Public utilities	762	3,216	11.5
	Social health	934		
Administrative equipment	Administration	870	870	3.1
	Total		27,740	100.0
Investment target			26,400	

Source: As presented in *Plan Quadriennal 1970-1973: Rapport Général*, p. 30 — but after two serious corrections have been made by this writer in the French version (where two items have been missed). The Arabic version of this document has no errors.

impact), as well as the investment policies called for. In the case of agriculture, it is the development of water resources that gets the lion's share of investment — understandably, since the shortage of water is the major bottleneck in the sector. In industry (which also comprises oil, gas and mining), hydrocarbons were to receive more than one-third of the total allocations, while the four groups of metallurgy, mechanical and electrical industry, chemical industry and construction materials were together to receive 38 per cent. The mines, where the major investments had been already made, were to receive 6 per cent only. The rest goes to electricity (6 per cent), textiles, foodstuffs and miscellaneous industries.

It is noteworthy that, in what is termed 'not directly productive investments', research should receive 6.4 per cent of total investment, mainly in the oil and gas fields. Not surprisingly, eduation and training, housing and social health were to receive 11.9 per cent, 3.4 per cent and 5.5 per cent respectively, or just over one-fifth of total investment.

So far the presentation has dwelt on the distribution of allocations by sector or subsector. The phasing of allocations, or their distribution by year, shows a slight acceleration from year to year, with the annual totals rising (in billion dinars) from 6.4 to 6.7, 7.0 and 7.6 respectively for the four years. However, the phasing per sector varies from case to case. Thus it remains the same for industry, but rises fastest for agriculture, while it drops for transport – to take just three illustrations. The explanation for this variation lies in the absorptive capacity of each sector combined with its needs.

So much for the investment input. The output is presented both globally in terms of national product expectations, and in detail in terms of physical results. Increase in GDP is expected to be 44 per cent (or about 9.5 per cent compound rate per annum). Thus, GDP is to rise from an estimated DA14,640m for 1969, the base year, to DA21.1 billion for 1973. It is to be noted in this connection that the level of GDP actually reached in 1973 was much higher than the Plan estimate; it stood at DA29.8 billion. (It is not clear from the Plan document if value added in the public administration sector is included in the estimates. I have reason to believe that it is not, both because it is usually not included in Algerian official statistics, and because the size and growth expected of the services sectors where 'government' would normally be listed is too small to comprise the public sector.) The expected rise in the contribution of each of the sectors can be seen in Table 12.16.

The increase in value added expected in the main branches of activity, and the percentage share of each branch in this increase, as calculated from Table 12.16, are shown in Table 12.17.

In relating the total value added during the period of the Plan to total investment, we disregard for our limited purposes here time lags between the making of investment and the emergence of the resultant increment in output; especially because some output in the first year or two is attributable to investments made prior to the Plan, which would to some extent compensate for investments made in the last one or two years whose output will appear beyond the last Plan year. Thus the incremental capital-output ratio for the whole economy is about 4.3. This is not untenable, given the economy's stage of development and the nature of the investments projected.

It is unfortunate that evaluations of the actual performance of the economy under the Plan are not available (at least, not to this writer). But interviews with knowledgeable officials at the Secrétariat d'Etat au Plan and at the ministries dealing with economic matters have emphatically affirmed that the execution of the Plan has been largely successful, and that the growth expected has been actually achieved. (Indeed, it was surpassed in the hydrocarbons sector, owing mainly to institutional changes with regard to ownership and control.) There is good reason to accept these assertions as true, since the Three-Year Plan 1967-69 registered a high level of investment performance. This can be seen from the comparison of planned and actual investment in Table 12.18.

The experience gained during the implementation of the Three-Year Plan, and the improvement in planning methods, techniques and institutions, as well as in execution and

Table 12.16: Expected Value Added in the Base Year and Terminal Year of the Four-Year Plan (million dinars)

Sector		Base Year 1969		Terminal Year 1973
Agriculture		2,400		2,700
Transformation industries		2,040		3,425
Foodstuffs	1,000		1,290	
Mechanical and electrical industries	300		745	
Chemical and other industries	300		610	
Textiles and leather	300		540	
Construction materials	140		240	
Mining and quarrying		150		310
Energy		320		400
Hydrocarbons		2,610		4,600
Crude oil	2,100		3,300	
Refined oil	400		800	
Gas liquefaction	110		500	
Buildings and public works		1,020		2,300
Sub-total: Commodities		8,540		13,735
Transport and communication		600		750
Services		1,800		2,100
Trade		3,700		4,500
Sub-total: Services		6,100		7,350
Total Gross Domestic Product		14,640		21,085

Source: *Plan Quadriennal 1970-1973: Rapport Général,* p. 90. The French edition of the Plan document has a number of serious errors in sub-totalling, because of which the sub-totals together exceed the totals. The errors persist in the Arabic version as well. This table incorporates the corrections.

follow-up, have made it possible for the execution of the Four-Year Plan to be more satisfactory than that of its predecessor, both with regard to investment and to output, and to exceed plan expectations. Table 12.19 (based on data already presented above) provides firm evidence of this statement.

Algeria is currently implementing its second four-year plan for the years 1974-7, the SFYP. Understandably, the first four-year plan 1970-3, FFYP, which had been prepared towards the end of the sixties, did not reflect the new realities of the oil and gas sector — even those preceding the price increases in the autumn of 1973. When the SFYP was being prepared, the internal oil situation had been altered through nationalisation and expansion measures. Nevertheless, even the SFYP in its original contours did not take into account the new resource availabilities of October 1973 and thereafter.

In the original formulation, the SFYP[80] stipulated a total gross public investment of

Table 12.17: Expected Increase in Value Added, 1970-3

Branch	Increase (DA million)	Per Cent Share
Agriculture	300	4.6
Hydrocarbons	1,990	30.9
Transformation industry	1,385	21.5
Mining and quarrying	160	2.5
Energy	80	1.2
Buildings and public works	1,280	20.0
Sub-total: Commodities	5,195	80.7
Transport and communication	150	2.3
Services	300	4.6
Trade	800	12.4
Sub-total: Services	1,250	19.3
Total all branches	6,445	100.0

DA54 billion, which is a vast increase over planned investment in the FFYP of DA27.7 billion. The planners and political leadership felt confident that the resources needed for the investment programme for 1974-7 would be possible to obtain, mostly from domestic savings, but also partly from foreign capital inflows. They also felt confident of their ability to effect such a large investment programme, on the basis of their experience in the four years 1970-3.

However, since the preparation of the SFYP, events have outdistanced these earlier expectations and provisions. Consequently the SFYP has been steeply revised, and now stands at DA126,471m, out of which DA110,217m are designed to be invested during the plan period. The distribution by sector is given in Table 12.20.

It can readily be seen that an investment programme of this size can by itself absorb all oil revenue expected over the years 1974-7. This explains why Algeria felt financial strains by the end of 1974, to the point of seeking loans from abroad. Yet the country is justified in making a strenuous effort, and accepting certain sacrifices in consumption, since the expected reward is accelerated development and increased welfare.

4. PROSPECTS AND PROBLEMS OF DEVELOPMENT: CONCLUSION

In my opinion, Algeria has the most promising prospects for development in the whole Arab world — if by development we understand not merely the increase (and absolute level) of income per head, but that comprehensive process which involves political, social and economic liberation, mobilisation, participation and self-expression — phenomena which are reflected only partially in national product per head. A process of this magnitude and dynamism involves mastery over national resources by the nation's institutions and its

Algeria

Table 12.18: Comparison of Planned with Actual Investment, 1967-9

Year	Investment Planned (DA million)	Actual	Rate of Realisation (per cent)
1967	2,747	1,652	60.1
1968	3,322	3,174	95.5
1969	5,012	4,301	85.8
Total	11,081	9,127	82.4

Source: *Plan Quadriennal 1970-1973: Rapport Général*, p. 84.

Table 12.19: Expectations and Achievements under Four-Year Plan 1970-3

Year	Investment (DA billion) Planned	Actual	GDP Expected	(DA billion) Actual
1970	6.4	8.3	n.a.	22.9
1971	6.7	8.5	n.a.	23.5
1972	7.1	11.0	n.a.	27.4
1973	7.6	12.7	21.1	29.8

men and women, and their capacity to extract the optimum social product of these resources, while developing the resources at the same time. The environment embracing the unfolding of the process must at the same time be one which involves an improvement in the capability to make decisions, the widening of the base of decision-making, and the ability to put economic decisions into effect. At the risk of using superlatives, I would insist that no Arab country has gone as far as Algeria in providing the objective conditions for such a broad process of development to get started and to gain momentum.

We have had occasion to assess the progress made by Algeria in the twelve years of independence 1962-74, and to observe where, and in what respects, this progress differed fundamentally from that claimed for the country by the colonial power before independence. At this point, we want merely to highlight a few indicators which would serve as landmarks on the path of development and point to its rising trend. The first of these is income per head which, after suffering a sharp drop after the exodus of the Europeans, and after a few years of indecision and false starts, steadily and substantially rose to reach, by the end of 1973, a level which is probably some 125 per cent higher than that for the first year of independence. This is remarkable in itself, not merely reflecting the windfall revenue from the petroleum and gas sector but, more importantly, the clear thinking, planning and firm action within which this sector was made to operate — in addition to the gains made in the course of industrialisation.

The process throughout, even during the first three years of the independence decade,

Table 12.20: Distribution of Investment in Second Four-Year Plan, 1974-77

Sector	Investment (DA m)	Per Cent of Total
Industry	48,000	43.5
Agriculture	12,005	10.9
Water	4,600	4.2
Infrastructure	15,521	14.0
Fishing	115	0.1
Social services and housing	14,610	13.3
Education and training	9,947	9.0
Tourism	1,500	1.4
Administration	1,399	1.3
Research and contingencies	2,520	2.3
Total	110,217	100.0

Source: Middle East Research and Information Project, *MERIP Reports*, No. 35 (February 1975), 'State Capitalism in Algeria', p. 19 ff.

was subjected to deliberate direction, although the effectiveness of such direction only became distinctly evident after 1965. Yet, if the fruits reaped were commensurate with the effort put into the economic management of the country during this decade, it can be emphatically asserted that the second decade will witness further consolidation of the earlier gains, and movement beyond these gains, both within the field of production and of distribution. To look forward beyond 1974 in the present case is not a matter of crystal-bowl gazing. It is, instead, to take into account the social dynamics characterising and governing Algeria's behaviour and the management of its economy since independence, as well as the new realities of the seventies, and to project on this basis.

However, a few spots of anxiety blot this generally rosy picture. The first is that whereas one of the major objectives of economic strategy and policy, namely diversification, is being approached firmly, through the consolidation and expansion of the non-oil sectors, more particularly industry, exogenous factors have since 1974 been tending to make the oil and gas sector move even faster in relative terms. As a result, it may well be that diversification will prove in fact more difficult to achieve. Furthermore, it would be unwise to deliberately suppress the growth of the oil and gas sector merely to achieve that greater balance so insistently sought. What is essential here is to use the resources arising from this sector in a manner that would further consolidate and expand the other sectors, mainly industry and agriculture, however that could be achieved. The enormity of such a task can be seen from a comparison over time of the composition of Algeria's exports — another landmark to observe.

It is evident from this tabulation that more rather than less dependence over many years to come is expected to be placed on hydrocarbon products, and less rather than more on all other export groups. Further elaboration on this tendency and its serious implications is hardly necessary. The second source of anxiety is the persistent sluggishness in agricultural production, despite the serious efforts made on all fronts: mobilisation, reorganisation and restructuring, local self-government, technical aid, increased finance and the provision of

Algeria

Table 12.21: Algeria's Exports (Actual and Expected) (per cent)

Export Group	1969	1973 [a]	1973 [b]	1977 [a]	1980 [a]
Agricultural products	18.2	14.1	7.0	6.0	4.0
Mining products	3.2	3.9	3.0	2.0	2.0
Industrial products	4.2	6.6	5.0	5.0	5.0
Hydrocarbon products	74.4	75.4	85.0	87.0	89.0
Total	100.0	100.0	100.0	100.0	100.0

a. Projections.

Source: The data come from *Plan Quadriennal 1970-1973: Rapport Général*, p. 111, for 1969 and 1973a; and Fascicule 2, p. 35, in *Dossier pour la Préparation du IIe Plan Quadriennal 1974-1977*, 3 volumes, for 1973b, 1977 and 1980.

institutional facilities in general. (Even in the *Second Four-Year Plan 1974-77* the expected rate of growth in agriculture is the lowest for any sector; at 3 per cent per annum it stands below the rate of natural increase of the population.)[81] As the socialist or self-managed sector accounts for about three-fifths of production, the style and effectiveness of its operation ought to receive searching attention.

The same urgency applies in the case of the self-managed or socialist industrial sector where, as we have already seen, the performance (in terms of net returns) is not as satisfactory as in the private sector of industry. There is urgent need, then, to search for ways and means to raise the level of efficiency, and of production, of the socialist sector as a whole, and to promote the marketability of its output — particularly of industrial goods. The problem is probably one that blights socialist organisation of industry and agriculture in the world in general, and it relates to motivation and the choice of criteria of performance (whether of profitability as an accounting measuring rod or of the attainment of physical targets, or of these combined). The system in Algeria is flexible enough to permit adjustments purporting to improve the performance of the socialist sector, since 'ideological purity' does not seem to command blind obedience, and pragmatism is the general stamp of behaviour and attitudes.

The third and probably most serious blot on the rosy picture of the future is the intractability of the manpower problem. For, in spite of the ambitious projections of manpower absorption in new jobs in the FFYP and SFYP alike, the problem will remain forbidding in its dimensions. In each of the four-year plans, some 400,000—450,000 new jobs are expected to be created, which — at best — can absorb the incremental manpower during plan years. Even the fulfilment of these expectations would leave the bulk of unemployment and underemployment untouched. What should cause particular concern is the fact that the employment projections are much more elaborate and detailed for non-agricultural than for agricultural employment, though the former is much smaller in volume than the latter. This in itself reflects an admission that not much can be done for the 'theoretical' rural labour force.

The problem acquires its true proportions if it is recalled that in addition to the high level of unemployment and underemployment at home, there is a substantial Algerian work-force in Western Europe — mostly in France. This work-force is estimated for 1973 at 780,000 strong, which represents roughly one-third of the *active* labour force at home (or about one-sixth of the entire 'theoretical' labour force — that is, all those males and females who fall within the working age range and are not incapacitated). This emigration in search of work is a phenomenon of long standing, and the decade of independence has not changed the situation. The reverse is true: there is still net emigration, and this is expected to continue even into the rest of the seventies, though on a smaller scale. The prospects of a solution are dim, so long as the absorptive capacity of the largest employer — agriculture — remains limited, owing mainly to the limitation of the area of cultivable land, which in turn is governed by the scarcity of water. Indeed, the harnessing of much more rain-water in barrages and its use for substantially expanded irrigation remain matters for the distant future.

A fourth and last source of anxiety, which had already caused concern in the very first years of independence,[82] is the growing strength of bureaucrats and technocrats. Put differently, there is a serious questioning whether a large body of men who are essential for fast development (whether as administrators and executives or as technocrats) are not turning into a 'new class' with their own class interests and entrenched positions. If this tendency has taken place, as some observers contend,[83] then there is the danger that socialism may remain more as a slogan than an actual way of life and organisation, and that pragmatism may reach beyond a critical level which separates two states: pragmatism or flexibility in the application of socialism, and socialism in the service of pragmatism where socialism may deteriorate into a mere verbalism. As the *Charte d'Alger* put it in 1964, there is the danger of a

> 'new social layer' speedily forming which tends to intervene on the side of the instinctively anti-socialist thrust of the bureaucratic bourgeoisie which forms in the apparatus of the administration, the state and the economy, owing to the feeling of power which it gets from the exercise of power.

Perhaps things have not gone this far, but this is a latent danger which a society claiming to have opted for democracy, socialism and equality should guard against carefully.

To end the chapter with these reservations or questionings regarding the country's record of socio-economic development is not meant to leave the reader with scepticism concerning Algeria's performance. The reverse is intended. Indeed, I would like to emphasise my evaluation that this performance is generally commendable, and at many points brilliant, particularly when viewed against the harsh background and the heavy burdens inherited from the long and cruel era of colonialism. To record some reservations against achievements as praiseworthy as I have tried to demonstrate serves, it is hoped, to bring the achievements into relief, and at the same time to point to some of the major tasks that still lie ahead if Algeria is to maintain its thrust on the political, social and economic fronts alike.

NOTES

1. In tracing the broad steps of Algeria's development in the post-war period, but particularly the years from 1946 to mid-1962, I have relied mainly on the following sources: (a) Europa Publications, *The Middle East and North Africa 1971-72, 1972-73, 1973-74* and *1974-75* (London, annual issues), chapter on Algeria; (b) O. Norbye, 'The Economy of Algeria', in P. Robson and D. A. Lury (eds.), *The Economies of Africa* (London, 1969); (c) Samir Amin, *The Maghreb in the Modern World: Algeria, Tunisia, Morocco*, translated from the

Algeria

French by Michael Perl (Penguin Africa Library, 1970), parts on Algeria; (d) René Gallissot, *L'Economie de l'Afrique du Nord* (Presses Universitaires de France, Paris, 1961), relevant parts; (e) Statistique Générale de l'Algérie, *Tableaux de l'Economie Algérienne 1960*; (f) Richard M. Brace, *Morocco, Algeria, Tunisia* (Prentice-Hall, Inc., New Jersey, 1964); (g) A. Benachenhou, *Régime des Terres et Structures Agraires au Maghreb* (Editions Populaires de l'Armée, Algiers 1970); (h) A. Benachenhou, *Connaissance du Maghreb, Notions d'Ethnophraphie, d'Histoire et de Sociologie* (Editions Populaires de l'Armée, 1971); (i) A. Tiano, *Le Maghreb entre les Mythes* (Presses Universitaires de France, Paris, 1967); and (j) General Union of Chambers of Commerce, Industry, and Agriculture in the Arab Countries, *Arab Economic Report* (Beirut, 1971-4, annual issues; Arabic), chapter entitled 'Economic Development in Algeria'.

A number of other surveys and reference works were consulted but as they deal more particularly with the independence era, they will be cited under section 2 below. On the other hand, several of the items cited here also deal with the period beginning with 1962.

2. Rep. Alg. Democ. et Pop., Secrétariat d'Etat du Plan, Direction des Statistiques, *Annuaire Statistique de l'Algérie 1970*, p. 16.

3. Statistique Générale de l'Algérie, *Tableaux de l'Economie Algérienne, 1960*, p. 22.

4. Ibid., p. 25.

5. Ibid., p. 26.

6. Ibid., p. 31.

7. For the proportion relating to 1944, see Ministry of Information and Culture, *Education*, in the series *The Faces of Algeria* (Arabic version, 1970), p. 15. For data relating to 1954 and 1959, ratios are based on *Tableaux... 1960*, op. cit., pp. 22, 31 and diagram facing p. 30.

8. *Tableaux... 1960*, diagram facing p. 30 for secondary education. *Education*, op. cit., p. 16, for data on university education.

9. *Tableaux... 1960*, p. 31.

10. Sec. d'Etat au Plan, Direction des Statistiques, *Tableaux de l'Economie Algérienne 1971* (Algiers, March 1972), p. 17.

11. *Tableaux... 1960*, pp. 130-1, 132-5.

12. Ibid., pp. 142 and 144.

13. Ibid., pp. 26-7.

14. Norbye, loc. cit., p. 479, quoting *l'Agriculture Algérienne*, Numéro Spécial, Le Développement Africain (Paris, October 1961), p. 143.

15. See note 1 above.

16. Amin, Ch. 2, pp. 60-89. It ought to be pointed out here that there are some discrepancies between Tables 1, 2 and 11 in this chapter with respect both to the rural (agricultural) and non-rural (non-agricultural) income of each community.

17. The data and evaluation of the Plan are based on the *Plan de Constantine* itself, *Tableaux de l'Economie Algérienne 1960*, pp. 69-75; Amin, pp. 123-6; and Norbye, pp. 489-93.

18. *Tableaux... 1960*, p. 68.

19. Ibid., p. 69 (my translation).

20. Ibid. It is relevant in this connection to see what the leaders of independent Algeria saw in the Plan: a delaying tactic meant to use economic bait for the consolidation of France's political grip. See FLN-Commission Centrale d'Orientation, *La Charte d'Alger – Ensemble des Textes Adoptés par le Premier Congrès du Parti du Front de Libération Nationale (du 16 au 21 Avril 1964)*, p. 96.

21. Norbye, op. cit., p. 489.

22. Norbye's estimates of investments and rates of growth during the Plan period differ widely from Amin's. (Compare Norbye, op. cit., pp. 490 and 491 with Amin, op. cit., p. 124.)

23. Amin, op. cit., pp. 124-6.

24. *La Charte d'Alger...* (p. 94-5) draws another, much more grim picture of population sufferings and dislocations, including: over one million *chouhada* (martyrs, killed in the war of liberation); 300,000 fighters in the *maquis*; about 3 million 'regrouped', i.e., 'torn away from their houses and villages to be landed in centres created especially for the purpose, virtually resembling concentration camps, where in addition to uprooting, they were forced to submit to atrocious conditions of life'; 400,000 detained or interned; 300,000 refugees, mainly in Tunisia and in Morocco; 700,000 emigrants from the countryside to the cities; 8,000 villages completely destroyed.

25. Amin, op. cit., p. 128.

26. The following works have been used as general references in the preparation of section 2, which deals with the independence decade – in addition to items (a), (b), (c), (i) and (j) in note 1 above: (a) Gérard Viratelle, *L'Algérie Algérienne* (Les Editions Ouvrières, Paris, 1970); (b) Ch. Debbasch et al. *Les Economies Maghrébines: L'Indépendance à l'Epreuve du Développement Economique* (Centre National de la Recherche Scientifique, Paris, 1971), pp. 9-87; (c) Institut d'Etude du Développement Economique et Social, *Problèmes de l'Algérie Indépendante*, a collection of 10 essays prepared by François Perroux (Presses Universitaires de France, Paris, 1963), a study which at the start of independence attempted to look at such problems as the new leaders were actually to witness in the years to follow; (d) J.F. de Laulanie, 'La Croissance de l'Economie Algérienne (1963-1968)', *Revue Algérienne des Sciences Juridiques Economiques et Politiques*, Volume VIII, No. 1, March 1971 (a quarterly published in French by the Faculty of Law and Economic Science in Algiers University); (e) 'The Maghreb: A Survey', *The Economist*, 11 March 1972 (prepared by Michael Wall in collaboration with Sue Dearden); (f) The Government of Algeria, Ministry of Information and Culture, *The Algerian Revolution: Facts and Prospects* (a highly informative illustrated volume published on the 10th anniversary of independence; printed in Madrid, 1972); (g) Chamber of Commerce and Industry in Algeria, surveys for various individual years, ending 1972/3, of the economy entitled *Algérie: situation économique* (Algiers; Arabic or French); and (h) *Tableaux de l'économie algérienne 1973* (July 1974). Several other basic references have proved of great value, but as these deal with specific aspects of the period under consideration, they will be indicated at the appropriate occasion.

27. There is no official count of the number of non-Algerians in the country around the end of 1962. However Amin (p. 129) agrees with the estimate made generally by knowledgeable observers that some 800,000 persons left the country (out of over one million). The latest census conducted in 1966 registered 196,500 non-Algerians in residence, or some 1.6 per cent of the total

population. (See République Algérienne Démocratique et Populaire, Secrétariat d'Etat au Plan, Direction des Statistiques, *Annuaire Statistique de l'Algérie 1970*, p. 16.) The number of non-Algerians in 1966 was just about equal to what it had been in 1856 (180,330). Thus the settlement of foreigners in the country, which had been rising in the intervening 110 years to reach a ceiling of about 1,060,000 on the eve of independence, shot downwards at meteoric speed in a few months and wiped away the demographic build-up of foreigners of over a century. (For 1856 data, see *Annuaire Statistique de l'Algérie 1970*, op. cit., p. 16.)

28. Amin, op. cit., pp. 129-33.

29. Europa..., *1971/72*, p. 152. However, according to *La Charte d'Alger*... (p. 97), 90 per cent of the Europeans left, including 300,000 in the active labour force. This last group comprised: 33,000 heads of 'exploitations', 15,000 top cadres and members of the liberal professions; 100,000 intermediate cadres and employees; and 35,000 highly skilled workers.

30. The Algerians officially admit this, but hasten to associate this phase with the rule of President Ben Bella, which ended on 19 June 1965 upon a bloodless take-over by the then Chief-of-Staff Col. Boumedienne, who has been President of the Republic ever since. See, for instance, *The Algerian Revolution: Facts and Prospects*, a volume published by the Ministry of Information and Culture in 1972; p. 48. See also statements by the new Council of the Revolution in the weeks immediately following the fall of Ben Bella, as they appeared in the local press (both French and Arabic).

31. Both under Ben Bella and briefly under Boumedienne a certain measure of internal political strife and discord continued – mainly between military and/or civilian groups contending for supremacy and power. But these do not involve us directly here, and, in any case, political life has been orderly and strife-free for several years now.

32. *The Algerian Revolution: Facts and Prospects*, pp. 52-3. (Unless otherwise indicated, all references are to the first edition.)

33. For 1960, see Europa..., *1971-72*, p. 159; for 1963, see *Annuaire... 1970*, p. 139. (Also Europa, op. cit., p. 165.)

34. Norbye, loc. cit., pp. 477-84.

35. For pre-independence estimates, see ibid. p. 479, and for 1963/4 see Amin, op. cit., pp. 136/7.

36. See for instance J.F. de Laulanie, loc. cit., pp. 86 and 89.

37. Ministry of Information and Culture, *1962-1972: Algeria in Numbers* (Madrid, 1972), Table 2.1, p. 19.

38. See, in connection with agrarian reform or agrarian revolution (apart from the general sources cited earlier), the following: (a) G. Destanne de Bernis in Ch. Debbasch *et al.*, op. cit.; (b) 'La révolution agraire: Rapport de synthèse adopté par le Conseil National Economique et Social, Alger (2me Session 1970)', *Revue Algérienne...*, Vol. VIII, No. 1, March 1971, pp. 207-44; (c) Ministry of Orientation, *Une Année de Révolution Socialiste*, (i.e., 5 July 1962 – 5 July 1963), pp. 49-60 on 'L'agriculture et le réforme agraire'; (d) Abdelaziz Zerdani, 'Les taches de l'édification du socialisme en Algérie', *Revue Algérienne...*, No. 2, June 1967, pp. 369-78; (e) André Tiano, 'L'Expérience du secteur public de production au Maghreb depuis l'indépendance', *Revue Algérienne...*, Vol. V, No. 2, June 1968, pp. 330-43 for Algeria; and 'L'avant-projet de révolution agraire' (of August 1966), pp. 505-32 in the same issue of the *Revue;* (f) Serge Koulytchizky, 'Comment sont prises les décisions dans l'autogestion Algérienne', in *Revue Algérienne...*, Vol. VI, No. 4, December 1969, pp. 1151-94; (g) Ministry of Information, *Self-Management*, one of a series of booklets entitled 'The Faces of Algeria' (a series which commands respect for precision, notwithstanding its glossy paper and illustrations); (h) Claudine Chaulet, *La Mitidja Autogérée* (a case study of an Algerian region under self-management), SNED (Algiers, 1971); (i) Ministry of Agriculture and Agrarian Reform, *Secteur Socialiste Agricole* (under the series of 'Ordonnances et Decrets'), containing the relevant decrees and ordinances issued between 1968 and 1971; and (j) Ministry of Information and Culture, Dossier Documentaires series, No. 17, on 'La Charte de la Révolution Agraire' of 8 Nov. 1971, comprising also Ordinance No. 71-73 of 8 November 1971 setting out the law governing the agrarian revolution. (Also published separately as *Révolution Agraire* by the Présidence du Conseil.)

39. This is a theme frequently encountered. But for an explicit reference to this 'path', see Zerdani (Minister of Labour), loc. cit. (item (d) in note 38 above). For earlier claims to a specifically Algerian style, see *La Charte d'Alger...*

40. See *Tableaux de l'Economie Algérienne 1971*, p. 82 (for distribution of the active labour force by sector), and p. 120 for employment in the socialist sector. These data derive from the 1966 census. See also *La Charte de la Révolution Agraire...*, p. 5. This latter source also contains information on the distribution of holdings by area, which appears in the text further down in the present chapter.

41. *La Charte...*, p. 5.

42. The discussion of the Agrarian Revolution in all its aspects draws on the law of 8 November 1971. See *La Charte de la Révolution Agraire*.

43. For evaluation and suggestions, see especially items (b), which is a report by the Conseil National Economique et Social containing valuable suggestions, (e) and (f) in note 38. For a more recent evaluation, see Al-Hashimi Bounajjar (Adviser to the Ministry of Labour and Social Affairs, Algeria) in a lecture on the Agrarian Revolution delivered on 6 February 1975 at the Center for Social Sciences at the Lebanese University, Beirut. The lecture was reproduced in *An-Nahar* (Beirut daily; Arabic) on 23 February 1975. It is from this lecture that the data on land distributed and expropriated till the end of 1974 (which are reported further down in the text) are taken. Also see Europa..., *1974-75*, pp. 206-7, and Middle East Research and Information Project, *MERIP Reports*, No. 35 (February 1975), 'State Capitalism in Algeria', pp. 15-19.

44. Data on and references to area cultivated, volume of production, and use of farm machinery come from: *Tableaux de l'Economie Algérienne 1960* (pp. 128-51) for the pre-independence era, and from *1962-1972: Algeria in Numbers* (pp. 48-52) and *Annuaire Statistique de l'Algérie 1970* (pp. 87-112) for the sixties. For references to the contribution of agriculture to national product see: for pre-independence years Chambre de Commerce et

Algeria

d'Industrie d'Alger, *Situation Economique de l'Algérie 1968*, p. 27, and for the sixties *Arab Economic Report 1971*, p. 13. The data reported further down in the text on irrigated and total cultivated area is from FAO, *Production Yearbook 1973*, p. 3, while the data on production indices of agricultural and food production (total and *per capita*) are from FAO, *Production Yearbook 1967*, pp. 27-30 and *Production Yearbook 1973*, pp. 25-32.

45. Calculated from *Situation Economique de l'Algérie en 1968*, p. 27 where data for industry, construction and public works are combined, and from Ch. Debbasch *et al.*, p. 11, for relative share of industry by itself. For pre-independence years, see *Arab Economic Report 1971*, p. 13.

46. *1962-1972: Algeria in Numbers*, Table 5.4.1, p. 64, up to 1971, and Europa Publications, *The Middle East and North Africa 1974-75*, p. 207, for 1972 and 1973.

47. *1962-1972: Algeria in Numbers*, Table 5.3.1, p. 62, for 1969-71, and *Annuaire Statistique de l'Algérie 1970* for 1961-9. (The first source gives data in kwh; the second in index numbers. I have calculated the level for 1971 by using 1969 – which is common in both sources – as a base. For 1972 production, see Europa..., *1974-75*, p. 210.

48. *1962-1972: Algeria in Numbers*, Tables 5.4.1 – 5.5.1, pp. 64-73.

49. See items (a), (e) and (f) in note 38. See also Michel Miaille, 'Contribution à une Reflexion Théorique sur l'Entreprise Socialiste Algérienne', *Revue Algérienne...*, Vol. IX, No. 3, September 1972, pp. 653-93. (For an official admission of problems in the self-managed sector, see Zerdani, loc. cit.)

50. See Ministry of Information and Culture, *Basic Industries* (No. 17 in the series 'The Faces of Algeria'; Algeria, 1971); Chambre de Commerce et d'Industrie d'Alger, *Situation Economique de l'Algérie 1970/71* (Algiers, 1972), Part I on 'Industry'; and *The Algerian Revolution*, op. cit., Ch. 6. For the most recent reporting on new industries set up, or under construction, between 1970 and end of 1974, see Europa..., *1974-75*, pp. 209-10, and *Middle East Economic Survey* (weekly, Beirut) for the period under cover.

51. *Annuaire Statistique... 1970*, p. 121.

52. *Situation Economique... 1970/71, Part I* (no page numbers in this volume).

53. Ibid.

54. See Ministry of Information and Culture, 'Dossiers Documentaires' Series, *L'Organization Socialiste des Entreprises* (containing the Charter and two Ordinances; February 1972).

55. In addition to general reference and survey works where the sector is discussed, see *The Algerian Revolution*, op. cit., Ch. 2; *Hydrocarbons* in 'The Faces of Algeria' series; Sonatrach, *SONATRACH* (undated, but presumably published in 1972 as it includes data for 1971; Arabic); and Atif Sulaiman, 'Oil and Gas Nationalizations in Algeria: Highlights on Some of Their Legal and Economic Aspects', paper for the Eighth Arab Petroleum Congress held in Algiers, 28 May–3 June 1972 (Sonatrach, Algiers).

56. For 1958, see Europa..., *1971-72*, p. 160, and *Arab Economic Report*, p. 31. For 1972 and 1973 production data, see the British Petroleum Company Limited, *BP Statistical Review of the World Oil Industry 1973*. The production estimate for 1974, as well as the data on revenue for 1972 and 1973, and revenue estimate for 1974, all come from Nicolas Sarkis, 'The Energy Crisis and the Challenge of Development in the Arab Countries', Paper No. 132 (A-1) submitted to the Ninth Arab Petroleum Congress, Dubai, 10-16 March 1975, Table 1, p. 16, and Table 2, p. 17.

57. Sonatrach, op. cit., p. 35.

58. Sarkis, op. cit., Table 1, p. 16.

59. For a lucid discussion of the controversy, and an evaluation of the French arguments, see Sulaiman, op. cit.

60. Ibid., p. 6.

61. Sonatrach, op. cit., p. 36.

62. See Chambre de Commerce et d'Industrie d'Alger, *Situation Economique de l'Algérie 1968*, p. 27 for national product data up to 1968, and *IFS*, December 1974, for 1973 GDP.

63. For the balance of payments surplus of 1963, see Norbye, op. cit., p. 517. G. Destanne de Bernis in Ch. Debbasch *et al.*, p. 15, presents different figures of gold and foreign reserves, thus:

End of Year	Million Algerian Dinars
1962	911
1963	1,131
1964	n.a.
1965	835
1966	1,221
1967	1,924
1968	2,204

Likewise data in *IFS*, op. cit., vary from those in the text for the years 1965-70, and from those of Debbasch *et al.*

64. The information on education and public health has been drawn largely from: (a) *Annuaire Statistique de l'Algérie 1970*, Chs. 5-7; (b) *Tableaux de l'Economie Algérienne 1971*, Part 2; (c) *1962-1972: Algeria in Numbers*, Sections 10-14; (d) *The Algerian Revolution*, Ch. 7, 'The Cultural Revolution'; and (e) *The Public Health, Education, and Public Works*, Nos. 2, 7 and 11 in 'The Faces of Algeria' series.

For the content of curricula and education reform, the following sources were consulted: (a) Ministry of National Education, *Introduction à la Réforme de l'Enseignement* (1969); (b) Ministry of Primary and Secondary Education, Institut Pédagogique National, *Directives et Conseils Pédagogiques: Horaires, Programmes, Instructions* (1971). (c) Ministry of Primary and Secondary Education, *Horaires et Programmes de l'Enseignement Technique* (1972); and (d) Ministry of Primary and Secondary Education, *Institut de Technologie de l'Education: Enseignements Elémentaire et Moyen* (French and Arabic; not dated).

Information for 1972 and 1973 is collected from: *Arab Economic Report* (1974), chapter on Algeria; and Europa..., *1974-75*, chapter on Algeria.

65. *1962-1972: Algeria in Numbers*, p. 146.

66. UNESCO, Paris (published by the Regional Center for Educational Planning and Administration, Beirut), *Comparative Statistical Data on Education in the Arab States: An Analysis: 1960-61 – 1967-68* (Beirut, 1969), p. 49.

67. *1962-1972: Algeria in Numbers*, p. 108; and subsequent pages for the statistics that follow.

68. The official sources are: Ministère des Finances et du Plan, *Tableaux de l'Economie Algérienne 1967*, and Caisse Centrale de Cooperation Economique, *Eléments d'Information Economique sur l'Algérie*, published in January 1970. The private sources are: A. de Lepine, *Financement des Investissements et Incitation à Investir en Algérie* (thesis at Paris University, 1967); and R.E. Farrel, 'L'Algérie sept ans après', in the monthly *Expansion*, April 1969. (The latter estimates are reproduced in Chambre de Commerce et d'Industrie d'Alger, *Situation Economique de l'Algérie 1968*.) The IMF data appear in *International Financial Statistics (IFS)*. (It is worth noting that *Tableaux... 1971*, p. 258, which is the most recent on hand, quotes 'la production intérieure brute' for 1969 — which is GDP *less* the value added in the government sector — as being DA14.6 billion. Even accounting for this omission, the GDP would be well below the estimate given in *IFS*.)

69. J. François de Laulanie (p. 88), whose article examines the series to which reference has just been made, errs grossly in calculating the rate of growth. The error arises from his claim that the rise in prices for the years 1963-8 ought to be deducted from the growth calculated for these years, although (a) in fact the 1966-8 figures are at constant (1965) prices, and (b) 1963 is the first year in his series, and therefore serves as the base in the calculation of growth between the two terminal years. Indeed, if — as the writer claims — the prices rose all through the six years, then deflating the data for 1963 (in relation to some antecedent base) would result in a *higher*, not lower, growth rate.

70. These observations are based on the full, six-year tables 2 and 3 in de Laulanie, op. cit., pp. 89 and 90. However, the data for 1972 and 1973 are from *MERIP Reports*, No. 35 (February 1975), 'State Capitalism in Algeria', p. 13.

71. MERIP, op. cit., p. 22.

72. For a discussion of RNPW, see Simon Kuznets, 'Quantitative Aspects of the Economic Growth of Nations: II. Industrial Distribution of National Product and Labour Force', *Economic Development and Cultural Change*, Supplement to Vol. V, No. 4, July 1957, especially pp. 5-16, 36, 41 and 44. (See note 21 in chapter on Jordan in this book for other references to writings on the same subject.)

73. Laulanie, p. 95, for 1963-6; *IFS*, December 1974 for 1967-73. The former source (quoting *Expansion*, April 1969) under-estimates investment considerably, compared with the more recent data in *IFS*. The volume of investment in the two sources is presented below:

	de Laulanie	IFS
1967	2.0	3.2
1968	2.2	4.7
1969	not estimated	6.1

74. Data on net official capital flows have been collected from the following sources: (a) OECD, *The Flow of Financial Resources to Less-Developed Countries 1961-65*, p. 155 for the period July 1962 — December 1965: (b) OECD, *Development Assistance: Efforts and Policies of the Members of the Development Assistance Committee, 1969 Review*, pp. 170-1, for 1966-9; (c) OECD, *Development Co-operation: Efforts..., 1973 Review*, for 1970-3; (d) US Department of State, *Communist States and Developing Countries: Aid and Trade in 1970* (Washington, 1971) for the years ending December 1970; (e) UN *Statistical Yearbook 1973*, p. 715, for aid from centrally planned countries, till end of 1972; and (f) KFAED, *Annual Report 1973-74*, Table 3, p. 24, till end of March 1974.

75. The evolution of planning ideas and structures is described in *The Algerian Revolution*, Ch. 4. See also *The Four-Year Plan* in 'The Faces of Algeria' series (December 1970), and Republique Algérienne Démocratique et Populaire, *Plan Quadriennal 1970-73: Rapport Général* (January 1970).

76. *The Algerian Revolution*, p. 118.

77. *Arab Economic Report 1971*, p. 49.

78. De Bernis, op. cit., p. 20 (my translation).

79. *The Four-Year Plan* in 'The Faces of Algeria' series, pp. 28-31.

80. The Secrétariat d'Etat au Plan kindly allowed me in February 1973 to have an advance full copy (including 8 'Fascicules') of the 1974-7 Plan, although it was still not published. The full title of the Plan document was *Dossier pour la Préparation du IIe Plan Quadriennal, 1974-1977*, in 3 volumes.

81. *Dossier...*, Fascicule 2, p. 18.

82. See *La Charte d'Alger...*, p. 39; MERIP, op. cit.; and Bounajjar in *An-Nahar*, op. cit.

83. For example, Samir Amin, op. cit., pp. 189-98.

13 MOROCCO

We come now to the westernmost and the last of the twelve Arab countries examined in this book.[1] Morocco, like its three Maghreb and seven of its Mashreq sisters, suffered foreign rule in its recent past. (Saudi Arabia stands out as the one exception to this statement, since the Ottoman rule over it had receded with the defeat of Turkey in World War One.) But unlike the Mashreq countries, Morocco and its three neighbours to the east suffered that special form of foreign occupation which is *settler* colonialism, with massive settlement by the colonising Europeans. Its road to independence from French 'protection' — for the form of occupation applied stipulated that Morocco was a French 'protectorate' — was through struggle and bloodshed, like the road of Algeria, Libya and Tunisia.

Morocco became a protectorate in 1912, after years of European interference in its affairs, competition for its resources and straight military action, interspersed by treaties and special arrangements. But before that, Spain had succeeded in taking hold of two Moroccan zones, one in the north-west and north-east and the other in the south: in the littoral facing the Atlantic, and in the Sahara further south bordering on Mauritania and touching the south-western tip of Saharan Algeria. Likewise, before the protectorate was established, Morocco had been 'internationalised' economically, in the sense that its economy was to be open to all foreign powers, unsheltered by protection or any other measures restrictive to trade with Western Europe. But with the arrival of 1912, France triumphed over its opponents: the territories ruled by Spain were slightly diminished and were now granted by the French, not the Moroccan ruler, the Sultan; Britain was made to forgo any claims to Morocco against the promise of a free hand in Egypt; and Germany's approval of the setting up of the protectorate was bartered for the occupation by the latter of a certain zone in the Congo.

To complete the story and make the European rivals all happy, Tangier in the north-west, at the door both of the Mediterranean and the Atlantic and forming the southern point of the Strait of Gibraltar, was declared international, with Europeans enjoying political privileges, tax exemptions and juridical immunity under the 'Capitulations' system. The administration of the city was to be undertaken by a council of foreign consuls. This régime, like the dual occupation by the French and the Spaniards, was to remain in force until independence in March 1956, and one part of it, the Spanish occupation of the southern Saharan slice of the country, continues until today, in early 1975.

Observers looking critically at the four Maghreb economies as they stood immediately after World War Two are in agreement that Morocco was the one most generously endowed in natural resources, with the richest mineral deposits (predominantly phosphates, as petroleum had not yet been discovered in the region); the most abundant supply of river water with several all-the-year-round rivers or *oueds;* a not insignificant area of fertile plains in the west, a generally temperate climate; and beautiful scenery. Poorest in endowment (at that time) was Libya, the easternmost of the Maghreb countries, with regard to which King Victor Emmanuel III is reported to have stated: 'We have got the bone of the chop.'[2] This early comparison, which is favourable to Morocco, stands in some contrast with the current realities, as both Algeria and Libya have discovered, and exploited, rich hydrocarbon resources to their great advantage, and have therefore been able to achieve higher rates of growth than Morocco since their independence. Compared with the remaining nine countries, Morocco stands with those with lower performance. Only Sudan shows a poorer record of growth since its independence.

The obvious harshness in this judgement does not derive from the modesty of Morocco's post-independence growth record as much as it does from the fact that this record was expected to be distinctly better in view of the country's pre-independence relatively high record. As we shall see later, the rate of growth in the post-war decade was a comfortable 5 per cent per annum on average, a rate which only a few countries covered in this study achieved during the same period.

Both the relative economic superiority of colonial days and the relative modesty of the performance in the independence era can predominantly be explained in terms of political, institutional and manpower factors. The country owed its early prosperity mainly to the energy of its artisans and craftsmen who had originally been Moors expelled from Spain in the days of the fanatical Inquisition, and to the sizeable Sephardic Jewish minority which had also been expelled from Spain and which came to excel in financial activities, jewellery and metal work, and clerical skills in general. It also owed a large part to the investments made by European businessmen and by the protectorate government in physical infrastructure, and to the creation of a modern sector incorporating agriculture, transport, mining, light industry and power. However, the post-war political, institutional and manpower factors were considerably different and less conducive to development, as will be realised later.

The country's special features in the post-war decade leading to independence included, in addition to the relatively satisfactory endowment in natural resources to which reference has been made, a dual economy, with a small but efficient modern sector owned and operated largely by Europeans and a large but much less efficient traditional and primitive sector owned and operated by nationals; a plural society (to use Charles Stewart's term) which comprised not only hundreds of thousands of Europeans and of Jews (the latter feeling separate though formally Moroccans), but also reflected a serious division of the population into Arabs and Berbers with variations of language and way of life.

Another special and paradoxical feature that has not failed to create contradictions in the society and economy is the presence on the one hand of a strong and deeply rooted monarchy, which has provided continuity, a powerful oligarchy (both landed and urban) and a tough army, along on the other hand with a multiplicity of political parties and a strong trade union movement. The political system which outwardly suggests a reasonable degree of political participation has none the less failed to provide strong initiative in the drive for development or, in the words of a perceptive political scientist, the system has provided 'tension . . . with stalemate, and the recognized need for action . . . with a pervasive lack of initiative'.[3] These latter observations relate more to the independence era, but have their root in the several decades preceding 1956. There will be occasion in the rest of the chapter to substantiate these judgements from the economic evidence available.

1. THE PRE-INDEPENDENCE DECADE: THE COLONIALIST LEGACY

The legacy bequeathed by European settler colonialism to Libya, Tunisia and Algeria was likewise bequeathed to Morocco. We have had occasion elsewhere to be acquainted with this legacy, its minor accidental benefits and its major deliberate deprivations, hardships and handicaps. Yet it will be useful to indicate the special nature and dimensions of the impact of 44 years of direct European colonisation on Morocco.

As elsewhere, this impact was felt in the fields of transport and communications, mining, agriculture, industry, banking and trade, political authority and government service, and in manpower, education and health.[4] The performance of the Europeans is generally mixed, ranging from 'good' to discreditable, with the Spanish influence being in general less beneficial and more deleterious than even the French was.

The first point of tangency between coloniser and colonised is, understandably, political. Here it can be found that the French, after first occupying the coastline region in the west, infiltrated further inland and ended by establishing their authority over the whole of the country by 1934 (except for the Spanish-held areas and Tangier). This was only achieved after very bitter fighting stretching, on and off, over 22 years, but climaxed in the tough rebellion carried on by Rif tribesmen, led by the legendary Abd al-Krim, in the years 1921-6. Furthermore, on more than one occasion the French had to help the Spaniards establish their authority in the regions over which they claimed suzerainty, where they too met with determined armed resistance. The protectorate era cannot be discussed without reference to the formidable and able Resident-General who held formal authority and wielded actual and very real power from 1912 to 1925: Marshal Lyautey. To him and to his paternalistic tendencies go the credit for establishing the administration and building the basic parts of the system of transport and communications that were to influence the society and the economy for decades to come.

The form which political structure and organisation took was essentially dualistic in nature: a Moroccan administration headed by the Sultan with very little real power, and a French administration which handled the more important matters of defence, foreign affairs, finance and national economy. This pattern determined one aspect of the colonialist legacy, which was the insulation of the Moroccans both from substantive political decision-making and from administration at the higher echelons, as well as from the training that comes with the exercise of authority and decision-making. Consequently, by the time independence was achieved, and in spite of the loosening of the grip of the protecting power in the post-war years (upon the defeat of the Vichy French, the entry of American forces during the latter years of World War Two into Morocco, and the undertaking by the Allies to grant the country its independence) Morocco was to find itself unable to govern its territory and administer its affairs alone.

Another aspect of foreign rule was the promotion of social fragmentation, or the nurturing of plurality in society. This was characterised, *inter alia,* by the encouragement of a considerable measure of self-rule among the Berber tribes (especially in the mountain regions), or what is known as the *jema'a* rule where local governing councils and voting procedures played an important part in local administrative participation. Simultaneously with local Berber self-rule there was direct rule of the Arab urban and rural areas via *caids* who acted on behalf of the central government, with the help of the *ulemas* who administered *shari'a* law in matters governed by the tenets of the Koran. The third element in this mosaic was the Jewish community, whose affairs were governed by the French. This community identified in part with the Moroccans, in part with the Europeans. Finally, there was the European community which was totally immune to the judiciary and taxation systems applicable to the Moslem Moroccans, and in whose favour economic legislation and policies were formulated and shaped to ensure rich economic rewards and the security of these rewards.

To proceed with the description of the scenario as it was at independence, we find that the work-force had a very low level of training, and the population at large a very low level of education. The discussion will later provide some objective evidence in support of these generalisations. It is sufficient for the present purpose of drawing the broad features of the colonialist legacy to add that as a result of these low levels of education and training, and of the primitiveness of production technology and the relative scarcity of capital in the Moroccan sector in general, this sector was traditional in methods and structure and inefficient in performance. This was as true of Moroccan agriculture as of industry (the latter being mainly restricted to handicrafts), and of financial and other services.

In contrast, the European sector, which comprised agriculture and irrigation, transport, power, mining, industry, banking, foreign trade and other services, was modern and efficient. (Tourism was of negligible significance in pre-independence days.) Furthermore, while the traditional sector catered to the subsistence needs of the producers to a considerable extent, the modern sector was a money economy and essentially catered to the export market in general and the French market in particular. It would be an exaggeration to pretend that the two sectors were totally divorced, for no doubt some complementarity existed. But it is certain from the evidence that any such complementarity was designed to favour the modern sector and was allowed to develop only that far. Likewise, the benefits that spilled over to reach the traditional sector from investments made in the modern sector were largely incidental and were not intended to be made in the interest of the traditional sector.

The best illustration of this assertion was the well-developed transport and communications system, the main purpose of which was to service the military and administrative, as well as the economic needs of the French administration and the European modern sector, although the traditional Moroccan sector could not fail to benefit from this system. Another illustration was that the Moroccan population certainly received a boost to its income and purchasing power from the military expenditures made by the French, but this was a frail silver lining to the dark and ominous cloud of colonialism. (One might also add that the occupation itself had the beneficial effect of bringing Berber and Arab closer together in their joint struggle for independence. This greater communication between the two communities was socio-cultural, as well as economic.)

Population and Manpower

No official estimates are available of the size of the Moroccan population when the country became a protectorate. However, according to one careful student of Moroccan affairs, 'the consensus seems to hover around 3,500,000 persons' in 1912.[5] It is not clear whether or not this total included the Jewish minority, but that would not affect the total substantially. The next estimates relate to the year 1920, when the population is variously reported as ranging between 5.2m and 5.5m.[6] The lower estimate seems to this writer to be more defensible — though still exaggerated — in view of the size of the estimate for 1912. The rate of population increase should have been much higher than it was then to permit a total increase of about 50 per cent in the eight intervening years.[7]

Whatever the correct starting population estimate, there is agreement among researchers that this population was mainly concentrated in the north and north-western part of the country. Only about 11.5 per cent (some 600,000 persons) were urban in 1920, and one-third of this modest proportion consisted of Europeans. Yet the European community had consisted merely of 3,000 in 1912 (excluding the armed forces), and these were mostly missionaries, traders, consuls and some 'court advisers'. The traders were in the cities in the western littoral, but managed to be represented inland by *semsars* (brokers or intermediaries), who were mostly Jewish. In 1921, the Jewish community numbered about 91,000, with heavy concentration in the cities, but also with a presence, no matter how modest, in many villages. By 1955, according to one source, the total population had risen to 10.4m, while the urban component had risen to 2.4m or 23 per cent, but about half a million of these were 'non-Moslem'.[8]

The official population estimate nearest to the date of independence relates to mid-1956, when the total was 10,065,000. This estimate relates to the 'Southern Zone', the 'Northern Zone' and Tangier, the first of which became the Kingdom of Morocco upon independence. The Southern Zone included the regions of Agadir, Casablanca, Fez, Marrakesh, Meknes, Oujda and Rabat, and its population numbered 8.72m. The Northern Zone included the regions of Chaouen, Larache, Nador, Tetouan and Rif, and had 1.17m inhabitants, while the Tangier International Zone had 175,000 inhabitants. The estimate for mid-1956 included about 200,000 Moroccan Jews and 575,000 Europeans, over half of whom were French.[9] The European community in Morocco was distinctly smaller than in Algeria both in absolute and in relative terms, and smaller than in Tunisia in relative terms. Furthermore, the Europeans in pre-independence Algeria comprised a much larger component of small farmers and urban proletariat. Broadly speaking, in Morocco there was a heavy concentration of Frenchmen in big business (entrepreneurs, investors, top executives), in large-scale farming, and in government, while other Europeans numbered heavily as overseers and foremen, and Jews – as already indicated – specialised in finance, commerce, clerical and book-keeping work, and as jewellers, goldsmiths and tinsmiths.[10]

No information is available with respect to the size and structure of the working population upon independence, the nearest census to that date being for 1951 for foreigners, and for 1952 for Moroccans (including Jews). In both instances, the information relates to the Southern Zone. The total working population in the Southern Zone for the year 1951/2 was 3,088,896, or 38.6 per cent of the population of just over 8m at the time. This is a high proportion, and it certainly exaggerates the participation of Moroccan women on the one hand (of whom over 771,000 are recorded as active in the agricultural sector alone), and likewise of men in agriculture. In both instances this exaggeration arises from the liberal definition used which does not deflate the data for unemployment and disguised unemployment, and which seems to include all persons of working age.

Given this definition, it can be seen that agriculture and related activities in the primary sector (livestock, forestry and fishing) absorb about 70 per cent of the working population. The breakdown per sector, sex and national group is summarised in Table 13.1.[11]

Several interesting features characterise the structure of the three groups. The first relates to the difference in concentration of women between the Moroccan and the foreign communities. The largest single component of foreign working women is to be found in administration and liberal professions, followed by personal and health services, trade, handicrafts and manufacturing – these groups together accounting for over three-quarters of the total. On the other hand, most Moroccan women were in agriculture (82.8 per cent of the total), with handicrafts and manufacturing and personal and health services together accounting for 14.2 per cent.

Taking the two national groups regardless of sex differentiation we notice the second feature, namely that the structure is very different, with a preponderant concentration of Moroccans in agriculture, even after discounting the fact of heavy underemployment in this sector. Much behind is the proportion of Moroccans in handicrafts and manufacturing and of transport, a fact which indicates the insignificance of these activities, especially that

Table 13.1: Working Population in Morocco[a]

Sector	Moroccans[b]				Foreigners[c]			
	Men	Women	Total	Per Cent of Total	Men	Women	Total	Per Cent of Total
Fishing and forestry	8,523	35	8,558	0.3	1,138	12	1,150	0.8
Agriculture	1,284,460	771,171	2,055,631	69.6	7,920	462	8,382	6.2
Mining and quarrying	18,237	605	18,842	0.6	2,354	12	2,366	1.7
Handicrafts and manufacturing	226,293	85,675	311,968	10.6	32,939	3,578	36,517	26.9
Transport, port administration	252,453	22,119	274,572	9.3	12,129	754	12,883	9.5
Trade	115,884	3,076	118,960	4.0	11,413	3,848	15,261	11.2
Personal services, health	26,319	46,872	73,191	2.5	4,105	4,853	8,958	6.6
Administration, liberal professions	63,236	1,807	65,043	2.2	21,464	13,948	35,412	26.1
Guards, watchmen	26,212	163	26,375	0.9	10,173	78	10,251	7.6
Not classified	–	–	–	–	2,367	2,209	4,576	3.4
Total	2,021,617	931,523	2,953,140	100.0	106,002	29,754	135,756	100.0

a. The data refer to the Southern Zone only.
b. The data for 'Moroccans' were obtained through a census in 1952. They include information on the Jewish working population. This information is not shown separately in the source indicated below, but is to be found in *Annuaire statistique de la zone française du Maroc, 1952*, pp. 26,27. According to this publication, the Jews in the work-force totalled 53,685, divided as follows:

	Number	Per Cent of Total
Fishing and forestry	113	0.2
Agriculture	476	0.9
Mining and quarrying	47	0.1
Handicrafts and manufacturing	25,693	47.9
Transportation, port administration	2,347	4.4
Trade	12,400	23.1
Personal services, health	4,506	8.4
Administration, liberal professions	4,143	7.7
Guards, watchmen	55	0.1
Not classified	3,905	7.2
Total	53,685	100.0

c. The data on 'Foreigners' relate to a census undertaken in 1951.
Source: *Annuaire Statistique du Maroc: 1955-1956*, pp. 34 and 35.

Morocco

the vast majority of those in the secondary sector were in actual fact in the traditional subsector of handicrafts, not modern industry. On the other hand, the European working force was concentrated in modern industry, and in administration and liberal professions. The last-named, that is administration and the liberal professions, absorbed 26.1 per cent of working Europeans, but only 2.2 per cent of Moroccans. In the third place, trade occupies only 4 per cent of the Moroccan working population, but 11.2 per cent of the European. In fact, the discrepancy between the two groups is much more glaring for the service sectors taken together: 18.9 per cent for Moroccans and 64.4 per cent for Europeans.

An additional observation can be made if the structure of the Jewish work-force is examined as it appears in note (b) to Table 13.1. Almost half of this force used to be engaged in handicrafts and manufacturing, and almost a quarter in trade. The proportion is higher in either case than its counterpart for Moslem Moroccans and for Europeans alike.

The feature to be finally described can be seen not in Table 13.1, but in the source from which the material given here has been taken. This relates to the nature of the work or the status of the worker, whether employer, manager, principal or self-employed *(patron)*, salaried or wage employee, or independent worker. The distribution is interesting and suggestive enough to warrant reproduction below.

Table 13.2: Status of Members of the Working Population 1951/2

	Moroccans			Foreigners		
	Men	Women	Total	Men	Women	Total
Agriculture						
Employers	466,406	388,260	854,666	4,014	382	4,396
Salaried employees	329,512	18,611	348,123	3,628	68	3,696
Independent workers	488,542	364,300	852,842	278	12	290
Total	1,284,460	771,171	2,055,631	7,920	462	8,382
Other sectors						
Employers	80,202	5,786	85,988	12,365	2,881	15,246
Salaried employees	508,787	101,094	609,881	78,830	21,373	100,203
Independent workers	148,168	53,472	201,640	6,887	5,038	11,925
Total	737,157	160,352	897,509	98,082	29,292	127,374

Source: *Annuaire Statistique du Maroc 1955-1956*, pp. 34 and 35.

The most prominent feature of this structure is the minute proportion of Europeans as independent workers in agriculture, and the modest proportion of the same group in non-agricultural sectors. The ratios of *patrons* to the salaried and wage employees are noticeably close to each other in non-agricultural sectors, and not strikingly different in agriculture. This dual observation suggests that the European business activity was distinctly more collectivised, thus leaving less room for independent workers.

Before this part of the discussion is closed it is necessary to point out that Morocco, like Algeria and Tunisia, has always suffered from a heavy problem of unemployment and underemployment. As part solution, Moroccans began to seek employment in France beginning with World War One, and continue to do so. The only difference today is that there are many thousands of workers in other West European countries, particularly Federal Germany.

Land, Agriculture and Irrigation

The examination of the land, agriculture and water situation in the pre-independence decade calls for some qualifications regarding the area involved. Thus, Spain held territories in the north-western, north-eastern, south-western and Saharan parts of the country (Ceuta, Melilla, the Ifni region, and Rio de Oro and Saguia al Hamra respectively). Together, these add up to about 285,000 square kilometres — over 90 per cent of which is a desert. Secondly, there was a long-standing frontier dispute with Algeria over certain Saharan areas. Thirdly, Morocco laid claim to the territory which was much later to become the independent republic of Mauritania. And finally, there was the International Zone of Tangier.

All these disputes (except the one relating to the Spanish Sahara) were settled by the summer of 1974, and Tangier's international status has been terminated. Today, the land area of the Kingdom is recorded as 459,000 square kilometres,[12] and it will be this figure which will constitute our base.

Data on land use in Morocco vary from one source to another, as they often do in other countries, owing to definitional difficulties and inconsistencies. For pre-independence Morocco, there is the added problem of the inclusion of the Southern (French) Zone only in official statistics. However, this Zone comprises virtually all the agricultural land that needs to be considered, and includes what Lyautey had called 'useful Morocco'. This agricultural land exceeded 15m hectares (150,000 sq. km.) upon independence, divided as follows:

Over 5 mn ha of cultivated land, of which 500,000 were devoted to fruit trees and practically all the rest to cereals;

2.5 mn ha of fallow land ('en jachère'), of which about 2 mn ha were marginal land; and

8 mn ha of pastureland.[13]

Roughly speaking, and without adjusting for quality differentials of land, this total area allowed about 2.4 ha for each rural inhabitant, on the assumption that the rural population constituted three-fourths of the total upon independence. This man/land ratio is slightly more favourable than that in Algeria (and in effect noticeably so owing to Morocco's more abundant water resources), but distinctly less favourable than that in Tunisia. However, a more meaningful ratio relates to the combination of arable land plus land under permanent crops, according to the terminology in FAO's *Production Yearbook*. If this area is taken by itself, with permanent meadows and pastures excluded, then the ratio would drop to about 1.1 ha per head of the rural population. This likewise stands more favourably than in Algeria and distinctly less so than in Tunisia. Furthermore, the ratio of arable land to total land area is largest in Tunisia, smaller in Algeria and smallest in Morocco.[14] (These generalisations are as true today as they were when each of these countries acquired independence.)

As in the other three Maghreb countries subjected to European settler colonialism, land acquisition by the Europeans was one of the very first, if not the first, manifestation of encroachment on the economic rights and interests of the occupied country. Again as elsewhere, the acquisition of land took overt illegal forms as well as thinly disguised legal

Morocco

forms. The choice of method depended on the region, the phase of the relationship between the French and the Moroccans, and the type of tenure prevailing in the area concerned.

The land tenure system was similar to that in the other countries surveyed in this work, although the nomenclature differs at times. Thus there were *melk* or privately owned land, private and public *habous* (endowment) land as in Tunisia and Algeria (called *waqf* land in the Mashreq), domanial land belonging in name to the state but in practice subject to the Sultan's decision (including *guich* land where ownership was vested in the state, but the right of exploitation was allowed to the tribes — mainly Arab — against their performance of military service), and *arch* or collective land, mainly in the mountainous and arid areas. *Melk* land was the smallest category in area.

Much of the private land fell under absentee landlordship, in a system called *khammes* as in the Mashreq countries. Only the terms of share-tenancy differed from country to country, with the tenant almost invariably exploited under share-tenancy arrangements. In the *khammes* system, the share-tenant obtained one-fifth of the produce, but this was the minimum; a larger share could be obtained if the tenant's contribution went beyond his labour.[15]

Apart from the exploitation of the tenant by the absentee landlord, there was the additional hardship caused by taxation and the heavy demands made by the *caid*, the representative of the central government. According to an observation made late in the last century, 'Grasshoppers come sometimes, droughts often, and the *caids* always.'[16] To this must also be added the primitiveness of technology, the shortage of investment and working capital, the heavy rural indebtedness, the problems of marketing and the inordinately large cuts made by middlemen, and the grossly underdeveloped irrigation facilities, for the degree of poverty of the small land holding and of the share-tenant to be appreciated.

However, in addition to all this, some of the best-located and most fertile land was being slowly transferred from Moroccan to European hands even before the start of the protectorate. Such transfers were not permissible then except with the consent of the Sultan, but Europeans circumvented this impediment through registering purchases in the name of Moroccans acting as 'straw men', or through entry into association with Moroccans. But after 1912, the Sultan's permission ceased to be mandatory, and transfers increased, taking — as already indicated — various forms ranging from the outright confiscatory to the straightforward sale, with different shades of illegality and coercion in between. (We need not reproduce here what is now widely known of the ingenious mechanisms for the dispossession of Moroccans — and other North Africans — by the Europeans.) Thus, from an area of some 80,000 hectares of European-held land in 1912 (owned in European names, apart from areas held under the names of or in association with Moroccans), the total rose to some 904,000 ha on 31 December 1955. (Some 824,000 ha were registered in the names of Europeans — over 95 per cent of whom were French, and over 98 per cent of the total area was rural — between 1915 and the end of 1956.) Even during 1956 itself, the year of independence, title was registered in foreign names to 4,929 ha (including 99 ha of urban land). If the period 1915-56 alone is taken, it will be found that a transfer of 819,270 ha of rural land was effected. This area covered 14,829 properties (13,173 French, and 1,656 'other' foreign), amounting to an average of 55.2 ha per property. Against this, there were at the end of 1956 only 61,542 registered Moroccan rural properties (excluding collectively-held land and *habous* land) with a total area of 1,099,967 ha, or an average of 17.9 ha per property.[17]

Enormous as the difference in area was in 1956 between foreign-held and Moroccan-held private rural land, it did not convey the full impact of colonisation. Two qualifications have to be made here. The first is that the foreign-held land was generally far superior in inherent quality and in productivity. The second is that, generally speaking, there is a much heavier concentration of medium and large Moroccan holdings among those registered, since registration calls for financial resources and access to government departments much more readily available to the more substantial landlord. Hence, if information were available for the whole country, it would probably show that the average Moroccan holding of rural land stood well below the average area just indicated.

With regard to the first point, there is evidence that two-thirds of foreign-held land was cultivable and cultivated, whereas Moroccan land was divided half and half between cultivable and uncultivable.[18] Stewart describes the situation strikingly by indicating that in 1953 the European-held land totalled 6.5 per cent of arable land, 10 per cent of total crop land, 23 per cent of orchards and vineyards, and only 4 per cent of fallow and range land — and this when the *rural* European community was only just over 1 per cent of the total rural population.[19] On a *per capita* basis, and considering the total Moroccan-held area of about 14.4m ha, a rural Moroccan had just under 2 hectares, of which under one hectare was cultivable, while the rural foreigner had 12 ha of which 8 ha were cultivable — and in addition the smaller area was in general much poorer in quality and much less provided with capital, machines and equipment, irrigation and institutional facilities. These differences reflected themselves, *inter alia*, in average income per farmer, as we will see towards the end of this section.

European circles were in the habit of defending themselves against criticism relating to the colonisation of agricultural land by pointing to their contribution to the physical infrastructure in the country, the market that foreigners provided for Moroccan agricultural produce, and the 'demonstration effect' of the distinctly more advanced European agriculture. There is no denying any of these points in principle, but in practice these advantages were all heavily qualified and/or limited in scope. Thus, the infrastructure was of incidental benefit, and in any case it was locationally concentrated where it was of primary benefit to the Europeans. The Moroccans did not have much to market anyway (about 70 per cent of the produce being in the subsistence subsector), and when their produce found its way to European buyers or to the export market it was on terms favourable to the buyers and mostly discriminatory, owing to the weak bargaining power of the Moroccan farmers. Finally, the demonstration or example effect was very restricted, because of the reluctance of the Europeans to allow the 'natives' to look over their shoulders. To all this must be added the fact that good agricultural land was increasingly passing from Moroccan to European hands at the same time as the population was increasing. This resulted in the ousting of thousands of small landowners and the creation of a large 'rural proletariat'.[20]

In fairness it ought to be stated that occasionally consciousness erupted that dispossession was becoming a serious problem, especially as a result of the forfeiture of land upon the default on rural debt repayment. Thus, a *dahir* (decree) was issued in 1945 setting the 'bien de famille' (family patrimony, or *lot viable*) at 8 ha, as '... a minimum ... which could be neither alienated nor seized, nor even rented'. This minimum was 4 hectares less than an area recommended as early as 1928 'for a Moroccan family settled on good land, and 12 hectares less than that for a family on mediocre land'.[21] But it was too late by then: a huge exodus had by the end of World War Two carried scores of thousands of Moroccans into the misery and squalor of the 'bidonvilles' that mushroomed on the outskirts of towns and cities.

The factors leading to this unhealthy and immoral development were exacerbated by the agricultural land tax known as the *tertib* which fell as a fixed rate (of 5 per cent) on the gross value of the crop. Understandably, this frequently led to the forced sale of land, and to the rushed sale of crops at the wrong moment when supply was at its largest. Rebates were allowed for improved and modern methods of cultivation, which in effect meant further discrimination against the Moroccans in favour of Europeans. Hence the *tertib* amounted to a subsidy by the Moroccans to the Europeans, as objective research has shown.

Information is not available with respect to the distribution of land by size of holding, but it is known that it was markedly skewed, with a concentration of very large holdings in few hands. (The maldistribution was more pronounced than in Algeria or Tunisia.) Again according to the careful research of Stewart, 'there were thousands of holdings of less than 5 hectares. Furthermore, it was estimated that 60 percent of the rural population was either farm labour or *khammes*.'[22] Inevitably, the maldistribution of land resulted in maldistribution of income. This phenomenon was intensified by the operation by Europeans of considerable areas *rented* from Moroccans who owned the land either privately or collectively.

Unfortunately, the construction of irrigation facilities in the pre-independence decades lagged far behind the possibilities, judged by the availability of surface water. Whatever facilities provided were initially in regions heavily colonised, but even then the areas actually involved were extremely small. Thus, in 1938-9, these totalled a mere 9,360 ha, and by 1955-6 had risen to only 65,718 ha.[23] Only in 1939 was a relatively large project undertaken to benefit Moroccan land. The expansion in irrigated area between 1939 and 1956, slow as it was, showed even more modest results than the area by itself would suggest.

According to students of the Moroccan economy and to informed Moroccans, the large dams constructed were excessively costly, technically deficient, insufficiently accompanied by adequate distribution systems and drainage facilities, and, additionally, designed mainly to serve the holdings of large influential landlords.[24] It remains to be added that official estimates show that by 1 January 1957 the irrigable area lying around the irrigation system totalled 132,450 ha, while the area for which irrigation facilities had been provided was 76,887 ha. Thus, the area actually irrigated constituted half of what could be irrigated, given the water availability. It was also estimated at the time of independence that the total irrigable area in the whole Southern Zone (the Kingdom of Morocco), was 455,500 ha.[25] The discrepancy between the potential and the achievements is a stern judgement of the failings of the protecting power after 44 years of occupation.

Repeated reference has been made to dualism in its general aspects. It can now be added that dualism took its most severe form in agriculture, where it manifested itself in such features as the size of holding, the location of agricultural land, the kind of crops sown, the techniques used, the degree of mechanisation, the capital invested and worked with, the marketing facilities enjoyed, and the institutional and organisational instruments and arrangements adopted. In brief, the much smaller group of European land-holders produced out of their small proportion of land (about one-eighth of total area) and through the adoption of an efficient, modern style of activity, an agricultural output far in excess of what their numbers or the areas exploited warranted. According to an estimate made for 1956 and quoted by Albert Waterston, who has examined the planning experience of Morocco carefully, the modern agricultural sector accounted for 'about 25 percent of the gross value of all crops, 80 percent of the wine and citrus fruits, about 33 percent of the vegetables and legumes, and 15 percent of the cereals'.[26] Stewart also quotes a Moroccan newspaper as claiming in 1956 'on the basis of official figures' that '28 percent of the value of all agricultural land and 29 percent of the value of all agricultural land, buildings, equipment, and livestock were represented by European holdings.'[27]

These proportions must be read in conjunction with the proportion of rural Europeans to the total rural population and that of European-held to total agricultural land. But the significance of the enormous discrepancy between the two sets of proportions is not merely quantitative nor even merely economic. For, like dualism everywhere in the formerly colonised world (as it has come to be understood), this phenomenon is the product of, is reflected in and perpetuates a pattern of sharp social and political differentiation between the coloniser and the colonised community in favour of the first.

The French administration began on the close of World War Two more seriously to consider and implement some corrective land measures (as it did with respect to the protection of the tenure of small land-holders through the *dahir* of 1945 to which reference has been made). But its measures came slowly, belatedly, and in small doses, with the result that they remained largely ineffectual. This was in sharp contrast with the active concern of the French with European land-holders and farms, expressed in concrete measures and institutions such as credit and marketing co-operatives and banks, experimental services, tax rebates, export facilities and the like. It cannot be denied that all these types of services were also available to Moroccan farmers, but this was a theoretical availability, since neither the extent and location of the services nor their human and other resources were capable of coping with the needs of the large mass of Moroccan farmers. Furthermore, they were largely unprepared, in terms of education, training and attitude, to seek or make satisfactory use of the services, were these to be accessible and in sufficient supply.

Credit provision was one illustration. Because of various impediments and constraints to which allusion has been made, Moroccan farmers had to resort to loans from usurers and loan sharks, at very high rates of interest. (The ultimate results of forced sale of land upon default, and rushed and disadvantageous disposal of crops to avoid default, have already been mentioned.) Evidence of the shortage of institutional agricultural credit comes in an official publication relating to 1952. It is reported that total credit advanced to Moroccans by the Sociétés Marocaines de Prévoyance (SOMAP) which were founded first in 1917, amounted to 7.7 billion old francs for the whole period 1917–1952/3. This amounts to $22m at the official rate prevailing then of 350 old Moroccan francs to the United States dollar. On average the credit extended annually amounted only to about $626,000. In the year 1952/3, these societies had almost 1.5m members, but their loans totalled about 1.5 billion francs for the year, or some 1,000 francs per borrower — less than 3 United States dollars on the average. As Stewart points out, the actual average loan was higher than the mechanistic division would suggest, as 'it has been asserted that 822 farmers who qualified as "modern" received the bulk of the credit granted to Moroccans during this period. This means that the great mass of the fellahin were getting no assistance at all from the SOMAP,'[28] although every *tertib* taxpayer had to be a member and to make an annual contribution to the working capital of the SOMAP to which he belonged.

Among the post-war corrective measures adopted with the aim of advancing modern methods among the farmers were demonstration or model farms set up under a new agency called Secteurs de Modernisation du Paysanat, SMP (Rural Modernisation Sectors). These farms themselves undertook or participated in work with demonstrative intent, in the hope of influencing the neighbours and urging them to imitate the new methods. The work was conducted under French supervisors, and control of the land thus turned into model farms was taken out of the hands of the original owners. (By independence, these lands had not yet been returned to the owners.) The impact of the SMP was minimal, as there was hesitation to adopt the new methods, often because the ancillary facilities were not available, and attitudes had not changed enough in the appropriate direction. Furthermore, the total area involved did not exceed 18,000 ha by the end of 1953. Thus by independence, all the factors related to traditional agriculture worked against its advance and increased productivity: size of holdings, inadequacy of credit and other services, insignificance of irrigation facilities, favouritism towards Europeans, ineffectual extension services, and above all, the absence of a national government truly devoted to the welfare of the rural population and capable of translating its devotion into concrete measures.

Industry and Mining

Industry was slow-moving in Morocco all through the years of the protectorate,[29] but not more so than elsewhere in pre-independence days in the other countries covered in this study. Thus, by 1956, the contribution of industry and handicrafts to gross domestic product at market (1960) prices was 11 per cent, rising from 10 per cent in 1951. Admittedly, handicrafts were responsible for a not insignificant part of this contribution – probably about 2 per cent of GDP.[30] Modern and traditional industry together employed about 312,000 Moroccans in 1951, and some 36,500 foreigners in 1952. The women constituted over 27 per cent of the total Moroccan industrial labour force, but only about 10 per cent of its foreign counterpart. This fact, plus the enormous size of the Moroccan industrial labour for a sector as small as modern industry was, together suggest the large volume of employment in handicrafts. The mission of the International Bank for Reconstruction and Development suggested in its report on Morocco that Moroccan craftsmen and their dependants totalled about 250,000,[31] but it would seem that this estimate is far too cautious. Understandably, it is extremely difficult to make a count of craftsmen engaged in handicrafts in their own homes, especially those who are not full-time craftsmen but undertake other part-time work. However, it is worth noting that the share of industry and handicrafts in the GDP was almost identical with their share in the labour force for 1951: 10 per cent versus 10.6 per cent. It is tenable to suggest that as the contribution to GDP did not change much by 1956, the share in the labour force did not change much either.

But of greater significance here is the allotment of shares to the Moroccans and Europeans in the magnitude and performance of modern industry. Writing soon after independence, a scholar noted that the share of Moroccans in the capital of large industries did not exceed 5 per cent of the total, with another 5 per cent going to non-French, Western interests, and a whole block of 90 per cent to Frenchmen.[32] However, this massive French involvement did not reflect continuous and consistent enthusiasm for industry. Thus, it was only by the end of World War Two that the French lost some of their hesitation and reluctance to invest in Morocco – an attitude that had been created by the fear of competition. (This was in sharp contrast with the French attitude towards industrial investments in Algeria.)

Greater interest in industry in Morocco was expressed in the post-war period. This was reflected both in the setting up of independent industries in the protectorate and in the establishment of branches or subsidiaries to mother companies in Metropolitan France. However, this revival did not last long: by 1955 the flight of capital became a problem of enormous dimensions reaching, according to Cowan, 35 billion francs in 1955 and 100 billion francs in 1956.[33] (Although we do not have data on investment by sector in the post-war decade, this flight of capital cannot but be considered sizeable in its own right.) It is this dramatic upsurge between 1945 and 1953 that gave the impression of a Moroccan 'industrial boom', to use Amin's phrase,[34] although in fact industrial expansion in Algeria and Tunisia was more solid and significant if examined within a longer time horizon.

Expressed numerically, the upsurge means a rise in the index of production in all branches of manufacturing industry from 157 in 1948, with 1938 as a base, to 284 in 1956, or an increase of 80 per cent in eight years. The largest jumps, however, were between 1948 and 1951, when the increase was from 157 to 216 index points, and between 1952 and 1953, from 227 to 257.

The rates of growth of the major branches of industry diverged widely, with metal and metal transformation industries, and chemical and chemical products industries leading (an index for 1956 of 479 and 475 respectively), followed by construction materials industries (an index of 378), textile and leather goods industries (294), and foodstuff and agricultural industries (lagging behind with an index of 217). Modern industry grew faster between 1938 and 1956 than either agriculture or construction, but much slower than mining or energy.[35]

Most manufacturing in pre-independence Morocco was of a simple nature, mainly for local consumption. The two notable exceptions were wine-making (designed mostly for French consumers, as the Moroccans on the whole were teetotallers, 'addicted' to their delicious and delicate mint tea), and canning (largely of sardines for export). The other industries included flour-milling, sugar, cement, textiles, some phosphate processing and petroleum-refining, and a narrow base of chemical, metal and engineering industries. It is indicative of the inadequacy even of modern manufacturing that in the field of light uncomplicated industry, where self-sufficiency could be easily achieved, the country remained dependent on imports for a substantial part of its total consumption.

In spite of the slow growth of manufacturing industry over the decades preceding independence, the traditional, handicraft 'industry' was being eased out relentlessly. This occurred under the competition of foreign manufactured substitutes. It was still too early in 1956 for the revival of interest in traditional handicrafts and of the 'rustic' in general, a phenomenon which is closely associated with the European and American tourist of today whose interest is a form of escape from the machine and its products. (The same applies to the rich Westernised national, in Morocco as elsewhere, who now relishes the hand-made slippers, rugs or copper pots.) But long before the incursion of manufacturing industry into the domain of the craftsman — indeed, as early as 1918 in the days of Lyautey — there was concern over the fate of handicrafts and the poverty of craftsmen. It was then believed that improvements in design, the organisation of craftsmen, the supply of work materials and tools at reasonable prices, and efficient marketing would help improve the conditions of handicrafts. To this end an Office des Industries d'Arts Indigènes was established in 1918 (later transformed into the Service des Métiers et Arts Marocains). But this agency was never very effective in bringing about a revival. Traditional industry continued on its course of stagnation, if not extinction.

As energy is frequently considered a branch of industry, it will receive brief examination here. This branch consistently contributed 2 per cent of GDP in the several years preceding independence. The sources included, as they do today, thermal and hydro-electric generators, coal-burning generators, coal, and petroleum and petroleum products. The country was well-equipped with facilities for the production and distribution of electricity, although consumption *per capita* was low at independence. Thus, a total of 935.1m kwh was produced in 1956, while consumption amounted to 781.3m kwh which is equivalent to only 78 kwh per person. Considering that only 226.9m kwh were consumed by households, *per capita* consumption was extremely low in 1956, and must have been restricted to the houses of the very rich, mainly in urban centres.[36]

Morocco is unique in the Arab world in the fact that it has always and until this day obtained most of its electric power from hydro-electric sources. In 1956, 85 per cent of total electric production was generated in this manner.[37] The small balance came from fuel-burning and coal-burning generators in the ratio of nine to one. On the other hand, coal is used rather extensively in Morocco. Thus, while production was about 500,000 tons (largely anthracite) in 1956, total consumption amounted to over 343,000 tons, all of which, except for 69,200 tons, was from local production. The largest users were the cement industry and electricity generators, consuming 36 per cent and 22.7 per cent respectively.[38]

Morocco's economy is largely associated with mining, and more particularly with phosphates. Yet the mining and quarrying sector rather consistently accounted for only 5 per cent of GDP in the years 1950-6, thus tailing the list of sectors except for energy. The association arises mainly from the long-standing importance of mining, which attracted the notice of foreign powers several years before Morocco became a French protectorate. The years immediately preceding and following 1912 witnessed a frenzied rush by West Europeans for mining concessions, and these were often awarded under duress, which was not always even thinly disguised.

Legislation enacted in 1914 purportedly in order to regulate the granting, operation and control of the concessions was biased in such a way as to favour French companies. It is ironic that phosphate mining, which, like all mining, was to be submitted to bids, was withdrawn from bidding arrangements in order to leave the horizon clear for French interests. Thus, according to a quotation in Stewart, rich deposits south-east of Casablanca were not submitted to bids in accordance with the *dahir* of 1914 since 'to abandon [these deposits] to the hazards of tenders would have risked the consequence of their cession ... to foreign interests'.[39] Lyautey 'nationalised' phosphate reserves in 1920 and placed mining and marketing activities under the Bureau Chérifien des Phosphates, which was the successor authority to the Bureau des Mines.

Later in 1928 another institution was established, the Bureau de Recherches et de Participation Minières, BRPM, with the functions of exploration and exploitation of all minerals except phosphates (which, however, came under the jurisdiction of the BRPM in 1938). This arrangement continued until 1951, when ownership of *all* underground minerals was vested in the state. But until then, the Palace, the BRPM, foreign (mainly French) interests, and some other local private interests owned the mineral wealth of the country. The government's direct reward was in the revenue it obtained as profit and export taxes. The two brought in 12.9 billion francs in 1956, or 14 per cent of total revenue. (Phosphate exports were valued at 37.7 billion francs for that year.)[40]

Morocco's mineral wealth goes beyond phosphates, though these are by far the most significant in terms of deposits, production and export. The more important items, with production and value in 1956, are listed in Table 13.3.

Production has fluctuated over the decades, with ups and downs reflecting world prices and general world political conditions. Regarding the latter factor, all mineral production suffered during World War Two. Thus, with 1938 as base year, the index for all minerals including phosphates dropped to a trough of 35 in 1941 (but to 29 without phosphates, for the year 1942). However, with 1949 as base year for a new series, it is found that the expansion in phosphate production was slower than for the other minerals combined. Thus the index for all minerals rose from 100 for 1949 to 182.9 for 1956, but to 235 if phosphates are excluded. The labour force registered in the mining sector in 1956 totalled 32,816.[41] This number differs substantially from that recorded for 1951 and 1952, where

Table 13.3: Mineral Production, 1956

	Tons	Million Francs
Phosphates	5,521,817	24,493.3
Iron ore	489,690	736.7
Anthracite	482,000	2,516.0
Metallurgical manganese	383,115	2,820.5
Lead	120,047	7,216.7
Chemical manganese	38,294	502.2
Zinc	70,921	1,903.7
Cobalt	6,438	575.1
Copper	2,863	134.0

Source: Royaume de Maroc, Ministère de l'Economie Nationale, Service Central des Statistiques, *Annuaire Statistique du Maroc (Ex-Zone Sud) 1955-1956*, p. 269.

Moroccans and foreigners in the mining and quarrying sector totalled less than 22,000. (See Table 13.1 above.)

With the exception of coal and petroleum, most mineral production in Morocco finds its way to export markets. On the other hand, only a small proportion of coal, and no petroleum, is exported. (Indeed, petroleum was a very insignificant item in mining, with production being a little over 97,000 tons in 1956.) Furthermore, most minerals are exported in their raw state. The country did not have the industrial facilities to process a substantial part of the raw minerals, and this was in turn probably a matter of policy, designed to reserve the processing activity to the importing countries. By independence, only some 100,000 tons of phosphates were retained in the country and processed as superphosphates and hyperphosphates for domestic use.

However, the place of phosphate goes much beyond the employment and the income, and the export and profit tax revenue it generates. In addition, substantial income is created for the railways and the ports since the phosphate industry is their largest client. Furthermore, there is the great contribution of phosphates to commodity exports, exceeding one-third of their total value. But the full significance of phosphates was far from being attained in 1956, since despite the huge volume of production and exports, the unit net return was low. The country could earn much more yet by increasing the value added in the phosphate extractive industry through processing a much larger volume than it had been doing until independence. The potential acquires its enormity from the fact that Morocco was then the world's third-largest producer (after USA and USSR),[42] and the demand for fertilisers derived from phosphates is expanding at a very fast rate. Moroccan agriculture itself will require much more than it actually uses.

The Service Sectors

The commodity sectors grouped together contributed 54 per cent of GDP in 1956, leaving 46 per cent to the service or tertiary sectors. A detailed examination of each of these sectors will not be undertaken, but brief space will be devoted to transport and communication, foreign trade, money and banking, and the government, including public finance. (Tourism is left out as it was insignificant in those days.)

Motivated by their own military and economic interests, the French turned their attention to the construction of railways and ports immediately they formalised their take-over of the country in 1912. These two categories, plus the highways, provided the country by 1956 with an adequate, efficient and well-equipped system. The traveller can immediately see the proof of this by using the public means of transport, between urban centres and within them. Some quantitative indicators will gauge the extent of the development of the transport system in the 44 years of French rule:[43]

- Some 50,000 km. of highways were built, of which 13,700 km. were asphalted by the end of 1956.
- 1,756 km. of railway were built, 706 km. of which were served by electric locomotives, the rest being diesel- or steam-run. The railways system had 116 locomotives and a total of 6,212 carriages for passengers and cargo, which handled 5.85m passengers and 9.95m tons in 1956.
- The country is served by 8 ports; total tonnage handled was 62.3m tons in 1956.
- Even as far back as 1956 the country had 7 airports which handled 13,776 take-offs and landings, involving about 256,000 passengers and 6,569 tons of air freight.
- Although telephone and postal services were small on a *per capita* basis in 1956, the equipment was relatively well-installed and efficiently operated. The services included facilities for savings accounts at the post offices.
- Finally, the urban centres were well-provided with roads, public lighting, public transport (using electricity and diesel), post offices, railway stations and a water piping and drainage system quite adequate for those days.

The public sector of transport and communications relied to a considerable extent on foreign (mainly French) operators. For instance, they numbered 3,682 out of a total of 8,293 in the railways in 1956, and 1,793 out of the 10,187 officers and crew of boats registered in Morocco. The port installations also relied heavily on foreign technicians and executives.

According to Amin, the commodity foreign trade of Morocco grew considerably between 1920 and 1955. Thus, with 1920 as the base and at 1955 prices, exports rose by a net 1,170 per cent and imports by 500 per cent. However, despite the much faster rate of growth of exports, there was always a trade deficit owing to the initially higher absolute level of imports (33 billion francs versus 10 billion for exports in 1920).[44] The largest single group of imports consisted in 1956 of capital goods for the industrial sector, the next-largest was foodstuffs, followed by products of mineral origin, then by equipment for the agricultural sector. Together these constituted about five-sixths of total imports. On the other hand, the largest group of exports was agricultural produce — mainly foodstuff — followed by minerals (predominantly phosphates). Together these two groups constituted four-fifths of the total.[45]

Understandably, Morocco's largest trading partner was France and other countries in the franc zone, both for imports and for exports. The second place was occupied by the United States and dollar zone importers, and the third by Britain and sterling zone countries — all for imports. However, this pattern was reversed for exports. These three groups of trading partners among them accounted for almost three-fourths of imports and of exports.

The data so far have related to the former Southern Zone, thus excluding the Spanish and the Tangier International Zones. The latter imported goods worth 10.9 billion francs and exported 2.3 billion francs in 1956, against about 161 billion and 119 billion francs respectively for the Southern Zone. No information is available for the Spanish Zone.

The persistent trade deficit was in part met by the net sale of services and net factor receipts from abroad (including the remittances of Moroccan workers in France), in part by grants and other forms of capital flows from France and, since World War Two, from the United States, which made payments for the use of certain military bases. French contributions constituted the largest single item among the receipts of foreign exchange and factor earnings. (However, a substantial part of these contributions originated in transfers made by the United States under the Marshall Plan in aid of Morocco and the two other French protectorates in North Africa.) But over and above the current earnings and international transfers there remained a large deficit during the 5 years 1950-4, which averaged around 30 billion francs.[46] This gap was bridged by foreign indebtedness.

However, as the FAO Report on Morocco pointed out, 1955 and 1956 (as well as 1957) showed a dramatically reversed trend. Thus, these years experienced a substantial surplus on current account, which stood at 4 billion francs for 1955, but rose to 41 billion for 1956 and 43 billion for 1957. This is in sharp contrast with the preceding five years when the deficit on current account averaged over 25 billion francs.

Nevertheless, despite the large surpluses and large net capital inflows to the public sector (amounting to 19.7, 23.2 and 37.1 billion francs for the three years 1955-7), the general situation of the country did not benefit much because the same three years witnessed a huge outflow of *private* capital from Morocco to France. This outflow, which was caused by the expectation and later the materialisation of independence, totalled 133 billion francs for the three years.[47] The outflow, plus the hesitation to invest inside the country, and the general atmosphere of indecision and confusion, all led to a drop in GDP for 1956 (and much more for 1957) at constant prices. The drop in domestic and national product in turn led to a shrinkage of the availability of resources for further investment. How this cycle was broken in the independence era can be seen when the uninterrupted GDP series for the years 1951-73 is presented in the next section.

Before independence, and indeed until October 1959, Morocco's currency was closely tied to the French franc, and the country was part of the franc zone. When the Moroccan franc was introduced as an act of sovereignty, it was at par with the French franc. Then in 1959 the unit of money became the Moroccan dirham, equivalent to 100 old francs. The issue authority used to be the Banque d'Etat du Maroc (established under international status, but formed as a corporation subject to French law).[48] French interests held a majority share in the capital and therefore had a majority of seats in the board of directors.

As member of the French franc zone, the protectorate was influenced primarily by the policies and decisions of the French monetary authorities. Membership gave the country access to the franc pool, including the availability to this pool of other foreign currencies, and it also meant the free movement of the franc among the members of the zone. However, submission of the country's national economic policy to considerations determined beyond national frontiers limited Morocco's ability to design and implement those monetary (and banking) policies which it would have deemed appropriate to its growth and economic interest in general.

The protectorate was relatively well-equipped with banking institutions, including a few (not always called banks but Funds or 'Caisses') that were designed to provide medium- and long-term credit to agriculture, construction and industry. However, the Europeans were largely the beneficiaries of credit facilities, for reasons that have already been mentioned in connection with agricultural credit.

The degree of monetisation in the country as a whole was low in the period immediately following the war, although money in circulation and money supply both witnessed a notable expansion during the war. By the end of 1949, the money in circulation stood at 27.7 billion francs, but it rose to 65.4 billion at the end of February 1956, and to 70.1 billion at the end of 1956 (equivalent to $76.3m for 1949, and $200m for the end of 1956).[49] On a *per capita* basis, this amounts to $8.9 for 1949 and $19.2 for 1956 – a very small amount indeed.

Compared with other Arab countries at an equally early phase of their independence and economic evolution, Morocco showed more strongly established banking habits. Thus, for 1949 and 1956 respectively, bank deposits amounted to 50.4 and 85.6 billion francs respectively. If to this are added post office savings the totals would rise to 54 billion and 98.2 billion for the two years. In addition, the country was already used to treasury bonds in 1949. Unfortunately, information is not available on the lending activities of the various categories of banks (commercial and developmental) for the period under examination.

The government sector and the liberal professions combined occupied over 100,000 of the labour force in 1951/2, with the foreigners constituting over one-third of the total. It can safely be presumed that the numbers did not decrease by 1956 – the civil service almost never shrinks in size, although the services it renders to the population may well deteriorate in quality, as some underdeveloped countries have good reason to know! In 1956, there were some 28,000 Frenchmen in the civil service (40,000 according to another estimate), including a large component at the intermediate and higher administrative and technical skills, and a large number of schoolteachers.[50] According to Amin, 23,000 Moslems were employed in 1955 as 'petty officials'.[51] One can only surmise that in all there were upon independence 55,000–65,000 officials (presumably) in the central government, more than half of whom were non-Moroccans. This is not a heavily laden civil service for a country with over 10 million inhabitants.

Government revenues and expenditures over the ten years 1947-56 rose considerably – from 19.3 billion francs to 142.6 billion francs. A balanced budget was always prepared. (The net increase of 639 per cent in a decade ran parallel with a net increase in the cost of living for Moroccans and non-Moroccans of 52 and 74 per cent respectively.)[52] Roughly one-fifth of the revenues came in the latter years from direct taxes, while customs duties accounted for slightly over one-fifth, and indirect taxes and other fees and transfers from public enterprises (like the Office Chérifien des Phosphates and the Régie Co-Intéressée des Tabacs) together accounted for the balance, that is, for more than half of total revenues. The *tertib* tax, which fell heavily on the Moroccan peasantry, accounted for about 7 per cent of *all* revenues in 1956, and one-third of all direct taxes. The French government made grants to the general budget as the occasion demanded in order to balance the budget. But the other side of the arrangement must be remembered in this connection, namely that French businesses and officials were a major beneficiary of the public expenditures made – the very expenditures which caused the deficit in the first place.

Taking the 1947-56 decade as a whole into account, it is found that allocations for development work (the 'Second Part' of the budget and the allocations to the 'Fonds de Modernisation et d'Equipement' which began to be made in 1949) accounted for about 30 per cent of all allocations under the general budget. Developmental allocations were designated as the 'extraordinary budget'. The proportion was noticeably lower in 1948, and somewhat lower in 1956, but otherwise rather steadily kept. The largest single developmental allocation in 1956 went to irrigation and agriculture (about one-third), followed by transport and communications, housing, education, energy and health – in that order. The other beneficiaries together accounted for less than 15 per cent. (We will soon have occasion to examine the size of investment in the public and private sectors in the context of the examination of the evolution of national product.)

The recurrent expenditures consumed the bulk of the general budget. Among these, the largest beneficiary was, typically, the Ministry of the Interior, followed, in that order, by finance and 'common expenditures' ('charges communes'), education, defence, public health, public works and agriculture — each of which had an allocation in excess of 5 billion francs, and together accounting for almost 85 per cent of the total.

Education and Training

Like its three Maghreb neighbours to the east, Morocco suffered the results of a policy of extreme sluggishness in the field of public education and vocational training. The French were keen on keeping the pace of education slow in order all the more easily to delay the infiltration of modern ideas and the shouldering by Moroccans of much more of the functions of their economy. However, two factors operated in the post-war years to counteract this tendency: the contact which the war had provided with other foreign groups and the promise of independence it carried, and the pressure by the Moroccan authorities to have increasing allocations directed to education. (As we have just seen, these amounted to about one-fifth of recurrent expenditures and 11 per cent of capital expenditures for 1956.)

The pressures were undoubtedly the product both of a spontaneous desire by the Moroccan political leaders to raise the level of education in the country and a response to the increasing demand by people for educational and training facilities for their children. The two forces could not but have been strengthened by the improvement in communication and contact with the outside world.

Apart from an old traditional, Islamic 'university', Al-Qarawiyin University of Fez founded in the middle of the ninth century, the protectorate had no institutions for higher education. The total student body in the public system of education (including the schools of the Alliance israélite universelle and the *franco-israélite* schools which are grouped with the public sector) rose from 309,433 to 361,979 between 1953 and 1954, then fell to 353,242 in 1955 owing mainly to a large drop in the number of students in primary and secondary Islamic schools, and a much smaller drop in the *franco-israélite* and the Alliance schools.[53] However, the year of independence witnessed a considerable expansion in the enrolment of Moslem students in the public system at all levels: from 223,827 to 335,465. As the latter figure represents the Moslem student body on 10 November 1956, it takes account of the new political situation, and no doubt reflects the new surge towards education consequent upon independence. The distribution of the school population by type and level of education, and by community, was as shown in Table 13.4 on 10 November 1956.

Before we proceed to the analysis of the data presented in Table 13.4, it ought to be pointed out that private education occupied a very minor place in the country. Thus, in all there were 10,237 pupils in private schools in 1955, but the number is shown as nil in 1956. It is not clear whether these schools were closed down, whether the statistics just ignored them, or whether they failed to record them.

The tabulated information calls for several comments. There is, first, the relative size of the three groups: Moslem Moroccan, Israelite (Jewish) Moroccan, and foreign (mainly French). To appreciate this, we have to start by defining our universe. This amounted to an estimated total of 8,720,000 inhabitants in mid-1956 in the Southern Zone which is relevant to our analysis. Of this total, 440,000 persons were non-Moroccan, and the Moroccan Jews (who had numbered about 200,000 in 1951-2) were probably fewer in

Table 13.4: School Population by Type and Level of Education, by Community, and by Sex on 10 November 1956

Type and Level	Moroccans								Foreigners						Grand Total	
		Moslems		Jews			French			Other			All Communities		
	Total	Male	Female	Total	Male	Female	Total	Male	Female	Total	Male	Female	Total	Male	Female
Higher[a]	2,477	2,274	203	272	240	32	1,024	747	277	19	15	4	3,792	3,276	516
Secondary European[b]	1,767	1,242	525	1,958	917	1,041	11,681	5,596	6,085	1,079	515	564	16,485	8,270	8,215
Secondary European: teacher training	30	30	—	16	6	10	152	94	58	8	6	2	206	136	70
Secondary technical	1,314	867	447	548	300	248	5,037	3,115	1,922	720	457	263	7,619	4,739	2,880
Secondary Moslem[c]	10,420	9,922	498	3	3	—	62	50	12	5	5	—	10,490	9,980	510
Primary European[d]	6,761	3,417	3,344	3,698	1,793	1,905	46,732	24,218	22,514	8,499	4,387	4,112	65,690	33,815	31,875
Primary Moslem[e]	312,505	225,076	87,429	509	297	212	5,741	4,329	1,412	240	215	25	318,995	229,917	89,078
Jewish: franco-israélite	97	2	95	2,474	1,073	1,401	73	17	56	133	—	133	2,777	1,092	1,685
Alliance israélite universelle[f]	94	60	34	27,752	13,950	13,802	253	139	114	367	174	193	28,466	14,323	14,143
Total	335,465	242,890	92,575	37,230	18,579	18,651	70,755	38,305	32,450	11,070	5,774	5,296	454,520	305,548	148,972

a. Includes (a) Centre d'Etudes Supérieures Scientifiques (323M, 135F), (b) Centre d'Etudes Juridiques (734M, 127F), and (c) Institut de Hautes Etudes Marocaines (2,219M, 254F).
b. Includes teacher training, but details are not given explicitly. It has been presumed here that this sub-category is designated as 'catégorie supérieure', and has been shown above as 'Secondary European: teacher training'.
c. Includes teacher training: 43 Moslem girls.
d. Includes primary vocational training:

Moslems	175 M	
	38 F	
Jewish	18 M	
	35 F	
French	709 M	
	404 F	
Other foreign	110 M	
	75 F	
Total	1,012 M	
	552 F	

e. Includes primary vocational training:

Moslems	3,820 M	
	3,542 F	
Jews	18 M	
	59 F	
French	354 M	
	104 F	
Other foreign	86 M	
	1 F	
Total	4,278 M	
	3,706 F	

f. Includes only primary and kindergartens. Also includes primary vocational training:

Moslems	4 M	
	7 F	11
Jews	497 M	
	459 F	956
French	24 M	
	24 F	48
Other foreign	8 M	
	9 F	17
Total	533 M	
	499 F	1,032

Source: *Annuaire Statistique... 1955-1956*, Part I, 'Enseignements', Table I and IV *bis*.

mid-1956 owing to the emigration of some 25,000—50,000 in the intervening period, to Israel mainly, but also to Europe.[54] Likewise, a number of foreigners, though most probably a smaller proportion, emigrated when independence came.

In the absence of any estimates of the number in November 1956, the date to which school enrolment figures relate, we can only make some free-hand estimates of the size of each community. We also assume that the potential school population constitutes some 30 per cent of the total, as this proportion falls within the age groups 5-16 years. According to our assumptions, the total and school-age populations stood as shown in Table 13.5 in November 1956.

Table 13.5: Total and School-Age Population, November 1956

Community	Total	School-Age Group
Moroccan Moslem	8,150,000	2,445,000
Jewish	175,000	52,500
Foreign	400,000	120,000
Total	8,725,000	2,617,500

It can be seen right away that the actual school enrolment was slightly over one-sixth of the school-age population. There was a discrepancy in each case, but by far the most glaring, even scandalous, case was that of Moslems. Thus, while the school attendance rate was 68.2 per cent for foreigners, and 70.9 per cent for Jews, it fell steeply to 13.7 per cent for Moroccan Moslems. This is not a condemnation of this community, although there may have been islands of hesitation or even reluctance to send children — especially girls — to schools. It is instead a stern but justified condemnation of the colonialist system which was very remiss in providing enough school facilities for the millions of Moroccans. Thus, while the European and Jewish school systems were adequate and absorbed the bulk of school-age children, the public school system designed to cater mainly to the Moroccan Moslems was scandalously inadequate, particularly far from the urban centres. There was in addition a stronger European and Jewish than Moslem motivation to send girls to school, as can be read in the enrolment data distributed by sex.

Another sad observation is the very small proportion of Moroccan Moslem children who went on from the primary to the secondary cycle. In all, there were 12,217 of these in the secondary system (European and Moslem, excluding those in secondary teacher training who numbered 30, and those in secondary technical schools who numbered 1,314). The Moslem student body in secondary schools accounted for a mere 3.8 per cent of total Moslem enrolment in the first cycle. The proportion for foreigners and Jews amounted to 20.7 and 5.7 per cent respectively. Although the proportion for the Jews was also low, it was not as low as that for the Moslems. It is possible that Jewish youth in the age groups suited for secondary education had been reduced in numbers, owing to the emigration of younger people. We have no other explanation for this phenomenon, since the total going into secondary teacher training and technical training was only 564 (16 and 548 respectively).

The third comment relates to the student body in technical and vocational training.

This totalled 9,548 in primary vocational training (7,575 Moslem, 130 Jewish and 1,843 foreign) and 7,619 in secondary technical training (1,314 Moslem, 548 Jewish and 5,757 foreign). Here again the disproportion between Moslems and foreigners was enormous, and although it may have in part reflected a reluctance on the part of Moslems to go to vocational and technical schools, essentially it reflects a failure on the part of the French to provide enough facilities and incentives for the Moroccans.

Finally, the absence of a modern national university is another cause for condemnation of the educational policy of the 'protecting power'. In this instance, as in that of pre-university education, it was the national *independent* government that took steps to correct the imbalance. Thus, as we have already indicated, in 1956 alone the enrolment of Moroccan Moslems in the two first cycles of education rose by 49.9 per cent, including a tangible increase in the proportion of girls. While it is true that the enrolment in 1955 had dropped by 4.8 per cent below that in 1954, it is also true that the notable increase in 1954 over 1953 had been of the order of 23.2 per cent. Thus 1956 marks steep acceleration in enrolment even above 1954. Furthermore, the year 1957 came to confirm the vast expansion in Moslem (including female) school enrolment, with an increase of 32.5 per cent over 1956. (The expansion was to continue in the following decade and a half.)[55] This clearly suggests that colonialism constituted in great part a constraint which reined in the Moroccans' desire for education.

Furthermore, shortage of resources could not be used as an excuse, since the protecting power was called upon to invest in education and other social services and had the means to do so: the protectorate was not merely a mine to exploit (in the figurative and literal senses alike), or a cow to milk; it was also a trust to protect and develop. An authority which could find the resources to build a modern transport system and provide its *colons* with considerable financial support, and which could invest handsomely in mining and industry, could also build the schools and health facilities needed for the development of manpower.

In self-defence, the French frequently refer to their budget support to Morocco, and to the thousands of French teachers in the European and Moroccan school systems, as evidence of good-will and a sense of educational (and other developmental) responsibility. The budget support (for recurrent and/or developmental expenditures) and the engagement of Frenchmen in teaching are undeniable facts (though a considerable proportion of the funds for the capital budget had originated in Marshall Plan post-war transfers). However, the relevant question here relates to the motivation behind these facts, and to their degree of adequacy in the face of the enormity of the country's needs. Naturally, the trust of 'protecting' Morocco was not only to involve a one-way flow of benefits: northwards to France, but a two-way flow.[56]

Education in Morocco faced a number of problems like those faced by its counterpart in the other Maghreb countries: inadequacy of school facilities, shortage of national teaching personnel and the resort to French teachers in large numbers to fill the gap, and the language of instruction. With respect to the last point, Morocco was less handicapped than Algeria where French was made to replace Arabic much more drastically. None the less, Arabic was placed in a position distinctly more modest than it deserved. For, though the population comprised a large component of Berbers who had their own dialect (or dialects), most of these spoke Arabic, and many of the educated Berbers had received their education through the medium of Arabic.

Morocco had the unsettling experience of two languages struggling for supremacy, which in some instances resulted superficially in a happy marriage that produced bilingualism.

Yet no doubt this marriage carried with it the strains and pulls of two cultures each claiming full or at least main allegiance, and each trying to have the mental constructs of the bilingual Moroccan formed in its own medium. In addition to this, there was the struggle for use as a *de facto* official language in government publications, and as the language in book-keeping records and other correspondence in the private sector, as in everyday conversation. While being national Moroccan, these problems had a significance that went beyond national frontiers, in the sense that they related also to Morocco's identification with the Arab and Islamic worlds, an identification that suffered distortion to the extent that Arabic was suppressed and French boosted as a language of instruction, government usage and general intercourse.

One final point which is related to education will be made to render more concrete the evidence of the failure of the French to prepare the population for self-rule, in contrast with their considerable work in agriculture (mainly irrigation), mining, transport, industry and power, and housing and urban utilities — even if this work was largely motivated by self-interest. We refer here to the civil service. Although official information is not available, careful students of the period all agree that this service was predominantly French. The verdict is best summed up by Waterston, who says:

> When the Protectorate ended in March 1956, about 40,000 Frenchman were occupying most of the posts, often down to minor positions, in government. An additional 10,000 held important positions in public and semi-public agencies operating public utilities, railroads, and ports.[57]

Obviously, the failure should also extend to take account of the shortage of skilled Moroccans to replace many of the tens of thousands of Europeans who worked in different capacities and at various levels of skill in sectors other than the civil service and public utilities. One point needs special mention here; this is the recourse to French teachers. This was obviously necessary, in view of the shortage of Moroccan teachers. But the shortage itself should be regretted as a shortcoming on the part of the French. It is not clear if Waterston had included the teachers in the estimate of 40,000 Frenchmen in the civil service. In any case, it is useful to indicate the size of the teacher body. Thus, 5,132 French teachers were engaged in European schools and in Moslem schools, in addition to 309 in Jewish schools — as against 5,805 and 592 Moroccans respectively.[58]

There can be few, if any, attenuating circumstances for a 'protecting power' that fails to train nationals, after 44 years of rule, to man a sizeable proportion of government and teaching posts, and of the administrative and technical manpower of the modern sector. This failure was not an isolated phenomenon connected solely with the political and administrative management of the country. For there is enough evidence to prove that apart from leaving the Sultan some prestige and certain outward trimmings of supremacy (but very little of the real political power which the Resident-General and the French government in Metropolitan France exercised in Moroccan affairs), the French tried not to 'disturb' the political and social structure. This was deliberate. It was designed to create the impression of minimal interference in internal affairs, but in fact it was meant to minimise *effective* political expectations by the élite. To soothe, or more honestly to bribe, the Moroccan élite was necessary and proved feasible. Even those elements in the élite that had the opportunity of education were made to desire to identify with the French, to emulate them culturally, socially, and in modes of thought and ways of life. The mechanism was the discriminate award of favours, whether in the form of land, irrigation water, government posts, 'accept-

Morocco

ance' by the ruling French socially, or political *entrée* and a listening ear to the requests of the élite.

It is no wonder therefore that one careful scholar is able to say:

> Morocco is unique in that so much of the traditional governmental and political system survived the half century of direct French rule relatively intact. Certain social groups, such as the tribes or the urban bourgeoisie, were in many instances carefully protected by the French, and even the sultan was, in a way, put in mothballs, to be resurrected at the time of independence in 1955.

Linking this observation with the attitudes in the independence era, the writer goes on to say: 'Many habits of political action that had yet to be unlearned seemed peculiarly appropriate in the post-protectorate years.'[59]

Economic Growth

It is now necessary to look at the course of growth of national product in the pre-independence decade, in order to appreciate the combined effect of the factors so far examined, plus others that have not received attention in this section. However, the examination will be brief, because it promises to be more meaningful to examine the course for the whole period for which information is now available, namely 1951-73, in the next section.

There is a handicap to contend with in respect to the years 1951-6. This is that the data available vary and make comparison difficult. Thus, the earliest series on hand appears in the *Annuaire Statistique du Maroc 1955-1956*, for the years 1951-7. But the series is presented here in terms of current prices. On the other hand, there is a series in the FAO report on Morocco for the same years, but at constant 1952 prices.[60] Presumably the GDP for 1952 should be equal in both series, but instead there is a difference of 29 billion francs. A more recent series is presented in IMF's *International Financial Statistics, Supplement to 1967/68 Issues*, but here again the data are different from those in either of the series just referred to. Both this series and the population data published in conjunction with it refer to the whole of Morocco, not just the Southern Zone (or French protectorate) to which the two other series for 1951-7 refer.[61] As the *IFS* series is the most recent of the three and as later issues of the *IFS* provide us with data stretching from 1952 to 1973, we have opted for the national accounts as they appear in this publication.

The 1951-73 series will be reproduced in full in the next section. (Actually, the *IFS* starts with 1952.) It is sufficient here to attempt three tasks: to examine the magnitude of the growth achieved from 1951 to 1956; to explore the factors behind and the mechanisms influencing this growth (including a brief reference to planning, leaving to a later section the more careful examination of planning); and to acquire more intimate understanding of the dualism in the economy, and how the inherent differences between the modern and the traditional sectors reflected themselves in sectoral incomes and income distribution between Moroccans and Europeans.

According to the *IFS* series, gross domestic product at current prices rose from 6.08 billion dirhams in 1952 to 6.92 billion in 1955 and 7.49 billion in 1956. (The dirham was introduced in October 1959, as equal to 100 old Moroccan (or French) francs. Its use before 1959 is merely to provide continuity and uniformity in the data.) This represents a total net rise of 13.8 per cent between 1952 and 1955, and of 23.2 per cent through 1956. (As we have been designating 1956 as the year of independence, we will treat it here as the terminal year in the era under examination, especially as the development plan then in implementation was to run till 1957; and outlays under this plan continued in spite of formal independence.) The cost-of-living index rose by 10.8 per cent during the period 1952-6, while the price index is reported by the *IFS Supplement* to have remained unchanged. There is reason to distrust the former for pre-independence years, though for subsequent years its quality improved and it moved roughly along the same path as that of the price index. Consequently we will try to reconcile the two indices for deflating the GDP. Though arbitrary, this measure gives this writer greater confidence in the results than the use of either index by itself.

Consequently, the growth of GDP at current prices will be deflated by 5 per cent for the years 1952-6. The result will be a total growth of 17.3 per cent in real terms, or about 4 per cent per annum on the average. However, this result needs some qualification, as the years 1952 and 1953, and to a lesser extent 1954, benefited from the sharp rise in the selling price of minerals as a result of the Korean war, while the years 1955 and 1956 (and subsequently 1957) felt the adverse effect of approaching independence on investment, foreign exchange availability, and national product. Indeed, GDP dropped consistently from 1954 to 1955, then to 1956 (and to 1957) according to the FAO series already referred to. (The *IFS* series confirms this course except for 1956 when a positive real growth of 2.4 per cent is reported.) It is essential to add that data are not available for the years earlier than 1951. But it is generally believed that were the eleven years 1946-56 to be taken together, the sluggishness witnessed in the last two or three years would be less damaging to the average rate of growth than it proves to be in the context of the shorter period 1952-6. It would therefore be warranted to suggest that the rate of real growth for the whole period 1946-56 could not have been less than 5 per cent. Indeed, this rate is often quoted in the literature. It is quite credible in the judgement of this writer. Furthermore, it is creditable for the period concerned, as few Arab countries achieved such a rate in a comparable phase of their recent economic history.

The rate of population increase in the years under survey is said to have been 2 per cent per annum on the average, that is, much below the level it came to reach in the succeeding years until the present. According to official estimates, the population of the French protectorate alone increased by 716,000 from the census of 1951/2 (when the total was 8,004,000) to the middle of 1956, when the total was estimated at 8,720,000.[62] This constitutes a net total increase of 8.9 per cent, or about 2.1 or 2.2 per cent per annum on the average.

However, what is relevant for our purposes is to assess the rate of population increase for the country as a whole, not just the Southern Zone (the French protectorate), as the GDP data adopted by us relate to the whole country. According to the *IFS Supplement to 1967/68*, which is the source of the long GDP series to be adopted here, the population rose from 9.3m in 1952 to 10.4m in 1956. This seems to be overestimated, if compared with the estimate of 10m for mid-1956 as recorded in the *Annuaire Statistique... 1955-1956* (already referred to). The *IFS* estimates, adjusted to take into account the increase from mid-1956 to December 1956, show a net total increase of 11.8 per cent, of 2.8 per cent per annum. Though high for those days, this rate is more consistent with the very high rate, hovering around 3.2 or 3.3 per cent, that prevails now, than the low rates of 2—2.2 per cent often quoted for the mid-fifties. This judgement is based essentially on the unlikely premiss that the net rate has risen by 1 or 1.2 per cent in 10 or 15 years, even assuming improvement in sanitation and hygiene. (As a matter of fact, no tangible improvement occurred, as the country lost a large number of physicians and medical technicians in the years imme-

Morocco 605

diately following independence.)

Consistent with the adoption of the GDP and population data in the *IFS* (but with the adjustment of population size to agree with the official mid-1956 estimate), the GDP for 1956 in real terms (that is, deflated only slightly for price increases) would be about 7.13 billion dirhams while population stood at 10.2m. Thus, GDP *per capita* would have risen from 65,376.3 old francs (or $186.8 at the rate of 350 francs/dirhams to the US dollar) for 1952, to 70,000 old francs (or $200) for 1956. This represents 7.1 per cent growth *per capita* for the period, or about 1.75 per cent per annum on the average. But were the rate of growth of 5 per cent suggested for the *whole* post-war period to be taken as the base of calculation, the *per capita* rate of growth would amount to 2.7 per cent on the average. This would constitute a satisfactory record for the period under discussion. It ought to be remembered, though, that an average income of about $200 *per capita* was far from being representative of the income received by the mass of the population. However, we will have occasion shortly to examine the question of income distribution and its unevenness.

Investment and Planning

Information on investment by the private and public sectors separately is available at constant (1952) prices for the years 1951-7, but without a breakdown by sector. A second source gives total gross investment at current prices made over the same years, but with a very large difference from the data in the first source. Yet a third source gives another set of figures, covering the years 1949-57 for the public sector alone (excluding quasi-public authorities), which differs from either of the two other sets. No explanation is available which makes a reconciliation of these three sets possible.[63] Given this confusion, we will present here the first set (the FAO data) for the years 1951-6, and compare its particulars aggregated for the whole economy with the data in the second *(Annuaire Statistique . . . 1955-1956)* source, and finally we will present the information in the third source (Waterston) within the context of *planned* investment in the public sector.

The FAO data of gross fixed investment are given in Table 13.6.

Table 13.6: Gross Investment by Source, 1949-57 (billion francs at 1952 prices)

Year	Private	Public	Total	Per Cent of GDP
1949	n.a.	n.a.	92.1	
1950	n.a.	n.a.	n.a.	
1951	93.0	27.0	120.0	24.7
1952	98.0	28.0	126.0	24.4
1953	87.0	25.0	112.0	19.7
1954	77.0	28.0	105.0	17.9
1955	65.0	27.0	92.0	15.9
1956	44.0	27.0	71.0	12.5
1957	34.0	19.0	53.0	10.1
Average 1951-56			104.3	19.2
1951-57			97.0	17.5

The totals are quite suggestive of the direct association between the political mood and the volume of private sector investments. The consistent decline in this volume, except for 1952 when the Korean war boosted expectations in the high profits of mineral exports, is adequate testimony to our assertion. However, public investment was less sensitive to psychological factors and profit expectations, and expresses an autonomous, deliberate policy position. The volume of investment by this sector continued largely unchanged, except for 1957 when Morocco had to depend relatively and absolutely less on French loans and grants-in-aid.

It remains to be added that the average investment for the years 1951-6, which amounted to 19.2 per cent of GDP (all in real terms), produced a rate of real growth, as we saw earlier, of about 4 per cent per annum on the average. These results suggest an inordinately high capital-output ratio. But this is largely explainable in the relatively large proportion of investment directed to infrastructure, both economic and social. Investments in this field have slow fruition, even when output is easily imputable to investment. As we will have occasion to see presently, a large proportion of investment, whether private or public, originated outside Moroccan territory, either in the sense that the resources came directly from France (or via France), or that a large part of investment decisions (which belonged to the modern sector) were made by Frenchmen residing in Morocco, but taking into account their economic interests in and connections with mother establishments in Metropolitan France, and thus moving their funds back and forth in that fashion which seemed to them to optimise the returns.

The total investments made over the years 1951-6 amounted in real terms to 626 billion francs according to the FAO data (or to 679 billion, if 1957 is included). Against this, *Annuaire Statistique . . . 1955-1956* records a total investment of 664.7 billion francs (or 740.4 billion) respectively, but at current prices. The difference more or less accounts for the rise in the cost of living. However, year-by-year variations are noticeably larger than the net difference for the whole period would suggest. The largest discrepancy is to be found instead between the first two sources, on the one hand, and the data in Waterston, on the other. Thus, according to the third set of data, public actual investments over the years 1949 to 1953 amounted to 146.3 billion francs, while those planned for the years 1954 to 1957 totalled 224.7 billion. Together the two investment programmes total 371 billion francs.

It is not possible to compare this last total with the totals in either of the first two sets, as the years covered are not comparable. However, we can contrast the investment data for the years 1954-7, which are common to all three sets. According to the FAO data, public investments for these four years totalled 101 billion francs – a sum which is much smaller than that in Waterston. Likewise, if we consider total investment as recorded in *Annuaire Statistique . . .1955-1956,* and deduct from it private investment (duly adjusted for price increases) as recorded in the FAO publication, we would still come up with a large discrepancy. It can only be surmised that there actually was a serious shortfall between planned and achieved investment in the years 1954-7, which is a perfectly legitimate development to expect for those years, with political uncertainty and psychological hesitation resulting in economic shrinkage.

The two investment programmes detailed in Waterston constituted the first and second Plan de Modernisation et d'Equipement, the first spreading over the years 1949-52, but later extended to cover 1953 in order to complete the projected investment, and the latter spreading over the years 1954-7. The total outlay involved was, as already indicated, 371 billion francs. The programming was made possible when in 1948 funds were made available by the Marshall Plan for the three North African countries (to the tune of 375 billion francs). The programmes involved the public sector only, but it was hoped that the substantial investment to be made in infrastructure under the two plans would provide strong promotive encouragement to private investors. Consistent with this expectation, industry was largely left out as the preserve of private entrepreneurs. Other features of the programmes are clear from Table 13.7.

Table 13.7: Investment Programmes of the Modernisation and Investment Plans 1949-53 and 1954-57 (in billions of current francs)

Sector	First Plan Total	First Plan Per Cent of Total	Second Plan Total	Second Plan Per Cent of Total	Both Plans Total	Both Plans Per Cent of Total
Transportation	32.5	22.2	27.3	12.1	59.8	16.1
Communications	10.0	6.9	9.7	4.3	19.7	5.3
Irrigation	27.7	18.9	40.7	18.1	68.4	18.4
Electric power	21.3	14.6	19.5[a]	8.7	40.8	11.0
Agriculture and forestry	6.3	4.3	32.0	14.2	38.3	10.3
Fishing, merchant marine and industry	—	—	1.3	0.6	1.3	0.4
Mining	2.2	1.5	12.7	5.7	14.9	4.0
Education	17.6	12.0	15.8	7.0	33.4	9.0
Housing	10.0	6.8	29.2	13.0	39.2	10.6
Public health	9.1	6.2	8.0	3.6	17.1	4.6
Public buildings	6.2	4.3	8.5	3.8	14.7	4.0
Municipal works	—	—	19.6	8.7	19.6	5.3
Miscellaneous	3.4	2.3	0.4[b]	0.2	3.8	1.0
Total	146.3	100.0	224.7	100.0	371.0	100.0

a. In the Second Plan this item includes coal and oil as well.
b. In the Second Plan this item is specified as 'tourism'.

Source: Albert Waterston, *Planning in Morocco: Organization and Implementation* (Baltimore, 1962), Appendix A for the First Plan, and Appendix B for the Second Plan, quoting *Deuxième Plan de Modernisation et d'Equipement*, p. 335, Table b, and pp. 289-97 respectively.

The third task set for this part of the discussion is to examine the distribution of income by community and by type (that is, whether modern or traditional). The two are not unrelated, as the Europeans virtually owned and controlled the modern sector, while the traditional sector was virtually all Moroccan.

We have had occasion to refer to the relative shares of the two sectors in agricultural production, and in certain other fields of activity. Understandably, estimates cannot be very precise because of definitional difficulties, the existence of a certain overlap in some border areas of activity, and the greater poverty in statistical information where the traditional sector is concerned — whether because it is largely a subsistence sector, or because it relates to outlying regions rather far from the arm of the statistician, or for other reasons. It is therefore no wonder that estimates of the respective shares in production vary. Thus, Amin,

Stewart and Waterston, to whom we have had repeated occasion to refer, have different estimates, although the general drift of their observations is the same. These writers are also in agreement regarding the nature of the causes behind the difference in the performance of the two sectors, whether these are political-institutional, technological, financial, organisational or attitudinal.

Notwithstanding the caution necessitated here in the nature of the question, it is well worth quoting an attempt made in the FAO report on Morocco already referred to, with respect to the contribution of each of the sectors to GDP, and the share of each in the labour force, as an average for the three years 1952-4.[64] The findings are summarised in Table 13.8 as tabulated in the report, in relative rather than in absolute terms.

Table 13.8: Comparison between the Modern and the Traditional Sectors

Sector	Share in GDP 1952-4 Average	Share in Labour Force, 1952		
		Moroccans[a]	Europeans	Total
Modern Sector	67.9	26.0	100.0	29.3
Agriculture etc.	5.8	2.4	7.1	2.6
Mining	5.6	1.2	3.3	1.3
Manufacturing industry[b]	12.8	2.9[c]	23.6	3.8
Building and construction	8.3	3.1	6.6	3.3
Electricity, water	1.1	–	1.5	0.1
Transport and communications, trade	27.7	13.4	35.9	14.4
Administration and defence	6.5	3.0	22.1	3.8
Traditional Sector	32.1	74.0	–	70.7
Urban traditional handicrafts	2.7	5.2	–	4.9
Moroccan agriculture:				
Market	8.8[d]	68.8	–	65.7
Subsistence	20.5[d]			
Total both sectors[e]	100.0	100.0	100.0	100.0
	Billion francs	Thousands		
Modern sector	377	755.0	135.8	890.8
Traditional sector	178	2,145.0	–	2,145.0
Total	555	2,900.0	135.8	3,035.8

a. Both Moslem and Jewish.
b. An estimate, since data on manufacturing industry and handicrafts had been combined in the original source. (See Source below.)
c. Of whom 35,000 to 40,000 have permanent employment.
d. On the assumption that 30 per cent of the produce is for the market.
e. Totals do not all add because of rounding.

Source: FAO, *Maroc*, Table II-7, p. II-54. Source presents data in monetary and manpower terms only. The calculations for percentages are the writer's.

Table 13.8 is quite eloquent in expressing the imbalance in the economy and society. Thus, although the modern sector contributes two-thirds of GDP, it is mainly owned and operated by Europeans, the participation of Moroccans in this sector being minimal both in the sense that only a quarter of the active Moroccan population is engaged in this sector, and that there are relatively fewer Moroccans than Europeans engaged in each of the activities in the modern sector. As against this, the whole European active population is engaged in the modern sector, and all those engaged in the traditional sector are Moroccans. The latter group constitutes about three-quarters of the Moroccan labour force, and produces about one-third of GDP.

Another pertinent observation is that more than two-thirds of the whole active Moroccan population are engaged in agriculture, with a large majority of these in the subsistence subsector of agriculture. There is no breakdown of the 68.8 per cent of Moroccans in agriculture between the market and the subsistence subsectors, but it can safely be assumed that the activities of most of these are still conducted on a barter, non-monetised basis. In fact, it can also safely be assumed that the agricultural production of the 1,995,000 Moroccans in traditional agriculture could be undertaken by less than a quarter of these were they to have the means and methods that workers in the modern sector have. The implications of this are serious and enormous: the situation shelters a state of massive disguised unemployment (and considerable underemployment); furthermore, were the techniques of cultivation and related operations to improve, and the necessary capital and servicing institutions and resources to become adequate, the country would be faced with a problem of starkly undisguised (as well as disguised) unemployment of truly unmanageable proportions in the short and medium term.

There is no need to draw inferences in detail through a sector-by-sector analysis. But it is necessary in conclusion to draw attention to the fact that the modern sector, which engages the whole of the European labour force, was weakly related to the traditional sector, interacting with it minimally. And, furthermore, the European community which wielded such enormous economic (and political) power in the country, constituted only 5 per cent of the total population in the mid-fifties, and owned about one-eighth of cultivable land.

The picture becomes more complete if we go beyond the aggregates presented in Table 13.8 to examine the average income of members of the various work groups. Here again, estimates vary, but agree with respect to the general pattern prevailing. According to Waterston, the output of one farmer in modern agriculture was about 500,000 francs, while that of the farmer in traditional agriculture was less than 30,000. Even traditional craftsmen whose income was higher than that of farmers, and of the national average of 80,000 francs, earned less than Moroccan workers in mining or industry whose average income was two-and-a-half to three times as high. But even the latter, relatively privileged group had an average income well below that of Europeans engaged in the *same* fields of activity. Amin reaches much more drastic conclusions, but ones with the same general drift. According to him, the average income of non-Moslems was 305,000 francs per head in 1955, while that of Moslems was a little over 44,000 francs (32,000 for rural and 61,000 for non-rural workers). In addition, the average for Moroccans is misleading, inasmuch as it conceals serious maldistribution. In practice, the bulk of the rural population and the urban proletariat received an income per head much below the community average.

The same pattern applied in Algeria and Tunisia, though the levels for each category were slightly lower than in Morocco. Likewise, the three countries had more or less the same pattern of urban stratification with regard to the distribution of the labour force in the various sectors, and the distribution of the workers in each sector among manual and other unskilled or minimally skilled workers, white-collar workers, middle-income groups and upper-income groups. Invariably, the upper-income group was much more thinly populated than its European counterpart.[65]

The protectorate era came to an end on 2 March 1956, and an economic stock-taking at that moment would have found Morocco burdened with a heavy colonialist legacy, but also well-equipped physically in several parts of its infrastructure, and relatively well-endowed in land, water and minerals. Where it was least satisfactorily equipped was precisely in those areas which constitute a *sine qua non* for development: a well-educated population and trained and experienced manpower, a large enough civil service well-prepared for its many tasks, a development-oriented political leadership with the power *and* the desire to curb the pressures of the political élite to continue enjoying favours and privileges and power well beyond its size or right.

Still, compared with its two Maghreb sisters ruled by France, Morocco found itself with the advantage in 1955-6 of a slightly better economic performance. Amin presents data that indicate in all their aspects (except that of a higher rate of population increase in Morocco than in Tunisia and Algeria) a tangible advantage for Morocco. The annual rate of growth in each of the Maghreb countries is shown in Table 13.9.

Table 13.9: Annual Growth Rate, Algeria, Tunisia and Morocco (per cent)

	Algeria 1880-1955	Tunisia 1910-55	Morocco 1920-55
Agriculture	1.5	2.0	2.6
Industry	3.1	3.1	6.0
Services	2.0	2.4	3.7
Total production	1.9	2.5	3.7
Population	1.6	1.8	2.0
Production per head	0.3	0.7	1.7

Source: Samir Amin, *The Maghreb in the Modern World: Algeria, Tunisia, Morocco* (Penguin Books, 1970), p. 46, table.

This advantage by itself, given the other factors of physical endowment and infrastructure, ought to have enabled Morocco to maintain and consolidate its lead. Algeria's considerable gas and oil resources that were in the sixties and early seventies to give its economy a great push forward are certainly a new factor that was not in the picture before 1955. But, as the years since 1956 have proved, Morocco's performance has not kept pace with its good start. The evidence of this and why it has occurred will occupy us in the next section, even though deeper insight into the causes for the slowing down or even stagnation in the Moroccan economy will be gained in the analysis to come in Volume II of this study. For the present, it is enough to say that Morocco has not capitalised on the modest advantage it had by the end of 1955, and that this was probably not beyond the control of its decision-makers.

2. DECOLONISATION MOROCCAN STYLE

The Moroccan economy did not, and could not, proceed on its independent course in March 1956, like a ship suddenly controlled by a new captain with a new destination and a new navigation map. The links that tied the newly independent economy to its colonialist past were too strong to be abruptly severed.

More significantly, the 'new captain' did not want the links to be abruptly severed. Independent Morocco, or more precisely the new political leadership, now master of its own affairs in economic and other fields (at least outwardly and superficially) did not believe in sudden and sharp alterations in the course of the economy's motion; instead, this leadership distrusted abrupt *de facto* decolonisation while insisting on a clear-cut *de jure* decolonisation. In other words, they feared the disruptive and adverse large-scale exodus of French (and other European) residents on whom the economy had so heavily depended in all its leading sectors, and at most administrative and technical levels, both in government and in the private sector of the economy. It equally feared a greater drop in investment and a larger outflow of capital than had occurred in 1954-6.

The same attitude applied to the Moroccanisation of productive assets: the transfer of *colon* land to Moroccan hands, and the transfer likewise of industrial and other interests to Moroccan or mainly Moroccan ownership. The government preferred a slow process of transfer, in order to minimise the shock to the economy and the loss of the manpower and skills, the capital and the technology, and possibly the lucrative market connections which the colonialist relationship had provided. This amounted to taking a calculated risk, and the authorities felt that the 'gain and loss' analysis of the two courses of action open to them indicated that the loss would be minimised if decolonisation proceeded slowly and the European community was frightened minimally.

Likewise, the leadership was careful not to scare the Jewish community and make it opt for emigration: as it was, a substantial number of Jews, with a heavy concentration of persons in the age brackets of economic (and military) activity had emigrated to Israel. The number is estimated at 50,000 from the establishment of Israel in 1948 to 1956. The authorities wanted the Jews to stay for two reasons. First, because they were Moroccan nationals, and on grounds of principle the government wanted them to feel as sheltered and secure as Moroccan Moslems were. This desire was made concrete in official policies and attitude, despite some hostility among the population, beginning with the establishment of Israel and the expulsion of a large proportion of the Arabs from Palestine, then during the tripartite – British/French/Israeli – attack on Egypt in October 1956, later during the Arab-Israeli June war of 1967, and finally during the October war of 1973. The second consideration was one of pragmatism. The government was aware of the value of the skills of the Jewish community, particularly in the fields of finance, trade, office management and accounting, and craftsmanship. This value went clearly beyond the community's relative size.

The same pragmatism characterised the official approach to Arabisation, or the substitution of Arabic for French as a language of instruction, government records and correspondence, as well as a commercial medium in the private sector, and as the medium of conversation among the inhabitants, especially the middle and upper classes.

However, all along, the pragmatism which was adopted under economic and administrative motivation, that is, on grounds of economic and administrative self-interest, was in sharp contrast with the nationalist urge to speed the process of Moroccanisation and Arabisation, and in some contrast with the desire of part of the moneyed classes to buy out the

Europeans and take possession of their properties at reduced prices. The political pressure for speed came from within the ruling circles, but much more so from the ranks of the opposition whose message wove together the two main strands of nationalism and radicalism, with nationalism taking into account not just Moroccan but Arab nationalism at large, and with radicalism based on the premiss that only with true economic independence could the exploitation and greed of colonialism be curbed and the genuine and rightful socio-economic interests of the masses promoted and assured.

The two forces of pragmatism on the one hand, and nationalism-cum-radicalism on the other hand, pulled in opposite directions in 1956 under King Mohammed V, as they do today under his son King Hassan II. However, it can be argued forcefully that the contradiction was more superficial or illusory than real. Indeed, the relationship of the two forces is, or ought to be seen as being, of a dialectical nature, since what seems outwardly an irreconcilable conflict between the two is no more than a mutual challenge which can ultimately lead to accommodation and interaction embodied in one strand of policy. It seems to this writer quite clear that the plea for pragmatism arising from concern over the immediate problems fails to take into account the longer-term interests of the society and economy, and amounts to a shying away from the creative challenges of Moroccanisation and Arabisation. On the other hand, the plea for nationalism/radicalism can also become counter-productive if it does not keep sight of the concrete problems that an over-speedy process of Moroccanisation and Arabisation would necessarily bring to the fore. It is perhaps the failure to achieve the appropriate synthesis, and in effect (though not in official pronouncements) the precedence given to pragmatism, that is behind the indecision in the mapping of the society's and economy's course of action, and in the movement along that course. The failure is also probably essentially answerable for an economic and social performance since 1956 which is less creditworthy than would have been expected given the country's start in the pre-independence decade. It is to the manifestations of the indecisiveness of the course of decolonisation that we will now turn.

The first of these manifestations is the persistent demographic composition of the population. It is seen in this connection, according to the census of 1960, that four years after independence, there were still 395,893 non-Moroccans residing in the country, including 175,090 Frenchmen, 92,901 Spaniards and 93,026 Algerians. (The Moroccan population included 162,420 Jews.)[66] Thus the European community totalled some 268,000, or over half its size at the time of independence. This suggests a slow exodus of non-Arab foreigners, distinctly unlike the process that was to be experienced in Algeria shortly afterwards. Even by the time of the census of July 1971, there were still 112,000 foreigners in the country.[67]

It is noteworthy that 93 per cent of the French and Spanish residents were in urban centres but this component, although very large for the two groups of Europeans, constituted only 7.3 per cent of the total urban population in Morocco. (This points to the fast urbanisation of the Moslem population over the short span of four years of independence.) The urban European community was still active in the same fields as before, though in different proportions. There were still some 20,000 in government service according to one estimate,[68] and many in mining, energy, manufacturing establishments and the liberal professions, as well as owners of larger farms.

Despite the energetic steps taken in the field of education, the country stood as a net loser with respect to many skills, owing to the inability to train replacements for the Europeans who left — let alone improving on the ratio of these skills to total population. The country suffered most with regard to professional men (notably physicians and medical technicians) and teachers. Many physicians had left, leaving behind one to every 10,000 inhabitants. Furthermore, Moroccan physicians constituted then a very small proportion of the total, and medical students training abroad in France and Spain totalled only 150 at that time.[69] What made matters still worse was the very uneven distribution of physicians (as of dentists, pharmacists, qualified midwives and nurses, and medical technicians). These were heavily concentrated in cities, and among the cities, heavily concentrated in Casablanca. The drop in medical and related personnel can be seen from Table 13.10. Only the number of physicians rose by 1971 to exceed what it had been at the end of 1955.

Table 13.10: Numbers of Medical Personnel, 1955-71

	Doctors	Dentists	Pharmacists	Midwives
Number on 31 December 1955	948	169	364	100
31 December 1956	866	175	347	102
31 December 1971	1,218	163	345	61

Sources: *Annuaire Statistique... 1955-1956*, pp. 108 and 109, and *Annuaire Statistique... 1971*, pp. 29 and 30.

The exodus of Frenchmen particularly was an illustration of the inability to acclimatise to new political realities: psychologically to adjust to a situation of an ordinary resident, after having been a member of the ruling group. This was true of most Frenchmen, though it was also true that prospering economic conditions in France at the time had a pull effect on many Frenchmen overseas.

Decolonisation in the agricultural sector was considerably slower. It never took the form of official policy, translated in legislation, and executed. But it is none the less known that quite a sizeable proportion of French-held rural land has passed to Moroccan hands on a private basis. The buyers have been mostly urban people, and are basically absentee landlords. Even when the radical National Union of Popular Forces was briefly in power in 1960, it was unable to expropriate foreign landowners. Afraid of such a measure, the 3,000-odd French landowners acted quickly and, with the support of the French government, managed to obtain assurances from the government with regard to the safety of their ownerships. Nor have these landowners been menaced by land reform involving the setting of a low ceiling on ownership, since no such reform had by then (or, for that matter, ever) been decreed. The only land reform measures taken have referred to rain-fed government land, and to irrigation schemes on public land. Indeed, it was only in March 1973 that the government 'announced that 250,000 hectares of agricultural land owned by foreigners would be nationalized. About 2,000 settlers, mostly French, are involved.'[70] The source reporting the nationalisation goes on to say: 'The question of compensation is still being studied, so that the nationalization decree will take effect only when a policy on compensation has been drawn up.' By the summer of 1974, this policy was not yet laid down. It remains to be added that the nationalisation decree suggests that about three-quarters of formerly foreign-held land had already passed hands through private arrangements.

The impact of decolonisation has had two aspects: one favourable to Moroccans, in that it provided them with housing units, good, well-developed land, shares in industrial and other establishments, greater scope for work in the field of professions and of teaching, and more posts in the civil service. The other aspect is unfavourable, to the extent that a variety of skills became in short supply, even if at a slow pace, thus causing hardship economically, socially, and in public administration. What made the shortage more serious was the sluggishness of Morocco's response to the challenge of decolonisation. This attitude stands in contrast with that of Algeria and even of Tunisia, much to the chagrin of a large body of articulate intellectuals, trade unionists, students, and lower-middle-class educated Moroccans.

The slowness to take the challenge afforded by independence and to develop manpower skills and take over the productive assets owned by the Europeans made Morocco miss a golden opportunity. This is probably behind the feeling of general loss in the years immediately following independence, and the absence of a feeling of mission. These factors have had a tangible effect on the performance of the economy, which was outright low in the few years after 1956, and which has only recently begun to become satisfactory. However, in fairness, it ought to be added that neither of the two other Maghreb countries formerly under French rule was successful in shaking off the effect of colonisation and in marking good economic progress before the passage of three or four years after independence.

3. THE ECONOMY 1956-74

The 19 years of independence 1956-74 will be treated together in the context of the examination of economic developments in the country. Morocco has not witnessed changes of marked significance which can constitute turning points for the economy and which therefore justify the division of the period into distinct phases. This is not to say that the independence era is a smooth uniform stretch of time. During this era, King Hassan II ascended the throne in January 1961, upon the death of his father Mohammed V. This political landmark almost overlapped with an economic landmark: the introduction in November 1960 of the Five-Year Plan 1960-64. The Plan is considered a landmark by observers as well as by the planning authorities themselves, who said in a 'Note aux Lecteurs' in the Plan document:

> The Five-Year Plan 1960-64 can be considered as the first Moroccan experience with true economic planning, going in fact beyond the stage of simple multi-annual programmes of investment, [based] on public funds such as the last four-year plans carried out under the Protectorate or the two-year transitional plan 1958-1959 ...[71]

The *dahir* dated 17 November 1960 (the Plan Law) was the beginning of a new phase in the development effort of the country — a phase which not only was to be marked by a somewhat more satisfactory economic performance than the years 1956 to 1960 or 1961, but also one which was characterised by more serious planning and improvement in the techniques of planning, and plan evaluation. On the political level, the *dahir* was one of the last major measures to be taken by King Mohammed V, while the execution of the Plan was one of the first tasks to which the new king turned his attention.

No other attempt will be made here to suggest the parcelling of the independence period into stages. The few spells of violent political strife will not occupy us, even though they have had a direct bearing on the investment and expectations climate prevailing. In the rest of this section we will examine the major developments in the economy, including structural and institutional changes, and we will assess both the promotive and the inhibiting factors in the course of development. Planning will occupy the following section.[72]

Morocco was ushered into independence basically somewhat better off in certain respects than many other former colonies upon the disappearance of the colonial power — whether this power called the territory under its rule a colony, a mandated area, a protectorate or a dominion. Yet Morocco found itself among those Arab countries left with one of the heaviest legacies: a deteriorating situation during the last pre-independence years summed up in the stagnation and then the decline in national product at constant prices; a flight of foreign (and some domestic) capital of grave dimensions; a large drop in investment which was to adversely influence the course of growth for a few years to come; the exodus of technicians, administrators and teachers, and of businessmen in the various sectors, which, though not taking the form of a stampede, was harmful to the economy none the less (and which, equally bad, was to be compensated for from domestic human resources only slowly); a distinct rise in the already high levels of unemployment and underemployment; and a voluminous exodus from the countryside to the urban centres before these could be prepared for an inflow of the size experienced.[73]

These core problems were to beset the economy for years. While the flight of capital, the drop in gross investment and the exodus of Europeans were problems of a more transitory nature, the other problems have proved more intractable. However, that was not all. Certain new impediments to development emerged along with, and in some instances because of, the passing of political power from foreign to national hands. Thus, the shortage of resources for investment continues to plague the efforts to achieve substantial growth and to make necessary the resort to considerable foreign financing with all that this entails in the encumbrance of political strings and the burden of debt-servicing. Greater attention to health conditions and to education has led to a drop in death rates, but has also led to an inordinately high and demanding net increase in population, estimated currently at no less than 3.3 per cent per annum. The political unrest and the slowness to achieve political consensus around basic national questions (including among others decolonisation and Arabisation) have likewise added new and very serious burdens that slow down the movement towards greater development.

Finally, a certain degree of indecisiveness earlier on with respect to the objectives and strategies of development has slowed down the pace of industrialisation. There is no need to proceed further with the cataloguing of the 'growing and independence pains' of Morocco. Yet the assertion with regard to the existence and persistence of these pains must not be construed to mean a denial of the success in several directions, including those where movement has been slow and beset by handicaps.

The Course of Growth

It might be useful to start with an examination of the economy's performance via the evolution of the national product. This evolution will be traced over the whole period for which comparable data are available, namely 1951-73. We have had occasion to mention the rate of growth achieved in the five pre-independence years, but not to record the year-by-year size of GDP and GNP. This will be done in Table 13.11.

As can be seen from the tabulated data, the conversion of the series from current to constant prices has been achieved through the use of the cost-of-living index, in spite of some misgivings about the reliability of this index in the earlier half-dozen years. However, it seems to this writer the best index available under the circumstances. Obviously, the conversion can be made for the whole period on the basis of the extension of either of the two index number series: the one with 1958, and the other with 1963 as base year, so as to serve the whole period 1951-73. A compromise has been attempted in Table 13.11, namely to calculate the index numbers for the years 1963-73 on the basis of the 1958

616 Morocco

Table 13.11: Gross Domestic Product and Gross National Product 1951-73 at Current and at Constant Prices[a] (billions of francs (dirhams))[b]

Year[c] (1)	GDP Current Prices (2)	Current Prices[d] (3)	GNP Constant 1958=100 (4)	Prices 1963=100 (5)	Rate of Growth GNP (per cent) 1958=100 (6)	1963=100 (7)
1951	4.87	4.50	6.08			
1952	6.08	5.76	6.94		14.1	
1953	6.59	6.29	7.40		6.6	
1954	6.88	6.58	7.83		5.8	
1955	6.92	6.55	7.53		−3.8	
1956	7.49	7.03	7.64		1.5	
1957	7.64	7.22	7.44		−2.6	
1958	8.51	8.17	8.17		9.8	
1959	8.53	8.26	8.26		1.1	
1960	9.09	8.92	8.41		1.8	
1961	9.04	8.97	8.31		−1.2	
1962	10.62	10.59	9.37		12.7	
1963	11.86	11.95	9.96	11.95	6.3	
1964	12.49	12.58	10.06	12.09	1.0	1.2
1965	13.16	13.25	10.27	12.27	2.1	1.5
1966	12.84	12.88	10.14	12.15	−1.3	−1.0
1967	13.60	13.71	10.81	12.97	6.6	6.7
1968	15.31	15.36	12.06	14.48	11.6	11.6
1969	15.92	16.12	12.29	14.75	1.9	1.9
1970	16.96	17.20	12.95	15.54	5.4	5.4
1971	18.57	19.00	13.73	16.48	6.0	6.0
1972	20.15	20.41[e]	14.22	17.06	3.6	3.5
1973	18.80	n.a.	13.75	15.27	−3.3	−10.0

a. The data in the sources are at current prices. I have used the cost-of-living index as deflator, although this index for 1951-6 was not very satisfactory, as indicated in section 1. Two series have been linked, one with 1958 and the other with 1963 as base. The results with the 1958 base are shown in columns (4) and (6). I have also calculated the GNP at constant (1963) prices from 1963 onwards; the results appear in columns (5) and (7). If the jump in GNP at constant prices from the 1958 to the 1963 base is ignored and the annual growth rates are then calculated, the differences are insignificant. The average annual rate would in either case be 4.2 per cent.
b. The currency unit used is the 'new' franc or dirham (which came into use in October 1959). The pre-1959 francs were converted into new francs at 100 old for 1 new franc/dirham.
c. Owing to the adjustments made from time to time, as the *Annuaire Statistique* and *IFS* series show, I have — wherever applicable — used the more recent, adjusted figures.
d. No calculation for GDP at constant prices has been attempted here, as I have considered the GNP more significant as representing the economy's own (internal) performance.
e. *IFS* March and December 1974 do not give GNP for 1972. I have obtained it by adding net factor payments abroad to GDP, as recorded in Banque Nationale pour le Développement Economique, *Minutes of the Ordinary General Assembly Held on 28 June 1973 at Rabat, Morocco* (Rabat; Arabic), p. 54.

Sources: The basic sources used for GDP, GNP and cost-of-living index data are: *IFS Supplement to 1967/68 Issues, IFS* September 1967, *IFS* November 1968, and *IFS* March and December 1974, except for 1951. The *Annuaire Statistique . . . 1955-1956, Annuaire Statistique . . . 1964-1965*, and *Annuaire Statistique . . . 1970* were also used for comparison. GNP for 1951 is from *Annuaire Statistique . . . 1955-1956*, p. 468.

series, and, side by side with that, to deflate by the 1963 index number series from 1963 onwards. Understandably, the big jump in the rate of growth for 1963 caused by the transition from one index series to the other (whereby GNP for 1963 at current prices becomes GNP at constant prices for the new series) must be disregarded; and in any case, from 1963 onwards, the annual rates of growth — expectedly — are virtually the same whichever series is used for deflating current prices.

The end result of the calculation is an average compound rate of real growth of about 4.1 per cent per annum for the years 1951-73. However, if the period is divided into pre-independence and independence eras, the average rates would be 4.84 per cent and 4 per cent respectively.

The division is useful in demonstrating the decline of the growth rate after 1956. This is mainly due to the low rates characterising the years 1956-61 in general (with the exception of 1958 which was a year with an exceptionally good agricultural harvest), and later the three years 1964-6. From 1967 onwards the growth record is less erratic than in any comparable group of years before 1967. This is true in spite of the fact that the contribution of agriculture to national product continued to fluctuate, even widely sometimes. This strongly suggests the expansion and the consolidation of other sectors on firmer grounds, which permits a greater steadiness in the performance of the economy beginning with the latter years of the sixties.

The question of the development of individual sectors relates to the structure of the economy, which will be examined later. The relative importance of agriculture over the years will then become better understood. For the present, it is sufficient to emphasise two findings as predominant: that the overall performance since 1956 has been rather poor; but that the last five or six years have shown signs of stabilisation at a distinctly higher level of performance, with the rate of growth averaging 5.85 per cent per annum — except for 1973, when a sharp decline was registered.

The poor performance of the economy becomes a cause for greater concern when related to the fast-increasing population. Thus, in dollar equivalents the GNP in real terms amounted to $217 for 1951, $216.9 for 1956, and $226 for 1972 (at selling rate) or $231.2 (if trade conversion factor is used for calculation).[74] The failure of GNP *per capita* to rise between 1951 and 1956 arises from the dip in 1955 and the very slight rise in 1956. However, taking the whole period into consideration, there would still be only a very small improvement which is not even worth calculating. Indeed, the margin of error in the GNP series (and in the deflating factor) is certainly so large as to swallow the minute percentage rise in *per capita* GNP.

Yet the result is different if the average rate of net increase in population for the 23 years, say 2.8 per cent per annum, is allowed for in the average rate of growth of 4.1 per cent. Here the improvement in GNP *per capita* would be 1.3 per cent on average. Two comments are in place here. First, that taking the initial and the terminal years for comparison is, obviously, misleading. Secondly, making the comparison between 1951 and 1972 or 1973 in dollar equivalents subjects the results to the vagaries of changes in exchange rates. Thus, if we were to restrict the comparison to dirhams, the real GNP *per capita* would amount to 759.6, 764 and 1,077 dirhams for 1951, 1956 and 1972 respectively. Again, there is stagnation between 1951 and 1956, but a rise of 41.8 per cent from 1951 to 1972, or just over 1.5 per cent per annum. (Were the GNP at constant 1958 prices to be used for calculation all through, the net total increase for the 22 years 1951-72 would be 18.3 per cent *per capita*, or about 0.8 per cent per annum.)

Owing to the quality of the data involved, it can be safely said that the 'true' rate of growth *per capita* hovers around 1 per cent per annum on the average — taking into account the difference in the two GNP series, as recorded in Table 13.11 above. It is sufficient to say that this rate, or something in its neighbourhood, does not permit a tangible improvement in the level of living of Moroccans, assuming the pattern of product distribution has not worsened over the years. Obviously, if this pattern has become characterised with a larger degree of egalitarianism then the modesty of the rise in level of GNP *per capita* would become slightly less disturbing from the standpoint of welfare than the size of the rate of increase would by itself suggest.

There is no information available to this writer on productivity and its evolution over the years. Common sense would suggest a deterioration lasting for several years after 1956, as a result of the loss of thousands of Europeans and Jews with superior skills in their fields, and the entry into the stream of employment of Moroccan replacements insufficiently trained and experienced. Furthermore, the dislocation befalling organisation and management (with respect to capital ownership and the locus of authority and decision-making) must have exacted its toll on productivity. We have no way of determining whether such (assumed) damage to productivity has in the more recent years been made good. The impact of investment on growth remains the only variable available for examination.

For the sake of consistency, the information on gross fixed capital formation will be derived from the same source as that on national product, namely the *International Financial Statistics* series. The volume of capital formation and its relation to GNP will be presented in Table 13.12. The data relate investment to GNP and not to GDP.

Gross fixed investment at both current and constant prices has been recorded in the table, in absolute values, and as a proportion of GNP. Two sets of calculations have been made: one relating investment at current prices to GNP at current prices, and the second relating the one to the other at constant prices. The results are detailed in Table 13.12, as well as summarised there. The differences between the two sets of proportions are not significant. In either case, the gross fixed investment in the years 1951-6 amounts to about one-sixth of GNP, while it is slightly less than one-eighth for the period 1956-73, and slightly over one-eighth for the whole period 1951-73.

The pattern is reproduced in the rates of real growth for the periods indicated, thus the highest-investment phase 1951-6 has the highest growth rate of 4.84 per cent, the lowest-investment phase 1956-73 has the lowest growth rate of 4 per cent, and the 1951-73 period with investment in an intermediary position has a growth rate of 4.1 per cent. The average capital/output ratios are 3.4, 3 and 3.1 for the three periods or phases respectively. The earliest period and the one with the highest ratio was also the one which experienced a greater relative concentration of investment in infrastructure.

Unfortunately information is not available with respect to the sectoral distribution of investment in the years of independence. This information could be collected from various annual reports, but what is needed is a series where the data are uniformly calculated and presented. The national accounts section of the *Annuaire Statistique* do not contain such a series. Nevertheless we will have occasion in the next section on 'Planning' to examine the pattern of planned investment by sector. There will also be some opportunity for the assessment of the degree of plan implementation in this respect. Likewise, there will be occasion then to see how the total investment was divided between the public and the private sectors. It will be sufficient for the present purpose to stress the modesty of the resources that the economy has been directing to investment. To this must be added the fact that though the bulk of this investment has come from domestic saving, the country usually receives a not inconsiderable volume of foreign aid in the form of grants and loans.

Morocco

Table 13.12: Gross Fixed Investment at Current and at Constant Prices Related to GNP at Current Prices 1951-73 (billions of dirhams)

Year	Investment (billion dirhams)		Investment/GNP (per cent)	
	Current	Constant	Current	Constant
1951	0.98	1.32	21.78	21.71
1952	1.18	1.42	20.49	20.46
1953	1.15	1.35	18.28	18.24
1954	1.02	1.21	15.50	15.45
1955	0.93	1.07	14.20	14.21
1956	0.79	0.86	11.24	11.26
1957	0.69	0.71	9.56	9.54
1958	0.82	0.82	10.04	10.04
1959	0.76	0.76	9.20	9.20
1960	0.92	0.87	10.31	10.34
1961	1.05	0.97	11.70	11.67
1962	1.15	1.02	10.86	10.88
1963	1.41	1.41	11.80	11.80
1964	1.39	1.34	11.05	11.08
1965	1.44	1.33	10.87	10.84
1966	1.53	1.44	11.88	11.85
1967	1.89	1.79	13.78	13.80
1968	1.97	1.86	12.83	12.85
1969	2.18	1.99	13.52	13.49
1970	2.61	2.36	15.17	15.19
1971	2.70	2.34	14.21	14.20
1972	2.67	2.23	13.08	13.07
1973	2.90	2.36	n.a.	n.a.
Average 1951-6	1.01	1.21	16.48	16.65
1956-73	1.60	1.47	12.27	12.21
1951-73	1.48	1.42	12.94	13.07

Note: (1) The deflator used for 1951-62 has 1958 as base; that for 1963-72 has 1963 as base.
(2) Averages for last two columns do not go beyond 1972, as GNP for 1973 is not available.

Sources: For investment 1952-73, *IFS Supplement to 1967/68 Issues*, *IFS*, September 1967, *IFS* November 1968, and *IFS* March and December 1974. Percentages and averages are calculated from data in Tables 13.11 and 13.12. Investment for 1951 is obtained from *Annuaire Statistique... 1955-1956*, pp. 466 and 467.

(The inflow of aid will be discussed in connection with the external sector.)

The examination of the structure of the economy and its change over time is also handicapped owing to the absence of information on the contribution of the various sectors to GNP or GDP. Moroccan statistics provide information on the individual sectors' contribution to 'Gross Domestic Production' (GDProduction), in accordance with French methodology copied in Morocco, which is GDP minus salaries and wages paid by the public sector. The inclusion of the share of the government sector would change the relationships among the various sectors. The structure can therefore only be examined for gross domestic production, but as this procedure will apply to the whole period, consistency will be preserved and some inferences can be drawn from the comparison of the structure at different points of time.

Table 13.13: Relative Contribution to Gross Domestic Production of the Various Sectors, 1951, 1956, 1967 and 1972 (per cent)

Sector	1951	1956	1967	1972
Agriculture, fishing, forestry, livestock	38.8	38.9	30.3	31.0
Energy	1.1	1.5	2.8	3.3
Mining and quarrying	6.5	6.9	5.7	5.7
Industry and crafts	15.6	17.0	14.2	13.9
Building and public works	8.7	6.4	5.8	5.6
Commodity sectors	70.7	70.7	58.8	59.5
Transport and services	10.4	12.0	18.6	18.1
Trade	18.9	17.3	22.6	22.4
Service sectors	29.3	29.3	41.2	40.5
Total all sectors	100.0	100.0	100.0	100.0

Strictly speaking, the figures are not comparable, since they differ in designation from year to year. Thus, for 1951 and 1956, the data are quoted in 1952 prices, while for 1967 they are at 1960 prices. Finally, 1972 data are at current prices. The differences notwithstanding, it is still possible to make some meaningful observations with regard to structure for the four years selected.

Sources: For 1951 and 1956, *Annuaire Statistique . . . 1955-1956;* for 1967, A. A. Belal and A. Agourram, loc. cit., p. 145; and for 1972, Banque Nationale pour le Développement Economique, p. 7. In all instances except for 1972 the original data were expressed in monetary terms and the percentages were calculated by the writer. (Sectoral details of GDP for 1973 are not available, although global GDP is.)

It is clear from this table that a marked change in the structure has occurred between the first half-decade and the last half-decade of the 1951-72 period. The largest component of this change in percentage points is the drop by almost a quarter of the contribution of agriculture to GDProduction. However, in relative terms, the increase in the contribution of energy (water and electricity) is by far the largest, since this contribution tripled between 1951 and 1972, and almost doubled between 1956 and 1967. Yet this change accounts only for 2.2 percentage points, against about 8 points in the case of agriculture. Furthermore, energy has a special place in that it is the only commodity sector whose contribution rose in relative terms, whereas the general trend for all other commodity sectors, in spite of occasional deviations, was downward. Thus, mining and quarrying dropped gently, and the drop constitutes a small fraction of the base magnitude. The same is true, *mutatis mutandis,* of industry (manufacturing plus handicrafts). However, while building and public works move in the same direction, the magnitude of the drop here is larger than in mining and in industry, both in number of points and in the relative size of the drop related to the initial year; the change in the contribution of this last sector is nearest in significance to that in agriculture.

Together, the commodity sectors have lost ground, with their contribution dropping from about seven-tenths to about six-tenths of GDProduction. The decline of over 10 percentage points has been gained by the service sectors. These are grouped under two titles: transport and other services (excluding trade), and trade. (The government sector, as already indicated, does not form part of the concept of Gross Domestic Production.) Both sectors have gained in relative importance, particularly 'transport and services', which gained more percentage points than trade. Indeed, the contribution of this sector rose by over 63 per cent on the average for the last half-decade over that for the first half-decade of the 22-year period under examination, while the comparable rise in the contribution of trade is less than 25 per cent. It is most probable that were the contribution of the government sector to be included in the table, the gain of the service sectors between 1951 and 1972 would be distinctly greater than the 10 or 11 percentage points indicated in Table 13.13. The basis for this statement is the fourfold expansion in the size of the civil service and necessarily in the total salary and wage bill.

This 'phenomenon' of relative shrinkage in the commodity sectors as a group versus service sectors can be witnessed in several, if not all, the countries surveyed in this study. One aspect of this development is healthy, to the extent that the vast expansion in the contribution of certain service sectors which are of fundamental significance for development is concerned (such as transport and communication, education, banking and the like). Yet another aspect is largely regrettable though unavoidable, to the extent that the inflation in the government sector does not represent a proportionate improvement and/or expansion in the service which the government offers the citizenry. What really happens is often in part a mere quantitative inflationary phenomenon caused by various factors such as the award of jobs and benefits to party members, relatives, fellow tribesmen or retainers, or is simply caused by the dictates of the 'Parkinsonian law of administration'. Furthermore, another unhealthy aspect of the relative growth of the tertiary group of sectors is the growth of those personal services that are largely associated with the enlargement of the bourgeoisie, whether this group consists of the traditional elements of the bourgeoisie (the large landlords, the tribal chiefs and top executives), or is enlarged to include newly emerging industrial barons, substantial merchants, well-paid technocrats, senior government officials, and members of the liberal professions.

What is more significant than the dry and bare expressions of change in structure in monetary or relative terms is the change that has actually taken place in the scope and efficiency of each of the sectors. This means the variety and quality of products turned out, the organisation of establishments and efficiency of labour, and the technology used in each of the sectors. We are not in possession of sufficient information on these several matters to enable us to survey and evaluate the progress made in them. The data as presented in Table 13.13 by themselves could have more than one meaning. The change in the structure as analysed in the last few paragraphs could have come about through a vast expansion in every sector which shaped the interrelations between the sectors as they seem to have been shaped. On the other hand, these interrelations could have been thus shaped with a low platform of economic performance which is just modestly better than stagnation.

In the case of Morocco, the latter explanation is the more applicable. The various sectors have grown modestly, with their divergent rates of growth creating the pattern witnessed in the year 1972. However, there is one exception to this generalisation. This is tourism, which has grown at a very fast rate from very modest beginnings in the late fifties or early sixties, although in absolute terms it still constitutes a small sector in its contribution to national product.

The External Sector

It has been stated that loans and grants are an important ingredient in the financing of investment, given the insufficiency of domestic savings to meet the resource requirements of even the rather low level of investment in the country. It is worthwhile in this connection to examine the whole external sector and its position in the Moroccan economy.

This economy was very closely tied to France in pre-independence days, and has continued to be so tied, though more loosely and less intensively since independence. The special relationship took and still takes the form of relatively intensive trade relations, a large-sized Moroccan labour force in France (which sends sizeable remittances back home), grants-in-aid from the French government to its protectorate as well as help for it to obtain loans on foreign money markets, and since independence continued financial ties as a result of the flow of some French aid and the unsettled question of compensation to be paid to Frenchmen for the surrender of *colon* lands. However, as the years passed, the predominance which French aid possessed has lapsed, as the United States, as well as Federal Germany and the World Bank and the Kuwait Fund for Arab Economic Development came to play very important parts in the supply of investment funds to Morocco. The combined effect of this inflow of foreign capital can be clearly seen through the structure and development of the country's balance of international payments.

This balance had two conflicting trends in the years before independence: a deficit on current account compensated for in the capital account in the first few years of the fifties, and a surplus on current account in 1955 and 1956 which was more than counteracted by the outflow of private capital.[75] The situation in the years 1956-73 fluctuated considerably. We need not reproduce here a complete annual balance of payments series for these 18 years, since a presentation of the main features of the annual balances in Table 13.14 will suffice for present purposes.

One of the most salient features of the picture in Table 13.14 is the shift in the country's position on current account, from one showing a surplus in the first five years to one showing a deficit in all but one of the remaining 13 years. As far as the transfers are concerned, which constitute a second important aspect, it can be seen that private transfers have gained significance since the early sixties, but what is more important, there has been a shift from rather large net transfers abroad to much larger net transfers into the country after the mid-sixties. The final point to draw attention to is the consistently large and inward-flowing net capital movement on government account, except for 1972 when the inflow dropped, and 1973 when it almost disappeared. In other words, the central government has all through independence been a recipient of relatively large capital inflows. The global volume of these transfers is larger than the total of the amounts indicated in the last column in Table 13.14, since these amounts are net receipts, after outflows and servicing of debt have been accounted for. This qualification notwithstanding, the total of the column indicated is 4.1 billion dirhams, or about $855m.

Indeed, an attempt to calculate the aid received by Morocco from July 1945 (in the case of US aid) to the end of 1972 estimates the amount at $1,469m. This sum includes loans and grants coming from OECD sources. In addition, economic aid from the USSR amounted to $93m in the period 1955 through 1972. And aid from Kuwait Fund for Arab Economic Development totals KD10.91m ($36.9m at current rates) for the years 1962—March

Morocco

Table 13.14: Main Features of the Balance of Payments 1956-73 (millions of dirhams: minus sign indicates debit)

Year	Goods and Services	Transfers		Capital Movements	
		Private	Government	Private	Government
1956	385	–	44	67	140
1957	428	12	20	38	189
1958	394	7	58	23	113
1959	541	5	29	17	136
1960	176	–89	130	4	202
1961	–463	–130	220	7	227
1962	–382	–97	11	–1	211
1963	–431	–117	183	11	210
1964	–22	–217	110	12	285
1965	120	–190	91	21	490
1966	–297	67	–27	–16	212
1967	–525	202	–29	4	249
1968	–528	142	96	–76	234
1969	–416	293	56	–35	198
1970	–993	348	20	277	449
1971	–786	536	15	145	407
1972	–424	634	–	–95	148
1973	–636	1,012	68	–313	9

Notes: Data for 1968-73 are expressed in US dollars in the source. They have been converted at the rates indicated in the source for the various years. ('Trade conversion rate' for first column, and 'exchange rate' for other columns.)

Sources: *IFS Supplement to 1967/68 Issues* for 1956-60, *IFS*, November 1968 for 1961-7, and *IFS* March and October 1975 for 1968-73.

1974.[76] Much of the amounts included in the total for OECD countries aid is shown as net capital movements and transfers, which indicates that the gross inflow has been larger. Furthermore, the data do not include aid from multilateral agencies. Nor do they include inflows of grants and loans from France in the period 1945-56.

Not much can be drawn as inference from these amounts, as against those indicated in the last column of Table 13.14. This column referred totally to capital movements, whereas a part of the aid from OECD countries is grants and falls under a separate category, as unrequited transfers. Furthermore, there are many qualifications regarding the comparability of components of the totals and the legitimacy of aggregating the components.[77] However, one broad generalisation can be made. This is that a total net inflow of, say 1.6 billion US dollars over the years 1945-72 is far from being a very potent factor of development in a country whose population over this period has averaged about 12m inhabitants. Taking into account the number of years during which the flow has taken place, the annual aid would amount to 4.8 US dollars *per capita*. Again, assuming all of it was directed to investment – a very heroic assumption – there would be an increase of national product of 1.6 dollars per head. It is obvious that for foreign aid to create a substantial push to development, it

624 Morocco

has to come in much larger volume, to form a regular and predictable flow, and finally to be mostly directed to investment in conformity with a rational and intelligent system of priorities.

The emphasis placed here on foreign aid is not misplaced or exaggerated, inasmuch as the country's own earnings of foreign exchange are not growing fast enough to remove the need for large capital inflows. The total net increase for commodity exports, as for commodities and services combined, has been 213 per cent; thus a compound rate of growth of slightly over 6 per cent per annum on the average has been achieved. This performance exceeds the increase in imports, where the total net increase in commodity exports was 108 per cent, and that for commodities and services combined 154 per cent. The average annual rates of growth have been 3.6 per cent and 5 per cent respectively.

The major individual exports have marked a faster rate of growth than the total exports. Thus, phosphates, citrus and tourism have achieved a total net increase of 278, 1,092 and 458 per cent respectively. Though not the fastest-growing item, tourism has none the less become the first earner of foreign exchange in absolute terms. However, the superior earnings of tourism are counteracted by travel abroad, as Table 13.15 shows.

Table 13.15: Foreign Exchange Receipts and Payments (million dirhams)

	1953	1963	1972
Total exports, goods and services	1,407	2,469	4,396
Total commodity exports	943	1,944	2,953
Phosphates	178	461	673
Citrus	36	258	429
Tourism (receipts)	160	218	893
Total imports, goods and services	1,909	2,947	4,811
Total commodity imports	1,711	2,264	3,564
Tourism (payments)	165	186	388

Sources: Data for 1953 are drawn from: *IFS Supplement to 1967/68 Issues;* FAO, *Maroc,* Table II-10, p. II-57, and *Annuaire Statistique . . . 1955-1956,* p. 211. For 1963 and 1972, the data are drawn from *IFS,* September 1967 and March 1974, respectively, from Table 5.11, p. 324 in IBRD, *The Economic Development of Morocco* (Baltimore, 1966), and from Banque Nationale pour le Développement Economique, op. cit., p. 54.

This tabulation must be clear evidence that though the exports of goods and services have grown faster than imports over the 20-year period, nevertheless there is still a large deficit in the current account, and the size of this deficit has not varied much since 1961 (except for 1965). The difference between *commodity* imports and exports has fluctuated more widely. Indeed, it would be pertinent to conclude that the imports ought to grow much faster, thus creating a much larger import surplus, and that the growth in imports ought to be mainly caused by the importation of capital goods for development work, if the economy is to move ahead faster.

However, such a move would lead to the faster accumulation of foreign debt — since capital inflow will have to finance the expanded import surplus, unless substantial grants are received. Here lies a problem that has caused concern ever since independence, since the external requirements of development, though legitimate, create an equally legitimate fear that the foreign debt may become unmanageable over the years, so long as foreign assets fall seriously short of foreign liabilities. Morocco had a total foreign debt (direct as well as guaranteed by the government) of 122.7m old francs, or 1.2m dirhams, by the end of 1953. But it had foreign assets at the same time (for the government and the commercial banks) totalling 406m dirhams. The total for debt and assets by the end of 1956 was 1.9m dirhams and 308m dirhams respectively. However, by the end of 1972 the situation had been reversed and became distinctly serious. Thus, net foreign assets were 1,453m dirhams for 1973, while foreign debt had risen to 4,018m dirhams for 1972.[78] This debt amounts to a quarter of the GNP of the country for 1972. Its servicing is a heavy burden on the external sector. The burden would become more seriously heavy if foreign indebtedness were to increase considerably. However, if the increase were to be called for by the needs of financing development, it would be justifiable and even prudent. In any case, the situation as presented reflects the difficulties the country faces as it struggles to raise its rate of growth. The bright spot in this situation is the distinct tendency for the rate to rise over the years 1967-72. (However, it declined sharply in 1973.) Unfortunately, no such tendency is visible in the current account of the balance of payments, where the deficit does not seem to show a declining tendency in the seven-year period 1967-73.

Finance

In addition to the sizeable foreign debt, there was a domestic debt of 2,349m dirhams at the end of 1972. In itself, this reflects the serious limitations the government would suffer if it were to rely more heavily on domestic resources in financing development. (The domestic debt doubled between 1967 and 1972.)[79] This indebtedness has accompanied a vast expansion in the budget of the country. The three 'chapters' of the budget totalled 193m dirhams (19.3 billion old francs) in 1947, both for receipts and expenditures, as the budget used to be drawn on the basis of balance between the two sides. The budget totalled 1,425m dirhams for 1956, or about 7.4 times that for 1947. (In both instances, the allocations included the 'extraordinary' or capital budget, which amounted to 40.2m and 309m dirhams respectively.)[80]

However, the pace of expansion slowed during the years of independence. This was the result of a deliberate policy of compression in expenditure along with the increase of revenues. This was achieved through better tax assessment and collection procedures, the imposition in 1971 of a surtax on personal income, and the improved exploitation of government-owned enterprises and mines. Thus, the receipts estimated for 1972 amounted to 4,733m dirhams, while the expenditure estimates were 5,202m dirhams (including 1,608m dirhams for public investment). If to the budget of the central government are added the 'appended' and 'special' budgets, the grand total for revenues and expenditures would rise to 5,865m and 6,263m dirhams respectively, leaving a deficit of 398m dirhams. The closed accounts showed a shortfall of 610m dirhams in revenue, but a saving of 117m dirhams in current expenditures and another of 324m dirhams in development allocations. This left a larger gap than the 398m originally estimated. It is worth noting that 'direct taxes and fees' have declined slightly over the last five years, from about 25 per cent of the ordinary (as distinct from the extraordinary, including foreign-financed) revenues, to about 22 per cent. Ordinary revenues represent one-sixth of national income, while direct taxes and fees represent 3.6 per cent. Customs duties and indirect taxes together account for about two-thirds of ordinary revenues. The remaining items account for the balance of about 8 per cent.[81]

Population, Manpower and Education

Between 1956 and the middle of 1973 the population is reported to have risen by 57.4 per cent, from 10.06 to 16.31 million inhabitants. If these estimates are correct, then the rate of population increase is 2.9 per cent per annum on the average, which is clearly below the rate which is generally considered to be operative, namely 3.2 or 3.3 per cent. It would be tenable to consider the 1973 estimate more reliable than that for 1956, since the census taken on 20 July 1971 — which is believed to have a high degree of reliability — showed the population then to be 15.38m. (An official estimate for mid-1970 put the population at 15.52m.)[82] Whatever estimates are correct, and we need not devote more time to the issue here, it seems clear from studies of annual demographic changes that the Moroccan population is a fast-growing one. We tend to accept the higher estimate of natural increase of about 3.2–3.3 per cent,[83] rather than the lower one of 2.9 per cent which our calculations have shown. Furthermore, this population has a very high component of young persons below twenty — reportedly 57 per cent of the total. This is not out of line with the situation in several other Arab countries, and the implications for development are the same with respect to the unduly high rate of dependency involved, the heavy burden of education necessarily to be shouldered, and the urgency of finding many more new jobs each year than if the increase were slower.

Tables 13.1 and 13.2 in section 1 presented information on the active population in 1951 and 1952. Since then, there have been two attempts to collect and present material on manpower for the whole country: the census of 1960, and that of 1971. Unfortunately, the detailed final results of the latter census are not available. Consequently, the results of the 1960 census will be examined in detail, while aggregates relating to 1972 will be used for comparison.

According to the census of 1960, the total population numbered 11,626,232 inhabitants, including 395,883 foreigners (mostly Europeans) and 162,420 'Israelites' (i.e. Jews). The active population was 3,254,379, or 28 per cent of the total. In contrast, the number of persons *actually* employed in 1972 was 3,638,000 out of a population of 15.83m — or 23 per cent of the total.[84] The bulk of the active population in 1960 was in rural areas (though not all were engaged in agricultural activity). The ratio between the rural and the urban components of the work-force was 70.30 to 29.70, though those engaged in agriculture, who constituted 56 per cent of the total, included a small component of urban inhabitants. Indeed, there is no one sector which draws all its labour from either rural areas or urban centres; there is overlap in every instance. Yet this does not mean that there is a uniform distribution of urban and rural workers: indeed, the reverse is true, owing to the heavy concentration of foreigners (mainly Europeans) and Jews in urban centres, and the concentration of these communities in activities generally located in or around urban centres, and, conversely, owing to the heavy concentration of Moroccan Moslems in rural areas and in agricultural activity alike. The dissimilar distribution of the three groups between urban and rural, which is very striking, is shown in Table 13.16.

The Moslem component of the work-force numbered 3,071,090 in 1960, or 27.7 per cent of all Moslems. The proportion is almost equal to that for the whole population but slightly below that for the foreigners and Jews taken together, which stood at 32.8 per cent. However, the size of the active population and its relationship to total population must not be allotted more than a reasonable degree of credibility. This is because the active population is known to have included a not inconsiderable number of persons only partially employed. (though 1.2m occasional women workers in agriculture were not included in the statistics) and a fewer number of unemployed though able-bodied persons. Thus, the inflation of

Morocco

Table 13.16: Geographical Distribution of Nationalities (per cent)

	Rural	Urban
Moslems	73.69	26.31
Moroccan Jews	5.25	94.75
Foreigners	38.11	61.89
Non-Moslems (foreigners and Jews)	10.54	89.46

Source: *Annuaire Statistique... 1964-1965*, p. 28.

the size of the work-force is much less serious than it had been when the census of 1951/2 was taken. At that earlier date the work-force was reported as constituting 38.6 per cent of the population. The absurdity of the earlier findings can be directly seen from a comparison of the magnitudes. Thus, the active population (for all communities) numbered 3,088,896 in 1951/2, in a population of just over 8m. In 1960, the active population exceeded that of 1951/2 only by 5.4 per cent, although the total population had increased by 45.3 per cent. It is obvious that the 1960 census was much more representative of the true situation than the one held nine years before, particularly if it is remembered that education and training had progressed and made it possible for a higher proportion of the population to participate in employment. The data for 1972 are both the most reliable and the most meaningful. The first attribute arises from the fact that the data come from the more recent and more precise census of July 1971, while the second arises from the fact that the 1972 data refer to persons in active employment, not to the 'theoretical' labour force as in 1960.

The distribution of the active population in 1960 by sector of economic activity and by type of residence (whether rural or urban) is presented in Table 13.17, while the 1972 aggregates will be included as a general note at the end of the table. Admittedly, the data for 1960 do not command a very high degree of reliability. Nevertheless, they are clearly suggestive of the structure of the labour force at the time. If the unemployed are deducted, this would leave an employed work-force constituting just over a quarter of the population — which is probably on the high side. The labour force is distributed among the various sectors very much as would be expected in a country like Morocco, at its level of development then and with its resource endowment.

None the less, the distribution has a few striking features worth noting. The first is the insignificance of the force in industry properly speaking. Even including handicrafts (designated 'manufacturing industry — consumption' in the source), the whole sector engages a mere 8.6 per cent of active population, but less than half of this proportion is in mechanised industry, as handicrafts absorb the vast majority of 'industrial' workers. An equally baffling feature is the distinct modesty of the labour component in construction and public works, considering that a high proportion of gross investment goes into these two categories of activity, and that they are labour-intensive. The secondary sectors together (that is, all commodity sectors except agriculture) engage 11.8 per cent of the active population — a low proportion indeed. In contrast, the secondary sectors employed 18.1 per cent in 1972.

Those engaged in services constituted a rather small proportion in 1960 — 22.6 per cent of the total, against 26.1 per cent for 1972. Obviously, agriculture and other activities of a primary nature have an inordinately large share of the work-force. This share dropped signi-

Table 13.17: Distribution of Active Population by Sex, Type of Residence and Economic Sector (1960 Census, and estimates for 1972)

Sector	Rural Male	Rural Female [a]	Rural Both Sexes [a]	Urban Male	Urban Female	Urban Both Sexes	Total All Categories	Per Cent of Total
1. Agriculture	1,652,737	140,297	1,793,034	38,247	2,478	40,725	1,833,759	56.35
2. Electricity and water	1,562	20	1,582	6,287	304	6,591	8,173	0.25
3. Mining	18,226	257	18,483	15,468	490	15,958	34,441	1.06
4. Extractive industries (energy)	494	2	496	4,382	68	4,450	4,946	0.15
5. Construction and public works	22,711	49	22,760	33,043	350	33,393	56,153	1.73
6. Transformation industry	9,408	44	9,452	28,635	596	29,231	38,683	1.19
7. Manufacturing industry (consumption)[b]	36,815	27,277	64,092	111,184	52,344	163,528	227,620	6.99
8. Industry[c]	411	17	428	9,340	2,717	12,057	12,485	0.38
9. Transport and communication	12,823	115	12,938	64,532	2,603	67,135	80,073	2.46
10. Trade, banking, insurance	66,406	1,968	68,374	147,363	10,727	158,090	226,464	6.96
11. Other services[d]	60,912	17,033	77,945	97,385	68,039	165,424	243,369	7.48
12. Police and armed forces	16,268	73	16,341	60,871	1,697	62,568	78,909	2.42
13. Undetermined activity	63,264	4,037	67,301	35,443	5,045	40,488	107,789	3.31
14. Unemployed	121,240	1,665	122,905	173,155	5,455	178,610	301,515	9.26
Total	2,083,277	192,854	2,276,131	825,335	152,913	978,248	3,254,379	100.00[e]

a. Excluding 1,231,550 undeclared females who assist in agricultural work.
b. Mainly handicrafts. The designation here is identical with that in the source.
c. Presumably industrial branches other than (6) and (7).
d. Includes a large component of civil servants.
e. Total rounded.

General Note: The recently published *Plan de développement économique et social 1973-1977* (Vol. I, p.121) has a summary distribution of the active population in *actual* employment which differs from that presented above. According to the *Plan*, the employed represented 23 per cent of total population in 1972 (below the proportion claimed for 1960). The number and its distribution stood as follows:

	Number	Per Cent
Primary sectors	2,030,000	55.8
Secondary sectors	660,000	18.1
Tertiary sectors	680,000	18.7
Administration	268,000	7.4
Total	3,638,000	100.0

Source: *Annuaire Statistique... 1964-1965*, p.34. Last two columns added.

Morocco

ficantly between 1960 and 1972. (However, the structure seems to have changed noticeably inasmuch as the secondary and tertiary groups of sectors are concerned. This can be seen from the general note in Table 13.17.) However, it ought to be remembered that the 1960 data included the unemployed, estimated at 9.26 per cent of the active population. If this item were deleted, the distribution of those in active employment would differ somewhat. Thus, the three groups of sectors would stand as shown in Table 13.18.

Table 13.18: Distribution by Sector of Work-Force in Employment (per cent)

	1960	1972
Primary sectors	62.1	55.8
Secondary sectors	12.9	18.1
Tertiary sector (including administration)	25.0	26.1
Total	100.0	100.0

Source: Table 13.17 and 'General Note' in it.

Though there has been a shift between the primary and secondary groups, their total has remained almost unchanged over the 13-year span.

A comparison of the structure of the work-force with that of the sectoral contribution to Gross Domestic Production (as it was presented in Table 13.13 above) shows that workers in agriculture, as a group, have a low productivity, inasmuch as their share in the labour force is much larger than their contribution to GDProduction. On the other hand, to the extent that the labour data are reasonably correct, workers in all the secondary and the tertiary sectors have a high level of productivity, as their contribution to GDProduction is superior to their relative participation in the labour force. This conclusion can be accepted in its broad lines, and it suggests the urgent need for the improvement of the performance of labour in agriculture, if the returns to agricultural operators are not to remain on the average far below those in secondary and tertiary activities. This improvement will have to come about not only through training and the use of better seeds and supporting capital, but also through institutional reform including more efficient extension services, credit facilities, and marketing arrangements.

However, the most urgent task for the Moroccan economy, society, and government is to make a veritable breakthrough in employment as a whole. Indeed, the failure to create nearly as many new jobs as there are new job-seekers is the major failure in all the succeeding development plans that have been implemented.[85] Even if one does not subscribe to the extreme gloom expressed by some students of the economy who maintain that in the late sixties urban unemployment was between 30 and 50 per cent, and that rural underemployment was over 60 per cent of the work-force,[86] it is still possible to consider the problem as intractable after 17 years of independence. And this is true although emigration to Western Europe siphons out thousands of workers every year. The difficulty of absorbing a large part of the unemployment in existence is compounded with the continuously recurring shortfall between new jobs created and new job-seekers joining the labour market — a shortfall currently exceeding 40,000 workers every year.

The search for work opportunities must naturally move in the direction of the secondary and tertiary sectors, since agriculture is already excessively overpopulated. The secondary sectors, as we have seen, currently account for about 18 per cent of those in active employment. For employment here to rise to a substantial level would require a substantial expansion and investment. The service sectors, particularly the civil service, do not have much scope for absorption, unless more padding were to be resorted to and underemployment were allowed to become high. The hope of the country obviously lies, on the one hand, in speedy development on all fronts (especially in labour-intensive activities), along with development-oriented training for the young, and, on the other hand, in the speedy application of family planning and management and the compression of the rate of population increase until it reaches manageable limits.

Like many of the other Arab countries surveyed in this study, Morocco has devoted a great deal of energy and resources to the expansion of education. And, at least quantitatively, remarkable success has been made and the glaring failure of the French has been compensated for. This can be seen at a glance on comparing the school population in November 1956, with that in 1972-3. The number of all students at all levels, in the public and private systems, totalled 454,520, as Table 13.3 showed. The number rose to 1,628,619 in 1972-3.[87] This represents a total net increase of 258 per cent in the intervening 16 years, which amounts to an average compound rate of growth of about 8.5 per cent per annum. The numbers indicated for 1972-3 do not include students in technical training whose precise numbers are not available but are known to exceed 10,000 males and females.

The information for 1972-3 is not available in detail. The most recent detailed breakdown of school population relates to 1971-2, and although the data are a few years old now, they are worthwhile reproducing in Table 13.19.

The country's achievements in the field of education have taken several forms, and can be assessed in different ways. The most obvious is the numerical expansion, with all that this implies in the construction and equipping of hundreds of new school buildings and the training of thousands of teachers. This has imposed a heavy financial burden on the government, absorbing on average between a fifth and a quarter of the recurrent budget.

To gauge the quantitative achievement, one has also to relate school enrolment to school-age population. While enrolment in 1956 was slightly over one-sixth of school-age youth for the country, and less than one-seventh for Moslems, in 1971-2 it was slightly over one-third for Moroccans. In other words, the proportion multiplied 2.4 times in 15 years, while the population was rising at the same time. However, the education of females for the country as a whole did not make any progress, with the female component remaining about one-third of the total. Yet if the Moroccans are taken alone, there appears to be a rise by about 5 percentage points in female enrolment. One sharp contrast worth recording relates to the size of enrolment in secondary education. In 1956, this enrolment was negligible for Moroccan Moslems in absolute terms (only 12,217 boys and girls), and it constituted a mere 3.8 per cent of the enrolment at the primary level. By 1971-2, there were 313,424 secondary school students, and their number amounted to 25.4 per cent of enrolment in primary schools.

Not much progress has been achieved with respect to self-reliance in teachers; in other words, the country depended in 1971-2 on a much larger body of foreign (mainly French) teachers than in 1956. Part of the explanation lies in the vast numerical expansion in the student body and in the need for teachers. (However, there is differentiation in the picture, as the number of foreign teachers has dropped considerably at the primary level, but multiplied several times at the secondary level, between November 1956 and 1971-2.) But part

Table 13.19: Students at Three Levels of Education, 1971-2

Level	Public System			Private System			Total		
	Male	Female	Total	Male	Female	Total	Male	Female	Total
Primary:									
Modern	775,245	396,062	1,171,307	—	—	—	775,245	396,062	1,171,307
Moslem	—	—	—	21,629	13,758	35,387	21,629	13,758	35,387
Ittihad	—	—	—	1,465	1,029	2,494	1,465	1,029	2,494
MUCF[a]	—	—	—	6,286	6,281	12,567	6,286	6,281	12,567
Other[b]	—	—	—	4,306	5,875	10,181	4,306	5,875	10,181
	775,245	396,062	1,171,307	33,686	26,943	60,629	808,931	423,005	1,231,936
Secondary:									
Modern	197,491	77,727	275,218	—	—	—	197,491	77,727	275,218
ERI[c]	1,354	523	1,877	—	—	—	1,354	523	1,877
Traditional	5,534	1,747	7,281	—	—	—	5,534	1,747	7,281
Moslem	—	—	—	6,665	3,290	9,955	6,665	3,290	9,955
Ittihad	—	—	—	1,227	1,106	2,333	1,227	1,106	2,333
MUCF[a]	—	—	—	6,435	5,530	11,965	6,435	5,530	11,965
Other	—	—	—	2,712	2,083	4,795	2,712	2,083	4,795
	204,379	79,997	284,376	17,039	12,009	29,048	221,418	92,006	313,424
Higher:[d]									
Modern	12,022	2,378	14,400	—	—	—	12,022	2,378	14,400
Traditional	703	45	748	—	—	—	703	45	748
	12,725	2,423	15,148	—	—	—	12,725	2,423	15,148
Total all levels	992,349	478,482	1,470,831	50,725	38,952	89,677	1,043,074	517,434	1,560,508

a. French Cultural Mission.
b. Includes private Jewish schools (such as the Alliance Israélite Universelle).
c. Ecoles Régionales d'Instituteurs.
d. Excludes researchers and trainers at centres and institutes of higher learning.

Source: *Annuaire Statistique...1971*, p.18.

also lies in the failure to train enough Moroccan teachers in the meantime.[88] (In absolute terms, there has been a dramatic increase in the number of Moroccan teachers, both at the primary and secondary levels, but not enough to cope with the expansion in student enrolment.)

This aspect is closely related to Arabisation. No doubt the country has made notable advances in this direction, but there is a long distance yet to cover. The progress made enables the schools to give instruction in the first primary years solely in Arabic, introducing French beyond that (with English as the first additional language). There has also been progress in the Arabisation of technical terms, with the help of an Inter-Arab institute established for the purpose in Rabat by the League of Arab States. Nevertheless, there is still greater fluency in French than in Arabic among government officials, particularly at the higher and the technical levels, and official publications, whenever bilingual, show much greater precision and command of language in the French than the Arabic version.

Another aspect of the qualitative change witnessed in the field of education is the establishment of two universities, the first of which, the Mohammed V University in Rabat, was founded in 1957. The second was founded in 1972 in Marrakesh under the name of the University of Ben Youssef of Marrakesh. Most of the education given in the several arts, sciences, and technical and professional faculties is in French, though now there are some parallel programmes in Arabic, as in the case of law. However, Arabic literature and history programmes, understandably, use Arabic as the language of instruction. In addition to the universities, there are several institutes of higher learning which specialise in such fields as business administration, agriculture, law, mining, economics and statistics. The country is also the seat of the African Center for Research into Administrative Training for Development which was established in 1964 as a joint effort between UNESCO and the UN Economic Commission for Africa.

No information is in hand to indicate firmly how much progress has been achieved with respect to technical and vocational training. However, it is known[89] that there has been some progress here, with country-wide programmes established under the Ministry of Education as well as under specific economic ministries. The fields in which such training is possible are varied, and include agriculture, industry, hotel operation, commerce and office skills, with branches in all these. The training takes place at two levels, primary and secondary. (There are no complete statistics on the number of technical trainees in all fields in 1971-2; however, there were 5,398 training in commercial, industrial and hotel-keeping skills. This does not indicate satisfactory expansion over 1956.)

Yet another contrast to be drawn is that between the respective roles of traditional and modern schools between 1956 and 1971-2. While 97.8 per cent of Moslem students were in 'Moslem' or 'traditional' schools in 1956, the proportion dropped to 3.8 per cent in 1971-2; the gain has been made totally in favour of the modern system. It is also noteworthy that the whole primary public system is now described as 'modern'; most students having traditional and Moslem education are in the private sector, with only one-seventh in public secondary schools. The private sector also includes the schools of the French Cultural Mission, and other private Moslem and Jewish schools.

Morocco has not undertaken as far-reaching a probe into its educational system as have Tunisia and Algeria, but it has nevertheless re-examined this system. Some measures of reform have been designed and implemented since the late sixties, with respect to teacher training colleges or schools, content of curricula, language of instruction, and the allocation of course-hours in daily school programmes. But a great deal still needs to be done, and much more investment has yet to be made in laboratory and other equipment and facilities.

Furthermore, even quantitatively there is scope for much more expansion, if the high rate of illiteracy reportedly still prevailing is to be substantially lowered.

Land, Irrigation and Rural Revival

In a sense, at the same time much and little has been done with respect to land development, irrigation and rural revival. The title of a chapter in Amin's book *The Maghreb in the Modern World*, 'Morocco — Hesitation and Contradiction' sums up the situation.[90] Thus, a number of measures have been taken, and institutions built, and plans formulated, with only modest concrete results. This contradiction arises because the measures have been slow to come, or very marginal and therefore ineffectual, or yet because the institutions have been insufficiently equipped with funds, personnel or direction and policy guidelines to cope with the objectives set for them, or finally because the plans formulated for rural development have not been based on a solid foundation of resources, manpower, technology and — above all — mobilisation of the rural masses. The brief discussion that follows is meant to give a factual basis for these assertions.[91]

The area of total cultivable and cultivated land involved in this examination remained relatively unchanged during the period 1956-72. The most prominent advance was in the extension of irrigation to about 150,000 new hectares by the end of 1972, over and above the 64,000 ha irrigated in mid-1956. Yet there are indications and allusions in the *Plan ... 1973-1977* where the situation by the end of 1972 is described, that not the whole area of 214,650 ha said to be 'equipped' for irrigation by that date was all *completely* equipped.[92] Clearly irrigation does not cover a vast area, if related to total cultivated, or even to total irrigable area. (The 1973-77 Plan itself projects irrigation to extend to another 108,990 ha by 1977, which would not constitute a vast expansion.)

One important distinction that can be made between 1956 and the present has been the transfer into Moroccan possession of about 750,000 ha of mostly superior-quality land originally in the possession of Europeans. (It will be recalled that another 250,000 was still in European hands in mid-1974.) However, this transfer is not an operation for which the government can claim credit, since it was effected by Europeans and Moroccans consummating transfer deals directly. Furthermore, much of the land has gone into the possession of absentee landlords. Thus the transfer, which outwardly seems to be a propitious development, may indeed have made true agrarian reform more rather than less difficult, and may not have advanced the cause of large-scale farming either, since the owners are mostly townsmen not excessively moved by zeal for promoting agricultural activity, which remains marginal to their economic and political interests.

The government's philosophy of Promotion Nationale as it relates to the rural sector involved several ideas and measures — mainly the expansion of credit facilities, the promotion of co-operative societies or some variant of these, the improvement of farming techniques, the setting up of certain institutions involving rural revival and development, irrigation and reform of the system of agricultural taxation. If an inventory were to be made of the specific measures and institutions, it would indeed be impressive, although it would still have two large gaps. These are the absence of agrarian reform involving land redistribution — or more correctly, the limitation of such a reform measure to land benefiting from new irrigation schemes and to domainal land; but the area of these together is very marginal. The second gap refers to the failure to nationalise European-owned land. There is also a qualification to this second 'gap'. It relates to the collective land leased to Europeans under the protectorate, some 45,000 ha in area, at extremely low rent. According to Stewart, the average annual rent per hectare was 170 old francs, with cases where it did not exceed 5 francs. Under a decree issued in mid-1959, part of this land was taken back immediately, part was to continue being leased for 3-5 years but to revert to government thereafter, and part was to remain in lease though at higher rent.[93]

What has been said is enough to show that no significant change was effected in the system of land tenure, the redistribution of land being restricted to a very small area that cannot be considered anything but marginal. In addition, it became clear by 1959, thanks to some small surveys on land ownership and size of holding, that the situation was even worse than had been expected. The smallness of the small holdings, and the proportion these represented depicted a situation grimmer than expected. The conclusion was clear that the vast majority of landowners had holdings well below the size believed to be required for the minimal necessities of life. In addition, the small holdings were fragmented, which meant waste and higher cost in operation.[94]

As we have seen, substantial expansion was achieved in irrigation, but this was *only* in relation to the very modest base. Altogether, the area currently under irrigation is well below half the irrigable area estimated to be 500,000. If the irrigated area is related to that currently thought to be irrigable, namely 1,095,000 hectares, then the achievement would shrink yet further.[95]

But this is only one qualification, and probably a minor one. More serious complaints are levelled against the whole system. These relate to bad planning, seriously inadequate drainage, high cost, and insufficient training of farmers in newly irrigated areas to help them adjust to the new cultures made feasible through the availability of water. Still more seriously, the whole policy of the location and size of the dams has come under harsh criticism. Admittedly, much of this criticism has come from opposition circles.[96] Although this calls for caution, it does not justify a total discrediting of the charges made. These have included, in addition to what has been said here, the accusation that the location of barrages and canal systems has in some instances been influenced by powerful notables who are large landlords, in such a way as to have the irrigation canals fall in or close to their land. To the extent that this accusation is true, it means that the benefit to the rural population is limited, since the holdings using the water will not be very numerous, though individually extensive in area.

Another accusation has been that the privileged landlords have had early access to information about sites being considered for the construction of dams and irrigation canals, and have bought land in the localities concerned in anticipation of the appreciation of land prices. From a perusal of some of the memoranda and newspaper articles on this subject, and from intensive interviewing, this writer feels that the accusations are valid at least in part.

There is, however, a very strong official counter-argument in favour of the barrage policy — particularly that relating to large barrages. This is that in addition to the irrigation water they make available, they expand the electricity-generating capacity of the country. Considering that power obtained from hydraulic sources constituted 56 per cent of total power generated in 1971 (but was 68 per cent in 1970), this point is very telling. Furthermore, the rise in the demand for water in urban centres is currently growing at about 5 per cent per annum, and these centres can only be supplied by the water they increasingly need if barrages are built and more water is stored rather than dissipated or left unused. It was supposed in the Five-Year Plan 1968-72 that if the hydraulic policy of the country were fully implemented, by the end of 1972 half of the total mobilisable water of the country, which was estimated at 16 billion cubic metres, would be effectively utilised.

It is the government's conviction of the correctness of its policy that has made it push ahead with dam construction. Thus there are currently 22 dams (against 12 by 1956), though some works are still under completion in three or four of them. With the works completed for all the country's dams, the authorities believe that agricultural production will quadruple, and so will the income of the rural population. However, while this may be true on the basis of a comparison between the returns to a rain-fed against an irrigated hectare, it cannot be taken to be true of the whole county.[97] A thorough study of cost-return relations will have to be undertaken before such statements can be accepted. Besides, the fact that *one* hectare will bring in four times the returns it used to bring in before irrigation does not mean that the rural population will have four times as much income as before. The question of income distribution will have to be considered before such a rosy picture can be accepted as true of the situation. In any case, at the time of writing, the gross returns of the agricultural sector are far from the level that the official document expected for them. Thus, value added in the agricultural sector rose from 1,822m dirhams in 1956 to 4,090m dirhams in 1972, at current prices. The latter figure is just over 2.2 times the former (or 2.0 times on the basis of constant prices). Exaggerated optimism must have coloured the official statement in question, in addition to its being a victim of the 'fallacy of composition'!

Finally, the major charge against the barrage policy is that it essentially serves modern agriculture, leaving traditional farming — especially where small holdings and fragmentation prevail — largely outside the pale of irrigation benefits. Here again, the charge seems to be easy to substantiate. Even official documents place irrigation within the context of modern agriculture, and the location of most of the dams confirms this association.

The controversy around barrages in Morocco is a very major one, and unless it is resolved there will continue to be a feeling that the economy will not move along a clear and sound course. This is so because agriculture is still the largest contributor to national product, and it engages the activities of well over half the active population. Furthermore, the Five-Year Plan 1968-72 devoted 65 per cent of all public investment in agriculture to dams and works directly associated with them, while the Plan for Economic and Social Development 1973-7 allocated 44 per cent (but in fact a large absolute amount). The implications of the controversy, like its causes, are economic as well as social and political in nature. The socio-political dimension in particular requires urgent attention.

Another aspect of agricultural policy has been the amendment of the *tertib* tax, which, it is recalled, used to be levied on gross produce at a flat 5 per cent rate, with rebates allowable to modern agriculture. This resulted in a clear bias in favour of European agriculture. After pressure by opposition parties and the Union Marocaine de l'Agriculture in the early independence years, some amendments were made. These related to the exemption allowances, the coverage of the rebates, and finally to the rates. The amendments constituted improvements, yet they were all very modest in reach. It was in the summer of 1961 that the *tertib* was finally abolished. Here again the hesitation and the half-hearted measures affecting the poor, rural masses added to the feeling of frustration and made the mobilisation of the people behind development work that much more difficult.

Several legislative and institutional steps aiming at agrarian reform had been initiated by the early sixties, but the first major organisational step was taken in 1965 upon the issue of a number of decrees defining this reform, its scope, and the procedures of its implementation. The next major landmark, but one which was to be of even wider coverage, was the issue in July 1969 of the Code for Agricultural Investment (Le Code des Investissements Agricoles) which attempted, in an integrated fashion, to provide the economic, legal and organisational framework for investment in the rural sector. This Code was given a great deal of publicity, especially as the 1965 measures of agrarian reform were felt to have remained largely frozen.

The Code aimed at making investments by the state in the land maximally profitable, whether these were in equipment, irrigation facilities, crop rotation, industrial crops, mechanisation, or in the spread of improved farming techniques. Against public investment, there was to be private investment in the areas benefiting from government investment or subsidies. Thus the landowners were to bear 15 per cent of the cost incurred by the government. Reimbursement was to be by instalment. The institutional and organisational changes provided for in the legislation (that is to say, in the whole set of 49 legislative texts to which reference was made before) were to serve the overall objectives. However, no provisions were made for the limitation of large land holdings. Instead, as Belal and Agourram indicate, there was a clear trend to emphasise the consolidation of holdings as a corrective measure for fragmentation.[98] In line with this, the minimum allowable size was 5 ha of irrigated land.

Published information cannot yet give sufficiently firm ground for an assessment of the effect of the Code. However, it is claimed that it has promoted investment and helped in the development of agricultural production. This is not reflected in the data for the three years 1970-2, where the pattern of growth is no different from the several preceding years, apart from the fluctuations between bad and good harvest years. But it is probably too early to judge.

Some criticism has been levied at the Code. It is maintained that it addresses itself mainly to irrigated and to-be-irrigated areas, and to other areas where agriculture is already successful or obviously has great promise. Almost by definition, this means some bias in favour of the modern subsector with its medium- and large-sized holdings, and a further handicap in the way of the small operation in the traditional subsector attempting to narrow the wide gap between itself and the large operation. Another criticism centres around the inadequacy of the financial and technical means put at the disposal of the institutions meant to serve agriculture and to help farmers improve their methods. This writer feels that the criticism is not unfounded on either score.

The final group of measures undertaken to be discussed here includes the various institutions built since independence in order to achieve the Promotion Nationale in the rural sector. Many such institutions are involved, some new, some reorganised. The detailed step-by-step survey of the life history of these institutions makes tedious reading, and will not be undertaken here. It will instead be sufficient to name the major organisations and to assess their effectiveness in the pursuit of their objectives.

The first is Opération Labour, or Operation Tillage (or Ploughing), conducted under the auspices of La Centrale des Travaux Agricoles, which was designed to replace the unsuccessful Secteurs de Modernisation du Paysanat, SMP, that were first established in 1945, and of which 62 were set up. Opération Labour did not take control of the land directly like its predecessor, but aimed at increasing output through help extended to land-holders in mechanical ploughing, in the use of the right seeds and fertilisers and of machinery, and in the improvement of methods in general. The Opération also involved help in improving social conditions. Part of the task was undertaken by the 100 or so Works Centres set up under the programme, the rest by the farmer himself. The financial burden was also shared, with the overheads borne by the government, and the cost of inputs by the farmers.

The Opération in its old form came to an end when in January 1962 a new body was set up under the name of Office Nationale de la Modernisation Rurale, ONMR. In its five years of life, Opération Labour covered a maximum of 290,000 ha, but the area declined thereafter to reach 94,000 ha in 1961-2.[99] However, it was not only the area served that dropped from year to year, but the yield per hectare as well. This was true of the land under Opération Labour as well as land adjoining it ('zones témoins', which were supposed to benefit from the 'demonstration effect'). The yield of the first category dropped to about half its original volume in three years, while that of the second dropped to about 61 per cent, though from a lower level to start with. However, there was still a net gain over and above the original yield before the programme had been started.[100]

The blame for these results must be shared between the farmers, who were not enthusiastic enough to keep the programme alive and flourishing, and the government, which did not give it enough financial support and sought to make it financially self-supporting prematurely. Furthermore, neither the technical staff of the programme, nor the experienced personnel of the co-operatives (where these existed) were adequate for the tasks involved.

The ONMR had as tasks the promotion of agricultural activity and the raising of livestock. (Morocco has a large population of livestock: some 11.7m sheep, 2.7m cattle and 5.6m goats.[101]) The Office is empowered to evolve programmes of action and draft the necessary legislation, as well as to 'condition the physical environment, put the agricultural "exploitations" in a state fit to undertake production, organize and develop production, participate in the vocational training of farmers' and 'to put into effect the operations decided on by government in matters related to land and development, especially on land domain and collective land' — as the decree setting up the ONMR stipulated.

Once again the achievements were modest. And experimentation with organisational forms continued, with little substantive difference, and as little difference in results. Thus, the ONMR was first reorganised in 1965, then replaced by the Office de Mise en Valeur Agricole, OMVA, itself to be later abolished and replaced by regional offices. Essentially the basic weaknesses were the same. The smaller and the poorer the farmer, the more modest the real help (be it technical, supervisory or financial) that he received. The lion's share went to the large, and by definition to the modern and already superior farms. Even students of the Moroccan economy, who are generally charitable in their assessment of government efforts, on the whole concede that the results of these measures have been very modest indeed, particularly where the traditional sector was concerned. It is arguable that the high turnover of organisations is itself a sign that the authorities are equally aware of this.

The same judgement can be passed on credit institutions. In protectorate days, agricultural credit was provided by the Sociétés Indigènes de Prévoyance, SIP, renamed in 1954 Sociétés Marocaines de Prévoyance, SOMAP, then Sociétés de Crédit Agricole et de Prévoyance, SOCAP — apart from private credit-extending institutions. The Sociétés were fed with financial facilities by the Caisse Centrale de Crédit et de Prévoyance. (This structure continued into the early sixties, when it was reformed.) Parallel with the old system were the Caisses Régionales d'Epargne et de Crédit, CREC, which extended credit to a few sectors including agriculture. Likewise, there were the Sociétés Coopérative Agricoles Marocaines, SCAM, whose activities included the provision of credit. In all instances, the loans were short-term or medium-term. In the year 1956-7, total credit extended was about 82m dirhams.[102] However, the beneficiaries were essentially not the small farmers, the most needy group. The larger the operation (and, almost automatically, the more influential the landlord), the likelier and the larger the loan.

This judgement continues to be correct (though to a lesser extent). The improvement is imputable to two factors. The first is the larger resources now (in the early seventies) available to the main organisation, the Caisse Nationale de Crédit Agricole, CNCA, with its own capital and working capital together more than twice the volume available in 1956.[103] The second is the easing of collateral and other lending requirements to make it possible for small farms to obtain credit.

The first and major measure of reform in the agricultural credit system came in 1961, when the CNCA was established. Since then several regional and many local branches have been set up, but the main bottlenecks remain the insufficiency of resources for lending (though these have more than doubled since independence), and the insufficiency of technical and extension staff. In an official report dated May 1972 it is stated that in the first four years of the Five-Year Plan 1968-72, 2,297 persons had been trained as engineers and veterinary officers, practical engineers (that is, not licensed as engineers), technical assistants and technical agents. While the Plan had provided for 1,901 of these, the needs of the country amounted to 3,561 persons in the four categories of skill. Furthermore, there was a discrepancy between plan provisions and achievements. The Plan for Economic and Social Development 1973-7 does not provide a quantified comparison between needs and availability of technical personnel, but it is clear from the context that there is still a wide gap in the account.[104] Furthermore the framework is still faulty, with the traditional subsector which is needier than its modern counterpart continuing to benefit relatively less from the financial facilities, even though the CNCA already has a dozen years of experience behind it.

There is one more organisation that will be referred to here, out of several that have been established but will not be examined owing to space limitations and to the modesty of their role. This is the Office National des Irrigations, ONI, which was established in 1960 to take over and merge together the individual administrations controlling individual barrage areas. Its functions include the conception and planning of irrigation projects and their networks (though it is the Ministry of Public Works that undertakes actual construction), the management of the works, including the aspect of irrigation and that of generation of power where this is relevant, the elaboration of new patterns of crop rotation and, in conjunction with other competent bodies, the transformation of cultivation in irrigated areas. The Office has been rather successful within the framework of its powers. The misgivings relating to the whole barrage policy must not be projected to include the Office itself, since the final decision on sites rests with the government. The government is a political body, while the Office is essentially technical and administrative. In any case, the Office disappeared in 1965, where, along with the ONMR, it was replaced by the OMVA (already referred to).

The Evolution of Major Areas of Activity

Land, irrigation and rural development in general were given more space here than the other sectors will receive. This is because the rural sector is of considerable importance on economic, social and political grounds, and because its problems, like those of unemployment and underemployment (which are closely linked with agriculture anyway) are the most intractable in the whole economy.

What will be attempted now is an examination of the course of evolution of the major areas of activity, namely agriculture, industry, mining, energy and tourism.

We saw in Table 13.11 above that GNP (at constant prices) rose by 86 per cent between 1956 and 1972. However, the three groups of sectors — the primary, the secondary and the tertiary — moved at different rates of growth, and the individual sectors diverged from each other even more. The following tabulation will attempt to show this divergence, sector by sector, using the values for 1956 as the base, and deflating the values for 1972 in the same manner used in Table 13.11 in order to find the indices of real growth by the terminal year.

Morocco

Table 13.20: Indices of Real Growth in Each Sector, 1956-72 (1956 = 100)

Sector	1972
Agriculture, livestock, forestry and fishing	152.8
Energy (water and electricity)	406.9
Mining (and quarrying)	159.4
Industry and handicrafts	157.8
Construction and public works	169.1
Transport, services	290.7
Trade	279.4
All sectors listed above	191.8

Note: The index for the sectors combined is slightly higher than that for GNP, which is 186.1. The discrepancy arises from the fact that GNP includes the 'contribution' of government to national product, whereas this table does not.

Source: For 1956 data, *Annuaire Statistique . . . 1955-1956*, p. 466; for 1972 data, BNDE, op. cit., p. 7. The 1956 data were at constant (1952) prices, while the 1972 data were at current prices. Consequently the cost-of-living index which was originally used for deflation in Table 13.11 was used for the 1956 and 1972 values.

If we consider the index for the sectors combined as the dividing line between the fast-growing and the slow-growing sectors, then only one commodity sector, energy, emerges as growing satisfactorily. Indeed, it is the fastest-growing, but it does not influence the average rate of growth much because its contribution is very modest (in fact, by far the smallest) in absolute terms. Both categories of service sectors listed are likewise fast-growing. Every other sector is slow-growing, with the primary group — agriculture, livestock, forestry and fishing — being distinctly the most sluggish.

The performance of agriculture is all the more unsatisfactory because for many years it has been the beneficiary of a relatively large share of public investment. This will become clear in the next section when the various plans will be examined. Yet disappointing as the results are, they make for persistence in diverting large investments to land a very high priority. However, that by itself will not be capable of improving the performance, if the errors of omission and of commission in land policy are not corrected. It is not necessary to repeat these since they have received sufficient attention already.

Furthermore, nothing much more need be said with respect to the evolution of the sector's activities. We have seen that the area under cultivation has not varied between 1956 and 1972, but that the area under irrigation has expanded considerably. We need only add that some new cultures have been introduced, such as sugar beet, sunflower and other crops producing vegetable oils. Other crops, particularly citrus fruits, have recorded substantial expansion both in the volume and the value of production and of exports. (Production has averaged 812,000 tons for the three years 1970-2, and the value of exports has averaged 389m dirhams.)[105]

Table 13.21 sums up the evolution of the country's agricultural performance. The changes in total production and of foodstuff production (and likewise the change *per capita*) are presented in the form of index numbers, based on data in the FAO *Production Yearbook* for 1967 and 1972.

These data are quite eloquent. They reveal serious deterioration with respect both to general agricultural production and food production between the early fifties and 1966,

Table 13.21: Total Agricultural Production and Foodstuff Production, 1952-6 and 1961-5

Total Agricultural Production	
1952-6 as base (=100)	Index for 1966: 106
1961-5 as base (=100)	Index for 1972: 146
Production of Foodstuff	
1952-6 as base	Index for 1966: 108
1961-5 as base	Index for 1972: 146
Per capita Production	
Total Agricultural Production	
1952-6 as base	Index for 1966: 76
1961-5 as base	Index for 1972: 113
Foodstuff Production	
1952-6 as base	Index for 1966: 77
1961-5 as base	Index for 1972: 113

Source: FAO, *Production Yearbook*, 1967 and 1972 (Chapter III).

but some improvement between the early sixties and 1972. Total production marked very modest progress in the first period, while *per capita* production by 1966 actually fell to three-fourths its base level — in other words, it lagged behind population increase. However, even in the second, more recent period, *per capita* production rose only slightly (by 13 per cent) over its level in the base years.

The country's livestock wealth has not changed much over the years. The dairy and meat industry is far from developed, and the country satisfies only about 40 per cent of its requirements in dairy products. Although self-sufficient in meats, Morocco has not modernised its slaughterhouses except in the large urban centres. The livestock branch of activity could expand considerably if it were to receive and diligently use the resources necessary for such expansion.

Energy stands at the other extreme with respect to rate of growth. The only branches of energy of significance are electricity and coal; petroleum production is dwindling fast, with only 25,400 tons recovered in 1972, and natural gas production is equally insignificant. Coal production has been rising since 1969, after it dipped during the preceding few years. It stood at 547,000 tons in 1972. However, it is electricity generation that has made the largest gain over the years of independence, rising from 935.1m kwh in 1956 to 2,337m kwh in 1972 — a net rise of 150 per cent. This would allow for about 148 kwh per person per year, or a net rise of 58 per cent *per capita* in the whole period. Though the improvement is tangible, it is by no means satisfactory, especially when a considerable part of the power produced is used outside households. One limitation on production is the desire by the government to keep their main reliance on hydro-electric generators, which still account for about 70 per cent of production.[106]

Mining has been the next-slowest sector — almost as slow-moving as agriculture. (If phosphate extraction, which is fast-growing, is excluded, the rate of growth would be even lower.) However, although it has had some fluctuation, the trend is rising, in terms of the volume of production and of exports, and of the value of exports. Phosphates are still by far the most significant among the components of the sector, and outweigh all the other components combined, whether in volume or in value. (Phosphate production totalled 14.97m tons in 1972, and 17.08m tons in 1973, while the other products combined totalled 1.13m and 1.07m, apart from coal, respectively. On the other hand, total exports of crude mining products totalled a little over 877m and 1 billion dirhams, of which phosphates alone accounted for 673m and 788m respectively.)[107] If there is one major lesson that these few statistics suggest, it is the scope for vast expansion in the value added in the mining sector, through a transition from the export of most ores in a crude form to the processing of much of these ores. A beginning, though very modest (involving the production of some 150,000 tons of hyperphosphates and superphosphates) has been made in this direction, as already indicated earlier, but what has been done represents a modest proportion of the country's potential.

The prospecting for minerals and the research and planning relating to minerals is still under the Bureau de Recherches et de Participations Minières, BRPM, which had been founded in 1928 and which continues to exist.[108] The actual exploitation and marketing of phosphates, the most important mineral, is in the hands of the Office Chérifien des Phosphates, to which reference was made in the first section of this chapter. (It will be remembered that Morocco is the second-largest producer of phosphates in the world, but the largest exporter.) These two institutions are probably the most active of their type in Morocco. This is mainly because they have autonomy in operation and they deal in marketable products, the production and sale of which is profitable. It is to be recalled that mineral wealth became state property in 1951, while it used before that to be owned jointly by private interests (virtually all foreign) and the government. The BRPM has extensive shares in 32 companies that are active in the field of mining. This participation ranges widely, from about one-sixteenth to about two-thirds of capital. The private interests include a high proportion of foreign capital.

The last to be considered in the commodity group of sectors is industry. This activity includes both the modern and traditional subsectors. The latter has been stagnant, to the point that official statistics do not give it separate treatment. It is even probable that it has stagnated at its level in absolute terms, which would mean a decline in relative terms. The stagnation arises from factors largely beyond the control of government or the craftsmen, such as the preference for manufactured substitutes to handicrafts products. (There is still a Bureau that looks after the 'artisanat', as well as a special 'Caisse' to extend loans to artisans.) Its decline notwithstanding, traditional industry remains exceedingly important as an employer of manpower, engaging as it does many more men and women than the modern subsector. This in itself should call for special treatment.

The major branches of modern industry and their growth indices by 1972 (1958=100) are listed in Table 13.22. The unweighted average for these groups is 191, which is about equal to the index for all sectors as recorded in Table 13.20. However, the index for 'industry and handicrafts' is only 157.8. While it is quite possible that weighting would bring down the average, it is also tenable that the inclusion of handicrafts, which constitute a stagnating subsector, may well have had a strong effect in pulling the whole index downwards.

In any case, the conclusion cannot be avoided that the advances made in industry are very modest, even when compared with those in many other Arab countries. Morocco is one of the few cases where *both* agriculture and industry have been sluggish — in fact, the most

Table 13.22: Growth Indices of Industry, 1972

Branch	Index in 1972
Mineral ore processing	150
Ceramics and construction materials	239
Chemical products	232
Oils and fats	177
Foodstuffs	166
Textiles	321
Tanning, leather and leather goods	109
Paper and cardboard	155
Miscellaneous	174

Source: BNDE, op. cit., p. 99.

sluggish sectors in the economy. This in itself suggests the vast scope for growth in the industrial sector. However, it must be stated that the last five years covered, namely 1968-72, or the years of the last plan fully implemented, are reported to have witnessed an average rate of growth of about 5.7 per cent per annum. Though not substantial, this rate compares very favourably with that achieved in the decade 1958 to 1967. Indeed, the total growth achieved in the last five years is greater than that achieved in the preceding ten. (The year 1973 alone witnessed a rate of growth of 11.7 per cent.) There are individual exceptions to this generalisation. These are the leather, paper and cardboard industries, where there has been a marked slackening, and textiles, where the slackening has been more moderate. In this last case, which constitutes the branch growing fastest in the sector, the slackening is the result of a natural slowing down, following speedy expansion. The industry is probably passing through a gestation period now in order to absorb its vast investments in the last decade.

Modern industry has received great impetus since independence. First a Bureau d'Etudes et de Participations Industrielles, BEPI, was established in 1958, to be as active as BRPM in its field. However, BEPI has been quite inactive for almost a decade. An Industrial Investment Code was enacted in 1961, to provide incentives for industry. Furthermore, credit is extended by more than one institution — most eminently the BNDE (Banque Nationale pour le Développement Economique), which extended 145m dirhams from 1961 to 1972. This constitutes 64 per cent of its total loans for the dozen years.[109] The picture has, however, to be seriously qualified. In so far as the ownership of industry is concerned, foreign interests still owned a large proportion of industrial capital. Only in 1971 did Moroccanisation begin to be effected very gradually. In March 1973 the King ordered acceleration, with a deadline for the completion of the process in April 1974. (Moroccanisation of banks, insurance companies, import agencies and trading establishments was to be completed by April 1975.[110]) Another qualification relates to the shortage of Moroccan industrial entrepreneurs, the inadequacy of pre-investment studies, and — as far as planning is concerned — the over-optimism and over-estimation of the reaction of entrepreneurs to plan projections (and of consumers to locally manufactured goods).

Lastly, there remains one sector to consider, which falls in the tertiary group. This is tourism. It is unfortunate that this sector is not shown separately in the national accounts, but is grouped with transport and other services. Nor are its earnings in foreign exchange in the current account of the balance of payments distinguishable from the other components of the item 'travel' into and out of the country. However, its fast growth can be gauged from the evolution in the number of tourists visiting Morocco. This has exceeded the one million mark for 1972, and 1.2m for 1973, although tourism began to acquire significance in the early sixties.

The government fully recognises the potential of tourism. Together with agriculture and manpower training it constitutes the three-lane approach to development in the recent conception of the planners. Whether the strategy of development can depend heavily on tourism is a debatable question.[111] But it remains true that tourism can be a substantial contributor to the foreign exchange pool of the country (as we had occasion to see earlier), and to the national product. This contribution can be made much larger, if the investments envisaged in the sector can be made, and made within the right system of priorities. The country is still poorly equipped for the big tourist business it could draw, or even for the business it now has. By the end of 1970, there were only 31,318 beds of all classes in the country's hotels. These had to meet the demand by residents travelling or vacationing inside the country, as well as foreigners coming on business and pleasure. Furthermore, judging by the distribution of hotels by 'class', the country over-emphasises the rich tourist. Future expansion must cater to the middle and lower middle classes more emphatically.

One thing is certain: Morocco has the natural endowments, in terms of sunshine, lovely climate and beautiful scenery, that can make it a major attraction for people on vacation. Yet optimism as far as foreign exchange and national product are concerned must be tempered where employment is concerned. Only a fraction (less than one-fifth) of the jobs expected to be created by new investments in the sector have actually materialised. However, the results of the Five-Year Plan 1968-72 are not available to assess the extent of increase in employment thanks to the substantial new investments made in tourist facilities.

It is appropriate to end this section with the observation that Morocco, probably more than any other country included in this study, has built specialised institutions and organisations which stand parallel to the respective ministries and undertake certain functions, presumably unfettered (or only slightly fettered) by the routine and bureaucracy of ministries. True, this has not always been the case: jealousies have often immobilised these autonomous or semi-autonomous institutions, activities have been hampered by insufficient staff, funds or powers, but in most cases the legislative instruments establishing them have given them the powers that are meant to enable them to function adequately. Yet, from their inception, and even today, most of them have suffered from shortage of trained personnel and/or of funds, and in several instances they have been bypassed, and exist as deserted structures showing in their outward façade glories past, which contrast sadly with their present state of neglect.

We have had occasion to refer to several such institutions — in the fields of agriculture, industry and mining, as well as finance. Many others exist elsewhere, complete with legislative framework, offices, impressive names and initials. But only few are active and successful. This minority includes some of the financial institutions and the BRPM and OCP. The most important financial institution is the BNDE. Together, the financial institutions had 1,630 million dirhams as working capital by the end of 1970, including 198 million of external loans.[112] Their loans to the economy were 1,800m in 1972 and to public collective bodies 257m at that date. In addition, their portfolio amounted to 104m. Short-term loans amounted to about 12 per cent of the total, while medium-term loans accounted for one-third, and the balance was in long-term credit. Industry was the largest beneficiary, followed closely by hotels, then by agriculture, housing and trade. (These data exclude the loans extended by the institutions known as Fonds d'Equipement Communal of which there are several, but for which data are not available to this writer.) A complete list of the specialised financial institutions to which reference is being made follows:

Banque Nationale pour le Développement Economique, BNDE. Capital 20m dirhams, owned by the government, the private sector — Moroccan banks, insurance companies and agencies, as well as members of the board of directors and other individuals — and by foreign groups including banks and insurance companies, foreign finance institutions and the IBRD.

Caisse de Dépot et de Gestion, CDG, charged with the management of the 'institutions de prévoyance et de solidarité', encouragement of savings, direct investment, and extension of credit to communal collectivities. Its working capital comes from its own capital and reserves, the deposits at its disposal (especially from the Caisse d'Epargne Nationale, CEN and the Caisse Nationale de Securité Sociale, CNSS and other institutional deposits).

Caisse Nationale de Crédit Agricole, CNCA, whose capital consists of credits from the government, a loan from the IBRD, credit from the Banque du Maroc, and creditor current accounts from depositors.

Crédit Immobilier et Hotelier, CIH, founded in 1920 but continuing into the present under the name CIH du Maroc, with capital owned by the CDG, Banque du Maroc, Moroccan banks and insurance companies, and bearer-shares. In addition, it has received loans from the IBRD and the proceeds of local loans.

Caisse Marocaine des Marchés, CMM, founded in 1950, is a marketing fund with capital currently owned mainly by BNDE, CDG and Banque Marocaine pour le Commerce Extérieur. Its basic role is to help the financing of public markets or such private markets considered a public interest.

4. PLANNING AND PLANS IN MOROCCO[113]

Morocco has had experience with planning since 1949, as we saw in section 1. This experience has run without interruption until the present, the quality and comprehensiveness of the plans apart. Thus there were two plans under the protectorate, the 1949-53 and the 1954-7 plans. A sort of interim plan was formulated to bridge the gap between the 1954-7 plan and the fully-fledged plan that was to be formulated as soon as feasible. Thus the Biennial Investment Plan for 1958-9 was formulated. Since then, there have been four plans: the Five-Year Plan 1960-4, the Three-Year Plan 1965-7, the Five-Year Plan 1968-72, and the current one, the Plan for Economic and Social Development 1973-7.

Upon independence, Morocco adopted the French planning (and the national accounting) concepts, techniques and approaches, and the structure of the planning organisms as they were experienced under the protectorate and as they were known to stand in France after independence. Naturally, in many respects this adoption was not the most sound or appropriate thing, in so far as the statistical data available, the skills available, and the stage of development in the country differed from those in France and called for adjustments in conception, methodology and type and sophistication of planning. This observation apart, Morocco was fortunate in the sense that its desire to imitate the French experience was an added impetus for continuing with the practice of planning unbroken, even if the planners

Morocco 645

paid the price that emulation usually exacts. This price was to spend several years of trial and error before they could steer much of their own course in the light of their own experience and their country's reality. It can be said that by the mid-sixties, the planners were convinced that the best course of action was 'learning through doing', and this conviction and the lesson it represents brought in the dividend of a much improved and realistic planning, particularly beginning with the 1968-72 Plan.

The planning machinery set up upon independence was essentially a continuation of the machinery the protectorate government had had, with a change in nomenclature. Initially there was a Planning Office attached to the Office of the Secretary-General of the protectorate. Upon independence, the latter became the Secretary-General of the government, and the Planning Office was attached to him, as well as the Service Central de Statistiques and the Bureau des Publications et Graphiques. However, on 2 September 1957 a Ministry of National Economy and Finance was created, and the planning authority was transferred to it, under the name Division de la Coordination Economique et du Plan, DCEP. More than 80 per cent of the staff of 60 were French — the Moroccans numbered two, plus an Algerian and a few UN advisers.[114] The DCEP was to prepare a transitional two-year plan for 1958 and 1959, and the law stipulating this plan also charged the planning authority with the preparation of a five-year plan for the years 1960-4 by a date not later than 1 October 1959.

Finally, this law (which was enacted on 22 June 1957) set up a Conseil Supérieur du Plan, CSP, which was to be headed by the head of the government and to include among its 24 members a number of Ministers and senior officials as well as some members of the National Consultative Assembly, and finally three members to represent the agricultural sector, three to represent the unions, and one each for handicrafts, industry and commerce.[115] The CSP was not active in the area for which it had been designed, namely examination of the broad structure of the plan, but busied itself with political and ideological conflicts among its members. Thus, the Conseil 'was permitted to expire', in Waterston's words. Its demise occurred in the early sixties.[116]

What is significant is that the law stipulated that many commissions should be created to help broaden the planning process and widen the base of consultation and discussion prior to the formulation of the plan. These included a series of commissions specialised in various aspects of planning; Provincial Economic Commissions (Commissions Economiques Provinciales) to provide regional and local depth and protect the plan from the danger of being solely an exercise by technicians and bureaucrats in the central government; and a Central Research and Financing Commission (Commission Centrale d'Etudes et de Financement) which was to assess the financing requirements and explore how to meet them. This elaborate structure remained largely and literally a chart on paper, with the Central Research and Financing Commission being no more than a shadow without much substance or power, and with no Provincial Commissions. These in fact were never formed, while the specialised commissions, of which 15 were formed, never functioned properly; they were headed by bureaucrats and technicians whose reports rarely reflected what the non-government members said or the lessons of experience they brought with them.

The DCEP continued to occupy its place, at least on organisational charts, down to the late sixties. The Five-Year Plans 1968-72 and 1973-77 appear under its imprint. However, it had been relegated to a very minor place by the early sixties, and in fact the DCEP

was not even involved in the formulation of the Three-Year Plan 1965-67. The Plan was prepared by technicians from the *French Commissariat Général du Plan* in conjunction with government officials appointed by the Government to a series of sectoral and other commissions.[117]

Today, with the break-up of the Ministry of National Economy and Finance and the reallocation of its functions to separate ministries (finance; trade, industry, mines and merchant shipping; agriculture and agrarian reform; and tourism — apart from other ministries less closely related to economic affairs), the planning function is vested in the Secretary of State at the Prime Minister's Office for Planning, Regional Development and Professional Training. However, there are other authorities with overlapping functions, such as the Ministry of Town Planning, Housing and the Environment; and the Secretary of State at the Prime Minister's Office for National Promotion, National Co-operation and Crafts — to say nothing of the BRPM and the BEPI.

We need not go into the various changes in the organisation and structure of the planning authority, as these followed the general pattern of organisational change and reformulation with which we became familiar in the last section of this chapter. But it is important to stress the fluctuations in the degree of seriousness with which planning has been taken and in the philosophy underlying all planning activity. Thus, the transitional Two-Year Investment Plan 1958-59 was meant merely as a continuation of the 1954-57 Plan, emphasising the completion of the projects initiated earlier but not completed. The Five-Year Plan 1960-64 began under one philosophy but changed course and adopted another soon after. Thus, initially, in its first version (published in November 1960, the same month when the *dahir* enacting it as law appeared) this Plan emphasised industry and based the strategy of development on industrialisation. The government under which the Plan was formulated and finalised was radical in attitude and intent on achieving decolonisation speedily. But soon afterwards this government was replaced by another, distinctly less radical. Thus, a second version of the Plan was published which shifted the emphasis from industrialisation to combating unemployment — from a positive to a negative policy, as it were. Furthermore, the authorities reverted to their fundamental liberalism, which was reflected, outside the contents of the Plan, in the new Industrial Investment Code of 1961 which opened the doors wide to foreign investment and to local private entrepreneurship. By 1962, the Plan was dead for all practical purposes, and the government kept the hollow structure until the next plan was formulated.[118] It is to be noted incidentally that the years 1960-4 were years of near stagnation in the economy. This may be no more than an association, but it is worth bearing in mind.

The subsequent plans fared a little better, but invariably there was a shortfall in overall investment coupled with variations in outlook and emphasis. Although each of the last three plans — 1965-7, 1968-72 and 1973-7 — devotes some sections to an examination of the performance of the preceding plan, we do not have the opportunity to set down the detailed objectives and quantitative targets side by side with the performance, for a well-based evaluation. Consequently, in what remains of this section we shall present the broad features of the plans, from the Two-Year Investment Plan 1958-59, to the Five Year Plan 1973-77,[119] and finally present an overall evaluation of the planning experience of the country and of the impact of planning on development.

The investment programme of the Two-Year Investment Plan 1958-59 was all centred in the public sector, and it totalled the equivalent of 895m dirhams (89.5 billion old francs). The programme allocated the investments in the manner shown in Table 13.23. The emphasis was primarily on the rural sector, with allocations for it exceeding one-third of the total. On the other hand, industry received a very small percentage, since together with energy and trade it accounted for 6.5 per cent only. This is explained in the fact that the pro-

Morocco

Table 13.23: Planned Investment, 1958-9

Sector	Million Dirhams	Per Cent
Agriculture	173	19.3
Irrigation	141	15.7
Energy, industry and trade	58	6.5
Transport and communications	135	15.1
Housing	149	16.7
Education, culture and social services	124	13.9
Administrative investments	80	8.9
Miscellaneous	35	3.9
Total	895	100.0

gramme was one of public investment, and the expectation was that the private sector would provide almost all the resources necessary for industrial development. The government preferred to rely more on industrial promotive policies than on direct investment in industry. Housing, as can be seen, received a relatively high proportion, a fact that was not to be repeated in the plans to follow. Education and training were also to receive strong support through the investment programme.

The actual investment constituted a small proportion of the total projected, particularly in agriculture. In fact, the two years covered, particularly the second, witnessed a sharp drop in investment, with practically no private resources going into capital formation. Yet this year also witnessed some important institutional developments: the formation of the Banque du Maroc, and of the BNDE, and the independence of the country's currency (and commercial policy) from the franc and French commercial policy. This in itself constituted a platform from which to launch policies promotive to industry. Furthermore, though project implementation was slow, owing in part to the inexperience of the national bodies in charge of execution and evaluation, and in part to the inadequate preparation of project studies, the plan period served as a phase of apprenticeship for the years to come.

In terms of financing, the country showed some promise in that the bulk of the plan was financed from domestic sources, although some foreign aid flowed into the country. However, the investment programme was not excessively large. This had a conflicting significance: it lightened the load of foreign indebtedness, but it also failed to have a strong impact on development. Yet a much larger programme would have failed to have a much larger impact, because the administrative and technical and supervisory machinery in the government was not capable of coping with many more projects.

The formulation of the Five-Year Plan 1960-64 was completed in November 1960, after a very large number of meetings by the specialised commissions and many working groups and subcommittees. (It is reported that about 1,500 persons in all were involved, one way or another, in the preparation of the Plan.) In the meantime, the government had been reshuffled, and in consequence the broad guidelines of the Plan had to be changed a few months before the final draft.

The Plan was comprehensive: taking into account economic and social development, and projecting the investment activities of the private as well as the public sector. It laid down those institutional, economic and financial policies considered necessary to make the private sector behave as expected in the projections. None the less, owing to the harsh limitations that financing, manpower skills and experience imposed, the Plan remained modest in magnitude. The total gross investment stipulated was 8.5 billion dirhams (the net investment was to be 6.6 billion), or an average of 1.7 billion dirhams annually, equivalent to $340m at the rate of exchange then prevailing. The rate of growth expected was 6.2 per cent per annum.

The Plan had two major objectives: (a) to achieve a large measure of self-sufficiency in manpower skills, capital and outlets for local production, and (b) to reduce the degree of dualism in the economy. These objectives were to be achieved through energetic and far-reaching educational and training programmes; measures of agricultural reform and modernisation in the traditional sector; the establishment of a base of heavy industry (mainly in the steel and chemical industries), while leaving wide open the opportunity for private enterprise to enter into industry at large; and reforming of public administration and reducing the foreign element in it in order to speed the implementation of the Plan. The Plan was to be followed by more detailed elaborations on the parts of the Plan that related to the regions, and the Plan document also announced subsequent publications to deal with modifications as the need arose, and with sectoral plans. The sectoral plans did appear, but not much was done with respect to the regional plans.

Before we proceed any further, it is necessary to state that the initiation of the Plan was delayed, partly because the directives and policies necessary for implementation were not issued, and partly because of personnel shortages at almost every level of action. Furthermore, revisions, the need for which was already evident, were difficult to make because of the shortage of statistical information and the very limited co-operation of the business community with the Statistical Service in its efforts to collect data. The Plan was finally divided into two halves, the first to consist mainly of the completion of projects already in the pipeline, and of preparatory measures for the second part, which was to incorporate many more of the projects originally included. However, the second part was never implemented *as a Plan,* or as a coherent whole, and the Plan lapsed in 1962. The planners began preparing for the next document, the Three-Year Plan 1965-7.

The investment programme is mainly of historical interest, since the Plan was left largely unimplemented. Nevertheless, we will present it below in detail, but we will not go into any other projections (such as those relating to the balance of payments, employment, or individual sectors). The values all refer to net investment, as the Plan document does not present gross investment.

It is not very significant to evaluate a Plan which was less than half implemented, whether in terms of its life span, or its investment programme. Nevertheless, it will be useful to point to the major defects and shortcomings experienced in the years 1960-4.

To begin with, the gross investment envisaged, namely 8.5 billion dirhams, was not achieved. Table 13.12 shows that a total of 5.61 billion were invested over the five years, or two-thirds of the total projected. (The chapter describing the situation before the Three-Year Plan 1965-7 in the Plan document itself states that expected investment was 7.68 billion dirhams, while actual investment totalled 5.38 billion, or 70 per cent. The discrepancy in the data is not explained.) By itself, this is a satisfactory performance, But it must be remembered that much of this investment had not been planned. The divergence was large, both from year to year and from sector to sector. Thus, there were simultaneously movements in opposite directions: underspending in many instances because of the shortage in skilled manpower, experience and pre-investment studies; and spending on projects not in

Table 13.24: Net Investment Under the Five-Year Plan 1960-4

Sector	State		Local		Semi-Public		Private		Total	
	Million Dirhams	Per Cent	Million Dirhams	Per Cent	Million Dirhams	Per Cent	Million Dirhams	Per Cent	Million Dirhams	Per Cent
Totals	2,589.7	39.2	395.0	6.0	158.2	2.4	3,457.8	52.4	6,600.7	100.0
Agriculture	830.9	32.0	—	—	—	—	1,223.2	35.3	2,054.1	31.2
Industry	289.5	11.2	—	—	158.3	100.0	1,426.0	41.2	1,873.8	28.4
Handicrafts	11.4	0.5	—	—	—	—	44.1	1.3	55.5	0.8
Electric power	51.5	2.1	—	—	—	—	38.0	1.1	89.5	1.3
Infrastructure	550.9	21.5	—	—	—	—	—	—	550.9	8.3
Rural and urban development	314.5	12.2	395.0	100.0	—	—	640.0	18.6	1,349.5	20.5
Services	7.7	0.3	—	—	—	—	86.5	2.5	94.2	1.5
Social investment	413.2	16.1	—	—	—	—	—	—	413.2	6.1
Administrative investment	120.0	4.1	—	—	—	—	—	—	120.0	1.9
Total	2,589.6	100.0	395.0	100.0	158.3	100.0	3,457.8	100.0	6,600.7	100.0

Source: Condensed from the *Five-Year Plan 1960-64*, pp.30-4.

the Plan at all (in satisfaction of promises spontaneously made by Ministers or other dignitaries — promises that had to be honoured by the provision of new allocations).[120]

Furthermore, the division of labour was hazy between authorities undertaking development work, and duplication often occurred, with co-ordination being very poor and limited in scope. (Such bodies included the National Development Board entrusted with the task of 'Promotion Nationale', and the BEPI and BRPM.)

The end result in terms of growth achieved was well below expectations. The average rate of growth was 4 per cent annually, which was superior to the rate prevailing in the preceding several years. On the other hand, the expectation of the Plan to achieve a rate of 6.2 per cent was unrealistic, given the many bottlenecks in the economy and the very low performance in the decade before. The bottlenecks were not unknown to the planners, since they devoted substantial space to describe them and to explain how they operate and slow down the pace of growth.

The document of the Three-Year Plan 1965-67 starts with an examination of the previous Plan and of the causes for its shortcomings and failure. Indeed, the King himself was very critical of the way in which the Five-Year Plan 1960-64 stumbled and prematurely expired, in two speeches he made at the Supreme Council for National Promotion and Planning. He also drew attention to the logic of the experience, which led the planners to emphasise the development of infrastructure and basic activities during the unfolding of the Three-Year Plan 1965-67, in order for the country to be spared a repetition of its recent experience with the Five-Year Plan. Finally, he indicated his preference that the planning document be considered more of a programme than a plan, as it was intended as a transitional instrument between the 1960-64 Plan, and a forthcoming plan for which preparations were to be set afoot at an early stage, namely the Five-Year Plan 1968-72.

The priorities of the 1965-67 Plan were: the development and modernisation of agriculture; the promotion of tourism; and the formation of skilled cadres. The first of these priorities included the fight against unemployment and underemployment in the rural sector, and generally the promotion of agriculture, whether rain-fed or irrigated.

It is observed in the Plan document[121] that industrial growth in the years 1960-4 did not help in the attainment of the objectives of the Five-Year Plan, and that this was attributable to the inability of industry to find domestic markets for its products. This conviction seems to have led the planners to the adoption of the line of least resistance: the investment pre-eminently in consumer goods for which local markets are assured, and the assurance of these markets through protection, government intervention and subvention. This course was far from being a forceful course of industrialisation and the facing of the challenges to which industry was subjected.

No detailed presentation of the Plan will be undertaken here. It is sufficient that the Plan document lays stress on balance, whether this is between regions and localities, or between sectors. The investment programme that was to bring about the transformations envisaged totalled 3.5 billion dirhams, allocated by sector and by source, as can be seen in Table 13.25.

The Plan document warns the reader that the investment programme is approximate, and that the Plan is indicative. This explains why no projections are included in Table 13.25 for private-sector investment in certain fields. To this note of realism must be added another note: the modesty of the rate of growth expected. This is 3.7 per cent. And the reader is reminded again that it would be meaningless to aim at a much higher but unrealistic and unfeasible rate which cannot be warranted by the economy's expected performance.

The Plan document did not foresee full domestic financing of the investment programme.

Morocco

Table 13.25: Investment Programme of the Three-Year Plan 1965-67 (million dirhams)

Sector	Public Sector	Quasi-Public Sector	Private Sector	Total	Per Cent
Agriculture	851.6	—	a	851.6	24.4
Tourism	134.0	—	90.0	224.0	6.4
Training of cadres	117.7	—	a	117.7	3.4
Infrastructure	389.3	—	a	389.3	11.2
Energy	120.0	120.0	—	240.0	6.9
Productive sectors[b]	532.5	352.3	459.6	1,344.4	38.6
Education and social services	151.9	—	—	151.9	4.4
Administration (equipment)	124.1	—	a	124.1	3.6
Extraordinary expenditure	40.0	—	a	40.0	1.1
Total	2,461.1	472.3	549.6	3,483.0	100.0

a. Indicated as 'reminder' only. Since the Plan was an indicative plan, no projections are made for private sector investments in certain fields — either because these fields are not relevant to private sector activity, or because no projection is possible (as in the case of agriculture).
b. These include the following:

Mining	44.6	352.3	146.6	543.5	
Industry	485.0	—	313.0	798.0	
Traditional industry	1.7	—	a	1.7	
Fishing and merchant marine	1.2	—	a	1.2	
Total productive sectors	532.5	352.3	459.6	1,344.4	

Source: *Three-Year Plan 1965-1967* (Arabic), pp. 54-64.

Domestic financing was set at 1.57 billion dirhams, and foreign financing at 0.52 billion, totalling 2.09 billion. The shortfall was to be sought from foreign sources, in addition to the magnitude of 0.52 billion explicitly stated as foreign-financed.

This Plan encountered more or less the same types of problems as its predecessor, but the severity of the hardships was milder. The Plan ran its course, but it was understood right from the start as a mere bridge leading to the next plan that was to be a fully-fledged plan. The performance in the years 1965-7 was mixed. Actual investments (at constant prices) were in excess of 4.5 billion dirhams, or more than 30 per cent over planned investment. This is in part explainable in the fact that the two magnitudes are not comparable: the planned investment did not include private sector investments in agriculture, whereas actual expenditure included all categories, regardless of source or agent. Another partial explanation is that many investments were made for which the Plan had not provided. The average rate of growth achieved between 1965 and 1967 was about 2.5 per cent, or about two-thirds the rate expected. Indeed, the average capital-output ratio for the three years amounts to 8.2:1 — a ratio too high even for a plan that has a large component of infrastructural investment. The explanation must lie in part in the low level of efficiency of the other factors of production, and in the inadequacy of the framework.

652 Morocco

The Five-Year Plan 1968-72 document is prefaced by a brief evaluation of the performance under the Three-Year Plan 1965-7. This performance is measured in terms of investments actually made out of total allocations for each of the sectors. The proportion of realised investments varies from sector to sector, as the following summing-up shows, but it is 68 per cent for the economy as a whole. (This contradicts what we stated earlier — namely that actual exceeded planned total investment. The reader is referred to the explanation attempted there.) The total allocations are slightly lower than the total investment programme, including private-sector investments anticipated, but more than the sum of the planned investment by the public and quasi-public sectors (3,134m versus 3,012m dirhams for actual and planned investment, respectively).[122] Furthermore, as can be seen from a comparison of the data in Table 13.25 with those to follow immediately, the credits actually made available to each of the sectors differ from those planned.

Table 13.26: Investments Used from Allocations under Three-Year Plan 1965-67

Sector	Credits Available (million dirhams)	Credits Used (million dirhams)	Performance Per Cent
Agriculture	988	585	59
Tourism	102	54	53
Infrastructure	528	405	77
Industry, mining, energy	850	548	64
Education, training, health, housing	416	321	77
Administration (equipment)	189	158	84
'Promotion Nationale'	61	61	100
Total/average	3,134	2,132	68

The mere spending of allocations is no better an indicator of the level of performance under planning in Morocco than anywhere else, but it is the only indicator available to us. Furthermore, to examine the performance through physical indicators, even were the particulars available, would entail a degree of detail which it is not advisable to usher here.

The Five-Year Plan 1968-72 is the first plan which is worthy of the name. It had comprehensive coverage and was allowed to run its full five years, though it experienced certain deviations between planned investment (by sector, programme and project), allocations in the annual budgets, and actual investments made. Furthermore, this is also the first plan which has been instrumental in bringing about sustained growth at a reasonably satisfactory level. (Yet this itself will be qualified in due course.)

The planners took into account the physical and material pressures in formulating the objectives of the Plan. Foremost among these pressures is the population increase which weighs increasingly heavily on the economy, the sluggishness of agriculture, and the low level of domestic savings and of private investments. With these problems in mind, a set of priorities was adopted which does not differ from that encountered before, namely: achievement of a rate of agricultural production clearly superior to that of population increase; expansion of tourist facilities; and continuation with acceleration of the manpower

Morocco 653

training programmes initiated earlier, with a view to the better equipping of the country with the technical and scientific apparatus needed for training, and the harmonisation between the training provided and the country's requirements.

In addition, three other priorities were underlined: confrontation with the population problem through family planning, provision of many more new jobs, fight against the *bidonvilles* mainly through the Promotion Nationale project, and resort to temporary emigration; promotion of industrial development, though agriculture continues to have top priority; and encouragement of saving through the elaboration of saving-promoting institutions, expansion in self-financing through the ploughing back of business profits, improvement in the taxation system with a view to the skimming of more income by the treasury, and the encouragement of the inflow of foreign capital. All through, regional and local planning were to receive all the attention and resources they merited, so that the development effort may be well spread out and balance may be achieved.

Table 13.27 presents the investment programme of the Five-Year Plan. This investment programme was hoped to raise Gross Domestic Production by 2,720m dirhams,[123] which means that the incremental capital-output ratio for the whole economy was to average 4.2:1. It is to be noted that all through in the plans, this ratio has been found to be high. This is understandable in view of the content of the investment programmes (with a heavy emphasis on infrastructure), and the low labour productivity of the large mass of workers.

The growth rates expected to be achieved varied from sector to sector, and varied also from those relating to the Three-Year Plan 1965-67. According to the Plan document, the rates achieved 1964-8 and expected for 1968-73 are shown in Table 13.28. It is worth noting that the two basic sectors of agriculture and industry were to achieve the most modest growth, the first distinctly below the average rate for the economy. Nor was the structure expected to vary much during the span of the Five-Year Plan. Indeed, according to the Plan document the period 1968-73 [*sic*] was not to witness significant structural change, as Table 13.29 shows.

The early ups and downs in the contribution of agriculture are more the result of climatic conditions than of deliberate investment policy. However, the expected drop between 1968 and 1973 was hoped to be achieved as a result of the investment programme and policies aiming at structural change. But the change is small, particularly where the other sectors are concerned. This is essentially a reflection of the philosophy underlying development planning and effort in Morocco, which is to bring about improvements in the sectors as they stand, though with occasional drastic changes in the relative position of one or two sectors. We have tourism in mind here, and mining to some extent. Industry has not at any time been adopted as a leading sector with which to spearhead the developmental operation.

The Plan expectations largely materialised with respect to investment (where 94 per cent of the investment projections were actually made),[124] although the fluctuations by sector and by financing agent were much wider. Likewise, the growth rate achieved was 93 per cent of that expected (4 per cent versus 4.3 per cent). However, official publications refer to a growth rate of 5.6 per cent.[125] This is obtained by relating 1972 to *1967*, which is not a legitimate procedure. The procedure was adopted probably because the GDP and GNP in 1967 were notably lower than in 1968, and this would show a good performance when 1967 is taken as the base year. The comparison between the projections for 1968-73 and the achievements for 1967-72 in Table 13.30 shows that all sectors except for 'construction and public works' had a better performance than earlier expected.[126] However, the comparison is rather misleading, since the reference periods are not strictly comparable. (This shift in years occurs frequently, and on the whole seems deliberately used to show the

Table 13.27: Investment Programme Under the Five-Year Plan 1968-72 (million dirhams)

Sector	Government			Business and Households			Total	
	State Budget	Other Budgets	Total	Quasi-Public Sector	Private Sector	Total	Million Dirhams	Per Cent
Agriculture	1,550	55	1,605		160	160	1,765	15.5
Barrages	746		746				746	6.5
Promotion Nationale project	120	30	150				150	1.2
Tourism	171	10	181	230	349	579	760	6.6
Energy	214		214	296		296	510	4.5
Mining	300		300	829	133	962	1,262	11.0
Industry	290		290	465	666	1,131	1,421	12.4
Handicrafts	22		22				22	0.2
Trade and services					90	90	90	0.8
Education and training	276		276				276	2.4
Youth and sports	20	5	25				25	0.2
Public health	101		101				101	0.9
Transport	554	10	564	57	72	129	693	6.1
Telecommunications	170		170	21		21	191	1.7
Housing – urban water	181	83	264	15	1,000	1,015	1,279	11.2
Administration (equipment)	196	2	198				198	1.7
Total new investment	4,911	195	5,106	1,913	2,470	4,383	9,489	82.9
Renewal of equipment		205	205	317	1,300	1,617	1,822	15.9
Adjustments (against advances for work preceding 1968)	139		139				139	1.2
Grand total	5,050	400	5,450	2,230	3,770	6,000	11,450	100.0

Source: *Plan Quinquennal 1968-1972*, Vol. I, pp.51 and 54.

Table 13.28: Growth Rate Achieved, 1964-8, and Expected, 1968-73

	1964-8	1968-73
Agriculture	1.9	2.1
Energy and mining	2.0	7.0
Industry and handicrafts	2.9	4.3
Construction and public works	5.5	8.5
Transport, trade, services	3.6	4.6
Total economy	2.9	4.3

Source: *Plan Quinquennal 1968-1972*, Vol. I, Ch. 1, p. 48.

Table 13.29: Share of Major Sectors in Gross Domestic Production (per cent)

	1960	1964	1968	1973
Agriculture	32.3	29.6	28.6	25.6
Energy and mining	8.8	8.5	8.2	9.2
Industry and handicrafts	13.4	15.7	15.7	15.6
Construction and public works	3.9	4.7	5.3	6.4
Transport, trade and services	41.6	41.5	42.2	43.2
Total	100.0	100.0	100.0	100.0

Source: *Plan Quinquennal 1968-1972*, Vol. I, p. 56.

performance as being good.)

No doubt the most satisfactory aspect of the performance was that relating to agriculture, traditionally the most sluggish of the sectors. This, plus other aspects of the economy's performance in recent years together constitute a new source of hope that the Moroccan economy has at last begun to move ahead at a satisfactory rate, although it has very far to go before it can achieve self-sustaining growth.

There are several major obstacles to be overcome before the blissful state of self-sustained growth is reached. One of these to which we will draw attention here is the dearth of domestic savings compared with the investments called for, and the inevitable heavy dependence on foreign financing of development. In the Five-Year Plan 1968-72, foreign financing was to account for more than half of total financing of public-sector investment, as the breakdown in Table 13.31 shows.

As things turned out, foreign financing was less significant than expected, or 1,733m dirhams out of a total investment of 5,630 million. (However, in the breakdown of this total, only 4,870 million are accounted for.)[127] Although some improvement is manifest here, there is still extensive recourse to deficit-financing.

Table 13.30: Comparison between Projections for 1968-73 and Achievements for 1967-72 (per cent)

Sector	Projections 1968-73	Achievements 1967-72
Agriculture, livestock, fishing	2.1	6.0
Energy and mining	7.0	7.2
Industry and handicrafts	4.3	5.3
Construction and public works	8.5	7.8
Trade, transport and other services	4.6	5.0
Gross Domestic Production	4.3	5.6

Table 13.31: Sources of Finance for Public-Sector Investment (million dirhams)

Foreign resources	1,940
Treasury	626
Regional Development Funds	565
New domestic resources (identified)	330
Sub-total	3,461
New domestic and foreign resources (unidentified)	1,589
Total	5,050

Source: *Plan Quinquennal 1968-1972*, Vol. I, p. 76.

The least satisfying aspect of the performance has been in the field of employment. Thus, whereas the Five-Year Plan 1968-72 had envisaged the provision of 485,000 new jobs with a shortfall of 115,000 job-seekers, in fact, according to a population and housing census undertaken in July 1971, there were 350,000 unemployed job-seekers. But this was not all, as the Plan for Economic and Social Development 1973-77 goes on to emphasise.[128] The census did not include as underemployed or unemployed 700,000 persons who worked during 1971, but for less than 6 months. Furthermore, the timing of the census in mid-summer disguised a large part of the underemployment, as hundreds of thousands would then have been remuneratively engaged in the countryside, who would not be gainful workers in much of the remainder of the year. The Plan document estimates urban unemployment alone to have been 15.4 per cent of the urban active population, apart from that in the rural sector.

The latest plan for the years 1973-7 seems to show greater concern with social development than the earlier plans (as its title itself suggests, in addition to its content). Indeed, one of the two major orientations set forth is the distribution of the national product 'within the framework of true social justice'.[129] The other orientation is the expansion in national product. This expansion is projected at an average of 7.5 per cent per annum (as against 4.7 per cent envisaged for the years 1969-73). However, the breakdown of this overall average varies substantially from the achievements of the previous Plan which covered the years 1968-72. The 1973-77 Plan projects the rates shown in Table 13.32.[130]

Table 13.32: Predicted Expansion, 1973-77 Plan (per cent)

Primary activities	3.6
Secondary activities	11.0
Tertiary activities	6.9
Gross Domestic Production	7.5

Source: *Plan... 1973-1977*, Vol. I, p. 71.

This pattern of growth reflects itself in the changes expected in the structure of the economy, with the share of primary activities in Gross Domestic Production dropping by 2.5 percentage points, that of secondary activities rising by 2.9 points, and that of tertiary activities dropping by 1.3 points.

The investment programme is very ambitious, with 26.3 billion dirhams for the five years, about 2.3 times that for 1968-72. The public sector is to provide 42.5 per cent of the total, while the quasi-public sector accounts for 12.4 per cent, the private sector for 20.7 per cent, and bank credit for 24.4 per cent. We need not go into as much detail here as in the case of the Five-Year Plan 1968-72, with regard to the breakdown of investment by sector and by agent of financing, but will simply give the percentage share of each of the sectors in the investment projected in Table 13.33.

Table 13.33: Projected Investment, 1968-72 Plan (per cent)

Agriculture	15.8
Industry	37.2
Infrastructure	8.6
Education and training	6.2
Social and cultural equipment	23.6
General administration	4.4
Regional development	4.2
Total	100.0

Source: *Plan... 1973-1977*, Vol. I, p. 81.

As can be seen, this is the first plan that allots more resources to industry than to any other sector. This reflects a change in the priority system which used to emphasise agriculture among the productive sectors. Another noticeable feature is the high proportion directed to housing (included in 'social and cultural equipment'), which comes after a poor performance in the previous Plan. In the 1968-72 Plan, 20,000 urban housing units had been projected for construction, but only 7,100 were actually built. In the countryside, out of 60,000 projected (in some 400 villages to be built in the irrigation areas), only 20,000 were actually constructed. Renovation of decrepit housing fared even worse, with 3,000 out of 30,000 units actually renovated.[131] Consequently, the 1973-77 Plan directs large allocations to housing in order to finish the largely unfinished tasks undertaken in the previous Plan.

It is too early to assess the degree of realism in the capability of the country to find enough resources to meet the huge investment programme foreseen. It is true that the mobilisation of domestic resources in the 1968-72 period proceeded better than had been expected. But the performance in absolute terms does not justify the large-scale optimism involving the mobilisation of a substantially larger volume of finance, not just a marginally larger volume. The answer will be extremely difficult to find in foreign financing, since this is expected to be 11.3 billion dirhams — about $2.8 billion at the exchange rate prevailing in 1973. This is far in excess of the aid Morocco had ever received in a comparable span of time. Furthermore, although the formation of cadres is moving ahead satisfactorily, there are still serious gaps and shortages at various professional and technical levels, and there is still an inadequacy of pre-investment studies.

The likelihood is great, in this writer's view, that the 1973-77 Plan as a whole will prove over-ambitious and that the human and financial resources available to the country will prove incapable of meeting the requirements of such a plan. (In fact, 1973 showed a decline in GDP, or negative growth, as indicated earlier.) The over-optimism may have arisen from the euphoria brought about by the reported success of the 1968-72 Plan — a success, it must again be said, which only appears if the year 1967 is taken as the reference year instead of 1968, the initial year in the Plan. In any case, the 'jump' from an investment programme totalling 11.4 to one totalling 26.3 billion dirhams is one which cannot be warranted on the grounds of the earlier 'success'.

5. CONCLUSION

There is no call for a detailed evaluation of the planning experience and performance of Morocco; such an evaluation has already been undertaken during the examination of the individual plans. It is sufficient here to record the marked improvement in planning methods and in the statistical basis on which the plans are formulated, as well as in the staffing of planning agencies. However, there is still some proliferation in agencies, as observed earlier. Furthermore, there has been rather excessive experimentation with the setting up of new institutions related to planning, or with the refurbishing of old institutions, in such a manner that hesitation and indecision have inevitably resulted. In addition, the ministries and other agencies entrusted with plan execution have on the whole been inadequately equipped to spend all the allocations made available to them. This is true especially of the period preceding 1965. In view of these and other factors (foremost among which is the inadequacy of skilled manpower), the growth rates projected have on the whole been far too optimistic and unrealistic.

Yet this evaluation is rather technical and to a certain extent simplistic, and it concerns itself with the phenomena and factors that float on the surface of the situation. What is more significant, and more deeply embedded — and therefore more difficult to quantify — is the social and institutional framework. This includes the poor mobilisation behind planning and the plans, which in turn is caused by the pattern of the distribution of power in the country, as seen by the intelligentsia and socio-political associations. The distrust that a number of the educated and semi-educated feel towards the development policy is understandable, though at times it may reach the limits of absurdity and be based on nothing better than political gossip.

Morocco is now equipping itself fast with skilled manpower, even though the unemployment and underemployment problem remains largely intractable. It is also equipping itself with the infrastructure and the other productive assets its economy needs for satisfactory development. What remains to be added to this mix is the all-important socio-political factor: a socially oriented political authority which feels as much anxiety about social justice and true political participation as it does about mechanistic development in terms of economic growth. The problem of external financing may become insignificant once these conditions are satisfied. For external finance is no more difficult to obtain, with Arab funds abundant and accessible, thanks to the developments in the oil sector after October 1973. The returns to investment will probably become tangibly greater once the social and institutional stage is adjusted.

Going beyond planning and the evaluation of plans and their impact to a general evaluation of the economy since independence, this writer feels he cannot do better than quote at length from the conclusions of two Moroccan economists quoted more than once in this chapter, namely Belal and Agourram. Here is how they see the economy and society in the independence era:

> The most notable transformation which has marked the evolution of the Moroccan society and economy since independence does not consist of a decisive change in the structure of the economy and its connections with the outside world, but rather of the 'transfer' of a part of national income and capital, previously held by foreigners, to nationals — thanks to the 'Moroccanisation' of the administration and of a part of the economy.
>
> Social differentiation is more stressed now, but the new bourgeois layers have only a very weak propensity towards productive investment. The enormous tasks of creation of employment, education and the training of cadres, and improvement in the level of living of the mass of the population continue and are aggravated by demographic increase.
>
> The coming generations which have had access so far to secondary education manifest anxiety with respect to their future, and increasingly challenge the economic and social options of the authorities.
>
> There is no doubt that in the future their weight will be felt increasingly in the search for a more efficient path to development, whose achievement implies profound upheavals in the economic and social structures inherited from the past. There is notably also the problem posed by the rural structures which constitute a fundamental block to development. Likewise, there is the problem of capital formation which remains mortgaged to the burden of all sorts of transfers to the outside, to the wasteful and unproductive use of savings, the behaviour of the ruling class, etc. To sum up, what is involved is the creation of the social, political and cultural conditions of a true 'take-off'.[132]

NOTES

1. The examination relating to the background of the present period and to the protectorate or pre-independence years relies mostly on the following sources: (a) Carleton S. Coon, *Caravan: The Story of the Middle East* (New York, 1951); (b) L. Gray Cowan, *The Economic Development of Morocco* (Santa Monica, 1958); (c) Rom Landau, *The Moroccan Drama 1900-1955* (London, 1956); (d) J. and S. Lacouture, *Le Maroc à l'Epreuve* (Paris, 1958); (e) Neville Barbour (ed.), *A Survey of North Africa* (New York, 1959); (f) Food and Agricultural Organization, Project FAO du Développement Méditerranéen, *Maroc: Rapport National* (Rome, 1959); (g) Douglas E. Ashford, *Political Change in Morocco* (Princeton, 1961); (h) F. Perroux and R. Barre, *Développement, Croissance, Progrès – Maroc-Tunisie* (Paris, 1961); (i) René Gallissot, *L'Economie de l'Afrique du Nord* (Paris, 1961); (j) André Tiano, *La Politique Economique et Financière du Maroc Independant* (Paris, 1963); (k) Charles F. Stewart, *The Economy of Morocco 1912-1962* (Cambridge, Mass.,1964); (l) Neville Barbour, *Morocco* (London, 1964); (m) The International Bank for Reconstruction and Development, *The Economic Development of Morocco* (Baltimore, 1966); (n) KFAED, *Report on the Structure of the Moroccan Economy* (Kuwait, Arabic; for limited internal circulation; 1967); (o) Samir Amin, *The Maghreb in the Modern World: Algeria, Tunisia, Morocco* (Penguin Books, 1970); (p) John Waterbury, *The Commander of the Faithful: The Moroccan Political Elite* (London, 1970); (q) Ch. Debbasch et al., *Les économies maghrébines de l'indépendance à l'épreuve du développement économique* (Paris, 1971); and (r) Europa Publications, *The Middle East and North Africa 1971-72, 1972-73, 1973-74* and *1974-75* (London, 1972, 1973, 1974, 1975), chapter on Morocco. It is to be emphasised that most of these sources cover the independence era (or parts of it) as well.

2. Stewart, op. cit., p. 5, quoting Alan Houghton Broderick, *North Africa* (Paris, 1949).

3. Waterbury, pp. 3-4.

4. I am mainly (and extensively) indebted to Stewart and Amin for much of the material relating to the period preceding independence and for the evaluation of the situation when independence arrived.

5. Stewart, op. cit., p. 16.

6. Amin, op. cit., p. 33, for the lower estimate, and KFAED, op. cit., p. 6, for the higher. The latter source relies on a few sources.

7. Stewart (p. 60) quotes a total of 4,334,000 inhabitants (including Jews and Europeans, with Algerian Moslems incorporated in the latter group). But this total refers only to the French Zone of Morocco. Presumably the Spanish Zone and the Tangier International Zone accounted for the difference which ranges between about 1m and 1.2m. (Stewart's source is Gouvernement Chérifien, Service Central des Statistiques, *Annuaire statistique de la zone française du Maroc, 1952.)*

8. Amin, op. cit., p. 33, for the urban-rural distribution in 1920 and 1955, and Stewart, op. cit., p. 60, for the number of Europeans in 1912 and of Jews in 1921. (However, official estimates for mid-1956 are below Amin's for 1955. See note 9 below.)

9. Royaume de Maroc, Ministère de L'Economie Nationale, Service Central des Statistiques, *Annuaire Statistique du Maroc (Ex-Zone Sud) 1955-1956*, p. 24. For the information on the Northern Zone and Tangier, See FAO, Table II-1, p. II-45.

10. Stewart, op. cit., pp. 67-8.

11. All the information on the working population for 1951/2 is from *Annuaire Statistique du Maroc 1955-1956*, pp. 34 and 35.

12. *Annuaire Statistique du Maroc 1971*, p. 15. However, the Europa 1973-74 edition (p. 517) gives the area as 446,550 sq. km.; and the FAO *Production Yearbook 1972* (p. 7) states the area as 445,050 sq. km.

13. FAO, p. I-13. According to the *Annuaire Statistique du Maroc 1955-1956* (p. 161), the areas indicated in the text were in 1955-6 4.77m ha, 2.97m ha, and 7.57m ha respectively (a total of 15.31m ha), apart from the esparto grass zone of 2.2m ha.

14. FAO, *Production Yearbook 1972*, pp. 6 and 7 for areas and 21 and 22 for agricultural population.

15. See A. Benachenhou, *Régimes des Terres et Structures Agraires au Maghreb* (Rabat, 1970) for a thorough examination of the whole question of land tenure.

16. Quoted in Stewart, op. cit., p. 18.

17. Stewart, op. cit., p. 18, for the area in 1912, and *Annuaire Statistique du Maroc 1955-1956*, pp. 387 and 389 for data on 31 December 1955 and for 1956.

18. Stewart, op. cit., p. 81.

19. Ibid., p. 77. The Moroccan ownership per capita varies slightly from the size quoted before, owing to a difference between the total area taken as the basis for calculation.

20. Ibid., Chs. I and III and Amin, Part I.

21. Stewart, op. cit., p. 81.

22. Ibid., and Amin, op. cit., p. 66.

23. *Annuaire Statistique du Maroc 1955-1956*, p. 196.

24. Stewart, op. cit., pp. 113-114, and personal interviews conducted by the writer in June 1972.

25. *Annuaire Statistique du Maroc 1955-1956*, p. 196.

26. Albert Waterston, *Planning in Morocco: Organization and Implementation* (Baltimore, 1962), p. 4.

27. Stewart, op. cit., fn 14, p. 219, quoting *Le Petit Casablancais* (Moroccan newspaper) on 24 March 1956, p. 1.

28. *Annuaire statistique de la zone française du Maroc, 1952*, pp. 344-5, for data on 1951-2 and 1952-3; Stewart, op. cit., pp. 107-9 for cumulative credit for the period 1917-1952/3.

29. See IBRD, Chs. 2 and 9, as well as Stewart and Cowan for the background survey of industry and mining.

30. Roughly calculated from data on 'gross domestic production' in *Annuaire Statistique... 1955-1956*, p. 465. IBRD (p. 197) states that the value added of handicrafts was 100m dirhams, 'or 2 percent of Gross National Product'. However, see percentages attributed to handicrafts and manufacturing in Table 13.7 further down.

31. IBRD, op. cit., p. 197, for the estimate of the number of craftsmen and their dependants, and Table

13.1 for data on the industrial labour force in 1951/2. However, FAO, *Maroc*, counts 150,000 Moroccans as urban craftsmen. See Table 13.7 in our text.

32. Cowan, *The Economic Development of Morocco* (Santa Monica, 1958), pp. 44-5.

33. Ibid., p. 45, quoting *Le Petit Casablancais* of 13 April 1957, p. 1.

34. Amin, op. cit., p. 42.

35. FAO, *Maroc*, p. II-63, Table II-16.

36. *Annuaire Statistique... 1955-1956*, pp. 259 and 260.

37. Ibid., p. 259.

38. Ibid., p. 262.

39. Stewart (p. 119) quoting René Hoffherr, *L'économie marocaine* (Paris, 1932), p. 201.

40. *Annuaire Statistique... 1955-1956*, p. 450 for taxes and revenue, and p. 215 for exports.

41. Ibid., pp. 269-72 and 276.

42. UN *Statistical Yearbook 1973*, p. 194.

43. All data with respect to transport and communication come from that Chapter (Part III, 'Transport and Communications') in *Annuaire Statistique... 1955-1956*.

44. Amin, op. cit., p. 47. Only in 1941 was there a trade surplus.

45. Information regarding trade in 1956 comes from ibid., Part III, 'Foreign Trade'.

46. See FAO, *Maroc*, Table II-10, p. II-57.

47. Ibid., and Table II-18, p. II-65, and pp. 36-7.

48. I have drawn in the description of the monetary system on FAO, *Maroc*, pp. II-26 to II-29.

49. Data on money and banking for the pre-independence period come from *Annuaire Statistique... 1955-1956*, Part III, 'Monnaie, Crédit, Banques'.

50. Stewart, op. cit., p. 167 and Waterston, op. cit., p. 5, for the smaller and the larger estimate respectively.

51. Amin, op. cit., p. 75.

52. Data come from *Annuaire Statistique... 1955-1956*, Part V, 'Finances Publiques'. For cost-of-living increase, p. 311. (The index rose from 2,175 to 3,308 and from 1,509 to 2,621 for Moroccans and foreigners, from 1949 to 1956, respectively, with 1939 = 100.)

53. Ibid., Part I, 'Enseignement' for all data on schooling.

54. Ibid., p. 24, for the estimate for mid-1956. See Stewart, op. cit., pp. 167-8 regarding Jewish and European emigration.

55. The analysis draws on information in Table 13.4, while the reference to 1957 is based on data in FAO, *Maroc*, Table II-12, p. II-59.

56. In much of this analysis and that of the problems of education I have benefited from discussions held with many Moroccans and a few Frenchmen in a few cities, in June 1972.

57. Waterston, op. cit., p. 5.

58. *Annuaire Statistique... 1955-1956*, p. 91.

59. Waterbury, op. cit., p. 317 with respect to the élite. The quotation comes from p. 4.

60. See p. 468 in the *Annuaire Statistique... 1955-1956*, and Table II-15, p. II-62 in FAO, *Maroc*.

61. IMF, *International Financial Statistics, Supplement to 1967/68* (hereafter referred to as *IFS Supplement*), p. 237 for national accounts and p. 236 for cost-of-living series.

62. *Annuaire Statistique... 1955-1956*, p. 24.

63. The first set appears in FAO, *Maroc*, Table II-15, p. II-62; the second in *Annuaire Statistique... 1955-1956*, p. 466; and the third in Waterston, Appendix A and Appendix B. (The sources will be referred to as 'FAO', 'Annuaire 1955-1956', and 'Waterston'.) It ought to be pointed out that total annual investments shown in the text above differ from those in FAO, owing to the fact that the FAO totals come from a UN source noted in Table II-15, while the details for public and private investment come from an official Moroccan publication. However, the divergence is not serious.

64. FAO, *Maroc*, Table II-7, p. II-54.

65. Waterston, op. cit., pp. 4-5; Amin, op. cit., pp. 61 and 68 ff.

66. *Annuaire Statistique du Maroc 1964-1965*, p. 28.

67. Reported in *Europa..., 1973-74*, p. 517.

68. Waterston, op. cit., p. 5.

69. Stewart, op. cit., p. 168, quoting the paper *La Vie Economique*, 12 February 1960, p. 1.

70. *Europa..., 1973-74*, p. 512. See also Amin, op. cit., p. 68.

71. Ministère de l'Economie Nationale, Division de la Coordination Economique et du Plan, *Plan Quinquennal 1960-1964*, unnumbered page at the end of the volume.

72. The examination and assessment depend extensively on (a) intensive interviews held in Morocco in June 1972, (b) those sources listed in note 1 above that relate to a substantial part of the independence era, and (c) a few other sources not listed in note 1. The last group will be referred to as the occasion arises.

73. See, for instance, A. A. Belal and A. Agourram, 'L'économie marocaine depuis l'indépendance', in Ch. Debbasch *et al.*, op. cit., pp. 141-64, especially pp. 141-4. (Much of the material in this article appears also in *Bulletin Economique et Social du Maroc*, Vol. XXXII, No. 116, January-March 1970.)

74. The population estimate for 1972 is 15.83m. The 'selling rate' of conversion is 4.77 dirhams to the US dollar, or 4.661 dirhams if the 'trade conversion factor' is adopted. See *IFS*, March 1974 for this information. For more recent data, see *IFS*, October 1975.

75. See Tables II-10 and II-18 appended to Ch. II in FAO, *Maroc*.

76. The sources from which the information has been attained are: (a) *Time* magazine, Vol. LXXXI, No. 13, 29 March 1963 (p. 13), for US economic aid from 1 July 1945 to 30 June 1962, quoting official US sources; (b) OECD, *The Flow of Financial Resources to Less-Developed Countries 1961-1964* (p. 155) for 1962-5; (c) OECD, *Development Assistance: Efforts and Policies of the Members of the Development Assistance Committee, 1969 Review* (p. 170) for 1965-8; (d) OECD, *Development Cooperation: Efforts and Policies of the Members of the Development Assistance Committee, 1973 Review* (pp. 216-7) for 1969-71, and UN *Statistical Yearbook 1973* (p. 716) for 1972; (e) *Arab Economist* (Beirut monthly), No. 53, June 1973, p. 47 (quoting US Department of State), *Communist States and Developing Countries: Aid and Trade in 1970* (Washington, 1971) for Soviet aid, and UN *Statistical Yearbook 1973* (p. 715) for 1971 and 1972; and (f) KFAED, *Annual Reports* over the years 1963-1973/4.

77. It is sufficient for this to be realised, to attempt a comparison of the balance of payments data for the same years in, say, IBRD, *Economic Development of Morocco*, A. A. Belal and A. Agourram, the *Annuaire Statistique*, and *IFS* series.

78. Data on foreign debt for 1953 and 1956 come from *Annuaire Statistique... 1955-1956*, p. 446, while data on assets come from FAO, *Maroc*, Table II-14, p. II-61. Information for 1972 and 1973 is from *IFS*, December 1974. (Foreign debt for 1973 is not available.)

79. *IFS*, June 1974.

80. *Annuaire Statistique... 1955-1956*, p. 449.

81. BNDE, op. cit., pp. 30-8.

82. *IFS*, June 1974 for the 1972 estimate, *Annuaire Statistique... 1970* (p. 14) for the estimate of mid-1970, and *Annuaire Statistique... 1955-1956* (p. 24) for the 1956 estimates.

83. Among others, see A. A. Belal and A. Agourram, op. cit., p. 150, regarding the rate of 3.3 per cent.

84. All information on population and employment recorded in the 1960 Census comes from *Annuaire Statistique... 1964-1965*, Ch. II, 'Population'. For 1972, see *Plan de développement économique et social*, Vol. I, p. 121.

85. The intractable problem of large-sized unemployment and underemployment is one of the few points on which all studies and reports agree. See, for instance, the relevant sections in Stewart, Tiano, Belal and Agourram, IBRD and Amin.

86. Belal and Agourram, op. cit., p. 150.

87. Europa..., *1973-74*, p. 521. The number of students in institutions of higher education is not given for 1972-3, because of being 'not available'. In 1970-1 it was 13,572 and in 1971-2, 15,148. I assumed the number for 1972-3 to be 16,000, which suggests a more modest increase than that between the two preceding years.

88. Foreign teachers at the primary and the secondary levels together numbered 6,608 men and women in 1956, but 8,962 in 1971-2. The number of Moroccans was 5,817 and 47,593 for the two years respectively. See *Annuaire Statistique... 1955-1956*, p. 91, and *Annuaire Statistique... 1971*, pp. 25 and 26.

89. Impression gathered from interviews conducted in Morocco in June 1972. A stronger affirmative evaluation is made in *Plan... 1973-1977*, Vol. I, pp. 21-2 and Vol. II, pp. 741-2.

90. Amin, op. cit., Ch. 6.

91. The main special works consulted for an understanding of the government's policy with respect to land, irrigation, agriculture and rural reform in general are the following: (a) Royaume du Maroc, Ministère de l'Agriculture et de la Réforme Agraire, *Principaux aspects de l'économie agricole marocaine* (May, 1972; mimeographed); (b) Ministère des Travaux Publics et des Communications, 'Le programme d'irrigation du million d'hectares et la construction des grandes retenues d'accumulations: la politique des barrages' (mimeographed statement, May 1972); (c) Ministère de l'Agriculture et de la Réforme Agraire, *Objectifs généraux visés par le gouvernement de Sa Majesté le Roi en matière de politique agricole* (December 1971); (d) *Al-'Alam* (daily newspaper, Rabat; Arabic), series of articles on dams and water use and management during June 1972; (e) Michel Villeneuve, *La situation de l'agriculture et son avenir dans l'économie marocaine* (Paris, 1971); (f) Caisse Nationale de Crédit Agricole, *Rapport* (annual reports, beginning with the year 1962-3 and down to 1971-2); (g) Kingdom of Morocco, *Documents Relating to the Code of Agricultural Investment* (Collection of 49 *Dahirs*, Decrees and Orders issued all on 25 July 1969, dealing in an integrated manner with agricultural development. Arabic; Rabat, 1969); (h) Caisse Nationale de Crédit Agricole, *Le crédit agricole du Maroc* (special report; mimeographed; 1964); and (i) André Tiano, *La politique économique et financière du Maroc indépendant* (Paris, 1963), especially Part One, Ch. 4 and Part Three, Ch. 1. In addition to these sources, I have referred to the relevant parts in Stewart, Cowan, Amin, and Belal and Agourram.

92. *Plan de développement économique et social 1973-1977*, Vol. I, pp. 23-4, and Vol. II, pp. 17-18. For the programme of irrigation for 1973-7, see ibid., Vol. I, p. 128.

93. Stewart, op. cit., p. 178, and fn 37.

94. There are many references to these surveys and their findings (see, for instance, Stewart, op. cit., pp. 177 ff). During the interviews I conducted I got the same impressions as those imparted by Stewart and others. But I was unable to come across the original studies. Stewart quotes figures. The most significant are attributed to the Ministry of Agriculture which 'estimated that 50 percent of the rural families had less than 3 hectares; 25 percent had no land at all; and only the remaining 25 percent had "viable" farms.' In contrast, under the protectorate the 'viable' farm was supposed to average 17 ha in area, with 8 ha being cultivable. On the other hand, it is reported in *Objectifs généraux...*, p. 10, that holdings up to 10 ha in size total 2.8m ha or two-thirds of *melk*, i.e. privately owned land.

95. 'Le programme d'irrigation du million d'hectares...', p. 1.

96. There is polite criticism in some of the sources referred to in notes 1 and 91 above. The harshest criticism has appeared in a number of memoranda prepared by independent economists and by Istiqlal circles.

97. 'Le programme d'irrigation du million d'hectares...', p. 10. Tiano (p. 168) quotes figures that indicate net returns per hectare slightly over four times the net returns before irrigation.

98. Belal and Agourram, op. cit., p. 157. For a full appreciation of the comprehensiveness of the legislation, see *Documents Relating to the Code of Agricultural Investment*, op. cit.

99. Tiano, op. cit., p. 178.

100. Ibid., p. 179.

101. *Annuaire Statistique... 1970*, p. 43. More recent information is not available in the 1971 issue, or in the 1968-72 or 1973-77 Plans.

102. Tiano, op. cit., pp. 269-71.

103. Ibid., p. 27, for the resources by the end of 1956, and Caisse Nationale de Crédit Agricole, *Rapport d'Activité 1970-1971*, p. 76.

104. *Principaux aspects de l'économie agricole marocaine*, p. 34. See also *Plan... 1973-1977*, Vol. II, pp. 12-13 and 209-16.

105. BNDE, op. cit., p. 82 for production and *IFS*, June 1974, for value of exports.

106. *Annuaire Statistique... 1955-1956*, p. 258 for 1956, and BNDE, op. cit., pp. 91 and 93 for 1972. However, according to *Annuaire Statistique... 1971*, the proportion was 56.3 per cent in 1971. (See ibid., p. 72.)

107. BNDE, op. cit., p. 96, for volume of production in 1972 and p. 41 for total value of exports of crude minerals, but *IFS*, June 1974, for value of phosphates exports by themselves, to 1972. For 1973, see General Union of Arab Chambers of Commerce, Industry, and Agriculture, *Arab Economic Report*, 1974, pp. 527 and 534.

108. See booklet entitled *Le Bureau de Recherches et de Participations Minières* (undated, publisher not indicated but thought to be the BRPM itself) for a discussion of the structure of the Bureau and its activities which include research, exploitation and marketing.

109. BNDE, op. cit., p. 118. For facilities extended to investors, see Cabinet Royal, Centre d'Accueil et d' Orientation des Investisseurs (Investment Orientation Center), *Investment in Morocco* (Rabat, July 1969); and the Ministry of Trade, Industry, Mining and Merchant Marine, Bureau d'Etudes Interministériel, Morocco: *Guidelines for Investors* (Rabat, undated, but presumably published late 1970 or 1971 since it contains information down to July 1970).

110. Europa... , *1973-74*, p. 514.

111. Belal and Agourram question the wisdom of the choice of tourism as an 'engine of development' (p. 159).

112. All information has been obtained from Banque du Maroc, Etudes Economiques, 'Vue d'ensemble des organismes financières specialisés au Maroc' (mimeographed memorandum, August 1971).

113. For the discussion of the background of planning in Morocco, planning administration, and the country's experience in planning I have drawn mainly on: (a) Albert Waterston, *Planning in Morocco: Organization and Implementation* (Baltimore, 1962); (b) Albert Waterston, *Development Planning: Lessons of Experience* (Baltimore, 1965); (c) Douglas Elliott Ashford, *Morocco – Tunisia: Politics and Planning* (Syracuse, 1965); (d) Douglas E. Ashford, *National Development and Local Reform: Political Participation in Morocco, Tunisia, and Pakistan* (Princeton, 1967); (e) T. Bencheiki, 'Planification et politique agricole', *Bulletin Economique et Social du Maroc*, Vol. XXXI, Nos. 112-13, January-June 1969; and (f) Habib el-Malki, 'Le financement des plans marocains depuis 1960', *Bulletin Economique et Social du Maroc*, Vol. XXXII, No. 117, April-June 1970. I have also benefited greatly from several interviews centring around planning, conducted in June 1972.

114. Waterston, *Planning in Morocco*, pp. 13-14, and Waterston, *Development Planning...*, p. 380.

115. Waterston, *Planning in Morocco*, pp. 14-15.

116. Waterston, *Development Planning...*, p. 462.

117. Ibid., p. 375 n.

118. See Amin, pp. 180 ff; Waterston, *Development Planning*, also has many sporadic references (though not expressed in ideological terms) to the same failings of the planning process and the fluctuations in conceptions behind it, as well as the political and administrative dislocations accompanying it.

119. I have relied in this presentation on the actual texts of the plans, except for the Two-Year Investment Plan 1958-59 (Plan Biennal d'Equipement, 1958-1959), where I have used the data in Waterston, *Planning in Morocco*, Appendix D.

120. Ashford, *Development Planning...*, p. 319.

121. *The Three-Year Plan 1965-1967* (Arabic), pp. 30-1.

122. *Plan Quinquennal 1968-1972*, Volume I, Ch. I, p. 18, for the information on the proportion of the investment programme executed.

123. Ibid., p. 60.

124. See Table 13.12 for gross investment made in the five years 1968-72.

125. See Table 13.11 for GDP and GNP for the years 1968-72. See BNDE, op. cit., p. 5, where the average growth rate is given as 5.5 per cent; and the last plan, *Plan de développement économique et social 1973-1977*, Vol. I, p. 13, where the rate is quoted as 5.6 per cent.

126. *Plan... 1973-1977*, Vol. I, p. 13.

127. Ibid., p. 18.

128. Ibid., pp. 20-1.

129. Ibid., p. 46.

130. It is to be noted here that the previous reference period is given as 1969-73, which again causes confusion since this differs from the two periods quoted earlier in the context of the Five-Year Plan 1968-72, namely 1967-72 and 1968-73.

131. Ibid., pp. 33-4

132. Belal and Agourram, op. cit., p. 164 (my translation).

14 ARAB DEVELOPMENT IN ITS REGIONAL FRAMEWORK

Since the Arab-Israeli war of October 1973 and the vast increase in the price of oil and oil revenues, the Arab region has come to a recognised position of economic prominence in the world. The huge foreign assets accumulated as a result of crude oil exports, the steeply increased imports of consumer and capital goods and of military hardware made possible, the large volume of foreign aid extended to Third World countries, and the possession of more than half of the world's proven oil reserves have together suddenly placed the Arabs in a strong, and no doubt envied, position in the worlds of energy and money. This position has enabled them to exercise a degree of political influence never before experienced in their recent history, but it has also exposed them to attack in certain quarters of the industrial world, which being the main consumer and importer of oil, is therefore the party called upon to make substantial transfers of real income for the oil imports.

The sudden opulence is an indication neither of considerably improved performance in the Arab economies nor of long-term assured well-being, nor yet of a uniform good fortune. For the opulence is still associated with underdevelopment; the massive financial resources are the result of the export of a depleting resource; and the good fortune is still largely restricted to the oil-producing and oil-exporting countries whose populations constitute only about a quarter of the total population of the region, in addition to the fact that within each country there are excessive disparities in income and wealth among individuals. (The regional inequality of income distribution can be readily seen from a few indicators. Thus, GNP *per capita* for 1974, according to this writer's calculations, is about $893, whereas it stands at $2,500 for the oil-exporting countries but $286 for the other countries, including Egypt.)

These serious qualifications notwithstanding, it can be said that the oil revenues are in large part beginning to be put to proper use. They are being translated into development inside the oil economies through the acceleration of capital formation, education, technological transformation and institutional change – a process which will produce favourable results in a few years' time. Even the sizeable imports of arms and military equipment can be justified by necessity, as the Arab-Israeli conflict continues and the Arab countries feel that they have to protect their development gains and achievements against Israel's military might and its territorial incursions, and to liberate the territories already occupied. Furthermore, the unevenness in fortune among the oil and non-oil countries is corrected to a certain modest extent through the aid being extended from the first to the second group of countries. And, although vast internal inequalities of wealth and income continue to exist, and have certainly grown in the post-war period, economic and social development is expected to raise the floor of income and wealth and to increase and widen economic opportunities for the poorer groups.

This picture, which can on the whole be said to be rather bright, has not been uniformly so in the post-war period. Indeed, what has been said about it relates mainly to its most recent phase – the short period subsequent to October 1973 – and only to the outward, partial manifestations of development. The few decades preceding this period were much less reassuring. The evaluation of the thirty years between the end of World War Two and the beginning of 1975 which occupies the rest of this chapter will therefore trace the transformation that has occurred in the features and performance of the economies of the Arab region. On the other hand, the deeper aspects of development and the prospects for the future will be examined in Volume II (the companion volume) when the determinants of development will be identified and assessed.

The economic features of the Arab region and its level of development do not distinguish it unmistakably from other developing regions of the world, nor do they constitute a common stamp which marks and differentiates the Arab group of countries in West Asia and North Africa from other regions. Rather, the basis of differentiation must be sought in socio-cultural and institutional features, in a long history lived jointly, and in feelings of identification and affinity. It is largely these non-economic characteristics which tie the Arab countries together and set the Arab region apart from other regions, as well as a world-view and a set of political hopes and expectations commonly shared, that together justify the regional approach of this book.

Yet the assertion that it is not common economic features that essentially unite the Arab world and distinguish it from other regions does not imply the absence of regional economic peculiarities or the futility of the attempt to identify and analyse such peculiarities as exist. This chapter sets out to perform the function of identification and analysis, and to report on the major developments of the post-war period. Necessarily the presentation will be skeletal. The preceding chapters of the present volume have provided the detail which constitutes the underpinning of many of the generalisations of this chapter.

1. BROAD FEATURES

With the exception of Lebanon, Kuwait, Saudi Arabia and Libya, it was the agricultural sector which until 1973 occupied first place as a contributor to national product among the twelve countries covered in this book. In the case of Lebanon, the 'place of honour' was taken by the trade sector, while in the case of the other three countries it was petroleum. (If the whole region is taken into account, then the list of countries depending mainly on the oil sector becomes longer with the inclusion of Abu Dhabi and Dubai in the United Arab Emirates, Bahrain, Qatar and Oman.)

However, apart from this structural feature, it is important to note the predominance of rural society in the region as a whole. Thus, in spite of the high degree of urbanisation existing by the mid-seventies as against the mid-forties, and in spite of the slow but sure signs of a structural shift in many of the country economies towards the sectors of manufacturing industry, transport, finance, government and non-personal services (at the expense of agriculture, personal services and real estate), a little over 55 per cent of the people live in the countryside and draw the bulk of their livelihood from agricultural pursuits, as Table 14.1 shows.

The data in Table 14.1 must be considered merely suggestive. This is because they depend on rough estimates, and no differentiation is made between the proportion of the population which is agricultural and that of the economically active population engaged in agriculture, though the two can, andprobably do, diverge. In spite of these serious qualifications, it can be said that Arab society is still predominantly rural, but that the ratio of rural to urban population has declined noticeably over the years. Indeed, in one decade it seems to have declined by 6 percentage points, but it must have declined much more sub-

Table 14.1: Agricultural Population and Economically Active Population in Agriculture, 1960 and 1970

Country	Year	Agricultural Population and Economically Active Population in Agriculture Per Cent of Total
Iraq	1960	53.2
	1970	46.6
Kuwait	1960	1.5
	1970	1.0
Saudi Arabia	1960	71.5
	1970	60.5
Jordan	1960	43.9
	1970	38.7
Syria	1960	54.3
	1970	48.8
Lebanon	1960	52.9
	1970	47.4
Egypt	1960	58.5
	1970	54.8
Sudan	1960	85.7
	1970	79.9
Libya	1960	55.5
	1970	42.6
Tunisia	1960	56.5
	1970	46.4
Algeria	1960	66.8
	1970	55.7
Morocco	1960	63.7
	1970	60.6
12 Countries	1960	63.9
	1970	57.7

Source: FAO, *Production Yearbook 1973*, pp. 17-19.

stantially between 1945 and 1975. Over the thirty years in question, the ratio may well have dropped from some 70 per cent to some 55 per cent.

This distinct process of urbanisation is universal the world over, as are its causes and implications. However, it is essential at this point to indicate that the heavy dependence on agriculture is accompanied with some basic structural and operational weaknesses in the sector of agriculture in the Arab countries, without exception but with some variations of degree and quality. Yet, predominant as rural society and agricultural activity are, and serious though their problems are, they have not received the national attention and efforts that they rightly merit. Furthermore, the agricultural sector, on which there is substantial dependence in virtually all the economies under consideration, suffers from a number of problems.

To begin with, there is a regional shortage and marked seasonality of rainfall, resulting in the drastic limitation of cultivable land. Admittedly, the concept of 'cultivable land' does not lend itself to precise definition and quantification, even if it is related strictly to the pattern of technology and resources available to each country at the present time. Furthermore, no acceptable estimates are on record for a few of the countries covered by this study, while for the rest confusion arises from the multiplicity of estimates for each country without uniformity in the bases of estimation. Nevertheless, in spite of the substantial definitional and measurement problems, it is safe to say that for the twelve countries covered, the cultivable area constitutes a small proportion of the total land area, some 9.4 per cent, out of a land area of 11.1m square kilometres, as Table 14.2 shows. (For the entire Arab region, the figures are estimated at 8 per cent and 13.6m square kilometres respectively.)

Modest as this proportion is, it is still vastly larger than the ratio of actually cultivated to total land area, which is about 3.9 per cent. (Though the area of cultivated land is easier to establish than that of cultivable land, it is still subject to wide variation. This is essentially due to non-uniformity with respect to the inclusion or exclusion of land lying fallow in any one year, and of some pasture land. We have all through attempted to exclude pasture land, but to include temporarily fallow land.) And finally, irrigated land makes up some 0.79 per cent of total land area, or 20.02 per cent of cultivated area. (The figures are 3.4, 0.66 and 19.45 per cent, respectively, for the whole Arab region, comprising 20 states.)

The proportions recorded in Table 14.2 have wide variations behind them. Nevertheless, on the whole the low overall ratios of cultivable and cultivated to total land are very depressing, especially when the supposedly cultivable land itself, though more than double the cultivated land, would still be unable to provide comfort were the bulk of it to be actually reclaimed and cropped, given the supportive factors of labour and capital. The exceptions to these gloomy observations are few in number, and include countries of modest total area like Lebanon, Syria and Tunisia, where the difference between cultivated and cultivable land in absolute terms is not substantial, and where the prospects for irrigation are modest (except for Syria).

Two countries stand out with distinct and large potential with respect to the scope for the extension of cultivated land which now represents a small proportion of cultivable land, thanks to the excellent prospects for the expansion of irrigation. These are Iraq and Sudan. For the region as a whole, the extreme modesty of irrigation potential and facilities constitutes a serious constraint on the area under the plough or capable of being brought under the plough, and on agricultural production and the range of produce. The inadequacy and seasonality of rainfall accentuate the problem. The constraint is especially limiting in the long, dry summer season. (It ought to be added that Iraq and Egypt alone account for almost three-quarters of the total irrigated area in the twelve countries surveyed. This means that the irrigated area in the remaining ten countries is very small indeed, both in absolute terms and as a proportion of total cultivated land, but especially as a proportion of total land area.)

The land-man ratio is frequently measured by relating total land area to total population. Such a measure would be grossly misleading in the case of the Arab region, since it suggests that there are 10 hectares of land per inhabitant for the 20 Arab states together, or almost 9 ha per person for the 12 states surveyed in this book, while in fact less than one-tenth of the total area of the region is cultivable, the rest consisting mainly of desert and other arid

Table 14.2: Total, Cultivable, Cultivated and Irrigated Land

Country	Total Area (thousand ha)	Cultivable Land Area (thousand ha)	Cultivable Land Area Per Cent of Total	Cultivated Land Area (thousand ha)	Cultivated Land Area Per Cent of Total	Irrigated Land Area (thousand ha)	Irrigated Land Area Per Cent of Total	Irrigated Land Area Per Cent of Cultivated Area
Iraq	43,492	12,100	27.8	5,750	13.2	3,675	8.45	63.91
Kuwait	1,782	2.7	0.15	0.6	0.03	0.6	0.03	100.00
Saudi Arabia	214,969	1,500	0.7	910	0.4	176	0.08	19.34
Jordan	9,774	1,200	12.3	1,132	11.6	60	0.61	5.30
Syria	18,518	8,415	45.4	5,612	30.3	485	2.62	8.64
Lebanon	1,040	330	31.7	240	23.1	68	6.54	28.33
Egypt	100,145	4,420	4.4	2,852	2.8	2,852	2.85	100.00
Sudan	250,581	45,000	18.0	7,100	2.8	711	0.28	10.01
Libya	175,954	8,800	5.0	2,377	1.3	125	0.07	5.26
Tunisia	16,361	5,000	30.6	4,510	27.6	80	0.49	1.77
Algeria	238,174	10,000	4.2	6,240	2.6	270	0.11	4.33
Morocco	44,655	8,000	17.9	7,076	15.8	265	0.59	3.75
Total 12 States	1,115,445	104,767.7	9.4	43,799.6	3.9	8,767.6	0.79	20.02
Add: Remaining 8 States	246,973	4,000	1.6	2,710	1.1	277	0.11	10.22
Total all Arab States	1,362,418	108,767.7	8.0	46,509.6	3.4	9,044.6	0.66	19.45

Notes: (1) 'Cultivated land' is designated as 'arable land' in the FAO source. Arable land is one component (along with 'Land under permanent crops' and 'permanent meadows and pastures') of 'agricultural land'.
(2) No data are available from the FAO source on 'cultivable land'.
(3) The actually cultivated or arable category includes land lying fallow in the FAO source.
(4) There is a small difference in some cases between 'total area' and 'total land area' of countries, which is accounted for by the area of inland water bodies, i.e. rivers and lakes.
(5) The data on cultivated and irrigated land differ in some instances from their counterpart in country chapters. However, we have adopted the FAO data in the table, for the sake of uniformity.

Sources: For all columns except that of 'cultivable area': FAO, *Production Yearbook 1973*, pp.3, 5 and 435-6; for 'cultivable area', country chapters for the 12 countries enumerated; and for the 8 countries grouped together, rough estimates from various sources.

types of terrain. It is thus the cultivable area that can provide a proper resource to relate to population, or, given the confusion surrounding the definition and measurement of cultivable land, it is the area actually cultivated which should be set against the size of population, if the true weight of the pressure of population on land resources is to be appreciated.

An aggregate population in 1974 of 127.5 million (or 140 million if the 20 Arab states are taken into account) draws about one-third of its livelihood from agricultural activity, which means that roughly 290 persons depend on one square kilometre of cultivated land, or less than a quarter of one hectare per person. This pressure is lowest in Syria, Iraq, Sudan and the North African countries, and highest in Kuwait, Egypt and Saudi Arabia. The availability of water bodies usable for irrigation governs the ranking of the various countries with respect to population pressure on land resources (and foodstuffs).

So far we have concentrated on a major handicap to agricultural development, namely the very limited area of cultivable and cultivated land. A second handicap arises from the limited endowment in internal water bodies. (Egypt, Sudan, Iraq and Syria constitute notable exceptions in the whole of the Arab region, with relative abundance in river water.) The shortage of rainfall, plus its seasonality and unpredictability, makes agriculture seriously vulnerable to the vagaries of climatic conditions and imposes a severe constraint on the volume of production. Between a good and a bad year, total agricultural production in countries depending mainly on rainfall may vary by as much as one-third. This obviously means a sharp and discontinuous drop or rise in national product from one year to another, particularly in cases where agriculture is the major sector.

These handicaps are compounded by low labour productivity, backward farming techniques, inadequate investment in land and water resources, and the resulting low yields and small income of share-tenants and wage-farmers who constitute a large part of the rural population. The substantial investments effected in the post-war period in dams and irrigation (and to some extent drainage) systems, and in mechanisation — though significant in themselves — still fall distinctly short of solving the problem of water and technology. This is particularly so in view of the sluggish efforts to bring about transformation in rural manpower via improved training, better farming techniques, greater use of co-operative societies and appropriate change in attitudes and motivation, as well as to increase employment opportunities noticeably.

Finally, the rural society as a whole, including the agricultural sector as one area of major economic activity, has never featured as high in the priorities of the decision-makers as it should. Industrialisation has a glamour which agricultural development does not possess, and shining new factories seem to rank higher than efficient farms as show-pieces in the eyes of ministers of information and of national economy alike. Often this lopsided view ignores the size and economic significance of rural society and of agriculture. The oversight has had drastic results, headed by the sluggishness of food production and the necessity of vast food imports at the expense of badly needed foreign exchange resources. The ambitious and far-reaching measures of agrarian reform instituted have on the whole produced very modest tangible results, for reasons that have been exposed in the country chapters on Iraq, Syria and Egypt. (More on this subject later.)

Emphasis is placed in this part of the chapter on agriculture as the backbone of most Arab economies. This is not to belittle the significance of other sectors, nor is it to underestimate the transformation in the structure of Arab economies in the direction of non-agricultural activities during the post-war period. It is essentially to underline this writer's firm conviction that for many more years to come, development in the Arab world must primarily be taken to mean rural and agricultural rejuvenation so that the essence and manifestations of development may reach the poorest farmer in the remotest village, as Gunnar Myrdal rightly emphasises in his *Asian Drama* and *The Challenge of World Poverty*.

The sketch made so far, while true of the state of agriculture in general, should not hide the fact that some impressive advances have been made in certain parts of Arab agriculture, such as the extension of cultivated area, the construction or expansion of irrigation systems, the widening of the range of agricultural produce, the rise in land yields and in labour productivity, or the introduction of radical measures of agrarian reform. Such islands of achievement, however, merely serve to accentuate the vast expanses still in need of basic transformation and tangible development, whether in technology, institutions, organisation or performance. That this is so can be evidenced by the very sluggish advances made in food production, where by and large population increase has fallen short of the increase in food production by only 10-15 per cent during the thirty post-war years, leaving too small a margin for comfort. If to this is added the rise in consumption expenditure and the diversification in food items consumed, it will become clear why there has been need to resort to increased food imports, even in countries that used to be surplus areas. Thus, the twelve countries included in this study imported $2.8 billion worth of food products in 1973, which constituted 19.4 per cent of their total imports of $13.9 billion for the year. The imports almost doubled in 1974, reaching a value of $24.3 billion. They rose further still to about $37 billion for 1975, with food imports totalling about $4.5 billion, or some 12 per cent of the total. (This supports the thesis that the marginal propensity to consume food declines with income increases. With domestic food production marking little change, the propensity to import food products becomes all significant.)

It was pointed out earlier that the weight of population pressure on land resources should take into account the very limited area of cultivated land. We must now add the second component of the pressure: population. The assessment of the pressure would be quite different were the *quality* of the population to be different, given the factor of land and the size of the labour force. Thus a healthier, better-trained, more strongly motivated and more technically advanced population would produce a new man-land 'mix' which would suggest that the pressure was weak, or that the Arab world even suffers from underpopulation. As it is, the low level of education of the bulk of the population of the region, the unsatisfactory health conditions, the poverty and low nutritional levels, certain restrictive cultural forces related to work, the traditional social organisation and general traditionalism and slow acceptance of technical innovation by rural society — all are factors the combination of which is as responsible for the high pressure of man on land resources as the modesty of the ratio of cultivable and cultivated land to total land area. Indeed, the ratio is largely a function of the quality of the population and the capital in its hands. However, these retarding factors are not necessarily the expression of deliberate decisions by the working population; often they are the product of the institutional framework within which work skills are formed and work is conducted.

But to stop at this point with respect to the broad characteristics of the populations at large and manpower more specifically would be unfair for the region's record in the fields of social development and technological change. Education and health services have moved in large, brisk strides in the post-war years, and the level of literacy has risen considerably, although nobody can tell precisely by how much. The university population of the twelve countries covered in this study is today close to 600,000 (including students in Europe, North America and socialist countries). Serious efforts are being made in most countries to expand vocational and technical training.

First- and second-cycle education deserve separate treatment. The twelve countries that occupy us in this book had over 18.3m pupils in pre-university institutions. (The information available for Bahrain, Oman, Qatar, the United Arab Emirates and Yemen Arab Republic shows that they had over 300,000 pupils. No data are on hand regarding university students in these states, and no information on education at all is available to this writer with respect to Mauritania and Somalia.[2])

However, commendable as the advances in education have been, they still call for a few substantial qualifications. The first relates to the spread of education. Schooling is provided currently for about 53 per cent only of boys and girls of school age, and the opportunities for female education are distinctly narrower than for males. Furthermore, the countryside is still substantially less equipped with schools than the urban centres. And even where schools exist in rural areas, they are not adequately adapted to the needs of the agricultural community. Finally, the immense expansion in the number of men and women attending university has not been matched by improvement in quality. And, as we have had occasion to say in country chapters, and will discuss in Volume II, the educational systems are still far from being directly relevant to the developmental needs of the region, in addition to being slow in adapting their methods and approaches to the urgency of problem-solving and to the vast advances made in educational methods and techniques in the more developed countries.

Health conditions have also improved considerably, as the country-by-country statistics regarding medical services testify. Social organisation is changing, particularly in urban centres, under the influences of education, industrialisation, and urbanisation itself. And the islands of advanced technology are expanding in size all the time, particularly in the oil-exporting countries in recent years, and in such countries as Egypt and Lebanon, where important centres of learning have been in operation for many decades.

Another aspect of the broad subject of population that deserves some examination is manpower and the active labour force. As the relevant statistics and discussion in the country chapters have shown, information on labour supply and active labour force is scanty and unsatisfactory. The definitional base differs between countries, reaching its maximum absurdity in those cases where all members of the population 5 years of age and over are counted as members of the (potential) labour force. In other instances the lower age limit is more reasonable, but the statistics of employment do not differentiate between *potential* and *actual* employment.

Steering our way through this confusion, we find that the active labour force in the Arab world constitutes a small proportion of the population, probably around only a quarter. The proportion is highest in Lebanon, but we cannot determine where it is lowest. The low degree of labour participation is mostly a reflection of underdevelopment. (We disregard the level of *per capita* income when this income does not reflect the performance of the economy and society, as in the case of most of the oil-producing and -exporting countries.) It is also partly a reflection of the marked youthfulness of Arab populations, where 50 per cent are below 20 years of age, and partly of the exclusion of most women.

Manpower statistics betray a contradiction when it comes to the counting in of women. Thus, in some instances the size of the potential labour force is relatively small because women are left out of account. In the opposite case, employment, particularly in the sector of agriculture, is inflated because virtually all the females of working age (however that is determined) are considered in employment on the basis of the very occasional agricultural or pastoral tasks they undertake. But, generally speaking, most women of working age are not included in the estimation of the labour force.

The country peculiarities apart, one generalisation emerges with respect to employment, which is true of all the countries surveyed with the possible exception of Lebanon. This is that there is a high level of unemployment in each of the economies, but more so in the rural sector. Furthermore, there is substantial underemployment or disguised unemployment both in urban and rural communities, though this is more pressing in the latter. The advances made in investment and development, the expansion in many of the sectors, and the emergence of some new sectors and subsectors and industries have together remained incapable of absorbing the increasing labour force.

The problem has been exacerbated by several factors: the fast rate of natural increase of population, averaging 2.8–3 per cent for the region; marked concentration of investment in capital-intensive sectors and projects and the slow creation of job opportunities; the increasing pace of mechanisation and of fragmentation in agriculture, with its depressive effect on employment; and the emergence of a 'new class' of unemployed educated young men who, superficially, seem to be equipped to work with school diplomas in their pockets but, in actual fact, find themselves largely unemployable because their 'equipment' mostly consists of general education with no vocational skills — to name just a few factors. Notwithstanding the Utopian declarations and promises in official statements and development plans, the problem of unemployment (and underemployment) remains intractable for the region as a whole, particularly with the rate of population increase being as high as it currently is. This writer estimates the reservoir of underutilised Arabs to be no less than 15 million, mostly in the rural areas but increasingly in urban centres as well. The problem represents one of the major challenges to development and planning in the Arab world. And the challenge will be the more difficult to be faced, the longer the philosophy and conceptualisation of development remain obsessed with aggregates and inane statistics and neglect the real needs of real human beings.

The predominance of agriculture in certain countries, and of the petroleum sectors in others, has been pointed out. We do not need to discuss the structure of Arab economies in detail or sector by sector. But it is necessary to draw the broad features of this structure. Three major developments will claim our attention: the expansion and rise to prominence of oil production and export; the building of infrastructure; and the drive towards industrialisation.

The discovery and exploitation of oil resources predates World War Two in some of the countries surveyed here, but the post-war period witnessed the substantial — indeed the dramatic — growth of the oil sector. (We use the term 'oil' to mean in fact oil and gas, or hydrocarbons.) Thus, oil production totalled some 14m tons in 1946, with only three of the five major producers — namely, Iraq, Kuwait and Saudi Arabia — in the production phase then, and Libya and Algeria many years before that phase. In contrast, the five countries produced 768m tons in 1974, while all the Arab oil-producing countries (that is, including those not covered by this study, and some others that are included, but which are minor producers and exporters, namely Egypt, Syria and Tunisia) produced an estimated 908m tons, or 31.7 per cent of the world's total of 2,851m tons.[3]

The rise in revenues from the export of crude oil has been even steeper and more dramatic than that in production, with revenues estimated at $61.8 billion for 1974 ($53.3 billion for the five countries enumerated earlier). The much faster rate of growth of revenue is not the reflection of mere economic fortune. It is instead the outcome of a protracted struggle between the major oil concessionary companies operating in the region and the major oil-producing countries. The struggle has centred essentially around oil prices and government take from each barrel of crude exported, as well as the acquisition by the countries of the assets of the companies, whether under participation in capital or outright nationalisation. After many years of almost fruitless dialogue, with the oil countries in a weak position (basically because of their political weakness *vis-à-vis* the companies and the Western countries to which they belong), the situation became one of confrontation between equals, before it ended in the early seventies by becoming one in which the oil countries virtually dictated their terms and extended their sovereignty to the oil sector.

This is not the appropriate place for a thorough examination of developments in the struggle for the control of the oil industry, in the Arab world and elsewhere; there is an abundance of serious and impartial works on the subject. It is none the less necessary to trace the phases of this struggle, even if briefly. Three phases can be identified. The first stretches from the early days of the industry and the award of concessions, often under duress in fact if not outwardly, to the late fifties or early sixties. During this period, the oil companies took all the decisions themselves without reference to the oil countries. The main decisions involved related to the pricing of oil, the expenses deductible from the sale price, the share of the governments in royalties and in profits, the volume of production, the destination of exports, and generally all top managerial matters.

While it is true that the setting of the royalty was the product of negotiation preceding the award of the concession, in fact it was the companies that determined the royalty. Furthermore, the oil countries did achieve a relatively notable success during this first phase, when in the early fifties they acquired the companies' approval of a fifty-fifty sharing of net profits. However, the companies in conceding the issue did not accept anything economically very damaging, considering the low level of prices then prevailing, and the fact that, thanks to the integration of their operations, they were the main buyers of the oil they produced and thus obtained a cheap input for their refining and other industrial uses.

The second phase was one in which the governments had a larger share in decision-making, though they remained 'junior partners' in this process. The change came as a result of the establishment of an oil producers' association bringing together the major Arab and non-Arab producers of the Third World. This was achieved in 1960, upon the formation of OPEC, the Organization of Petroleum Exporting Countries. (Although in 1968 the Arab producers formed an association of their own, OAPEC, the Organization of Arab Petroleum Exporting Countries, it was the former that succeeded in taking the major steps relating to pricing, sharing of revenues, volume of production, and like matters.) The significance of this association was that it formed some sort of countervailing power to face the close *de facto* association of the major oil companies. The impetus leading to OPEC's formation came from the decline in oil prices, and therefore oil revenues for the countries, in the late fifties.

Less than a decade passed after OPEC came into existence when some of its members, notably Algeria, Libya and Iraq (to restrict the reference to Arab countries) began to press for improvement in financial terms and participation in the companies' capital (or acquisition of part of the assets engaged in the production activity). By the late sixties and the early seventies, several bold measures had been taken by the countries just enumerated, and the third phase was ushered in. This last phase reached its maturity on 16 October 1973, when the six members of OPEC located around the Arabian Gulf met in Kuwait and decided, unilaterally, to raise the posted price of oil by 70 per cent. Then again on 23 December of the same year the price was raised further, to reach a level approximately four times as high as it had been immediately before the October meeting. Parallel with this significant meeting came another on 17 October by the Arab Ministers of oil, also in Kuwait. This latter meeting extended the area of national control over the oil industry by deciding to use oil exports as a political lever in the Arab-Israeli war, which was then raging. Oil was to serve as a pressure mechanism through a mixed system of embargo on exports to certain countries and production cuts in general, to restrict the exports to most other countries in order to influence their attitude with respect to the Arab-Israeli conflict. In addition to these developments, the third phase has witnessed an extension of the process of government participation in the ownership of the companies' capital, more nationalisations, and further increases in the share of governments in net profits.

Obviously, these were most significant landmarks in the history of the oil industry in the Arab region. But equally significant has been the immense financial wealth that has resulted. The sudden rise in prices, the subsequent transfer of immense financial resources from oil-importing to oil-exporting countries, the pressure sustained by the importers' balances of payments, the increase in production costs as a result of oil price increases, and the anxiety of the industrial countries that their money markets might be subjected to strains and dislocations because of the movements of capital seeking investment opportunities — these and like issues troubled the Western world and strained relations with OPEC countries. But these issues will not detain us here. We are primarily concerned with the developmental impact of the new financial resources made available to the Arabs since October 1973.

In looking at their new wealth, the Arab leaders and intellectuals have focused on four points. First, that the oil revenues were not in fact a form of income, since they arose from the sale of a depleting resource. Indeed, the revenues were no more than one form of capital obtained through the surrender of another form, namely the natural resource petroleum. Second, because oil is a depleting resource, and its sale by itself represents no assured future flow of income, oil revenues ought to be put, as fast and as effectively as possible, into productive investment, so that the oil-exporting countries may be able to possess an income-generating economy capable of compensating for oil revenue as this begins to decline.

In the third place, the oil producers came to the sound conclusion that only enough oil should be produced as would meet the essential needs of the importers. In taking this position, the producers have been motivated both by self-interest and international responsibility. For it is in the interest of the oil countries to have their oil last as long as possible and to serve their own industrialisation, which is sought with determination. Such service is viewed not merely, or even predominantly, through the use of oil as fuel, but through the use of oil and gas in developing petrochemical industries. And it is in the interest of the international community not to exhaust oil resources quickly because these have a price advantage over other sources of energy, but to activate their search for alternative resources and to develop them as speedily as possible.[4]

The fourth point of focus in the oil-producing countries has been the necessity not only to achieve development themselves, but to help other countries in their drive for development through grants and loans. The policy of economic aid has aimed primarily at other Arab countries in need, and further afield at Islamic, and non-Arab, non-Moslem Asian and African countries. This aid has gone even further to help certain industrial countries in financial difficulties, and to support the World Bank activities, the International Monetary Fund's oil facility, and FAO's fund for food. Loans for development programmes and projects have been substantially increased since October 1973, and several Arab development funds are now in operation to manage and extend economic aid. These are the Kuwait Fund for Arab Economic Development, the Arab Fund for Economic and Social Development, and the newer Funds of Saudi Arabia, Abu Dhabi and Iraq. We will have occasion to refer again to these important instruments of development further down.

Emphasis in the Arab countries on the construction and equipping of infrastructure has been a marked feature of development in the post-war period. Even before central planning had become a well-established instrument of resource allocation among the uses enjoying priority, a common-sense approach had suggested to the economic decision-makers that the economies needed first of all a strong underpinning before the directly productive sectors could be promoted. The underpinning is being provided through the expansion and modernisation of transport and communication facilities, power, irrigation and drainage works, storage facilities, urban utilities (water, sewerage, etc.), and social services. This economic and social infrastructure has until recently received the largest share of investment resources in most countries, since only the Maghreb countries formerly under French rule have inherited a relatively adequate economic infrastructure. (Against this limited advantage, these latter countries were grossly underequipped in terms of education.)

However, the direction of resources towards infrastructural investment does not mean that the Arab economies are well-equipped with the relevant facilities. Indeed, with few exceptions, these facilities are still short of existing needs, and far short of the estimated needs of the years immediately ahead. The shortage is discernible both inside each of the countries and between countries. In fact, the excitement which has accompanied the accumulation of large financial reserves as a result of the recent rise in oil prices and revenues should be sobered considerably by the thought of the vast funds that have to be invested in road and railway building, the expansion and qualitative improvement of telecommunications, the construction of silos and warehouses, the increase in electric power generation, and the extension of irrigation networks and drainage systems.

The inventory of priority programmes and projects in the area of infrastructure is long and very expensive to fulfil, and the financial reserves on hand will be under great pressure if this inventory is all to be fulfilled in the next decade. The costliness of infrastructural investment is well-known, as is its high capital-output ratio. This is particularly true of the countries that have large land areas (including deserts or semi-deserts) where to connect habitation centres it would be necessary to undertake huge investments, which could benefit generally small population concentrations. The cost per head of population becomes perforce very high. Saudi Arabia, Sudan, Libya, Morocco, Iraq — to name the most notable illustrations — will have to take this high unit cost into account in planning the development of infrastructure.

The last aspect to examine in the present section of the chapter is the place of industry in the structure of Arab economies. To preface the examination, it will be useful to recapitulate and summarise what we saw in the individual country chapters. It was found then that the countries under discussion fall into two groups, plus one individual case. The first group are non-oil countries with agriculture making the largest single contribution to national product. This share hovers around 25 per cent of GNP on the average, with a range between 20 and 30 per cent. In the second group, the major oil countries, it is the oil sector that makes the largest single contribution, with its share currently (at the beginning of 1975) exceeding 50 per cent of national product in Kuwait, Saudi Arabia and Libya (as well as in the oil-producing countries of the Arabian Gulf which are not included in this study). Finally, Lebanon is in a category by itself, with the largest contribution to national product made by trade, as already stated elsewhere.

The sectoral structure has witnessed some important changes in the post-war years. The most substantial both in absolute and relative terms has been the rise in the contribution of the oil sector, where applicable. However, this structural shift does not reflect a comparable improvement in the performance of the oil economies, inasmuch as the oil exports were achieved irrespective of the level at which the rest of the economy stood. Another change has been the considerable expansion in the government sector — an expansion which has been legitimately necessitated by the undertaking by the newly independent governments of many new and complex tasks in the military, political, economic, social and administrative fields. But part of the expansion has been the product of 'bureaucratic elephantiasis', in confirmation of the Parkinsonian Law of administration. Where socialism has prevailed (or, as the critics of Arab socialism prefer to say, where state capitalism has prevailed), as well as in most countries adhering to a system of private enterprise, the public sector has grown considerably on taking over many new economic functions. And finally, the growth in size of Arab armies has also contributed considerably to the rise in the 'contribution' of the government sector. Needless to say, not all this growth is a healthy sign or an indicator of a healthy shift in structure. It remains to be said here that the shift that interests us at this point is that involving the increase in the share of industry.

Industrialisation has made considerable progress in the Arab world, particularly in Egypt, Lebanon, Algeria, Syria and Iraq. But nothing like an 'industrial revolution' has occurred. The contribution of manufacturing industry (which in some countries is defined to include the generation of electricity) is at its largest in Egypt, where it is over 22 per cent of GNP. At its lowest, it is only a few percentage points in Kuwait and Libya. In most other countries the contribution of manufacturing industry hovers around 10 per cent.

However, the size of the contribution is not a sufficient indicator of the real significance of manufacturing industry. For a large share can fail to be accompanied by many of the supportive activities and the attitudes indicative of a true transformation in the economy, while a small share can be thus accompanied, at least in the short and medium terms. In the context of the Arab region, it can be said that industrialisation has not turned into 'industrialism' yet, to borrow the term and its content from Kerr, Harbison, Dunlop and Myers in their book *Industrialism and Industrial Man*. In other words, what is taking place in the Arab world is, with hardly any exception, a mere transplanting of factories and industrial technology from developed to developing countries. The theoretical and applied research that goes with industrial innovation is still largely missing; factory organisation, institutionalised industrial relations and labour discipline are still in their first stages; scientism and awareness of cause-effect relationships are making their first steps, with still a large measure of fatalism and the spill-over both of agricultural mentality and mercantile mentality; industrial entrepreneurship, with all that goes with it in terms of innovation and adaptation, and adoption of the forms of organisation and the patterns of division of authority appropriate to industry, is still at its early stages of evolution; and finally, only a beginning has been made in the manufacture of producers' goods — the machines that make the manufactured products. It is painful, with respect to the last point, that a region that now claims some of the most modern and technologically advanced refineries and petrochemical factories cannot itself design and make a machine that can produce needles and pins.

Egypt, Lebanon and Algeria lead the list of twelve countries in the variety of industrial products which their factories turn out, with Egypt and Algeria claiming more heavy industry than Lebanon. Algeria has probably been achieving the fastest rate in industrialisation over the decade 1965-74, with more emphasis on engineering industry than anywhere else. By and large, and until recently, much of the investment has gone into import-substituting industries. But over the past few years, huge investments have been (and are increasingly being) directed towards industries that are predominantly export-oriented.

This last category is represented mainly in the many branches of the petrochemical industry, into which the oil countries are going. Saudi Arabia in particular has committed enormous funds over the two years 1973/4 and 1974/5 for the development of petrochemical and metallurgical industry, in addition to large investments made earlier. Furthermore, Kuwait, Algeria, Iraq, Libya, and to some extent Syria have directed substantial investments into refining and petrochemical industry. The range of industries also includes traditional and obvious lines such as food processing, soft drinks, tobacco, cement, sugar-refining, household equipment, leather goods and clothing. Of importance are some capital goods (mainly produced in assembly plants in association with foreign internationally known firms) like trucks and tractors; some household durables like radios, refrigerators, gas ovens, air-conditioners; and some other products like paints, pharmaceuticals and rubber tyres.

An inventory like this one is reassuring and promising. However, it leaves untold the listing of growing pains that Arab industry has had with respect to design, construction, manpower training, industrial relations, management, competitiveness, duplication of plants and success in export markets. The country chapters have dwelt on many of these problems which need not be recapitulated here. It is only necessary to add, as a final observation, that for industry to acquire a central and firm place in Arab economies, it is essential that the proper industrial environment be provided. Its components include investment in research and design, industrial entrepreneurship, adequate financing, adequate training of manpower, the appropriate economic, fiscal and commercial policies, and regional Arab co-operation in the context of the Arab Common Market and other mechanisms set up for the promotion and intensification of intra-Arab regional relations.

2. ECONOMIC DEVELOPMENT AND SOCIAL JUSTICE

The countries of the Arab world with the exception of Saudi Arabia and Yemen were still under some form of foreign rule or patronage by the end of World War Two. All but the Aden protectorate and the Trucial Coast (as they were then designated) and Algeria were fully independent states by the end of 1961. They share with scores of other Asian and African countries the problems of newly acquired independence as well as the desire to achieve speedy material and social progress.

The fervent nationalism which dominates the thoughts and actions of most leaders in the Arab world (espousal of socialist ideas notwithstanding, as these ideas remain subservient to nationalism) has come to have a distinct socio-economic content. This content emphasises development and vast improvement in the performance of the economy; more satisfactory services in the fields of health care, education and housing; the provision of employment opportunities and of social insurance; and social justice broadly defined. The more recent constitutions or provisional constitutions, such as those of Egypt, Syria, Iraq, Yemen People's Democratic Republic, Tunisia, Algeria and Libya, emphasise social welfare and social justice as an area of government action. In doing this they reflect the general mood of the times and serve as a source of authority for relevant legislation, development planning and appropriate executive action.

Another strongly underlined aspect of the drive for development and modernisation is industrialisation. It symbolises a break with the past: a break with traditional, slow-changing economies, with primitive technology, and with the role of supplier of primary commodities and buyer of manufactured goods from foreign industrial countries. Beyond being a symbol of economic liberation, industrialisation is designed to create greater balance in the growth and structure of the region's economies by making them less dependent on the dominant agricultural and hydrocarbons sectors. Furthermore, industrialisation is expected to expand opportunities for employment and to absorb some of the surplus labour of the countryside and urban centres.

Notwithstanding the urge to industrialise, the underdeveloped state of transport and communications, irrigation and water resources and power has made politicians and economic planners allocate the largest share of public expenditures over the past generation to these sectors — as already indicated. Social services as one group have ranked next in importance, along with land reclamation and agricultural services. Manufacturing industry, though hailed as a most important sector, has generally ranked next as a recipient of development funds, except in the past two or three years.

The military establishments have also been a major recipient of public funds. Partly because of the frequent association between independence and national armies, but mainly because of the unresolved Arab-Israeli conflict arising from the loss of Palestine, a large outlay is made on military establishments. Some 6.6 per cent of the aggregate national product of the Arab region as a whole is spent on the armies and military *matériel*, but this proportion is greatly exceeded in the countries adjoining Israel, for which it averages about 10.4 per cent. (Defence outlays for 1974 totalled $8,209m for the whole region except Mauritania and Somalia. The estimated aggregate GNP is about $116 billion,[5] while my own estimate is $125 billion.)

The State and Development

The socio-economic systems in the region have undergone considerable change over the thirty-year period under consideration. The end result is socialism in certain countries, private enterprise in some others, and a mixed system in a third group. However, the lines of demarcation have become quite hazy and indistinct, despite the persistence of some basic differences. Thus, the first group allows wide scope for capitalism and private enterprise, while in the second group the state is a very active partner of private enterprise. In short, the prevailing feature is the mixed economy, with nuances of difference depending on the ideology which the leadership basically espouses.

These assertions can be readily supported. Thus, the socialist fervour of Egypt in the sixties, and to some extent of Syria, Iraq and Algeria, has given place to a much more open system — though in the case of Algeria there is probably more socialist content now than under Ben Bella, while there was more vocal assertion then of socialist orientation. Tunisia's claim to socialism is difficult to substantiate in any case, while Libya's efforts to establish socialism are no less a manifestation of state capitalism than elsewhere in the region. At the other extreme, Saudi Arabia's profession of hostility to all collective systems, socialism included, has not stopped it from putting in the hands of the public sector most of the country's productive assets and of its large projects, in addition to the oil sector itself. Kuwait, another country espousing private enterprise, has a large joint sector, as well as a substantial public sector which controls the oil industry. Furthermore, Kuwait and Saudi Arabia, like their socialist sisters, have evolved a form of 'welfare state' which is probably more generous in what it offers in the fields of education, medical care, low-income housing and other public services and subventions. On balance, it is probably Lebanon, Jordan and Morocco which exemplify the system of private enterprise most.

The government's role in development comprises many components, as it does anywhere in the world. These include economic legislation; economic, fiscal, financial and commercial policy; the setting up of development banks — in addition to components that relate less directly to development. Probably planning is the most comprehensive and far-reaching manifestation of the government's involvement in development. Today, all the countries included in this study have explicit development plans, with the exception of Kuwait, whose National Assembly has never approved a plan submitted to it, but where, in any case, there is sectoral planning at the ministry level.

Arab plans vary in comprehensiveness and sophistication, as we have had occasion to see in the country chapters. Likewise, the plans require different degrees of commitment to plan targets by the public and private sectors, and allow widely different scopes for private investment. The most comprehensive plans, such as those of Egypt, Syria, Iraq and the Maghreb countries (including Libya) take into account the availability of all resources, private as well as public, and internal as well as external; they also formulate investment programmes in detail, and make explicit the monetary and physical targets set for the plans.

As we shall see when we discuss planning as a determinant in development further down in the companion volume (Volume II), the experience of the Arab countries has not uniformly been highly rewarding, although on balance it has been useful in all countries. This is because it has created an awareness of the totality of resource availability and resource use, of bottlenecks and surpluses in physical and human resources, of the need to set up priorities and to think seriously of development targets, of the importance of formulating a development strategy, and generally of injecting rationality into the deployment of resources with a view to optimising returns to the economy and society.

The negative aspects of the evaluation arise in part from factors extraneous to the planning agencies and the planning function proper (such as political instability, the power of private interests resisting the philosophy and practice of planning, war, and such matters), as from internal factors. The latter include insufficient experience; shortage of the appropriate skills in economics, statistics and social and manpower matters; excessive optimism; frequent alterations in the plans; extreme centralisation, and insufficient background and supportive studies.

Economic Performance

Though good by Asian and African standards, the overall economic performance of most Arab countries is very low by Western and USSR standards. In stating this, we abstract from the level of GNP *per capita* in, say, 1974, which is about $893 on the average for the whole Arab world, since this relatively high level has been attained after October 1973 and the steep rise in oil prices and revenues. (The oil revenue alone accounts for about 55 per cent of the current aggregate GNP of the region.) Furthermore, the sudden rise in income is no indication of a parallel rise in economic performance.

The national product *per capita* varies from country to country, but right before the October oil price increases it averaged around $400-425 for the region. This average is deceptive in that it hides the gross inequality in distribution between the oil and non-oil countries covered by this study. The first group which then had about a quarter of the aggregate population accounted for 57 per cent of the national product, while the latter group accounted for three-quarters of the population and 43 per cent of the national product. By the end of 1974, the discrepancy had grown wider as a result of the much steeper rise in national product in the oil countries, as Table 14.3 demonstrates. Today, the rich quarter of aggregate Arab population accounts for three-quarters of aggregate national product. The impact of oil on the pattern of distribution is even stronger than these few statistics suggest, as the aggregate national product just before October 1973 also included a considerable component arising from oil revenues and their income multiplier.

The performance of Arab economies is not to be gauged merely from income data. Indeed, there is ample visual evidence which the observer cannot fail to see in the Arab countries, even if this evidence is not always impressive in the countryside. What has acted to make the concrete, physical impact of development less obvious is the combined effect of a fast increase in population and gross inequality in distribution inside most countries. The effect of these two factors has led to the seemingly paradoxical phenomenon of a statistically satisfactory rate of growth, with evidence all round of poverty and underprivilege — particularly in the countryside of most countries and in the mass of the urban centres.

Yet the critical tone of this comment ought to be tempered by the recollection that early in the post-war period the average regional income per head was considerably lower, especially when oil revenues started to be of some significance only beginning with 1952, and then only in a few of today's oil-producing countries. Indeed, it would not be rash to estimate the income per head in the year preceding October 1973 as being four times as high as it had been in 1946, and in 1974 to be eight to nine times as high.[6]

The rates of growth achieved in the various countries, which prior to October 1973 may have averaged 5-6 per cent of GNP for the twelve countries included here, were only in part attributable to oil revenues. These must have influenced the course of growth in the oil countries themselves, where growth rates of 8-10 per cent were recorded for a number of years (except in Iraq, where the rates were distinctly lower in the late sixties and somewhat lower in the early seventies). But the influence was restricted to the local economies themselves, the spill-over effects into sister Arab economies being minimal. Beginning with 1974, the situation has changed considerably, as we will have occasion to see when we examine inter-Arab economic co-operation.

Outside the oil countries credit for growth achieved must therefore go primarily to the marshalling of domestic savings and their investment. While it is true that development has experienced many false starts, misallocation of resources, waste, insufficiently planned and studied investments, confused priorities — to name a few of the 'growing pains' of economies — it is also true that by and large the rates of growth attained have been satisfactory on the whole by Third World standards. However, the growth achieved in most of the non-oil countries does not permit confidence and comfort because of the high rates of population increase prevailing. For some countries like Egypt, Morocco and Sudan, where population growth is high and economic growth is sluggish, the race between the two remains uncomfortably close. Furthermore, the regional growth rates attained do not mean that the results have been satisfactory from the point of view of overall, integrated development, which is much more comprehensive and meaningful than the narrower concept of economic growth. For the time being, the evaluation is restricted to growth in the 'statistical, quantitative' sense.

The resources saved domestically and directed to investment in the twelve countries, whether or not oil-exporting, have during the post-war period averaged about 12 per cent of GNP. About a quarter as much has come in as official foreign aid: grants and loans from developed market economies and from centrally planned (socialist) economies. The two sources together put into the stream of investment the equivalent of 15 per cent of GNP during the post-war period on average. (The country chapters provide some detailed information both on investment and on foreign aid.) In absolute figures, total investment was in the magnitude of $60 billion dollars between 1946 and 1973, of which $14-16 billion came

Table 14.3: Arab Countries' Population and Gross National Product 1974

Country	Population (million)	GNP ($ billion)	GNP Per Capita $
Iraq	10.75	13.00	1,209
Kuwait	0.92	11.50	12,500
Saudi Arabia	6.00	38.25	6,375
Jordan	2.65	1.00	377
Syria	7.30	2.85	390
Lebanon	2.65	3.15	1,189
Egypt	37.00	9.20	249
Sudan	17.50	2.50	143
Libya	2.30	9.80	4,261
Tunisia	5.75	2.90	504
Algeria	16.30	12.30	755
Morocco	16.90	6.30	373
Sub-Total or Average	126.02	112.75	895
Bahrain	0.24	0.36	1,500
Qatar	0.19	2.35	12,368
United Arab Emirates	0.33	6.25	18,939
Oman	0.77	1.10	1,429
Yemen, A. R.	6.40	1.10	172
Yemen, P. D. R.	1.65	0.65	394
Somalia	3.10	0.22	71
Mauritania	1.30	0.22	169
Sub-Total or Average	13.98	12.25	876
Total or Average	140.00	125.00	893

Note: Data on population are more dependable than on GNP, despite the large margin of error in the former especially for Saudi Arabia, Lebanon, and most of the eight countries not included in this study.

Sources: For population: *IFS*, October 1975; General Union of Chambers of Commerce ... etc., *Arab Economic Report*, 1974 edition; and Europa Publications, the 1974-75 edition. For GNP, *IFS* and *Arab Economic Report*, as well as UN *Monthly Bulletin of Statistics*, June 1975; The International Institute for Strategic Studies, *The Military Balance 1974-1975* (London, 1974), pp. 32-39; MEFIS, *Middle East Attitudes and Strategies*, updating No. 2, 1975. All but the last source have data for 1972 or 1973. I have adjusted the information to cover 1974. For the oil countries, the adjustment took into account the increased oil revenue plus its (assumed) GNP multiplier, plus the growth in the non-oil sectors. The multiplier assumed varied from country to country, depending on my general knowledge of the relative importance of the oil sector contribution in each of the economies concerned. Understandably, the resulting data must be considered as tentative and only broadly suggestive.

from external sources. (Foreign investments in oil and other sectors are excluded from this account.)

Obviously, these aggregates must be accepted with great reserve and caution, for at least three reasons. The first is the dearth of statistics in the Arab countries, while the second is the relative secrecy with which aid from the centrally planned economies to the major recipients (Egypt, Algeria, Syria and Iraq) has been shrouded. Finally, even where Western aid is concerned (but the point also applies to aid from the socialist countries) the information is not all consistent, as sometimes it relates to commitments, sometimes to actual disbursements.

Since 1974 the picture has changed radically. Foreign, non-Arab aid has proportionately declined considerably for various reasons. Two of these are worth registering. The first is the coming into financial prominence of the Arab oil countries which are now capable of directing a large volume of economic aid to their needy sister countries. The second is the growing hesitation of many Western countries to advance grants and loans to the Third World. The United States, traditionally the major supplier in absolute terms, is presently one of the least enthusiastic, as a recent report of the OECD shows.[7] This phenomenon is attributed to 'disenchantment' with the philosophy and results of aid in the donor countries. Basically, the disenchantment relates to the meagre political dividends which the United States has been reaping. There is no shortage of evidence to the effect that what is really at issue is the failure of aid to make the recipients align themselves with the politics and policies of the donors, and the subsequent impatience of legislatures and executive authorities alike in the Western industrial countries.[8] Thus, even if the first reason were to be absent, we would still be witnessing today a relatively smaller flow of external resources for development into the Arab world. Under the circumstances, the sudden affluence of the Arab oil countries has been a stroke of good fortune for the non-oil countries.

Social Justice

The title of the present section combined economic development and social justice, thus emphasising the close connection and interaction between the two. Indeed, it is here believed that true development can be achieved only if there is a dialectical relationship between improvement in the productive capability of a country and improvement (that is, less inequality) in the pattern of wealth and income distribution among the citizens, each serving the other and leading to further improvements in it.

The measures of social justice undertaken in the countries under examination have centred on several areas of action. Some were supposed to act indirectly, some directly. The first group included the supply free or at subsidised prices of public services like education, health care, recreation and popular housing. More direct in their operation were such measures as progressive direct taxation, mainly of income, profits, inheritance and some capital assets such as land, but more particularly buildings. The most direct were supposed to deal with the redistribution of wealth and productive assets and of income. This last category, which primarily comprised agrarian reform and nationalisation of the major productive establishments, constituted the core of the drive for social justice as envisaged by some of the Arab countries. These consisted mainly of Egypt, Syria, Iraq, Algeria and Libya, but Sudan and Tunisia can be added though the reach of their measures was limited. (If the region as a whole is considered, the Yemen People's Democratic Republic will have to be added.) Some space will be devoted here to agrarian reform and nationalisation.

It is first necessary to set the background to agrarian reform. The system of land tenure varied little from country to country as the decade of the fifties set in, particularly in the Mashreq. A common legal heritage shaped mostly by the tenets of Islam and originating in the previous Ottoman rule of most of the region was at the base of these systems. Broadly speaking, three main features characterised land tenure before the reforms of the 1950s, the early 1960s, and the early 1970s (the last being in Algeria). These were: a small number of very large land holdings, comprising a great deal of absenteeism; a very large number of very small land holdings (mostly uneconomical to operate) resulting from the system of inheritance combined with excessive fragmentation of holdings; and share-tenancy in conditions of insecurity for the tenants, an unduly large share of crops for landlords, and heavy dependence of tenants on landlords for tenure, credit and — in many cases — protection.

To make matters worse, a sizeable proportion of medium and large estates consisted of several units which were often not in close proximity to each other. Thus, on the whole, the system did not provide the advantages of large-scale operation indicated by the concentration of ownership, nor the advantages of small-scale operations associated with family farms consisting of adequately-sized whole areas. Absenteeism among large landlords encouraged their agents to neglect the land and exploit the share-tenants, and additionally raised the cost of agricultural produce to the urban centres as the middleman's share was much larger than the service he rendered to the production and distribution processes. Furthermore, the absentee landlords (with notable exceptions in Egypt and post-war Syria) did not make substantial investments in the land. Consequently, though production of almost all crops increased considerably during the ten or twelve years after 1946, the bulk of this rise was attributable more to increased acreage than to increased productivity per acre or per farmer.

However, the situation with regard to tenure institutions and relationships in the countries concerned was substantially different by the end of the sixties. This change was the result of the implementation of land reform measures, which, in addition to setting upper limits to the size of land holdings per individual or family, regulated share-tenancy conditions and stipulated for the institution of agricultural co-operative societies and the spread of their various services in the reform areas.

Looking back, we see that agrarian reform measures have indeed put land in the possession of thousands of hitherto landless peasants, or peasants with minute holdings; have resulted in the emergence of a pattern of tenure relations (rent rates, length of lease, and so on) superior from the standpoint of equity and security to that prevailing previously; and have involved the formation of many more co-operative societies and the extension of agricultural services (cheap and supervised credit, extension services, grading and packing, marketing, research) beyond those experienced before. Yet, owing to the relative modesty of the number of those benefiting from land redistribution, to the inability to extend agricultural services far enough and to manage the land covered by land reform efficiently, and to the serious delays in the expropriation and redistribution of excess areas, as in the case of Syria but more so of Iraq; to the severe limitations on the areas of cultivable and cultivated land, as in the case of Egypt and Jordan; and to the insufficiency of the number and experience of technical cadres to guide the farmers in their work — owing to all these factors, on balance the rise in productivity and in production for the countries concerned has been noticeably limited. Indeed, there have been cases where total production has actually declined.

The main exception to this judgement is that tenure relations have distinctly improved for the tenants. Otherwise, it can be said that the improvement arising from agrarian reform as a whole has mainly been in the institutional, social and political realms. The class structure of the countries enumerated has changed almost beyond recognition. This change has totally altered the locus of power in such a way that the ruling classes of pre-reform days have been disenfranchised and real power has shifted from the upper classes — of whom the large landlords constituted a prominent component — mainly to the middle and lower middle classes. That a 'New Class' has emerged in the sense in which Milovan Djilas uses the term in his *The New Class* is undeniable.

Nationalisations have been taken to mean socialist transformation in the countries that have effected them. Most of these nationalisations have occurred in the sixties. Since the beginning of this decade, Egypt, Algeria, Syria, Iraq and Libya (and to a lesser extent Tunisia and Sudan) have enacted legislation involving the passage of ownership of banks, insurance companies, transportation facilities, large industry and public utilities to the government. Other measures relating to non-agricultural establishments have been the limitation of individual capital ownership in corporations, the imposition of steeper rates of income and profit taxes, the raising of the floor of wages, and provision for participation of labour in the direction of corporations. These measures were considered socialist by the governments. This is a matter which is in dispute among Arab socialists, since, in many instances, the measures taken had political but not ideological motivation behind them.

Socialism or not, Egypt and Algeria seem to have gone furthest along the course of nationalisation and public sector economic participation. In the case of Egypt, small housing, small business, personal services and land remain in private hands, leaving the bulk of productive assets in the public sector. While Egypt was urged in this direction initially by the desire of its government to better control the use of resources and to increase investment, and while the country set out on the road to socialism in a pragmatic way, there was a clear shift towards ideological justification and commitment by mid-1962. (This shift has been somewhat reversed since 1971.)

In Algeria and in Tunisia many of the measures taken had political motivation behind them, in the sense that the nationalisations were directed against the French, who had been the owners of most of the establishments nationalised, although the measures came to be declared 'steps towards socialism'. In the Sudan, it was the government's desire to own and run the large industrial firms (particularly as these had substantial foreign ownership) that prompted the nationalisations; again here, the motives were in reality more pragmatic than ideological. In brief, much of the socialism supposed to prevail in certain Arab countries is essentially what we can call 'socialism by baptism'. That is to say, the measures of state capitalism have been named 'socialism' even where the designation did not fit.

An overall evaluation of the extent of social justice achieved will run very much along the same lines as that undertaken earlier for development and economic performance. There have been areas of improvement, but no even improvement across the countries concerned and their peoples. Often, the legal and institutional framework has been established, but the real centres of power have not undergone that conversion in their conscience and attitudes to make them effect the reform measures honestly and uniformly, or the civil services have not been radicalised and de-bureaucratised enough to implement the measures. And, in addition to these negative factors, there have been others related to insufficient studies preceding the measures to make them solidly grounded, or insufficient public consciousness to guarantee implementation, or yet insufficient organisation among the masses to enable them to have and to exercise power (or at least the power to ask the leaders to account for their promises) for the implementation of social measures. Where the masses are concerned, whether they are rural or urban, social justice legislation and institutions have conferred peripheral benefits only. Development in the full sense of the term remains spotty both in the sense that it is not comprehensive and that it is not even geographically uniform among the various components of the population.

As far as population masses are concerned, mention must be made of the substantially increased urbanisation, with all that is associated with it in terms of economic and social dislocations. Changes in the degree of urbanisation cannot be measured with certainty, owing both to insufficient and unreliable statistics, and to the different definitions of 'urban centres' adopted in the different countries. However, generally speaking, it can safely be said that the urban population is now larger in relative terms by over half, having risen in the post-war period from an estimated 30 per cent of the total to around 45 per cent. The factors behind this shift are many, including the heavy pressure on cultivable and cultivated land resources to begin with; fragmentation; low productivity and low income in the countryside; mechanisation; the more glaring insufficiency of education and health services in the countryside than in the urban centres; the seemingly smaller availability of job opportunities in the rural sector; and in general the social lure of cities with their recreational attractions and promise for those peasant elements with greater sensitivity to the urges of social mobility. To these push and pull factors must be added the spread of the 'education ethos' and of education itself in the countryside, where schools generally stop at the elementary level and parents wanting intermediate and secondary education for their children have little alternative to moving to an urban centre for the sake of their children's future.

However, the expectations of newly urbanised peasants have remained far from fulfilled. The towns and cities have offered fewer employment opportunities than hoped for; the schools and health care facilities have not been expanded enough to cope with the growing needs; the public utilities (urban transport, housing, water and power supplies, and the like) have fallen short of the new requirements. This is not to say that job opportunities, social facilities, public utilities and housing have not grown in the urban centres. It is merely to emphasise that in spite of the growth in the areas indicated, this growth has been slower than the rate of urbanisation. Of special relevance is the fact that the expansion of the sector of manufacturing industry, even where it has been marked, has proved incapable of absorbing a sizeable part of the displaced agricultural labour.

The influx into towns and cities has created strains not only quantitatively, but also qualitatively, that is with respect to the growth of discontent, delinquency, crime, overcrowding, unemployment and underemployment, as well as the loss of the aesthetic appeal of the older urban centres. The slums have in consequence multiplied, and the 'bidonvilles' have become a common feature of many Arab cities. That this whole process of deterioration is common to the Third World at large does not make it any less painful and regrettable.

We have dealt with 'economic performance' and 'social justice' separately, though we had indicated their interdependence at the outset. It is now hoped that the discussion of the attempts to achieve each of these targets has revealed not only the successes registered and the shortcomings and difficulties experienced, but also that neither of the two desiderata is achievable in a profound sense without the other. Thus there can be little real satisfaction in the pursuit of distributive justice if the economic performance is poor, and little significance for the population if economic performance is satisfactory but social justice is neglected. Indeed, the two are mutually supportive and contribute to each other's achievement. This is the fundamental lesson that some of the region's countries have failed to absorb adequately and whose misreading has led to the faltering of the pursuit of one or the other objective, and to long-run damage to both.

3. ECONOMIC RELATIONS BETWEEN THE REGION AND THE REST OF THE WORLD

We are more interested in this chapter in the intraregional economic relations than in those of the region as one unit with other parts of the world. However, the latter, or the region's international relations, will be looked into, even if very briefly, so that the intraregional relations may be placed in their broader context and evaluated accordingly.

The region's international economic relations are vast and of long standing. Like other former colonised areas, the Arab region has had its economies tied to those of the Western colonial system, and of the powers ruling it in particular. The most obvious and comprehensive form of relationship has been physical occupation itself, involving the presence of military personnel, administrators, professional men and businessmen. This presence varied from country to country, being densest in the Maghreb countries and in Palestine. (The Zionist incursion into Palestine, representing a severe form of settler colonialism, and the uprooting of the majority of the Arab population will not occupy us here, though it has been a very harsh colonial incursion and continues to weigh heavily on the Arabs at large.)

The economic presence was felt, among other things, in investment and trade, and generally in the shaping of economic activities in such a way as to serve the economic interests of the colonising power. The fields of investment drawing the most substantial volume of resources have been petroleum, gas and mineral resources, particularly phosphates, though manufacturing industry, transport and communications have also been the recipients of considerable investment.

Independence did not bring about drastic change in this pattern immediately: indeed, economic transactions between the formerly colonial and the formerly colonised rose in volume and value for about a decade after World War Two, but these transactions were conducted within a new legal and political framework. However, the pattern changed after the mid-fifties upon the economic entry of the USSR (and other members of the socialist community) into the region, but then mainly for the Arab countries that adopted a socialist ideology and system, like Egypt, Syria, Algeria and Iraq. (The region's trade with the socialist countries tripled in the decade 1955-64, but still represented no more than one-seventh of the trade with the Western countries by the end of the decade, or one-eleventh of total external trade.) The change in the pattern lasted roughly another decade, since which economic transactions with the Western countries have again risen considerably, particularly with the rise, and subsequently the acceleration, of the value of oil exports and of oil revenues in the early seventies, and the consequent acceleration in imports into the region.

The greater part of the trade of the region is not intraregional but with other parts of the world, as Table 14.4 shows. Intraregional trade constituted a mere 6.37 per cent of total imports and 3.50 per cent of total exports for the twelve countries covered for 1973, the most recent year for which detailed and final information is available. (The proportion is even smaller for the 20 Arab states.) Early estimates suggest that the proportion has dropped further in 1974. For, although the value of total imports for the twelve countries with which we are primarily concerned rose from $12.8 billion in 1973 to an estimated $24.0 billion for 1974, exports rose much more steeply, from $23.1 billion to an estimated $74.9 billion.[9] However, the bulk of the increase in both instances represented goods imported from, or exported to, non-Arab countries. Thus intraregional trade for 1974 is most certainly an insignificant part of the region's total trade, a mere few percentage points for imports, and much less for exports (probably below 2 per cent) where petroleum constitutes by far the largest single component.

Table 14.4: Intraregional and International Trade of Arab Countries, 1973 (in millions of US dollars)

Country	(1) Total	EXPORTS (2) To Arab World	(3) (2) ÷ (1) Per Cent	(4) Total	IMPORTS (5) From Arab World	(6) (5) ÷ (4) Per Cent
Iraq	1,726.6	57.1	3.31	953.5	46.5	4.88
Kuwait	3,062.8	22.7	0.74	1,009.7	110.7	10.96
Saudi Arabia	7,615.7	50.4	0.66	1,893.3	151.9	8.02
Jordan	57.3	30.2	52.70	327.7	71.2	21.73
Syria	339.0	72.9	21.50	593.3	86.1	14.51
Lebanon	645.3	291.2	45.13	1,482.8	121.1	8.17
Egypt	1,030.9	80.4	7.79	1,350.8	77.8	5.76
Sudan	437.0	50.1	11.46	436.1	27.2	5.24
Libya	3,596.5	12.0	0.33	1,904.0	119.4	6.27
Tunisia	384.3	30.8	8.01	606.2	28.9	4.77
Algeria	1,772.7	12.9	0.73	2,245.4	15.4	0.68
Morocco	862.3	42.5	4.93	1,117.9	30.9	2.76
Sub-Total	21,529.8	753.2	3.50	13,920.7	887.1	6.37
Bahrain	231.8	0.4	0.17	248.1	2.0	0.81
Qatar	447.3	7.7	1.72	170.3	11.2	6.58
United Arab Emirates	1,509.7	0.5	0.03	783.7	9.1	1.16
Oman	390.5	0.4	0.10	147.2	0.8	0.54
Yemen A.R.	8.0	2.1	26.25	125.4	26.1	20.81
Yemen P.D.R.	97.9	15.3	15.63	100.5	19.9	19.80
Somalia	40.5	24.3	60.00	132.7	2.3	1.73
Mauritania	159.9	2.2	1.38	107.5	1.0	0.95
Sub-Total	2,885.6	52.9	1.83	1,815.4	72.4	3.99
Total 20 Countries	24,415.4	806.1	3.30	15,736.1	959.5	6.10

Note: Data on imports and exports from the source indicated below differ — sometimes considerably — from those in *International Financial Statistics* or UN *Monthly Bulletin of Statistics*. In each case, they are subject to error arising from various sources, as the introductory notes in *Directions of Trade* suggest. We have opted for DOT data because they contain the detail needed for our purposes and, in any case, as details and aggregates come from the same source, their errors are likely to be uniform and the proportions (in columns 3 and 6 in the table) are likely to be minimally affected.

Source: IMF and IBRD, *Directions of Trade: Annual 1969-73,* No. 9, country pages.

The rise in the volume and value of external trade has been considerable since the end of World War Two, for several reasons. The most important of these, on the side of imports, is the tremendous drive for development, especially since the sixties, necessitating the importation of industrial raw materials, intermediate goods, machines and equipment. The importation of manufactured consumer goods and household durables has also risen alongside that of capital goods. For the region as a whole, imports in 1958, for instance, were more than five times their value in 1938, and over one and a half times their value immediately following the war. In 1966, the value of imports was about 50 per cent higher than in 1958, while imports for 1973 were 136 per cent higher than for 1966 for the twelve countries under examination. (The inclusion of the region's other countries qualifies these contrasts only marginally.) Vast though the rise in total imports has been between 1966 and 1973, the region's share in world imports fell from 2.9 per cent to 2.4 per cent. The drop in this share over the preceding two decades, 1946-66, was larger, because the region's means for financing imports prior to the late sixties were distinctly more scarce.

On the other hand, the share of the region's exports in world exports rose between 1966 and 1973, from 4 to 4.9 per cent, thanks to the vast expansion in oil exports. The rise is even sharper for 1974, both for imports and exports, owing to the substantial increase in the value of oil exports for this year. The region's imports represented 2.9 per cent of the world's total imports in 1974, but its exports accounted for 10.1 per cent of the world's total.[10] (It is important to note that oil exports represented over 87 per cent of the region's total exports in 1974. But for oil, the region's exports would have constituted less than 1.5 per cent of world exports.)

The region as a whole, which had a large surplus on trade as well as current account in 1973, and a much larger one in 1974, would have had a large deficit in the absence of oil exports. Obviously the volume of imports itself would have been vastly different but for oil, and the region's trade would represent a much tinier proportion of world trade.

However, the fact that the region enjoys a substantial surplus on current account does not mean that balance of payments hardships do not exist in individual countries. This is not true today of non-oil countries, nor was it true earlier in the post-war period. But such hardships have become lighter and redress easier in the seventies, owing to the larger flow of financial resources from the oil-rich to the hardship countries. Even Egypt, which is probably the worst-off in the present context, has been able to meet its most pressing import requirements thanks to capital transfers from the major oil-exporting countries, and has been additionally enabled recently (in August 1975) to repay about $1.4 billion of foreign debts.[11]

Widespread efforts to achieve speedy industrialisation, to build infrastructure, and generally to modernise non-manufacturing commodity and service sectors have required heavy dependence on imports. Such countries as Egypt, Syria, Lebanon and Iraq, as well as the Maghreb countries formerly under French hegemony, were able in the initial years of their independence to finance a large proportion of their imports from foreign assets accumulated during World War Two (and in subsequent years, for the Maghreb). However, these assets were soon totally wiped out, while the need for foreign exchange resources kept growing. The export of primary commodities, and to a lesser extent of services, has financed the bulk of imports. But the needs of development and consumption combined have grown faster than production, and exports — except for oil — have grown less fast than imports. Foreign economic aid in the form of grants and loans has bridged the gap between required and available resources.

External economic relations are by no means restricted to commodity trade, though this has been over the decades the most significant component. In addition, these relations include services and capital flows like travel and tourism, the training of tens of thousands of men and women in institutions of higher learning in Western and socialist countries, insurance, banking, and the flow of technical assistance and technology from advanced to Arab countries, as well as investments and foreign aid. The relative value of these items has changed drastically over time, with deposits and investments in Western countries growing fastest in volume after October 1973, and foreign (non-Arab) aid dropping proportionately. The rise and the drop, respectively, are the result of the same factor, namely the steep rise in oil prices and therefore in Arab oil revenues and aid capability. This has, on the one hand, made the region, taken as one unit, self-sufficient in terms of the availability of foreign exchange resources, and, on the other, made foreign 'donor' countries advance much less aid to some of the region's needy countries. (We are ignoring here the factor of reduced enthusiasm on the part of the donors, particularly the United States, to which reference was made earlier.)

In fact, however, the vast financial resources available since October 1973 have not solved the problem of capital-hunger, as the bulk of these resources have gone to the Western money markets and investments, leaving the region's needs for capital investments considerably less than fully satisfied. This point can be appreciated from the fact that the international reserves of the twelve countries surveyed rose to $28.4 billion by the end of 1974 from a total of $11.9 billion for 1973.[12] This is apart from investments in projects and equity. Only a small proportion of the total — about 10 per cent — was in the Arab world.

The gap between resource availability and needs cannot be filled by non-Arab aid, in view of the general climate of hesitation in the major donor countries, and the feeling that the Arab members of OPEC, particularly Saudi Arabia, Kuwait, the United Arab Emirates, Qatar and Libya, whose absorptive capacity is still below the level of their resources, ought themselves to satisfy the capital needs of the non-oil countries. The pattern of regional resource re-allocation *required* will claim our attention in Volume II. What ought to be indicated here refers to what has *actually* taken place, and this will be attempted in the next section of the chapter. It is sufficient at this point to say that in spite of the inadequacy of Arab capital flows inside the region, these flows have become much more substantial, and promise to grow further in volume, using many new forms and modalities. Before long, Arab capital flows should make it unnecessary for capital-short countries to seek aid from sources external to the region. This would be one step towards self-reliance in the drive for development, which should also entail the generation inside the region of more of the critical development forces needed, such as technological adaptation, science and education, high-level manpower and planning techniques.

We have had occasion to refer to official foreign aid to the Arab region as a whole in the present chapter, and indicated that a total of $14-16 billion came in from advanced market and centrally-planned economies, and from multilateral agencies. It is difficult, if not impossible, to venture an estimate as to the source allocation of this sum. But, as a broad order of magnitude, we can suggest that a little over half came from market economies, with the balance divided equally between centrally planned economies and multilateral agencies. A further $6 billion to $7 billion has come from private foreign sources, mainly to be invested in the petroleum industry. (Total gross investment in this industry by 1974 was about $8-9 billion, approximately 60 per cent of which is in Iraq and the Arabian Peninsula.) The aggregate flow is not impressive, when related to the area, the population, and the investment opportunities of the region. On a *per capita* basis for the thirty years under examination, foreign aid has amounted to a mere 5 US dollars per year. The paucity of this sum can be seen if it is remembered that, on an incremental basis and assuming it is all invested, *per capita* aid is capable of producing about 1.5 dollars more of national product per annum per person. (In contrast, Israel alone received around $18 billion of foreign economic aid between 1949 and the end of 1974, or about $346 *per capita* per annum.)

Like foreign aid anywhere in the world, that flowing into the Arab region has been influenced by political factors and alignments, both in its abundance and in its scarcity. In addition, it has favoured those investment ends that best serve, or at least accommodate, the interests of the donors. Investment in the oil sector, which constituted about one-third of all inflows − bilateral, multilateral and private combined − was directed to one specific sector and did not directly aim at broad development.

The region did not, and still does not, handle foreign aid *as a region*, but country by country and haphazardly. Nor does it address itself, as one region, to the broad issues arising from and associated with external economic relations, like trade, industrialisation, capital flows, technological transfers and the brain drain. The single but significant exception to this generalisation regarding a fragmented approach is the Arab members of OPEC in their dealings with the rest of the world with respect to the volume of oil production and oil prices, but even here this group approach is recent, and its effectiveness only dates back to October 1973. The Arab world, like the rest of the Third World, still has to travel the long journey of intraregional solidarity before it can correct the imbalance between itself and the industrial countries, and put itself firmly on the road to internally generated and sustained development as we understand it in this book.

4. INTRAREGIONAL ECONOMIC RELATIONS AND CO-OPERATION

Economic relations between the Mashreq countries are of long standing; in some instances, as internally between the parts of the Fertile Crescent, or between Lebanon, Syria and Palestine on the one hand, and Egypt on the other, they are ancient. However, since World War Two, intraregional economic relations have not grown parallel with the growth of the region's total external relations and of its development pace. The relations take many forms and raise many issues. In the present context, we will restrict ourselves to the recording and evaluation of the existing relations, leaving the discussion of Arab economic co-operation as a determinant of development to Volume II.

Trade and the movement of persons across frontiers have, at least since the turn of the century and down into the mid-forties, been the major form intraregional relations have taken. Since then, there have been new forms. These include formalised arrangements for co-operation − some even aiming at integration or unity − and other institutions, whether under the aegis of the League of Arab States or undertaken outside the framework of the League bilaterally and multilaterally, or by the private sector. They also include capital flows, investments, and aid extended by specialised agencies or funds, as well as professional unions formed on syndical bases. While economic interaction and co-operation moved slowly in the early post-war period, today in the mid-seventies it is accelerated, is expressed in many forms, and uses so many instruments that there is the danger of excessive proliferation. (See Table 14.5 below.)

The categories of economic relations together form an increasingly spreading and tightening web of relations, but they are not mutually exclusive as listed further down, although there are nuances of difference between them. In order to facilitate the analysis, we will concentrate in the rest of this section on the major categories.

Trade

Intraregional trade was characterised earlier as forming an insignificant part of the region's total trade, particularly with respect to exports. Table 14.4 presented a detailed picture of the pattern of inter-country trade for 1973, from which a few salient generalisations can now be derived. The first is the overall characterisation just cited, namely that inter-country imports constitute 6.4 per cent of total imports, as against 3.5 per cent for exports. Even if oil exports are excluded, the proportion only rises to about 12 per cent. These modest proportions reflect three factors: the long and established pattern which had been shaped under conditions of dependency in colonial days; the state of underdevelopment itself which, in the Arab region as elsewhere in the Third World, leads to a limitation of exchange transactions among the member countries; and the broad similarity of the exportable products and the import needs of these countries, coupled with the narrowness of the range of locally produced agricultural and manufactured goods. Much of what the countries have for sale finds readier markets outside the region; most of what they badly need to buy can best be provided by suppliers in the advanced countries outside the region.

Table 14.5: Major Arab Organisations, Unions and Projects with Economic and Social Objectives as of End of 1974

A. Arab Official Organisations (Specialised Agencies) Formed Within the Framework of the League of Arab States

1. Council of Arab Economic Unity
2. Arab Educational, Cultural, and Scientific Organization
3. Arab Regional Literacy Organization
4. Institute of Arab Research and Studies
5. Permanent Bureau for the Coordination of Arabization in the Arab World
6. Industrial Development Center for the Arab States
7. Arab Boycott Office
8. Arab Financial Institution for Economic Development (in practice, superseded by the next body)
9. Arab Fund for Economic and Social Development
10. Arab Postal Union
11. Arab Telecommunications Union
12. Arab Labour Organization
13. Arab Organization for Standardization and Metrology
14. Arab Air Carriers' Organization
15. Arab Cities' Organization
16. Arab Organization for Administrative Sciences
17. Arab Center for Studies on Arid and Desert Regions
18. Arab Organization for Agricultural Development
19. Arab Institute on Forests
20. Arab Academy for Maritime Transport
21. Arab Science Council for the Utilization of Atomic Energy for Peaceful Uses
22. Arab Union for Tourism
23. Board for the Utilization of the River Jordan and Its Tributaries
24. Arab Union of Automobile Clubs and Tourist Societies
25. Administrative Tribunal of the Arab League

26. International Arab Organization for Social Defence, comprising:
    a. The International Arab Bureau for Narcotics
    b. The International Arab Bureau for the Prevention of Crime
    c. The International Arab Bureau of Criminal Police
27. Arab Institution for the Insurance of Investments
28. Organization of Arab Petroleum Exporting Countries, comprising the following joint Arab projects:
    a. Arab Maritime Petroleum Transport Company
    b. Arab Shipbuilding and Repair Company
    c. Arab Petroleum Investment Company
    d. Arab Petroleum Services Company

B. Maghreb Organisations, Unions and Committees Formed Within the Framework of the Maghreb Permanent Consultative Committee, Parallel to Arab League Activities

1. Maghreb Center for Industrial Studies
2. Maghreb Alfa Bureau
3. Maghreb Committee on Tourism
4. Maghreb Committee on Postal and Telecommunications Coordination
5. Maghreb Commission for Transport and Communications (including separate committees for air transport, railways, shipping and road transport)
6. Maghreb Committee on National Accounts and Statistics
7. Maghreb Committee on Employment and Labour
8. Maghreb Committee on Standardization
9. Maghreb Committee on Insurance and Re-Insurance
10. Maghreb Committee on Pharmaceutical Products
11. Maghreb Committee on Electric Power

C. Arab Professional (Syndical) Unions

1. General Union of Arab Chambers of Commerce, Industry, and Agriculture for the Arab Countries
2. Federation of Arab Economists
3. Federation of Arab Bankers
4. Federation of Arab Labourers
5. Federation of Arab Engineers
6. Union of Arab Insurance Companies
7. Arab Union of Iron and Steel
8. Arab Union of Textile Industries
9. Arab Union of Chemical Industries

D. Arab Companies

1. Arab Potash Company, Limited
2. Arab Tankers Company
3. Arab Company for Re-Insurance
4. Arab Maritime Transport Company

Notes: 1. Many of the institutions listed above, categories A to D, are inactive, or have not even gone beyond the stage of resolutions taken to be formed officially. Among those actually formed, several are totally or largely stagnant.
2. Category D comprises companies formed by general Arab participation in capital. The list can be enlarged to include other joint undertakings. However, the latter have a smaller number of participants than the four companies under D.
3. Joint Arab projects undertaken by the private sector do not appear under D.

Source: Data collected from the records of the General Union of Chambers of Commerce . . . etc. and of OAPEC.

The second generalisation to draw from Table 14.4 is that wide variations characterise country-by-country intraregional commodity trade. The countries with the largest proportion of intraregional trade are Jordan, Lebanon and Syria, followed distantly by Sudan, Egypt and Tunisia, although the proportion differs widely between imports and exports. Thirdly, trade between the Maghreb and the Mashreq countries is virtually non-existent. This does not emerge from Table 14.4, because it is not detailed enough. In the Maghreb, it is Tunisia which trades most with other Maghreb partners. A fourth generalisation can be added, though this too is not to be gleaned from the table. This is the drop over the years of intraregional trade, which in the mid-fifties (when ten of the twelve countries surveyed had obtained their independence) stood at about one-eighth of total imports and one-twelfth of total exports. In other words, intraregional trade has lagged considerably behind growth in total trade, particularly where exports are concerned.

In addition to commodity trade, there is normally substantial intraregional exchange of services, particularly in the Mashreq. As in the case of trade in goods, the pattern is very uneven, with some countries being much more active in the sale and purchase of services than others. Thus Lebanon has a large transit, entrepôt, and re-export trade as well as flourishing tourist, air transport, contracting and banking activities which provide services to a large number of non-residents. Egypt, like Lebanon, normally receives hundreds of thousands of visitors each year whose main motive is holiday-making; and Jordan, until the Arab-Israeli war of June 1967, also had a large number of tourists coming to visit the historical sites and the holy places of the country. In the latter case, the motive is a mixture of holidaying and sight-seeing, and religious 'pilgrimage' by Christians. Iraq also has a certain pilgrimage activity, with many thousand of pious Moslem Shi'ites going there (mainly from Iran) to visit shrines and holy places. But the most impressive pilgrimage activity is witnessed annually by Saudi Arabia, into which around one million Moslems come to observe the pilgrimage rites.

The educational institutions of Egypt and Lebanon, and to a lesser extent of Iraq, Syria and Algeria, attract many thousands of Arab students who, although no large spenders, account for some of the region's economic exchanges. The largest single component of Arab students studying in other Arab countries consists of Palestinians. Homeless, they have to seek education in institutions that are open to them and have adequate facilities. In 1970, there were some 56,000 Arab students in universities in the region outside their own countries. The number is estimated at least one-third larger now in the academic year 1974/5.

Intraregional Manpower Mobility

Travel for education is but one aspect of the movement of Arabs across national frontiers. The intraregional movement of manpower for work is likewise neither negligible nor a new phenomenon. Long before the oil industry acquired the predominance it now has and, with its ramifications, became a relatively large employer of skilled labour, the area witnessed substantial movements of persons in search of work or refuge. Thus, Lebanese (and to some extent Syrian) professional men, administrators and journalists, as well as merchants and craftsmen, started to go to Egypt and the Sudan early in the twentieth century, and to a lesser extent to Palestine during the British Mandate. For many years, tens of thousands of Egyptian teachers and technicians have gone to work in Iraq, Saudi Arabia, Kuwait, the Arabian Gulf area, Syria, Yemen and Lebanon. More recently, since the mid-fifties and early sixties, thousands have gone to Libya and Algeria, and even further afield in Moslem non-Arab countries.

The oil industry broadly defined, as well as manufacturing industry, employs in each of the oil-producing countries a substantial contingent of Palestinians, Jordanians (many of whom are in effect Palestinians holding Jordanian citizenship) and Lebanese. Furthermore, large numbers of Palestinians (and of Lebanese and Syrians) work outside the oil industry, in Saudi Arabia, the Gulf area, Iraq and Libya. Jordan, Syria and Lebanon are also hosts to large Palestinian groups, refugee since the establishment of the state of Israel and their expulsion from their homeland in 1948, and again since the war of June 1967 in which the eastern part of Palestine (which, since 1950, came to be known as the West Bank of Jordan) was occupied. In addition to employment in public services such as education and health in some host countries, and in public works, the Palestinian refugees have gone into private business as merchants, craftsmen and repair workmen. They are also to be found in numbers as teachers and professional men and women. They constitute the largest single group of expatriate Arabs in the oil countries. Remittances to refugee families concentrated in East Jordan, the West Bank, Lebanon and Syria from relatives working in the oil-rich host countries are substantial in the aggregate and help to improve the living conditions of the beneficiaries.

Two prominent factors have enabled the Palestinians to participate so intensively in the development and everyday work of the host countries: their high level of education in contrast with their hosts (and, indeed, in comparison with other expatriate groups); and their eagerness to distinguish themselves in compensation for the loss of homeland and means of livelihood in Palestine.

Population statistics for the twelve countries covered by this study are not available in enough detail to enable us to construct a clear and precise picture of the size of manpower movements across state frontiers in the region. But the collation of fragmentary information from many of the countries (with the exception of Saudi Arabia, Sudan and Egypt) enables us to conclude that some 2.3 million Arabs, including Palestinians, are residents of countries not their own. If the Palestinians are excluded, the number would be about 600,000. The labour force among these constitutes a relatively larger proportion than it normally does in the countries of origin; the present writer estimates the labour force to be about 35 per cent of the total number of expatriates (as against around 25 per cent in the countries of origin on the average). The higher proportion among expatriates is explainable by the fact that people go to other countries essentially in order to seek employment and therefore contain a large contingent of persons of working age. Indeed, in most cases in the oil countries, expatriate workers first came by themselves, then, as their residence continued, they brought their dependants along to live with them. This is seen most clearly in Kuwait, where the percentage of males among the expatriates dropped from the very high level of 78.5 per cent in 1957 to the still high level of 58.5 per cent in 1973, with a parallel movement in the size of the expatriate labour force related to the total expatriate community.

Intraregional Capital Flows

Like the movement of manpower inside the region, the movement of capital is an old phenomenon, though its dimensions remained modest until the oil industry acquired prominence. But long before this, some investments were made by the Lebanese in Egypt, Syria, Jordan and Iraq; and by the Syrians in Lebanon, Egypt and Jordan. However, the bulk of investment and its direction shifted in the early fifties. The capital outflow gathered volume fast as oil revenues rose noticeably. Most of the outflow was initially from Kuwait, Saudi Arabia and to some extent Iraq, in the direction of Lebanon, and less so Egypt, Jordan and Syria. And, subsequent to the Israeli-Anglo-French joint Suez campaign in 1956, and to the socialisation or nationalisation measures taken in Egypt, Syria and Iraq in the early 1960s, a significant volume of flight capital moved from these countries into Lebanon. Most of this capital has been directed to the acquisition of real estate and into bank deposits, and to trade to a smaller extent. The inflow into Lebanon rose further in volume in the mid- and late sixties, as some of the Trucial States of the Arabian Gulf began to receive substantial oil revenues.

Towards the end of the sixties more of the capital outflow from the oil countries in the Arabian Peninsula moved not inside the region but in the direction of the Western money markets — mainly London and New York. Accurate statistics are not available, but a cautious guess would put the figure at $600m a year. (The international reserves of the five major oil governments amounted to about $2.6 billion by the end of 1969;[13] probably no more than 30 per cent of this sum was invested in, loaned to or deposited in the region.) The picture has dramatically changed since October 1973, both because oil revenues have risen very steeply, and a much larger volume of oil money than ever before has been channelled to other Arab countries. Table 14.6 contains an attempt to group together the various types of published intraregional official capital flow (whether bilateral, institutional, or in the form of joint projects). The period covered is October 1973 to the end of 1974.

It ought to be pointed out that substantial capital flows have been effected which do not appear in published material; these are grants made mainly to Egypt, Syria and Jordan, the 'confrontation' or front-line countries in the Arab-Israeli conflict. It is difficult to classify such flows; they can be considered either military or economic aid. The present writer hesitates to make a distinction, in the Arab context or elsewhere, inasmuch as military aid can replace resources which the recipient country would otherwise have had to direct to the military complex, thus releasing an equivalent volume of resources to be directed to economic purposes. As Table 14.6 shows, the total intraregional capital flow is in the range of $7 billion for the period in question.

Though unprecedented in its volume, a transfer of this size, effectively in one year, since very little was effected in the last quarter of 1973, may well become a normal flow in the several years to come. The significance of resources totalling say $6-7 billion for the seven recipient countries that are non-oil producers or only modest producers (that is, excepting Iraq, Kuwait, Saudi Arabia, Libya and Algeria) can be appreciated if it is remembered that GNP in these seven countries for 1974 was $28 billion only. (See Table 14.3.) The inflow of $6 billion, especially if it were to be directed to infrastructure and directly productive investment, would be decisive for the course of development. Such economic aid would constitute about one-fifth of aggregate GNP. This is capable of generating an incremental GNP of 7 per cent per annum, which in itself would represent a respectable rate of growth, to be added to the average of 5 per cent achieved out of domestic savings. (We assume an incremental capital-output ratio of 3, although this is probably very low in view of the large component of infrastructural and slow-fructifying productive investments being made.)

While of the utmost importance for the recipient countries, the resource transfer would represent a mere 10-12 per cent of the oil revenues of the five oil-rich donor countries at the current levels. If it is recalled that a much larger volume of financial capital was transferred to the Western economies during 1974 — mostly for the purchase of bonds and stocks and for deposit in banks — it would be realised that annual intraregional flows of $6 billion are in the realm of the desirable *and* the possible. Indeed, if the oil-exporting countries that are not included in the study were also to be involved in our calculations, the flow could easily be raised to $7 billion under the same assumptions.

In the longer run, a much larger intraregional flow must be encouraged and envisaged,

Table 14.6: Intraregional Flow of Official Capital October 1973 – End December 1974 ($ million)

Donor / Recipient	Iraq	Kuwait	Saudi Arabia	United Arab Emirates and Abu Dhabi	Qatar	Oman	Bahrain	Libya	Algeria	Arab Oil Assistance Fund	KFAED	AFESD	ADFAED	IFED	SADF	TOTAL
Egypt	875.00	615.00	1,045.00	319.50	161.50			10.00			57.50	22.00	2.50		161.00	3,269.00
Syria	50.00	225.00	500.00	162.25				100.00	20.00		40.36	6.80	12.25			1,116.66
Jordan		56.00	57.00	21.63							23.70		6.63			164.96
Bahrain				70.00									10.13			80.13
Yemen (North)			2.10	1.00				16.00		11.00			1.00	5.00		36.10
Yemen (South)	5.00									11.30	14.20	10.90		5.00		46.40
Sudan	10.00		205.00							37.30		27.00		10.00		289.30
Tunisia				10.40	10.00						16.39	6.80	10.36			53.95
Algeria												20.30				20.30
Morocco										8.20	8.30					16.50
Somalia										7.30				2.50		9.80
Mauritania										4.70				2.50		7.20
Front-Line Countries	100.00	400.00	400.00	300.00	150.00	15.00	4.00									1,369.00
OAPEC Joint Projects	50.23	91.21	91.21	91.21	57.55		15.14	54.45	20.65							471.65
OAPEC Oil Assistance Fund	16.00	16.90		10.00												42.90
Total Flow	1,106.23	1,404.11	2,300.31	985.99	379.05	15.00	19.14	180.45	40.65	79.80	160.45	93.80	42.87	25.00	161.00	6,993.85

Notes: 1. Contributions to 'front-line countries' were made to Egypt, Syria, Jordan, and – to a much lesser extent – the Palestine Liberation Organization. The breakdown is not available. Nor is it known if Libya and Algeria have paid their share.
2. Payments to Egypt, Syria and Jordan by Saudi Arabia (shown opposite the names of these countries) include $507m described as 'contribution to front-line countries' ($250m, $200m and $57m respectively.) Besides the sums referred to in Notes 1 and 2, it was reported in the Arabic press after the October 1973 war that $3–4 billion were paid to Egypt and Syria to help them defray the costs of their war effort. The donors were Saudi Arabia, Kuwait, Iraq, UAE, Qatar, Libya and Algeria. No official confirmation has since been made either by the presumed donors or recipients.
3. Some transfers have been reported, but their details are not available. One of these is the $80m paid into the Arab Oil Assistance Fund by members of OAPEC (Organization of Arab Petroleum Exporting Countries). The contributions of Iraq, Kuwait and Abu Dhabi (UAE) are known and shown individually above. (The table contains some double counting to this extent, since the Fund got its resources from donors and advanced loans to recipients. The recording of both categories involves duplication, but this is necessary in order to produce as complete a picture of the process as possible.)
4. Egypt and Syria, as OAPEC members, have paid their shares in the capital of OAPEC's joint projects. However, as these countries are recipient countries on the whole, their shares do not appear in the columns above.
5. The transfers recorded have probably not all been effected. Credits extended may not have been totally drawn on; commitments are not always completely fulfilled. Conversely, some transfers reported in the daily press are not recorded in the sources to this table. The gaps relate mostly to some large transfers by UAE, Qatar, Libya and Algeria. On balance, perhaps a total of $5–6 billion was in fact transferred; this is a high proportion of the grand total shown in the table.
6. The transfers recorded include grants, loans and participations in the share capital of projects. The grants account for about 40 per cent of the grand total of $6,994m.
7. The data shown above do not include country participations in the share capital of the Islamic Development Bank of $1,087m, or in Arab-African and Arab-European banks, although some Arab countries have benefitted from the operations of these institutions.

Sources: Various issues of *Middle East Economic Survey* (Beirut weekly) and *Arab Oil and Gas* (Beirut fortnightly) between October 1973 and end December 1974.

probably not less than $8-10 billion annually, even while taking into account the development and consumption demands of the oil-exporting countries. The assertion may sound unrealistic and unwarranted in the light of the huge spending programmes of these countries as formulated in 1974 and 1975 for the several years to come. However, it is the present writer's reasoned conviction that such programmes are grossly exaggerated and well beyond the actual spending capacity of the three surplus countries among the five oil producers, namely Kuwait, Saudi Arabia and Libya. (Iraq and Algeria are capable of absorbing virtually all their oil revenue.) Furthermore, a substantial volume of resources has been diverted to arms purchases and to heavy initial outlays, or commitments, for the launching of petrochemical and engineering industries. Such outlays cannot be considered recurrent, appearing year after year, apart from the question of the size of outlays contrasted with the more limited execution capacity of most of the oil countries.

Four features of the pattern of intraregional capital flows must be examined for an adequate understanding of it. These are government-to-government transfers (whether grants, loans or bank guarantees); transfers by public and semi-public companies or authorities in the mixed sector, in whose share or working capital the public and the private sectors participate; private transfers; and transfers by development funds. (The funds are governmental institutions but will be treated as a separate item owing to their importance.) The examination will have to remain concentrated and brief, mainly because we have had occasion to refer to some of these four sources of capital flows in the country chapters, but also because we do not have complete information on some of the institutions in the second and third categories.

1. Government-to-Government Transfers: Two difficulties arise in the process of assessing these transfers: the insufficiency of published information, and the mixture of military and economic objectives. However, as indicated earlier, we opt for a unified definition whereby all such transfers are considered forms of economic aid, either directly or indirectly. Bilateral transfers do not date only from October 1973, but go back to 1957; nor are they restricted to the oil countries as donors, since in the fifties Jordan received financial support from three governments, two of which had no oil production at the time: Egypt, Syria and Saudi Arabia. However, bilateral capital transfers became significant in volume after the Arab-Israeli war of June 1967, when they were made by three oil countries: Saudi Arabia, Kuwait and Libya. In addition, Kuwait made substantial transfers before October 1973, totalling at least KD135m, which were directed to several countries suffering economic strains.

The volume of bilateral transfers was considerably intensified subsequent to the Arab-Israeli war of October 1973. The commitments were made either individually by each donor country alone, or jointly by general agreement in Arab summit conferences. The objectives were partly to help the front-line countries (Egypt, Syria and Jordan, plus the Palestine Liberation Organization) meet their military burdens, partly to help their economies. Bilateral transfers in aid of other capital-short Arab economies have also been effected between some of the oil countries (notably Kuwait, Saudi Arabia, Iraq and Libya) and a few needy countries, notably Sudan, Yemen Arab Republic and Yemen People's Democratic Republic. (Abu Dhabi and Qatar have also made substantial contributions and loans both under summit arrangements and separately.)

2. Transfers by the Mixed Sector or Autonomous Agencies: Capital flows have been increasingly effected by autonomous agencies, mostly in the mixed sector, since the October war.

This form has been mainly used by Kuwait, and to a much lesser extent by Saudi Arabia. Kuwait has developed several mixed companies, or has directed substantial working capital to ones in existence, and these companies (or consortia, in some instances) have entered into a substantial number of large undertakings jointly with recipient countries. The most conspicuous examples of such mixed institutions are the Kuwait Investment Company and the Kuwait Foreign Trading, Contracting and Investment Company, the Kuwait International Investment Company, and the Consortium of Real Estate Companies. The country receiving most credit or investment capital is Egypt.

Another channel of capital transfer has been joint banks, some of which are purely Arab, while some others have foreign participation. The large establishments are mixed Arab and foreign. There are five of these: Union de Banques Arabes et Françaises, Banque Arabe et Internationale d'Investissement, Arab European Bank, Saudi International Bank, and Union Méditerranéenne de Banques. The last two have one Arab partner each, Algerian and Saudi respectively. In addition to the banks, there are several financial institutions, mainly in Kuwait and Lebanon, and in Egypt. However, one distressing generalisation can be made with regard to all these banks and institutions: they mostly siphon financial resources out of the Arab region and into the Western economies. Their operations in the Arab world itself are hardly 10 per cent of the total, according to well-informed bankers.

Capital transfers under the present category are channelled through different forms. These include investment in existing or new undertakings; participation in institutions formed jointly by the donor and recipient countries; the pooling of credit facilities (as in the case of joint banks); the promotion of new projects and the underwriting and/or management of bond issues; and the provision of bank guarantees for imports by the recipient country. In the case of the Kuwaiti Consortium of Real Estate Companies – an institution which has $700m working capital put at its disposal by government – the flow takes the form of investment in housing schemes with the recipient country's participation consisting mainly of counterpart contributions (like land sites for construction) but also of share capital participation. In most instances, the undertakings or joint projects, or credit provision, are devoted to single projects; only in a few cases is the capital flow directed to a sector or programme, as in the case of the Consortium.

Joint undertakings or projects, and joint institutions – whether involving mixed-sector or merely private sector participation in the donor country – are acquiring greater developmental significance in those parts of the region where they exist, although bilateral transfers are of much larger magnitude. The significance is at least twofold: such joint action, in addition to tapping a wider range of investment funds and opportunities, injects the dynamism of the private sector without losing sight of social needs, thus combining efficiency with need satisfaction. The combination is possible because the joint action usually involves substantial enough resources to compel the attention of the governments, and to make them subject the undertaking to the priority requirements stipulated in their development strategies. On the other hand, the participation of profit-seeking individuals or corporate bodies ensures the application of efficiency standards.

3. *Private, Non-Institutional Capital Flows:* This is the form of flow about which least is known, whether the source is private individuals or business establishments. In the past, these flows went mainly to real estate or to banking accounts. A good part of them probably still follow the same path, but with an increasing volume going towards joint projects with private-sector partners in the recipient country. Most transfers emanate from Kuwait, the Gulf and Saudi Arabia, inasmuch as Iraq, Libya and Algeria apply rigorous

constraints to the outflow of private funds. Furthermore, in the case of Algeria, no substantial private fortunes are being made.

Private flows in general are losing their significance, as institutionalisation is becoming increasingly necessary and desirable. This arises both from scale considerations, as projects require more and more capital, and from the greater recourse to pre-investment feasibility studies and consultancy services which large institutions are more able to afford and more eager to obtain. However, despite the growth of the role of mixed institutions and of governments in the transfer of resources, private transfers in the present context will continue to be valuable to Arab economic co-operation, as they widen the web of relations and involve more influential persons in joint projects. In the final analysis, economic interlocking and intermeshing is more conducive to regional unity than political decisions taken at the top in the extremely narrow centres of authority.

4. Transfers by Development Funds: The Kuwait Fund for Arab Economic Development, KFAED, has distinction in this field on three counts. First, it is the oldest fund of the kind in the whole region. Secondly, it has the largest capital to work with (KD1,000m, plus the power to borrow twice as much for operations); and thirdly, it has had its mandate widened in March 1974 to include non-Arab Third World countries in need of development capital.

The formation of KFAED at the end of 1961 was a bold undertaking, after years of Arab hesitation and indecision, when the possibility of attracting loan money from the oil-producing countries, as well as from the oil concessionary companies, was being considered and sought, but to no avail. Even after a finance agency was established in 1957 by the League of Arab States (approved initially by eight states) formally known as the Arab Financial Institution for Economic Development, the act remained symbolic and was never translated into reality. Initial resistance to the schemes suggested for the joint establishment of a development agency by oil producers and companies came mainly from the companies, although the countries themselves showed less enthusiasm for the idea. The main reasons for official resistance, respectively explicit and covert, were the internal need for all oil revenues received, and the desire to claim individual credit for any loans made rather than risk anonymity if the loans were made through a regional institution.

Had such a regional fund come into existence, it was to provide finance for several regional projects, apart from national projects. The former category as seen by the supporters of the fund idea was to lie mostly in the fields of transport and communication (including a trans-Arab highway linking Lebanon, Syria, Jordan, Iraq and Kuwait), an integrated Arab airways company, an Arab merchant ship company, and a tanker fleet. The possibility of setting up large joint Arab industrial complexes in certain countries was also considered.

The establishment and actual launching of a regional fund had to wait until 1972 to materialise, with the formation and funding of the Arab Fund for Economic and Social Development. (AFESD was formally established in 1968.) This Fund started with a share capital of KD100m, subscribed to fully by all the Arab countries but two, though only in part paid up by the end of 1974. (All twenty Arab countries and the Palestine Liberation Organization had joined the Fund and bought shares in its capital by the end of March 1975.) Owing to the acceleration of the Fund's operations and the commitment of the resources available to it, the Board of Governors approved the increase of the capital to KD400m in April 1975. According to resolutions taken, the initial capital is to be all fully paid before February 1976, while the increased capital is to be gradually funded beginning February 1977, to be paid up within eight years. By the end of March 1975, AFESD had extended loans to seven countries totalling KD37.1m.

Like KFAED, AFESD has aimed at and attained very high standards in the appraisal of projects, the drawing out of loan agreements, and in loan administration. AFESD has further distinguished itself in four respects: (a) directing loans to whole sectors or programmes, including infrastructural investment; (b) acting as a catalytic agent in providing financing (or financing commitments) well beyond its own means, by providing through its own participation the security required by other bilateral or international lending agencies to make them participate too — a process which has enabled AFESD to arrange a volume of development finance four times its own allocations; (c) promoting joint projects involving two or more Arab countries, and generally emphasising this aspect of its activities; and (d) the devotion of attention and resources to the study of development opportunities, including project identification and feasibility studies.

In order to give joint projects greater impetus and resources, AFESD has designed a large, six-year co-operative programme for the identification and preparation of projects, with the United Nations Development Programme on the one hand, and the twenty Arab governments on the other, involving a total outlay of $19.2m. The programme will have AFESD as Executing Agency.[14]

Two of the three remaining funds have come into existence since the October war. The first and oldest (established in July 1971, but only activated later) is the Abu Dhabi Fund for Arab Economic Development, ADFAED, with an initial capital of $125m, raised subsequently in May 1974 to $500m. The second is the Saudi Development Fund, SDF, established in September 1974. SDF has a capital of $2.8 billion, and a mandate to give loans to developing countries in general, not just Arab. Finally, Iraq established the Iraq Fund for External Development, IFED, in June 1974, with a capital of ID50m, or $169m. Information on the loans extended is available only in part for these funds, being fullest for ADFAED, which seems to have been the most active so far. It is believed that the other two have yet to get into a proper operational stage, although the Saudi Fund has had its law passed and its board and management appointed for a full year now.[15]

Five other types of economic effort at the Arab regional level, or the Arab-African level, deserve reporting here. The first is the Arab African Oil Assistance Fund which was set up by OAPEC members in June 1974 with the object of helping the African countries pay for their petroleum imports. A sum of $200m was assigned for the purpose. (A similar sum has since been set for 1975.) The second type is meant to benefit the technological progress of the African countries, most of which supported the Arabs in the October war diplomatically and politically. An institution has been set up for the purpose, under Arab League auspices. This is the fund for Technical Assistance to African States, with a working capital of $25m. The third type is the Arab Bank for Industrial and Agricultural Development in Africa, ABIADA, established in November 1973 with an initial capital of $125m. Its mandate is to extend credits to needy African countries for development purposes. Since its formation, its share capital has been raised to $230m.[16]

The fourth type of effort is neither regional nor purely Arab; it groups together 17 Arab and 7 non-Arab Moslem countries. This is the Islamic Development Bank which was set up in August 1974. Its capital of $900m, later raised to $1,087m, is subscribed to by the 24 countries, but mainly by the Arab members. The Bank is part of the activities of the Islamic Conference which was formally established in 1971, and it embodies some of the Islamic religious tenets, mainly the prohibition of the levy of interest. It is still to be seen what mechanism the Bank will use to allocate its limited resources, if it is not to charge interest. Most probably a charge will be made which will presumably represent a reward to the Bank out of the (expected or realised) profits or surpluses made by the borrower. (Profit-sharing is permitted, unlike interest, by orthodox believers.) The final type of regional effort is purely Arab. It is the Arab Oil Assistance Fund, a facility of $80m set up in June 1974 by OAPEC members, to assist non-oil Arab countries meet the rising cost of oil imports. (This sum has been also approved for 1975.) AFESD administers this fund.

The benefits of Arab financing accruing to non-Arab countries through the institutions set up for the purpose will supplement the other economic aid efforts proffered by the Arab oil countries to several Third World countries in Asia and Africa. It is worth noting in this connection that KFAED's mandate was extended in March 1974 to permit it to extend development assistance to non-Arab countries, at the same time as its capital was raised from KD200m to KD1,000m. By the summer of 1975, several such countries had already been accorded KFAED loans.

This brief reference to Arab aid to non-Arab countries does not do justice to the full volume of such aid, or to the sense of responsibility that the Arab oil countries have revealed since October 1973. Arab oil governments have entered into several preferential arrangements involving billions of United States dollars, for the purpose of easing the financing of oil imports, the financing of development work, or the undertaking of joint projects, in addition to the impetus provided for some of the more advanced Third World countries (such as South Korea and India) through the importation of certain capital or goods from them and their participation in contract work in certain industrial endeavours in the Arab oil countries. Furthermore, these oil countries have shown their sense of responsibility through adequate participation in the International Fund for Agricultural Development and the undertaking to shoulder more than their proportionate share in the establishment of new special funds for Third World development, as well as in the share capital of the institutions of the World Bank Group. (Contributions to this Group include subscription to the IMF Special Oil Facility and to the working capital of the IBRD.) This broad effort must receive particular stress at the time when the advanced industrial countries as a group are offering a fraction of 1 per cent of their combined national product for international development. In contrast, the combined contributions of the Arab oil countries constitute about 10 per cent of their aggregate GNP for 1974.

Organization of Arab Petroleum Exporting Countries, OAPEC
Important as Arab oil has come to be in several aspects of intraregional economic relations, it promises to play a much more prominent role in the future. The central impact of oil radiates into many areas of life and activity, and also promises to reach much further as the resources made accessible through increased oil revenues will help the drive for development and technological change in the region. However, by themselves, oil revenues do not constitute an insurance policy or a guarantee that development will be accelerated and that it will have the proper content. Several conditions will have to be satisfied for this to happen, as we will attempt to show in the companion volume (Volume II).

One of these conditions in this writer's view is the evolving of a regional view of oil and development within an institutional framework capable of propagating this view and of giving it substance. The Organization of Petroleum Exporting Countries, OPEC, neither became nor pretended to be the appropriate institutional framework; its objectives were not development-oriented, and its constituency was not purely Arab. It was OAPEC, the Organization of *Arab* Petroleum Exporting Countries, which was to meet these requirements. This organisation was formed in 1968 and today groups together ten Arab countries — all the oil exporters except Oman and Tunisia.

It can be said that until the autumn of 1973 OAPEC had a very modest role as a focus of

Arab positions with regard to oil policies, as a promoter of joint projects, or as a seeding mechanism for the evolving of ideas and policies for the oil sector and its development as an integral part of the Arab economies. Likewise, its activity in preparing technical and economic studies for its members was modest. However, in the brief period since the October war, OAPEC has — under new leadership — chiselled a new role for itself. This role is characterised by the initiation of studies concerned with the development of national and joint regional projects related to hydrocarbons, to manpower in the oil industry, and to other areas of interest; the strengthening of its professional staff in order to be better enabled to prepare studies of greater sophistication; the organising of training seminars for oil officials in member countries; participation in and initiation of international meetings centring around the areas of its broad interest; active interest in the Arab-European dialogue for economic and technological co-operation; and initiative in the establishment of joint projects in the oil sector.

Four such projects are currently in existence, only the first of which had been established before the October war. The projects are: The Arab Maritime Petroleum Transport Company (founded in January 1973), with an authorised share capital of $500m; The Arab Shipbuilding and Repair Yard Company, with a capital of $100m; The Arab Petroleum Investments Company, with a capital of $1,028m, and the Arab Petroleum Services Company, with a capital of $338m.[17]

These activities notwithstanding, OAPEC still has far to go if it is to undertake a more aggressive role and to take strong initiative in the formulation of oil strategies and policies. The lag in its movement in this direction is not a reflection of subjective weakness, but rather of two factors external to the organisation as such. The first is the prior assumption by OPEC, which came into existence eight years before OAPEC and groups together thirteen members (including seven Arab countries) of such a role, at least with respect to relations with the concessionary oil companies and oil prices. In the second place, OAPEC cannot appropriate to itself powers held to tightly by the individual governments, especially on sensitive matters which they are eager to retain for their discretion and decision-making. This is a problem which all regional (and other supra-national) bodies have to face, where decision-making in certain critical matters is considered an integral part of sovereignty that cannot be delegated. As such, the problem has to be lived with, and dealt with delicately and patiently. In the final analysis, no regional organisation can have powers that go beyond the degree of true regional identification by the members, and beyond their willingness to allow a body which represents them to take decisions binding on them.

Nevertheless, OAPEC's present areas of activity are probably no less important basically than being able to be party to the more glamorous political and strategic decisions of the industry. And certainly, even within the present constraints, OAPEC is fulfilling a significant function in the drive for development, in the oil sector and the region as a whole.

Economic Co-operation Under the Auspices of the League of Arab States

The operative word 'co-operation' can be defined in more than one way; thus there cannot be one determinate assessment of the achievement registered. The multiplicity of definitions largely reflects what different analysts cherish as the desirable format and content of co-operation, given their ideologies, interests, fears and personal predilections in general. For our purposes, the concept is used as a generic term to cover a wide gamut, from mere economic exchange with some preferential treatment, to economic unity at the other end, with gradations in between including the creation of a free trade area, of a common market, and of joint institutions and projects, as well as the free movement of factors across national frontiers and the promotion of complementarity between Arab economies. Likewise, the content varies, from being restricted to trade, to being so comprehensive as to embrace all aspects of economic exchange and activity.

At one time or another, the Arab states, whether bilaterally or multilaterally, have taken steps towards each of the points on the scale, though in certain critical instances, the steps have merely been resolutions taken, or pledges made, with no serious intent of implementation. The oldest instances of co-operation in modern times formalised in trade agreements can be encountered in the pre-independence era. These were between Syria and Lebanon when they were under French Mandate and formed one customs union, between Syria and Palestine, Transjordan and Syria, Transjordan and Palestine, Transjordan and Hejaz (part of today's Saudi Arabia), Egypt and Syria, and Egypt and Palestine – all in the 1920s.[18] All but the Syro-Lebanese customs union were disrupted and discontinued in the years preceding World War Two. The Union itself was broken in 1950.

The only case of multilateral co-operation preceding the formation of the League of Arab States was the Middle East Supply Centre, set up in 1940 by Great Britain, to be joined two years later by the United States. The MESC included 18 political entities, 6 of which were non-Arab. It stretched its coverage from Iran east, to Malta west, and from Iraq and Syria north to Somaliland and Ethiopa south. Its objectives were to assure and regulate the imports of essential commodities to the region, to provide the necessary shipping in stringent wartime conditions, and to promote local production and intraregional exchanges and thus reduce the need for imports. To achieve these ends, the MESC developed planning, control, guidance and assistance functions and mechanisms in its headquarters in Cairo and in its branch offices in the region. What is worth noting in this connection and with respect to the bilateral trade agreements referred to before is that all these instances of co-operation materialised under the aegis of a foreign power which imposed its will. The lesson to be derived is not that Arab economic co-operation cannot proceed far without foreign domination, but that co-operation cannot be honestly pursued and materialise without the political will to bring it about at the highest decision-making level.

There has never been outright hostility to and rejection of the principle of economic co-operation among the Arab countries by governments, political and other pressure groups, or serious individuals, although certain misgivings have been voiced with regard to specific aspects of co-operation. The arguments submitted in favour of co-operation, like those marshalled against it, have been economic as well as political and ideological. Often these arguments are expressed in general terms, encompassing the various forms of co-operation; as often the real reasons for the positions taken, for but mostly against, have been implicit and concealed. But, as an overall assessment, it can be said that co-operation represents the mainstream of Arab thinking and feeling.

Evidence for this last statement comes from the fact that, as early as 1944 and 1945 when the Protocol forming the League of Arab States, and then its Charter, were drawn up and signed, it was stipulated that the League would undertake to bring about economic co-operation and organise it among the member states, and between these as a group and the group of non-members. Subsequent major documents, beginning with the Treaty for Joint Defence and Economic Cooperation, included clauses specifically stressing the pursuit of such co-operation. One of these clauses was of particular significance, as it stipulated for the formation of the Arab Economic Council which, in co-operation with the Economic Committee which the Charter had brought into being, was to suggest the ways and means for economic development, co-operation and organisation and co-ordination.[19]

The Economic Council remained rather ineffectual, as its meetings were sparse and its machinery minimal, until in 1959 it was given autonomy. Two years before, the Council drew and approved a convention for economic unity. It took five years, from 1957 to 1962, before the Council formed an autonomous body to implement the Agreement of Arab Economic Unity, namely the Council for Arab Economic Unity, CAEU, and another two years before the latter Council had enough members sign its agreement and ratify it to make it binding. Thus it was in 1964 that the CAEU became operational, and it was in the same year that the Council established an Arab Common Market to mark the first step towards economic unity through the liberalisation of trade among the members of the Council and the ACM. There is hardly need to emphasise the slow pace of the process of co-operation; the passage of twenty years between the Alexandria Protocol and the formation of the CAEU is enough evidence of that. But what is of greater significance is the meagreness of the practical results achieved and the half-hearted implementation of the agreements entered into regarding economic unity and the setting up of the ACM.[20]

In 1953, and before the CAEU had been formed, the Council of the Arab League, which is the highest body in the League, had decided to draw the Convention for Facilitating Trade and Regulating Transit, CFTRT, among member countries. This agreement, which has since been followed by several amendments, stipulated for the full exemption of Arab agricultural products exchanged from customs duties, and for the phased exemption of manufactured goods. The extent of exemption for the latter group was to depend on the proportion of value added arising in the exporting country.[21] The transit aspect of the agreement had to wait till 1959 before being incorporated in a special Transit Convention, between Lebanon, Jordan, Saudi Arabia and Syria. Finally, in this connection, the Agreement to Establish Unified Customs Duties Schedules was entered into in 1956 among the signatories of the CFTRT with the exception of Yemen.

Parallel with the CFTRT, the Agreement for the Settlement of Payments for Current Transactions and the Transfer of Capital, ASPTC was formulated in 1953. Its objective, as the title suggests, was to provide the foreign exchange facilities for settling accounts among trading partners. These facilities were all the more necessary owing to the existence of exchange controls in most of the countries of the region, and the hardships that several of these experienced with respect to exchange availability.

We need not go into detail in evaluating these various trade, transit and payments agreements and their numerous amendments. What needs to be said is simply that they worked very poorly: they were not all implemented, the payments agreement remaining a dead letter; the trade and transit agreements were very slowly implemented, well behind the schedules set for them; the implementation has remained all through at the mercy of the political climate and therefore has witnessed severe discontinuities as a result of the erratic course of political relations; and the administrative powers which the agreements stipulated for and which permitted the temporary freezing of the clauses of the agreements proved in fact not the exception but the rule, and turned out to be at times much more powerful than the contractual obligations themselves. In short, the agreements have even to this day witnessed only partial implementation and are still subject to serious interruptions and financial and quantitative restrictions that can only be called arbitrary.[22] In addition, the supplementary payments arrangements necessary for the proper operation of trade agreements are still absent. However, these agreements have been rendered obsolete and superseded by the Economic Unity Agreement and its offshoot the Arab Common Market Agreement, which came into being later.

The Economic Council of the League has formed a large number of organisations, syndical bodies and economic projects, as Table 14.5 shows. We have had occasion to observe that most of these have been still-born, or have remained dormant. No further evaluation will therefore be undertaken at this point, particularly as reference will be made to the institutions under question when a general appraisal is made of the steps taken by the Arab League towards economic co-operation.

As we saw earlier, the Council for Arab Economic Unity has concentrated on the Arab Economic Unity Agreement entered into under its auspices, and the Arab Common Market subsequently established as a first unitary step. These 'achievements', modest as they are, were registered many years after the appearance of the League in 1944. Today, over thirty years later, even the ACM is still a very lame institution of limited coverage, comprising seven countries (with one that refused to join the EUA and another that has failed so far to ratify the ACM agreement). However, the ACM has taken a number of appropriate decisions and organisational and procedural steps, but it remains for the national policies of the member countries to conform to these steps and to give them substance. In practice, what has been achieved is even more modest than a common market: it is a free trade area. Standardisation of tariffs *vis-à-vis* the 'outside world' has yet to be undertaken, before a common market is truly launched.

Before this survey is concluded, it ought to be pointed out that the Maghreb countries have largely kept outside the structures and activities of the Arab League in the present context. The Maghreb has concentrated on its own co-operative structure and formed a number of institutions to that end (as Table 14.5 shows). The body at the head of this structure is the Maghreb Permanent Consultative Committee, MPCC. This Committee was formed in 1964 by the Ministers of national economy of the Maghreb countries, in order to achieve economic co-operation and co-ordination. (Libya withdrew from the MPCC and all its institutions in 1970.)

The Maghreb countries have not been more purposeful than the Mashreq countries that have sought co-operation under League auspices.[23] Furthermore, the two groupings have done very little to combine efforts or to co-ordinate activities in the area of economic co-operation. However, Maghreb countries have joined several League institutions, including the Organization of Arab Petroleum Exporting Countries and the Arab Fund for Economic and Social Development. On the other hand, they are not members of the ACM, a position which probably reflects the fact that trade between Maghreb and Mashreq countries is virtually non-existent.

The main causes behind the very limited co-operation between the Maghreb and the Mashreq groups are examined by Burhan Dajani, the Secretary-General of the General Union of Chambers of Commerce, Industry, and Agriculture in the Arab Countries. He undertakes the examination in the context of a paper submitted to a regional seminar on industrial development policies held early in 1971. In his view, five reasons account for the fact that there is little economic exchange between the Mashreq and the Maghreb, and that the Maghreb has shown little interest in some of the agreements reached under Arab League or CAEU auspices. These are:

1. Economic co-operation within the framework of the League was started before the Maghreb countries obtained independence and joined League membership.
2. Mashreq countries had relations among themselves not shared by Maghreb countries which were barred by the French and Italian colonial governments from participation in these relations.
3. The French had tied the Maghreb economies firmly to their own, and the ties continued under independence.

4. The means of transport, especially by sea, between Mashreq and Maghreb are underdeveloped.
5. The Arab countries, like other developing countries, tend to have more intensified economic exchanges with the advanced industrial countries than among themselves.[24]

It ought finally to be pointed out that the low level of co-operation observed between the two groups of countries also prevailed inside each of the groups. Thus, it is striking that the Arab countries have resorted to bilateral agreements outside the framework of the CFTRT, instead of co-operating within the multilateral agreement. About twenty bilateral agreements (mainly relating to trade) have been concluded over the years, which suggests a greater readiness to conclude such agreements and to co-operate within them. This can probably be explained by the fact that they are more responsive to the special circumstances of the partners than multilateral arrangements. The latter have to account for many more pulls, pressures and strains.

Attempts at Arab economic co-operation have taken many forms and spread over several sectors. These include trade, payments, manpower and capital mobility across national frontiers, co-ordination of and co-operation in undertakings in the fields of industry, mining, land transport, shipping and aviation, as well as those of administrative development, standards and measurements, and professional and syndical association. A look at Table 14.5, along with the subsequent discussion of the steps taken under the aegis of the League of Arab States, will be sufficient to reveal the breadth of the area comprised by the attempts at co-operation.

However, the full breadth and the ambition of these attempts can best be seen in the wide coverage of the Agreement of Arab Economic Unity concluded under the auspices of the Council of Arab Economic Unity. This Agreement in effect stipulates for the unification or else standardisation of all aspects of economic life. Taxation systems, monetary and fiscal systems and laws, business laws, foreign exchange regulations, inheritance, equal rights to undertake business and to own property, and all other institutional regulators of economic activity are to be co-ordinated and standardised towards the outside world, and to permit complete mobility and interaction within the Agreement area. Co-ordination of the strategies and policies of agricultural, industrial and commercial development was also to be undertaken. It would qualify the judgement of over-ambition only partially to say that the signatories of this Agreement were aware of the dictates of realism, and therefore lowered their sights in starting the long march towards unity by taking the initial step of an Arab Common Market. Even this target has, in practice, been made more modest.

The over-ambition, qualified seriously by the initiation of more modest measures, and even then the implementation of these only slowly and imperfectly, is a phenomenon in Arab life well worth examination. It would require analysis using the tools of social psychology to explain why the League members should repeatedly take solemn joint decisions, and make pledges, which they know fully well will not be put into effect, and conversely drag their feet in the implementation of the much more modest measures which they end by opting for. But this is not the place for such analysis, nor does the writer pretend to be qualified to undertake it.

However, two observations are in place here. In itself, the act of adopting resolutions aiming at intensified co-operation, or complementarity, or yet total unity is often a response to what the politicians believe to be popular among certain important groups in their constituencies, and even to embody Arab nationalist *public* sentiment. Yet withdrawal from such resolutions takes place as soon as expedient, upon which they are substituted by much more modest measures, the scale and reach of which satisfy the truly insular and non-co-operative tendencies of most political decision-makers. The deliberate frustration of the broader expectations is often a reflection of a misguided understanding of the notion of political sovereignty, and/or a misunderstanding of the significance of economic co-operation for *all* the parties involved. To these points must be added certain implicit or explicit arguments against co-operation.

The most common arguments relate to the difference in socio-economic systems prevailing in the various Arab countries. This is presumed to render co-operation near impossible, even if restricted to the free flow of intraregional goods and services. Another complaint states that the disparate levels of economic development and performance favour some and handicap other countries. A third point often raised is the similarity of products that can be exchanged, which in the nature of the case makes for a low level of exchange. And finally, the argument is advanced that to seek complementarity, or to streamline economic and business laws and regulations, would be an infringement on sovereignty and effectively tantamount to political unity, even if partially, while such unity does not yet have a ready soil.

These and like arguments may have some truth in them, but they are essentially rationalisations, and they can mostly be rebutted. There have been a number of such rebuttals, as well as positive expositions of the merits of earnest co-operation. Perhaps the one body which deserves special mention for its consistent and long-standing efforts in advocating co-operation and arguing the case for its merits is the General Union of Chambers of Commerce, Industry, and Agriculture in the Arab Countries. A large body of literature has been produced by the General Union, most of which has been prepared directly by or under the direction of its Secretary-General, Burham Dajani, to whom reference has been made. He is singled out in order to record his major contributions to the cause of co-operation.

The counter-arguments advanced in support of co-operation emphasise the point that differences in socio-economic systems are no bar to smooth and large-scale exchanges of goods and services, as evidenced by the expanding trade between advanced market and centrally planned countries. Indeed, it is added, the latter act as importers and exporters the way these groups would act in a system of private enterprise. Nor should the disparate levels of economic performance operate against co-operation and even co-ordination and complementarity, since the wide range of possible investments in the fields of industry, agriculture and transport make it possible to have a far-reaching pattern of division of labour among countries which takes into account the different capabilities of these countries.

Likewise, the similarity of products is no excuse for the freezing of co-operation. For, on the one hand, it would be absurd to suggest that regions in the same country with similar industries or agricultural products should pull apart to become separate sovereign entities because of this similarity. On the other hand, the similarity is often more apparent than real, owing to differences of specifications, quality, or maturing date between seemingly identical foodstuffs such as wheat, vegetables, fruits or industrial crops such as cotton or tobacco.

Finally, sovereignty must not be understood as something sacrosanct in a rigid, literal manner. All agreements constitute in effect some infringement on sovereignty, since they limit the freedom of action of the sovereign entity. What is more relevant here is to enquire whether the limitation is, on balance, in the national interest. This is precisely where the argument for co-operation and complementarity is strongest, since it can manifest that *all* parties in co-operation are better off than without co-operation, although the benefits accruing may well vary from one party to another. The benefits derive from scale considerations, division of labour, greater possibilities of research and technological improvement, greater bargaining power and salutary competition.

However, it ought to be admitted in the present context that insufficient examination has been made of this very point. The studies undertaken around co-operation, complementarity and unity have been general, often assertive, and wanting in profundity and sophistication. The writers have satisfied themselves largely with their intuitive 'feel' of the overwhelming strength of the case for co-operation and with the case as made convincingly for other regions in the world.[25] The study of the issue in the Arab context has been mainly restricted to a few works relating to the impact of CFTRT, the inter-Arab trade agreement of 1953, and of the merger between Egypt and Syria from February 1958 to September 1961 with its eight-fold increase in commodity trade between the two countries.

An overall survey and evaluation would reveal that emphasis has shifted over the years from one course of action to another, as most conducive to co-operation broadly defined. Initially, the emphasis was on co-operation and co-ordination of policies and activities. In the late fifties, unity was underlined. In the early and mid-sixties, the Arab Common Market became the focus of attention and effort. Much more recently, a more pragmatic approach has been pursued, emphasising the establishment of joint projects as the best way for building unity 'from the foundations upwards'. This is in contrast with agreements reached at the top which often represent a thin layer of co-operation with no understructure to withstand the disruptive pressures that usually weigh heavily on it.

The last pragmatic approach has found support in the success of some of the institutions created under the League's umbrella, such as OAPEC, the Industrial Development Center of the Arab States, the Arab Fund for Economic and Social Development, and the Arab Labour Organization. Indeed, it is argued, joint undertakings need not even be formed under the aegis of the League, and many have in effect emerged outside its framework. Most joint ventures of the type referred to earlier in this chapter are bilateral efforts, particularly those formed after October 1973 thanks to capital flows recorded in Table 14.6. This does not dishearten the advocates of the pragmatic, project-by-project and institution-by-institution approach, who maintain that the emergence of a large number of such projects and institutions will bring about concrete complementarity and co-operation, even a certain degree of unity which will force itself on the consciousness of the politicians and make them ultimately opt for some form of *formal* unity. Thus unity will become the end result of the process, rather than the initial step that would hopefully be followed later on by the underpinnings.

This approach does not pass unchallenged. The fundamental complaint against it is that it involves haphazard co-operation, whereas the pursuit of co-operation ought to proceed along well-mapped paths of co-ordination, complementarity of development plans, and a deliberate, clearly defined division of labour among the Arab countries. It is complementarity that receives the boldest underlining currently, and it benefits from the support that the intensified capital flows in the region bring about. These flows are believed to encourage and permit at the same time the insistence on complementarity, and the means to make this complementarity concrete. If it is not realistic to achieve co-ordination and complementarity at the ambitious level of whole economies, through the deliberate meshing of comprehensive development plans, it is yet realistic and possible to achieve the objective at the sector, or even industry level. Thus, certain key sectors are mentioned as possible areas of meshing, such as transport and communication, and industry. The individual industries advanced as possible areas of complementarity are petro-chemicals; fertilisers (both nitrogenous and phosphates); iron and steel; spinning and weaving; paper, paper pulp, and synthetic silk; and machinery, including tractors. The complementarity may take the form of horizontal or vertical integration, as each case may require for optimisation.

Recently the CAEU has attempted, in a resolution taken in December 1973,[26] to lay down a broad strategy for Arab economic action. The basic principles adopted were: (a) the achievement of balanced development based on self-capability and self-reliance; (b) complementarity; (c) the elaboration of one unified, comprehensive plan where economic co-ordination is tied to investment policy in a manner which provides guarantees for the investments made and assures benefits both to individual countries and to the region as a whole; and (d) while treating the Arab Economic Unity Agreement as a broad framework for action, the adoption of phased partial steps within it in order to approach the objectives soundly and realistically.

In closing, there are a few overall lessons to be drawn from the thirty-year experience of the Arab countries in the field of co-operation. The first is that much less has been achieved than aimed at or undertaken in agreements and arrangements under Arab League auspices. In the second place, most of the impediments to co-operation are not economic but political, socio-psychological, the result of misconceptions or misunderstandings by political leaders, or the making of particularistic vested interests that see in co-operation a menace to themselves. In addition, the impediments have included the suspicion by several countries, especially those with rich oil resources, that any form of close co-operation would in effect lead to, if not aim at, depriving them of their fortunes. This feeling is made more inhibiting by the superiority of many of the 'have-nots' in manpower skills, which generates increased fear among the 'haves'.

Thirdly, the few bright instances of success among institutions formed under League auspices have been characterised by at least two special features. The first is their large measure of autonomy, and therefore freedom from the heavy bureaucracy and lack of imagination 'distinguishing' the Secretariat of the League. The second is the high quality of leadership enjoyed by these institutions, which combines motivation and drive, modern-mindedness, innate capability and a broad Arab nationalist horizon embracing the whole Arab world.

Finally, co-operation has been approached via multiple avenues. This is sensible and appropriate. But the distribution of emphasis among these avenues has been largely accidental and haphazard, instead of being deliberate in the light of aprioristic perception and continuous re-examination.

5. THE PALESTINE QUESTION AND REGIONAL DEVELOPMENT

No discourse on the Palestine problem is included in this book, although this problem is central in Arab concern and of strong impact on all aspects of Arab life, and Palestine is an integral part of the Arab region which the book embraces. However, it would be a gross oversight not to examine — even if briefly — the economic impact of the Palestine problem and the broader Arab-Israeli conflict. As far as possible, the examination will be undertaken in isolation from the political overtones of the problem.

The conflict of the Palestinian Arabs with the world Zionist movement, but particularly with the Zionists in Palestine, which goes back to the turn of the twentieth century, like the broader Arab-Israeli conflict which dates from the establishment of the state of Israel against Arab will in mid-May 1948 and the involvement of the Arab states in the Palestinian-Zionist conflict, have brought and continue to bring in their trail serious economic problems. They have also had some developmental implications.

To begin with, the establishment of Israel, which prevented the Palestinian Arab majority from exercising self-determination and fulfilment as a political entity and a coherent community, also broke the geographic continuity of the Arab world and severed its circuit of social, cultural and economic life. Furthermore, it resulted directly in the uprooting in 1948, and in the sudden impoverishment, of about 53 per cent of the Palestinian Arabs, or 750,000 persons; and of a further 250,000 in the June 1967 war between Israel and the Arab states. The total number of displaced persons (including the natural population increase of both groups at 3.33 per cent per annum) stood at the end of 1974 at no less than 1,750,000. An almost equal number of Palestinians still live under Israeli occupation, on Palestinian soil in the originally mandated area.[27] This area stretches from Lebanon and Syria north to the Gulf of Aqaba south, and from the River Jordan east to the Mediterranean west. The displaced Palestinians who are outside Palestinian territory constitute about 52 per cent of the total community of about 3.4 million.

The property that the refugees who fled the country during communal clashes in 1947/8 left behind was that of a community which had been well-off in regional terms and whose economy was a going concern. This property consisted of land, buildings, offices, businesses, industry, equipment, means of transport, services, living quarters, personal effects and other assets. Detailed estimates of the value of these assets reach a total of 757 million Palestine pounds (or pounds sterling, worth $4 each at the time), at 1948 prices. In addition, the income forgone (calculated and extrapolated from the few preceding years) totalled some £P 46 million for 1948 for the refugees.[28] If these aggregates are adjusted for price rises and for growth, and the income series is extended, they would exceed £4 billion (sterling) by the end of 1974.

On the Israeli side, the establishment of Israel resulted in massive immigration, including large numbers of Jews from Iraq, Yemen and North Africa. These inflows, which were attracted and encouraged by Israel, imposed heavy financial and social responsibilities on the state. However, they proved of great demographic (and military) value and they also put in its hands vast assets, consisting first of the assets of the refugees;[29] secondly of a sizeable portion of land belonging to Palestinian Arabs who never left their homeland;[30] thirdly, of all public property, whether it was land, buildings, transport means and facilities, or public services; and fourthly, of a vast inflow of foreign aid which reached some $18 billion between 1948 and the end of 1974.[31]

The United Nations formally assumed responsibility for the needs of relief-receiving refugees. First, an agency was set up in 1950 under the title United Nations Relief for Palestine Refugees. Then, the following year, a new body was formed, which has carried the responsibility since then. It is the United Nations Relief and Works Agency for Palestine Refugees in the Near East, UNRWA. The budget initially allotted provided no more than the equivalent of 7 cents per day for each refugee — a sum which had to account for food, education, shelter and other aid items, as well as administration. Today, with inflationary pressures, the budget has risen to about $86m for 1973/4, and to about $120m for 1974/5. With 1,583,646 relief-receiving refugees in 1974, the budget allows for about 22 cents a day per refugee, on average.[32] (Some 570,000 refugees are in camps, the rest living on their own. Relief is not uniform for all recipients, but depends on the economic situation of the recipient.)

The Arab host countries have also had to bear a considerable burden as a result of the refugee influx. These countries are basically Jordan, Lebanon and Syria, where the large concentrations of Palestinians are to be found. (The 'Gaza Strip', which has a very high concentration of refugees and the most meagre resources, is a part of Palestine.) The total cash contributions of the Arab states (hosts and others) have been not inconsiderable, probably not below $250m until the middle of 1975. In addition, important aid in various other forms has been extended by these states. This includes services in kind, such as education, medical care, customs exemptions for relief supplies, rent-free premises and camp sites. In addition, economic opportunities in the host countries have been opened to the refugees, in spite of the generally high rates of unemployment for nationals and the prevailing state of underdevelopment.

However, it must be added as a serious qualification that tens of thousands of Palestinians brought with them vocational, professional and administrative skills not originally available, or in short supply. The beneficiaries are Jordan, Saudi Arabia, Kuwait and the other oil-producing sheikhdoms in the Arabian Gulf, and Libya, but also Lebanon and Syria. Indeed, the development of the oil region, and of Jordan, owes a major debt to Palestinian manpower, as the country chapters and the discussion of manpower movements across national frontiers earlier on in this chapter have indicated.[33]

Another economic aspect of the conflict is the boycott of Israel by the Arab states. This boycott has taken the form of a ban on the exchange of goods and services, on travel across armistice lines, on the flow of Arab oil to Israeli destinations, and on the passage of Israeli ships (or other ships carrying cargoes for or from Israel) through Arab-controlled waterways. It also involves the boycott of all foreign concerns which establish subsidiaries or assembly plants in Israel, and of ships that call at Israeli ports.

The boycott has deprived Israel of convenient markets and sources of supply, hampered Israeli trade with East Africa and Asia in spite of Israel's access to the Gulf of Aqaba after the Suez war in 1956, and again after the June 1967 war, and limited investment by foreign companies in assembly plants or subsidiaries and branches in Israel. Until Israel got hold of Egypt's oilfields in Sinai during the war of June 1967, the boycott also raised the cost of oil imports to Israel beyond what it would have been had oil been imported from, say, Iraq or Saudi Arabia.

On the other hand, the boycott has deprived Jordan of the convenient port of Haifa in Israel and has forced it to use the more distant ports of Beirut and Aqaba. For a few years and until the oil flowing to Haifa was diverted to Lebanon and Syria, Iraq suffered from a slowing down in the expansion in oil exports and revenues, as a result of the stoppage of oil flow in the Iraq-Haifa pipeline. And, to the degree that trade with Israel would have represented a net gain to the Arab countries, the boycott has been harmful to the Arabs. This degree, however, is very modest since the Israeli market is small, and Arab exports find much larger markets elsewhere; and since the importation of manufactured goods for consumption and production purposes from the industrially advanced countries presents advantages of quality and price not paralleled by Israeli goods.

On balance, the damage to the Arab economies as a result of the boycott has been minimal and negligible, but it has been real and substantial to Israel. But more damaging to the latter than the costs actually incurred, or the dislocations forced as a result of the boycott, have been the benefits involuntarily forgone by Israel. Were it not for the boycott, Israeli capital, technicians, industry, financial houses and the many branches of activity would have made immense business in and reaped considerable profits from the Arab markets.[34] The excessive degree of economic vulnerability and dependence on foreign aid that has characterised Israel all through the years would have been considerably reduced were economic exchanges to be open between Israel and the Arab world. As the matter stands, Israel's GNP has over the years 1948-74 been just about equal to consumption (private and public) plus depreciation, and investment has had to be totally financed from the import surplus which is made possible by foreign aid.[35]

The last economic aspect of the conflict to be referred to is the military outlay necessitated by the state of war and the continued tension existing between the two parties, culminating so far in four wars. Considering the enormous demands of development in the Arab world, the diversion of a sizeable proportion of total resources to the military machine cannot but be a heavy drain on scarce resources. This outlay involves serious dislocation of resources and constitutes a high proportion of the budgets of Israel, Egypt, Syria and Jordan, as well as a high proportion of GNP. (See Table 14.7.) Even assuming that a certain military outlay is inevitable whether or not the conflict existed, it remains true that the actual size of the outlay is considerably larger than it would normally be without the conflict. For the Arab region as a whole, it is about $8.2 billion, or 6.6 per cent of aggregate GNP, while for Israel alone it is $3.7 billion or 42 per cent of GNP for 1974.

On the other side of the account, it is important to note that the military establishment is the largest single employer in most countries, and that it contributes to the development of transport and communications and to manufacturing, with the latter activity resulting in the production of certain civilian manufactures at the factories for armaments. Furthermore, the armies have been a significant instrument for the education and vocational training of hundreds of thousands of young men. Admittedly, to justify the large armies and substantial defence budgets by the roads built or the sewing machines and bicycles manufactured would be pretty absurd. None the less, the contribution of the military to civilian production is an offsetting item in the account. The military outlay would be much less strongly criticised if the armies were to be citizens' armies in the true sense, holding the rifle in one hand and the plough in the other, so to speak. In this case, they could contribute substantially to all lines of production, particularly housing, agriculture and the building of irrigation and drainage systems. The fact that the Arab armies are the largest reservoir of skilled manpower that is trained in the use of machines and adept in such technical occupations like plumbing, welding and soldering, electricity and electronics, and repairs and maintenance work, makes it potentially a valuable asset for development. An army thus occupied would constitute less of a misallocation of human resources. The allocational amelioration, even if limited, would be significant in the context of the Arab world where there is both underutilisation (or wrong utilisation) of manpower, and a shortage in skills essential for development.

An attempt has been made in this chapter to trace the process of development in its regional context. This has involved the identification of development trends of regional reach and dimensions, and the drawing of comparisons among the region's political components. But, to a greater extent, the attempt has involved the identification and brief examination of collective or co-operative economic action of developmental significance. This has referred to the various efforts, whether inside or outside the framework of the League of Arab States. On balance, the results of these efforts seem to have been modest, both with regard to regional co-operation achieved and to the developmental impact of this co-operation. Side by side with this sobering conclusion a brighter realisation emerges. The focus of this realisation is that the region has great developmental potential, and that this potential can better be brought into existence and made real through collective, co-operative action based on complementarity among the various Arab economies. Furthermore, the region now, for the first time, has the capital funds that can be utilised for development.

The bright prospects are not unmixed with limitations. These include a wide array of

Table 14.7: Defence Expenditures by the Arab States and Israel for 1974, Related to Gross National Product

Country	Defence Budget $ Million	GNP $ Billion	Defence As Percentage of GNP
Iraq	803	13.00	6.18
Kuwait	162	11.50	1.41
Saudi Arabia	1,808	38.25	5.61
Jordan	142	1.00	14.20
Syria	460	2.85	16.14
Lebanon	133	3.15	4.22
Egypt	3,117	9.20	33.88
Sudan	118	2.50	4.72
Libya	402	9.80	4.10
Tunisia	43	2.90	1.48
Algeria	404	12.30	3.28
Morocco	190	6.30	3.02
Sub-Total	7,782	112.75	6.90
United Arab Emirates	140	6.25	2.24
Bahrain	8	0.36	2.22
Qatar	23	2.35	0.98
Oman	169	1.10	15.36
Yemen, A. R.	58	1.10	5.27
Yemen, P. D. R.	29	0.65	4.46
Somalia	n.a.	0.22	n.a.
Mauritania	n.a.	0.22	n.a.
Sub-Total	427	12.25	3.49
Total, Arab States	8,209	125.00	6.56
Israel	3,688	8.8	42.0

Sources: For defence expenditure, Middle East Financial and Industrial Services (MEFIS), *Middle East Investment Attitudes and Strategies*, Updating No. 2:1975; for GNP, Table 14.3 above. It is to be noted that GNP estimates reported in MEFIS differ slightly from those in this table, but the effect on the proportion of GNP spent on defence (the last column) is negligible except in the case of Jordan and Yemen Arab Republic, where MEFIS reports 10.9 and 3.6 per cent respectively.

impediments to development that are not substantially different from those characterising most parts of the Third World. But what is particular to the Arab world is the marked hesitancy among the oil-rich countries, minor exceptions notwithstanding, to direct the bulk of their surplus funds to developmental investment in their sister Arab countries, both in national and in regional projects. This is in sharp contrast with the crisp readiness with which they 'export' a much larger volume of financial resources to the Western economies where it mainly takes the form of stocks and bonds and bank deposits, and to a smaller extent direct investments in real estate and industry. This contrast is all the more baffling and frustrating considering the erosion of the value of the foreign currencies in which the funds are placed in the Western money markets, and the hostile reception which has met these placements since October 1973. On the other hand, investments in the Arab world have a warm welcome, satisfactory financial rewards, and immunity from the erosion experienced by placements in non-Arab money markets. In addition, to invest Arab money in Arab economies is to show concrete national solidarity, while to place it in the West is to strengthen the states and the economies that for so long ruled the Arab world and exploited it economically, and that continue to give support to Israel. Yet, if this point is to end on a note of optimism, it can be said that the intraregional capital flows during 1974, estimated earlier at about $7 billion, constitute a substantial increase over anything experienced before, although they still represent a small proportion of the funds available for use in destinations outside the domestic markets where they are generated.

NOTES

1. The calculation of food imports is based on data on total imports for 1973 from *IFS* and from a study on 'Middle East Imports and Japan's Exports to that Area, 1970-74' prepared by the Economic Research Institute for the Middle East of Tokyo, as reported in *Middle East Economic Survey (MEES)*, Vol. XVIII, No. 46, of 5 September 1975. Food imports were reported partly in *Arab Economic Report* of January 1974 (published in Beirut in Arabic by the General Union of Arab Chambers of Commerce, Industry, and Agriculture for the Arab Countries) and partly in Europa, *The Middle East and North Africa 1974-75*. In those few instances where the food imports related to 1972, I have adjusted them for 1973. Data for 1974 and 1975 have been obtained from FAO in 1977.

2. The data on education are collated from the country chapters and Europa, op. cit., statistical survey for each country.

3. Nicolas Sarkis, 'The Energy Crisis and the Challenge of Development in the Arab Countries', paper No. 132 (A-1) submitted to the Ninth Arab Petroleum Congress held in Dubai, 10-16 March 1975; Table 1, p. 16 (Table 2, p. 17 for revenues). Sarkis's estimates have been largely confirmed by later records. See The British Petroleum Company Limited, *BP Statistical Review of the World Oil Industry, 1974*.

4. See Yusif A. Sayigh, 'Arab Oil Policies: Self-Interest Versus International Responsibility', *Journal of Palestine Studies*, Vol. IV, No. 3, Spring 1975, pp. 59-73.

5. Data from Middle East Financial and Industrial Services, *Middle East Investment Attitudes and Strategies*, Updating No. 2, 1975, and The International Institute for Strategic Studies, *The Military Balance 1974-1975* (London, 1974), pp. 32-9.

6. See Sarkis, loc. cit., Table 4, p. 19 (and the sources of this table) for GNP in 1972 or 1973. Estimates for 1974 are mine, based on Sarkis's table plus adjustments that take into account the incremental oil revenue till the end of 1974 plus the income multiplier of this revenue (assumed to be only 33 per cent over and above the revenue itself, owing to the considerable leakages and the fact that investments made out of oil revenue had not begun to fructify by the end of 1974).

7. OECD, *Development Cooperation, Efforts and Policies of the Members of the Development Assistance Committee, 1974 Review* (November 1974). This Report sums up the situation (p. 11) by stating: 'The DAC countries over the past ten years have increased their national product by about two-thirds in real terms ... But during this ten year period, the real value of official development assistance from DAC Member countries decreased by about 7 per cent ...' Regarding the drop in the contribution of the United States in real terms, see p. 14, Table VII-1, p. 116, and p. 133.

8. The reader is particularly referred to the Dag Hammarskjöld Foundation (Upsala, Sweden), in their *1975 Dag Hammarskjöld Report, What Now* (Upsala, 1975), prepared on the occasion of the Seventh Special Session of the United Nations General Assembly. For rich source material on aid and other matters relating to international co-operation in the solution of the economic and social problems of the globe, see the documents of the Sixth and Seventh Special Sessions of the United Nations General Assembly, New York, April/May 1974 and September 1975, and those of the Fourth Summit Conference of the Non-Aligned Countries held in Algiers in September 1973.

9. These data on trade for 1973 and 1974 are reported in UN, *Monthly Bulletin of Statistics*, June 1975, Table 52, pp. 110-17. They differ from data in *IFS* or in *DOT*. However, we have adopted them because nowhere else were data available for 1974 for comparison purposes. Furthermore, the differences are not important enough to influence the point that is made in the text with regard to the steep rise in the value of exports in 1974.

10. Calculations based on ibid., Table B, p. xiv, and Table 52, pp. 110-17.

11. According to several reports in the Lebanese

daily press late in August 1975.

12. UN, *Monthly Bulletin of Statistics*, June 1975, Table 68, pp. 226-37. The reserves consist of gold, position in IMF, foreign exchange and SDRs.

13. Ibid.

14. AFESD, *Annual Report 1973* and *Annual Report 1974* (both in Arabic), and the memorandum relating to the AFESD-UNDP Project entitled 'Programme for the Identification and Preparation of Intercountry Investment Projects and Related Feasibility Studies'.

15. By Decree No. M/48 of 1 September 1974, reported in *MEES*, Vol. XVII, No. 50, of 4 October 1974.

16. Information on the various efforts collated from various issues of *MEES* and *AOG*, for the relevant dates.

17. Information obtained from OAPEC Secretariat in Kuwait.

18. Alfred G. Musrey, *An Arab Common Market: A Study in Inter-Arab Trade Relations, 1920-67* (New York, 1969), Ch. 1. See also Chs. 2 and 3 for a survey of the Syro-Lebanese Customs Union and of the Middle East Supply Center. For a useful reference list relating to Arab economic co-operation, see ibid., especially pp. 271-4.

19. The League of Arab States, *Collection of Economic Treaties and Agreements Entered Into Within the Framework of the League of Arab States* (Cairo, 1969; Arabic), for the relevant texts.

20. For a survey and evaluation of the ACM, see Musrey, op. cit., and Yahya Arawdaky, *The Arab Common Market* (Damascus, 1970; Arabic).

21. Muhammed A. Diab, *Inter-Arab Economic Cooperation 1951-1960* (Beirut, 1963) has the fullest empirical study of the CFTRT of 1953.

22. For an evaluation of these agreements (as of most of the organisations and projects formed by the Arab League), see the relevant chapters in the annual issues of the *Arab Economic Report* to which reference has been made. See also: (a) Burhan al-Dajani, *Analysis of Some of the Aspects of Economic Relations Among the Arab Countries* (Cairo, 1962), the relevant sections; (b) Musrey, op. cit.; (c) Diab, op. cit., and (d) Muhammed A. Diab, 'Arab Economic Cooperation Between Theory and Application', and Burhan Dajani, 'Arab Economic Cooperation: Practical and Historical Aspects', both in *The Day of Arab Economic Cooperation, 23 March 1972* (Lectures printed together along with five commentaries; Kuwait, 1972; Arabic).

23. For a full examination of the principles governing Maghreb countries' co-operation, and the steps taken – with special emphasis on industry – see 'Memorandum by the Maghreb Permanent Consultative Committee on the Occasion of Its Participation in the Meeting of the Board of the Industrial Development Center of the Arab States in Cairo, 27 November – 7 December 1969', reproduced in *Arab Economic Report, 1969*, pp. 134-62.

24. The points are taken almost verbatim from Dajani's. See *Arab Economic Report, 1971*, pp. 60-74 for the memorandum (pp. 63/4 for the five points).

25. The writings of Bela Balassa, R. G. Lipsey, J. E. Meade, Raymond F. Mikesell and E. A. G. Robinson are often quoted or referred to. So are studies on the centrally planned economies, the EEC, and Latin America.

26. Resolution No. 634/D 22, taken during the 22nd Ordinary Meeting held in Cairo 28 November – 3 December 1973. See *Arab Economic Report, 1974*, pp. 166-80 for the text of the most important resolutions of the meeting.

27. The total number of Palestinians and of refugees has been the subject of controversy between the Zionists on the one hand and the United Nations and Arabs on the other, with the Zionists claiming a much smaller number than the others. For data confirming my estimates, see: (a) Government of Palestine, *Village Statistics 1945: A Classification of Land and Area Ownership in Palestine* (Jerusalem, 1945); (b) Government of Palestine, *A Survey of Palestine, 1945-1946* (Jerusalem, 1946), Vols. I and II, plus Supp.; (c) UN Economic Survey Mission for the Middle East, *Final Report of the United Nations Economic Survey Mission for the Middle East* (New York, 1949), Vols. I and II, pp. 22-3; (d) Fayez Sayegh, *The Palestine Refugees* (New York, 1952); (e) Yusif A. Sayigh, *The Economic Impact of the Refugee Problem on Lebanon, Syria, and Jordan* (Karachi, 1954), Appendix on population; (f) Fayez Sayegh, *The Arab Israeli Conflict* (New York, 1956); (g) UNRWA, *UNRWA Reviews: A Background Information Series* (Beirut, 1962), especially Information Paper 6 which deals with the rectification of UNRWA records during 1950-62; and (h) UNRWA, *Quarterly Bulletin of Economic Development*, especially Nos. 11 and 13.

For the Zionist point of view, see: (a) S. Thecknessee, *Arab Refugees, A Survey of Resettlement Possibilities* (RIIA, London, 1949), Ch. 2, where the total of 1948 refugees is given as 713,000; (b) The Institute for Mediterranean Affairs, *The Palestine Refugee Problem: A New Approach and A Plan for A Solution* (New York, 1958), Appendix 5; (c) Walter Pinner, *How Many Arab Refugees?* (London, 1959); and (d) Israeli Government, Ministry of Foreign Affairs, *Arab Refugees: Arab Statements and the Facts* (Jerusalem, 1961), pp. 41-8. It is worth emphasising that the Arabs, who numbered 1,415,000 in May 1948, would have reached about 3.4m by the end of 1974 at a compound rate of net increase of 3.33 per cent per annum. This is the total arrived at independently by estimating the number of Palestinian groups in their various abodes in 1974. The estimate was made by Edward Hagopian and A. B. Zahlan, 'Palestine's Arab Population: The Demography of the Palestinians', in *Journal of Palestine Studies*, Vol. III, No. 4, Summer 1974.

28. See Yusif A. Sayigh, *The Israeli Economy* (The Palestine Research Center, PRC, Beirut, 1966; Arabic), Ch. 3. See also B. C. Loftus, *National Income of Palestine, 1945* (Jerusalem, 1947).

29. Israel's first President, Chaim Weizmann, called this 'windfall' of assets 'a miraculous simplification of Israel's tasks', as quoted in James McDonald, first United States ambassador to Israel, in *My Mission to Israel* (New York, 1951), p. 176.

30. For an early examination of the confiscatory measures adopted by Israel against the Arabs, see: (a) Don Peretz, *Israel and the Palestine Arabs* (Washington, 1959); (b) Walter Schwartz, *The Arabs in Israel* (London, 1959); (c) Sabri Jiryis, *The Arabs in Israel* (Institute for Palestine Studies, Beirut, 1969), originally appeared in Hebrew in Israel; (d) Sabri Jiryis, 'The Legal Structure

for the Expropriation and Absorption of Arab Lands in Israel', in *Journal of Palestine Studies*, Vol. II, No. 4, Summer 1973; (e) *New Outlook* (an Israeli periodical), Special Issues on the Arabs in Israel, March/April, 1962, pp. 64-71; and (f) *Jerusalem Post* (an Israeli daily), 19 January 1956, where D. Ben Gurion, the then Prime Minister, stated that Israeli authorities had by January 1956 expropriated 200,000 hectares (some 500,000 acres) of land belonging to Arabs still living in Israel.

31. Data collected mainly from balance of payments data in Bank of Israel *Annual Report* for the various years covered. See also *IFS* balance of payments data for Israel; and various publications of the Falk Project for Economic Research in Israel, particularly *Fourth Report 1957 and 1958*, with an essay on *The Israeli Economy: The First Decade* by Don Patinkin (Jerusalem, 1959).

32. For details, see UNRWA, *Annual Report of the Commissioner-General of the United Nations Relief and Works Agency for Palestine Refugees in the Near East*, for the various years. Until recently, the *Report* was prepared by the Director-General, before his title was changed into Commissioner-General.

33. For education and high-level manpower among the Palestinians, which are of direct relevance to the developmental capability and contributions of this community, see: (a) Nazeeh Koura, *The Education of Palestinians: Facts and Problems* (PRC, Beirut, 1975; Arabic); (b) Nabil Shaath, 'High Level Palestinian Manpower', in *Journal of Palestine Studies*, Vol. 1, No. 2, Winter 1972; (c) Ibrahim Abu Lughod, 'Educating A Community in Exile: The Palestinian Experience', in *Journal of Palestine Studies*, Vol. II, No. 3, Spring 1973; and, for a background study relating to the Mandate period, (d) Nabil Ayoub Badran, *Education and Modernization in Palestine, 1918-1948* (PRC, Beirut, 1969).

34. For a discussion of the boycott and its impact, see: (a) Marwan Iskandar, *The Arab Boycott of Israel* (PRC, Beirut, 1966); (b) Joseph Moughayzil, *The Arab Boycott and International Law* (PRC, Beirut, 1968; Arabic); (c) Michael Shefer, 'Les conséquences du boycottage arabe sur les économies arabes et israéliennes', in *Les Temps Modernes*, Special Issue on *Le Conflict Israélo-Arabe* 22e Année, No. 253 bis, 1967, pp. 925-67; (d) Amer Sharif, *A Statistical Study on the Arab Boycott of Israel* (The Institute for Palestine Studies, Beirut; 1970); (e) 'The Arab Boycott', in *The Economist* (London), 1 August 1970; (f) D. Losman, 'The Arab Boycott of Israel', in *The International Journal of Middle East Studies*, Vol. 3, No. 2, April 1972; and (g) 'The Arab Boycott', a panel discussion reported in *Shu'un Falastiniyya* (Palestine Affairs, a monthly published by the PRC, Beirut; Arabic), No. 46, June 1975, pp. 132-60.

35. See note 31 above for the sources for this statement. Patinkin has made the point most potently for the years 1948-58; nevertheless the subsequent years have seen no relaxation but greater hardship in Israel's economic situation.

INDEX

NOTE: entries under each country are provided only for major topics. For full references see specific subjects which are subdivided by country, e.g. desalination: Kuwait

AGIP 148
Abu Dhabi Fund for Arab Economic Development 701
Adelman, Irma 13, 290
Agourram, A. 636, 659
agrarian reform *see* land reform
Agreement for the settlement of Payments for current Transactions and the Transfer of Capital 705
Agreement of Arab Economic Unity 707
agricultural banks and credit: Egypt 325, 332; Libya 430; Iraq 54-5; Jordan 209-11, 218; Morocco 590, 637-8; Saudi Arabia 161; Sudan 402
agricultural co-operative societies: Algeria 522; Egypt 332, 336-7; in Iraq 55, 62, 65; Jordan 209-11, Morocco 633; Sudan 401; Syria 241, 259
Agricultural Credit Corporation (Jordan) 209-11, 218
agricultural machinery: Algeria 543, 546; Iraq 42, 66; Jordan 209; Morocco 595; Saudi Arabia 160-61; Sudan 387; Syria 238, 246
agriculture 118, 666-71, 679; Algeria 525-6, 530, 535-43 *passim*, 544, 546, 547, 568, 572-3; Egypt 318, 323, 349, 351, 360; Iraq 26, 31-6, 42, 49, 59-66, 77n; Jordan 191, 193-5, 195-6, 207, 208-15, 219, 220, 224; Kuwait 101, 103; Lebanon 281, 287, 291, 301, 292-4; Libya 420, 425, 428, 430, 435, 443, 446, 451, 452, 455-6, 459, 460, 464, 466, 467; Morocco 580, 581, 582, 583, 586-91, 592, 597, 598, 602, 607, 609, 613, 617, 620, 626, 627-8, 633-8 *passim*, 639, 644, 648, 651, 652, 655, 657; Saudi Arabia 134, 137, 140, 155-61, 169, 170; Sudan 377, 378, 379-87 *passim*, 39-2, 398, 399, 401, 405, 410, 411; Syria 231, 235, 237-8, 241,

245-7, 260, 264; Tunisia 472, 474-5, 478, 481, 485-9, 490, 494, 497, 499-500, 510, 511 *see also* collective farms *and* land reform
aid 665, 675-6, 681-3, 689, 690-91, 696, 711-12, 715n; from Abu Dhabi 397; from Egypt 191, 425, 431; from Kuwait 89, 107, 117-20, 191, 197, 198, 357, 397, 402, 698-9; from Libya 191, 197, 397, 402; from Qatar 357; from Saudi Arabia 171-2, 191, 197, 198, 357, 397, 402; from Syria 191; from the United Arab Emirates 357; from the West 191, 198, 213, 270, 339-40, 397, 402, 425, 480, 622; from USSR 361-3, 402, 622; to Algeria 119, 564, 570; to Egypt 118, 119, 171, 339-40, 348, 357, 358-9, 361-3, 371-2, 373, 699; to Iraq 119; to Jordan 118, 119, 171, 188, 191, 197, 198, 222, 223, 608; to Libya 419, 425-31, 432, 443; to Morocco 618, 622-3, 647, 651, 655, 659; to Sudan 118, 395, 402-10 *passim*, 415; to Syria 118, 119, 229, 238, 239, 262, 268-70; to the Arabian Gulf 119; to Tunisia 479-80, 495-6, 511; to Yemen 119
airways *see* transport and communications
al-Dahiri, Abdul-Wahhab Mutar 27, 63
Alexander, Sydney, S. 11
Algeria 521-78; Algeria Charter 522; Arabisation in 558-9; Assemblée Populaire Communale Elargie 538-9; *autogestion* 533, 535, 536; colonial period 521-30; Front de Libération National 522, 540; industrialisation 543-54; Office National de la Réforme Agraire 535; planning and development 559-74; SONATRACH 535, 547, 550, 551; transformation of 530-59; welfare services 554-9;

workers in France 573-4
al-Manoufi, Ali 23
al-Razzaz, Munif 59
American University of Beirut, Economic Research Institute 192, 282
Amin, Galal A. 11
Amin, S. 505, 527, 529, 530, 531, 534, 591, 597, 607-8, 610, 633
Arab African Oil Assistance Fund 701
Arab Bank for Industrial and Agricultural Development in Africa 701
Arab Common Market Agreement 705-6
Arab Economic Council 704-5
Arab European Bank 699
Arab Fund for Economic and Social Development 107, 117-18, 362, 396, 397-8, 404, 411, 700, 706, 709
Arab-Israeli war 675, 698, 710-13; Egypt 342, 357, 358; Iraq 20, 21; Jordan 188, 221; Kuwait 119-20; Libya 439; Saudi Arabia 145; Syria 244
Arab Labour Organisation 709
Arab Land Bank 218
Arab Maritime Petroleum Transport Co. 703
Arab Oil Assistance Fund 702
Arab Petroleum Investments Co. 703
Arab Petroleum Services Co. 703
Arab Shipbuilding and Repair Yard
Arab unity *see* co-operation, Arab economic
Arabian American Oil Company (ARAMCO) 84, 143, 162, 285
Arabian Drilling Co. 148
Arabian Geophysical and Surveying Co. 148
Arabian Oil Co. 86
Arabisation 611-12, 632
army, the *see* defence expenditure
artificial fibres industry: Iraq 43

720 Index

artificial silk industry: Iraq 41, 42
Asfour, Edmond 130, 133

Badre, Albert 282
balance of payments 675, 689, 707; Algeria 553-4, 577n; Egypt 325-6, 339, 342, 353, 354, 355, 358, 360-61, 371-2, 373, 689; Iraq 53; Jordan 189, 198-9, 220, 223; Kuwait 103, 112-13; Lebanon 296-7, 298-9, 307-9; Libya 443, 458; Morocco 596, 622-5, 643; Sudan 397, 388, 395, 397, 402-4, 410, 415; Syria 252-3; Tunisia 494, 496, 497, 501, 511, 516
Bank Misr (Egypt) 319, 325
banks and banking 666, 679, 685, 690, 699; Egypt 319, 323, 349, 354, 367, 368; Iraq 38, 49, 53-5; Jordan 192, 193, 196, 218-19; Kuwait 105, 113; Lebanon 286, 287, 288-90, 291, 296-8, 304, 305, 310; Libya 434, 455, 460; Morocco 581, 582, 596-7, 642-4; in Saudi Arabia 134, 142, 166-8; Sudan 392, 399, 401-2, 424; Syria 231-3, 252, 272, 273; Tunisia 501; see also specific banks and types of bank
Banque Arabe et Internationale d'Investissement 699
Banque de Crédit Agricole, Industriel et Foncier (Lebanon) 297
barrages see dams
Basrah Petroleum Co. 18, 19, 36
bedouin, the see nomads
Belal, A. A. 636, 659
Ben Bella, President 532, 576
Ben Saleh, Ahmad 501, 505-6
beverages and drinks industry see food and drink industries
Boecke, J. H. 398
books 274, 279n
Boumedienne, President 532, 576n
Bourguiba, President 472, 479, 498, 503, 506
budgets, state: Morocco 597, 625; Algeria 556; Egypt 326, 371; Iraq 18, 55-7; Jordan 201, 223; Kuwait 85-8, 93, 94, 109-12, 121-2, 176; Libya 424; Saudi Arabia 135, 137, 168-70, 172, 182n; Sudan 404; Syria 252, 276; Tunisia 502

capital formation: Libya 446; Jordan 199; Morocco 618; Saudi Arabia 131, 135-7; Syria 263
capital-output ratio 676; Egypt 349; Iraq 51; Kuwait 110-11, 116; Libya 451; Morocco 606; Saudi Arabia 135-7, 154; Sudan 405, 410; Syria 247
cement industry 678; Iraq 41, 53;

Jordan 217; Morocco 592; Saudi Arabia 156; Syria 237
central banks: Iraq 54; Jordan 218; Kuwait 106, 115; Sudan 401; Syria 239, 252; Tunisia 480
Charter of National Action (Iraq) 59
chemicals industry: Algeria 529, 567; Egypt 343; Iraq 43; Morocco 592, 648; Tunisia 493; Syria 243
citrus fruit 624, 639
civil servants: Egypt 321; Kuwait 97, 121; Lebanon 311; Syria 233
civil service see public administration
clothing industry 678; Iraq 43, 53; Jordan 217; Tunisia 490
coal industry: Morocco 592, 593, 640
collective farms: Iraq 65; Tunisia 506-7
colonialism 11, 687; Algeria 521-30; Egypt 320-21; Libya 419, 420-22, 465; Morocco 579-611, 587-8, 614-15; Tunisia 471, 472-5, 486
commercial banks: Kuwait 106; Libya 460
communications see transport and communications
Compagnie Général de Geophysique 148
Consortium of Real Estate Companies (Kuwait) 699
construction industry: Algeria 545, 561, 562; Egypt 319, 323, 341; Iraq 40, 52; Jordan 195-6, 217; Kuwait 98, 103, 116; Lebanon 285, 295, 303; Libya 426, 429, 430, 434, 443, 455, 456-7, 460, 462; Morocco 620-21; Saudi Arabia 140, 151; Sudan 391-2, 401; Syria 231-3, 237, 247; Tunisia 475, 485, 511
construction materials industry: Algeria 544, 546, 547, 567; Egypt 343; Iraq 41, 43, 53; in Kuwait 103; Morocco 592; Tunisia 475
consultants, foreign 104
consumption and consumer goods 689; Algeria 543, 544, 545, 570; Egypt 349, 353, 354, 355, 375; Lebanon 295, 298, 308, 309; Libya 458; Saudi Arabia 137-8; Syria 268
Convention for Facilitating Trade and Regulating transit 705, 707, 708
Cooper, Charles, A. 11
co-operation, Arab economic 104, 678; Kuwait and 115, 117-20; Libya and 434-5; Syria 264, 266; Tunisia 497-8; see also intraregional economic relations
corruption 311
cotton cultivation: Egypt 318, 349,

365, 368, 378; Sudan 387-8; Syria 237, 239
cotton-ginning: Iraq 40; Syria 274
Council for Arab Economic Unity 705, 707, 710
coups d'etat 289, 304, 317, 433
craft industries: Algeria 528; Libya 43, 464; Morocco 580, 582, 585, 591, 592, 609, 620, 627; Sudan 392, 399; Tunisia 490-91, 509, 518n
cultural development: Lebanon 290; Syria 229, 267, 276
currency devaluation 145, 172

Dajani, Burhan 706-7, 708
dams 670; Egypt 344, 349, 364-6, 383-4; Iraq 29-30; Morocco 589, 634-5, 638; Saudi Arabia 159; Sudan 405; Syria 245; Tunisia 487
date processing: Iraq 40, 53
debt, personal 209-11
defence expenditure 665, 677, 679, 698, 713, 714; Egypt 327, 344, 358, 359, 372; Iraq 38, 49, 57; Jordan 191, 196, 222; Libya 455; Saudi Arabia 134, 169, 170; Sudan 404; Syria 253
de Gaulle, General 528
desalination: Kuwait 101; Libya 461; in Saudi Arabia 159-60
development 11-12, 689; Algeria 528, 559-74; concept of 12-13; defined 15; Egypt 327; Kuwait 88, 109, 110; Lebanon 290, 312; oil revenues for 40; Saudi Arabia 127; Sudan 379, 397; Tunisia 516-17 see also planning, economic
development administration: Morocco 645-6, 650, 658; Egypt 345-54 passim; in Iraq 41, 43, 66-74; Jordan 219-25; Kuwait 85, 115-16; Libya 426, 430; Saudi Arabia 129, 130, 177-80; Sudan 408; Syria 260-72; Tunisia 515-16
development budget see budgets
development funds 700-702; see also specific funds
dualistic economies: Morocco 580, 589, 603, 648; Tunisia 478, 590. Algeria 521-2
diversification: Iraq 43; Kuwait 105-6, 107, 115; Saudi Arabia 148, 178, 180
Doxiadis Associates 165

East Ghor canal 213-15
East Jordan Valley, A Social and Economic Survey 213
economic growth 13, 680-83; Algeria 529, 565, 566, 580; Egypt 345-54; Iraq 47-53, 73-5, 187; Jordan 187, 192-7; Kuwait 115; Lebanon

Index

282-6, 290; 314; Libya 454-5, 580; Morocco 603-5, 615-22, 638-43 *passim*, 650, 653, 655, 658; Saudi Arabia 130-38; Sudan 391, 410; Syria 229, 246, 253; Tunisia 483, 510, 513-14, 516
economic management and policy: Egypt 359, 364; Iraq 17-18; Kuwait 164; Lebanon 286, 287; Saudi Arabia 154; Tunisia 496
Económic Organisation (Iraq) 58
education 119, 671, 672, 676, 678, 683, 686, 694; Algeria 523-4, 528, 536, 540, 556-9, 568; Egypt 202, 322-3, 369, 471; Iraq 17, 23, 36, 44-5; Jordan 189, 202-3, 220; Kuwait 88, 89, 93-4, 110, 116, 202; Lebanon 202, 288, 290, 298, 299-300, 312; Libya 202, 421, 424, 425, 428-9, 443, 444, 451, 452, 455, 461, 462; Morocco 581, 582, 590, 597, 598-603, 610, 612, 615, 630-33, 647, 648, 659; Sudan 398, 399, 404, 413-14; Saudi Arabia 137, 138, 141-2, 169, 172-5, 180, 202; Sudan 202; Syria 241, 248-50, 267, 276; Tunisia 471, 472-3, 480, 483, 500, 501-4, 514, 516, 519n
Egypt 317-76; *Charter, The* 327, 367; Economic Organisation 367; Egyptianisation 338-9; High Dam 364-6; industrialisation 339-45; land reform 328-38; planning 345-54; revolution 326-8; socialism 366-72; socio-economic structure 317-26
electrical equipment industry: Algeria 544, 546, 547, 567; Iraq 43
electricity supply 118; Algeria 528-9, 545, 568; Egypt 343, 344, 365; Iraq 42, 43, 49; Jordan 204-5, 217; Kuwait 101, 102, 103, 110, 116; Lebanon 286, 293; Libya 429-30, 443, 452, 455, 461; Morocco 592-3, 597, 620, 640; Saudi Arabia 137, 151, 155, 164-5; Sudan 391, 396-7, 398, 410, 412; Syria 241, 243, 245, 248, 274; Tunisia 475, 493, 506
El Ghonemy, Riad 334-5
emigration: Jordan 207; Syria 277; Tunisia 499
employment *see* manpower and employment *and* unemployment
energy *see* electricity supply
engineering industry 698; Algeria 544, 546; Egypt 343; Iraq 43; Morocco 592
entrepreneurship *see* private enterprise
l'Enterprise de Recherches et d'Activités Petroliers 21
Euphrates High Dam 245, 266
European Economic Community 496
expatriate manpower 694-5; Algeria 575-6n, 420; Kuwait 84, 88, 92, 97, 98, 103-4, 121, 122-3, 420; Libya 420, 426, 429, 434, 465-5; Saudi Arabia 154, 175, 176, 420
exports 677, 687-8, 692, 694; Algeria 526, 553-4, 572; Egypt 318, 339, 342, 343, 354; Iraq 53; Jordan 222; Lebanon 294, 295; Libya 458; Morocco 593-4; Saudi Arabia 127, 140; Sudan 387-8, 393, 405, 412, 432; Syria 238, 239, 242, 264, 266, 268; Tunisia 491-2, 494, 497
external trade 687-91; Algeria 553-4; Egypt 367; Iraq 53; Jordan 197-200, 223; Kuwait 81, 112-13; Lebanon 298-9, 305; Libya 458; Morocco 582, 595-6, 622-5; Saudi Arabia 170-72; Sudan 402-4; Tunisia 474, 475, 494-8

Faisal, Crown Prince 128-30, 135;
family planning: Egypt 366, 371; Morocco 653
farming *see* agriculture
Farrell, R. E. 560
Fenelon, K. G. 18, 23, 47
fertiliser industry 709; Morocco 594; Algeria 543; Egypt 318, 336; Iraq 43; Jordan 209; Lebanon 293; Saudi Arabia 149, 160; Syria 244, 246, 260; Tunisia 493, 496
fishing: Kuwait 82; Morocco 583, 639; Sudan 378, 391-2, 399, 401, 411-12; Saudi Arabia 139, 140, 160
flour milling: Iraq 40; Morocco 592
Food and Agriculture Organisation 31, 193, 235
food and drink industries 677; Algeria 543, 568; Egypt 343; Iraq 40, 41, 43, 53; Jordan 187-8, 190, 192, 217; Morocco 592, 595; Saudi Arabia 153, 154; Syria 237, 252; Tunisia 489-90
footwear industry: Saudi Arabia 153
foreign aid *see* aid
foreign assets and investment 695-702, 714-15; Kuwait 106-7, 108, 117; Libya 441
foreign capital (in Arab countries) 707, 709; Algeria 504; intra-regional flows 695-702; Lebanon 286, 298-9, 309; Libya 425; Morocco 646; Saudi Arabia 152, 182n; Sudan 397; Tunisia 495
foreign exchange *see* balance of payments
foreign loans *see* aid
forestry: Libya 443; Morocco 583, 639; Saudi Arabia 140, 160; Sudan 377, 391-2, 399, 411
France 431; and Algeria 521-78 *passim*; and Morocco 579-663 *passim*;
furniture industry: Egypt 343; Jordan 192, 217; Saudi Arabia 154; Syria 243

gas industry 687; Algeria 530, 533, 543, 545, 546, 547, 549-54, 561, 562, 565, 568, 571; Iraq 42, 49; Kuwait 103, 116; Libya 455; Saudi Arabia 134, 140; Sudan 394; Tunisia 475, 506
General Authority for the South and Arabia Gulf 117, 119
General Union of Chambers of Commerce, Industry and Agriculture in the Arab Countries 708
Germany 579, 622
Ghaddafi, Colonel 434
glass industry: Iraq 42; Syria 237; Tunisia 493;
governments *see* state, the
grain industry: Iraq 53; Jordan 217
gross domestic product: Algeria 526, 529, 553, 559-63; Egypt 319-20, 322, 323, 340, 343, 345-54, 357, 358, 372; Iraq 48, 50-52; Jordan 192-6, 197, 207, 208, 223; Kuwait 90-92, 103, 105, 124n; Lebanon 282, 301, 303, 305, 308, 309; Libya 427-8, 442, 453-6; Morocco 603-5, 615-22, 629, 653, 657; Saudi Arabia 132-4, 139, 152, 155, 166, 178; Sudan 378, 382, 392, 407; Syria 264, 267; Tunisia 475, 476-7, 480-85, 488, 499-500, 502, 511, 514-15; *see also* economic growth
gross national product 665, 680-83, 696, 713; Algeria 530; Egypt 323-5, 345-54, 355; Iraq 17, 36-7, 48-53; Jordan 188, 192-6, 197, 203, 221, 223; Kuwait 38, 86-7, 90-92, 116, 124n, 126n; Lebanon 195, 281, 282; Libya 38, 427, 441-2, 470n; Morocco 616-17, 638, 643; Saudi Arabia 38, 130-38, 167; Sudan 389-91, 399-401; Syria 242-3, 261; Tunisia 480-81, 494, 510

Hagen, Everett 13
Haikal, Mohammed Hassanein 327
Hansen, Bent 319, 350, 354
Harbison, F. H. 290
Haseeb, Khair el-Din 48
Hashem, Jawad 23, 24, 25, 31, 40-41, 44
health care 119, 671, 672, 678, 683, 686; Algeria 555, 568; Egypt 322, 325, 353, 369, 371-2; Iraq 45-8; Jordan 204, 220; Kuwait 88, 94-5,

110; Lebanon 288, 290, 298; Libya 425, 429, 430, 443, 444, 452, 455, 461; Morocco 581, 597, 598, 612-13, 615; Saudi Arabia 139, 175-177; Sudan 399, 404; Syria 229-31, 248-50, 267, 276; Tunisia 471, 504
Higgins, Benjamin 419, 444
High Dam 344, 349, 364, 375n, 383
higher education 671; Algeria 557-8; Egypt 325, 369, 370; Iraq 45; Jordan 202; Kuwait 94; Lebanon 299-300; Libya 429, 462-3; Morocco 598, 632; Saudi Arabia 175; Syria 249-50; Tunisia 503
Himadeh, Sa'id B. 12
Hosni, A. 320, 322
housing 678, 683; Algeria 528, 555, 568, 597; Egypt 349, 369, 371; Iraq 34, 46-7, 52-3, 58, 70; Jordan 190, 196, 203-4, 220; Kuwait 96, 101, 116; Lebanon 291, 295; Libya 426, 429, 430, 443, 445, 447, 451, 452, 455, 462; Morocco 602, 613, 644, 647, 658; Saudi Arabia 134, 137, 177; Sudan 399, 402, 405; Syria 321-3, 241, 250-51, 267, 276
hydrocarbons see gas industry and oil resources and production

ideology 679, 685; Algeria 533, 543, 573; Egypt 328; Tunisia 504-8 passim
illiteracy and literacy 671; Egypt 320, 322; Iraq 23, 138; Jordan 202, 229, 250; Kuwait 93, 97-8, 250; Lebanon 229; Libya 138, 250, 424; Morocco 138; Saudi Arabia 138, 161, 250; Sudan 379, 413; Syria 229, 250, 262; Tunisia 250
import-export trade: Lebanon 298-9; Syria 272
imports 687-8, 692, 694; Algeria 554; Egypt 325, 344, 345, 368; Iraq 53; Jordan 197-200; Kuwait 112; Lebanon 294, 298, 305, 308-9; Libya 426, 449, 458; Morocco 592, 595, 624, 642; Saudi Arabia 155, 157, 170; Sudan 402; Syria 239, 242, 268, 274
income distribution 665, 681, 683; Algeria 526-8, 534, 565, 609; Egypt 336, 367, 368, 369; Iraq 17; Kuwait 96, 115; Libya 460; Morocco 589, 607-10, 635; Syria 266; Tunisia 473-4, 509, 609
income per capita 680-83; Algeria 534, 559-60, 571; Egypt 319-20, 322; Iraq 48; Jordan 189, 203, 220; Kuwait 82; Lebanon 282;

Libya 421; Saudi Arabia 127; Sudan 377, 391, 401; Syria 229-30
income tax see taxation
Industrial Bank of Kuwait 105
industrial banks: Iraq 41, 42, 44, 54; Kuwait 104, 105; Libya 430; Sudan 394, 402; Egypt 325
Industrial Development Center of the Arab States 709
industrial estates: Kuwait 102, 104-5; Saudi Arabia 151
industrialisation 670, 677, 678-9, 689; Algeria 145-6, 543-9, 591; Egypt 339-45, 366; Iraq 42; Libya 435; Saudi Arabia 127, 150-51; Syria 240, 241-2, 261; Tunisia 510, 591
industry 676-7, 685, 707, 709; Algeria 522, 528, 530, 543-9, 561, 562, 572, 677; Egypt 323, 339-45 passim, 349, 367, 368, 677; Iraq 40-44; Jordan 215-19; Kuwait 102-9; Lebanon 286, 287, 294-5, 301, 677; Libya 443, 445, 446, 451, 459, 460, 464; Morocco 580, 581, 591-3, 602, 620, 641-2, 644, 646-7, 648, 657; Saudi Arabia 150-51; Sudan 405, 410, 411; Syria 241, 243-4, 260, 266, 272, 273; Tunisia 474, 475, 478, 485, 489-94; see also specific industries
inflation 108, 145, 172; Algeria 578n; Egypt 354-5, 357-8; Iraq 55; Jordan 193; Lebanon 283; Libya 441, 449, 468; Morocco 606; Saudi Arabia 130; Sudan 390, 405, 409; Syria 251-2, 261
infrastructure 676, 689; Algeria 521, 555; Kuwait 88, 90, 101-2, 115; Lebanon 286-7; Libya 420, 421, 443, 445, 449, 460, 466; Morocco 580, 588, 606; Sudan 412; Saudi Arabia 161-5; Tunisia 471; Syria 237, 240, 262
Institut de Recherches et de Formation en Vue de Développement 287, 288
insurance 685, 690; Egypt 367, 369; Iraq 20, 38, 49, 58; Jordan 192, 196; Kuwait 105; Lebanon 291; Libya 434, 455; Morocco 642; Saudi Arabia 134; Syria 242
International Bank for Reconstruction and Development (studies): Iraq 24-5, 27, 31; Jordan 191, 192, 204, 219-20; Libya 419, 422, 431, 444; Morocco 591; Saudi Arabia 129; Sudan 386; Syria 237, 241, 248, 250-51, 260
International Monetary Fund 560
International Ore and Fertilizers Co. 149
intraregional economic relations 691-710
investment 670, 677, 680, 681, 690, 712; Algeria 528-30, 563-70, 571;

allocation 70-71; capacity to absorb 42, 73-4, 168-9, 178-9, 262, 441, 690; Egypt 336, 339-41, 344-57, 358, 371; Iraq 16, 17, 29, 35-6, 42, 43, 48, 50-53, 67-74; Jordan 218-25; Kuwait 108, 110-11, 116, 121; Lebanon 285-6, 297, 308-9; Libya 425-8, 441, 443, 445-52, 459-60, 461, 469n; Morocco 580, 591, 596, 605-10, 615, 618-19, 623, 627, 635, 636, 639, 644-58; Saudi Arabia 151, 168-9, 178-9; Sudan 391, 393-4, 398, 405-10 passim; Syria 238, 242-3, 244, 247, 248, 262, 268-70, 275-6; Tunisia 475, 479, 484-5, 491, 494-5, 508, 510-15; see also capital formation and foreign assets and investment
Iraq 17-80; agrarian and land reform 20, 57, 59-66; agriculture 31-6; Board of Trade Survey 18; Development Board 18, 66; development planning 66-74; external trade 53; factors affecting economic performance 72-6; Kurds and 18, 20-21; land 24-9; manufacturing industry 40-44; population and manpower 22-4; public finance 55-7; recent history 18-22; water resources 29-31;
Iraq National Minerals Co. 40
Iraq National Oil Co. 21
Iraq Petroleum Co. 18, 19, 20, 21, 36, 38, 57, 73
iron and steel industry 710; Algeria 544, 546, 565; Egypt 343; Iraq 43; Morocco 648; Saudi Arabia 149-50; Syria 244; Tunisia 492
irrigation 668, 670, 676, 679; Algeria 543, 574; Egypt 318, 330, 333, 338, 365; Iraq 29-31, 66, 77n; Jordan 189, 192, 197, 213-14, 220; Kuwait 116; Lebanon 293-4; Morocco 582, 589, 597, 602, 634, 638; Saudi Arabia 157-9; Sudan 383-4, 386-7, 398, 405, 411; Syria 237, 239, 241, 244-5, 246, 260, 262; Tunisia 474, 487
Islamic Development Bank 701
Israel 213-14; see also Arab-Israeli war
Issawi, Charles 317, 319, 321, 336
Italy 425

joint enterprise see mixed sector (of the economy)
Jordan 187-228; agriculture 208-15; Development Board 218, 219-21; economic growth 192-7; Economic Security Committee 222; external trade 197-200; Industrial Development Fund 218; industry 215-19; manpower 205-7;

Index 723

National Planning Council 223; planning 219-25; population 189-90, 200-202; problems of 225; recent history 188-92; *see also* Palestine expellees
Jordan Central Co-operative 209-11
Jordan Electricity Authority 218
Jordan Valley Land Tenure Survey 213

Kuwait 81-126; Arab states and 117-20; budgets 109-12; development planning in 115-16; economic system 113-15; education in 93-4; external trade 112-13; health care in 94-5; Industrial Development Committee 104; industries 102-9; infrastructure 101-2; land and housing 99-101; manpower in 96-9; national income 90-92; population of 92; problems of 120-24; recent history 81-90; Shuaiba Industrial Zone 102, 104-5; social welfare in 95-6
Kuwait Airways Corporation 115
Kuwait Cement Co. 102, 113
Kuwait Chemical Fertiliser Co. 102, 105, 113
Kuwait Foreign Trade, Contracting and Investment Co. 106, 699
Kuwait Fund for Arab Economic Development 86, 117, 270, 362, 396, 397, 495, 564-5, 622, 700-702
Kuwait International Investment Co. 106, 699
Kuwait National Petroleum Co. 86, 102, 105
Kuwait Oil Co. 82
Kuwait Oil Tanker Co. 106, 113
Kuwait Oxygen Co. 102
Kuwait Petrochemical Industries Co. 102, 113
Kuwait Shipping Co. 105-6
Kuznets, S. 195, 217

labour *see* manpower and employment
land ownership and purchase: Algeria 523, 524; Egypt 317-18, 321, 327, 328-38 *passim*; Iraq 18, 26-8, 58; Jordan 208, 212-16 *passim*; Kuwait 99-101, 109, 111, 121; Libya 423; Morocco 586-9, 662n; Saudi Arabia 134, 159, 165; Sudan 384; Syria 60, 253-60; Tunisia 472, 474, 481, 485-7
land reclamation 158, 679; Egypt 333, 337-8, 368; Libya 435; Sudan 398; Syria 237, 240, 262, 273
land reform 683-5; Algeria 522, 525, 533-43; Egypt 256-7, 328-38, 366, 367, 368, 369; Iraq 20, 57,

59-66, 256-7; Jordan 212; Libya 445; Morocco 613, 633-6; Sudan 384-5; Syria 239, 241, 242, 254-60, 275; Tunisia 486-8, 506
land resources 668-71; Iraq 17, 18, 24-9, 668; Jordan 187, 188-9, 191-2, 226n; Lebanon 293; Libya 421, 422-3, 461, 485-9; Morocco 586-91, 610, 633-8; Saudi Arabia 157; Sudan 377-8, 381-6, 410-11, 668; Syria 237-8, 241, 245, 266
League of Arab States 703-10
leather industry 678; Algeria 545; Iraq 42, 53; Morocco 592; Tunisia 490
Lebanon 281-315; customs union with Syria 281-2, 285; economic growth 282-6; economic structure 300-310; position of 290-91; sectoral developments 291-300
Libya 419-70; aid to 425-31; colonisation 420-22; development of 453-65; National Planning Council 444; oil resources 435-42; Petroleum Commission 436; planning 442-52; republican government 433-5;
Libyan American Reconstruction Commission 426, 432, 443
Libyan Development Council 426, 428, 432, 443
Libyan Finance Corporation 443
Libyan Oil Corporation 438
Libyan Petroleum General Authority 438
Libyan Public Development and Stabilization Agency 426, 432, 443
Litani Project (Lebanon) 293-4
literacy *see* illiteracy and literacy
livestock: Morocco 583, 639, 640; Saudi Arabia 139, 140, 160; Sudan 377, 392-3, 398, 399, 411
loans *see* aid

machinery *see* mechanical engineering
Maghreb Permanent Consultative Committee 706
Maniakin, V. 48
manpower and employment 672-3, 678, 679, 686, 707, 712; Algeria 523, 526, 528, 531-2, 537-8, 541, 559, 563, 573; Egypt 323, 326, 332, 336, 343, 344, 349, 358, 359-60; intraregional mobility 694-5; Iraq 22-4, 42-3, 76n; Jordan 196, 205-7, 223; Kuwait 93, 96-9, 100, 103, 115, 116, 121-2; Lebanon 282-3, 290, 302, 672; Libya 425, 429, 451-2, 452, 456, 463-5, 467; Morocco 581, 582-6, 593-4, 595, 597, 602, 609,

610, 629-30, 643, 656, 658, 659; Saudi Arabia 138-42, 153-5, 177, 178; Sudan 379-81, 386, 405, 410; Syria 233-7, 264-5, 266, 268; Tunisia 473, 478-9, 483, 488-9, 491, 498-504, 510, 511, 515; *see also* expatriate manpower, technical skills and training *and* unemployment
manufacturing industry 118, 666, 677, 679, 687; Algeria 281; Egypt 40, 281, 232, 339, 343, 344, 349; Iraq 23-4, 40-44, 49, 53; Jordan 187, 195-6, 207, 217, 219, 220; Kuwait 98, 103-5, 116; Lebanon 281, 285-6, 295; Libya 434, 455-6, 464; Morocco 592, 620; Saudi Arabia 140, 150-55; Sudan 392, 393-5; Tunisia 474, 490, 506; Syria 40, 231-3, 237, 240, 244, 247
Marzouk, G. A. 319, 350, 354
match industry: Iraq 40; Jordan 217; Syria 237
Mazur, M. P. 191, 206
mechanical engineering industry: Algeria 544, 546, 567; Iraq 53; Saudi Arabia 153
metal piping industry: Kuwait 103; metals industry: Algeria 546, 567; Egypt 343, 367; Iraq 41, 42, 53; Morocco 592; Saudi Arabia 154
Middle East Supply Centre 704
mineral resources 687; Algeria 565; Iraq 40, 43; Jordan 215-16; Libya 451; Morocco 579, 610; Saudi Arabia 146, 150; Sudan 378; Syria 243-4; Tunisia 475, 491-4, 496
mining 707; Algeria 522, 530, 533, 543, 545, 546, 547, 561, 562, 565; Egypt 349; Jordan 191, 195-6, 217, 219, 220; Libya 455, 464; Morocco 580, 581, 582, 593-4, 602, 620, 624, 640-41; Saudi Arabia 134, 139, 140; Sudan 392, 399; Syria 231-3, 241, 247; Tunisia 474, 475, 481, 490, 492, 506
mixed sector (of the economy) 699; Egypt 367; Iraq 42; Kuwait 90, 108, 113-14, 116; Saudi Arabia 151; Tunisia 514
Mobil Co. 149
modernisation: Algeria 521, 540; Morocco 648; Tunisia 477;
money *see* banks and banking *and* budgets, state
money supply: Egypt 54; Iraq 54; Jordan 189; Lebanon 54; Libya 427; Saudi Arabia 167; Sudan 401; Syria 252; Tunisia 511, 596-7
Morocco 579-663; Banque Nationale

724 Index

pour le Développement Economique 642, 643-4, 647; Berbers 581, 582, 601; Bureau de Recherches et de Participation Minières 593, 641; Bureau d'Etudes et de Participations Industrielles 642; Caisse National de Crédit Agricole 637-8; colonisation of 579-611; decolonisation 611-14; economic growth 603-5, 615-22; education 598-603, 630-33; external sector 622-5; industry 591-4, 638-44; investment 605-10; land resources 586-91, 633-8; migration of workers to France 586; Office Nationale des Irrigations 638; Office Nationale de la Modernisation Rurale 636-7; Operation Labour 636; planning 605-10, 644-58; population and manpower 582-6, 626-8; service industries 594-8
mortgage banks: Iraq 54; Sudan 402
Morris, Cynthia 13, 290
Mosul Petroleum Co. 18, 36
Myers, C. A. 290

Nasser, President 317, 321-2, 327-8, 352, 364, 372; National bank for Industrial and Touristic Development 297-8
National Bank of Iraq 54
national banks: Algeria 535; Egypt 325; Libya 430, 443; Morocco 644, 647; Tunisia 506
national income: Algeria 534; Egypt 319-20, 322; Iraq 47-53, 73; Jordan 189, 192, 203, 220, 226n; Kuwait 82; Lebanon 282-6, 300-303, 305; Saudi Arabia 127; Sudan 378, 388-91, 399; Syria 229-30, 237-8, 261, 263, 266
nationalisation 683, 685; Algeria 521, 533, 541, 685; Egypt 366-9, 685; Iraq 19, 20, 21-2, 39, 42, 43, 52, 58, 73; Libya 434, 438; Syria 240, 242, 253, 272; Sudan 685; Tunisia 685
nationalism, Arab 12, 289, 612, 678, 707-8
natural resources: Iraq 17; Kuwait 103; Morocco 580; Saudi Arabia 145-6, 154; Syria 264; see also specific resources
net domestic product: Sudan 386; Syria 263-72
nomads: Jordan 189, 203; Libya 242; Saudi Arabia 139, 155, 160, 175, 181; Syria 238
O'Brien, Patrick 367-8, 369
oil exploration: Egypt 343; Iraq 21; Libya 419, 425, 436-7; Syria 241; Tunisia 493
oil refining 678; Algeria 529, 546; Iraq 38, 42, 43, 49; Jordan 217; Morocco 592; Saudi Arabia 145, 149, 152; Syria 244, 260; Tunisia 493
oil resources and production 666, 673-5, 676, 687, 694-5; Algeria 530, 533, 546, 547, 549-54, 562, 565, 566, 567; Egypt 343-4; Iraq 17, 39, 49, 53; Kuwait 49, 84-5, 86, 103, 107-8, 116, 676; Libya 420, 430, 435-42, 449, 452, 455, 466, 676; Morocco 640; Saudi Arabia 49, 84, 127, 139-50, 180-81, 676; Sudan 394; Syria 229, 231, 244; Tunisia 491-4, 506, 511
oil revenues 289, 297, 304, 397, 665, 673-5, 680-81; Algeria 39, 543, 549, 552-3, 571-2; Iraq 18, 19, 36-40, 52, 56, 66, 67; Kuwait 38, 39, 82-3, 86-7, 107-8, 109, 111, 121-2; Libya 38, 39, 426, 432, 439-41, 444, 449, 460; Saudi Arabia 38, 39, 127-8, 134, 143-4, 168; Tunisia 489, 496
Omar, Hussein 23
organisations, Arab 692-3 see also names of specific organisations
Organization of Petroleum Exporting Countries (OPEC) 86, 143, 552, 674, 690
Organization of Arab Petroleum Exporting Countries (OAPEC) 702-3, 706, 709
ownership of dwellings see housing

paint industry 678; Algeria 545, 546; Pakistan 425, 431
Palestine Liberation Organisation 119-20
Palestine 710-13
Palestine expellees 187, 190, 196, 205, 226n, 695, 711-12, 715n; Lebanon and 282, 284-5, 289, 304
Palestine resistance movement 191
paper industry 710; Iraq 41, 42; Syria 243
pearl fishing 81, 82
peasants see land reform
petrochemicals industry 675, 678, 698, 709; Algeria 544, 546; Egypt 343; Iraq 42; Kuwait 103; Libya 437; Saudi Arabia 149
PETROMAR 150
Petromin 140, 146-50
Petromin-AGIP 143
Petromin Lubricating Oils Co. 149
Petromin Sulfuric Acid Co. 149
Petromin Sulfur Co. 149
pharmaceuticals industry 678; Egypt 343; Iraq 42
phosphates see mineral resources
pilgrimage: Saudi Arabia 166

pipelines: Algeria 528, 551; Egypt 343-4; Lebanon 285; Syria 247-8
planning, economic 676, 680; Algeria 271, 528-9, 546, 559-70; Egypt 271, 339, 345-54, 375-6n; Iraq 18, 19, 41-2, 58-9, 66-74, 115-16; Jordan 219-25; Kuwait 680; Lebanon 286-7, 312; Libya 442-52; Morocco 271, 605-10, 614, 635, 644-58; Saudi Arabia 178-80; Sudan 405-10; Syria 241, 260-72, 345; Tunisia 271, 481-3, 496, 508-16
plastics industry: Egypt 343
politics 680, 691, 707-8; Algeria 521-30 passim, 532, 534-5, 576; Egypt 321-2, 327, 366-72, passim; Iraq 17, 19, 22, 76; Kuwait 120; Lebanon 304, 311; Libya 422, 431, 432-5, 452, 466; Morocco 580, 602, 610, 659; Sudan 397, 408-9, 413; Syria 240, 246; Tunisia 471-2, 504-8, 516
population 670, 671, 673, 681; Algeria 523; Egypt 317-18, 319, 349, 353, 354, 359, 360, 366; Iraq 17, 22-4, 32; Jordan 188, 190, 200-202; Kuwait 87-9, 92, 123, 124n; Lebanon 282-3; Libya 423-4, 451, 459, 461; Morocco 581, 582-6, 604-5, 612, 617, 626-8, 652, 660n; Saudi Arabia 127, 138-9, 182n; Sudan 378, 379-81, 413; Syria 229, 264-5; Tunisia 478-9, 489, 502
Porter, R.S. 192
ports: Jordan 217; Saudi Arabia 162-3
poverty and the poor: Egypt 320; Iraq 17, 28; see also income distribution
power, political: Algeria 522; Egypt 321-2, 336; Iraq 17, 58; Morocco 658-9; Syria 253
printing industry: Algeria 546; Iraq 40
private enterprise 679, 680, 699-700; Algeria 530, 545, 547-8, 566; Egypt 352, 363-4, 366, 373; Iraq 42, 43; Jordan 221, 223, 679; Kuwait 113, 114, 116; Lebanon 281, 285-6, 291, 297, 303-10, 679; Libya 431, 449, 459; Morocco 606-7, 636, 642, 647, 648, 651, 652, 679; Saudi Arabia 137, 148, 151; Sudan 405, 415; Syria 237-8, 240, 241, 242-3, 265, 270-71, 276-7; Tunisia 501, 505-6, 514
productivity and production 670, 671, 686; Algeria 525-6, 533,

Index   725

542-3, 545, 552-3, 561, 563, 572-3; Egypt 318, 336, 342, 343, 345, 355, 360; Iraq 28, 44, 50, 62, 73; Jordan 207; Libya 440-41, 458, 467; Morocco 592, 593, 613, 629, 639-40, 644-58 *passim*; Saudi Arabia 135, 139-40, 141, 161; Sudan 381, 401; Syria 237, 264, 266, 268, 276; Tunisia 475, 488-9, 493, 494, 506, 509; *see also* gross domestic product

profits and profit sharing: Algeria 545, 548; Egypt 345, 353, 368; Iraq 58; Lebanon 305; Syria 275

public administration 666, 677, 707; Algeria 523, 540-41, 559, 562, 574; Egypt 353-4, 363, 372, 373; Iraq 19, 38, 49, 63; Jordan 187-8, 196; Kuwait 84, 85-6, 90, 109, 121, 122, 123; Lebanon 287-8, 304; Saudi Arabia 134, 138, 170, 181; Libya 431, 433, 452, 455; Morocco 581, 585, 597, 610, 613, 621, 630, 643, 645-6, 648; Sudan 399, 404, 412-13; Syria 231-3; Tunisia 478, 480, 505, 509, 516

public finance *see* budgets, state

public sector (of the economy) 677, 680; Algeria 545, 547-8; Egypt 355, 366-72 *passim*, 373; Iraq 41, 43; Jordan 220, 223, Kuwait 113, 114-15, 116; Lebanon 291, 297; Libya 449, 460; Morocco 606, 636, 639, 647, 652; Saudi Arabia 151, 178; Sudan 405, 409; Syria 241, 243, 260-63; Tunisia 505, 506, 514; *see also* nationalisation

public utilities *see* infrastructure *and* services and service industries

public works *see* construction industry

quarrying: Iraq 49; Libya 455, 464; Morocco 620; Saudi Arabia 134, 139, 140; Syria 243

railways *see* transport and communications
rainfall *see* water resources
real estate *see* land and land ownership
refrigeration industry: Jordan 192
relative national product per worker: Algeria 563; Lebanon 302-3
roads *see* transport and communications
Rodinson, Maxime 327
Rostow, W.W. 13
rubber industry 678; Iraq 42, 43
rural society 666-71, *see also* agriculture

Salter, Lord 31
sanitation *see* health care
Saud, King 128
Saudi Arabia 127-85; agriculture and water 155-61; banking 166-8; budgets 168-70; Central Planning Organisation 130; Committee for Economic Development 129; development planning 177-80; education 172-5; external trade 170-72; gross national product 130-38; health 175-7; Industrial Development Fund 167; Industrial studies and Development Centre 152; infrastructure 161-4; manufacturing industry 150-55; oil resources 142-50; population and manpower 138-42; problems of 180-81; recent history 127-30
Saudi Arabian Airlines 163
Saudi Arabian Fertilizers Co. 149
Saudi Arabian Monetary Agency 128, 129, 135, 137, 148, 152, 167, 168, 179, 184n
Saudi Credit Bank 168
Saudi Development Fund 701
Saudi International Bank 699
Saudi Marine Petroleum Construction Co. 149
savings *see* investment
Schumpeter, J.A. 13
science and technology 559
services, and service industries 666, 690, 694; Egypt 319, 320-21, 349; Iraq 38, 70; Jordan 187-8, 195-6, 207, 220, 223; Kuwait 90, 97, 98, 103, 105, 109, 116; Lebanon 286, 300-303, 303-310 *passim*, 694; Libya 429, 457, 460, 464; Morocco 594-8, 602, 621, 627, 630; Saudi Arabia 134, 140, 164-5; Sudan 399, 405; Syria 231-3, 276; Tunisia 481, 485, 499, 562
Shell Co. 149
Shell (Kuwait) Co. 86
shipbuilding: Kuwait 81
shipping: Kuwait 81, 82, 105-6
shoe industry: Iraq 40, 43; Jordan 217
Sinclair Arabian Oil Company 143
skilled manpower *see* technical skills and training
soap industry: Iraq 40; Jordan 217; Syria 237
social justice 678, 683-6; Egypt 327; Libya 467; Lebanon 288; Morocco 656-7; Syria 275-6; Tunisia 506
social problems: Egypt 344; Kuwait 120-21; Lebanon 300; Sudan 413-14
social structure 684-5; Algeria

533-4; Iraq 17; Kuwait 81-2, 88-9; Morocco 602, 658-9; Saudi Arabia 127; Syria 240, Tunisia 471-2
social welfare 676, 678, 679; Egypt 369; Iraq 46, 58; Jordan 187-8, 190, 196, 203; Kuwait 95-6, 114, 116; Lebanon 312; Libya 451, 461, 467; Saudi Arabia 177; Sudan 404, 405; Syria 242, 248-50, 264; Tunisia 477, 506
socialism 677, 679, 687; Algeria 522, 533, 536, 537, 543-4, 548-9, 573, 574, 679; Egypt 304, 328, 336, 363-4, 366-72, 679; Iraq 58-9, 64; Kuwait 679; Lebanon 306, 312; Libya 434; Saudi Arabia 679; Syria 242, 243, 253-76 *passim*, 304; Tunisia 497, 501, 504-8 *passim*, 679
Societe Auxiliaire de l'Enterprise de Recherches et d'Activities Petrolières 143, 148
Spain 579
Spengler, J.J. 13
state, the: Iraq 34-5; Lebanon 286, 287, 306, 309, 310-11; Saudi Arabia 181; Syria 233, 238-9 *see also* politics
state farms: Algeria 533, 537-40, 548
steel *see* iron and steel industry
Stewart, C.F. 589, 607-8
storage industry 118, 676; Iraq 53; Libya 449; Sudan 397
Sudan 377-417; Agricultural Reform Corporation 387; development plans 405-10; dual economy 398-402, 414-15; economic performance 388-404; external sector 402-4; Industrial Development Corporation 394, 408; socio-economic structure 377-9
Suez Canal 338-9, 358
sugar industry 678; Iraq 41; Morocco 592; Syria 237
sulphur extraction industry: Iraq 42, 53
Supreme Agricultural Council (Iraq) 64
Syria 229-79; Agrarian Reform Agency 254; economic performance 251-3, 271-2; merchant tractorists 238, 240, 256; merger with Egypt 240-42, 272-5 *passim;* nationalisation 272-5; planning 260-72; recent history 237-53; socialism 253-76

tanning industry: Iraq 40
Tapline Co. 162
taxation 56-7, 683, 685; Egypt 368; Iraq 17; Kuwait 103, 121-2;

Lebanon 309, 310; Libya 428, 460-61; Morocco 597, 625, 635; Saudi Arabia 181; Sudan 404; Syria 242, 276
technical assistance 118, 690; Iraq 43; Jordan 199-200; Kuwait 104; Libya 425
technical skills and training 671, 673, 680; Algeria 528, 533, 541, 550, 551, 558, 559, 565; Egypt 344, 351, 354; Iraq 36, 42; Jordan 187, 188, 189, 203, 207; Kuwait 89, 115; Lebanon 288; Libya 429, 431, 443, 465; Morocco 600-601, 602, 612-14, 630, 632, 648, 650, 652-3, 659; Saudi Arabia 141-2, 148, 150, 151, 154, 161, 180; Sudan 410, 413; Syria 264
textiles industry 710; Algeria 545, 546, 568; Egypt 343; Iraq 40, 42, 43, 53; Jordan 217; Morocco 592; Saudi Arabia 153; Syria 237; Tunisia 490, 506
tobacco industry 677; Iraq 40, 43, 53; Jordan 192, 217, 222; Saudi Arabia 153; Syria 237
tourism 690; Egypt 319, 358, 694; Jordan 218, 219, 220, 694; Lebanon 298, 305, 315n; Libya 443; Sudan 397; Morocco 582, 621-2, 624, 643, 644, 650, 652; Tunisia 494-5, 497, 511
town planning: Lebanon 295
trade 687, 707; Algeria 522, 562; Egypt 319, 323, 349; intra-regional 692-4; Jordan 193, 195-6; Kuwait 98; Lebanon 281, 286, 289, 296-7, 298-9, 301-2, 666; Libya 456; Morocco 581, 585, 621, 642, 644; Saudi Arabia 134, 142; Sudan 391; Syria 231-3, 241, 266-7; Tunisia 481, 511; *see also* external trade
trade unions: Algeria 549
training *see* education
transport and communications 118, 666, 676, 679, 687, 707, 709; Algeria 528, 555, 562; Egypt 323, 349, 358, 367, 368; Iraq 53, 70, 73; Jordan 196-7, 217-18, 219, 220; in Kuwait 105, 110, 116; Lebanon 286, 194, 195-6, 298, 299, 305, 311; Libya 421, 424, 429, 430, 434, 435, 443, 445, 451, 455, 460, 461; Morocco 580, 581, 582, 594, 595, 597, 602, 621; Saudi Arabia 137, 142, 151, 154, 161-5, 169, 170; Sudan, 391, 395-6, 397, 398, 399, 412; Syria 231-3, 237, 241, 247, 260, 273; Tunisia 474, 475, 478, 481, 506, 511
transport equipment industry:

Egypt 343, 398; Saudi Arabia 154
Tunisia 471-519; agriculture 485-9; colonisation of 471-5; Compagnie Financière et Touristique 496; economic performance 480-85; external sector 494-8; industry 489-94; manpower 498-504; mineral resources 491-4; National Bureau for Handicrafts 491; *Perspectives Décannales de Developpment 1962-1971* 481-3, 508-9; planning 508-16; Société Nationale d'Investissement 496; transformation of 504-8
Turkey 425, 431
tyre industry: Iran 43

USSR: aid from 361-3, 687; technical assistance from 43, 364-6
underdevelopment 13
unemployment 673; Algeria 523, 528, 529, 538, 573; Egypt 319, 359; Iraq 24; Jordan 190-91, 204, 205-6, 221, 226n; Libya 464; Morocco 585-6, 609, 615, 650, 656, 659; Saudi Arabia 139; Syria 236-7, 264-5; Tunisia 473, 479, 480, 498-9, 500, 503, 515
Union de Banques Arabes et Française 699
Union Mediterranéene de Banques 699
United Kingdom 198, 419, 425, 597
United Nations 425, 443, 701, 711
United States 198, 213, 404, 419, 425, 431, 479, 622, 683
urbanisation 667, 686; Iraq 22, 24; Libya 461; Morocco 612, 626; Saudi Arabia 165; Syria 276; Tunisia 478-9

vegetable oil industry: Syria 237
vehicle industry: Algeria 545, 546

Warriner, Doreen, 24, 27, 29, 31, 238
water resources 668-71, 679; Algeria 567, 574; Iraq 17, 18, 25, 29-31, 49; Jordan 191, 192, 208, 212-15, 220; Lebanon 293; Libya 435; Morocco 579, 610, 620; Saudi Arabia 146, 155-61, 169, 170; Sudan 377-8, 383-4, 386-7, 410-11; Syria 213-14, 266; Tunisia 474-5, 485-9 *passim*. *see also* irrigation
water supply industry 676; Egypt 325, 369; Jordan 204-5, 217; Kuwait 103, 110, 116; Lebanon 286, 311; Libya 430, 443, 447, 461; Sudan 391; Saudi Arabia 137, 159-60, 164; Tunisia 506

Waterston, Albert 589, 602, 606, 607-8, 609
wealth: Egypt 321-2, 327; Iraq 17; Kuwait 96; *see also* income distribution
women 672; Jordan 207; Kuwait 98, 116; Libya 463, 464; Morocco 583, 591, 601, 630; Saudi Arabia 138-9, 172, 173, 181; Syria 234; Tunisia 477, 501
woollen industry: Iraq 40, 41, 53

Zeeland, Paul Van 303

Middle East & North Africa

Conical Orthomorphic Projection
Origin 27½° N; Standard parallels 16° N. & 38° N.